ASTON VILLA
THE
COMPLETE RECORD

ROB BISHOP & FRANK HOLT

A TWOCAN PUBLICATION
ISBN: 978-1-915571-27-4

© 2022. Rob Bishop & Frank Holt.

All rights reserved. No part of this publication may be reproduced, stored in a retrieval system, or transmitted in any form, or by any means, electronic, mechanical, photocopying, recording or otherwise without the prior permission in writing of the copyright holders, nor be otherwise circulated in any form or binding or cover other than in which it is published and without a similar condition being imposed on the subsequent publisher.

Every effort has been made to ensure the accuracy of information within this publication but the publishers cannot be held responsible for any errors or omissions. Views expressed are those of the authors and do not necessarily represent those of the publishers or the football club.

PICTURE CREDITS:
Action Images, Alamy, Press Association, Aston Villa FC.

CONTENTS

Introduction	4
The History of Aston Villa	6
Villa Park - A Special Place	84
Programmed for Success	92
A Great Game!	94
Club Legends	140
Villa Stars A-Z	144
Managers / Head Coaches	268
League Seasons	290
Club Honours & Records	554
Appearances During WW2	556
Player Records	558
Roll of Honour	598

ACKNOWLEDGEMENTS

The material for this book has been researched over many years, and many people have helped with the project.

Brian Archer, whose family have been involved with the club for over a century, has patiently and unfailingly answered a stream of questions and queries.

The club programme, the Villa News & Record, has been a constant source of reference, as have hundreds of newspapers and periodicals.

The staff at history libraries nationwide have been more than helpful, with Peter Drake, Phil McMullan and Pat at the Birmingham Central Library, providing invaluable assistance, along with staff at the Special Collections library at the University of Birmingham.

Members of the Association of Football Statisticians have assisted over the years, and we would also like to thank Tony Brown and Brian Tabner for permission to make use of their research material for match attendance figures.

Others who have helped include Jon Farrelly, Ian Nannestad, Reg Thacker, Nadine Lees, Keith Morris and Paul Vanes. The authors would also like acknowledge the support they have received from their families.

ATTENDANCE FIGURES

Some of the attendance figures shown in this book may differ from those previously published. Numerous sources have been consulted and the figures are based on the most accurate record available.

During football's formative years, attendances were often difficult to obtain, with reporters often estimating the number of spectators based on takings at the gate. It was only from 1925 that the Football League required clubs to submit official match attendance figures.

A great deal of research has been carried out by experts Tony Brown and Brian Tabner, who has had access to the official ledgers from 1925. We are grateful to Tony and Brian for their permission to use their information.

INTRODUCTION

Seismic change has taken place over the past decade, to football in general and to Aston Villa in particular.

Who could have envisaged, when the previous edition of the Complete Record was published in 2010, that technology would come to play such a crucial role with the introduction of the Video Assistant Referee system, and that we would be forced to play competitive domestic football during the summer - and behind closed doors? But both things came to pass, the former by order of the game's governing bodies, the latter because of the Covid-19 pandemic.

For Villa, the past twelve years have been something of a roller-coaster ride. When the last edition was published, the club had just achieved three consecutive top-six finishes in the Premier League and made two trips to Wembley in the space of six weeks.

But the shock resignation of manager Martin O'Neill in August 2010 changed everything. In the first season after his departure, a solid start and a strong finish ensured a top-half place, but from that point it was a slow, painful slide towards relegation in 2016.

All this was played out against doubts over the club's ownership as Randy Lerner gradually pulled back from his original commitment. The one high spot during these difficult years was when Villa reached the FA Cup final for the eleventh time. But the long wait for an eighth victory in the competition continued after a 4-0 defeat by Arsenal.

Adjustment to life in the second tier proved difficult, and in 2018 the very existence of the club was under threat before new owners Nassef Sawiris and Wes Edens provided the platform for things to start moving in the right direction again. Thanks to the heavy investment of these two gentlemen, Villa have returned to the Premier League.

Premier League action behind closed doors at Villa Park following the outbreak of the COVID-19 pandemic.

INTRODUCTION

Peter Withe celebrates his European Cup-winning goal v Bayern Munich.

This updated edition of the Complete Record includes reviews of every competitive season in the club's history, together with results, scorers, attendances and line-ups from every league and cup game plus profiles of every manager and nearly 200 key players.

Since the previous edition, around 150 players have worn the famous claret-and-blue shirt, while there have been nine men in charge, the current boss carrying the title head coach rather than manager. And where there had previously just been one change of chairman from 1982 until 2006, when Doug Ellis was succeeded by Randy Lerner, there have subsequently been two more. Six years ago, Lerner was succeeded by Tony Xia, whose brief reign ended in 2019 when Nassef Sawiris and Wes Edens were appointed executive chairman and chairman respectively.

The decade has also seen the loss of some of key figures in the club's history, including Ellis, Ron Saunders, Graham Taylor and Tommy Docherty. And to huge sadness, several important players have died prematurely, including Dalian Atkinson, Ugo Ehiogu, Jlloyd Samuel and Peter Whittingham.

In this midst of so much change, one thing has remained constant. The statistics which are so essential to any organisation have been faithfully updated by my co-author Frank Holt, whose meticulous attention to detail never ceases to amaze me. We hope you will find this book both informative and entertaining.

Rob Bishop

August 2022

John Carew.

ASTON VILLA · THE COMPLETE RECORD

THE HISTORY OF ASTON VILLA

1874/75 - Birth of a football club

In 1874 members of the Male Adult Bible Class, meeting at the Aston Villa Wesleyan Chapel in Villa Cross in Handsworth, looked at forming a football section. They already had a thriving cricket club and members wanted a winter sporting activity.

The first question they considered was whether to adopt the Rugby code or Association football. One of the members, William B Mason was due to play in a rugby match at Heathfield Park between Handsworth and Grasshoppers and a group consisting of John Hughes, William H Price, George Matthews and William H Scattergood were asked to go along to watch the game and give their opinion.

On the way back from the match, the quartet stopped under a lamp at the top of Heathfield Road to discuss the situation. They decided that Rugby was a little too rough for them and that they should adopt the Association rules. The most probable date for that momentous meeting was Saturday 21st November 1874.

Other members agreed with the decision and a ball was hired from Clapshaw and Cleve for 1s 6d (seven and a half-pence) for a Saturday afternoon practice session in Westminster Road, where Westminster Church was later built.

At the end of the practice match there was a whip-round, and 16 players put 1s (5p) each into a hat to purchase a ball. The group then moved to the formation of the club and the election of officers. W H Price was appointed captain with Charles H Midgley elected as secretary.

Club colours were adopted - royal blue caps and stockings, scarlet and royal blue striped jerseys and white shorts (or knicks as they were known). A club rule stated that 'no member can take part in a match unless in the above uniform'.

One of the initial difficulties was finding opponents, as there were very few football clubs in Birmingham at the time. They had played cricket against Aston Brook St Mary's several times during the previous summer and there was a good relationship between the clubs, so a football challenge was issued to St Mary's.

However, a further difficulty arose in that St Mary's played rugby, not association football. The clubs reached a compromise, and it was decided that the first half would be played under Rugby rules and the second half under Association-Sheffield rules.

The game took place on Saturday 13 March 1875 on land belonging to a Mr Wilson in Birchfield, where Wilson Road now stands, consisting of 15 players on each side.

It started with an oval ball and although Villa played little football in the first half, the time being taken up with lining up, throwing in and scrimmaging, the defence excelled and half-time was reached without any score. Villa then produced their round ball and a much better second half ensued. Twenty-five minutes into the second-half, the ball was played down the centre to John Hughes who, running towards goal took a shot. The ball hit the goalkeeper and Hughes scored the club's first-ever goal from the rebound to give Villa a 1-0 victory.

The Villa team comprised; goalkeeper William H Scattergood, three backs, William H Price (captain), William Weiss and Fred Knight; four half-backs, Edward B Lee, George Matthews, Harry Matthews and Charles H Midgley and seven forwards, John Hughes, William Such, Harry Whateley, George Page, Alfred Robbins, William B Mason and William B Sothers.

That was the only match played in the first season. At the time, football was not played after March and Aston Villa returned to cricket. But the foundations had been laid...

1876 - George Burrell Ramsay

In 1876, a most significant event occurred in the history of Aston Villa, one which would shape the whole future of the club.

George Burrell Ramsay, a Scot who had learned his football in Glasgow, and was one of the greatest dribblers of his time, came across Villa players as they practised in Aston Park. At some stage Ramsay joined in, amazing the players with his skill, his close dribbling, deft touches, swerves and feints.

William McGregor, who would also play an important part in the development of the game, later told of the first meeting between Ramsay and the raw Villa players.

"I have heard some of the old members speak of the fascination which Ramsay's dextrous manipulation of the ball had for them," he recalled. "They had never seen anything like it. He had it so completely under control that it seemed impossible for them to tackle him. The members were ready to thrust all sorts of honours upon him, and he was literally compelled to take the captaincy".

McGregor also wrote: "It was George Ramsay who first moulded the style of the club's play, and the Aston Villa team have never lost the reputation they gained for short quick passing under Ramsay's direction".

Ramsay was captain of Villa from 1876 to 1880. He always wore a small polo cap and long shorts and was a star the crowds loved. Under Ramsay's remarkable influence, the club made rapid progress and he remained with the club as player, secretary, consultant and vice-president until his death in 1935.

1878/79 - Archie Hunter

The next significant event in the club's history was the arrival of Archie Hunter. As an 18-year-old, Hunter arrived in Birmingham from Scotland on Saturday 8 August 1878 without knowing a single person in the town. Within a few years, he would become one of the most well-known players in the country.

Back home, Hunter had become acquainted with the Calthorpe Football Club, which used to travel to Scotland to play the second team of the strong Queen's Park, and he decided to join them when he arrived in Birmingham.

However, before he could locate Calthorpe, a work colleague, George Uzzell, mentioned Aston Villa and asked Hunter to become a member. Initially, unsure about taking his friend's advice, Hunter decided to join on being told that a fellow Scot - George Burrell Ramsay - was the Villa captain.

1879/80 · The first trophy

In 1879, Aston Villa entered the FA Cup for the first time. Archie Hunter's younger brother Andy, who had come down from Scotland to join him, had the distinction of scoring Villa's first goal in the competition.

After receiving a bye in the first round, Villa drew 1-1 away against Stafford Road on 13 December 1879 before winning the replay 3-1 at Wellington Road six weeks later with a brace from William Mason and a goal from Sammy Law.

Villa were then drawn away to Oxford University, three times finalists and winners in 1874, but to everyone's surprise they scratched from the competition.

It is difficult now to understand quite why Villa took this decision, although they were having a good run in the Birmingham Senior Cup at the time. They may well have decided to concentrate on winning a competition in which their chances were good, rather than face almost certain defeat at the hands of the strong University side. It proved to be the correct decision, because Villa went on to win their first trophy.

Having received a walkover in the first round of the Birmingham Senior Cup when Harborne Unity scratched, they beat Excelsior 8-1 at Wellington Road before beating Newport 7-0 away on St Valentine's Day 1880.

In round four, Villa played Aston Unity at Aston Lower Grounds and progressed by a single goal to meet Walsall Swifts, again at the Lower Grounds in the semi-final. A 2-1 victory took them through to play Saltley College in the final at the same venue on 3 April.

Saltley had the benefit of a strong wind, but it was Villa who took a 30th-minute lead when Archie Hunter dribbled through and passed to Eli Davis to score.

From the restart, the ball was taken up field and from a scrimmage, Elgin equalised, but after the break Villa pressed forward and skipper George Ramsay quickly restored the lead. Almost immediately, Davis took the ball down the left wing and centred for Bill Mason to make the score 3-1 and give Villa their first cup success.

Even so, Villa were not totally satisfied. They later complained about the quality of the medals, which were subsequently replaced.

The first of many trophies - Villa's players display the Birmingham Senior Cup. Back row: J Hughes (umpire), W McGregor (vice-president), William Mason, Ted Lee, Harry Simmonds, Tom Pank, Eli Davis, F Johnstone (vice-president), H Jefferies (secretary). Front: Andy Hunter, George Ramsay, W Ellis (president), Archie Hunter, Charlie Johnstone. On ground: Sammy Law, John Ball.

1880/81 · Heart of the matter

There were some notable victories during the 1880/81 season. On New Year's Day, Villa beat Heart of Midlothian 4-2 at Perry Barr and the following week, a crowd of over 5,000 saw them gain a convincing 4-0 victory over Darwen in a match between the holders of the Challenge Cup for their respective district associations.

In the FA Cup, Villa overcame Wednesbury Strollers and Nottingham Forest before gaining a 3-1 third-round victory at Notts County, thanks to a brace from Andy Hunter and a goal from his brother Archie. But Stafford Road avenged the previous season's defeat by Villa, winning 3-2 at Perry Barr.

Villa again reached the final of the Birmingham Senior Cup, scoring 24 goals and conceding just one along the way, including a fine 6-0 quarter-final victory over Wednesbury Old Athletic at Aston Lower Grounds. During the game, the roof of the dressing room gave way due to the weight of people standing on it, but fortunately no-one was seriously injured.

Having reached the final in such fine style, though, Villa surprisingly lost to Walsall Swifts at the Lower Grounds where a 7,000 crowd saw Yates score the only goal in the first half.

On the way to the game the Walsall brake had been involved in an accident and some of the players were shaken by this. On being told of the incident, Villa were asked to spare the opposition, the order being given not to press them too hard. Walsall fell back in defence after scoring and held on despite intense Villa pressure.

Partial revenge was gained a week later with a 4-1 victory over the Swifts at Stoke in the Staffordshire Cup final, Archie Hunter hitting a hat-trick. Villa played a total of 25 games that season, winning 21, drawing one and suffering just three defeats.

1881/82 · No stroll for Clarke

Villa defeated Nottingham Forest 4-1 in the first round of the FA Cup, with a brace each from Oliver Whateley and Arthur Brown, received a bye in round two, and then met Notts County in round three. After a 2-2 draw at home on New Year's Eve, the replay resulted in the same scoreline and Villa then went through 4-1 at Perry Barr in the second replay.

At the time, Archie Hunter was often unable to play because of business commitments in Scotland, although he travelled down whenever possible for important games. In January, Hunter travelled overnight from Ayr for the fourth-round match away to Wednesbury Old Athletic. Oliver Vaughton gave Villa the lead, but the 'Old Urns' went on to win 4-2 despite a second Villa goal from Hunter.

Disaster struck at the end of January when goalkeeper Billy Clarke broke his leg in a game against Wednesbury Strollers.

Villa beat Glasgow Rangers 3-2 on the Scottish club's first visit to Birmingham in a match played under English rules in the first half when Rangers scored twice, and Scottish rules in the second half when Villa hit three goals.

Once again, Villa gained some consolation for the FA Cup defeat, by beating Wednesbury Old Athletic 2-1 in April to again lift the Birmingham Senior Cup.

The following week, Villa travelled to Scotland, with mixed results. Heart of Midlothian were beaten 6-1 in Edinburgh, but Glasgow Rangers triumphed 7-1. On Saturday 24 April, Villa reached the final of the inaugural Mayor of Birmingham Charity Cup by beating Wednesbury Old Athletic 2-0 in the semi-final.

Villa beat Walsall Swifts 4-1 in the final on 6 May when a bumper crowd brought in more than £200 for charity.

In the Birmingham Senior Cup, Villa again reached the final, scoring 21 goals with just one against and went on to win the trophy with a 2-1 victory over Black Country rivals Wednesbury Old Athletic.

1882/83 · The hand of Harry

In a season which started with an 8-0 victory over Stafford Road - a benefit match for the local Birchfield Harriers athletics club - Villa went on to enjoy their best FA Cup run to date.

Walsall Swifts and Wednesbury Old Athletic were both beaten 4-1, while Aston Unity were overcome 3-1 before Villa beat Walsall Town on a quagmire of a pitch at Perry Barr. The Walsall side included Gershom Cox who would later join Villa, go on to captain the side and have the unenviable distinction of scoring the first own-goal in the Football League.

Eight thousand Villa supporters travelled to Notts County for the quarter-final. Archie Hunter, now captain, opened the scoring on 30 minutes. But County equalised through Harry Cursham before half-time and after the break, Cursham completed his hat-trick to put County 3-1 up before Oliver Whateley pulled a goal back for Villa and Arthur Brown brought the scores level at 3-3 - only for William Gunn to grab County's winner.

Villa claimed the result should have been a draw, protesting that a goal-bound first-half shot had been fisted out by Cursham. A Villa delegation travelled to London for the appeal with witnesses who said that the ball had been fisted out illegally. The referee advised that he had not seen anything wrong and the result stood. The game was referred to as 'the long arm match' for some years afterwards.

It was a case of déjà vu in the Birmingham Senior Cup, Villa once again beating Wednesbury Old Athletic in the final, this time by 3-2. They scored a total of 50 goals throughout the competition, conceding just two.

1883/84 · Taking the high road

Villa were drawn away in each of their FA Cup matches, defeating Walsall Swifts, Stafford Road and Wednesbury Old Athletic before meeting Queen's Park in Glasgow.

The opposition were due to play a Scottish Association Cup-tie against Hibernian on the date scheduled for the fourth round and Villa were asked to play the match a week earlier. With several players injured, however, Villa declined to bring the game forward.

The tie was in doubt until the Scottish FA agreed to the SFA Cup match being postponed, but there was a tremendous amount of interest in the game. Special trains were run from Birmingham to Glasgow and the Villa team were given a tremendous reception both on their departure and on their arrival in Scotland.

Even so, it was not the most successful of trips. Queen's Park were far too strong, running out 6-1 winners. The only consolation was that when Oliver Whateley scored just before the end, it was the first time Villa had scored against the leading Scottish club who went on to reach the FA Cup Final and lifted the Scottish Association Cup for the seventh time later that season.

The Birmingham Senior Cup was won outright following a third consecutive victory as Villa beat Walsall Swifts 4-0. Villa won 27 of their 40 matches, with two drawn games and eleven defeats.

1884/85 · First victory over Queen's Park

Villa reached the FA Cup third round, winning 4-1 against Wednesbury Town in thick fog, and gaining a 2-0 away win at Walsall Town.

They then met West Bromwich Albion in January and, after a goalless draw at Perry Barr, lost the replay 3-0 as Albion adapted far better to the atrocious conditions.

Queen's Park travelled down from Glasgow on 8 January and the match generated enormous interest. Over 12,000 people saw the visitors go ahead just before the break, but second-half goals from Arthur Brown and Albert Brown gave Villa a 2-1 win - their first victory over the leading Scottish side of the day. The reaction in Birmingham could not have been greater if the FA Cup had been won. Villa again won the Birmingham Senior Cup, beating Walsall Swifts in the final to lift the new trophy.

1885/86 · A Derby defeat

The FA Cup campaign came to a swift end. After a convincing 5-0 win against Walsall Town, during which play was stopped following a pitch invasion, Villa went out 2-0 away to Derby County in the second round.

In friendly games, Gloucester County were beaten 11-1, and in four games over the Christmas period, Villa won 13-1 against Acton and 7-0 against London Scottish before losing by the odd goal of seven against London Casuals and drawing 2-2 with Queen's Park on New Year's Day.

Victories against Notts County and Oxford University further strengthened Villa's growing reputation, while the Mayor of Birmingham's Charity Cup was again won, a 7-0 semi-final victory over Aston Unity being followed by a 4-1 win against Wednesbury Old Athletic in the final.

1886/87 · Champagne football

Villa's FA Cup run of 1886-87 exploded into life with a 13-0 first-round win against Wednesbury Old Athletic - still the club's record Cup victory - followed by a 6-0 win over Derby Midland to take Villa to a third-round tie at home to Wolverhampton Wanderers.

The game ended 2-2 and when the replay also finished all square at one goal each, Villa were unhappy with an FA decision that the second replay should take place at Wolves' ground. Nevertheless, they gained another draw, this time 3-3, and third replay took place at Perry Barr. Freddie Dawson settled any nerves when he put the home side in front inside ten minutes, and a second goal from Archie Hunter put Villa through on a 2-0 scoreline.

Stars in stripes - Villa's 1886/87 team, who gave the club their first FA Cup triumph. Back row: Frank Coulton, Jimmy Warner, Frankie Dawson, Harry Simmonds, Albert Allen. Front: Richmond Davies, Albert Brown, Archie Hunter, Howard Vaughton, Dennis Hodgetts. On ground: Harry Yates, Jack Burton.

A bye in round four and an easy 5-0 win over Horncastle brought a strong Darwen side to Perry Barr for the quarter-final.

Villa were three-up by half-time, when champagne was produced and the players were invited to enjoy a drink! The interval indulgence almost proved costly as Darwen quickly pulled two goals back before Villa held on to reach the semi-finals for the first time.

The semi-final draw paired Preston North End with West Bromwich Albion, while Villa faced Glasgow Rangers at Crewe. It was a game spoken of by many spectators as the finest they had witnessed.

Rangers, strengthened by players from other Scottish sides, comprised practically a Scottish representative team. But Villa arrived in Crewe straight from a week's training at Holt Fleet and within ten minutes Archie Hunter gave them the lead.

Rangers equalised, but Hunter restored the advantage in the second half before Albert Brown made the game safe at 3-1. Meanwhile, Albion beat Preston by the same score, which meant a derby in the final at Kennington Oval.

Villa returned to Holt Fleet for training the week before the final, while Albion made Ascot their training headquarters. After the unexpected win against Preston, Albion were favourites to win this first all-Midlands final, but the general feeling was that the Cup would go to the team scoring first.

This proved to be the case. There was no score at the interval, but ten minutes after the break, Hunter and Richmond Davis combined to supply Dennis Hodgetts, who drove his shot past Bob Roberts to put Villa 1-0 up. As Albion faded, Hunter scored a second goal after 88 minutes to become the first Villa captain to lift the FA Cup.

An artist's impression of the 1887 Cup Final.

1887/88 · Not so friendly

Villa seemed well on the way to retaining the FA Cup. After beating Oldbury Town 4-0 in the first round and Small Heath Alliance by the same score in round two, they received a bye into the fourth round, where Shankhouse were thrashed 9-0. Preston North End were Villa's fifth-round opponents and the team again went into special training at Holt Fleet to prepare for the tie.

A huge crowd was expected and the committee asked the local police superintendent for mounted police to guarantee that spectators would be kept in check. But no-one anticipated just how large the attendance would be and it proved impossible to keep order.

Archie Hunter gave Villa an early lead, but shortly afterwards the game was held up when spectators swarmed onto the pitch. Villa players were asked to help clear the crowd and Hunter appealed for the pitch to be cleared, but it was obviously a vain hope that order could be restored.

The captains, with agreement of the referee and umpires, decided that, with the likelihood of further disruption, it would be impossible to continue with the cup tie and the match should continue as a friendly.

Playing conditions were chaotic as Preston went on to win 3-1. The situation was considered by the FA who decided that the result must stand, indicating that adequate arrangements had not been made. Villa were out of the Cup.

But football was about to change forever. On 2 March 1888, William McGregor circulated several clubs with his suggestion that the most prominent clubs in England arrange home and away fixtures. A meeting was arranged in London later that month. On Tuesday 17 April 1888, the Football League was born.

1888/89 · Second in the First

Villa achieved runners-up position in the first season of League football behind Preston North End, who remained unbeaten throughout the inaugural campaign.

The club's opening game took place on Saturday 8 September against Wolverhampton Wanderers at Dudley Road. Playing uphill in the first half, Villa found themselves behind after 29 minutes when the ball struck full-back Gershom Cox and went in for the Football League's first own-goal. Tommy Green equalised a minute before the break and that historic game ended 1-1.

Archie Hunter was missing from the opening-day line-up following the death of his brother Andy, but he returned the following week when Villa came from a goal behind at half-time against Stoke to win 5-1 at Wellington Road.

This was followed by a 2-1 victory over Everton before Villa met Notts County at the end of September. Playing in an all-white kit, Villa went ahead after five minutes through Albert Allen, who went on to score a hat-trick in a runaway 9-1 win. The first defeat came a week later at Anfield Road where Everton won 2-0.

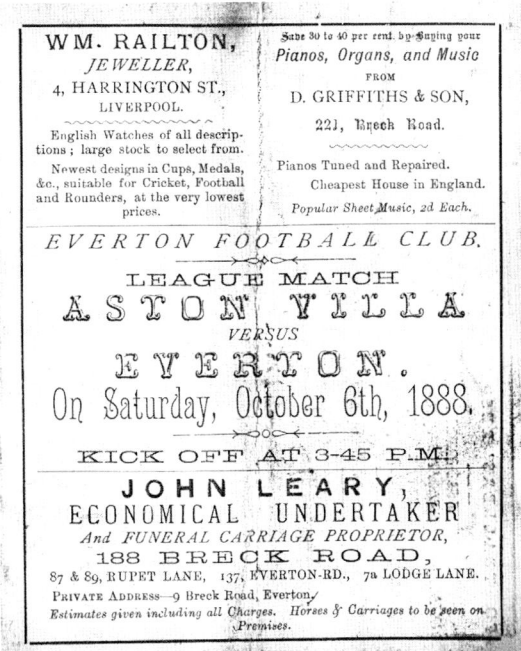

The programme for Villa's first League visit to Everton. It is the most-played League fixture in the country.

Archie Goodall, signed from Preston North End in October, scored on his debut, a 6-1 home win against Blackburn Rovers before Villa gained their first away win a week later, a 3-2 victory over Bolton Wanderers at Pikes Lane. Tommy Green scored an 88th-minute equaliser at Deepdale on 10 November in the only match Preston failed to win at home all season, although it was not until a Football League meeting in Birmingham on 21 November that a system of points was decided - two points for a win and one for a draw - which meant Villa were second behind Preston, despite suffering a 5-1 reversal at Blackburn four days earlier.

There was an amazing game at Turf Moor on the first Saturday of January. Although the kick-off was delayed, there were only eight Villa players on the pitch when Burnley kicked off. Two more men arrived after five minutes, but Villa played the remainder of the game with only ten men, Hunter being absent. Not surprisingly they went down 4-0.

In the FA Cup, home wins against Witton (Blackburn) 3-2 and Derby County 5-3, gave Villa a third-round tie against Blackburn Rovers at Leamington Road. Tom Green and Archie Hunter both played despite being injured and Villa suffered their record FA Cup defeat, going down 8-1. It was the last Cup match for Hunter, who had been the first Villa captain to lift the trophy.

1889/90 · End of the road for Archie

New signings included Vale of Leven defender James Cowan, who would go on to play a major part in the club's success over the next twelve years, and Billy Dickson from Sunderland.

The season started brightly and after a 2-2 draw against Burnley and a 1-1 result against Notts County when Dickson scored on his debut, Villa inflicted Preston's first-ever league defeat, winning 5-3 at Wellington Road. A week earlier, the champions and FA Cup holders had beaten Stoke 10-0.

Subsequent results were variable. A 3-0 defeat at West Bromwich Albion was followed by a 6-2 victory at Burnley, while a 7-1 home success against Derby County took Villa up to third place before they were brought down to earth by a 7-0 drubbing from Blackburn Rovers. Villa gained revenge against Albion with a 1-0 victory before Ike Moore scored two goals on his debut against Wolves to turn an interval deficit into a 2-1 win.

Sadly, Archie Hunter's playing career came to an end in dreadful playing conditions at Anfield Road on 4 January 1890. There were pools of water several inches deep plus mud and slush above the players' ankles. Villa lodged a formal protest over the state of the pitch with Mr Gregson, the referee and it was agreed to play only 35 minutes each way. But Hunter collapsed into a pool of water and, following medical treatment, was advised to retire from playing. Villa lost 7-0 - a sad end to the career of 'the famous Villa captain'.

The following month, Villa went out of the FA Cup, losing 4-1 to Notts County and although the season finished on a high note with a 3-0 success over high-flying Blackburn Rovers, the team's eighth-place finish was a disappointment.

1890/91 · Challenging times

Villa opened their campaign at Molineux. Full-back Walter Evans made his debut, as did Fred Marshall, who replaced Dennis Hodgetts on the left wing. Albert A Brown put the visitors ahead on 35 minutes, but second-half goals from Sammy Thomson and Arthur Worrall gave Wolves the points.

Hodgetts returned the following Saturday when Villa won 3-2 against Notts County at Wellington Road, but it would be the last Saturday in October before Villa gained a second victory, beating Derby County 4-0.

A five-match unbeaten run ended abruptly with a 7-1 defeat against Notts County at the end of November, followed by a 5-1 reversal at the hands of Blackburn Rovers. After drawn games at home to Blackburn and Sunderland, January brought away defeats at Everton, Sunderland and Preston.

Charlie Athersmith, who made his debut when Villa lost the return game against Preston on 9 March, went on to net a hat-trick five days later in a 6-2 victory over Wolves. Villa rounded off the season with a 3-1 win at Accrington a week later, but finished a very disappointing ninth.

In the FA Cup, a 13-1 home win against Casuals was followed by a second-round 3-0 defeat by Stoke who were then playing in the Football Alliance, having lost their league status the previous season.

1891/92 · John Devey arrives

John Devey, who had arrived from Birmingham St George's in March, scored a brace on his debut in the opening match against Blackburn Rovers and went on to net five goals in the first four league games as Villa stormed to the top of the table.

Defeats followed at the hands of Derby, Bolton and Burnley before a run of five victories restored Villa's title ambitions. Although a visit to champions Everton resulted in a 5-1 reversal, Villa recovered with a 6-1 win against Burnley.

On Boxing Day, Villa defeated Darwen 7-0, but the highs and lows of football can be illustrated by games on two consecutive Saturdays in March. On the 12th of the month Villa became the first team to net a dozen goals in a league match, winning 12-2 against Accrington

John Devey

- a club record which still stands. But seven days later they lost 3-0 to West Bromwich Albion in the FA Cup final.

Villa went into the final as firm favourites, especially after a magnificent 4-1 win against Sunderland in the semi-final, but in the last final to be played at Kennington Oval, a record crowd of 32,810 saw Jasper Geddes give Albion a fourth-minute lead from which Villa never recovered.

Many supporters blamed goalkeeper Jimmy Warner for the defeat and smashed the windows of his pub in Spring Hill. Warner never played for the club again. Outfield player George Campbell played in goal the following week and Edwin Diver then came in for the final three league games. Villa finished fourth, their highest position since the inaugural season.

1892/93 · An extended league

The Football League had been extended to 28 teams and two divisions, 16 teams in the First Division and 12 in the Second.

Villa won their opening-day fixture for the first time, beating Burnley 2-0 at Turf Moor, with five players making their debuts - goalkeeper Willie Dunning signed from Bootle as a replacement for Warner, full-back Archie Stokes, John Ramsey, Peter Dowd and James Fleming.

Five days later, Fleming hit a brace on his home debut as Villa beat Everton 4-1 and victory at Stoke by a single goal put Villa top of the table. Following this excellent start, however, things started to go wrong. The Villa committee suspended Dowds for a month for 'failing to keep himself fit' and the following Saturday champions Sunderland arrived at Wellington Road and were three-up before the break, eventually winning 6-1.

Two days later, Villa visited Stoney Lane for the re-staging of a fixture they had won 1-0, but which had been declared a friendly because the appointed referee had failed to arrive. At the second time of asking Albion overturned Villa's interval advantage to win 3-2, and there were further setbacks by Bolton, Everton and Wolves.

Thereafter, the highlights of the season were a 6-1 victory over Derby, while five goals were scored against Albion, Nottingham Forest, Sheffield Wednesday and FA Cup winners Wolves. In a thrilling encounter with Accrington, Villa overcame a 3-1 deficit at the break to win 6-4, Albert Woolley scoring twice on his debut.

1893/94 · We are the champions

Improvements to Wellington Road for the first match of the season against West Bromwich Albion included the erection of small iron railings around the enclosure, designed to keep back the crowd and prevent spectators from going on the pitch.

Making his debut against his old club, Jack 'Baldy' Reynolds gave Villa the lead from the penalty spot and a thrilling game was only decided when Albert Woolley's goal in the dying seconds gave Villa a 3-2 verdict. Another debutant against Albion was full-back James Elliott, from Middlesbrough Ironopolis - the second signing from the Teesside club in four months, following Bob Chatt.

Champions for the first time - the title-winning squad of 1893/94. Back row: G Ramsay, J Margoschis, J Dunkley, John Baird, W McGregor, F Cooper, J Lees, James Cowan, Bill Dunning, W Marsh, James Elliott, C Johnstone, Jimmy Welford, I Whitehouse, J Grierson (trainer) F Rinder. Front: Charlie Athersmith, Bob Chatt, Stephen Smith, John Devey, Albert Woolley, Dennis Hodgetts, Willie Groves, Jack Reynolds.

A 1-1 away draw with champions Sunderland, followed by a 5-1 success at home to Stoke took Villa to the top of the league, and although they dropped down to third place after a 3-0 defeat by Sheffield United at Bramall Lane in October, they went top again before the month was out, following a 6-3 away win at Albion and a 4-0 home win against Burnley.

They never looked back. In November, Villa started a run of six consecutive league wins, the club's best winning sequence to date. A packed Boxing Day crowd saw Villa triumph 9-0 against Darwen and Villa twice scored six away from home, beating both Albion and Burnley 6-3.

The title was won with six more points and a better goal average than runners-up Sunderland. John Devey was top scorer for the third consecutive season, netting 22 league and cup goals.

In the FA Cup, following victories over Wolves and Sunderland, Villa went out in extra-time at Sheffield Wednesday.

1894/95 · Cup glory at the Palace

The FA Cup final returned to London for the first time since Albion's triumph over Villa at Kennington Oval three years earlier. The finalists were the same, but the outcome, in the first final to be played at the Crystal Palace, was totally different.

Villa were by far the superior side, although the match was decided as early as the first minute. Indeed, many of the 42,560 crowd were still taking up their positions when Charlie Athersmith provided the pass for Bob Chatt to beat goalkeeper Joe Reader for the only goal of the game.

Villa scored 17 goals on their way to the final, beating Derby County, Newcastle United and Nottingham Forest before meeting Sunderland in the semi-final at Ewood Park, where two second-half goals from Stephen Smith secured a 2-1 win.

In the league, Villa opened the season at home to newly-promoted Small Heath, later to become Birmingham City, winning this first-ever league meeting between the clubs 2-1 thanks to goals from Steve Smith and Bob Gordon on his debut. Gordon, signed from Heart of Midlothian, was yet another Middlesbrough Ironopolis 'old boy'.

In October, Howard Spencer made his debut in a 3-1 victory over Albion at Wellington Road. The full-back, who went on to captain both club and country, would be very much part of Villa for the next 42 years.

The football world was shocked and deeply saddened by the death of Archie Hunter on 29 November at the age of just 35. The famous Villa captain never fully recovered after collapsing at Everton.

Villa went into 1895 as leaders following a 6-0 home win against Stoke on Boxing Day, but then came the distraction of the FA Cup run and the team slipped down to third.

Even so, Villa were getting into the habit of winning trophies and with just a single home defeat, at the hands of the champions Sunderland, and only 12 league goals conceded compared with 51 scored, Wellington Road was becoming a fortress.

Our turn this time - Villa's players proudly parade the FA Cup after beating Albion in the third final between the clubs in the space of nine seasons.
Standing: J Grierson (trainer), J Dunkley, Jack Reynolds, C Johnstone, Howard Spencer, John Devey, Tom Wilkes, J Lees, Jimmy Welford, F Rinder, J Margoschis (chairman). Seated: G Ramsay (secretary), Charlie Athersmith, Bob Chatt, James Cowan, George Russell, Dennis Hodgetts, Stephen Smith.

1895/96 · Back at the top

Villa started the season with three major signings. Following a great deal of persistence by the committee, centre-forward John Campbell was finally secured from Glasgow Celtic, while Jimmy Crabtree was purchased from Burnley for a record £250 and John Cowan was signed from Glasgow Rangers, joining his brother James.

Villa started with a victory over Albion, John Devey scoring the only goal after 14 minutes. The season burst into life the following Saturday when Small Heath visited Perry Barr. A baking hot day became even hotter for the Heathens when Villa hit five first-half goals and eventually ran out 7-3 winners with Campbell netting four.

John Cowan's opportunity came against Derby in September, following an injury to Steve Smith. Cowan scored on his debut in a 4-1 win, with his brother James also on the scoresheet.

Champions again. The 1895/96 title-winning squad. Back row: G Ramsay, Dr V Jones, J Grierson (trainer), Howard Spencer, Mr Cook, Tom Wilkes, J Ansell (president), Dennis Hodgetts, J Marcoschis (chairman), Charlie Johnstone, Jimmy Welford, I Whitehouse, W McGregor, J Lees, F Rinder. Front: Bob Chatt, Jimmy Crabtree, Jack Reynolds, James Cowan, John Devey, Frank Burton, Charlie Athersmith, John Campbell. On ground: Stephen Smith, John Cowan.

When a 4-3 win against Everton was followed by victory over Sunderland on the first Saturday in October, Villa's title ambitions were clear. The team remained in the top two for the rest of the season.

Results were consistent rather than spectacular, but Villa remained unbeaten from the beginning of December until the third Saturday in March when they lost 5-3 to Bury at Gigg Lane. This run included six consecutive victories, starting against Wolves at Molineux when goals from Steve Smith and Howard Spencer clinched a 2-1 success.

Derby County also had title ambitions and a week after knocking Villa out of the FA Cup, the teams met again at Derby in the league. Special excursions from Birmingham were arranged and the huge Villa following were silenced when the home side took a two-goal lead. But John Devey scored right on the interval and Charlie Athersmith grabbed a vital point with a second-half equaliser.

Villa went on to take the championship with four more points than the Rams, who finished runners-up. John Campbell netted 26 goals in as many league appearances, with John Devey contributing 16.

We won the Cup - and then lost it! Even a £10 reward - a substantial sum in those days - failed to retrieve the trophy after it was stolen while on display in a shop window in September 1895.

1896/97 - At the double...

Villa's achievement of league and FA Cup double cannot be over-emphasised. Only Preston, in the league's inaugural season, had achieved this feat and it would be another 64 years before it was repeated by Tottenham in 1961.

A replacement was needed for Dennis Hodgetts who was coming to the end of his Villa career, so Fred Wheldon was signed from Small Heath for a record £350. The fee was paid with a deposit of £100 and a guarantee of a further £250 from the proceeds of a game between the sides.

Jimmy Whitehouse arrived from Grimsby Town for £200 - a record fee for a goalkeeper. Although these big-money buys were significant, the signing of Albert Evans from Barnard Castle would, arguably, have the greatest long-term benefit.

It would not happen in the modern game, but Villa faced Small Heath in a friendly on the evening before opening the league season. Playing against his old club, Wheldon scored twice early in the game which seemed to take the interest out of the match. With about 15 minutes left, in failing light, the referee called an early halt to the game, with Villa leading 3-1.

The following night Stoke were beaten 2-1 in the opening league game, but there was a shock three days later when Villa visited Stoney Lane for Albion's first home game. Villa started confidently enough and led at the interval with a goal from Devey, but the Baggies ran out 3-1 winners.

The points were then shared in a 2-2 draw with Sheffield United, and the following Saturday about 1,000 spectators travelled to Everton to see Devey give Villa an early lead and Campbell add a second before the break. Although Taylor pulled a goal back for the Toffees, Campbell restored Villa's advantage before Alf Milward netted a consolation goal, Villa winning 3-2.

After this splendid victory, there was a disappointment when Everton won 2-1 at Perry Barr the following week, but a goalless draw at Sheffield United was the start of a 12-match unbeaten run which included nine wins.

Following a 2-1 success against Wolves on Boxing Day, Villa once more entered the new year at the top of the table. They then suffered defeats by Burnley and Sunderland, but dropped only one more point, winning ten of the last eleven league games.

In the Cup, Newcastle United were swept aside 5-0 before victories against Notts County and Preston - in a second replay at Bramall Lane - saw Villa return to Sheffield ten days later for the semi-final against Liverpool. John Cowan put them in front after 20 minutes and scored again six minutes into the second half, with Charlie Athersmith hitting a third.

Such was their lead that Villa had already effectively secured the league championship when they travelled to Crystal Palace to meet Everton in the final. Campbell put Villa in front after 18 minutes with a swerving shot, only for Jack Bell to break clear five minutes later and slip the ball past Whitehouse for the equaliser. Boyle put Everton ahead on 28 minutes, but Villa's lead was restored before the break with goals from Wheldon and Jimmy Crabtree, whose header proved to be the winner.

After the game came the news that Derby County - the only team that could mathematically catch Villa - had lost to Bury and Villa achieved the unique distinction of winning both League and FA Cup on the same day.

The double achievement also marked the end of an era. The Wellington Road ground in Perry Barr was left behind with the opening of a new home at Aston Lower Grounds - which later became known as Villa Park.

Campbell had the distinction of scoring the first goal at the new ground as Villa beat Blackburn Rovers 3-0 before going on to beat Wolves and Preston to finish the season with eleven points more than runners-up Sheffield United.

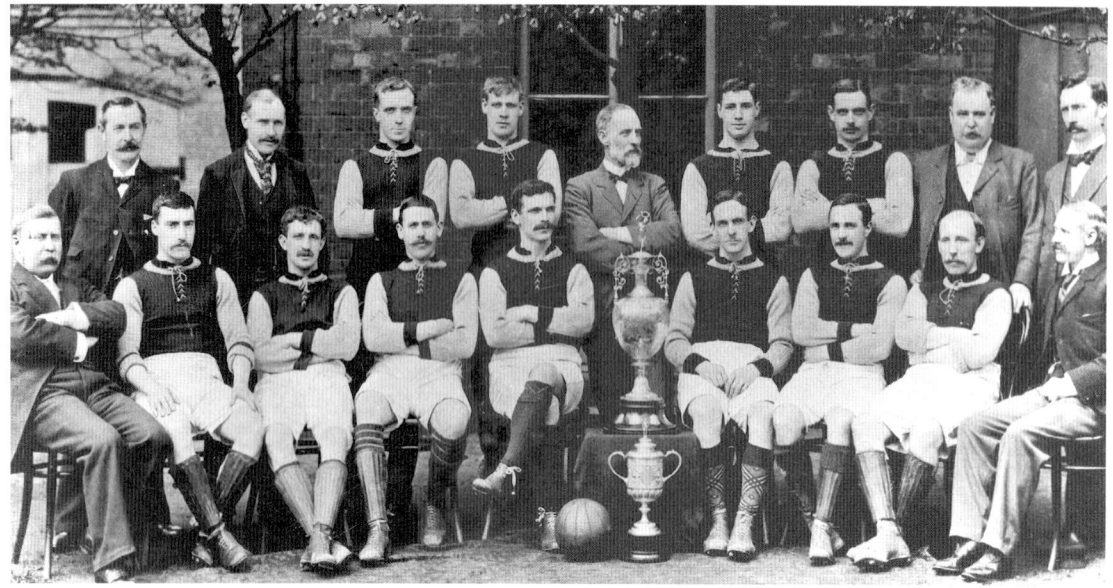

At the double - Villa become the second team, after Preston North End in 1889, to win the League Championship and the FA Cup. Back row: G Ramsay, J Grierson (trainer), Howard Spencer, Jimmy Whitehouse, J Margoschis (chairman), Albert Evans, Jimmy Crabtree, J Lees, C Johnstone. Front: Dr V Jones, James Cowan, Charlie Athersmith, John Campbell, John Devey, Fred Wheldon, John Cowan, Jack Reynolds, F Rinder.

1897/98 - Agony for Spencer

Following the success of five league and cup trophies in just four years, this season proved to be an anti-climax.

John Campbell, who had scored 43 goals in 63 league and cup appearances, departed for Glasgow Celtic, along with Jack Reynolds and Jimmy Welford. Scotsman James Fisher, meanwhile, was brought down from St Bernard's and netted five times before leaving for Celtic.

Villa made a better start than the previous season, recording four straight wins against Sheffield Wednesday, Albion, Notts County and Bury.

Hopes were high, but they then lost 4-3 at Blackburn and disaster followed two days later at Olive Grove in the return game with Sheffield Wednesday. Howard Spencer was injured, and Villa's ten men went down by three clear goals. The injury was costly - it would be 17 months before Spencer was fit enough to return to the side.

The team bounced back at home to Bolton Wanderers, where the Sharp brothers, Jack and Bert, made their debuts. Two-down at the interval, Villa hit back to win with three second half goals in five minutes, Jack Sharp netting a brace before Wheldon claimed the winner.

After beating Blackburn 5-1 on the second Sunday of December, it was February before Villa gained their next win, beating Preston 4-0. Although this prompted a mini revival, Villa won only one of the last five matches - the final game of the season against Nottingham Forest, in which George Johnson scored on his debut.

Villa went out of the Cup at the first hurdle, losing 1-0 in front of a packed crowd at Derby where the gates were locked 20 minutes before kick-off.

1898/99 - A four-month match...

Villa's determination to return to the top soon became obvious, and only one of the first dozen games was lost. This run included seven straight wins and there were fireworks for Derby on Bonfire Night, Villa winning 7-1 after hitting the Rams with a five-goal first-half blitz.

At the end of November, Villa played Sheffield Wednesday at Olive Grove and the kick-off was delayed due to the late arrival of Mr Scragg, the referee.

Villa were 3-1 down with ten and a half minutes to play when the official blew for time due to failing light. The League Management Committee decided that the remaining time would have to be played and four months later, on 13 March 1899 Villa returned to finish the match. Goalscorer Frank Bedingfield did not play in the resumed fixture, his place going to George Johnson, while Billy Garraty replaced John Devey. Fred Spiksley added a goal for Wednesday, the final score being 4-1. It could be argued that Johnson and Garraty were Villa's first substitutes.

In January, Villa again made a quick exit from the FA Cup, losing 2-1 at Nottingham Forest, followed by a run of just one win in nine games. Villa then came back strongly, winning 6-1 against Notts County and beating Albion 7-1 before meeting fellow title-challengers Liverpool in the last match of the season.

Both sides had the same points, but goal average favoured defensive teams. Although Villa's average was superior, a 1-0 Liverpool win would have taken the title to Merseyside. As it turned out, the mathematics were soon forgotten. John Devey put Villa in front on four minutes and by the 35th minute Villa led by five clear goals. The title was back at Villa Park.

THE HISTORY OF ASTON VILLA

Villa parade an array of trophies in 1898/99, the most important of which was the League Championship. Back row: W McGregor, Tommy Bowman, Jimmy Crabtree, Billy Garratty, F Cooper, J Ansell, F Rinder (chairman), J Lees, C Johnstone, Dr V Jones, J Grierson (trainer), Howard Spencer, Billy George, Albert Evans, I Whitehouse. Front: Dr C Griffiths, George Johnson, Charlie Athersmith, John Devey, Fred Wheldon, James Cowan, Stephen Smith, W Cooke.

1899/1900 · Retaining the title

Villa opened the season with a fine win at Sunderland, Billy Garraty scoring the only goal, and two days they later, faced newly-promoted Glossop at Villa Park. After beating Burnley in their first-ever Division One match, the Derbyshire side must have been reasonably confident, even though they were up against the champions. Their confidence was misplaced. Villa scored six in the opening 23 minutes and went on to win 9-0, Billy Garraty netting four.

Villa were brought back to earth the following Saturday when Albion inflicted a 2-0 home defeat, but they resumed winning ways with victories at Everton and at home to Blackburn. The team did not then drop below third place all season.

In November, Villa met the famous Corinthians team for the Sheriff of London Charity Shield at Crystal Palace. Garraty headed Villa in front only for RE Foster to equalise before the break. With 12 minutes remaining, GO Smith hit the winner for Corinthians.

Villa beat Preston 5-0 at Deepdale at the beginning of December, but there was a surprise later that month. Glossop had problems when Villa visited for their return game, having gone nine games without a win and having had two of their players go missing following a dispute over wages. Another Villa win seemed certain, but it was not to be, Alex Davidson scoring after eight minutes to give the home side the points.

There was a 50,000 Villa Park crowd for the game with Sheffield United on the first Saturday in March. Villa led the table with the Blades one point behind, but having two games in hand. Walter Bennett put the visitors ahead just before the break, but Villa, no doubt inspired by the

A new century – and Villa are champions for the fifth time in seven seasons. Standing: J Grierson (trainer), Frank Burton, John Cowan, F Cooper, Jimmy Crabtree, G Ramsay (secretary), Mr Hart (president), Mr Cook, W McGregor, J Lees, Billy George, I Whitehouse, Howard Spencer, Albert Evans, F Rinder. Seated: Albert Wilkes, James Cowan, Fred Wheldon, John Devey, Charlie Athersmith, Billy Brawn, Stephen Smith, A Eyre.

17

Blackpool Lifeboat Band playing 'Rule Britannia' during the interval, equalised through Garraty.

Bobby Templeton hit the only goal of the game at Wolves in Villa's last match of the season to give them a four-point lead and a better goal average over United who still had two games to play, against Wolves at Molineux the following night and at Burnley the following week.

After beating Wolves 2-1, the Blades needed to score at least eight against Burnley, but surprisingly lost 1-0 and Villa were champions for the fifth time in seven years.

There was, however, disappointment in the FA Cup. After beating Manchester City and Bristol City, Villa went out to Millwall from the Southern League in a second replay at Reading.

1900/01 · Champions on the slide

The second half of the season must have left the Villa Park faithful hugely disappointed after the previous period of success as the reigning champions slid down the table to finish 15th out of 18.

It all started so promisingly, as Stoke were defeated 2-0 and Preston 4-0, followed by victory at The Hawthorns where George Johnson scored the only goal of the game. Bury then arrived at Villa Park and left empty handed following a John Devey strike.

At that juncture, Villa occupied their customary position at the top of the table and bounced back from a 2-1 home defeat by Everton with a credible goalless draw at Sunderland and victory over Derby.

Villa won 2-0 at Preston in mid October without the services of Devey, Crabtree and Johnson and Manchester City were beaten 7-1 on the first Saturday in December.

The team entered 1901 in second place following a 3-0 win against Bolton on Boxing Day and a goalless draw at Stoke, but it was all downhill from there.

Villa would gain only one more league win during the remainder of the season, 2-1 at home to Sheffield Wednesday in March with goals from Garraty and Frank Lloyd, who was making his debut.

The most significant signing was Joe Bache who joined Villa from Stourbridge. The 20-year-old was not able to make much impact that season, but went on to play 474 games and score 184 goals before his career was curtailed by the Great War.

In the first round of the FA Cup, which was delayed following the death of Queen Victoria, Villa gained revenge for the previous year by beating Millwall 5-0. Nottingham Forest were beaten in round two, Villa winning 3-1 after extra-time following a goalless draw at Villa Park. Many supporters boycotted the third-round game at Small Heath, upset at the Heathens decision to cash in by doubling the admission charge to a shilling (5p). There was no score and Villa charged normal admission prices for the replay four days later which was won by a Billy Garraty header near the end of extra-time.

Villa eventually lost 3-0 to Sheffield United in a semi-final replay at Derby following a 2-2 draw at Nottingham. Villa again met Corinthians at Crystal Palace for the Sheriff of London's Charity Shield, Charlie Athersmith scoring a second-half goal to take the Shield.

1901/02 · Welcome Jasper

Of the players signed by Villa in 1901 as they attempted to stem the slide, Jasper McLuckie from Bury had the biggest initial impact. The first nine games had produced only two wins - although the second was a welcome 2-0 victory at Small Heath - when McLuckie made his debut against Sheffield Wednesday on the last Saturday in October.

The striker hit a brace in a 4-1 win and went on to score seven goals in his first four games - a feat that would only be bettered by Dion Dublin 97 years later.

Villa line up for the 1901/02 campaign. Back row: W Cooke, H Toney, F Cooper, G Ramsay (secretary), Dr V Jones, F Rinder (chairman), Billy George, J Lees, J Margoschis, W Strange, J Grierson (trainer). Front: Bobby Templeton, George Johnson, Joe Bache, Jimmy Crabtree, Jasper McLuckie, Albert Wilkes, Tommy Niblo, Billy Garratty. On ground: Tom Perry, Arthur Millar, Willie Clarke, Alf Wood.

THE HISTORY OF ASTON VILLA

Willie Clarke - the first black player to score a Football League goal.

McLuckie hit a hat-trick in December in a 4-1 win against Grimsby and the only goal of the match at home to Small Heath on Boxing Day.

On Christmas Day, another summer signing Willie Clarke had made a piece of football history when he became the first black player to score in a Football League game, a 3-2 victory at Everton.

The change in fortunes was such that Villa entered 1902 at the top of the table. Unfortunately, their title hopes were immediately dispelled by a 6-0 defeat at Sheffield United on New Year's Day and although they came back with a 2-0 win against Bury three days later, only two further matches were won, against Derby at home and Wolves away.

The team finished in a disappointing eighth place, but McLuckie's contribution of 16 goals in 21 games had been vital. The second highest scorer was Joe Bache with eight.

Villa were out of luck in the FA Cup. Leading 2-1 at Stoke, they were pegged back by a late Freddie Johnson equaliser for the Potters. Travel delays when the team returned from their training headquarters in Blackpool for the replay resulted in Villa only arriving just before kick-off.

Stoke went ahead with a goal that was initially disallowed for offside, but the referee changed the decision following protests by the Potters. Although Billy Garraty produced an equaliser, Villa went out 2-1 in extra-time.

1902/03 · A late title challenge

Villa started the season where they had left off, the first six games producing only one win, and any title challenge appeared to be over.

Right up until the end of March, performances were very inconsistent. A run of three victories from mid-November, including a 7-0 thrashing of Newcastle on a pitch made treacherous by a week of rain, brought the team up to 12th place, but Villa then slipped back following defeats at Wolves and at home to Liverpool.

Boxing Day brought a vital win over Sheffield Wednesday, thanks to a Billy Garraty penalty, as Villa were reduced to ten men after Evans was badly injured, but the Owls gained ample revenge with a 4-0 win on New Year's Day.

Bobby Templeton departed for Newcastle in the new year for a record £400 fee after making 71 appearances. Having already lost Evans for the season, there was a further blow at the beginning of March when Joe Bache was sidelined for the remainder of the campaign.

Villa went into April in eighth place with 29 points, ten behind leaders Sheffield Wednesday. With two points for a win, Villa knew they would have to win every game to have any hope of winning the title - but they nearly pulled it off. Six of the last seven games were won, the solitary defeat coming during a terrible storm at Anfield where the referee insisted that play must continue. Meanwhile, Wednesday picked up only three more points. Villa had a better goal average than the Owls and just one more point would have given them the title. In the event they had to be content with runners-up spot.

There was plenty of excitement in the FA Cup. A Villa Park crowd estimated at 60,000 saw Villa triumph 4-1 against Sunderland in round one, despite having Billy Garraty carried off. Villa were then drawn away to Barnsley but paid the Tykes £250 plus half the proceeds of the gate to switch the venue and won 4 -1, McLuckie netting a hat-trick.

Tottenham away was the next stop and such was Villa's drawing power that Spurs doubled the admission prices without any impact on the gate. Villa won 3-2, but lost 3-0 in the semi-final to Bury, who beat Derby 6-0 in the final - a record which remained unequalled until Manchester City repeated it against Watford in the 2019 final.

1903/04 · Abandoned hope

Only Howard Spencer and Albert Evans now remained from the double-winning team and there were no new signings in the side that visited Newcastle for the first match of the season. Joe Bache earned Villa a draw with an 84th-minute equaliser, but there was no reprieve at Roker Park three days later, when Sunderland triumphed 6-1.

Villa won 3-1 against Albion the following week, but despite going into 1904 in second place, they finished a disappointing fifth, six points behind the champions Sheffield Wednesday.

Albert Hall and Freddie Miles made their debuts in a 7-3 win at Nottingham Forest in December, when Villa were without Evans, Johnson, Garraty and McLuckie. A 2-1 victory over Wednesday on Boxing

19

Day followed during an unbeaten run that extended to six matches, but performances were generally inconsistent.

Villa went out of the Cup in unfortunate circumstances. After winning 3-2 at Stoke, they were again drawn away at Tottenham and the Southern League club, again wishing to cash in on their visitors' popularity, placed benches near the touchline to accommodate extra spectators. Joe Bache gave Villa a first-half lead, but during the interval spectators from the benches walked on to the pitch followed by many from the terraces. Spectators remained on the pitch at the start of the second half and the game had to be abandoned with Villa leading 1-0.

Tottenham were fined following an enquiry, and the match was ordered to be replayed at Villa Park the following Thursday, Spurs winning 1-0.

1904/05 · Hampton's Cup glory

Harry Hampton scores Villa's first goal in the 1905 Cup Final.

Villa won the FA Cup for the fourth time in a season that was a particular triumph for two players, Howard Spencer and Harry Hampton.

Spencer, out of the side in mid-season, was recalled in February and the skipper went on to gain a record third FA Cup winner's medal with the club.

Hampton made his league debut against Manchester City in November, having been signed from Wellington Town earlier in the year, and went on to top Villa's goal chart with 22, including the two which won the Cup.

The Cup campaign opened with a 5-1 home win against Leicester Fosse. Next up were Bury and Villa gained revenge for the semi-final defeat two years earlier, winning 3-2 after Bache and Garraty hit the Shakers with two goals in a minute during the first half.

A 5-0 victory in round three against Southern League Fulham set up a semi-final date with Everton at Stoke. Albert Hall gave Villa the lead ten minutes after the break, but with just six minutes remaining, Jack Sharp equalised against his former club. The replay took place at Nottingham four days later and goals from Hampton and Garraty sent Villa to the Palace with a 2-1 win.

In the final, Villa attacked right from the start and inside two minutes Hampton planted a left-foot shot into the corner of the net. With 14 minutes to go the centre-forward struck again to clinch a 2-0 win. The consolation for the Magpies came at the end of the month with the League Championship, while Villa finished a respectable fourth.

Villa met Woolwich Arsenal for the first time in October when a record Manor Road crowd saw the Gunners triumph 1-0, but Villa made amends in the return fixture on Boxing Day with a 3-1 win. Small Heath were defeated both home and away in the last season before changing their name to Birmingham.

Cup winners for the fourth time. The triumphant 1905 team. Back row: J Margoschis, J Whitehouse, F Cooper, J Devey, W McGregor, J Ansell (president), Howard Spencer, F Rinder (chairman), Billy George, Freddie Miles, E Strange, W Brown, Dr Jessop, A Wilkes, J Grierson (trainer). Front: H Toney, G Ramsay (secretary), Dr V Jones, Billy Brawn, Billy Garratty, Harry Hampton, Jack Windmill, Joe Pearson, Alex Leake, Joe Bache, Albert Hall, J Lees.

1905/06 - In aid of Howard Spencer

Villa began the defence of the FA Cup at home to King's Lynn from the Norfolk & Suffolk League, Charlie Millington hitting four goals in an 11-0 romp.

A less-than-convincing performance followed in a goalless home draw with Plymouth Argyle, but Garratt, Garraty and Bache struck in the first nine minutes of the replay and Villa went on to win 5-1. The Cup run then ended against Second Division Manchester United at Bank Street. Jock Peddie gave the home side a seventh-minute lead with a shot deflected by a defender and although Hall produced an equaliser, United went on to win 5-1.

In the league, Villa led the table on various occasions during the season, but finished a disappointing eighth. A run of four defeats from the end of December and again from mid-March killed off any title ambitions.

These were changing times as 13 players made their league debuts during the season, including Joe Walters who went on to score 42 goals in 114 league games and James Logan, who played 157 games before returning to Scotland when he signed for Glasgow Rangers in 1912.

Sam Greenhalgh made his league debut in a 3-1 win against Nottingham Forest in February, a game reserved for Howard Spencer's Benefit from which the directors were able to hand over a cheque for just over £711.

1906/07 - Villa News & Record

Villa won the opening season's league fixture for the first time in the 20th century, winning 4-2 against Blackburn Rovers. As welcome as this was, there was a bonus, because supporters now had their own match-day programme. The Villa News & Record was published for the first time, edited by a well-known sports journalist, Edwin W Cox.

The close season had seen an exodus of Villa players to the south with George Johnson moving to Plymouth Argyle along with Garratt and Noon, while Elston and Hisbent went to Portsmouth and Kingaby left for Fulham

There had been no new faces for the Blackburn match, but Chris Buckley, who would later become chairman, made his debut in a 2-0 win at Stoke two days later.

Five of the first six matches were won, including a 4-1 destruction of Birmingham - Villa's first league victory over their close neighbours since the name change - and Villa sat on top of the league once more.

From the start of the season, though, the directors embarked on a policy of experimenting with team selection - the same side did not play more than two consecutive games - and this policy appeared to have a detrimental effect on results.

There was a run of six games without defeat in December, including five wins, and a further run of four successive league victories from the end of January, which took Villa up to third place and gave hope of a title challenge. But results fell away and the team finished fifth.

In the FA Cup, Villa beat Second Division Burnley 3-1, but went out with a poor display at Bolton on a pitch covered by sand. The home side went ahead after three minutes when a slip by Billy George gave Albert Shepherd the easiest of chances and the Trotters went on to win 2-0.

1907/08 - Runners-up spot

The season started without Albert Wilkes, who had departed to Fulham after nine years, and Howard Spencer, who retired. However, Spencer took part in the pre-season practice match and announced that, if at any time the club need his services, he would oblige. The board took him up on his offer and the full-back, who would later become a Villa director, turned out in three league games in November.

The decision was taken to no longer run the third team, due to travelling costs. This was a pity as earlier in the year, Haydn Price had the unique honour of gaining an international cap while playing for Villa's third team, playing for Wales in their victory over Scotland. There were, however, 33 professionals to start the season.

Villa plunged to their biggest opening day defeat to date, losing 4-1 at home to Manchester United. Charlie Wallace, a £500 capture from Crystal Palace who would go on to spend over 50 years with Villa, made his debut, but the side was reduced to ten men after half-an-hour when Chris Buckley suffered a fractured right ankle which would keep him out for the season.

Buckley's misfortune was the first of an ever-growing number of injuries and illnesses to hit players in the first half of the season, with even long-standing goalkeeper Billy George missing ten games through lumbago.

Runners-up spot was achieved thanks to some good performances towards the end of the season - only three of the last 14 games were lost. Joe Bache, who scored all four goals against Nottingham Forest on Christmas Day, hit three hat-tricks during this period and finished with 24 goals in 32 league games.

In the penultimate game, Villa won at Manchester United, but it was too late; United had already taken the title and Villa had to settle for second.

1908/09 - Where are the goals?

The team hit a goal slump in the 1908-09 campaign. Joe Bache consistently hit the target early on, but then the goals dried up and he finished with only eleven, while Harry Hampton's 30 league games brought only nine goals - his lowest total to date.

Villa started at Liverpool and it took James Logan only two minutes to open the scoring. The home side came back to win 3-2, but this was the only defeat in the first eight games.

From that juncture, though, the team were unable to put a decent run together as the directors continued to experiment with team selection.

On Boxing Day, George Travers hit a hat-trick in the first half-hour of his debut, but made only three more appearances, finishing with four goals in as many games.

For only the second time in the history of the club, Villa went out of the FA Cup without scoring a goal, losing 2-0 at Nottingham Forest a week after Forest had triumphed at Villa Park in the league.

Villa and Manchester City were level on points when the teams met at Villa Park on the last Saturday of the season, with both sides in danger of relegation. With time running out, the scores were level at 1-1, with little prospect of a winner from either side, when Joe Walters hooked a shot against the bar. The ball then bounced down and curled over the line - and Villa were safe.

Villa shot up to seventh place two days later by beating champions Newcastle United 3-0 to complete a double over the Magpies and give an indication of better things to come.

1909/10 · Champions again

What brought the transformation from relegation candidates to champions? It could be said that the many team alterations made by the directors in a search for a winning formula paid off. The side were certainly more settled, with only 18 players used.

There was only one new signing, Billy Gerrish being plucked from Southern League Bristol Rovers. The only other player to make his debut was Arthur Moss who stood in for the injured Chris Buckley in a 4-3 win against Blackburn Rovers in January - a victory which took Villa to the top, where they remained for the rest of the campaign.

The season started with a 5-1 home win against Woolwich Arsenal followed by a 2-1 victory at Bolton. Villa then travelled to Plumstead for the return game with Arsenal and found themselves 3-1 down with 13 minutes left when the game was abandoned due to bad light.

They then beat Chelsea 4-1 with a Gerrish hat-trick to go second behind the early leaders Manchester United before losing by the odd goal of five at Blackburn.

A week before Christmas, Villa beat Liverpool 3-1 at home to start a 15-match unbeaten league run, which included a 7-1 thrashing of Manchester United and a 5-0 win against Sheffield Wednesday in March. By the end of the month, with six games to play, Villa had established a seven-point lead over their nearest rivals Liverpool.

With three wins and a draw in the run-in, Villa took the title by five points. Harry Hampton contributed 26 league goals while Joe Bache hit 20 and Charlie Wallace became the first Villa player for eight years to appear in every match.

In the FA Cup, Villa beat Oldham 2-1 away and Derby 6-1 at home before going down 2-1 at home to Manchester City.

What no-one could have predicted is that there would be two World Wars, relegation to a Third Division which was not even in existence at the time, and 71 years would pass before Villa were champions again.

1910/11 · So near yet so far

It was exactly twelve years since the climax to the season had been so exiting. On the last Saturday of the 1898/99 season, Villa had clinched the title with a 5-0 win over Liverpool; now it was Liverpool who would snatch the crown from Villa's grasp.

A week earlier, Villa had put themselves firmly in the driving seat by beating title contenders Manchester United 4-2 to go top at a packed Villa Park, where hundreds of spectators were locked out. Although the margin was only goal average, Villa had two games to play while United, who had led the table for most of the season, had just one match, against high-flying Sunderland.

Two days later at Blackburn, Charlie Wallace missed a penalty and the

Champions for the sixth time. Back row: Tommy Lyons, A Layton, J Logan, Billy George, A Cartridge, Freddie Miles, J Kearns, Joe Grierson (trainer). Middle row: E Strange, P Bate, H Spencer, F Cooper, J Ansell (president), F Rinder (chairman), J Margoschis, Dr H Jessop, H Doe, G Ramsay (secretary). Front: Billy Gerrish, G Hunter, E Eyre, Joe Bache, G Tranter, Chris Buckley, Albert Hall. On ground: Joe Walters, A Moss, Harry Hampton, Charlie Wallace.

game ended goalless, so Villa were just a point clear going into the last game at Anfield.

Ronald Orr gave Liverpool a two-goal advantage, but Joe Walters pulled a goal back before the break and the match was only settled three minutes before the end when John McDonald scored a third goal for the home side.

We can only guess how the players felt when they trooped off to hear that Manchester United had won 5-1 to become champions.

1911/12 · Rebuilding the team

After missing out on the title, it was obvious the directors were determined to seek a winning formula once again, no fewer than 13 players making debuts in a season during which 32 players were used.

Goalkeeper was one position that needed to be addressed, Billy George having taken up the post as player/trainer with Birmingham after making over 400 Villa appearances. Dr Lee Richmond Roose started the season between the posts, but departed for Arsenal after ten games. Brendel Anstey returned, having played nine times the previous season. And when Anstey was injured in March, Albert Lindon turned out at Tottenham before amateur Len Richards played in the last six games.

Those problems paled into insignificance, though, alongside the death on 20 December, at the age of 64, of club legend William McGregor, the man responsible for the formation of the Football League.

Testimonials were in vogue. Villa's home game against Sunderland on 7 October was set aside as a testimonial for George Burrell Ramsay, but Chris Buckley was not happy with the choice of opposition he was given for his testimonial and wanted the Bradford City game. The directors would not agree to his request and on the evening before the game at Manchester United in November a telegram was received at the Villa offices: "Decided not to play tomorrow - Buckley".

At one stage, the player was suspended sine die and although everything seemed to be smoothed over, Buckley did not arrive at the station for Villa's Scottish tour in April.

There were some good performances, resulting in a sixth-place finish. Six goals were scored against both Manchester clubs while Harry Hampton hit four in a 6-1 Boxing Day win against Oldham. Villa did the double over Liverpool, scoring five without reply at Villa Park and five goals were also scored against Bury and Notts County.

In the FA Cup, after a comfortable 6-0 win against Walsall, Villa met Southern League Reading at Villa Park. Hampton gave Villa a first-half lead, but Joe Bailey equalised and Reading won the replay 1-0.

1912/13 · Clem Stephenson's dream

Four expensive signings of real quality were on view for the opening-day victory against Chelsea. Goalkeeper Sam Hardy and Jimmy Harrop arrived from Liverpool, while Andy Ducat signed from Woolwich Arsenal and Harold Halse from Manchester United.

It was not surprising, therefore, that Villa had the league and FA Cup double firmly in their sights, although Sunderland also had the same lofty ambitions. In the end Villa won the FA Cup, beating the Wearsiders in the final, while Sunderland took the league title with Villa as runners-up.

Unfortunately, Ducat suffered a broken leg at Manchester City four games into the season and did not play again until 1915. The Buckley dispute rumbled on despite the fact he had received a benefit cheque for £450. After playing in the first match of the season, Buckley was suspended by the league until 30 April 1914 and never played for Villa again.

Despite these setbacks, there were some tremendous performances. In October, Sheffield Wednesday were beaten 10-0, Hampton netting five. Hampton was injured for the next home match and Halse took his centre-forward position, promptly repeating the feat as he scored all Villa's goals in a 5-1 win against Derby.

Ready for action – Villa's players line up in the goalmouth before the 1913 Cup Final against Sunderland at the Crystal Palace: Charlie Wallace, Joe Bache, Jimmy Leach, Jimmy Harrop, Tommy Lyons, Harold Halse, Harry Hampton, Sam Gardy, Tommy Weston, Clem Stephenson, Tommy Barber.

Oldham Athletic were beaten 7-1 on Boxing Day during a 16-match unbeaten run which saw Villa at the top of the league and through to the semi-finals of the Cup.

The Cup run had started with a 3-1 win at Derby, following which Villa scored five goals without reply against West Ham United, Crystal Palace and Bradford. A week before the semi-final against Oldham, Villa crashed 4-0 at Manchester United, losing their top spot to Sunderland, but they recovered from this shock to reach the Palace, overcoming Oldham Athletic at Blackburn with a Clem Stephenson goal.

Fifteen minutes into the final, a record crowd of 121,919 - some on the roofs of the stands, others watching from trees - saw Charlie Wallace hit his penalty wide after Stephenson had been brought down.

There was no need for Villa to worry; Stephenson had already disclosed to Sunderland's Charlie Buchan that Villa would win with a goal headed by Tommy Barber - he had seen it in a dream the previous night.

There's hardly a Villa player in sight as Tommy Barber's late header wins the 1913 Cup Final.

Even when goalkeeper Sam Hardy had to leave the field for a time in the second half with a knee injury, leaving Jimmy Harrop in goal and Hampton at centre-half, this conviction continued. Sure enough, with eleven minutes to play, Wallace's corner was headed in powerfully by Barber and the Cup was won.

The destination of the league title still had to be decided and when the teams met again at Villa Park the following Wednesday it was estimated that there were 30,000 people outside when the gates were locked 45 minutes before kick-off. Anstey played in goal as Hardy had not recovered and Villa lost Tommy Lyons for part of the second half. The game ended 1-1 and despite winning the two remaining matches, Villa had to settle for runners-up spot.

1913/14 · Big plans for Villa Park

The directors gave approval at the 1913 AGM to a scheme submitted by chairman Frederick Rinder to extend and improve Villa Park. Rinder's ambition was to build a ground that would comfortably hold 104,000 spectators. Unfortunately, events in Europe the following year would prevent this ambitious plan coming to fruition.

Harold Halse departed for Chelsea after just one season having scored 28 goals in his 36 appearances. Harry Hampton was suspended for the first month of the season along with Sunderland's Charlie Thomson following events at the FA Cup final. The match referee was also suspended for not maintaining order.

Unlike the previous year there were no new faces in the team and although it was a good season - Villa again finished runners-up in the league and reached the Cup semi-final - it fell short of expectations.

By the end of October, only two games had been won and the title appeared to be out of reach following a three-goal defeat by Sheffield United on New Year's Day, which left the club in eleventh place, ten points behind the leaders, Blackburn.

But that was followed by a 14-match unbeaten run which took the team up to second place and through to semi-finals. When Villa met Liverpool at White Hart Lane, hopes were raised that the double was again a possibility. It was not to be. A Jimmy Nicholl brace put Villa out of the Cup and this was followed by three straight league defeats.

The league double was then completed over Liverpool with Bache scoring the only goal of the game at Anfield, followed by victories against Derby and Tottenham. But the season then ended with a 3-1 home defeat to Middlesbrough which gave Boro third place.

1914/15 · The Great War

The season opened with the nation at war. Villa's directors debated whether to carry on playing football, but agreed with the general feeling that 'it is in the best interests of the community that the game should proceed'.

Unsurprisingly, given the uncertain times, there were no significant new signings, the decision having been taken to rely on home-grown players rather than pay transfer fees.

A crowd of only 8,000 turned up at Villa Park to see a 2-1 win against newly-promoted Notts County. Defeats then followed at home to Sunderland and away at Sheffield Wednesday.

The Great War continued to cast a grave shadow over everything, the decision to continue playing was continually challenged and interest waned. The Under Secretary of War indicated that professional footballers should find employment in His Majesty's Forces and the Villa News & Record regularly carried reports on what players were doing for their country.

Recruitment drives were made at each game and adverts advised that all recruits were entitled to draw three shillings (15p) per day after enlisting, as well as being allowed to return home until called by their unit. The directors, meanwhile, arranged for military training on a regular basis for all players and made such facilities available at the ground. Each man was provided with a service rifle and additional miniature rifles were provided for shooting practice at the club's rifle range.

Results on the pitch were mixed, and the team finished 14th. On Boxing Day, Villa suffered their highest home league defeat so far, losing 7-1 to Bolton Wanderers. Down to ten men after less than five minutes when John McLachlan was carried off while making his first appearance of the season, Villa were further hampered by injuries to Ducat and Leach.

Clem Stephenson gave the home side the lead, but the Trotters stormed back, with Joe Smith in devastating form as he hit four goals.

The best displays came against Liverpool when six goals were scored both home and away. Villa won 6-3 at Anfield in November with six different scorers while debut boy Harry Nash and Harry Hampton each hit a hat-trick in the return match.

At the end of the season, the Football League and the FA Cup competitions ended for the remainder of the war.

1919/20 · Six of the best

It had been four years since their last league match, but Villa had only two new players on view in the opening day defeat at Sunderland - Ernie Blackburn and Dickie York. Hubert Bourne, a close-season signing from Manchester United, made his debut against Derby County two days later and scored in a 2-2 draw.

Fixtures were arranged so that teams faced each other home and away on alternate weekends - and occasionally back-to-back - and Villa found it difficult to get used to the new system. Only one point was gained from the first seven games and the team slid to the foot of the table.

The first Saturday in October brought the first win, Clem Stephenson scoring the only goal against Bradford Park Avenue, a week after a 6-1 away defeat by the same opposition.

The need to strengthen the side was well recognised and a great deal of transfer activity ensued. Three players were bought at the auction of the defunct Leeds City team - Billy Kirton (who went on to play 261 games) John Hampson and George Stephenson. It would be two years before Stephenson made a first-team appearance, but a total of 21 players made debuts during the season.

The player who had the most immediate impact was centre-half Frank Barson, at £2,850 a record signing from Barnsley.

Barson added strength to the defence and his overall dominating personality provided a tremendous confidence boost to the whole team. Barson made his debut in a 4-1 win at Middlesbrough and by the time Villa beat Chelsea 5-2 on Christmas morning they had pulled up to seventh place. But the new year brought only limited success.

Harry Hampton played only seven games and failed to add to his record as Villa's top goalscorer before departing for Birmingham. Amazingly, at the time of the centre-forward's departure, the crowd already had a new goalscoring hero. Billy Walker had made his debut.

It was in the FA Cup that Villa excelled. After winning 2-1 at home to QPR, with a brace from Walker, Villa found themselves a goal down at the break against Manchester United. Eleven minutes after the re-start Clem Stephenson equalised and with just nine minutes remaining, Walker hit the winner.

There was an unprecedented demand for tickets for the home third round tie against Sunderland and with the ground still not complete after alterations started before the War, there were concerns that the reduced capacity of 60,000 was not sufficient. The decision was taken to double the minimum admission price - not as a means of cashing in, the club was anxious to stress, but as a way of keeping down the crowd 'in the interests of the game and the public themselves'.

The ploy was successful - the attendance was the lowest of Villa's six Cup games, Clem Stephenson scoring the only goal after 36 minutes.

The fourth-round tie at Tottenham was settled after six minutes when Billy Kirton's centre was turned into his own net by Tommy Clay and then it was on to Bramall Lane to meet Chelsea in the semi-final. Villa triumphed 3-1 with a Billy Walker brace and a goal from Harold Edgley. But tragedy struck five days later when the teams met at Stamford Bridge in the league, Edgley suffering a broken leg which ended his Villa career.

The Cup Final against Huddersfield Town remained goalless after 90 minutes, the deciding goal coming seven minutes into extra-time when Kirton headed in from a corner to give Villa a record six FA Cup wins.

It's ours again! Villa proudly parade the FA Cup after their sixth triumph in the competition. Back row: R Leeson, William Boyman, A Young, Tommy Ball, J Lee, W Parkes, Howard Humphries, Jack Thompson, Jimmy Leach. Third row: H Cooch, W Smith, Hubert Bourne, Dicky York, John Hampson, Arthur Davies, Jack Pendleton, Dave Reid, Ernie Blackburn, Clive Wigmore, Arthur Dorrell. Second row: G Ramsay (secretary), Dr H Jessop, H Doe, J Devey, P Bate, F Rinder (chairman), J Ansell (president), H Spencer, J Jones, Dr V Jones, Freddie Miles (trainer), F Cooper, E Strange. Front: Sam Hardy, Charlie Wallace, Jimmy Stephenson, Frank Moss, Billy Walker, Andy Ducat, Tommy Smart, Billy Kirton, Clem Stephenson, Jimmy Harrop, Tommy Weston, Frank Barson. On ground: Harry Nash, W Toone, George Hadley, Jimmy Lawrence.

1920/21 · No place like Brum

Huge transfer fees were being paid by clubs in 1920 in an explosion of activity. But the Villa directors decided they had a squad capable of winning both league and cup so there were no new additions to start the season. It looked as though they might be right when Villa hit five goals without reply in the opening game against Arsenal at Villa Park and Walker showed he was already chasing Hampton's record by netting four.

After winning four out of the first five games, the team were top of the table, but a major problem arose when the board decided that all players must live within easy access to the ground. This was resisted by several senior players who lived and had business interests elsewhere.

Barson, who lived in Sheffield, and Clem Stephenson, in Newcastle-upon-Tyne, were selected to play at Bolton the following Wednesday, but failed to turn up, while Hardy, Ducat and Wallace produced medical certificates for their absence. The team lost 5-0 and Barson and Stephenson were suspended for two weeks and given a month in which to arrange a move to Birmingham.

The problem did not go away; they were not the only players who did not fancy a house move to Brum and four of the five were no longer with the club by the start of the following campaign. Barson, meanwhile, remained for just one more season before refusing to re-sign.

In mid-October, Sam Hardy was carried off at Preston and Villa crashed 6-1. It would be New Year's Day before the goalkeeper would return, by which time Villa were down to seventh place.

The team suffered a series of injury problems. In January, Villa played most of the match against Everton with only nine players as both Hampson and Tommy Weston were forced to leave the field. Leading 1-0 at half-time, Villa lost 3-1, two of the Toffees' goals coming in the last five minutes.

The injury crisis continued right to the end of the season; Walker was carried off with a broken collarbone against Derby in the final away match and Frank Moss was off the field for the greater part of the second half the following week against the same opposition. It was reported in the Birmingham Mail that Moss had sustained a wound to his knee joint while on active service and either a piece of shrapnel or a bullet was lodged in it.

By early April, the team were down to 15th in the table, although they finished a respectable tenth by winning the final five games.

In the FA Cup, Tottenham gained revenge for the previous year's defeat winning 1-0 at White Hart Lane in round four.

It was revealed that the proposed improvements to Villa Park would have to be scaled back due to escalating costs following the Great War. Frederick Rinder's grand plan for the stadium never reached fruition.

1921/22 · Thanks for the memories

There were some familiar faces missing when the players assembled for the 1921-22 campaign. Earlier in the year, Clem Stephenson and James Harrop had departed for Huddersfield Town and Sheffield United respectively as a result of the decision on players being required to reside in Birmingham, and now the captain, Andy Ducat, who wanted to live in London, had joined Fulham.

Sam Hardy announced his retirement from first class football (although he went on to play over 100 games for Nottingham Forest), Charlie Wallace joined Oldham after 14 years with the club and Jimmy Lee was transferred to Stoke. Other departures included Jack Thompson to Brighton, Jimmy Stephenson to Sunderland, John Hampson to Port Vale. Harold Edgley, who never fully recovered from his horrific injury against Chelsea, joined QPR.

Following criticism that Villa were not entering the transfer market to replace the departed big-name players, Rinder explained that the club would not pay big sums for transfers and were pursuing a policy of rearing their own players.

In the circumstances, a fifth-place finish was commendable. The system of playing home and away games against the same opposition in successive weeks continued with results often being reversed. Notably, a 5-0 defeat at Middlesbrough was followed by a 6-2 win the following week. After losing 3-2 at Bradford City on Bonfire Night, Villa won 7-1 a week later. They did, however, record a couple of doubles in December, against Newcastle and Sheffield United.

The team appeared to be heading for a good run in the FA Cup. Walker hit a hat-trick in a 6-1 win against Derby County in round one and scored the only goal against Luton Town in the second round.

After a goalless draw at Stoke, it was the turn of Ian Dickson to hit three in the replay, Walker again being on target in a 4-0 win in front of 53,385 supporters on a Wednesday afternoon.

Villa then visited Notts County in round four and led twice, but the home side hit back with equalisers, the second coming a minute before the end. The replay stood at 3-3 at the end of 90 minutes, but Jack Cock put Villa out with a goal extra-time.

1922/23 · An amateur replacement

There were no major signings to start a season which opened with Frank Barson appointed captain in succession to Andy Ducat, who was still in dispute with the club. Barson refused to re-sign and stayed home in Sheffield. Although the centre-half had clashed with the Villa hierarchy on several occasions, his value to the side was readily acknowledged, and the club were reluctant to let him go.

When Manchester United made enquiries, a price of £6,000 was placed on his head. This was negotiated down to £5,000 and Barson left for Old Trafford with United's agreement that he could continue to live in Sheffield.

Villa looked to an unusual source for a replacement. An amateur, W E Barnie-Adshead, captain of the Birmingham University team, was asked to play against Blackburn and Cardiff. The move was not a success and Villa lost both games, although Barnie-Adshead did score. Tommy Ball then came in and held the centre-half position until his death the following year.

THE HISTORY OF ASTON VILLA

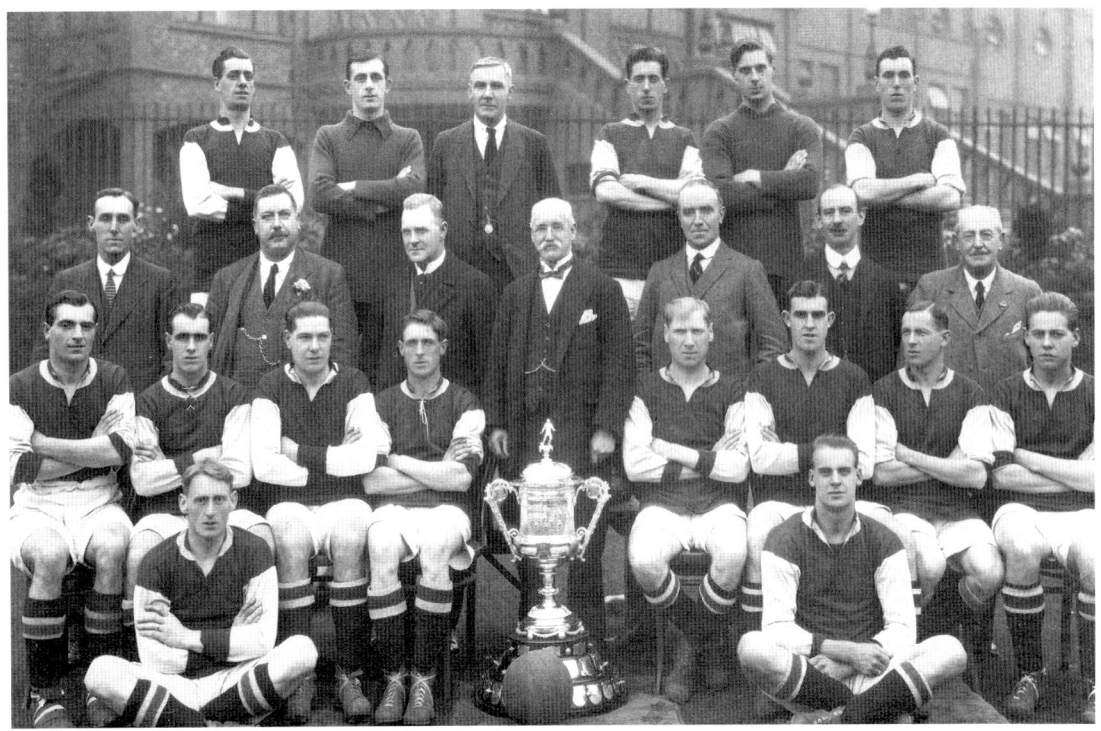

Villa 1922/23. Back row: Percy Jones, Tommy Jackson, H Cooch, Jock Johnstone, Cyril Spiers, Tommy Smart. Second row: Freddie Miles (trainer), Capt B Bate, J Jones, F Rinder (chairman), H Spencer, E Strange, G Ramsay (secretary). Front: Dicky York, Billy Kirton, I Dickinson, Len Capewell, Frank Moss, Tommy Ball, Arthur Dorrell, George Blackburn. On ground: Tommy Mort, Billy Walker.

At the end of September, only Stoke kept Villa off the bottom of the table, but the team recovered with five wins in six games, including a double over Spurs. Progress was then steady rather than spectacular, York scored the first hat-trick of the season on Boxing Day and Walker was still finding the net regularly, finishing with 23 goals.

John Roxburgh came into the side at Manchester City in February and scored twice on his home debut the following week as Villa hit six against Stoke. A Walker hat-trick helped Villa to an exciting 5-3 win at Huddersfield in March, which put the team in fourth place and the next home games produced wins against Birmingham and Chelsea. But it was too late for a serious title challenge and the team eventually finished sixth.

In the first round of the Cup, Villa were reduced to ten men at home to Blackburn Rovers when George Blackburn was carried off early in the game with concussion. A Dickie Bond penalty put the visitors through.

1923/24 · Murder and Wembley

Villa started with a 3-0 defeat at Birmingham and tragic though this may have seemed at the time, it was nothing compared to the real-life tragedy which followed two-and-a-half months later.

After playing a major part in Villa's victory at Notts County, centre-half Tommy Ball was shot dead the following day, killed by his landlord and neighbour, George Stagg on the night of 11th November.

The shooting and subsequent trial obviously overshadowed the whole season. Stagg was sentenced to death, but this was subsequently commuted to penal servitude for life. Not surprisingly, the remainder of the league season was largely unspectacular with Villa again finishing sixth in the league.

It was a different story in the FA Cup. The campaign began in ankle deep mud at Portland Park, Ashington where the teams had to endure snow followed by torrential rain before Villa came away with a 5-1 win.

A 2-0 victory at Swansea Town was followed by a comfortable 3-0 home win against Leeds United before Albion were then beaten by two clear goals at The Hawthorns. Villa were through to meet Burnley in the semi-final.

A record attendance of 54,531 was set at Bramall Lane, Sheffield, and despite an injury suffered by Kirton who opened the scoring, the team went on to reach Wembley for the first time, winning 3-0 with York adding two more goals in the second half.

In the final - the club's first visit to the new Wembley Stadium - Newcastle United pressed from the outset, but Villa then came into the match, with a barrage of shots on the opposition goal before the break. At one stage, Walker was knocked out following a collision with a goalpost while making a desperate attempt to score.

The match remained goalless until five minutes from time when Neil Harris followed up a shot from Billy Cowan to put Newcastle in front. Stan Seymour added a second goal shortly afterwards.

Villa 1924/25. Back row: George Blackburn, Freddie Miles (trainer), Tommy Smart, Frank Moss, Tommy Jackson, Vic Milne, Jock Johnstone, George Ramsay (secretary), George Stephenson. Front: Dicky York, Billy Kirton, Len Capewell, Billy Walker, Arthur Dorrell, Tommy Mort.

1924/25 · Victories in the dark

A 4-2 opening-day win against Liverpool at Anfield may have raised hopes, but the season was not a success. Villa finished 15th, their lowest position for 24 years.

Many players suffered from loss of form and with the directors retaining their policy of refusing to finance big-money transfers, the team came under increasing criticism from supporters. Centre-forward became a particular problem with Len Capewell, scorer of 26 the previous campaign, finding goals hard to come by in addition to suffering injury problems. Percy Varco, Albert Surtees, 'Ginger' Phoenix, Walter Harris and Billy Dinsdale were all given the job of leading the attack as the squad was shuffled.

The heaviest defeat of the season came on Christmas Day, a 6-0 thumping at Leeds, but a Phoenix brace on Boxing Day gave Villa a 2-1 revenge win. There was, however, only one more league victory before April - Len Capewell scored the only goal against Birmingham - by which time the team were down to 19th.

A Wednesday night home game against Arsenal on 1st April ended in semi-darkness, but with a welcome 4-0 win. But it was back to earth at Villa Park the following Saturday when Sunderland triumphed 4-1. After the win in the dark against the Gunners, perhaps Villa thought they had found a new formula for success when they decided an evening kick-off for the Good Friday fixture, rather than a traditional daytime start. If so, it worked. Villa scored a 2-1 win over Manchester City, although the players had to forego their half-time break so the match could finish.

In the FA Cup, Villa were 1-0 down at half-time against Port Vale in the first round before coming back to win 7-2 with a Walker hat-trick and four goals from Capewell. Swansea were beaten 3-1 at Vetch Field to set up a third-round meeting with Albion.

There were over 64,000 packed into The Hawthorns when Joe Carter gave the home team the lead, but Villa came back in the second half and Walker charged goalkeeper George Ashmore, and the ball, over the line for the equaliser. Phoenix gave Villa the lead in the replay four days later, but two second half goals saw Albion through.

1925/26 · A flying start

The season was most notable for Villa's 10-0 opening-day win against Burnley. Len Capewell announced he was back with a bang as he became only the third Villa player to score five in a single game. It was a tasty appetiser to a prolific campaign for the striker.

In September, Capewell began a run of scoring in eight consecutive league games and finished the season with 34 league and cup goals. Walker hit the net 22 times while York netted 20. Villa also equalled their second-best league tally to date with 86 goals, although they conceded 76 - more than ever before.

At the end of September came the sad news of the death of Tommy Barber, scorer of Villa's 'dream goal' in the 1913 FA Cup final. Barber served in the Footballers' Battalion during the Great War, a traumatic experience from which he never recovered.

On the playing side, it was very much a case of 'as you were'. Only two new players were introduced all season. Outside-left Reg Chester came

Villa 1925/26. Back row: Tommy Smart, E Strange, Jock Johnstone, Alec Talbot, Cyril Spiers, Frank Moss, Tommy Jones, George Blackburn, H Cooch, Teddy Bowen. Front: Dicky York, George Stephenson, Billy Kirton, Billy Walker, Len Capewell, Arthur Dorrell, Tommy Mort. On ground: Cecil Harris, Joe Corbett, Tommy Muldoon.

in for the Manchester United home game in September and went on to make three appearances, scoring once, while Fred Norris played in the final six matches, scoring twice on his home debut.

In October, Villa led 3-0 at home to Birmingham with only ten minutes remaining. Most of the visiting supporters had departed when Villa goalkeeper Cyril Spiers sparked a Blues revival by throwing the ball into his own net. Joe Bradford then scored twice and the game ended 3-3.

Despite the previous year's success, Villa reverted to an afternoon kick-off for the Good Friday match against Arsenal, but they achieved the same outcome, winning 3-0.

In the FA Cup, Villa met Albion at The Hawthorns for the third successive season. In an exciting finish - the goals all came in the last six minutes - Walker put the visitors in front and Joe Carter equalised before Billy Kirton grabbed a last-minute winner and a fifth-round place at home to Arsenal.

The tie against the Gunners ended 1-1. In the replay the following Wednesday afternoon Arsenal scored twice in the first 14 minutes to end Villa's run.

1926/27 - A record signing

Once again there were no new big signings to start the season as Villa stuck to their transfer policy. The only player to make his debut in the opening fixture at Newcastle was centre-forward Joe Nicholson who had arrived from Cardiff in an exchange deal involving George Blackburn. Cardiff had the better deal; while Blackburn went on to make 115 league appearances for the Bluebirds, Villa crashed 4-0 at Newcastle and Nicholson did not play for the club again.

A 5-1 defeat at Leicester on the last Saturday of November (Arthur Chandler scored all the Foxes goals) left the team in 20th place, but Len Capewell then netted a hat-trick against Everton as Villa hit back from 3-1 down at half-time to win 5-3 and start a run of four consecutive wins.

By the end of January, Villa were still in the bottom half of the table and out of the FA Cup after losing 2-1 to Cardiff. The only consolation in this defeat was that the Welshmen went on to win the trophy, taking the FA Cup out of England for the only time.

Capewell scored the only goal of the game against Bury at Gigg Lane on the first Saturday in February to start a run of seven wins through to the end of March. The sequence was only interrupted by a 6-2 defeat at Albion, a setback tempered by a 4-2 victory over Birmingham the following week. Unfortunately, the last seven games brought only one win and a tenth-place finish.

The policy on transfers had to change, and in February striker Billy Cook was signed from Huddersfield Town. Then in April, in a complete reversal of policy, the club paid a record £7,500 for Scottish international Jimmy Gibson from Partick Thistle. The Scot made his debut in the last game of the season, a goalless draw at Huddersfield and went on to make 227 appearances before retiring in 1936.

1927/28 · Pongo's arrival

The main talk around Villa Park prior to start of the season was whether a white ball should replace the traditional brown, and if shirts should be numbered. The season opened without either innovation being adopted.

On the playing side, Jimmy Gibson made his home debut in the opening game against Leicester City, but it was not a happy one as the team went down 3-0. Villa then became the first visitors to Fratton Park for a top-flight league game following Pompey's promotion, suffering a 3-1 defeat.

After these setbacks, centre-forward Joe Beresford, who had signed from Mansfield Town in May, made his debut in a goalless draw at Liverpool, but then scored a hat-trick in a 7-2 demolition of Portsmouth on his first home appearance two days later.

Nine players were brought into the first-team during the season as the directors searched for a winning combination. Joe Tate would go on to make 193 appearances over the next six years, although his debut ended in a 5-0 defeat at Derby on Boxing Day.

Five goalkeepers were used. Joe Hickman made his debut in a 5-4 home win over Sheffield Wednesday on Christmas Eve and was also between the posts for the 5-0 defeat by the Rams two days later. After conceding nine goals in two games, he did not have another first-team opportunity.

The transfer which really captured supporters' imagination came in February when club secretary Billy Smith was despatched to Birkenhead to sign Tranmere Rovers' centre-forward Tom 'Pongo' Waring 'for the most reasonable fee he could'.

Smith duly obliged, although the £4,700 fee was a record for a Third Division player and £200 more than Liverpool had offered. Waring's Villa debut came in a 6-2 reserve-team victory over Birmingham, in which he netted a first-half hat-trick in front of a crowd of 23,600. While the striker was making his debut for the reserves, Villa went out of the FA Cup in the fifth round at Arsenal after earlier wins at Burnley and at home to Crewe.

Waring then scored on his first-team debut, a 3-2 win against Sunderland at Roker Park seven days later, before scoring again in a 7-2 friendly win over Scottish club Airdrie and netting twice in the next league game, an incredible encounter at Newcastle United. Villa eventually lost 7-5 as the teams endured a fierce snowstorm at the start of the second half. Jimmy Gibson finished the game in goal after Ben Olney was injured.

Nearly, but not quite. The 1928/29 squad, who finished third in the table and reached the FA Cup semi-finals. Back row: Billy Kingdon, Teddy Bowen, Vic Milne, Ben Olney, Alec Talbot, Tommy Smart, Frank Moss. Middle: H Bourne, W Malins, J Jones (chairman), J Devey, H Spencer, S Smith (secretary). Front: Dicky York, Jimmy Gibson, Tommy Mort, Arthur Dorrell, Billy Walker, Tom "Pongo" Waring, Reg Chester. On ground: Fred Tully, Billy Cook, Len Capewell, Joe Beresford.

1928/29 · Third place and a semi-final

The season would set the pattern for the following six years; Villa would come close to a trophy, but would end up with nothing. Although they were the top-flight's highest scorers with 98 goals, and won more games than any team in the division, Villa had to settle for third place. Ironically, champions Sheffield Wednesday had only avoided relegation by beating Villa in the last match of the previous season.

The league campaign took a while to get going, with only one victory in the first six games. Then came three wins, culminating with a 7-1 victory over Bury, but it was followed by a remarkable home game with Bolton Wanderers which illustrated frailties in defence. Villa, two-down inside 12 minutes, fought back with a brace from Walker and a goal from Arthur Dorrell to lead 3-2 at the interval. This advantage was retained until the 70th minute when the Trotters scored three times in four minutes to win 5-3.

Villa bounced back the following week against Birmingham at St Andrews. Although Waring scored after three minutes, Villa found themselves 2-1 down at the break. But a second-half brace from Walker in between a strike from Joe Beresford secured a 4-2 win. Remarkably, only one player made his debut that season, Norman Swales deputising for Joe Tate in seven league and cup games.

In the FA Cup, Villa gained revenge for their 1927 defeat with a 6-1 win against Cardiff. Clapton Orient then came to Villa Park in round four and their goalkeeper Arthur Wood was invincible in a goalless draw before Villa hit eight without reply in the replay, including a Waring hat-trick.

Reading were beaten in round five before Villa made up for the previous year's defeat by knocking out Arsenal at Villa Park with an 87th-minute goal from Waring.

The semi-final against Portsmouth was preceded by three straight league defeats and Villa's luck was out at Highbury. When a penalty was awarded against Teddy Bowen for handling, Ben Olney could only push Jack Smith's spot kick onto the bar and over the line. Another Cup run was over.

1929/30 · All-out attack

It was almost a case of 'as you were". In a similar league campaign to the previous season, Villa finished fourth, scoring 92 goals and conceding 83.

The big game of the season was a fourth-round FA Cup tie against Walsall in the FA Cup. When Walsall's name came out first in the draw, the Third Division South team asked the FA for the game to be switched to Villa Park. This request was agreed and a then record 74,600 people watched the match with many more locked out.

Walker headed home inside four minutes and doubled this 20 minutes later, heading in a York corner, but Villa were pulled back just before the break by winger Joe Johnson, playing his only game for the Saddlers. The result was then in doubt until the last few minutes when George Brown settled the issue to clinch a 3-1 win.

Tom 'Pongo' Waring

There was an additional bonus from this Cup tie. Walsall goalkeeper Fred Biddlestone impressed Villa so much that the following Saturday he was signed, remaining at Villa Park until 1939.

There were 70,000 at Villa Park to see the side progress to round six by beating Blackburn Rovers 4-1 and the draw gave Villa a home match with Huddersfield. Walker played despite suffering from an illness which would keep him out of action until the end of April. With the scores level after an hour, Ben Olney dropped the ball at the feet of Alex Jackson to present the Huddersfield player the easy task of tapping the ball into the net for the winner. Waring missed a large part of the season and did not play in the Cup run.

Villa had a new striker playing alongside the ex-Tranmere man in the opening day 2-1 league win against Birmingham. George Brown, a close season signing from Huddersfield, finished the season with a goal haul of 36. He scored a hat-trick in a 5-2 win against Arsenal in September and repeated the feat when Everton were beaten by the same score the following month. But Billy Walker went one better, notching four goals in a 5-1 win over Sheffield United in December.

On the first Saturday in January, Eric Houghton made his debut in a 4-3 home defeat at the hands of Leeds United. Villa were two-down when Billy Walker was fouled in the area and entrusted the 19-year-old with the spot-kick. Houghton was distraught when his penalty was saved by Jimmy Potts, but Walker told him not to worry, insisting he would not miss his next one. Houghton always remembered his captain's advice and went on to become Villa's all-time penalty king.

In March, Jack Mandley was signed from Port Vale and he scored on his debut in a 5-3 win against Huddersfield.

1930/31 · Goals, goals, goals!

Villa scored 128 goals - still a top-flight record - but had to settle for runners-up spot behind Arsenal, who also knocked them out of the FA Cup.

Even so, the goal statistics for the season are amazing; Villa scored in every home game - a total of 86 league goals at Villa Park - and failed to score in only three away matches. They also netted four or more goals in 20 league games.

Pongo Waring set the pace with four in a 4-3 win at Manchester United on the opening day and then repeated the feat the following Saturday at Villa Park in a 6-1 win against West Ham.

Waring scored in each of the first seven games, by which time he had netted 13 times, and he went on to score a club record 49 goals in 39 league games. A strike against Arsenal in his only FA Cup match brought the centre-forward's tally to 50, while winger Eric Houghton contributed 30.

During a seven-game winning run from the end of January, cumulating in a 5-1 romp against Arsenal in mid-March, a total of 33 goals were scored. Twelve of them were contributed by Waring, including another four-goal salvo in a 4-2 win against Sunderland.

Despite the fine win over the Gunners, though, Villa were unable to catch Arsenal and had to settle for second place.

In November 1930, lance-corporal Harry Morton was in goal for the Army team in the annual fixture which Villa won 7-0. Such was Morton's performance that Villa bought him out of the Army and signed him as a professional. He went on to play over 200 first-team games.

1931/32 · Another century of goals

After a record goal haul, there were high hopes that Villa would go one place higher and take the title. Although 104 goals were scored, however, the title eluded them.

Villa occupied third place in January behind newly-promoted Everton and West Bromwich Albion and while Everton went on to take the crown, Villa and Albion fell away, finishing fifth and sixth respectively. Ironically, Villa's previous season's points haul would have taken the title by three clear points.

Reg Miles had moved to Millwall with Fred Biddlestone taking over in goal. Although Dai Astley had been signed from Charlton, his opportunity would come later in the season and there were no new signings in the side for the first game at home to Leicester, which Villa won 3-2.

The goal machine! The 1930/31 squad scored a top-flight record of 128 goals. Back row: Teddy Bowen, H Cooch, Alec Talbot, Fred Biddlestone, Tommy Smart, Jimmy Gibson, Billy Walker, Joe Tate, Dicky York. Front: Jack Mandley, Tommy Mort, Arthur Dorrell, Pongo Waring, Reg Chester, George Brown, Eric Houghton. On ground: Billy Kingdon, Joe Beresford.

After a draw at Huddersfield and defeat at Liverpool, Villa hit a rich vein of form, beating Grimsby 7-0, Chelsea 6-3 and West Ham 5-2. Pongo Waring hit four in each of the games against the London clubs.

Although the side scored a lot of goals, they were unable to put together a decent run. In November, Villa beat Blackpool 5-1, Waring scoring another hat-trick, but then went down 3-0 to Albion. The following month, there was a 5-4 defeat at Sheffield United and a 5-1 home defeat by Blackburn before Villa recovered with a 7-1 Christmas Day win against Middlesbrough.

George Brown stood in for Waring on the first Saturday in January and amazingly hit five goals in an 8-3 win at Leicester - the only Villa player to achieve the feat in an away fixture. Brown followed up with four more in the next league game as Villa crushed Liverpool 6-1 and between times, he netted the winner at The Hawthorns to put holders Albion out of the FA Cup. Villa lost to Portsmouth in the following round.

1932/33 · Out-gunned once more

Everyone who bought the Aston Villa Annual was given the opportunity of winning a £10 note by predicting where the team would stand in the league table on 31st December. It should not have been too difficult - they were second, which was where they finished the season, again as runners-up to Arsenal.

Pongo Waring did not play until January, when he came back with a brace in a 5-2 win against Liverpool, but he made only four more league appearances and played just one FA Cup match. He was suspended by the FA for 28 days from 22 February for ungentlemanly conduct following an incident in a 3-0 defeat at Leicester and did not appear again all season.

George Brown led the attack, scoring 35 goals in 40 league and cup matches, including four against Bolton at the beginning of September and another quartet at Blackburn in the final away game.

Early in the season, it looked as though it would be Villa's year. A 3-1 win against Chelsea on the first Saturday in October consolidated their position at the top, and they were the only unbeaten team in the division. It was not until the twelfth game of the season, away at Albion, that the run was ended.

Villa immediately bounced back with a 6-2 win against Blackpool, while a magnificent 5-3 win against Arsenal in the next home game left them on top once more. Years later, former Villa secretary Fred Archer recalled this match as one of the most exciting he had ever seen at Villa Park.

No-one could have predicted after such an epic encounter that it would be many years before Villa would again hold that lofty position. The following week, defeat by Manchester City left the team in second place and the top spot continued to elude them.

Christmas followed the usual pattern. The home game against Wolves on Boxing Day ended in defeat, but the following day Villa won 4-2 at Molineux, where full-back Joe Nibloe made his debut.

After a 2-2 draw at Bradford City in the third round of the Cup, Villa won the replay 2-1, Ernie 'Mush' Callaghan making his first senior appearance. Callaghan went on to play for the club until 1947 and when he retired, he remained on the ground-staff for many years.

Danny Blair tackles Arsenal's Jack Lambert at Highbury, 1 April 1933.

Unfortunately, the side then crashed out of the Cup, losing 3-0 at home to Sunderland.

Villa travelled to Highbury on April Fools Day, three points behind their rivals, but with two games in hand. But Arsenal gained revenge for their defeat earlier in the season with a 5-0 win to effectively kill off Villa's title challenge.

The final away game against Blackburn was won 5-0, Brown's four goals coming in the space of seven minutes. The club then caused something of a sensation in the football world by signing Arthur Cunliffe and Ronnie Dix from Rovers for a fee described as 'considerable'. Both players made their first appearance in the final game, Cunliffe scoring as Villa signed off with a 2-0 win against Derby County.

1933/34 · Taking to the skies

The club decided that this was their Diamond Jubilee season and after coming close in the past five years were looking to celebrate with some silverware. It was also when Villa decided they needed to move with the times and for supporters to take to the skies. Early in 1934, the club invited applications for the post of team manager, while air travel was arranged to take shareholders to away games.

On the pitch, Waring was back, but there was disappointment at Villa Park when the season opened with a defeat by a Leicester side who had only just avoided relegation the previous season.

The poor form continued, and Villa's 13th-place finish was their second lowest since football had resumed after the Great War. Although the team were still scoring plenty of goals (their total of 78 was three more than champions Arsenal), defensive frailties continued, with 75 goals conceded.

Strangely enough, reports often blamed the forwards for not scoring enough! It seemed that the attitude was to go for goal and simply attempt to score more than the opposition. The cavalier approach resulted in exciting football, but results were unpredictable. For example, a crowd approaching 60,000 saw Villa beat Wolves 6-2 at Villa Park on Christmas Day, but the following day the team suffered a 4-3 reversal in the Molineux fog.

There was only one new face introduced into the side all season, half-back Tommy Gardner arriving from Hull City in February.

If the league title was out the question, the FA Cup gave supporters hope of a trophy. Villa beat Chesterfield after a draw at Saltergate, and then recorded a fine 7-2 victory over Sunderland with four goals from Astley and three strikes from Houghton.

It was then off to Tottenham where an Astley goal on the hour mark was enough send Villa back to North London for a quarter-final against their old rivals, Arsenal. Astley was on target again at Highbury and Houghton doubled the lead before Peter Dougal scored a consolation goal for the Gunners. But the cup run came to an embarrassing end in the semi-final at Huddersfield. Manchester City went ahead in the fourth minute and had scored six times before Astley kept up his personal record of scoring in every round.

The only consolation was the report that many applications had been received for the post of team manager from men whose names were well known in the game. On Friday 29 June 1934 at the 59th annual meeting, James McMullan was introduced as Villa's first manager.

1934/35 · New boss, same old problems

It was obvious that the defence needed to be strengthened and along with a manager, Jimmy McMullan, two new players were unveiled at St Andrews on the opening day of the season - full-back George Beeson from Sheffield Wednesday and defender Jimmy Allen, a £10,775 club record signing from Portsmouth.

A 2-1 defeat by Birmingham was not a good start, but the manager had to wait only a further two days for his first win, a 2-1 victory over Wolves. There was an air of optimism that the appointment would transform Villa's fortunes, but the early signs were not good. The return game against Wolves was lost 5-2 and five goals were again conceded

A new era. The 1934/35 squad photo included the club's first team-manager Jimmy McMullan. Back row: H Cooch, Tommy Gardner, Jimmy Allen, Dai Astley, Harry Morton, Alec Talbot, Jimmy Gibson, Danny Blair. Front: George Brown, Tommy Mort, Pongo Waring, J McMullan (manager), Ronnie Dix, Tommy Wood, George Beeson.

the following Saturday against Leicester, this time without reply.

In September, former captain John Devey, who first played for the club in 1891 and had been a director for 33 years, resigned his position on the board for health reasons and was replaced by another old boy, Albert Wilkes.

McMullen went back to his old club Manchester City in December, and signed James McLuckie. Unfortunately, after making his first appearance at Middlesbrough, injury forced McLuckie to miss the remainder of the season.

Villa referred the matter to the Football League Management Committee as they were not satisfied that the player's full medical condition had been disclosed at the time of transfer, but the commission ruled that nothing had been withheld by City and the appeal was not upheld.

Left-back Fred Butcher came into the side for two games at the end of September, but suffered a fractured leg in January while playing at Derby in the Mid-Week League and never made another first-team appearance. Villa players did not have much luck in the Mid-Week League, Freddie Haycock suffering a broken fibula in his left leg in a match at Burton.

The team finished 13th, the same position as the previous year and there was not even a cup run to excite supporters. Villa went out 3-1 at home to Bradford City who were 14th in the Second Division at the time - and even the solitary Villa goal was farcical. When Houghton's shot was punched away by goalkeeper George Swindin, the ball hit Bantams defender Robert Hamilton on his back and rebounded into the net.

Frank Broome, a signing from Berkhamstead Town, came into the side in April and scored twice on his home debut, a 4-2 win against Liverpool.

1935/36 - Relegated for the first time

Such was the enthusiasm for the new campaign that 16,000 turned up at Villa Park for the pre-season public practice match. But the supporters' dedication would be tested to the full, long before the season ended. McMullan's reign as manager was over after just eleven games. In October Albion humiliated Villa at Villa Park, scoring seven without reply to leave goalkeeper Fred Biddlestone shell-shocked in his first game since November 1931.

McMullan resigned before the 4-2 defeat at Leeds the following week, while Pongo Waring asked for a transfer and was sold to Barnsley the following month. Frank Barson was appointed coach and the team were despatched to Rhyl for a week of intensive training. It did not help; the players returned to a 6-2 drubbing by Grimsby Town which left them at the bottom of the table.

The directors set about the task of strengthening the squad with a vengeance. Villa's spending over the next two months went into football folklore as seven expensive signings were made in an effort turn the position around. Tommy Griffiths, George Cummings, Jack Palethorpe, Jackie Williams, Alex Massie, Gordon Hodgson and Charlie Phillips cost around £36,000 in total, a massive figure at the time.

These were, indeed, dark days at Villa; in early October they mourned the death of George Burrell Ramsay who had been a huge part of the club for 59 years.

As the depression continued, Ted Drake scored all of Arsenal's goals in a 7-1 win at Villa Park on 14 December, the middle game of three in which 17 goals were conceded. The side struggled to get out of the bottom two, but there were a few signs of hope at the start of 1936.

A New Year's Day win at top of the table Sunderland was followed by success against Portsmouth three days later, while victory at high-flying Derby the first Saturday in February edged the team off the bottom.

A 2-1 victory over Birmingham at the end of March was followed by a win against Albion at The Hawthorns. The band played Auld Lang Syne as the teams ran onto the pitch, but this seemed premature as the victory brought nine points out of a possible twelve. A 4-2 win over Wolves on Good Friday lifted Villa out of the bottom two, but this was to be their last victory and relegation became a certainty after a home defeat by bottom club Blackburn Rovers in the final game of the season. It meant the only two original members of the Football League not to have been relegated went down together.

1936/37 - A new approach

Villa were greeted by large enthusiastic crowds for their first league games outside the top division. At Swansea on the opening day, the players were introduced to the mayor and the teams stood in the centre while the Welsh national anthem was sung. After the first six games the team topped the table, having dropped only two points.

There was a new man in charge. During the summer Fred Rinder had been over to Germany and persuaded James Hogan, coach of the Austrian team at the Berlin Olympics, to become Villa manager.

The new boss brought a new style of play, with more emphasis on ball control and tactical awareness, but supporters were warned that the results of his coaching would not immediately come to fruition.

This proved to be the case, and late September brought a reality check - a 3-0 home defeat by Fulham followed by defeat at Doncaster. The next four months yielded only five wins and defeat at Coventry on the first Saturday in February left the team in ninth place.

There were further changes in personnel. Bob Iverson, a signing from Wolves made his debut against Norwich City in December when Freddie Haycock also played his first game, and Ronnie Starling arrived from Sheffield Wednesday the following month.

One of the criticisms the previous season had been that players were just being bought on reputation, without consideration of the team's requirements. This was now being corrected, with more thought given to team building. Signings were being made to strengthen specific positions and to fit the team ethic.

A good run of eight wins in nine games took Villa up to fourth place on Easter Saturday and the prospects for promotion looked good. Three days later, over 65,000 were at Villa Park to see the return game with Newcastle, a side Villa had beaten 2-0 at St James' Park on Good Friday.

But the result was reversed, and the final six games were all lost as the team finished in a disappointing ninth place. Nevertheless, the directors were pleased with the way the season had gone; the signs were good for the future and there was a much better level of discipline at the club.

The Second Division champions of 1936/37. Back row: Ronnie Starling, Alex Massie, Ernie "Mush" Callaghan, Jimmy Allen, Fred Biddlestone, George Cummings, Bob Iverson, Eric Houghton. Front: H Bourne, J Riley, J Broughton, F Normansell (chairman), F Rinder, C Buckley, J Hogan (manager). Front: Freddie Haycock, Frank Broome, Frank Shell, Jack Maund.

1937/38 · Promoted as champions

Champions of the Second Division, only two defeats at Villa Park, where 50 goals were scored, and semi-finalists in the FA Cup. This was the season when the good times returned. The crowds were up, too, Villa enjoying the highest average attendance for any season so far. Certainly, a new style of football was being played; for the first time ever, Villa had the best defensive record in the country.

The measure of support to be expected was demonstrated when 15,000 turned up for a pre-season public trial game and over 50,000 saw Villa kick-off the league campaign with a 2-0 win over West Ham.

One of the features was the rivalry with Coventry City who topped the table for a large part of the season. In the 1-1 draw at Villa Park all gates were closed 15 minutes before the start, while a record crowd at Highfield Road saw Ronnie Starling score the only goal of the game.

Seven goals were scored against Stockport County in December and on Boxing Day, Villa became the first visiting team to take maximum points at Bradford Park Avenue.

The FA Cup campaign started with a 3-2 win at Norwich, while 69,000 were at Villa Park to see Blackpool defeated 4-0. Then three games against Charlton Athletic attracted a combined total of over 202,000. A 1-1 draw at The Valley and 2-2 draw at Villa Park four days later resulted in a second replay at Highbury, where Villa came back from a goal down to win 4-1 with a hat-trick from Frank Broome.

A club record of 75,540 was set for the home sixth-round clash with champions Manchester City, Villa winning an action-packed game 3-2.

Shell scored after only three minutes of the semi-final at Bramall Lane, the only goal conceded by Preston in the competition, but George Mutch equalised shortly afterwards, and Hugh O'Donnell hit Preston's winner.

The side bounced back with a fine performance and a 3-0 win against Manchester United and the final four matches were all won. When the season finished with a 2-0 home success against Norwich, Villa were already champions.

Villa then left for a three-match tour of Germany, playing games in Berlin, Düsseldorf and Stuttgart. Two of the three games were won, including a 3-2 victory over a German Select XI at the Reichssportfeld watched by a crowd of 110,000.

At the club's AGM, a profit of £17,172 was reported after a record 1,100,000 spectators watched first-team games at Villa Park. The good times were certainly back.

THE HISTORY OF ASTON VILLA

Villa's players line up in Berlin before their 3-2 victory over a Germany/Austria Select XI in May 1938.

1938/39 · Back in the big time

Frederick Rinder had predicted the team would have an easier time back in the First Division, as every game played by Villa over the past two years had been equivalent of a cup-tie. The side settled down to life back in the top flight, but in the last complete season before the Second World War, enthusiasm for football was not quite the same.

There was a massive outpouring of emotion by all 50,000 present before the game with Portsmouth on the first Saturday in October, following Neville Chamberlain's return from meeting Adolph Hitler in Munich. Directors, officials and players from both clubs gathered round the centre circle along with match officials while Villa's chairman gave an address and expressed appreciation to Mr Chamberlain for his efforts to ensure peace. The band played 'O God, our help in ages past' and the National Anthem was sung. Even so, the threat of war hung over the season.

Villa scored a total of 71 goals and there were some excellent home wins, but Villa Park was not the fortress it had been, and there were also seven defeats. Bob Iverson set a record by scoring after 9.6 seconds in a 2-0 win against Charlton Athletic, but Frederick Rinder died on Christmas Day, ending a link back to the beginnings of the club and the origin of The Football League.

The transfer market was generally quiet in view of the political situation, but the club showed their determination to strengthen the team by paying Blackpool £10,500 for centre-forward Frank O'Donnell in November while goalkeeper Joe Rutherford came from Southport the following March.

In the FA Cup, Third Division Ipswich Town, playing their first season in the Football League, came to Villa Park and gained a credible draw. Four days later Villa won 2-1 at Portman Road, Haycock netting the winner with two minutes to go. Villa's cup ambitions then ended in the mud at Deepdale, where they lost to Preston for the second year running, this time by two clear goals.

The season ended on a bright note when an O'Donnell hat-trick at Ipswich brought Villa back from two-down to win the Ipswich Hospital Cup. The following week, the team beat Coventry City to take the Lord Mayor of Birmingham's Charity Cup.

1939/40 · A nation at war

Villa played Albion prior to the start of the season in a match for the Football League Jubilee Trust Fund and the result was a repeat of the previous year's game, a 1-1 draw.

The following week, the season opened with players wearing numbered shirts in a league match for the first time. Villa beat Middlesbrough 2-0 with goals from Jackie Martin and George Edwards. On 3 September, after two further games had been played, war was declared and three days later the Football League suspended all fixtures.

Players' contracts were also suspended, with players allowed to turn out for any club in Britain. The Villa players were paid off by the club with two weeks money.

Although regional competitions were then arranged, Villa and five other clubs decided to close down completely. In November, the War Office took over Villa Park and it became a hive of activity for the war effort. Work on expanding the Holte End terrace had started early in 1939 and special permission was granted for this to be completed.

In April, Villa played a testimonial match at St. Andrews for Birmingham's long-serving goalkeeper Harry Hibbs, who had announced his retirement. The maximum permitted wartime crowd of 15,000 saw Villa lose 2-1. Two weeks later, Villa played a friendly at Chelmsford City, where they wore white in the first half, but changed to their own colours for the second.

1940/41 · Birmingham & District League

Villa still did not take part in the Regional League, but entered the Birmingham & District League, and also played in local competitions, using Solihull Town's ground for home games. There were often problems in raising a team which, initially usually comprised reserve players with the addition of any available first-team men.

In December, when Villa travelled to Worcester City with only ten players, the home side's player/manager Syd Gibbons sportingly turned out for Villa at right-half. This sportsmanship did not however extend to the result, Worcester won 3-2. Villa finished seventh.

1941/42 · Back to Villa Park

Villa Park was returned to the club in September 1941, although parts of the ground were rented out to aid the war effort, and the dressing rooms were occupied by fire watchers. Villa swept all before them, taking the Birmingham League title and winning several local trophies.

There were some convincing victories even though attendances were modest. Dicky Davis, guesting for the club, scored 19 goals in nine league games, including six in an 8-1 win at Worcester City.

Davis, though, was not in the team on 21 March 1942, when the highest-ever score at Villa Park was recorded, a 19-2 win against RAF Lichfield. Broome, Harry Parkes and Billy Goffin each scored four times in front of just 750 people.

Alex Massie scored five and Broome hit four in a 14-1 Birmingham League Cup win against RAF Hednesford in January and Albert Kerr netted a hat-trick in a 7-0 league win against the same opposition in February. It was Larry Canning's turn to hit a hat-trick in April, in a 9-0 win against RAF Lichfield. There were also a couple of challenge matches against Albion, both of which were won.

1942/43 · The enemy at Villa Park

On 29 August, Villa played their first game in the Football League (North) Competition, winning 2-0 against Wolves at Villa Park with goals from Parkes and Edwards. Birmingham also entered the competition - and used Villa Park for their home games.

Villa were in difficulties with the league over admission prices. The club were charging 1/6d (7.5 pence) rather than the required 1/3d (6.25 pence) but they were admitting service men free when they should have been charging 7d (almost 3 pence.) The League ruled that they should charge the correct amount, but rather than do so, Villa decided to also admit women free of charge!

In September, centre-half Ernie 'Mush' Callaghan was awarded the British Empire Medal for gallantry during an air raid.

There were useful wins, including an 8-2 victory over Albion, before the final game in the First Championship on Christmas Day when a 5-2 win against Leicester placed Villa 14th out of 48 teams.

Villa won through the qualifying rounds of the Football League War Cup and then knocked out Wolves, Stoke and Bristol City to meet Blackpool in the semi-finals. After the Seasiders won 3-1 at Bloomfield Road there were 50,000 at Villa Park for an exciting second-leg match which saw Villa fight back to win 2-1, but just miss out on a final place.

1943/44 · War Cup winners

Villa gained revenge for the previous year's defeat to Blackpool in the Football League War Cup, beating the Seasiders in the two-leg final. Blackpool won 2-1 at Bloomfield Road and the return game at Villa Park opened sensationally when Frank Broome scored after 40 seconds to bring the aggregate scores level - only for ex-Villa player Ronnie Dix to restore the visitors' advantage 35 seconds later.

George Edwards scored a second Villa goal on ten minutes, but again Blackpool came back, Tommy Pearson netting five minutes later. Bob Iverson put Villa in front once more on 38 minutes and when Broome netted five minutes after the break there was no way back for the Seasiders, Villa winning 5-4 on aggregate.

The cup run created tremendous interest. In April, 600 Villa supporters spent the night on Bath railway station to ensure they did not miss the second leg of the quarter-final against Bath City.

There had been welcome news prior to the start of the season when the FA lifted the sine die suspension of George Cummings, imposed following incidents against Leicester the previous Christmas.

War Cup winners 1944. Back row: P Hunt (trainer), Ronnie Starling, J Broughton, F Normansell (chairman), C Buckley, Ernie Callaghan, Alan Wakeman. Front: H Smith, Bob Iverson, Alex Massie, George Cummings, Harry Parkes, E Smith. On ground: George Edwards, Vic Potts, Frank Broome, Eric Hougton.

Villa announced that they would no longer be playing guest players, although Birmingham-born full-back Vic Potts continued to appear, signing permanently on 30 August 1945.

The season ended with Villa, the Football League North Cup winners, meeting Charlton Athletic, the Southern winners, at Stamford Bridge for King George's Fund for Sailors. Eric Houghton put Villa ahead, but Charlie Revell produced a late equaliser and the game ended 1-1. The First Lord of the Admiralty presented both sides with a trophy.

1944/45 · Bids, please, for the cup!

In August, 35,000 were at Tynecastle Park to see Villa win 4-3 against an Edinburgh Select XI in the Edinburgh Charity Cup. With 13 minutes to go, Villa led 3-0 with goals from Frank Broome, Eric Houghton and Bob Iverson. The hosts then scored three in four minutes before Broome hit an 86th-minute winner.

Villa finished fourth in the Football League (North) First Championship, losing only three times and finishing with a seven-match winning sequence.

Villa held a mock auction in October for the cup they had won the previous season, raising £450 for Red Cross funds, although the trophy did not leave Villa Park.

In the Second Championship, Villa won all eight of their games played in January and February. Starting with a 3-1 win at Albion, Villa completed the double with a 6-2 victory and went on to gain doubles over Birmingham, Coventry City and Walsall. In April, Leicester City were beaten 7-2 and the following month, George Edwards hit four in a 9-2 romp against Coventry City.

1945/46 · A record attendance

The end of World War Two brought the crowds back, and a Villa Park record attendance was set as the FA Cup made a welcome return. For the first and only time, the competition was organised on a two-leg basis, while the Football League was still not back to normal, First and Second Division clubs competing in regionalised sections.

The club also had a new boss. Just before the start of the season it was announced that captain Alex Massie - who was still playing - would be taking over as manager. Massie played in the first three league games, his final appearance being a 7-1 win against Luton Town. In October Villa paid their first big fee since before the war when they acquired Leslie Smith from Brentford for £7,500.

When Villa met Coventry City at Highfield Road in the third round of the FA Cup, they were on an incredible run of eleven consecutive league wins, followed by two drawn games, but the undefeated run came to an end when Dennis Simpson grabbed an 86th-minute winner for the home side. Three days later, goals from Smith and Billy Goffin saw Villa through on aggregate to face Millwall in round four.

A 4-2 victory at Cold Blow Lane was followed by a 9-1 home win. Villa were 5-1 up at the break and six players shared the goals, Frank Broome contributing a hat-trick. Broome scored the only goal of the first leg in the fifth round at Chelsea, where Joe Payne - who holds the record of scoring ten goals in a league game - missed a penalty for the home side.

A record 76,588 Villa Park crowd watched the quarter final home game against Derby County. Villa led 3-2 with only four minutes to play, thanks to goals from George Edwards, Bob Iverson and Broome, but Peter Doherty equalised and Sammy Crooks snatched Derby's winner. The second leg ended in a draw, Broome giving Villa the lead only for Raich Carter to head the equaliser.

Villa finished top goalscorers in the Football League's South Section with 106, but finished runners-up to Birmingham City on goal average.

1946/47 - League football is back

The Football League was restored with the same fixtures and teams as for the aborted 1939/40 season, and 50,000 attended Villa's opening game against Middlesbrough. In 1939, Villa had beaten Boro 2-0, but an 88th-minute goal from Wilf Mannion gave the visitors the points this time around.

Joe Rutherford, George Cummings, Ernie 'Mush' Callaghan, Frank Broome and George Edwards had all played in the 1939 fixture, but it was Broome's last game before joining Derby County. As for other members of the original team, Alex Massie was now manager, Bob Iverson and Jackie Martin were still with the club, Frank O'Donnell had joined Nottingham Forest, Freddie Haycock was playing for Wrexham and Jimmy Allen had retired.

After another home defeat by Everton, Villa's first win came at Derby on the second Saturday, and they then completed a double over Wolves.

Although Villa finished eighth, their home record was unusually poor, but they attracted large crowds on their travels. There were 63,896 at Stamford Bridge when they beat Chelsea 3-1 and almost 60,000 at Highbury for a 2-0 success against Arsenal.

The club had stuck by many of their pre-war players, and it was obvious the side would need rebuilding if they were to achieve honours. Dickie Dorsett was signed from Wolves and went on to play 271 games over the next seven years, scoring 35 goals. In January, Villa broke their transfer record when they paid Swansea Town £12,000 for Trevor Ford, who finished top goalscorer in each of his three full seasons at the club, netting 60 goals in 120 league games.

Among the players who were emerging, Johnny Dixon would go on to make 430 appearances and lift the FA Cup at Wembley before retiring in 1961, while Harry Parkes, a regular member of the side during the war, went on to play in every position for the club - including emergency goalkeeper - before retiring in 1955. Eddie Lowe, meanwhile, became the club's first post-war England international.

On Boxing Day, Eric Houghton, who had signed professional forms on 24 August 1927, played his last match for the club, a Central League fixture against Huddersfield Town. He scored from the penalty spot with the last kick of the match before signing for Notts County.

1947/48 - A Cup classic

Villa started with practically the same staff as the previous season and finished sixth, two places higher, partly because of a marked improvement in home form, with 13 wins and only three defeats. In October, Bert 'Sailor' Brown was signed from Nottingham Forest and his debut came in a 2-0 home win against Sheffield United.

Back to Football League action, as Villa prepare for the 1946/47 campaign. Back row: Leslie Smith, Eddie Lowe, Alan Wakeman, Con Martin, Ronnie Starling, Joe Rutherford, Frank Moss, Harry Parkes. Front: H Bourne (trainer), George Edwards, Dickie Dorsett, George Cummings, Bob Iverson, Vic Potts, Alex Massie (manager). On ground: Derek Ashton, Trevor Ford, Johnny Dixon, Amos Moss, Mush Callaghan.

The only other players to be introduced were left-back Albert Vinall and right-half Harold Chapman who both made their debuts in a Good Friday draw against Charlton Athletic at The Valley.

On Boxing Day, a Villa Park record league attendance of 68,099 saw an injury-hit Villa put up a gallant performance against Wolves. Dennis Westcott gave the visitors the lead after only two minutes and when Joe Rutherford dislocated his finger diving at the feet of the same player on 40 minutes, Harry Parkes went in goal until the interval.

Brown, who had suffered a thigh injury, then took over as custodian for the second half and George Edwards equalised, only for Johnny Hancocks to grab Wolves' winner. Nineteen-year-old lance-corporal Keith Jones made his debut in goal for the return game at Molineux the following day as Villa went down 4-1.

There were high hopes of a decent FA Cup run when Villa met Manchester United at home in the third round, particularly when George Edwards gave the home side the lead inside 14 seconds.

The visitors recovered to lead 5-1 at the break, but cheered on by a 58,683 crowd, Villa staged a tremendous second-half fight back to bring the score to 5-4 after 81 minutes. Then a Trevor Ford shot hit the bar, but Stan Pearson's last-minute goal completed an incredible 6-4 win for United in one of the finest games ever played at Villa Park.

1948/49 · A remarkable finish

Trevor Ford gave Villa the best possible start to the season with a goal after 30 seconds at Villa Park in the opening match against Liverpool. The striker scored his second before the break and Villa ran out 2-1 winners.

But the optimism generated by this victory was soon dispelled. It was the only win in the first ten games and by the end of September, Villa were bottom of the league with just four points.

There was an obvious need for changes. Larry Canning, Derrick Ashton and Ambrose Mulraney were introduced to the side, in addition to the versatile Con Martin, who arrived from Leeds. Martin made his debut in a 4-3 home win against Sheffield United on the first Saturday in October. The following week, Sailor Brown was injured in the game against Portsmouth and never played league football again.

In December, Villa again broke their transfer record by paying Queen's Park Rangers £17,500 for Ivor Powell. The Welsh international wing-half made his debut in a 1-1 draw at Liverpool in what was a vastly improved performance from the previous week's 6-0 defeat at Middlesbrough.

Following a 4-0 Christmas Day defeat by Wolves, 63,769 were at Villa Park on Boxing Day for the return fixture and there was a complete reversal of fortunes as Villa, with four goals from Trevor Ford, trounced the Molineux men 5-1. It was the first time since the Football League had been restored that a Villa player had scored more than two in any match.

Villa met Bolton Wanderers in three FA Cup games before Herbie Smith's 102nd-minute winner in the second replay put Villa through. There were 70,718 at Villa Park for the fourth-round tie against Cardiff City which Villa led at the break. Trevor Ford then shot wide from the penalty spot before the Bluebirds hit back to win 2-1.

Larry Canning, 1948.

The Cup had provided a welcome respite from the league struggle, the Bolton games giving manager Massie the opportunity to reorganise his side and to rethink his tactics. With a half-back line of Powell, Martin and Frank Moss Junior, and instructions to the forwards to concentrate on force, the close-passing style previously adopted was abandoned.

There was a complete transformation. Assisted by another big-money signing, Colin H Gibson from Newcastle United, the team lost only one league game and dropped only eight points from New Year's Day until the end of the season. The final league position of tenth was remarkable, considering Villa had spent the first five months in the relegation zone.

1949/50 · Without a manager again

At the end of July came the shock announcement that Alex Massie had resigned as manager. The board indicated that they were not immediately seeking a replacement and it was December of the following year before a new boss was appointed.

The previous season's spending spree had resulted in the club recording a financial loss, despite record receipts, and the only player bought during the summer was Jimmy Harrison, a full-back from Leicester City who had played in the FA Cup final against Wolves three months earlier.

Unlike the previous season, there was no fear of relegation, but neither was there much prospect of a title challenge. The team finished twelfth with 42 points, the same number as the previous season.

No boss! Villa, minus a manager, line up before a match during the 1949/50 season. Back row: H Bourne (trainer), Colin Gibson, Jim Harrison, Joe Rutherford, Harry Parkes, Frank Moss, Con Martin. Front: Billy Goffin, Trevor Ford, Ivor Powell, Dickie Dorsett, Leslie Smith.

Manchester United, although only finishing fourth, were a Villa bugbear, winning 4-0 at Villa Park on a gloomy mid-October Saturday and 7-0 at Old Trafford on a Wednesday afternoon in March. That game was watched by only 24,072 spectators, and Villa were without Con Martin who was playing for Ireland and Trevor Ford who was turning out for Wales. To complete a miserable afternoon, Colin Gibson had a penalty saved by Jack Crompton. With the internationals back in the side the following Saturday the team returned form, beating Liverpool 2-0 at Villa Park.

The season ended with a 5-1 defeat at Portsmouth, where Villa's consolation goal was a Dickie Dorsett penalty a minute from the end. May also saw the departure of Eddie Lowe to Fulham, along with his younger brother Reg.

1950/51 · George Martin arrives

Top of the table after the first two games, down to 21st on Armistice Day, a relegation battle through to March, and then up to a 15th place finish. It was a fluctuating season, to say the least. There was a new manager, too. In mid-December, Newcastle United boss George Martin was appointed.

The season started with a 2-0 home win against Albion, followed by a 3-1 success against Sunderland two days later. Unfortunately, there were only two further victories before the New Year, against Newcastle and Chelsea.

Goalkeeper Jack Hindle arrived from Barrow and made his debut in a goalless draw against Manchester United at Old Trafford in September, but more significant was the £15,000 purchase later in the month of Tommy 'Toucher' Thompson from Newcastle. Thompson would go on to gain England international honours the following year.

In October, Stan Lynn, a £10,000 acquisition from Accrington Stanley, became the second of Villa's 1957 FA Cup-winning team to make his debut.

After Trevor Ford was transferred to Sunderland for £30,000 early in the season, Edwards, Gibson, Craddock and Lynn all led the attack before Dave Walsh became Martin's first signing, arriving from West Bromwich Albion for £25,000.

Danny Blanchflower was the next big buy, a £15,000 signing from Barnsley in March. It was just a pity that it was Tottenham, and not Villa, that he would later lead to the first league and FA Cup double of the 20th century.

1951/52 - Best start for two decades

George Martin's first full season in charge saw Villa finish in the top six for the second time since the war - and for a while they were even dreaming about the title. A 5-2 opening-day defeat at Bolton looked ominous, but it turned out to be a rarity during the opening weeks of the campaign. By mid-September, Villa had won six, drawn one and suffered just that single setback at Burnden Park.

Their 13-point haul from eight games was the club's best start for 19 years. Not even when winning the Second Division championship in 1937/38 had they launched the season in such impressive style.

Even a surprise midweek defeat away to struggling Huddersfield Town failed to throw them out of their stride. The following Saturday, they climbed to the top of the table with a 2-0 home win over Liverpool, courtesy of goals from Billy Goffin and Tommy Thompson. Frustratingly, they then fell away alarmingly, losing six of their next seven matches, and any thoughts of becoming champions evaporated.

Even so, Villa certainly derived a great deal of pleasure from completing a double over Albion, and there was also a Boxing Day victory over Wolves at Molineux. Rather more significant, though, was the previous day's 3-3 draw between the sides - the last Christmas Day match to be staged at Villa Park.

Villa also enjoyed their biggest win in the First Division for 21 years when they thrashed Chelsea 7-1 towards the end of April, although they signed off with a 6-1 defeat at Newcastle.

1952/53 - The long-range header

If it was otherwise a fairly uneventful season, the 1952/53 campaign was significant for producing one of the strangest goals in Villa's history. It happened in Villa's second home game on the evening of Monday 1 September, a 3-0 victory over Sunderland, and it was the only senior goal ever scored by Peter Aldis, even though he made 295 appearances for the club.

Most headed goals are scored at close range; occasionally you might see one which loops in from the edge of the penalty area; this one was from 35 yards!

This is how Dick Knight described it in the Birmingham Mail: "It was left-back Peter Aldis who got the second to claim his first goal in senior football. In the 74th minute, from 35 yards out, he headed towards goal. Threadgold, with an eye on the challenging Walsh, was deceived by the bounce, which took the ball over his outstretched arm and into the net".

It was as well Villa won that night, because it was another eight games before they claimed their next victory, a far-from-convincing 1-0 success over Middlesbrough.

The Teessiders were beaten in more emphatic fashion when they returned to Villa Park in January. By then, it had become evident that Villa's best hope of glory was the FA Cup and goals from Johnny Dixon, Tommy Thompson and Colin H Gibson secured a 3-1 victory.

As the team's league form fluctuated - they eventually finished eleventh - they then overcame lower division opponents Brentford and Rotherham United, only for their Wembley dream to be ended by Dave Hickson's goal in a 1-0 quarter-final home defeat by Everton.

1953/54 - Houghton back as boss

The first decisive action of 1953/54 took part two weeks before the season got under way, and there was not a football in sight. George Martin, who had been in charge since December 1950, was sacked after he refused to resign 'because his style did not fit'.

It certainly seemed a harsh move by the board, given that Villa had finished the previous campaign in mid-table, but even as Martin was being dismissed, it became evident that former player Eric Houghton was being lined up as his successor. A statement from the club suggested an appointment would be made within 'the next few days', but in the event, it was almost a month before Houghton, who had been managing Notts County, returned to his spiritual home.

His first season at the helm, it must be said, was hardly a major success. Villa had lost three of their first six matches, and although Houghton's return inspired a run of four straight wins and elevation to fourth in the table, the team were unable to maintain that form. They managed only a single point from the subsequent half dozen matches and from that juncture, their form was very up and down.

Among the brighter moments were a 2-1 victory over Wolves at Molineux (although the scoreline was reversed at Villa Park on Boxing Day) and late-season 6-1 thrashing of Albion.

But Wolves went on to become champions, while Albion finished runners-up and lifted the FA Cup. Villa had to settle for 13th place in the final table.

1954/55 - A marathon cup-tie

The 1954/55 campaign was significant for several reasons. Danny Blanchflower was transferred to Tottenham Hotspur; Harry Parkes retired; chairman Fred Normansell died at the age of 68.

It was, indeed, a time to reflect on the departure of two fine players and the passing of an outstanding club servant. For a while, too, the melancholy mood seemed to rub off on the players. Following a 4-2 defeat at Leicester on the last weekend of March, Villa stood 16th in the table and there seemed little prospect of them climbing much higher. Then they embarked on a superb run-in which brought seven wins, a draw and just one defeat from their last nine games to claim sixth place.

That late surge was something of a relief after the inconsistency which had gone before. There were times when Eric Houghton's men looked formidable, and they twice put together three-match winning runs, although it was only in springtime that they really blossomed.

The loss of the classy Blanchflower was a particularly hard blow, his value to the side being underlined by the fact that Villa initially wanted £40,000 for him. He eventually became Tottenham's £30,000 record signing when he moved to White Hart Lane in December.

The transfer meant he was not involved when Villa engaged in one of the longest sagas in FA Cup history. Having overcome Brighton in round three, their fourth-round tie lasted a staggering five matches and eight-and-a-half hours before Doncaster Rovers won the fourth replay at The Hawthorns.

The teams had previously met at Belle Vue, Villa Park, Maine Road and Sheffield Wednesday, where extra-time had not been possible because of bad light.

1955/56 · Hanging on in there...

Inconsistency has been a perennial problem for Villa and never was it more evident than during the 1955/56 campaign. After a top-six finish the previous season, how on earth do you explain a slump to 20th just 12 months later? Ultimately, Eric Houghton's men won their last three matches to avoid relegation on goal average from Huddersfield Town, who went down with Sheffield United.

In an era when clubs changed their strips only infrequently, Villa switched to jerseys reminiscent of those worn by pre-war players - and it was a backward step in more ways than one. By the end of August, they had twice lost to Sunderland, conceding nine goals in the process.

There were, admittedly, a few memorable moments, including a classic 4-4 home draw against a Manchester United side who would go on to become champions. Generally, though, there was little to cheer the claret and blue faithful, despite Houghton's assertion that Villa were "one of the hardest-training teams in the country".

Not surprisingly, the local Sports Argus newspaper attempted to analyse the team's failings, concluding that the players were ageing and that no youngsters were coming through from the reserves.

Villa hit rock bottom early in the New Year, leaking ten goals in consecutive defeats by Blackpool and Chelsea and there were calls for the board to go.

After a 4-3 defeat at Tottenham, the Argus headline declared 'Almost Goodbye Villa', suggesting it was virtually impossible for them to avoid the drop. Three weeks later, the paper proclaimed 'a miracle' after wins over Sheffield United, Preston and Albion ensured safety.

1956/57 · Wembley wonders

The season would end in glory, with Villa celebrating their seventh triumph in the FA Cup, but there was no indication of what lay ahead when shareholders gathered for the club's 81st annual meeting at Birmingham's Grand Hotel in July 1956.

There was unrest in the wake of the previous season's flirtation with relegation and a move was made to remove directors Norman Smith and W E Lovsey. The duo were re-elected, however, and Villa embarked on a campaign which would see a marked improvement in their league position as well as their first major trophy for 37 years.

While there were very few changes in personnel, the team were much more consistent this time around and may well have finished higher than tenth, but for bad weather during the winter months.

Villa 1955/56. Back row: W Hunt, C Nickes, Peter Aldis, Trevor Birch, Pat Saward, Amos Moss, Dickie Dorsett, Arthur Proudler, Johnny Dixon, Roy Pritchard, Ray Hogg, Billy Myerscough. Middle: J Easson, J Whitear, Joe Tyrell, Bill Baxter, Dennis Parsons, Keith Jones, Stan Lynn, Vic Crowe, Peter McParland, Dennis Jackson, J Hogan. Front: Bill Moore (trainer), Tommy Southren, Colin Gibson, Con Martin, Eric Houghton (manager), Eddie Follan, Ken Roberts, Norman Lockhart, Nobby Clark, Mr Hunt.

THE HISTORY OF ASTON VILLA

Seventh heaven - Villa's players with the FA Cup after the club's seventh triumph in the competition in 1957. Back row: Peter Aldis, Stan Lynn, Nigel Sims, Stan Crowther, Peter McParland. Front: Eric Houghton (manager), Jackie Sewell, Billy Myerscough, Johnny Dixon, Les Smith, Bill Moore (trainer). On ground: Jimmy Dugdale, Pat Saward.

Postponements meant they had a gruelling schedule of ten matches in the space of 25 days during April - and with a Wembley date against Manchester United looming, it was hardly surprising that their league form faltered.

Defeats by Wolves and Luton Town in the last two matches were forgotten, though, as Peter McParland's two second half goals secured a 2-1 Wembley victory over the Busby Babes. Like so many Cup triumphs, it was very nearly all over at the first hurdle. With just nine minutes remaining on a quagmire of a pitch at Kenilworth Road, Villa trailed Luton 2-1 and seemed to be on the way out.

But Peter McParland's goal forced a replay which Villa won 48 hours later, courtesy of a Johnny Dixon brace and the team then overcame Second Division opposition in the next two rounds, beating Middlesbrough 3-2 at Ayresome Park and Bristol City 2-1 at home.

The quarter-final draw paired Villa with the tie they least wanted - Burnley away - but a battling performance and a McParland goal earned them a 1-1 draw at Turf Moor before they emerged 2-0 winners in the replay thanks to goals from Dixon and McParland.

Trailing twice to neighbours Albion in the semi-final at Molineux, Villa hit back with two McParland goals for a 2-2 draw, Billy Myerscough heading the only goal in the replay at St Andrew's.

McParland took his Cup haul to seven goals with the brace which secured a 2-1 Wembley triumph over United - and Dixon proudly received the Cup from Her Majesty the Queen. That acrimonious annual meeting had long since been forgotten.

Skipper Johnny Dixon leads the players on a Wembley lap of honour.

45

1957/58 - A storming finish

Villa's FA Cup triumph had given Midlands football a tremendous lift, but it was not about to alleviate the inconsistency which had dogged them since the end of the war. After the glory of Wembley, 1957/58 was very much an anti-climax, Eric Houghton's men sliding to 14th in the table and making their Cup exit at the first hurdle when they went down 2-0 to Stoke City in a third-round second replay at Molineux.

Defeat in the Second City derby at St Andrew's on the opening day was not quite what the boys in claret and blue had in mind after their lap of honour around Wembley nearly four months earlier. Apart from three wins over Christmas and into the New Year, they never really settled into a decent run of form - at least, not until a finishing sequence of six games without defeat dispelled any fears of relegation. Before that run of four wins and two draws, they had been only two points above the danger zone.

If that storming finish merely papered over the cracks, though, there were, at least, a few moments to savour. Villa enjoyed three five-goal triumphs, against Leicester City, Sheffield Wednesday and Sunderland, the latter on the day that central-defender Jimmy Dugdale suffered two broken ribs but returned on the left wing before finally being forced out of the action 15 minutes from time.

Another defender, full-back Stan Lynn, also made his mark that day when he netted a hat-trick, two of his goals coming from the penalty spot.

1958/59 - Blinded by the light

A new £35,000 floodlighting system was installed at Villa Park during the summer of 1958, but the lights served only to illuminate the team's shortcomings. They were switched on at half-time in the match against Portsmouth on Monday 25 August and Villa's 3-2 victory that night offered hope of a promising campaign.

By mid-September, though, it looked a forlorn hope as Eric Houghton's side suffered six straight defeats, conceding 24 goals in the process. The first of those setbacks, 7-2 at the hands of newly-promoted West Ham, clearly had a demoralising effect on morale in the dressing room.

That dismal sequence left the team second from bottom, which was the position they would occupy when the curtain fell on a depressing season. Villa, FA Cup winners just two years earlier, were relegated for only the second time in the club's history.

Their fate was sealed in the final match of the season. Victory over neighbours West Bromwich Albion at The Hawthorns would have kept them in the First Division and a 65th-minute Gerry Hitchens goal seemed to have done the trick. But two minutes from time, Ronnie Allen equalised for the Baggies, and with fellow relegation contenders Manchester City beating Leicester City on the same night, Villa were down.

One of the saddest aspects of the season was the departure in November of Eric Houghton after five years as manager which had included FA Cup glory. He was succeeded by Joe Mercer at Christmas, and three consecutive wins in early March lifted Villa five points clear of the relegation zone - but they failed to win again in their remaining nine games.

At least there was some consolation on the Cup front, Mercer's men overcoming Rotherham, Chelsea, Everton and Burnley before losing 1-0 in the semi-final to a Nottingham Forest team managed by Villa legend Billy Walker.

1959/60 - Bouncing back

Villa splashed out £30,000 on four players during the summer and it proved to be money well spent. Jimmy MacEwan, Bobby Thomson and John Neal were all regulars in the side who stormed to the Second Division title, while Jimmy Adam made 21 appearances and scored three goals as Villa were promoted at the first time of asking.

From the outset, it was clear Mercer's men meant business. True, they lost to Sunderland in their second match after winning at Brighton on the opening day, but they then embarked on a 14-match unbeaten sequence, mainly consisting of victories, which saw them sitting pretty at the top of the table.

That excellent run was brought to an end by a 2-1 set-back at Liverpool, where one-time Villa player Dave Hickson scored on his debut. But Villa responded with a vengeance. During the week leading up to the home match against Charlton Athletic on Saturday 14 November, the Birmingham Mail ran a story headlined: 'Mercer: I must have goals', reporter Eric Woodward (who would later become the club's commercial manager) pointing out that Gerry Hitchens, Thomson and Wylie had all struggled to find the net in recent matches. Hitchens, in fact, was under threat of losing his place.

Gerry and his pals certainly came up trumps against the Londoners. Hitchens hit five, Thomson two and Wylie one as Villa clocked up a record Villa Park win of 11-1. It did not end there, either. The following Saturday, Hitchens hit a hat-trick in a 5-2 success at Bristol City and then he netted twice in a 5-0 home victory over Scunthorpe United.

From then on, a return to the First Division was never in doubt, Villa clinching promotion with a 2-1 home win over Bristol City on the second Saturday in April. They fared well in the Cup, too, knocking out Leeds United, Chelsea, Port Vale and Preston before losing 1-0 to Wolves in the semi-final at The Hawthorns.

1960/61 - Unfinished business

Back in the First Division after just one season, there was never any question of Villa slipping down again as they acquitted themselves well to finish in the top half of the table.

While the team's league form was highly satisfactory, though, 1960/61 is best remembered as the season when a new competition was introduced to English football. And four years after lifting the FA Cup, Villa were only too happy to be the first club to get their hands on the Football League Cup.

It would be several years before some clubs showed any interest, but Villa embraced the new competition right from the outset. Mercer's

THE HISTORY OF ASTON VILLA

A notable Villa first - the squad who won the inaugural League Cup in 1961. Back row: Alan O'Neill, Harry Burrows, Jimmy MacEwan, Geoff Sidebottom, Alan Deakin, John Neal, Ralph Brown. Middle: Joe Mercer (manager), Ray Shaw (coach), Ron Wylie, Stan Lynn, Nigel Sims, Gordon Lee, Jimmy Dugdale, Bobby Thomson, F Archer (secretary). Front: J Heath, N Smith, Vic Crowe, C Buckley (chairman), Peter McParland, D Normansell, W Lovesey.

Minors, as the young team were popularly known, kicked off the League Cup in round two with a 4-1 home win over Huddersfield Town in October, when Gerry Hitchens scored Villa's first goal in the competition.

They then needed a replay to dispose of Preston North End while three games were required against Plymouth Argyle before the Pilgrims were overcome 5-3 in a second replay.

The fifth round was more straightforward, Villa beating Wrexham 3-0, but a replay was again required after the two-leg semi-final against Burnley had finished 3-3 on aggregate.

A Stan Lynn penalty and a Hitchens goal eventually saw Villa through 2-1 in the replay at Old Trafford in early May, in a match watched by just 7,953, and with Villa due to fly out to Russia the following week, the final against Rotherham United was held over until the start of the following season.

Mercer's side also needed replays in the FA Cup to overcome Bristol Rovers and Peterborough United before they went down 2-0 at home to Tottenham Hotspur, who went on to become the first team since Villa in 1897 to complete the double. The Peterborough replay attracted a crowd of 64,531 and even that figure was eclipsed for the Spurs tie, which was watched by 69,672.

On the league front, Villa opened with a 3-2 home win over Chelsea before they were brought down to earth with defeats by West Ham and Blackpool, but they settled down well to finish a respectable ninth.

The end of the season proved to be a time of farewells for the club. Johnny Dixon, who had been with Villa since 1944, retired after scoring in the final game of the season against Sheffield Wednesday, while Gerry Hitchens headed off to Italy in the summer to join Inter Milan.

1961/62 · League Cup winners

Villa's love affair with the League Cup had blossomed in the competition's inaugural campaign, but they had to wait until the start of the 1961/62 season before the relationship was consummated.

They must have wondered, though, if the summer break ahead of the first final would prove costly. They faced an uphill task after losing 2-0 in the first leg at Rotherham, where Stan Lynn missed a penalty, but lifted the trophy after a compelling return match at Villa Park.

The game was deadlocked until Alan O'Neill opened the scoring in the 67th minute, and two minutes later Harry Burrows made it 2-0 to take the tie to extra-time. With just ten minutes remaining, Peter McParland drove home the winner and Villa had written themselves into the record books as the first winners of the Football League Cup.

With a trophy in the cabinet by the first week of September, Villa fared well in the league, too. Having finished ninth on their return to the top flight, they moved up to seventh and would have been higher, but for a poor finish which yielded only one point from the last three matches.

Before that, however, entertainment had been very much on the agenda, Villa scoring 21 goals in the space of five matches, including an 8-3 thrashing of Leicester City which was followed 48 hours later by a 5-1 Easter Monday triumph over Nottingham Forest. There had also been a thrilling 5-4 win at Arsenal three weeks earlier as Joe Mercer's side hit a fee-scoring springtime surge.

Villa enjoyed an extended FA cup run for the second consecutive season, too, this time reaching the quarter-finals before, once more, their hopes were ended by the eventual winners Tottenham.

Any hopes of more League Cup glory, meanwhile, were dashed in November, when Villa lost at home to Ipswich Town in the third round.

1962/63 · Fading dreams

If ever a football team flattered to deceive, it was Aston Villa in August 1962. For only the eighth time in the club's history, they kicked off with three consecutive league victories - and the claret-and-blue faithful believed anything was possible when their favourites beat Tottenham for the first time since the war in front of over 64,000.

Yet by the following May, Villa had tailed off so badly that they finished a disappointing 15th, setting a trend of mediocrity which would culminate seven years later in relegation to the old Third Division.

Exactly how Mercer's men lost their way is difficult to pinpoint, such was the euphoria around Villa Park during that breathtaking opening week. True, the team looked vulnerable at the back on occasions but after a home win over Leyton Orient in October they stood sixth in the table,

just two points behind leaders Everton. While the Merseysiders went on to lift the title, though, Villa slowly drifted away and even the arrival of Wales international inside-forward Phil Woosnam in November brought the slide to only a temporary halt.

In fairness, they suffered more than most from the Big Freeze which gripped the nation that winter. During January and February they played just twice, failing to score in either game, and although they resumed with two straight wins in March, including a 4-0 thumping of Birmingham City, that was followed by miserable sequence of eleven defeats.

At least the League Cup brought a little respite - for a while, anyway. Villa battled their way to the final for the second time in three seasons, only to lose 3-1 on aggregate to the old enemy from across the city.

1963/64 · Farewell Joe Mercer

Villa kicked off with an excellent away win at Nottingham Forest - but it went downhill from there. If Tony Hateley's winner at the City Ground raised hopes of success, it was very much a false dawn. There were a few bright spots during the first couple of months, notably a 4-0 win at Blackpool and a 2-0 home verdict over Chelsea, but by the end of October, Villa were languishing in 19th place - the position in which they would finish the season.

Typically, there were moments which made fans wonder why Villa were not pushing towards the top of the table, rather than looking anxiously over their shoulders. Arsenal were beaten 2-1 at Villa Park; Manchester United were sent packing 4-0 on the day Denis Law was sent off for kicking Alan Deakin; Nottingham Forest were comprehensively beaten.

If only the team could have produced such results on a more regular basis, they would have achieved mid-table respectability at the very

The Villa squad who started the 1962/63 campaign so well before losing their way after the Big Freeze. Back row: Gordon Lee, Alan O'Neill, Jimmy Dugdale, Nigel Sims, John Sleeuwenhoek, Geoff Sidebottom, Charlie Aitken, Derek Dougan, Alan Deakin. Front: Ray Shaw (coach), John Neal, Ron Wylie, Vic Crowe, Tommy Ewing, Harry Burrows, Bobby Thomson, Jimmy MacEwan, Joe Mercer (manager). On ground: Mike Tindall, Allan Baker, Jimmy McMorran.

least. But an over-reliance on Hateley meant their goal supply was severely restricted and they were low on confidence for long spells. That was never more evident than when they were dumped out of the FA Cup by Aldershot, losing a third-round replay 2-1 at the Recreation Ground following a goalless draw at home to their Fourth Division opponents.

Ultimately, Villa had the luxury of losing their final three games and still staying up, but it was the end of the road for Joe Mercer. The man who had taken the club to two League Cup finals and two FA Cup semi-finals, as well as steering them back to the First Division, parted company with the club in July 1964.

1964/65 · West Midlands mediocrity

With the Mercer era at an end, his assistant Dick Taylor was the man charged with the task of reviving the club's flagging fortunes. From the outset, it was clear Taylor was fighting an uphill battle.

The notion that a new manager might give the team fresh impetus was dispelled by the end of the first week of the campaign as Villa slipped to three consecutive defeats. It was not until the eighth game, against Sunderland in mid-September, that they recorded their first victory.

In fairness, the new boss was severely hampered by injury problems, with John Sleeuwenhoek, Alan Deakin, Phil Woosnam, Mike Tindall and Lew Chatterley all absent at one stage or another.

Villa eventually hauled themselves away from the danger zone to finish 16th in what was a dismal campaign for West Midlands clubs. The 'big four' had all enjoyed top-flight status from 1959 onwards, but West Bromwich Albion finished only two places above Villa - and both Wolves and Birmingham City were relegated.

Villa achieved relative respectability by virtue of remaining unbeaten in their final eight matches, an impressive sequence which culminated with a 2-1 home victory over champions Manchester United.

The club's best efforts were in the cups. They reached the fifth round of the FA Cup before losing to Wolves in a second replay at The Hawthorns, while the League Cup saw them progress to the semi-finals before they went out 4-3 on aggregate to Chelsea.

The competition had still failed to capture the public's imagination, though - barely 12,000 witnessed the first leg at Villa Park.

Villa 1965/66. Back row: John Sleeuwenhoek, Charlie Aitken, Colin Withers, Dave Pountney, Graham Parker, Willie Hamilton. Front: John MacLeod, Mick Wright, Tony Hateley, Phil Woosnam, Tony Scott.

1965/66 - Repeat performance

It was very much a case of 'as you were' in 1965/66. For the second year running, Leeds United were the first visitors to Villa Park; once again, the Yorkshire club went home with the points. Once again, Villa had to be content with a finishing position of 16th. It was proving to be a depressing trend.

Yet after a faltering start, the club's immediate prospects looked bright when a run of five wins in six games carried them into the top half of the table. After a 3-2 home win over Tottenham in late September, they stood a very respectable ninth.

Tony Hateley, unfortunately, was injured that afternoon and although he missed only three matches, the momentum was lost during his absence. The striker's importance to the team was underlined when he returned to action and scored in consecutive wins over Nottingham Forest and Sheffield Wednesday, results which took Villa up to eighth.

But that was as good as it got. From that point on, the team were dogged by inconsistency, even with Hateley remaining a permanent member of the line-up.

A crowd of 40,694 - then a record for the competition - witnessed Villa's exit from the League Cup in the quarter-finals against neighbours West Bromwich Albion at The Hawthorns, and the team's league form was erratic. How else can you describe a 5-2 home defeat by Fulham, followed immediately by a 5-5 draw at Tottenham? And that draw was earned after Villa had trailed 5-1!

At least Villa ended on a high note, beating Chelsea at Stamford Bridge, although one of their scorers, skipper Phil Woosnam, subsequently put in a transfer request.

1966/67 - Post-World Cup blues

The nation was still on a high from England's World Cup triumph as the season unfolded, but the euphoria soon started to wear off at Villa Park. If 16th place in the two previous campaigns had hardly been anything to shout about, Dick Taylor's third season at the helm proved disastrous as the club suffered relegation to Division Two for the third time in their history.

And unlike the previous occasions, when they had returned to the top division after just two years and twelve months respectively, this time they would endure a painfully long passage of time outside the top flight.

The indications were discouraging from the outset as Villa won just two of their opening ten league games and were dumped out of the League Cup in a 6-1 battering by West Bromwich Albion at The Hawthorns.

The team were pitifully weak up front and the Albion setback exposed vulnerability at the back. They conceded another six at home to Chelsea the following Saturday and were then thrashed 5-0 by Leicester, for whom Derek Dougan hit a hat-trick.

Strangely enough, goalkeeper Colin Withers granted an interview about the humiliating defeats to the Daily Mail, describing the business of being beaten 17 times in three matches as 'a bit disheartening'.

Although Villa won four of their next ten league fixtures, they were still too close to the danger zone for comfort. A 2-1 home win over a Manchester United side who went on to become champions should have provided a massive confidence boost. Instead, an outstanding victory was followed by a 6-1 drubbing at Stoke, where ex-Villa man Harry Burrows helped himself to a hat-trick.

Ironically, Villa's final win was when they took revenge on the Potters in late March. After their 2-1 success, there were four teams below them, but their form was appalling over the last nine matches - seven defeats and two draws,

Relegation was confirmed in a 4-2 home defeat by Everton in the penultimate game and it was no surprise when Taylor was sacked three days later. At least he was spared another six-goal mauling at Southampton on the final day.

1967/68 - No summer of love

It is famously remembered as the Summer of Love, but there was not much harmony around Villa Park. It was bad enough that the club had just been relegated for the second time in nine seasons; worse still that new manager Tommy Cummings should arrive against a backdrop of discontent as the Shareholders Association made a bid to get two of their members appointed to the Villa board.

Cummings vowed not to let the boardroom battle affect his team's performances, but from the opening weeks, it was evident there would be no quick promotion. The opening six matches yielded just one win and five defeats and Villa were facing a battle to climb away from the lower reaches of their new surroundings.

Cummings was bold and brave enough to write a regular column in the Sports Argus, but Villa could not get things right on the pitch. They may well have faced relegation, in fact, but for an impressive mid-winter sequence of six wins in seven matches which was, in all honesty, out of character with the rest of the campaign.

Ironically, the team's best form came at a time when the club's power struggle raged more strongly than ever, before the directors fought off a bid to have them all removed from office. Ultimately, the season petered out in tame fashion, Villa finishing 16th after losing their final match to QPR - who were promoted to the First Division as a result.

1968/69 - Doug and Doc's revolution

The Beatles sang 'Revolution' in 1968 - and there was revolution in the air down Witton way. Supporters had expected a big improvement on the previous season, but there was never any indication that it would happen.

From the outset, it was clear Villa were destined for another campaign of struggle, and just one success in the opening ten league matches left them firmly in the relegation zone, with only Carlisle United below them.

They won the next match, but then went another seven without victory. After a 1-0 home defeat by Preston on the second weekend of November plunged the team to the bottom of the table, the fans decided enough

THE HISTORY OF ASTON VILLA

Villa 1968/69. Back row: Peter Broadbent, Dick Edwards, John Dunn, Fred Turnbull, Charlie Aitken, Mike Ferguson. Front: David Rudge, Mick Wright, Brian Godfrey, Brian Tiler, Lionel Martin, Brian Greenhalgh, Willie Anderson.

was enough. Angry supporters in a crowd of just 13,374 staged a demonstration against the board at the ground and then descended on Birmingham city centre to vent their feelings about Villa's demise.

The outcome, the following Monday, was the sack for Tommy Cummings, who became the club's fourth managerial casualty in ten years. With assistant manager Malcolm Musgrove also dismissed, trainer Arthur Cox took temporary charge - and immediately faced a headache when Barrie Hole was suspended by the club for walking out of Villa Park after being told he would be dropped for the next match at Portsmouth.

Jimmy Brown - Villa's youngest-ever player at 15 years and 349 days in September 1969.

Villa were in turmoil and the next six weeks were dominated by speculation, before five of the six directors were replaced in a takeover which saw travel agency chief Doug Ellis installed as chairman on 16 December. Two days later, Tommy Docherty was appointed manager, and suddenly there was optimism. The following Saturday, nearly 20,000 witnessed a 2-1 home win over Norwich City - and on Boxing Day, more than 41,000 saw Villa beat Cardiff City 2-0.

From that juncture, Villa could do little wrong as they secured Second Division safety by losing just once in a 13-match sequence. They reached the fifth round of the FA Cup, too, their fourth-round replay victory over Southampton attracting over 59,000, before they bravely went down 3-2 to Tottenham at White Hart Lane.

Villa's form did, admittedly, fall away over the past few weeks and a finishing position of 18th was hardly what the club had had in mind nine months earlier. Even so, it was a lot better than it might have been.

1969/70 · Sinking to a new low

Tommy Docherty pledged in his programme notes on the opening day that Villa would get out of the Second Division that season. They did, but there was no sign of celebration around Villa Park. On Wednesday 14 April, the unthinkable happened when Villa, founder members of the Football League and six-times champions, were relegated to the old Third Division.

Their fate was sealed 24 hours later after hopes had been raised by victory over Sheffield United in their final match of the campaign. Charlton Athletic, themselves in danger of going down, beat Bristol City 2-1 - and the boys in claret and blue were condemned to the lowest point in their history.

Docherty was not even on the scene when relegation was confirmed, having been sacked in January and succeeded in the managerial hot seat by one of the club's former players, Vic Crowe. The new boss was fighting an almost impossible battle from day one, Villa lying bottom of the table with just four wins and 17 points from 26 matches, By late February, relegation looked unavoidable.

The team clung on bravely, signing off with three wins and a draw in their last five matches. When they beat the Blades in front of more than 32,000 in the final game, there was a brief glimmer of hope - but it was snuffed out all too quickly.

The damage had been done by early November, Villa managing only two wins in their first 18 matches. And they did not even manage a league goal at Villa Park until the fourth home match of the season, a 2-2 draw against Millwall.

Andy Lochhead heads Villa's equaliser in the second leg of the League Cup semi-final against Manchester United.

1970/71 · We're going to Wembley

Having sunk to the lowest point of their 97-year existence, surely the only way was up for Villa as they contemplated the prospect of trips to places like Chesterfield, Rochdale and Torquay? It was not that simple.

Villa discovered that getting out of the Third Division was nowhere near as easy as many supporters believed, and while a finishing place of fourth indicated that the team had at least consolidated after the disasters of recent seasons, that was not exactly what the claret-and-blue faithful had in mind. For most supporters, only an immediate return to Division Two was good enough, so the team fell short of expectations.

Wembley bound - the Third Division squad who took Villa to the 1971 League Cup final. Back row: Keith Bradley, Ian 'Chico' Hamilton, Charlie Aitken, Pat McMahon, George Curtis, Lew Chatterley. Middle row: Ron Wylie (coach), Bruce Roich, Andy Lochhead, John Dunn, Fred Turnbull, Mick Wright, Vic Crowe (manager). Front: Jimmy Brown, David Gibson, Brian Godfrey, Brian Tiler, Willie Anderson.

But there's no doubt that Villa captured the imagination of the nation as they battled their way to the League Cup final, scoring an unforgettable semi-final victory over a Manchester United side which included three of the game's legends, George Best, Bobby Charlton and Denis Law.

To be fair, it was nothing new for a Third Division team to reach Wembley in this competition and Villa were less successful than their predecessors. QPR had won the inaugural Wembley final against West Bromwich Albion in 1967 while Swindon Town had followed suit by beating Arsenal two years later. Villa might easily have made it a hat-trick of lower division triumphs, but after outplaying Tottenham Hotspur for most of the final, they ultimately went down 2-0 to a Martin Chivers brace in the last twelve minutes.

On the league front, Villa were always in contention for a quick return to the Second Division, but lacked the consistency required to claim one of the promotion places. Their hopes were finally dashed in a 2-0 defeat at Mansfield in the final away match.

1971/72 · Encounters of the Third kind

After years of decline, lightened only by the previous season's League Cup adventure, Villa really captured supporters' imagination as they stormed back to the second tier as Third Division champions. The team failed to score in only five of their 46 league matches and the average attendance at Villa Park was only just short of 32,000, the highest for a decade.

That figure was boosted by an incredible turnout of 48,110 - a record at the time for a Third Division match - against fellow promotion contenders Bournemouth, while they topped the 40,000 mark on another three occasions, against Walsall, Bristol Rovers and Chesterfield.

It was a crusade with a purpose from the opening day, when Villa ignored a thunderstorm which left the playing surface saturated and made constructive football impossible. It certainly was not what you would expect in August, but Villa announced their intentions for the next nine months as Plymouth Argyle were beaten 3-1 by goals from Geoff Vowden, Pat McMahon and a Willie Anderson penalty.

There were, inevitably, a few slips along the way, and early season defeats by Bolton Wanderers and Mansfield Town meant it was late September before Vic Crowe's side hit the top of the table for the first time. Even then, three defeats during October raised doubts over the team's ability to sustain a promotion challenge, but the answer was loud and clear. Just one setback in the next 20 matches heralded the fact that Villa were on their way back up the English football ladder.

That impressive run featured a 6-0 victory at Oldham - the club's biggest away win since the Second World War - and a crucial 2-1 home success over Bournemouth in arguably the most exciting match of the season. The visitors led through their free-scoring Ted MacDougall - later to join Manchester United - and were the better team for much of the match, but Villa took the points with goals from Geoff Vowden and Andy Lochhead.

Promotion was eventually clinched by Vowden's goal in a 1-1 draw at Mansfield before the title was secured by a 5-1 thrashing of Torquay. And as a nice finishing touch, a 1-0 home win over Chesterfield in the final game gave Villa a total of 70 points - a Third Division record in the days of two points for a win.

On the way back - Villa face the camera ahead of their return to the second tier. Back row: Ian Ross, Ray Graydon, Jimmy Cumbes, Chris Nicholl, Tommy Hughes, Charlie Aitken, Malcolm Beard. Middle: David Rudge, Brian Tiler, Andy Lochhead, Fred Turnbull, Neil Rioch, Keith Bradley, Jimmy Brown, Pat McMahon, Alun Evans. Front: Ron Wylie (coach), Brian Little, Harry Gregory, Geoff Vowden, Chico Hamilton, Bruce Rioch, Mick Wright, Willie Anderson, Vic Crowe (manager).

1972/73 - A flying start

There was a spring in Villa's step as they launched the 1972/73 campaign and for a while they even looked capable of a second consecutive promotion. Of the opening ten Second Division matches, seven were won, two were drawn and only one resulted in defeat. It was an even more impressive start than they had made in the lower grade twelve months earlier.

Behind the scenes, there was boardroom upheaval, Harry Parkes being replaced by former England cricketer Alan Smith while Doug Ellis was elected chairman. But that certainly did not affect the buoyancy on the pitch as an eager Villa side went about their business in determined fashion. The storming start, unfortunately, was hard to maintain and the team were given a reality check as they slipped 2-0 at Fulham in early October and then 1-0 at home to QPR the following Saturday.

The defeats were repeated in the return matches the following March, and with Villa also suffering a double setback at the hands of Burnley, promotion was always out of reach after those euphoric opening weeks.

While Burnley went up as champions, Crowe's men were eleven points adrift of runners-up QPR, although third place was a commendable finish to the club's first season back in Division Two.

1973/74 - Farewell Vic Crowe

After finishing third the previous season, the 1973/74 campaign was decidedly ordinary for Vic Crowe's side. A promising start saw them remain unbeaten in the opening seven matches - albeit winning only two of them - and they recovered from the setback of two straight defeats to string together a six-match unbeaten sequence which featured five wins.

But from early November onwards, victories proved hard to come by as the goals dried up. It was, indeed, a bleak midwinter as Villa went twelve league matches without a win, a dismal run which yielded just five points and even fewer goals. The rot was stopped when Ray Graydon's goal secured a 1-0 win at Cardiff City on 23 February, although there was a depressing feeling all around Villa Park two weeks later when neighbours West Bromwich Albion won 3-1 to complete a double over Villa.

That match attracted a crowd of over 37,000, but the next game, at home to Carlisle United, drew barely 12,000. Those who bothered to turn up saw Villa record a 2-1 success - the first of four consecutive victories. The team generally lacked consistency, though, and their final position of 14th prompted Crowe's departure.

The highlight of the campaign was undoubtedly a fourth-round FA Cup victory over Arsenal. Sammy Morgan's goal earned a 1-1 draw at Highbury before he was sent off, leaving Villa to hang on in determined fashion. Nearly 48,000 packed into Villa Park the following Wednesday to see Morgan and Alun Evans give Crowe's men a 2-0 win in the replay.

1974/75 - A Centenary double

Villa appointed a new boss in the summer of 1974 - and by the end of the season, he had been named Manager of the Year. That was hardly surprising, given the incredible success Ron Saunders achieved during his debut campaign at Villa Park.

Not only were the club promoted back to the First Division, finishing runners-up to Manchester United, they also had a piece of silverware to show for their efforts after beating Norwich City 1-0 at Wembley in a League Cup final contested by two Second Division clubs.

Yet there was little to suggest, during the opening week of the season, that Villa would enjoy glory on two fronts. The opening three matches, away to York City and Hull City, and at home to Norwich, all ended in 1-1 draws.

Any notion that this might be a season of mediocrity, though, was dispelled when Hull visited Villa Park for the return clash. Sammy Morgan netted a hat-trick, Villa won 6-0, and the fuse was smouldering on an explosive campaign.

The team's free-flowing style delighted supporters and while they were blighted by inconsistency during the first half of the season, suffering eight defeats by the end of December, that all changed in the new year.

They lost just one of the remaining 18 league matches, finishing the campaign with a run of eight straight victories. The goals kept flowing, too. Villa scored 79 in the league - 13 more than United - plus nine in the FA Cup before making a fifth-round exit to Ipswich Town, and 22 in the League Cup.

True, they made hard work of overcoming lowly Chester in the semi-final, edging through 3-2 in the second leg at Villa Park after a 2-2 draw at Sealand Road.

But Ray Graydon's Wembley winner, scored on the rebound after Norwich goalkeeper Kevin Keelan had pushed his penalty onto a post, gave Villa their second League Cup triumph - and better was to follow as they marched back to the top division. What a way to celebrate the club's Centenary!

1975/76 - Home sweet home

This was the season when Villa made their home ground a fortress to ensure that their place in the First Division was consolidated. Ron Saunders' side failed to win a single match on their travels all season, yet were never in any danger of being relegated, even during a depressing run of just one win in 17 matches.

That was because they were beaten only twice at Villa Park in the league throughout the campaign, by Leeds United on the opening day and Queens Park Rangers in January. Even during the disappointing 17-game sequence, they managed ten draws which were invaluable in the days of two points for a win.

It was just a pity they could not find an away win or two to hoist themselves towards a mid-table finish. That elusive away success looked like it might materialise when they led in stoppage time at Upton Park, only for West Ham to grab a last-gasp equaliser for a 2-2 draw.

While Villa were formidable on home soil in the league, unfortunately, their dominance did not extend to the cups. This was the club's first season of European competition, but it was soon over.

Having lost 4-1 in the first leg of their opening round UEFA Cup tie in Antwerp, they went down 1-0 at home to the Belgians in the return leg.

THE HISTORY OF ASTON VILLA

Then, after beating Oldham in the second round of the League Cup, they went out 2-1 to Manchester United in the third. And to complete a hat-trick of exits, they slipped 2-1 at home to Southampton in a third round FA Cup replay, having led into stoppage time at The Dell the previous Saturday. The Saints marched on to win the Cup, beating Manchester United at Wembley.

1976/77 · Extra-time drama

Ron Saunders' vision of a brave new Villa really began to take shape in 1976/77. It was memorable in so many ways - the team finished fourth in the table, scored more than a century of goals in all competitions and lifted the League Cup for the second time in three seasons.

They achieved the latter feat in dramatic style, too. After an uneventful, goalless contest against Everton at Wembley, the final replay at Hillsborough was not much better, ending in a 1-1 draw. But the second replay at Old Trafford more than made amends for the drudgery which had gone before.

Everton led at half-time through a Bob Latchford goal and the Merseysiders' advantage was still intact with eight minutes remaining. Then Chris Nichol equalised with a superb long range shot before Brian Little squeezed the ball home from a narrow angle to put Villa in front - only for a Mike Lyons goal to take the tie to extra-time. With less than two minutes to go, a third stalemate looked inevitable, but Little popped up with the goal which gave Villa the trophy for the third time.

If the League Cup final replay overflowed with drama, it was against the other major Merseyside club that Saunders' men produced their best performance of the season - and one which has rarely been matched since.

Gordon Smith, skipper Chris Nicholl and Brian Little salute Villa supporters after the dramatic League Cup victory over Everton at Old Trafford.

On the evening of 15 December, the boys in claret and blue destroyed Liverpool - who would go on to retain the title - with a scintillating display which saw them lead 5-1 at half-time. There were no further goals in the second half, but it remains one of the most talked-about games in Villa's history.

Arsenal also left Villa Park on the receiving end of a 5-1 drubbing that season and Ipswich were beaten 5-2, while Villa scored four against West Ham, Derby County, Sunderland and West Bromwich Albion. It was, indeed, a vintage campaign.

The 1977 League Cup-winning squad. Back row: Charlie Young, Ray Graydon, John Deehan, John Burridge, Jake Findlay, Andy Gray, Frank Carrodus, Brian Little, Roy MacLaren (coach). Front: Gordon Cowans, Dennis Mortimer, John Gidman, Leighton Phillips, Ron Saunders (manager), Chris Nicholl, Alex Cropley, John Robson, Gordon Smith.

1977/78 · Back on the Euro trail

If their initial venture into Europe two years earlier had been something of a disaster, Villa were much better equipped when they embarked on the UEFA Cup trail in September 1977.

This time they swept aside Turkish club Fenerbahce 6-0 on aggregate in the opening round before recording more modest, but equally impressive, victories over Polish outfit Gornik Zabrze and Spanish club Athletic Bilbao, both on a 3-1 aggregate which featured a win on home soil followed by a disciplined away draw.

For the fourth consecutive round, they were drawn at home first when they were paired with Barcelona in quarter-final. This time, they hit back from two-down with only four minutes remaining to force a 2-2 draw in front of 49,619 - the highest-ever Villa Park attendance for a European tie - before losing 2-1 at the Camp Nou.

The home tie was significant in that it was the first truly great night of European football to take place at Villa Park, featuring a superlative display from Barcelona's legendary Johann Cruyff. It was after the Dutch master had been substituted in the 82nd minute that Saunders' men staged their remarkable comeback.

On the domestic front, Villa were dogged by inconsistency for most of the campaign, although victories in five of the last six matches saw them climb to eighth place in the final table. One depressing statistic, though, was the fact that Villa suffered six defeats on home soil - more than the combined total of Villa Park setbacks over the three previous seasons.

1978/79 · Cutting the ticker tape

There was a ticker tape welcome for two significant summer signings at White Hart Lane on the evening of Wednesday 23 August, but Villa assumed the role of party-poopers. Although Tottenham supporters turned out in force to welcome Argentine duo Ossie Ardiles and Ricardo Villa, Ron Saunders' men displayed scant regard for the two South Americans, reducing the north London venue to silence with a 4-1 victory.

Two of the goals came from players who would later manage the club - John Gregory and Brian Little - and it was perhaps as well Villa were in such impressive form that night.

They had opened the season with a 1-0 home victory over Wolves four days earlier, but by the end of October only two more league wins had been recorded as the squad was decimated by injury problems.

All was not well behind the scenes, either. The season got under way against a backdrop of boardroom unrest, created by a division over whether Saunders should be handed a longer contract in recognition of his achievements of the past few campaigns. It was a dispute which culminated in the resignation of chairman Sir William Dugdale, along with directors Harry Cressman and Alan Smith.

Ultimately, though, Villa at least pulled things around on the pitch. From November onwards they began to climb the table, eventually finishing eighth - and there were a couple of particularly sweet moments in April.

An inspired performance yielded a 3-1 victory over a Liverpool side who went on to become champions, and nine days later, Gary Shelton netted a hat-trick in a 5-1 thrashing of Arsenal.

1979/80 · Farewell Mr Ellis

There was further unrest behind the scenes as the 1979/80 season unfolded - a boardroom battle which was prompted by Doug Ellis's call for an EGM to remove chairman Harry Kartz, vice-chairman Ron Bendall and Bendall's son Donald. The move failed, leaving Ellis and his main supporter, fellow director Eric Houghton, no alternative but to resign.

With club politics providing an uneasy backdrop, it speaks volumes for the team that they came through a difficult season with credit, finishing seventh in the table and reaching the quarter-finals of the FA Cup, where they went down 1-0 at West Ham United to Ray Stewart's controversial late penalty.

Villa would, in fact, have fared much better, but for their dearth of goals. They averaged barely one per match and the leading scorer was Gary Shaw with a modest total of nine. For all that, there were some fine wins, notably 3-0 at home to both Southampton and Coventry City, 3-1 at Derby and 3-1 at Bristol City, where Shaw netted a hat-trick.

Arguably the most significant result of the season, though, was a 3-1 home win over Bolton Wanderers on the first weekend of November. It was the first match after the dust had settled on the boardroom battle and Villa's line-up featured ten of the players who would play such important parts in the glory days of the subsequent two campaigns. One of the most successful teams in the club's history was rapidly taking shape.

1980/81 · Countdown to the title

Never in Aston Villa's history has a defeat been greeted by such jubilant scenes. Ron Saunders' side lost 2-0 at Arsenal in the final game of the season on Saturday 2 May, but there were celebrations on the terraces of Highbury's famous Clock End. As news of Ipswich Town's 2-1 defeat at Middlesbrough filtered through, one thing became abundantly clear - Villa were champions for the first time in 71 years.

As far as the national press were concerned, the title had been won almost by default, and any praise for Villa's magnificent achievement was given only grudgingly. But who cared? The league table that Saturday evening showed Villa on top of the table, which reflected nine-and-a-half months of endeavour rather than 90 minutes on one afternoon.

Forget the notion that Villa relied on the misfortune of their closest rivals to claim the title. The table showed they had lost only eight of their 42 games and had accumulated more points than any other team.

The feat was all the more commendable in that Saunders used only 14 players all season, with seven of them - Jimmy Rimmer, Gordon Cowans, Dennis Mortimer, Ken McNaught, Des Bremner, Tony Morley and Kenny Swain - playing in every match.

THE HISTORY OF ASTON VILLA

The fantastic 14 - and their boss. Villa's 1980/81 title-winning squad. Back row: Eamonn Deacy, Ken McNaught, Jimmy Rimmer, David Geddis, Gary Williams. Middle: Des Bremner, Colin Gibson, Tony Morley, Gordon Cowans. Front: Allan Evans, Gary Shaw, Ron Saunders (manager), Dennis Mortimer, Kenny Swain, Peter Withe.

Gary Shaw and Allan Evans, meanwhile, missed only a handful between them, while Peter Withe was ruled out of half-a-dozen, and Colin Gibson and Gary Williams effectively shared the left-back berth. The only other players to feature in the first-team were David Geddis and Eamonn Deacy.

Yet Villa started the campaign by becoming the first team to concede a goal in the top flight when they went behind inside two minutes of their opening match at Leeds. The game at Elland Road was eventually won 2-1 and by mid-November the team had lost only twice.

A few doubts began to creep in when Villa then lost three times in five games, but a Boxing Day victory over Stoke City launched a ten-match unbeaten run (including eight wins) which announced in no uncertain terms that this team really meant business.

There were question marks once again after Ipswich won 2-1 at Villa Park on 14 April to complete a double (they also knocked Villa out of the FA Cup) but Saunders confidently declared after that setback that his team would still be champions. So it proved. Victory over Nottingham Forest and a draw at Stoke City steered Villa back on course as Ipswich began to falter, and a 3-0 home win over Middlesbrough in the final home match put the title within touching distance.

Little could anyone have imagined, as Peter Withe scored his 20th league goal of the season, that Boro would do Villa such a massive favour seven days later. Yugoslav striker Bosko Jankovic, who scored both Boro goals against Ipswich, died in November 1993 at the age of 42, but as Dave Woodhall points out in his 2002 book 'From One Season To The Next': "Never has a player done so much for the club without signing for them".

1981/82 · The road to Rotterdam

On the basis that statistics can prove anything, you could argue that Villa endured something of an anti-climax in the season immediately after their championship triumph. From pole position, they slid to a very modest eleventh place in the table and while there was early success on the domestic cup front, the team progressed no further than round five in both the FA Cup and the League Cup.

But the claret and blue faithful were not overly concerned with their team's unremarkable performances on the home front - they were cheering all the way to Rotterdam.

57

ASTON VILLA · THE COMPLETE RECORD

On the brink of glory - Villa's players line up in Rotterdam before the 1982 European Cup final. Back row: Peter Withe, Andy Blair, Nigel Spink, Pat Heard, Gary Shaw, Ken McNaught, Allan Evans, Dennis Mortimer, Jimmy Rimmer. Front: David Geddis, Colin Gibson, Gordon Cowans, Gary Williams, Tony Morley, Des Bremner, Kenny Swain.

It was very much a case of 'into the unknown' as Villa embarked on the European Cup trail for the first time. By the following May, they were celebrating the finest achievement in the club's history as Villa beat German giants Bayern Munich in Rotterdam's De Kuip stadium to become champions of Europe.

There was a very gentle introduction to the continent's most prestigious competition in the form of a first round draw against Icelandic champions Valur, who were duly brushed aside 7-0 on aggregate as Terry Donovan and Peter Withe each netted twice in the first leg and Gary Shaw followed suit in the return match in Reykjavik.

Next up was a trip behind the Iron Curtain to East Germany. This time it was Tony Morley's turn to score twice as Villa won 2-1 away to Dynamo Berlin, and even though the second leg resulted in a 1-0 home defeat, progress was achieved on the away goals rule.

A battling goalless draw away to Soviet champions Dynamo Kiev laid the foundations for a quarter-final victory which was secured by first-half goals at Villa Park from Shaw and Ken McNaught. Suddenly, just one hurdle stood between Villa and a place in the final and that was duly overcome as Morley's classic finish at Villa Park proved enough to knock out Belgians Anderlecht.

And so to Rotterdam, where rookie goalkeeper Nigel Spink performed heroics after replacing the injured Jimmy Rimmer and Peter Withe scored the most important goal in the club's history.

The European Cup-winning season is also significant in that it signalled the end for Ron Saunders, who left the club in February and was succeeded by Tony Barton.

While the season ended in Euro glory, it should be remembered that it also started with a trophy. Villa drew 2-2 with FA Cup winners Tottenham Hotspur at Wembley in August and the two clubs held the Charity Shield for six months each.

Champions of Europe! Skipper Dennis Mortimer, manager Tony Barton and match-winner Peter Withe celebrate victory over Bayern Munich in Rotterdam.

THE HISTORY OF ASTON VILLA

1982/83 - Super Cup glory

Emulating a European Cup triumph was always going to be a difficult task, but Villa performed admirably the following season, finishing sixth in the table - an improvement of five places - and reaching the quarter-finals of the FA Cup.

They also fared well against foreign opposition, beating Barcelona over two legs to lift the European Super Cup in January 1983 and reaching the last eight in their defence of the European Cup. Victories over Turkish club Besiktas and Romanians Dinamo Bucharest raised hopes that there may even be a repeat of the triumph in Rotterdam, but the quarter-final against Juventus proved a hurdle too far. The Italian aristocrats displayed their class with a 2-1 success at Villa Park in the first leg and then completed a comprehensive aggregate success with a 3-1 result in Turin two weeks later. There was one other international competition, too, Villa losing 2-0 to Uruguayan side Penarol in the World Club Championship in Tokyo.

On the domestic front, Villa's status as European champions made them the team to beat in the First Division. A 3-1 opening-day home defeat by Sunderland was followed by a 5-0 drubbing at Everton, and when the team also lost at Southampton in the third match, the alarm bells started ringing.

Thankfully, Tony Barton's side rectified the situation with four straight wins, and although they made an early exit from the League Cup, their league form was subsequently good enough for a top six finish.

The highlight of the season, though, was the Super Cup victory over Barcelona in January. With both sides determined to claim the title of the best in Europe, it was an ill-tempered affair. Over the two legs, the Spaniards had two players sent off and six booked, while Villa picked up two bookings and had Allan Evans dismissed. Barca won the first leg 1-0 at the Nou Camp, but Gary Shaw brought the scores level at Villa Park before Gordon Cowans and Ken McNaught secured a 3-1 aggregate victory.

The other significant event had taken place the previous month, when Doug Ellis bought out Ron Bendall's controlling share in the club to return as chairman, three years after his resignation from the board.

1983/84 - Mid-table 'failure'

Such were Villa's expectations at the start of the season that the team's finishing position of tenth was considered a failure - to the extent that it cost Tony Barton in his job. In May 1984, just two years after leading the club to European Cup glory in Rotterdam, Barton was sacked.

Public sympathy was very much with Ron Saunders' former number two. His dismissal was an unsavoury end to a season which, while never approaching the heights of the past few campaigns, was nevertheless satisfactory.

Villa finished in the top half of the table and reached the League Cup semi-finals - and it would have been a much healthier situation, but for

All set for the 1983/84 season, with the UEFA Super Cup they had won the previous season. Back row: Tony Morley, Paul Rideout, Mark Walters, Andy Blair, Allan Evans, Alan Curbishley. Middle: Jim Williams (physio), Ray Walker, Mark Jones, Nigel Spink, Colin Gibson, Gary Williams, Gordon Cowans, Roy MacLaren (coach). Front: Ken McNaught, Des Bremner, Steve McMahon, Tony Barton (manager), Gary Shaw, Peter Withe, Dennis Mortimer.

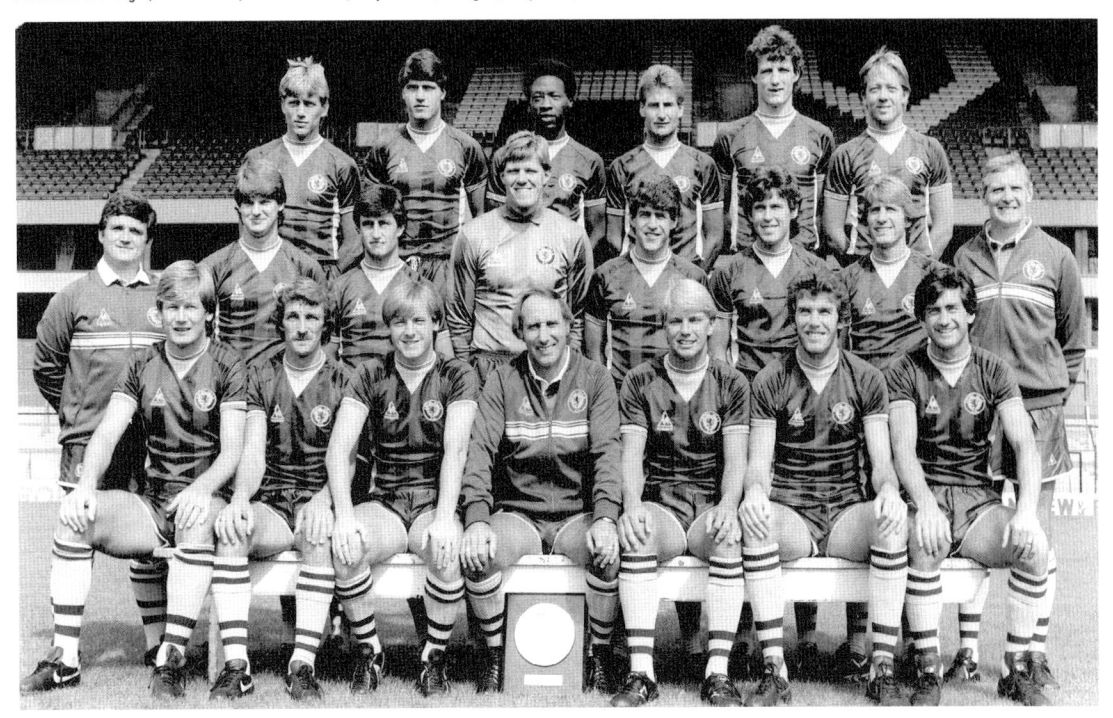

the team's travel sickness. They won only three times in away matches, although one of those victories was one which would be savoured for many a year afterwards. Peter Withe's brace lit up Old Trafford for Villa on Bonfire Night and secured a memorable 2-1 victory.

Typical of the team's inconsistency, though, that magnificent victory was preceded by a 6-2 Villa Park drubbing by Arsenal and followed by a home draw with Stoke.

The team's home form, thankfully, was excellent. Apart from the Arsenal debacle, they only suffered three other setbacks in their own back yard.

Villa also beat Everton at Villa Park in the second leg of the League Cup semi-final, a match which attracted the club's highest attendance of the season. Unfortunately, they had lost the first leg 2-0 at Goodison Park and it was the Merseysiders who went to Wembley.

1984/85 · Six of the best, briefly...

Following the departure of Tony Barton, Villa appointed the youngest manager in their history. Graham Turner was 36 when he took charge in the summer of 1984 and his debut campaign was reasonably successful. While the team made rapid exits from both cup competitions, they at least finished in a respectable tenth place for the second consecutive season.

There were undoubtedly some low points, and Turner described the second half of a 5-0 home drubbing by Nottingham Forest in September as the most humiliating 45 minutes he had ever endured. Yet Villa followed up with a 4-2 victory over Chelsea three days later - and in early October, they produced a performance which suggested they were still capable of being a major force in English football.

Didier Six, one of the stars of France's 1984 European Championship triumph, was signed from Mulhouse, and his debut coincided with a stunning display which destroyed Manchester United 3-0 at Villa Park.

Sadly, it was very much a one-off for Six, who was never anywhere near as effective again. He made just 16 appearances before returning to France the following year.

Villa, meanwhile, were unable to reproduce their exhilarating form against United on a regular basis, although Newcastle and Sunderland were both beaten 4-0 at Villa Park and QPR were sent packing to the tune of 5-2.

1985/86 · Supporters stay away

Villa have endured worse campaigns, but 1985/86 was undoubtedly one the most depressing chapters in the club's history. Thousands of supporters, disillusioned by the club's decline and worried by the spread of hooliganism, simply stayed away.

The Heysel Disaster of a few months earlier had sickened people to the extent that barely 20,000 turned up for the opening home game against

Villa 1985/86. Back row: Tony Dorigo, Andy Gray, Nigel Spink, Kevin Poole, Brendan Ormsby, Dean Glover. Middle: Jim Williams (physio), David Norton, Mark Walters, Gary Shaw, Steve McMahon, Gary Williams, Malcolm Beard (coach). Front: Tony Daley, Darren Bradley, Allan Evans, Graham Turner (manager), Ray Walker, Colin Gibson, Paul Kerr.

1986/87 - Doom, gloom and relegation

It may seem inconceivable, but five years after being crowned champions of Europe, Villa were relegated from English football's top flight in what was little short of a shambles of a season. And they went down under the stewardship of three managers.

Graham Turner was in charge for the first half dozen matches, which yielded just three points before he was dismissed after a 6-0 humiliation at Nottingham Forest in mid-September.

Turner's successor Billy McNeill had started the campaign at Manchester City - another club destined for the drop - and he briefly sparked a revival which raised hopes of survival before Villa's form after Christmas dipped alarmingly.

After beating Charlton Athletic at home on Boxing Day, they did not win again until the last Saturday in March, Paul Birch's solitary goal securing victory over Midland rivals Coventry City. By the time the team lost 3-1 at Manchester United on the final day, Frank Upton was in temporary charge, McNeill having departed after relegation had been confirmed by a 2-1 home defeat at the hands of Sheffield Wednesday five days earlier.

The Bank Holiday game against Wednesday was played on the 30th anniversary of the club's last FA Cup triumph. In stark contrast to the jubilant scenes at Wembley three decades later, Villa Park was like a morgue.

Only 15,007 witnessed the final nail being driven into Villa's coffin and even that depressing figure was an improvement on some of the low attendances which had populated the famous venue as relegation became increasingly likely. Among the few highlights were 3-3 draws against Liverpool away and Manchester United at home, plus a 4-0 romp against West Ham at the end of April.

Paul Elliot in Villa Park action v West Ham United, April 1987

Liverpool. By the end of August, that figure had almost halved to 10,524 for the visit of Luton Town. A goalless draw against Southampton in February attracted a pitiful 8,456. The average home attendance for the season was 15,237 - the lowest at Villa Park since the First World War.

In fairness, it was a period when football in general was at a depressingly low ebb, particularly in the West Midlands. At one stage, it looked very much as if all three local top-flight clubs would be relegated and Blues and Albion did, indeed, go down. At the same time, Wolves dropped into the old Fourth Division.

It was scant consolation to Villa supporters that their team were the best of the bunch. A finishing position of 16th, achieved by a six-match unbeaten run from later March onwards, was much better than many fans had feared, but the team from the glory years continued to be dismantled.

Gordon Cowans moved to Italian club Bari, Dennis Mortimer joined Brighton, Peter Withe followed his former teammate Ken McNaught to Sheffield United - and Graham Turner's young side struggled to cope.

At least they reached the League Cup semi-finals for the second time in three seasons, losing 4-3 on aggregate to Oxford United, who went on to beat QPR in the final.

1987/88 - Sorting out the shambles

If no-one else had dared mention it, Graham Taylor had no qualms about highlighting Villa's decline when he took over as manager in May 1987.

He pulled no punches, pointing out that the whole set-up needed restructuring and describing the club as 'a shambles'. But Taylor also stressed that it was his job to sort things out - and by the end of his first season he had gone a long way to achieving his objective.

Promotion was not exactly gained in convincing fashion - as Taylor later observed, "We did it by the skin of our teeth" - but that hardly mattered. For a long time, it looked as if Villa might have to participate in the Play-Offs and at one stage towards the end of the campaign they even dropped out of that group of contenders. But they eventually recovered to claim the second automatic promotion place behind champions Millwall after an afternoon of drama on the final day.

While Taylor's men were nervously drawing 0-0 at Swindon Town, their rivals Bradford City and Middlesbrough both lost at home. That left Villa and Boro both on 78 points with exactly the same goal difference - but Villa clinched second place by virtue of having scored five more goals than the Teessiders.

We're on the way up. Villa, on course for promotion, face the camera in 1988, shortly after the arrival of David Platt from Crewe. Back row: Martin Keown, Gary Shaw, Tom Bennett, Mark Lillis, Gareth Williams, Garry Thompson, David Hunt, Kevin Gage, Stuart Gray. Middle: Jim Walker (physio), Andy Blair, Alan McInally, John Ward (assistant manager), Nigel Spink, Lee Butler, Dave Richardson (assistant manager), Neale Cooper, Andy Gray, Bobby Downes (youth team coach). Front: Tony Daley, Paul Birch, Bernie Gallacher, Allan Evans, Graham Taylor (manager), Steve Sims, Warren Aspinall, David Norton, David Platt.

The most crucial result of all, though, was undoubtedly the one against Bradford five days earlier. The Yorkshire club had arrived at Villa Park with a four-point advantage over Taylor's side and a win that day would have given them automatic elevation to the top flight. But David Platt, signed from Crewe earlier in the year, scored the only goal in front of a tension-charged crowd of 36,423 to take the promotion race down to the wire.

1988/89 · Too close for comfort

Gaining promotion was all very well; staying in the top flight was quite another matter. Taylor's men managed it - but only just. Survival was achieved, in fact, after Villa's kit had been packed away for the summer.

After completing a gruelling schedule with a point at home to Midland rivals Coventry City on the final Saturday, all Villa could do was await the results of West Ham's two outstanding fixtures. The Hammers won at Nottingham Forest to set Villa nerves on edge, but then lost 5-1 to Liverpool at Anfield. The Hammers were down and Villa were safe, but it had been a hard slog.

Yet the campaign had begun promisingly. A 2-2 home draw against Millwall was a modest start, but Villa then won 3-2 at Arsenal and drew 1-1 at home to Liverpool before Alan McInally scored twice in a 2-2 draw at West Ham, taking his goal haul to six in four games.

After five games, Villa were unbeaten, and despite the reality check of back-to-back defeats by Sheffield Wednesday and Wimbledon, there were some encouraging results, notably home wins over Everton, Tottenham Hotspur and Norwich City.

When McInally took his total to 19 goals in as many league and cup games with a brace in the Boxing Day victory over QPR, Villa stood tenth in the table, but poor form from New Year onwards left everyone biting their nails at the end.

At least there was no question about the Second City bragging rights. Three games against Blues - two legs of a second-round League Cup tie plus a Simod Cup game - resulted in an embarrassingly comfortable 13-0 aggregate.

1989/90 · England calling...

Villa hardly fired their supporters' imagination when their two biggest signings during the summer of 1989 were both central defenders - for combined fees which were less than the £1.1m received from Bayern Munich for striker Alan McInally. Yet Kent Nielsen and Paul McGrath, together with Derek Mountfield, who had arrived the previous year, were to play crucial roles in the club's best league campaign since the title triumph nine years earlier.

THE HISTORY OF ASTON VILLA

The squad who finished runners-up to Liverpool in 1989/90. Back row: Derek Mountfield, Gareth Williams, Dean Spink, Ian Olney, Kent Nielsen, Ian Ormondroyd, Steve Sims, Mark Lillis, Nigel Callaghan, Mark Parrott. Middle: Gordon Cowans, Paul McGrath, Darrell Duffy, Nigel Spink, Bobby Downes (youth team coach), Dennis Booth (coach), Jim Walker (physio), Lee Butler, Kevin Gage, David Jones, Mark Blake. Front: Paul Birch, Tony Daley, Bernie Gallacher, John Ward (assistant manager), Graham Taylor (manager), Dave Richardson (assistant manager), Stuart Gray, Chris Price, David Platt.

From late November onwards, the trio formed the backbone of a 3-5-2 formation which took the First Division by storm and carried Villa to runners-up spot behind Liverpool. It was an inspired strategy by Graham Taylor, yet the manager may well have been out of a job by the end of September!

An indifferent start left Villa in the bottom four as they faced Derby County, and regardless of any decision by the board, Taylor had begun to consider his own position. Had they lost to the Rams he would almost certainly have resigned; as it was, David Platt's solitary goal persuaded him to stay on.

From that juncture, there were only occasional setbacks. The Derby victory was the first of five straight wins, and despite a 2-0 reversal at Norwich, the momentum was quickly regained with a 4-1 thrashing of Coventry City, followed by a 2-0 win at Wimbledon, where Taylor deployed Nielsen, McGrath and Mountfield as his three-man back line.

The team were beaten only once in the league between then and late February, when a superb 2-0 midweek success at Tottenham prompted the national press to talk about Villa as prospective champions.

Sadly, the title bid began to falter with a shock 3-0 home defeat the following Saturday - ironically at the hands of Wimbledon - and Villa scored only eight goals in the course of twelve matches which included a 3-0 FA Cup quarter-final defeat on Oldham's synthetic pitch.

The goals started flowing again in the last two games, although the 3-3 home draw with Norwich handed the title to Liverpool.

Even so, it had been a season to savour. No wonder Graham Taylor was being touted as the next England manager.

1990/91 - Czeching our Doctor Jo

All sorts of speculation preceded the appointment of Graham Taylor's successor, but when it finally happened, it caught everyone by surprise. Dr Jozef Venglos had taken the Czech Republic to the World Cup quarter-finals that summer, but he was hardly a household name in this country and no-one recognised him when chairman Doug Ellis introduced him to the media.

It was a bold decision by Ellis to go for an overseas manager for the first time in Villa's history but sadly, it was far from successful. While Venglos's vast knowledge of the game was undisputed, he had considerable difficulty in motivating English footballers. By the end of the season, with relegation having been only narrowly avoided, he parted company with the club by mutual consent.

While his spell in charge was hardly memorable, though, it did contain a few highlights, particularly in the early stages. After overcoming Banik Ostrava in the first round of the UEFA Cup, Villa achieved a truly momentous result when they beat Italian giants Internazionale 2-0 in the first leg of a second-round tie. Indeed, an unbeaten seven-match league and cup run earned Venglos the Manager of the Month award for October, although it was very much downhill from there.

63

ASTON VILLA · THE COMPLETE RECORD

The first overseas boss - new manager Dr Jozef Venglos joins his players for the 1990/91 photo-call. Back row: Derek Mountfield, Darrell Duffy, Ian Ormondroyd, Lee Butler, Paul McGrath, Tony Cascarino, Kent Nielsen, Nigel Spink, Ian Olney, Andy Comyn, Gareth Williams. Middle: David Platt, Nigel Callaghan, Richard Money (coach), Bobby Downes (youth teamcoach), John Ward (assistant manager), Jo Venglos (manager), Dave Richardson (assistant manager), Jim Walker (physio), Dennis Booth (coach), Kevin Gage, Gordon Cowans. Front: Paul Birch, Bernie Gallacher, David Jones, Mark Blake, Stuart Gray, Chris Price, Tony Daley, Mark Parrott, Dwight Yorke.

Villa crashed 3-0 in the return match at the San Siro and the team's league form also went into decline. Even the return of European Cup hero Peter Withe, who was appointed assistant to Venglos in succession to the sacked John Ward, did little to halt the slide. In the end, safety was mathematically assured by a 2-1 home win over Norwich City in the penultimate match, but by then it was widely acknowledged that Villa would be looking for a new manager during the summer.

1991/92 · Ron rings the changes

Ron Atkinson had been touted as a Villa manager on numerous occasions and in the summer of 1991 it finally came to fruition. Atkinson, who had been on the club's books as a youngster, was a hugely popular choice when he took over in the wake of the failed Jo Venglos venture.

Big Ron had made his name as a player with Oxford United and a manager with Manchester United. When he arrived from Sheffield Wednesday, there had rarely been such eager anticipation at Villa Park.

His debut campaign was hugely enjoyable, too, Villa setting the tone for some exciting performances on an unforgettable opening day. By an amazing quirk of fate, the club's first game was away to Sheffield Wednesday, and Atkinson had to endure a barrage of abuse from Owls fans still seething over his departure from Hillsborough. He was grim faced as his former team took a two-goal lead, but was all smiles when Villa hit back to win 3-2.

The goals came from three of his summer signings - Steve Staunton, Cyrille Regis and Dalian Atkinson - and the line-up included three other new recruits, Kevin Richardson, Shaun Teale and Paul Mortimer. Another trio of signings, Darius Kubicki, Ugo Ehiogu and Les Sealey would make their debuts further down the line. These were, indeed, changing times.

It was also the season in which Dwight Yorke started to make an impact, the youngster from Tobago scoring a superb individual goal against Nottingham Forest in September and adding ten more in the league by the end of the season.

He was even more prolific in the FA Cup, scoring five in as many appearances, including a fourth-round hat-trick at Derby, as Villa reached the quarter-finals before going out at Liverpool.

And just imagine how much higher the team would have finished but for a mid-winter slump which saw them win only once and score just twice in the first dozen league games of 1992.

1992/93 · Second in the Premier

Football history was made in August 1992 when the FA Premier League was launched, and the new concept was very much to Villa's liking. Ron Atkinson's men were runners-up to Manchester United in the league's inaugural season. And although they ultimately trailed the Red Devils by ten points, it was only on the penultimate weekend that their title hopes were finally extinguished by a 1-0 home defeat at the hands of Oldham Athletic.

THE HISTORY OF ASTON VILLA

Villa 1991/92. Back row: Richard Money (coach), Peter Withe (coach), Ugo Ehiogu, Ian Ormondroyd, Kent Nielsen, Les Sealey, Nigel Spink, Glen Livingstone, Ivo Stas, Neil Cox, Darrell Duffy, Dave Richardson (director of youth), Roger Spry (fitness consultant). Second row: Jim Walker (physio), Jim Barron (coach), Nigel Callaghan, Shaun Teale, Ian Olney, Dalian Atkinson, Cyrille Regis, Kevin Gage, Mark Blake, Bryan Small, Steve Staunton, Andy Gray (assistant manager). Front: Derek Mountfield, Kevin Richardson, Dwight Yorke, Martin Carruthers, Stuart Gray, Ron Atkinson (manager), Gary Penrice, Gordon Cowans, Tony Daley, Chris Price, Paul Mortimer. On ground: Chris Boden, David Jones, Mark Parrott, Steve Froggatt David Farrell, Richard Crisp, Neil Davis.

The club's first Premier League match was a 1-1 draw at Ipswich Town on Saturday 15 August, a result which was subsequently repeated at Villa Park against Leeds United and Southampton, Dalian Atkinson scoring in all three games.

Villa's first victory was at Bramall Lane, where Garry Parker's brace secured a 2-0 success over Sheffield United, although it was after Dean Saunders had arrived from Liverpool that the season really took off. Saunders cost a club record £2.3m, but it proved a sound investment as he immediately forged a lethal partnership with Atkinson. The Welsh striker scored twice on his home debut - ironically against Liverpool - with his strike partner also on target in a 4-2 victory, and the duo simply could not stop scoring over the next couple of months.

Sadly, Atkinson was then laid low by a stomach injury which kept him out of action for four months and his extended absence undoubtedly had a strong bearing on Villa missing out on top spot.

The cause was not helped, either, by a man who had enjoyed two spells at Villa Park and who would return for a third the following season. Unfortunately for Villa, Gordon Cowans was playing for Blackburn Rovers on the evening of Wednesday 21 April and was instrumental in inflicting a 3-0 defeat on his former teammates. Four days later, Oldham won at Villa Park and United were crowned champions. All the same, it had been a season to savour.

1993/94 - Spot on for cup glory

Repeating the outstanding feat of finishing runners-up in the inaugural campaign was always going to be a tall order and Villa had to settle for a more modest tenth place as the new league decided it should be known as the Premiership - a name which would remain in existence until it reverted to the Premier League in 2007.

If league performances fell short of the high standards set the previous season, though, Villa really turned on the style in the League Cup to lift the trophy for the fourth time.

A two-leg victory over neighbours Birmingham City in the second round was followed by a flattering 4-1 success at Sunderland and well-merited successes in north London, first against Arsenal and then Tottenham.

When the semi-final draw paired Villa with Tranmere Rovers, a passage to Wembley looked a formality. Instead, the scene was set for one of the most thrilling encounters in the club's history.

Dalian Atkinson opens the scoring in the 1994 League Cup Final

ASTON VILLA · THE COMPLETE RECORD

Wembley wonders - Villa's 1994 League Cup-winning squad. Back row: Guy Whittingham, Neil Cox, Dalian, Atkinson, Paul McGrath, Ugo Ehiogu, Mark Bosnich, Nigel Spink, Andy Townsend, Shaun Teale, Steve Staunton, Bryan Small, Steve Froggatt. Front: Jim Walker (physio), Ray Houghton, Graham Fenton, Kevin Richardson, Ron Atkinson (manager), Earl Barrett, Dean Saunders, Tony Daley, Jim Barron (assistant manager).

Tranmere led 3-0 in the first leg at Prenton Park and suddenly the dream seemed to be over. But Dalian Atkinson's late goal at least gave Villa hope and the same player also scored in the dying minutes at Villa Park to bring the aggregate score level at 4-4 before Ron Atkinson's men won a penalty shoot-out in which goalkeeper Mark Bosnich saved three spot-kicks.

Villa were very much the underdogs in the final against a Manchester United side who would go on to win a league and FA Cup double. But there was never any question of the Red Devils making it a treble as another Atkinson goal, plus two from Dean Saunders, clinched a magnificent 3-1 Villa triumph.

The club started well in the UEFA Cup, beating Slovan Bratislava in the opening round before going out to Deportivo La Coruna despite drawing the first leg in Spain.

1994/95 · The great escape

A reduction in Premiership numbers from 22 to 20 meant that four clubs had to be relegated at the end of 1994/95 - and Villa were very nearly among the unfortunate quartet. Only on the final day was the club's continued top-flight residence secured.

Villa 1994/95 - Back row: Dave Farrell, Ugo Ehiogu, Paul McGrath, John Fashanu, Shaun Teale, Andy Townsend, Garry Parker. Middle: Jim Walker (physio), Graham Fenton, Guy Whittingham, Nigel Spink, Mark Bosnich, Michael Oakes, Bryan Small, Earl Barrett, Jim Barron (assistant manager). Front: Dwight Yorke, Nii Lamptey, Ray Houghton, Kevin Richardson, Ron Atkinson (manager), Dean Saunders, Dalian Atkinson, Phil King, Steve Staunton.

Going into the final match of the season, Villa needed a draw against already-condemned Norwich City to be assured of safety. They achieved it with a Steve Staunton goal which secured a 1-1 result while Crystal Palace lost at Newcastle and went down along with Norwich, Leicester City and Ipswich Town.

For all the late concern, however, there was an abundance of optimism when Villa were unbeaten in their first five matches and then knocked Italian giants Internazionale out of the UEFA Cup in dramatic fashion. After losing to a Dennis Bergkamp penalty at the San Siro stadium, Ray Houghton's goal in the second leg brought the aggregate score level. Villa won a nerve-tingling penalty shoot-out, full-back Phil King blasting the match-winning spot kick past Inter's Villa supporting keeper Gianluca Paglucia.

Having claimed such a major scalp, it was something of a shock when Villa fell at the next hurdle to Turkish outfit Trabzonspor - and by then they had also plummeted down the Premiership table. A 4-3 defeat at Wimbledon in early November left them without a win in nine league games and cost manager Ron Atkinson his job, even though the team had been playing much better than their lowly position suggested.

Ironically, the depressing run came to an end with a 4-3 win at Tottenham in caretaker manager Jim Barron's only match in charge, before former Holte End hero Brian Little was appointed as Atkinson's successor.

From that juncture, survival was the name of the game. It was achieved - but only just.

1995/96 - Success all the way

Of all the Premier League campaigns to date, this was undoubtedly Villa's most successful. True, they did not quite emulate the achievement of finishing runners-up in the inaugural season, but an excellent fourth-place finish was accompanied by a League Cup triumph and progress to the FA Cup semi-finals for the first time since 1960.

The massive improvement was due in no small part to the three major signings made by manager Brian Little during the summer - Gareth Southgate from Crystal Palace, Savo Milosevic from Partizan Belgrade and Mark Draper from Leicester City. The combined outlay for that trio was just short of £10million, but it was money well spent.

Southgate, switched from midfield to central defence even before the opening game, was so impressive that he broke into the England side and played in Euro 96, Draper offered creativity in the middle ground and Milosevic, despite a faltering start, still contributed a dozen league goals, including a hat-trick against Coventry City. Even those three, however, were outshone by Dwight Yorke, who netted 25 goals and was in irrepressible mood all season.

From the 3-1 opening-day victory over Manchester United (who went on to become champions) it was clear something special was afoot. Villa were consistent in the league, holding fourth place from early February onwards, and resourceful in the cups. Two-nil down in the first leg of the League Cup semi-final at Arsenal, there seemed little prospect of reaching Wembley - but two goals from Dwight Yorke earned a 2-2 draw and a goalless return match took Villa through on the away goals rule.

In the final, they overwhelmed Leeds United, winning 3-0 with goals from Milosevic, Ian Taylor and Yorke.

Seven days later, their hopes of a cup double evaporated in a 3-0 defeat by Liverpool in the FA Cup semi-final at Old Trafford, but it was certainly a season supporters recall with great affection.

1996/97 - Yorke hits the top 20

There was no trophy this time around, while Villa's UEFA Cup adventure was over almost as soon as it began, but 1996/97 was nevertheless a highly satisfying campaign. Brian Little's side maintained a consistency which earned them a very creditable finishing position of fifth, and it was just a pity they could not have overcome what appeared to be an easy hurdle in Europe.

After an opening-day defeat at Sheffield Wednesday, Villa remained unbeaten in eight matches - two of them against Helsingborgs in the first round of the UEFA Cup. Unfortunately, a 1-1 scoreline at Villa Park and a goalless encounter in the second leg meant the Swedish part-timers went through to round two on the away goals rule.

There was not much joy on the domestic cup front, either, Villa getting through just one round before making their exit in both the League Cup and the FA Cup - defeat in the latter coming at the hands of a Derby County side inspired by Paul McGrath, who had moved to the Baseball Ground a few months earlier.

Dwight Yorke

Villa line up before the 1996/97 season, proudly displaying the League Cup they had won in March for the second time in three seasons. Back row: Scott Murray, Phil King, Neil Davis, Gareth Farrelly, Carl Tiler, Riccardo Scimeca, Darren Byfield, Lee Hendrie, Fernando Nelson. Middle: Paul Barron (coach), Paul McGrath, Gareth Southgate, Ugo Ehiogu, Michael Oakes, Mark Bosnich, Ian Taylor, Gary Charles, Tommy Johnson, Jim Walker (physio). Front: Julian Joachim, Steve Staunton, Franz Carr, Mark Draper, Allan Evans (coach), Brian Little (manager), John Gregory (coach), Savo Milosevic, Dwight Yorke, Andy Townsend, Alan Wright.

McGrath was also in the Derby side when they beat Villa 2-1 in April, on the day goalkeeper Mark Bosnich stormed away from the ground after being told he was not in the starting line-up, but by and large it was a fairly successful season.

Dwight Yorke hit the 20-goal mark for the second year running and should really have had one more. He netted a hat-trick in a 4-3 defeat at Newcastle and video evidence subsequently proved that his disallowed effort at St James' Park should have counted.

1997/98 - A European adventure

It was a case of great expectations around Villa Park in the summer of 1997. The club almost doubled their record transfer fee by paying £7million for Stan Collymore and season ticket sales climbed to more than 24,000. But, by late August, those expectations had well and truly evaporated. Four straight defeats represented Villa's worst-ever start to a league campaign, and they did not even score in the first three.

Thankfully, the depression was short-lived, and three consecutive wins sent Brian Little's men shooting up to mid-table respectability at the same time that their best European campaign since the early eighties was taking shape. The team excelled in the UEFA Cup, knocking out Girondins de Bordeaux, Athletic Bilbao and Steaua Bucharest to reach the last eight.

By the time the quarter-finals rolled round, though, there had been a dramatic development, with Little resigning and John Gregory taking over barely 24 hours later.

Little's departure was something of a mystery, for while Villa had suffered a shock FA Cup fifth-round home defeat by Coventry City and were uncomfortably close to the Premiership danger zone, his position appeared to be under no pressure.

Whatever the reasons, though, the change of manager could hardly have had a more positive effect.

True, Villa went out of the UEFA Cup despite a brave, battling effort against Atletico Madrid, but from potential relegation candidates they were transformed into European qualifiers for the following season by winning nine of their final eleven league matches. Victory over Arsenal in the final game, on the day Gareth Barry made his full debut, was enough to secure seventh place - and fourth-placed Chelsea's victory over VfB Stuttgart in the Cup Winners' Cup final a few days later meant Gregory's boys could look forward to further European action a few months later.

1998/99 - Record-breaking start

Sometimes there's just no logic in football and that was never truer for Villa than during the first few months of 1998/99. Throughout the summer, the club had been beset by problems, not least of which was the transfer of Dwight Yorke to Manchester United. As manager John Gregory observed, he seemed to spend all his time 'putting out fires'.

Yet against this backdrop of apparent discontent, Villa contrived to make their best-ever start to a league campaign. When they romped to a 4-1 win at Southampton in early November, it completed a sequence of twelve Premiership games without defeat. Better still, eight wins and four draws gave them a formidable total of 28 points and top spot in the Premiership - a position from which they were not dislodged until Boxing Day.

And those cynics who suggested Yorke's departure indicated Villa were a 'selling club' were put in their place as Paul Merson was recruited from Middlesbrough for £6.75million and striker Dion Dublin followed from Coventry City for £5.75million. Both players were instrumental in the team's superb first half of the season, and Dublin's return of seven

THE HISTORY OF ASTON VILLA

Villa 1998/99. Back row: Darren Byfield, Fabio Ferraresi, Gary Charles, Alan Lee, Ugo Ehiogu, David Hughes, David Unsworth, Lee Collins, Ben Petty, Richard Walker, Darius Vassell. Middle: Jim Walker (physio), Simon Grayson, Riccardo Scimeca, Ian Taylor, Matthew Ghent, Michael Oakes, Mark Bosnich, Adam Rachel, Gareth Southgate, Alan Thompson, Gareth Barry, Gordon Cowans (coach). Front: Kevin MacDonald (coach), Lee Hendrie, Mark Draper, Stan Collymore, Paul Barron (coach), John Gregory (manager), Steve Harrison (coach), Dwight Yorke, Julian Joachim, Alan Wright, Malcolm Beard (coach).

goals in his first three games was unprecedented in Villa's history. Even after the Boxing Day defeat at Blackburn, Gregory's boys were briefly back in pole position going into the New Year, but then it all went horribly wrong. Stan Collymore was admitted to the Priory Clinic suffering from depression, Merson was also having problems off the pitch and then, after a shock FA Cup defeat at home to a Fulham side from two divisions below Villa, Ugo Ehiogu suffered a fractured eye socket during a 2-1 setback at Newcastle.

A season which had opened so brightly then stuttered inconsistently towards its conclusion and although sixth place was respectable enough, it was several rungs below what the Villa faithful had envisaged at Christmas. To rub salt in the wounds, where seventh had been sufficient for UEFA Cup qualification twelve months earlier, circumstances conspired to ensure that sixth was not good enough this time around.

1999/2000 - Goodbye old Wembley

The season which heralded the dawn of a new Millennium could not have been more eventful for Villa. It was a campaign in which John Gregory's position seemed to be in jeopardy following a run of nine league matches without a win, yet ultimately, the board's decision to show faith in their manager was more than justified.

It was arguably an earlier-than-usual third round FA Cup-tie against Darlington which turned around Villa's fortunes. The Quakers had already been knocked out once, but were drawn as 'lucky losers' to make up the numbers following Manchester United's controversial decision to withdraw from the Cup in order to play in the World Club Championship.

Defeat by Darlington might well have signalled the end of Gregory's reign, but Villa came through 2-1 to secure a fourth round place. And even though they lost on penalties in a League Cup quarter-final at West Ham the following Wednesday, they were subsequently re-instated after it was discovered the Hammers had fielded an ineligible player.

When the tie was re-staged a month later, Villa won 3-1 in extra-time and by then they were back on course on two other fronts. Apart from steadily climbing the Premiership table with an unbeaten sequence which would eventually extend to twelve matches, they were also through to the fifth round of the FA Cup - and that path eventually led to Wembley for the last final to be staged beneath the old stadium's famous twin towers. While the historic occasion ended in the bitter disappointment of a 1-0 defeat by Chelsea, you could not argue with the team's achievements - FA Cup finalists, League Cup semi-finalists, sixth in the Premiership.

It was also the season in which temperamental Benito Carbone joined the club on a short-term contract, and the Italian midfielder lit up Villa Park with some mesmerising displays. His finest achievement was a hat-trick in a 3-2 fifth-round Cup victory over Leeds United after Villa had twice trailed in a pulsating tie.

2000/01 - The Angel has landed

Anxious to build on their success in reaching the Cup Final, Villa made a bold venture into the transfer market, signing flamboyant Frenchman David Ginola from Tottenham Hotspur for £3million. It was a move which sparked unprecedented interest among the claret and blue faithful, Ginola having to fight his way through a crowd of around 1,000 supporters who turned up at Villa Park on the day he was unveiled to the media.

There was a strong suspicion, though, that the signing was the brainchild of chairman Doug Ellis rather than John Gregory, and the manager was reluctant to use his expensive new purchase on a regular basis. Ginola was restricted to just 14 league starting appearances in his debut season, going on as substitute on 13 other occasions.

If that signing seemed extravagant, though, it was nothing compared with the arrival of Colombian striker Juan Pablo Angel for a club record

£9.5million during the January transfer window. This time Gregory was the prime mover in the deal, although once again, it was hardly an instant success, Angel struggling to settle in and having to wait until the final home game, a 3-2 victory over Coventry City, before scoring his first goal.

A more memorable first goal was the spectacular angled volley by Luc Nilis on his league debut against Chelsea at the end of August. Sadly, it was the Belgian striker's only one in claret and blue. His career was ended when he suffered a double fracture of his leg in a collision with Ipswich goalkeeper Richard Wright at Portman Road two weeks later. A finishing position of eighth was reasonable enough, although they would surely have been in the top six with a sharper cutting edge.

Villa also entered the Intertoto Cup for the first time, beating Marila Pribram (formerly Dukla Prague) in the first round before going out to Celta Vigo.

Peter Schmeichel - the club's oldest scorer!

2001/02 - Schmeichel on target

Villa claimed two pieces of silverware in 2001/02 - one right at the start of the season and one right at the end. An early start - 14 July to be precise - was rewarded as John Gregory's men lifted the Intertoto Cup, overcoming Croatians Slaven Belupo and French club Stade Rennais before beating Swiss outfit Basel in the final.

And a combined crowd of nearly 34,000 watched the two-leg FA Youth Cup final in which Villa's youngsters scored a 4-2 aggregate victory over an Everton side spearheaded by Wayne Rooney. Sadly, the senior cup competitions brought nothing but disappointment as Villa made early exits from the UEFA Cup, League Cup and FA Cup.

At least the team's league form was encouraging, wins over Southampton and Chelsea in the last two matches lifting them up to a respectable finishing position of eighth. Villa had actually led the table after beating Bolton in October, and were seventh after winning at Charlton in January, in a game which turned out to be Gregory's last in charge.

In the aftermath of his departure, Stuart Gray and John Deehan took over briefly on a caretaker basis before Graham Taylor returned for a second spell at the helm.

Danish goalkeeper Peter Schmeichel made a piece of club history in a 3-2 defeat at Everton in October when he became both the first goalkeeper to score in a competitive Villa game and also the club's oldest-ever scorer.

2002/03 - Second City blues

The previous time Graham Taylor had left the club, it had been to take charge of the England team; this time around, he decided it was best to step aside after just one full season at the helm, a season which he publicly described as 'lousy'.

Right from the outset, the signs were ominous. Following an Intertoto Cup defeat at the hands of French club Lille, Villa's opening four league games all finished 1-0 - three of them in favour of the opposition. And although a 2-0 victory over Charlton Athletic appeared to have provided a welcome pick-me-up, everyone of claret-and-blue persuasion plummeted to the depths of despair on the night of a 3-0 reversal at St Andrew's. As if that were not bad enough, Birmingham City also won the return match 2-0 at Villa Park on a night when Dion Dublin and Icelandic midfielder Joey Gudjonsson were both sent off.

There was little to raise Villa spirits in between times, either. A decent League Cup run ended with a dramatic 4-3 home defeat by Liverpool, but it was the end of January before the team recorded their only Premiership away success. Almost incredibly, it was achieved by a 5-2 scoreline against a Middlesbrough side who were previously unbeaten at home.

As a largely unsatisfactory season stuttered towards its conclusion, a goal from Swedish striker Marcus Allback against Sunderland secured safety in the final home match.

2003/04 - Climbing the table

David O'Leary was quickly appointed as Graham Taylor's successor and by the time the campaign got under way, he had recruited goalkeeper Thomas Sorensen and midfielder Gavin McCann from relegated Sunderland.

The two new signings became the 100th and 101st players to represent Villa in the Premier League when they made their debuts on the opening day at Fratton Park, but it was not the best of starts as Portsmouth kicked-off their first Premiership campaign with a 2-1 victory.

After three matches, Villa had mustered only a single point and by late November Villa were languishing in the relegation zone. Ultimately, though, it turned out to be a successful season, with a finishing position of sixth and progress to the semi-finals of the League Cup, where Bolton's 5-2 first-leg win proved to be too big a hurdle to overcome despite a battling effort in the return match at Villa Park.

Such was the team's improvement in the second half of the season that they even occupied a Champions League position, albeit for only an hour. Having beaten Tottenham Hotspur on the first Sunday of May, O'Leary's side stood fourth in the table, only to slip back to fifth when Liverpool beat Middlesbrough at Anfield. A week later, any lingering prospect of Champions League qualification was removed from the agenda in a 1-1 draw at Southampton, while defeat at home to Manchester United on the final day meant that even UEFA Cup football was just beyond reach as Villa finished sixth on goal difference behind Newcastle United.

Villa's youth team, meanwhile, reached the final of the FA Youth Cup, helped by six goals by Luke Moore and five from Gabriel Agbonlahor, before losing to Middlesbrough in the final.

2004/05 - Champions League dreamers

For the second year running, Villa nurtured hopes of European qualification, only to see them destroyed during the closing weeks. Twelve months earlier, sixth place in the table had not proved sufficient to secure a UEFA Cup spot; this time around, seventh would have been enough, and it remained a distinct possibility going into May.

Despite having just been held to draws in consecutive home matches against Charlton Athletic and Bolton Wanderers, David O'Leary's men still had Europe in their sights as they travelled to White Hart Lane - only to suffer a 5-1 thrashing by Tottenham Hotspur.

Six days later, the dream was well and truly extinguished in a 2-1 home reversal at the hands of Manchester City, so it hardly mattered that the final game, against Liverpool at Anfield, was also lost by the same margin.

Two points from a possible 15 left Villa supporters bemoaning a catastrophic end to a campaign which had begun so promisingly and had seen the team climb to fifth in November with consecutive victories over Portsmouth, Bolton Wanderers and Tottenham.

At that stage, optimists began talking about the possibility of Champions League qualification, although the notion was quickly dispelled as Villa finished 2004 with just one point from their subsequent six games.

£3million Martin Laursen signed from AC Milan

Having gone out of the League Cup to Burnley in October, there was also a quick exit from the FA Cup, again at the hands of lower division opposition, as Sheffield United triumphed 3-1 at Bramall Lane.

The club's most significant signing was Danish defender Martin Laursen for £3million from AC Milan, although a knee injury restricted him to just twelve appearances.

2005/06 - Beating the Blues

They say that every cloud has a silver lining, and Villa found two in the midst of a disappointing 2005/06 campaign. David O'Leary's side mustered only ten league wins, but two of them went a long way to easing the pain of so many setbacks.

A 1-0 success in October was followed by a 3-1 win exactly six months later, with Birmingham City the opponents on each occasion. A Kevin Phillips goal secured all three points at St Andrew's to give Villa their first Premiership victory over the old enemy from across the city, while Milan Baros (2) and Gary Cahill were on target at Villa Park in April. Phillips and Baros had arrived the previous summer for vastly contrasting fees. While Phillips had been snapped up for a bargain £750,000 from Southampton, the Czech international had cost almost ten times as much as O'Leary took a £7m gamble to boost his team's strike force.

Villa also recruited another Czech, midfielder Patrik Berger, plus Dutch left-back Wilfred Bouma, right-back Aaron Hughes and goalkeeper Stuart Taylor, but it was a campaign when the new boys never really gelled.

A piece of club history was made on the opening day, when all four goals in a 2-2 draw against Bolton Wanderers were scored in the first nine minutes, but that explosive start can hardly be said to have ignited Villa's season. There was, at least, an incredible 8-3 League Cup win at Wycombe to savour (after Villa had trailed 3-1 at half-time) while progress to the fifth round represented the club's best FA Cup run since their final appearance six years earlier.

2006/07 - Atlantic crossing

This was the club's most significant season for many years, and not necessarily because of anything which happened on the pitch - although Villa still performed considerably better than they had over the previous two campaigns.

The summer departure of David O'Leary was followed by a genuine managerial coup in the appointment of Martin O'Neill, a man regarded as one of the top bosses in the game. His arrival at Villa Park was greeted by such jubilant scenes that secretary Steve Stride, who drove the new manager to Villa Park for his official unveiling, commented that he now knew how the Beatles must have felt when crowds of delirious fans gathered to welcome them!

Sadly, it was to be the last season at Villa Park for Stride, who had worked for the club since 1972, had been secretary since 1979 and a director for almost a decade. But long before his resignation in May 2007, Villa's hierarchy had undergone an even more dramatic change.

A few years earlier, the prospect of Villa without Doug Ellis had been almost unthinkable, but a new chairman was installed in September 2006 when Ellis sold his controlling interest to American businessman Randy Lerner.

Subsequently, the new owner bought out Villa's other shareholders and after nine years as Aston Villa plc, the club reverted to Aston Villa FC. Work on the new £13million training facility at Bodymoor Heath was also completed, while a re-branding programme, featuring a new badge and fresh signage around the stadium, was also undertaken.

These were, indeed, changing times, and O'Neill's arrival inspired a nine-match unbeaten start to the Premiership season. A mid-winter slump saw Villa briefly looking anxiously over their shoulders before they recovered with another nine-match unbeaten sequence to finish in a respectable eleventh place.

Midfielder Stiliyan Petrov became Villa's first Bulgarian player when he signed from Celtic for £6.5million just before the August transfer deadline, while O'Neill recruited three more new signings during the January window - England under-21 international Ashley Young from Watford for an initial £8million, Norwegian striker John Carew from French champions Lyon in exchange for Milan Baros, and Scottish midfielder Shaun Maloney from Celtic for £1million.

But the stars of the season were home-grown striker Gabriel Agbonlahor, who headed the scorechart with ten goals in his first full campaign, and Gareth Barry, who marked his appointment as captain by converting six penalties. In doing so, Barry became only the 13th player in Villa's history to score ten or more spot kicks.

2007/08 - Let us entertain you

Villa Park attendances soared to a 58-year high in 2007/08 - and supporters were undeniably rewarded for their loyalty. The average home attendance of 40,375 was Villa's best since 1949/50 and the third highest in the club's history - and the players responded to the tremendous level of support.

They accumulated 60 points, the club's highest total for eleven years, and scored 71 goals - more than any Villa team since the title-winning side of 1980/81. And while a top six position in the league was not quite enough to secure UEFA Cup qualification, Villa at least returned to Europe by claiming an Intertoto Cup place.

Before the final match at West Ham, there was even a slim chance of finishing fifth. In the event, any such notion was ruled out as Villa drew 2-2 at Upton Park while Everton beat Newcastle United to secure an automatic UEFA Cup spot alongside FA Cup winners Portsmouth and League Cup winners Tottenham Hotspur. There's no doubt, though, that the Villa faithful received excellent value for money for the vast majority of the season.

Among the team's impressive away wins were 3-0 at Middlesbrough, 4-0 at Blackburn and 6-0 at Derby County, plus 4-4 draws at Tottenham and Chelsea. The result at Pride Park was Villa's biggest top-flight away success since a win by the same margin at Manchester United in 1914, while Stiliyan Petrov's 45-yard goal was the longest in the club's history.

The team performed admirably at home, too, scoring four times against both Newcastle United and Bolton Wanderers - and John Carew's three second-half goals against the Magpies made him the seventh Villa player to hit a Premier League hat-trick.

Then there was a double in the Second City derby. Villa won 2-1 at St Andrew's in November, courtesy of Liam Ridgewell's own-goal and a late header from Gabby Agbonlahor, before handing a 5-1 drubbing to the old enemy at Villa Park in April. Agbonlahor was also on target in that match, completing an emphatic victory after Ashley Young and Carew had both scored twice.

John Carew climbs to head home in a 5-1 thrashing of Birmingham City, April 2008.

A continental-style team group as Villa face the camera before their UEFA Cup game away to Slavia Prague in November 2008. Back: Ashley Young, John Carew, Gabby Agbonlahor, Carlos Cuellar, Zat Knight, Brad Guzan. Front: Craig Gardner, Nicky Shorey, Steve Sidwell, Curtis Davies, Moustapha Salifou.

2008/09 - Away the lads

The bare statistics show that Villa finished sixth in the table for the second year running, albeit with two more points than in the previous season. But mere statistics do not even begin to tell the story of an eventful campaign which was packed with drama, records and promise - even though the promise was ultimately unfulfilled.

Villa's final position was good enough for qualification to the play-off round in the new Europa League, but at one stage everyone was convinced that Champions League football was within grasp.

Indeed, when Chelsea visited Villa Park on the third weekend of February, Martin O'Neill's men stood third and held a seven-point advantage over fifth-place Arsenal. Surely, fourth was as low as the team were going to finish?

In the event, Frank Lampard's winning goal that afternoon saw Villa leapfrogged by Chelsea - and from that juncture they managed only two more wins as their advantage over the Gunners was gradually eroded.

But those disappointing closing weeks should not overshadow what had gone before. From the outset, it seemed we were destined for something special as Gabby Agbonlahor netted an eight-minute hat-trick in the opening league game against Manchester City. It was the second fastest hat-trick ever scored in the Premier League (behind Robbie Fowler's treble for Liverpool against Arsenal in 1994) and it was also the first time a Villa player had scored three times on the opening day for 78 years.

By Christmas, MON's men were really flying. A 1-0 success at West Ham lifted them to third in the festive table, and they had also qualified for the knockout stages of the UEFA Cup, having scored a memorable victory over Dutch masters Ajax during the group phase.

There was also progress on the FA Cup front as Villa disposed of Gillingham and Doncaster Rovers to reach the fifth round, while a 2-0 success at Blackburn in early February established a club record of seven consecutive league away wins.

On the same evening there was another club record when six players - Gareth Barry, Emile Heskey, Gabby Agbonlahor, James Milner, Ashley Young and Luke Young - were called up for the England squad. Villa were starting to look invincible, but exits from the FA Cup and UEFA Cup in quick succession had an adverse effect on the team's league form as their confidence drained away. Even so, it was a season to savour.

2009/10 - Back down Wembley Way

The 2009/10 campaign was one of Villa's most successful of the Premier League era. Not only did Martin O'Neill's side finish sixth for the third consecutive season, they were also involved in two exciting cup runs.

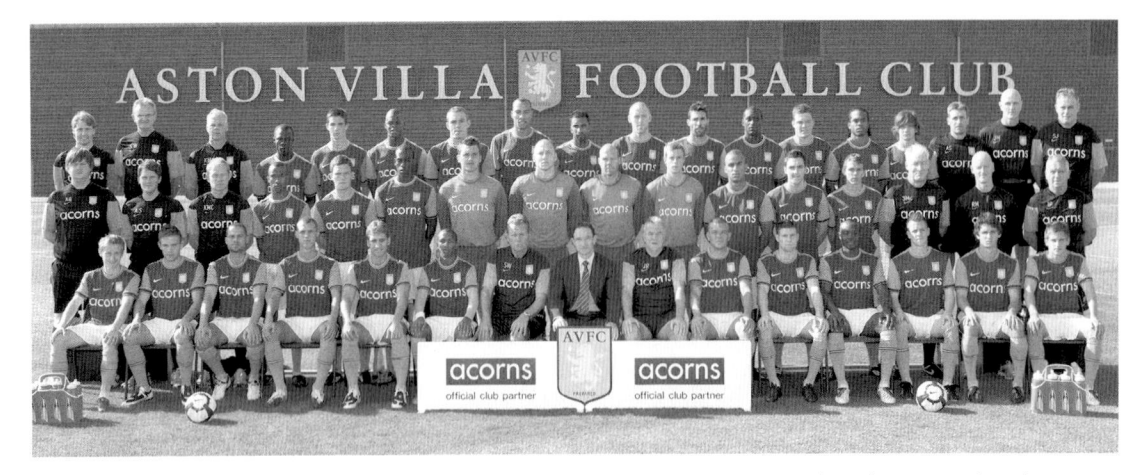

The 2009/10 squad who achieved a top six Premier League finish and made two visits to Wembley. Back row: Patrick Riley (analyst), Stuart Walker (physio), Kevin MacDonald (coach), Moustapha Salifou, Ciaran Clark, Marlon Harewood, Richard Dunne, John Carew, Habib Beye, James Collins, Carlos Cuellar, Emile Heskey, Shane Lowry, Nathan Delfouneso, Chris Herd, Alan Smith (physio), Jim Henry (fitness coach), Steve Jones (kit assistant). Middle: Alex Butler, Andy Smith (masseurs), Kenny McMillan (fitness coach), Fabian Delph, Craig Gardner, Isaiah Osbourne, Andy Marshall, Brad Guzan, Brad Friedel, Elliott Parrish, Gabby Agbonlahor, Stewart Downing, Stephen Warnock, Seamus McDonagh (coach), Roddy Macdonald (medical officer), Ian Paul (kit manager). Front: Barry Bannan, Andreas Weimann, Luke Young, Steve Sidwell, Stiliyan Petrov, Ashley Young, Steve Walford (coach), Martin O'Neill (manager), John Robertson (assistant manager), Wilfred Bouma, James Milner, Nigel Reo-Coker, Nicky Shorey, Eric Lichaj, Marc Albrighton.

The club's previous Wembley visit had been a decade earlier for the last FA Cup final played at the old stadium. Now they were back down Wembley Way twice in the space of six weeks.

Having overcome Cardiff City, Sunderland and Portsmouth in the Carling Cup, they secured their place in the final with an exhilarating 6-4 second-leg victory over Blackburn Rovers in the semi-final.

And although the final ended in a 2-1 defeat to Manchester United, Villa were adamant they were denied a sixth triumph in the competition by a controversial incident in the opening minutes. James Milner converted a penalty after Gabby Agbonlahor was brought down by Nemanja Vidic, but Martin O'Neill's men - as well as most neutral observers - felt the Serbian defender should have been sent off. Villa would surely have gone on to win against ten men, but in the event, Michael Owen equalised and Wayne Rooney headed a 74th-minute winner.

A week after the final, Villa booked a return ticket to Wembley in the FA Cup when John Carew's second-half hat-trick helped secure a 4-2 win at Reading in the sixth round. The semi-final at Wembley was evenly balanced for over an hour, but Chelsea went on to win 3-0.

There were several changes of personnel. Long-serving midfielder Gareth Barry joined Manchester City during the summer, while Villa recruited defenders Richard Dunne, James Collins, Stephen Warnock and Habib Beye, midfielder Fabian Delph and winger Stewart Downing, who had to wait until November for his debut because of a serious foot injury.

Despite the jolt of an opening-day home defeat by Wigan Athletic and an early exit from the new Europa League, the team put good results together and it was only on the penultimate weekend that their hopes of Champions League qualification were extinguished. Their points total of 64 was the club's highest since the Premier League was reduced to 20 teams in 1995/96.

2010/11 · Fighting a losing battle

Any prospect of a repeat of the successful 2009/10 campaign was effectively wrecked even before a ball had been kicked. Martin O'Neill, unhappy that his spending power was being curtailed, announced his resignation as manager just five days before the start of the season, leaving everyone at the club in a state of shock.

Something had to be done quickly - and reserve coach Kevin MacDonald was promptly put in charge on a caretaker basis. For a while, at least, it looked as if Villa had resolved a difficult situation without having to look elsewhere.

They were convincing 3-0 home winners against West Ham on the opening day, and although they suffered a crushing 6-0 defeat at Newcastle the following week, another home win - 1-0 against Everton - had people talking about MacDonald as a permanent replacement for O'Neill.

After the caretaker boss ruled himself out, though, the club recruited experienced Frenchman Gerard Houllier, and for a while the situation looked promising as the team maintained a top ten position. But a poor run in November and December, when they recorded only two wins, left Villa just above the relegation zone. It was time for drastic action, and Villa splashed out a club record £18million for Sunderland striker Darren Bent in a bid to halt the decline.

It worked. Bent scored the winner on his debut against Manchester City and went on to score eight more, including two in a 2-1 win over Arsenal at the Emirates Stadium on the penultimate weekend of the season.

That result, followed by an equally unlikely 1-0 home success over Liverpool on the final day, secured a slightly flattering position of ninth in the final table.

2011/12 · So sad for Stiliyan

Gerard Houllier's ill-health towards the end of the previous season had resulted in his assistant Gary McAllister taking charge for the last few games. And when the Frenchman decided it was time to retire, Villa were once again forced to look for a new manager.

The board's decision to appoint Birmingham City boss Alex McLeish was unpopular, to say the least. Yet Villa's start was hugely encouraging. It was mid-October - and the eighth game of the season - before they tasted defeat in the Premier League. True, they had not exactly been flying, but wins over Blackburn Rovers and Wigan Athletic, plus five draws, at least represented a stable launch to the campaign.

Unfortunately, the 4-1 setback in Manchester was the start of a depressing run of just one win in eleven games, a sequence which was ended by a brilliant 3-1 success at Chelsea on New Year's Eve, when goals from Stephen Ireland, Stiliyan Petrov and Darren Bent prompted early celebrations for 2012.

Sadly, it did not last. Despite a 3-2 win against Wolverhampton Wanderers at Molineux, where on-loan Irish striker Robbie Keane scored two spectacular goals against the club with whom he had started his career, Villa continued to struggle.

But even disappointing results on the pitch paled into insignificance by comparison with the devastating news in March that skipper Stiliyan Petrov had been diagnosed with acute leukaemia.

Villa effectively limped to the finishing line. After a 1-0 home win against Fulham - in what proved to be Petrov's final competitive match at Villa Park - the team failed to record a win in their remaining ten games, finishing just two points above the relegation zone. That seven-match unbeaten start proved to be a valuable insurance policy.

2012/13 · Gabby top of the Premier chart

Boosted by the arrival of new manager Paul Lambert, plus summer signings Ron Vlaar, Matt Lowton, Karim El Ahmadi and Brett Holman, Villa were optimistic ahead of the 2012/13 campaign, although it was not long before everyone was brought down to earth.

A 1-0 opening-day defeat at West Ham was followed by a 3-1 setback by Everton in the first home match. Those defeats had the manager diving into the market during transfer deadline week, with Christian Benteke, Ashley Westwood, Joe Bennett, Jordan Bowery added to the squad.

Initially, at least, the new signings had the desired effect when Villa recorded their first Premier League win, 2-0 against Swansea City, courtesy of a spectacular Lowton volley and a late clincher from debut boy Benteke. Suddenly everything looked rosy, particularly when Darren Bent's goal established an interval lead at Southampton the following week.

But a second-half collapse saw Villa beaten 4-1, setting the pattern for a season of inconsistency. That was never more evident than in December, when a superb 3-1 success at Liverpool was followed by three crushing festive defeats - 8-0 at Chelsea, 4-0 at home to Tottenham and 3-0 at home to Wigan Athletic.

Despite their erratic league form, Villa progressed to the semi-finals of the League Cup and were hot favourites for a trip to Wembley when they were drawn against Bradford City. Sadly, it all went horribly wrong, the League One side winning 4-3 on aggregate.

The remainder of the season was largely disappointing, with a couple of notable exceptions. Lowton's volley in a 3-1 win at Stoke City was even better than his effort against Swansea, while Benteke netted a hat-trick in a 6-1 thumping of Sunderland on the night Gabby Agbonlahor overtook Dwight Yorke as the club's highest Premier League scorer.

Villa 2012/13. Back row: Steve Jones (assistant kit manager), Mark Brittan (analyst), Terry Gennoe (coach), Jordan Bowery, Richard Dunne, Nathan Baker, Shay Given, Brad Guzan, Andy Marshall, Christian Benteke, Ciaran Clark, Eric Lichaj, Alan Smith (physio), John Hartley (physio), Alex Butler (masseur). Middle: Adrian Lamb (fitness coach), Paddy Riley (head of recruitment), Ian Paul, Tom Allen (analyst), Roddy MacDonald (club doctor), Karim El Ahmadi, Gary Gardner, Gabby Agbonlahor, Enda Stevens, Andreas Weimann, Stephen Ireland, Brett Holman, Paul Rastrick (physio), Ryan Williams (facilities assistant), Gordon Cowans (coach), Andy Smith (masseur), Gareth Payne (analyst). Front: Ashley Westwood, Fabian Delph, Matt Lowton, Chris Herd, Darren Bent, Gary Karsa (football operations director), Paul Lambert (manager), Ian Culverhouse (assistant manager), Ron Vlaar, Charles N'Zogbia, Joe Bennett, Marc Albrighton, Barry Bannan.

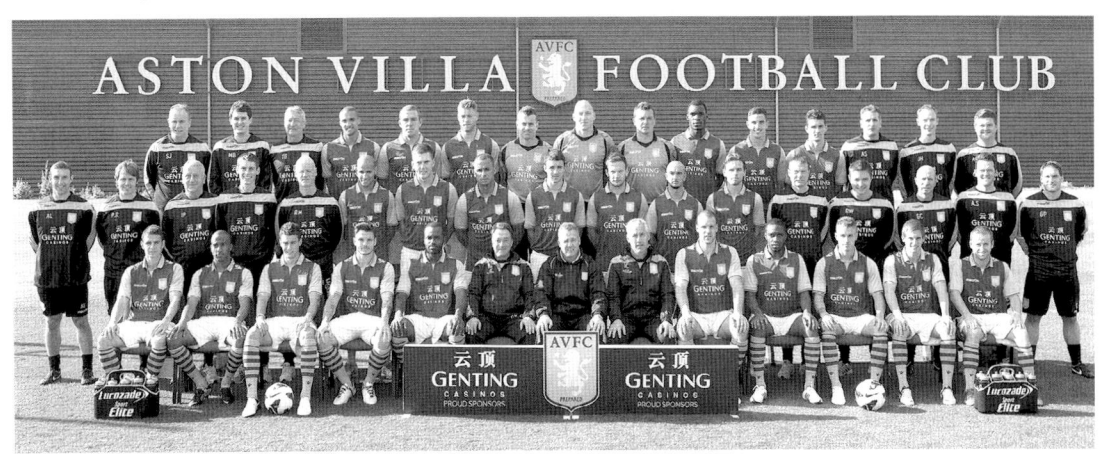

2013/14 · Capital start, then a struggle

Villa's form at the start of the season could not have been more impressive. A 3-1 victory over Arsenal on the opening day, courtesy of two Christian Benteke goals plus one from debut boy Antonio Luna, was followed by another equally fine performance in the capital a few nights later. True, they lost 2-1 to Chelsea, but Paul Lambert's side were worth at least a point and probably all three on a night when nothing went right for them.

Unfortunately, the promising start proved to be a false dawn. In 17 subsequent Premier League matches before the turn of the year, the team mustered just four wins, including an unlikely 3-2 success at home to Manchester City and victory by the same margin at Southampton when they had less than 30 per cent possession.

Thankfully, there was a marked improvement in January. Gabby Agbonlahor's goal ensured a 1-0 win on a wet New Year's Day at Sunderland; Benteke and Andreas Weimann were on target in a 2-2 draw at Liverpool; and neighbours West Bromwich Albion were beaten 4-3 in a thriller settled by Benteke's cheeky penalty.

Once again, though, Villa were unable to maintain their form, scoring just once in four February games which yielded a single point before back-to-back home wins over Norwich City and Chelsea raised hopes of a revival.

It did not happen. One point from the following six games - earned in a goalless Villa Park draw against Southampton - left the team with what was effectively a 'must win' final home match against Hull City. They responded with a 3-1 verdict which all-but ensured survival before ending the campaign with emphatic defeats at Manchester City and Tottenham Hotspur.

2014/15 · Wembley delight - and despair

For the second year running, Villa started the campaign well, only to fall away alarmingly. An Andreas Weimann goal secured maximum points at Stoke City on the opening day, and Paul Lambert's side followed up with a goalless home draw against Newcastle United, a 2-1 verdict against Hull City and an unlikely 1-0 win at Liverpool, where Gabby Agbonlahor's close-range goal silenced the Kop.

Going into the fifth game of the season, Villa stood second in the table, two points behind Chelsea. Half-a-dozen defeats later, during which they scored just once and conceded 15, they had slid to just above the relegation zone.

There was, at least, an improvement through November and December, when Villa recorded back-to-back wins against Crystal Palace and Leicester City, as well as drawing five other games.

But the team's lack of fire power was exposed over the festive season, a 1-0 Boxing Day setback at Swansea being followed by goalless home encounters against Sunderland and Crystal Place, games attended by former Italy international goalkeeper and Villa supporter Gianluca Pagliuca.

Cool finish – Christian Benteke's penalty gives Villa a thrilling 4-3 victory over West Bromwich Albion

THE HISTORY OF ASTON VILLA

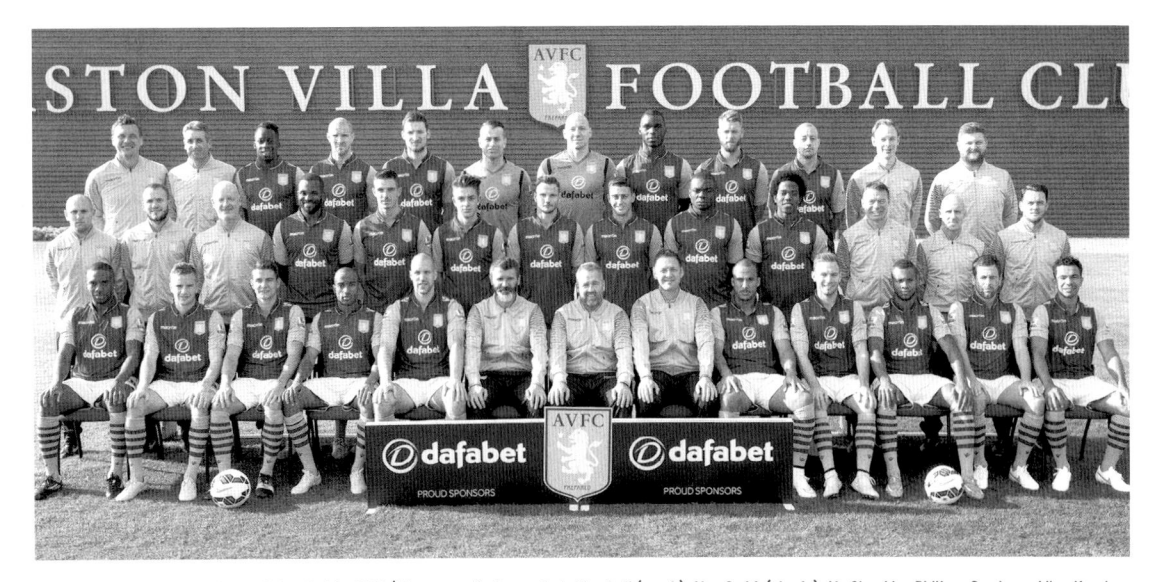

Bound for Wembley - the Villa squad ahead of the 2014/15 season. Back row: Andy Marshall (coach), Alan Smith (physio), Aly Cissokho, Philippe Senderos, Libor Kozak, Shay Given, Brad Guzan, Christian Benteke, Nathan Baker, Alan Hutton, John Hartley (physio), Alex Butler (masseur). Middle: Chris Lorkin (conditioning coach), Mike Watts (head of performance), Roddy MacDonald (club doctor), Darren Bent, Ciaran Clark, Jack Grealish, Chris Herd, Matt Lowton, Jores Okore, Carlos Sanchez, Paul Rastrick, David Henderson (physios), Andy Smith (masseur). Front: Charles N'Zogbia, Tom Clevereley, Ashley Westwood, Fabian Delph, Ron Vlaar, Roy Keane (assistant manager), Paul Lambert (manager), Scott Marshall (coach), Gabby Agbonlahor, Andreas Weimann, Leandro Bacuna, Joe Cole, Kieran Richardson.

If Pagliuca was disappointed not to see his favourite team score, at least he did not see them lose, which was their fate in the following five league games, culminating in Lambert's dismissal as manager on 11 February.

The one bright spot was an FA Cup run, which started under Lambert with wins against Blackpool and Bournemouth and continued with a fifth-round victory over Leicester City after manager-in-waiting Tim Sherwood popped into the home dressing room at half-time to deliver an inspired team-talk.

Even then, the team's Premier League losing run extended to seven games before two Villa Park successes over West Bromwich Albion in the space of five days stopped the rot in the league and then ensured a semi-final place.

The performance against Liverpool at Wembley, where goals from Christian Benteke and Fabian Delph clinched a 2-1 win after the Merseysiders had gone ahead, was arguably Villa's best of the decade, but it proved to be a hard act to follow. After wins over Everton and West Ham had eased relegation fears, safety was ironically ensured by results elsewhere on the day Villa were thrashed 6-1 at Southampton. And sadly, there was still another humiliation to come - a 4-0 Wembley mauling by Arsenal in the Cup final.

Villa's players salute Fabian Delph's Wembley winner against Liverpool in the FA Cup semi-final.

2015/16 · Leicester champions; Villa down

Villa had spent four seasons battling against relegation and in 2016 it finally happened. In what was by some distance the most catastrophic campaign in the club's history, Villa finished rock bottom with a miserly 17 points - the club's lowest-ever haul. And who could have predicted it would happen in the season that Leicester City won the title for the first time in their history?

77

Villa mustered just three Premier League victories - including one on the first day of the season. For the third year running, they got off to a winning start, beating promoted Bournemouth 1-0 at Dean Court with a header from debut boy Rudy Gestede. There was also an early-season boost in the form of a Scott Sinclair hat-trick in a 5-3 League Cup win over Notts County, while another Gestede header raised the roof as Birmingham City were knocked out in the third round.

But after the optimism generated by that opening-day success on the south coast, Tim Sherwood's side simply could not buy a league win. The closest they came was at Leicester, where Jack Grealish's first goal for the club plus a superb curling shot from Spanish midfielder Carles Gil established a 2-0 lead just past the hour mark. But a late collapse resulted in a 3-2 defeat to a team who, against all expectations, went on to become champions.

For Villa, meanwhile, the pain showed no sign of easing. A League Cup exit at Southampton proved to be Sherwood's last game in charge, and although a goalless home draw against Manchester City was an encouraging start for his successor Remi Garde, it was merely a brief respite. Home wins against Crystal Palace and Norwich City early in the new year offered a glimmer of hope, but any notion of a revival was cruelly crushed in a 6-0 Valentine's Day massacre by Liverpool at Villa Park - the first of eleven consecutive defeats.

Relegation was confirmed by a 1-0 setback at Manchester United in mid-April, by which time coach Eric Black was in temporary charge, Garde having departed at the end of March.

2016/17 · No easy way back

There was an air of optimism around Villa Park as Villa prepared for their first taste of second-tier football for 29 years. Former Italian star Roberto Di Matteo, the man who had guided Chelsea to Champions League glory in 2012, had been appointed manager during the summer and had signed nine new players, including James Chester, Jonathan Kodjia, Albert Adomah and Tommy Elphick.

But it soon became apparent that an immediate return to the Premier League was going to be far from easy. An opening-day defeat at Sheffield Wednesday was followed by an encouraging 3-0 victory over Rotherham United in the first Villa Park action of the season and, for a while at least, the team produced some attractive football. Unfortunately, they also developed a habit of conceding late goals, and their confidence drained. A dismal 2-0 defeat at Preston left Villa 19th in the table with just ten points from the first eleven games. Two days later, Di Matteo's brief reign was at an end, with Steve Bruce taking over in the managerial hot seat.

By the turn of the year, Villa's season was back on track as half-a-dozen wins lifted them into mid-table with their sights fixed firmly on a Play-Off place. Despite the arrival of another seven new signings during the January transfer window, though, it was the last week of February before they recorded their first success of 2017.

The 1-0 victory over Derby County, to be fair, was the start of an impressive sequence which yielded seven wins in eight games as Kodjia took his season's total to 19 goals. But Villa managed only one more win from the final six games - Gabby Agbonlahor's goal securing a 1-0 success in the Second City derby - and they had to settle for a modest finishing position of 13th.

2017/18 · So near yet so far

Villa were just 90 minutes from promotion at the end of an absorbing campaign. In the end, it all came down to a Play-Off final against Fulham at Wembley, where a 23rd-minute Tom Cairney goal meant the Cottagers, and not Steve Bruce's team, would spend the summer preparing for Premier League football.

To be fair, Villa supporters might have accepted that scenario after the first three Championship games. Gabby Agbonlahor scored what proved to be his last goal for the club to earn a 1-1 home draw against Hull City in the opening match, but back-to-back defeats at Cardiff City and Reading were anything but encouraging. There was a big improvement, though, once Norwich City had been dispatched 4-2 by a Conor Hourihane hat-trick plus Andre Green's first goal for the senior side.

That was the first of an eight-match unbeaten league run which ended with a 2-0 defeat at Molineux on the day we began to appreciate that Wolves were by far the best team in the division. Early in the new year, though, supporters began to dream of the second automatic promotion place. Starting at Middlesbrough in the final match of 2017, Villa put together a seven-match winning run which sent them shooting up to second place.

Once again, unfortunately, they were brought down to earth by a 2-0 setback, this time at Fulham, and the team's inconsistency was highlighted when their best performance of the season - a stunning 4-1 Villa Park victory over Wolves - was followed by a 3-1 home defeat by QPR and a 1-0 defeat at Bolton.

Jack Grealish's sensational volley - a goal witnessed by HRH Prince William - clinched a 1-0 victory over Cardiff City, while Leeds United were beaten by the same score a few nights later. But even a 4-0 verdict at Ipswich was not enough to lift Villa back into the automatic places, so it was down to the Play-Offs. Mile Jedinak's goal in the first leg at The Riverside was enough to see off Middlesbrough on aggregate in the semi-final, but the trip to Wembley brought only disappointment.

2018/19 · A Wembley wonderland

The Wembley woe of 2018 was replaced twelve months later by what can only be described as a Wembley wonderland. Villa once again reached the Championship Play-Off final - and this time it ended with promotion back to the Premier League after a three-year absence.

Dean Smith's men were 2-1 winners against Derby County, thanks to goals from Anwar El Ghazi and John McGinn, and the atmosphere before, during, and most notably after the game, had to be experienced to be believed. The national stadium had seen nothing like it for a long time. Such a fantastic finale had seemed highly unlikely just three months earlier. At the end of February, Villa were in the bottom half of the table, with little prospect of making the Play-Offs.

THE HISTORY OF ASTON VILLA

Villa's promotion-winning squad on parade early in the 2018/19 season. Back row: Ahmed Elmohamady, Jonathan Kodjia, Mile Jedinak, Andre Moreira, Orjan Nyland, Mark Bunn, Tammy Abraham, Keinan Davis, Anwar El Ghazi. Middle: Gary Walsh (coach), Axel Tuanzebe, Scott Hogan, Birkir Bjarnason, Jack Grealish, Yannick Bolasie, Glenn Whelan, Albert Adomah, Henri Lansbury, James Bree, Stephen Clemence (coach). Front: Neil Taylor, John McGinn, James Chester, Steve Agnew (coach), Steve Bruce (manager), Colin Calderwood (coach), Alan Hutton, Conor Hourihane, Rushian Hepburn-Murphy.

But Jack Grealish was appointed captain on his return from a lengthy injury lay-off, and by half-time Villa were 4-0 up against Derby at Villa Park. It was the start of a club record ten-match winning sequence which carried Villa from 13th place a finishing position of fifth.

The season could not have started any better, Villa winning 3-1 at Hull City and following up with a 3-2 home win over Wigan Athletic. Those wins were followed by three consecutive draws, only for Villa to be sliced apart in a humiliating 4-1 defeat at Sheffield United. By the end of September, just 14 points had been collected from ten games, and many supporters had become publicly critical of manager Steve Bruce's tactics. A 3-3 home draw against Preston North End at the start of October proved to be the last match for Bruce, who was sacked the following day.

The appointment of Dean Smith, a lifelong Villa supporter, provided just the tonic the team needed and their form improved dramatically, featuring emphatic away wins over high-riding Derby County and Middlesbrough plus a 4-2 success in the Second City derby.

Villa's fortunes dipped again in the new year, with just one win in nine games during January and February. But what a difference Grealish's return made. Qualification for the Play-Offs was assured with two games to spare, and after a penalty shoot-out success over Albion in the semi-final, Villa were determined not to slip at the final hurdle.

Tammy Abraham's penalty gives Villa a 2-1 victory over West Brom in the first leg of the Championship play-off semi-final

2019/20 · VAR, Coronavirus – and survival

It was a season like no other, not only for Villa, but for the whole of the football world. First there was the introduction of the Video Assistant Referee, which seemed to create more problems than it solved, and in March, the campaign was put on hold because of the spread of the Covid-19 disease.

Not surprisingly, it was tough going for Villa, despite a summer spending spree which brought in a host of new signings, including Bjorn Engels, Trezeguet, Matt Targett, Jota, keeper Tom Heaton and the club's first Brazilian players, midfielder Douglas Luiz and striker Wesley, who arrived for a club record £22million. French full-back Frederic Guilbert was another new face, having been signed during the January transfer window and loaned back to Caen.

An opening-day defeat at Tottenham was perhaps no great surprise, but a home defeat by Bournemouth the following weekend emphasised just how difficult life at the top was going to be.

Early season highlights included home wins over Everton and Newcastle United, plus a 5-1 romp at Norwich City, watched by Princes William and George, but by the turn of the year, Villa were entrenched in a relegation battle. January victories over Burnley and Watford eased the pressure, and there was also a memorable victory over Leicester City in the Carabao Cup semi-final before Villa did themselves proud in a narrow Wembley defeat by Manchester City in the final.

By then, Villa had been deprived of the services of Heaton and Wesley, both seriously injured at Burnley on New Year's Day, although another

Matt Targett gets away from Arsenal's Eddie Nketiah during the 1-0 win at Villa Park, as play resumed behind closed doors following the outbreak of the coronavirus pandemic, 21 July 2020.

new striker, Ally Samatta, became the first Tanzanian to score in both the Premier League and a Wembley final.

When the season came to a halt, Villa were in the bottom three and they showed little sign of improving their precarious position as football resumed behind closed doors in June. Four defeats and two draws left them five points from safety, but an amazing revival saw them collect eight points from the final four games to secure survival.

Villa's 2020/21 squad. Back row: Keinan Davis, Kortney Hause, Ezri Konsa, Jed Steer, Tom Heaton, Lovre Kalinic, Emiliano Martinez, Tyrone Mings, Bjorn Engels, Wesley. Middle row: Neil Cutler (goalkeeper coach), Jacob Ramsey, Frederic Guilbert, Neil Taylor, Ollie Watkins, Ross Barkley, Douglas Luiz, Trezeguet, Matt Targett, Anwar El Ghazi, Conor Hourihane, Jeremy Oliver (head of performance). Front: Marvelous Nakamba, Matty Cash, Jack Grealish, John Terry (assistant head coach), Dean Smith (head coach), Craig Shakespeare, Richard O'Kelly (assistant head coaches), John McGinn, Ahmed Elmohamady, Bertrand Traore.

2020/21 · A season of progress

Hat-trick hero - Ezri Konsa is the first to congratulate Ollie Watkins after the new boy completed a hat-trick in the 7-2 demolition of Liverpool - with Jack Grealish and Matty Cash racing to join the celebrations.

The bookies get it right more often than not, and they were spot on in making newly-promoted Fulham and West Bromwich Albion two of their three tips for relegation. But when it came to the third team destined for the drop, they could not have been more wrong.

In the light of Villa's narrow escape in July 2020, it was not altogether surprising that Dean Smith's men were strongly fancied to go down. But any such notion was effectively dispelled by Christmas, and at one stage there was even talk of qualification for the Europa League.

Ultimately, they fell well short of that target, largely because of Jack Grealish's lengthy absence with a shin injury, but a final position of eleventh represented the club's highest placing in English football for a decade. The season could hardly have started any better, Villa kicking-off with four consecutive wins for only the fifth time in the club's history - and the previous occasion had been 90 years earlier.

That blistering start included an incredible 7-2 victory over champions Liverpool, featuring a hat-trick from record signing Ollie Watkins, and with fellow new boys Emiliano Martinez, Matty Cash and the on-loan Ross Barkley all settling in nicely, supporters were already dreaming of Europe.

Successive home defeats by Leeds United and Southampton brought everyone back down to earth, but Villa continued to pick up valuable points, including eleven from five games during an unbeaten December, to ensure there would be no concerns about a return to the Championship.

It was just a pity that Grealish's three-month absence had such a big impact. The brilliant midfielder missed twelve games, of which Villa won just three, and the points dropped during that period were the difference between European qualification and mid-table.

Like many Premier League teams, Villa's season was disrupted by Covid-19. An outbreak among the first-team squad and staff in January resulted in back-to-back home games against Tottenham and Everton being postponed at a time when confidence was sky-high.

The pandemic also forced the club to field under-23 and under-18 players for a third-round FA Cup tie against Liverpool. Despite a not-unexpected 4-1 defeat, they made history as Villa's youngest-ever first team.

There were also a couple of other notable achievements. Martinez kept 15 clean sheets, equaling Brad Friedel's Premier League club record in 2009/10, while Watkins' 14-goal total equalled Villa's highest by an English player during the Premier League era, previously achieved by Julian Joachim in 1998/99.

Ollie Watkins celebrates scoring the winner with Jack Grealish as Villa left Tottenham with all three points, 19 May 2021.

2021/22 · Promises, promises...

Villa Park was rocking again in football's initial post-pandemic season, even if supporters were left with a feeling of unfulfilled promise - sometimes in the space of a single afternoon.

Nothing encapsulated the team's inconsistency more than the Midland derby at home to Wolves. Villa were dominant and delightful - and two up through Danny Ings and John McGinn - only to finish in disarray as the visitors plundered three goals in the closing ten minutes.

It was also a time when the club parted company with two of its favourite sons. Even before a ball was kicked, Jack Grealish joined Manchester City for a British record £100million and in November head coach Dean Smith - another lifelong Villan - was dismissed after a run of five straight defeats.

Villa had earlier bounced back from a shock opening-day setback at Watford to record some decent results, including a first victory over Manchester United since 2009.

But that depressing five-match losing sequence persuaded the club's owners that it was time for a change, and the appointment of a new head coach had the desired effect. Villa won four of their first four matches under Steven Gerrard, and for a while we even harboured thoughts of European qualification.

Once again, though, it proved difficult to maintain the winning habit, even with the arrival from Barcelona of Philppe Coutinho, who had been the world's most expensive player when moving from Liverpool to the Camp Nou.

That was never more evident than when Villa won consecutive matches against Brighton, Southampton and Leeds United, only to follow up by losing four in a row.

Ollie Watkins

Gerrard almost did his former club Liverpool a favour on the final day, when Villa led 2-0 against Manchester City through Matty Cash and Coutinho, only for the home side to score three quick goals and pip their Merseyside rivals to the title.

If a 14th-place finish was something of a disappointment, at least there were some personal highlights. Emi Martinez was impressive in goal, Ollie Watkins enjoyed a double-figure goal-haul for the second consecutive season and Cash made his international debut for Poland.

The 2021/22 squad on parade. Back row: Keinan Davis, Carney Chukwuemeka, Kortney Hause, Viljami Sinsalo, Emiliano Martinez, Jed Steer, Ezri Konsa, Axel Tuanzebe, Anwar El Ghazi. Middle row: Ricky Shamji (head of medical services), Trezeguet, Jacob Ramsey, Morgan Sanson, Matt Targett, Ollie Watkins, Leon Bailey, Douglas Luiz, Danny Ings, Jaden Philogene-Bidace, Cameron Archer, Matty Cash, Jeremy Oliver (performance director). Front: Neil Cutler, (goalkeeping coach), Marvelous Nakamba, Emiliano Buendia, Tyrone Mings, Craig Shakespeare (assistant head coach), Dean Smith (head coach), Aaron Danks (first team coach), John McGinn, Ashley Young, Bertrand Traore, Austin MacPhee (set-piece coach).

THE HISTORY OF ASTON VILLA

Left: Emi Martinez. Above: Matty Cash. Below: Philppe Coutinho.

ASTON VILLA - THE COMPLETE RECORD

VILLA PARK - A SPECIAL PLACE

Even the name has a special ring to it, so much so that Hollywood megastar Tom Hanks imagined it being located on Italy's Amalfi coast. The actual location, in the Witton area of Birmingham, is nowhere near as aesthetically pleasing as that popular holiday destination. Yet for many people, it is equally romantic.

As Simon Inglis observed in his 1997 book Villa Park, 100 Years: "There are football grounds and football grounds. And then there is Villa Park." Inglis is a lifelong supporter, so he is obviously biased, but his opinion is shared by thousands of people whose allegiances lie elsewhere. If Wembley is English football's spiritual home, Villa Park is not far behind, even though the club did not take up residence until they had been in existence for more than two decades.

Before their move to Villa Park in 1897, Villa had occupied four other 'home' grounds during their formative years - including one which they used for just a single match. The fixture generally acknowledged as Villa's first-ever game took place in March 1875 on a field in Birchfield.

During the following year, Villa also played at Aston Park and at the Lower Grounds - on an area known as The Meadow. But in the autumn of 1876, the club established a more permanent base at Wellington Road in Perry Barr. The first gate receipts, for a match against Wednesbury Town on 30 September, amounted to 5s 3d, around 26p in today's money.

It was a modest start, but this would be Villa's home for the next 21 years as they became known as the Perry Barr Pets and enjoyed success in both the FA Cup and the newly-formed Football League. Wellington Road had a capacity of almost 27,000 and in January 1888, a crowd of 26,849 packed in the ground for an FA Cup tie against Preston North End. Unofficially, the attendance was estimated at 35,000.

The overcrowding resulted in the police and mounted soldiers having to control disturbances among the spectators, who constantly spilled onto the pitch. With Villa leading 1-0, the teams agreed that the match should continue as a friendly, Preston going on to win 3-1. Unfortunately, Villa were blamed for what happened and the FA ruled that the result should stand. Villa, the Cup holders, were out of the competition.

Although the facilities at Wellington Road were primitive, Villa hosted several important games at their Perry Barr home, including FA Cup semi-finals and an England v Ireland international in 1893.

Four years later, after becoming football's double winners, Villa played their first match at what would later become known as Villa Park, a 3-0

A view from the Witton End in 1907

VILLA PARK - A SPECIAL PLACE

The Trinity Road stand in the early 1930s

victory over Blackburn Rovers on Saturday 17 April 1897. Little could anyone present that afternoon imagine that it would evolve into a magnificent all-seater arena.

And it happened without Villa Park ever losing its charm. While it boasts facilities to match those at any purpose-built stadium, Villa Park has retained the distinguishing features of a traditional football ground - four individual stands, each with its own character.

The newest of these is the magnificent Trinity Road stand, which was officially opened by Prince Charles in 2001, although it is the vast, imposing Holte End for which the venue is best-known. Formerly the largest behind-the-goal terrace in Europe, the Holte is now a spectacular double-decker structure capable of accommodating over 13,000 home supporters.

Quite apart from its tradition and atmosphere, though, Villa Park is also one of the most ideally located sporting arenas in the country. Situated in the centre of England, it is barely a mile from the M6 motorway.

It is no stranger to major events, either, having hosted matches at both the 1966 World Cup finals and the 1996 European Championship. Numerous other international fixtures have been staged there, and it was a regular venue for FA Cup semi-finals before they were moved to Wembley. Villa Park also had the honour of staging the last-ever UEFA Cup Winners' Cup final in 1999, when Italians Lazio beat Spanish club Real Mallorca. No-one could have envisaged, when the ground opened, that just over a century later a major European final would be played in this corner of Birmingham.

Then again, the site had hosted international entertainment before a football was ever kicked in anger. The Aston Lower Grounds was a popular amusement park and gardens which attracted visitors from far and wide, and which welcomed Buffalo Bill's famous Wild West show in 1887. Villa also played on the site during their formative years, on an adjacent area known as the Magnificent Meadow, which was also used for cricket, cycling and athletics. But it was not until Easter Saturday in 1897 that the club staged their first match at the new, enclosed arena, still known at the time as the Lower Grounds. A week earlier, they had become only the second team to achieve the double, beating Everton in the Cup Final at the Crystal Palace on the same day the League title became a mathematical certainty.

Any hopes of a large crowd for the opening match at the club's new home were dashed by torrential rain which restricted the attendance to around 14,000 – and many spectators were soaked to the skin because large sections of the Witton Lane stand roof had not been completed.

The distinctive barrel roof of the Witton Lane stand in 1958.

Lighting up time – August 1958.

At least the sodden supporters witnessed a 3-0 victory over Blackburn Rovers. Two days later, the crowd was 35,000 for an Easter Monday double-header – a cycling tournament on the 20ft-wide track which surrounded the pitch, followed by a derby against Wolves at 5.00pm, which Villa won 5-0.

It is unclear exactly when the ground became known as Villa Park, although the name was certainly being used frequently by the early part of the 20th century. During that era, the dressing rooms were located in the main Witton Lane stand, which was opposite covered terracing on Trinity Road. The capacity was 50,000, including 10,000 seats.

By 1914, there were plans to create a huge stadium capable of holding 104,000, but the grand scheme was curtailed by the First World War. Even so, the first phase of chairman Fred Rinder's masterplan – the rebuilding of both end terraces – was completed before the outbreak of hostilities with Germany. During the war, the ground – now minus its cycle track – was offered to the army for billeting, and when peacetime resumed in 1918, the most pressing project was a new stand on the Trinity Road side of the arena. Escalating building costs meant this had to be delayed for a few years but a decision to proceed was finally taken in April 1922. The impressive new structure, which now housed the dressing rooms, was in use by the end of the following year, and received a Royal visit from the Duke of York for a game against Bolton Wanderers in January 1924.

The capacity increased still further when the huge Holte End terrace was built even higher during the 1930s, and development continued even during the Second World War, when the Trinity Road stand was used as an air-raid shelter and the home dressing room was occupied by a rifle company of the 9th Battalion Royal Warwickshire Regiment.

Football experienced a boom time in the immediate post-war years, and Villa Park attendances reflected the game's immense popularity. In March 1946, a record crowd of 76, 588 witnessed an FA Cup quarter-final against Derby County and in 1948-49 the average League attendance soared to an all-time high of 47,168.

But it was from the 1950s that supporters saw the dramatic changes which have ultimately shaped the Villa Park of the 21st century. Floodlights were installed in 1958, the first system comprising 180ft-high pylons in all four corners of the ground, each holding 48 1500-watt lamps. They were switched on for the first time at half-time in a Monday evening match against Portsmouth on 25 August, Johnny Dixon having the distinction of being the first player to score a goal illuminated by the lights. In October that year, they were officially 'switched on' at a friendly against Swedish club GAIS.

ASTON VILLA · THE COMPLETE RECORD

A covered Holte End in the 1970s - with the famous AV floodlights.

Four years later, the Holte End was covered and 12 months after that, the distinctive barrel-shaped roof of the Witton Lane stand was dismantled to be replaced by a modern if rather less charming cover. In 1966, there was a temporary change when 6,000 seats were installed on the open Witton End terrace for the staging of three World Cup games, involving Argentina, Spain and West Germany.

That seating was subsequently removed, and 11 years later the terrace itself ceased to exist, being replaced by what became known as the North Stand. Not only did the new structure contain seats offering a superb downfield view from its upper tier, with terracing below, it also featured executive boxes and smart new offices.

The next major changes were by necessity rather than choice. In April 1989, football mourned the deaths of 96 people who were crushed during the Liverpool v Nottingham Forest FA Cup semi-final at Hillsborough, and the subsequent Lord Justice Taylor report ruled that all top clubs should transform their grounds into all-seater stadiums.

For Villa, the directive signalled the end of an era. The Holte End, one of the most famous terraces in the world, was demolished after the final game of the 1993/94 season, and seven months later a replacement double-decker stand was in use for the first time. In the meantime, there had been another significant change, the relatively small Witton Lane stand being replaced by a two-tier construction named after chairman Doug Ellis.

All that then remained from Villa's bygone era was the 1923 Trinity Road stand, which was bulldozed in the summer of 2000 to make way for a three-tier structure housing nearly 13,000 seats. The new stand was used in full for the first time when Villa hosted an England v Spain friendly early the following year, with the official opening ceremony being performed by HRH The Prince of Wales in November 2001.

View from the Witton End terrace in 1974.

VILLA PARK - A SPECIAL PLACE

Above - The North Stand and Doug Ellis stand.

Below - The current Holte End and Trinity Road stand.

An aerial view, not long before the Trinity Road stand was demolished.

Villa Park has staged 55 FA Cup semi-finals and semi-final replays - more than any other ground. The first was Tottenham's 4-0 victory over West Bromwich Albion in 1901 and the last was Manchester United's 4-1 win against Watford in 2007. It was also the venue for Liverpool's 2-1 win against West Ham in the 1981 League Cup final replay.

The ground has hosted eleven England internationals, spread across three different centuries. The first was the 2-1 win over Scotland in April 1899 and the last was a goalless draw against Holland in February 2005. In addition, it hosted four games between the Football League and the Scottish League, between 1898 and 1962.

Three World Cup group games were played at Villa Park in 1966, plus three group games in Euro '96 plus the quarter-final between the Czech Republic and Portugal.

Apart from football, Villa Park has also been a venue for boxing, American Football, religious gatherings and rock concerts.

VILLA PARK - A SPECIAL PLACE

Villa Park hosts the group match between West Germany and Spain during the 1966 World Cup Finals.

PROGRAMMED FOR SUCCESS

Villa supporters have become accustomed to centenary celebrations down the years. In 1974, it was the 100th anniversary of the club; 1997 marked a century at Villa Park; and 2006 was the centenary of the official programme.

It was a milestone marked throughout the 2006/07 season by a cover design based on the line drawing of Villa Park against a light blue background, which graced the Villa News & Record from 1949 to the mid-1960s. The centenary was also celebrated by a season-long series dedicated to Villa programmes from the past.

Until the early part of the 20th century, the club did not produce a programme, although match cards featuring team line-ups and fixtures were occasionally available. But in September 1906, the first issue of the Villa News & Record was published for the opening match against Blackburn Rovers. The new publication got off to an encouraging start, too, with around 5,000 copies sold.

Since those early days, the programme has undergone many changes, but it is still regarded as one of the best in the country, being voted Programme of the Year on eight occasions. The awards were first made in 1966, and we had to wait five years before Villa topped the charts for the first time. But the club's 1971 triumph was repeated in 1972, 1973, 1977, 1978, 1990, 1992 and 2005. It has also finished as runner-up several times and received various awards for continued excellence.

The foundations for this success were laid in 1969, when the News & Record was re-launched as a magazine-style publication by commercial manager Eric Woodward. It proved to be an astute switch.

Two years later, after the first award from the British Programme Collectors' Club, chairman Doug Ellis wrote in his annual report: "The profit on the News & Record continues to be excellent - over £10,600 this time. What gives us even greater cause for satisfaction is that this money was not made by cutting costs, but by providing a superior product".

At the time, Villa were playing in the old Third Division so the achievement was all the more impressive, and the success was repeated twelve months later. By 1972, three clubs - Villa, Chelsea and Coventry City - had won the best programme award twice. The Villa News & Record was setting new standards, and the following year, a hat-trick of triumphs was completed.

Villa just missed out for the following three years, finishing second on each occasion, but in 1977 the trophy was back in the club cabinet. Winners four times and runners-up three times was a record that could not be rivalled by any other programme in the country.

And even after a switch to a larger format in 1977/78, the honours kept rolling in as the club enjoyed a fifth victory in the space of eight seasons.

By the time of the next award in 1990, the competition was organised by the Football League Executive Staffs Association, Villa returning to top spot after five seasons as runners-up to Everton. Another triumph followed two years later, and in 2005 the Villa publication was voted No.1 by the Football Programme Directory.

A decade later, there was quite a coup for the Villa News & Record when thriller writer Lee Child stepped in as a guest editor for the issue against Leicester City in January 2016. Fittingly, the cover design was based on one of the famous author's Jack Reacher novels.

There was a significant change the following year when the programme reverted to a smaller size, but the 84-page perfect-bound issues continued to provide supporters with informative and entertaining content.

Even when football was forced behind closed doors by the Covid-19 outbreak in 2020, many supporters took out subscriptions for the final six home issues of 2019/20 and for the whole of the 2020/21 campaign.

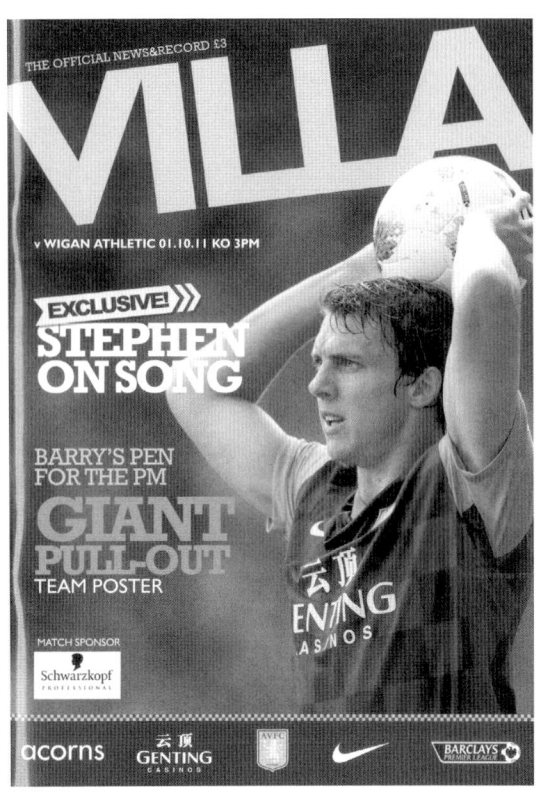

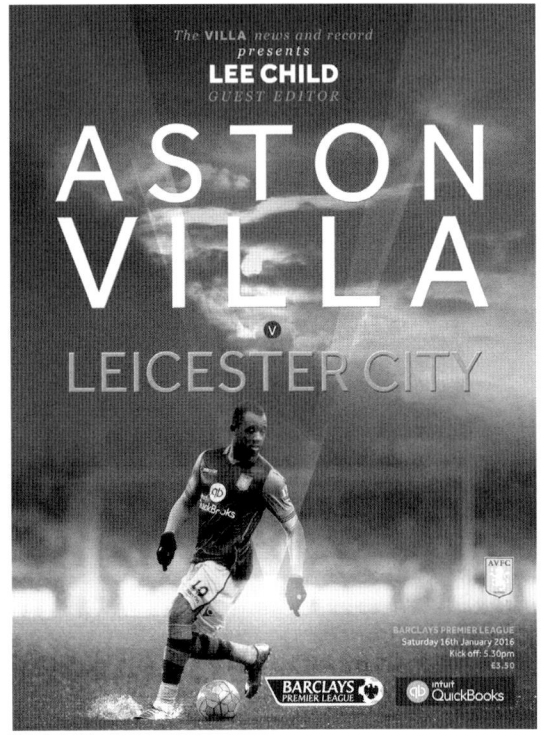

A GREAT GAME!

Memorable Villa matches through the years

VILLA 2-0 ALBION
2 APRIL 1887

Villa won the FA Cup for the first time in this first all-Midland final while Albion were runners-up the second year running. The game was a personal triumph for skipper Archie Hunter, who was central to Villa's success.

In a pre-match briefing, Hunter set out his requirements for every player, and the plan worked perfectly. FA President Major Marindin, who was the referee, said the game was won by Archie Hunter's captaincy.

For the first 20 minutes Albion held the advantage. Kicking down the slope from the Kennington Oval gas works with a strong wind behind them, they kept the Villa goal under constant pressure. But Villa backs Frank Coulton and Joey Simmonds were in superb form and with goalkeeper Jimmy Warner looking unbeatable, the threat faded.

Villa gradually got on top, and after the interval it was one-way traffic, with Dennis Hodgetts and Howard Vaughton dominating.

The breakthrough came on 55 minutes. Hunter passed to Richmond Davis who fed Hodgetts for the winger to hit a well-directed shot past goalkeeper Bob Roberts.

This was just the boost Villa needed, while Albion appeared to lose heart. Victory was finally sealed two minutes from time when Hunter's persistence paid off. The centre-forward gained possession, eluded the full-backs and headed for goal. As Roberts came out, Hunter threw himself full length onto the ground to jab the ball over the line.

Villa were originally set to return on Monday, but a last-minute change of plan saw the team arriving back at New Street at half-past three on the Sunday morning to be greeted by a tremendous crowd with a band playing 'See The Conquering Hero Comes'.

Villa: Warner, Coulton, Simmonds, Yates, Dawson, Burton, Davis, Brown, Hunter, Vaughton, Hodgetts.

Albion: Roberts, H. Green, Aldridge, Horton, Perry, Timmins, Woodhall, T. Green, Bayliss, Paddock, Pearson.

Attendance: 15,500

Bayliss (West Bromwich Albion) heads towards goal during the 1887 FA Cup Final.

A GREAT GAME!

General view of the FA Cup final between Aston Villa v Everton final played at the Crystal Palace before a crowd of over 65,000.

VILLA 3-2 EVERTON

10 APRIL 1897

Two years after their second FA Cup victory, Villa were back at the Crystal Palace with the double firmly in their sights. It was even reported that local tradesmen were offering unlimited presents of clothing, spirits, liquor and cigars to the players if they won the final!

The game started at a blistering pace. Jack 'Baldy' Reynolds, Fred Wheldon and Charlie Athersmith all had chances before Villa opened the scoring on 18 minutes. Athersmith and John Devey combined well down the right wing before the latter supplied John Campbell, who hit a swerving shot from 25 yards.

Five minutes later, Jack Bell took a pass from Abe Hartley and calmly beat keeper Jimmy Whitehouse for the equaliser. Inside a further five minutes Everton were in front, James Cowan giving away a free kick, from which Richard Boyle scored direct.

Five minutes later, Wheldon headed Villa level from Jimmy Crabtree's free-kick and four minutes before the break, Villa were in front once more. Athersmith took a corner and he and Reynolds exchanged passes before the latter centred for Crabtree to send a powerful header past goalkeeper Menham for what proved to be the winner.

The day had started with only Derby County having a mathematical chance of overtaking Villa in the race for the league title, but news came through that the Rams had been beaten by Bury - so Villa had won the league championship and the FA Cup on the same day.

Villa: Whitehouse, Spencer, Evans, Reynolds, James Cowan, Crabtree, Athersmith, Devey, Campbell, Wheldon, John Cowan.

Everton: Menham, Meecham, Storrier, Boyle, Holt, Stewart, Taylor, Bell, Hartley, Chadwick, Milward.

Attendance: 65,891

VILLA 2-0 NEWCASTLE UNITED
15 APRIL 1905

Villa were playing in their fifth FA Cup final with their captain, Howard Spencer, returning to Crystal Palace after picking up a winner's medal eight years earlier. Newcastle had never reached the final, but pre-match opinion was divided as to which team were favourites.

Villa attacked right from the kick-off and were ahead after just two minutes. A Newcastle attack was broken up by Spencer and the ball was crossed to the left where Albert Hall swung over a fine centre. When Joe Bache failed to connect, Harry Hampton pounced to send a left foot shot wide of goalkeeper Jimmy Lawrence.

Newcastle then took up the running but with Spencer prominent and Billy George ever alert, the danger was repelled. As Villa regained the upper hand, Lawrence did well to turn the ball behind from Hampton and the centre-forward then missed a golden opportunity with only the keeper to beat. Villa continued to look dangerous making full use of the wide pitch with long sweeping passes. A shot by Bill Brawn hit the post while Joe Bache missed two chances of adding to the score.

After the action of the first half, the second period opened quietly, but Villa soon returned to the attack, Bache having three chances and Hampton heading over.

With 14 minutes to go, Hall cleverly beat Magpies full-back Andy McCombie to let fly with a sizzling left foot shot which Lawrence could not hold. The alert Hampton seized on the rebound and calmly netted his second goal.

Villa: George, Spencer, Miles, Pearson, Leake, Windmill, Brawn, Garraty, Hampton, Bache, Hall.

Newcastle United: Lawrence, McCombie, Carr, Gardner, Aitken, McWilliam, Rutherford, Howie, Appleyard, Veitch, Gosnell.

Attendance: 101,117

Villa's Harry Hampton scores the opening goal past Newcastle United goalkeeper Jimmy Lawrence.

Right: A scramble in the Newcastle United goalmouth.

A GREAT GAME!

ASTON VILLA · THE COMPLETE RECORD

VILLA 1-0 SUNDERLAND

19 APRIL 1913

One Sunderland supporter put his house on the outcome of the 1913 Cup final - which is why the property bears the name Aston Villa! You will find the building in Front Street, Quarrington Hill, County Durham and it once belonged to businessman Albert Gillett, co-owner of the G & B bus company.

Mr Gillett, an avid follower of the Wearside club, was so confident his favourites would win the 1913 Cup final that he publicly declared that his new home would be named after the cup winners. He was as good as his word, reluctantly calling the house Aston Villa after Tommy Barber's late goal secured victory over a Sunderland team who would go on to become league champions.

It was the club's fifth Cup triumph, and the second time in a decade that Villa had beaten that season's champions in the final, having also denied Newcastle United the double in 1905.

If the 1913 final deserves its place among Villa's greatest moments, though, it certainly was not a contest noted for attractive football. A record crowd of nearly 122,000 at the Crystal Palace witnessed what was, at times, a brutal confrontation between two of the country's leading clubs.

Villa's prolific scorer Harry Hampton was among those singled out by the Wearsiders for harsh treatment, while goalkeeper Sam Hardy had to go off for a spell, leaving Villa down to ten men as Jimmy Harrop took over between the posts.

It was a testing time, with Sunderland clearly intent on making the most of their numerical supremacy, but Villa held firm.

Apart from Hardy's injury, Villa had also suffered an early blow when Charlie Wallace shot wide from the penalty spot after Clem Stephenson had been brought down.

But Wallace made up for his miss when he produced the corner which led to Villa's winning goal. With all his teammates closely marked in the goalmouth, Wallace played his flag kick behind them - and Barber met it with a header which left goalkeeper Joe Butler helpless.

Villa: Hardy, Lyons, Weston, Barber, Harrop, Leach, Wallace, Halse, Hampton, Stephenson, Bache.

Sunderland: Butler, Gladwin, Ness, Cuggy, Thomson, Low, Mordue, Buchan, Richardson, Holley, Martin.

Attendance: 121,919

Tommy Barber's last-minute winning goal in the 1913 FA Cup final.

VILLA 4-2 BLACKPOOL

6 MAY 1944

Any self-respecting Villa supporter will tell you the club have won the FA Cup seven times. But it's often forgotten that Villa were also cup winners in 1944, lifting the Football League North Cup.

And while the final was not played at a neutral ground, it was arguably more exhilarating than any of Villa's triumphs in the 'official' Cup. They took on Blackpool, who had won the trophy the previous year, and emerged 5-4 aggregate winners over the course of two absorbing games.

Billy Goffin opened the scoring just after half-time in the first leg at Bloomfield Road, only for the Seasiders to pounce twice in the last eight minutes for a 2-1 win.

Such was the level of interest in the second leg that thousands of supporters were locked out. Those lucky enough to gain admission witnessed a match which was described by Bert Fogg in the following day's Sunday Empire News as 'remarkable and memorable'.

Depending on which reports you believe, Villa were ahead in either 29 or 40 seconds, while the visitors were level before the game was 90 seconds old – and Fogg suspected that neither should really have been allowed!

He felt Bob Iverson was offside before setting up Frank Broome for Villa's opener and was adamant Jock Dodds was also offside as Blackpool equalised straight from the restart. Dodds' shot was parried by goalkeeper Alan Wakeman, and former Villa man Ronnie Dix collected the rebound to score with a shot which deflected in off George Cummings.

Villa were back in front in the tenth minute through George Edwards and although Blackpool were level again five minutes later, the home side were in front for a third time on 38 minutes, Bob Iverson scoring after an Eric Houghton shot had been parried.

It was breathtaking entertainment, and with the aggregate scores level at 4-4 at half-time, the final could have gone either way. As it was, Broome claimed his second goal early in the second half and Villa savoured their first cup glory since beating Huddersfield Town in the 1920 Cup final.

Villa: Wakeman, Potts, Cummings, Massie, Callaghan, Starling, Broome, Edwards, Parkes, Iverson, Houghton.

Blackpool: Savage, Pope, Kinsell, Johnston, Hayward, Jones, Matthews, Dix, Dodds, Finan, Pearson.

Attendance: 54,824

George Cummings, one of the stars of Villa's wartime cup final win over Blackpool.

A GREAT GAME!

Villa captain Johnny Dixon leads his team down the steps after collecting the FA Cup.

VILLA 2-1 MANCHESTER UNITED

4 MAY 1957

Villa had previously played only once at Wembley, losing the 1924 FA Cup final to Newcastle United, but they returned in triumph in 1957.

Just twelve months after staving off relegation, Eric Houghton's side made football history by winning the Cup for a record seventh time.

It was an incredible year for West Midlands football, with three local clubs - Villa, West Bromwich Albion and Birmingham City - reaching the semi-finals, an unprecedented feat which has never been repeated.

As it was, Villa were the only one of the trio to make it to Wembley, beating Albion in a replay at St Andrew's while Blues went down to Manchester United in the other semi-final.

By the time the final rolled around, United had been crowned champions and were looking to become the first club in the 20th century to achieve a league and cup double.

The Reds certainly started as hot favourites, but their hopes suffered a major blow after just six minutes when their goalkeeper Ray Wood suffered a fractured jaw in a collision with Villa winger Peter McParland.

But that should not detract from a fine performance by Villa, who kept Jackie Blanchflower busy, the stand-in keeper saving well from Les Smith, Jackie Sewell and McParland before Villa's Irish international took centre stage with two goals.

His crucial breakthrough arrived when he lunged to meet skipper Johnny Dixon's cross and send a bullet header flying past the helpless Blanchflower, and he drove home number two from close range after Billy Myerscough's shot had hit the bar.

United reduced the deficit with a looping header from Tommy Taylor eight minutes from time.

Villa: Sims, Lynn, Aldis, Crowther, Dugdale, Saward, Smith, Sewell, Myerscough, Dixon, McParland.

United: Wood, Foulkes, Byrne, Colman, Blanchflower, Edwards, Berry, Whelan, Taylor, Charlton, Pegg.

Attendance: 99,225.

101

ASTON VILLA · THE COMPLETE RECORD

A GREAT GAME!

Skipper Johnny Dixon proudly holds aloft the FA Cup after Villa's 1957 Wembley triumph.

VILLA 11-1 CHARLTON ATHLETIC

14 NOVEMBER 1959

Has there ever been a more prophetic pre-match pep talk, or a better example of a football team repaying the faith shown in them by their manager?

On Wednesday 11 November 1959, four days after Villa had lost at Liverpool, manager Joe Mercer boldly declared they would be unchanged for the weekend visit of Charlton Athletic.

It had been, he admitted, a difficult decision to make, particularly as his forwards were not scoring. Even star striker Gerry Hitchens had endured a relatively barren spell of four league games.

The manager was particularly sympathetic towards Hitchens, whose place was believed to be under threat from a youngster called Ken Price.

But Hitchens and his pals could hardly have responded in better fashion to their manager's challenge.

Hitchens hit five, Bobby Thomson two and Ron Wylie one, while wingers Jimmy MacEwan and Peter McParland also put their names on the score sheet, the Irishman netting the final two goals. It was exhilarating stuff, indeed, although there had been no sign of what was to come when Dennis Edwards equalised for the Londoners in the 22nd minute.

It was just a pity that fewer than 22,000 braved the rain to witness Villa's goal feast.

Charlton were handicapped from the hour mark, to be fair, by the loss of goalkeeper Willie Duff because of a damaged finger, but by then Hitchens had just hooked home his fifth goal.

Villa: Sims, Lynn, Neal, Crowe, Dugdale, Saward, MacEwan, Thomson, Hitchens, Wylie, McParland.

Charlton: Duff, Sewell, Townsend, Hinton, Ufton, Kiernan, Lawrie, Lucas, Leary, Edwards, Summers.

Attendance: 21,291

Two-goal Bobby Thomson (below) and five-goal Gerry Hitchens (right).

VILLA 3-0 ROTHERHAM UNITED

5 SEPTEMBER 1961

While other top-flight clubs were initially reluctant to get involved in the Football League Cup, Villa embraced the new competition from its inception.

It was a decision which paid dividends as Joe Mercer's side became the inaugural winners - but they had to play the waiting game before getting their hands on the trophy.

Their first-round tie against Huddersfield Town was played in October 1960, and it was eleven months later before the final was staged.

Fixture congestion at the end of the 1960/61 campaign meant the two-leg clash against Second Division Rotherham had to be held over until the start of the following season, and Villa played four league matches before the second leg of the League Cup final.

The first leg at Millmooor was a night to forget from a Villa perspective. Having lost the opening league match at Everton the previous Saturday, they were lethargic in the extreme, going down 2-0 to early second-half goals from Barry Webster and Alan Kirkman. Stan Lynn had the chance to reduce the deficit 16 minutes from time, but the normally deadly penalty-taker had his spot kick saved by goalkeeper Roy Ironside. That left Villa with a massive task on home soil, but by the time the second leg rolled around two weeks later, they were in much better shape, having won two league matches and drawn another.

Mercer's men attacked from the outset, although by half-time they had been unable to make a breakthrough. But their pressure was rewarded in the 67th minute, Alan O'Neill evading a challenge from two defenders before firing past Ironside.

It was just the fillip Villa needed and two minutes later the tie was all square as Harry Burrows hit number two with a low shot which took a deflection.

There was no further score in normal time, but after 19 minutes of extra-time, Jimmy MacEwan's centre led to a scramble in the visitors' defence before Peter McParland hammered his shot into the roof of the net.

For the second time in just over four years, the Irishman was a Villa cup-winner!

Villa: Sidebottom, Neal, Lee, Crowe, Dugdale, Deakin, MacEwan, O'Neill, McParland, Thomson, Burrows.

Rotherham: Ironside, Perry, Morgan, Lambert, Madden, Waterhouse, Webster, Weston, Houghton, Kirkman, Bambridge.

Attendance: 31,201

Jimmy MacEwan hooks the ball across the face of the Rotherham goal.

TOTTENHAM HOTSPUR 5-5 VILLA

19 MARCH 1966

It's always a stirring occasion when a team hit back from three or four goals down to salvage something from a match, although such feats are usually achieved on home soil with the backing of a fervent crowd.

When Villa produced one of the greatest recoveries in their history in March 1966, they did it in the unlikeliest of settings.

When a strong Tottenham side established a 5-1 lead against Dick Taylor's side by the 52nd minute at White Hart Lane, you would have bet your mortgage on the fact there was no way back.

Spurs went ahead after just two minutes through Alan Gilzean, with Jimmy Greaves and Frank Saul taking the score to 3-0 inside the first quarter of an hour

Tony Hateley pulled one back for the visitors following some good approach work from Alan Baker, but by the end of an embarrassingly one-sided opening period Laurie Brown had made it 4-1. When Jimmy Robertson dived to head in number five early in the second half, a double-figure trouncing looked possible, but Villa suddenly got their act together.

In the 55th minute, Hateley set up Alan Deakin for a ten-yard shot and then Villa's leading scorer took over, scoring twice in barely a minute.

At 5-1, Villa had looked finished; at 5-4 there was everything to play for - and Hateley duly brought the scores level with a header which gave him his fourth goal.

The visitors almost grabbed victory, too, when Deakin took the ball around goalkeeper Pat Jennings and looked certain to score until Alan Mullery cleared off the line. It was an exhilarating comeback.

Tottenham: Jennings, Mullery, Knowles, Clayton, Brown, Mackay, Robertson, Possee, Saul, Gilzean, Greaves.

Villa: Withers, Wright, Tindall, Sleeuwnhoek, Aitken, Baker, Pountney, Deakin, MacEwan, W Hamilton, Hateley.

Attendance: 28,371

Tony Hateley nets Villa's third goal past Tottenham Hotspur goalkeeper Pat Jennings.

A GREAT GAME!

Andy Lochhead beats United's Ian Ure in the air to head the equaliser.

VILLA 2-1 MANCHESTER UNITED

23 DECEMBER 1970

For a period quite rightly considered the nadir of Villa's history, the club's days in the old Third Division are still fondly recalled by people who lived through the experience. It was an exciting new adventure for many supporters, who travelled to grounds they had never previously visited.

The match which stands out from that period, though, and the one which former secretary Steve Stride regards as his favourite Villa game, was against more familiar opposition in the second leg of the 1970/71 League Cup semi-final.

Having overcome Notts County, Burnley, Northampton Town, Carlisle United and Bristol Rovers, Villa's dreams of reaching Wembley appeared to be over when they were paired with mighty Manchester United in the two-leg semi-final.

It was just two-and-a-half years after United had become the first English team to win the European Cup, and their line-up featured three of the greatest names in the Reds' history - Bobby Charlton, George Best and Dennis Law. Then there was goalkeeper Jimmy Rimmer - later to play for Villa - plus Paddy Crerand, Tony Dunne and Brian Kidd.

From no hope at all before the first leg, though, suddenly there was a glimmer as Villa staged a battling rearguard at Old Trafford to force a 1-1 draw, courtesy of an Andy Lochhead goal.

Vic Crowe's men were still very much the underdogs in the second leg, and when Kidd opened the scoring on 14 minutes, most of the 62,500 crowd were convinced it was curtains. But the home side refused to submit and in the 37th minute they were level, Lochhead outjumping Ian Ure to head Brian Godfrey's cross into the roof of the net.

And Villa Park simply erupted in the 72nd minute. Brian Godfrey crossed from the right and the ball skidded off Lochhead's head, but Willie Anderson lobbed back into the goalmouth for Pat McMahon to head home near the far post.

Villa had performed one of English football's greatest giant-killing acts to make it a truly magical Christmas.

Villa: Dunn, Bradley, Aitken, Godfrey, Turnbull, Tiler, McMahon, Gibson, Lochhead, I Hamilton, Anderson.

United: Rimmer, Fitzpatrick, Dunne, Crerand, Ure, Sadler, Morgan, Best, Charlton, Kidd, Law.

Attendance: 62,500

ASTON VILLA · THE COMPLETE RECORD

A GREAT GAME!

Villa Park dressing room celebrations after the 2-1 victory.

VILLA 5-1 LIVERPOOL

15 DECEMBER 1976

If Villa's unexpected League Cup victory over Manchester United provided a perfect Christmas present in 1970, this match had the same effect six years later.

During the build-up to the festive season Ron Saunders' side, by then re-established in the top flight, were in sparkling form as they tore apart a Liverpool side who had powered their way to the title the previous season and would be champions again the following May.

Villa had already handed five-goal thrashings to Ipswich Town and Arsenal at Villa Park, but the team's first-half demolition of the men from Anfield was something to behold.

Villa's victory all the more remarkable because all the goals were scored in a whirlwind first half. Andy Gray opened the scoring after nine minutes, netting his 19th goal of the season following a flowing move between Alex Cropley, John Deehan and John Robson, whose cross from the left was met by a long, hanging header by the Scottish striker.

Two minutes later, Deehan moved on to a pass from Dennis Mortimer before firing home through goalkeeper Ray Clemence's legs and the same player made it 3-0. Just past the half-hour mark, John Gidman's darting run down the right set up Brian Little for an angled shot into the far corner, and Liverpool were totally demoralised.

Paisley's men managed to reduce the arrears, but even then, there was time for Gray to head home Villa's fifth from a Mortimer corner.

It was something of a surprise that there was no further scoring, although there could have been more as Villa attacked the Holte End in the second half.

Villa: Findlay, Gidman, Robson, Phillips, Young, Mortimer, Deehan, Little, Gray, Cropley (Buttress 54), Carrodus.

Liverpool: Clemence, Neal, Thompson, Kennedy, Jones, Hughes, Keegan, McDermott, Callaghan, Johnson, Heighway.

Attendance: 42,851

Celebration time for John Gidman, Andy Gray and scorer Brian Little.

Right: John Deehan fires home his second and Villa's third goal.

A GREAT GAME!

VILLA 3-2 EVERTON

13 APRIL 1977

If you're looking for a classic football tale of the unexpected, look no further than the second replay of the 1977 League Cup final.

Villa and Everton had given absolutely no indication, during a drab goalless draw at Wembley or in a 1-1 replay stalemate at Hillsborough, of the drama which would unfold when they met for a third time at Old Trafford.

Indeed, the original game, ranks as one of the worst finals ever to be staged at Wembley. It was described by Brian Glanville in the Sunday Times as being 'as dull and uneventful as a seaside town in winter'.

Villa thought they had won the first replay at Sheffield when Roger Kenyon's own-goal gave them a 79th-minute lead, only for Bob Latchford to snatch an equaliser 90 seconds from the end.

None of which prepared a 54,749 crowd for the twists and turns of the third game. There was no cynicism in the press this time, Jeff Farmer declaring in the Daily Mail that 'the League Cup final came belatedly but gloriously to life in a second half of momentous excitement'.

Ron Saunders' side were a goal down at the interval, with Latchford again on target for the Merseysiders, and that situation still existed going into the final ten minutes.

But just when it seemed Villa would never reap the rewards of their positive football, they suddenly scored twice in the space of barely a minute. First, skipper Chris Nicholl cut in from the right-hand touchline to deliver a swerving 35-yard shot which flew just inside a post, and then Brian Little somehow screwed home a shot from a tight angle after he had brilliantly evaded two challenges.

Everton were not finished, though, and three minutes later the scores were level again as Mike Lyons headed in at close range.

Extra-time looked like ending in deadlock, but right at the death, substitute Gordon Smith's cross from the right was deflected across the goalmouth. It was the sort of chance Little did not miss and he duly stroked the ball past stranded goalkeeper David Lawson from six yards.

Villa: Burridge, Gidman (Smith 103) Nicholl, Phillips, Robson, Graydon, Mortimer, Cowans, Cropley, Deehan, Little.

Everton: Lawson, Robinson, McNaught, Darracott, Lyons, Hamilton, Dobson, Pearson, Goodlass, King, Latchford.

Attendance: 54,749

Brian Little nets the winning goal past Everton goalkeeper David Lawson.

Right: John Burridge and Chris Nicholl celebrate with the trophy.

A GREAT GAME!

VILLA 1-0 BAYERN MUNICH

26 MAY 1982

Oh, it must be. And it is! Peter Withe!

The words, uttered by ITV commentator Brian Moore, provide an indelible memento of the club's finest hour. You could hear the jubilation in Moore's voice as he described Withe's 67th-minute winner in the 1982 European Cup final - and you could certainly hear it from around 12,000 Villa supporters massed behind that goal in Rotterdam's De Kuip stadium.

Around 23 minutes plus stoppage time later, the noise grew into a crescendo as French referee Georges Konrath blew the final whistle. Having been crowned First Division champions twelve months earlier for the first time in 71 years, Villa were champions of Europe!

After a gentle stroll against Valur of Iceland in the first round, they confounded their critics by overcoming Dynamo Berlin, Dynamo Kiev and Anderlecht - all formidable opponents - to reach the final against Bayern Munich. The West German giants, boasting a line-up packed with world class players, were hot favourites, even more so when Villa goalkeeper Jimmy Rimmer was forced out of the action with a neck injury after just nine minutes.

Thankfully for Villa, his replacement produced the sort of inspired performance all footballers dream about. Reserve goalkeeper Nigel Spink had previously played just one senior game, but he was equal to everything Bayern could throw at him as the Germans pressed forward relentlessly.

If Spink was the hero at one end of the pitch, though, the ultimate glory belonged to Withe. It was hardly a classic finish, the ball hitting his shin and then a post before going in, but it may never be eclipsed as the most important goal in Villa's history.

The move actually began in Villa's goalmouth, where Allan Evans intercepted a centre before Des Bremner touched the ball back to Spink, who threw it out to Gary Williams on the left.

The full-back passed inside to Gordon Cowans, who pushed it forward to Withe, just inside the Bayern half. Easing away from a challenge, the striker touched it back to skipper Dennis Mortimer, who continued the patient build-up with a forward pass to Gary Shaw.

Drifting to the left-hand touchline, Shaw produced a clever turn and a piercing through ball to Tony Morley, who turned his marker inside out before crossing low to the far post. As Brian Moore uttered, it must be, and it is - Peter Withe!

Villa: Rimmer (Spink, 9); Swain, Evans, McNaught, Williams; Bremner, Mortimer, Cowans, Morley; Shaw, Withe.

Bayern: Muller, Dremmler, Horsmann, Weiner, Augenthaler, Kraus (Niedermayer), Durnberger, Brietner, Hoeness, Mathy (Guttler), Rummenigge.

Attendance: 39,776

Peter Withe shoots past Muller in the Bayern Munich goal to win the European Cup.

A GREAT GAME!

115

ASTON VILLA · THE COMPLETE RECORD

A GREAT GAME!

Gary Shaw, Tony Morley and winning goalscorer Peter Withe proudly show off the cup to Villa fans.

VILLA 3-1 TRANMERE ROVERS

27 FEBRUARY 1994

The bare scoreline does not even begin to describe the sheer drama which unfolded one Sunday afternoon at Villa Park in February 1994.

This game was the 'second half' of a League Cup semi-final, but it turned into a saga which ran and ran before Ron Atkinson's men clinched their place in the final.

The story had begun at Prenton Park eleven days earlier, when Villa's dreams of cup glory appeared to have evaporated as they trailed 3-0 to underdogs Tranmere going into stoppage time.

Dalian Atkinson's last-gasp volley at least provided a glimmer of hope for the return leg, although even then the manager conceded it would take a 'superhuman effort' from his players to overturn the deficit.

By the 23rd minute at Villa Park, getting to Wembley looked nowhere near as daunting a prospect following an opportunist close-range effort from Dean Saunders and a stunning diving header from central defender Shaun Teale.

At 3-3 on aggregate and with home advantage, Villa were suddenly the team in the driving seat, but it was not quite that simple. Six minutes later, the Merseysiders edged back in front with a penalty from veteran striker John Aldridge and an hour later there was still no change in the situation. But two minutes from time, Tony Daley's right-wing cross was met by a firm Dalian Atkinson header and the aggregate score was level again.

Extra-time failed to produce an outcome, so it was down to the nerve-tingling business of a penalty shoot-out - and the tension eclipsed anything which had happened during the previous 120 minutes.

The first five spot kicks were converted before Mark Bosnich saved from Ged Brannan to leave Villa 3-2 ahead. At 4-3, though, Ugo Ehiogu hit the bar, and Tranmere drew level through Aldridge. When skipper Kevin Richardson fired over with Villa's next kick, Liam O'Brien had the chance to send Tranmere to Wembley.

O'Brien's penalty was brilliantly saved by Bosnich, though, and after Daley had made it 5-4, Bosnich wrote himself into Villa folklore by making his third save of the shoot-out, this time from Ian Nolan.

A month later, Villa beat United 3-1 in the final to lift the trophy for the sixth time, but the game supporters always talk about is the semi-final. Rarely have a Villa Park crowd experienced such a range of emotions.

Villa: Bosnich, Cox (Fenton, 77), McGrath, Teale, Barrett; Houghton (Ehiogu, 90), Richardson, Townsend, Daley; Saunders, Atkinson.

Tranmere: Nixon, McGreal, Hughes (Thomas, 90), Higgins, Nolan, Nevin (Morrissey, 98), O'Brien, Irons, Brannan, Malkin, Aldridge.

Attendance: 40,593

Dean Saunders celebrates with teammates Dalian Atkinson and Earl Barrett.

A GREAT GAME!

Inter the next round - Phil King thumps home the decisive penalty.

VILLA 1-0 INTER MILAN
29 SEPTEMBER 1994

Never has the term Penalty King been more appropriate...

Seven months after the drama of their League Cup showdown against Tranmere, Villa again had to endure a nerve-tingling penalty shoot-out after their first round UEFA Cup-tie against Italian giants Internazionale finished level on aggregate.

And the man who converted the spot kick which carried Ron Atkinson's men through to the second round was Phil King, a left-back who made only 23 appearances in claret and blue, but had the perfect temperament to handle intense pressure.

King, signed from Sheffield Wednesday for £250,000 that summer, was a cheerful, easy-going character who simply refused to be intimidated by the occasion.

As he made his way to take the crucial kick which could ensure a famous victory, Steve Staunton and Ugo Ehiogu both reminded him that if he scored, Villa were through. To which he replied: "I don't know if I can be bothered".

A few seconds later, he was standing with his arms raised in triumph as his shot crashed past goalkeeper Gianluca Pagliuca and into the roof of the net.

Garry Parker, Staunton and Andy Townsend had also converted Villa's first three penalties to cancel out conversions from Giovanni Bia, Dennis Berkkamp and Andrea Seno.

Then Davide Fontolan missed, only for Guy Whittingham's kick to be saved by Pagliuca and leave the score at 3-3.

Next up was Ruben Sosa, but nerves also got to the Uruguayan striker as he crashed his shot against the bar. King had no such problems.

But it was not just the spot-kick drama which made this such a memorable night. Four years earlier, Villa had lost 3-2 on aggregate to Inter in the same competition after a magnificent 2-0 win at Villa Park - and they again faced a potential exit when Bergkamp's 75th minute penalty gave the Serie A team a first-leg lead.

The return match was a pulsating, compelling contest, won 1-0 by Ray Houghton's 41st-minute goal before extra-time failed to produce an outcome.

Villa had matched one of the leading sides in Europe over two games, and King's winner prompted manager Atkinson to describe it as "my greatest result".

Villa: Spink, Barrett, Staunton, Ehiogu, McGrath, Richardson (Parker 98), Houghton, Townsend, Saunders (Whittingham 18), Atkinson, King

Inter: Pagliuca, Bergomi, Festa, Bia, Conte (Fontolan 62), Paganin, Berti, Seno, Bergkamp, Sosa, Pancev (Orlandini 112).

Attendance: 30,533

Two strikes from Graham Fenton helped Villa lead 3-0 before the half hour mark.

TOTTENHAM HOTSPUR 3-4 VILLA

19 NOVEMBER 1994

There have been some unlikely scorelines at White Hart Lane over the past three decades, including a 5-2 Villa win in 1992 and a 4-2 success in 2000, Tottenham having gone two-up on both occasions.

But this win was surely the most unlikely result of all between two sides whose meetings have frequently overflowed with open, entertaining football and plenty of goals.

Villa had failed to win in nine matches, a dismal sequence which had cost manager Ron Atkinson his job; Andy Townsend was starting a six-match suspension; Spurs were in buoyant mood after appointing former England captain Gerry Francis as their new boss.

If ever there was a banker home win, this was it - yet before the game was half-an-hour old, Villa were three-up!

Just eight minutes had elapsed when Dalian Atkinson headed the opening goal before young midfielder Graham Fenton, deputising for Townsend, took centre stage.

In the 21st and 27th minutes, the eager Geordie produced almost carbon copy goals, bursting into the Spurs penalty area to beat goalkeeper Ian Walker with two shots into the same corner of the net.

Until five minutes before half-time, the visitors were still well in control but the whole complexion of the game altered dramatically as Teddy Sheringham reduced the deficit before German striker Jurgen Klinsmann netted twice, including a penalty, to bring the scores level by the 71st minute.

But the visitors settled down again before coming up with a stunning stoppage-time winner. Garry Parker sent a perfectly weighted pass for Dean Saunders to chase and the Welsh marksman brushed aside Gary Mabbutt's challenge before sending an unstoppable drive past Walker.

It was an incredible finale which left caretaker boss Jim Barron as the only manager in Villa history with a 100 per cent record!

Tottenham: Walker, Kerslake (Nethercott, HT), Calderwood, Campbell, Mabbutt, Anderton, Popescu, Howells, Caskey (Barmby, 46), Klinsmann, Sheringham.

Villa: Bosnich, Barrett, Ehiogu, McGrath, King, Houghton, Parker, Richardson, Fenton, Saunders, Atkinson (Lamptey, 53).

Attendance: 26,899

VILLA 3-2 ARSENAL

13 DECEMBER 1998

One-nil to the Arsenal became something of a catchphrase throughout the late 1990s. Quite simply, if you went a goal down to the Gunners, you could forget about winning.

So when Dutch master Dennis Bergkamp scored his second Arsenal goal on the stroke of half-time at Villa Park, the home side faced what most observers regarded as Mission Impossible.

There was something special about Villa's class of 1998, though. The team had enjoyed a club record start to the campaign of twelve unbeaten matches and although they had subsequently lost to Liverpool and Chelsea, they were still second in the table going into this match, having been knocked off the top by Manchester United 24 hours earlier.

At the interval, it looked very much as if John Gregory's side were destined to remain in second place and the subdued mood around Villa Park became one of sheer horror when a half-time parachute drop went horribly wrong.

Flt-Sgt Nigel Rogoff suffered multiple injuries when, after experiencing problems with his approach, he was unable to avoid the roof of the Trinity Road stand and plunged on to the track surrounding the pitch. It was a sickening sight and the start of the second half was delayed as medical men tended to Rogoff before he was rushed to hospital. There would certainly have been no complaints had Villa gone through the motions in the second half after such a dreadful incident.

With less than half-an-hour remaining, they were still two-down, but suddenly there was hope as Stan Collymore and Lee Hendrie combined to create a chance for Julian Joachim, who calmly stroked the ball past David Seaman with the outside of his boot.

Within three minutes, Villa were level. Alan Thompson's shot was going wide before Dion Dublin stabbed it past Seaman from close range - and the Holte End erupted on 83 minutes when Dublin, surprisingly finding himself in space when Thompson's corner dropped at his feet, drove the winner into the roof of the net.

Villa had completed a remarkable comeback - and were re-instated at the top of the table.

Villa: Oakes, Watson, Ehiogu, Southgate, Wright, Hendrie, Taylor, Barry (Collymore, 53), Thompson; Joachim (Grayson, 86), Dublin.

Arsenal: Seaman, Dixon, Bould, Keown, Vivas, Parlour (Boa-Morte, 89), Ljungberg (Grimandi, 67), Vieira, Overmars, Bergkamp, Anelka.

Attendance: 39,217

Seven minutes to go when Dion Dublin thumps home the winner.

VILLA 3-2 BOLTON WANDERERS
27 OCTOBER 2001

Villa climbed to the top of the Premier League for the first time in the 21st century with this narrow victory against a Bolton side who trailed them by just three points at kick-off time.

Indeed, the newly-promoted Trotters must have fancied their chances at Villa Park, having beaten Manchester United 2-1 at Old Trafford the previous week. On the same afternoon, Peter Schmeichel had created two records, becoming the first goalkeeper to score a competitive Villa goal and at the same time establishing himself as the club's oldest-ever scorer, only for John Gregory's men to suffer their first league defeat of the season.

Villa's response to a 3-2 setback at Everton could not have been any better. A midweek victory over Charlton Athletic lifted them to third, and three days later, they were in pole position.

There were fears Bolton would repeat their Old Trafford victory when former Walsall striker Michael Ricketts put them ahead in the second minute, but Juan Pablo Angel had the perfect response as he equalised with a downward header from Steve Staunton's 13th-minute corner.

Three minutes before half-time, Villa were in front, Angel's flick setting up Darius Vassell for a clinical finish as he shrugged off his marker and drilled a low 15-yard shot just inside the right-hand post.

A minute after the break it was 3-1, Angel converting the club's first penalty for more than a year after Riccardo Gardner had been adjudged to have pushed Moustapha Hadji.

There were some anxious moments for Villa after Ricketts had tapped in Bolton's second a quarter-of-an-hour before the end, but Gregory's boys held on to go top of the table.

Villa: Schmeichel, Delaney, Alpay, Staunton, Wright, Hadji, Boateng, Hendrie (Taylor, 86), Kachloul, Angel (Dublin, 72), Vassell (Merson, 73).

Bolton: Banks, N'Gotty (Barness 90) Bergsson, Hansen (Wallace, HT), Charlton, Frandsen, Gardner (Holdsworth, 72), Farrelly, Nolan, Diawara, Ricketts.

Attendance: 33,599

Juan Pablo Angel celebrates after scoring his second goal from the penalty spot.

A GREAT GAME!

VILLA 5-1 BIRMINGHAM CITY
20 APRIL 2008

Villa's Class of 2007/08 scored goals with a frequency reminiscent of the immediate pre-war and post-war years and their most prolific spell produced 15 in three consecutive games during April.

Bolton Wanderers were comprehensively beaten 4-0 at Villa Park before Martin O'Neill's side went to Derby and thrashed the relegation-bound Rams 6-0 - Villa's biggest top flight away win since 1912.

While those two emphatic victories were deeply satisfying, though, Villa's players knew the game in which they really had to deliver was the Second City showdown against the old enemy from the other side of Birmingham.

They certainly did not disappoint, recording the club's biggest league win over Blues since the early 1960s.

The only surprise was that it took them nearly half-an-hour to make a breakthrough. A flowing 28th-minute move down the right, involving Gareth Barry and Nigel Reo-Coker, ended with Olof Mellberg hitting the ball across the edge of the penalty area for Ashley Young to drive right footed into the bottom corner.

Three minutes before half-time it was 2-0 as John Carew met Young's free-kick with a glancing header - and the Norwegian striker grabbed his second on 53 minutes with a simple tap-in following Barry's inviting pass.

Just past the hour mark, Villa made it four, Young thumping home the rebound after Maik Taylor had parried his initial shot.

And although Mikael Forssell grabbed a consolation goal for the visitors, Gabby Agbonlahor fired home number five in the 77th minute. It was, indeed, a five-star show!

Villa: Carson, Mellberg (Harewood, 85), Knight, Laursen, Bouma, Young, Reo-Coker, Barry, Petrov, Carew, Agbonlahor.

Birmingham City: Taylor, Kelly, Ridgewell, Jerome (Kapo, 58), Muamba, Jaidi, Nafti, McSheffrey, Murphy, Zarate (Forsell, 58) McFadden.

Attendance: 42,584

Ashley Young opens the scoring for Villa.

Right: Jubilant John Carew after netting the second.

A GREAT GAME!

VILLA 6-4 BLACKBURN ROVERS
20 JANUARY 2010

Ten-goal Villa games are something of a rarity, and this one was simply incredible as Villa carried their supporters through a range of emotions before reaching the League Cup final for the eighth time.

There was an air of confidence at the start, which was hardly surprising given that Martin O'Neill's men held a 1-0 lead from the first leg of the semi-final. That gave way to depression as Blackburn dominated the opening half-hour and established a two-goal advantage, but Villa then turned on the style to lead 5-2 before the visitors staged a spirited revival.

Finally, there was an air of euphoria as Ashley Young's late goal put the issue beyond any lingering doubt and carried Villa to Wembley.

You could feel the confidence drain from a packed Holte End as Rovers striker Nikola Kalinic pounced twice by the 26th minute, but the home side got the goal they desperately needed after half an hour. Stephen Warnock's clinical close-range conversion of Young's right-wing cross was special because it was his first for the club - and it breathed life back into Villa.

James Milner restored parity with a well-struck 39th-minute penalty after Gabby Agbonlahor had been hauled to the ground by Chris Samba, and with the Rovers centre-back sent off for the offence, the pendulum swung strongly towards Villa.

Richard Dunne forced Steven Nzonzi into an own-goal, Milner's 25-yard shot deflected in off Agbonlahor and then Holte Enders rose to salute Emile Heskey as the England striker calmly eased past goalkeeper Paul Robinson before slotting home his first goal in front of the famous terrace.

At 5-2 on the night, with another goal in the bank, surely it was all over? Ten-man Blackburn thought otherwise, strikes from Martin Olsson and Brett Emerton reducing the aggregate deficit to two.

The word breathtaking is perhaps overused in football, but this one certainly took the breath away - until Young darted to the edge of the penalty area and curled a low right-foot shot past Robinson.

Villa: Guzan, Cuellar, Collins, Dunne, Warnock, A Young, Petrov, Milner, Downing (Sidwell, 85), Agbonlahor, Heskey.

Blackburn: Robinson, Chimbonda, Samba, Nelsen, Givet, Dunn (McCarthy, 54), Emerton, Nzonzi (Reid, 61), Olsson, Pedersen, Kalinic (Di Santo, 72).

Attendance: 40,406

Richard Dunne and Gabriel Agbonlahor celebrate Villa's third goal.

Right: Ashley Young celebrates after scoring Villa's sixth and putting the tie beyond doubt.

A GREAT GAME!

ASTON VILLA · THE COMPLETE RECORD

VILLA 4-3 WEST BROMWICH ALBION
29 JANUARY 2014

For the second time in 2013/14, Villa were required to recover from an early two-goal deficit against the Baggies, having drawn 2-2 at The Hawthorns. But the claret-and-blue rapid response unit were equal to the task, ultimately emerging with the club's 300th Premier League victory in a compelling contest which had drama, fabulous goals and entertaining football in constantly driving rain.

Only four minutes had elapsed when Albion skipper Chris Brunt sent a stunning left-foot angled drive into the top corner from almost 30 yards.

Villa boss Paul Lambert described that one as a 'wonder strike', but he was understandably less tolerant of the visitors' second, the unfortunate Fabian Delph slicing the ball into his own net.

Four minutes later, though, Villa were back in contention when Brad Guzan's long free kick took a flick off Albion defender Diego Lugano as Christian Benteke challenged. Andi Weimann was a picture of composure as lobbed sublimely over Ben Foster from just inside the box.

It was all-square on 24 minutes. Matt Lowton crossed low from the right and although Leandro Bacuna did not make the best of contacts, he did enough to scoop the ball over the line.

An amazing turnaround was complete when Fabian Delph put Villa ahead with a goal every bit as good as Brunt's opener. Benteke headed on Ashley Westwood's long high ball from deep in the home half, and Delph cleverly slipped away from Steven Reid on the left-hand edge of the area to hammer an unstoppable left-footer in off the underside of the bar.

Benteke almost made it 4-2 which went off Foster's legs for a corner, but in the 43rd minute, the Baggies were back on level terms Mulumbu stroking a low shot past Guzan.

There was only one goal after the break, but it was enough to make Villa only the sixth club to achieve 300 Premier League wins. After being brought down by Lugano in the 65th minute, Benteke cleverly tricked Foster into diving left before stroking his penalty into the other side of the goal.

Villa: Guzan, Lowton (Holt 65), Vlaar, Clark, Bertrand, Bacuna, El Ahmadi (Sylla 76), Westwood, Delph, Weimann (Baker 79), Benteke.

Albion: Foster, Reid (Berahino 76), Lugano, Olsson, Ridgewell, Mulumbu, Yacob, Morrison, Brunt, Anelka (Amalfitano 26), Anichebe (Vydra 80).

Attendance: 36,083

Christian Benteke celebrates scoring Villa's fourth from the penalty spot. Left: A jubilant Brad Guzan.

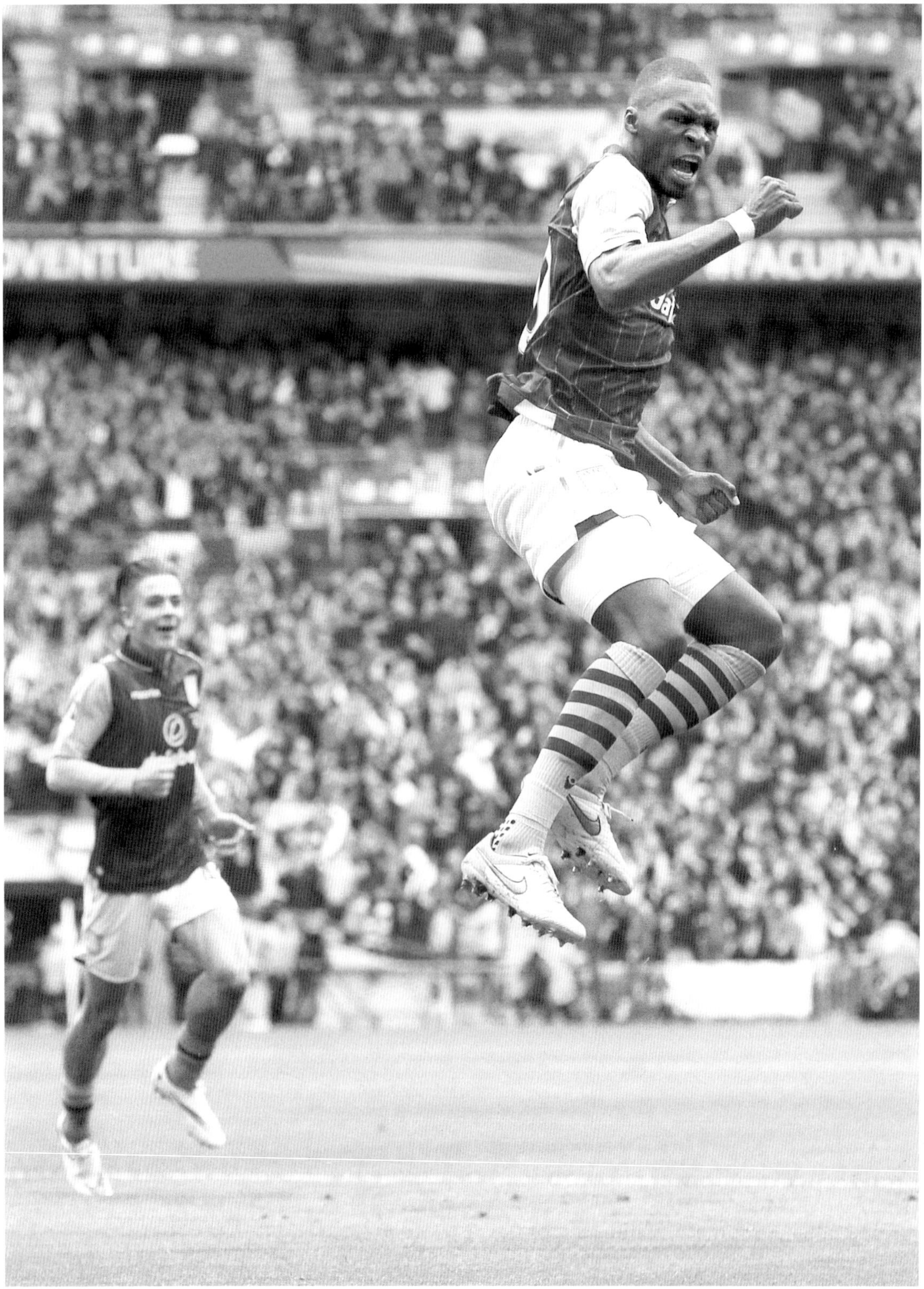

VILLA 2-1 LIVERPOOL

19 APRIL 2015

Villa have made numerous visits to the 'new' Wembley Stadium, but none so memorable as the 2015 FA Cup semi-final.

The team took time out from their battle against relegation to take on a Liverpool side who stood fifth in the Premier League and were red hot favourites to reach the final.

But this was a day when Villa, released from the day-to-day worries of top-flight survival, reveled in the role of underdogs. That much was evident even as the teams lined up in the tunnel. The weight of expectation was etched on Liverpool skipper Steven Gerrard's face; to his left, Shay Given was grinning from ear to ear.

Villa approached the game in a positive mood which mirrored the keeper's broad smile - until they were disrupted by the 26th-minute departure of Nathan Baker. Sub Jores Okore had hardly settled when he and Delph were both unable to clear following a Liverpool attack down the left, paving the way for an opening goal from Philippe Coutinho against the run of play.

It was a demoralising blow, but six minutes later, Delph and Grealish combined effectively to set up Benteke for a sublime equaliser as the Belgian striker stroked a right-foot shot beyond Simon Mignolet.

Nine minutes after the interval, Benteke and Grealish did likewise for what proved to be the winner from Delph, who tucked away his low right-foot shot with all the aplomb of a seasoned striker.

"Not a lot of people gave us a chance", said manager Steve Sherwood. "But we believed it and when we stepped out onto the pitch, we realised our fans believed it too".

Villa: Given, Bacuna, Vlaar, Baker (Okore 26), Richardson, Westwood, Delph, Cleverley, N'Zogbia (Sinclair 75), Benteke, Grealish (Cole 83), Benteke.

Liverpool: Mignolet, Can, Skrtel, Lovren, Markovic (Balotelli HT), Henderson, Allen (Johnson 77), Moreno (Lambert 90), Gerrard, Coutinho, Sterling.

Attendance: 85,416

Fabian Delph celebrates with teammates after hitting the winning goal.   Left: Christian Benteke opens Villa's account.

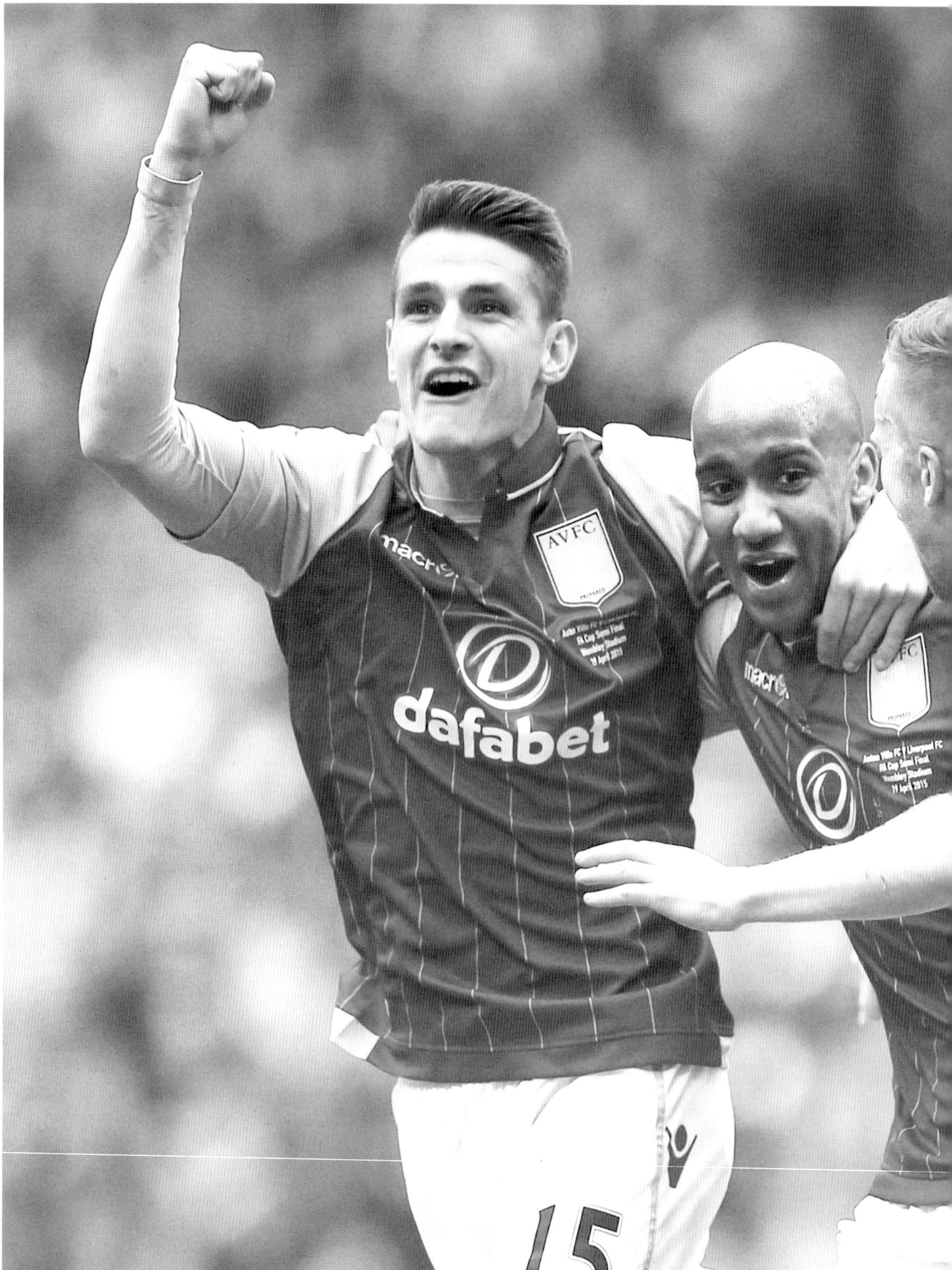
AVFC
dafabet
15

A GREAT GAME!

Fabian Delph is mobbed by teammates, Ashley Westwood, Tom Cleverley and Jack Grealish after hitting the winning goal.

VILLA 5-5 NOTTINGHAM FOREST
28 NOVEMBER 2018

Most of the 32,000-plus crowd who turned up at Villa Park on a Wednesday evening in November 2018 were no doubt aware of the incredible 5-5 draw which unfolded when Villa visited White Hart Lane a few months before the 1966 World Cup finals.

But little could they have imagined they would witness a repeat of that incredible scoreline during the game's modern era - even on the back of a 4-2 Villa victory in the Second City derby three days earlier. Dean Smith's men trailed three times to an impressive Forest outfit, but were still disappointed not to win.

On a truly surreal night, Forest were two-up inside six minutes with neat finishes from former Villa loanee Lewis Grabban and Joao Carvalho, but eight minutes later, Villa were back on level terms.

Tammy Abraham reduced the deficit with a stunning header, and then equalised when he diverted the ball past Costel Pantilimon after Jonathan Kodjia's shot had been blocked on the line.

Matty Cash restored the visitors' lead before Abraham completed his hat-trick by sending Pantilimon the wrong way from the penalty spot to make it 3-3 at half-time.

Forest were in front yet again six minutes after the interval, thanks to Joe Lolley's unstoppable 25-yard drive, but when Tobias Figueiredo was sent off for a crude challenge on John McGinn, Grealish swung in the resultant free-kick and Abraham sent a header inside the near post. It was the first time since David Platt in 1988 that a Villa player had scored four goals in a single game.

Sub Anwar El Ghazi put Smith's men ahead for the first time with a superb left-foot shot from Neil Taylor's cross, only for Grabban to squeeze home his second from a tight angle eight minutes from the end.

Villa: Nyland, Hutton, Tuanzebe, Chester, Taylor, McGinn (Whelan 78), Hourihane, Grealish, Bolasie (Elmohamdy 82), Abraham, Kodjia (El Ghazi 66).

Forest: Pantilimon, Figueiredo, Cash (Dias 77), Robinson, Dawson, Lolley, Yacob, Colback, Darikwa, Carvalho (Hafele 70), Grabban (Ansarifard 89).

Attendance: 32,368

Anwar El Ghazi celebrates scoring Villa's fifth with Alan Hutton and four-goal Tammy Abraham.

Right: A delighted Tammy Abraham after his fourth strike.

A GREAT GAME!

VILLA 7-2 LIVERPOOL
4 OCTOBER 2020

Of all the unexpected results in Villa's history, this was surely the most unlikely of the lot. How on earth did Dean Smith's side, who had narrowly escaped relegation the previous reason, record such an emphatic victory over the team who had won the Premier League title by a country mile?

A hard-earned point was as much as most supporters dared hope for as Jurgen Klopp's team arrived at Villa Park after launching the defence of their title with three straight wins. Instead, a positive approach from the home side reaped incredible rewards. Liverpool enjoyed greater possession, but Smith's slick operators looked capable of scoring every time they attacked. As Klopp said to Smith at the final whistle: "Wow!"

Just four minutes had elapsed when a mistake by Liverpool keeper Adrian enabled Jack Grealish to set up record signing Ollie Watkins for his first goal at this level. That one was a simple tap-in, but Watkins' second was a sight to behold as he moved in to Grealish's astute through ball, cut inside from the left and sent a rising right-foot drive into the far corner. Mo Salah reduced the deficit, but by half-time John McGinn scored with a long-range drive and Watkins completed his hat-trick with a close-range header from Trezeguet's cross.

On-loan midfielder Ross Barkley, who might easily have scored twice in the opening period, marked his debut by taking the score to 5-1 following another Grealish assist, and although Salah again reduced the deficit with a cool finish, Villa were not finished.

Grealish got in on the scoring act, first with a shot which deflected in off Fabinho and then a cheeky chip past the advancing Adrian following McGinn's magnificent pass. With Watkins also volleying against the bar, and both keepers making some fine saves, it might easily have finished 12-7. What a pity this unbelievable encounter was played against the backdrop of an empty stadium because of the Covid-19 pandemic.

Villa: Martinez, Cash (Elmohamady 80), Konsa, Mings, Targett, Luiz (Nakamba 80), McGinn, Trezeguet (Traore 87), Barkley, Grealish, Watkins.

Liverpool: Adrian, Alexander-Arnold, Gomez (Jones 61), Van Dijk, Robertson, Keita (Miramino HT), Fabinho, Wijnaldum, Salah, Firmino (Milner 68), Jota.

Hat-trick hero Ollie Watkins is chased by Roberto Firmino and Takumi Minamino.

Right: Emiliano Martinez celebrates against the backdrop of empty terraces.

A GREAT GAME!

ASTON VILLA · THE COMPLETE RECORD

Ross Barkley celebrates scoring Villa's fifth goal with Ezri Konsa and Jack Grealish.

A GREAT GAME!

ASTON VILLA LEGENDS

GEORGE BURRELL RAMSAY

George Ramsay was a football pioneer whose reputation was world-wide. His service to Villa spanned 59 years as player, secretary, consultant and vice-president.

The circumstances of Ramsay's introduction to Aston Villa have long passed into folklore. Born in Glasgow in March 1855, where he learned his football and became a master of ball control, Ramsay was one of the greatest dribblers of his time.

After moving to Birmingham to take up a clerical post, he was walking in Aston Park in 1876 when he came across Villa players, who invited him to join in a practice match. Later, William McGregor described that first meeting and how the players were bewildered by Ramsay's dextrous manipulation of the ball.

"They had never seen anything like it", said McGregor. "He had it so completely under control that it seemed impossible to tackle him. The members were ready to thrust all sorts of honours upon him, and he was literally compelled to take the captaincy".

Ramsay, wearing a small round polo cap and long pants, was a star the crowds loved. Along with John Lindsay, he found and negotiated the purchase of the Wellington Road ground in Perry Barr. He played in the first match at the ground and also later claimed to be the first man to kick a ball at Villa Park.

In 1878, he represented Birmingham in a 2-1 defeat of Nottingham in the first match played in the city under electric lights. Ramsay then led Villa to their first trophy success, the Birmingham Cup in 1880, scoring in the 3-1 defeat of Saltley College in the final.

Unfortunately, he was forced to retire from playing due to injury but his value to Villa continued. He was appointed secretary - and the position was much more than the title implies. His incredible football knowledge was instrumental in bringing tremendous success to Villa. Ramsay's reputation was such that he was able to attract star players, but he could also spot potential and his determination to sign a player was well-known and respected.

Granted a benefit match by Villa, as well as two Football League Service medals, Ramsay retired as secretary on 28 June 1926, but was retained as consultant and was also made vice-president. He died on 7 October 1935.

WILLIAM McGREGGOR

William McGregor was born in Braco, Perthshire on 27 January 1846. He first saw football being played by stonemasons, when he was around the age of seven. In 1870, McGregor moved to Birmingham, then in the midst of a trade boom brought on by the Franco-Prussian War.

A lifelong teetotaller, a dedicated Methodist and active member of the local Liberal Association, McGregor started to watch football at Aston Lower Grounds where the Birmingham Cricket and Football Club, 'The Quilters' played.

But they kicked off too late for him to watch all the game and return to the linen draper's shop he ran in Summer Lane with his brother Peter, in time for Saturday evening opening. McGregor wrote to a local paper urging earlier kick-off times and he then began to watch Birmingham Calthorpe on Bristol Road before news of Aston Villa's Scottish connection took him to Wellington Road.

From 1877, he went on to hold every office with the club. He even acted as umpire on many occasions and, after earlier misgivings, helped to secure the recognition of professionalism.

It is impossible to overestimate the tremendous debt football, and the players of the 21st century, owe to William McGregor. At the time of his now-famous letter leading to the formation of the Football League, the game was in danger of dying out as a spectator sport.

McGregor was instrumental in taking a British pastime and helping to turn it into the world's number one sport. He recognised that Villa needed to be put on a more business-like footing and in January 1889, he proposed that the club be converted to a limited liability company. He then fought hard to bring this to fruition, achieving his target in January 1896.

Following the formation of the Football League, McGregor was appointed its first chairman, becoming President in 1892. In September 1894, the Football League played Aston Villa in a testimonial match for his benefit, and during the same year, he was elected the league's first Life-President.

A member of the FA council and the International Selection Committee, he was presented, just two weeks before his death, with the Football Association long-service gold medal.

McGregor died on 20 December 1911. Nearly a century later, in November 2009, a magnificent statue of the great man was unveiled by Lord Mawhinney, chairman of the Football League, outside the main entrance to the Trinity Road stand.

FREDERICK RINDER

Fred Rinder was born in Liverpool in July 1858. He played rugby for Leeds Grammar School and was also a useful mile runner who excelled at the high jump. But it was his tremendous flair for organisation and financial management that brought great benefit to football in general, and Aston Villa in particular.

Rinder moved to Birmingham in 1876 to join the Birmingham City Surveyor staff, and quickly became associated with Villa.

Elected as a member of the club in 1881, he was very much part of the club for 57 years, providing magnificent service.

In 1892, Rinder became dissatisfied with the way the club was being run. He also suspected the gatemen of fraud, obtaining sufficient support to call a special meeting at Barwick Street where he criticised the men in control, reminding them that they were throwing away the future of a fine football club. He carried the meeting, forced the committee to resign and took over as financial secretary of the new committee.

This meeting has gone down as one of the defining moments in the history of the club. Rinder pledged to put Villa on the map, and this

proved to be an understatement as the club embarked on a period of unparalleled success, known as the 'golden age'. Two years after the Barwick Street meeting, Rinder was elected chairman.

He was not always an easy man to get on with, but proved himself to be the strong man Villa needed. He introduced turnstiles in 1895 and this immediately led to an increase in gate receipts. He also negotiated the purchase of the new ground that would become Villa Park and developed the stadium, along with architect Teddy Holmes.

In 1914, he put forward his grand plan for the further development of Villa Park, with a design by Archibald Leitch, to accommodate a minimum of 104,000 spectators. Work started, but the Great War interrupted the development. After the war, unfortunately, costs spiralled and the project had to be scaled down.

In July 1925, following criticism of the eventual cost of the splendid Trinity Road stand, Rinder resigned. He returned to the Board in 1936 and one of his first tasks was to bring Jimmy Hogan back from Europe as team manager.

Rinder held senior positions at both the Football League and the Football Association. He was the longest survivor of the original gathering to form the league, missing only one of the first 50 annual meetings. He also served the FA as an international selector, leading an England tour to Sweden and Finland at the age of 79.

Taken ill while watching a Villa Mid-Week League game at the Alexander Stadium in Perry Barr, he died on Christmas Day 1938.

SIR DOUG ELLIS

It could be argued that Doug Ellis had an influence on Aston Villa from the moment he first drew breath. He was born in Cheshire on 3 January 1924 - and Villa went on to reach the FA Cup final that year!

It was from the late 1960s, though, that Ellis really began to make an impact at Villa Park. Having made his fortune in the travel industry, he was appointed Villa chairman in December 1968.

When he took over at the helm for the first time, the club were on the brink of disaster, with a poor team struggling in the old Second Division, falling attendances, heavy financial losses and a ground badly in need of repair. The new chairman's initial tasks were to bring in the charismatic Tommy Docherty as manager and to instigate a share issue which generated desperately needed funds.

By the end of the following season, when Villa were relegated to English football's third tier for the first time, Docherty had been sacked, although Ellis's next two appointments were considerably more successful. Between them, Vic Crowe and his successor Ron Saunders, guided Villa to two League Cup triumphs and back to the top flight.

Ellis resigned as chairman in 1975 and four years later he departed from the board. But he returned as chairman in 1982 and remained in charge until he sold the club to American entrepreneur Randy Lerner in 2006.

By the time he took up his honorary position as President Emeritus, a total of 13 managers had served under him, including Graham Taylor, Ron Atkinson, Brian Little and John Gregory.

He also appointed Martin O'Neill in August 2006, shortly before stepping aside to make way for the club's new American owner.

Ellis also had three years as a Birmingham City director from 1965 and had earlier been co-promoter of Birmingham Speedway.

His main sporting interest outside football was salmon fishing, which earned him his nickname, from former England international Jimmy Greaves, of 'Deadly'.

A former member of the FA's international, finance and Charity Shield committee, as well as FIFA's media and television committee, Ellis was also the founder chairman of the technical control board at the FA and the Football League.

Awarded an OBE in the 2005 New Year's Honours list, he was knighted in 2012 for his charitable services. He died in October 2018.

VILLA STARS A-Z

A selection of players who have shaped the club's history

GABBY AGBONLAHOR

BIRTHPLACE: Birmingham
DATE OF BIRTH: 13 October 1986
DEBUT: Everton (A), 18 March 2006
VILLA TOTALS: 391 appearances / 87 goals

Gabriel Agbonlahor was a product of Villa's Academy, making a name for himself as a prolific scorer (including 40 in one season for the youth team) before being handed his debut by David O'Leary in March 2006.

Villa were struggling at the time and were on the receiving end of a 4-1 drubbing by Everton, although the Goodison Park gloom was lifted somewhat by a stunning goal from the debut boy, who made two more starting appearances that season before really making his presence felt during Martin O'Neill's first campaign in charge. Named in the opening-day line-up against Arsenal at the new Emirates Stadium, he started all but one of the club's 42 league and cup matches - and went on as a substitute in the other.

He ultimately played all but 77 minutes of Villa's season, and justified O'Neill's faith by finishing as top scorer with ten goals, nine in the Premier League and one in the FA Cup.

The following season, he was missing from the starting line-up just once. This time he finished with eleven goals and was named Barclays Player of the Month for November as well as breaking into Fabio Capello's England squad.

On the opening day of 2008/09, he hit a hat-trick in eight minutes as Villa beat Manchester City 4-2. It was the fastest hat-trick since Robbie Fowler's for Liverpool against Arsenal in 1994 - and the first Villa opening-day hat-trick since Pongo Waring hit four against Manchester United in 1930. He finished with 13 goals, and his impressive formed earned the former under-21 international his first full cap against Germany in Berlin.

Agbonlahor maintained his impressive scoring form in 2009/10, hitting a personal best total of 16, and although he was never as prolific again, his goal against Sunderland in April 2013 made him Villa's record Premier League marksman with 61 goals. He went on to reach 74, plus 13 in cup ties, before Villa's relegation to the Championship three years later. He left the club at the end of the 2017/18 season.

CHARLIE AITKEN

BIRTHPLACE: Edinburgh
DATE OF BIRTH: 1 May 1942
DEBUT: Sheffield Wednesday (H), 29 April 1961
VILLA TOTALS: 660 appearances (club record) / 16 goals

No player has worn the Villa shirt more often and it's quite likely that no-one ever will. During a Villa Park career which spanned 17 seasons, Charlie Aitken made a club record 660 appearances - 657 starts plus three as a substitute. He played for Villa in three different divisions, as well as the FA Cup, the League Cup, the Charity Shield and the UEFA Cup. And while his European adventure was restricted to just two games, he was in the club's first-ever UEFA Cup line-up against Antwerp in 1975. He also played three times for Scotland under-23s.

A defender with outstanding positional sense, Aitken timed his challenges superbly, rarely making a reckless tackle. Having played junior football north of the border, he joined Villa in August 1959, but had to wait until the final match of the 1960/61 season to make his debut in a 4-1 home win against Sheffield Wednesday. Coincidentally, it was the day another Aston Villa great, Johnny Dixon, made his final appearance for the club.

The following season, Aitken established himself as Villa's regular left-back, a position he held until January 1976, when he played his final game against QPR.

He missed very few matches during his time in claret and blue and was an ever-present in five seasons. His finest moments were the club's Wembley victory over Norwich City in the 1975 League Cup final, the Third Division championship in 1972 and promotion back to the First Division in 1975, when he was named Midland Footballer of the Year.

Having passed Billy Walker's Villa appearance record in December 1973, he remained at Villa Park for a further two-and-a-half years before joining New York Cosmos in the North American Soccer League in the summer of 1976.

MARC ALBRIGHTON

BIRTHPLACE: Tamworth
DATE OF BIRTH: 18 November 1989
DEBUT: CSKA Moscow (A), 26 February 2009
VILLA TOTALS: 102 appearances / 9 goals

Not many English footballers can claim to have made their first-team debut in Russia, but Marc Albrighton did. Not that it was in the best of circumstances. When the winger played his first senior Villa game against CSKA Moscow, it was on a night when manager Martin O'Neill fielded a weakened team, and Villa went out of the UEFA Cup.

Albrighton's Premier League debut was also a day to forget, a substitute appearance in a 2-0 home defeat to Wigan on the opening day of the 2009/10 campaign. Even so, those two games hold a special place in the heart of a player who has been a Villa supporter since childhood.

Having graduated through Villa's youth ranks, he reveled in the opportunity to exhibit his skills on the first-team stage. On the opening day of 2010/11 he excelled on his first Premier League starting appearance, setting up two goals in a 3-0 victory over West Ham.

Albrighton scored his first Villa goal in October that year, and a month later he signed a contract extension designed to keep him at Villa Park for the following three-and-a-half years. That was precisely how things unfolded, Albrighton being released by manager Paul Lambert in the summer of 2014. Less than two years later, he was part of the Leicester City side who won the Premier League title.

Apart from his creative skills, Albrighton was on target nine times for Villa, including the Premier League's 20,000th goal. His shot against Arsenal in December 2011 earned him a £20,000 cheque for the charity of his choice, Acorns Children's Hospice.

In May 2022, Albrighton was awarded Honorary Freedom of the Borough of Tamworth for his services to the local community.

PETER ALDIS

BIRTHPLACE: Birmingham
DATE OF BIRTH: 11 April 1927
DEBUT: Arsenal (A), 10 March 1951
VILLA TOTALS: 295 appearances / 1 goal

Even for a full-back, a ratio of just one goal in nearly 300 appearances is modest. But the single goal Peter Aldis contributed to the Villa cause seems destined to remain forever in the record books. He scored it in a 3-0 Villa Park victory over Sunderland in September 1952, and it was no ordinary goal - it was a header from 35 yards!

If that remains arguably Aldis's personal highlight of his time in claret and blue, however, he made a far greater impact nearly five years later, playing in all nine games as Villa fought their way to Wembley in the FA Cup and beat Manchester United 2-1 in the final.

And while there was rarely much prospect of him adding to his long-range header, which bounced over a distracted Sunderland keeper, Aldis gave the club exceptional service at left-back over an eight-year period.

The former Cadbury's chocolate maker joined the club in 1948, turning professional early the following year and making his debut against Arsenal at Highbury in March 1951.

After overcoming a cartilage injury, Aldis was a regular member of the side from the start of the 1953/54 season. He left Villa Park in 1960 and played in Australia for several years, being named that country's Footballer of the Year in 1966. He died in November 2008.

WILLIE ANDERSON

BIRTHPLACE: Liverpool
DATE OF BIRTH: 24 January 1947
DEBUT: Chelsea (A), 21 January 1967
VILLA TOTALS: 267 appearances / 44 goals

Every club would have loved George Best in their line-up during the 1960s, and Villa had the next best thing. With his mop of dark hair and teasing talents, winger Willie Anderson resembled the Manchester United legend in both looks and playing style. And while he could never hope to emulate Best's brilliance, he served Villa well.

In different circumstances, in fact, he might have forged his career at Old Trafford, where he was in the same FA Youth Cup-winning team as Best and was later understudy to the Irish wizard in United's first-team squad.

But where his personal prospects were bleak in Manchester, they blossomed once he had made the move to Villa Park in 1967 in what proved to be a bargain £20,000 transfer.

His misfortune was that he joined Villa after they had been relegated to the old Second Division and it got even worse when they were relegated to Division Three in 1970. But Anderson stood out in a poor team and things finally came good for him when he helped the club to the 1971 League Cup final and the Third Division championship twelve months later, when he netted 15 league and cup goals. Anderson had notched 267 Villa appearances and scored 44 goals by the time he joined Cardiff City in February 1973.

JUAN PABLO ANGEL

BIRTHPLACE: Medellin, Colombia
DATE OF BIRTH: 24 October 1975
DEBUT: Manchester United (A), 20 January 2001
VILLA TOTALS: 205 appearances / 62 goals

It took Juan Pablo Angel a while to justify his £9.5m club record price tag but he eventually evolved into one of Villa's most popular players of the modern era.

Signed from Argentine giants River Plate in January 2001, the Colombian striker took a while to settle in this country, not least because his wife was seriously ill during his first few months with the club.

It was not until the final home game of the season, a dramatic 3-2 victory over Coventry City, that Angel scored his first goal in claret and blue - the first of an impressive haul of 62 in over 200 appearances.

Quick, deceptively strong and clinical in the penalty area, he developed into one of the most dangerous strikers in the Premier League, scoring some magnificent goals. None was better, arguably, than his darting run through the heart of Chelsea's defence before drilling home a stunning low shot from just outside the penalty area.

The memorable strike, in December 2003, helped Villa to a 2-1 League Cup quarter-final victory during a season when they also finished sixth in the table. That was due in no small measure to Angel's 16 goals, while he also hit another seven in cup ties.

He was less prolific over the next couple of seasons and eventually headed back across the Atlantic to join New York Red Bulls in April 2007.

DAI ASTLEY

BIRTHPLACE: Dowlais, Wales
DATE OF BIRTH: 11 October 1909
DEBUT: Portsmouth (A), 17 October 1931
VILLA TOTALS: 173 appearances / 100 goals

Villa were certainly not short of fire power when Dai Astley arrived at the club, boasting a prolific scoring trio in Pongo Waring, Billy Walker and Eric Houghton. But the new boy ensured that the trio became a quartet - for a while, at least - and his addition ensured that the goals kept flowing over the course of the next few seasons.

After signing from Charlton Athletic, Astley started as he intended to continue, netting on his debut in a 3-0 victory over Portsmouth and although he made only 15 appearances during his initial campaign, he became a regular the following season, hitting the target on numerous occasions.

Even when the club were relegated in 1935/36, it was not for the lack of goals, including 21 from Astley who, by then, had emerged as Villa's leading marksman.

By the time he left for Derby County in November 1936, he had scored exactly a century of goals - a ratio of more than one every two games. Capped 17 times by Wales, he later made a name for himself as a coach on the continent, working in Italy, Sweden and France. He died in 1989.

CHARLIE ATHERSMITH

BIRTHPLACE: Bloxwich
DATE OF BIRTH: 10 May 1872
DEBUT: Preston North End (H), 9 March 1891
VILLA TOTALS: 311 appearances / 86 goals

A winger with tremendous pace and a showman who was always able to rise to the big occasion, Charlie Athersmith performed with tremendous consistency over ten years with Villa. Signed in February 1891 from Unity Gas at Saltley, he gained an FA Cup runners-up medal the following year and then collected five League Championship and two FA Cup winner's medals in six years between 1894 and 1900.

Exhibiting excellent ball control, the sight of Athersmith embarking on a dazzling run and delivering a centre with lightning speed was a sight to behold. In 1896/97 he won every honour in the game.

In addition to the League and FA Cup double he played for England three times, scoring in a 6-0 win against Ireland. Athersmith was capped a total of twelve times, scoring three goals, and represented the Football League nine times.

In 1901, he joined newly-promoted Small Heath. He later became trainer at Sheffield United and died in September 1910.

DALIAN ATKINSON

BIRTHPLACE: Shrewsbury
DATE OF BIRTH: 21 March 1968
DEBUT: Sheffield Wednesday (A), 17 August 1991
VILLA TOTALS: 114 appearances / 36 goals

His time at Villa was disrupted by injuries and inconsistency, but Dalian Atkinson still averaged a goal every three games, as well as producing some significant and memorable moments.

Signed from Spanish club Real Sociedad in 1991, he scored on his debut in a 3-2 victory away to one of his former clubs, Sheffield Wednesday, on the opening day of the season. It was his only goal during a debut season blighted by injury, but twelve months later he had the satisfaction of scoring Villa's first goal in the new Premier League, in a 1-1 draw at Ipswich Town.

He was on target 13 times that season - including one which is widely regarded as Villa's best goal of the Premier League era. Sprinting from his own half against Wimbledon at Selhurst Park, he shrugged off challenge after challenge before steering a delicate chip over goalkeeper Hans Segers from just outside the penalty area. It was voted BBC's goal of the season.

Atkinson's third season at Villa was his most impressive. He played 44 league and cup games and was on target 15 times, including the opening goal in Villa's 3-1 League Cup final victory over Manchester United.

He joined Turkish club Fenerbahce in 1995, but did not settle in Turkey, and later played in Saudi Arabia and South Korea. Atkinson died in August 2016, suffering a cardiac arrest after being tasered by West Mercia Police following an incident near his father's house in Telford.

JOE BACHE

BIRTHPLACE: Stourbridge
DATE OF BIRTH: 8 February 1880
DEBUT: Notts County (A), 16 February 1901
VILLA TOTALS: 474 appearances / 184 goals

There could be no greater tribute to a true Villa legend than that given in the Villa News & Record at the time of Joe Bache's death in November 1960. He was described as 'one of the greatest players ever to don a football jersey'.

Bache joined Villa from Stourbridge in December 1900 and he scored in his first senior game, a 6-2 friendly win against a Berlin Select XI in January 1901. He made his league debut against Notts County the following month and quickly became a firm favourite with the Villa Park crowd. Called up by England in 1903, Bache scored in each of his first four internationals.

Bache, who was at home in any forward position, played inside-left when Villa won the FA Cup in 1905. He was appointed captain in 1906 and played on the left wing in the 1913 FA Cup-winning side.

He was also a member of the Villa team who won the League Championship in 1910. His 184 goals included nine hat-tricks and his treble in the 6-0 away win against Manchester United at the age of 34 in March 1914 makes him Villa's oldest hat-trick hero.

Bache was Villa's skipper when the Great War brought football to a halt. On the resumption in August 1919 he became player-manager of Mid-Rhondda and then had a spell as player/coach of Grimsby Town, turning out for the Mariners at the age of 40. In 1927, Bache returned to Villa Park in a coaching capacity. He died in November 1960.

TOMMY BALL

BIRTHPLACE: Chester-le-Street
DATE OF BIRTH: February 1899
DEBUT: Bolton Wanderers (H), 7 April 1920
VILLA TOTALS: 77 appearances / 0 goals

The name Tommy Ball is etched in Villa folklore as arguably the most tragic character in Villa's history. In November 1923, at the age of just 24, Ball was shot dead by a neighbour following an argument, and you can find a memorial to him in the grounds of St John's Church in Perry Barr.

It's an enduring tribute to a powerful player who would surely have gone on to achieve great things in the game. Indeed, he would almost certainly have played in the 1924 FA Cup final, which was played just a few months after his death. Villa lost at Wembley to Newcastle United, but that would have been a special moment for a player who was being tipped for England recognition.

Although his first-team appearances were initially restricted, he took over from the legendary Frank Barson as a regular at the heart of Villa's defence from the start of the 1922/23 campaign.

Ball made 36 appearances that season and had missed only two of Villa's first 16 games the following season before the tragedy occurred on Sunday 11 November, the day after he had produced an outstanding performance in a 1-0 win at Notts County.

BARRY BANNAN

BIRTHPLACE: Airdrie, Scotland
DATE OF BIRTH: 1 December 1989
DEBUT: SV Hamburg (A), 17 December 2008
VILLA TOTALS: 83 appearances / 2 goals

A competitive and classy midfielder, Barry Bannan's sublime passing skills prompted one radio reporter to describe his left foot as being like a wand. It was an apt description for a player capable of winning the ball and then spraying passes to all areas of the pitch.

Having played for Celtic Boys Club as a youngster, he opted to join Villa's Academy at the age of 14, making a big impression as Villa won a youth competition in Germany, where he was named player of the tournament.

He maintained his progress with some excellent displays for the club's Academy and reserve teams during the 2007-08 campaign and was rewarded with a professional contract.

Ironically, his first two games for the senior side were both in the UEFA Cup. He went on as a sub for Craig Gardner for his debut against SV Hamburg in December 2008 and the following March made his first starting appearance in the second leg of the quarter-final away to CSKA Moscow.

After loan spells at Derby County and Blackpool, Bannan returned to Villa Park for the 2010-11 season, getting his first Premier League action as a late substitute in the opening day victory over West Ham and scoring against Rapid Vienna in the Europa League a few days later.

After being given a run of games by manager Gerard Houllier, Bannan was briefly on loan at Leeds United, but he returned to make over 60 appearances over the course of the following two seasons. He joined Crystal Palace in 2013.

TOMMY BARBER

BIRTHPLACE: West Stanley
DATE OF BIRTH: 22 July 1886
DEBUT: Bradford City (A), 28 December 1912
VILLA TOTALS: 68 appearances / 10 goals

A quick glance at Tommy Barber's statistics in claret and blue hardly suggest a player to rank among the club's greats. If his time at Villa Park was brief, though, he literally made a dream come true - and it was not even his own dream!

On the night before the 1913 FA Cup final against Sunderland, his teammate Clem Stephenson dreamt that Barber would score the winning goal with his head. Barber did exactly that in front of 121,919 spectators at the Crystal Palace to give Villa a 1-0 victory over a Sunderland side who were crowned league champions that season.

Barber's Cup Final drama came less than four months after he joined the club from Bolton Wanderers, having moved to the Midlands on Christmas Eve 1912.

He was a regular in the side for the remainder of that campaign and also played 33 games the following season, although his appearances were less frequent in 1914/15 as football limped on following the outbreak of the Great War. He died from TB in 1925.

EARL BARRETT

BIRTHPLACE: Rochdale
DATE OF BIRTH: 28 April 1967
DEBUT: Manchester City (A), 29 February 1992
VILLA TOTALS: 150 appearances / 2 goals

Classy and athletic, Earl Barrett added genuine quality to Villa's line-up over a period of nearly three years - and his two full seasons in claret and blue rank among the most successful of the club's Premier League era. The right-back was an ever-present as Villa finished runners-up to Manchester United in the inaugural Premier campaign of 1992/93.

His cultured, assured displays that season earned him Ron Atkinson's personal vote as Villa's player of the season and underlined what an astute signing the manager had made when recruiting Barrett from Oldham Athletic for a club record £1.7million the previous February.

The following season, Barrett was in the team who won the League Cup, producing a stylish, assured performance in the 3-1 Wembley victory over United. Cool and composed under pressure, his quality shone through as he invariably kept opposition wingers quiet as well as distributing the ball effectively and intelligently.

Capped three times by England, he enjoyed getting forward, too, even though he managed only two goals during his time at Villa Park.

Barrett was again a regular in the line-up at the start of the following season, but new manager Brian Little, who replaced Atkinson in November, reluctantly sold him to Everton at the end of January.

GARETH BARRY

BIRTHPLACE: Hastings
DATE OF BIRTH: 23 February 1981
DEBUT: Sheffield Wednesday (A), 2 May 1998
VILLA TOTALS: 440 appearances / 52 goals

In the words of journalist and Villa supporter Richard Whitehead, Gareth Barry evolved 'from the coolest teenager on the planet to a fully matured leader of men'.

It's hard to imagine a more accurate description of a player who emerged from nowhere when he made his Villa debut in 1998, but became one of the greatest players in the club's history.

Barry grew up, in a football sense, as a schoolboy with Brighton & Hove Albion, but in 1997 he joined Villa's Academy.

It was a decision which ultimately cost the club £1million in compensation, but the outlay ultimately looked no more than small change.

He signed professional on turning 17 in February 1998 - and at the end of that season had his first taste of senior football, going on as a substitute for the injured Ian Taylor in a 3-1 win at Hillsborough.

Barry played that day in midfield - the position where he would make his biggest impact in claret and blue. Yet his early days were mainly spent as a central-defender for Villa and a left-back for England after he broke into the national team while still only 19.

A member of the Villa side in the 2000 FA Cup final defeat by Chelsea, Barry's midfield influence over the following years was such that Villa invariably struggled in his absence.

His desire for Champions League football almost led to a move to Liverpool in the summer of 2008. That deal did not materialise, but in May 2009, he left Villa to join Manchester City for £12million.

DARREN BENT

BIRTHPLACE: London
DATE OF BIRTH: 6 February 1984
DEBUT: Manchester City (H), 22 January 2011
VILLA TOTALS: 72 appearances / 25 goals

Villa were languishing near the foot of the Premier League table in January 2011 and it was clear that drastic measures were required to maintain top-flight status. Manager Gerard Houllier's solution was to splash out a club record £18million on Sunderland striker Darren Bent. And while the fee was 50 per cent more than that paid for previous record signing James Milner, it proved to be money well spent.

The former England international made an immediate impact, scoring the only goal on his debut against Manchester City, and by the end of the season he had added eight more goals to lift Villa to an unlikely finishing position of ninth. Despite playing only 16 games, he was club's joint-leading scorer along with Ashley Young.

Having scored nine in the second half of his debut campaign, Bent maintained his prolific marksmanship with ten by the end of January 2012, including one in a fourth-round FA Cup tie at Arsenal.

But a serious ankle injury at Wigan ruled him out of action for the remainder of the season and effectively ended his chances of playing for England in that summer's European Championship finals. Even so, he was Villa's highest scorer for the second consecutive season.

Bent was briefly appointed captain at the start of the following campaign, although he managed only six goals in 2012/13 before joining Fulham on a season-long loan in the summer of 2013. He subsequently had loan spells with Brighton & Hove Albion and Derby County, making a permanent move to Pride Park after being released by Villa in 2015.

CHRISTIAN BENTEKE

BIRTHPLACE: Kinshasa, Zaire
DATE OF BIRTH: 3 December 1990
DEBUT: Swansea City (H), 15 September 2012
VILLA TOTALS: 101 appearances / 49 goals

Football clubs and players sometimes fit perfectly, and that was certainly the case with Aston Villa and Christian Benteke. In three seasons at Villa Park, the towering Belgium international simply could not stop scoring as he became an idol with fans.

His ratio of virtually a goal every two games was one he had produced over a shorter timescale during his second spell with Belgian club Genk, but a feat he never came close to achieving at either Liverpool or Crystal Palace following his departure from Villa Park.

Signed from Genk on transfer deadline day in 2012, Benteke made an explosive start to life in claret and blue, scoring Villa's second goal against Swansea City on his debut after going on as a substitute and producing a performance described by manager Paul Lambert as 'unplayable'.

Benteke went on to score 23 league and cup goals, including two in a superb 3-1 win at Liverpool. There was also a hat-trick in a 6-1 thrashing of Sunderland, and Benteke was nominated for the PFA Young Player of the Year award, finishing runner-up to Gareth Bale.

His second season started in equally stunning fashion - two goals in a 3-1 opening-day victory at Arsenal - and despite a hip injury and a ruptured Achilles tendon at different stages, he was on target eleven times in 28 appearances.

Unfortunately, an Achilles injury caused him to miss the 2014 World Cup finals plus the start of the following season. But he still netted 15 goals in 34 games, including the equaliser at Wembley as Villa hit back to beat Liverpool 2-1 in the FA Cup semi-final. His final game for Villa was the Cup Final against Arsenal. In July 2015 he joined Liverpool for £32.5million.

JOE BERESFORD

BIRTHPLACE: Chesterfield
DATE OF BIRTH: 26 February 1906
DEBUT: Liverpool (A), 3 September 1927
VILLA TOTALS: 251 appearances / 73 goals

Other players may have scored more goals, but Joe Beresford's contribution to the cause during Villa's heady days of the late 1920s and early 1930s was invaluable. While colleagues such as Billy Walker and Pongo Waring made the headlines with their incredible scoring feats, Beresford was regarded as the team's engine because of his incredible work-rate.

An inside-forward or centre-forward, he also possessed a powerful right foot, which meant he always weighed in with his fair share of goals. In 1930/31, for instance, he was only the fourth highest scorer, behind Waring, Eric Houghton and Walker - but still hit 14 as Villa chalked up a record 128 goals in a single season.

Signed from Mansfield Town, Beresford made his debut in a goalless draw at Anfield, but a week later he gave Villa supporters an indication of his lethal finishing by netting a hat-trick, including a penalty, in a 7-2 drubbing of Portsmouth at Villa Park. He was on target eight more times before the end of that season and was also in double figures over the course of the following four campaigns.

He continued to be a regular, as well as being capped once by England, up to the start of 1935/36, when he joined Preston, for whom he played in the 1937 FA Cup final against Sunderland. He died in 1978.

PAUL BIRCH

BIRTHPLACE: West Bromwich
DATE OF BIRTH: 6 November 1962
DEBUT: Barcelona (H), 26 January 1983
VILLA TOTALS: 223 appearances / 25 goals

Not many players can claim to have won a medal on their debut. But it happened to Paul Birch. In January 1983, eight months after the club's European Cup triumph, Villa faced Spanish giants Barcelona in the UEFA Super Cup. Although they lost the first leg 1-0 at the Camp Nou, a 3-0 second-leg victory at Villa Park gave them the trophy. And Birch, who had gone on as a substitute for Gary Shaw, was clutching a winner's medal after his first experience of senior football.

It was quite a start for a young man who had begun his career as apprentice three years earlier after joining Villa straight from school. And while he never scaled such dizzy heights again, Birch was an invaluable member of the squad over the following eight years.

He averaged more than 20 league appearances a season from 1983/84 onwards, reaching a peak in the Second Division promotion campaign of 1987/88, when he played in more than 40 league and cup matches.

Birch, who joined Midland neighbours Wolverhampton Wanderers in 1991, died in February 2009.

DANNY BLANCHFLOWER

BIRTHPLACE: Belfast
DATE OF BIRTH: 10 February 1926
DEBUT: Burnley (H), 17 March 1951
VILLA TOTALS: 155 appearances / 10 goals

Danny Blanchflower was one of the classiest players ever to pull on a claret-and-blue shirt. A master of his trade, his poise and balance were allied to an ability to make precision passes, even on the most difficult of surfaces.

A man of great integrity, Belfast-born Blanchflower joined Villa from Barnsley in 1951 and over the next three-and-a-half years he produced some immaculate performances as an attacking wing-half, also contributing ten goals.

During his three full seasons at Villa Park, he missed just three league matches, and was an ever-present as the team finished sixth in 1951/52.

It was at White Hart Lane, however, that honours came his way. He joined Tottenham Hotspur for £30,000 in 1954 and was captain of the double-winning team of 1961 and the side who retained the FA Cup the following year. Ironically, Villa were among Spurs' Cup victims on both occasions, losing at home in the fifth round in 1961 and in a quarter-final in north London the following year.

Capped 56 times by Northern Ireland, Blanchflower was also voted FWA Footballer of the Year in 1958 and 1961. He died in December 1993.

MARK BOSNICH

BIRTHPLACE: Fairfield, Australia
DATE OF BIRTH: 13 January 1972
DEBUT: Luton Town (A), 25 April 1992
VILLA TOTALS: 228 appearances / 0 goals

His time at Villa Park was laced with controversy, but Mark Bosnich was one of the club's most successful goalkeepers - and certainly the best at saving penalties.

The Australian international was the man between the posts when Villa won the League Cup in 1994 and 1996 and was almost single-handedly responsible for Ron Atkinson's men reaching the first of those Wembley finals. In arguably the most dramatic contest of the decade at Villa Park, Bozzie made three saves during a tension-charged penalty shoot-out after the semi-final against Tranmere Rovers had finished 4-4 on aggregate. Amazingly, he saved two more spot kicks in a 2-0 win at Tottenham a few days later and that season he kept out five of the penalties fired at him during normal play, as well as the trio which took Villa to Wembley.

His best penalty save was undoubtedly the one against Deportivo La Coruna in a first leg UEFA Cup match in Spain, when Bosnich was almost horizontal as he dived to his left to tip away a well-struck kick from Brazilian star Bebeto.

There were times, though, when Bosnich was more a villain than a hero. Villa were fined £20,000, for instance, over payments to Bosnich's agent Graham Smith at the time of the player's arrival from Sydney Croatia, while the keeper stormed out of Derby's Baseball Ground after learning he was not in the starting line-up for a match against the Rams in 1997. He joined Manchester United two years later.

DES BREMNER

BIRTHPLACE: Aberchirder, Scotland
DATE OF BIRTH: 7 September 1952
DEBUT: Arsenal (H), 22 September 1979
VILLA TOTALS: 227 appearances / 10 goals

Des Bremner's contribution to Villa's glory years of the early 1980s was immense. Essentially a right-sided midfielder, his unselfish non-stop running was a key feature of Villa's attacks during their charge to the championship in 1981 and the European Cup a year later.

He was equally comfortable, though, at full-back or in central defence, which proved invaluable when he deputised for the injured Allan Evans in the away leg of the European Cup quarter-final against Dynamo Kiev.

And although goalkeeping hero Nigel Spink and match-winner Peter Withe made all the headlines in the European Cup final in Rotterdam, Bremner's tireless work and crunching tackles were responsible for frustrating Bayern Munich's star players.

The hard-working Scot began his career as a defender with Hibernian, but he was converted into a midfielder, scoring 22 goals before joining Villa in 1979.

His goal haul in claret and blue was more modest, but where he had narrowly missed out on major honours north of the border, he more than made amends in the Midlands, enjoying triumphs in the League Championship, European Cup and European Super Cup.

His all-action style epitomised Villa's success during that heady period. A non-stop grafter, he simply got on with the job, content with his role as a vital cog in a smooth-running machine.

Described by manager Ron Saunders as 'the most underrated footballer I ever purchased', Bremner was every inch a team man. It was hardly surprising, then, that Saunders took him to Birmingham City when his Villa days came to an end in October 1984.

FRANK BROOME

BIRTHPLACE: Berkhamstead
DATE OF BIRTH: 11 June 1915
DEBUT: Portsmouth (A), 6 April 1935
VILLA TOTALS: 151 appearances / 91 goals

Frank Broome may have been small and looked frail, but his scoring ability was incredible. His stunning ratio of 91 in 151 games does not even include all the goals he scored for Villa during the war years, including two in the League War Cup final against Blackpool in 1944.

That was nearly a decade after he had arrived at Villa Park and he was still playing in claret and blue when League action resumed after the war, albeit making just one appearance in 1946/47 before moving to Derby County.

By the time of his departure, he had given Villa outstanding service and it had been clear from the outset that here was a player whose positional sense and timing more than compensated for his lack of physique.

Signed from his hometown club Berkhamstead in November 1934, Broome made his debut the following spring and it was clear that the club had acquired someone special. A week after making his debut at Fratton Park, he was on target twice in a 4-2 home win over Liverpool. And although his eleven goals in 16 league outings failed to prevent relegation the following season, Broome made himself a permanent fixture.

He played in 38 league games in the club's seasons in the lower grade, hitting 28 goals in 1936/37 and 20 as Villa won the title the following year, when he was also on target six times in seven FA Cup-ties.

That was followed by 16 in 1938/39, making him the club's leading scorer for the third consecutive season before League football went on hold in September 1939. He continued in similar prolific fashion throughout the war years and was also one of Villa's scorers in a 4-3 FA Cup defeat by Derby in March 1946. He died in September 1994.

GEORGE BROWN

BIRTHPLACE: Mickley, Northumberland
DATE OF BIRTH: 22 June 1903
DEBUT: Birmingham (H), 31 August 1929
VILLA TOTALS: 126 appearances / 89 goals

Long before West Bromwich Albion's record scorer Tony Brown assumed the nickname, Villa had their own Bomber Brown. George Brown was already a household name in English football by the time he joined Villa. A skilful player with a powerful left foot, he invariably struck fear into the hearts of opposition defenders.

A former miner, he broke into professional football when he asked Huddersfield Town for a trial while he was on strike. Instead of mining for coal, he was suddenly digging deep for goals, hitting 143 goals for the Leeds Road club, whom he helped to a hat-trick of title triumphs.

He also played eight times for England during that period and although he added only one cap to his collection while at Villa Park, his contribution was invaluable.

In his first season alone, Brown headed the scorechart with 36 league and cup goals and he was only one short of that figure in 1932/33. But it was during a generally less productive 1931/32 campaign that he really hit the headlines, despite making only 17 appearances that season.

In January 1932, he netted five in an 8-3 away win at Leicester City and the following week hit four in a 6-1 Villa Park romp against Liverpool. Brown, who was transferred to Burnley in 1934, died in 1948.

ERNIE 'MUSH' CALLAGHAN

BIRTHPLACE: Birmingham
DATE OF BIRTH: 29 July 1907
DEBUT: Bradford City (H), FA Cup, 18 January 1933
VILLA TOTALS: 142 appearances / 0 goals

If ever there was a true Villa man, it was surely 'Mush' Callaghan. Born within walking distance of Villa Park, he served the club for more than 40 years, latterly as a maintenance man.

It is for his years as a player, though, that Callaghan wrote himself into claret and blue folklore. Having made his name in non-League circles, he was recommended to the club by former Villa star John Devey, signing professional in September 1930.

HARRY BURROWS

BIRTHPLACE: Haydock
DATE OF BIRTH: 17 March 1941
DEBUT: Hull City (A), 26 December 1959
VILLA TOTALS: 181 appearances / 73 goals

Harry Burrows quite literally lit up Villa Park when he played his first senior game for the club. Although he had to wait until the following season for his official debut, a Boxing Day victory in Villa's Second Division title season of 1959/60, he was given his first outing in October 1958 - on the night the Villa Park floodlights were officially opened. A friendly against Swedish club GAIS was arranged to mark the occasion and Burrows netted one of the goals in a 3-0 victory.

The game at Hull was his only game of the season, but Burrows, who had arrived as an amateur in 1956, started to make his mark with five goals in 17 games in 1960/61. He then won a medal as Villa beat Rotherham United in the inaugural League Cup final which was held over until the start of the 1961/62 campaign, and that season established himself as the team's regular left-winger.

A fast, forceful player with a powerful shot, Burrows was a firm favourite with the claret and blue faithful over the next few seasons. Popularly known as 'The Blast', he also became Villa's penalty-taker and won a cap for England under-23s. In March 1965, Burrows joined Stoke City where he continued his scoring exploits.

It was more than two-and-a-half years before he made his senior debut, but it was the first of nearly 300 appearances for the club, more than half of them in unofficial wartime games.

He scored his only goal for Villa during the hostilities, in a Football League War Cup semi-final against Blackpool in 1943; more importantly, he produced consistently solid displays, initially in the centre of defence and as a wing-half, and later at right-back.

Callaghan was nearly 29 when Villa were relegated for the first time in their history in 1935/36 and, having played only 21 games at that stage of his career, he felt his future may lie elsewhere. But he stayed to help Villa back to the First Division in 1937/38 and was then an ever-present in the last full season before League football went on hold for seven years.

Having signed up with the Police Reserve, he continued playing regularly for Villa during the war, but his appearances were limited to just eleven when League football resumed. Even so, he became the oldest player to represent Villa in a competitive match when he played his final game against Grimsby Town at the age of 39 years and 257 days in April 1947. It was a record which stood until 2011, when it was surpassed by goalkeeper Brad Friedel.

Callaghan worked as the club's odd-job man until his retirement in 1971 and he was subsequently awarded a testimonial. He died in March 1972.

LEN CAPEWELL

BIRTHPLACE: Birmingham
DATE OF BIRTH: 8 June 1895
DEBUT: Blackburn Rovers (A), 1 April 1922
VILLA TOTALS: 157 appearances / 100 goals

It took Len Capewell just 20 seconds to open the scoring on the first day of the 1925/26 season and by the end of the match he had netted five times in a 10-0 defeat of Burnley. A week later, he was on target at Leeds United to start a record run of scoring in eight consecutive league games. Scoring goals was second nature to Capewell, who finished his Villa career with 100 in his 157 games.

Capewell, who had served in the Royal Engineers during the Great War, joined Villa from Wellington Town in January 1922, having already gained a reputation as a prolific marksman. He netted a hat-trick when making his debut in a reserve game against Bolton Wanderers and then scored on his league debut, a 2-1 win at Blackburn Rovers.

Capewell quickly became established at Villa and collected an FA Cup runners-up medal in April 1924, finishing that season with 26 goals.

His appearances the following season were restricted by injury. He scored four goals in an FA Cup match against Port Vale, but on 29 January 1925, Capewell was devastated by the death of his young son.

His best season came in 1925/26 when he scored 32 goals in 34 league games. On 1 April 1929, seven years to the day after making his debut, Capewell marked his last league appearance with a goal at Leicester City.

He continued to score regularly for the reserves until joining Walsall in February 1930. He died in 1978.

JOHN CAREW

BIRTHPLACE: Strommen, Norway
DATE OF BIRTH: 5 September 1979
DEBUT: Newcastle United (A), 31 January 2007
VILLA TOTALS: 131 appearances / 48 goals

"John Carew, Carew, he's bigger than me and you, he's gonna score one or two..." There's no doubt that the 6ft 4in Norwegian striker was one of Villa's most popular players of the early 21st century, with supporters singing his song to the tune of Que Sera.

Although he was little known on these shores before his arrival at Villa Park, that changed rapidly once he donned a claret and blue shirt and became the club's leading scorer for two consecutive seasons.

By the time he joined Villa, he had played for several clubs, including Valencia, AS Roma, Besiktas and Lyon, from whom he joined Villa as part of a deal which saw Czech striker Milan Baros move to France.

The towering Carew immediately made his presence felt. Despite a 3-1 defeat on his debut, he hit the post with one header at St James' Park and hit the net with another, only to have his effort harshly disallowed for pushing.

But he got off the mark with the winner against West Ham on his first home appearance the following Saturday and scored twice more by the end of his first campaign. That was the prelude to some prolific scoring over the next couple of seasons as he headed Villa's goal chart with 13 in 2007/08 and 15 the following campaign. And he achieved his tag of leading scorer despite lengthy injury absence during both seasons.

He was once again the leading scorer the following season, this time with a total of 17, including three at Reading in the FA Cup. It was the club's first FA Cup quarter-final hat-trick since Harry Hampton hit three at Bradford in 1913. The Norwegian's appearances were limited at the start of the 2010/11 campaign and in January 2011 he joined Stoke City on loan. His Villa contract expired at the end of the season and he subsequently signed for West Ham.

VILLA STARS A-Z

TONY CASCARINO

BIRTHPLACE: Orpington, Kent
DATE OF BIRTH: 1 September 1962
DEBUT: Derby County (A), 17 March 1990
VILLA TOTALS: 54 appearances / 12 goals

Tony Cascarino was Villa's record signing by some distance when he arrived from Millwall in March 1990, his £1.5m fee far outstripping the £650,000 paid to Bradford City for Ian Ormondroyd 13 months earlier.

Manager Graham Taylor made the bold swoop in a bid to clinch the First Division title, but it was a move which backfired. Although Villa won at Derby on Cascarino's debut - with Ormonroyd, ironically, scoring the only goal - their challenge fell away in the closing weeks and the crown went to Liverpool.

It was not until the final two matches, in fact, that Cascarino - who had been a prolific marksman alongside Teddy Sheringham at The Den - scored his first goals for the club.

His output was much improved in his second season, when he was on target ten times, including one against his former club in the League Cup, but it was a campaign of struggle for Villa, who only narrowly avoided relegation under Jo Venglos.

A Republic of Ireland international, Cascarino was sold to Celtic following Ron Atkinson's appointment as manager that summer. He later moved to Chelsea and subsequently had successful spells with French clubs Olympique Marseille and AS Nancy.

FRANK CARRODUS

BIRTHPLACE: Altrincham
DATE OF BIRTH: 31 May 1949
DEBUT: York City (A), 17 August 1974
VILLA TOTALS: 197 appearances / 10 goals

Frank Carrodus learned his trade the hard way, playing initially for his hometown club Altrincham before being snapped up by Manchester City in 1969. Five years later, he arrived at Villa Park for almost £100,000 and in his first season he paid back a fair amount of the club's investment by playing 36 games and scoring three goals as Ron Saunders' side won promotion back to the top division.

A cool, composed midfielder, Carrodus also played in all but one of the ten games which culminated in a League Cup final victory over Norwich City at Wembley.

He remained an integral figure in Villa's midfield over the next three seasons as they re-established themselves in the First Division, and was back at Wembley for the 1977 League Cup final against Everton.

He also played in the replay at Hillsborough, but missed the dramatic second replay at Old Trafford, where Villa won 3-2 after extra-time. He joined Wrexham in December 1979.

163

BOB CHATT

BIRTHPLACE: Barnard Castle
DATE OF BIRTH: August 1870
DEBUT: Accrington (A), 15 April 1893
VILLA TOTALS: 95 appearances / 27 goals

Bob Chatt scored the fastest goal ever to win the FA Cup when he hit the winner for Villa against West Bromwich Albion after just 30 seconds of the 1895 final. When Chatt hit home Charlie Athersmith's pass at the Crystal Palace, many people were unaware the match had kicked off - including some members of the press. In the confusion, some initial reports credited the goal to John Devey.

Born just two miles from the birthplace of full-back Albert Evans, Chatt started his career with Middlesbrough Ironopolis, where his scoring ability brought him to the notice of Villa. His debut at Accrington was the Lancashire club's last Football League match.

Although he began his career as a centre-forward, Chatt filled a variety of positions with distinction at Villa, and he played centre-half for the Football League against the Irish League in November 1895. Having helped Villa to the League Championship title in 1894, further Championship medals followed in 1896 and 1897.

In June 1898, Chatt returned to his native North East, reverting to amateur status with Stockton, and in 1899 added an FA Amateur Cup winner's medal to his collection. He is one of only two players to have gained both FA Cup and FA Amateur Cup winners' medals. He died in 1955.

CIARAN CLARK

BIRTHPLACE: Harrow
DATE OF BIRTH: 26 September 1989
DEBUT: Fulham (H), 30 August 2009
VILLA TOTALS: 160 appearances / 10 goals

Ciaran Clark was one of the club's understated players during the second decade of the 21st century. Although he never completed an ever-present season in the Premier League, he was a dependable figure at the heart of Villa's defence for several seasons. A centre-back who could also operate at left-back, Clark graduated through Villa's youth ranks from the age of eleven before making his first-team debut in 2009.

It was his only senior appearance that season, but he was selected more frequently the following campaign, when his hard tackling earned him the unwanted distinction of becoming the first Premier League player to be booked in six consecutive games.

He also scored his first two goals, both against Arsenal in a 4-2 home defeat, and while they provided little consolation, he headed a stoppage-time equaliser in a thrilling 3-3 draw at Chelsea in early January.

Clark claimed his first FA Cup goal with a fine solo effort at Bristol Rovers in January 2012, and he also was captain on the odd occasion, including a 4-1 League Cup quarter-final win at Norwich City. Following Villa's relegation to the Championship, he was transferred to Newcastle United in August 2016.

JAMES COLLINS

BIRTHPLACE: Newport, Wales
DATE OF BIRTH: 23 August 1983
DEBUT: Birmingham City (A), 13 September 2009
VILLA TOTALS: 108 appearances / 6 goals

James Collins signed for Villa on the same 2009 deadline day as Richard Dunne, and the duo formed a sound central-defensive partnership. The Wales international arrived from West Ham with a reputation for his uncompromising defending, and he maintained that image during his time at Villa Park.

He and Dunne helped to ensure that Villa conceded very few goals during their debut campaign, which culminated in Villa finishing sixth in the Premier League as well as reaching the League Cup final and FA Cup semi-finals.

Collins scored the first of his six goals for Villa when he netted the winner against Chelsea just a few weeks after signing, although he was better known for his reliability at the back, particularly during two seasons when the club battled to avoid relegation.

The former Cardiff City player returned to West Ham in August 2012 and nearly followed in Steve Staunton's footsteps as only the second Villa player to have two spells with two clubs. Following his release by the Hammers, Collins signed a short-term contract with Villa early in the 2018/19 campaign, but ripped it up after suffering a calf injury in his first training session. He later explained that he would have been embarrassed to stay because he would have been injured for the duration of the six-week agreement.

JAMES COWAN

BIRTHPLACE: Jamestown, Scotland
DATE OF BIRTH: 17 October 1868
DEBUT: Burnley (H), 7 September 1889
VILLA TOTALS: 356 appearances / 27 goals

James Cowan was playing for Vale of Leven reserves when Warwick County FC, playing at the County Cricket Ground at Edgbaston, invited him to Birmingham for a trial. The ever-alert George Ramsay heard that Cowan was in the city and talked him into signing for Villa.

And what a signing! Cowan, an ever-present in his first season, went on to become the outstanding centre-half of his day. A magnificent tackler with great powers of anticipation and a shrewd tactician, he believed in playing the ball from the back through the half-backs rather than adopting the 'big-boot' tactics favoured by most teams at the time.

During 13 years with Villa, Cowan gained two FA Cup winners' medals (1895 and 1897), a runners-up medal in 1892 and five League Championship medals (1894, 1896, 1897, 1899, 1900). He possessed magnificent ball control, but very seldom headed the ball, believing the game should be played on the ground.

Despite Anglo-Scots not being in favour with the Scottish selectors at the time, Cowan won three caps.

A fast runner, Cowan fancied in the autumn of 1895 that he could win the Annual Powderhall Handicap 130 yards professional sprint in Edinburgh the following January. He entered for the race under an assumed name and then feigned a back injury so he could return to Scotland to 'recuperate'.

The full extent to which he hoodwinked the Villa committee has passed into folklore, but Cowan spent the time well, undertaking extensive training before winning the race and a prize of £80.

On his return, Cowan was faced with a furious Villa committee who initially suspended him for four weeks. However, Fred Rinder saw the funny side and the suspension was quickly lifted, enabling Cowan to return and help Villa take the league title again. Cowan retired in 1902 and became QPR's first manager in 1906. He died in December 1918.

GORDON COWANS

BIRTHPLACE: Durham
DATE OF BIRTH: 27 October 1958
DEBUT: Manchester City (A), 7 February 1976
VILLA TOTALS: 527 appearances / 59 goals

Few players throughout Villa's history can match the sheer quality of Gordon Cowans' passing. Over 15 yards or 50, the midfielder's delivery of a football oozed poise and precision, and invariably set a dangerous attack in motion. Indeed, David Platt went on record as saying he would not have been the player he was without the immaculate service he received from the man popularly known as Sid.

Gordon Sidney Cowans will also be remembered as Villa's Prodigal Son. He left the club three times - and on each occasion he returned, latterly as a youth coach. He was always destined to wear claret and blue, having been on schoolboy forms at Villa Park from the age of twelve. On leaving school, he graduated through Villa's youth and reserve teams before being handed his first taste of senior football in 1976, when he went on as a substitute against Manchester City at Maine Road.

By the end of the following season he was a first-team regular as well as winning a League Cup medal in a dramatic victory over Everton in the second replay of the marathon 1977 final.

Between 1979 and 1983, he did not miss a single match as he became an integral figure in the most successful period of the club's history, adding League Championship, European Cup and European Super Cup medals to his collection. His long unbroken appearance run came to an end when he broke his leg in a pre-season friendly, causing him to miss the whole of the 1983/84 campaign.

In 1985, he joined Italian club Bari, but was brought back to Villa Park by Graham Taylor three years later. Once again, he excelled, helping Villa to finish runners-up to Liverpool in 1990. Later that year, Taylor, having been appointed England manager, handed Cowans his tenth and final cap, but in 1991, the midfield man was sold to Blackburn Rovers. In 1993 he returned for a third spell before joining Derby County.

JIMMY CRABTREE

BIRTHPLACE: Burnley
DATE OF BIRTH: 23 December 1871
DEBUT: West Bromwich Albion (H), 2 September 1895
VILLA TOTALS: 202 appearances / 8 goals

Cup holders Villa paid more than double their previous transfer fee when securing the services of Burnley's Jimmy Crabtree for £250 in 1895. Already an international, having gained his first cap the previous year, Crabtree became one of England's greatest players in the period up to 1902, finishing with 14 caps, eleven of them gained while with Villa.

A naturally gifted, versatile player, who excelled as a half-back, he was arguably better still when playing full-back. A keen, skilful tackler, Crabtree was at the peak of his career during his time at Villa Park.

Crabtree gained a League Championship winning medal at the end of his first season with Villa and went on to gain further league title-winning medals in 1897, 1899 and 1900. In 1897, he also gained an FA Cup winner's medal as Villa won the double.

Having already skippered the Clarets, Crabtree also captained both Villa and England. His final first-team appearance was at Grimsby Town in April 1902 and after leaving Villa Park he had a short spell with Plymouth Argyle before becoming a licensee in Lozells. Just six years after his career ended, Crabtree died at the age of just 36.

ALEX CROPLEY

BIRTHPLACE: Aldershot
DATE OF BIRTH: 16 January 1951
DEBUT: Leicester City (H), 25 September 1976
VILLA TOTALS: 83 appearances / 7 goals

Alex Cropley fell short of a century of appearances for Villa and his scoring record was modest, to say the least, yet he was one of the most gifted footballers ever to wear a claret and blue shirt. The reason his statistics are relatively unimpressive is simple. Apart from being one of the club's most talented players, he was also one of the unluckiest, spending a year out of action with a broken leg.

Although he was born in Surrey, Cropley was brought up in Edinburgh, starting his career with Hibernian before joining Arsenal in 1974. Two years later, he moved to Villa for £125,000 and in his first season he helped the club to League Cup glory.

Unfortunately, Villa were robbed of his creative spark when he suffered a broken leg against West Bromwich Albion, an injury which kept him sidelined for the following twelve months. Although he was a regular at the end of the 1978/79 campaign, he never fully recaptured the form he had displayed before his injury.

After spells on loan with Newcastle United and Toronto Blizzard, he left the club in September 1981 to join Portsmouth. Despite being born in England, he qualified to play for Scotland, winning two caps.

VIC CROWE

BIRTHPLACE: Abercynon, Wales
DATE OF BIRTH: 31 January 1932
DEBUT: Manchester City (A), 16 October 1954
VILLA TOTALS: 351 appearances / 12 goals

It was something of a consolation prize for Vic Crowe when Villa became the inaugural winners of the League Cup in 1961. Proud as he was of the club's achievement, he must have reflected on the greater glory which had passed him by four years earlier.

Although he had established himself as a regular member of Villa's first team in the mid-fifties, Crowe was restricted by injury to just one match throughout the 1956/57 campaign. While he was going through the recovery process, his teammates embarked on the trail which ended with an FA Cup triumph.

Crowe signed professional for Villa in the summer of 1952, although he had to wait more than two years for his first-team breakthrough, finally being handed his chance following Danny Blanchflower's departure to Tottenham Hotspur. It was an opportunity he grabbed with both hands and over the next two seasons, Villa Park regulars witnessed the emergence of a totally committed wing-half who never shirked a challenge.

Unfortunately, he was inactive for all but 90 minutes of that memorable 1956/57 campaign, but mid-way through the following season he was back to full fitness - and back in the line-up.

After the disappointment of relegation of 1959, he missed only one match as Villa bounced back to the First Division at the first time of asking, and then enjoyed success in the historic first League Cup final against Rotherham United.

His impressive playing career in claret and blue came to an end when he joined Peterborough United in 1964, but he was back at Villa Park for a successful spell as manager six years later. He died in January 2009.

CARLOS CUELLAR

BIRTHPLACE: Madrid, Spain
DATE OF BIRTH: 23 August 1981
DEBUT: Litex Lovech (A), 18 September 2008
VILLA TOTALS: 121 appearances / 3 goals

Carlos Cuellar was hugely popular, both with the claret and blue faithful and his teammates, during his time at Villa Park.

The Spanish central defender, who could also operate as a full-back, was a dependable figure throughout his four seasons with the club.

Having learned his trade with Osasuna in his homeland, the man from Madrid enjoyed a hugely successful debut campaign with Glasgow Rangers in 2007/08, making a club record 65 appearances in a single season for the Ibrox club. He joined Villa at the start of the following season, making his debut in Bulgaria in a 3-1 UEFA Cup win over Litex Lovech before getting his first taste of Premier League football as a late substitute in a 2-1 derby victory over West Bromwich Albion at The Hawthorns.

Most of his appearances that season were at right-back because of the impressive form of centre-backs Martin Laursen and Curtis Davies, and his versatility enabled him to continue performing solidly in that role following the arrival at Richard Dunne and James Collins in 2009.

Cuellar scored his first Villa goal in a 5-1 home victory over Bolton Wanderers in November that year, and later that season he played at Wembley twice, in the League Cup final against Manchester United and the FA Cup semi-final against Chelsea. He left in the summer of 2012, joining his former Villa manager Martin O'Neill at Sunderland.

JIM CUMBES

BIRTHPLACE: Manchester
DATE OF BIRTH: 4 May 1944
DEBUT: Oldham Athletic (A), 27 November 1971
VILLA TOTALS: 183 appearances / 0 goals

If ever a debut went virtually unnoticed, it was surely Jimmy Cumbes' first game for Villa. All the action was at the other end of the pitch as Vic Crowe's side, with the help of an Andy Lochhead hat-trick, hammered Oldham Athletic 6-0 at Boundary Park to record the club's biggest post-war away win.

Cumbes, though, gained a degree of satisfaction from the fact that he kept a clean sheet, a feat he achieved on numerous other occasions over the next few months. By the end of that season, the former Tranmere Rovers and West Bromwich Albion keeper was the proud possessor of a Third Division championship medal, having remained an ever-present between the posts following his arrival from The Hawthorns in November.

He also played in every match as Villa finished third in Division Two the following season and missed only one in 1973-74. And while he was absent for four consecutive games early in the 1974-75 campaign, he ultimately experienced double glory, helping Villa to promotion plus a League Cup triumph over Norwich City at Wembley.

Cumbes, who also made a name for himself as a fast bowler for Worcestershire County Cricket Club, left Villa in March 1976, having been replaced by John Burridge earlier that season. He again linked up with Vic Crowe who, by then was coach of Portland Timbers in the North American Soccer League.

GEORGE CUMMINGS

BIRTHPLACE: Falkirk
DATE OF BIRTH: 5 June 1913
DEBUT: Chelsea (H), 16 November 1935
VILLA TOTALS: 232 appearances / 0 goals

George Cummings had broken into the Scotland team by the time he joined Villa from Partick Thistle in November 1935 and his quality shone through during his 14-year association with the club. Sadly, it included the war years, or Cummings would have amassed over 400 appearances in claret and blue, rather than his official figure of 232. He also played in more than 180 wartime games.

The fact that he never hit the target for Villa in league or cup action only serves to underline the fact that he concentrated on what he knew best - keeping opposition wingers quiet. A solid, resolute full-back, he was nicknamed 'The Icicle' because of his ability to remain calm under pressure.

That was never more evident than when he subdued the great Stanley Matthews as Villa beat Blackpool in the 1944 League North Cup final.

When he joined Villa, they were struggling at the foot of the table, and while he became a firm favourite with supporters in the second half of that season, he was unable to prevent relegation for the first time in the club's history.

A knee injury restricted him to just a dozen games the following season but he returned to action on a regular basis in 1937/38, helping Villa to the Second Division championship. He missed only two games during the last full season before the war, and when League football returned he took over as captain, producing consistent performances until 1949, when he hung up his boots to concentrate on coaching Villa's youngsters. He died in 1987.

TONY DALEY

BIRTHPLACE: Birmingham
DATE OF BIRTH: 18 October 1967
DEBUT: Southampton (A), 20 April 1985
VILLA TOTALS: 290 appearances / 38 goals

If Tony Daley never quite fulfilled his immense potential, it was only because he was beset by injuries throughout his career. When fully fit, he was a delight to watch as his pace and skill down either flank made him a constant menace to opposition full-backs.

He was a winger whose runs and crosses set up countless openings for his teammates, not to mention a healthy number of goals for himself, many of them spectacular efforts which had Villa supporters in raptures.

Daley joined Villa as an apprentice in 1983, signing professional two years later, not long after making his first-team debut. He also played in four other games at the end of that season and he continued to make progress over the next couple of years until injuries restricted him to just eleven starts during Villa's promotion campaign of 1987/88.

Significantly, he made his highest number of league appearances in 1989/90, when Villa finished runners-up to Liverpool in the First Division title race. His form that season, and again in 1991/92, prompted his former club manager Graham Taylor to hand him his first England cap and he went on to play seven times for his country, including the 1992 European Championship finals in Sweden.

Daley was also a member of the Villa side who beat Manchester United 3-1 in the 1994 League Cup final at Wembley before joining Wolves for £1.25million that summer.

ALAN DEAKIN

BIRTHPLACE: Birmingham
DATE OF BIRTH: 27 November 1941
DEBUT: Rotherham United (A), 5 December 1959
VILLA TOTALS: 270 appearances / 9 goals

There was disappointment for Alan Deakin when he made his Villa debut during the club's Second Division title campaign of 1959/60. His lone appearance that season was in a 2-1 defeat at Rotherham United - but it was against the same opponents 22 months later that he helped Villa to become the inaugural winners of the League Cup.

The two-leg final against the Yorkshire outfit was staged in the opening weeks of 1961/62, a season which ranks as Deakin's most successful in claret and blue. Apart from the League Cup triumph, he also played in 40 league matches as Villa finished a creditable seventh in only their second season back in the First Division.

Although the remainder of the sixties saw Villa on a downward spiral, Deakin maintained the form which had made him arguably the most naturally talented of the crop of teenage players known as Mercer's Minors.

He also won half-a-dozen England under-23 caps, only to suffer a broken ankle during the 1964/65 season, when a call-up to the full national side looked a distinct possibility.

Deakin had the bitter taste of relegation in 1967, but his devotion to the cause was never in question. After 270 appearances over the course of a decade, he moved to Walsall in October 1969. He died in January 2018.

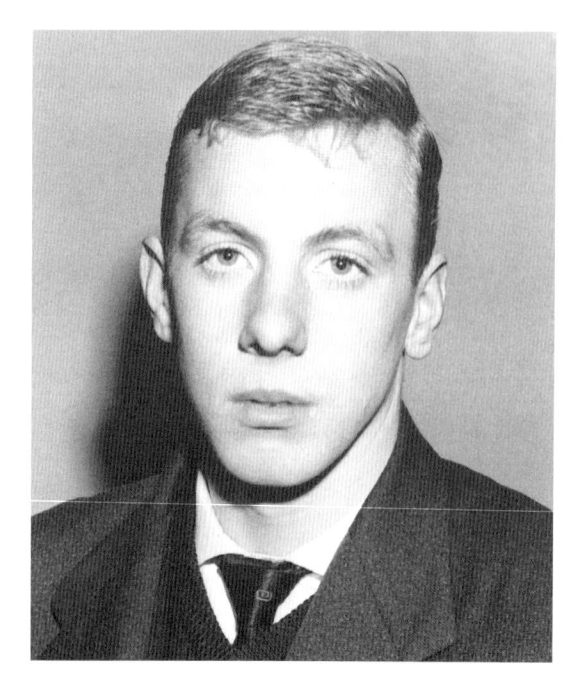

JOHN DEEHAN

BIRTHPLACE: Solihull
DATE OF BIRTH: 6 August 1957
DEBUT: Ipswich Town (A), 1 November 1975
VILLA TOTALS: 139 appearances / 50 goals

Many strikers are opportunists. But John Deehan worked hard to create openings, both for himself and his teammates, during a four-year run in Villa's first team. His endeavours were productive, his half century of goals coming in a relatively small number of appearances - 135, plus four as sub - for an average slightly better than a goal every three games.

Having joined Villa as an apprentice in 1973, he broke into the senior side for the first time at Portman Road in November 1975. Villa lost 3-0, but a week later, home supporters had a glimpse of what lay in store when he scored in a 5-1 victory over Sheffield United.

He was on target seven times that season and really clicked into gear over the next two campaigns for a combined haul of 34.

His personal best of 18 goals in claret and blue helped the club to a League Cup triumph and fourth place in the table in 1976-77. He displayed a liking for European football, too, scoring five times in seven games as Villa reached the UEFA Cup quarter-finals in 1977-78.

Capped seven times by England under-21s, his Villa playing days came to an end with a move to West Bromwich Albion in September 1979, although he returned to the club in 2001 as assistant manager to John Gregory.

MARK DELANEY

BIRTHPLACE: Haverfordwest
DATE OF BIRTH: 13 May 1976
DEBUT: Nottingham Forest (H), 24 April 1999
VILLA TOTALS: 193 appearances / 2 goals

One of the saddest moments of Villa's Premier League years was the announcement in August 2007 that Mark Delaney had been forced to retire because of a serious knee injury. The Welsh full-back been out of action since an FA Cup-tie against Manchester City 18 months earlier, but his departure at the age of 31 was still a bitter blow. Over the course of seven seasons, he had served Villa extremely well at right-back with his solid, dependable, understated performances.

A former packer in a wool factory, he joined Villa from Cardiff City in March 1999, making a couple of substitute appearances before the end of that season, but the following year he was a regular in the Villa side who reached the FA Cup final.

Early in the 2000/01 season, Delaney suffered the first of what turned out to be a series of knee problems. Even so, he still played in nearly 200 games for the club and the figure would surely have been nearer 300 had he managed to maintain peak fitness.

Delaney, capped 36 times by Wales, scored only two goals for Villa. But that hardly mattered when you consider his reliability at right-back and, when the need arose, in central defence.

Following his enforced retirement, Delaney took up coaching, initially looking after Villa's youth team and then the under-23s. In January 2021, after an outbreak of Covid-19 among the first-team squad and staff, he took charge of a young Villa side in a third-round FA Cup tie against Liverpool.

FABIAN DELPH

BIRTHPLACE: Bradford
DATE OF BIRTH: 21 November 1989
DEBUT: Wigan Athletic (H), 15 August 2009
VILLA TOTALS: 134 appearances / 8 goals

A host of clubs were lining up to sign Fabian Delph after Leeds United failed to gain promotion from League One in 2009, and it was hardly surprising. The combative youngster had emerged as a key figure in the Yorkshire club's midfield and clearly had a bright future.

Delph opted for a move to Villa Park, although it was a while before he was able to make an impact on the Premier League stage. He was frequently on the bench during his debut campaign, which was curtailed when he suffered a cruciate knee ligament injury during training in April - a setback which kept him out of action until Boxing Day.

After being in and out of the team for the remainder of 2010/11 and the start of the following season, he returned to Leeds on loan in January 2012, only to suffer an injury which meant another early finish.

It was during Paul Lambert's first season as manager that Delph started to establish himself as a first-team regular and the following year he really blossomed, being voted Villa's player of the month for August, September and October. His form was so impressive that on 3 September, he became the 72nd Villa player to represent England, going on as a substitute in a 1-0 win over Norway.

He was voted Villa's player of the season for 2013/14 and towards the end of the following campaign he was appointed captain. He scored the winning goal as Villa beat Liverpool 2-1 in the FA Cup semi-final, but the 4-0 defeat by Arsenal in the final proved to be his final game for the club before he joined Manchester City.

JOHN DEVEY

BIRTHPLACE: Birmingham
DATE OF BIRTH: 26 December 1866
DEBUT: Blackburn Rovers (H), 5 September 1891
VILLA TOTALS: 311 appearances / 183 goals

John Devey gained a reputation in local football, having represented the Football Alliance when with Birmingham St Georges. Hardly a week went by without his name being linked with Villa before he finally arrived in 1891 at the age of 24.

Devey scored twice on his league debut, a 5-1 win against Blackburn Rovers at Wellington Road and went on to win five League Championship medals, in 1894, 1896, 1897, 1899 and 1900, in addition to FA Cup winner's medals in 1895 and 1897 plus a runners-up medal in 1892.

A prolific scorer, Devey was the complete footballer; he was an intelligent player who read the game well. Possessing good pace, he was alert to everything on the field, and was excellent with his head as well as both feet. He relied on skill rather than strength and was noted for suddenly pivoting on his heel and then shooting.

Devey went on to captain Villa through the club's golden age, including the double-winning season of 1896/97. Amazingly, he was only capped twice by England, scoring once. Devey was also a fine cricketer, hitting over 6,500 runs for Warwickshire, including eight centuries. He received Benefits from both Villa and Warwickshire.

After scoring in his final league match, a 4-1 win against Grimsby Town in December 1901, he played his last senior game, an FA Cup third-round tie against Stoke in January 1902, before winding down his Villa career three months later in a Birmingham League match. He then became a Villa director, remaining on the board until 1934. He died in October 1940.

JOHNNY DIXON

BIRTHPLACE: Hebburn-on-Tyne
DATE OF BIRTH: 10 December 1923
DEBUT: Derby County (H), 6 April 1946
VILLA TOTALS: 430 appearances / 144 goals

The biggest tragedy of Johnny Dixon's later life was that he could not remember his greatest triumph. Dixon suffered from Alzheimer's disease before his death in January 2009 at the age of 85 and had no recollection of the glorious day at Wembley half a century earlier when he proudly held the FA Cup aloft.

Thankfully, the occasion will always be cherished by Villa folk. Although it was the club's seventh Cup triumph, it was their first at Wembley - and their last of the 20th century.

A few years before his death, the popular Geordie described just how much it meant to him, describing how he was almost in tears a few minutes before the final whistle when he imagined the feeling of being presented with the trophy. "It was fantastic when I went up to collect the Cup," he said. "The Queen handed me the Cup and I turned away from her to hold it up. To do something like that just once in a lifetime is tremendous".

Dixon's Villa career had begun a decade earlier when he wrote for a trial because he liked the club's name! He arrived during the war, in August 1944, and 20 months later he scored on his debut against Derby County in the Football League (South). After scoring three goals in five games, he established himself as a regular in the Villa line-up when league football resumed in 1946/47, going on to make an impressive 430 appearances before his retirement in 1961.

He also scored 144 goals, including five during the 1957 Cup run, and was on target in a 4-1 victory over Sheffield Wednesday in his farewell game. A classy inside-forward, he was Villa's leading scorer four times, including the 1951/52 campaign, when he hit a personal best 28.

Dixon also helped Villa to the Second Division title in 1959/60 after they had been relegated the previous season for only the second time in the club's history. Following his retirement, he coached the club's youngsters for six years.

ARTHUR DORRELL

BIRTHPLACE: Birmingham
DATE OF BIRTH: 30 March 1898
DEBUT: Derby County (A), 8 September 1919
VILLA TOTALS: 390 appearances / 65 goals

The son of Billy Dorrell who played for Villa in the 1890s, Arthur joined the club in May 1919 following Army service. He collected an FA Cup-winner's medal in his first season at Villa Park after initially sharing the left-wing berth with Arthur Edgley who broke his leg in a league match at Stamford Bridge a week after the semi-final win against Chelsea.

Dorrell came in to make the position his own, becoming a fixture throughout the 1920s and forming a renowned left-wing partnership with Billy Walker. Cool in any situation, he made his second FA Cup final appearance against Newcastle United in 1924, but had to be content with a runners-up medal.

In December that year, Dorrell made the first of his four international appearances, forming England's left wing with Billy Walker in a 4-0 win against Belgium at The Hawthorns. He scored once for England, in a 3-2 win against France in Paris, and played twice for the Football League, scoring in a 5-1 win against the Irish League in 1925.

His final Villa appearance came in a 1-1 draw at Birmingham on the last Saturday of 1929. At the end of the season, Dorrell joined Port Vale along with Dicky York, who had played on the right-wing over the same period. Dorrell died in September 1942.

DICKIE DORSETT

BIRTHPLACE: Brownhills
DATE OF BIRTH: 3 December 1919
DEBUT: Portsmouth (H), 12 October 1946
VILLA TOTALS: 271 appearances / 35 goals

Dickie Dorsett was well known to Villa supporters long before he joined the club. Before the war he had been a prolific scorer for neighbours Wolves, scoring more than 70 goals in 110 appearances for the Molineux club, including their consolation goal in an FA Cup final defeat by Portsmouth in 1939.

Having guested for numerous clubs in between his RAF duties, he was still with Wolves when League football resumed in August 1946, but early that season he moved across the Midlands, making his debut for Villa in a 1-1 home draw against Pompey. At that stage of his career, Dorsett was still operating as a forward, and he finished his debut campaign as leading scorer with 13 goals, hitting another eleven two seasons later.

By then, though, he had been converted to a more defensive wing-half role and he excelled in that position, as well as at left-back, as he amassed a total of more than 250 games in claret and blue.

Even when he was involved in a serious car accident in January 1950, he was quickly back in action, missing only three games, and although he never managed an ever-present season, he was an automatic choice throughout his seven seasons at Villa Park.

Popular with both his teammates and Villa supporters, he retired at the end of the 1952/53 campaign to coach Villa's youngsters. He died in 1999.

DEREK DOUGAN

BIRTHPLACE: Belfast
DATE OF BIRTH: 20 January 1938
DEBUT: Everton (A), 19 August 1961
VILLA TOTALS: 60 appearances / 26 goals

He was better known for his exploits in the gold and black of Villa's West Midland neighbours Wolves in the late 1960s, but Derek Dougan left an indelible impression during two seasons at Villa Park. His extrovert nature ensured his name will remain forever in Villa folklore.

He stepped out for his debut at Goodison Park with a completely shaved head - something almost unheard of in those days - and was never far from controversy throughout his colourful career.

Indeed, he had shocked the football world by asking Blackburn Rovers for a transfer the day before the 1960 FA Cup final, which the Lancashire club lost 3-0 to Wolves, although it was the following summer before Joe Mercer made him a Villa player for £15,000.

Dougan was signed as a replacement for the prolific Gerry Hitchens, who had joined Inter Milan, and it was always going to be a hard act to follow. As it was, he managed almost a goal every two games, helping Villa to finish seventh in his debut campaign before making an explosive start to 1962/63. On target in an opening-day victory over West Ham, he netted both goals the following Monday as a crowd of 64,751 witnessed Villa's first victory over Tottenham Hotspur since the Second World War.

A Northern Ireland international, Dougan was transferred to Peterborough United in the summer of 1963. He died in 2007.

STEWART DOWNING

BIRTHPLACE: Middlesbrough
DATE OF BIRTH: 22 July 1984
DEBUT: Burnley (A), 21 November 2009
VILLA TOTALS: 79 appearances / 11 goals

Stewart Downing was so highly rated by Martin O'Neill that the manager signed him knowing that he would be sidelined for several months. The winger needed an operation on a foot injury sustained in a tackle with Villa's Stiliyan Petrov as Middlesbrough battled in vain to avoid relegation at the end of 2008/09.

It was clear that Downing faced a lengthy lay-off beyond the close-season break, but that did not stop O'Neill from making him his first signing of the summer transfer window - and the manager's faith was justified. It was the third Saturday of November before his first action, a 20-minute substitute appearance at Burnley, but it soon became evident what a shrewd signing he was. He quickly made an impact, scoring his first Villa goal in a 4-2 League Cup quarter-final win at Portsmouth and then helping Villa to beat Manchester United at Old Trafford for the first time since 1983.

By the end of that season, he had been instrumental in Villa reaching both the League Cup final and FA Cup semi-finals, as well as achieving a sixth-place finish for the third consecutive year.

The 2010/11 was a personal triumph for Downing, who played in 44 matches and scored eight goals, including Villa's first and last of the season. He opened the scoring at Villa Park in a 3-0 win over West Ham on the opening day and hit the only goal in the 1-0 home victory over Liverpool on the final day. That was his last game before he moved to Anfield in July 2011.

MARK DRAPER

BIRTHPLACE: Long Eaton
DATE OF BIRTH: 11 November 1970
DEBUT: Manchester United (H), 19 August 1995
VILLA TOTALS: 155 appearances / 11 goals

Mark Draper made the art of passing seem almost effortless as he stroked the ball around Villa's midfield for four seasons. Signed by Brian Little from Leicester City for £3.25million, he quickly settled at Villa Park and was on target on his debut in a famous 3-1 opening-day victory over Manchester United.

His classy performances were a key feature as Villa won the League Cup, reached the FA Cup semi-finals and finished fourth in the table in his debut season - and he also scored an amazing goal against Peterborough in the League Cup.

Controlling the ball on his thigh after Andy Townsend had flicked a cheeky free-kick, he sent a 20-yard volley just under the bar.

The following season his place came under threat from £4million record signing Sasa Curcic, and Draper's cause was not helped when he was sent off in an early season 4-3 defeat at Newcastle, although he still made more appearances than his Serbian midfield rival.

He was again Villa's main playmaker throughout an eventful 1997/98 campaign, when Villa qualified for the UEFA Cup, although the following season his appearances were restricted by an ankle injury which required surgery.

Although he re-established himself as a regular at the end of that season, he lost his place at the start of the 1999/00 campaign, making just one substitute appearance before joining Spanish club Rayo Vallecano on loan in January 2000.

DION DUBLIN

BIRTHPLACE: Leicester
DATE OF BIRTH: 22 April 1969
DEBUT: Tottenham Hotspur (H), 7 November 1998
VILLA TOTALS: 189 appearances / 59 goals

No player has made a more explosive start to his Villa career than Dion Dublin. Signed from Coventry City for £5.75million in November 1998, the former Cambridge and Manchester United striker simply could not stop scoring in his first three games for the club.

On target after half an hour against Tottenham, he scored again four minutes later to inspire a 3-2 victory. A week later at Southampton, the new boy helped himself to a hat-trick in a 4-1 victory which extended the team's unbeaten league start to 12 matches - the best in Villa's history.

And although his double-strike failed to prevent a 4-2 home defeat by Liverpool in the following match, it gave him an incredible start of seven goals in three games, an achievement unprecedented by any Villa man.

The problem was that it was impossible to maintain such a ratio and by the end of that first season in claret and blue his goal haul was a relatively modest eleven as he was hampered by a hernia and then a knee injury.

Those problems were nothing, though, compared with the fate which befell Dublin just before Christmas the following season. An accidental collision with Sheffield Wednesday's Gerald Sibon left him needing a four-hour operation on a crushed vertebra.

Only the swift action of physio Jim Walker averted the threat of paralysis, yet Dublin was back in action just over three months later. He even scored the penalty which gave Villa an FA Cup semi-final victory over Bolton at Wembley and despite his lengthy absence he still finished as the club's leading scorer with 15 goals.

By the time he left Villa Park four years later, Dublin had scored 59 league and cup goals. He was also natural leader who was an inspiration to the club's younger players.

JIMMY DUGDALE

BIRTHPLACE: Liverpool
DATE OF BIRTH: 15 January 1932
DEBUT: Arsenal (H), 11 February 1956
VILLA TOTALS: 255 appearances / 3 goals

Not many footballers can claim to have won FA Cup medals with two different West Midlands clubs, but Jimmy Dugdale did. A solid, dependable centre-half, he was in the West Bromwich Albion side who beat Preston 3-2 in the 1954 final and was back at Wembley three years later, inspiring Villa to a 2-1 victory over hot favourites Manchester United.

While two-goal Peter McParland was hailed as the hero, many people regarded Dugdale as the man-of-the-match after he kept dangerman Tommy Taylor quiet until the striker finally managed to head home United's late consolation goal.

Dugdale had begun his career at The Hawthorns as an amateur in 1950, turning professional two years later. Having savoured Cup glory with the Baggies, he made the four-mile journey to Villa Park for £25,000 in February 1956.

Villa were struggling at the time, but Dugdale's performances over the final 14 games were instrumental in the club retaining First Division status. The following season, when he missed just two games, they climbed to tenth in the table and reached the Cup final, Dugdale playing in every tie before excelling at Wembley.

He was captain during 1958/59, when Villa were relegated, but was again a key figure as they bounced back at the first attempt. With FA Cup and Second Division championship medals under his belt, Dugdale added another to his collection when Villa won the inaugural League Cup in 1961 before joining QPR the following year. He died in February 2008.

RICHARD DUNNE

BIRTHPLACE: Dublin
DATE OF BIRTH: 21 September 1979
DEBUT: Birmingham City (A), 13 September 2009
VILLA TOTALS: 111 appearances / 5 goals

Some deadline-day transfers go right to the wire; when Richard Dunne joined Villa, the wire was stretched beyond the limit. Negotiations for the central-defender's move from Manchester City continued all day at Bodymoor Heath as members of the club's media staff waited patiently to announce the signing.

The deal was finally concluded at 4.59pm - just a minute before the window closed - but even then, it could not be formally announced until it had been ratified by the FA the following morning.

If the Republic of Ireland international arrived in dramatic circumstances, though, it was not long before his experience had a settling effect on a revamped Villa defence, which also featured two more new boys, James Collins and Stephen Warnock.

All three made their debuts in the Second City derby, helping Martin O'Neill's side to a 1-0 win, and less than a month later, Dunne was on target in consecutive home games against his former club Manchester City and Chelsea.

By the end of the season, he had played at Wembley twice for Villa, in the League Cup final and FA Cup semi-final, and his form was so consistent that he was named in the PFA Team of the Year.

Dunne remained a regular until he injured his shoulder in a collision with Manchester City keeper Joe Hart in February 2012. But his value to the team was underlined when he returned to action ahead of schedule for the last three games to help Villa secure Premier League safety. He was released by manager Paul Lambert in May 2013 and joined QPR two months later.

GEORGE EDWARDS

BIRTHPLACE: Great Yarmouth
DATE OF BIRTH: 1 April 1918
DEBUT: Manchester United (H), 5 November 1938
VILLA TOTALS: 152 appearances / 41 goals

George Edwards was the man who ignited one of the most famous games in Villa's history with one of the quickest goals ever scored. He was on target after just 14 seconds of a third-round FA Cup-tie at home to Manchester United in January 1948, an epic contest which Villa eventually lost 6-4 after trailing 5-1 at half-time.

That was just one of 41 goals officially credited to a player who operated either as a centre-forward or an inside-forward. He scored more than double that amount in unofficial wartime games, including 39 Football League South goals in the transitional campaign of 1945/46. He was also on target four times in FA Cup-ties that season, one of them in another significant match - the 4-3 quarter-final defeat by Derby County in front of Villa Park's record crowd of 76,558.

Edwards arrived at Villa Park from Norwich City in 1938, although his involvement in the final full season before the war was restricted to just three games by an ankle injury.

He helped Villa to victory over Blackpool in the 1944 war cup final, and turned out as a guest for numerous other clubs during the hostilities, as well as making over 100 appearances in claret and blue. When League football resumed, he was a regular in the Villa side over the next five years before moving into non-League football in 1951. He died in 1993.

UGO EHIOGU

BIRTHPLACE: Hackney
DATE OF BIRTH: 3 November 1972
DEBUT: Arsenal (H), 24 August 1991
VILLA TOTALS: 302 appearances / 15 goals

People used to joke that Villa would never sell Ugo Ehiogu - because they would have to hand over a sizeable chunk of the fee to his previous club West Bromwich Albion. The powerful defender had cost Villa just £45,000 when he arrived from The Hawthorns in the summer of 1991, but while that was a bargain price, the Baggies clearly had their eye to business. A hefty sell-on clause was written into the contract, so that when Ehiogu joined Middlesbrough for £8million in October 2000, around £3million went to Albion.

If Villa's profit was not what it might have been, they certainly received outstanding value from the quietly spoken Londoner. He was signed by Ron Atkinson, who had seen his potential while manager at The Hawthorns, and although Ehiogu's first-team appearances were initially restricted, he gradually developed into one of the most solid centre-backs in the country.

His first season as a regular, ironically, was the 1994/95 campaign in which Villa only narrowly avoided relegation, but twelve months later he was a member of the side who won the League Cup, finished fourth in the Premier League, and reached the FA Cup semi-finals.

Ehiogu continued to be a tower of strength, winning the first of four full England caps in May 1996 and missing only one league game over the course of the following two seasons.

He was also in the Villa side who reached the 2000 FA Cup final, but subsequently made it clear he wanted to leave, eventually moving to Teesside. Ehiogu later coached Tottenham's under-23 side, but died after suffering a cardiac arrest at Spurs' training ground in April 2017.

VILLA STARS A-Z

ALLAN EVANS

BIRTHPLACE: Polbeth, Edinburgh
DATE OF BIRTH: 12 October 1956
DEBUT: Barcelona (H), 1 March 1978
VILLA TOTALS: 475 appearances / 62 goals

Allan Evans played a crucial role at the heart of the defence during Villa's championship and European Cup triumphs. Yet, it was as a striker that he had arrived at Villa Park from Dunfermline Athletic in May 1977. He scored 15 goals for the Scottish club, although his Dunfermline debut was one to forget - he suffered a broken leg against Glasgow Rangers.

After his move to Villa, he was regularly on target for the reserves and played up front in his first three senior games, scoring against Newcastle United. By the end of that season, though, he had been converted to a central defender, a position in which he served the club so well over the next decade. Solid and consistent, he was a fine tackler and a commanding header of the ball and was parsimonious in the extreme when it came to keeping out forwards. During the League Championship campaign of 1980/81, his impressive form ensured that Villa conceded only 40 goals in their 42 games. His predatory instincts also meant he was always a threat to opposition defences - he was on target seven times that season.

His excellent form also earned him four Scotland caps, and it was not until the second half of the club's relegation season of 1986/87 that he ceased to be a first-team regular. Even then, he fought his way back into the team twelve months later to become a pivotal figure in Villa's promotion from the old Second Division.

He also made 26 appearances in the club's first season back in the First Division before joining Leicester City on a free transfer in August 1989, and later moving to Australia. He also had spells as an assistant manager to Brian Little at both Leicester and Villa.

ALBERT EVANS

BIRTHPLACE: Barnard Castle
DATE OF BIRTH: 18 March 1874
DEBUT: Bury (H), 7 November 1896
VILLA TOTALS: 206 appearances / 0 goals

Full-back Albert Evans made his Villa debut at Wellington Road in November 1896 and by the end of the season he was the holder of both FA Cup-winner's and League Championship medals, going on to help Villa to two more titles in 1899 and 1900.

Introduced to Villa by their former player Bob Chatt, who had spotted him playing in the North East, Evans formed a fine full-back partnership with Howard Spencer. He represented the Football League once, but amazingly did not win an England cap. Evans suffered a series of injuries including breaking a leg twice while playing for Villa, the second one causing him to miss out on the 1905 FA Cup triumph.

After he recovered from a third broken leg, sustained when jumping over a drain, the directors decided to grant him part of the proceeds of the league game against Bristol City in October 1907 as a benefit, guaranteeing at least £250. They also granted him a free transfer and payment of wages until the end of the season. Evans picked up his cheque - and signed for West Bromwich Albion the following day!

The last surviving member of the 1897 double-winning team and the only one still living when Villa lifted the FA Cup for a record seventh time 60 years later, Albert and his wife celebrated their golden wedding on 25 September 1965. He died in March the following year.

183

TREVOR FORD

BIRTHPLACE: Swansea
DATE OF BIRTH: 1 October 1923
DEBUT: Arsenal (A), 18 January 1947
VILLA TOTALS: 128 appearances / 61 goals

If there was a half chance of a goal - or possibly even less - Trevor Ford was willing to throw himself in where it hurt. Strong and courageous, he reveled in battles against opposition defenders, and loved the business of scoring. During his time with Villa, he was one of the most prolific marksmen in the club's history, falling only marginally short of a goal every two games.

Originally a full-back, Ford began his professional career with his hometown club Swansea immediately after the war before joining Villa for £12,000 in January 1947. A week after his first game, a 2-0 win against Arsenal at Highbury, he marked his home debut with Villa's goal in a 1-1 draw with Blackpool; by the end of the season, he had hit the target nine times in as many games.

For the next three seasons, he was in double figures, heading Villa's goal chart on each occasion. A fearless centre-forward, he could shoot powerfully with both feet and Villa fans really took him to their hearts. Indeed, he was described by Charlton Athletic defender Derek Ufton as 'the most complete centre-forward I have played against'.

His value certainly increased during his spell at Villa Park. The club's outlay for him was no mean figure in those days, but it proved to be a wise investment - they received £30,000 from Sunderland when he moved to Roker Park in October 1950.

Ford, who subsequently spent three years with Dutch club PSV Eindhoven, won 39 Welsh caps and became the first player to score more than 30 goals for his country.
He died in May 2003.

BRAD FRIEDEL

BIRTHPLACE: Lakewood, USA
DATE OF BIRTH: 18 May 1971
DEBUT: Hafnarfjordur (A), UEFA Cup, 14 August 2008
VILLA TOTALS: 131 appearances / 0 goals

Brad Friedel has the distinction of being the oldest player in Villa's history. The American goalkeeper eclipsed Mush Callaghan's record when he played at Manchester United in February 2011 at the age of 39 years and 259 days - and he was four days past his 40th birthday when he made his final appearance for the club against Liverpool on the final day of that season.

Friedel joined Villa in the summer of 2008, having previously played for Turkish club Galatasaray, Americans Columbus Crew, Liverpool and Blackburn Rovers. After eight years and over 300 appearances for the Ewood Park club, it was something of a surprise when, at the age of 37, the former USA international was tempted to Villa Park by manager Martin O'Neill.

But he insisted he was looking for a new challenge, and certainly did not disappoint the claret and blue faithful, who were delighted to have a permanent keeper following Scott Carson's season-long loan from Liverpool in 2007/08.

Friedel's vast experience gave enormous confidence to the defenders in front of him and he was an ever-present in the Barclays Premier League for two consecutive seasons, being rested for only a few cup-ties.

In November 2008, Friedel played his 167th consecutive Premier League match, breaking a record previously held by former Villa goalkeeper David James - and by the end of the 2009/10 season, he had extended the sequence to 228.

A member of USA's 1994 World Cup finals squad, Friedel also played for his country against England at the Wembley Stadium that year, and he returned to the new Wembley for the Carling Cup final and an FA Cup semi-final in 2010. By the time he left Villa to join Tottenham Hotspur in the summer of 2011, Friedel had made a record 266 consecutive Premier League appearances, a figure he extended to 310 during his time at White Hart Lane.

BILLY GARRATY

BIRTHPLACE: Saltley, Birmingham
DATE OF BIRTH: 6 October 1878
DEBUT: Stoke (H) 2 April 1898
VILLA TOTALS: 260 appearances / 112 goals

Billy Garraty helped Villa to the league title for the fifth time in 1900, finishing top scorer in the country as he hit 27 goals in 33 league games. He opened the season by netting the only goal at Sunderland and then hitting four in a 9-0 romp against Glossop in Villa's first home game. The striker also scored a hat-trick in a 6-2 home win against Notts County.

Garraty joined Villa during the 1896/97 season, having played many games in his younger days for Lozells on The Meadow, which would later form a large part of Villa Park. The following season, he and George Johnson became the first 'substitutes' in league football when the pair replaced John Devey and Frank Bedingfield in a resumed game against Sheffield Wednesday, the referee having blown the final whistle too early in the original fixture.

An industrious, never-say-die inside or centre-forward with great energy, Garraty collected an FA Cup winners' medal in 1905. Just as he looked set for an international career, injury intervened, although he earned one cap, in a 2-1 win against Wales in 1903.

The last two years of Garraty's career were mainly played out in the reserves, his final first-team game coming at Bristol City in March 1908. He was retained for the following season and it was announced in September that the club were to grant him a benefit when he suddenly departed for Leicester Fosse. Equally suddenly, he left the Foxes for West Bromwich Albion at the end of October. He later became a delivery driver for Ansells Brewery until his death in May 1931.

COLIN H GIBSON

BIRTHPLACE: Normanby-on-Tees
DATE OF BIRTH: 16 September 1923
DEBUT: Huddersfield Town (A), 12 February 1949
VILLA TOTALS: 167 appearances / 26 goals

Colin H Gibson was a classic example of a player being signed on the strength of performances against the club he ultimately joins. In the space of five days in September 1948, he twice excelled for Newcastle United against Villa as the Geordies came out on top 2-1 at St James' Park and 4-2 in the return match at Villa Park.

Those displays left a lasting impression on Villa manager Alex Massie, who signed Gibson from the Tyneside club for £17,000 the following February. It was money well spent, the speedy, skilful winger doing a good job in claret and blue over the course of the next five-and-a-half years.

Although he was born in the North East, Gibson was living in South Wales when he embarked on his professional career, playing more than 150 games and scoring 40 goals for Cardiff City before joining Newcastle in 1948. His spell with the Magpies was short-lived, comprising just 23 appearances, but those performances against Villa secured him a move which saw him flourish.

While at Villa Park, he played for England B and toured Scandinavia with the FA. But after playing the first half dozen games of the 1955/56 he found himself out of favour, making just one more appearance before moving to Lincoln City in January 1956. He died in 1992.

BILLY GEORGE

BIRTHPLACE: Atcham
DATE OF BIRTH: 29 June 1874
DEBUT: West Bromwich Albion (A), 9 October 1897
VILLA TOTALS: 403 appearances / 0 goals

Only Nigel Spink has played more games in goal for Villa than Billy George, whose record of 103 clean sheets in 360 league games was a remarkable total in an era of attacking football. Villa were league and FA Cup double winners when, in 1897, they signed George, a regular soldier serving in the Royal Artillery.

Villa had first been alerted to George when he played against them for Bristol & District. But the signing infringed FA regulations, with chairman Fred Rinder, secretary George Ramsay and George all suspended for a month. The club were also fined £50 and severely censured.

This was, however, a cheap price to pay for a fine sportsman who became one of the greatest Villa goalkeepers. George had a massive impact on the club, collecting League Championship medals in 1899 and 1900 and an FA Cup-winner's medal in 1905.

In 1901, George played for the Football League in a 9-0 win against the Irish League. He was capped three times for England in 1902 and also played against Scotland at Ibrox Park in a game abandoned when disaster struck as terraces collapsed. George, also a fine County cricketer, retired in 1911, saving Ernest Ower's penalty in his final home game, a 2-0 win against Bristol City. George was then appointed trainer at Birmingham. He died on 4 December 1933.

COLIN GIBSON

BIRTHPLACE: Bridport
DATE OF BIRTH: 6 April 1960
DEBUT: Bristol City (H), 18 November 1978
VILLA TOTALS: 238 appearances / 17 goals

Although he ultimately had to settle for a watching brief, Colin Gibson's contribution to Villa's finest achievement should not be underestimated. Despite being consigned to the substitutes' bench from the quarter-final onwards, he played in the first four matches of Villa's 1981/82 European Cup campaign, including the tough second round tie against Dynamo Berlin.

He actually warmed up towards the end of the final against Bayern Munich after Gary Williams suffered a knock, but was relieved not to be required in Rotterdam because he had not played for over three months.

Gibson had been Villa's regular left-back for the first half of that season, having shared the role with Williams during the title-winning campaign of 1980/81.

Before joining Villa as an apprentice in 1976, Gibson was an associated schoolboy with his local club Portsmouth. He turned professional two years after arriving at Villa Park, getting his first taste of senior football as a substitute in a home win over Bristol City.

That was the first of well over 200 appearances in claret and blue. Even after Williams took over at left-back, Gibson made several appearances in midfield before joining Manchester United in November 1985. He also played for England at under-21 and B level.

JIMMY GIBSON

BIRTHPLACE: Larkhall, Lanarkshire
DATE OF BIRTH: 12 June 1901
DEBUT: Huddersfield Town (A), 7 May 1927
VILLA TOTALS: 227 appearances / 10 goals

Villa paid a record fee of £7,500 for Scottish international Jimmy Gibson from Partick Thistle in April 1927. Gibson, almost 6ft 3in tall, teamed up with Alec Talbot and Joe Tate to form a giant half-back line nicknamed 'wind, sleet and snow' during a Villa career spanning nine seasons.

The son of former Scotland player Neil Gibson, he won a further four caps while with Villa to bring his international total to eight. Along with former teammate and future Villa boss James McMillan, he scored one of the goals as Scotland's brilliant Wembley Wizards thrashed England 5-1 in 1928.

Unfortunately, there were no cup medals during Gibson's time with the club - Villa finished runners-up twice - although he was a member of the side which set a record of 128 goals in 1930/31. There were, however, many fine performances, perhaps none better than against Arsenal in November 1932 when Villa and the Gunners were battling for the title. In a scintillating match, Villa came back twice from behind to win 5-3 and Gibson, playing centre-half in the absence of Talbot, scored the first equaliser. This match demonstrated his versatility; he was at home in several positions and was also called upon as emergency goalkeeper.

With his long legs, Gibson was able to bring the ball under control from the most acute of angles and, despite his size, he was an excellent ball player and a fine dribbler. He retired in May 1936 and later worked at ICI in Witton. He died on New Year's Day 1978.

JOHN GIDMAN

BIRTHPLACE: Liverpool
DATE OF BIRTH: 10 January 1954
DEBUT: Carlisle United (H), 29 August 1972
VILLA TOTALS: 243 appearances / 9 goals

Liverpool's loss turned out to be Villa's gain after John Gidman was released by the Anfield club as a youngster. After being discarded by the Reds, he moved to Villa Park in 1970, turning professional a year later.

A member of the team who won the FA Youth Cup in 1972, the attacking full-back made his debut at home to Carlisle United early the following season. In 1973/74, he won the Terrace Trophy when he was voted player of the year by Villa supporters, but the following November, he suffered a serious eye injury when a firework exploded in his face.

He was restricted to just 17 games that season and was still recovering from his injury when Villa beat Norwich City in the 1975 League Cup final.

But Gidman re-established himself as a regular the following season and also helped Villa to victory over Everton in the 1977 final.

An England international, he moved back to Merseyside in October 1979 when he joined the Goodison Park club in a £650,000 deal which saw Pat Heard move in the opposite direction. After two seasons at Everton, he became Ron Atkinson's first signing for Manchester United, with whom he won an FA Cup medal in 1985.

BRIAN GODFREY

BIRTHPLACE: Flint, North Wales
DATE OF BIRTH: 1 May 1940
DEBUT: Middlesbrough (A), 30 September 1967
VILLA TOTALS: 160 appearances / 25 goals

Although he played for Villa during some of the club's darkest days, Brian Godfrey ultimately had the satisfaction of being captain of the side who faced Tottenham Hotspur in the 1971 League Cup final.

Villa, then in the old Third Division, lost 2-0. But along with his teammates, Godfrey emerged with universal acclaim for an excellent performance against a star-studded Spurs outfit. It made amends for Godfrey's disappointment seven years earlier when he was left out of the Preston team to face West Ham in the FA Cup final after helping them to a semi-final victory over Swansea at Villa Park.

An inside-forward, he certainly made an impact when he arrived from Deepdale in September 1967, scoring in each of his first three games and finishing his first season with 13 goals. Although he was never as prolific again, he was one of the more successful members of a struggling team who slipped from 16th to 18th to 21st in his first three seasons with the club. His fourth and final campaign was much more productive. Apart from helping Villa to the League Cup final, he also played in all but two of their Third Division matches.

Godfrey, who was capped three times for Wales during his time at Preston, moved to Bristol Rovers in the summer of 1971 in a deal which saw winger Ray Graydon move in the opposite direction. He died in February 2010.

BILLY GOFFIN

BIRTHPLACE: Amington
DATE OF BIRTH: 12 February 1920
DEBUT: Coventry City (H), FA Cup, 8 January 1946
VILLA TOTALS: 173 appearances / 42 goals

Billy Goffin made two debuts for Villa - and scored on both occasions. Having signed professional with the club in 1937, he was given his first taste of senior football in a wartime Birmingham & District League match at Hednesford in September 1940.

Although Villa lost 6-1, Goffin netted their only goal, but it was not nearly as satisfying as the one he scored on his official debut in a third-round FA Cup-tie against Coventry City more than five years later.

That one secured a 2-0 victory after the Sky Blues had won the first leg 2-1, and Goffin hit four more goals as Villa reached the quarter-finals, where the home leg against Derby County took place in front of a Villa Park record gate of 76,588.

The left-winger's appearances were limited to just nine when League football resumed the following season, yet he still scored three times, and from 1947/48 onwards was a big favourite with supporters.

Nicknamed 'Cowboy', Goffin joined Walsall after leaving Villa, retiring in 1958. He died in 1987.

ANDY GRAY

BIRTHPLACE: Glasgow
DATE OF BIRTH: 30 November 1955
DEBUT: Middlesbrough (A), 4 October 1975
VILLA TOTALS: 210 appearances / 78 goals

Powerful, courageous, forceful, charismatic - there are any number of adjectives to describe Andy Gray. More than anything, though, he was best known as a warhorse who was willing to go in where it hurt. His bravery sometimes resulted in injuries, but it also yielded 78 goals during two spells as a Villa player, the majority during a successful first session in claret and blue following his £110,000 transfer from Dundee United in September 1975.

His debut against Middlesbrough at Ayresome Park ended in a goalless draw, but the following week he gave Villa Park regulars a taste of things to come when he was on target against Tottenham Hotspur in his first home match. Although Villa struggled on their travels that season, failing to record a single away win, Gray's double-figure goal-haul helped Ron Saunders' men to comfortably retain top flight status, and the following campaign he contributed 29 goals as Villa finished fourth in the table and won the League Cup. Such was his impact that he was voted both PFA Footballer of the Year and Young Player of the Year.

He also won the first of his 20 Scotland caps while at Villa Park, his fearless approach bringing him six goals for his country by the time he made his final appearance a decade later.

In September 1979, Gray moved across the West Midlands to join Wolves for £1.469m and the goals continued to flow. He scored the winner as Wolves won the League Cup the following year and was also on target for Everton in their 1984 FA Cup final triumph over Watford.

He was returned to the club in 1985 and although Villa were in decline, he still contributed some important goals before moving to West Bromwich Albion and subsequently Glasgow Rangers. Gray also had a season as assistant to Villa manager Ron Atkinson in 1991/92 before leaving to pursue a television career.

VILLA STARS A-Z

STUART GRAY

BIRTHPLACE: Withernsea
DATE OF BIRTH: 19 April 1960
DEBUT: Bradford City (A), 28 November 1987
VILLA TOTALS: 132 appearances / 15 goals

Stuart Gray made one of Villa's truly memorable debuts. Signed from Barnsley in November 1987, he made an immediate impact by scoring twice in a 4-2 victory against Second Division promotion rivals Bradford City at Valley Parade.

Villa's bid for a rapid return to the top tier had already been gaining momentum, but manager Graham Taylor's astute piece of transfer business sent it into overdrive. In eleven league games following Gray's arrival, Villa won eight and drew three, and although he missed four of them through injury, his invaluable contribution was evident. By the end of that season, he had scored five goals in 19 games to help Villa to runners-up spot behind Millwall.

The following season, he added a further four goals in 35 appearances, making a successful switch to left-back from November onwards as Villa just avoided relegation, and he was also a member of the side who finished second behind Liverpool in 1989/90. He was appointed captain by Taylor, although he and his teammates struggled under Jo Venglos in a 1990/91 campaign which brought another scrape with relegation.

Gray joined Southampton at the start of the following season, only for his career to be ended by a serious Achilles tendon problem in 1993. He subsequently managed the Saints and was also assistant manager of Villa for a while, taking charge along with John Deehan on a caretaker basis following John Gregory's departure in January 2002.

RAY GRAYDON

BIRTHPLACE: Bristol
DATE OF BIRTH: 21 July 1947
DEBUT: Plymouth Argyle (H), 14 August 1971
VILLA TOTALS: 232 appearances / 81 goals

Ray Graydon missed a penalty at Wembley in 1975 and it turned out to be the greatest moment of his career. His spot kick was turned against a post by Norwich City goalkeeper Kevin Keelan, but the free-scoring winger hammered home the rebound to give Villa their second League Cup triumph.

If that was Graydon's personal best achievement in claret and blue, it was by no means the only one. Villa's victory earned them qualification for the UEFA Cup, and Graydon had the distinction of being the scorer of the club's first goal in European competition, albeit in a 4-1 defeat by Belgian club Antwerp.

Although his appearances were restricted during his final season at Villa Park, he was a member of the team who lifted the League Cup again in 1977 by beating Everton in a dramatic second replay of the final at Old Trafford.

It would be wrong, though, to label Ray Graydon as a player who excelled only in cup ties. When he was signed from his hometown club Bristol Rovers in the summer of 1971, in an exchange deal involving Brian Godfrey, Villa were in the old Third Division. By the time he moved to Coventry City six years later, they were back in the top flight.

In his first season, Graydon missed only one game and scored 14 times as Villa won the Third Division title - and his 19-goal league haul helped secure promotion from the old Second Division in the same season they won the League Cup. Graydon later went into football management, having spells in charge of Walsall and Bristol Rovers.

191

JACK GREALISH

BIRTHPLACE: Birmingham
DATE OF BIRTH: 10 September 1995
DEBUT: Manchester City (A), 7 May 2014
VILLA TOTALS: 213 appearances / 32 goals

Having grown up as a Villa fan and graduated through the club's youth and reserve ranks, Jack Grealish's flamboyant style and ability to create something out of nothing quickly endeared him to supporters.

His creative flair yielded an abundance of 'assists' plus a fair sprinkling of goals. And despite being a constant target for frustrated defenders, he simply picked himself up after being fouled and got on with the business of dancing past opponents and making incisive passes.

Grealish made his debut as a late substitute in a 4-0 Premier League defeat at Manchester City in May 2014, having spent most of the season on loan at Notts County. His Villa first starting appearance was in a 1-0 FA Cup victory over Blackpool the following January, and by the end of that season he had played in 24 games, helping Villa to the Cup Final when he set up Fabian Delph for the winning goal in a 2-1 semi-final victory over Liverpool at Wembley.

His first goal for the club came in a 3-2 setback at Leicester City in September 2015 and he ended the 2015/16 campaign with the unenviable record of being on the losing side in every one of his 16 appearances as Villa were relegated to the Championship.

It was his return from injury, in March 2019, which sparked the team's return to the Premier League. Appointed captain, he inspired a club record sequence of ten consecutive wins as Villa went from also-rans to promotion contenders before beating Derby County 2-1 in the Play-off final.

Grealish also scored ten goals - including a crucial last-day strike at West Ham United - as Dean Smith's men narrowly avoided going straight back down. He starred in an amazing 7-2 victory over Liverpool in October 2020, as well as breaking into the England team, before joining Manchester City for a British record of £100million in the summer of 2021.

VILLA STARS A-Z

BRAD GUZAN

BIRTHPLACE: Chicago
DATE OF BIRTH: 9 September 1984
DEBUT: QPR (H), 24 September 2008
VILLA TOTALS: 171 appearances / 0 goals

Until July 2008, Villa had never signed an American goalkeeper. Then two came along in the space of a couple of weeks - and both were named Bradley. Already in the process of trying to lure Brad Friedel from Blackburn Rovers, manager Martin O'Neill reached out across the Atlantic to recruit Brad Guzan from Chivas USA. And although Friedel went on to become the club's oldest player, his understudy eventually made more appearances.

Born in the Chicago suburb of Evergreen Park, Guzan joined Villa after competing for the USA in the Olympic Games in Beijing. His appearances were initially restricted by both Friedel and Shay Given, who arrived in 2011, and he was released at the end of the following season.

But he was re-signed during the summer of 2012, and gradually took over as Villa's first-choice keeper during the 2012/13 campaign. At the end of that season, in fact, he was voted the club's Player of the Year for his contribution to Villa avoiding relegation.

Guzan remained the regular keeper over the course of the following three years before joining Middlesbrough on a free transfer following Villa's relegation in 2016. The highlight his Villa career was arguably a goalless League Cup tie at Sunderland in October 2009, when he saved a penalty in normal time - and three more as Villa won 3-1 in the shoot-out.

ALBERT HALL

BIRTHPLACE: Stourbridge
DATE OF BIRTH: 21 January 1882
DEBUT: Nottingham Forest (A), 19 December 1903
VILLA TOTALS: 215 appearances / 61 goals

Albert Hall scored on his debut at the City Ground in December 1903 in a game to remember - Villa went on a 7-3 romp against Nottingham Forest. Signed from Stourbridge, he initially played alongside right-winger Billy Brawn before switching to the left-wing, where he had a marvellous understanding with his inside partner Joe Bache.

Hall's name in Villa folklore was established in September 1906 with a remarkable goal in a 4-1 win against Birmingham - a long dipping shot that flew past astonished keeper Nat Robinson.

In 1907, he represented the Football League alongside Bache at Ibrox and further representative honours against the Scottish League came at Villa Park the following February. He was fast, lively, elusive with close ball control, and was able to cross with unerring precision as well as being dangerous near goal.

Hall gained an FA Cup-winner's medal in 1905, producing an outstanding performance against Newcastle in the final, and a League Championship medal in 1910, the same year he won his only England cap.

A talented cricketer and billiards player, Hall moved to Millwall at the end of 1913 and retired during the Great War. He then returned to Stourbridge where he was in business as an enamelware manufacturer. He died in October 1957.

The midfielder's appearances that season were sporadic, but in his second campaign he played a total of 55 games, scoring twelve goals, as Villa finished fourth in the table and became the third team from Division Three to reach the League Cup final, which they lost 2-0 to Tottenham Hotspur.

The following season, Hamilton helped them back to the Second Division, and he was also an integral member of the team who won promotion back to the top tier in 1974/75, when he was back at Wembley for another League Cup final. This time he collected a winner's medal as Villa beat Norwich City 1-0.

Hamilton played 50 league and cup games that season, hitting 13 goals, and he was also involved in 31 of Villa's matches on their first season back in the First Division. He joined Sheffield United in July 1976.

HARRY HAMPTON

BIRTHPLACE: Wellington, Shropshire
DATE OF BIRTH: 21 April 1885
DEBUT: Manchester City (A), 9 November 1904
VILLA TOTALS: 372 appearances / 242 goals

Hampton - popularly known as 'Appy 'Arry - terrorised opposition defences in the decade before the Great War. Robust and fearless, Hampton was famous for the way he bundled goalkeepers - a legitimate tactic at the time.

His fame spread when, at Stamford Bridge in 1913, he charged Scotland goalkeeper James Brownlie over the line with the ball in his hands for the only goal of the match.

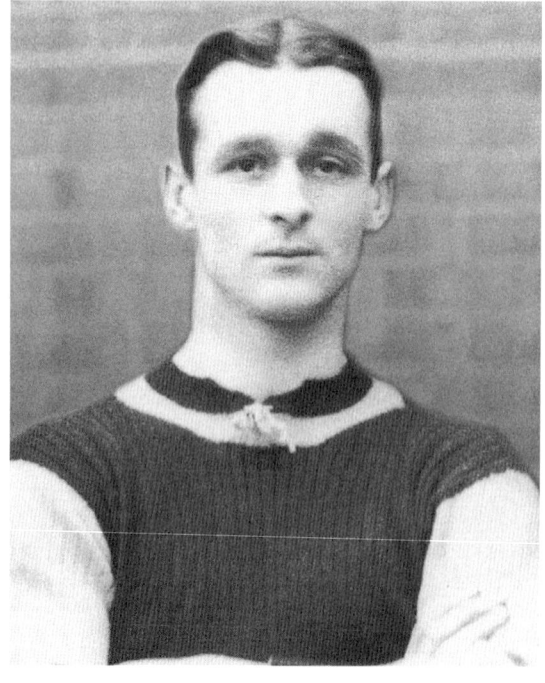

IAN HAMILTON

BIRTHPLACE: Streatham
DATE OF BIRTH: 31 October 1950
DEBUT: Norwich City (H), 9 August 1969
VILLA TOTALS: 252 appearances / 48 goals

Popularly known as Chico, Hamilton served Villa well for nearly seven years, even if his debut season in claret and blue was one to forget. Having been on Chelsea's books as a youngster, he joined Villa from Southend United for £40,000 in July 1969. By the following summer, the club were preparing for Third Division football for the first time in their history.

Two weeks later, he won a second FA Cup-winners medal as Villa defeated Sunderland 1-0 in the final, his first having been won in 1905 when he netted in every round and scored both goals in the final against Newcastle United.

Hampton joined Villa in April 1904, having netted 54 goals for Wellington in two seasons, and quickly became a crowd-pleaser. He holds the club's league scoring record with 215 goals and won a League Championship medal in 1910, scoring 26 times in his 32 league games.

Hampton scored twice in his four England games and represented the Football League three times, scoring seven goals.

In October 1912, he became the first Villa player to score five goals in a league game, a 10-0 victory over Sheffield Wednesday. In April 1915, Hampton extended his hat-trick record in league and cup to 14 in a 6-2 win against Liverpool, who had also been the opponents for his first hat-trick in 1905.

When football resumed in 1919 following the Great War, Hampton played seven games and then moved to Birmingham, where he was top scorer as Blues won the Second Division title in 1921. He died in March 1963.

SAM HARDY

BIRTHPLACE: Newbold, Chesterfield
DATE OF BIRTH: 26 August 1883
DEBUT: Chelsea (H), 2 September 1912
VILLA TOTALS: 183 appearances / 0 goals

Villa signed Sam Hardy from Liverpool in May 1912 and the England international goalkeeper capped a fine first season with an FA Cup-winner's medal, keeping a clean sheet against Sunderland in the 1913 final. Even so, it was a painful experience as he spent some time off the field after being injured. The season ended with Villa as runners-up in the league, a position in which they also finished the following year.

A League Championship medal winner with Liverpool in 1906, Hardy served in the Royal Navy during the Great War returning to gain a second FA Cup-winner's medal as Villa defeated Huddersfield Town 1-0 in the 1920 final.

He won a further seven caps with Villa to bring his international total to 21 over a period of more than 13 years. Hardy also represented the Football League ten times.

The legendary Charlie Buchan rated Hardy the finest keeper he ever played against and remarked that he never saw him dive full length - a tribute to his anticipation and positional sense.

Hardy lived in Chesterfield where he had business interests, and with the directors pressing for players to live close to Villa Park, he announced his retirement at the end of the 1920/21 campaign.

However, he turned out for Nottingham Forest the following season winning a Second Division championship medal and playing 102 league games before retiring in October 1924. Hardy, who was named in the 100 League Legends by the FA, died in October 1966.

TONY HATELEY

BIRTHPLACE: Derby
DATE OF BIRTH: 13 June 1941
DEBUT: Nottingham Forest (A), 24 August 1963
VILLA TOTALS: 148 appearances / 86 goals

If Tony Hateley had been fortunate enough to play in a successful Villa team, who knows how many goals he might have scored? As it was, his ratio was slightly better than one every two games, which is incredible when you consider he played for Villa during the lean years which culminated in relegation in 1967. Hateley had departed by the time the drop into Division Two was confirmed, having joined Chelsea for £100,000 in October 1966.

We can only speculate on whether Villa would have survived if Hateley had stayed. Based on his prolific scoring over the previous three seasons, it's fair to assume they would have had a fighting chance. Even in a struggling side, the former Notts County striker had no difficulty in hitting the target.

Having hit the only goal of the game on his debut at Nottingham Forest on the opening day of 1963/64, he finished that season with 17 - and those goals were crucial to Villa staying above the relegation zone.

An ever-present in 1964/65, his league haul rose to 20 - plus a further 14 in cup-ties, including four in a 7-1 League Cup romp against Bradford City. And although he missed three games the following season, his league total was a phenomenal 27, including four in a 5-5 draw at Tottenham. Hateley died in February 2014.

JIMMY HARROP

BIRTHPLACE: Sheffield
DATE OF BIRTH: September 1884
DEBUT: Chelsea (H), 2 September 1912
VILLA TOTALS: 170 appearances / 4 goals

Centre-half Jimmy Harrop had the distinction of collecting one FA Cup-winner's medal for Villa and he would surely have picked up a second, but for injury. A member of the team who beat Sunderland 1-0 in the 1913 final at the Crystal Palace, the Yorkshireman helped Villa through four rounds in 1920 before being missing both the semi-final victory over Chelsea at Bramall Lane and the final against Huddersfield Town at Stamford Bridge.

Harrop played 139 games for Liverpool before joining Villa in May 1912. His first season in claret and blue was a great success. He made 35 league appearances as Villa finished runners-up to Sunderland, and although he missed a couple of the early cup-ties, he was a key figure in the Cup Final triumph over the Wearsiders.

He remained a regular at the heart of the defence until football was curtailed because of the First World War at the end of the 1914/15 campaign. When the Football League resumed in 1919/20, he was again a commanding figure until injury robbed him of a second slice of Cup glory. The following season his appearances were less frequent, although he still played 23 games before joining Sheffield United in the summer of 1921.

LEE HENDRIE

BIRTHPLACE: Birmingham
DATE OF BIRTH: 18 May 1977
DEBUT: QPR (A), 23 December 1995
VILLA TOTALS: 308 appearances / 32 goals

Lee Hendrie could hardly have made a more controversial start to his first-team career. The midfielder was sent off on his debut - and he did not even start the match! Having replaced the injured Mark Draper after 33 minutes of Villa's game against QPR at Loftus Road just before Christmas 1995, Hendrie was twice booked for innocuous offences, the second of which earned him a red card in stoppage time.

It was a tough start for a young man who had supported Villa as a boy, although it was not the only contentious incident during a turbulent career. He even managed to pick up a booking on his final appearance for the club, despite being on the pitch for only the final seven minutes of a 1-1 draw at Arsenal on the opening day of the 2006/07 campaign.

For all that, he served Villa well for more than a decade and became one of a select band of players who have made more than 300 appearances for the club.

Unfortunately, frequent injury problems meant he never managed an ever-present season, although he started 32 games as Villa finished sixth in 2003/04. He was also a late substitute in the 2000 FA Cup final against Chelsea.

His long association with the club ended in September 2006 when he moved to Stoke City on loan for the remainder of that season, subsequently joining Sheffield United.

EMILE HESKEY

BIRTHPLACE: Leicester
DATE OF BIRTH: 11 January 1978
DEBUT: Portsmouth (A), 27 January 2009
VILLA TOTALS: 110 appearances / 14 goals

He was not a prolific striker, but there's no doubt that Emile Heskey made an immense contribution to all the clubs he represented. His power and pace caused problems for opposition defenders, and his sheer presence also helped to create scoring situations for his teammates.

Villa were aware of his threat from his time with his hometown club Leicester City. He was one of the few players that Gareth Southgate struggled against, and it was no great surprise when Liverpool signed him for a club record £11million in 2000.

He subsequently played for Birmingham City and Wigan Athletic before Martin O'Neill took him to Villa in January 2009. Four days after signing, he hit the winner in a 1-0 victory at Portsmouth, although his only other goal before the end of the season was at home to West Ham, when Villa played in white after the referee refused the Hammers permission to use their second kit.

The following season Heskey was on target five times, including two goals in League Cup ties as Villa reached the final against Manchester United at Wembley, where he was in the starting line-up. Capped 62 times by England, he spent two more seasons at Villa Park before being released in May 2012 and moving to Australian club Newcastle Jets.

GERRY HITCHENS

BIRTHPLACE: Rawnsley, Staffordshire
DATE OF BIRTH: 8 October 1934
DEBUT: Birmingham City (H) 21 December 1957
VILLA TOTALS: 160 appearances / 96 goals

Gerry Hitchens played for Villa during an era when football was still very much based on attack. Even so, his ratio of 96 goals in 160 games was an incredible achievement. He wore claret and blue for just three-and-a-half seasons, but he topped the goal chart in each of his three full campaigns, including a haul of 42 in 1960/61 - the highest figure by any Villa player since Pongo Waring's club record 50 in 1930/31.

Hitchens began his career with non-League Kidderminster Harriers before joining Cardiff City in 1955. He was the Bluebirds' leading scorer two years running before moving to Villa Park for £22,500 in December 1957.

His debut was one he would have wanted to forget, a 2-0 home defeat by the old enemy from across the city, but he was on target in a 3-0 Boxing Day victory over Arsenal and then netted both goals in a 2-1 success at Everton.

By the end of the 1957/58 campaign, he had hit eleven league and cup goals, and then really got into his stride, even though his 16-goal haul the following season could not stave off relegation.

There was no such problem as Villa responded by gaining promotion at the first attempt by winning the Second Division title with the help of 23 Hitchens goals - five of them in an 11-1 romp against Charlton Athletic - and then came the free-scoring 1960/61 campaign which earned him the first of seven England caps.

Unfortunately for Villa, it also prompted interest from abroad and he joined Inter Milan that summer. Hitchens, who spent eight years in Italy, died in 1983 while playing in a charity game.

THOMAS HITZLSPERGER

BIRTHPLACE: Munich, Germany
DATE OF BIRTH: 5 April 1982
DEBUT: Liverpool (H), 13 January 2001
VILLA TOTALS: 114 appearances / 12 goals

Born the month before the 1982 European Cup final, Thomas Hitzlsperger could never have imagined that he would one day play for both his home city club and the team who beat them on that famous night in Rotterdam.

As it was, he had not broken into Bayern's first team before he was snapped up by Villa.

Nicknamed 'Der Hammer' because of his powerful shot, he quickly became a cult hero with Villa supporters, who were sorry to see him leave when he returned to his home country with VfB Stuttgart five years later.

Recruited on a free transfer in August 2000, Hitzlsperger was restricted to a single first-team appearance in his initial campaign - as a substitute in a 3-0 defeat by Liverpool on the day Juan Pablo Angel was paraded at Villa Park. But he played in a dozen games the following season netting his first goal with a right-foot drive in a 2-2 draw against Leicester City at Filbert Street. That goal remained special to Hitzlsperger, although it was with his left foot that he proved more lethal.

Two of his best goals for the club were the duo he delivered in his final season, a last-minute volley at Bolton and an even better effort at Portsmouth when he flicked the ball up to knee height before thumping home an unstoppable shot.

Hitzlsperger continued to impress with Stuttgart and became a regular Germany international, being selected for his country's 2006 World Cup squad and helping them to the final of Euro 2008.

DENNIS HODGETTS

BIRTHPLACE: Birmingham
DATE OF BIRTH: 28 November 1863
DEBUT: Wednesbury Old Athletic, FA Cup (H), 30 October 1886
VILLA TOTALS: 218 appearances / 90 goals

Dennis Hodgetts became the first Villa player to score a goal in an FA Cup final when he put Villa ahead in their 2-0 victory over West Bromwich Albion in 1887. A hat-trick on his Villa FA Cup debut the previous October had contributed to a 13-0 victory that still stands as Villa's highest win.

Hodgetts, who made his name with Birmingham St George's, joined Villa in February 1886 and quickly became a firm favourite with the Perry Barr crowd. Strong, well-built, powerful and proficient with both feet, Hodgetts packed a terrific shot. His ball distribution was exceptional, as was his scoring ability. With his immaculately waxed moustache and his parted hair, he oozed star quality.

Hodgetts followed up his FA Cup success with a second triumph in 1895 having collected a runners-up medal in 1892. He also won two League Championship medals (1894 & 1896) as well as being capped six times for England and representing the Football League.

Very much part of the Villa set-up for over a decade before moving to Small Heath in October 1896, he later returned to Villa to coach the young players. In 1910, he became a publican in Birmingham and in June 1930 he was elected vice-president of the club, a position he still held at the time of his death on in March 1945.

ERIC HOUGHTON

BIRTHPLACE: Billingborough, Lincolnshire
DATE OF BIRTH: 29 June 1910
DEBUT: Leeds United (H), 4 January 1930
VILLA TOTALS: 392 appearances / 170 goals

Eric Houghton inflicted considerable damage on Villa's opponents - and he did it in the best possible way. He was never sent off and there is no record of him being cautioned, but while he was every inch the gentleman footballer, he possessed a shot like a bullet.

It was an asset which produced 170 goals in official games alone, plus a further 87 throughout the war years. And while most players prefer to hit a moving ball, Houghton was at his most fearsome at set-pieces. Opposition defenders quivered whenever he stepped up to take a free-kick, and he was deadly from the penalty spot, netting nearly 80 penalties at all levels during his time with Villa - including one on his farewell appearance, a reserve game against Huddersfield Town on Boxing Day 1946.

That was almost 17 years after his first-team debut in January 1930, Houghton having joined Villa as a youngster in 1927. He gave a hint of what was to come by scoring twelve times in 19 games in his first season in the senior side - and then he really took off.

In 1930/31, Villa simply could not stop scoring, hitting a top-flight record 128 goals. A staggering 49 of those came from centre-forward Pongo

Waring, but Houghton contributed 30. He followed up with 24 in 1931/32 and was in double figures for ten consecutive seasons before the outbreak of the Second World War.

Villa were twice runners-up to Arsenal during that period, although Houghton also experienced anguish in 1935/36, when his 15 goals failed to prevent the club's first relegation.

Even so, he helped Villa back to the First Division two years later and was also a member of the team who won the War Cup in 1944.

Houghton's time in claret and blue came to an end in 1946 when he joined Notts County, but he was back seven years later to establish himself as one of Villa's greatest managers.

RAY HOUGHTON

BIRTHPLACE: Glasgow
DATE OF BIRTH: 9 January 1962
DEBUT: Ipswich Town (A), 15 August 1992
VILLA TOTALS: 121 appearances / 11 goals

Ray Houghton spent less than three seasons with Villa, but he ranks among the club's most accomplished players during the Premier League years.

His contribution to the club's early days in the new league was considerable. A player who combined guile with graft, he arrived from Liverpool in the summer of 1992, having won a League Championship and two FA Cup medals with the Merseysiders. He made his debut as a member of the team who launched the inaugural Premier League campaign with a 1-1 draw at Ipswich and his excellent performances helped Ron Atkinson's men to finish runners-up to Manchester United.

The following season, he helped Villa to reach the League Cup final, although he had to settle for the role of an unused substitute in the 3-1 Wembley victory over United. Along with Steve Staunton, Paul McGrath and Andy Townsend, he played for Ireland in that summer's World Cup finals in America.

Early the following season, he produced his best performance in claret and blue. With Villa trailing 1-0 from the first leg of a UEFA Cup-tie against Inter Milan, Houghton's goal took the tie to extra-time, Atkinson's side eventually winning on penalties. He joined Crystal Palace on transfer deadline day in 1995.

ARCHIE HUNTER

BIRTHPLACE: Joppa, Scotland
DATE OF BIRTH: 23 September 1859
DEBUT: Burton Robin Hood (A), 12 October 1878
VILLA TOTALS: 74 appearances / 43 goals

The appearance and goals figures can neither reflect Archie Hunter's career, most of which was played before the formation of the Football League, nor his colossal impact on Villa.

Hunter arrived in Birmingham from Scotland on 8 August 1878 'without a single friend in town', but very soon he was the most well-known and well-respected player around. Hunter looked to join Calthorpe, a club he knew from their tour to Scotland, but was persuaded to join Villa by George Uzzell, a work colleague.

A member of the Villa team who won the club's first trophy, the Birmingham Challenge Cup, in 1880, Hunter took over as skipper from George Burrell Ramsay and became the first Villa captain to lift the FA Cup, scoring his side's second goal in a 2-0 win against Albion in 1887. So vital was Hunter to Villa they once chartered a special train to take him to an away game when work commitments prevented him travelling with his teammates.

Hunter, the club's record FA Cup scorer with 34 goals, led Villa into league football, helping them finish runners-up to Preston North End in the inaugural season. The end of his playing career came in dreadful conditions against Everton at Anfield on 4 January 1890 when he suffered a heart attack. He was taken to hospital and advised to retire.

Hunter never fully recovered, and he died on 29 November 1894. More than a century after his death, Hunter was included in the 100 League Legends unveiled by the Football League as part of their centenary celebrations.

ALAN HUTTON

BIRTHPLACE: Glasgow
DATE OF BIRTH: 30 November 1984
DEBUT: Everton (A), 10 September 2011
VILLA TOTALS: 202 appearances / 3 goals

Few Villa players have been more enigmatic than Alan Hutton. The full-back could do nothing right in supporters' eyes at one point, yet ended up being hailed as the Scottish Cafu! Comparisons with the Brazilian ace were a touch tongue-in-cheek, but they underlined what a cult figure Hutton had become with the Villa faithful, who gradually came to appreciate his solid performances and unselfish attitude.

The former Glasgow Rangers defender was in the spotlight at the start of his Villa career. Signed from Tottenham Hotspur on transfer deadline day in August 2011, he was interviewed on the pitch by AVTV that night, under the Villa Park floodlights, along with loan signing Jermaine Jenas.

Although he helped Villa to a 2-2 draw on his debut at Everton, his first season was largely disappointing as he failed to reproduce the form he had previously shown under manager Alex McLeish, both at Ibrox Park and for Scotland.

It got worse, too, when McLeish's successor Paul Lambert signed Matt Lowton in 2012, and Hutton spent the following two seasons on loan at Nottingham Forest, Spanish club Real Mallorca and Bolton Wanderers.

By the summer of 2014, his appearances amounted to the 34 he had made in his first season, but an impressive start to the 2014/15 campaign earned him a three-year contract, which was extended for a further twelve months in June 2018 after four consecutive seasons as a regular in the side. He was limited to 21 games in his final campaign with the club, but it was notable for his memorable solo goal in a 4-2 home victory over Birmingham City. That moment alone cemented his place in claret-and-blue folklore.

BOB IVERSON

BIRTHPLACE: Folkestone
DATE OF BIRTH: 17 October 1910
DEBUT: Norwich City (H), 19 December 1936
VILLA TOTALS: 153 appearances / 12 goals

Just nine seconds had elapsed in Villa's home game against Charlton Athletic in December 1938 when Bob Iverson opened the scoring. Villa went on to win 2-0, but of far greater significance is the fact that Iverson's goal is the fastest ever recorded by a Villa player.

But that single moment does not even begin to tell the contribution he made to the Villa cause. Signed from Wolves in December 1936, the Kent-born utility man played well over 300 games for the club, although more than half of his appearances were unofficial games during the war, when he won a War Cup medal following Villa's two-leg final victory over Blackpool in 1944.

He arrived at Villa Park when the club were playing in the old Second Division for the first time in their history and was a regular member of the team who won the title in 1937/38. He was then an ever-present during Villa's first season back in the top division, and although he could operate in a number of positions, he was at his best as a left-half.

Iverson continued to turn out regularly for Villa during the war and was also a regular in the first season that League football resumed following the hostilities. After playing in the first three games of the 1947/48 campaign, Iverson retired to concentrate on coaching Villa's youngsters. He died in 1953.

TOMMY JACKSON

BIRTHPLACE: Newcastle-upon-Tyne
DATE OF BIRTH: 16 March 1897
DEBUT: Sunderland (A), 23 February 1921
VILLA TOTALS: 186 appearances / 0 goals

When Tommy Jackson was asked if he would like to play for Villa, he thought he was being asked to play for local side Bolden Villa! The Northumberland University student declined because Norman Anderson, the Bolden keeper, was one the best in the area. In fact, the person asking the question was Billy Wright, Aston Villa's North East scout.

Jackson still turned Wright down as he couldn't see how he could displace the legendary Sam Hardy and did not wish to interrupt his studies. But Wright continued to pursue Jackson until he signed, initially on amateur forms. Jackson met up with the reserves for a Central League game at Nelson in November 1920 and the following February made his first-team debut at Sunderland. Villa won 1-0 at Roker Park with Jackson saving one shot from Charlie Buchan by heading the ball out for a corner!

Hardy surprisingly announced his retirement at the end of the season and Jackson became established as first choice. He was in the first Villa team to play at Wembley, collecting an FA Cup runners-up medal in 1924. He studied the technique of penalty takers, once winning a five-shilling (25p) bet with Hughie Gallagher during a match with Newcastle that he would save Frankie Hudspeth's spot kick.

Jackson competed with Cyril Spires and then Ben Olney throughout the 1920s, although his last two seasons were played mainly in the reserves. His last senior appearance came at Sunderland in February 1930. He was released at the season end but went out on a high when Villa clinched the Central League title in his farewell game.

Jackson continued his link with football, reporting Central League matches for the Sports Argus. He died in 1975 but many years later he was name-checked in an episode of the BBC TV drama Peaky Blinders.

DAVID JAMES

BIRTHPLACE: Welwyn
DATE OF BIRTH: 1 August 1970
DEBUT: Newcastle United (A), 7 August 1999
VILLA TOTALS: 84 appearances / 0 goals

David James was a larger-than-life character who spent only two seasons at Villa Park, but made a big impact. When he left for West Ham in 2001, Villa received a fee of £3.6m - double what they had paid Liverpool for him.

Many people remember him for the error which handed Chelsea their winning goal in the 2000 FA Cup final, but without him, Villa would not have appeared in English football's showpiece occasion. His saves from Bolton's Allan Johnston and Michael Johansen in the semi-final penalty shoot-out were crucial to John Gregory's men heading back down Wembley Way seven weeks later.

Unfortunately, James's failure to hold Gianfranco Zola's cross presented Roberto Di Matteo with the winner in a final every Villa supporter would prefer to forget.

James arrived from Anfield in the summer of 1999 with a reputation as an outstanding shot-stopper and he certainly did not disappoint, even though his first season was disrupted by injuries.

His absences restricted him to 38 league and cup games during his debut campaign, but he bounced back from his Cup Final disappointment to enjoy an ever-present second season.

VILLA STARS A-Z

BILLY KINGDON

BIRTHPLACE: Worcester
DATE OF BIRTH: 25 June 1905
DEBUT: Burnley (H), 4 September 1926
VILLA TOTALS: 242 appearances / 5 goals

Billy Kingdon was a classic example of a player who refused to submit to misfortune. Even when he was out of favour for the best part of two-and-a-half seasons, he went about his business without complaint.

The reward for his diligence was that he emerged from his lengthy spell in the reserves to re-establish himself in Villa's first team and ultimately make 242 appearances.

Although he was small for a wing-half, Kingdon more than made amends with his tenacious approach. Having played non-League football for Kidderminster Harriers, he signed professional for Villa in March 1926, making his debut later that year. He also scored a couple of goals during that debut campaign, although he endured an eight-year wait before getting on the scoresheet for a third time.

Such was his impressive form that he played nearly 120 games during his first four seasons before effectively becoming the club's forgotten man in the early 1930s.

But he regained his place in the 1932/33 campaign and remained a regular member of the team until 1935. He was transferred to Southampton in June 1936. Kingdon, who later managed Yeovil Town, died in 1977.

MARTIN KEOWN

BIRTHPLACE: Oxford
DATE OF BIRTH: 24 July 1966
DEBUT: Queens Park Rangers (A), 30 August 1986
VILLA TOTALS: 132 appearances / 3 goals

He is better known for his time with Arsenal, where he started his career and later had an extended, successful spell. But Martin Keown also made his mark as a Villa player during three eventful seasons with the club.

Signed from the Gunners in 1986, the rugged central defender was immediately thrust into a relegation battle as Villa won just one of their opening eight league games, which led to the departure of manager Graham Turner. For the remainder of that season, he was one of the few players to impress under new boss Billy McNeill, but it was no great surprise when Villa went down.

It was a different story the following season, Keown forming a solid defensive partnership, initially with Steve Sims and later with Allan Evans, as Villa bounced back at the first attempt under the management of Graham Taylor. The dependable defender missed only the final two games of the promotion campaign and also scored three goals, including the winner against Ipswich Town in January.

Keown was again a regular throughout the 1988/89 campaign and although Villa only narrowly avoided relegation, his consistent displays attracted attention from other clubs. He moved to Everton that summer, but later rejoined Arsenal, where he enjoyed considerable success before pursuing a media career.

EZRI KONSA

BIRTHPLACE: Newham, London
DATE OF BIRTH: 23 October 1997
DEBUT: Crewe Alexandra (A), 27 August 2019
VILLA TOTALS: 99 appearances / 6 goals

Many Villa supporters were unaware of Ezri Konsa when he joined the club in July 2019, but over the course of three seasons he become a firm favourite.

Initially limited to a peripheral role because of Bjorn Engels' partnership with Tyrone Mings, he has established himself as a solid, reliable centre-back alongside Mings at the heart of the defence, and has also contributed some important goals.

Konsa was on target on his debut in a 6-1 League Cup win at Crewe, although his second goal was far more significant. It earned a point in a 1-1 draw at Everton as Villa secured Premier League survival at the end of his first season.

He also netted both goals in a 2-1 home win over Leicester City in December 2021, becoming the first Villa defender to score twice in a Premier League match since Ciaran Clark more than eleven years earlier.

Having been with Charlton Athletic from his school days, he was signed by Brentford manager Dean Smith in June 2018, and Smith was only too happy to take him to Villa Park the following summer.

VILLA STARS A-Z

ALEX LEAKE

BIRTHPLACE: Small Heath, Birmingham
DATE OF BIRTH: 11 July 1871
DEBUT: Nottingham Forest (a) 13 September 1902
VILLA TOTALS: 142 appearances / 10 goals

Alex Leake was 31 when he made his Villa debut after being transferred from Small Heath, and many supporters assumed he was past his best. But he confounded his critics by performing better than ever. Noted for his unfailing good humour and sunny disposition, he proved to be of immense service to Villa with an incredible work rate ethic.

Hard to beat in the tackle and able to read the game to perfection, Leake gained his reputation both as a centre-half and left-half and was a natural defender. Capped in March 1904, he went on to play five consecutive internationals during which England were unbeaten, and in 1905, he represented the Football League in a 3-2 win against the Scottish League at Hampden Park. He was also a member of the Villa side who beat Newcastle United 2-0 in the FA Cup final that year.

Leake, who was a useful cricketer, played his last Villa league game on 9 November 1907 and was transferred to Burnley the following month, remaining at Turf Moor until May 1910 before eventually winding down his playing career at Wednesbury Old Athletic in 1912. He died on 29 March 1938.

MARTIN LAURSEN

BIRTHPLACE: Silkeborg, Denmark
DATE OF BIRTH: 26 July 1977
DEBUT: Southampton (H), 14 August 2004
VILLA TOTALS: 91 appearances / 11 goals

Villa lost the services of a true professional when Martin Laursen was forced to admit defeat in his battle against injury in April 2009. Throughout five seasons at Villa Park, the Danish international had been dogged by knee problems which restricted him to a dozen games in his debut season and just one in his second.

By the end of his third season, in fact, he had not managed 30 appearances - but then we discovered just why Villa had paid Italian giants Milan £3million for him. The 2007/08 campaign was an unqualified success for Laursen, who was not only an ever-present in the Premier League, but also weighed in with half-a-dozen goals.

His commanding performances and scoring feats earned him the Supporters' Player of the Year award - and it got even better. Appointed captain at the start of the 2008/09 campaign, he was a colossus at the heart of the defence as Villa broke into the top four and made progress in the UEFA Cup. He continued scoring, too, including the crucial early opening goal against Ajax in a UEFA Cup group game.

But another knee injury at West Ham just before Christmas proved to the beginning of the end. Laursen returned for the home game against West Bromwich Albion three weeks later, but it proved to be his last appearance before his premature retirement.

than his last-gasp extra-time winner against Everton in the second replay of a marathon 1977 League Cup final. Little was on target twice at Old Trafford that night in what was the crowning glory of a season in which he scored 26 league and cup goals.

His goal haul that season, which included a hat-trick in the League Cup semi-final second replay against QPR, was two more than he had managed a couple of seasons earlier, when he had helped Villa to promotion and League Cup glory.

Born less than a mile from Newcastle United's St James' Park, Little joined Villa as an apprentice in 1969, signing professional two years later and helping the club to an FA Youth Cup triumph in 1972. By then, he had made his first-team debut and the following season he featured more frequently in the senior side, making 20 appearances.

After establishing himself as a key member of the team over the next two seasons, he missed more than half the 1975/76 campaign through injury - but started more than 100 games over the course of the subsequent two seasons. Frustratingly, he received only one England cap, going on as a late substitute for Mick Channon against Wales at Wembley in 1975.

At the end of his playing career, he became Villa's youth team coach and later moved into management, guiding Villa to victory over Leeds United in the 1996 League Cup final.

ANDY LOCHHEAD

BIRTHPLACE: Milngavie, Scotland
DATE OF BIRTH: 9 March 1941
DEBUT: Bristol City (h) 21 February 1970
VILLA TOTALS: 154 appearances / 44 goals

Andy Lochhead's thinning hair hardly gave him the look of a professional footballer, but his cutting edge brought him more than 150 goals throughout a career which spanned 17 years. Although his time at Villa Park was relatively brief, he wrote himself into claret and blue folklore with some brave, fearless displays as Villa climbed back from the depths of the darkest days in the club's history.

Having established himself in another claret and blue shirt at Burnley, the Scottish striker had a spell with Leicester City, for whom he played in the 1969 FA Cup final, before joining Villa in February 1970. Two months later, after he had failed to score in a dozen appearances, Villa were relegated from the Second Division.

The following season, he rediscovered his goal touch, helping Villa to the League Cup final - and in 1971/72 he missed only one league game, heading the score chart with 19 as the club won the Third Division title.

His total goal haul that season was 25, a figure few players have achieved since, and it included the winner against promotion rivals Bournemouth in front of a Villa Park crowd of 48,110, then a record attendance for that division. After scoring six goals in Villa's first season back in Division Two, he moved to Oldham Athletic in August 1973. Lochhead died in March 2022.

BRIAN LITTLE

BIRTHPLACE: Newcastle-on-Tyne
DATE OF BIRTH: 25 November 1953
DEBUT: Blackburn Rovers (H), 30 October 1971
VILLA TOTALS: 302 appearances / 82 goals

It's difficult to equate the refined gentleman who later managed the club with the cavalier footballer who was such an integral figure in Villa's line-up for most of the seventies. Brian Little was a striker who endeared himself to the crowd with his flair and ability to do something out of the ordinary.

Quick and intelligent, he was a delight to watch. His innovative approach brought him plenty of goals too, none more important or more dramatic

EDDIE LOWE

BIRTHPLACE: Halesowen
DATE OF BIRTH: 11 July 1925
DEBUT: Coventry City (A), 5 January 1946
VILLA TOTALS: 117 appearances / 3 goals

Eddie Lowe holds the distinction of being the first Villa player to be capped by England after the Second World War, making his international debut against France at Highbury in May 1947.

Although he was born in the West Midlands, Lowe moved to London during the war, making guest appearances for Millwall, Finchley and Walthamstow Avenue before joining Villa in May 1945. His first appearance for the club was at Plymouth in the Football League South in November that year and he went on to make 24 appearances in the competition.

His official debut, though, was in a third-round FA Cup-tie at Coventry the following January. Villa lost 2-1, but that season's cup-ties were played over two legs and Alex Massie's side went through on aggregate and reached the quarter-final before losing to Derby County.

His impressive displays in the first post-war season of League football earned him his England call-up and he also represented his country twice more while at Villa. A tenacious tackler and hard worker, Lowe remained a first-team regular until the end of 1948, but was then limited to infrequent appearances before joining Fulham in the summer of 1950. He died in March 2009.

DOUGLAS LUIZ

BIRTHPLACE: Rio de Janiero
DATE OF BIRTH: 5 May 1998
DEBUT: Tottenham Hotspur (A), 10 August 2019
VILLA TOTALS: 111 appearances / 5 goals

Villa had never signed a Brazilian player until the summer of 2019, and then two arrived within the space of a few weeks. And while the club record signing of striker Wesley understandably generated more interest, the lesser-known Douglas Luiz proved to be a more astute acquisition.

While Wesley struggled to settle in the Premier League, his countryman established himself as an important member of the squad, clocking up over 100 appearances by the end of the 2021/22 campaign. A midfielder capable of winning possession and making defence-splitting passes, Luiz also contributed a handful of goals, none more spectacular than his stunning strike on his home debut against Bournemouth.

A product of the Vasco da Gama academy in Rio, he joined Manchester City in 2017, but never made an appearance for the Etihad club because of work permit issues. He was loaned to Spanish club Girona, but then signed for Villa, finally being granted a work permit in time for the club's first match back in the Premier League after a three-year absence.

A Brazil international, Luiz won a gold medal when his country beat Spain 2-1 in the 2020 Olympics football final, which was delayed by twelve months by the Covid-19 pandemic.

STAN LYNN

BIRTHPLACE: Bolton
DATE OF BIRTH: 18 June 1928
DEBUT: Huddersfield Town (A), 14 October 1950
VILLA TOTALS: 324 appearances / 38 goals

It's difficult to know whether Stan Lynn was best known for his solid, hard-tackling performances at full-back or his thunderbolt shot. The answer is probably both. While he served Villa superbly in a defensive role for over a decade, his powerful shooting was always a big talking point among Villa folk.

His 38 goals in claret and blue gave him an average of more than one every ten games - and he became the first full-back to score a First Division hat-trick when he scored three, including two penalties, in a 5-2 victory over Sunderland in January 1958.

He remains, in fact, one of the highest-scoring full-backs in football history, having hit a total of 70 goals during a career which spanned more than 500 games.

Signed by Villa from Accrington Stanley in March 1950, he was on target three times before the end of that season, two of his goals coming when he operated as an emergency centre-forward. Throughout the course of the next ten seasons, Lynn was Villa's regular right-back, although injury problems meant that he was an ever-present only once - when Villa won the Second Division title in 1959/60.

By then he had helped the club to FA Cup glory over Manchester United in the 1957 final, and he was also in the line-up for the first leg of the 1961 League Cup final against Rotherham United. Ironically, he picked up another League Cup winner's medal two years later, when Birmingham City beat Villa in the 1963 final, having moved across the city to join the club's biggest rivals in October 1961. He died in 2002.

TOMMY LYONS

BIRTHPLACE: Hednesford
DATE OF BIRTH: 5 July 1885
DEBUT: Liverpool (A) 7 December 1907
VILLA TOTALS: 237 appearances / 0 goals

When Tommy Lyons joined Villa from Bridgetown Amateurs in 1906, he was described in Villa News & Record as 'another strapping player from Hednesford'. He started his career in Villa's third team, but was soon given a senior outing against Cambridge University.

Lyons' Football League debut the following season was a baptism of fire as Villa went down 5-0 to Liverpool at Anfield. Even so, he did enough to retain his place for the remainder of the season as Villa finished runners-up, and he went on to form a fine full-back partnership with Freddie Miles, collecting a League Championship medal in 1910 and an FA Cup-winner's medal in 1913.

Strong and fearless in a tackle, Miles also possessed a fine football brain. He was very much part of the Villa Park scene right up to the Great War, his last appearance coming in April 1915 at Bradford Park Avenue where, despite having taken a knock, he went in goal when Sam Hardy was injured. After the war, Lyons played for Port Vale and later joined Walsall as a coach, turning out for the Saddlers in a league game in 1923. He died in October 1938.

JIM MacEWAN

BIRTHPLACE: Dundee
DATE OF BIRTH: 22 March 1929
DEBUT: Brighton (A), 22 August 1959
VILLA TOTALS: 181 appearances / 32 goals

Many a burly full-back must have given Jimmy MacEwan a look of disdain at kick-off, only to regret it by the end of the match. MacEwan's fragile appearance disguised a talent which bemused many a defender as he exhibited his skills down the right touchline as well as providing a regular supply of goals.

The Scottish star had turned 30 when he joined Villa in 1959, having previously enjoyed a successful career north of the border with Arbroath and Raith Rovers. Taking over from FA Cup-winner Les Smith, who had been forced to retire through injury, MacEwan marked his debut with a goal in a 2-1 win on the opening day of 1959/60 and by the end of that season he had helped Villa to the Second Division title.

In the club's first season back in the top tier, he was on target ten times in league and cup matches and he was also a key figure in the side who became the first winners of the League Cup.

He remained at Villa Park until 1966, when he joined Walsall, and although his appearances were limited over his final two seasons following the arrival of Johnny MacLeod, he remained a popular figure with supporters. MacEwan died in November 2017.

CON MARTIN

BIRTHPLACE: Dublin
DATE OF BIRTH: 20 March 1923
DEBUT: Sheffield United (H), 2 October 1948
VILLA TOTALS: 213 appearances / 1 goal

There was a time when players were permitted to represent both Northern Ireland and the Republic of Ireland - and in 1949, Con Martin became the first player to turn out for both in the same year. He scored the first goal from the penalty spot for the history-making Republic team who won 2-0 at Goodison Park in September that year to become the first overseas opposition to beat England on home soil.

By then, he had already started to make a name for himself in claret and blue, having joined Villa from Leeds United just over twelve months earlier. He was rated at the time as one of the best centre-halves in the country and he enhanced his reputation at Villa Park.

In 1951/52 he started the season at left-back, but then played 27 games as Villa's goalkeeper when Joe Rutherford was injured. His best position, though, was at the heart of the defence, and he performed admirably throughout his time with the club. Although he did not manage an ever-present campaign, he was virtually an automatic choice over a period of eight seasons, apart from 1953/54, when injury restricted him to just four games.

He scored only once for Villa, a penalty in a 4-1 win at Charlton in April 1950, but that was of no consequence, given his heroics at the other end of the pitch. Martin left Villa in 1956, returning to his homeland to take over as player-manager of Waterford. He died in 2013.

ALEX MASSIE

BIRTHPLACE: Glasgow
DATE OF BIRTH: 13 March 1906
DEBUT: Manchester City (A), 7 December 1935
VILLA TOTALS: 152 appearances / 5 goals

Even ardent Villa supporters must have thought Alex Massie must have taken leave of his senses when he joined the club in December 1935 - and Massie himself was surely thinking along the same lines.

His debut was made in a 5-0 defeat at Manchester City; his first home game was the infamous 7-1 thrashing by Arsenal on the day Ted Drake scored all seven of the Gunners' goals; a week later there was a 5-1 drubbing at Blackburn.

The new signing quickly became aware he was engrossed in a desperate relegation battle, and it was one Villa lost as the club went down for the first time in their history. But from there, it got better for both player and club. The Scotland international was a classy wing-half whose passing was a delight to watch, and his quality shone through as Villa regained top-flight status by winning the Second Division title under his leadership two years later.

Massie had already captained his country by the time he arrived at Villa Park for £6,000 from Hearts, so it was no great surprise when he assumed the role of Villa skipper.

In 1938/39, he was an ever-present and would no doubt have continued to be so for many years, but for the intervention of the war. As it was, he never made another official appearance for the club, even though he played regularly during the war years. He also turned out in the first three Football League (South) games in 1945 before retiring to become the club's first post-war manager. He died in 1977.

JOHN McGINN

BIRTHPLACE: Glasgow
DATE OF BIRTH: 18 October 1984
DEBUT: Wigan Athletic (H), 11 August 2018
VILLA TOTALS: 147 appearances / 16 goals

Few people in England were aware of John McGinn when he joined Villa from Scottish club Hibernian. But the tenacious midfielder has certainly made a massive impact during his time in claret and blue. He is adored by Villa supporters, who serenade him with the words: "We've got McGinn, super John McGinn...".

It certainly did not take him long to earn the respect of the Villa faithful. From the outset, it was clear that he was a player who worked tirelessly, was hard to knock off the ball - and scored goals which were often sensational. His first, against Sheffield Wednesday in September 2018 was so special that it was voted the ELF Championship goal of the season, McGinn sending a perfect volley into the top corner with the outside of his right foot from 25 yards.

By the end of the season, he had scored another five Championship goals and he crowned a memorable debut season with the header which secured 2-1 win over Derby County in the Play-Off final at Wembley.

The hard-working Scot, who began his career with St Mirren, also scored Villa's first goal back in the Premier League and was as comfortable in the Premier League as he had been in the Championship. Unfortunately, he had a severe setback just before Christmas when he suffered a fractured ankle - but he was back in action for the final ten games to help Dean Smith's men avoid relegation.

It took a while for McGinn to regain full fitness but he developed into one of the most effective midfielders in the country, as well as helping Scotland to qualify for the 2021 European Championship finals.

PAUL McGRATH

BIRTHPLACE: Ealing, London
DATE OF BIRTH: 4 December 1959
DEBUT: Nottingham Forest (A), 19 August 1989
VILLA TOTALS: 323 appearances / 9 goals

Not only is he the most revered Villa star of the modern era, Paul McGrath is also regarded as one of the greatest players in the club's history. Yet the man who conjured up pure genius and turned the business of defending into an art form hardly made the most impressive of starts in claret and blue.

Signed by Graham Taylor from Manchester United in the summer of 1989, the Republic of Ireland international cost £425,000 and it seemed the investment was doomed to failure when his first few months at Villa Park were blighted by his much-publicised off-the-field problems. By the end of that season, though, it was clear the money had been well spent. With McGrath operating alongside Derek Mountfield and Kent Nielsen in a three-man defence, Villa finished runners-up to Liverpool and were back in Europe following a five-year ban on English clubs.

By 1993, Macca had been voted the club's Player of the Year for the fourth consecutive season and he was also voted PFA Footballer of the Year as Villa finished second again, this time to Manchester United in the inaugural Premier League campaign.

The following year, despite needing pain-killing injections in a frozen shoulder, he helped Villa to League Cup glory against his former club United; two years later, he was back at Wembley for an emphatic 3-0 victory over Leeds in the 1996 final.

He also won 51 of his 83 Irish caps while at Villa Park, where he played the best football of his career. He left Villa for Derby County in 1996.

ALAN McINALLY

BIRTHPLACE: Ayrshire
DATE OF BIRTH: 10 February 1963
DEBUT: Blackburn Rovers (H), 30 September 1987
VILLA TOTALS: 71 appearances / 28 goals

He spent only two seasons at Villa Park, but Alan McInally was a huge favourite with supporters. His bustling, direct style in the No.9 shirt made him a Holte End hero in the mould of Andy Gray and Peter Withe, and he frequently urged supporters on that massive terrace to get behind the team at a time when attendances were sparse and noise levels were subdued.

The son of former Kilmarnock player Jackie McInally, the powerful Scot joined Villa from Celtic in the summer of 1987 as manager Graham Taylor attempted to build a squad capable of bouncing back from Division Two following the club's relegation.

Taylor saw his £225,000 capture as the man to score the goals which would fire Villa to promotion at the first attempt, making the point that he was also signing a player who did not get injured. Ironically, McInally took a knock in the team's first pre-season match in Sweden and missed the first ten games of the campaign!

His contribution that season was a modest four league goals plus two in cup-ties, although his strong physique proved invaluable as Villa finished second behind Millwall.

It was in his second season, though, that he really came into his own. Known as Rambo, he found the First Division very much to his liking, scoring six times in the opening four games.

Although his output tailed off after Christmas, his 14 goals ensured that Villa retained First Division status. Capped by Scotland during that period, he also scored eight cup goals including a superb solo effort against Millwall in the League Cup.

His impressive scoring exploits earned him a £1.1million move to German giants Bayern Munich in 1989. He later pursued a TV career.

PAT McMAHON

BIRTHPLACE: Glasgow
DATE OF BIRTH: 19 September 1945
DEBUT: Norwich City (H), 9 August 1969
VILLA TOTALS: 150 appearances / 30 goals

Pat McMahon must have wondered if he had made a mistake when he joined Villa from his boyhood favourites Celtic in the summer of 1969. Although he had made only fleeting appearances for the Parkhead club's first team, he had to settle for the role of substitute in Villa's opening game of the new season. He was involved in the action against Norwich City that afternoon, but a 1-0 Villa Park defeat set the tone for what was to be the nadir of the club's existence.

McMahon played in 24 Second Division games in his debut campaign, scoring four goals, but was unable to halt Villa's slide into the Third Division for the first time in their history.

The following season, the classy midfielder chalked up 47 appearances and scored twelve goals as Villa finished fourth in Division Three and reached the League Cup final, where he was a member of the side who acquitted themselves so well against Tottenham Hotspur at Wembley.

His involvement in 1971/72 was a more modest 18 games and five goals, but he collected a championship medal as the club won the Third Division title. He continued to impress over the next couple of seasons, but played only twice during Villa's promotion from the Second Division in 1974/75. The following year he moved to American club Portland Timbers.

The son of former Scottish international Willie McNaught, he joined Everton as an apprentice in 1972 and made 86 appearances for the Merseysiders before his move to Villa Park.

Along with six other players, he enjoyed an ever-present campaign as Villa won the title in 1980/81, and although a knee injury meant he missed most of the first half of the following season, he was back in time for the later stages of the European Cup.

Indeed, he scored Villa's second goal with a close-range header in the second leg of the quarter-final against Dynamo Kiev, while he and Evans were towers of strength against Bayern Munich in the final. He was also in the side who won the UEFA Super Cup by beating Barcelona in 1983. In August that year he was transferred to neighbours West Bromwich Albion. In more recent times, he ran the Former Villa Players Club.

PETER McPARLAND

BIRTHPLACE: Newry
DATE OF BIRTH: 25 April 1934
DEBUT: Wolves (H), 15 September 1952
VILLA TOTALS: 341 appearances / 121 goals

Whenever the 1957 FA Cup final is mentioned, one name immediately comes to mind. Peter McParland was the man most responsible for Villa's famous Wembley victory over favourites Manchester United, scoring two second half goals to give Eric Houghton's underdogs a 2-1 verdict.

KEN McNAUGHT

BIRTHPLACE: Kirkcaldy
DATE OF BIRTH: 11 January 1955
DEBUT: Queens Park Rangers (A), 20 August 1977
VILLA TOTALS: 260 appearances / 13 goals

Ken McNaught's first experience of an Aston Villa triumph was hardly one to savour. He was in the Everton team beaten by Ron Saunders' men in the 1977 League Cup final. If McNaught was an extra-time loser in the epic second replay at Old Trafford, though, Saunders clearly saw him as a player who could help bring success to Villa.

The club paid Everton £200,000 for McNaught's services that summer and although the central defender struggled to settle in, he gradually established himself as an integral part of the team who would go on to enjoy League Championship and European Cup glory. His initial defensive colleague was Leighton Phillips, but by the start of the 1978/79 campaign, he had forged a partnership with fellow Scot Allan Evans which would form the backbone of Villa's domestic and continental triumphs.

The Northern Ireland international is also remembered, of course, for his unfortunate collision with Ray Wood, which left United's goalkeeper with a fractured jaw and the Manchester club down to ten men for long periods. But McParland's contribution to the Villa cause extended far beyond the events of that memorable afternoon.

He scored a total of seven FA Cup goals that season, and his winner's medal certainly was not the only one the free-scoring winger collected during a decade in claret and blue. He also helped Villa to the Second Division title in 1959/60 - and scored the extra-time winner which secured a 3-2 aggregate victory over Rotherham United in the inaugural League Cup final in 1961, giving him the distinction of being the first player to score in both an FA Cup and League Cup final.

McParland joined Villa from Irish club Dundalk in 1952 and even manager George Martin could not have envisaged the impact he would make at Villa Park. He won the first of his 34 international caps while still a teenager, scoring twice on his debut against Wales in 1954, and represented his country at the 1958 World Cup finals in Sweden.

Equally at home at centre-forward as on the left wing, McParland was a prolific scorer, hitting the target 121 times for Villa, including 25 league and cup goals during the 1959/60 campaign. After nearly ten years with the club, he moved across the West Midlands to join Wolves for £35,000 in January 1962.

OLOF MELLBERG

BIRTHPLACE: Gullspang
DATE OF BIRTH: 3 September 1977
DEBUT: Tottenham Hotspur (A), 18 August 2001
VILLA TOTALS: 263 appearances / 8 goals

Villa supporters were left with a lasting impression of Olof Mellberg. In May 2008, the Swedish international arranged for every one of the 3,200 supporters who made the trip to West Ham for his farewell match to be presented with a replica shirt as his parting gift. It was the central defender's way of thanking the fans for the backing they had given him throughout his time in claret and blue, although by then he had long since repaid the £5.6million Villa had paid for him.

Arriving from Spanish club Racing Santander the summer of 2001, Mellberg made an outstanding debut in an opening-day goalless draw at Tottenham and remained a dominant figure at the heart of Villa's defence for seven seasons, rarely making a mistake as he constantly produced commanding displays. Even after he had signed a pre-contract agreement to join Italian giants Juventus, he continued to perform consistently.

He was, almost incredibly, dropped for the opening game of the 2003/04 season at Portsmouth, but new manager David O'Leary quickly realised the error of his ways, reinstating Mellberg and subsequently appointing him captain. Villa went on to finish sixth.

Mellberg also operated effectively at right-back, as well as netting a few vital goals. He was the first player to score a competitive goal at the Emirates Stadium when Villa drew 1-1 with Arsenal in the opening match of 2006/07.

PAUL MERSON

BIRTHPLACE: Northolt, Middlesex
DATE OF BIRTH: 20 March 1968
DEBUT: Wimbledon (H), 12 September 1998
VILLA TOTALS: 144 appearances / 19 goals

Despite his many off-the-field problems, Paul Merson charmed Villa supporters with his exquisite skills. The former Arsenal idol was 30 by the time he arrived from Middlesbrough for £6.75million but those cynics who felt Villa had paid over the top were soon silenced. The sight of Merson stroking a ball with the outside of his foot over distances up to 50 yards was one to savour.

Even when his personal life was in turmoil, his level of performance was immaculate and in 2000, when he helped Villa to the FA Cup final, he was voted both Players' and Supporters' Player of the Year.

At one stage, it seemed that if Merse was on song, so were Villa. That was never more evident than in a fifth-round Cup-tie against Leeds United. At the time the Yorkshire club were riding high in the Premiership and they led twice before Benito Carbone completed a superb hat-trick to take Villa into the quarter finals.

Yet the real star was the irrepressible 'Magic Man' who was not even on the pitch for the final 20 minutes. A delightful display culminated with him suffering a nasty wound and concussion in a clash of heads with Michael Duberry as he knocked the ball across goal for Carbone to claim the winner.

An England international, Merson left Villa in 2002, helping Portsmouth to promotion the following season. He later played for, and managed, Walsall.

VIC MILNE

BIRTHPLACE: Aberdeen
DATE OF BIRTH: 22 June 1897
DEBUT: Chelsea (H), 15 September 1923
VILLA TOTALS: 175 appearances / 1 goal

Some footballers become coaches when they hang up their boots; others go into management. Vic Milne took a rather different course. When his playing career came to an end in 1929, he was appointed as Villa's medical officer! A couple of years before joining the club, he had qualified as a doctor, so it was Dr Vic Milne who signed for Villa from his hometown club Aberdeen in 1923.

Milne went on to establish himself as Villa's regular centre-half for the best part of six seasons, although he got his big break in tragic circumstances. Signed as cover for Tommy Ball, he took over as first choice in November 1923 after Ball was murdered by a neighbour.

Milne, who had reached the Scottish Cup semi-finals with Aberdeen in 1922, had made only two first-team appearances when Ball was shot dead. But he stepped into the breach and was virtually a permanent fixture for the remainder of the season, helping Villa to the FA Cup final, which they lost 2-0 to Newcastle United.

Milne had served his country during the Great War, and he showed equal disrespect to opposing centre-forwards as he had to the Germans. Even the prolific Dixie Dean, of Everton and England, never relished the prospect of Dr Milne's medicine.

Forced to retire because of injury at the end of the 1928/29 season, he returned to Villa Park in 1930 in his medical capacity, a post he held for three years. He died in 1971.

FREDDIE MILES

BIRTHPLACE: Birmingham
DATE OF BIRTH: January 1884
DEBUT: Nottingham Forest (A), 19 December 1903
VILLA TOTALS: 269 appearances / 0 goals

Freddie Miles was a classic example of a local hero. Born near Villa Park, he was hugely popular with supporters over the course of more than a decade - and had the distinction of helping the club to FA Cup glory and a League Championship triumph.

A left-back, Miles partnered Howard Spencer during the early part of his Villa career, although it was his full-back pairing with Tommy Lyons which subsequently proved so successful.

Miles broke into the Villa first team at the end of 1903, and less than 18 months later, he was in the team who beat Newcastle United 2-0 in the 1905 FA Cup final at The Crystal Palace.

Villa regularly challenged near the top of the table throughout Miles' time in the team, and in 1909/10 he made 27 appearances as they became champions.

He also captained the side several times before retiring, and then worked at Villa Park throughout the Great War. When football resumed in 1919, he became Villa's trainer, and was in that role when the team lost to Newcastle in the 1924 Cup Final. He died in 1926.

JAMES MILNER

BIRTHPLACE: Leeds
DATE OF BIRTH: 4 January 1986
DEBUT: West Ham (A), 12 September 2005
VILLA TOTALS: 126 appearances / 22 goals

James Milner became Villa's record signing when he arrived from Newcastle United for a reported £12million in August 2008 - but it was a transfer which should really have happened two years earlier. Just before the 2006 transfer window closed, the midfielder was in new manager Martin O'Neill's office, ready to complete a switch from Tyneside, when he was recalled by Newcastle and the deal was abandoned.

Milner had spent most of the previous season on loan at Villa Park under O'Neill's predecessor David O'Leary, scoring on his home debut against Tottenham Hotspur and making a total of 31 appearances in claret and blue. The former Leeds United player was so impressive that O'Neill wanted to make it a permanent move - something which finally happened a couple of years later.

In his first season as a fully-fledged Villan, Milner helped his new club to a top-six finish and the last 32 of the UEFA Cup. He made 43 league and cup appearances for Villa that season, scoring six goals, and having become the most-capped England under-21 international with 46 appearances, he broke into the full national side at the start of the 2009/10 campaign.

Milner's last game for Villa was on the opening day of the 2010/11 campaign, when he scored in a 3-0 home win over West Ham. Four days later, he signed for Manchester City. He later joined Liverpool.

SAVO MILOSEVIC

BIRTHPLACE: Bijeljina, Yugoslavia
DATE OF BIRTH: 2 September 1973
DEBUT: Manchester United (H), 19 August 1995
VILLA TOTALS: 117 appearances / 33 goals

An unsavoury spitting incident at Blackburn in 1998 completely soured Savo Milosevic's relationship with Villa supporters, and he hardly endeared himself to manager Brian Little shortly afterwards by refusing to be a substitute for a game at Derby. From that juncture, the Serbian striker's departure was inevitable, and he headed off to Spain that summer to join Real Zaragoza.

For two-and-a-half years before that, however, he had delighted the fans with his deft touch and eye for goal. Having been signed from Partizan Belgrade for a club record £3.5million on the strength of a video which illustrated his scoring ability, Milosevic's first Villa goal was laced with irony, although we did not know it at the time.

After scoring against Blackburn at Ewood Park, he raced the length of the pitch to celebrate with Villa supporters at the same Darwen End where he would eventually insult them.

By the end of his first season, he had inspired Villa to League Cup glory, hitting a superb dipping shot to open the scoring in the 1996 final against Leeds United at Wembley. Despite his ultimate unpopularity, he still averaged almost a goal every third league appearance - 28 in 90 games - as well as hitting five in cup-ties. He was also Villa's first £1m-plus player on which the club recouped their outlay when he left. He later managed both the Serbia national team and Partizan, where he had started his career.

TYRONE MINGS

BIRTHPLACE: Bath
DATE OF BIRTH: 13 March 1993
DEBUT: Reading (A), 2 February 2019
VILLA TOTALS: 128 appearances / 7 goals

Several factors were instrumental in Villa's return to the Premier League in 2019, most notably Jack Grealish's return from injury and the prolific scoring of on-loan Chelsea striker Tammy Abraham. But the arrival of Tyrone Mings undoubtedly had a major bearing on the promotion bid.

Signed on loan from Bournemouth for the remainder of the season, the stylish centre-back was responsible for tightening up a previously leaky defence. Not that the transformation was instantaneous. After a goalless draw on his debut at Reading, Mings and his new teammates found themselves three-down to Sheffield United in his first Villa Park appearance. But with just eight minutes to go, and many supporters having left, Mings scored with a header which sparked a late revival and a 3-3 draw.

It was during the team's record-breaking ten-match winning run, though, that Mings really came into his own. Villa kept a clean sheet in five of those games and conceded just one goal in the other five.

After helping the team to victory over Derby County in the Championship Play-Off final at Wembley, Mings signed on a permanent basis in July 2019 and has continued to be a key part of the club's re-emergence in the Premier League. His impressive form was rewarded when former Villa defender Gareth Southgate handed him his first England cap in October 2019.

Mings also has a big reputation off the pitch. During his time at Ipswich Town, he bought shirts bearing his new No.3 for supporters who had purchased shirts with his previous No.15 on the back - and he spent Christmas Day 2013 helping to feed homeless people.

TONY MORLEY

BIRTHPLACE: Orsmskirk
DATE OF BIRTH: 26 August 1954
DEBUT: Bolton Wanderers (A), 18 August 1979
VILLA TOTALS: 180 appearances / 34 goals

Villa's triumphs of the early 1980s were built essentially on teamwork, but Tony Morley was always guaranteed to throw in a touch of flamboyance. Supporters rose to their feet in anticipation whenever the flying winger was in possession of the ball - and his pace and silky skills rarely disappointed them.

For sheer showmanship, Morley's twisting and turning before he crossed for Peter Withe to hit the European Cup winner is a moment which is still vivid for Villa supporters who either witnessed it at the time or have subsequently watched video footage.

Apart from his creative ability, Morley also contributed a fair number of goals. He was on target ten times during the title-winning campaign of 1980/81 - including a spectacular Goal of the Season against Everton at Goodison Park. And although his six-goal league return the following season was relatively modest, he was Villa's leading European Cup scorer with four goals.

His second against Dynamo in Berlin, when he raced the length of the pitch before slotting home a low shot, ranks among the club's all-time great goals, while his sublime left foot shot against Anderlecht carried Villa to the final.

Signed from Burnley for £200,000 in the summer of 1979, Morley spent four successful years at Villa Park before being transferred to West Bromwich Albion in December 1983. He served under manager Ron Saunders at three different clubs - Villa, Birmingham City and Albion during a second spell at The Hawthorns. He was also a member of the Villa side who beat Barcelona in the UEFA Super Cup, as well as winning six England caps.

TOMMY MORT

BIRTHPLACE: Kearsley
DATE OF BIRTH: 1 December 1897
DEBUT: Bolton Wanderers (H), 15 April 1922
VILLA TOTALS: 369 appearances / 2 goals

With all the excitement surrounding plans for the building of the Trinity Road Stand, it was perhaps excusable that Tommy Mort's debut on Easter Saturday in 1922 did not receive a great deal of attention, even though it came against his hometown club. The Villa News & Record merely noted Mort as 'a full-back from Rochdale, making a promising appearance as partner to (Tommy) Smart."

That was something of an understatement - it was the start of a famous ten-year partnership in which the two players ideally complemented each other.

Mort, a fine exponent of the sliding tackle and the more mobile of the two, was a firm believer in safety-first tactics and would remain at Villa Park until 1935.

Mort was a popular player, collecting an FA Cup runners-up medal against Newcastle in 1924. Having made his England debut against Wales the previous month, when he partnered Smart, he went on to gain three international caps.

The dependable full-back scored just two goals and even he was surprised by the first, volleying from the centre-circle to put Villa ahead against Bury in March 1926. His second strike came on Christmas Day 1932, when he netted the final goal in a 7-1 romp against Middlesbrough.

Mort made his last senior appearance at the age of 37, a 5-1 home win against Leicester City, in January 1935. He died in June 1967.

DENNIS MORTIMER

BIRTHPLACE: Liverpool
DATE OF BIRTH: 5 April 1952
DEBUT: West Ham (h) 26 December 1975
VILLA TOTALS: 406 appearances / 36 goals

The image is one which remains etched on the mind of any Villa supporter, even those too young to remember it. Dennis Mortimer stood proudly at the Feyenoord Stadium in Rotterdam on the night of 26 May 1982, holding aloft the European Cup, football's most prestigious club trophy.

Mortimer was captain of the team which achieved a feat that even the most ardent Villa supporter could not have envisaged. He was also skipper of the side who, twelve months earlier, had become Football League champions for the first time since 1910.

Those achievements alone make him one of the greatest players in Villa history, although he served the club for much longer than two glorious seasons, making over 400 appearances during a decade in claret and blue.

Signed from Coventry City for £175,000 on Christmas Eve 1975, the forceful midfielder made an immediate impact on his debut against West Ham on Boxing Day, helping Villa to a 4-1 victory over West Ham. Over the course of the following two seasons, Mortimer played more than 100 games, and was a member of the Villa team who beat Everton in the marathon 1977 League Cup final.

Although Jimmy Rimmer and Peter Withe were older, Morty was also the father figure of the team who were crowned champions and European Cup winners in consecutive seasons at the dawn of the 1980s. He was the longest-serving member of that all-conquering team and was the undisputed driving force, making great demands on himself and his colleagues as well as producing powerful runs which struck fear into the hearts of opposition defenders. Surprisingly, he never played for the full England team, having to settle for youth, under-23 and B caps.

Mortimer left Villa to join Brighton in 1985 and by the time he retired two years later he had amassed more than 700 appearances for his various clubs.

HARRY MORTON

BIRTHPLACE: Oldham
DATE OF BIRTH: 7 January 1909
DEBUT: Manchester City (A), 28 November 1931
VILLA TOTALS: 207 appearances / 0 goals

The phrase 'if you're good enough, you're big enough' is not often applied to goalkeepers, but it was certainly apt for Harry Morton. Although he was relatively short for a keeper, standing less than 5ft 10in, and weighed barely eleven stone, he was brave and decisive, commanding his area with authority.

His big break came in 1930 when, as Corporal Harry Morton, he played against Villa in a friendly for an Army team. Although Villa won comfortably, he impressed so much that he was invited for a trial, turning professional the following March.

In November that year, he was handed his first-team debut, taking over from Fred Biddlestone. He remained in the side for the remainder of that season and by the end of the 1934/35 campaign, he had missed just one game, helping Villa to the FA Cup semi-finals in 1934.

During the subsequent two seasons, when he shared the goalkeeping duties with Biddlestone, he amassed a further 39 appearances, taking his total number of Villa games to more than 200 before his transfer to Everton in March 1937. He died in the mid-1970s.

FRANK MOSS (Senior)

BIRTHPLACE: Aston
DATE OF BIRTH: 17 April 1895
DEBUT: Notts County (A), 5 April 1915
VILLA TOTALS: 281 appearances / 8 goals

Frank Moss was the first player to captain both England and a club side at Wembley when, in 1924, he led England in their first international at the stadium and two weeks later captained Villa in the FA Cup Final. Already the holder of a Cup-winner's medal following Villa's triumph over Huddersfield Town in 1920, Moss had to settle for a runners-up medal as Villa lost 2-0 to Newcastle in only the second final to be staged at Wembley.

Moss played for Walsall before joining Villa in February 1914 and managed only two appearances before the Great War brought football to a halt. He then served in the 4th Lincolnshire Regiment and suffered a career-threatening severe wound to his left knee in 1917.

But after an outstanding display against Chelsea in the FA Cup semi-final in March 1920, his place in the team was established. Moss was a driving force who became a master of wing-half play both in attack and defence, as well as being excellent in the air. He went on to gain five England caps and twice represented the Football League. He made the last of his 281 appearances against Manchester United in August 1928 before joining Cardiff City the following January.

But that was not the end of the family connection with the club. His sons Frank (junior) and Amos later served Villa with distinction. Moss died in Worcester on 15 September 1965.

FRANK MOSS (Junior)

BIRTHPLACE: Birmingham
DATE OF BIRTH: 16 September 1917
DEBUT: Everton (H), 5 September 1938
VILLA TOTALS: 314 appearances / 3 goals

Individually, they are outnumbered by several players, but no family have accumulated more appearances for Villa than the Mosses of Birmingham.

Frank Moss and his sons Frank and Amos played more than 700 games between them - and Frank junior went one better than his father by joining Villa's exclusive 300 Club.

And just imagine how much higher his figure would have been but for the intervention of the Second World War. After joining Villa from Sheffield Wednesday in May 1938, Moss played just twice the following season before heading off to serve his country in the Royal Navy. On his return, though, he settled down to the business of serving his club as a committed and reliable centre-half.

Over the course of eight consecutive seasons, he was virtually an automatic choice at the heart of the defence. In each of those seasons, he made 30-plus appearances and was an ever-present in 1949/50.

He scored only three goals, including the winner against Manchester City in December 1949, but produced consistently sound performances at the back.

It was not until 1954/55 that his career began to wind down, and even then, he remained at Villa Park as a coach to the club's youngsters for one more season.

DEREK MOUNTFIELD

BIRTHPLACE: Liverpool
DATE OF BIRTH: 2 November 1962
DEBUT: West Ham (A), 17 September 1988
VILLA TOTALS: 120 appearances / 17 goals

Derek Mountfield was essentially the 'third man' in a Villa central defensive trio which provided the foundation for the team's 1989/90 title challenge. While many people immediately think of Paul McGrath and Kent Nielsen, Mountfield is often overlooked, yet his contribution to the 3-5-2 formation adapted by manager Graham Taylor was equally important.

It was just a pity Villa eventually missed out to Liverpool in the title race, because the solid, dependable centre-back had already amassed several medals with their Merseyside rivals Everton.

Having started his career with Tranmere Rovers, he moved to Goodison Park in 1982 and within five years he had helped Everton to two league titles, the FA Cup and the European Cup Winners' Cup.

After more than 150 games for Everton, he joined Villa for £450,000 in June 1988 to bolster a side who had just been promoted back to the top flight. His debut season was disrupted by injury problems, but after McGrath and Nielsen had arrived the following summer, he revealed the qualities which had prompted Taylor to sign him.

A regular in the side over the next two seasons, he also chipped in with his fair share of goals and was on target in both legs of the 1990 UEFA Cup-tie against Banik Ostrava.

Like Nielsen, he found himself out of favour following Ron Atkinson's appointment, and made only two appearances in 1991/92, having a spell on loan with Wolves before signing for the Molineux club in March 1992.

CHRIS NICHOLL

BIRTHPLACE: Wilmslow
DATE OF BIRTH: 12 October 1946
DEBUT: Rotherham United (A), 11 March 1972
VILLA TOTALS: 252 appearances / 20 goals

Chris Nicholl was a dominant figure at the heart of Villa's defence for more than five seasons, yet he is best remembered for his scoring achievements. He was not prolific, but he scored some unusual and spectacular goals.

At Filbert Street in March 1976, for instance, he contrived to score all four goals - two into his own net - to create a top-flight record as Villa drew 2-2 with Leicester City.

And 13 months later, he was on target with an amazing dipping shot from at least 35 yards in a dramatic 3-2 victory over Everton in the second replay of the League Cup final. He had been appointed captain by then, and proudly held the trophy aloft at Old Trafford after one of the greatest games in Villa's history.

A gritty, uncompromising defender, Nicholl was signed from Luton Town in March 1972 and was on target in only his second match, going on to make 13 appearances as Villa became Third Division champions.

Over the next four seasons, he barely missed a game, helping the club to League Cup glory and promotion from Division Two in 1975.

Powerful in the air, he was a strong tackler who also had excellent positional sense. His Villa days came to an end in the summer of 1977 when he joined Southampton, a club he later managed. He also had a spell in charge of Walsall as well as working as assistant to his former Saints boss Lawrie McMenemy with Northern Ireland.

KENT NIELSEN

BIRTHPLACE: Frederiksberg, Denmark
DATE OF BIRTH: 28 December 1961
DEBUT: Nottingham Forest (A), 19 August 1989
VILLA TOTALS: 102 appearances / 5 goals

Former Villa secretary Steve Stride tells an amusing tale of how he and manager Graham Taylor engaged in an imaginary game of cricket at Brondby's training ground while waiting for a decision from the Danish club's officials over Kent Nielsen's proposed transfer to Villa.

Thankfully, the deal went through - and the £500,000 fee proved to be money well spent. Despite a low-key start to life in claret and blue, Nielsen really came into his own when he, Paul McGrath and Derek Mountfield were employed by Taylor as a three-man central defence against Wimbledon at Plough Lane in November. The tactic worked superbly as Villa scored a 2-0 victory over their bogey team, and the trio played an integral role as Villa mounted a strong title challenge, finishing runners-up to Liverpool.

It earned Villa UEFA Cup qualification the following season, and in October 1990, Nielsen enjoyed his finest moment as a Villa player, scoring with a stunning volley from outside the penalty area in a 2-0 victory over Inter Milan. Villa lost the return leg 3-0 at the San Siro Stadium, but Nielsen's strike remains one of the club's most memorable post-war goals.

He missed only one league match that season, although Villa struggled under the management of Jozef Venglos and only narrowly avoided relegation - and he figured only occasionally after Ron Atkinson was appointed manager ahead of the 1991/92 campaign.

Nielsen returned to Denmark to join Aarhuus that season - and went on to help his country to a Euro 1992 triumph in Sweden.

DEREK PACE

BIRTHPLACE: Bloxwich
DATE OF BIRTH: 11 March 1932
DEBUT: Burnley (H), 17 March 1951
VILLA TOTALS: 107 appearances / 42 goals

Liverpool's David Fairclough is always recalled as football's first 'super sub', but if substitutes had been allowed in the 1950s, the honour would surely have belonged to Derek Pace. Instead, the man fondly known as 'Doc', had to settle for a relatively small number of first-team appearances during eight seasons at Villa Park - but he delivered an impressive ratio of almost a goal every other game.

We can only imagine what his goal haul had subs existed. After scoring regularly in junior football, Pace signed professional for Villa in September 1949 and 18 months later scored on his debut in a 3-2 home victory over Burnley. Over the next few seasons, he regularly came up with goals whenever first-team opportunities presented themselves, and his nine goals in 19 league appearances during the 1955/56 campaign were instrumental in helping the club to avoid relegation.

The following season, he was not quite as prolific in the league, scoring six in 21 games, but he played in Villa's first six FA Cup-ties, netting twice as they reached the semi-finals. He then lost his place to Billy Myerscough, who scored the winner in the semi-final replay against Albion at St Andrew's and was preferred to Pace in the final against Manchester United.

After leaving Villa in 1957, Pace scored 150 goals for Sheffield United. He died in 1989.

HARRY PARKES

BIRTHPLACE: Birmingham
DATE OF BIRTH: 4 January 1920
DEBUT: Coventry City (A), FA Cup, 5 January 1946
VILLA TOTALS: 345 appearances / 4 goals

Harry Parkes's statistics tell only part of the Erdington-born player's time at Villa Park. While he is one of an elite group to have made more than 300 league and cup appearances for the club, you can add to his official figure a further 134 wartime games. And although his goal haul during the post-war years amounted to less than a handful, he had netted 41 before peace was declared.

It was during the hostilities that Parkes won his only medal, helping Villa to victory over Blackpool in the Football League North Cup final of 1944.

His prolific output of goals during that period was largely because he played mainly at inside-left, although such was his versatility that he was willing to operate almost anywhere. He occupied eight different positions throughout the course of his career, although he was at his most effective in a full-back role. He retired in 1955 to concentrate on his successful sports shop in Birmingham and sat on Villa's board of directors in the late 1960s and 1970s.

One of the club's most popular players of all time, Parkes was voted Villa's Player of the Decade for the 1940s in a poll among supporters at the turn of the 21st century. He died in March 2009.

STILIYAN PETROV

BIRTHPLACE: Sofia, Bulgaria
DATE OF BIRTH: 5 July 1979
DEBUT: West Ham (A), 10 September 2006
VILLA TOTALS: 219 appearances / 12 goals

Everyone connected with Villa - and, indeed, the wider football community - was shocked when the club announced on Friday 30 March 2012 that Stiliyan Petrov had been diagnosed with acute leukemia.

Villa's captain had complained about a lack of energy in the previous Saturday's match at Arsenal, but the news stunned everyone. It was difficult to comprehend that such a fit athlete, who had served the club so well over the previous six years, could suffer such a disease. For the remainder of that season, and for a long time afterwards, supporters applauded in the 19th minute of every game to show their support for a man who had worn the number 19 shirt with such distinction.

Petrov had made an immediate impression when he arrived from Celtic just before the 2006 transfer window closed, although it took him a while to justify the £6.5million fee which made him Martin O'Neill's first major signing. The Bulgarian midfielder enjoyed an outstanding debut in a 1-1 draw at West Ham, but then struggled to reproduce the form which had made him such an effective player at Parkhead.

It was a similar story for much of his second campaign at Villa, but a sensational goal from the centre-circle against Derby at Pride Park in April proved to be the turning point. It was a strike which propelled him into Villa folklore, and the following season, he barely put a foot wrong, controlling the midfield as O'Neill's team challenged for a Champions League place as well as reaching the last 32 of the UEFA Cup. He was voted Players' Player of the Year, Supporters' Player of the Year and Lions Club Player of the Year.

A natural leader, Petrov was appointed captain at the start of the 2009/10 season following Martin Laursen's retirement and led out Villa for the first time at the new Wembley Stadium when they reached the 2010 League Cup final.

Sadly, the game at Arsenal just before his diagnosis proved to be his last competitive Villa appearance. He made a full recovery and trained with the team ahead of the 2016/17 season, although he was not offered a contract by new manager Roberto di Matteo.

LEIGHTON PHILLIPS

BIRTHPLACE: Swansea
DATE OF BIRTH: 25 September 1949
DEBUT: Millwall (H), 21 September 1974
VILLA TOTALS: 175 appearances / 4 goals

When it comes to football versatility, Leighton Phillips had few peers. Throughout the course of an 18-year professional career, the Welshman played in eight different positions, ranging from full-back to striker.

Although he was born near Swansea, it was at the Swans' big rivals Cardiff City that he began his career, joining the Ninian Park club straight from school and making over 200 appearances for the Bluebirds.

He joined Villa for £100,000 in September 1974, making his debut as a substitute in a 3-0 home victory over Millwall, and he soon became a regular in the line-up. Phillips helped Villa to promotion from the old Second Division, although he missed out on the team's League Cup run because he was cup-tied.

Over the next three seasons he was virtually an automatic choice as Villa re-established themselves in the First Division, and his disappointment at missing out on League Cup glory in 1975 was erased when he played in every round in 1976/77, forming a fine partnership alongside Chris Nicholl as the team's run culminated with the famous second replay victory over Everton at Old Trafford.

His time at Villa came to an end in November 1978 when he joined Swansea, helping his hometown club from the old Third Division to the top tier of English football.

Platt had come to the notice of clubs all over Europe during the World Cup finals in Italy the previous year when he became an overnight sensation with a spectacular which gave England a dramatic victory over Belgium.

Platt joined his boyhood favourites Manchester United straight from school, but was released in 1985 as part of a cost-cutting exercise at Old Trafford. If that was a bitter disappointment, though, a move to Fourth Division Crewe put his career back on track and he was regularly on target for the Gresty Road club.

His move to Villa could hardly have worked out better. Platt scored on his debut in a 3-2 defeat away to promotion rivals Blackburn Rovers, and by the end of the season he had hit five goals, including a headed winner against another of the main contenders, Bradford City.

The following season, his 15 goals helped Villa to retain top-flight status during a traumatic season under Jo Venglos, and Platt then headed the scorechart with 24 in two consecutive seasons before heading to Bari. He was also voted PFA Player of the Year for 1989/90.

CHRIS PRICE

BIRTHPLACE: Hereford
DATE OF BIRTH: 30 March 1960
DEBUT: Millwall (H), 27 August 1988
VILLA TOTALS: 144 appearances / 2 goals

A reliable right-back, Chris Price arrived from Blackburn Rovers in the summer of 1988 as one of the players signed by Graham Taylor following Villa's promotion. Over the course of three seasons, the Hereford-born defender's steady performances were one of the key features of a team who became embroiled in two relegation battles - with a title challenge in between.

DAVID PLATT

BIRTHPLACE: Chadderton
DATE OF BIRTH: 10 June 1966
DEBUT: Blackburn Rovers (A), 20 February 1988
VILLA TOTALS: 155 appearances / 68 goals

Graham Taylor claimed he paid over the odds when he recruited David Platt from Crewe Alexandra for £200,000 early in 1988, matching a bid made by his former assistant Steve Harrison, who was by then manager of Watford.

The Villa boss, though, was aware it was still an astute piece of business. Operating as an attacking midfielder, Platt was a prolific marksman for three-and-a-half seasons in claret and blue, and when he left for Italian club Bari in the summer of 1991, he netted Villa a club record incoming fee of £5.5million.

He missed only eight games during that period and was an ever-present in 1990/91, playing in all 38 First Division games plus eleven cup-ties, including four in the UEFA Cup.

Popular with Holte Enders, who serenaded him affectionately about his lack of hair, Price scored only a couple of goals, although one of them was the winner against Arsenal at Highbury in April 1990 as Villa mounted a title bid before missing out to Liverpool.

The arrival of Ron Atkinson as manager signalled the beginning of the end of Price's career in claret and blue and he made only three more appearances before returning to Blackburn early in 1992.

CYRILLE REGIS

BIRTHPLACE: French Guiana
DATE OF BIRTH: 9 February 1958
DEBUT: Sheffield Wednesday (A), 17 August 1991
VILLA TOTALS: 63 appearances / 12 goals

Not many footballers can claim to have represented four major West Midlands clubs, but Cyrille Regis did. And while his best days were undoubtedly with West Bromwich Albion and Coventry City, he did an excellent job for Villa following the appointment of Ron Atkinson, who had also been one of his bosses at The Hawthorns.

Born in French Guiana, Regis was brought up in London from the age of four and initially played non-League football before being spotted by former Albion star Ronnie Allen, who was scouting for the Baggies at the time.

He was a prolific scorer for the successful Albion team of the late 1970s and early 1980s, winning the PFA Young Player of the Year award in 1978, before joining Coventry in 1984 and helping them to FA Cup glory three years later.

In 1991, he became Atkinson's first signing for Villa, arriving from Highfield Road on a free transfer, and he made an immediate impact. One of six players making his debut at Sheffield Wednesday on the opening day of the season, he was also one of the three new boys - along with Dalian Atkinson and Steve Staunton - to score in a 3-2 victory.

He played more than 40 games that season, helping Villa to seventh place in the final table and the quarter-finals of the FA Cup. He was also the club's eleven-goal joint leading league scorer, along with Dwight Yorke. His second season was not so successful, his appearances restricted by the arrival of £2.3million club record signing Dean Saunders, and he was also laid low in the middle of the season after undergoing Achilles tendon surgery.

Following an amicable departure from Villa Park, he spent the 1993/94 season with Wolves. Capped five times by England, he was awarded the MBE in 2008. Regis died in January 2018.

JACK REYNOLDS

BIRTHPLACE: Blackburn
DATE OF BIRTH: 21 February 1869
DEBUT: West Bromwich Albion (H), 2 September 1893
VILLA TOTALS: 110 appearances / 17 goals

Collecting trophies was second nature to 'Baldy' Reynolds, who picked up three League Championship medals and two FA Cup-winner's medals in four seasons with Villa. One of the great players of the 1890s, he was fast, strong, capable with both feet and a fine header of the ball. He also possessed a powerful shot.

Having spent his youth in Ireland before returning to Blackburn in 1884, Reynolds joined the East Lancashire Regiment two years later and was posted back to Ireland. After playing for the Regimental Team, he joined Distillery and then Ulster, reaching the Irish Cup Final.

Capped five times for Ireland, he scored against England before his English birth was discovered and he went on to gain a further seven caps and score three goals for England between 1892 and 1897.

In 1891, Reynolds joined West Bromwich Albion, helping them to FA Cup glory the following March - when he scored the third goal in a 3-0 defeat of Villa in the final.

In 1893, Reynolds joined Villa and made his debut against Albion, scoring the opening goal with a penalty in a 3-2 win. By the end of the season he had won a League Championship medal and in April 1895, he picked up his second FA Cup-winner's medal as Villa beat Albion 1-0 in the final.

1896 brought a further league title and the following season, Reynolds was part of Villa's double team. He then departed for Celtic, but after just four league games, moved to Southampton. At the time of his death on 12 March 1917, Reynolds was working as a collier in the Sheffield area.

Such was his notoriety and legendary status that even in the 21st century, his life and exploits are still the subject of lectures at the University of Ulster.

KEVIN RICHARDSON

BIRTHPLACE: Newcastle-on-Tyne
DATE OF BIRTH: 4 December 1962
DEBUT: Sheffield Wednesday (A), 17 August 1991
VILLA TOTALS: 180 appearances / 16 goals

Kevin Richardson was a footballer who went about his business without ever commanding massive headlines. He was described in the 1993 Aston Villa Review as the 'quiet man who prefers to lead by example'.

A grafting midfielder, he constantly helped to break up opposition attacks before providing sensible passes to more creative teammates. If he was never a star, however, the unassuming Geordie's contribution was essential, both to Villa and the clubs for whom he played before and after his time in claret and blue.

Having helped Everton to the title in 1985, he repeated the feat with Arsenal four years later. And when Villa challenged strongly for the inaugural Premier League crown in 1992/93, he was frequently talked about as potentially the first player to win championship medals with three different clubs.

That third medal eluded him as Villa finished runners-up to Manchester United, but he added another honour to his collection the following season when he captained the side to a 3-1 victory over the Red Devils in the 1994 League Cup final.

He returned to the twin towers in May that year for his only England appearance in a 5-0 victory over Greece, and by the end of the season he had missed only two Villa games since his arrival from Spanish club Real Sociedad in the summer of 1991.

As Villa struggled in 1994/95, however, he lost his place after Ron Atkinson had been replaced by Brian Little. He subsequently followed Big Ron to Coventry City.

VILLA STARS A-Z

JIMMY RIMMER

BIRTHPLACE: Southport
DATE OF BIRTH: 10 February 1948
DEBUT: Queens Park Rangers (A), 20 August 1977
VILLA TOTALS: 287 appearances / 0 goals

Not everyone in the Villa camp was jubilant on the night of 26 May 1982. The European Cup final against Bayern Munich left Jimmy Rimmer feeling devastated rather than delighted. Although he was as happy as anyone with the outcome, his own involvement in what should have been the greatest night of his football life was over after just nine minutes.

A recurrence of a neck injury suffered in the final league game against Swansea the previous Friday forced Rimmer to make the hardest decision of his career and indicate that he was unable to continue.

While substitute Nigel Spink performed heroics to keep Bayern at bay, Rimmer was in tears as he received treatment from club doctor David Targett in the dressing room, although he did manage to return to the dug-out in time to witness Peter Withe's winning goal.

His misfortune meant he holds the distinction of having won European Cup medals with two different clubs - despite not being on the pitch at the end of either final. He had been on the bench when Manchester United beat Benfica in the 1968 final at Wembley. Despite the cruel blow of his injury in Rotterdam, though, Rimmer had the satisfaction of being one of only five Villa players to start all nine European Cup matches that season.

Having forged his early career with United, Rimmer had a spell on loan with Swansea City and then joined Arsenal before moving to Villa for £65,000 in 1977. Over the course of the next five seasons, he was a model of consistency, missing only one game and helping Villa to the title in 1980/81. He returned to Swansea in 1983.

233

BRUCE RIOCH

BIRTHPLACE: Aldershot
DATE OF BIRTH: 6 September 1947
DEBUT: Norwich City (H), 9 August 1969
VILLA TOTALS: 176 appearances / 37 goals

Signed from Luton Town in the summer of 1969, along with his brother Neil, Bruce Rioch must have wondered by the end of his first season at Villa Park if he had made a bad career move. Although he was an ever-present, he was unable to prevent Villa from sliding into the old Third Division for the first time in their history. He also witnessed the departure of Tommy Docherty, the manager who had signed him.

If that debut campaign was one to forget, he found himself at Wembley less than twelve months later as Villa reached the League Cup final, which they lost 2-0 to Tottenham Hotspur. His appearances that season were restricted by injury, but in 1971/72 he missed only six of the 46 league games as Villa stormed to the Third Division title. A forceful midfielder, Rioch also had a penchant for long-distance goals and was on target nine times during the title-winning campaign.

He was also a prominent member of the side as Villa finished third on their first season back in Division Two, but the following season he was reluctantly sold to Derby County for £200,000.

It turned out to be good business for both the club and the player. While Villa won promotion back to the top flight in 1974/75, Rioch's first full season at the Baseball Ground saw the Rams crowned League champions.

He later had spells as manager of Middlesbrough, Millwall, Bolton Wanderers and Arsenal. Rioch, whose father was Scottish, also had the distinction of being the first English-born player to captain Scotland in a full international match.

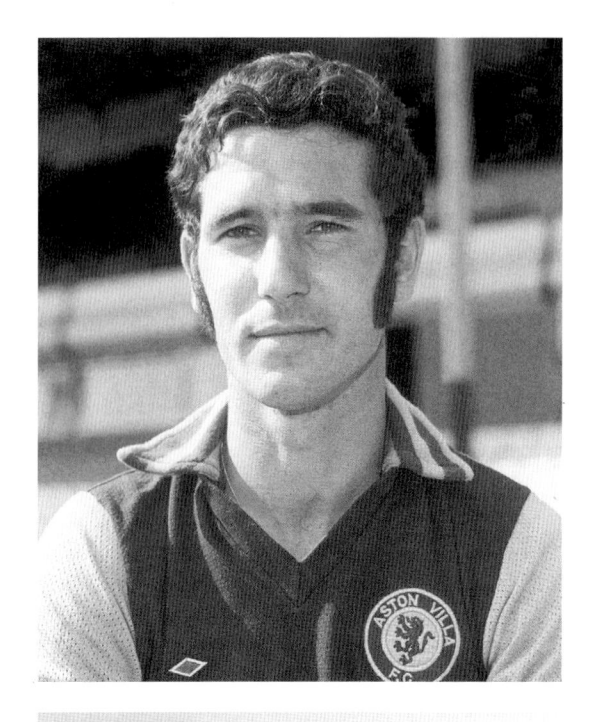

JOHN ROBSON

BIRTHPLACE: Consett
DATE OF BIRTH: 15 July 1950
DEBUT: Sheffield Wednesday (A), 23 December 1972
VILLA TOTALS: 176 appearances / 1 goal

John Robson's story is one of the most tragic of Villa's history. An accomplished full-back who was transformed into an equally fine midfielder, his career was curtailed by multiple sclerosis in 1978 and his long battle against the disease sadly culminated in his death in May 2004.

His passing was mourned by Villa supporters who had admired his quality performances in claret and blue during the 1970s.

Robson had played more than 200 games for Derby County when manager Vic Crowe brought him to Villa Park just before Christmas 1972 and he quickly settled into the full-back role he had occupied at the Baseball Ground.

The following season he moved into midfield following the emergence of John Gidman at right-back and was restricted to only a dozen appearances. But during the triumphant 1974-75 campaign he missed just one of Villa's 55 league and cup matches as they won promotion back to the First Division and lifted the League Cup.

Robson continued to serve Villa well at English football's top level and was a member of the team who repeated their League Cup success with victory over Everton in the 1977 final. Sadly, he played just three games at the start of the following season before being forced into retirement. The club staged a testimonial match for him in October 1978.

IAN ROSS

BIRTHPLACE: Glasgow
DATE OF BIRTH: 26 January 1947
DEBUT: Port Vale (H), 26 February 1972
VILLA TOTALS: 205 appearances / 3 goals

Like so many youngsters on Liverpool's books down the years, Ian Ross had the misfortune to be in the presence of top-class players. Even so, he made 68 appearances for the Reds before moving to Villa for £70,000 in February 1972.

At the time, it may have seemed a backward move to leave one of the leading clubs in the country for a Villa side then in the Third Division, but it could hardly have worked out better.

A totally committed footballer, he helped Villa to the Third Division title within a few months of his arrival and captained the team who won the League Cup and promotion from the Second Division in 1974/75.

Ross's consistent performances were an integral part of many a Villa victory during that successful period. He was an ever-present in both 1973/74 and 1974/75 and missed only four games during the team's first season back in the First Division.

He lost his place at the start of the 1976/77 campaign and after loan spells with Notts County, Northampton Town and Peterborough United, he made a permanent move to London Road in December 1976. Ross died in February 2019.

JOE RUTHERFORD

BIRTHPLACE: Fatfield, County Durham
DATE OF BIRTH: 20 September 1914
DEBUT: Birmingham City (H), 4 March 1939
VILLA TOTALS: 156 appearances / 0 goals

Joe Rutherford was the man between Villa's posts at the outbreak of the Second World War - and he still occupied the position when League football resumed seven years later.

A fearless keeper, Rutherford arrived from Southport early in 1939, making his debut in a 5-1 thrashing of Birmingham City. He missed only one game during the remainder of that season, but when the hostilities with Germany began, he served in the RASC. As well as being stationed in Italy, he was also based at Mansfield, making several guest appearances for Nottingham Forest.

But at the end of the war, he returned to Villa, remaining the club's first choice keeper until the early 1950s, when he retired and formed his own business. Rutherford played a total of 148 league games, plus eight FA Cup-ties. He died in 1994.

JLLOYD SAMUEL

BIRTHPLACE: San Fernando, Trinidad
DATE OF BIRTH: 15 May 1984
DEBUT: Chester City (H), 21 September 1999
VILLA TOTALS: 200 appearances / 3 goals

Some players slip under the radar when it comes to recognition, and Jlloyd Samuel was a prime example. During his time at Villa Park, he was quiet and unassuming both on and off the pitch yet when he was in form there were few better defenders.

Better still, his qualities at the back, either as a left-back or a wing-back, were complemented by his ability to push forward down the left flank and offer Villa's attacks an extra dimension. Such was his versatility that he also played at right-back on occasions - and he made his Premier League debut in central defence when Gareth Southgate was ruled out of a 2-0 home win over Derby County in March 2000.

Born in Trinidad but raised in London, Samuel played in the same Sunday League team as future England internationals John Terry and Jermain Defoe and was an Academy youngster with Charlton Athletic and West Ham before moving to Villa. Having made 17 appearances, he was loaned to Gillingham, returning to Villa in 2001 and taking over at right-back when Mark Delaney was injured.

His most notable campaign was the 2013/14, when he played every single minute, helping Villa to a sixth-place finish and the semi-finals of the League Cup. He also scored all three of his Villa goals that season, netting both home and away against Charlton plus one against Bolton Wanderers in the second leg of the League Cup semi-final.

He remained a regular over the following three seasons, but played just five games in 2007/08 before joining Bolton. Tragically, he was killed in a car crash in May 2018.

DEAN SAUNDERS

BIRTHPLACE: Swansea
DATE OF BIRTH: 21 June 1964
DEBUT: Leeds United (A), 13 September 1992
VILLA TOTALS: 144 appearances / 49 goals

Dean Saunders was one of the most engaging characters ever to wear a Villa shirt. While he charmed supporters, though, he had a ruthless streak when it came to opposition defenders. Although he spent only three seasons at Villa Park, he was the club's leading scorer on each occasion.

Having been on manager Ron Atkinson's wanted list for several months, he arrived from Liverpool for a club record £2.3million a few weeks into the 1992/93 campaign.

He did not score on his debut at Elland Road, but his first home game saw him line up against Liverpool - and how he revelled in scoring twice in a 4-2 victory against the club he had just left.

It was by no means a one-off. During the next few weeks, Deano and his striking partner Dalian Atkinson could not stop scoring. Atkinson's output dried up after he was sidelined by injury in December, but Saunders went on to score 16 league and cup goals, including the winner in front of the Kop as Villa beat Liverpool 2-1 at Anfield to complete a double over the Reds.

He repeated that 16-goal haul the following season, when he became the first Villa player to score a Premier League hat-trick, and was also on target twice in the 3-1 League Cup final triumph over Manchester United at Wembley. Although Villa were engaged in a battle against relegation in 1994/95, Saunders went one better with his personal haul, his 17 goals playing a significant part in the club's top-flight survival before joining Turkish club Galatasaray.

Sward was again a regular member of the side in 1957/58, missing only two games, but was restricted to just 14 appearances as Villa were relegated twelve months later.

Significantly, he made 40 league appearances as Joe Mercer's men bounced back at the first attempt by winning the Second Division title in 1959/60, although he played only another eleven games before moving to Huddersfield Town in March 1961.

Despite being a late starter in the game, Saward played 18 times for his country. He was later player-coach at Coventry City and manager of Brighton. He died in September 2002.

JACKIE SEWELL

BIRTHPLACE: Whitehaven
DATE OF BIRTH: 24 January 1927
DEBUT: Sheffield United (A), 3 December 1955
VILLA TOTALS: 145 appearances / 40 goals

Jackie Sewell was not exactly a bargain basement signing when he joined Villa in December 1955, costing the club a sizeable £20,000 fee from Sheffield Wednesday. Even so, it was a modest outlay by comparison with the £34,500 he had cost Wednesday from Notts County four years earlier, when he was the most expensive player in the country.

PAT SAWARD

BIRTHPLACE: Cobh, Republic of Ireland
DATE OF BIRTH: 17 August 1928
DEBUT: Manchester United (H), 15 October 1955
VILLA TOTALS: 170 appearances / 2 goals

Pat Saward must have realised he was on the brink of something special when he made his Villa debut. Having signed from Millwall, he scored in his first game, a thrilling 4-4 draw against Manchester United.

That was one of only half a dozen appearances made by the Republic of Ireland wing-half during his inaugural campaign as Villa only just retained First Division status. But it was the following season that he really came into his own, missing only one league game and playing in all nine cup-ties as Villa finished a respectable tenth in the table and won the FA Cup.

During his time at Hillsborough, he also became established as an England international and was one of the scorers in the infamous 6-3 Wembley defeat by Hungary in 1953. His international days were over by the time he arrived at Villa Park, although he certainly proved good value for money.

Although the team were threatened by relegation during his first season, he missed only a handful of games in the following campaign, hitting a total of 18 goals as Eric Houghton's men finished in the top half of the table and won the FA Cup.

He continued to be a regular at inside-right for Villa over the subsequent two seasons, but played only twice more for the club following relegation in 1959. After losing his place to Bobby Thomson, he was transferred to Hull City in October 1959, subsequently taking up a player-coach role with Lusaka City of Zambia. He died in September 2016.

GARY SHAW

BIRTHPLACE: Kingshurst
DATE OF BIRTH: 21 January 1961
DEBUT: Bristol City (A), 26 August 1978
VILLA TOTALS: 213 appearances / 79 goals

Gary Shaw was the golden boy of Villa's golden era. Holte Enders easily identified with the blond-haired local lad who hit the target on a regular basis. Shaw's partnership with Peter Withe struck fear into the heart of opposition defences during the title-winning campaign of 1980/81 and the European Cup trail the following season.

While Withe provided the power, Shaw's pace and anticipation completed a lethal duo, earning him accolades far beyond Villa Park. In 1981, having contributed 18 goals to Villa's League Championship triumph, he was voted PFA Young Player of the Year. And twelve months later his talents were acknowledged on the continent as he received the accolade of European Young Footballer of the Year.

Shaw began his apprenticeship with Villa in 1977 and by the end of the following year he had been given his first taste of senior football, making his debut as a substitute at Bristol City before having a couple of starting appearances.

He signed professional on his 18th birthday and established himself as a first-team regular in 1979/80 before missing only two league games during Villa's march to the title the following season.

His Euro award was the result of some outstanding performances along the road to Rotterdam, including the crucial breakthrough goal from a tight angle in the quarter-final against Dynamo Kiev.

He remained a regular during the 1982/83 season, during which he won a European Super Cup medal, but then, sadly, became the victim of a series of injury problems which seriously curtailed his appearances. He was given a free transfer in 1988, later playing in Denmark, Austria and Hong Kong.

NIGEL SIMS

BIRTHPLACE: Coton-in-the-Elms, Derbyshire
DATE OF BIRTH: 9 August 1931
DEBUT: Burnley (h) 19 March 1956
VILLA TOTALS: 310 appearances / 0 goals

A move across the West Midlands proved to be the making of Nigel Sims. Before his transfer from Wolves to Villa in March 1956, he had been restricted to just 39 appearances during eight years at Molineux, where he had been the understudy to England goalkeeper Bert Williams. But once he was out of Williams' shadow, his career really blossomed.

He stayed with Villa for roughly the same time he had been at Molineux, but during that period he amassed 310 appearances and won an FA Cup medal. Although the club were engaged in a battle against relegation immediately after his arrival, he and his teammates really came into their own the following season.

Sims missed only four league games as Villa made a significant improvement to finish tenth - and he was between the posts in all nine of their Cup ties, culminating in victory over Manchester United in the final.

Brave and self-confident, Sims performed consistently over the next few seasons, and although he tasted the disappointment of relegation in 1959, he conceded only just over a goal a game as Villa stormed straight back to the First Division twelve months later.

He also played in the first leg of the inaugural League Cup final against Rotherham United, missing the return match at Villa Park through injury.

It was his replacement in that match, Geoff Sidebottom, who eventually took his place. Sims was granted a free transfer in 1964 and joined Peterborough United. He died in January 2018.

TOMMY SMART

BIRTHPLACE: Blackheath, Staffordshire
DATE OF BIRTH: 20 September 1897
DEBUT: Everton (H), 14 February 1920
VILLA TOTALS: 451 appearances / 8 goals

Full-back Tommy Smart was a true Black Country character who had a commanding physical presence on the field, so much so that some of the best wingers around at the time were reputed to be afraid of him! Despite his size and appearance, though, Smart was not deliberately rough and had brilliant kicking, heading and positional qualities.

Signed from Halesowen in January 1920, he quickly became established in the Villa team, partnering Tommy Weston, and in April that year he gained an FA Cup-winner's medal as Villa beat Huddersfield Town 1-0 in the final at Stamford Bridge. Following the departure of Weston in 1922, Smart went on to form a fine full-back partnership with Tommy Mort, the pair being popularly known as 'Death and Glory'.

Smart won five England caps in an international career spanning eight years and also represented the Football League. He added an FA Cup runners-up medal in 1924 and was a member of the team who finished runners-up in 1930/31. His last league game was at Blackpool in March 1933 - more than 13 years after his debut. He played for Brierley Hill Alliance the following year, retiring in 1936. He died in June 1968.

JOHN SLEEUWENHOEK

BIRTHPLACE: Wednesfield
DATE OF BIRTH: 26 February 1944
DEBUT: Bolton Wanderers (h) 4 April 1961
VILLA TOTALS: 260 appearances / 1 goal

Popularly known as 'Tulip', John Sleeuwenhoek was the son of a Dutch paratrooper, although he was born in the Black Country. After winning England Schoolboy honours, he signed professional for Villa in February 1961 at the age of 17, making his first-team debut at home to Bolton Wanderers a couple of months later.

Although that was his only senior appearance that season, he established himself as Villa's regular centre-half in 1961/62 with some commanding, hard-tackling performances, and remained an integral member of the team for six seasons.

Unfortunately, his only ever-present campaign was when Villa were relegated in 1966/67, when he also scored his only goal for the club in a 2-1 victory over Stoke City. Although he was Villa's centre-half at the start of their initial Second Division campaign, he was sold to Birmingham City in November 1967. Capped twice by England under-23s, Sleeuwenhoek died in 1989.

LES SMITH

BIRTHPLACE: Halesowen
DATE OF BIRTH: 24 December 1927
DEBUT: Arsenal (H), 11 February 1956
VILLA TOTALS: 130 appearances / 25 goals

Had he joined Villa earlier, Les Smith would surely have made hundreds of appearances in claret and blue. It was his misfortune, though, to have previously been with Wolves at a time when the Molineux club were blessed with two of the finest wingers in the country.

Despite spending a decade at Molineux, he was restricted to less than 90 games because of the presence of Johnny Hancocks and Jimmy Mullen, and it was only after moving to Villa Park that he finally became a regular first-team player.

Arriving around the same time as Jimmy Dugdale, Smith made his debut on the same day as the former Albion defender and that season the duo helped Villa to avoid relegation. Twelve months later, it was a different story as they were both in the team who beat Manchester United in the FA Cup final, right-winger Smith scoring one of his 25 goals for the club in a fourth-round victory at Middlesbrough.

He was a regular over the next two seasons too, but was forced into retirement after suffering a ruptured Achilles tendon towards the end of the 1958/59 campaign. He died in March 2008.

LESLIE SMITH

BIRTHPLACE: Ealing
DATE OF BIRTH: 13 May 1918
DEBUT: Plymouth Argyle (A), 3 November 1945
VILLA TOTALS: 197 appearances / 37 goals

Like his namesake, Leslie Smith was also a winger, although he operated on the left. Signed from Brentford in October 1945, his first games for Villa were in the Football League South before league football officially returned the following season.

An ever-present in the first two post-war campaigns, he was also a regular over the course of the next three seasons, delighting Villa supporters with his excellent ball control. He also contributed his fair share of goals, and his total of 37 in nearly 200 league cup matches was a decent return for a player who was primarily a provider of chances.

In his first season with the club, he was a key member of the side who reached the quarter-final of the Cup in 1946. It was just a pity that such a talented player did not win any honours with Villa, although he had previously helped Brentford to the London Wartime Cup in 1942, as well as being capped by England both before and during the war. Smith returned to Griffin Park in 1952 and later had a spell as player-manager of Kidderminster Harriers. He died in May 1995.

STEPHEN SMITH

BIRTHPLACE: Abbots Bromley, Staffordshire
DATE OF BIRTH: 7 January 1874
DEBUT: Burnley (H), 28 October 1893
VILLA TOTALS: 187 appearances / 43 goals

Stephen Smith was working at the Cannock & Rugeley Colliery when he was signed by Fred Rinder at the coalface in 1893, making his league debut in a 4-0 home win against Burnley in October that year. Noted for the accuracy of his passing, he won a League Championship medal in his first season, and helped Villa to four more league titles, in 1896, 1897, 1899 and 1900.

In addition, he gained an FA Cup winner's medal in 1895, two weeks after scoring for England in his only international, a 3-0 victory over Scotland.

Smith had a fine turn of speed and was a particularly close dribbler who opponents found extremely difficult to dispossess. He also had a terrific shot, but being on the small size, he suffered from physical treatment handed out by opposition defenders and received more than his fair share of injuries.

Quiet and unassuming, Smith was a modest winner and a good loser. After his last appearance at Derby County in April 1901, he moved to Portsmouth. Later in life, he took over Roke Stores in Benson, Oxfordshire where he remained until his death in May 1935.

GARETH SOUTHGATE

BIRTHPLACE: Watford
DATE OF BIRTH: 3 September 1970
DEBUT: Manchester United (h) 19 August 1995
VILLA TOTALS: 242 appearances / 9 goals

He will be remembered by most people for the penalty miss which cost England a place in the final of Euro '96, but Gareth Southgate deserves far better than that. He was one of the most cultured defenders ever to wear a Villa shirt, giving the club superb service over a six-year period. Even after he had asked for a transfer in the summer of 2000, he still performed immaculately the following season before finally moving to Middlesbrough.

Southgate joined Villa from Crystal Palace in 1995, briefly having the distinction of being the club's record signing before his £2.5million was surpassed by a £3.5million outlay for Savo Milosevic the following week.

He arrived essentially as a midfielder, but by the opening match of the season, he had been converted to a central defender, a switch which was to prove beneficial to both club and country.

He immediately struck up a fine understanding with Paul McGrath and Ugo Ehiogu in a three-man defence, providing the backbone to a successful debut campaign in which Villa won the League Cup, finished fourth in the Premiership and reached the FA cup semi-finals.

Southgate also won the first of his 57 England caps that season and was a key figure in England's run to the semi-finals of the European Championships before his weak penalty against Germany ended hopes of the nation's first major triumph since the 1966 World Cup.

It was a blow from which Southgate quickly recovered and his form over the next few seasons was outstanding, notably when Villa reached the quarter-finals of the UEFA Cup in 1997/98.

Appointed club captain following Andy Townsend's departure to Middlesbrough, Southgate led Villa to the 2000 FA Cup final, the last at the old Wembley Stadium, where they lost 1-0 to Chelsea.

His transfer request on the eve of Euro 2000 made him unpopular with supporters, but he continued to produce excellent performances before heading for Teesside.

Following his retirement as a player, Southgate moved into management with Middlesbrough, and was appointed England coach in 2016, leading the team to the 2018 World Cup semi-finals and the Euro 2020 final, which was delayed by twelve months because of the Covid-19 pandemic.

HOWARD SPENCER

BIRTHPLACE: Edgbaston, Birmingham
DATE OF BIRTH: 23 August 1875
DEBUT: West Bromwich Albion (H), 13 October 1894
VILLA TOTALS: 294 appearances / 2 goals

Full-back Howard Spencer, one of the most well-respected players at the turn of the 20th century, played a leading part in Villa's golden era. Scrupulously fair, Spencer's skill and sportsmanship earned him the title of 'prince of full-backs'. Standing out with his blond, wavy hair, his classic features and his stylish play, Spencer captained both Villa and England.

He signed for Villa from Birchfield Trinity and made his debut in a 3-1 win against West Bromwich Albion at Wellington Road in October 1894. At the end of his first season, and still only 18, Spencer collected the first of his three FA Cup-winner's medals, the second arriving in the double year of 1897. Then, in 1905, he led Villa to another FA Cup triumph against Newcastle United at the Crystal Palace.

Spencer initially partnered Jimmy Welford and then formed an excellent partnership with Albert Evans. He collected four League Championship medals (1896, 1897, 1899, and 1900) and gained six full England caps in addition to representing the Football League nine times. In February 1906, Spencer was granted a second benefit, the first having been awarded six years earlier.

Although announcing his retirement in the 1907 close season, Spencer still took part in pre-season training, advising the club that if any time they needed his services, he would oblige. Spencer was taken up on this offer and turned out in three league games, making his final appearance against Newcastle United at Villa Park on 30 November.

In 1909, Howard Spencer was elected to the Villa board following the death of vice-president Howard Toney and he remained a director until 1936. Even then, his Villa association continued.

After declining a request to become a Life Member, Spencer became a vice-president at that year's annual meeting. A successful coal merchant, Spencer died in January 1940.

NIGEL SPINK

BIRTHPLACE: Chelmsford
DATE OF BIRTH: 8 August 1958
DEBUT: Nottingham Forest (A), 26 December 1979
VILLA TOTALS: 460 appearances / 0 goals

Nigel Spink made more appearances for Villa than any other goalkeeper, and there were some historic moments over the course of his 460 games for the club. He had the distinction, for instance, of being Villa's keeper in the club's first-ever Premier League match, a 1-1 draw at Ipswich Town in August 1992.

Spink, though, will always be best remembered for his inspired performance a decade earlier, when he went on as a substitute for the injured Jimmy Rimmer in the European Cup final. Less than ten minutes into the game, Rimmer was forced to go off with a shoulder problem and it looked bleak for Villa as the regular number one was replaced by a player who had made only one first-team appearance.

But Spink became the hero of Rotterdam with a succession of brilliant saves which denied hot favourites Bayern Munich before Peter Withe grabbed the winning goal.

That was one of five occasions on which Spink went on as a substitute. The other four were all in Premier League matches - including two in his last season at Villa Park, by which time he had become second choice to Mark Bosnich. His final game, in fact, was as an outfield player when he replaced the injured Ian Taylor in the last minute of a 1-0 defeat at QPR in December 1995.

Five weeks later he joined West Bromwich Albion on a free transfer, ending a magnificent 19-year Villa career. For much of that time, he was Villa's first choice goalkeeper, and he also helped the club to victory over Barcelona in the 1983 European Super Cup as well as making a substitute appearance for England against Australia in June that year.

STEVE STAUNTON

BIRTHPLACE: Drogheda, Ireland
DATE OF BIRTH: 19 January 1969
DEBUT: Sheffield Wednesday (A), 17 August 1991
VILLA TOTALS: 350 appearances / 20 goals

Football programmes regularly feature footballers who 'played for both clubs' and Steve Staunton knows all about that. The Republic of Ireland international did not just play for both Liverpool and Villa - he did it twice!

Staunton was a key figure the Reds line-up from 1988 until the summer of 1991, when he became one of Ron Atkinson's first signings in a £1.1million transfer.

After 263 appearances in claret and blue, he returned to Merseyside when his Villa contract expired in June 1998, but was brought back to the Midlands by John Gregory in December 2000. This time around, he was seemingly in the twilight of his career, arriving on a free transfer for what many believed would amount to little more than a fringe role.

No-one could have imagined that he would enjoy such a successful second spell in Villa colours. Over the next two-and-a-half seasons, he took his Villa appearances to 350.

Throughout both his spells with Villa, Staunton was a consummate professional who performed admirably at left-back, as a central defender or in midfield. Having been a member of Liverpool's 1989 FA Cup-winning side, he helped Villa to a League Cup triumph over Manchester United in 1994.

Staunton, Villa's most-capped player with 102 appearances for Ireland, left the club in August 2003, and subsequently played for Coventry City and Walsall before being taking over as manager of the country he had represented at three World Cup finals.

CLEM STEPHENSON

BIRTHPLACE: New Delaval, County Durham
DATE OF BIRTH: 6 January 1890
DEBUT: Tottenham Hotspur (H), 25 February 1911
VILLA TOTALS: 217 appearances / 96 goals

Clem Stephenson was confident he would pick up a winner's medal going into the 1913 FA Cup Final. He had dreamed the night before that Tommy Barber would head the winning goal, which is exactly what happened.

Signed for £165 from Durham City in 1910, Stephenson was loaned to Stourbridge before making his debut against Tottenham Hotspur in February 1911 when he scored in a 4-0 home win.

The following season, Stephenson established a regular place in the team. He was equally at home on the left, could also operate on the wing and proved the perfect link between half-back and forwards as well as being a regular scorer. In March 1912, he recorded his first hat-trick in a 6-0 win against Manchester United.

Stephenson's career was interrupted by the Great War, but he finished 1919/20 as top scorer with 29 goals, including a hat-trick in a 3-2 win against Middlesbrough and all the goals in a 4-0 win against Sheffield United later the same month. He also collected a second FA Cup winner's medal.

Even so, all was not well. Stephenson lived in Newcastle-on-Tyne and in March 1921, he joined an exodus of players who left the club following the decision of the directors that players must reside in Birmingham. He was suspended in September 1920 when he failed to arrive for a game at Bolton.

Stephenson was transferred to Huddersfield, where he had a glittering career, picking up three League Championship medals plus FA Cup-winner's and runners-up medals. He also made his England debut and went on to manage the club from 1929 until 1942.

Stephenson, who died in October 1961, was named in the 100 League Legends as part of The Football League centenary celebrations. His brother George also played for Villa.

KENNY SWAIN

BIRTHPLACE: Birkenhead
DATE OF BIRTH: 28 January 1952
DEBUT: Norwich City (H), 16 December 1978
VILLA TOTALS: 179 appearances / 5 goals

He brought a touch of culture to his full-back role with Villa, which is hardly surprising because Kenny Swain would have been equally comfortable in a classroom. Before being offered his big chance by Chelsea in 1973, he was all set to become a PE teacher.

Education's loss was football's gain. Swain helped Chelsea to promotion from the old Second Division in 1977 and by the time he arrived at Villa Park in December 1978, he had scored 30 goals in 127 league and cup games for the Stamford Bridge club.

At that stage of his career, he played as either a midfielder or a striker, scoring four times in 25 games by the end of his first season with the club. The following season, though, he challenged John Gidman for the right-back spot, making the position his own following Gidman's transfer to Everton.

Not surprisingly, his goal output dried up after that, but over the next three seasons he missed only four games, boasting an ever-present record in the title-winning campaign of 1980/81.

He also took over the captaincy whenever Dennis Mortimer was absent and played in all but one of the ties as Villa won the European Cup in 1982. He joined Nottingham Forest in August 1983.

ALEC TALBOT

BIRTHPLACE: Cannock
DATE OF BIRTH: 13 July 1902
DEBUT: Swansea Town (A), FA Cup, 2 February 1924
VILLA TOTALS: 263 appearances / 7 goals

Alec Talbot was the pivotal figure in Villa's famous Gibson-Talbot-Tate half-back line and was the longest serving of the trio, turning out for the first team for more than a decade - not bad for a player who cost just £100 from non-League Hednesford Town in 1923.

The former miner played only once during the 1923/24 campaign, helping Villa to a 2-0 FA Cup win at Swansea, and made only infrequent appearances during the next few seasons. But in 1928/29, he made the centre-half position his own as he, Jimmy Gibson and Joe Tate laid the foundations for one of the most successful defensive partnerships in Villa's history.

While the forwards earned all the accolades in the early 1930s, Talbot and his pals were impressive at the back. He missed only three league games from 1929 until the end of the 1931/32 campaign, and made 136 consecutive appearances between September 1929 and November 1933. While his most important attribute was his solid defensive work, Talbot was also a stylish player with excellent distribution.

It was just a pity he did not win a major honour for the club, twice featuring in sides that finished runners-up as well as being a beaten semi-finalist on two occasions. Talbot had a brief spell with Bradford Park Avenue after leaving Villa in 1935, but then returned to the Midlands to revisit his non-League roots with Brierley Hill and Stourbridge. He died in 1975.

JOE TATE

BIRTHPLACE: Old Hill
DATE OF BIRTH: 4 August 1904
DEBUT: Derby County (A), 26 December 1927
VILLA TOTALS: 193 appearances / 4 goals

The man on the left of the famous Gibson-Talbot-Tate half-back line, Joe Tate evolved from an inside-forward to a more defensive-minded wing-half, and he was a defender with class.

A strong player with a fine tactical brain, he rarely resorted to booting the ball clear, preferring to play it on the ground and instigate moves which would often put the opposition under pressure. Villa certainly had no complaints on their return for the £400 they paid Cradley Heath for him in 1925.

It was two-and-a-half years before he broke into the first team, making his debut in a 5-0 drubbing at Derby on Boxing Day 1927 and he made only four senior appearances that season. But over the next five seasons, he was pretty much an automatic choice. He missed just two games in 1929/30 and was an ever-present the following season. It was at that time that he won his three England caps. Although he scored only four goals for Villa, one of them was against Birmingham City in a 4-0 win at St Andrew's in February 1931.

His first-team involvement, unfortunately, was curtailed by a series of knee, ankle and back problems, and he played only one game in 1933/34, dropping into the reserves before leaving in May 1935 to become player manager of Brierley Hill Alliance. He died in 1973.

IAN TAYLOR

BIRTHPLACE: Birmingham
DATE OF BIRTH: 4 June 1968
DEBUT: Arsenal (A), 26 December 1994
VILLA TOTALS: 290 appearances / 42 goals

Few players can claim the special affinity with Villa supporters which Ian Taylor holds. He stood on the Holte End when he was a boy, he cheered the team to League Cup glory over Manchester United in 1994 and was back at Wembley two years later.

This time he was on the pitch, scoring the crucial second goal as they beat Leeds United in the 1996 final. And whenever he was out of the team through injury, he was frequently spotted among the fans, both home and away.

He was a magnificent servant to the club. Maybe he arrived at Villa Park later than he would have liked, initially playing non-League football for Moor Green before making his mark with Port Vale and Sheffield Wednesday, but his contribution to the claret and blue cause was phenomenal.

For nearly nine years, Taylor was an integral part of Villa's midfield, producing non-stop graft which was so beneficial to his teammates. Essentially, he was a player's player, but the fans loved him, too, appreciating that he was realising all their dreams of wearing the famous shirt.

That was never more evident than when he scored with a header at the Holte End on his home debut just after Christmas 1994, in a 3-0 victory over Chelsea. That was a special moment for Taylor, matched only by his left-foot volley against Leeds in the 1996 final.

There were two more Wembley trips in 2000, for the FA Cup semi-final against Bolton and the final against Chelsea, before he left Villa in 2003. He subsequently became the club's official ambassador.

SHAUN TEALE

BIRTHPLACE: Southport
DATE OF BIRTH: 10 March 1964
DEBUT: Sheffield Wednesday (A), 17 August 1991
VILLA TOTALS: 181 appearances / 5 goals

There were more glamorous signings during Ron's Revolution in the summer of 1991, but arguably none more crucial than Shaun Teale. New manager Ron Atkinson was aware the arrival of Teale, snapped up from Bournemouth for a relatively modest £300,000, was not likely to boost Villa Park season ticket sales. But the manager was adamant that the uncompromising centre-back would bring much-needed defensive stability.

Teale, a former painter and decorator, was tenacious and tough, slotting in perfectly alongside the cultured Paul McGrath and making 51 appearances as Villa finished seventh in the final season of the old First Division. Teale missed four games through suspension the following season, but still helped Villa to runners-up spot behind Manchester United in the inaugural Premier League campaign.

A further twelve months down the line, he was a member of the side who beat Manchester United 3-1 in the League Cup final at Wembley.

Injuries restricted his appearances in 1994/95 - when Villa only narrowly avoided going down - and his time with the club came to an end that summer, when he moved to Tranmere Rovers.

GARRY THOMPSON

BIRTHPLACE: Birmingham
DATE OF BIRTH: 7 October 1959
DEBUT: Tottenham Hotspur (H), 23 August 1986
VILLA TOTALS: 73 appearances / 19 goals

One of football's most engaging personalities, Garry Thompson will tell anyone who cares to listen that he single-handedly got Villa promoted in 1987/88. The remark is made very much tongue-in-cheek, yet it is not without justification.

Ruled out by injury from the start of the season until late November, the King's Heath-born striker scored eleven goals in the remaining 24 Second Division games as Graham Taylor's team returned to the old First Division.

Thompson played for nine clubs and played 584 games during a career which spanned two decades, but there was never any question about where his heart lay. As a Villa supporter, it was a dream come true when he signed from Sheffield Wednesday in 1986, having previously been a prolific scorer for Coventry City and West Bromwich Albion.

Unfortunately, he arrived at a time when the club were in decline, and he hit the target just six times in league matches as Villa were relegated. But following his lengthy lay-off at the start of the following season, he was back with a vengeance and his two headers in the Second City derby at St Andrew's elevated him to a Holte End cult hero.

He later played for Watford, Crystal Palace, QPR, Cardiff City and Northampton Town, and also had spells as manager of Bristol Rovers.

TOMMY THOMPSON

BIRTHPLACE: Fencehouses, County Durham
DATE OF BIRTH: 10 November 1928
DEBUT: Blackpool (A), 23 September 1950
VILLA TOTALS: 165 appearances / 76 goals

When Tommy Thompson retired from football in 1964, he boasted an impressive haul of more than 200 goals for his various clubs. Villa supporters of the early 1950s were treated to a sizeable proportion of that total. From his arrival in 1950 until his departure five years later, Thompson delighted the Villa faithful with his clever footwork and ability to put the ball in the net.

He began his career with Newcastle United, before moving to Villa for £12,500 in September 1950 - and his value had doubled to £25,000 when he left the club to join Preston North End.

Thompson scored on his home debut against Tottenham Hotspur, going on to reach double figures by the end of his first season. He maintained a steady output over the next four years, netting 21 goals, all in the league, in 1953/54 and a total of 20 the following season.

Capped twice by England, he joined Preston in the summer of 1955 and subsequently played for Stoke City, helping the Potters to promotion to the First Division in 1963. He died in 2015.

BOBBY THOMSON

BIRTHPLACE: Dundee
DATE OF BIRTH: 21 March 1937
DEBUT: Sunderland (H), 31 August 1959
VILLA TOTALS: 172 appearances / 70 goals

His surname was slightly different, but Bobby Thomson had a great deal in common with Tommy Thompson. He, too, was a prolific marksman and if his ratio was not quite as impressive, it was not far behind. He joined Villa from Wolves in 1959, having found his opportunities limited at Molineux by the likes of Denis Wilshaw, Roy Swinbourne and Jimmy Murray.

But he had no problems in settling at Villa Park, stepping into a side who had been relegated the previous season and making an immediate impact with a goal on his debut in a 3-0 victory over Sunderland. That was just one of 20 he scored as Villa won the Second Division title in 1959/60, and while goals became harder to come by in the top flight, he contributed a dozen in each of Villa's first three seasons back in the First Division.

He was also a member of the Villa team who won the inaugural League Cup completion, as well as being in the side who were beaten finalists in 1963. In September that year, the rugged, hard-working Scot joined Birmingham City before finishing his professional career with Stockport County.

MIKE TINDALL

BIRTHPLACE: Birmingham
DATE OF BIRTH: 5 April 1941
DEBUT: Hull City (H), 28 December 1959
VILLA TOTALS: 136 appearances / 9 goals

Although Mike Tindall was never regarded as a regular, he gave excellent service to the club during a decade as a professional at Villa Park. His misfortune was that he had so much competition, both at wing-half and inside-forward. But his sheer enthusiasm and willingness to work hard for the team made him popular with supporters.

He joined the club straight from school in 1956 and signed his first contract two years later, impressing in Villa's youth and reserve teams as well as winning several England Youth caps.

He was given his initial taste of first-team football in a couple of games during the 1959/60 Second Division championship campaign, although he then had to wait until the early part of the 1961/62 season for his next selection.

After recovering from a broken leg in 1964, he enjoyed his most regular spell in the team in 1965/66 and 1966/67, making 29 and 28 appearances respectively.

But the following season he was largely out of favour, playing in only half a dozen games, and in 1968 he joined Walsall, for whom he played for a season before retiring from the professional game. He died in August 2020.

ANDY TOWNSEND

BIRTHPLACE: Maidstone
DATE OF BIRTH: 27 July 1963
DEBUT: QPR (H), 14 August 1993
VILLA TOTALS: 176 appearances / 11 goals

Two medals in the space of two years transformed Andy Townsend from one of football's nearly men into a winner. Before joining Villa from Chelsea in the summer of 1993, the Republic of Ireland international had played in five semi-finals and had lost them all.

But where he had missed out with Southampton, Norwich City and Chelsea, he hit the jackpot in 1994 when Villa beat Manchester United in the League Cup final - and he was captain when they outclassed Leeds United in the 1996 final.

A few eyebrows were raised at Villa's outlay of £2.1million for a 30-year-old, but he immediately justified the fee as his midfield dominance and powerful runs gave the side a vital edge they had previously lacked.

He also scored some crucial goals. In his first season at Villa Park, he was on target four times and each one was a winner - against Ipswich Town, Leeds United, Arsenal and Slovan Bratislava, in a UEFA Cup tie. Villa invariably struggled when he was not in the team, although the fact that he always wore his heart on his sleeve meant he occasionally had to endure a lengthy absence.

During his second season, he served a six-match suspension following a series of bookings and a red card in a 4-3 defeat by Wimbledon in what proved to be Atkinson's final match. Townsend returned to the line-up at Arsenal on Boxing Day - and promptly earned himself another two-match ban by being sent off again!

Villa only narrowly avoided relegation that season, but the following campaign was the club's most successful of the Premier League era. Apart from winning the League Cup - Townsend described receiving the trophy as the most satisfying feeling of his career - they finished fourth in the table and reached the FA Cup semi-finals. He joined Middlesbrough in August 1997.

VILLA STARS A-Z

DARIUS VASSELL

BIRTHPLACE: Birmingham
DATE OF BIRTH: 30 June 1980
DEBUT: Middlesbrough (H), 23 August 1998
VILLA TOTALS: 201 appearances / 45 goals

Few Villa players have been as explosive coming off the bench as Darius Vassell. Although he made over 200 appearances for the club, more than a third of them were as a substitute. But that did not stop the local boy from making a massive impact at Villa Park. In only his third appearance for the club, Vassell was a hero on a night everything seemed to be going wrong.

Villa were 2-0 down to Norwegian part-timers Stromsgodset in a first round UEFA Cup-tie in September 1998 when he replaced Darren Byfield ten minutes from time at Villa Park. Three minutes later, Gary Charles reduced the deficit - and in stoppage time, Vassell netted twice to clinch a dramatic 3-2 victory and make himself a Holte End hero.

Injuries meant he had to wait nearly two-and-a-half years for his second goal - the winner in an FA Cup replay against Newcastle United in January 2001.

Even after he had burst on to the international scene, scoring a spectacular goal on his England debut against Holland and earning a place in Sven Goran Eriksson's squad for the 2002 World Cup finals, his substitute appearances still outnumbered his starts until the early stages of 2002/03.

Vassell continued to knock in the goals on a regular basis until 2004/05, which was his last season for the club. In May 2005, he joined Manchester City.

FRED TURNBULL

BIRTHPLACE: Wallsend-on-Tyne
DATE OF BIRTH: 28 August 1946
DEBUT: Middlesbrough (A), 30 September 1967
VILLA TOTALS: 183 appearances / 3 goals

Such was the high regard in which Fred Turnbull was held at Villa Park, he was granted a testimonial in 1976, two years after he had been forced to retire because of persistent injury problems. His time in claret and blue coincided with some of the leanest years of the club's history but the wholehearted central defender at least had two major achievements to savour.

He was a member of the team who reached the 1971 League Cup final with a memorable semi-final victory over Manchester United, and twelve months later he helped Villa to the Third Division title.

Turnbull arrived on a two-month trial in 1966 and was almost immediately handed a professional contract. The following year he had his initial taste of first-team football and over the next couple of seasons he gradually established himself, with the help of a loan spell at Halifax Town.

It was after Villa's relegation in 1970 that his career really blossomed, Turnbull missing only a handful of games during the Third Division days - and he also made 21 appearances in the club's first season back in Division Two. Unfortunately, he lost his fitness battle and was forced to hang up his boots after playing only ten games in 1973/74.

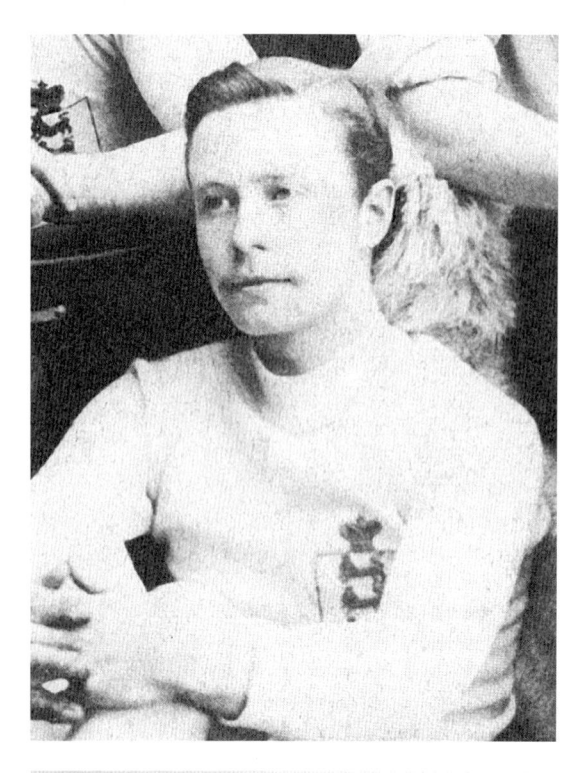

HOWARD VAUGHTON

BIRTHPLACE: Aston
DATE OF BIRTH: 9 January 1861
DEBUT: Wednesbury Strollers (H), FA Cup, 30 October 1880
VILLA TOTALS: 30 appearances / 15 goals

The bald statistics showing only FA Cup games cannot truly reflect the immense contribution Oliver Howard Vaughton made to Aston Villa. The son of prominent Villa supporter, 19-year-old Howard joined Villa in August 1880. In addition to many friendlies, he also played in numerous local cup-ties.

A fine inside-left, Vaughton partnered Eli Davis, later linking up with Oliver Whateley on the right before returning to the left with Dennis Hodgetts. An exponent of close ball control, Vaughton played with skill and style, even if his shooting was inclined to be erratic.

In February 1882, Vaughton and Arthur Brown became the club's first internationals, being capped by England against Ireland in Belfast. Vaughton hit five goals and Brown contributed four to England's 13-0 victory.

He went on to add a further four caps over the next two years, and also excelled at roller and ice-skating, swimming and cycling, as well as being a County cricketer with Warwickshire and Staffordshire and a County hockey player. He was described in the Villa News & Record as 'the finest all-round athlete the Midlands has produced during the past half-century'.

Vaughton gained an FA Cup-winner's medal following a 2-0 win against West Bromwich Albion in the 1887 final, but a serious thigh injury forced him was forced to retire on the eve of League football in 1888. He then began his own silversmith's business in the Birmingham jewellery quarter, and his firm made the replacement FA Cup after the original trophy had been stolen from a shop window in Newtown Row in 1895.

Vaughton was made a Villa vice-president in 1923, became president in June 1924 and was elected to the board in September that year. It was a position he held until ill-health forced his retirement in December 1932. The following February, Vaughton was made a Life Member of the club. He died in January 1937.

RON VLAAR

BIRTHPLACE: Hensbroek, Netherlands
DATE OF BIRTH: 16 February 1985
DEBUT: West Ham United (A), 18 August 2012
VILLA TOTALS: 88 appearances / 2 goals

He was known as Concrete Ron, and the description could not have been more accurate. Ron Vlaar was as solid as concrete at the heart of Villa's defence. Strong in the tackle, and noted for his sensible, no-nonsense distribution, the Dutch centre-back arrived at Villa Park at a time when everyone at the club was still coming to terms with the absence of Stiliyan Petrov, who had been diagnosed with acute leukemia a few months earlier.

Richard Dunne had taken over as captain for the remainder of the previous season, while record signing Darren Bent briefly wore the armband at the start of the 2012/13 campaign.

But after only a handful of matches, Vlaar did enough to convince new manager Paul Lambert that he was a natural leader. His first game as captain was a 2-0 home win over Swansea City in September and despite Villa struggling to avoid relegation, his commanding performances were instrumental in their survival. His first goal for the club was one to savour, too, a stunning long-range drive which paved the way for a 6-1 victory over Sunderland at the end of April.

Vlaar maintained his consistency throughout the following season, which culminated with him being a member of the Netherlands team that reached the 2014 World Cup semi-finals in Brazil. Less than twelve months later, he helped Villa to the FA Cup final, but subsequently became a free agent. In December that year, he rejoined AZ Alkmaar, where he had started his career. He announced his retirement in 2021.

BILLY WALKER

BIRTHPLACE: Wednesbury
DATE OF BIRTH: 29 October 1897
DEBUT: QPR (H), FA Cup, 10 January 1920
VILLA TOTALS: 531 appearances / 244 goals

Billy Walker scored both goals in a 2-1 FA Cup first-round victory on his senior debut in January 1920 and by the end of the season he had collected an FA Cup-winner's medal as Villa beat Huddersfield Town 1-0 in the final.

Walker joined the club in 1915 and remained with Villa until his retirement in November 1933. He had a massive impact at Villa Park and made his final appearance at Portsmouth having set a club record of 531 appearances, which stood until it was passed by Charlie Aitken in December 1973. Walker's overall record of 244 goals still stands.

After scoring on his international debut in October 1920, Walker was capped 18 times, hitting nine goals, and had the distinction of scoring England's first-ever goal at Wembley. Two weeks later he was back at the stadium with Villa. Unfortunately, they lost the 1924 FA Cup final 2-0 to Newcastle United, and he was knocked out after crashing into a goalpost.

Walker, who went on to captain both Villa and England, could shoot with either foot and also possessed superb heading ability as well as being Villa's deputy goalkeeper, a role he filled for England when deputising for the injured Fred Fox in a 3-2 win over France in 1925. He also represented the Football League six times.

Walker netted double figures in twelve consecutive seasons from 1919/20 and was the first player to score a hat-trick of penalties when Villa beat Bradford City 7-1 in November 1921. He netted twelve league and FA Cup hat-tricks, including four goals in a 5-0 home win against Arsenal in August 1920 and four again in a 5-1 win at Villa Park against Sheffield United in December 1929.

Following retirement, he went into management and became only the second person to have played in and then managed an FA Cup-winning team, leading Sheffield Wednesday to FA Cup success in 1935 and repeating the feat with Nottingham Forest in 1959. He died in November 1964.

CHARLIE WALLACE

BIRTHPLACE: Southwick, County Durham
DATE OF BIRTH: 20 January 1885
DEBUT: Manchester United (H), 2 September 1907
VILLA TOTALS: 349 appearances / 58 goals

Charlie Wallace spent over 50 years with Villa after joining the club from Crystal Palace in May 1907. He quickly became a fixture on the right wing and was a firm crowd favourite.

Villa finished runners-up in his first season and went on to take the title in 1909/10. An FA Cup-winner's medal followed in 1913 as Villa chased a league and cup double. Wallace had the misfortune to shoot wide from the penalty spot in the final against Sunderland, but supplied the corner from which Tommy Barber headed the only goal. In the league, Villa were again runners-up, the position in which they finished on four occasions while Wallace was with the club.

He picked up a second FA Cup-winner's medal in the 1920 final - the first after the Great War - and won the last of three caps as England hit back from 4-2 down at half-time for a famous 5-4 victory over Scotland. Wallace also represented the Football League five times.

He joined Oldham Athletic in May 1921, but subsequently returned to Villa Park where he held a range of positions, including junior team coach, boot-room attendant, kit-man, scout, steward and odd-job man. He also worked as a painter and decorator. Wallace died in January 1970.

DAVE WALSH

BIRTHPLACE: Waterford
DATE OF BIRTH: 28 April 1923
DEBUT: Fulham (H), 13 January 1951
VILLA TOTALS: 114 appearances / 40 goals

Despite having a hard act to follow, Dave Walsh was a huge favourite with Villa supporters and ultimately became as popular as Trevor Ford. Although his scoring ratio was not quite as prolific as that of his predecessor, he averaged a goal every three games throughout the early 1950s, and his figure would have been higher, but for a slow start.

After becoming the club's £25,000 record signing in December 1950, the Irishman did not get off the mark until the end of March, when he was on target in a 2-1 victory over Sheffield Wednesday. He then hit two more in a 6-2 thrashing of Stoke City on the final day and from that point, his output made him one of Villa's leading scorers over the following three seasons.

Having played for several clubs in Ireland, Walsh really made his presence felt with Villa's neighbours West Bromwich Albion, netting 100 goals for the Baggies and helping them to promotion in 1949.

He scored in his first six Albion games, a sequence he was never likely to repeat in claret and blue. Even so, he was very much a fans' favourite until his transfer to Walsall in 1955.

A dual Irish international, he won 29 caps for Northern Ireland and the Republic. He died in March 2016.

MARK WALTERS

BIRTHPLACE: Birmingham
DATE OF BIRTH: 2 June 1964
DEBUT: Leeds United (H), 28 April 1982
VILLA TOTALS: 225 appearances / 48 goals

Mark Walters was relatively unknown when he made his Villa debut as a 17-year-old, going on as a substitute against Leeds United a month before the European Cup final. But it was not long before the pace and skill he had displayed in Villa's 1980 FA Youth Cup triumph made him a firm favourite with supporters.

The fast-raiding left-winger was in the team on a frequent basis the following season - including a substitute appearance in the UEFA Super Cup victory over Barcelona - and from the 1983/84 campaign, his career went into overdrive as he constantly tormented opposition full-backs as well as scoring his fair share of goals.

Although Villa went into decline in the mid-1980s, Walters was one of the team's genuine stars during that bleak period, and in 1985/86 he played a total of 53 league and cup goals, scoring 13 goals.

He also made several appearances for England under-21s, although he was restricted to 21 Villa games and just three league goals as the club suffered relegation in 1987.

Despite being back in the side on a regular basis during the first half of Villa's promotion campaign, he was unhappy with life in the Second Division and was transferred to Glasgow Rangers in December 1987.

After winning all three domestic honours north of the border, he joined Liverpool in 1991.

TOM 'PONGO' WARING

BIRTHPLACE: High Tranmere
DATE OF BIRTH: 12 October 1906
DEBUT: Sunderland (A), 25 February 1928
VILLA TOTALS: 225 appearances / 167 goals

Pongo Waring's goalscoring record at Villa was remarkable, a ratio of three goals every four matches. He opened season 1930/31 by scoring all four in a 4-3 win against Manchester United at Old Trafford and repeated the feat a week later in a 6-1 victory over West Ham.

He scored in each of Villa's first seven games and by the end of the season had netted 49 league goals (in 39 games) as Villa hit a record 128 goals. The strike in his only FA Cup game gave him a season total of 50, a club record. Waring also scored on his England debut in Paris, going on to hit four goals in five international appearances.

When he joined Villa from Tranmere Rovers in February 1928 for £4,700 (a record Third Division fee) 23,600 turned up for his first game a reserve match against Birmingham. The crowd were not disappointed - he hit a first-half hat-trick in a 6-2 win, and followed this up with a goal on his league debut the following Saturday as Villa won 3-2 at Sunderland.

Waring was a natural footballer. He had effortless ball control, was commanding in the air and could score with either foot. He used his height and weight to good effect, and opposition defenders always knew they were in for a torrid time. Rated one of the most dangerous centre-forwards between the wars, Pongo was loved by the Villa Park crowd and he was certainly a colourful character.

But in October 1935, Villa hit the bottom of the table, manager James McMullan left the club and Waring asked for a transfer, joining Barnsley the following month. Waring died in December 1980.

STEPHEN WARNOCK

BIRTHPLACE: Ormskirk
DATE OF BIRTH: 12 December 1981
DEBUT: Birmingham City (A), 13 September 2009
VILLA TOTALS: 101 appearances / 3 goals

Stephen Warnock was a role model for any aspiring young footballer; he was professional in everything he did and refused to wilt in the face of adversity. That was never more evident than during his second season at Villa Park. Signed from Blackburn Rovers 15 months earlier, the former Liverpool defender was out of favour with Martin O'Neill's successor Gerard Houllier, being forced to train with the reserve squad.

But another managerial change resulted in an upturn in his fortunes. New boss Alex McLeish restored him to the team and praised his 'phenomenal' attitude in getting on with the job in difficult circumstances. The outcome was that Warnock went on to make over 100 appearances for the club before moving to Leeds United in January 2013.

The accomplished left-back was one of three key defensive signings, along with Richard Dunne and James Collins, made by O'Neill early in the 2009/10 season. All three made their debuts as Villa won the Second City derby 1-0 at St Andrew's and their solid defending helped the club to a sixth-place finish, plus the League Cup final and FA Cup semi-finals.

Warnock also scored the occasional goal for the club, including one which sparked a comeback against his former club Blackburn in the second leg of a League Cup semi-final. Having won the first leg 1-0 at Ewood Park, Villa quickly trailed 2-0 in the return match, but Warnock's goal set the tone for an amazing 6-4 victory.

VILLA STARS A-Z

TOMMY WESTON

BIRTHPLACE: Halesowen
DATE OF BIRTH: August 1890
DEBUT: Manchester City (H), 20 January 1912
VILLA TOTALS: 178 appearances / 0 goals

During the summer of 2007, Eddie Weston made a sentimental visit to Villa Park, stepping on to the famous Villa Park pitch which his father Tommy had graced almost a century earlier. It was an emotional moment for 89-year-old Eddie, who described how Tommy had never boasted about his days as a footballer. "Dad was proud of his achievements," said Eddie, clutching one of his dad's FA Cup medals, "but he never bragged about his achievements".

Yet Tommy Weston could have been forgiven for doing so. After all, not many players can claim to have gained two FA Cup winner's medals either side of a world war! Weston, a proud Black Countryman, did exactly that as he helped Villa to victory over Sunderland in front of 121,919 at the Crystal Palace in the 1913 final, and was also in the side who beat Huddersfield Town at Stamford Bridge in 1920 in the first final after the Great War. There was very nearly a third final appearance, too, Villa reaching the 1914 semi-finals before they lost to Liverpool.

Those big occasions were just three of the 178 games he played for the club, having previously made an impression on the local non-League scene. He and Tommy Lyons provided Villa's regular full-back pairing for three seasons leading up to the outbreak of the First World War and he also played for three seasons after the hostilities, before joining Stoke City in 1922 and retiring two years later. He died in 1973.

ANDREAS WEIMANN

BIRTHPLACE: Vienna
DATE OF BIRTH: 5 August 1991
DEBUT: West Ham United (H), 14 August 2010
VILLA TOTALS: 129 appearances / 24 goals

Popularly known as Andi, Weimann served Villa well over the course of five seasons and had a knack of scoring crucial goals - including his first for the senior side. Villa were battling to climb away from the Premier League danger zone in March 2012 and were heading for a goalless home draw against Fulham until he bravely flung himself forward in stoppage time to force the ball over the line.

In December that year, he was on target twice in a 4-1 win at Norwich in a League Cup quarter-final, and the following season he netted the winner in a famous 3-2 victory over Manchester City before his brace against Hull City helped to secure top-flight survival.

The Austrian striker began his career with the junior ranks of Rapid Vienna before joining Villa's Academy three years later and was a regular scorer for the youth team and reserves before breaking into the first team.

Ironically, he was injured in a Europa League tie against Rapid in only his second game, being ruled out until the following January, when he joined Watford on loan. After being used mostly as a substitute for the 2011/12 campaign, he established himself as a regular the following season and remained a key member of the squad until his transfer to Derby County in June 2015.

259

ASHLEY WESTWOOD

BIRTHPLACE: Nantwich
DATE OF BIRTH: 1 April 1990
DEBUT: Swansea City (H), 15 September 2012
VILLA TOTALS: 162 appearances / 5 goals

His birth date might suggest otherwise, but Ashley Westwood was nobody's fool, producing sound performances in Villa's midfield for four-and-a-half seasons. He went about his job with minimum fuss, describing himself as 'someone who keeps out of the limelight and keeps it simple'. When it came to the business to retaining possession and laying the ball off to teammates, Westwood rarely put a foot wrong in his role as a deep-lying playmaker.

Signed from Crewe Alexandra on the final day of the 2012 summer transfer window, Westwood made his debut on the same day as Christian Benteke, both players going on as substitutes against Swansea City at Villa Park. Having made a leap from the fourth to the top tier of English football, he had to wait until November before making his first starting appearance in a 1-0 win at Sunderland.

But once he had established himself, Westwood maintained a consistently high standard, and despite his deep role, he even contributed a handful of goals, including one in the opening minute against Hull City as Villa won 3-1 in May 2014 to avoid relegation.

He also helped Villa to reach the 2015 FA Cup final, but was unable to prevent them from going down to the Championship twelve months later. After playing in the lower tier for the first half of the 2016/17 season, he was back in the Premier League following a move to Burnley in January 2017.

FREDDIE WHELDON

BIRTHPLACE: Langley Green
DATE OF BIRTH: 1 November 1871
DEBUT: Stoke (H), 2 September 1896
VILLA TOTALS: 139 appearances / 75 goals

George Frederick Wheldon was a brilliant inside-left, noted not only for his goalscoring prowess, but also for the opportunities he created for others. Villa broke their transfer record in obtaining his services from neighbours Small Heath in June 1896, the fee being made up of £100 plus the guarantee of £250 from a game.

Having already won a Second Division championship medal, Wheldon immediately gave Villa fans a taste of what they could expect, scoring twice in 3-1 victory against the Heathens at Perry Barr. He went on to net 23 goals during the season as Villa won the double, including the equaliser against Everton at Crystal Palace in the FA Cup final.

Wheldon certainly lived up to his nickname, Diamond, when he moved across the city. He was top scorer again the following season and in 1899 and 1900, he claimed his second and third League Championship medals

In 1897, Wheldon was called up by England and netted a hat-trick on his international debut, going on to score six goals in four appearances. Wheldon was also a fine cricketer, scoring 4,938 runs for Worcestershire, including three centuries, and taking 93 catches as wicket keeper.

In July 1900, Wheldon moved on to West Bromwich Albion. In his later life, he became an innkeeper in Worcester, where he died in January 1924.

ALBERT WILKES

BIRTHPLACE: Birmingham
DATE OF BIRTH: October 1875
DEBUT: Stoke (H), 3 September 1898
VILLA TOTALS: 159 appearances / 8 goals

"Neat, skilful and scrupulously fair, being on the light side - and yet, withal, magnificently proportioned - he has no use for the heavy lunges occasionally resorted to by players who contribute weight in place of skill."

This is how Albert Wilkes was described in the Villa News & Record in 1907. A wing-half, he was strong in the tackle and possessed the skill and vision to set up openings for his forwards. He started his career with Oldbury Town, joining Villa from Walsall for whom he was centre-half in the first opposition team to win at Villa Park as the Saddlers beat Villa's double-winning team to take the Lord Mayor of Birmingham's Charity Cup in 1897.

Wilkes made his debut in September 1898 and Villa went on to take the league title at the end of his first season. A League Championship medal followed in 1900. Renowned for his never-say-die attitude and for his capacity for hard work, Wilkes represented England in five consecutive internationals during 1901 and 1902, scoring once. He also took up refereeing, and was an excellent singer who delighted thousands in the Music Halls with his baritone voice. He was awarded the Royal Humane Society's Award for rescuing from drowning, a boy who had fallen through the ice at Dartmouth Park, his daughter receiving the same award after saving a child from drowning in the sea at Aberdovey.

Wilkes established a flourishing photographic business, specialising in team groups, individual player profiles and action shots, that was subsequently run by his son Albert junior. Appointed to the Villa board in 1934, Wilkes travelled many thousands of miles seeking new players. Sadly, he was taken ill after watching a game in November 1936 and died of pneumonia eleven days later.

Williams made 43 appearances that season, and although he missed both legs of the opening round against Valur, he then became an integral part of the side who went on to conquer Europe.

A versatile footballer, capable of operating in any number of positions, Williams was at his best as a steady left-back. He joined Villa as an apprentice in 1975, turning professional three years later and making his debut as a substitute against Everton early in the 1978/79 campaign. He played 23 games that season, only for his progress to be halted by an injury which restricted him to just one starting appearance in 1979/80 - although he did have nine games for Walsall during a loan spell in which he helped the Saddlers to promotion from the old Fourth Division.

Then came the glory years, Williams also adding a UEFA Super Cup medal to his league and European Cup honours, and he continued to serve Villa well during the leaner years of the mid-eighties before joining Leeds United in 1987.

PETER WITHE

BIRTHPLACE: Liverpool
DATE OF BIRTH: 30 August 1951
DEBUT: Leeds United (A), 16 August 1980
VILLA TOTALS: 233 appearances / 92 goals

Manager Ron Saunders described Peter Withe as 'the last piece in the jigsaw' when he signed the much-travelled striker from Newcastle United in the summer of 1980. But even the astute Saunders could not have imagined how perfectly Withe would fit into the Villa picture. Within two years, the forceful marksman had more than repaid the club record £500,000 which Villa invested to bring him from St James' Park.

In his debut campaign in claret and blue, Withe scored 20 league goals to inspire Villa to the club's first League Championship crown for 71 years. And while his league output was reduced by 50 per cent the following season, he hit the most important goal in Villa's history to clinch victory over Bayern Munich in the European Cup final.

A powerful, bustling centre-forward, Withe perfectly complemented the pace and anticipation of his striking partner Gary Shaw throughout a glorious chapter of the Villa story. He maintained a high scoring ratio over subsequent seasons, too, and had contributed 92 goals by the time he moved to Sheffield United in 1985.

His prolific output was not the only reason he was so popular. Always a showman, he ran to the Holte terracing at the end of every match to collect a bag of sweets from a supporter.

Withe was 28 when he joined Villa and had already won a championship medal with Nottingham Forest under Brian Clough's management. He had the option of joining several clubs, including his boyhood favourites Everton, but decided Villa Park offered the best prospect of a second medal. His vision could not have been more accurate, and he also won eleven England caps, scoring once.

He later had a spell as Villa's assistant manager when Jozef Venglos was in charge, and subsequently enjoyed considerable success as coach of the Thailand national team.

GARY WILLIAMS

BIRTHPLACE: Wolverhampton
DATE OF BIRTH: 17 June 1960
DEBUT: Everton (H), 16 September 1978
VILLA TOTALS: 302 appearances / 2 goals

Gary Williams could hardly have picked a more opportune time to establish himself as a Villa regular. He played half the games during the title-winning campaign of 1980/81 and really came into his own as the team followed up with their European Cup triumph a year later.

COLIN WITHERS

BIRTHPLACE: Erdington
DATE OF BIRTH: 21 March 1940
DEBUT: Tottenham Hotspur (A), 21 November 1964
VILLA TOTALS: 163 appearances / 0 goals

Goalkeeper Colin Withers had the misfortune to play for Villa during one of the most depressing periods of the club's history - and the picture would have been even bleaker but for his outstanding form. An England schoolboy international, he joined a struggling Villa side in November 1964 and they continued to find the going tough, despite his heroics between the posts.

Fondly known as 'Tiny', his endeavours were not lost on supporters, even though he had previously played for the old enemy Birmingham City. The fans acknowledged just how important Withers was to the team by awarding him the Terrace Trophy in both 1966 and 1967.

The award was of little consolation on the second occasion, Villa being relegated to the old Second Division. At least Withers was spared the ignominy of a second relegation when Villa slipped down to the Third Division in 1970. He had left the club the previous summer to join Lincoln City, subsequently playing in Holland for Go Ahead Eagles. Withers died in December 2020.

PHIL WOOSNAM

BIRTHPLACE: Caersws
DATE OF BIRTH: 22 December 1932
DEBUT: Bolton Wanderers (H), 1 December 1962
VILLA TOTALS: 125 appearances / 29 goals

The term 'thinking man's footballer' could have been invented for Phil Woosnam. Before turning professional with Leyton Orient in 1957, he taught physics in an East London School, having gained a BSc at Bangor University. Once he had committed himself to a career in football, he applied his scientific mind to his activities on the pitch - and threw in a generous helping of artistry. The Welsh midfielder's sublime skills provided a creative spark which set up countless goals for his teammates.

At Villa Park, the main man to benefit was Tony Hateley, who arrived at the club nine months after Woosnam and was Villa's leading scorer for each of the three full seasons the duo played together.

After making the short journey from Orient to West Ham United, Woosnam was a key figure at Upton Park for four years before joining Villa in November 1962. His intelligent passing and vision immediately endeared him to supporters.

He was unfortunate in that Villa were going through a lean period during him time with the club, but his silky skills made him a delight to watch. He was a decent marksman, too. During his final season he hit the target on 20 occasions, and only Hateley scored more.

In the summer of 1966, Woosnam became coach of Atlanta Chiefs and was later appointed commissioner of the North American Soccer League. He died in 2013.

ALAN WRIGHT

BIRTHPLACE: Ashton-under-Lyne
DATE OF BIRTH: 28 September 1971
DEBUT: West Ham United (H), 18 March 1995
VILLA TOTALS: 329 appearances / 5 goals

Alan Wright is a member of an elite band of players to have played more than 300 games for Villa, including two cup finals. A steady full-back, he was in the side who thrashed Leeds United 3-0 in the 1996 League Cup final and was back at Wembley four years later for the last FA Cup final to be played at the old stadium. That one, sadly, ended in a 1-0 defeat by Chelsea.

Wright joined Villa from Blackburn Rovers for £900,000 just before the 1995 transfer deadline, leaving a club who were destined for the Premiership title to help Brian Little's team avoid relegation. Having achieved that objective, he enjoyed considerable success over the next few seasons. Apart from two Wembley finals, there was also an FA Cup semi-final in 1996 and a League Cup semi-final in 2000, plus numerous ventures into Europe.

But he saved his handful of goals for league matches. With a slight variation here and there, all five were unstoppable shots from either the edge of the penalty area or from just outside.

MICK WRIGHT

BIRTHPLACE: Ellesmere Port
DATE OF BIRTH: 25 September 1946
DEBUT: Blackpool (A), 7 September 1963
VILLA TOTALS: 318 appearances / 1 goal

Mick Wright was a loyal servant to Villa for almost a decade, clocking up over 300 appearances, but had the misfortune to be at the club during some of its darkest days. During his lengthy spell at Villa Park, his reliable full-back performances stood out among the mediocrity as Villa were relegated to the Second Division and then to the Third.

At least he had the satisfaction of making a substantial contribution to the team's Third Division championship campaign of 1971/72, although he was denied the opportunity of playing regularly again at a higher level. After the first two matches of the following season, he made way for John Gidman, and eventually retired through injury in May 1973.

Wright joined the club as an apprentice in the summer of 1962, making his debut at Blackpool 14 months later before he had even signed professional.

He played 35 games that season and continued to be Villa's regular right-back throughout the remainder of the 1960s. An England youth international, he scored only one goal for Villa, hitting the target in a 3-0 victory over Manchester City in September 1966. He was granted a testimonial by the club following his enforced retirement.

RON WYLIE

BIRTHPLACE: Glasgow
DATE OF BIRTH: 6 August 1933
DEBUT: Preston North End (H), 22 November 1958
VILLA TOTALS: 244 appearances / 27 goals

Ron Wylie was effectively a farewell gift to Villa from manager Eric Houghton. Having given the Scottish inside-forward his baptism in league football when they were together at Notts County in 1951, Houghton signed Wylie from County for just over £9,000 in November 1958.

A few days later the new boy impressed in his first game for the club, a Villa Park floodlight friendly against Hearts, after which it was announced that Houghton was parting company with the club he had led to FA Cup glory 18 months earlier.

It meant the club were without a manager when Wylie made his league debut, but when Joe Mercer arrived a month later, it quickly became evident that the new boss was as impressed with Wylie as his predecessor had been. Although Villa went down that season, Wylie was a key member of the team who won promotion back to the top flight at the first attempt and followed up with League Cup glory in 1961.

He continued to be a regular until the summer of 1965, when he moved across the city to join Blues, but not before he had collected that season's Terrace Trophy award as well as being voted Midland Footballer of the Year.

In later years, Wylie served Villa as an assistant manager, reserve team coach, scout and community liaison officer, but it is for his playing days in the late 1950s and early 1960s that he is best remembered. He died in April 2020.

DWIGHT YORKE

BIRTHPLACE: Tobago
DATE OF BIRTH: 3 November 1971
DEBUT: Crystal Palace (A), 24 March 1990
VILLA TOTALS: 287 appearances / 98 goals

Dwight Yorke ranks among the greatest players in the club's history - and it's debatable if anyone has been more flamboyant. Signed by Graham Taylor following a Villa trip to Trinidad & Tobago in 1989, the Calypso Kid developed into a world class footballer who simply oozed talent and always played with a smile on his face.

There was even a song recorded in his honour, an adapted version of 'New York, New York' and Holte Enders were only too happy to serenade him with the words: 'It's up to you, Dwight Yorke, Dwight Yorke'.

DICKY YORK

BIRTHPLACE: Birmingham
DATE OF BIRTH: 25 April 1899
DEBUT: Sunderland (A), 30 August 1919
VILLA TOTALS: 390 appearances / 87 goals

If he had not been a footballer, Dicky York would surely have been a successful athlete or rugby player. He ran for Birchfield Harriers at the age of eight and preferred the oval ball to the round one during his school days.

But his turn of speed was eventually put to good use in claret and blue. Having served with the Royal Flying Corps during the First World War, when he played as a guest for Chelsea, he signed for Villa in May 1919 and made his debut in the opening game of the first post-war campaign.

Initially operating as right-half, his appearances were limited over his first couple of seasons, and he was not involved at all in Villa's victorious 1920 FA Cup run. But it was as a right-winger that he made his biggest impression. From the start of 1921/22, he was effectively an automatic choice for nine consecutive seasons and was an ever-present in 1926/27 and 1928/29.

York also won two England caps during that period, as well as playing for Villa in the 1924 FA Cup final. By the time he moved to Port Vale in 1931, he had made nearly 400 appearances and scored 87 goals. He died in 1969.

It was all a long way from his low-key arrival at Villa Park in 1989, after manager Graham Taylor had been impressed with him during a Villa tour to Trinidad and Tobago. At first, despite his obvious talent, Yorke was held back by his slender frame. But once he had settled in there was simply no stopping him.

Some of his goals were outrageous, too, the best of them arguably against Nottingham Forest in 1991. He sprinted through Forest's defence before leaving a defender on his backside with a delightful turn and sending an exquisite chip over goalkeeper Mark Crossley from the edge of the penalty area. Yorke was also on target with the final goal in the 3-0 demolition of Leeds United in the 1996 League Cup final at Wembley. That was just one of 98 goals he scored for Villa, 60 of them in the Premier League.

And for sheer audacity, who can forget his impudent chip from the penalty spot in an FA Cup-tie at Sheffield United in January 1996? Or the (almost) carbon copy against Arsenal's David Seaman at Villa Park a couple of years later? It was so good, he did it twice.

ASHLEY YOUNG

BIRTHPLACE: Stevenage
DATE OF BIRTH: 9 July 1985
DEBUT: Newcastle United (A), 31 January 2007
VILLA TOTALS: 215 appearances / 38 goals

It seemed a hefty outlay when Villa paid Watford a reported initial £8million for the relatively unproven Ashley Young during the January 2007 transfer window; within twelve months it began to look an astute piece of business. Despite scoring on his debut in a 3-1 defeat at Newcastle, Young was only moderately successfully during his first few months in claret and blue, but from then on, he made a massive impact.

Having switched from the role of striker to wide midfielder shortly after his arrival, Young was a regular throughout his first full season, missing only one league match, through suspension, and scoring nine goals. Operating either as a winger or in a free role just behind the strikers, he was a constant threat to opposition defences and his outstanding form earned him his first England cap in November 2007.

But it was during the 2008/09 campaign that he really blossomed, and apart from regular England selections he collected three prestigious awards. He was voted Barclays Player of the Month for both September and December, and was later acclaimed PFA Young Player of the Year.

There was an air of anticipation among Villa fans whenever he was in possession of the ball, and statistics revealed that he led the way for Premier League wide players in terms of goals, assists and crosses. The highlight of a season in which he missed only two league games was his dramatic stoppage-time winner against Everton at Goodison Park, just seconds after the home side had equalised.

It was his second goal of the game, and he again finished the season with nine, a figure he achieved for four consecutive seasons before joining Manchester United in June 2011. After a decade at Old Trafford and a short spell with Inter Milan, Young returned to Villa Park on a free transfer in June 2021.

ASTON VILLA MANAGERS

JIMMY McMULLAN

VILLA MANAGER: June 1934 - October 1935

BIRTHPLACE: Denny, Scotland

DATE OF BIRTH: 26 March 1895 - 28 November 1964

PLAYING CAREER: Third Lanark 1912-1913, Partick Thistle 1913-1921 and 1923-1926, Maidstone United (player-manager) 1921-1923, Manchester City 1926-1933. Scotland international, 16 caps

MANAGERIAL CAREER: Oldham Athletic 1933-1934, Notts County 1936, Sheffield Wednesday 1937-1939

While numerous other clubs had been operating with a team manager for several years, Villa declined to do so until 1934 when, as the club programme revealed: "Aston Villa's methods are to move with the times, as all methods must." The man handed the responsibility of being the club's first manager was Jimmy McMullan, a former Scotland international who had played in two FA Cup finals for Manchester City as well as winning the Scottish Cup with Partick Thistle.

McMullan's pedigree as a player was beyond dispute, and he had translated his intelligence on the pitch into a season in charge of Oldham Athletic before Villa recruited him. He was described in the Villa News & Record as 'a quiet man, with a humorous twinkle in his eye and knowledge of what he wants'.

The same article suggested McMullan would not only be popular, but would achieve the purpose for which for which he had been appointed. Unfortunately, it didn't turn out that way. Villa's first ever game with a manager in charge resulted in a 2-1 defeat by Birmingham at St. Andrew's on 25 August 1934, although his 'home debut' two days later brought a 2-1 victory over Wolves. It was, however, no more than a moderate season, Villa finishing in the same 13th position they had occupied a year earlier, when the team had been picked by the directors.

If McMullan's initial campaign was something of a disappointment, it was nothing compared with the traumatic start to the following season. Villa won only three of their opening eleven games and the manager resigned in the wake of a 7-0 home defeat by West Bromwich Albion. These were clearly troubled times, the board also being rocked by a transfer request from Pongo Waring, one of Villa's finest-ever players.

While Waring subsequently joined Barnsley, Villa's directors were forced to concede that their initial choice of boss had simply not worked out. Although it would be unfair to blame McMullan for the team's continued poor form without his leadership, the end of the season brought only heartache as Villa were relegated for the first time in their history. McMullan died in November 1964.

JIMMY HOGAN

VILLA MANAGER: August 1936 - September 1939

BIRTHPLACE: Nelson

DATE OF BIRTH: 16 October 1882 - 30 January 1974

PLAYING CAREER: Burnley Belvedere 1898, Nelson 1900, Rochdale Town 1901, Burnley 1903, Fulham 1905, Swindon Town 1908, Bolton Wanderers October 1908, Dordecht (Holland) coach 1910. Hogan subsequently had coaching appointments with the Austrian and Swiss national teams, plus MTK (Hungary) Dresden (Germany), Racing Club de France and Lausanne (Switzerland)

MANAGERIAL CAREER: Fulham 1934-35, Austrian national team 1935-36

It would be 54 years before Villa appointed their first foreign manager, but the arrival of Jozef Venglos in 1990 wasn't the first time the club had recruited a new boss from overseas.

Although he was a Lancastrian, Jimmy Hogan had enjoyed considerable success as a coach in Switzerland and Austria and had guided the Austrian national team to the 1936 Olympic final not long before taking over at Villa Park.

ALEX MASSIE

VILLA MANAGER: September 1945 - July 1949

BIRTHPLACE: Possilpark, Scotland
DATE OF BIRTH: 13 March 1906 - 20 September 1977
PLAYING CAREER: Bury 1927-1928, Bethlehem Steel 1928-1930, Hearts 1930-1935, Villa 1935-1939. Scotland international, 18 caps
MANAGERIAL CAREER: Torquay United 1950-1951, Hereford United 1951-1952.

When football resumed on a nationwide basis after the Second World War, Villa needed a new manager. The man they chose was former player Alex Massie, who had helped the club to promotion in 1937/38, three years after being signed from Scottish club Hearts.

Massie actually played in the opening three matches of the 1945/46 campaign before hanging up his boots to concentrate on management. He quickly adapted to the role, leading Villa to runners-up spot in the Football League South as well as guiding them to the quarter-finals of the first post-war FA Cup competition. He was the man in charge, in fact, when a record crowd of 76,588 packed into Villa Park for the quarter-final home leg against Derby County.

With league football back on the agenda the following season, Massie had every reason to feel well satisfied with his achievements. Over the course of thee seasons, Villa finished eighth, sixth and tenth respectively, and he signed some excellent players, including Trevor Ford, Dickie Dorsett, Leslie Smith, Colin H Gibson and Con Martin.

The appointment of a man regarded as one of the finest coaches in football history showed a lot of foresight by Villa's directors. The season was in full flow by the time Hogan arrived and he initially made little impact, Villa falling away to ninth in the Second Division after losing their final six games. But his second campaign at the helm was a resounding success.

Cheered on by average home crowds of around 42,000, Villa took the Second Division by storm to gain promotion as champions and reached the FA Cup semi-finals before going down to Preston North End at Bramall Lane.

Those heady days, featuring a 69,208 attendance for a fourth round Cup-tie against Blackpool and 75,540 for the quarter-final against Manchester City, more than vindicated the board's decision to choose a man whose methods were ahead of his time, but were not always appreciated by English players.

Even so, Villa finished a respectable sixth on their return to the top flight in 1938/39 and we will never know what else Hogan might have achieved. His time as manager was curtailed by the outbreak of the Second World War, which resulted in the 1939/40 season being abandoned after just three matches.

After the war, Hogan worked for Celtic and Brentford as well as having a brief spell back at Villa Park before moving to Hungary, whose national team benefited enormously from his input as they thrashed England 6-3 at Wembley in 1953 and 7-1 in Budapest the following year.

Massie had launched his playing career with Partick Thistle before joining Bury from Ayr United in 1927. The following year he moved to the United States, where he played for Bethlehem Steel in the American Soccer League.

He returned to these shores in 1930 for a brief spell with Dublin club Dolphins before joining Hearts, where his classy performances won him international recognition.

Moving to Villa for £6,000 in December 1935, he was unable to prevent the club's first relegation, but captained the side as they won the Second Division title two years later.

He left the club in July 1949 and was later appointed manager of Torquay United. He also managed Hereford United before retiring from the professional game.

GEORGE MARTIN

VILLA MANAGER: December 1950 - August 1953

BIRTHPLACE: Bathgate, Scotland

DATE OF BIRTH: 14 July 1899 - 6 November 1972

PLAYING CAREER: Hamilton Academical 1920-21, Bo'ness 1921, Hull City 1922-28, Everton 1928-32, Middlesbrough 1932-33, Luton Town 1933-37

MANAGERIAL CAREER: Luton Town 1939-47, Newcastle United 1947-50

George Martin's tenancy as Villa manager has been described in some publications as being less than successful, which is a somewhat harsh appraisal of his time in charge.

While there was no suggestion of Villa challenging for honours while Martin was the boss, their record was comparable with anything achieved at Villa Park during the immediate post-war years.

The team did, to be fair flounder in the bottom half of the table in Martin's first season, but it should not be forgotten that they were already struggling when he took over in December 1950, having won only four games by that stage. The grim situation continued into the New Year - and became considerably worse with five straight defeats during February and March. At that juncture, relegation looked a distinct possibility, but Martin rallied his troops to the point where they lost only once in their final eleven games, climbing to the safety of 15th place.

That was Villa's lowest position since their promotion back to the First Division, but the following season, despite the jolt of a 5-2 opening-day thrashing at Bolton, they eventually finished sixth - the club's highest position for six years. And while that was followed by a mid-table finish twelve months later, the modest league position was accompanied by an FA Cup run which took Villa to the quarter-finals, the furthest they had been in the competition since 1946.

Martin also made a significant signing that season, bringing in Peter McParland from Irish club Dundalk, so his contribution to the Villa story is more than many people give him credit for. In August 1953, he left the club and became a scout for Luton Town, a club he had previously managed and, indeed, would again for a short spell in the sixties.

ERIC HOUGHTON

VILLA MANAGER: September 1953 - November 1958

BIRTHPLACE: Billingsborough
DATE OF BIRTH: 29 June 1910 - 1 May 1996
PLAYING CAREER: Villa 1927-1946, Notts County 1946-49
England international, 7 caps
MANAGERIAL CAREER: Notts County 1949-53

Anyone privileged enough to have been in Eric Houghton's company during his later years will have marvelled at his entertaining and absorbing recollections of life at Villa Park.

There was certainly plenty to recall. Here was a man who did it all (with the exception of becoming chairman) during an association with the club that spanned more than 60 years.

Initially a player with a fearsome shot (see the Villa A-Z) he subsequently served on the board before being appointed senior vice-president in 1983.

More than anything, though, he is best remembered as the manager who led Villa to FA Cup glory over favourites Manchester United at Wembley in 1957. Not that Houghton's early years at the helm were quite so successful.

After taking over from George Martin in September 1953, his debut campaign saw Villa finish a modest 13th, although there was a big improvement a year later as they climbed into the top six.

If Houghton felt he had discovered a winning formula, he was bitterly disappointed. The upward trend ground to a halt in 1955-56, when Villa only narrowly avoided relegation and their immediate prospects looked bleak. But that near-disaster was followed by a triumph which was not repeated by Villa throughout the remainder of the 20th century.

While the team's league form was stabilised to the extent that they occupied a respectable position in the top half of the table, it was their FA Cup run, culminating in Peter McParland's two match-winning goals against United, which captured supporters' imagination.

Apart from guiding the side to the Cup, Houghton was also the man who signed Gerry Hitchens, one of the club's most revered strikers, although the manager would not be around to reap the benefit of Hitchens' most prolific period in claret and blue.

A disappointing 1957-58 campaign saw Villa slip down to 14th in the league and a catastrophic start to the following season resulted in Houghton being sacked in November 1958.

He will always be fondly remembered, though, for that famous Wembley victory over United. He will forever hold the distinction of being the first Villa manager to lead the club to FA Cup glory.

JOE MERCER

VILLA MANAGER: December 1958 - July 1964

BIRTHPLACE: Ellesmere Port
DATE OF BIRTH: 9 August 1914 - 9 August 1990
PLAYING CAREER: Everton 1932-46, Arsenal 1946-54, England international, 5 caps (plus 27 wartime)
MANAGERIAL CAREER: Sheffield United 1955-58, Manchester City 1965-1972, England (caretaker) 1977

Although they would never attain the legendary status of Manchester United's Busby Babes, the Villa team nurtured under Joe Mercer's management also leaned heavily towards youth.

Like Matt Busby at Old Trafford, Mercer had a great belief in developing his club's talented youngsters, who became popularly known in the early sixties as Mercer's Minors.

Mercer's first task as boss, however, was to fight a relegation battle and, for the second time in his early managerial career, it was a battle he lost, having also gone down in his first season in charge of Sheffield United.

When he succeeded Eric Houghton in December 1958, Villa were bottom of the First Division and despite a minor recovery in March, when they won three consecutive matches, their fate was sealed by Ronnie Allen's infamous late equaliser for Albion in the final game.

The new manager did, however, steer his struggling team to the FA cup semi-finals - a feat they repeated 12 months later, during a campaign which saw them bounce back to the top flight as Second Division champions.

It was over the course of the following two seasons that Mercer assembled his 'Minors', introducing players such as Alan Deakin, John Sleeuwenhoek, Alan Baker, Jimmy McMorran and a young Scot by the name of Charlie Aitken, who would go on to become Villa's record appearance holder.

The youth policy paid dividends, too. In their first season back in the top division, Villa finished ninth and were the inaugural winners of the League Cup; the following season they moved up to seventh and were FA Cup quarter-finalists; twelve months later, despite a disappointing league campaign, they again reached the League Cup final before losing on aggregate to Birmingham City.

But 1963-64 proved to be one season too far for Mercer. Against the backdrop of declining league form (Villa slid to 19th) there were early exits from both cup competitions. The strain was beginning to take its toll and in July, Mercer stood down because of ill-health.

It was a sad conclusion for someone who was an immensely popular figure and who had also enjoyed a hugely successful playing career, but there was plenty of life after Villa for Joe Mercer.

After a year out of the game, he returned as manager of Manchester City, a club he led to the First Division title, the FA Cup, the League Cup and the European Cup Winners' Cup. He also had a brief spell as caretaker manager of England following Sir Alf Ramsey's departure in 1974.

DICK TAYLOR

VILLA MANAGER: July 1964 - May 1967

BIRTHPLACE: Wolverhampton
DATE OF BIRTH: 9 April 1918 - 28 January 1995
PLAYING CAREER: Wolverhampton Wanderers 1934, Grimsby Town 1935-48, Scunthorpe United 1948-54

Dick Taylor was a natural successor to Joe Mercer in the managerial hot seat. He had been Mercer's assistant for the previous six years and was well-acquainted with the former manager's methods.

If the directors' decision to promote from within the club initially appeared to make a great deal of sense, however, it was hardly a successful move.

In each of Taylor's first two seasons, Villa had to settle for a modest final place of 16th, although they did reach the League Cup semi-finals in 1965 before going out 4-3 on aggregate to Chelsea.

Sadly, the notion that Villa were at least established as a top flight club was crushed unceremoniously two years later. While English football

TOMMY CUMMINGS

VILLA MANAGER: July 1967 - November 1968

BIRTHPLACE: Sunderland
DATE OF BIRTH: 12 December 1928 - 12 July 2009
PLAYING CAREER: Burnley 1947-1963, Mansfield Town 1963-64
MANAGERIAL CAREER: Mansfield Town 1963-1967

Tommy Cummings was a huge success in claret and blue. Unfortunately for Villa, he is best remembered for his defensive feats with Burnley, rather than as manager at Villa Park.

A solid centre-half during his playing days, Cummings made more than 400 appearances in Burnley's claret and blue, helping the Lancashire club to the First Division title in 1960.

He then moved into management with Mansfield Town, initially in a player-manager capacity as the Stags won promotion from the Fourth Division in his first season at Field Mill.

But his switch to Villa Park in the summer of 1967 hardly had the effect the club's directors were hoping for. Not for the first time in football history, a relegated team struggled in the lower tier and Villa had to settle for 16th place in Division Two as their average attendance slipped below 20,000 for the first time since the war.

When the team again struggled at the start of the 1968-69 campaign, the writing was on the wall for Cummings, who was sacked after a depressing sequence which yielded just two wins from the first 18 league matches and left Villa entrenched in the relegation zone.

To be fair, the manager was not the only one to pay the price of failure and it wasn't long afterwards that a boardroom upheaval resulted in Doug Ellis being installed as the Villa's new chairman.

Cummings had been in the job for merely 16 months. It would have been no consolation to him that his successor would not last that long.

was generally on a high following the nation's World Cup triumph, the feelgood factor failed to transmit itself to Villa Park.

Taylor, noted for his dedication and hard work, was unable to prevent relegation for only the third time in the club's history as Villa suffered some humiliating defeats and finished second from bottom.

In hindsight, the manager's biggest mistake was probably the sale of Tony Hateley to Chelsea in October 1966. Hateley had been the club's leading marksman for the previous three seasons - he scored 27 in 1965-66 - and without his invaluable contribution, the team struggled badly in front of goal.

It was no real surprise when Taylor was dismissed, although no-one could have imagined at the time that he would do Villa a great service 20 years later.

In 1987 he acted as an intermediary when his namesake Graham Taylor was appointed as manager, having formed a lifelong friendship with Graham's father Tom during his days as a coach at Scunthorpe United in the early fifties.

It was a gesture Dick Taylor was delighted to make. Although he left the club's employment in 1967, he subsequently ran a sports shop in Witton, not far from the ground, and was a season ticket holder at Villa Park until his death at the age of 76.

TOMMY DOCHERTY

VILLA MANAGER: December 1968 - January 1970

BIRTHPLACE: Glasgow

DATE OF BIRTH: 24 April 1928 - 31 December 2020

PLAYING CAREER: Celtic 1947-1949, Preston North End 1949-1958, Arsenal 1958-1961, Chelsea 1961-1962. Scotland international, 25 caps

MANAGERIAL CAREER: Chelsea 1961-1967, Rotherham Utd 1967-1968, QPR 1968, Porto 1970-1971, Scotland 1971-1972, Manchester United 1972-1977, Derby County 1977-1979, QPR 1979-1980, Sydney Olympic 1981, Preston North End 1981-1982, South Melbourne 1982-1983, Sydney Olympic 1983, Wolverhampton Wanderers 1984-1985, Altrincham 1987-1988

Tommy Docherty was in charge at Villa Park for just 13 months. Yet if you were to ask any supporter to name all of the club's managers, his name would undoubtedly be among the first to be mentioned.

His time at Villa may have been short, but it was never dull. The controversial, outspoken, sometimes inspirational former Scotland international left an indelible mark on this famous club.

He was quick-witted, too, and some of his one-liners have become part of Villa folklore. Assured by Doug Ellis that "I'm right behind you, Tommy," the Doc responded: "I want you right in front of me, chairman, so I can see what you're doing!"

While that remark still raises a laugh four decades later, it gave an indication of the uneasy relationship between chairman and manager.

Yet it could all have been so different. Having cut his managerial teeth over a six-year period at Chelsea, Docherty had spent a year with Rotherham United before spending just 28 days as boss of QPR.

He arrived at Villa just before Christmas 1968, shortly after Ellis had been elected chairman and it seemed to be a marriage made in Heaven as a team who had seemed destined for relegation made a miraculous recovery.

Starting with a 2-1 home win over Norwich City, Villa enjoyed a 13-match run in which they lost only once, and safety was assured. The fans responded, too. Where gates had been falling, more than 41,000 turned up for the Boxing Day victory over Cardiff City, while 59,084 packed into Villa Park for a fourth-round FA Cup replay against Southampton.

The momentum, unfortunately, was not maintained. Although supporters kept the faith, Docherty's initial impact was not sustained the following season and it was late September before the team recorded their first league win.

There was no happy Christmas this time around. On 19th January, with Villa rooted to the bottom of the Second Division, Docherty was sacked and an incredible chapter of Villa's history was at and end.

Docherty's career certainly wasn't. During the course of the next 18 years he was in charge of nine different club sides as well as having a spell as Scotland manager. That preceded five years at Manchester United, who he led to FA Cup glory against Liverpool in 1977.

He also managed in Australia, as well as having spells with charge of Preston North End and Wolves. He died in December 2020.

VIC CROWE

VILLA MANAGER: January 1970 - May 1974

BIRTHPLACE: Abercynon, Glamorgan

DATE OF BIRTH: 31 January 1932 - 21 January 2009

PLAYING CAREER: Villa 1954-64, Peterborough United 1964-67, Wales international, 16 caps

MANAGERIAL CAREER: Portland Timbers 1975-76 and 1980-82

Vic Crowe embarked on what was effectively Mission Impossible when he took over as manager early in 1970. Villa were bottom of the Second Division, having won just four games, and were staring relegation in the face, even with four months of the season remaining.

And while Crowe had been an outstanding servant to the club as a player and had returned the previous year in a coaching capacity, the task was simply too much.

Circumstances conspired to give Vic Crowe the unwanted distinction of being the man who took Villa into the old Third Division for the first time

RON SAUNDERS

VILLA MANAGER: June 1974 - February 1982

BIRTHPLACE: Birkenhead
DATE OF BIRTH: 6 November 1932 - 7 December 2019
PLAYING CAREER: Everton 1951-55, Tonbridge 1955-57, Gillingham 1957-58, Portsmouth 1958-64, Watford 1964-65, Charlton Athletic 1965-67
MANAGERIAL CAREER: Yeovil Town 1967-69, Oxford United 1969, Norwich City 1969-1973, Manchester City 1973-74, Birmingham City 1982-1986, West Bromwich Albion 1986-1987

Ron Saunders is regarded by many supporters as the best manager in Villa's history - and he was undisputedly the most successful.

Under Saunders, the business of winning trophies was almost taken for granted at Villa Park. The club were playing in the old Second Division when he was appointed; by the time he left they were champions of England and on the threshold of European Cup glory.

Those feats were recognised when, at the age of 74, was guest of honour at Villa's game against Manchester United in December 2006. He was also present the following May at the celebrations to mark the 25th anniversary of the 1982 European Cup triumph.

It would, indeed, have been fitting had he remained in charge of the team he had built when they enjoyed Villa's finest hour – victory over German giants Bayern Munich in Rotterdam. Unfortunately, he left in February that year following a dispute with the Board over his contract.

Even the unfortunate manner of his exit, though, could not detract from his achievements over the previous eight years.

in their history – yet he was also in charge through a period which is remembered fondly by many supporters.

In his first full season, he took them to fourth place in the lower tier, and if many people had hoped for an immediate return to Division Two, there was, at least, the consolation of an unforgettable League Cup run.

If Crowe is cruelly referred to as the manager who took Villa to their lowest point, he is also the inspiration as they scaled one of their greatest heights – a 3-2 aggregate win over Manchester United in the League Cup semi-final.

There was no disgrace in a 2-0 Wembley defeat by Tottenham in the final, either, and the following season Villa took the league by storm as they became champions with an average home attendance of nearly 32,000, including 48,110 – a record for the Third Division – for the 2-1 home win over Bournemouth.

Crowe derived great satisfaction, too, as Villa finished third in Division Two in 1973. Unfortunately they were unable to maintain the momentum, sliding to 14th the following year, and Crowe was sacked.

Having previously coached Atlanta Chiefs, he headed back to America after leaving Villa, this time as chief coach to Portland Timbers, with whom he had a second spell in the early 1980s.

He died in January 2009 at the age of 76.

275

In his first season, he guided Villa to promotion back to the top flight plus a League Cup final victory over Norwich City, and his reward for the "double" was the accolade of Manager of the Year.

Villa were back at Wembley for another League Cup final in 1977, this time against Everton. After a goalless stalemate under the twin towers, the teams drew 1-1 in the replay at Hillsborough before Villa emerged 3-2 winners after extra-time in the second replay at Old Trafford.

If two trophies in the space of three seasons satisfied the fans' desire for a quick fix of success, Saunders was constantly striving for even greater honours and in 1980-81 he led Villa to the First Division title for the first time in 71 years.

The club employed a squad of just 14 players that season, and although the following campaign was disappointing on the home front, those players carried Villa to the European Cup quarter-finals before Saunders' untimely departure shortly before the clash against Dynamo Kiev.

As a player, Saunders had been a prolific goalscorer, netting more than 200 goals during a 13-year career – and his success continued into management. He guided Norwich to the Second Division title in 1972 and the League Cup the following year before taking Manchester City to the 1974 final.

After leaving Villa, he remained in the West Midlands, spending four years with Birmingham City before ending his career at West Bromwich Albion.

He died in December 2019 at the age of 87.

TONY BARTON

VILLA MANAGER: April 1982 - June 1984

BIRTHPLACE: Sutton, Surrey
DATE OF BIRTH: 8 April 1937 - 20 August 1993
PLAYING CAREER: Fulham 1954-59, Nottingham Forest 1959-61, Portsmouth 1961-67
MANAGERIAL CAREER: Northampton Town 1984-85, Portsmouth (caretaker) 1991

If Ron Saunders was the manager who paved the way for Villa's European Cup triumph, Tony Barton was the man who ensured that the task was completed. Having previously been manager's assistant, he took over as caretaker when Saunders resigned and quickly convinced the Board that he was the man for job.

After some impressive Villa performances during February and March, including a European Cup quarter-final victory over Dynamo Kiev, Barton's appointment on a permanent basis was announced on 1 April, a couple of days after a 2-1 victory over neighbours West Bromwich Albion.

It proved to be a prudent decision. The Albion result was the first in a run of four straight league wins which saw Villa turn around a generally below-par First Division campaign to eventually finish eleventh.

More important still, it galvanised the squad in readiness for their priority of European Cup success. The first game after Barton officially took control was the first leg of the semi-final against Anderlecht,

one of the top clubs on the continent, and Tony Morley's superb goal secured a 1-0 lead which Villa defended resolutely throughout a turbulent return match in Brussels.

It has been suggested that Barton had no great influence over the greatest achievement in Villa's history, that he merely allowed the players to continue with the methods they had employed under Saunders as they went on to beat Bayern Munich in the final in Rotterdam.

If that is so, it was a sign of good management as the team responded to his low-key approach, and Barton certainly made his mark the following season as Villa rediscovered their league form to climb back into the top six.

In hindsight, the 1983-84 was no great disaster, either, Villa finishing tenth in the table and reaching the League Cup semi-finals before going out to Everton. The problem for Barton was that it fell a long way short of the championship and European Cup triumphs of 1981 and 1982 and he was relieved of his duties.

He subsequently managed Northampton Town and also had a spell as caretaker boss of Portsmouth. He died after suffering a heart attack at the age of 56 in 1993.

GRAHAM TURNER

VILLA MANAGER: July 1984 - September 1986

BIRTHPLACE: Ellesmere Port

DATE OF BIRTH: 5 October 1947

PLAYING CAREER: Wrexham 1964-68, Chester City 1968-73, Shrewsbury Town 1973-83

MANAGERIAL CAREER: Shrewsbury Town 1978-84, Wolverhampton Wanderers 1986-94, Hereford United 1995-2009 and 2010, Shrewsbury Town 2010-2014

Graham Turner was a manager whose ability to work on a shoestring budget made him a huge success at Shrewsbury Town before his time with Villa and again afterwards with both Wolves and Hereford United.

His spell in charge of Villa, unfortunately, was rather less remarkable, mainly because he was not nearly as comfortable dealing with high-earning top flight footballers as he was at discovering and nurturing young talent.

After taking over from Tony Barton in the summer of 1984, Turner could hardly have wished for a better start to his Villa managerial career, his team kicking-off the season with back-to-back wins over Midland rivals Coventry City and Stoke City.

He was quickly reminded of the size of his task when Villa were brought down to earth with heavy defeats by Newcastle United and Nottingham Forest, although his first season as boss wasn't without its moments, the team finishing a respectable tenth.

If Turner hoped to use his moderate debut campaign success as a springboard to bigger and better things, he was bitterly disappointed.

His second season kicked off with a 4-0 thumping at Manchester United and Villa slid to a final position of 16th, although they did manage to reach the League Cup semi-finals before going down 4-3 on aggregate to Oxford United.

The European Cup-winners of just four years earlier were now a club very much in decline, and the 1986-87 season was just six matches old when Turner was sacked. After four defeats and one win in the opening five fixtures, a humiliating 6-0 setback at Nottingham Forest proved to be a defeat too far for the former England youth international.

As player-manager at Gay Meadow, he had led Shrewsbury Town to the Third Division title in 1978-79, while he later guided Wolves from Division Four to Division Two in consecutive seasons as well as leading the Molineux club to a Sherpa Van Trophy triumph over Burnley at Wembley in 1988.

He subsequently steered Hereford back into the Football League after several seasons in the Conference before ending his career with a second spell in charge at Shrewsbury.

BILLY McNEILL

VILLA MANAGER: September 1986 - May 1987

BIRTHPLACE: Bellshill, Scotland
DATE OF BIRTH: 2 March 1940 - 22 April 2019
PLAYING CAREER: Celtic 1957-1975. Scotland international, 29 caps
MANAGERIAL CAREER: Clyde 1977, Aberdeen 1977-78, Celtic 1978-83 and 1987-91, Manchester City 1983-86, Hibernian (caretaker) 1998

Billy McNeill is jokingly referred to as the manager who took two clubs down in the same season. That's not strictly true because he left Manchester City with the campaign only a few weeks old and can hardly be held accountable for their demise after his departure.

But, having taken over from Graham Turner in September and having initially turned Villa's fortunes around, he was the man at the helm as the club suffered relegation for the first time since sliding into the Third Division 17 years earlier.

At the time, McNeill's eight-month tenure made him the club's shortest-serving manager, other than caretaker bosses, and he is certainly not remembered with any great affection.

Yet his record north of the border, both as a player and a manager, is outstanding. Regarded by many as Celtic's greatest captain, he led the Parkhead side to nine Scottish titles, seven Scottish Cups and six Scottish League Cups, as well as becoming the first British player to hold aloft the European Cup when Celtic's 'Lisbon Lions' beat Inter Milan 2-1 in the 1967 final.

When he returned to Parkhead in a managerial role, the Glasgow giants won the championship three times and the Scottish Cup and League Cup once each.

There was further success, too, when he left Villa and headed back to Scotland in 1987, Celtic winning a league and cup double in their centenary year, followed by another cup triumph the following year.

Other than winning promotion with Manchester City, though, he had nothing to show for his endeavours at either Maine Road or Villa Park. He died at the age of 79 in April 2019.

GRAHAM TAYLOR

VILLA MANAGER: May 1987 - June 1990 & Feb 2002 - May 2003

BIRTHPLACE: Worksop
DATE OF BIRTH: 15 September 1944 - 12 January 2017
PLAYING CAREER: Grimsby Town 1962-68, Lincoln City 1968-72
MANAGERIAL CAREER: Lincoln City 1972-77, Watford 1977-87, England 1990-93, Wolverhampton Wanderers 1994-95, Watford 1996 and 1997-2001

Villa pulled off a major coup when they lured Graham Taylor away from Watford in the summer of 1987. He effectively had a job for life at Vicarage Road, having steered the Hornets from the Fourth Division to the top flight in the space of five seasons. Even more impressive, Watford had finished runners-up in 1983 to secure UEFA Cup qualification and had then reached the 1984 FA Cup final before going down to Everton.

It was a track record which made Taylor, who had also won the Fourth Division title while in charge at Lincoln City, one of the most respected managers in English football. Watford's rock-star owner Elton John had even dedicated a song to Taylor on one of his albums and it was difficult to envisage the manager ever following anything other than the Yellow Brick Road.

But by the time Villa came calling, Taylor clearly felt he had achieved as much as possible with Watford and the claret and blue army were delighted when chairman Doug Ellis managed to lure him up the M1 to Villa Park. Not that the new boss pulled any punches about the state of the club who had recruited his services.

Alarmed at Villa's decline since their 1982 European Cup triumph - they had just been relegated to the old Second Division - he spent several weeks assessing what he had inherited and publicly declared the club as 'a shambles.'

Taylor's initial task was to restore some semblance of order to a club which was undeniably in decline and he did so with great effect. By the end of his first season, Villa were back in the First Division, clinching promotion as runners-up to Millwall.

Getting back to the top division was one thing, staying there was quite another matter, as Taylor discovered the following season. Although he had considerably strengthened the squad, Villa struggled for much of the 1988-89 campaign and only avoided relegation when West Ham lost at Liverpool after Taylor's men had completed their own programme.

ASTON VILLA MANAGERS

With the addition of Paul McGrath and Kent Nielsen, though, the team fared much better the following season, finishing runners-up to Liverpool and reaching the quarter-finals of the FA Cup. Unfortunately, there was a price to pay - Taylor's achievements brought him to the attention of the Football Association, who were looking for a replacement for Bobby Robson after the 1990 World Cup finals.

Ellis reluctantly let him go, although chairman and manager were reunited eleven years later. After his time with England, Taylor took charge of Wolverhampton Wanderers and subsequently returned to Watford, guiding the Hornets to the Premiership.

He resigned after Watford were relegated after just one season, and in 2001, he took on a role as a non-executive director of Villa. When John Gregory left the following February, Taylor became the first Villa manager to be appointed for a second time, although this time around he was nowhere near as successful.

After consolidating during the remaining months of 2001-02, Villa could manage only 16th place the following season and he decided it was time to leave. Taylor, who later worked as a co-commentator for BBC Radio 5 Live, died in January 2017 after suffering a heart attack.

JOZEF VENGLOS

VILLA MANAGER: July 1990 - May 1991

BIRTHPLACE: Ruzombroek, Czechoslovakia

DATE OF BIRTH: 18 February 1936 - 26 January 2021

PLAYING CAREER: Slovan Bratislava 1954-1966

MANAGERIAL CAREER: Prague Sydney 1966, New South Wales 1966-67, Australia 1967-69, VSS Kosice 1969-71, Czech under-23s 1970-72, Slovan Bratislava 1973-76, Czechoslovakia 1978-82 and 1988-90,Sporting Club de Portugal 1983-84, Kuala Lumpur 1985-87, Malaysia 1986-88, Fenerbahche 1991-93, Slovakia 1993-95, Oman 1995-97, Celtic 1998-99, JEF United Ichihara 2002

Dr Jozef Venglos made a piece of Villa history in the summer of 1990 when he became the club's first overseas manager. It was certainly a bold move in the wake of Graham Taylor's departure to become England coach, but one which was doomed to failure.

Although Venglos had vast knowledge and experience, and had just led Czechoslovakia to the World Cup quarter-finals, his methods simply didn't suit the English game.

A strict disciplinarian who was passionate about his work, he could not understand when his players were not completely distraught following a defeat or enjoyed a beer after a match.

Although there was no question about his pedigree - he had enjoyed two league championship successes during his time in charge of Slovan Bratislava - there was never any prospect of a repeat at Villa Park.

Although the 1990-91 campaign was punctuated by some fine performances - most notably a 2-0 first-leg success over Inter Milan in the UEFA Cup - it was generally one long struggle, with Villa only narrowly avoiding relegation.

The team seemed unable to respond to his coaching methods, and after a humiliating 5-1 home defeat by Manchester City in late April, the Birmingham Mail ran a back page headline pleading: 'For God's sake go, Dr Jo'.

It was a piece of sensationalism which was met by condemnation from within the club, but a parting of the ways was inevitable. Venglos, aware that things were not working out, even told chairman Doug Ellis, he should do what he believed to be right for the club. The club's first overseas managerial adventure was over after just one season. He died in January 2021.

RON ATKINSON

VILLA MANAGER: June 1991 - November 1994

BIRTHPLACE: Liverpool
DATE OF BIRTH: 18 March 1939
PLAYING CAREER: Oxford United 1959-71
MANAGERIAL CAREER: Kettering Town 1971-74, Cambridge United 1974-78, West Bromwich Albion 1978-81 and 1987-88, Manchester United 1981-86, Atletico Madrid 1988-89, Sheffield Wednesday 1989-91 and 1997-98, Coventry City 1995-96, Nottingham Forest 1999

Originally on Villa's books as a teenager, Ron Atkinson made his name as a long-serving member of the Oxford United team who rose from the Southern League to the Football League Second Division in the space of six years.

He then embarked on a successful managerial career and was mentioned as a potential Villa boss on numerous occasions before it came to fruition in the summer of 1991. After the low-key Jo Venglos, the club badly needed a high-profile figure, and Big Ron fitted the bill perfectly. He had steered West Bromwich Albion to the UEFA Cup quarter-finals of 1978-79, he had inspired Manchester United to two FA Cup triumphs (1983 and 1985), he had managed Spanish club Atletico Madrid - and he had just guided Sheffield Wednesday to a League Cup final victory over United.

Not for the first time in his career, though, he courted controversy by accepting the Villa job after assuring Sheffield Wednesday he was happy to remain at Hillsborough. Ironically, the fixtures for the following season threw up Wednesday v Villa on the opening day and he had to endure a vitriolic reception on his return to South Yorkshire. Even so, he had the last laugh as Villa hit back from two-down to record a 3-2 win which laid the foundation for a successful campaign in which Villa finished seventh and reached the FA Cup quarter-finals.

Atkinson's second season in charge was better still. He had the distinction of being the club's first manager in the new FA Premier League and guided them to runners-up spot, albeit ten points behind Manchester United.

The master of witty one-liners, Big Ron insisted that his teams play with a touch of flamboyance and while their league form was inconsistent, the following season he led them to League Cup glory. Three years earlier he had masterminded Wednesday's success over his former club United at Wembley; now he repeated the feat as he tactically outwitted Alex Ferguson in the 1994 final. His introduction of 19-year-old Graham Fenton into a five-man midfield worked wonders as Villa ran out 3-1 winners.

The remainder of the season, unfortunately, was very much an anti-climax, Villa winning only twice in their last nine games, and the trend spilled over into the 1994-95 campaign.

Despite a five-match unbeaten start and a memorable UEFA Cup victory over Inter Milan, Villa endured a dismal league sequence which yielded just one point from a possible 27. It was all the more infuriating because they were still, by and large, playing attractive football, but chairman Doug Ellis's patience was running thin. The day after Villa lost 4-3 to Wimbledon at Selhurst Park, having held a 3-1 lead, Atkinson was informed his services were no longer required.

BRIAN LITTLE

VILLA MANAGER: November 1994 - February 1998

BIRTHPLACE: Newcastle-upon-Tyne
DATE OF BIRTH: 25 November 1953
PLAYING CAREER: Aston Villa 1970-79. England international, 1 cap
MANAGERIAL CAREER: Wolverhampton Wanderers 1986, Darlington 1989-91, Leicester City 1991-94, Stoke City 1998-99, West Bromwich Albion 1999-2000, Hull City 2000-02, Tranmere Rovers 2003-06, Wrexham 2007

If Brian Little's arrival at Villa Park as a player had been straightforward, his return to the club in the manager's chair 24 years later could hardly have been more controversial.

In the wake of Ron Atkinson's departure, the club quickly identified Little as the man to revive their fortunes, but this business of getting him away from Leicester City, the club he had guided back to the top flight, was no easy matter.

Leicester were adamant they would not release him from his contract and ultimately he was forced to walk out in order to fulfil his dream

ASTON VILLA MANAGERS

JOHN GREGORY

VILLA MANAGER: February 1998 - January 2002

BIRTHPLACE: Scunthorpe
DATE OF BIRTH: 11 May 1954
PLAYING CAREER: Northampton Town 1972-77, Villa 1977-79, Brighton & Hove Albion 1979-81, QPR 1981-85, Derby County 1985-88, Plymouth Argyle 1990, Bolton Wanderers 1990,
England international, 6 caps.
MANAGERIAL CAREER: Portsmouth 1989-90, Plymouth Argyle 1990, Wycombe Wanderers 1996-98, Derby County 2002-03, QPR 2006-07

Rarely in the history of football has there been such a quick appointment as that of John Gregory as Villa's manager. Barely 24 hours after Brian Little's departure, Villa unveiled their former midfielder and coach as his successor.

It was an announcement greeted with cynicism by the national press, many of whom regarded Gregory, who had previously been a coach under Little's management at both Leicester City and Villa, as nothing more than a panic appointment. Yet by the end of the season, he was being hailed as a miracle worker as Villa, having been looking over their shoulders towards the relegation zone when he arrived, climbed to seventh in the final table and qualified for the UEFA Cup.

It seemed Gregory could do no wrong. In his first match in charge, he inspired the expensive, but previously ineffective Stan Collymore to a two-goal performance in a 2-1 win over Liverpool, and Villa produced some delightful football as they won nine of their final 11 league games.

of managing Villa. And just like Atkinson before him, he had to endure a hostile reception at his former club when he took Villa to Filbert Street in only his third game in charge.

With Villa hovering around the relegation zone at the time of his appointment, Little's brief was simply to retain Premiership status with a team of quality, but ageing players. He achieved that objective as Villa secured safety with a 1-1 draw at Norwich City on the final day, and then set about reshaping the side around three major summer signings, defender Gareth Southgate, midfielder Mark Draper and Serbian striker Savo Milosevic.

Little did this to such good effect that the 1995-96 campaign turned out to be the club's most successful season of the Premier League era. They finished fourth in the league, reached the FA Cup semi-finals and won the League Cup with an emphatic 3-0 victory over Leeds United at Wembley, where Milosevic opened the scoring with a magnificent goal.

The League Cup triumph saw Villa return to European competition the following season, although they fell at the first hurdle to Swedish part-timers Helsingborgs, it was another good campaign on the domestic front.

Despite early exits from both the League Cup and FA Cup, Villa finished fifth to once again secure a UEFA Cup place - and Little underlined his ambitions by splashing out a club record £7m on striker Stan Collymore from Liverpool.

It was a bold move which, sadly, proved to be the beginning of the end for the manager.

Rather than inspiring the team to greatness, Collymore's arrival coincided with the worst start in the club's history - four straight defeats - and although the team recovered, they were still languishing in 15th place in February, when Little shocked everyone by resigning.

It got better, too, Villa opening the following campaign with a 12-match unbeaten sequence which represented the best start in the club's history. The manager even gathered his players for a celebratory team photo on the pitch at The Dell after they had broken the record with a 4-1 victory over Southampton.

With Villa still top of the table early in the New Year, there was even talk of Gregory as a possible England manager, yet by November his job was under threat.

Having fallen away to sixth place in 1998-99, Villa started the following season brightly before suffering a slump which saw them slide into the bottom half of the table. Gregory weathered the storm, though and Villa eventually finished sixth as well as battling their way to the last FA Cup final to be staged at the old Wembley Stadium.

Sadly, Villa's drab display in a 1-0 defeat by Chelsea reflected the more negative approach employed by the manager by this stage, and this was followed by another largely uninspiring campaign, albeit one in which Villa finished a respectable eighth.

They were briefly back on top of the table but Gregory's relationship with chairman Doug Ellis was uneasy, to say the least. Even so, it came as something of a surprise when he left the club in January after guiding Villa to consecutive wins over Derby and Charlton.

DAVID O'LEARY

VILLA MANAGER: May 2003 - July 2006

BIRTHPLACE: Stoke Newington
DATE OF BIRTH: 2 May 1958
PLAYING CAREER: Arsenal 1975-93, Leeds United 1993-95. Republic of Ireland international (68 caps)
MANAGERIAL CAREER: Leeds United 1998-2002

David O'Leary had been out of work for a year when he took over as Villa manager, but the former Republic of Ireland international certainly appeared to be an inspired choice.

The team had finished 16th the previous season, but with very few changes in playing personnel, he guided them to sixth in his first campaign at the helm. There was, admittedly, a spell when Villa hovered around the relegation zone, but they were ultimately in contention for UEFA Cup qualification and possibly even a Champions League place.

Neither objective was achieved, however, and he was not able to recapture the success of that initial season in charge. Despite a promising start, Villa slipped to tenth the following year - and by his third season, supporters had started to lose faith.

His popularity nosedived following an embarrassing 3-0 League Cup defeat at Doncaster in November, and although Villa enjoyed their best FA Cup run since the 2000 final, going out in a fifth round replay at Manchester City, the team's league form was erratic.

In the midst of some depressing defeats, there was a 3-1 victory over Birmingham City in the Second City derby at Villa Park (Villa had also won 1-0 at St. Andrew's earlier in the season), but a finishing position of 16th took O'Leary back to where he had started.

That summer, after rumours that a statement from the players criticising chairman Doug Ellis had been instigated by O'Leary, his contract was terminated.

It was a sad end for a man who had enjoyed a magnificent playing career as a central defender. Apart from holding Arsenal's all-time appearance record, he helped the Gunners to the title in 1989 and 1991 and to FA Cup glory in 1979 and 1993.

MARTIN O'NEILL

VILLA MANAGER: August 2006 - August 2010

BIRTHPLACE: Kilrea, Northern Ireland
DATE OF BIRTH: 1 March 1952
PLAYING CAREER: Nottingham Forest 1971-81, Norwich City 1981, Manchester City 1981-82, Norwich City 1982-83, Notts County 1983-85
MANAGERIAL CAREER: Grantham Town 1987-89, Shepshed Charterhouse 1989, Wycombe Wanderers 1990-95, Norwich City 1995, Leicester City 1995-2000, Celtic 2000-05

Rarely has the appointment of a football manager generated so much interest as when Martin O'Neill arrived at Villa Park on the first Friday of August 2006.

Around 2,000 supporters turned up in the hope of catching a glimpse of the new boss and their enthusiasm was undeniable. As club secretary Steve Stride observed, as he, chairman Doug Ellis and O'Neill stepped from their car outside the North Stand reception: "Now I know how The Beatles must have felt!"

O'Neill's arrival did, indeed, evoke images of the sort of welcome normally afforded to pop stars as supporters crowded around the vehicle, and security men had to create a path for him to get inside the ground.

The exuberant welcome was perfectly understandable. Although Ellis was in the process of selling the club to American businessman Randy Lerner, he had pulled off a major coup as his final act as chairman.

In Martin O'Neil, he had recruited one of the most respected managers in the business, a man who had enjoyed huge success with both Leicester City and Celtic and who had recently been interviewed for the England job.

If football fans in general were surprised that the FA declined to put O'Neill in charge of the national team, the claret and blue army could not disguise their delight that he had been tempted to Villa Park.

He immediately made his presence felt, too. Despite taking over just two weeks before the Premier League campaign got under way, he inspired Villa to their best start for eight years as they remained unbeaten in the first nine games. And even though the team suffered a mid-winter slump, another nine matches undefeated at the end of the season secured a respectable finish of eleventh.

It got even better the following season, Villa climbing to sixth and only narrowly missing out on automatic UEFA Cup qualification - and better still in 2008-09, when Villa finished sixth as well as reaching the round of 32 in the UEFA Cup.

O'Neill achieved a third consecutive sixth place finish in 2009-10, this time with Villa's highest points total since the Premier League was reduced from 22 teams to 20. He also led the club to two Wembley appearances in the space of six weeks - for the League Cup final and the FA Cup semi-final.

But just five days before the start of the following season, he resigned after learning that chairman Randy Lerner was not willing to finance massive transfer deals.

GERARD HOULLIER

VILLA MANAGER: September 2010 - June 2011

BIRTHPLACE: Therouanne, France
DATE OF BIRTH: 3 September 1947 - 14 December 2020
PLAYING CAREER: Hucquelliers 1969-71, Le Touquet 1971-76
MANAGERIAL CAREER: Le Touquet 1973-76,
Noeux-les Mines 1976-82, Lens 1982-85, Paris St Germain 1985-88, France 1992-93, Liverpool 1998-2004, Olympique Lyonnais 2005-07

In the wake of Martin O'Neill's shock departure, coach Kevin MacDonald stepped into the breach in the days leading up to Villa's opening game of the 2010-11 campaign.

And while kicking off the new campaign with a caretaker manager was hardly an ideal scenario, it was as good a situation as the club could have wished for. The Scot was hugely popular with the players, several of whom he had nurtured through the youth ranks, and there was a feelgood factor around Villa Park as West Ham were beaten 3-0 on the opening day.

By the end of August, though, MacDonald had intimated to the board that he doubted his ability to manage at English football's highest level, and chairman Randy Lerner moved swiftly to procure a permanent successor to O'Neill. The man chosen was Gerard Houllier, the Frenchman who had led Liverpool to a League Cup, FA Cup and UEFA Cup treble nine years earlier.

The announcement of Houllier's appointment was made on 8 September, although his commitments with the French Football Federation meant that it was later in the month before he took charge, with former Liverpool midfielder Gary McAllister arriving as his assistant.

It was a difficult time for the club. Villa were hit by a succession of injury problems, mustering only 20 points by the halfway stage in the Premier League and losing 2-1 to Birmingham City in the League Cup quarter-finals.

A home defeat by Sunderland in January left them in the relegation zone, and the manager acted swiftly to stop the rot, taking full-back Kyle Walker on loan from Tottenham Hotspur before smashing Villa's transfer record with a reported £18million outlay for Sunderland striker Darren Bent.

It was an expensive remedy, but one which worked perfectly, Bent scoring the only goal on his debut against Manchester City and netting eight more as Villa not only avoided the drop, but climbed to a final position of ninth with wins over Arsenal and Liverpool in their last two matches. By that stage, Houllier was manager in name only. After overseeing consecutive wins over Newcastle and West Ham, which considerably eased the club's relegation worries, he was admitted to hospital with heart problems.

McAllister took charge for the final five games and at the start of June, Houllier's eight-month reign as boss came to an end when he stepped down because of his health issues. He died in December 2020.

ALEX McLEISH

VILLA MANAGER: June 2011 - May 2012

BIRTHPLACE: Glasgow
DATE OF BIRTH: 21 January 1959
PLAYING CAREER: Aberdeen 1978-94, Motherwell 1994-95, Scotland international, 77 caps
MANAGERIAL CAREER: Motherwell 1994-98, Hibernian 1998-2001, Glasgow Rangers 2001-06, Scotland 2007, Birmingham City 2007-11, Nottingham Forest 2012-13, Genk 2014-15, Zamalek 2016, Scotland 2018-19

Of all the managerial appointments made by Aston Villa down the years, it's fair to say, Alex McLeish was the most unpopular with the claret-and-blue faithful. Supporters were incensed by the club's decision to look to a man who had just suffered relegation with Villa's bitter rivals Birmingham City, even though he had led Blues to League Cup glory earlier that year.

The fact that he had guided the old enemy to only their second major trophy cut no ice among supporters down Witton way. The news even prompted protests outside Villa Park.

There is no denying, though, that the former Scotland international made a promising start to his new job. Having recruited experienced Manchester City keeper Shay Given and French midfielder Charles N'Zogbia, McLeish kicked-off with a creditable goalless draw at Fulham and then even won over some of his critics with a 3-1 victory over Blackburn Rovers in his first home match.

That was followed by draws against Wolves, Everton, Newcastle United and QPR, and when Wigan Athletic were beaten 2-0 at Villa Park on the first weekend of October, the new manager boasted a seven-match unbeaten start to the Premier League campaign.

But the honeymoon period came to an abrupt end in the form of a 4-1 defeat at Manchester City and a 2-1 derby setback at home to West Bromwich Albion, and the remainder of the season was, with a few exceptions, a struggle for the manager.

Supporters became increasingly vocal about the team's lack of success, notably at Villa Park, where just four wins represented an unwanted club record.

A 2-0 defeat at Carrow Road on the final day of the season was played out against the backdrop of Villa supporters chanting for Norwich City boss Paul Lambert to be the club's next manager. McLeish was sacked 24 hours later, and that summer the fans got their wish.

PAUL LAMBERT

VILLA MANAGER: June 2012 - February 2015

BIRTHPLACE: Glasgow
DATE OF BIRTH: 7 August 1969
PLAYING CAREER: St Mirren 1986-93, Motherwell 1993-96, Borussia Dortmund 1996-97, Celtic 1997-2005, Livingston 2005-06, Scotland international, 40 caps
MANAGERIAL CAREER: Livingston 2005-06, Wycombe Wanderers 2006-08, Colchester United 2008-09, Norwich City 2009-12, Blackburn Rovers 2015-16, Wolverhampton Wanderers 2016-17, Stoke City 2018, Ipswich Town 2018-2021

Paul Lambert was very much the supporters' choice when he took over as Villa manager in the summer of 2012. The claret-and-blue faithful, impressed with his achievements on a modest budget at Norwich City, had chanted his name throughout Villa's 2-0 defeat at Carrow Road on the final day of the previous season.

Their wish was granted when the former Scotland international was appointed as Alex McLeish's successor on 2nd June, and the new boss wasted no time in strengthening the squad by signing Ron Vlaar, Matt Lowton and Karim El Ahmadi. Even so, it was not until after he had moved into the transfer market again - this time for Christian Benteke and Ashley Westwood - that Villa recorded their first Premier League win in mid-September, beating Swansea City 2-0.

By the end of 2012, though, supporters were beginning to have doubts, particularly after a disastrous festive programme which brought an 8-0 drubbing at Chelsea - the club's heaviest defeat in top-flight football - and emphatic home defeats by Tottenham Hotspur and Wigan Athletic.

The manager did, at least, guide his team to the League Cup semi-finals, only for them to suffer a 4-3 aggregate exit at the hands of League One outfit Bradford City, and Villa eventually had to settle for 15th in the final league table.

Despite a brilliant 3-1 success at Arsenal on the opening day of the following campaign, Villa again struggled, with Lambert criticised for his reliance on a counter-attacking style. A second-consecutive 15th-place finish did nothing to win over the doubters.

Lambert's third season at the helm could hardly have started better, Villa taking ten points from the first four league games, including a 1-0 win at Liverpool. But that fine start quickly evaporated as Villa suffered six successive defeats, failing to score in five of them.

The rot was stopped by three draws, followed by back-to-back wins against Crystal Palace and Leicester City, but there was still little sign of a sustained improvement. Although Lambert steered his team to the fifth round of the FA Cup with victories over Leicester City and Bournemouth, he was dismissed on 10th February, the day after a 2-0 setback at Hull City left Villa 18th in the table.

TIM SHERWOOD

VILLA MANAGER: February 2015 - October 2015

BIRTHPLACE: Borehamwood
DATE OF BIRTH: 6 February 1969
PLAYING CAREER: Watford 1987-89, Norwich City 1989-92, Blackburn Rovers 1992-99, Tottenham Hotspur 1999-2003, Portsmouth 2003-04, Coventry City 2004-05, England international, 3 caps
MANAGERIAL CAREER: Tottenham Hotspur 2013-14

Tim Sherwood's time in charge was relatively brief, but no Villa manager has ever had such a dramatic impact on his team before taking charge.

Having been appointed on the day before the fifth-round FA Cup tie against Leicester City, Sherwood watched from the stand, ready to commence his duties 48 hours later. But after Villa had struggled through the opening 45 minutes, he made an impromptu half-time visit to the dressing room for a brief pep talk which inspired a 2-1 victory and a place in the quarter-finals.

There was something of a reality check once Sherwood was officially installed. Villa, languishing in the lower reaches of the Premier League, conceded a stoppage-time goal in a 2-1 defeat to Stoke City the following Saturday and were then beaten 1-0 at Newcastle. But the first two weeks of March saw an amazing transformation.

In the space of five days, back-to-to back victories over neighbours West Bromwich Albion saw Villa both three points better off and looking forward to a Wembley trip for a Cup semi-final against Liverpool.

It got better, too, as Sherwood enjoyed two memorable afternoons in north London. A 1-0 win over his former club Tottenham Hotspur was a massive boost in the battle for top-flight survival and then he oversaw what was arguably Villa's best display of the decade as they hit back from a goal down to beat Liverpool at Wembley.

Premier League safety was all but secured by consecutive home wins over Everton and West Ham, although there was an ominous sign at Southampton the following Saturday. On the journey home from the south coast, the manager and his players learned they were staying up because Hull City had lost at Tottenham - but that was scant consolation for their own abysmal performance in a 6-1 humiliation at St Mary's.

The Cup Final brought further misery in the form of a 4-0 drubbing by Arsenal, and Villa struggled again at the start of the following season. A run of nine league games without a win - including six straight defeats - left the team in 19th place. Sherwood was sacked on 25th October, five days after Villa had been knocked out of the League Cup by Southampton.

REMI GARDE

VILLA MANAGER: November 2015 - March 2016

BIRTHPLACE: L'Arbresle, France
DATE OF BIRTH: 3 April 1966
PLAYING CAREER: Lyon 1987-93, Strasbourg 1993-96, Arsenal 1996-99. France international, 6 caps
MANAGERIAL CAREER: Lyon 2011-14, Montreal Impact 2017-19

The job of Villa manager certainly was not the most inviting prospect when Remi Garde became the club's second French boss. Garde, a former Arsenal player and Lyon manager, took over in November 2015 with Villa bottom of the Premier League after failing to win a league match since the opening day of the season.

It was a depressing trend the new boss was unable to reverse. Despite inspiring Villa to a goalless draw against leaders Manchester City in his first match in charge, Garde's strict disciplinarian approach failed to make any impact.

Although he oversaw home wins over Crystal Palace and Norwich City early in 2016, it was evident by the end of March that Villa were doomed to relegation and he left by mutual consent.

Garde's 23 league and cup games, with a win ratio of just 13 per cent, gave him the unwanted distinction of being the shortest-serving manager in Villa's history - for a while, at least...

ROBERTO DI MATTEO

VILLA MANAGER: June 2016 - October 2016

BIRTHPLACE: Schaffhausen, Switzerland
DATE OF BIRTH: 29 May 1970
PLAYING CAREER: Schaffhausen 1988-91, Zurich 1991-92, Aaru 1992-93, Lazio 1993-96, Chelsea 1996-2002. Italy international, 34 caps, 2 goals
MANAGERIAL CAREER: Milton Keynes Dons 2008-09, West Bromwich Albion 2009-11, Chelsea 2012, Schalke 2014-15

Scot Eric Black had been in temporary charge for the final weeks of the previous campaign, having the unenviable task of overseeing Villa's relegation to the Championship. But there was always going to be a fresh approach after it became evident that chairman Randy Lerner was about to sell the club to the Chinese-based Recon Group.

Hopes of a quick return to the Premier League were high following the arrival of Di Matteo, who had guided Chelsea to UEFA Champions League glory four years earlier, but it was not to be. Villa played some attractive football under Di Matteo - initially, at least - but were prone to late defensive errors which proved costly on numerous occasions.

It certainly was not what new chairman Tony Xia had in mind when making the appointment that summer. After just 12 games in charge, including a 3-1 League Cup defeat at Luton Town, Di Matteo was sacked on 3rd October.

Although Villa had lost only four times, he was effectively condemned by a win ratio of just 8.3 per cent as he became the shortest-serving manager in the club's history.

STEVE BRUCE

VILLA MANAGER: October 2016 - October 2018

BIRTHPLACE: Corbridge, Northumberland

DATE OF BIRTH: 31 December 1960

PLAYING CAREER: Gillingham 1979-84, Norwich City 1984-87, Manchester United 1987-96, Birmingham City 1996-98, Sheffield United 1998-99

MANAGERIAL CAREER: Sheffield United 1998-99, Huddersfield Town 1999-2000, Wigan Athletic 2001, Crystal Palace 2001, Birmingham City 2001-07, Wigan Athletic 2007-09, Sunderland 2009-11, Hull City 2012-16, Sheffield Wednesday 2019, Newcastle United 2019-2021, West Bromwich Albion 2022-

For the second time in five years, Villa supporters were less than impressed when the club announced the appointment of a new manager in October 2016. Unlike Alex McLeish, Steve Bruce did not arrive directly from St Andrew's, but the fact that he had previously managed Birmingham City meant he was never likely to be welcomed with open arms to Villa Park.

Yet Bruce, who had guided Hull City to promotion a few months earlier, soon began to win over the doubters as he set about arresting the slide suffered by Villa during Roberto di Matteo's brief reign.

He could not have made a better start. After a 1-1 draw against Wolves in his first game in charge, Villa were 2-1 winners at Reading - their first away success for 14 months. And while he was never as adventurous as his predecessor had been, Bruce continued to get results.

In 13 matches from his arrival until the end of 2016, Villa lost just twice and were looking strong contenders for a Play-Off spot. Then, against the backdrop of eight new signings during the January transfer window, they simply could not buy a win, collecting a solitary point from the first eight Championship games of 2017.

A run of seven wins in eight games stopped the rot, but the promotion dream was over, and Bruce turned his attentions to reshaping his squad with a busy summer in the transfer market, during which he made another seven new signings.

The outcome was a successful campaign in which automatic elevation to the Premier League looked a realistic proposition, particularly after a incredible sequence of seven consecutive wins from late December until the middle of February.

Ultimately, though, Villa had to settle for a place in the Play-Offs, which culminated with the disappointment of a 1-0 defeat to Fulham at Wembley.

Despite the club's financial problems during the summer of 2018, Bruce insisted that he wouldn't walk away, and he was subsequently backed by the club's new owners Nassef Sawiris and Wes Edens.

The new season started well, with back-to-back victories over Hull City and Wigan Athletic, and Villa were unbeaten in their first five Championship games. But there was a feeling of dissatisfaction over Bruce's cautious tactics and he was dismissed in October following a 3-3 home draw against struggling Preston North End.

DEAN SMITH

VILLA HEAD COACH: October 2018 - November 2021

BIRTHPLACE: West Bromwich
DATE OF BIRTH: 19 March 1971
PLAYING CAREER: Walsall 1989-94, Hereford United 1994-97, Leyton Orient 1997-2003, Sheffield Wednesday 2003-04, Port Vale 2004-05
MANAGERIAL CAREER: Walsall 2011-2015, Brentford 2015-2018, Norwich City 2021

Dean Smith became a different kind of Villa boss when he took over in October 2018. Unlike all his predecessors, his title was head coach, rather than manager. And although he was not as big a name as Ron Atkinson or Brian Little, Smith's appointment was greeted equally enthusiastically - possibly even more so, given the fact that he was "one of our own."

Throughout his career, Smith has made no secret that he had supported Villa since he was a boy. His love for the club, combined with an impressive managerial record on a shoestring budget at Brentford, made him the ideal contender to succeed Steve Bruce.

His impact at Villa Park could not have been greater. Seven months after his arrival, Villa gained promotion back to the Premier League by beating Derby County in the Championship Play-Off final at Wembley. It was not a straightforward journey back to the top flight. After an initial surge, Villa's form faltered early in the new year and by mid-February, their promotion hopes looked remote. But Smith never lost faith, and a club record sequence of ten consecutive wins carried them to the Play-Offs.

Life in the Premier League presented new challenges, and with Villa in the relegation zone when the country went into lockdown because of Covid-19, Smith was frequently criticised by supporters on social media. He came up with the perfect response, though, motivating his players to collect eight points from their final four matches to secure survival.

Smith made some astute signings ahead of Villa's second season back in the Premier League, including keeper Emiliano Martinez from Arsenal, striker Ollie Watkins from Brentford, full-back Matty Cash from Nottingham Forest and winger Bertrand Traore from Lyon. Villa's form was greatly improved, to the extent that Smith was voted the PL manager of the month after five unbeaten matches in December. It was the first time a Villa boss had won the award since Martin O'Neill a decade earlier, and the team went on to achieve a mid-table position.

Smith, who also led Villa to the 2020 Carabao Cup final, was dismissed in November 2021 following a run of five consecutive defeats.

STEVEN GERRARD

VILLA HEAD COACH: November 2021 -

BIRTHPLACE: Whiston, Merseyside
DATE OF BIRTH: 30 May 1980
PLAYING CAREER: Liverpool 1998-2015, LA Galaxy 2015-16 England international (114 caps, 16 goals)
MANAGERIAL CAREER: Glasgow Rangers 2018-2021

Just four days after Dean Smith's departure, Villa appointed one of England's best-ever players, persuading Steve Gerrard to leave Scottish champions Glasgow Rangers.

Six months earlier, Gerrard had led Rangers to their first league title for a decade, but the lure of the Premier League and the challenge of turning around Villa's fortunes were opportunities he could not resist.

His arrival at Villa Park inspired a 2-0 victory over Brighton which ended a run of five consecutive defeats, and subsequent wins against Crystal Palace, Leicester City and Norwich City ensured that Villa were well clear of the danger zone by the end of 2021.

Gerrard's pulling power was evident during the January transfer window, when he persuaded his former Liverpool teammate Philippe Coutinho to join Villa, initially on loan and then on a four-year contract, as well as signing Everton full-back Lucas Digne and Arsenal's versatile defender Calum Chambers.

Regarded as one of the greatest midfielders of his generation, Gerrard enjoyed a glittering playing career with Liverpool, scoring 185 goals in 710 games. He was Man of the Match as the Anfield club beat Milan on penalties after trailing 3-0 in the 2005 Champions League final, and he also helped the Reds to two FA Cup triumphs, three League Cups, the UEFA Cup and the UEFA Super Cup.

Voted the PFA Players' Player of the Year in 2006 and the FWA footballer of the year in 2009, he is also the fourth-most capped England international, representing his country in the World Cup finals of 2006, 2020 and 2014 as well as the European Championship finals of 2000, 2004 and 2012.

ASTON VILLA MANAGERS

1879-84

SEASON SNIPPETS

1879/80

Andy Hunter scored Villa's first ever FA Cup goal, providing the equaliser at Stafford Road after Charles Crump had put the home side ahead.

George Ramsay won the toss in his only FA Cup match, the replay with Stafford Road on 24 January 1880. After winning the match Villa scratched from the competition.

On 3 April 1880, Ramsay led Villa to victory to gain their first trophy, the Birmingham Cup, defeating Saltley College 3-1 in the final. Eli Davis, George Ramsay and Bill Mason were Villa's scorers.

1880/81

Because of the difficulty over work commitments, Archie Hunter would often be shown as 'Centre' and Andy Hunter as 'Wright'.

1881/82

Interest was certainly increasing. For the fourth round tie against Wednesbury Old Athletic, three special trains were laid on to take supporters from Birmingham to Bescot for the game at Wood Green Oval.

1882/83

The fifth round tie with Notts County was known for a long time afterwards as 'the long-armed match' as Villa claimed that it was the long arm of Harry Cursham that fisted the ball out, with County goalkeeper Gillett beaten, denying them a fourth goal. The appeal was later taken to the FA, but this was dismissed and the result stood.

1883/84

Queen's Park had originally been due to play their Scottish FA Cup match on 19 January and asked for the fourth round tie to be brought forward. Villa declined the request and the Scottish FA agreed that the match with Villa could take precedence.

PRE-LEAGUE FA CUP

MANAGER: Committee

FA CUP 1879/80

MATCH	DATE	VENUE	OPPONENTS	RESULT	HT SCORE	SCORE	SCORERS	ATT
1			Bye					
2	Dec 13	A	Stafford Road	D	0 0	1 1	Andy Hunter	2,000
R	Jan 24	H	Stafford Road	W	1 0	3 1	Mason 2, Law	2,000
3		A	Oxford University				Villa scratched from the Competition	

Appearances
Goals

FA CUP 1880/81

MATCH	DATE	VENUE	OPPONENTS	RESULT	HT SCORE	SCORE	SCORERS	ATT
1	Oct 30	H	Wednesbury Strollers	W	1 3	5 3	Goalscorers Not Available	2,000
2	Dec 4	A	Nottingham Forest	W	1 0	2 1	Andy Hunter, Vaughton	2,500
3	Feb 12	A	Notts County	W	1 1	3 1	Andy Hunter 2, Archie Hunter	4,500
4	19	H	Stafford Road	L	1 1	2 3	Vaughton 2	5,000

Appearances
Goals

FA CUP 1881/82

MATCH	DATE	VENUE	OPPONENTS	RESULT	HT SCORE	SCORE	SCORERS	ATT
1	Nov 5	H	Nottingham Forest	W	1 1	4 1	Whateley 2, Arthur Brown 2	6,000
2			Bye					
3	Dec 31	H	Notts County *	D	2 1	2 2	Davis, Whateley	5,000
R	Jan 7	H	Notts County **	D	0 1	2 2	Arthur Brown, Archie Hunter	8,000
2R	14	H	Notts County	W	2 0	4 1	Archie Hunter, Whateley, Arthur Brown, Dawson	10,000
4	21	A	Wednesbury Old Athletic	L	2 3	2 4	Vaughton, Archie Hunter	6,000

Appearances
Goals

* After extra-time   ** After extra-time - score at 90 minutes 1-1

FA CUP 1882/83

MATCH	DATE	VENUE	OPPONENTS	RESULT	HT SCORE	SCORE	SCORERS	ATT
1	Oct 21	H	Walsall Swifts	W	3 0	4 1	Arthur Brown 2, Vaughton, Archie Hunter	5,000
2	Nov 18	H	Wednesbury Old Athletic	W	2 1	4 1	Harvey, Archie Hunter, Vaughton, Whateley	6,000
3	Jan 6	H	Aston Unity	W	2 0	3 1	Davis, Vaughton, Archie Hunter	4,000
4	27	H	Walsall Town	W	1 1	2 1	Vaughton, Arthur Brown	5,000
5	Mar 3	A	Notts County	L	1 1	3 4	Archie Hunter, Whateley, Arthur Brown	10,000

Appearances
Goals

FA CUP 1883-84

MATCH	DATE	VENUE	OPPONENTS	RESULT	HT SCORE	SCORE	SCORERS	ATT
1	Nov 10	A	Walsall Swifts	W	1 0	5 1	Archie Hunter 3, Roberts, Vaughton	4,000
2	Dec 1	A	Stafford Road	W	2 0	5 0	Arthur Brown 2, Archie Hunter 2, Whateley	3,000
3	29	A	Wednesbury Old Athletic	W	2 3	7 4	Arthur Brown 2, Whateley, Vaughton 3, Archie Hunter	7,000
4	Jan 19	A	Queen's Park (Glasgow)	L	0 2	1 6	Vaughton	10,000

Appearances
Goals

290

Match 1

Player						
Ball JH						
Simmonds HR						
Pank T						
Law SR						
Lee EB						
Davis E						
Mason WB						
Hunter Archie						
Johnstone CS						
Crossland WS						
Hunter Andy						
Ramsay GB						

MATCH
- 1
- 2: 1 2 3 4 5 6 7 8 9 10 11
- R: 1 2 3 4 5 6 7 8 10 11 9
- 3

Totals: 2 2 2 2 2 2 2 1 2 2 1
          1   2   1

Match 2

Copley GH, Lee EB, Pank T, Law SR, Johnstone CS, Hunter Andy, Watts WH, Davis E, Vaughton OH, Hunter OH, Crossland WS, Simmonds HR, Brown Arthur

MATCH
- 1: 1 2 3 4 5 6 7 8 9 10 11
- 2: 1 4 3 5   8 7 11 10 6   2 9
- 3: 1 4 3 5   6 11 8 10 7 2 9
- 4: 1 5 4 3   6 11 10 9 7 2 8

Totals: 4 4 4 4 1 3 3 4 4 3 3 3
                  3   3 1

Match 3

Copley GH, Lee EB, Simmonds HR, Dawson JH, Pank T, Law SR, Davis E, Vaughton OH, Brown Arthur, Crossland WS, Whateley O, Clarke AW, Hunter Archie, Hunter Andy, Brooks F, Horton TA

MATCH
- 1: 1 2 3 4 5 6 7 8 9 10 11
- 2
- 3:   3 2 6 4 5 10 11 8   9 1 7
- R: 3 2 6 4 5   10   11 1 8 7 9
- 2R: 3 2 6 4 5 7 11 8   9 1 10
- 3:   3 2 6 4 5   10 8   9 1 7   11

Totals: 1 5 5 5 5 5 3 4 5 1 5 4 4 1 1 1
                      1 1 4   4 3

Match 4

Clarke AW, Simmonds JO, Bryan T, Anderson D, Harvey RA, Hunter Andy, Vaughton OH, Hunter Archie, Brown Arthur, Roberts WD, Davis E, Apperley CW, Whateley O, Mason TW, Lee EB

MATCH
- 1: 1 2 3 4 5 6 7 8 9 10 11
- 2: 1   2 4 3 6 11 8 9 10 5 7
- 3:   3   4 2 6 11 8 9 10 5 7 1
- 4:   2   4 3 7 11 9 8 10 5 6 1
- 5:   3   4   6 11 8 9 10 5 7 1 2

Totals: 2 4 2 5 4 5 5 5 5 1 5 4 3 1
              1   4 4 4 1 2

Match 5

Vale AF, Simmonds JO, Riddell TC, Dawson FHH, Price RO, Apperley CW, Whateley O, Vaughton OH, Hunter Archie, Roberts WD, Davis E, Brown Arthur, Clarke AW

MATCH
- 1: 1 2 3 4 5 6 7 8 9 10 11
- 2: 1 2 3 4   5 10 11 8 7 6 9
- 3:   3 4 2 5 10 11 9 6 7 8 1
- 4: 1 3 2 5   4 6 7 9 10 11 8

Totals: 3 3 4 4 2 4 4 4 4 4 4 3 1
                  2 5 6 1   4

1884-88

SEASON SNIPPETS

1884/85

Robert Price did not arrive until half-time on 6 December, so Villa played the first half with ten men. Walsall had two goals disallowed, one right on the half-time whistle, the other for offside and said that they would consider appealing the result.

1885/86

The FA Cup defeat by Derby County was the last Villa FA Cup match for Walter Jones, Thomas Riddell, Robert Price, Oliver Whateley, Charles Hobson and Arthur Brown.

1886/87

Villa were leading 3-0 at half-time against Darwen when Mr Amos Roe, president of the Moseley Rugby Football Club, brought onto the field the Midland Counties Challenge Cup won by his club and filled it with champagne which the players of each team were invited to drink. The second-half was very different, Darwen came back with two goals and had a third disallowed for offside.

The Glasgow Rangers team for the semi-final was strengthened by the inclusion of players from Hibernian, Vale of Leven, Queen's Park and Dumbarton.

1887/88

Such was the crowd for the fifth round tie with Preston that supporters continually broke onto the pitch. The position was such that with Villa leading 1-0, it was agreed by both captains that the game should not be played as a cup tie, but to play out the remainder of the match as a friendly. However, on winning 3-1 Preston claimed the tie and, on appeal, the FA agreed with Preston.

PRE-LEAGUE FA CUP

MANAGER: Committee

FA CUP 1884/85

MATCH	DATE	VENUE	OPPONENTS	RESULT	HT SCORE	SCORE	SCORERS	ATT
1	Nov 3	H	Wednesbury Town	W	2 1	4 1	Arthur Brown 2, Albert A Brown, Archie Hunter	4,000
2	Dec 6	A	Walsall Town	W	1 0	2 0	Whateley, Archie Hunter	5,000
3	Jan 3	H	West Bromwich Albion	D	0 0	0 0		22,000
R	10	A	West Bromwich Albion	L	0 2	0 3		10,000

Appearances
Goals

FA CUP 1885/86

MATCH	DATE	VENUE	OPPONENTS	RESULT	HT SCORE	SCORE	SCORERS	ATT
1	Oct 17	A	Walsall Town	W	4 0	5 0	Archie Hunter, Davis, Vaughton, Albert A Brown, Arthur Brown	7,000
2	Nov 14	A	Derby County	L	0 1	0 2		6,000

Appearances
Goals

FA CUP 1886/87

MATCH	DATE	VENUE	OPPONENTS	RESULT	HT SCORE	SCORE	SCORERS	ATT
1	Oct 30	H	Wednesbury Old Athletic	W	5 0	13 0	Hodgetts 2, Loach 2, Archie Hunter 3, Davis, Albert A Brown 3, Burton 2	4,000
2	Nov 20	H	Derby Midland	W	3 1	6 1	Hodgetts 2, Loach, Albert A Brown 2, Archie Hunter	5,000
3	Dec 11	H	Wolverhampton Wanderers *	D	1 0	2 2	Albert A Brown 2	6,000
R	Jan 15	A	Wolverhampton Wanderers *	D	1 1	1 1	Albert A Brown	7,000
2R	22	A	Wolverhampton Wanderers **	D	0 1	3 3	Vaughton, Albert A Brown 2	10,000
3R	29	H	Wolverhampton Wanderers	W	2 0	2 0	Dawson, Archie Hunter	12,000
4			Bye					
5	Feb 5	H	Horncastle	W	3 0	5 0	Davis, Albert A Brown 3, Archie Hunter	3,500
6	12	H	Darwen	W	3 0	3 2	Dawson, Archie Hunter, Hodgetts	10,000
SF	Mar 5	N	Glasgow Rangers ***	W	1 1	3 1	Archie Hunter 2, Albert A Brown	10,000
F	Apr 2	N	West Bromwich Albion ****	W	0 0	2 0	Hodgetts, Archie Hunter	15,500

Appearances
Goals

* After extra-time - score at 90 minutes 1-1
** After extra-time - score at 90 minutes 2-2
*** Played at Crewe
**** Played at Kennington Oval

FA CUP 1887/88

MATCH	DATE	VENUE	OPPONENTS	RESULT	HT SCORE	SCORE	SCORERS	ATT
1	Oct 15	A	Oldbury Town	A	1 0	4 0	Albert A Brown 2, Archie Hunter, Allen	3,500
2	Nov 5	A	Small Heath Alliance	A	2 0	4 0	Green 2, Albert A Brown, Allen	12,000
3			Bye					
4	Dec 17	A	Shankhouse	A	4 0	9 0	Archie Hunter 2, Allen 2, Albert A Brown 2, Green 2, Hodgetts	3,000
5	Jan 7	H	Preston North End	H	1 1	1 3	Archie Hunter	27,000

Appearances
Goals

292

Player	1	2	3	4	5	6	7	8	9	10	11		MATCH
Harvey WA	1												
Simmonds JO		2											
Riddell TC			3										
Price RO				4									
Robertson RR					5								
Whateley O						6							
Brown Albert A							7						
Hunter Archie								8					
Brown Arthur									9				
Vaughton OH										10			
Davis E											11		
Dawson FHH													

	1	2	3	4	5	6	7	8	9	10	11		
	1	2	3	4	5	6	7	8	9	10	11		1
	1	2	3	4		6	7	8	9	10	11	5	2
	1	2	3	4		6	7	9	8	10	11	5	3
	1	2	3	5		6	7	8	9	10	11	4	R

4	4	4	4	1	4	4	4	4	4	4	3	
						1	1	2	2			

Player
Hobson CSH
Jones WA
Riddell TC
Burton JH
Price RO
Whateley O
Brown Albert A
Hunter Archie
Brown Arthur
Vaughton OH
Davis R

	1	2	3	4	5	6	7	8	9	10	11		MATCH
	1	2	3	4	5	6	7	8	9	10	11		1
	1	2	3	4	5	6	7	8	9	10	11		2

2	2	2	2	2	2	2	2	2	2	2		
							2	1	2	1		

Player
Warner J
Coulton F
Simmonds JO
Yates HR
Robertson RR
Burton JH
Brown Albert A
Davis R
Hunter Archie
Loach AA
Hodgetts D
Dawson FHH
Vaughton OH

	1	2	3	4	5	6	7	8	9	10	11			MATCH
	1	2	3	4	5	6	7	8	9	10	11			1
	1	2	3	4		6	7	8	9	10	11	5		2
	1	2	3		5	6	7	8	9	10	11	4		3
	1	2	3	4		6	7	8	9		11	5	10	R
	1	2	3	4		6	7	8	9		11	5	10	2R
	1	2	3	4		6	7	8	9		11	5	10	3R
														4
	1	2	3	4		6	7	8	9		11	5	10	5
	1	2	3	4		6	7	8	9		11	5	10	6
	1	2	3	4		6	7	8	9		11	5	10	SF
	1	2	3	4		6	7	9			8	5	10	F

10	10	10	9	2	10	10	10	10	3	10	9	7	
					2	14	2	10	3	6	2	1	

Player
Warner J
Coulton F
Cox G
Yates HR
Devey HP
Burton JH
Brown Albert A
Green TW
Hunter Archie
Allen AA
Hodgetts D
Simmonds JO
Dawson FHH

	1	2	3	4	5	6	7	8	9	10	11		MATCH
	1	2	3	4	5	6	7	8	9	10	11		1
	1	2	3	4	5	6	7	8	9	10	11		2
													3
	1	2	3	6		4	7	8	9	10	11	5	4
	1	2	3	6		4	7	8	9	10	11	5	5

4	4	4	4	2	4	4	4	4	4	4	1	1	
						5	4	4	4	1			

1888/89

SEASON SNIPPETS

At Dudley Road on 8 September, Gershom Cox became the first player to score an 'own goal' in a league match in giving Wolves a 29th-minute lead. Tommy Green equalised a minute before the break.

The method of allocating points was resolved at a meeting in Birmingham on 21 November, two points for a win with one point for a draw. Villa were then placed second.

Villa took the field at Burnley in January with only eight men. Two more players arrived after eight minutes play, but Villa had only ten players for the remainder of the game.

Tommy Green played his last game on 9 February 1889 at home to Preston North End.

The Derby County match on 9 March was the last Villa game for Arthur Wollaston, Thomas Harrison and Archie Goodall.

The 8-1 defeat at Blackburn Rovers on 2 March remains Villa's heaviest FA Cup defeat. Archie Hunter suffered a badly damaged leg and could only hobble about the pitch in agony while Harry Yates suffered a knee injury which reduced his involvement to that of a spectator. It was the only first-team appearance for Bob Thomas.

DIVISION ONE

MANAGER: Committee

MATCH	DATE	VENUE	OPPONENTS	RESULT	HT SCORE	SCORE	SCORERS	ATT
1	Sep 8	A	Wolverhampton Wanderers	D	1 1	1 1	Green	2,500
2	15	H	Stoke	W	0 1	5 1	Dixon, Brown, Hunter, Green 2	4,000
3	22	H	Everton	W	2 0	2 1	Hodgetts 2	4,000
4	29	H	Notts County	W	4 0	9 1	Allen 3, Hunter 2, Hodgetts, Brown, Green 2	4,000
5	Oct 6	A	Everton	L	0 1	0 2		10,000
6	13	H	Blackburn Rovers	W	2 1	6 1	Green, Goodall, Brown, Allen 2, Hunter	5,000
7	20	A	Bolton Wanderers	W	0 0	3 2	Hodgetts, Hunter, Allen	8,000
8	27	H	Accrington	W	1 2	4 3	Allen, Brown 2, Hodgetts	7,000
9	Nov 3	A	Stoke	D	0 0	1 1	Allen	4,000
10	10	A	Preston North End	D	0 1	1 1	Green	10,000
11	17	A	Blackburn Rovers	L	1 1	1 5	Allen	9,500
12	24	H	Wolverhampton Wanderers	W	1 0	2 1	Goodall 2	6,000
13	Dec 8	A	Notts County	W	1 1	4 2	Brown, Goodall 2, Green	2,000
14	15	A	Accrington	D	1 1	1 1	Brown	2,000
15	22	H	Burnley	W	2 1	4 2	Green, Goodall, Hunter, Allen	2,000
16	29	H	Derby County	W	3 1	4 2	Green 2, Allen, Goodall	4,000
17	Jan 5	A	Burnley	L	0 1	0 4		6,000
18	12	H	Bolton Wanderers	W	1 1	6 2	Brown, Allen 2, Hodgetts, Hunter, Green	2,000
19	19	H	West Bromwich Albion	W	1 0	2 0	Hodgetts, Allen	10,000
20	26	A	West Bromwich Albion	D	1 3	3 3	Allen, Hodgetts, Green	8,515
21	Feb 9	H	Preston North End	L	0 0	0 2		10,000
22	Mar 9	A	Derby County	L	2 1	2 5	Allen 2	3,000

Final League Position: 2nd in Football League

Appearances
Goals

FA CUP

1	Feb 2	H	Witton	W	2 2	3 2	Allan, Hunter, Green	1,500
2	16	H	Derby County	W	2 2	5 3	Hunter 2, Hodgetts 2, Brown	2,000
3	Mar 2	A	Blackburn Rovers	L	0 3	1 8	Hodgetts	12,000

Appearances
Goals

Warner J	Cox G	Coulton F	Yates HR	Devey HP	Dawson FHH	Brown Albert A	Green TW	Allen AA	Garvey BW	Hodgetts D	Dixon AA	Hunter Archie	Ashmore W	Goodall AL	Burton JH	Wollaston AW	Harrison T	Thomas RS		MATCH
1	2	3	4	5	6	7	8	9	10	11										1
1	2	3	4	5		7	8	10		11	6	9								2
	2	3	6	5		7	8	10		11	4	9	1							3
1	2	3	6	5		7	8	10		11	4	9								4
1	2	3	6	5	4	7	8	10		11		9								5
1	2	3	4			7	8	10		11		9		5	6					6
1	2	3	6	5		7	8	10		11		9			4					7
1	2	3	6	5		7	8	10		11		9			4					8
1	2	3	4	5		7	8	10		11		9			6					9
1	2	3	6	5		7	8	10		11		9		4						10
1	2	3		5		7	8	10		11		9		4						11
1	2	3	4	5		7	8	11				9		10	6					12
1	2	3		5		7	8					9		10	6	4	11			13
1	2	3		5		7	8	11				9		10	6	4				14
1	2	3		5		7	8	11				9		10	6	4				15
1	2	3		5	6	7	8	11				9		10	4					16
1	2	3		5		7	8	10		11				4	6					17
1	2	3		5		7	8	10		11		9		4	6					18
1	2	3		5		7	8	10		11		9		6	4					19
1			4	5		7	8	10		11		9		2	6					20
1	3		6	5		7	8	10		11		9		2	4					21
1	3			5		7		10	8	9				2	6	4	11			22
21	22	19	13	21	3	22	21	21	2	17	3	19	1	14	16	4	2			
						8	13	17		8	1	7		7						

1	2	3		5		8	7	10		11		9		4	6					1
1	2	3	6	5		8	7	10		11		9		4						2
1	3		6	5		8	7	10		11		9		4			2			3
3	3	2	2	3		3	3	3		3		3		3	1		1			
						1	1	1		3		3								

FINAL LEAGUE TABLE

	P	W	D	L	F	A	P
Preston North End	22	18	4	0	74	15	40
Aston Villa	**22**	**12**	**5**	**5**	**61**	**43**	**29**
Wolverhampton W	22	12	4	6	51	37	28
Blackburn Rovers	22	10	6	6	66	45	26
Bolton Wanderers	22	10	2	10	63	59	22
West Bromwich A	22	10	2	10	40	46	22
Accrington	22	6	8	8	48	48	20
Everton	22	9	2	11	35	47	20
Burnley	22	7	3	12	42	62	17
Derby County	22	7	2	13	41	61	16
Notts County	22	5	2	15	40	73	12
Stoke	22	4	4	14	26	51	12

1889/90

SEASON SNIPPETS

Three players made their debut against Burnley in the first game of the season, Albert Aldridge, Thomas Clarkson and James Cowan.

The home game with Notts County on 14 September kicked-off 40 minutes late. Notts County arrived 30 minutes late, but Villa then had to change their colours as they had come onto the pitch in white. Notts County emerged also wearing white and so Villa had to go back and change to their old chocolate and blue kit. Billy Dickson made his debut.

Villa became the first team to defeat Preston North End in the Football League when they won 5-3 at Wellington Road on 21 September 1889.

Ike Moore scored two goals on his debut against Wolves on 2 November 1889. Moore was playing instead of Dennis Hodgetts who was in dispute with the Committee. It was quickly resolved - Hodgetts returned the following week!

Villa started the game at Derby County on 28 December with only ten men, Billy Dickson was absent. A telegraph was sent to Batty Garvey to fill the place and Garvey duly arrived 35 minutes after kick-off.

Archie Hunter lodged a formal protest with the referee regarding the state of the pitch before the start of the away game at Everton on 4 January. He was told that the matter would be considered at the next league meeting. Alas, Hunter collapsed in dreadful conditions when the whistle blew for half-time. He was taken to hospital and never played again.

William Dickie made his only appearance in the FA Cup round two match at Notts County.

DIVISION ONE

MANAGER: Directors

MATCH	DATE	VENUE	OPPONENTS	RESULT	HT SCORE	SCORE	SCORERS	ATT
1	Sep 7	H	Burnley	D	2 1	2 2	Hodgetts 2	4,000
2	14	H	Notts County	D	0 1	1 1	Hodgetts	6,500
3	21	H	Preston North End	W	3 1	5 3	Cowan 2, Dickson, Brown, Allen	8,000
4	28	A	West Bromwich Albion	L	0 2	0 3		8,000
5	Oct 5	A	Burnley	W	4 1	6 2	Allen 4, Hunter, Hodgetts	8,000
6	12	H	Derby County	W	5 0	7 1	Allen 3, Dickson, Hunter, Hodgetts, Brown	5,000
7	19	A	Blackburn Rovers	L	0 4	0 7		8,000
8	26	H	West Bromwich Albion	W	1 0	1 0	Brown	8,000
9	Nov 2	H	Wolverhampton Wanderers	W	0 1	2 1	Moore 2	10,000
10	9	A	Notts County	D	1 0	1 1	Dickson	4,000
11	16	A	Bolton Wanderers	L	0 1	0 2		8,000
12	23	H	Everton	L	1 1	1 2	Brown	6,000
13	30	A	Accrington	L	2 3	2 4	Allen 2	2,000
14	Dec 7	H	Stoke	W	2 0	6 1	Dickson 2, Garvey 3 Allen	4,000
15	21	A	Wolverhampton Wanderers	D	1 0	1 1	Hodgetts	8,000
16	25	A	Preston North End	L	2 1	2 3	Moore, Dickson	9,000
17	26	H	Accrington	L	1 1	1 2	Garvey	2,000
18	28	A	Derby County	L	0 1	0 5		8,000
19	Jan 4	A	Everton	L	0 4	0 7		10,000
20	25	H	Bolton Wanderers	L	1 1	1 2	Brown	5,000
21	Mar 17	A	Stoke	D	0 1	1 1	Allen	3,150
22	31	H	Blackburn Rovers	W	1 0	3 0	Campbell, Hodgetts, Brown	6,000

Final League Position: 8th in Football League

Appearances
Goals

FA CUP

1	Jan 18	A	South Shore (Blackpool)	W	2 0	4 2	Allen, Dickson, Hodgetts 2	1,500
2	Feb 1	A	Notts County	L	0 3	1 4	Hodgetts	15,000

Appearances
Goals

Match	Warner J	Coulton F	Aldridge A	Clarkson T	Cowan James	Devey HP	Brown Albert A	Allen AA	Hunter Archie	Garvey BW	Hodgetts D	Dickson WA	Gray FJS	Davis G	Cox G	Burton JH	Moore I	Hickton AJ	Yates HR	Connor J	Graham J	Campbell L	Dickie WA	Paton DJF
1	1	2	3	4	5	6	7	8	9	10	11													
2	1	3	2	4	5	6	7	8	9		11	10												
3	1	3	2	4	5	6	7	8	9			10	11											
4	1	3		2	4	5	6	7	8			10	9	11										
5				3	4	5	6	7	8	9	11	10			1	2								
6	1			3	4	5	6	7	8	9	11	10				2								
7				3	4	5	6	7	8	9	11	10				2								
8	1			3	4	5	6	7	8	9	11	10				2								
9	1			3		5	6	7	8	9		10				2	4	11						
10	1			3		5	6	7	8	9	11	10				2	4							
11	1		3	6		5	6	7	8	9	11	10				2	4							
12	1			3		5	6	7	8	9	11	10				2	4							
13	1			3			5	6	7		11	10				2	4	9						
14	1			3			5	7	11		10	9				2	6	8	4					
15	1	3	2		5	4	7	11	9		10	8				6								
16	1	3	2		5	6	7			11	9	8					4	10						
17	1	3			5	6	7			11	9	8				2	4	10						
18	1	3	2		5	6	7	8		11	9						4	10						
19	1	3			5	6	7	10	9		11	8				2	4							
20	1	3			5		7	9			8					2	4			6	10	11		
21	1	3			5	7	10			11	8					2	4						9	
22	1	3		4	5	6	7	8			10	9				2						11		
	21	12	17	10	22	19	22	20	13	12	22	19	2	1	18	10	5	1	1	1	1	2	1	
					2		6	12	2	4	7	6			4		3					1		

1		2			5	4	7	9			11	8			3	6	10							
2		2			5		8	10			11	9			3	6				7	4			

2	2				2	1	2	2			2	2			2	2	1			1	1			
								1			3	1												

FINAL LEAGUE TABLE

	P	W	D	L	F	A	P
Preston North End	22	15	3	4	71	30	33
Everton	22	14	3	5	65	40	31
Blackburn Rovers	22	12	3	7	78	41	27
Wolverhampton W	22	10	5	7	51	38	25
West Bromwich A	22	11	3	8	47	50	25
Accrington	22	9	6	7	53	56	24
Derby County	22	9	3	10	43	55	21
Aston Villa	**22**	**7**	**5**	**10**	**43**	**51**	**19**
Bolton Wanderers	22	9	1	12	54	65	19
Notts County	22	6	5	11	43	51	17
Burnley	22	4	5	13	36	65	13
Stoke	22	3	4	15	27	69	10

1890/91

SEASON SNIPPETS

Walter Evans made his debut in the first match of the season at Wolves, as did Fred Marshall who played in place of Dennis Hodgetts on the left-wing.

Leading 2-0 against Notts County on 13 September, debutant Tom McKnight thought he had made the score three. However, the 'goal' was disallowed and County immediately raced down the field and Andrew McGregor pulled a goal back. Nevertheless, Villa went on to win 3-2.

Charlie Harley made his only Villa appearance at Bolton Wanderers on 4 October 1890.

Daniel Paton injured his knee after 20 minutes of the game with Derby on 18 October and had to leave the field. Paton did not play for Villa again.

George Campbell and James Brown made their first Villa league appearances in the 4-0 win against Derby County on 25 October 1890.

Conditions at Deepdale for the game on 24 January were shocking. Snow had thawed rapidly and there were large pools of water scattered over the ground with a miniature river running down the centre of the pitch.

Charlie Athersmith made his debut against Preston North End at Wellington Road on 9 March 1891.

Before Villa's FA Cup first-round game started, The Casuals handed in a written protest against the ground which was hard and slippery on the surface.

DIVISION ONE

MANAGER: Committee

MATCH	DATE	VENUE	OPPONENTS	RESULT	HT SCORE	SCORE	SCORERS	ATT
1	Sep 6	A	Wolverhampton Wanderers	L	1 0	1 2	A Brown	4,000
2	13	H	Notts County	W	2 1	3 2	A Brown, Dickson, Graham	6,000
3	20	A	Burnley	L	0 1	1 2	L Campbell	10,000
4	27	H	West Bromwich Albion	L	0 2	0 4		8,000
5	Oct 4	A	Bolton Wanderers	L	0 2	0 4		5,000
6	11	H	Everton	D	1 1	2 2	Paton, L Campbell	12,000
7	18	A	Derby County	L	3 3	4 5	Hodgetts, Cowan 2, Graham	3,000
8	25	H	Derby County	W	0 0	4 0	Hodgetts 2, Cowan, A Brown	3,000
9	Nov 1	A	West Bromwich Albion	W	1 0	3 0	A Brown 2, Dickson	8,000
10	8	H	Burnley	D	2 3	4 4	Dickson, Cowan, A Brown, Graham	5,000
11	15	H	Accrington	W	0 0	3 1	Graham, Hodgetts, A Brown	8,000
12	22	H	Bolton Wanderers	W	2 0	5 0	A Brown 2, J Brown, G Campbell, Dickson	10,000
13	29	A	Notts County	L	1 4	1 7	Dickson	4,000
14	Dec 6	A	Blackburn Rovers	L	0 1	1 5	Dickson	5,000
15	13	H	Blackburn Rovers	D	1 2	2 2	Allen, A Brown	4,000
16	26	H	Sunderland	D	0 0	0 0		6,000
17	Jan 1	A	Everton	L	0 2	0 5		10,000
18	10	A	Sunderland	L	0 3	1 5	Graham	6,000
19	24	A	Preston North End	L	0 2	1 4	A Brown	2,000
20	Mar 9	H	Preston North End	L	0 0	0 1		5,000
21	14	H	Wolverhampton Wanderers	L	2 2	6 2	McNight, Dickson 2, Athersmith 3	5,000
22	21	A	Accrington	W	1 1	3 1	Burton, Dickson 2	1,500

Final League Position: 9th in Football League

Appearances
Goals

FA CUP

1	Jan 17	H	The Casuals	W	2 0	13 1	Graham 2, McNight, L Campbell 3, Hodgetts 4, A Brown 2	5,000
2	31	A	Stoke	L	0 0	0 3		7,000

Appearances
Goals

298

Warner J	Evans WG	Cox G	Devey HP	Cowan James	Connor J	Brown Albert A	Allen AA	Dickson WA	Graham J	Marshall FA	McKnight T	Hodgetts D	Clarkson T	Campbell L	Harley CC	Paton DJF	Campbell G	Brown JR	Burton JH	Athersmith WC			MATCH
1	2	3	4	5	6	7	8	9	10	11													1
1	2	3	4	5	6	7		9	10		8	11											2
1	3	2	4	5				9	10	7	8		6	11									3
1	3	2	4	5				9	10	7	8		6	11									4
1	2	3	4	5				9	10		8		6	11	7								5
1	2	3	4	5		7		8	10			11	6			9							6
1	2	3	4	5		7		8	10			11	6			9							7
1	2	3	5	9		7		8	10			11					4	6					8
1	2	3	5	8		7		9	10			11					4	6					9
1	2	3	5	8		7		9	10			11					4	6					10
1	3	2	5			7	8	9	10			11					4	6					11
1	3	2	5	8		7		9	10			11					4	6					12
1	3	2	5	8		7		9	10			11					4	6					13
1	2		5	8		7		9	10			11	6				3	4					14
1	3		5	8		7	10				9	11					2	6	4				15
1		2	5	8	3	7	10				9	11					4	6					16
1	2	3	5	8		7		9	10			11					6	4					17
1	2	3	4	5			8		10			9		11			6	7					18
1	3	2	5			7			10		8	9		11			6	4					19
1	2	3		5			8				9	11		10			6	4		7			20
1	2	3		5			8				9	11		10			6	4		7			21
1	2	3		5			8				9	11		10			6	4	7				22
22	21	20	19	20	3	16	8	18	17	3	10	18	6	8	1	2	15	15	2	2			
				5		11	1	10	5		1	4		1		1	1	1	1	3			

| 1 | 3 | 2 | | 5 | | 7 | | 10 | | | 8 | 9 | | 11 | | | 4 | 6 | | | | | 1 |
| 1 | 3 | 2 | 5 | | | 7 | | 10 | | | 8 | 9 | | 11 | | | 6 | 4 | | | | | 2 |

| 2 | 2 | 2 | 1 | 1 | | 2 | | 2 | | | 2 | 2 | | 2 | | | 2 | 2 | | | | | |
| | | | | | | | | 2 | | | 2 | 4 | | 3 | | | | | | | | | |

FINAL LEAGUE TABLE

	P	W	D	L	F	A	P
Everton	22	14	1	7	63	29	29
Preston North End	22	12	3	7	44	23	27
Notts County	22	11	4	7	52	35	26
Wolverhampton W	22	12	2	8	39	50	26
Bolton Wanderers	22	12	1	9	47	34	25
Blackburn Rovers	22	11	2	9	52	43	24
Sunderland	22	10	5	7	51	31	23
Burnley	22	9	3	10	52	63	21
Aston Villa	**22**	**7**	**4**	**11**	**45**	**58**	**18**
Accrington	22	6	4	12	28	50	16
Derby County	22	7	1	14	47	81	15
West Bromwich A	22	5	2	15	34	57	12

1891/92

SEASON SNIPPETS

John Devey and Percy Hislop made their debut in the first match of the season. Hislop netted the equalising goal and Devey contributed two goals in the 5-1 win against Blackburn Rovers.

Goalkeeper Jimmy Warner was injured during a scrimmage after 20 minutes at Burnley on 17 October and was taken off. George Campbell went in goal, Villa had to play with ten men.

Albert Hinchley played in goal for the eleven games Warner was absent, but the game at Notts County on 2 January was his last Villa match.

Charlie Hare scored twice on his league debut at Darwen on 31 October and was on target again on his home debut the following week against Notts County.

The game at Accrington on 12 December was abandoned due to a blizzard and replayed on Monday 4 January 1892.

Thomas Dutton made his only league appearance at Blackburn on 5 March. The game was also Jack Graham's last appearance.

Billy Dickson scored in his last game for Villa, the 6-3 defeat against Wolves on 18 April.

Villa spent a week training at Holt Fleet prior to the FA Cup second-round match with Darwen who had a short stay at Matlock.

The FA Cup final was the last to be played at Kennington Oval. The custom of presenting the cup and medals was changed and the presentation took place in one of the committee rooms!

The FA Cup final was the last game for Jimmy Warner. Outfield player George Campbell played in goal for the next league game before Edwin Diver came in for the final three league matches.

DIVISION ONE

MANAGER: Directors

MATCH	DATE		VENUE	OPPONENTS	RESULT	HT SCORE		SCORE		SCORERS	ATT
1	Sep	5	H	Blackburn Rovers	W	2	1	5	1	Hislop, J Devey 2, Dickson, Athersmith	10,000
2		12	H	West Bromwich Albion	W	0	1	5	1	Athersmith, J Devey 2, Hislop, Dickson	12,100
3		19	A	Preston North End	W	0	0	1	0	Hislop	9,000
4		28	H	Sunderland	W	4	1	5	3	Brown, Hodgetts, Dickson, J Devey, Athersmith	6,000
5	Oct	3	A	Derby County	L	1	2	2	4	Dickson 2	10,000
6		10	H	Bolton Wanderers	L	0	1	1	2	Hislop	3,000
7		17	A	Burnley	L	1	2	1	4	Dickson	5,000
8		24	A	Stoke	W	3	0	3	2	L.Campbell, J Devey, Dickson	7,000
9		31	A	Darwen	W	4	0	5	1	Hare 2, L Campbell 2, J Devey	4,000
10	Nov	7	H	Notts County	W	4	1	5	1	Hodgetts 2, Athersmith, J Devey, Hare	3,000
11		14	A	West Bromwich Albion	W	1	0	3	0	J Devey, L Campbell, Hare	10,000
12		21	H	Stoke	W	1	1	2	1	L Campbell, Brown	6,000
13		28	A	Everton	L	1	0	1	5	Hodgetts	8,000
14	Dec	5	H	Burnley	W	3	0	6	1	J Devey 4, Dickson, Brown	5,000
15		19	A	Wolverhampton Wanderers	L	0	1	0	2		8,000
16		26	H	Darwen	W	2	0	7	0	Hodgetts 3, L Campbell 2, Athersmith, J Devey	3,000
17		28	H	Everton	L	0	3	3	4	J Devey 2, Athersmith	14,000
18	Jan	2	A	Notts County	L	1	3	2	5	Athersmith, J Devey	7,000
19		4	A	Accrington	L	0	2	2	3	Athersmith, J Devey	3,500
20		9	H	Derby County	W	3	0	6	0	J Devey, Dickson, Hodgetts, L Campbell 2, Athersmith	5,000
21	Mar	5	A	Blackburn Rovers	L	2	1	3	4	L Cambell 3	5,000
22		12	H	Accrington	W	5	0	12	2	D Hodgetts 2, J Devey 4, Dickson 3, L Campbell 3	8,000
23		26	A	Sunderland	L	0	0	1	2	J Devey	18,000
24	Apr	2	H	Bolton Wanderers	W	1	0	2	1	J Devey, Dickson (pen)	10,000
25		16	H	Preston North End	W	2	0	3	1	Dickson, Hodgetts, H Devey	10,000
26		18	H	Wolverhampton Wanderers	L	2	5	3	6	Hodgetts, Dickson, J Devey	8,000

Final League Position: 4th in Football League

Appearances
Goals

FA CUP

1	Jan	16	H	Heanor Town	W	0	0	4	1	Hodgetts 3, J Devey	4,000
2		30	H	Darwen	W	1	0	2	0	J Devey, Hodgetts	6,000
3	Feb	13	A	Wolverhampton Wanderers	W	1	1	3	1	L Campbell, J Devey, Athersmith	24,400
SF		27	N	Sunderland*	W	1	1	4	1	J Devey, Dickson, Hodgetts 2	25,000
F	Mar	19	N	West Bromwich Albion **	L	0	2	0	3		32,810

Appearances
Goals

* Semi-final played at Bramall Lane, Sheffield
** Final played at Kennington Oval

300

	Warner J	Cox G	Evans WG	Brown JR	Cowan James	Campbell G	Athersmith WC	Dickson WA	Devey JHG	Hislop PD	Hodgetts D	Hinchley AA	Devey HP	Baird J	Campbell L	Hare CB	Coulton F	Dutton TT	Graham J	Diver EJ	MATCH
	1	2	3	4	5	6	7	8	9	10	11										1
	1	2	3	4	5	6	7	8	9	10	11										2
	1	2	3	4	5	6	7	8	9	10	11										3
	1	2	3	4	5	6	7	8	9	10	11										4
	1	2	3	4	5	6	7	8	9	10	11										5
	1	2	3	4	5	6	7	8	9	10	11										6
	1	2	3	4	5	6	7	8	9	10	11										7
		2	3	4	5		7	8	9		10	1		6	11						8
		2	3	4			7		9		10	1	5	6	11	8					9
			3	4	5	6	7		9		10	1		2	11	8					10
			2	4	5	6	7		9		10	1		3	11	8					11
			2	4	5	6	7		9		10	1		3	11	8					12
			2	4	5	6	7	8	9		10	1		3	11						13
		2	3	4	5	6			8	9	10	1			11	7					14
		2	3	4	5	6	7	8	9		10	1			11						15
				5	4	7		8	9		10	1	6	2	11						16
			2	4	5	6	7	8	9		10	1		3	11						17
			3	4	5	6	7		9		11	1		2	10	8					18
	1		2		5		7	8	9		11		4	6	10		3				19
	1			4	5		7	8	9		10		6	2	11		3				20
	1	3			5			9					4	6	11	7	2	8	10		21
	1	2	3		5		7	9	8		11		4	6	10						22
		3	2		5	1	7	9	8		10		4	6	11						23
		3			5	2	7	9	8				4	6	11	10			1		24
		2	3		5	4	7	9	8		10		6		11				1		25
		3	2		5	6	7	9	8		10		4		11				1		26
	11	17	23	18	25	20	24	21	25	7	24	11	10	15	19	8	3	1	1	3	
			3				9	15	26	4	12		1		15	4					

		2		5		7		9		10		4	6	11	8	3					1
	1		2	6	5		7	8	9		10			4	11		3				2
	1	3	2		5		7	9	8		10		4	6	11						3
	1	3	2		5		7	9	8		10		4	6	11						SF
	1	3	2		5		7	9	8		10		4	6	11						F

| | 5 | 3 | 5 | 1 | 5 | | 5 | 4 | 5 | | 5 | | 4 | 5 | 5 | 1 | 2 | | | | |
| | | | | | | | 1 | 1 | 4 | | 6 | | | | 1 | | | | | | |

FINAL LEAGUE TABLE

	P	W	D	L	F	A	P
Sunderland	26	21	0	5	93	36	42
Preston North End	26	18	1	7	61	31	37
Bolton Wanderers	26	17	2	7	51	37	36
Aston Villa	**26**	**15**	**0**	**11**	**89**	**56**	**30**
Everton	26	12	4	10	49	49	28
Wolverhampton W	26	11	4	11	59	46	26
Burnley	26	11	4	11	49	45	26
Notts County	26	11	4	11	55	51	26
Blackburn Rovers	26	10	6	10	58	65	26
Derby County	26	10	4	12	46	52	24
Accrington	26	8	4	14	40	78	20
West Bromwich A	26	6	6	14	51	58	18
Stoke	26	5	4	17	38	61	14
Darwen	26	4	3	19	38	112	11

1892/93

SEASON SNIPPETS

Villa had four players making their debut in the opening day win at Burnley, goalkeeper Bill Dunning, Arthur Stokes, James Brown and James Fleming.

Peter Dowds was suspended for a month by Aston Villa in September.

George Davis scored on his league debut against West Bromwich Albion on 19 September.

James Logan's first Villa game was on 15 October.

Frank Burton came in for his first game on 29 October.

Former West Bromwich Albion goalkeeper Bob Roberts made his Villa debut against Preston on 26 November.

David Skea marked his only Villa game with a goal at Notts County on 31 December.

Will Devey scored on his debut on 7 January.

The team left on the Friday and stayed overnight at the Roker Hotel prior to the game at Sunderland on 14 January. A whip round was made and each player was promised an additional £3 if they beat Sunderland. Alas, they lost 0-6.

Play was stopped for several minutes in the game against Notts county on 18 March due to the ball bursting.

Albert Woolley scored twice on his debut on 25 March.

Bob Chatt made his league debut on 15 April.

When Villa were drawn away at Darwen in the FA Cup, they offered the Lancashire team £150 to switch the fixture to Wellington Road, but Darwen demanded £300 which Villa declined.

DIVISION ONE

MANAGER: Directors

MATCH	DATE	VENUE	OPPONENTS	RESULT	HT SCORE	SCORE	SCORERS	ATT
1	Sep 5	A	Burnley	W	0 0	2 0	L Campbell, Hodgetts	8,000
2	10	H	Everton	W	1 0	4 1	Hodgetts, Fleming 2, J Devey	10,000
3	12	A	Stoke	W	0 0	1 0	L Campbell	4,500
4	17	H	Sunderland	L	0 3	1 6	Hodgetts	12,000
5	19	A	West Bromwich Albion	L	1 0	2 3	J Devey, Davis	11,239
6	24	A	Bolton Wanderers	L	0 1	0 5		7,000
7	Oct 1	H	Everton	L	0 0	0 1		12,000
8	8	A	Wolverhampton Wanderers	L	0 1	1 2	Hodgetts	8,000
9	10	H	Stoke	W	1 0	3 2	A Brown, L Campbell, J Devey	7,000
10	15	H	Nottingham Forest	W	1 0	1 0	A Brown	11,000
11	22	A	Preston North End	L	0 4	1 4	J Devey	6,000
12	29	H	Derby County	W	2 0	6 1	Athersmith 2, J Devey 2, Dowds, A Brown	8,000
13	Nov 5	A	West Bromwich Albion	W	2 0	5 2	A Brown 2, Hare, J Devey, Burton	15,000
14	12	A	Nottingham Forest	W	3 3	5 4	Athersmith, Hare, J Devey	10,000
15	19	A	Newton Heath	L	0 1	0 2		5,000
16	26	H	Preston North End	W	1 0	3 1	Hodgetts, A Brown, Dowds	6,000
17	Dec 3	A	Sheffield Wednesday	L	1 3	3 5	Dowds, J Devey 2	6,000
18	10	H	Blackburn Rovers	W	1 1	4 1	Athersmith, J Devey 2, A Brown	6,000
19	17	A	Derby County	L	1 0	1 2	Logan	5,000
20	24	H	Bolton Wanderers	D	1 1	1 1	Logan	3,000
21	31	H	Notts County	W	1 1	4 1	Athersmith, J Devey, Logan, Skea	3,000
22	Jan 7	H	Sheffield Wednesday	W	3 0	5 1	Logan 2, Hodgetts 2, W Devey	10,000
23	14	A	Sunderland	L	0 3	0 6		7,000
24	Feb 11	A	Blackburn Rovers	D	1 0	2 2	Athersmith 2	4,000
25	Mar 6	H	Newton Heath	W	2 0	2 0	Logan 2	6,000
26	18	H	Notts County	W	2 0	3 1	W Devey, J Devey 2	7,000
27	25	H	Accrington	W	1 3	6 4	J Devey 2, A Brown, Woolley 2, Athersmith	5,000
28	Apr 3	H	Wolverhampton Wanderers	W	2 0	5 0	Hodgetts, Devey, Woolley 2, A Brown	6,000
29	4	A	Burnley	L	1 0	1 3	J Devey	7,000
30	15	A	Accrington	D	0 0	1 1	J Devey	2,000

Final League Position: 4th in First Division

Appearances
Goals

FA CUP

| 1 | Jan 21 | A | Darwen | L | 1 3 | 4 5 | Athersmith, Cowan, J Devey, J Brown | 6,000 |

Appearances
Goals

302

Dunning JW	Stokes AW	Ramsey J	Dowds P	Cowan James	Brown JR	Athersmith WC	Devey JHG	Fleming J	Hodgetts D	Campbell L	Baird J	Campbell G	Paton JJ	Brown Albert A	Davis GA	Evans WG	Clarkson T	Logan J	Burton GF	Hare CB	Roberts RJ	Cox G	Devey HP	Skea DF	Devey W	Woolley A	Chatt RS	MATCH
1	2	3	4	5	6	7	8	9	10	11																		1
1	2	3	4	5	6	7	8	9	10	11																		2
1	2		4	5	6	7	8	9	10	11	3																	3
1	2	3		5	6	7	9		10	11		4	8															4
1	2			5	4				10	11	3	6		7	9													5
1	2	3		5	6	7	8	9	10	11		4																6
1	2			5	6	7	9		10	11		4		8		3												7
1	2			5	4	7	9		10	11		6		8		3												8
1	3			5	4	7	9		10	11				8		2	6											9
1			6	5	4	7	10		11		2			8		3		9										10
1			6	5	4	7	10		11		2			8		3		9										11
1			4	5		7	10		11			3		8		2		9	6									12
1			4	5		7	10		11			3		8		2		6	6	9								13
1	6			5		9	10		11			3		8		2		4	7									14
1			6	5		7	10		11			3		8		2		4	9									15
1	3		9	5	4		10		11			6		8		2			7	1								16
1			9	5	4	7	10		11			6		8		2				3								17
1			6	5	4	7	10		11					8		2		9		3								18
1			6	5	4	7	10		11					8		2				3								19
1				4	8		10		11		2	6				9			7	3	5							20
1	3				4	7	10		11			6				9				2	5	8						21
1	3		4			7	10		11							9	6			2	5		8					22
1			6		4	7	10		11					2		9				3	5		8					23
			6	5		9	10			11	2		7					1		3			8					24
1				5		7	10			11	2	6				9	4			3			8					25
			6	5		7	10		11		2			8		4		1	3				9					26
			6	5		7	9		10		3	2		8		4		1								11		27
1			6	5		7	9		10		2			8	3	4										11		28
1			6	5			9		10		2			8	3	4							7			11		29
1				5			9		10		2			8	3	4	7									11	6	30
26	13	4	19	26	18	26	30	4	28	11	12	15	1	20	1	17	1	10	12	6	4	10	4	1	6	4	1	
			3			10	20	2	8	3				9	1			7	1	2			1	2	4			

1	2		6	5	4	7	10		11					8				9		3							1
1	1		1	1	1	1	1		1					1		1		1		1							
					1	1	1																				

FINAL LEAGUE TABLE

	P	W	D	L	F	A	P
Sunderland	30	22	4	4	100	36	48
Preston North End	30	17	3	10	57	39	37
Everton	30	16	4	10	74	51	36
Aston Villa	**30**	**16**	**3**	**11**	**73**	**62**	**35**
Bolton Wanderers	30	13	6	11	56	55	32
Burnley	30	13	4	13	51	44	30
Stoke	30	12	5	13	58	48	29
West Bromwich A	30	12	5	13	58	69	29
Blackburn Rovers	30	8	13	9	47	56	29
Nottingham Forest	30	10	8	12	48	52	28
Wolverhampton W	30	12	4	14	47	68	28
Sheffield Wednesday	30	12	3	15	55	65	27
Derby County	30	9	9	12	52	64	27
Notts County	30	10	4	16	53	61	24
Accrington	30	6	11	13	57	81	23
Newton Heath	30	6	6	18	50	85	18

1893/94

SEASON SNIPPETS

Improvements to the ground for the opening-day match against West Bromwich Albion included the erection of small iron railings round the enclosure to keep the crowd back and prevent any breaking onto the pitch. Jack 'Baldy' Reynolds marked his debut by scoring a penalty against his old Club. James Elliott also made his debut, but there was difficulty over the signing of Willie Groves who had to be content with being a spectator.

There were two more new faces in the line up to meet Everton on 23 September - Jimmy Welford and James Gillan.

The situation regarding his transfer now resolved, Groves made his first appearance against Derby on 30 September.

Steve Smith made his debut against Burnley on 28 October.

Dunning and Reynolds were suspended by Aston Villa for the game at Bolton Wanderers on 18 November for 'going on a spree' earlier in the week. Lou Benwell played in goal and was particularly complemented for keeping a clean sheet in difficult conditions, blinding snow blowing across the pitch with howling winds in fitful gusts. Dunning was back the following week and this was Benwell's only first-team appearance.

George Russell came in for his first game at Newton Heath on 16 December.

Will Devey made his final Villa appearance against Bolton Wanderers on 3 March.

DIVISION ONE

MANAGER: Directors

MATCH	DATE	VENUE	OPPONENTS	RESULT	HT SCORE	SCORE	SCORERS	ATT
1	Sep 2	H	West Bromwich Albion	W	1 1	3 2	Reynolds (pen), J Devey, Woolley	15,000
2	9	A	Sunderland	D	1 0	1 1	Hodgetts	10,000
3	11	H	Stoke	W	3 1	5 1	Hodgetts 2, Logan, Woolley 2	8,000
4	16	A	Everton	L	0 3	2 4	Woolley, Athersmith	20,000
5	23	H	Everton	W	0 1	3 1	Woolley 2, Athersmith	10,000
6	30	H	Derby County	D	1 0	1 1	Reynolds	10,000
7	Oct 2	A	Sheffield United	L	0 1	0 3		10,000
8	7	A	Nottingham Forest	W	0 0	2 1	J Devey, Groves	12,000
9	14	A	Darwen	D	1 0	1 1	J Devey	3,000
10	16	A	Stoke	D	2 2	3 3	Clare (og), J Devey, Athersmith	4,000
11	21	A	West Bromwich Albion	W	5 1	6 3	J Devey 2, Cowan, Hare, Athersmith, Woolley	15,000
12	28	H	Burnley	W	2 0	4 0	Smith, Hare, J Devey, Athersmith	10,000
13	30	H	Sheffield United	W	3 0	4 0	Hare 3, Reynolds	9,500
14	Nov 4	A	Blackburn Rovers	L	0 1	0 2		8,000
15	11	H	Sunderland	W	0 0	2 1	J Devey, Reynods (pen)	15,000
16	18	A	Bolton Wanderers	W	1 0	1 0	Hare	4,500
17	25	H	Preston North End	W	1 0	2 0	J Devey, Hare	10,300
18	Dec 2	A	Derby County	W	0 0	3 0	Hodgetts 2, Athersmith	7,000
19	9	H	Sheffield Wednesday	W	0 0	3 0	Hodgetts, R Brown (og), Athersmith	8,000
20	16	A	Newton Heath	W	0 0	3 1	Mitchell 2 (og), J Devey	8,000
21	23	A	Wolverhampton Wanderers	L	0 1	0 3		14,000
22	26	H	Darwen	W	4 0	9 0	Brown, Smith, J Devey 2, Hodgetts 2, Reynolds, Athersmith 2	12,500
23	Jan 6	A	Sheffield Wednesday	D	1 2	2 2	Reynolds, Woolley	3,000
24	18	A	Preston North End	W	3 1	5 2	J Devey 2, Cowan 2, Hodgetts	4,000
25	Feb 3	H	Newton Heath	W	3 0	5 1	J Devey 3, Hodgetts, Reynolds	4,000
26	Mar 3	H	Bolton Wanderers	L	1 1	2 3	Chatt 2	8,000
27	24	H	Blackburn Rovers	W	1 1	2 1	Chatt 2	20,000
28	26	A	Wolverhampton Wanderers	D	1 0	1 1	Athersmith	15,000
29	Apr 7	A	Burnley	W	1 1	6 3	Groves 2, J Devey 2, Hodgetts 2	7,000
30	14	H	Nottingham Forest	W	0 1	3 1	Athersmith, Chatt, J Devey	4,700

Final League Position: 1st in First Division

4 Own-goals

Appearances
Goals

FA CUP

1	Jan 27	H	Wolverhampton Wanderers	W	3 0	4 2	Cowan, J Devey 2, Chatt	22,981
2	Feb 10	A	Sunderland *	D	0 2	2 2	Hodgetts, Cowan	22,000
R	21	H	Sunderland	W	1 0	3 1	Athersmith, Chatt, Hodgetts	25,000
3	24	A	Sheffield Wednesday *	L	1 1	2 3	Chatt 2	20,000

Appearances
Goals

* After extra-time - score at 90 minutes 2-2

304

Dunning JW	Elliott JAE	Baird J	Reynolds J	Cowan James	Chatt RS	Athersmith WC	Logan J	Devey JHG	Hodgetts D	Woolley A	Welford JW	Gillan JS	Devey W	Groves W	Hare CB	Smith S	Randle WW	Benwell LA	Burton GF	Brown Albert A	Russell G	Coulton F																															MATCH
1	2	3	4	5	6	7	8	9	10	11																																											1
1	2	3	4	5	6	7	9	8	10	11																																											2
1	2	3	4	5	6	7	9	8	10	11																																											3
1	2	3	4	5	6	7	9	8	10	11																																											4
1		2	4	5		7		9	10	11	3	6	8																																								5
1		2	4	5	6			8	10	11	3			7	9																																						6
		2	4	5	6			8	10	11	3			7	9																																						7
		2	4	5				8	10	11	3	6		9	7																																						8
		2	4	5		7		8	10	11	3	6		9																																							9
1	2		4	5	6	7		9	10	11	3				8																																						10
1		2	4	5		7		9	10	11	3				6	8																																					11
1		2	4	5		7		9	10		3				6	8	11																																				12
1		2	4	5		7		9	10		3				6	8	11																																				13
1		2	4	5		7		9	10		3				6	8	11																																				14
1		2	4	5				9	10		3				6	8	11	7																																			15
		2		5				9	10		3				6	8	11	1	4	7																																	16
1		2	4	5		7		9	10		3				6	8	11		4																																		17
		2	4	5		7		9	10		3				6	8	11																																				18
1		2	4	5		7		9	10		3				6		11			8																																	19
1		2	4	5		7		9	11		3			10						8	6																																20
1		2	4	5		7		9	10		3				6		11			8																																	21
1		2	4	5		7		9	10		3				6		11			8																																	22
1		2	4	5		7		9	10	11	3									8	6																																23
1	3	2	4	5	8	7		9	10	11											6																																24
1	3	2	4	5	8	7		9	10	11					6																																					25
	3	2		5	8	7							9	10			11			6		4	1																														26
1	3	2	4	5	8	7		9	10						6		11																																			27
1	3	2	4	5	8	7		9	10						6		11																																			28
1	3	2		5		7		9	10						8		11		4		6																																29
1	3	2	4	5	8	7		9	10						6		11																																				30
28	12	29	26	30	13	25	4	29	29	14	19	3	4	22	10	15	1	1	4	6	5	1																															
			7		3	5	11	1	20	12	8			3	7	2			1																																	

1	2	3	4	5	8	7		9	10	11				6																																						1
1	2	3	4	5	8	7		9	10	11				6																																						2
1	2	3	4	5	8	7		9	10	11				6																																						R
1	2	3	4	5	8	7		9	10	11				6																																						3
4	4	4	4	4	4	4		4	4	4				4																																						
				2	4	1		2	2																																											

FINAL LEAGUE TABLE

	P	W	D	L	F	A	P
Aston Villa	30	19	6	5	84	42	44
Sunderland	30	17	4	9	72	44	38
Derby County	30	16	4	10	73	62	36
Blackburn Rovers	30	16	2	12	69	53	34
Burnley	30	15	4	11	61	51	34
Everton	30	15	3	12	90	57	33
Nottingham Forest	30	14	4	12	57	48	32
West Bromwich A	30	14	4	12	66	59	32
Wolverhampton W	30	14	3	13	52	63	31
Sheffield United	30	13	5	12	47	61	31
Stoke	30	13	3	14	65	79	29
Sheffield Wednesday	30	9	8	13	48	57	26
Bolton Wanderers	30	10	4	16	38	52	24
Preston North End	30	10	3	17	44	56	23
Darwen	30	7	5	18	37	83	19
Newton Heath	30	6	2	22	36	72	14

1894/95

SEASON SNIPPETS

The opening-day fixture against Small Heath - later to become Birmingham City - was the first ever league meeting between the Clubs. Bob Gordon scored on his debut with goalkeeper Tom Wilkes also playing his first match.

Billy Dorrell made his debut at Liverpool on 8 September.

Aston Villa played the Football League at Perry Barr on 24 September 1894. This was a Testimonial game for William McGregor. Bob Gordon was on target for Villa in a 3-1 defeat.

George Kinsey made his first appearance on 6 October.

Howard Spencer, who would be part of the Club for the next 42 years, made his league debut against West Bromwich Albion on 13 October.

Tom Purslow scored against West Bromwich Albion on 17 November - his only league game.

Former captain Archie Hunter died on 29 November age 35.

Bill Dunning made the last of his 69 league and FA Cup appearances against Everton on 17 January.

John Baird played his last senior Villa game against Bolton Wanderers on 26 January 1895.

Billy Podmore made his only Villa appearance in the FA Cup first-round game with Derby County on 2 February.

George Russell made his final Villa league appearance in the game with Everton on 24 April.

Bob Chatt scored in the first minute of the FA Cup final. The goal came so quickly that many supporters had not realised that the game had started and there was confusion over the scorer with some initial reports crediting Devey.

DIVISION ONE

MANAGER: Committee

MATCH	DATE	VENUE	OPPONENTS	RESULT	HT SCORE	SCORE	SCORERS	ATT
1	Sep 1	H	Small Heath	W	2 1	2 1	Smith, Gordon	20,000
2	8	A	Liverpool	W	0 1	2 1	Smith, Chatt	15,000
3	15	H	Sunderland	L	1 1	1 2	Smith	15,000
4	22	H	Derby County	W	1 0	2 0	Chatt, Devey	8,000
5	29	A	Stoke	L	0 3	1 4	Chatt	4,000
6	Oct 6	A	Nottingham Forest	L	1 1	1 2	Devey	6,000
7	13	H	West Bromwich Albion	W	2 0	3 1	Hodgetts, Woolley, Chatt	15,000
8	20	A	Small Heath	D	1 1	2 2	Gordon, Hodgetts	15,000
9	22	A	Sheffield United	L	1 1	1 2	Cowan	6,000
10	27	H	Liverpool	W	2 0	5 0	Cowan, Reynolds 2 (1 pen), Dorrell, Hodgetts	4,000
11	Nov 3	A	Sheffield Wednesday	L	0 0	0 1		8,000
12	10	H	Preston North End	W	1 1	4 1	Devey, Dunn (og), Hodgetts, Chatt	10,000
13	12	H	Sheffield United	W	2 0	5 0	Chatt 2, Devey 2, Reynolds	7,000
14	17	A	West Bromwich Albion	L	0 2	2 3	Smith, Purslow	12,000
15	24	H	Nottingham Forest	W	1 1	4 1	Hodgetts, Devey 2, Cowan	8,000
16	Dec 1	A	Blackburn Rovers	W	1 1	3 1	Smith 3	10,000
17	3	H	Sheffield Wednesday	W	1 0	3 1	Russell, Devey, Reynolds (pen)	5,000
18	8	H	Blackburn Rovers	W	1 0	3 0	Athersmith, Devey 2	5,000
19	22	A	Wolverhampton Wanderers	W	2 0	4 0	Hodgetts 2 Athersmith, Devey	7,000
20	26	H	Stoke	W	2 0	6 0	Athersmith 3, Reynolds (pen), Chatt, Devey	11,000
21	Jan 2	A	Sunderland	D	3 2	4 4	Smith 2, Reynolds (pen), Devey	12,000
22	5	H	Derby County	W	2 0	4 0	Smith, Chatt, Hodgetts 2	8,000
23	12	A	Preston North End	W	1 0	1 0	Devey	5,000
24	17	A	Everton	L	0 3	2 4	Dorrell, Smith	15,000
25	26	H	Bolton Wanderers	W	1 0	2 1	Jones (og), Devey	5,000
26	Feb 23	A	Burnley	D	0 2	3 3	Chatt, Crabtree (og), Athersmith	7,000
27	Mar 23	A	Bolton Wanderers	L	1 2	3 4	Smith, Athersmith, Devey	7,000
28	Apr 6	H	Burnley	W	1 0	5 0	Dorrell 2, Athersmith, Hodgetts, Chatt	4,000
29	15	H	Wolverhampton Wanderers	D	1 2	2 2	Athersmith, Spencer	7,000
30	24	H	Everton	D	2 1	2 2	Athersmith, Smith	5,000

Final League Position: 3rd in First Division

3 Own-goals

Appearances
Goals

FA CUP

1	Feb 2	H	Derby County	W	1 0	2 1	Devey, Smith	6,000
2	16	H	Newcastle United	W	6 1	7 1	Dorrell 2, Athersmith 2, Devey 2, Russell	9,000
3	Mar 2	H	Nottingham Forest	W	3 1	6 2	Chatt 2, Russell, Smith 2, Cowan	20,000
SF	16	N	Sunderland*	W	0 1	2 1	Smith 2	14,000
F	Apr 20	N	West Bromwich Albion**	W	1 0	1 0	Chatt	42,562

Appearances
Goals

* Semi-final played at Ewood Park, Blackburn
** Final played at Crystal Palace

Player Appearances

	Wilkes TH	Baird J	Welford JW	Reynolds J	Cowan James	Russell G	Athersmith WC	Chatt RS	Gordon R	Hodgetts D	Smith S	Elliott JAE	Devey JHG	Dorrell W	Dunning JW	Kinsey G	Hare CB	Spencer H	Woolley A	Burton GF	Purslow T	Podmore WH	MATCH
1	2	3	4	5	6	7	8	9	10	11													1
1		3	4	5	6	7	8			10	2	9	11										2
1		3	4	5	6	7	8		10	11	2	9											3
1		3	4	5	6	7	8			10		9	11										4
1	2	3	4	5	6	7	8	10		11		9											5
	2	3	4	5		7				10		9	11	1	6	8							6
		3	4	5	6	7	8		10			9					2	11					7
		3		5	6	7	8	9	10					1			2	11	4				8
		3		5	6	7	8	9	10				11	1			2		4				9
1		3	4	5	6	7	9		10	8			11				2						10
1		3	4	5	6	7	9		10	8			11				2						11
1		3	4	5	6	7	8		10	11		9					2						12
1		3	4	5	6	7	8		10	11		9					2						13
1		3	4	5	6	7	8			11		9					2				10		14
1		3	4	5	6	7	8		10	11		9					2						15
1		3	4	5	6	7	8		10	11		9					2						16
1		3	4	5	6	7	8		10	11		9					2						17
1		3	4	5	6	7	8		10	11		9					2						18
		3	4	5	6	7	8		10	11		9		1			2						19
		3	4	5	6	7	8		10	11		9		1			2						20
		3	4	5	6	7	8		10	11		9		1			2						21
		3	4	5	6	7	8		10	11		9		1			2						22
		3	4	5	6	7	8		10	11		9		1			2						23
		3	4	5	6	7			10	11		9	8	1			2						24
1	2			5		7			10	11	3	9			6	8			4				25
1				5	6	7	8		10	11	3	9					2		4				26
1			4	5		7	8		10	11	3	9			6		2						27
1		3		5	6	7	8		10			9	11				2		4				28
1		3		5	6	7	8		10	11		9					2		4				29
1			4	5	6	7	8		10	11	3	9					2						30
20	5	26	24	30	27	30	27	4	25	26	6	25	8	10	3	2	23	2	6	1			
			6		4		1	9	11	2		10	13		16	4		1	1		1		

1			4	5	6	7			10	11	3	9				2			8			1
1		3	4	5	6	7			10	11		9	8			2						2
1		3		5	6	7	8		10	11	2	9						4				3
1		3	4	5	6	7	8		10	11		9				2						SF
1		3	4	5	6	7	8		10	11		9				2						F
5		4	4	5	5	5	3		5	5	2	5	1			4		1	1			
				1	2	2	3			5		3	2									

FINAL LEAGUE TABLE

	P	W	D	L	F	A	P
Sunderland	30	21	5	4	80	37	47
Everton	30	18	6	6	82	50	42
Aston Villa	**30**	**17**	**5**	**8**	**82**	**43**	**39**
Preston North End	30	15	5	10	62	46	35
Blackburn Rovers	30	11	10	9	59	49	32
Sheffield United	30	14	4	12	57	55	32
Nottingham Forest	30	13	5	12	50	56	31
Sheffield Wednesday	30	12	4	14	50	55	28
Burnley	30	11	4	15	44	56	26
Bolton Wanderers	30	9	7	14	61	62	25
Wolverhampton W	30	9	7	14	43	63	25
Small Heath	30	9	7	14	50	74	25
West Bromwich A	30	10	4	16	51	66	24
Stoke	30	9	6	15	50	67	24
Derby County	30	7	9	14	45	68	23
Liverpool	30	7	8	15	51	70	22

1895/96

SEASON SNIPPETS

The receipts of £505 18s 6d for the match with West Bromwich Albion on 2 September set a record for league games at Perry Barr. Jimmy Crabtree and Johnny Campbell both made their debut.

Steve Smith 'scored' direct from a corner during the 7 - 3 romp against Small Heath on 7 September, but the 'goal' was disallowed as the ball had not been touched by another player, a requirement at the time. After the game, George Ramsey discovered 2,017 tickets unaccounted for. The receipts were £327 17s.

John Cowan scored on his debut on 21 September.

James Elliott made his last appearance on 26 October.

Goalkeeper Edward Harris was carried off injured against Sheffield United on 16 November. It was his only league game. Bob Chatt took over in goal. This was also the last match for Billy Dorrell.

Jeremiah Griffiths played the first of his two Villa league games against Bury on 28 December.

After dropping down to second place, a goal from John Cowan against Preston on 11 January put Villa back on top where they remained for the rest of the season.

Dennis Hodgetts scored in his last game, the FA Cup defeat on 1 February.

DIVISION ONE

MANAGER: Directors

MATCH	DATE	VENUE	OPPONENTS	RESULT	HT SCORE	SCORE	SCORERS	ATT
1	Sep 2	H	West Bromwich Albion	W	1 0	1 0	Devey	18,150
2	7	H	Small Heath	W	5 0	7 3	Campbell 4, Devey 2, Jas Cowan	14,000
3	14	A	Sheffield United	L	1 0	1 2	Hodgetts	10,000
4	21	H	Derby County	W	2 0	4 1	John Cowan, Devey, Campbell, Jas Cowan	12,000
5	28	A	Blackburn Rovers	D	1 0	1 1	Campbell	15,000
6	30	H	Everton	W	3 1	4 3	Campbell 2, Athersmith, Devey	15,000
7	Oct 5	H	Sunderland	W	0 0	2 1	Campbell, John Cowan	15,000
8	12	A	West Bromwich Albion	D	1 0	1 1	Campbell	15,000
9	19	H	Blackburn Rovers	W	1 1	3 1	Crabtree, Dorrell, Hodgetts	18,000
10	26	A	Small Heath	W	0 0	4 1	Devey 2, Reynolds, Campbell	10,000
11	Nov 2	H	Burnley	W	1 0	5 1	Athersmith 3, Smith, Devey	6,000
12	9	A	Sunderland	L	0 1	1 2	Hodgetts	15,000
13	16	H	Sheffield United	D	0 2	2 2	John Cowan, Chatt	4,000
14	23	A	Burnley	W	3 3	4 3	Athersmith 2, Devey, Reynolds (pen)	6,000
15	Dec 7	A	Preston North End	L	1 3	3 4	Devey, Campbell 2	5,000
16	14	H	Bolton Wanderers	W	0 0	2 0	Welford, Campbell	8,000
17	21	A	Everton	L	0 1	0 2		30,000
18	26	A	Wolverhampton Wanderers	W	0 1	2 1	Smith, Spencer	22,200
19	28	H	Bury	W	1 0	2 0	Campbell 2	5,000
20	Jan 4	A	Stoke	W	2 0	2 1	Campbell 2	12,000
21	11	H	Preston North End	W	0 0	1 0	John Cowan	10,000
22	18	A	Sheffield Wednesday	W	1 1	3 1	John Cowan, Devey, Crabtree	15,000
23	25	H	Nottingham Forest	W	2 1	3 1	Chatt, Devey, John Cowan	5,000
24	Feb 8	A	Derby County	D	1 2	2 2	Devey, Athersmith	20,000
25	22	H	Stoke	W	2 1	5 2	Chatt, Campbell 3, Robertson (og)	15,000
26	Mar 7	A	Bolton Wanderers	D	0 1	2 2	Devey 2	14,364
27	14	H	Sheffield Wednesday	W	1 1	2 1	John Cowan, Campbell	10,000
28	21	A	Bury	L	1 3	3 5	Devey, Campbell, John Cowan	13,000
29	Apr 3	A	Nottingham Forest	W	0 0	2 0	Athersmith, Campbell	10,000
30	6	H	Wolverhampton Wanderers	W	1 0	4 1	Cowan, Campbell 2, Crabtree	15,000

Final League Position: 1st in First Division

1 Own-goal

Appearances
Goals

FA CUP

| 1 | Feb 1 | A | Derby County | L | 0 4 | 2 4 | Hodgetts, Burton | 25,000 |

Appearances
Goals

308

Wilkes TH	Spencer H	Welford JW	Reynolds J	Cowan James	Crabtree JW	Athersmith WC	Devey JHG	Campbell JJ	Hodgetts D	Smith S	Burton GF	Cowan John	Chatt RS	Dorrell W	Elliott JAE	Harris EJ	Griffiths JA		MATCH
1	2	3	4	5	6	7	8	9	10	11									1
1	2	3	4	5	6	7	8	9	10	11									2
1	2	3	4	5	6	7	8	9	10	11									3
1		3	4	5	2	7	8	9	10		6	11							4
1	2	3	4	5	6	7	8	9	10			11							5
1	2	3	4	5	6	7	8	9	10			11							6
1	2	3	4	5	6	7	8	9	10			11							7
1	2	3	4	5	6	7	8	9	10			11							8
1	2	3	4		6	7	9		10		8	5	11						9
1	2		4	5	6	7	8	9	10	11				3					10
1	2		4	5	3	8	9		10	7	6	11							11
1	2		4	5	3	7	8	9	10		6	11							12
	2	3		5	6		9		10		4	7	8	11	1				13
1	2	3	4	5	6	7	9			11		10	8						14
1	2	3	4		6	7	9	10		11		8	5						15
1	2	3	4		6	7	9	10	8	11		5							16
1	2	3	4		6	7	8	9	10	11		5							17
1	2	3	4		6	7	8	9	10	11		5							18
1	2	3			6	7	8	9	10	11		5					4		19
1	2	3			6	7	8	9	10		4	11	5						20
1	2			5	3	7	8	9	10		4	11	6						21
1	2			5	3	7	8	9	10		4	11	6						22
1	2			5	3	7	8	9	10		4	11	6						23
1	2	3	4	5			7	9	10		6	11	8						24
1	2	3		5	6	7	9		10		4	11	8						25
1	2	3	6	5			7	9	10		4	11	8						26
1	2	3	4	5	6	7	9	10				11	8						27
1	2	3			5	4	7	9	10		6	11	8						28
1	2	3	4	5	9	7	8	10			6	11							29
1	2	3	4	5	9	7	8	10			6	11							30
29	29	24	22	23	28	29	30	26	21	11	14	22	17	2	1	1	1		
	1		1	2	2	3	8	16	26	3	2		9	3	1				

1	2			5	3	7	8	9	10		4	11	6						1
1	1			1	1	1	1	1	1		1	1	1						
									1		1								

FINAL LEAGUE TABLE

	P	W	D	L	F	A	P
Aston Villa	30	20	5	5	78	45	45
Derby County	30	17	7	6	68	35	41
Everton	30	16	7	7	66	43	39
Bolton Wanderers	30	16	5	9	49	37	37
Sunderland	30	15	7	8	52	41	37
Stoke	30	15	0	15	56	47	30
Sheffield Wednesday	30	12	5	13	44	53	29
Blackburn Rovers	30	12	5	13	40	50	29
Preston North End	30	11	6	13	44	48	28
Burnley	30	10	7	13	48	44	27
Bury	30	12	3	15	50	54	27
Sheffield United	30	10	6	14	40	50	26
Nottingham Forest	30	11	3	16	42	57	25
Wolverhampton W	30	10	1	19	61	65	21
Small Heath	30	8	4	18	39	79	20
West Bromwich A	30	6	7	17	30	59	19

1896/97

SEASON SNIPPETS

On the evening before they opened their league season, Villa played a friendly against Small Heath at Perry Barr, winning 3-1. Fred Wheldon scored two of the goals against his old club, having joined Villa from the Heathens for a fee of £300. Jimmy Whitehouse was in goal following his record transfer from Grimsby Town. Whitehouse then made his Villa league debut on 5 September.

Villa won 2-1 against Derby County in a benefit match for captain John Devey on 5 October.

Dennis Hodgetts was transferred to Small Heath on 10 October.

Villa had an offer of £250 for England international Frank Becton turned down in November. Although the forward was on offer, Liverpool refused to allow him to join Villa.

Albert Evans made his debut on 7 November.

In February, Villa went away to Holt Fleet in Worcestershire to prepare for the league and cup games against Preston North End. Mr J T Lees and trainer Joe Grierson were in charge of the party.

A week after winning the FA Cup, Aston Villa opened their new Aston Lower Grounds stadium with a 3-0 win against Blackburn Rovers. Unfortunately, torrential rain kept the attendance down to 14,000.

Villa defeated West Bromwich Albion 3-1 on 28 April in a match played for the benefit of the Villa players in honour of their having won the 'double' of cup and league.

DIVISION ONE

MANAGER: Directors

MATCH	DATE		VENUE	OPPONENTS	RESULT	HT SCORE		SCORE		SCORERS	ATT
1	Sep	2	H	Stoke	W	2	0	2	1	John Cowan, Devey	6,000
2		5	A	West Bromwich Albion	L	1	0	1	3	Devey	12,000
3		12	H	Sheffield United	D	1	1	2	2	Burton Wheldon	10,000
4		19	A	Everton	W	2	0	3	2	Devey, Campbell 2	25,000
5		26	H	Everton	L	1	1	1	2	Devey	15,000
6	Oct	3	A	Sheffield United	D	0	0	0	0		12,000
7		10	H	West Bromwich Albion	W	2	0	2	0	Wheldon, Campbell	15,000
8		17	A	Derby County	W	1	1	3	1	Wheldon, Campbell, John Cowan	10,000
9		24	H	Derby County	W	0	0	2	1	John Cowan, Wheldon	10,000
10		31	A	Stoke	W	1	0	2	0	Wheldon, Smith	8,000
11	Nov	7	H	Bury	D	1	1	1	1	Athersmith	4,000
12		14	A	Sheffield Wednesday	W	1	0	3	1	Wheldon, Campbell, Athersmith	10,000
13		21	H	Sheffield Wednesday	W	0	0	4	0	Smith, Athersmith, Devey, Wheldon	12,000
14		28	A	Blackburn Rovers	W	1	0	5	1	Devey, Wheldon 3, Smith	5,000
15	Dec	19	H	Nottingham Forest	W	2	1	3	2	Reynolds, Devey, Athersmith	5,000
16		25	A	Liverpool	D	2	2	3	3	James Cowan, Wheldon, Athersmith	15,000
17		26	A	Wolverhampton Wanderers	W	2	1	2	1	Chatt, Athersmith	15,000
18	Jan	2	H	Burnley	L	0	1	0	3		12,000
19		9	A	Sunderland	L	1	1	2	4	Ferguson (og), Crabtree	10,000
20		16	H	Sunderland	W	0	0	2	1	Wheldon, Devey	15,000
21	Feb	6	A	Bury	W	2	0	2	0	Campbell 2	10,000
22		8	A	Burnley	W	3	2	4	3	Campbell, Devey 3	4,000
23		22	H	Preston North End	W	2	0	3	1	Devey 2, Athersmith	14,000
24	Mar	6	A	Nottingham Forest	W	1	0	4	2	Devey 2, John Cowan, Wheldon	10,000
25		13	A	Liverpool	D	0	0	0	0		18,000
26		22	H	Bolton Wanderers	W	0	2	6	2	Athersmith, Reynolds, Campbell, Wheldon 2, Devey	8,000
27		27	A	Bolton Wanderers	W	2	0	2	1	Wheldon 2	8,000
28	Apr	17	H	Blackburn Rovers	W	2	0	3	0	Campbell, John Cowan, Killean (og)	14,000
29		19	H	Wolverhampton Wanderers	W	1	0	5	0	John Cowan 2, Devey, Campbell 2	35,000
30		26	A	Preston North End	W	1	0	1	0	Wheldon	3,000

Final League Position: 1st in First Division

2 Own-goals

Appearances
Goals

FA CUP

1	Jan	30	H	Newcastle United	W	4	0	5	0	Athersmith, Wheldon 3, Smith	5,500
2	Feb	13	H	Notts County	W	1	1	2	1	Wheldon, Campbell	20,000
3		27	A	Preston North End	D	0	1	1	1	Campbell	14,000
R	Mar	3	H	Preston North End	D	0	0	0	0		12,000
2R		10	N	Preston North End *	W	1	0	3	2	Athersmith 2, Campbell	22,000
SF		20	N	Liverpool **	W	1	0	3	0	John Cowan 2, Athersmith	30,000
F	Apr	10	N	Everton ***	W	3	2	3	2	Campbell, Wheldon, Crabtree	65,891

Appearances
Goals

* Second replay played at Bramall Lane, Sheffield
** Semi-final played at Bramall Lane, Sheffield
*** Final played at the Crystal Palace

Wilkes TH	Spencer H	Welford JW	Reynolds J	Cowan James	Crabtree JW	Athersmith WC	Wheldon GF	Devey JHG	Campbell JJ	Cowan John	Whitehouse J	Burton GF	Smith S	Evans AJ	Chatt RS	Griffiths JA																						MATCH
1	2	3	4	5	6	7	8	9	10	11																												1
	2	3	4	5	6	7	8	9	10	11	1																											2
1	2		4	5	3	7	8	9	10	11		6																										3
	2		4	5	3	7	8	9	10	11	1	6																										4
		3	4	5	2	7	10	8	9	11	1	6																										5
	2		4	5	3	7	8	9	10	11	1	6																										6
	2	3	4	5	6	7	10	8	9	11	1																											7
	2	3	4	5	6	7	10	8	9	11	1																											8
	2	3	4	5	6	7	10	8	9	11	1																											9
	2	3	4	5		7	10	8	9		1	6	11																									10
		3	4	5	6	7	10	8	9		1		11	2																								11
	2	3		5	6	7	10	8	9		1		11		4																							12
	2	3		5	6	7	10	8	9		1		11		4																							13
	2			5	6	7	10	8	9		1		11	3	4																							14
	2		4	5	9	7	10	8			1		11	3		6																						15
	2		4	5	3	7	10	8	9		1		11			6																						16
	2		4	5	3	7	10	8	9		1		11																									17
	2		4	5		7	10	8	9		1		11	3		6																						18
	2			5	8	7	10		9		1	6	11	3		4																						19
1	2		6	5	3	7	10	8	9				11		4																							20
1	2			5	6	7	10	8	9				11	3	4																							21
1	2			5	6	7	10	8	9				11	3	4																							22
1	2		4	5	6	7	10	8	9				11	3																								23
1	2		4	5	6	7	10	8	9	11				3																								24
	2		4	5	6	7	10	8	9	11	1			3																								25
1	2		4	5		7	10	8	9				11	3		6																						26
	2		4	5		7	10	8	9	11	1	6		3																								27
	2		4	5	6	7	10	8	9	11	1			3																								28
	2		4	5		7	10	8	9	11	1	6		3																								29
	2		4	5	6	7	10	8	9	11	1			3																								30
8	28	10	24	30	25	30	30	29	29	15	22	8	15	15	11	1																						
		2		1	1	8	18	17	12	7		1	3		1																							

1	2			5	6	7	10	8	9				11	3	4																							1
1	2		4	5	6	7	10	8	9				11	3																								2
1	2		4	5	6	7	10	8	9				11	3																								3
1	2		4	5	6	7	10	8	9				11	3																								R
1	2		4	5	6	7	10	8	9	11				3																								2R
	2		4	5	6	7	10	8	9	11	1			3		6																						SF
	2		4	5	6	7	10	8	9	11	1			3																								F
5	7		6	7	6	7	7	7	7	3	2		4	7	1	1																						
				1	4	5			4	2			1																									

FINAL LEAGUE TABLE

	P	W	D	L	F	A	P
Aston Villa	30	21	5	4	73	38	47
Sheffield United	30	13	10	7	42	29	36
Derby County	30	16	4	10	70	50	36
Preston North End	30	11	12	7	55	40	34
Liverpool	30	12	9	9	46	38	33
Sheffield Wednesday	30	10	11	9	42	37	31
Everton	30	14	3	13	62	57	31
Bolton Wanderers	30	12	6	12	40	43	30
Bury	30	10	10	10	39	44	30
Wolverhampton W	30	11	6	13	45	41	28
Nottingham Forest	30	9	8	13	44	49	26
West Bromwich A	30	10	6	14	33	56	26
Stoke	30	11	3	16	48	59	25
Blackburn Rovers	30	11	3	16	35	62	25
Sunderland	30	7	9	14	34	47	23
Burnley	30	6	7	17	43	61	19

1897/98

SEASON SNIPPETS

James Fisher made his debut on 1 September.

Howard Spencer was injured at Sheffield Wednesday on 27 September and did not play again until 1899.

Brothers Bert and Jack Sharp made their debut against Bolton Wanderers on 2 October. Villa were two goals down when Jack scored twice to equalise, Fred Wheldon then netted the winner. The three goals came in five minutes.

Billy George made his first appearance on 9 October.

Howard Harvey scored twice in his first match on 27 November, the first goal coming in four minutes. The game was the first of only two played by James Suddick while Tommy Bowman also made his debut.

The morning kick-off for the match at Wolverhampton on 27 December had to be delayed as the Villa train was late arriving. The match started at 11.06am.

The 42,000 crowd for the home game with Sheffield United on 15 January was a record for the ground.

James Suddick signed off with a goal against Preston on 5 February, the second of his two Villa games.

Edmund Strange and Billy Garraty made their debut at home to Stoke on 2 April.

30 April was the last game for Jimmy Whitehouse, James Fisher, Bob Chatt and Frank Burton. Two Walsall players were given a trial, Charlie Aston and George Johnson who netted Villa's second goal. The Directors invited hundreds of schoolboys to watch the game.

DIVISION ONE

MANAGER: Directors

MATCH	DATE	VENUE	OPPONENTS	RESULT	HT SCORE	SCORE	SCORERS	ATT
1	Sep 1	H	Sheffield Wednesday	W	2 1	5 2	John Cowan, Wheldon 3, Athersmith	10,000
2	4	H	West Bromwich Albion	W	2 1	4 3	Wheldon 3, Fisher	12,000
3	11	A	Notts County	W	1 2	3 2	John Cowan 2, Devey	15,000
4	18	H	Bury	W	2 1	3 1	Fisher 2, Wheldon	12,000
5	25	A	Blackburn Rovers	L	0 0	3 4	John Cowan, Wheldon 2	10,000
6	27	A	Sheffield Wednesday	L	0 1	0 3		12,000
7	Oct 2	H	Bolton Wanderers	W	0 2	3 2	J Sharp 2, Wheldon	20,000
8	9	A	West Bromwich Albion	D	0 0	1 1	J Sharp	18,000
9	16	H	Notts County	W	3 1	4 2	Devey, J Sharp 2, Wheldon	20,000
10	23	A	Sunderland	D	0 0	0 0		20,000
11	30	H	Liverpool	W	2 0	3 1	Wheldon, Athersmith, Devey	20,000
12	Nov 6	A	Preston North End	L	1 2	1 3	Fisher	4,000
13	13	H	Everton	W	2 0	3 0	Wheldon 2, J Sharp	10,000
14	20	A	Bolton Wanderers	L	0 2	0 2		15,000
15	27	H	Sunderland	W	1 2	4 3	Harvey 2, Wheldon 2 (1 pen)	8,000
16	Dec 11	H	Blackburn Rovers	W	2 1	5 1	Crabtree, Athersmith, Wheldon, James Cowan, John Cowan	20,000
17	18	A	Stoke	D	0 0	0 0		11,000
18	25	H	Everton	L	0 2	1 2	Wheldon	25,000
19	27	A	Wolverhampton Wanderers	D	0 0	1 1	Athersmith	27,489
20	Jan 8	H	Sheffield United	L	0 1	0 1		20,000
21	15	H	Sheffield United	L	0 0	1 2	Wheldon	42,000
22	22	A	Derby County	L	1 2	1 3	B Sharp	12,000
23	Feb 5	H	Preston North End	W	3 0	4 0	Suddick, J Sharp, Wheldon, Athersmith	10,000
24	Mar 5	H	Derby County	W	3 0	4 1	Smith, J Sharp 2, Fisher	11,900
25	12	A	Bury	W	1 0	2 1	J Sharp, Wheldon	9,000
26	26	A	Nottingham Forest	L	0 3	1 3	Wheldon	5,000
27	Apr 2	H	Stoke	D	0 0	1 1	Harvey	10,000
28	11	H	Wolverhampton Wanderers	L	1 1	1 2	Wheldon	9,000
29	16	A	Liverpool	L	0 3	0 4		20,000
30	30	H	Nottingham Forest	W	2 0	2 0	Smith, Johnson	5,000

Final League Position: 6th in First Division

1 Own-goal

Appearances
Goals

FA CUP

| 1 | Jan 29 | A | Derby County | L | 0 0 | 0 1 | | 12,000 |

Appearances
Goals

Whitehouse J	Spencer H	Evans AJ	Chatt RS	Cowan James	Crabtree JW	Athersmith WC	Devey JHG	Fisher AJ	Wheldon GF	Cowan John	Wilkes TH	Burton GF	Sharp B	Sharp J	George W	Smith S	Bowman T	Harvey H	Suddick J	Strange EW	Garraty W	Aston CL	Johnson G																				MATCH
1	2	3	4	5	6	7	8	9	10	11																																1
1	2	3	4	5	6	7	8	9	10	11																																2
1	2	3	4	5	6	7	8	9	10	11																																3
	2	3	4	5	6	7	8	9	10	11	1																															4
	2	3		5	6	7	8	9	10	11	1	4																														5
	2	3	4	5	6	7	8	9	10	11	1																															6
		3	4	5		7	8		10	11	1	6	2	9																												7
		3	4	5		7	8		10	11		6	2	9	1																											8
		3		5	6	7	8		10		1	4	2	9		11																										9
		3		5	6	7	8		10			4	2	9	1	11																										10
		3		5	6	7	8		10	11		4	2	9	1																											11
		3		5	6	7	8	10		11		4	2	9	1																											12
		3	4	5	6	7	8		10	11			2	9	1																											13
		3	4	5		7	8	9	10	11			2		1																											14
		3		5	6	7			10	11		4			1		2	8	9																							15
1		3		5	6	7		9	10	11		4					2	8																								16
1		3		5	6	7		9	10	11		4					2	8																								17
1		3		5	6	7	9		10	11		4					2	8																								18
1		3		5	6	7	9		10	11		4					2	8																								19
1		3		5	6	7	9		10	11		4					2	8																								20
1		3		5	6	7	9		10	11		4					2	8																								21
1		3		5	6	7			10			4	9			11	2	8																								22
1		3	4	5	6	7			10					9		11	2		8																							23
1		3	4	5	6			10		7			8			11	2	9																								24
1		3	4	5	6	7		8	10					9		11	2																									25
1		3	4	5	6	7		8	10					9		11	2																									26
1		3	5				9			7		4	10			2	8			6	11																					27
1		3	4	5	6	7		8	10					9		11	2																									28
1		3	5						10	7			4	9			2	8		6	11																					29
1		2	4	5		7		8	10			6				11						3	9																			30
18	6	30	17	28	25	27	18	17	26	22	5	8	18	15	7	9	15	11	2	2	2	1	1																			
				1		1	5	3	5	23		5	1	10			2		3	1			1																			

| 1 | | 3 | | 5 | 6 | 7 | | | 10 | 8 | | | 4 | 9 | | 11 | 2 | | | | | | | | | | | | | | | | | | | | | | | | | 1 |

| 1 | | 1 | | 1 | 1 | 1 | | | 1 | 1 | | | 1 | 1 | | 1 | 1 | | | | | | | | | | | | | | | | | | | | | | | | | |

FINAL LEAGUE TABLE

	P	W	D	L	F	A	P
Sheffield United	30	17	8	5	56	31	42
Sunderland	30	16	5	9	43	30	37
Wolverhampton W	30	14	7	9	57	41	35
Everton	30	13	9	8	48	39	35
Sheffield Wednesday	30	15	3	12	51	42	33
Aston Villa	**30**	**14**	**5**	**11**	**61**	**51**	**33**
West Bromwich A	30	11	10	9	44	45	32
Nottingham Forest	30	11	9	10	47	49	31
Liverpool	30	11	6	13	48	45	28
Derby County	30	11	6	13	57	61	28
Bolton Wanderers	30	11	4	15	28	41	26
Preston North End	30	8	8	14	35	43	24
Notts County	30	8	8	14	36	46	24
Bury	30	8	8	14	39	51	24
Blackburn Rovers	30	7	10	13	39	54	24
Stoke	30	8	8	14	35	55	24

1898/99

SEASON SNIPPETS

Two players made their debut in the opening-day game against Stoke, Albert Wilkes and Richard Gaudie who scored Villa's third goal on 71 minutes.

William Haggart came in for his first game against Nottingham Forest on 22 October.

Frank Bedingfield scored on his debut at Sheffield Wednesday on 26 November. The game was abandoned with ten-and-a-half minutes remaining due to bad light, Sheffield were leading 3-1 at the time. When the matter was later considered by the Football League, the decision was that the remaining minutes must be played. Villa returned on 13 March 1899 when the ten-and-a-half minutes were played and Sheffield scored again, the result being 4-1. Bedingfield did not play in the resumed fixture and neither did John Devey, their places being taken by George Johnson and Billy Garraty while Wednesday had five different players. The original fixture was Bedingfield's only appearance.

Bert Sharp's last game was on 31 December.

After playing Burnley on 14 January, Villa did not play at home again until 25 March.

John Cowan played his last game on 4 February.

Jack Sharp's last game came on 18 February.

Bobby Templeton made his debut at Sunderland on 1 April. Villa were without Crabtree and Athersmith who were in Glasgow playing for the Football League against the Scottish League.

Walter Leigh made his only appearance on 15 April.

DIVISION ONE

MANAGER: Directors

MATCH	DATE	VENUE	OPPONENTS	RESULT	HT SCORE	SCORE	SCORERS	ATT
1	Sep 3	H	Stoke	W	1 1	3 1	Athersmith, Devey, Gaudie	19,002
2	10	A	Bury	L	0 1	1 2	Devey	7,000
3	17	A	Burnley	W	3 2	4 2	Smith 2, Johnson, Athersmith	9,000
4	24	H	Sheffield United	D	0 1	1 1	Devey	25,421
5	Oct 1	A	Newcastle United	D	0 1	1 1	Devey	27,500
6	8	H	Preston North End	W	3 2	4 2	Devey 2, James Cowan, Johnson	18,899
7	15	A	Liverpool	W	2 0	3 0	Johnson, Devey, Wheldon	20,000
8	22	H	Nottingham Forest	W	3 0	3 0	J Sharp 2, Devey	16,889
9	29	H	Bolton Wanderers	W	1 0	2 1	Wheldon, Devey	17,402
10	Nov 5	H	Derby County	W	5 1	7 1	Devey 2, Johnson 2, Wheldon 2, John Cowan	16,786
11	12	A	West Bromwich Albion	W	1 0	1 0	Johnson	18,000
12	19	H	Blackburn Rovers	W	2 0	3 1	Devey, Wheldon 2	21,220
13	26	A	Sheffield Wednesday	L	1 2	1 4	Bedingfield	10,000
14	Dec 3	H	Sunderland	W	1 0	2 0	J Sharp 2	24,983
15	10	A	Wolverhampton Wanderers	D	1 0	1 1	Crabtree	17,357
16	17	H	Everton	W	1 0	3 0	Wheldon, Devey, Johnson	21,335
17	24	A	Notts County	L	0 0	0 1		16,000
18	26	H	Newcastle United	W	1 0	1 0	Athersmith	30,000
19	31	A	Stoke	L	0 1	0 3		10,000
20	Jan 7	H	Bury	W	3 0	3 2	Wheldon, Devey 2	15,400
21	14	H	Burnley	W	3 0	4 0	Wheldon, Athersmith, Taylor (og), Bowman	21,000
22	21	A	Sheffield United	W	1 1	3 1	A Wilkes, Johnson, John Cowan	12,000
23	Feb 4	A	Preston North End	L	0 0	0 2		10,000
24	18	A	Nottingham Forest	L	0 1	0 1		16,000
25	Mar 4	A	Derby County	D	1 0	1 1	Johnson	10,000
26	18	A	Blackburn Rovers	D	0 0	0 0		14,000
27	25	H	Sheffield Wednesday	W	1 0	3 1	Wheldon, Garraty, Johnson	14,000
28	Apr 1	A	Sunderland	L	1 3	2 4	Devey, James Cowan	18,000
29	3	A	Wolverhampton Wanderers	L	0 3	0 4		18,000
30	15	A	Everton	D	0 0	1 1	Smith	15,000
31	17	A	Bolton Wanderers	D	0 0	0 0		7,000
32	22	H	Notts County	W	4 1	6 1	Devey 3, Wheldon, Garraty 2	18,900
33	24	H	West Bromwich Albion	W	3 0	7 1	Bowman, Wheldon 2, Garraty 3, James Cowan	12,500
34	29	H	Liverpool	W	5 0	5 0	Devey 2, Wheldon 2, Crabtree	41,000

Final League Position: 1st in First Division

1 Own-goal

Appearances
Goals

FA CUP

1	Jan 28	A	Nottingham Forest	L	1 2	1 2	Johnson	32,000

Appearances
Goals

Appearances Table

MATCH	Wilkes TH	Bowman T	Evans AJ	Wilkes A	Cowan James	Crabtree JW	Athersmith WC	Devey JHG	Johnson G	Gaudie R	Smith S	Wheldon GF	George W	Aston CL	Haggart W	Sharp J	Cowan John	Bedingfield F	Sharp B	Spencer H	Garraty W	Templeton RB	Leigh WH
1		2	3	4	5	6	7	8	9	10	11												
2	1	2		4	5	3	7	8	9	6	11	10											
3		2		4	5	3	7	8	9	6	11	10	1										
4		2		4	5	3	7	8	9	6	11	10	1										
5		2	3		5	4	7	8	9	6	11	10	1										
6		4	3		5	6	7	8	9		11	10	1	2									
7		4	3		5	6	7	8	9		11	10	1	2									
8		4			5	6		8	9		11	10	1	3	2	7							
9		4	3		5	6		8	9			10	1	2		7	11						
10		4	3	6	5			8	9			10	1	2		7	11						
11		4	3		5	6		8	9			10	1	2		7	11						
12		4	3		5	6	7	9				10	1	2		8	11						
13		4	3		5	6	7	8			11	10	1	2				9					
14		4	3		5	6	7		9		11	10	1	2		8							
15		4	3		5	6	7	8	9		11	10	1	2									
16		4	3	5		6	7	8	9		11	10	1						2				
17		4	3		5	6	7	8	9		11	10	1						2				
18		4	3		5	6	7	8	9		11	10	1						2				
19		4	3		5	6	7		9		11	10	1		8				2				
20		4	3	6	5	2	7	8	9		11	10	1										
21		4	3	6	5	2	7	8	9		11	10	1										
22		4	3	6	5	2	7	8	9			10	1				11						
23		4	3	6	5		7	8	9			10	1				11		2				
24		4	3	6	5			8	9		11	10	1		7				2				
25		4	3		5	6	7	8	9		11	10	1						2				
26		4			5	6	7		9		11	10	1	3					2	8			
27		4	3		5	6	7		9		11	10	1						2	8			
28		4	3		5			8			11	10	1	6					2	9	7		
29		4	3		5	6	7	8			11	10	1	2						9			
30		4	3		5	6	7				11	10	1						2	8		9	
31		4	3		5	6	7	8			11	10	1						2	9			
32		4	3		5	6	7	8			11	10	1						2	9			
33		4	3		5	6	7	8			11	10	1						2	9			
34		4	3		5	6	7	8			11	10	1						2	9			
Totals	2	34	29	11	33	30	28	30	24	5	28	33	32	13	1	8	6	1	4	11	9	1	1
Goals		2			1	3	2	4	21	10	1	3	15			4	2	1		6			

Cup

	4	3	6	5	2	7	8	9		11	10	1											1
	1	1	1	1	1	1	1	1	1		1	1	1										
								1															

FINAL LEAGUE TABLE

	P	W	D	L	F	A	P
Aston Villa	**34**	**19**	**7**	**8**	**76**	**40**	**45**
Liverpool	34	19	5	10	49	33	43
Burnley	34	15	9	10	45	47	39
Everton	34	15	8	11	48	41	38
Notts County	34	12	13	9	47	51	37
Blackburn Rovers	34	14	8	12	60	52	36
Sunderland	34	15	6	13	41	41	36
Wolverhampton W	34	14	7	13	54	48	35
Derby County	34	12	11	11	62	57	35
Bury	34	14	7	13	48	49	35
Nottingham Forest	34	11	11	12	42	42	33
Stoke	34	13	7	14	47	52	33
Newcastle United	34	11	8	15	49	48	30
West Bromwich A	34	12	6	16	42	57	30
Preston North End	34	10	9	15	44	47	29
Sheffield United	34	9	11	14	45	51	29
Bolton Wanderers	34	9	7	18	37	51	25
Sheffield Wednesday	34	8	8	18	32	61	24

1899/00

SEASON SNIPPETS

Villa's line up for the opening match was exactly the same as for the final match the previous season – the first time this has occurred since league football began.

William Haggard's last game came on 7 October.

Christopher Mann made his debut against Wolves on 11 November taking the place of James Cowan who was having treatment from a London Specialist after suffering knee damage the previous week against Newcastle. The Navy Brigade made a collection for the local Reservist Fund.

James Garfield scored after 35 minutes in his only Villa league game, a 2-0 win at Stoke, on 13 November.

Fred Wheldon failed to arrive at New Street Station to travel with the team to Liverpool on 18 November, but arrived at the ground later.

Michael Noon made his debut on 25 November against Burnley as Spencer was suffering from a damaged knee.

Charlie McEleny came in for his only Villa game at Preston on 2 December as Bowman was laid up with influenza.

At the end of the match against Blackburn on 20 January, the Villa party set off for Blackpool to spend the week training for the FA Cup tie with Manchester City.

Fred Watkins was capped twice for Wales whilst a Villa player, but his only appearance for the club came at Burnley on 31 March when he stood in for Steve Smith.

Fred Wheldon played his last Villa league game on 16 April.

DIVISION ONE

MANAGER: Directors

MATCH	DATE	VENUE	OPPONENTS	RESULT	HT SCORE	SCORE	SCORERS	ATT
1	Sep 2	A	Sunderland	W	0 0	1 0	Garraty	18,000
2	4	H	Glossop	W	6 0	9 0	Wheldon 2, Garraty 4, Smith, Athersmith, Devey	15,000
3	9	H	West Bromwich Albion	L	0 0	0 2		25,000
4	16	A	Everton	W	1 1	2 1	Wheldon, Garraty	30,000
5	23	H	Blackburn Rovers	W	1 1	3 1	Wheldon, Devey 2	15,000
6	30	A	Derby County	L	0 2	0 2		9,000
7	Oct 7	H	Bury	W	0 1	2 1	Wheldon, Johnson	18,000
8	14	A	Notts County	W	2 1	4 1	Johnson 3, Devey	10,000
9	21	H	Manchester City	W	1 1	2 1	Wheldon, Devey	25,000
10	28	A	Sheffield United	L	1 0	1 2	Smith	30,000
11	Nov 4	H	Newcastle United	W	2 0	2 1	Devey, Wheldon	12,000
12	11	H	Wolverhampton Wanderers	D	0 0	0 0		12,000
13	13	A	Stoke	W	2 0	2 0	Garfield, Devey	15,000
14	18	A	Liverpool	D	2 2	3 3	Templeton, Devey, Wilkes	15,000
15	25	H	Burnley	W	1 0	2 0	Wheldon, Templeton	20,000
16	Dec 2	A	Preston North End	W	3 0	5 0	Garraty, Smith 3, Dunn (og)	6,000
17	9	H	Nottingham Forest	D	1 1	2 2	Garraty, Devey	15,000
18	16	A	Glossop	L	0 1	0 1		6,000
19	23	H	Stoke	W	2 0	4 1	Smith, Garraty, Wheldon 2	5,000
20	30	H	Sunderland	W	2 0	4 2	Garraty 3, Johnson	60,000
21	Jan 1	A	Bury	L	0 2	0 2		14,266
22	6	A	West Bromwich Albion	W	1 0	2 0	Garraty 2	5,000
23	13	H	Everton	D	0 1	1 1	Athersmith	12,000
24	20	A	Blackburn Rovers	W	2 0	4 0	Garraty 2, Smith, Athersmith	8,000
25	Feb 3	H	Derby County	W	0 1	3 2	Garraty 2, Wheldon	7,000
26	17	H	Notts County	W	3 2	6 2	Garraty 3, Athersmith, Cowan, Devey	16,000
27	Mar 3	A	Sheffield United	D	0 1	1 1	Garraty	50,000
28	10	A	Newcastle United	L	1 2	2 3	Devey, Garraty	25,000
29	19	A	Manchester City	W	1 0	2 0	Garraty 2	15,000
30	24	H	Liverpool	W	0 0	1 0	Devey	12,000
31	31	A	Burnley	W	1 1	2 1	Wheldon, Devey	7,000
32	Apr 7	H	Preston North End	W	2 1	3 1	Garraty 2, Templeton	18,000
33	14	A	Nottingham Forest	D	1 1	1 1	Templeton	10,000
34	16	A	Wolverhampton Wanderers	W	1 0	1 0	Templeton	18,000

Final League Position: 1st in First Division

1 Own-goal

Appearances
Goals

FA CUP

1	Jan 27	A	Manchester City	D	0 1	1 1	Devey	30,000
R	31	H	Manchester City	W	1 0	3 0	Garraty 2, Wheldon	16,000
2	Feb 10	A	Bristol City	W	3 1	5 1	Garraty, Devey 4	12,000
3	24	A	Millwall	D	1 0	1 1	Wheldon	25,000
R	28	H	Millwall	D	0 0	0 0		15,000
2R	Mar 5	N	Millwall *	L	0 2	1 2	Johnson	15,000

Appearances
Goals

* Second replay played at Elm Park, Reading

FINAL LEAGUE TABLE

	P	W	D	L	F	A	P
Aston Villa	**34**	**22**	**6**	**6**	**77**	**35**	**50**
Sheffield United	34	18	12	4	63	33	48
Sunderland	34	19	3	12	50	35	41
Wolverhampton W	34	15	9	10	48	37	39
Newcastle United	34	13	10	11	53	43	36
Derby County	34	14	8	12	45	43	36
Manchester City	34	13	8	13	50	44	34
Nottingham Forest	34	13	8	13	56	55	34
Stoke	34	13	8	13	37	45	34
Liverpool	34	14	5	15	49	45	33
Everton	34	13	7	14	47	49	33
Bury	34	13	6	15	40	44	32
West Bromwich A	34	11	8	15	43	51	30
Blackburn Rovers	34	13	4	17	49	61	30
Notts County	34	9	11	14	46	60	29
Preston North End	34	12	4	18	38	48	28
Burnley	34	11	5	18	34	54	27
Glossop North End	34	4	10	20	31	74	18

317

1900/01

SEASON SNIPPETS

Albert F Brown scored two first-half goals on his league debut at Sheffield United on 24 November, but played only one more senior competitive Villa game.

Villa won 6-2 against Berlin FC on 7 January. Jimmy Crabtree scored three goals while Joe Bache, Albert F Brown and George Johnson netted a goal each. It was the first visit to Britain by a German team.

Joe Bache played the first of his 431 Villa league games against Notts County on 16 February, but it was the last match for Chris Mann, Willie Macaulay and Albert F Brown.

On 2 March 1901, Villa won 1-0 against Corinthians for the Sheriff of London's Charity Shield. Charlie Athersmith netted after 75 minutes.

Frank Lloyd scored on his Villa league debut against Sheffield Wednesday on 9 March.

The Villa team for the game on 16 March against Liverpool was depleted. Crabtree, Athersmith and Wilkes had travelled to Scotland for an Inter-League game, Spencer was injured, Steve Smith, Evans and Johnson all had influenza while Billy George pulled out at the last minute with a shoulder injury. Jack Whitley made his league debut in goal.

Alf Wood made his debut on 30 March.

Jimmy Murray made his debut against Wolves on 8 April.

On 17 April, Alf Gilson made his debut while Charlie Athersmith played his last game.

Steve Smith, Alf Gilson and Tommy Bowman all played their last Villa league game against Derby on 22 April.

Arthur Millar and Tom Watson both made their debut in the final match of the season.

First-round FA Cup matches were due to be played on 26 January, but were postponed due to the death of Queen Victoria.

A heavy snowstorm caused the third-round replay against Small Heath to be halted for four minutes.

318

DIVISION ONE

MANAGER: Directors

MATCH	DATE	VENUE	OPPONENTS	RESULT	HT SCORE	SCORE	SCORERS	ATT
1	Sep 1	H	Stoke	W	0 0	2 0	Athersmith, Smith	20,000
2	3	H	Preston North End	W	1 0	4 0	Devey 3, Garraty	12,000
3	8	A	West Bromwich Albion	W	1 0	1 0	Johnson	35,000
4	10	H	Bury	W	1 0	1 0	Devey	23,000
5	15	H	Everton	L	0 1	1 2	Devey	30,000
6	22	A	Sunderland	D	0 0	0 0		31,000
7	29	H	Derby County	W	1 0	2 1	Devey, Templeton	25,000
8	Oct 6	A	Bolton Wanderers	L	0 0	0 1		12,231
9	13	H	Notts County	L	0 0	1 2	Johnson	16,000
10	20	H	Preston North End	W	1 0	2 0	Smith, Garraty	9,000
11	27	H	Wolverhampton Wanderers	D	0 0	0 0		12,000
12	29	H	Blackburn Rovers	D	1 2	3 3	Templeton, Athersmith 2	14,000
13	Nov 3	A	Sheffield Wednesday	L	2 1	2 3	Johnson, Garraty	20,000
14	10	A	Liverpool	L	0 3	1 5	Johnson	18,000
15	17	H	Newcastle United	D	2 1	2 2	Johnson, Wilkes	20,000
16	24	A	Sheffield United	D	2 0	2 2	Brown 2	18,000
17	Dec 1	H	Manchester City	W	5 1	7 1	Johnson 4, Garraty, Wilkes, Devey	12,000
18	8	A	Bury	L	1 2	1 3	Smith	11,000
19	15	H	Nottingham Forest	W	2 0	2 1	Devey 2	30,000
20	22	A	Blackburn Rovers	D	0 0	2 2	Smith, Garraty	8,000
21	26	H	Bolton Wanderers	W	1 0	3 0	Devey 2, Athersmith	20,000
22	29	A	Stoke	D	0 0	0 0		12,000
23	Jan 5	H	West Bromwich Albion	L	0 0	0 1		25,000
24	12	A	Everton	L	1 2	1 2	Garraty	20,000
25	19	H	Sunderland	D	1 1	2 2	Devey, Garraty	16,000
26	Feb 16	A	Notts County	L	0 1	0 2		14,000
27	Mar 9	H	Sheffield Wednesday	W	1 0	2 1	Garraty, Lloyd	16,000
28	16	A	Liverpool	L	0 1	0 2		15,000
29	30	H	Sheffield United	D	0 0	0 0		12,000
30	Apr 8	A	Wolverhampton Wanderers	D	0 0	0 0		7,000
31	17	A	Newcastle United	L	0 1	0 3		18,000
32	20	H	Nottingham Forest	L	1 1	1 3	Bache	6,000
33	22	A	Derby County	L	0 2	0 3		6,000
34	27	A	Manchester City	L	0 1	0 4		16,000

Final League Position: 15th in First Division

Appearances
Goals

FA CUP

1	Feb 9	H	Millwall	W	3 0	5 0	Devey, Johnson 3, Smith	23,000
2	23	H	Nottingham Forest	D	0 0	0 0		45,000
R	27	A	Nottingham Forest *	W	0 1	3 1	Cowan, Garraty, Athersmith	30,000
3	Mar 23	A	Small Heath	D	0 0	0 0		15,000
R	27	H	Small Heath **	W	0 0	1 0	Garraty	15,000
SF	Apr 6	N	Sheffield United ***	D	1 2	2 2	Garraty, Devey	30,000
R	11	N	Sheffield United ****	L	0 1	0 3		25,000

Appearances
Goals

* After extra-time - score at 90 minutes 1-1
** After extra-time - score at 90 minutes 0-0
*** Played at City Ground, Nottingham
**** Played at Derby

FINAL LEAGUE TABLE

	P	W	D	L	F	A	P
Liverpool	34	19	7	8	59	35	45
Sunderland	34	15	13	6	57	26	43
Notts County	34	18	4	12	54	46	40
Nottingham Forest	34	16	7	11	53	36	39
Bury	34	16	7	11	53	37	39
Newcastle United	34	14	10	10	42	37	38
Everton	34	16	5	13	55	42	37
Sheffield Wednesday	34	13	10	11	52	42	36
Blackburn Rovers	34	12	9	13	39	47	33
Bolton Wanderers	34	13	7	14	39	55	33
Manchester City	34	13	6	15	48	58	32
Derby County	34	12	7	15	55	42	31
Wolverhampton W	34	9	13	12	39	55	31
Sheffield United	34	12	7	15	35	52	31
Aston Villa	**34**	**10**	**10**	**14**	**45**	**51**	**30**
Stoke	34	11	5	18	46	57	27
Preston North End	34	9	7	18	49	75	25
West Bromwich A	34	7	8	19	35	62	22

1901/02

SEASON SNIPPETS

Willie Clarke, who was signed to replace Athersmith, made his debut on 7 September along with Bert Banks.

George Smith played his first match on 9 September.

Albert Evans was taken off after 25 minutes against Sheffield United on 16 September with a knee injury and did not play again all season.

James Cowan had to go off with a thigh injury at Stoke on 21 September, his last Villa game.

Frank Lloyd was sent off for kicking Everton's Walter Abbott on 28 September.

Hartley Shutt and George Harris both made their first Villa appearances at Sunderland on 5 October.

Tom Perry played his first Villa game on 19 October.

Bill Marriott made his first appearance at home to Sheffield Wednesday on 26 October along with Jasper McLuckie who scored twice and hit seven goals in his first four matches.

Billy Brawn made his Villa debut at Blackburn on 11 January.

Tommy Niblo's first game came at Stoke on 18 January.

Harry Cooch made his debut at Newcastle United on 5 April deputising for Billy George who was in Glasgow playing for England in the tragic game when 25 people were killed when part of the terracing collapsed. Wilkes was also playing for England and Templeton represented Scotland. The International match was replayed at Villa Park on 3 May, the proceeds going to the Disaster Fund.

Villa's train journey to Grimsby for the final match took six hours and 20 minutes and the team only arrived 15 minutes before scheduled kick-off which was delayed by 10 minutes.

John Devey made his last appearance in the FA Cup replay against Stoke on 29 January.

DIVISION ONE

MANAGER: Directors

MATCH	DATE	VENUE	OPPONENTS	RESULT	HT SCORE	SCORE	SCORERS	ATT
1	Sep 7	A	Bury	D	0 0	0 0		13,000
2	9	H	Notts County	W	1 0	2 0	Bache, Garraty	15,000
3	14	H	Blackburn Rovers	D	1 0	1 1	Bache	20,000
4	16	H	Sheffield United	L	0 1	1 2	Wilkes	12,000
5	21	A	Stoke	L	0 0	0 1		8,000
6	28	H	Everton	D	0 0	1 1	Bache	15,000
7	Oct 5	A	Sunderland	L	0 0	0 1		8,000
8	12	A	Small Heath	W	0 0	2 0	Devey, Bache	25,000
9	19	A	Derby County	L	0 1	0 1		15,000
10	26	H	Sheffield Wednesday	W	1 0	4 1	McLuckie 2, Bache, Templeton	25,000
11	Nov 2	A	Notts County	W	1 0	3 0	McLuckie 2, Garraty	12,000
12	9	H	Bolton Wanderers	W	0 0	1 0	McLuckie	15,000
13	23	H	Wolverhampton Wanderers	W	1 0	2 1	McLuckie 2	20,000
14	30	A	Liverpool	L	0 0	0 1		20,000
15	Dec 7	H	Newcastle United	D	0 0	0 0		18,000
16	14	H	Grimsby Town	W	1 1	4 1	McLuckie 3, Devey	5,000
17	25	A	Everton	W	0 1	3 2	Garraty, Wood, Clarke	20,000
18	26	H	Small Heath	W	1 0	1 0	McLuckie	50,000
19	28	H	Nottingham Forest	W	1 0	3 0	Garraty, Clarke, McLuckie	14,000
20	Jan 1	A	Sheffield United	L	0 4	0 6		28,000
21	4	H	Bury	W	0 0	2 0	McLuckie, Clarke	15,000
22	11	A	Blackburn Rovers	L	0 1	0 4		20,000
23	18	A	Stoke	D	0 0	0 0		20,000
24	Feb 1	H	Sunderland	L	0 1	0 1		25,000
25	15	H	Derby County	W	2 1	3 2	Perry, Bache, Wood	20,000
26	17	A	Manchester City	L	0 0	0 1		17,000
27	22	A	Sheffield Wednesday	L	0 1	0 1		9,000
28	Mar 8	A	Bolton Wanderers	D	2 1	2 2	Johnson, McLuckie	10,000
29	22	A	Wolverhampton Wanderers	W	1 0	2 0	McLuckie, Bache	12,000
30	29	H	Liverpool	L	0 0	0 1		17,000
31	31	H	Manchester City	D	0 1	2 2	Johnson, McLuckie	20,000
32	Apr 1	A	Nottingham Forest	D	1 1	1 1	Niblo	8,000
33	5	A	Newcastle United	L	1 1	1 2	Niblo	12,000
34	12	A	Grimsby Town	L	0 2	1 4	Bache	6,000

Final League Position: 15th in First Division

Appearances
Goals

FA CUP

1	Jan 25	A	Stoke	D	1 1	2 2	Garraty 2	20,000
2	29	H	Stoke *	L	0 0	1 2	Garraty	22,000

Appearances
Goals

* After extra-time - score at 90 minutes 1-1

320

FINAL LEAGUE TABLE

	P	W	D	L	F	A	P
Sunderland	34	19	6	9	50	35	44
Everton	34	17	7	10	53	35	41
Newcastle United	34	14	9	11	48	34	37
Blackburn Rovers	34	15	6	13	52	48	36
Nottingham Forest	34	13	9	12	43	43	35
Derby County	34	13	9	12	39	41	35
Bury	34	13	8	13	44	38	34
Aston Villa	**34**	**13**	**8**	**13**	**42**	**40**	**34**
Sheffield Wednesday	34	13	8	13	48	52	34
Sheffield United	34	13	7	14	53	48	33
Liverpool	34	10	12	12	42	38	32
Bolton Wanderers	34	12	8	14	51	56	32
Notts County	34	14	4	16	51	57	32
Wolverhampton W	34	13	6	15	46	57	32
Grimsby Town	34	13	6	15	44	60	32
Stoke	34	11	9	14	45	55	31
Small Heath	34	11	8	15	47	45	30
Manchester City	34	11	6	17	42	58	28

1902/03

SEASON SNIPPETS

Alex Leake made his debut on 13 September following a transfer from Small Heath where he had been skipper.

Tom Perry's last game was at Blackburn on 27 September.

Harry Griffin played his first game against Sunderland on 4 October when unfortunately he was injured and did not get another opportunity.

Albert Fisher, a local lad who had done well in the reserves, was brought in against Bolton on 15 November, but it proved to be his only Villa league game.

There was confusion over Bobby Templeton's goal at Sheffield United on 20 December. A dog had run onto the pitch causing confusion and it was difficult to tell whether it was the dog or Templeton who actually scored.

Templeton played his last Villa league game on New Year's Day.

Oscar Evans came in for his first game at Bolton on 14 March as Bache was down with influenza.

Arthur Lockett made his debut on 27 April.

Villa were drawn away to Barnsley in the FA Cup second round, but paid £250 plus half the gate to switch the tie to Villa Park.

DIVISION ONE

MANAGER: Directors

MATCH	DATE	VENUE	OPPONENTS	RESULT	HT SCORE	SCORE	SCORERS	ATT
1	Sep 6	H	Derby County	D	0 0	0 0		20,000
2	13	A	Nottingham Forest	L	0 0	0 2		12,000
3	20	H	Bury	D	2 1	2 2	Bache, Johnson	15,000
4	27	A	Blackburn Rovers	W	1 0	2 0	Bache, Johnson	10,000
5	Oct 4	H	Sunderland	L	0 0	0 1		30,000
6	11	A	Stoke	L	0 1	0 1		7,000
7	18	H	Everton	W	1 0	2 1	Noon, Garraty	18,000
8	Nov 1	H	West Bromwich Albion	L	0 0	0 3		50,000
9	8	A	Notts County	L	1 2	1 2	Garraty	8,000
10	15	H	Bolton Wanderers	W	3 0	4 2	Garraty 2, Bache, Wilkes	10,000
11	22	A	Middlesbrough	W	0 1	2 1	Clarke, Bache	15,000
12	29	H	Newcastle United	W	4 0	7 0	Wood, Templeton, Johnson 2, Bache 2, Leake	12,000
13	Dec 6	A	Wolverhampton Wanderers	L	1 2	1 2	Bache	10,000
14	13	H	Liverpool	L	1 1	1 2	Bache	12,000
15	20	A	Sheffield United	W	2 1	4 2	McLuckie, Templeton, Garraty 2	14,000
16	26	H	Sheffield Wednesday	W	1 0	1 0	Garraty (pen)	30,000
17	27	H	Grimsby Town	D	1 1	2 2	Garraty 2	30,000
18	Jan 1	A	Sheffield Wednesday	L	0 2	0 4		28,000
19	3	A	Derby County	L	0 0	0 2		10,000
20	10	H	Nottingham Forest	W	2 0	3 1	Garraty 2 (1 pen), McLuckie	25,000
21	17	A	Bury	W	0 0	1 0	McLuckie	9,000
22	24	H	Blackburn Rovers	W	2 0	5 0	Brawn, Niblo, McLuckie 2, Garraty	20,000
23	31	A	Sunderland	L	0 1	0 1		22,000
24	Feb 14	A	Everton	W	1 0	1 0	Bache	20,000
25	28	A	West Bromwich Albion	W	1 1	2 1	McLuckie, Wood	35,000
26	Mar 14	A	Bolton Wanderers	W	0 0	1 0	Johnson	10,000
27	28	A	Newcastle United	L	0 0	0 2		20,000
28	Apr 4	H	Wolverhampton Wanderers	W	1 1	3 1	Johnson, McLuckie, Garraty	10,000
29	11	A	Liverpool	L	0 2	1 2	Garraty (pen)	15,000
30	13	H	Stoke	W	0 0	2 0	Clarke, Leake	10,000
31	15	H	Notts County	W	2 1	2 1	Brawn (pen), McLuckie	7,000
32	18	H	Sheffield United	W	1 0	4 2	Garraty, McLuckie 3	15,000
33	25	A	Grimsby Town	W	2 0	2 0	McLuckie 2	1,000
34	27	H	Middlesbrough	W	2 0	5 0	McLuckie 3, Leake, Wood	20,000

Final League Position: 2nd in First Division

Appearances
Goals

FA CUP

1	Feb 7	H	Sunderland	W	1 0	4 1	Bache, Johnson 2, Pearson	47,000
2	21	A	Barnsley *	W	2 0	4 1	McLuckie 3, Johnson	28,000
3	Mar 7	A	Tottenham Hotspur	W	1 1	3 2	Johnson, McLuckie 2	30,000
SF	21	N	Bury **	L	0 1	0 3		45,000

Appearances
Goals

* Drawn away but played at Villa Park
** Played at Goodison Park, Liverpool

322

George W	Shutt GH	Evans AJ	Perry T	Wood AJE	Wilkes A	Clarke WG	Garraty W	McLuckie J	Bache JW	Niblo TB	Leake A	Johnson G	Templeton RB	Spencer H	Noon MT	Harris GA	Griffin H	Fisher AW	Brawn WF	Cooch H	Pearson JF	Evans O	Lockett AH	MATCH
1	2	3	4	5	6	7	8	9	10	11														1
1	2	3	4		6	7	10	9	11		5	8												2
1	2	3	4	5	6		8		10	11			9	7										3
1		3	4	5	6		8		10	11			9		2	7								4
1		3		5	4		9		10	11					2	7	6	8						5
1		3		5	4	7	8	9	11	10	6				2									6
1		3		5		7	8	9	11	10	6				2	4								7
1		3		5		7	8	9	10		6		11		2	4								8
1		3		5		7	8		10	9	6		11		2	4								9
1		3		5	6	7	9		10	11					2	4		8						10
1		3		5	4	7	8		10		6	9	11	2										11
1		3		5	4	7	8		10		6	9	11	2										12
1		3		5	4	7			10		6	9	11	2										13
1		3		5	4		8		10	9	6		11	2				7						14
1		3		5	4		8	9	10		6		11	2				7						15
1		3		5		7	8		10		6	9	11	2	4									16
		3		5		7	8		10		6	9	11	2	4	6			1					17
		3				7	8		10		5	9	11	2	4	6			1					18
				5		7	8	9	10	11	6			2	3				1	4				19
1	2			5			8	9	10	11	6				3			7		4				20
1	2			5			8	9	10	11	6				3			7		4				21
1				5			8	9	10	11	6			2	3			7		4				22
1				5			8	9	10	11	6			2	3			7		4				23
1	2			5	6			9	10	11	3	8						7		4				24
1				5				9	10	11	6	8		2	3			7		4				25
1	2				5		8			11	6	9		2		3		7		4	10			26
	3			5	11	7	9				6	10		2					1	4				27
1	3			5	10		8	9			6	11		2				7		4				28
1	3			5	10		8	9			6	11		2				7		4				29
1	3			5	10	7		9			6	8		2				11		4				30
1	3			5		7		9			6	8		2				11		4	10			31
	3			5	4	7	8	9			6	10		2				11	1					32
1	3			5	4	7		9			6	8		2	10			11						33
1	3			5	4	8		9			6	10		2				7					11	34

| 29 | 15 | 18 | 4 | 31 | 21 | 20 | 28 | 21 | 25 | 17 | 28 | 20 | 11 | 27 | 16 | 4 | 1 | 1 | 16 | 5 | 13 | 2 | 1 | |
| | | | | 3 | 1 | 2 | 15 | 16 | 9 | 1 | 3 | 6 | 2 | | 1 | | | | 2 | | | | | |

1				5			8			10	11	6	9		2	3			7		4			
1				5				9	10	11	6	8		2	3			7		4				
1				5			8	9		11	6	10		2	3			7		4				

| 4 | | | | 4 | | | 2 | 3 | 3 | 4 | 4 | 4 | | 4 | 4 | | | 4 | | 4 | | | | |
| | | | | | | | | 5 | 1 | | | 4 | | | | | | | | 1 | | | | |

FINAL LEAGUE TABLE

	P	W	D	L	F	A	P
Sheffield Wednesday	34	19	4	11	54	36	42
Aston Villa	**34**	**19**	**3**	**12**	**61**	**40**	**41**
Sunderland	34	16	9	9	51	36	41
Sheffield United	34	17	5	12	58	44	39
Liverpool	34	17	4	13	68	49	38
Stoke	34	15	7	12	46	38	37
West Bromwich A	34	16	4	14	54	53	36
Bury	34	16	3	15	54	43	35
Derby County	34	16	3	15	50	47	35
Nottingham Forest	34	14	7	13	49	47	35
Wolverhampton W	34	14	5	15	48	57	33
Everton	34	13	6	15	45	47	32
Middlesbrough	34	14	4	16	41	50	32
Newcastle United	34	14	4	16	41	51	32
Notts County	34	12	7	15	41	49	31
Blackburn Rovers	34	12	5	17	44	63	29
Grimsby Town	34	8	9	17	43	62	25
Bolton Wanderers	34	8	3	23	37	73	19

1903/04

SEASON SNIPPETS

After playing Newcastle on 2 September, Villa spent two days training at Tynemouth prior the game at Sunderland on 5 September where they lost 6-1 and also lost the services of George Johnson through injury.

Hartley Shutt played his last Villa league game against Derby County on 10 October.

Jack Windmill came in for his first league game on 7 November against Newcastle United.

Freddie Miles made his debut at Nottingham on 19 December as did Albert Hall who scored in a 7-3 win.

Conditions were not good for the local derby with Small Heath on 16 January, snow, which was falling, covered the ground and the situation was made worse by a brisk wind.

Martin Watkins played his first game on 23 January.

Tommy Niblo played his last Villa game on 25 February.

Billy Matthews made his debut at Wolves on 12 March.

The half-time entertainment at Liverpool on 26 March included a brass band while over in one corner of the pitch an acrobat gave a display.

Jasper McLuckie's last Villa game came against Bury on 2 April. He recorded 46 goals in his 62 matches.

In the first round FA Cup match at Stoke on 6 February, Albert Evans fractured a small bone just above his ankle which put him out of action for the remainder of the season.

The second round FA Cup match at non-league Tottenham Hotspur was abandoned due to crowd trouble with Villa leading 1-0 with a goal from Joe Bache. The game was ordered to be replayed at Villa Park and the following Thursday, Spurs won 1-0 with an eighty-eighth-minute goal from Jack Jones.

DIVISION ONE

MANAGER: Directors

MATCH	DATE	VENUE	OPPONENTS	RESULT	HT SCORE	SCORE	SCORERS	ATT
1	Sep 2	A	Newcastle United	D	0 0	1 1	Bache	7,000
2	5	A	Sunderland	L	1 4	1 6	McLuckie	20,000
3	12	H	West Bromwich Albion	W	1 1	3 1	Garraty, McLuckie 2	35,000
4	19	A	Small Heath	D	2 0	2 2	Garraty, Pearson (pen)	20,000
5	26	H	Everton	W	1 0	3 1	Johnson, McLuckie, Wilkes	25,000
6	Oct 3	A	Stoke	L	0 0	0 2		12,000
7	10	H	Derby County	W	1 0	3 0	Niblo, Bache, McLuckie	15,000
8	17	A	Manchester City	L	0 0	0 1		30,000
9	24	H	Notts County	W	1 0	4 0	Garraty, Lockett, McLuckie, Johnson	20,000
10	31	A	Sheffield United	W	1 0	2 1	Johnson, Bache	20,000
11	Nov 7	H	Newcastle United	W	3 0	3 1	Bache 3	25,000
12	14	H	Wolverhampton Wanderers	W	0 0	2 0	Garraty 2 (1 pen)	20,000
13	21	A	Middlesbrough	L	1 1	1 2	Garraty (pen)	15,000
14	28	H	Liverpool	W	1 1	2 1	Brawn, Johnson	12,000
15	Dec 5	A	Bury	D	1 0	2 2	Bache 2	8,000
16	12	H	Blackburn Rovers	L	1 1	2 3	Bache, McLuckie	14,000
17	19	A	Nottingham Forest	W	3 2	7 3	Niblo 3, Leake, Hall, Bache 2,	10,000
18	26	H	Sheffield Wednesday	W	1 1	2 1	Niblo, Brawn	40,000
19	28	A	Derby County	D	2 0	2 2	Hall 2	22,000
20	Jan 2	H	Sunderland	W	1 0	2 0	Niblo, Lockett	30,000
21	9	A	West Bromwich Albion	W	2 1	3 1	Bache, Wood, Brawn (pen)	30,000
22	16	H	Small Heath	D	1 0	1 1	Brawn	20,000
23	23	A	Everton	L	0 1	0 1		30,000
24	30	H	Stoke	W	0 1	3 1	Harris, Watkins, Meredith (og)	12,000
25	Feb 13	A	Manchester City	L	0 0	0 1		12,000
26	27	H	Sheffield United	W	2 0	6 1	McLuckie 2, Hall, Brawn 2, Wood	20,000
27	Mar 12	A	Wolverhampton Wanderers	L	0 1	2 3	Hall 2	12,000
28	19	H	Middlesbrough	W	0 1	2 1	Bache 2	17,000
29	26	A	Liverpool	D	0 0	1 1	Leake	16,000
30	Apr 1	H	Notts County	D	0 0	0 0		15,000
31	2	H	Bury	L	0 0	0 2		15,000
32	9	A	Blackburn Rovers	W	0 0	3 0	Pearson, Garraty, Matthews	6,000
33	16	H	Nottingham Forest	W	2 1	3 1	Brawn, Garraty, Matthews	14,000
34	23	A	Sheffield Wednesday	L	0 3	2 4	Matthews, Garraty	14,000

Final League Position: 5th in First Division

1 Own-goal

Appearances
Goals

FA CUP

1	Feb 6	A	Stoke	W	2 1	3 2	Brawn (pen), Leake, Bache	10,000
2	25	H	Tottenham Hotspur *	L	0 0	0 1		33,000

Appearances
Goals

* After abandoned game at Tottenham

Match	George W	Spencer H	Noon MT	Wilkes A	Wood AJE	Leake A	Brawn WF	Johnson G	McLuckie J	Bache JW	Niblo TB	Garraty W	Lockett AH	Pearson JF	Cooch H	Shutt GH	Evans AJ	Windmill JW	Miles A	Hall AE	Watkins WM	Harris GA	Clarke WG	Matthews W
1	1	2	3	4	5	6	7	8	9	10	11													
2	1	2	3	4	5	6	7	8	9	10	11													
3	1	2	3	4	5	6	7		9	10		8	11											
4	1	2	3		6	5	7		9	10	11	8		4										
5	1	2	3	6	5		7	10	9		11	8		4										
6	1	2	3	6	5				7	9	10		8	11	4									
7					5	6	7	8	9	10	11			4	1	2	3							
8		2		4	5	6	7	8	9	10	11				1		3							
9		2			5	6		8	9	10		7	11	4	1		3							
10	1	2			5	6	7	8		10		9	11	4			3							
11	1	2				6	7	8		10		9	11	4			3	5						
12	1	2			5	6	7	8		10		9	11	4			3							
13	1	2			5	6	7			10		9	11	4			3							
14	1	2			5	6	7	8		10		9	11	4			3							
15		2			5	6	7	8		10		9	11	4	1		3							
16	1	2			5	6	7		9	10		8	11	4			3							
17	1	2				5	6	7		10	9		11	4					3	8				
18	1	2			5	6	7			10	9		11	4					3	8				
19	1				5	6	7			10	9		11	4			3		2	8				
20	1	2			5	6	7		9	10			11	4					3	8				
21	1	2				5	6	7	8	10	9		11	4			3							
22	1	2		6	5	3	7			10	9		11	4						8				
23	1		5		6	7				10	9		11	4			3		2	8	8			
24	1		5			6	7				9		11	4			3		2	8	10	6		
25	1			4	5	3	7				10	8	11						2		9	6		
26	1	2		4	5	6	7		9	10			11				3		3	8				
27			2	6	5				9				11	4	1		3		3	8		7	10	
28			2	5		6	7		9	10			11	4	1		3						8	
29			2	5		6	7		9	10			11		1		3						8	
30		2		4	5	6	7			10			11		1		3			9				
31		2			5	6	7		9				11	4	1		3	8					10	
32	1		2	6	5		9				8	11		4			3					7	10	
33	1		2	4	5	6	7			10		9	11				3						8	
34	1		2		5	6	7					9	11	4			3			10			8	
	25	23	12	18	29	28	32	13	15	27	15	16	28	26	9	1	14	1	16	9	5	2	2	8
				1	2	2	7	4	9	14	6	9	2						6	1	1		3	

1	1	2			4	5	6	7			10	11	9				3		8						
2	1	2			4	5	6	7			10	11	9				3	8							
	2	2			2	2	2	2			2	2	2				1		1	2					
							1	1			1														

FINAL LEAGUE TABLE

	P	W	D	L	F	A	P
Sheffield Wednesday	34	20	7	7	48	28	47
Manchester City	34	19	6	9	71	45	44
Everton	34	19	5	10	59	32	43
Newcastle United	34	18	6	10	58	45	42
Aston Villa	**34**	**17**	**7**	**10**	**70**	**48**	**41**
Sunderland	34	17	5	12	63	49	39
Sheffield United	34	15	8	11	62	57	38
Wolverhampton W	34	14	8	12	44	66	36
Nottingham Forest	34	11	9	14	57	57	31
Middlesbrough	34	9	12	13	46	47	30
Small Heath	34	11	8	15	39	52	30
Bury	34	7	15	12	40	53	29
Notts County	34	12	5	17	37	61	29
Derby County	34	9	10	15	58	60	28
Blackburn Rovers	34	11	6	17	48	60	28
Stoke	34	10	7	17	54	57	27
Liverpool	34	9	8	17	49	62	26
West Bromwich A	34	7	10	17	36	60	24

1904/05

SEASON SNIPPETS

Josiah Gray made his league debut on 3 September.

Walter Brown played his first game on 10 September.

Martin Watkins played his last game on 12 September.

The Derby County game on 15 October was the last match for both Alf Wood and Josiah Gray.

Harry Hampton made his debut at Manchester City on 9 November, but it was George Johnson's last game, he suffered a knee injury, missed the second-half and was forced to retire.

Jimmy Cantrell scored on his debut on 12 November.

Fog made it difficult to see on Christmas Eve when Villa met Bury, it was decided to make a start only because the crowd had turned up in large numbers.

The players left at 8.50am on 22 April for Bury and after the game went on to Ireland to meet Distillery on Monday and Dublin Bohemians on Tuesday before returning to play Wolves on Thursday 27th. The Wolves game was the last match for Willie Clarke and Arthur Lockett who scored.

Walter Corbett made his league debut at Middlesbrough on 8 April. Corbett would go on to gain an Olympic Gold Medal when playing for Great Britain in the 1908 games.

Celebrations were rather different in 1905, when Albert Hall put Villa ahead in the FA Cup semi-final it was reported that his hands were nearly shaken off by delighted colleagues.

While Newcastle United were playing in their first FA Cup final, Villa won the FA Cup for the fourth time. The trophy and medals were presented by Mrs Kenneth Kinnaird. It was Villa captain Howard Spencer's third winners medal. Receipts for the final were £7,785.

DIVISION ONE

MANAGER: Directors

MATCH	DATE	VENUE	OPPONENTS	RESULT	HT SCORE	SCORE	SCORERS	ATT
1	Sep 1	H	Preston North End	L	0 0	1 2	Brawn (pen)	15,000
2	3	H	Stoke	W	1 0	1 0	Hall, Bache 2	25,000
3	10	A	Blackburn Rovers	L	0 4	0 4		17,000
4	12	H	Everton	W	0 0	1 0	Brawn	5,000
5	17	H	Nottingham Forest	W	1 0	2 0	Mattews 2	25,000
6	24	A	Sheffield Wednesday	L	2 0	2 3	Bache, Matthews	16,000
7	Oct 1	H	Sunderland	D	2 1	2 2	Bache, Wood	30,000
8	8	A	Woolwich Arsenal	L	0 0	0 1		30,000
9	15	H	Derby County	L	0 1	0 2		30,000
10	22	A	Everton	L	1 1	2 3	Johnson, Garraty	25,000
11	29	H	Small Heath	W	0 1	2 1	Brawn (pen), Garraty	50,000
12	Nov 9	A	Manchester City	L	1 0	1 2	Lockett	15,000
13	12	H	Notts County	W	2 1	4 2	Lockett, Brawn, Cantrell, Hampton	20,000
14	19	A	Sheffield United	W	2 0	3 0	Hampton, Bache, Brawn (pen)	15,000
15	26	H	Newcastle United	L	0 1	0 1		12,000
16	Dec 3	A	Preston North End	W	1 2	3 2	Bache, Hampton, Garraty	12,000
17	10	H	Middlesbrough	D	0 0	0 0		8,000
18	17	A	Wolverhampton Wanderers	D	1 1	1 1	Hampton	10,000
19	24	H	Bury	W	2 0	2 0	Hampton 2	14,000
20	26	H	Woolwich Arsenal	W	2 1	3 1	Leake, Hampton, Bache	42,000
21	31	A	Stoke	W	1 0	4 1	Hampton 2, Garraty, Bache	7,000
22	Jan 7	H	Blackburn Rovers	W	2 0	3 0	Leake, Matthews, Bache	12,000
23	14	A	Nottingham Forest	D	1 0	1 1	Garraty (pen)	10,000
24	21	H	Sheffield Wednesday	L	0 0	0 2		20,000
25	28	A	Sunderland	W	1 2	3 2	Brawn, Hall, Bache	14,000
26	Feb 11	A	Derby County	W	1 0	2 0	Bache, Leake	7,000
27	25	A	Small Heath	W	0 0	3 0	Pearson, Hampton, Windmill	30,000
28	Mar 11	A	Notts County	W	2 1	2 1	Garraty, Pearson	4,000
29	18	H	Sheffield United	W	1 0	3 0	Hall, Bache, Hampton	15,000
30	Apr 5	A	Newcastle United	L	0 1	0 2		25,000
31	8	A	Middlesbrough	L	0 2	1 3	Hall	12,000
32	22	A	Bury	W	1 2	3 2	Hampton 2, Brawn	20,000
33	27	A	Wolverhampton Wanderers	W	2 0	3 0	Garraty, Hampton, Lockett	15,000
34	29	H	Manchester City	W	3 1	3 2	Garraty, Hampton, Hall	20,000

Final League Position: 4th in First Division

Appearances
Goals

FA CUP

1	Feb 4	H	Leicester Fosse	W	2 1	5 1	Bache 2, Hampton, Leake, Hall	25,000
2	18	H	Bury	W	2 1	3 2	Bache, Garraty, Hampton	32,000
3	Mar 4	H	Fulham	W	3 0	5 0	Pearson, Hampton 2, Hall, Bache	42,000
SF	25	N	Everton *	D	0 0	1 1	Hall	35,000
R	29	N	Everton **	W	1 0	2 1	Hampton, Garraty	25,000
F	Apr 15	N	Newcastle United ***	W	1 0	2 0	Hampton 2	101,117

Appearances
Goals

* Played at Victoria Ground, Stoke
** Played at The City Ground, Nottingham
*** Played at The Crystal Palace

FINAL LEAGUE TABLE

	P	W	D	L	F	A	P
Newcastle United	34	23	2	9	72	33	48
Everton	34	21	5	8	63	36	47
Manchester City	34	20	6	8	66	37	46
Aston Villa	**34**	**19**	**4**	**11**	**63**	**43**	**42**
Sunderland	34	16	8	10	60	44	40
Sheffield United	34	19	2	13	64	56	40
Small Heath	34	17	5	12	54	38	39
Preston North End	34	13	10	11	42	37	36
Sheffield Wednesday	34	14	5	15	61	57	33
Woolwich Arsenal	34	12	9	13	36	40	33
Derby County	34	12	8	14	37	48	32
Stoke	34	13	4	17	40	58	30
Blackburn Rovers	34	11	5	18	40	51	27
Wolverhampton W	34	11	4	19	47	73	26
Middlesbrough	34	9	8	17	36	56	26
Nottingham Forest	34	9	7	18	40	61	25
Bury	34	10	4	20	47	67	24
Notts County	34	5	8	21	36	69	18

1905/06

SEASON SNIPPETS

Charlie Millington made his debut at Nottingham Forest on 14 October as Harry Hampton was in Manchester playing for The Football League where he netted twice in a 4-0 win. Millington, who had recently scored a hat-trick for the reserves in a senior cup-tie, took only four minutes to score his first league goal.

Barney Allen scored after 26 minutes of his league debut against Middlesbrough on 4 November.

Harry Hadley played his first game on 11 November.

George Garratt made his debut on 18 November.

James Logan made his debut on 23 December.

Joe Walters came in for his first game on 30 December.

Walter Corbett had to go off at Bolton on 2 January with a knee injury and Villa played three-quarters of the game with ten men.

Albert Evans suffered a broken leg against Birmingham on 20 January which ended his Villa career.

A collection for Albert Evans at the Plymouth Argyle home FA Cup tie raised £33.

The game against Nottingham Forest on 17 February was a Benefit Match for Howard Spencer following which, the Directors handed over a cheque for £711 0s 9d. Sam Greenhalgh made his debut.

John Boden played his first Villa game against Manchester United in the FA Cup third round on 24 February.

Joe Hisbent made the first of his two appearances, at Sunderland on 28 February, while Arthur Elston had to leave the field injured in his only Villa game.

Bert Kingaby's debut came at Middlesbrough on 10 March.

Rowland Codling played his first game on 17 March.

Tom Riley made his first appearance at Woolwich Arsenal on 13 April following his transfer from Brentford.

DIVISION ONE

MANAGER: Directors

MATCH	DATE	VENUE	OPPONENTS	RESULT	HT SCORE	SCORE	SCORERS	ATT
1	Sep 2	A	Blackburn Rovers	D	1 1	1 1	Hampton	18,000
2	9	H	Sunderland	W	0 0	2 1	Garraty 2 (1 pen)	25,000
3	11	H	Liverpool	W	3 0	5 0	Hampton 3, West (og), Brawn	15,000
4	16	A	Birmingham	L	0 2	0 2		25,000
5	23	H	Everton	W	1 0	4 0	Bache, Garraty, Hampton, Hall	35,000
6	30	A	Derby County	L	0 0	0 1		18,000
7	Oct 7	H	Sheffield Wednesday	W	1 0	3 0	Brawn 2, Bache	28,000
8	14	A	Nottingham Forest	D	1 1	2 2	Millington, Garraty (pen)	13,000
9	21	H	Manchester City	W	1 0	2 1	Bache, Garraty (pen)	25,000
10	28	A	Bury	W	0 0	1 0	Bache	9,000
11	Nov 4	H	Middlesbrough	W	3 0	4 1	Hampton, Allen, Bache, Garraty (pen)	15,000
12	11	A	Preston North End	L	0 2	0 2		8,000
13	13	A	Stoke	W	0 0	1 0	Garraty	15,000
14	18	H	Newcastle United	L	0 2	0 3		30,000
15	25	H	Wolverhampton Wanderers	W	2 0	6 0	Cantrell 3, Garraty 2, Hampton	12,000
16	Dec 2	A	Liverpool	L	0 2	0 3		28,000
17	9	H	Sheffield United	W	0 1	4 1	Hall, Garraty 2, Hampton	12,000
18	16	H	Notts County	L	1 2	1 2	Hampton	9,000
19	23	H	Stoke	W	2 0	3 0	Hampton 2, Garraty	15,000
20	26	H	Bolton Wanderers	D	0 1	1 1	Bache	40,000
21	27	H	Woolwich Arsenal	W	2 1	2 1	Garraty, Hampton	30,000
22	30	H	Blackburn Rovers	L	0 1	0 1		20,000
23	Jan 2	A	Bolton Wanderers	L	0 1	1 4	Hampton	30,000
24	20	H	Birmingham	L	0 1	1 3	Bache	40,000
25	27	A	Everton	L	1 1	2 4	Matthews, Hampton	30,000
26	Feb 10	A	Sheffield Wednesday	D	1 0	2 2	Matthews, Hampton	8,000
27	17	H	Nottingham Forest	W	2 0	3 1	Garraty, Hall, Bache	23,000
28	28	A	Sunderland	L	0 0	0 2		20,000
29	Mar 3	A	Bury	D	3 2	3 3	Hampton 2, Hall	15,000
30	10	A	Middlesbrough	W	0 1	2 1	Boden, Garraty	12,000
31	14	H	Manchester City	W	2 1	4 1	Hampton 2, Bache, Garraty	20,000
32	17	H	Preston North End	L	0 1	0 1		20,000
33	24	A	Newcastle United	L	0 3	1 3	Matthews	17,000
34	31	H	Wolverhampton Wanderers	L	1 1	1 4	Bache	7,000
35	Apr 13	A	Woolwich Arsenal	L	0 2	1 2	Millington	25,000
36	14	A	Sheffield United	D	1 1	1 1	Bache	12,000
37	16	H	Derby County	W	2 0	6 0	Millington, Garraty, Walters, Matthews, Bache, Boden	10,000
38	21	H	Notts County	W	2 0	2 1	Bache, Walters	12,000

Final League Position: 8th in First Division

1 Own-goal

Appearances
Goals

FA CUP

1	Jan 13	H	King's Lynn	W	3 0	11 0	Hall 3, Wilkes, Millington 4, Garraty 2, Pearson	23,000
2	Feb 3	H	Plymouth Argyle	D	0 0	0 0		31,000
R	7	A	Plymouth Argyle	W	4 1	5 1	Garratt, Garraty 2, Bache, Hampton	22,843
3	24	A	Manchester United	L	1 2	1 5	Hall	36,000

Appearances
Goals

328

George W	Spencer H	Miles A	Pearson JF	Leake A	Windmill JW	Brawn WF	Garraty W	Hampton JH	Bache JW	Hall AE	Noon MT	Wilkes A	Cooch H	Evans AJ	Millington CJH	Allen WB	Hadley H	Garratt GT	Cantrell J	Logan JL	Corbett W	Walters J	Harris GA	Matthews W	Brown WG	Greenhalgh S	Hisbent JS	Elston AE	Boden JA	Kingaby HCL	Coding R	Riley T	MATCH
1	2	3	4	5	6	7	8	9	10	11																							1
1	2	3	4	5	6	7	8	9	10	11																							2
1		3	4	5	6	7	8	9	10	11	2																						3
1	2	3		5	6	7	8	9	10	11		4																					4
1	2	3	4	5	6	7	8	9	10	11																							5
1		3	4	5	6	7	8	9	10	11	2																						6
	2	3	4	5	6	7	8	9	10	11			1																				7
1	2		4	5	6	7	8		10	11				3	9																		8
1	2		4	5	6	7	8	9	10	11				3																			9
1	2		4	5	6	7	8	9	10	11				3																			10
1	2		4	5	6		8	9	10	11				3		7																	11
1	2		4	5		8	9	10	11					3		7	6																12
1	2		4	5			8	9	10	11				3		7	6																13
1	2		4	5			8	9		11	3			6	7	10																	14
1	2		4	5			8	9		11				3		6	7	10															15
1	2		4	5	6		8		10	11				3	9		7																16
1	2		4	5		8	9	10	11					3		6	7																17
1	2		4	5		7	8	9	10	11				3		6																	18
1	2		4			8	9		11			6		3			7	10	5														19
1	2		4			8	9	10	11			6		3			7		5														20
1			4		2	7	8	9	11			6		3				10	5														21
1			4	3		7	8	9				6						10	5	2	11												22
1			4	2		7	8	9						6				10	5	3	11												23
			4	5		7	8	9	10	11	2	6	1	3																			24
	2		4					9	10	11		5	1			6	7				3	8											25
1	2			5				9	10	11	3					4	7				6	8											26
1	2		4		6		8	9	10	11						7				3	5												27
1	2							9		8						4	7	10			6	5	3	11									28
1	2		4					9	11	8							7	10		3		5	6										29
1	2			3		8	9	10	11								6					4		5	7								30
1	2					8	9		11							6	7		3			4		5									31
1	2			3		8	9	10	11								7					4		5		6							32
1	2			3		8	9															4		5	7	6							33
1	2						9	10											11		10	4			5	7	6						34
1	2					8		10	11					9					6			4		5	7		3						35
	2					8		10					1			7		11	6	9		4		5			3						36
	2					8		10					1			7		11	6	9		4		5			3						37
	2					8		10									6	11		9		4		5			3						38
32	32	7	26	26	13	15	33	32	31	30	5	7	6	14	6	3	11	13	8	7	4	7	7	7	1	12	2	1	9	4	3	4	
						3	17	19	13	4			3	1		3		2		4				2									

1	2		4			8		10			6		3	9					11														1
1	2			5		8	9	10	11			6		4	7				3														2
1	2		4	5	6	8	9	10	11	3				7																			R
1	2		4		6	8	9	10	11					7		5							3										3
4	4		3	2	2	4	3	4	2	1	1	1	1	4	1	1			2				1				1						
				1			4	1	1	4			1			1																	

FINAL LEAGUE TABLE

	P	W	D	L	F	A	P
Liverpool	38	23	5	10	79	46	51
Preston North End	38	17	13	8	54	39	47
Sheffield Wednesday	38	18	8	12	63	52	44
Newcastle United	38	18	7	13	74	48	43
Manchester City	38	19	5	14	73	54	43
Bolton Wanderers	38	17	7	14	81	67	41
Birmingham City	38	17	7	14	65	59	41
Aston Villa	**38**	**17**	**6**	**15**	**72**	**56**	**40**
Blackburn Rovers	38	16	8	14	54	52	40
Stoke	38	16	7	15	54	55	39
Everton	38	15	7	16	70	66	37
Woolwich Arsenal	38	15	7	16	62	64	37
Sheffield United	38	15	6	17	57	62	36
Sunderland	38	15	5	18	61	70	35
Derby County	38	14	7	17	39	58	35
Notts County	38	11	12	15	55	71	34
Bury	38	11	10	17	57	74	32
Middlesbrough	38	10	11	17	56	71	31
Nottingham Forest	38	13	5	20	58	79	31
Wolverhampton W	38	8	7	23	58	99	23

1906/07

SEASON SNIPPETS

Villa News & Record was published for the first time for the Blackburn Rovers game on 1 September. Rovers arrived at the ground five minutes after the kick-off time of 3.30pm, but the game was not seriously delayed.

Chris Buckley made his debut at Stoke on 3 September.

The Manchester City game on 20 October was the last match for Billy Matthews and John Boden.

Joe Pearson played his last game against Middlesbrough on 27 October.

Robert Evans made his debut at Preston on 3 November. Evans made ten appearances for Wales between 1906-10 before it was discovered he was born in England and he was then capped four times for England, twice against Wales.

At kick-off time at Bolton on 22 December, Chris Buckley was the only Villa player to have arrived. Other players turned up fifteen minutes later minus Miles, whose place was taken by Alex Leake. Hall had to go off injured, but Villa won with ten men.

Fred Chapple came in for his first game against Preston on 24 December as Joe Bache was in bed with influenza.

After defeating Manchester United on Boxing Day, Villa were taken to their favourite training facility at Rhyl from where they travelled to Blackburn on 29 December, returning to Rhyl after the game until the return fixture with Manchester United on New Year's Day. Mr G B Ramsay was in charge.

The game against Sheffield Wednesday on 9 February was designated as a Benefit Match for Joe Pearson.

Alec Logan scored on his debut against Derby County on 23 March.

George Tranter came in for his first game against Notts County on 13 April.

Freddie Miles asked to stand down from the FA Cup game at Bolton on 2 February owing to the death of his father.

DIVISION ONE

MANAGER: Directors

MATCH	DATE	VENUE	OPPONENTS	RESULT	HT SCORE	SCORE	SCORERS	ATT
1	Sep 1	H	Blackburn Rovers	W	1 0	4 2	Bache, Hampton, Walters, Cantrell	30,000
2	3	A	Stoke	W	2 0	2 0	Hampton 2 (1 pen)	10,000
3	8	A	Sunderland	L	1 1	1 2	Bache	20,000
4	10	H	Stoke	W	0 0	1 0	Hall	12,000
5	15	H	Birmingham	W	1 0	4 1	Greenhalgh, Hall, Walters, Hampton (pen)	40,000
6	22	A	Everton	W	1 0	2 1	Hampton, Garraty	40,000
7	29	H	Woolwich Arsenal	D	1 1	2 2	Hampton, Bache	40,000
8	Oct 6	A	Sheffield Wednesday	L	0 2	1 2	Hampton	22,000
9	13	H	Bury	W	2 1	3 1	Millington, Matthews, Walters	25,000
10	20	A	Manchester City	L	1 1	2 4	Bache, Hall	35,000
11	27	H	Middlesbrough	L	0 0	2 3	Hampton 2	20,000
12	Nov 3	A	Preston North End	L	0 2	0 2		10,000
13	10	H	Newcastle United	D	0 0	0 0		30,000
14	17	A	Derby County	W	1 0	1 0	Garraty	8,000
15	24	H	Liverpool	L	1 2	2 5	Walters, Hall	25,000
16	Dec 1	H	Bristol City	W	2 0	3 2	Cantrell, Millington, Bache	27,000
17	8	A	Notts County	D	0 1	1 1	Buckley	10,000
18	15	H	Sheffield United	W	2 1	5 1	Hall (pen), Cantrell 3, Millington	20,000
19	22	A	Bolton Wanderers	W	1 1	2 1	Millington, Walters	18,000
20	24	H	Preston North End	W	1 0	3 0	Evans 2, Millington	20,000
21	26	H	Manchester United	W	1 0	2 0	Cantrell, Chapple	28,000
22	29	A	Blackburn Rovers	L	1 2	1 2	Cantrell	11,000
23	Jan 1	A	Manchester United	L	0 0	0 1		48,000
24	5	H	Sunderland	D	2 0	2 2	Bache, Evans	20,000
25	19	A	Birmingham	L	2 1	2 3	Chapple, Walters	60,000
26	26	H	Everton	W	1 1	2 1	Cantrell, Hampton	25,000
27	Feb 9	H	Sheffield Wednesday	W	3 1	8 1	Bache 2, Millington, Hampton 2, Cantrell 3	20,000
28	16	A	Bury	W	2 0	3 0	Cantrell, Hampton 2	10,000
29	23	H	Manchester City	W	2 1	4 1	Hampton 3, Hall	15,000
30	Mar 2	A	Middlesbrough	L	0 0	0 1		20,000
31	16	H	Newcastle United	L	1 3	2 3	Hall (pen), Cantrell	50,000
32	23	H	Derby County	W	0 0	2 0	Millington, A Logan	16,000
33	30	A	Liverpool	W	2 0	4 0	Hampton, Chapple, Hall 2	25,000
34	Apr 1	A	Woolwich Arsenal	L	1 0	1 3	Hall	18,000
35	6	A	Bristol City	W	2 0	4 2	Hampton 3, Hall	16,000
36	13	H	Notts County	D	0 0	0 0		15,000
37	20	A	Sheffield United	D	0 0	0 0		12,000
38	27	H	Bolton Wanderers	L	0 1	0 2		10,000

Final League Position: 5th in First Division

Appearances
Goals

FA CUP

| 1 | Jan 12 | A | Burnley | W | 1 1 | 3 1 | Cantrell, Bache 2 | 16,242 |
| 2 | Feb 2 | A | Bolton Wanderers | L | 0 2 | 0 2 | | 40,367 |

Appearances
Goals

FINAL LEAGUE TABLE

	P	W	D	L	F	A	P
Newcastle United	38	22	7	9	74	46	51
Bristol City	38	20	8	10	66	47	48
Everton	38	20	5	13	70	46	45
Sheffield United	38	17	11	10	57	55	45
Aston Villa	**38**	**19**	**6**	**13**	**78**	**52**	**44**
Bolton Wanderers	38	18	8	12	59	47	44
Woolwich Arsenal	38	20	4	14	66	59	44
Manchester United	38	17	8	13	53	56	42
Birmingham City	38	15	8	15	52	52	38
Sunderland	38	14	9	15	65	66	37
Middlesbrough	38	15	6	17	56	63	36
Blackburn Rovers	38	14	7	17	56	59	35
Sheffield Wednesday	38	12	11	15	49	60	35
Preston North End	38	14	7	17	44	57	35
Liverpool	38	13	7	18	64	65	33
Bury	38	13	6	19	58	68	32
Manchester City	38	10	12	16	53	77	32
Notts County	38	8	15	15	46	50	31
Derby County	38	9	9	20	41	59	27
Stoke	38	8	10	20	41	64	26

1907/08

SEASON SNIPPETS

James Logan inaugurated his captaincy by winning the toss against Manchester United on 2 September. Chris Buckley fractured his right ankle and missed the rest of the season. Charlie Wallace made his debut, but for Fred Chapple, who was playing because Walters had a sprained knee, it would be his last appearance.

Charlie Millington played his last game on 9 September.

Horace Turner made his debut on 14 September against Bolton as Billy George was suffering from lumbago. Rowland Harper also made his debut. Charlie Wallace was still not fit after being injured at Blackburn on 7 September.

George Tranter made his debut at home to Everton on 28 September as Sam Greenhalgh had been transferred to Bolton Wanderers the previous night.

Tom Riley's last game was on 5 October at Sunderland.

The Manchester City game on 9 November was Alex Leake's Benefit Match and also his last appearance. It was the last game also for Robert Evans.

John Wilcox made his debut on 16 November at Preston as Charlie Wallace injured his ankle the previous week.

George Reeves made his debut on 30 November.

Tommy Lyons made his debut on 7 December.

Walter Kimberley made his debut on 8 February.

Billy George was promised the whole of the proceeds of his Benefit Match which was the game against Sheffield Wednesday on 15 February. Unfortunately rain affected the attendance.

George Harris made his final appearance against Notts County on 2 March.

Billy Garraty's last Villa game was at Bristol City on 11 March.

Peter Kyle played his first Villa game against Preston on 14 March following a transfer from Woolwich Arsenal.

A gale sprang up shortly after 3.00pm during the FA Cup match with Manchester United, accompanied by blinding sheets of rain - the pitch was a quagmire. It was Jimmy Cantrell's last appearance.

DIVISION ONE

MANAGER: Directors

MATCH	DATE	VENUE	OPPONENTS	RESULT	HT SCORE	SCORE	SCORERS	ATT
1	Sep 2	H	Manchester United	L	0 2	1 4	Hampton (pen)	20,000
2	7	A	Blackburn Rovers	L	0 0	0 2		15,000
3	9	H	Sunderland	W	1 0	1 0	Greenhalgh	15,000
4	14	H	Bolton Wanderers	W	2 0	2 0	Hampton 2	18,000
5	21	A	Birmingham	W	0 1	3 2	Cantrell, Evans, Hall	50,000
6	28	H	Everton	L	0 0	0 2		25,000
7	Oct 5	A	Sunderland	L	0 2	0 3		25,000
8	12	H	Woolwich Arsenal	L	0 0	0 1		25,000
9	19	A	Sheffield Wednesday	W	0 1	3 2	Hampton 2, Hall (pen)	14,000
10	26	H	Bristol City	D	3 1	4 4	Hampton 2, Bache 2	20,000
11	Nov 2	A	Notts County	W	2 0	3 0	A Logan 2, Bache	12,000
12	9	H	Manchester City	D	2 1	2 2	Hampton 2 (1 pen)	15,000
13	16	A	Preston North End	L	0 3	0 3		12,000
14	23	H	Bury	D	1 1	2 2	Hall, A Logan	12,000
15	30	H	Newcastle United	D	1 2	3 3	A Logan, Bache, Hall	15,000
16	Dec 7	A	Liverpool	L	0 1	0 5		15,000
17	14	H	Middlesbrough	W	3 0	6 0	Cantrell 2, A Logan 2, Hall 2	10,000
18	21	A	Sheffield United	D	1 0	1 1	Hall	15,000
19	25	H	Nottingham Forest	W	0 0	4 0	Bache 4	20,000
20	26	A	Nottingham Forest	D	2 2	2 2	Cantrell 2	22,000
21	28	H	Chelsea	D	0 0	0 0		20,000
22	Jan 4	A	Blackburn Rovers	D	0 0	1 1	Bache	12,000
23	18	H	Birmingham	L	1 3	2 3	A Logan, Hall	35,000
24	25	A	Everton	L	0 0	0 1		25,000
25	Feb 8	H	Woolwich Arsenal	W	0 0	1 0	Bache	15,000
26	15	H	Sheffield Wednesday	W	3 0	5 0	Cantrell, Bache 3, Hampton	10,000
27	Mar 2	A	Notts County	W	3 1	5 1	Bache 3, Reeves, Hall (pen)	6,000
28	7	A	Manchester City	L	2 1	2 3	Hampton, Reeves	25,000
29	11	A	Bristol City	D	1 2	2 2	Hampton 2	18,000
30	14	H	Preston North End	W	1 0	3 0	Wallace 2, Reeves	20,000
31	21	A	Bury	L	0 2	1 2	Bache	10,000
32	Apr 4	H	Liverpool	W	1 0	5 1	Hampton 2, Bache 3	15,000
33	8	A	Newcastle United	W	2 1	5 2	Wallace 2, Bache 2, Hampton	15,000
34	11	A	Middlesbrough	W	0 0	1 0	Hampton	15,000
35	17	H	Bolton Wanderers	L	0 1	1 3	Bache	20,000
36	18	H	Sheffield United	W	0 0	1 0	Hampton	18,000
37	20	A	Manchester United	W	1 1	2 1	Hall 2 (1 pen)	10,000
38	25	A	Chelsea	W	2 0	3 1	Bache, Hall 2	25,000

Final League Position: 2nd in First Division

Appearances
Goals

FA CUP

1	Jan 11	H	Stockport County	W	3 0	3 0	Wallace, A Logan, Bache	16,000
2	Feb 1	H	Hull City	W	0 0	3 0	Hampton, Hall 2 (1 pen)	35,000
3	22	H	Manchester United	L	0 2	0 2		45,000

Appearances
Goals

332

	Cooch H	Miles A	Riley T	Buckley CS	Logan JL	Codling R	Wallace CW	Chapple FJ	Hampton JH	Bache JW	Hall AE	George W	Geenhalgh S	Cantrell J	Evans RE	Millington CJH	Turner HH	Harper RR	Walters J	Tranter GH	Windmill JW	Leake A	Logan A	Spencer H	Wilcox JM	Harris GA	Reeves G	Lyons AT	Garraty W	Kimberley WJ	Kyle P	MATCH
1	2	3	4	5	6	7	8	9	10	11																						1
	2	3		5	6	7		9		10	1	4	8	11																		2
	2	3		5	6			9		10	1	4	8	11	7																	3
	2	3		5	6			9		10		4	8	11		1	7															4
	2	3		5	6				10	9		4	8	11		1	7															5
	2	3		5					10	9			8	11		1	7	4	6													6
	3	2		5	6	7		9	10	8				11		1		4														7
	3			2	6	7		9		11			8			1		4		10	5											8
	3			5	6	7		9	10	11						1		4				2	8									9
	3			5	6	7		9	10	11						1		4				2	8									10
	3			5	6	7		9	10	11	1							4					8	2								11
	3			5	6	7		9	10		1			11				4				2	8									12
	3			5	6			9	10	11	1							4					8	2	7							13
	2			5	6			9	10	11	1							4					8		7	3						14
	3			5	6				10	11	1							4				9		2	7		8					15
	3			5	6	7			10	11	1							4				9					8	2				16
	3			5	6	7			10	11			8					4				9						2				17
	3			5	6	7			10	11			8					4				9						2	4			18
	3			5	6	7			10	11			8					4				9						2	4			19
	3			5	6	7			10	11			8					4				9						2	4			20
	3			5	6	7			10	11			8					4				9						2	4			21
	3			5		7			10	11			8					4				9			6			2	4			22
	3			5	6			8	10	11							7					9						2	4			23
	3			5	6	7		9	10	11	1							4									2	8				24
				5	6	7		9	10	11	1		8					4								3	2					25
				5	6	7		9	10	11	1		8					4								3	2					26
				5		7		9	10	11								4						6	8		2		3			27
	3			5	6	7		9	10	11								4									8	2				28
					6	7		9		11										10							8	2	5	3		29
	3			5	6	7		9		11	1							4									8	2			10	30
	3			5	6	7		9	10	11								4									8	2				31
	3			5	6	7		9	10	11								4										2			8	32
	3			5	6			9	10	11								4									8	2				33
	3			5	6			9	10	11								4					7				8	2			8	34
	3			5	6			9	10	11								4										8				35
	3			5	6			9	10	11	1							4					7				2				8	36
	3			5	6			9	10	11								4									8	2				37
	3			5	6	7		9	10	11								4									8	2				38

| 1 | 34 | 7 | 1 | 37 | 35 | 27 | 1 | 28 | 32 | 37 | 30 | 4 | 14 | 7 | 1 | 7 | 2 | 4 | 27 | 1 | 4 | 15 | 3 | 5 | 5 | 12 | 23 | 8 | 4 | 4 | | |
| | | | | | | 4 | | 18 | 24 | 13 | | 1 | 6 | 1 | | | | | | | | 7 | | | | 3 | | | | | | |

	3			5	6	7		8	10	11	1							4				9					2					1
	3			5	6	7		9	10	11	1							4									2	8				2
	3			5	6	7			10	11	1		8					4									2	9				3

| | 3 | | | 3 | 3 | 3 | | 2 | 3 | 3 | 3 | | 1 | | | | | 3 | | | | 1 | | | | | 3 | 2 | | | | |
| | | | | | | 1 | | 1 | 1 | 2 | | | 1 | | | | | | | | | 1 | | | | | | | | | | |

FINAL LEAGUE TABLE

	P	W	D	L	F	A	P
Manchester United	38	23	6	9	81	48	52
Aston Villa	**38**	**17**	**9**	**12**	**77**	**59**	**43**
Manchester City	38	16	11	11	62	54	43
Newcastle United	38	15	12	11	65	54	42
Sheffield Wednesday	38	19	4	15	73	64	42
Middlesbrough	38	17	7	14	54	45	41
Bury	38	14	11	13	58	61	39
Liverpool	38	16	6	16	68	61	38
Nottingham Forest	38	13	11	14	59	62	37
Bristol City	38	12	12	14	58	61	36
Everton	38	15	6	17	58	64	36
Preston North End	38	12	12	14	47	53	36
Chelsea	38	14	8	16	53	62	36
Blackburn Rovers	38	12	12	14	51	63	36
Woolwich Arsenal	38	12	12	14	51	63	36
Sunderland	38	16	3	19	78	75	35
Sheffield United	38	12	11	15	52	58	35
Notts County	38	13	8	17	39	51	34
Bolton Wanderers	38	14	5	19	52	58	33
Birmingham City	38	9	12	17	40	60	30

1908/09

SEASON SNIPPETS

Harry Hampton was out for the opening two matches after suffering a smashed finger sustained whilst playing cricket. Reserve Team skipper George Harris was suffering from a broken jaw caused by a rising cricket ball striking him in the face.

George Hunter made his debut on 12 September.

Jack Windmill's last game was on 19 September.

Samson Whittaker played his first game at Bradford City on 10 October.

Alfred Gittins made his only league appearance against Leicester Fosse on 31 October.

John McKenzie made his debut on 14 November against Notts County.

Edmund Eyre played his first game against Middlesbrough on 12 December following his transfer from Birmingham. It was Rowland Codling's last Villa match.

Arthur Layton and Frank Cornan made their debut at Manchester City on 19 December.

With their selection limited by illness and injury, the Directors decided to give George Travers a trial against Bury on Boxing Day, following his transfer from Birmingham. Travers responded with a hat-trick in the first twenty-five minutes of his debut.

Len Skiller made his debut on 9 January.

John Kearns became the fourth ex Birmingham player to make his Villa debut during the season when he played against Everton on 27 February.

Horace Turner was carried off injured after trying to stop Preston's third goal on 10 April, Walter Kimberley went in goal. Villa then acquired Arthur Cartlidge from Bristol Rovers and Cartlidge made his debut on 17 April at Middlesbrough.

DIVISION ONE

MANAGER: Directors

MATCH	DATE	VENUE	OPPONENTS	RESULT	HT SCORE	SCORE	SCORERS	ATT
1	Sep 1	A	Liverpool	L	1 1	2 3	J Logan, A Logan	20,000
2	5	H	Sheffield Wednesday	D	0 1	1 1	Walters	20,000
3	12	A	Nottingham Forest	W	1 1	2 1	Bache, Hampton	7,000
4	19	H	Sunderland	W	1 0	2 0	Hampton, Bache	20,000
5	26	A	Chelsea	W	1 0	2 0	Bache, Reeves	40,000
6	Oct 3	H	Blackburn Rovers	D	1 0	1 1	Bache	20,000
7	10	A	Bradford City	D	1 0	1 1	Bache	30,000
8	17	H	Manchester United	W	2 0	3 1	Reeves 2, Hampton	40,000
9	24	A	Everton	L	0 1	1 3	Reeves	40,000
10	31	H	Leicester Fosse	D	0 1	1 1	Bache	20,000
11	Nov 7	A	Woolwich Arsenal	W	0 0	1 0	Bache	15,000
12	14	H	Notts County	D	0 0	1 1	Tranter	12,000
13	21	A	Newcastle United	W	1 0	2 0	Wallace, Reeves	30,000
14	28	H	Bristol City	D	0 1	1 1	Bache	8,000
15	Dec 5	A	Preston North End	L	1 1	2 3	Wallace, Bache	10,000
16	12	H	Middlesbrough	L	0 2	0 3		15,000
17	19	A	Manchester City	L	0 0	0 2		12,000
18	25	H	Liverpool	D	0 1	1 1	A Logan	20,000
19	26	H	Bury	W	3 0	3 0	Travers 3	20,000
20	Jan 1	A	Bury	W	1 1	2 1	Reeves, Eyre	12,000
21	2	A	Sheffield Wednesday	L	0 1	2 4	Buckley, Reeves	18,000
22	9	H	Nottingham Forest	L	1 1	1 2	Hampton	15,000
23	23	A	Sunderland	L	1 2	3 4	Eyre, J Logan, A Logan	15,000
24	30	H	Chelsea	D	0 0	0 0		15,000
25	Feb 6	A	Sheffield United	L	1 3	1 3	Hampton	15,000
26	13	H	Bradford City	L	0 1	1 3	Wallace	20,000
27	15	A	Blackburn Rovers	L	1 1	1 3	Hampton	8,000
28	27	H	Everton	W	3 1	3 1	Hampton 2, Walters	10,000
29	Mar 13	H	Woolwich Arsenal	W	1 0	2 1	Eyre, Wallace (pen)	15,000
30	20	A	Notts County	D	1 1	1 1	Hall	6,000
31	27	A	Leicester Fosse	L	0 2	2 4	Walters 2	15,000
32	31	A	Manchester United	W	0 0	2 0	Walters, Hampton	4,000
33	Apr 3	H	Bristol City	D	0 0	0 0		16,000
34	9	H	Sheffield United	W	2 0	3 0	Walters, Eyre, Bache	12,000
35	10	A	Preston North End	L	1 3	2 4	Travers, Wallace (pen)	15,000
36	17	A	Middlesbrough	L	0 0	0 1		8,000
37	24	H	Manchester City	W	1 0	2 1	Wallace (pen), Walters	15,000
38	26	H	Newcastle United	W	1 0	3 0	Bache, Wallace 2 (1 pen)	9,000

Final League Position: 7th in First Division

Appearances
Goals

FA CUP

1	Jan 16	A	Nottingham Forest	L	0 1	0 2		14,000

Appearances
Goals

334

Match	George W	Lyons AT	Miles A	Tranter GH	Logan JL	Codling R	Wallace CW	Walters J	Logan A	Bache JW	Hall AE	Kyle P	Buckley CS	Hunter GC	Reeves G	Hampton JH	Windmill JW	Whittaker SS	Wilcox JM	Gittins AG	McKenzie JW	Kimberley WJ	Eyre E	Layton AED	Cornan F	Travers JE	Turner HH	Skiller LG	Kearns JH	Cartlidge A
1	1	2	3	4	5	6	7	8	9	10	11																			
2	1	2	3	4	5	6	7	8		10	11	9																		
3	1	2	3	4			7			10	11		5	6	8	9														
4	1	2	3	4			7			10	11		5		8	9	6													
5	1	2	3	4		6				10	11		5		8	9														
6	1	2	3	4		6	7	11		10			5		8	9														
7	1	2	3	4	6					10			5		8	9	7	11												
8	1	2	3	4	6		7			10	11		5		8	9														
9	1	2	3	4	6		7			10	11		5		8	9														
10	1	2	3	4	6		7			10	11		5			9			8											
11	1	2	3	4	6		7			10	11		5		8	9														
12	1		3	4	6		7			10	11		5		8	9					2									
13	1	2	3	4	6		7			10	11		5		8	9														
14	1	2	3	4	6		7			10	11		5		8	9														
15	1	2		4	6		7			10	11		5		8	9				3			11							
16	1	2	3		6	4	7			10			5		8	9							11	2	6					
17	1		3	4						10	7		5		8	9							11	2	6					
18	1		3					8		10	9		5	4			7							2	6	9				
19	1		3		7					10	11		5	4	8								11	3	6	9	1			
20		2			7					10			5	4	8								11	3	6	9	1			
21		2			7					10			5	4	8									2			1			
22			3		7					10	11		5	4	8	9				8			11							
23			3	4	6		7	10	9				5						8				11	2			1			
24	1		3	4	6		7	10	9				5								2			4						
25			3		6		7		9	10	11		5		8						2			4						
26	1		3		6		7	9		10	11		5																	
27	1	2	3		6					10	11		5	4	8	9														
28	1		3	4	5		7	10							8	9							11		6			2		
29	1		3	4	5		7	10							8	9							11		6			2		
30	1		3		5			10			8			4	7	9							11		6			2		
31	1		3	4	5		7	10							8	9							11		6			2		
32			3		5		7	10			8			6					4				11		6		1	2		
33			3		5		7	10	9					4	8								11		6		1	2		
34			3		5		7			10	11		5	4	8								11		6		9	1	2	
35			3		5		7							4					4											
36				5			7	10	9					4	8								11	2	6			3	1	
37			3		5		7	10	9					4	8								11	2	6				1	
38			3		5		7	10	9					4	8								11	2	6				1	
	27	18	34	21	28	5	34	15	6	31	23	1	26	15	23	30	1	4	1	5	3		17	9	16	4	7	1	9	3
					1		2		8	7	3	11	1		7	9								4		4				
			3		6		7		10			5	4	8	9								11	2	6					1
			1		1		1		1			1	1	1	1								1	1				1		

FINAL LEAGUE TABLE

	P	W	D	L	F	A	P
Newcastle United	38	24	5	9	65	41	53
Everton	38	18	10	10	82	57	46
Sunderland	38	21	2	15	78	63	44
Blackburn Rovers	38	14	13	11	61	50	41
Sheffield Wednesday	38	17	6	15	67	61	40
Woolwich Arsenal	38	14	10	14	52	49	38
Aston Villa	**38**	**14**	**10**	**14**	**58**	**56**	**38**
Bristol City	38	13	12	13	45	58	38
Middlesbrough	38	14	9	15	59	53	37
Preston North End	38	13	11	14	48	44	37
Chelsea	38	14	9	15	56	61	37
Sheffield United	38	14	9	15	51	59	37
Manchester United	38	15	7	16	58	68	37
Nottingham Forest	38	14	8	16	66	57	36
Notts County	38	14	8	16	51	48	36
Liverpool	38	15	6	17	57	65	36
Bury	38	14	8	16	63	77	36
Bradford City	38	12	10	16	47	47	34
Manchester City	38	15	4	19	67	69	34
Leicester Fosse	38	8	9	21	54	102	25

1909/10

SEASON SNIPPETS

On 1 September, an Appeal was started for the dependants of the late Arthur Brown who had died on 1 July, which subsequently raised £71 19s 4d.

Billy Gerrish, who had been signed from Bristol Rovers along with Arthur Cartlidge on 13 April, was brought in for his first league game against Woolwich Arsenal on 1 September and scored Villa's third goal on 22 minutes.

In the return game with Woolwich Arsenal on 6 September, Villa were 3-1 down when the match was abandoned after 77 minutes due to bad light.

Arthur Moss, only the second player to make his debut during the season, came into the team on 29 January against Blackburn Rovers in place of the injured Chris Buckley. Villa went to the top of the table after this game where they remained for the rest of the season. The 4-3 win came on a pitch that was in a dreadful state - melted snow left pools of water several inches deep on a rock-hard ground.

Harry Hampton scored a first-half hat-trick on Good Friday - his third goal came with an overhead kick with his back to the goal from a Wallace centre - and despite having to leave the field injured, he was back in action the following afternoon (26 March) when he again netted three times in the first-half to record his fifth hat-trick of the season.

DIVISION ONE

MANAGER: Directors

MATCH	DATE	VENUE	OPPONENTS	RESULT	HT SCORE	SCORE	SCORERS	ATT
1	Sep 1	H	Woolwich Arsenal	W	3 0	5 1	Bache 2, Hall, Gerrish, Walters	14,000
2	4	A	Bolton Wanderers	W	1 0	2 1	Wallace, Hall (pen)	20,000
3	11	H	Chelsea	W	3 0	4 1	Gerrish 3, Bache	20,000
4	18	A	Blackburn Rovers	L	0 1	2 3	Gerrish, Wallace	20,000
5	25	H	Nottingham Forest	D	0 0	0 0		30,000
6	Oct 2	A	Sunderland	D	0 0	1 1	Hall	20,000
7	9	H	Everton	W	2 1	3 1	Hampton 2, Hunter	30,000
8	16	A	Manchester United	L	0 0	0 2		15,000
9	23	H	Bradford City	W	1 1	3 1	Hampton, Gerrish, Hall	20,000
10	30	A	Sheffield Wednesday	L	1 1	2 3	Hampton 2	10,000
11	Nov 6	H	Bristol City	W	1 0	1 0	Gerrish	25,000
12	13	A	Bury	W	1 0	2 0	Bache 2	12,000
13	20	H	Tottenham Hotspur	W	1 1	3 2	Gerrish, Bache, Hampton	15,000
14	27	A	Preston North End	L	0 1	0 1		8,000
15	Dec 4	H	Notts County	D	0 0	1 1	Hampton	6,000
16	11	A	Newcastle United	L	0 0	0 1		15,000
17	18	H	Liverpool	W	1 0	3 1	Hampton, Bache 2	18,000
18	25	A	Sheffield United	W	1 0	1 0	Gerrish	25,000
19	27	H	Sheffield United	W	2 0	2 1	Hampton, Bache	25,000
20	Jan 1	A	Nottingham Forest	W	3 0	4 1	Bache, Hampton 3,	7,000
21	8	H	Bolton Wanderers	W	1 0	3 1	Bache 2, Gerrish	17,000
22	22	A	Chelsea	D	0 0	0 0		30,000
23	29	H	Blackburn Rovers	W	1 2	4 3	Hampton 3, Bache	12,000
24	Feb 12	H	Sunderland	W	1 1	3 2	Walters, Buckley, Gerrish	20,000
25	26	A	Manchester United	W	4 0	7 1	Gerrish 2, Walters 3, Hampton 2	20,000
26	Mar 5	A	Bradford City	W	2 1	2 1	Bache, Robinson (og)	22,000
27	12	H	Sheffield Wednesday	W	0 0	5 0	Hall 2, Wallace (pen), Bache 2	12,000
28	14	A	Everton	D	0 0	0 0		15,000
29	19	A	Bristol City	D	0 0	0 0		15,000
30	25	H	Middlesbrough	W	3 0	4 2	Hampton 3, Bache	30,000
31	26	H	Bury	W	3 1	4 1	Hampton 3, Walters	30,000
32	28	A	Middlesbrough	L	2 3	2 3	Wallace 2 (2 pens)	25,000
33	Apr 2	A	Tottenham Hotspur	D	1 1	1 1	Bache	35,000
34	9	H	Preston North End	W	0 0	3 0	Hampton, Bache, Gerrish	20,000
35	11	A	Woolwich Arsenal	L	0 0	0 1		8,000
36	16	H	Notts County	W	0 2	3 2	Eyre, Hampton, Wallace	11,000
37	27	H	Newcastle United	W	2 0	4 0	Bache, Wallace (pen), Eyre, Hampton	15,000
38	30	A	Liverpool	L	0 0	0 2		25,000

Final League Position: 1st in First Division

1 Own-goal

Appearances
Goals

FA CUP

1	Jan 15	A	Oldham Athletic	W	0 0	2 1	Bache, Hall	17,000
2	Feb 5	H	Derby County	W	3 0	6 1	Wallace, Hampton 3, Scattergood (og), Bache	45,000
3	19	H	Manchester City	L	0 2	1 2	Gerrish	45,000

1 Own-goal

Appearances
Goals

Cartlidge A	Lyons AT	Miles A	Logan JL	Buckley CS	Hunter GC	Wallace CW	Walters J	Gerrish WWW	Bache JW	Hall AE	Hampton JH	Tranter GH	Kearns JH	Layton AED	Eyre E	George W	Moss AJ		MATCH
1	2	3	4	5	6	7	8	9	10	11									1
1	2	3	4	5	6	7	8	9	10	11									2
1	2	3	4	5	6	7	8	9	10	11									3
1	2	3	4	5	6	7	8	9	10	11									4
1	2	3	4	5	6	7	8	9	10	11									5
1	2	3	4	5	6	7	8	9	10	11									6
1	2	3	4	5	6	7	8	10		11	9								7
1	2	3	4	5	6	7	8	10		11	9								8
1	2	3	4	5	6	7		8	10	11	9								9
1	2	3	4	5	6	7		8	10	11	9								10
1	2	3	4	5		7		8	10	11	9	6							11
1	2	3	4	5		7		8	10	11	9	6							12
1	2	3	4	5		7		8	10	11	9	6							13
1	2		4	5		7		8	10	11	9	6	3						14
1				5	6	7		8	10	11	9	4	3	2					15
1		2		5	6	7		8	10	11	9	4	3						16
1		2		5	6	7		8	10	11	9	4	3						17
1	2	3		5	6	7		8	10		9	4		11					18
1	2	3		5	6	7		8	10		9	4		11					19
	3			5	6	7		8	10		9	4		2	11	1			20
		3		5	6	7		8	10	11	9	4		2		1			21
	2	3		5	6	7		8	10	11	9	4				1			22
1	2	3			6	7		8	10	11	9	4					5		23
1	2	3		5	6	7	10	8			9	4		11					24
1	2	3		5	6	7	10	8			9	4		11					25
1	2	3		5	6	7		8	10		9	4		11					26
1	2	3		5	6	7	8		10	11	9	4							27
1	2			5	6	7		8	10	11	9	4	3						28
1	3			5	6	7		8	10		9	4		2	11				29
1	2	3		5	6	7		8	10	11	9	4							30
1	2			5	6	7	10	8			9	4	3	11					31
1	2	3		5	6	7		8	10	11	9	4							32
1	2			5	6	7	8		10	11	9	4	3						33
1	2	3		5	6	7		8	10		9	4		11					34
1	2			5	6	7	10	8			9	4	3	11					35
1	2			5	6	7		8	10		9	4	3	11					36
1	2		6	5		7		8	10		9	4	3	11					37
1	2		6	5		7		8	10		9	4	3	11					38

| 35 | 34 | 27 | 16 | 37 | 32 | 37 | 15 | 36 | 32 | 25 | 32 | 28 | 11 | 4 | 13 | 3 | 1 |
| | | | | 1 | 1 | | 7 | 6 | 14 | 20 | 6 | 26 | | | 2 | | |

	2	3		5	6	7		8	10	11	9	4			1				1
1	2	3		5	6	7		8	10	11	9	4							2
1	2	3		5	6	7		8	10	11	9	4							3

| 2 | 3 | 3 | | 3 | 3 | 3 | | 3 | 3 | 3 | 3 | 3 | | | 1 | | | |
| | | | | | | | | 1 | | 1 | 2 | 1 | 3 | | | | | |

FINAL LEAGUE TABLE

	P	W	D	L	F	A	P
Aston Villa	38	23	7	8	84	42	53
Liverpool	38	21	6	11	78	57	48
Blackburn Rovers	38	18	9	11	73	55	45
Newcastle United	38	19	7	12	70	56	45
Manchester United	38	19	7	12	69	61	45
Sheffield United	38	16	10	12	62	41	42
Bradford City	38	17	8	13	64	47	42
Sunderland	38	18	5	15	66	51	41
Notts County	38	15	10	13	67	59	40
Everton	38	16	8	14	51	56	40
Sheffield Wednesday	38	15	9	14	60	63	39
Preston North End	38	15	5	18	52	58	35
Bury	38	12	9	17	62	66	33
Nottingham Forest	38	11	11	16	54	72	33
Tottenham Hotspur	38	11	10	17	53	69	32
Bristol City	38	12	8	18	45	60	32
Middlesbrough	38	11	9	18	56	73	31
Woolwich Arsenal	38	11	9	18	37	67	31
Chelsea	38	11	7	20	47	70	29
Bolton Wanderers	38	9	6	23	44	71	24

1910/11

SEASON SNIPPETS

A banquet was held for the players at the Grand Hotel, Birmingham, five days before the season opened in, celebration of the previous season's title win.

Harry Hampton was carried from the field unconscious against Oldham on 3 September and had to be taken by horse ambulance to the house of the club surgeon. Hampton did not recover consciousness until 8.00pm and was out of action until 8 October.

Bill Rennéville made his debut on 10 September, but his only other appearance came the following week when he scored in a 3-0 win against Woolwich Arsenal.

Albert Hall was carried off following a collision with Andy Ducat on 17 September and did not play again until April 1912.

On 18 September, Charlie Athersmith died at Shiftnal age 38.

On 24 September, Walter Jones scored on his debut, but his only other appearance came the following week.

The 5-0 win against Middlesbrough on 26 November came after 60 men had been employed clearing the pitch of snow.

Horace Henshall made his debut on 10 December.

Arthur Cartlidge played his last game on 17 December.

Edmund Eyre played his last game on 7 January.

Horace Turner's last game was on 11 February.

Clem Stephenson scored on his debut against Tottenham Hotspur on 25 February.

Arthur Layton played his last game on 11 March.

Billy George suffered a thigh injury at Woolwich Arsenal on 15 March - his last Villa game.

Brendel Anstey made his debut as replacement for George at Newcastle on 18 March.

Charlie Wallace failed with a penalty at Blackburn on 24 April - a match crucial to Villa's title ambitions. In addition, the referee blew for time two minutes early and the players left the field but after protests from the crowd the players were recalled to finish the match.

DIVISION ONE

MANAGER: Directors

MATCH	DATE	VENUE	OPPONENTS	RESULT	HT SCORE	SCORE	SCORERS	ATT
1	Sep 3	H	Oldham Athletc	D	0 0	1 1	Gerrish	30,000
2	10	A	Sunderland	L	0 1	2 3	Logan, Bache	30,000
3	17	H	Woolwich Arsenal	W	2 0	3 0	Gerrish, Rennéville, Logan	28,000
4	24	A	Bradford City	W	1 1	2 1	Jones, Walters	25,000
5	Oct 1	H	Blackburn Rovers	D	2 0	2 2	Eyre, Bache	30,000
6	8	A	Nottingham Forest	L	1 1	1 3	Hampton	20,000
7	15	H	Manchester City	W	1 0	2 1	Bache, Walters	15,000
8	22	A	Everton	W	0 0	1 0	Walters	25,000
9	29	H	Sheffield Wednesday	W	1 1	2 1	Wallace, Bache	17,000
10	Nov 5	A	Bristol City	W	2 1	2 1	Bache, Walters	18,000
11	12	H	Newcastle United	W	3 2	3 2	Hampton 2, Walters	25,000
12	19	A	Tottenham Hotspur	W	0 0	2 1	Hampton, Walters	25,000
13	26	H	Middlesbrough	W	2 0	5 0	Bache 3, Hampton 2	15,000
14	Dec 3	A	Preston North End	W	0 0	1 0	Wallace (pen)	7,000
15	10	H	Notts County	W	2 0	3 1	Bache 2, Hampton	12,000
16	17	A	Manchester United	L	0 1	0 2		15,000
17	24	H	Liverpool	D	0 1	1 1	Hampton	16,000
18	26	H	Bury	W	3 0	4 1	Hampton, Henshall, Bache, Walters	35,000
19	28	A	Sheffield United	L	0 0	1 2	Walters	25,000
20	31	H	Oldham Athletic	D	1 0	1 1	Eyre	20,000
21	Jan 2	A	Bury	L	0 0	0 1		15,000
22	7	H	Sunderland	W	2 1	2 1	Bache 2	18,000
23	28	A	Bradford City	W	3 1	4 1	Walters, Hampton 2, Henshall	20,000
24	Feb 11	H	Nottingham Forest	W	1 1	3 1	Hampton, Henshall, Walters	20,000
25	18	A	Manchester City	D	1 1	1 1	Hampton	35,000
26	25	H	Tottenham Hotspur	W	2 0	4 0	Wallace, Bache, Stephenson, Hampton	8,000
27	Mar 4	A	Sheffield Wednesday	L	0 1	0 1		12,000
28	11	H	Bristol City	W	2 0	2 0	Stephenson, Wallace	18,000
29	15	A	Woolwich Arsenal	D	1 0	1 1	Stephenson	5,000
30	18	A	Newcastle United	L	0 0	0 1		20,000
31	27	H	Everton	W	0 1	2 1	Hampton, Walters	11,000
32	Apr 1	A	Middlesbrough	W	1 0	1 0	Henshall	18,000
33	8	H	Preston North End	L	0 0	0 2		12,000
34	14	H	Sheffield United	W	2 0	3 0	Wallace (pen), Hampton, Gerrish	30,000
35	15	A	Notts County	W	1 0	2 1	Hampton 2	18,000
36	22	H	Manchester United	W	2 1	4 2	Bache, Hampton, Henshall, Wallace (pen)	50,000
37	24	A	Blackburn Rovers	D	0 0	0 0		20,000
38	29	A	Liverpool	L	1 2	1 3	Walters	20,000

Final League Position: 2nd in First Division

Appearances
Goals

FA CUP

1	Jan 14	A	Portsmouth	W	1 0	4 1	Bache, Hampton 2, Thompson (og)	17,500
2	Feb 4	A	Manchester United	L	0 2	1 2	Henshall	65,100

1 Own Goal

Appearances
Goals

FA CHARITY SHIELD

	Sep 5	N	Brighton & Hove Albion *	L	0 0	0 1		15,000

Appearances
Goals

* Played at Stamford Bridge, London

FINAL LEAGUE TABLE

	P	W	D	L	F	A	P
Manchester United	38	22	8	8	72	40	52
Aston Villa	**38**	**22**	**7**	**9**	**69**	**41**	**51**
Sunderland	38	15	15	8	67	48	45
Everton	38	19	7	12	50	36	45
Bradford City	38	20	5	13	51	42	45
Sheffield Wednesday	38	17	8	13	47	48	42
Oldham Athletic	38	16	9	13	44	41	41
Newcastle United	38	15	10	13	61	43	40
Sheffield United	38	15	8	15	49	43	38
Woolwich Arsenal	38	13	12	13	41	49	38
Notts County	38	14	10	14	37	45	38
Blackburn Rovers	38	13	11	14	62	54	37
Liverpool	38	15	7	16	53	53	37
Preston North End	38	12	11	15	40	49	35
Tottenham Hotspur	38	13	6	19	52	63	32
Middlesbrough	38	11	10	17	49	63	32
Manchester City	38	9	13	16	43	58	31
Bury	38	9	11	18	43	71	29
Bristol City	38	11	5	22	43	66	27
Nottingham Forest	38	9	7	22	55	75	25

1911/12

SEASON SNIPPETS

Villa signed Welsh international Dr L R (Dick) Roose as a replacement for Billy George. Roose made his debut on 2 September against Bradford City, but went on to play only ten Villa games. Billy Askew also made his debut at Bradford, but played only once more.

Villa's game against Sunderland on 7 October was designated as a Benefit match for George Burrell Ramsay. Alfred Edwards made his debut as Buckley was injured.

Jimmy Birch scored both Villa goals on his debut against Sheffield Wednesday on 21 October.

Harold Edgley came in for his first appearance at Sheffield United on 23 October.

Bert Goode made his debut against Spurs on 18 November.

At about 5.00pm on 24 November, a telegram arrived at the Villa Offices from Chris Buckley 'Decided not to play tomorrow - Buckley'. Buckley was in dispute with the Club over the game allocated for his Benefit - he wanted the Bradford City game and refused to play unless this match was allocated to him. Buckley was suspended by the Club.

On 20 December, William McGregor died at Miss Storer's Nursing Home in Newhall Street, Birmingham, age 64.

George Hunter played his last game on 26 December.

Tommy Weston made his debut on 20 January.

Frank Mann's only Villa appearance was on 17 February.

Billy Gerrish and Jimmy Birch both played their last game on 24 February.

The game at Notts County on 11 November, which had been postponed due to fog, was eventually played on 13 March when Albert Ralphs made his only appearance.

Albert Lindon played his only Villa game on 23 March.

Len Richards became the fourth goalkeeper to be used during the season when he made his debut in a 6-0 win against Manchester United on 30 March. Walter Watson also played his first game.

William Littlewood made his debut at Liverpool on 6 April.

DIVISION ONE

MANAGER: Directors

MATCH	DATE	VENUE	OPPONENTS	RESULT	HT SCORE	SCORE	SCORERS	ATT
1	Sep 2	A	Bradford City	L	1 0	1 2	Hampton	20,000
2	4	H	West Bromwich Albion	L	0 1	0 3		20,000
3	9	H	Woolwich Arsenal	W	2 1	4 1	Walters, Hampton 2, Wallace (pen)	20,000
4	16	A	Manchester City	W	1 1	6 2	Walters, Bache 3, Hampton 2	30,000
5	23	H	Everton	W	1 0	3 0	Hampton, Wallace (pen), Walters	28,000
6	30	A	West Bromwich Albion	D	1 1	2 2	Hampton, Henshall	46,203
7	Oct 7	H	Sunderland	L	1 0	1 3	Wallace (pen)	30,000
8	14	A	Blackburn Rovers	L	0 3	1 3	Wallace (pen)	25,000
9	21	H	Sheffield Wednesday	L	1 0	2 3	Birch 2	18,000
10	23	A	Sheffield United	W	0 0	1 0	Walters	11,500
11	28	A	Bury	D	0 1	1 1	Walters	10,000
12	Nov 4	H	Middlesbrough	W	1 1	2 1	Wallace, Walters	20,000
13	18	H	Tottenham Hotspur	D	1 1	2 2	Hampton 2	16,000
14	25	A	Manchester United	L	0 1	1 3	Whittaker	12,000
15	Dec 2	H	Liverpool	W	1 0	5 0	Wallace 2 (1 pen), Goode 2, Bache	10,000
16	9	H	Preston North End	W	1 0	1 0	Bache	15,000
17	16	A	Newcastle United	L	2 3	2 6	Hampton, Bache	20,000
18	23	H	Sheffield United	W	0 0	1 0	Wallace	10,000
19	26	H	Oldham Athletc	W	3 1	6 1	Hampton 4, Stephenson 2	15,000
20	30	H	Bradford City	D	0 0	0 0		15,000
21	Jan 1	A	Bolton Wanderers	L	0 1	0 3		38,389
22	6	A	Woolwich Arsenal	D	1 0	2 2	Walters, Wallace	6,000
23	20	H	Manchester City	W	1 0	3 1	Wallace 2 (1 pen), Stephenson	11,760
24	27	A	Everton	D	1 0	1 1	Hampton	40,000
25	Feb 10	A	Sunderland	D	1 0	2 2	Stephenson, Henshall	15,000
26	17	H	Blackburn Rovers	L	0 1	0 3		28,000
27	24	A	Sheffield Wednesday	L	0 2	0 3		20,000
28	Mar 2	H	Bury	W	3 1	5 2	Hampton 4, Wallace	8,000
29	9	A	Middlesbrough	W	1 1	2 1	Wallace, Bache	12,000
30	13	A	Notts County	L	0 0	0 2		8,000
31	16	H	Notts County	W	4 0	5 1	Hampton 2, Stephenson, Goode, Wallace	15,000
32	23	A	Tottenham Hotspur	L	1 2	1 2	Edgley	20,000
33	30	H	Manchester United	W	1 0	6 0	Stephenson 3, Wallace 2, Hampton	15,000
34	Apr 5	H	Bolton Wanderers	L	0 0	0 1		20,000
35	6	A	Liverpool	W	1 0	2 1	Hampton, Stephenson	35,000
36	8	A	Oldham Athletc	W	1 1	2 1	Walters, Stephenson	10,000
37	13	A	Preston North End	L	0 3	1 4	Hampton	10,000
38	20	H	Newcastle United	W	0 0	2 0	Hampton, Hall	20,000

Final League Position: 6th in First Division

Appearances
Goals

FA CUP

1	Jan 13	H	Walsall	W	2 0	6 0	Bache, Henshall 2, Hampton 2, Wallace	18,000
2	Feb 3	H	Reading	D	1 0	1 1	Hampton	25,000
R	7	A	Reading	L	0 0	0 1		12,500

Appearances
Goals

340

FINAL LEAGUE TABLE

	P	W	D	L	F	A	P
Blackburn Rovers	38	20	9	9	60	43	49
Everton	38	20	6	12	46	42	46
Newcastle United	38	18	8	12	64	50	44
Bolton Wanderers	38	20	3	15	54	43	43
Sheffield Wednesday	38	16	9	13	69	49	41
Aston Villa	**38**	**17**	**7**	**14**	**76**	**63**	**41**
Middlesbrough	38	16	8	14	56	45	40
Sunderland	38	14	11	13	58	51	39
West Bromwich A	38	15	9	14	43	47	39
Woolwich Arsenal	38	15	8	15	55	59	38
Bradford City	38	15	8	15	46	50	38
Tottenham Hotspur	38	14	9	15	53	53	37
Manchester United	38	13	11	14	45	60	37
Sheffield United	38	13	10	15	63	56	36
Manchester City	38	13	9	16	56	58	35
Notts County	38	14	7	17	46	63	35
Liverpool	38	12	10	16	49	55	34
Oldham Athletic	38	12	10	16	46	54	34
Preston North End	38	13	7	18	40	57	33
Bury	38	6	9	23	32	59	21

341

1912/13

SEASON SNIPPETS

Sam Hardy, Andy Ducat, Jimmy Harrop and Harold Halse all made their debut against Chelsea on 2 September. It was Chris Buckley's last Villa game, he was still in dispute with the club over his Benefit and was suspended initially by Aston Villa and subsequently by the Football League and the Football Association until 30 April 1914. Buckley joined Arsenal in July 1914, but in later years would return to Villa as a Director and then Chairman.

After only four games, Andy Ducat broke his leg at Manchester City on 14 September and was out of action for two years.

John McLachlan made his debut on 16 September at Woolwich Arsenal.

On 5 October, Harry Hampton became the first Villa player to score five goals in a league game.

On 19 October, Harold Halse repeated Hampton's five-goal record.

Jimmy Leach came in for his first game on 14 December.

Tommy Barber played his first game at Bradford City on 28 December.

Arthur Dobson and Stuart Doncaster both made their debut at home to Blackburn Rovers on 15 February.

The third round FA Cup match against Derby County on 11 January was abandoned at half-time due to heavy snow with the score 1-1.

Charlie Wallace hit a penalty kick wide after 15 minutes of the FA Cup final. Sam Hardy was off the field injured for ten minutes in the second-half and so Jimmy Harrop went in goal. Tommy Barber headed the winner from a Wallace corner. Villa equalled the record of five FA Cup wins, while the attendance of 121,919 was also a record.

Harold Halse played his last game on 23 April.

On 30 April Villa played a Benefit Match at Stoke for Tom Wilkes who had won FA Cup and League Championship Medals with Villa. Stuart Doncaster scored twice in a 2-1 Villa win.

DIVISION ONE

MANAGER: Directors

MATCH	DATE	VENUE	OPPONENTS	RESULT	HT SCORE	SCORE	SCORERS	ATT
1	Sep 2	H	Chelsea	W	1 0	1 0	Stephenson	30,000
2	7	H	Bradford City	W	2 1	3 1	Halse, Bache, Hall	25,000
3	9	A	Oldham Athletic	D	1 1	2 2	Bache, Wallace (pen)	12,000
4	14	A	Manchester City	L	0 0	0 1		32,000
5	16	A	Woolwich Arsenal	W	1 0	3 0	Hampton 2, Stephenson	6,000
6	21	H	West Bromwich Albion	L	1 2	2 4	Bache 2	60,000
7	28	A	Everton	W	0 0	1 0	Halse	40,000
8	Oct 5	H	Sheffield Wednesday	W	6 0	10 0	Halse, Hampton 5, Stephenson 2, Bache 2	30,000
9	12	A	Blackburn Rovers	D	0 0	2 2	Halse 2	45,000
10	19	H	Derby County	W	2 1	5 1	Halse 5	20,000
11	26	A	Tottenham Hotspur	D	1 2	3 3	Halse 2, Stephenson	20,000
12	Nov 2	H	Middlesbrough	W	3 0	5 1	Hampton 2, Halse, Stephenson, Wallace (pen)	20,000
13	9	A	Notts County	D	1 1	1 1	Hampton	18,000
14	16	H	Manchester United	W	3 0	4 2	Bache, Hampton 2, Stephenson	20,000
15	23	A	Sunderland	L	0 2	1 3	Hampton	30,000
16	30	H	Liverpool	L	0 1	0 2		20,000
17	Dec 7	H	Bolton Wanderers	D	0 0	1 1	Wallace (pen)	20,000
18	14	A	Sheffield United	L	2 1	2 3	Halse 2	20,000
19	21	H	Newcastle United	W	2 1	3 1	Hampton, Bache, Wallace	15,000
20	26	A	Oldham Athletic	W	3 0	7 1	Hampton 3, Halse 2, Stephenson 2	15,000
21	28	A	Bradford City	D	1 1	1 1	Stephenson	25,000
22	Jan 4	H	Manchester City	W	1 0	2 0	Halse, Hampton	12,000
23	18	A	West Bromwich Albion	D	1 1	2 2	Hampton (pen), Harrop	50,000
24	25	H	Everton	D	1 0	1 1	Hampton	25,000
25	Feb 8	A	Sheffield Wednesday	D	1 1	1 1	Hall	40,000
26	15	H	Blackburn Rovers	D	1 1	1 1	Barber	18,000
27	Mar 1	H	Tottenham Hotspur	W	0 0	1 0	McLachlan	15,000
28	12	A	Derby County	W	1 0	1 0	Stephenson	6,000
29	15	H	Notts County	W	0 0	1 0	Stephenson	20,000
30	21	A	Chelsea	W	2 0	2 1	Hampton, Leach	65,000
31	22	A	Manchester United	L	0 2	0 4		30,000
32	24	H	Woolwich Arsenal	W	2 0	4 1	Halse 2, Bache, Hall	25,000
33	Apr 5	A	Liverpool	L	0 2	1 3	Doncaster	20,000
34	9	A	Middlesbrough	D	1 0	1 1	Hampton	10,000
35	12	A	Bolton Wanderers	W	0 2	3 2	Barber, Hampton, Stephenson	20,838
36	23	H	Sunderland	D	0 1	1 1	Halse	60,000
37	26	A	Newcastle United	W	3 0	3 2	Stephenson, Wallace, Hampton	20,000
38	28	H	Sheffield United	W	2 1	4 2	Wallace 2 (1 pen), McLachlan, Hampton	4,850

Final League Position: 2nd in First Division

Appearances
Goals

FA CUP

1	Jan 15	A	Derby County	W	3 1	3 1	Halse 2, Hampton	15,000
2	Feb 1	H	West Ham United	W	2 0	5 0	Morris, Halse 2, Hampton, Stephenson	51,024
3	22	H	Crystal Palace	W	3 0	5 0	Halse 2, Stephenson 2, Bache	44,500
4	Mar 8	A	Bradford Park Avenue	W	1 0	5 0	Hampton 3, Stephenson, Halse	24,000
SF	29	N	Oldham Athletic *	W	1 0	1 0	Stephenson	22,616
F	Apr 19	N	Sunderland **	W	0 0	1 0	Barber	121,919

Appearances
Goals

* Played at Ewood Park, Blackburn
** Played at The Crystal Palace

FINAL LEAGUE TABLE

	P	W	D	L	F	A	P
Sunderland	38	25	4	9	86	43	54
Aston Villa	**38**	**19**	**12**	**7**	**86**	**52**	**50**
Sheffield Wednesday	38	21	7	10	75	55	49
Manchester United	38	19	8	11	69	43	46
Blackburn Rovers	38	16	13	9	79	43	45
Manchester City	38	18	8	12	53	37	44
Derby County	38	17	8	13	69	66	42
Bolton Wanderers	38	16	10	12	62	63	42
Oldham Athletic	38	14	14	10	50	55	42
West Bromwich A	38	13	12	13	57	50	38
Everton	38	15	7	16	48	54	37
Liverpool	38	16	5	17	61	71	37
Bradford City	38	12	11	15	50	60	35
Newcastle United	38	13	8	17	47	47	34
Sheffield United	38	14	6	18	56	70	34
Middlesbrough	38	11	10	17	55	69	32
Tottenham Hotspur	38	12	6	20	45	72	30
Chelsea	38	11	6	21	51	73	28
Notts County	38	7	9	22	28	56	23
Woolwich Arsenal	38	3	12	23	26	74	18

1913/14

SEASON SNIPPETS

The Football Association announced on 5 July that they had suspended Mr A Adams, the Cup Final referee along with Charlie Thomson of Sunderland and Harry Hampton of Aston Villa following incidents in the Cup final in April. They were each suspended for a month from 1 September.

Charlie Slade made his debut on 20 September.

Albert Hall's last game was on 15 November, it was also Charlie Slade's last match.

Derby County doubled the admission prices for the game on Christmas Day. John McLaverty and John Laidlaw each made their first of only two appearances.

Robert Chandler kept a clean sheet in his only league game on Boxing Day when he came in for Sam Hardy who was injured at Derby the previous day.

John Laidlaw played his last game on 26 December.

Reg Boyne made his debut on 27 December.

George Tranter played his last first-team game against Blackburn Rovers on 3 January.

Archie Dyke made his debut at Sheffield Wednesday on 14 February as Charlie Wallace was playing for England.

The 6-0 win against Manchester United on 14 March was Freddie Miles' last first-team game. Miles suffered a leg injury against Birmingham Reserves on 11 April, but played out the game. The following Monday the doctor diagnosed a broken fibia bone in his leg. Joe Bache, at 34 years of age became the oldest Villa player to score a league hat-trick.

The game against Newcastle United on 4 April was Herbert Smart's only Villa league appearance.

Jack Burton, a member of Villa's first FA Cup-winning side in 1887, died on Good Friday morning, 10 April.

William Williams played his only league game against Derby County on 13 April.

Len Richards played his last game on 18 April.

DIVISION ONE

MANAGER: Directors

MATCH	DATE	VENUE	OPPONENTS	RESULT	HT SCORE	SCORE	SCORERS	ATT
1	Sep 1	H	Manchester City	D	0 1	1 1	Barber	10,000
2	6	A	Bradford City	D	0 0	0 0		30,000
3	13	H	Blackburn Rovers	L	0 2	1 3	Stephenson	40,000
4	20	A	Sunderland	L	0 0	0 2		30,000
5	27	H	Everton	W	2 1	3 1	Bache 2, Whittaker	45,000
6	Oct 4	A	West Bromwich Albion	L	0 0	0 1		48,057
7	11	H	Sheffield Wednesday	W	2 0	2 0	Barber, Hampton	20,000
8	18	A	Bolton Wanderers	L	0 2	0 3		30,130
9	25	H	Chelsea	L	0 1	1 2	Logan (og)	20,000
10	Nov 1	A	Oldham Athletic	W	0 0	1 0	Stephenson	15,000
11	8	H	Manchester United	W	2 1	3 1	Hampton (pen), Hall, Whittaker	25,000
12	15	A	Burnley	L	0 3	0 4		20,000
13	22	H	Preston North End	W	3 0	3 0	Hampton, Whittaker, Wallace	20,000
14	29	A	Newcastle United	D	2 1	2 2	Hampton, Stephenson	20,000
15	Dec 6	H	Liverpool	W	2 1	2 1	Hampton 2 (1 pen)	15,000
16	13	A	Tottenham Hotspur	D	1 2	3 3	Harrop, Whittaker, Hampton (pen)	15,000
17	20	H	Middlesbrough	L	1 3	2 5	Stephenson 2	15,000
18	25	H	Derby County	W	0 0	2 0	Hampton, Stephenson	10,000
19	26	H	Sheffield United	W	0 0	3 0	Hampton (pen), Barber, Wallace	40,000
20	27	H	Bradford City	L	0 1	0 1		20,000
21	Jan 1	A	Sheffield United	L	0 1	0 3		40,000
22	3	A	Blackburn Rovers	D	0 0	0 0		15,000
23	17	H	Sunderland	W	4 0	5 0	Bache 2, Edgley 2, Hampton	40,000
24	24	A	Everton	W	1 1	4 1	Hampton, Stephenson 2, Wallace	25,000
25	Feb 7	H	West Bromwich Albion	W	1 0	2 0	Wallace, Barber	40,000
26	14	A	Sheffield Wednesday	W	1 1	3 2	Stephenson, Hampton, Bache	30,000
27	25	H	Bolton Wanderers	W	1 0	1 0	Hampton	15,000
28	28	A	Chelsea	W	2 0	3 0	Stephenson, Hampton, Bache	60,000
29	Mar 14	A	Manchester United	W	2 0	6 0	Edgley, Bache 3, Hampton, Stephenson	30,000
30	18	H	Oldham Athletic	D	0 0	0 0		20,000
31	21	H	Burnley	W	1 0	1 0	Edgley	30,000
32	Apr 1	A	Preston North End	L	1 2	2 3	Stephenson, Hampton (pen)	16,000
33	4	H	Newcastle United	L	0 1	1 3	Wallace (pen)	20,000
34	10	A	Manchester City	L	1 2	1 3	Edgley	20,000
35	11	A	Liverpool	W	1 0	1 0	Bache	45,000
36	13	H	Derby County	W	2 2	3 2	Hampton 2 (1 pen), Bache	20,000
37	10	A	Tottenham Hotspur	W	1 0	2 0	J McLachlan, Hampton	30,000
38	25	H	Middlesbrough	L	0 2	1 3	Bache	25,000

Final League Position: 2nd in First Division | 1 Own Goal

Appearances
Goals

FA CUP

1	Jan 10	H	Stoke	W	2 0	4 0	Stephenson 2, Hampton 2	18,000
2	31	A	Exeter City	W	1 0	2 1	Hampton 2	9,600
3	Feb 21	H	West Bromwich Albion	W	1 1	2 1	Bache, Hampton	65,000
4	Mar 7	A	Sheffield Wednesday	W	1 0	1 0	Edgley	56,991
SF	28	N	Liverpool *	L	0 1	0 2		27,467

Appearances
Goals

* Played at White Hart lane

Hardy S	Lyons AT	Weston T	Tranter GH	Harrop J	Leach JM	Wallace CW	Whittaker SS	Barber T	Stephenson C	Bache JW	McLachlan JA	Slade HC	Littlewood WA	Hampton JH	Morris W	Hall AE	Anstey B	Miles A	McLaverty JG	Laidlaw JW	Edgley HH	Chandler R	Boyne R	McLachlan A	Dyke AS	Smart HH	Williams WH	Richards LJ	MATCH
1	2	3	4	5	6	7	8	9	10	11																			1
1	2	3	4	5	6	7		9	10	11	8																		2
1	2	3		5	6	7	9	4	10	11	8																		3
1	2	3		5	6	7		4	10	11	8	9																	4
1		3		5	6	7	8	4	10	11		9	2																5
1	2	3	4	5	6	7		8	10	11				9															6
1	2	3	4	5	6	7		8	10	11				9															7
1	2	3		5	6	7	4	8	10	11				9															8
1	2	3		5	6		7	8	10	11				9	4														9
1		3	4	5		7	8	6	10					9		11													10
	2	3	4	5		7	8	6	10					9		11	1												11
	2	3	4	5		8	6	10			9					11	1												12
1				5	6	7	8		10	11		2	9	4		3													13
1	2	3		5		7	6	10	11	8			9	4															14
1	2	3		5		7	8	6	10	11				9	4														15
1	2	3		5		7	8	6	10	11				9	4														16
1	2		4	5		7	8	6	10	11				9															17
1					6	7		4	10					9				2	3										18
	2			5	6	7		4	10	11				3	9				3	5	8	11							19
1	3			6	7			4	10					2	9					5		11	8						20
1	3			5	6	7			10	11				2	9								8	4					21
	2	3	4	5		7	6		10						9							11	8						22
1	2	3		5	6	7		4	8	10				9								11							23
1	2	3		5	6	7		4	8	10				9								11							24
1	2	3		5	6	7		4	8	10				9								11							25
	2				6			4	8	10				9	5		1		3			11		7					26
1	2			5	6	7		4	8					9	4				3			11		10					27
1	2	3		5	6	7		4	8	10				9								11							28
1	2			5	6			4	8	10				9					3			11		7					29
1	2	3		5	6			4	8	10				9								11		7					30
	2	3		5	6				10	8					4		1					11	9	7					31
1	2	3		5	6			4	8	10				9								11		7					32
	2	3		5		7	8			9					4		1					11		6		10			33
	2	3		5	6	7		4	8		10			9								11							34
1	2	3		5	6	7			8	10				9	4							11							35
	2			5	6	7		4	8	10				9	4		1					11			3				36
				5	6	7		4	8		10			9	4							11					1		37
1		3		5		7		8	10				2	9	4							11		6					38

| 30 | 34 | 28 | 9 | 35 | 28 | 32 | 14 | 28 | 36 | 28 | 8 | 3 | 7 | 30 | 13 | 3 | 6 | 2 | 2 | 19 | 1 | 4 | 3 | 6 | 1 | 1 | 1 | | |
| | | | | 1 | | | 5 | 4 | 4 | 12 | 12 | 1 | | 19 | | 1 | | | | 5 | | | | | | | | | |

1	2	3		5	6	7	8	4	10					9						11									1
1	2	3		5	6	7		4	8	10				9						11									2
1	2	3		5	6	7		4	8	10				9						11									3
1	2	3		5	6	7		4	8	10				9						11									4
1	2	3		5	6	7		4	8	10				9						11									SF

| 5 | 5 | 5 | | 5 | 5 | 5 | 1 | 5 | 5 | 4 | | | | 5 | | | | | | 5 | | | | | | | | | |
| | | | | | | | | | 2 | 1 | | | | 5 | | | | | | 1 | | | | | | | | | |

FINAL LEAGUE TABLE

	P	W	D	L	F	A	P
Blackburn Rovers	38	20	11	7	78	42	51
Aston Villa	**38**	**19**	**6**	**13**	**65**	**50**	**44**
Middlesbrough	38	19	5	14	77	60	43
Oldham Athletic	38	17	9	12	55	45	43
West Bromwich A	38	15	13	10	46	42	43
Bolton Wanderers	38	16	10	12	65	52	42
Sunderland	38	17	6	15	63	52	40
Chelsea	38	16	7	15	46	55	39
Bradford City	38	12	14	12	40	40	38
Sheffield United	38	16	5	17	63	60	37
Newcastle United	38	13	11	14	39	48	37
Burnley	38	12	12	14	61	53	36
Manchester City	38	14	8	16	51	53	36
Manchester United	38	15	6	17	52	62	36
Everton	38	12	11	15	46	55	35
Liverpool	38	14	7	17	46	62	35
Tottenham Hotspur	38	12	10	16	50	62	34
Sheffield Wednesday	38	13	8	17	53	70	34
Preston North End	38	12	6	20	52	69	30
Derby County	38	8	11	19	55	71	27

1914/15

SEASON SNIPPETS

The Country was at war when the season opened, the Great War having commenced in August and recruitment drives were made at all the games. Herbert Smart was one of the first Villa players to 'join the colours'.

The Directors arranged for Villa players to receive military training and this continued during the season.

Howard Humphries made his debut against Notts County on 2 September.

Jimmy Stephenson played his first senior game at Everton on 26 September.

In November came news that Walter Kimberley had been taken prisoner of war and was interned at Doeberitz while Stuart Doncaster, who had rejoined the Coldstream Guards, was invalided home having been wounded.

George Hampton made his debut on New Year's Day at Bolton.

Harry Nash scored a hat-trick against Liverpool on his debut on 3 April while Harry Hampton extended his hat-trick total to a record fourteen in league and cup.

On 21 April 1915, Harry Hampton scored two goals against Manchester City to bring his Villa league goalscoring total to a record 215 goals. These were his last Villa league goals.

At the end of the season, league football closed down for the remainder of the war. For twelve of the players, it would be their last season with Villa including Tommy Lyons, Joe Bache and Tommy Barber.

DIVISION ONE

MANAGER: Directors

MATCH	DATE	VENUE	OPPONENTS	RESULT	HT SCORE	SCORE	SCORERS	ATT
1	Sep 2	H	Notts County	W	1 0	2 1	Hampton 2 (1 pen)	10,000
2	5	H	Sunderland	L	1 2	1 3	Hampton	12,000
3	12	A	Sheffield Wednesday	L	0 4	2 5	Edgley, Humphries	10,000
4	19	H	West Bromwich Albion	W	2 0	2 1	C Stephenson, Harrop	30,000
5	26	A	Everton	D	0 0	0 0		25,000
6	Oct 3	H	Chelsea	W	2 1	2 1	Hampton (pen), C Stephenson	12,000
7	10	A	Bradford City	L	0 0	0 3		22,000
8	17	H	Burnley	D	1 2	3 3	Ducat (pen), Barber 2	16,000
9	24	A	Tottenham Hotspur	W	0 0	2 0	C Stephenson, Edgley	25,000
10	31	H	Newcastle United	W	0 0	2 1	Whittaker, Wallace	15,000
11	Nov 7	A	Middlesbrough	D	1 0	1 1	Bache	12,000
12	14	H	Sheffield United	W	0 0	1 0	Ducat	12,000
13	25	A	Manchester City	L	0 0	0 1		16,000
14	28	A	Liverpool	W	5 1	6 3	C Stephenson, Hampton, Barber, Bache, Edgley 2	15,000
15	Dec 5	H	Bradford Park Avenue	L	0 0	1 2	C Stephenson	10,000
16	12	A	Oldham Athletc	D	1 2	3 3	Edgley, Bache, Hampton	5,000
17	19	H	Manchester United	D	1 2	3 3	Edgley, Hampton 2	10,000
18	25	H	Blackburn Rovers	W	1 1	2 1	Edgley, Leach	15,000
19	26	A	Bolton Wanderers	L	1 4	1 7	C Stephenson	30,000
20	Jan 1	A	Bolton Wanderers	D	0 1	2 2	Hampton, Edgley	20,000
21	2	A	Sunderland	L	0 2	0 4		15,000
22	16	H	Sheffield Wednesday	D	0 0	0 0		8,000
23	23	A	West Bromwich Albion	L	0 0	0 2		30,000
24	Feb 6	A	Chelsea	L	1 1	1 3	C Stephenson	20,000
25	10	H	Everton	L	1 3	1 5	Hampton	7,000
26	13	H	Bradford City	D	0 0	0 0		5,000
27	22	A	Burnley	L	0 1	1 2	Leach	8,000
28	27	H	Tottenham Hotspur	W	0 0	3 1	Hampton 2, C Stephenson	25,000
29	Mar 13	A	Middlesbrough	W	2 0	5 0	Hampton 2, Harrop, C Stephenson 2	12,000
30	20	A	Sheffield United	L	0 3	0 3		17,000
31	Apr 2	H	Blackburn Rovers	W	1 1	2 1	Edgley, C Stephenson	10,000
32	3	H	Liverpool	W	5 0	6 2	Hampton 3, Nash 3	12,000
33	5	A	Notts County	D	1 1	1 1	Bache	12,000
34	10	A	Bradford Park Avenue	D	1 1	2 2	Ducat (pen), J Stephenson	12,000
35	17	H	Oldham Athletic	D	0 0	0 0		15,000
36	21	H	Manchester City	W	1 0	4 1	Nash 2, Hampton 2 (1 pen)	15,000
37	26	A	Manchester United	L	0 0	0 1		8,000
38	28	A	Newcastle United	L	0 0	0 3		10,000

Final League Position: 14th in First Division

Appearances
Goals

FA CUP

1	Jan 9	H	Exeter City	W	0 0	2 0	Bache, C Stephenson	13,000
2	30	A	Manchester City	L	0 0	0 1		29,661

Appearances
Goals

	Hardy S	Littlewood WA	Weston T	Barber T	Harrop J	Leach JM	Wallace CW	Stephenson C	Hampton JH	Humphries HJ	Edgley HH	Lyons AT	Ducat A	Dyke AS	Stephenson J	Tranter GH	Boyne R	Bache JW	Whittaker SS	Morris W	Anstey B	McLachlan JA	Hampton GH	Dobson HA	Nash HE	Moss F	MATCH
1	1	2	3	4	5	6	7	8	9	10	11																1
2	1	2	3	4	5	6	7	8	9	10	11																2
3			3	4	5	6	7	8	9	10	11	2															3
4	1	3		4	5	6	7	8	9	10	11	2															4
5	1		3	10	5	6		8			11	2	4	7	9												5
6	1	3		10	5	6		8	9		11	2	4	7													6
7	1	3		10	5			8			11	2	4		7	6	9										7
8	1	3		9	5	6		8			11	2	4		7			10									8
9	1	3		9	5	6		8			11	2	4		7			10									9
10	1	3			6	7	8				9		2		11			10	4	5							10
11	1	3			5	6	9	8			11	2	4		7			10									11
12		3			5	6	7	8	9		11	2	4					10			1						12
13	1	3		6			7	8	9		11	2	4					10		5							13
14	1	3		6			7	8	9		11	2	4					10		5							14
15	1	3			6	7	8	9			11	2	4					10		5							15
16	1	3			5	6	7	8	9		11	2	4					10									16
17	1	3			5	6	7	8	9		11	2	4					10									17
18	1	3			5	6	7	8	9		11	2	4					10									18
19	1	3			5	6	7	8	9		11		2					10				4					19
20	1	3			5		7	8	9		11							10		4			2	6			20
21	1	3			5		7	8	9		11							10		4			2	6			21
22	1	3		6				8	9		11	2			7		10			4				5			22
23	1	3		6	5		7	8	9		11	2	4				10										23
24	1	3			5	6	7	8	9	10	11	2												4			24
25	1	3			5	6		8	9	10		2			7			11						4			25
26	1	3			5	6			9		11		4	10	7		8			2							26
27	1	3			5	6	7	8	9		11		4					10		2							27
28	1	3			5	6	7	10	9		8		4					11		2							28
29	1	2	3		5		7	8	9		11		4					10		6							29
30	1	3			5	6	7	8	9		11							10	4	2							30
31	1	2	3		5	6	7	8	9		11		4					10									31
32	1	2	3		5	6	7	8	9		11		4												10		32
33	1		3				9	8			11	2	4		7			10		6		3				5	33
34	1				5	6	9	8			11	2	4		7			10									34
35	1	2	3		5		7	8	9				4					11		6					10		35
36	1	2	3		5		7	8	9		11		4							6					10		36
37	1	2	3		5	6	7	8	9		11														10	4	37
38	1	2	3	6	5		7	8	9									11		4					10		38

| | 37 | 34 | 12 | 14 | 32 | 26 | 30 | 37 | 30 | 6 | 35 | 21 | 26 | 3 | 11 | 1 | 4 | 24 | 2 | 16 | 1 | 1 | 3 | 5 | 5 | 2 | |
| | | | | | 3 | 2 | 2 | 1 | 11 | 19 | 1 | 9 | | 3 | 1 | | | 4 | 1 | | | | | | 5 | | |

| | 1 | 3 | | | 5 | | 7 | 8 | 9 | | 11 | 2 | 4 | | | | | 10 | | 6 | | | | | | | 1 |
| | 1 | 3 | | 6 | 5 | | 7 | 8 | 9 | 10 | | | 4 | | | | | 11 | 2 | | | | | | | | 2 |

| | 2 | 2 | | 1 | 2 | | 2 | 2 | 1 | 1 | 1 | 2 | | | | | | 2 | 1 | 1 | | | | | | | 1 |
| | | | | | | | | 1 | | | | | | | | | | 1 | | | | | | | | | 2 |

FINAL LEAGUE TABLE

	P	W	D	L	F	A	P
Everton	38	19	8	11	76	47	46
Oldham Athletic	38	17	11	10	70	56	45
Blackburn Rovers	38	18	7	13	83	61	43
Burnley	38	18	7	13	61	47	43
Manchester City	38	15	13	10	49	39	43
Sheffield United	38	15	13	10	49	41	43
Sheffield Wednesday	38	15	13	10	61	54	43
Sunderland	38	18	5	15	81	72	41
Bradford Park Av	38	17	7	14	69	65	41
West Bromwich A	38	15	10	13	49	43	40
Bradford City	38	13	14	11	55	49	40
Middlesbrough	38	13	12	13	62	74	38
Liverpool	38	14	9	15	65	75	37
Aston Villa	**38**	**13**	**11**	**14**	**62**	**72**	**37**
Newcastle United	38	11	10	17	46	48	32
Notts County	38	9	13	16	41	57	31
Bolton Wanderers	38	11	8	19	68	84	30
Manchester United	38	9	12	17	46	62	30
Chelsea	38	8	13	17	51	65	29
Tottenham Hotspur	38	8	12	18	57	90	28

1919/20

SEASON SNIPPETS

Dicky York and Ernie Blackburn both made their debut on 30 August against Sunderland.

Frank Barson made his debut against Middlesbrough on 25 October after his record £2,850 transfer from Barnsley. It was also Billy Kirton's first game.

Harry Hampton played his last Villa game on 3 January and was transferred to Birmingham the following month.

On 10 January, Billy Walker scored two goals on his debut - a first-round FA Cup match against Queen's Park Rangers.

Harold Edgley was carried off with a broken leg against Chelsea at Stamford Bridge on 2 April 1920, six days after scoring in a 3-1 FA Cup semi-final win against the same Club. Edgley not only missed the FA Cup final, but never played in Villa's first team again.

Villa won the FA Cup for a record sixth time on 24 April and after spending the weekend celebrating in London and Brighton, the players returned on the Monday evening and went straight to Villa Park to play Manchester City. Andy Ducat lead his team onto the pitch carrying the FA Cup, but three minutes after kick-off, Ducat was penalised for handling inside the penalty area and Tommy Browell scored the only goal of the match from the penalty spot for a City win. Frank Barson missed a penalty for Villa.

Freddie Miles had the distinction of training an FA Cup-winning team in his first year of office.

The FA Cup final was Arthur Dorrell's first FA Cup match.

DIVISION ONE

MANAGER: Directors

MATCH	DATE	VENUE	OPPONENTS	RESULT	HT SCORE	SCORE	SCORERS	ATT
1	Aug 30	A	Sunderland	L	0 2	1 2	C Stephenson	35,000
2	Sep 1	H	Derby County	D	0 0	2 2	Bourne, C Stephenson (pen)	20,000
3	6	H	Sunderland	L	0 3	0 3		40,000
4	8	A	Derby County	L	0 1	0 1		12,000
5	13	A	Liverpool	L	0 1	1 2	Bourne	35,000
6	20	H	Liverpool	L	0 1	0 1		30,000
7	27	A	Bradford Park Avenue	L	0 1	1 6	C Stephenson (pen)	15,000
8	Oct 4	H	Bradford Park Avenue	W	0 0	1 0	C Stephenson	30,000
9	11	A	Preston North End	L	0 2	0 3		12,000
10	18	H	Preston North End	L	1 2	2 4	C Stephenson, Dorrell	35,000
11	25	A	Middlesbrough	W	0 1	4 1	Boyman 3, Dorrell	18,000
12	Nov 1	H	Middlesbrough	W	2 3	5 3	C Stephenson 3, Dorrell, Boyman	40,000
13	10	A	West Bromwich Albion	W	2 1	2 1	C Stephenson, Boyman	20,000
14	15	H	West Bromwich Albion	L	1 1	2 4	Kirton, Boyman	60,000
15	22	A	Sheffield United	W	2 0	2 1	Kirton 2	25,000
16	29	H	Sheffield United	W	1 0	4 0	C Stephenson 4 (1 pen)	15,000
17	Dec 6	H	Manchester United	W	1 0	2 0	Kirton, Boyman	35,000
18	13	A	Manchester United	W	1 0	2 1	C Stephenson 2	30,000
19	20	H	Oldham Athletic	W	1 0	3 0	Kirton, Edgley, C Stephenson	30,000
20	25	H	Chelsea	W	2 2	5 2	Barson, Kirton, C Stephenson 2, Ducat	30,000
21	27	A	Oldham Athletic	W	2 0	3 0	Young 2, Kirton	10,000
22	Jan 1	A	Newcastle United	L	0 1	0 2		45,000
23	3	H	Burnley	D	1 1	2 2	C Stephenson 2	30,000
24	17	A	Burnley	D	0 0	0 0		25,000
25	24	A	Arsenal	W	1 0	1 0	C Stephenson	55,000
26	Feb 7	A	Everton	D	1 1	1 1	Walker	45,000
27	11	H	Arsenal	W	0 1	2 1	C Stephenson 2 (1 pen)	20,000
28	14	H	Everton	D	1 1	2 2	Walker, Kirton	40,000
29	28	H	Bradford City	W	0 0	3 1	Walker, C Stephenson, Kirton	40,000
30	Mar 13	H	Bolton Wanderers	L	0 1	1 2	Kirton	16,000
31	17	A	Bradford City	L	0 1	1 3	Barson (pen)	12,000
32	20	H	Blackburn Rovers	L	1 0	1 2	Walker	30,000
33	Apr 2	A	Chelsea	L	1 0	1 2	Kirton	70,000
34	3	H	Notts County	W	2 0	3 1	Boyman, Kirton, Barson (pen)	35,000
35	5	H	Newcastle United	W	2 0	4 0	Wallace, Walker 3	50,000
36	7	H	Bolton Wanderers	L	2 5	3 6	Stephenson, Walker, Barson (pen)	25,000
37	10	A	Notts County	L	0 2	1 2	Davis	18,000
38	15	A	Blackburn Rovers	L	0 2	1 5	York	15,000
39	17	H	Sheffield Wednesday	W	1 1	3 1	Kirton, Stephenson, Dorrell	30,000
40	26	H	Manchester City	L	0 1	0 1		45,000
41	29	A	Sheffield Wednesday	W	0 0	1 0	Stephenson	12,000
42	May 1	A	Manchester City	D	1 0	2 2	Kirton 2	30,000

Final League Position: 9th in First Division

Appearances
Goals

FA CUP

1	Jan 10	H	Queen's Park Rangers	W	1 0	2 1	Walker 2	33,000
2	31	A	Manchester United	W	0 1	2 1	C Stephenson, Walker	48,600
3	Feb 21	H	Sunderland	W	1 0	1 0	C Stephenson	31,784
4	Mar 6	A	Tottenham Hotspur	W	1 0	1 0	Clay (og)	52,179
SF	27	N	Chelsea *	W	1 0	3 1	Walker 2, Edgley	37,771
F	Apr 24	N	Huddersfield Town **	W	0 0	1 0	Kirton	50,018

Appearances
Goals

* Played at Bramall Lane, Sheffield
** Final played at Stamford Bridge, result after extra-time

FINAL LEAGUE TABLE

	P	W	D	L	F	A	P	
West Bromwich A	42	28	4	10	104	47	60	1
Burnley	42	21	9	12	65	59	51	2
Chelsea	42	22	5	15	56	51	49	3
Liverpool	42	19	10	13	59	44	48	4
Sunderland	42	22	4	16	72	59	48	SF
Bolton Wanderers	42	19	14	9	72	65	47	F
Manchester City	42	18	9	15	71	62	45	
Newcastle United	42	17	9	16	44	39	43	
Aston Villa	**42**	**18**	**6**	**18**	**75**	**73**	**42**	
Arsenal	42	15	12	15	56	58	42	
Bradford Park Av	42	15	12	15	60	63	42	
Manchester United	42	13	14	15	54	50	40	
Middlesbrough	42	15	10	17	61	65	40	
Sheffield United	42	16	8	18	59	69	40	
Bradford City	42	14	11	17	54	63	39	
Everton	42	12	14	16	69	68	38	
Oldham Athletic	42	15	8	19	49	52	38	
Derby County	42	13	12	17	47	57	38	
Preston North End	42	14	10	18	57	73	38	
Blackburn Rovers	42	13	11	18	64	77	37	
Notts County	42	12	12	18	56	74	36	
Sheffield Wednesday	42	7	9	26	28	64	23	

1920/21

SEASON SNIPPETS

When Billy Walker hit four goals against Arsenal on 28 August, he became the first Villa player to achieve this feat in the opening league game of a season.

The club decided to no longer admit boys to Villa Park for first-team games at half-price. The reasons given were that the ground was undergoing extensive alteration and also that there was a risk of personal injury to them in a large crowd.

Jimmy Lee made his last appearance at Liverpool on 18 December.

Goalkeeper Cyril Spiers made his debut in a 3-4 home defeat by Manchester United on Christmas Day and went on to play 112 games.

Edmund Wright was in goal for the 3-1 win in the return game with United at Old Trafford two days later, but Wright played only one further game.

The FA Cup defeat against Tottenham Hotspur was the last game for Clem Stephenson, Jimmy Stephenson, Jimmy Harrop and Jack Thompson.

Charlie Wallace scored in the last of his 349 Villa games, a 2-0 win against Bolton Wanderers on 7 May 1921. It was also the last game for goalkeeper Sam Hardy and John Hampson.

DIVISION ONE

MANAGER: Directors

MATCH	DATE	VENUE	OPPONENTS	RESULT	HT SCORE	SCORE	SCORERS	ATT
1	Aug 28	H	Arsenal	W	0 0	5 0	Walker 4, C Stephenson (pen)	45,000
2	30	A	Manchester City	L	1 2	1 3	Walker	35,000
3	Sep 4	A	Arsenal	W	0 0	1 0	Walker	45,000
4	6	H	Manchester City	W	1 1	3 1	Walker, J Stephenson, Dorrell	14,000
5	11	H	Tottenham Hotspur	W	3 0	4 2	Dorrell, Kirton, Walker 2	55,000
6	15	A	Bolton Wanderers	L	0 2	0 5		48,000
7	18	A	Tottenham Hotspur	W	1 0	2 1	Dorrell, Kirton	45,000
8	25	H	Oldham Athletic	W	0 0	3 0	Walker 2, Kirton	40,000
9	Oct 2	A	Oldham Athletic	D	1 1	1 1	Walker	23,000
10	9	H	Preston North End	W	1 0	1 0	Walker	40,000
11	16	A	Preston North End	L	0 3	1 6	Walker	22,000
12	23	H	Sheffield United	W	1 0	4 0	C Stephenson 2, Barson, Kirton	40,000
13	30	A	Sheffield United	D	0 0	0 0		40,000
14	Nov 6	H	West Bromwich Albion	D	0 0	0 0		70,000
15	13	A	West Bromwich Albion	L	0 0	1 2	C Stephenson (pen)	50,000
16	20	H	Bradford Park Avenue	W	2 1	4 1	Kirton, C Stephenson, Walker 2	30,000
17	27	A	Bradford Park Avenue	L	0 2	0 4		15,000
18	Dec 4	H	Newcastle United	L	1 1	1 2	Kirton	30,000
19	11	H	Newcastle United	D	0 0	0 0		35,000
20	18	A	Liverpool	L	1 1	1 4	Walker	40,000
21	25	H	Manchester United	L	1 0	3 4	Walker, C Stephenson 2	35,000
22	27	A	Manchester United	W	1 0	3 1	Walker 2, C Stephenson	70,504
23	Jan 1	H	Liverpool	L	0 2	0 2		40,000
24	15	H	Everton	L	1 0	1 3	Kirton	35,000
25	22	A	Everton	D	0 1	1 1	Kirton	40,000
26	Feb 5	A	Burnley	L	1 2	1 7	Humphries	40,000
27	9	H	Burnley	D	0 0	0 0		40,000
28	12	H	Sunderland	L	0 2	1 5	Boyman	35,000
29	23	A	Sunderland	W	0 0	1 0	Dorrell	40,000
30	26	H	Bradford City	L	0 1	1 2	Boyman	30,000
31	Mar 7	A	Bradford City	L	0 1	0 3		22,000
32	12	H	Huddersfield Town	D	0 0	0 0		55,000
33	19	A	Huddersfield Town	L	0 0	0 1		22,000
34	26	H	Middlesbrough	W	1 0	4 1	Walker 2, Young 2	25,000
35	28	H	Chelsea	W	1 0	3 0	Young, Walker, Dickson	30,000
36	29	A	Chelsea	L	0 3	1 5	Walker (pen)	32,000
37	Apr 2	H	Middlesbrough	L	0 1	0 1		30,000
38	9	A	Blackburn Rovers	W	1 0	1 0	Dickson	20,000
39	16	H	Blackburn Rovers	W	1 0	3 0	Moss, Walker, Barson (pen)	20,000
40	23	A	Derby County	W	1 0	3 2	Walker, Young 2	15,000
41	30	H	Derby County	W	1 0	1 0	Boyman	20,000
42	May 7	H	Bolton Wanderers	W	2 0	2 0	York, Wallace	15,000

Final League Position: 10th in First division

Appearances
Goals

FA CUP

1	Jan 8	H	Bristol City	W	2 0	2 0	C Stephenson (pen), Walker	49,734
2	29	A	Notts County	D	0 0	0 0		45,014
R	Feb 2	H	Notts County	W	0 0	1 0	Walker	49,491
3	19	H	Huddersfield Town	W	2 0	2 0	Walker 2	50,627
4	Mar 5	A	Tottenham Hotspur	L	0 1	0 1		52,000

Appearances
Goals

350

Player Appearances

Hardy S	Smart T	Weston T	Moss F	Barson F	Harrop J	Wallace CW	Kirton WJ	Walker WH	Stephenson C	Dorrell AR	Ducat A	Boyman WR	Stephenson J	Young A	Lee JT	Ball TE	Thompson JG	Spiers CH	Wright E	Hampson EJ	Leach JM	Humphries HJ	York RE	Jackson T	Blackburn RE	Blackburn GF	Dickson IW	Price LP	Bourne H	MATCH
1	2	3	4	5	6	7	8	9	10	11																				1
1	2	3	4	5	6	7	8	9	10	11																				2
1	2	3	6	5		7	8	9		11	4	10																		3
1	2	3		5	6		8	9		11	4		7	10																4
1	2	3	6	5			8	9	10	11	4		7																	5
	2	3	4		6		8	9		11			7	10	1	5														6
1	2	3			6		8	9		11	4		7	10		5														7
1		3	6				8	9		11	4		7			5	2													8
1	2	3	4	5	6		8	9	10	11			7																	9
1		3		5	6		8	9	10	11	4		7				2													10
1		3		5	6		8	9	10	11	4		7				2													11
	2	3	4	5	6		8		10	11		9	7		1															12
	2	3	6	5			8	9	10	11	4		7		1															13
		3	6	5			8	9		11			7	10	1		2													14
	2		6	5		7	8	9	10	11	4				1		3													15
	2	3			6	7	8	9	10	11	4				1	5														16
	2	3	4		6	7	8	9	10	11					1	5														17
	2	3	6			7	8	9	10	11	4				1	5														18
	2	3		5	6	7	8		10	11	4			9		1														19
	2	3		5	6	7	8	9		11	4					1														20
	2	3	4	5	6	7	8	9	10	11								1												21
	2	3	4	5	6	7	8	9	10	11								1												22
1	2	3		5	6	7	8	9	10	11				8																23
1	2	3		5	6	7	8	9	10	11									4											24
1				5	6	7	8	9		10	11	4																		25
1	2		4			5	8						7	9		3					6	10								26
1	3		6		5		8	9		11	4	10				2					7									27
1	3		6		5		8	9		11	4	10				2					7									28
	3							9	10	11	4		8	7		5	2						1							29
1	3			4	5			9	10	11			8	7		6	2													30
			6	5		7		9		11	4	8					3					2	10							31
1	2		6	5			8	10		11	4						3	7				9								32
1			4			7	8	9		11		10					3					2								33
		3		5		7		10			4			9				2			6			8	11					34
1	2	3	4	5				10						9				6			7			8	11					35
	2	3	6	5				10			4						1				7			8	11					36
1	2	3	6	5				10			4							7				9		8	11					37
1		3	4	5				10									6	9		7		2		8	11					38
	2	3	6	5			8										7	1				9	11	4						39
	2	3	6					10			4			9	5		7	1				8	11							40
1	2	3	4	5										10			6	7				9	8	11						41
1	2					7	8			11				10	9		5				4	3	6							42
25	37	28	32	29	20	18	31	37	21	34	24	10	15	13	10	13	9	2	2	6	1	5	11	3	4	5	8	8	1	
			1	2		1	8	26	8	4		3	1	5						1	1						2			

																														R
1	2	3	6			7	8	9	10	11	4																			1
1	2			3	5	6	7	8	9	10	11	4																		2
1	2			3	5	6	7	8	9	10	11	4																		3
1	3			6	5		7	8	9	10	11	4							2											4
1	3				5	6		8	9	10	11	4		7					2											
5	5	1		4	5	3	4	5	5	5	5			1					2											
									4	1																				

FINAL LEAGUE TABLE

	P	W	D	L	F	A	P
Burnley	42	23	13	6	79	36	59
Manchester City	42	24	6	12	70	50	54
Bolton Wanderers	42	19	14	9	77	53	52
Liverpool	42	18	15	9	63	35	51
Newcastle United	42	20	10	12	66	45	50
Tottenham Hotspur	42	19	9	14	70	48	47
Everton	42	17	13	12	66	55	47
Middlesbrough	42	17	12	13	53	53	46
Arsenal	42	15	14	13	59	63	44
Aston Villa	**42**	**18**	**7**	**17**	**63**	**70**	**43**
Blackburn Rovers	42	13	15	14	57	59	41
Sunderland	42	14	13	15	57	60	41
Manchester United	42	15	10	17	64	68	40
West Bromwich A	42	13	14	15	54	58	40
Bradford City	42	12	15	15	61	63	39
Preston North End	42	15	9	18	61	65	39
Huddersfield Town	42	15	9	18	42	49	39
Chelsea	42	13	13	16	48	58	39
Oldham Athletic	42	9	15	18	49	86	33
Sheffield United	42	6	18	18	42	68	30
Derby County	42	5	16	21	32	58	26
Bradford Park Av	42	8	8	26	43	76	24

1921/22

SEASON SNIPPETS

Martin Taylor played his only league game on 17 September.

Arthur Davis played his last game on 24 September.

The 5-0 defeat at Middlesbrough on 22 October was the last game for Jimmy Leach, Dick Boyman and Andy Young.

On 12 November 1921, Billy Walker became the first Villa player to score a hat-trick of penalties. Villa beat Bradford City 7-1 despite only having ten men for 55 minutes, George Blackburn having to leave the field injured following a collision with City's Cecil Kilborn.

George T Stephenson, who had arrived from Leeds City, made his debut on 3 December.

Percy Jones played his first game on 8 February.

On 11 March Tommy Weston played the last of his 178 games while 'Jock' Johnstone made his debut.

Len Capewell scored on his debut on 1 April.

George Harkus made his debut at Huddersfield on 5 April.

On 15 April, Tommy Mort made his debut in a 2-1 home win against Bolton Wanderers. Mort's first-team career would last for the next thirteen years and he would play 369 games.

Ernie Blackburn's last game was on 17 April.

Lew Price made his last appearance on 22 April.

The home game against Oldham Athletic on 29 April was Frank Barson's last match. Barson refused to re-sign for the 1922/23 season and was transferred to Manchester United in August 1922.

DIVISION ONE

MANAGER: Directors

MATCH	DATE	VENUE	OPPONENTS	RESULT	HT SCORE	SCORE	SCORERS	ATT
1	Aug 27	A	Manchester City	L	1 1	1 2	Walker	35,000
2	29	H	Cardiff City	W	1 0	2 1	Kirton, Young	30,000
3	Sep 3	H	Manchester City	W	2 0	4 0	Young 2, Kirton, Moss	35,000
4	5	A	Cardiff City	W	2 0	4 0	Barson 2 (1 pen), Moss, Dorrell	45,000
5	10	A	Preston North End	L	0 0	0 1		25,000
6	12	H	Blackburn Rovers	D	1 1	1 1	Walker	20,000
7	17	H	Preston North End	W	0 0	2 0	Walker 2	25,000
8	24	A	Tottenham Hotspur	L	1 1	1 3	Dickson	40,000
9	Oct 1	H	Tottenham Hotspur	W	1 0	2 1	Kirton, Dickson	40,000
10	8	A	West Bromwich Albion	W	1 0	1 0	Young	50,000
11	15	H	West Bromwich Albion	L	0 0	0 1		50,000
12	22	A	Middlesbrough	L	0 2	0 5		10,000
13	29	H	Middlesbrough	W	3 1	6 2	Dorrell, Dickson 2, Walker, Kirton, York	30,000
14	Nov 5	A	Bradford City	L	1 0	2 3	Walker 2	20,000
15	12	H	Bradford City	W	2 0	7 1	Walker 3 (3 pens), Dorrell 2, Dickson 2	35,000
16	19	H	Manchester United	W	1 0	3 1	Walker, Barson, Dickson	25,000
17	26	A	Manchester United	L	0 0	0 1		40,000
18	Dec 3	H	Liverpool	D	0 0	1 1	Dickson	25,000
19	10	A	Liverpool	L	0 1	0 2		40,000
20	17	A	Newcastle United	W	1 1	2 1	Walker, Dickson	35,000
21	24	H	Newcastle United	W	0 0	1 0	Dorrell	40,000
22	26	A	Sheffield United	W	2 1	3 2	Dickson, York, Barson	45,000
23	27	H	Sheffield United	W	3 2	5 3	Dickson 3, Kirton, Walker	35,000
24	31	A	Burnley	L	0 0	1 2	Moss	30,000
25	Jan 14	H	Burnley	W	0 0	2 0	Kirton, Walker	35,000
26	21	A	Everton	L	1 0	2 3	Kirton 2	30,000
27	Feb 4	A	Sunderland	W	2 1	4 1	Dickson 2, Walker (pen), Kirton	6,000
28	8	H	Everton	W	2 0	2 1	Kirton, Dickson	30,000
29	11	H	Sunderland	W	0 0	2 0	Walker, Dickson	30,000
30	25	H	Huddersfield Town	W	0 0	2 0	Kirton, Dickson	35,000
31	Mar 11	H	Birmingham	D	0 0	1 1	Dickson	42,000
32	15	A	Birmingham	L	0 1	0 1		30,000
33	18	H	Arsenal	W	2 0	2 0	Dickson, Walker (pen)	20,000
34	25	A	Arsenal	L	0 1	0 2		40,000
35	Apr 1	A	Blackburn Rovers	W	1 0	2 1	Capewell, Dorrell	15,000
36	5	A	Huddersfield Town	L	0 1	0 1		17,000
37	14	A	Chelsea	L	0 1	0 1		59,000
38	15	H	Bolton Wanderers	W	0 1	2 1	Walker 2 (1 pen)	25,000
39	17	H	Chelsea	L	0 1	1 4	Walker	20,000
40	22	A	Bolton Wanderers	L	0 1	0 1		20,000
41	29	H	Oldham Athletic	W	2 0	2 0	Walker, Capewell	20,000
42	May 6	A	Oldham Athletic	L	1 0	1 3	Capewell	12,000

Final League Position: 5th in First Division

Appearances
Goals

FA CUP

1	Jan 7	H	Derby County	W	5 0	6 1	Walker 3, Kirton 2, Dickson	41,000
2	28	H	Luton Town	W	1 0	1 0	Walker	53,832
3	Feb 18	A	Stoke	D	0 0	0 0		43,589
R	22	H	Stoke	W	3 0	4 0	Dickson 3, Walker	53,385
4	Mar 4	A	Notts County	D	1 1	2 2	Dickson 2	41,375
R	8	H	Notts County *	L	2 2	3 4	Walker, Dickson 2	40,161

Appearances
Goals

* After extra-time

FINAL LEAGUE TABLE

	P	W	D	L	F	A	P	
Liverpool	42	22	13	7	63	36	57	
Tottenham Hotspur	42	21	9	12	65	39	51	
Burnley	42	22	5	15	72	54	49	
Cardiff City	42	19	10	13	61	53	48	
Aston Villa	**42**	**22**	**3**	**17**	**74**	**55**	**47**	
Bolton Wanderers	42	20	7	15	68	59	47	
Newcastle United	42	18	10	14	59	45	46	
Middlesbrough	42	16	14	12	79	69	46	
Chelsea	42	17	12	13	40	43	46	
Manchester City	42	18	9	15	65	70	45	
Sheffield United	42	15	10	17	59	54	40	
Sunderland	42	16	8	18	60	62	40	
West Bromwich A	42	15	10	17	51	63	40	
Huddersfield Town	42	15	9	18	53	54	39	
Blackburn Rovers	42	13	12	17	54	57	38	
Preston North End	42	13	12	17	42	65	38	
Arsenal	42	15	7	20	47	56	37	
Birmingham City	42	15	7	20	48	60	37	
Oldham Athletic	42	13	11	18	38	50	37	
Everton	42	12	12	18	57	55	36	
Bradford City	42	11	10	21	48	72	32	
Manchester United	42	8	12	22	41	73	28	

1922/23

SEASON SNIPPETS

Following the departure of Frank Barson, Dr William Ewart Barnie-Adshead, an Amateur player who was captain of the Birmingham University team, agreed to play centre-half at Blackburn Rovers on 2 September and at home to Cardiff City two days later when he scored the Villa goal. A week earlier, Barnie-Adshead had been playing cricket in the Worcester County XI.

Cecil Harris made his debut at home to Newcastle United on 16 December.

George Harkus made his last appearance on 20 January.

John Roxburgh made his debut at Manchester City on 10 February, scored twice against Stoke on his home debut the following week, but played his last game on 5 May.

The FA Cup defeat by Blackburn Rovers on 13 January was the first time for fourteen years Villa had been eliminated at the first attempt.

DIVISION ONE

MANAGER: Directors

MATCH	DATE		VENUE	OPPONENTS	RESULT	HT SCORE		SCORE		SCORERS	ATT
1	Aug	26	H	Blackburn Rovers	W	1	0	2	0	Kirton, Walker	40,000
2		28	A	Cardiff City	L	0	2	0	3		45,000
3	Sep	2	A	Blackburn Rovers	L	1	3	2	4	York, Kirton	20,000
4		4	H	Cardiff City	L	1	2	1	3	Dr Barnie-Adshead	25,000
5		9	H	West Bromwich Albion	W	1	0	2	0	Moss, Capewell	40,000
6		16	A	West Bromwich Albion	L	0	2	0	3		35,000
7		23	H	Middlesbrough	D	1	0	2	2	Dickson, Dorrell	35,000
8		30	A	Middlesbrough	D	1	2	2	2	Kirton, Walker	25,000
9	Oct	7	H	Tottenham Hotspur	W	1	0	2	0	Dorrell 2	50,000
10		14	A	Tottenham Hotspur	W	0	1	2	1	Dickson, Walker	45,000
11		21	H	Bolton Wanderers	W	2	0	2	0	York, Walker (pen)	25,000
12		28	A	Bolton Wanderers	L	0	1	0	3		25,000
13	Nov	4	A	Oldham Athletic	W	1	0	2	0	Kirton, Walker	12,000
14		11	H	Oldham Athletic	W	1	0	3	0	York, Kirton 2	25,000
15		18	A	Liverpool	L	0	0	0	3		30,000
16		25	H	Liverpool	L	0	1	0	1		40,000
17	Dec	2	A	Sheffield United	D	0	0	1	1	Walker	18,000
18		9	H	Sheffield United	L	0	1	0	1		20,000
19		16	H	Newcastle United	D	1	1	1	1	York	17,000
20		23	A	Newcastle United	D	0	0	0	0		30,000
21		25	A	Burnley	D			1	1	York	27,000
22		26	H	Burnley	W	2	0	3	1	York 3	40,000
23		30	H	Preston North End	W	0	0	1	0	Walker	30,000
24	Jan	6	A	Preston North End	L	0	0	2	3	Walker 2	16,000
25		20	A	Nottingham Forest	L	1	2	1	3	Dorrell	15,000
26		27	H	Nottingham Forest	W	2	0	4	0	Dorrell, Dickson 2, Walker	20,000
27	Feb	3	H	Manchester City	W	0	0	2	0	York, Walker	20,000
28		10	A	Manchester City	D	1	0	1	1	Capewell	18,000
29		17	H	Stoke	W	4	0	6	0	Dickson 3, Roxburgh 2, Walker	30,000
30		24	A	Stoke	D	0	0	1	1	Walker	20,000
31	Mar	3	H	Huddersfield Town	W	2	1	2	1	Moss, Roxburgh	25,000
32		10	A	Huddersfield Town	W	2	2	5	3	Walker 3, Capewell, Dorrell	15,000
33		17	A	Birmingham	L	0	1	0	1		50,000
34		24	H	Birmingham	W	2	0	3	0	Capewell, Walker 2 (2 pens)	40,000
35		30	H	Chelsea	W	0	0	1	0	Walker (pen)	25,000
36		31	A	Arsenal	L	0	0	0	2		45,000
37	Apr	2	A	Chelsea	D	1	1	1	1	Walker	30,000
38		7	H	Arsenal	D	1	0	1	1	Walker	18,000
39		14	A	Everton	L	0	0	1	2	Capewell	30,000
40		21	H	Everton	W	3	0	3	0	Walker 2, Kirton	18,000
41		28	A	Sunderland	L	0	0	0	2		8,000
42	May	5	H	Sunderland	W	1	0	1	0	Dorrell	12,000

Final League Position: 6th in First Division

Appearances
Goals

FA CUP

1	Jan	13	H	Blackburn Rovers	L	0	1	0	1		47,000

Appearances
Goals

Player Appearances

Player	1	2	3	4	5	6	7	8	9	10	11	12	13	14	15	16	Match
Jackson T																	
Smart T																	
Mort T																	
Harkus GC																	
Moss F																	
Blackburn GF																	
York RE																	
Kirton WJ																	
Dickson IW																	
Walker WH																	
Dorrell AR																	
Johnstone JC																	
Capewell LK																	
Barnie-Adshead Dr WE																	
Ball TE																	
Spiers CH																	
Stephenson GT																	
Harris CV																	
Roxburgh JA																	
Jones PO																	

Match	Jackson T	Smart T	Mort T	Harkus GC	Moss F	Blackburn GF	York RE	Kirton WJ	Dickson IW	Walker WH	Dorrell AR	Johnstone JC	Capewell LK	Barnie-Adshead	Ball TE	Spiers CH	Stephenson GT	Harris CV	Roxburgh JA	Jones PO
1	1	2	3	4	5	6	7	8	9	10	11									
2	1	2	3	4	5		7	8		10	11	6	9							
3	1	2	3		4	6	7	8		10	11		9	5						
4	1	2	3		4	6	7	8		10	11		9	5						
5	1	2	3		4	6	7	8		10	11		9		5					
6	1	2	3		4	6	7	8		10	11		9		5					
7	1	2	3		4	6	7	8	9	10	11				5					
8		2	3		4	6	7	8	9	10	11				5	1				
9		2	3		4	6	7		9	10	11				5	1	8			
10		2	3		4	6	7	8	9	10					5	1	11			
11		2	3			6	7	8	9	10	11	4			5	1				
12		2	3			6	7	8	9	10	11	4			5	1				
13		2	3		4	6	7	8	9	10	11				5	1				
14		2	3		4	6	7	8	9	10	11				5	1				
15		2	3		4	6	7	8	9	10	11				5	1				
16		2	3		4	6	7	8		10	11		9		5	1				
17		2	3		4	6	7	8	9	10	11				5	1				
18		2	3		4	6	7	8	9	10	11				5	1				
19		2			6	7		8	10	11	4	9			5	1		3		
20		2	3			6		7	8	10	11	4			5	1	9			
21		2	3			6	9	7	8	10	11				5	1				
22		2	3			6	9	7	8	10	11	4			5	1				
23		2	3			6	9	7	8	10	11	4			5	1				
24		2	3			6	9	7	8	10	11	4			5	1				
25		2	3	6	4		7	8	9	10	11				5	1				
26		2	3		4	6	7	8	9	10	11					1				
27	1	2			4	6	7	8	9	10	11	5					3			
28		2			4	6	7		9		11		10		5	1	3	8		
29		2				6	7		9	10	11	4			5	1	3	8		
30		2			4	6	7		9	10	11				5	1	3	8		
31		2	3		4	6	7		9	5	11		10			1		8		
32		2	3		4	6	7			9	11		10		5	1		8		
33		2	3		4	6	7			9	11		10		5	1		8		
34		2	3		4	6	7			9	11		10		5	1		8		
35		2	3		4	6		7		10	11	9			5	1		8		
36		2	3			6	7	8	9	10	11	4			5	1				
37		2	3			6	7		9	10	11	4			5	1				
38		2	3		6		7			9	11	4	10		5	1		8		
39		2	3		6			7	8		11	4	9		5	1			10	
40		2			4	6		8	9	10	11				5	1	7			3
41		2			4	6		7	9	10	11			8	5	1				3
42		2			4	6		8		9	11		10		5	1			7	3

Totals: 8 | 42 | 34 | 3 | 31 | 38 | 36 | 31 | 30 | 40 | 41 | 15 | 17 | 2 | 35 | 34 | 5 | 5 | 12 | 3

Goals: | | | | 2 | | 9 | 7 | 7 | 23 | 7 | | 5 | 1 | | | | | | | 3

FINAL LEAGUE TABLE

	P	W	D	L	F	A	P
Liverpool	42	26	8	8	70	31	60
Sunderland	42	22	10	10	72	54	54
Huddersfield Town	42	21	11	10	60	32	53
Newcastle United	42	18	12	12	45	37	48
Everton	42	20	7	15	63	59	47
Aston Villa	**42**	**18**	**10**	**14**	**64**	**51**	**46**
West Bromwich A	42	17	11	14	58	49	45
Manchester City	42	17	11	14	50	49	45
Cardiff City	42	18	7	17	73	59	43
Sheffield United	42	16	10	16	68	64	42
Arsenal	42	16	10	16	61	62	42
Tottenham Hotspur	42	17	7	18	50	50	41
Bolton Wanderers	42	14	12	16	50	58	40
Blackburn Rovers	42	14	12	16	47	62	40
Burnley	42	16	6	20	58	59	38
Preston North End	42	13	11	18	60	64	37
Birmingham City	42	13	11	18	41	57	37
Middlesbrough	42	13	10	19	57	63	36
Chelsea	42	9	18	15	45	53	36
Nottingham Forest	42	13	8	21	41	70	34
Stoke	42	10	10	22	47	67	30
Oldham Athletic	42	10	10	22	35	65	30

1923/24

SEASON SNIPPETS

Dr Victor E Milne made his debut on 15 September.

Percy Jones played his last game on 22 September.

Shortly after 10.00pm on Sunday 11 November Tommy Ball was shot by his landlord, George Stagg, in Brick-Kiln Lane, Perry Barr. Ball died from his injuries and Stagg was later convicted of Murder.

On 8 December, Ian Dickson scored in his last match.

Norman Mackay made the first of his two appearances on 15 December.

Teddy Bowen made his debut on 5 January.

Villa welcomed the Duke of York, the future King George VI, to Villa Park for the game with Bolton Wanderers on 26 January. Chairman Fred Rinder led the Duke out onto the pitch where he was introduced to the two teams. It was the first time Royalty had watched a game at Villa Park.

Alec Talbot made his debut against Swansea Town in the FA Cup second round on 2 February.

Percy Varco and Alex McClure both made their debut at Sunderland on 13 February.

Bert Singleton made his debut against Arsenal on 12 March, but his last game came three days later against Spurs.

Billy Armfield and Archie Campbell both made their debut on 15 March.

Albert Surtees played his first game on 2 April.

Joseph Corbett made his debut on 12 April.

On 26 April, Frank Moss became the first player to have been captain of a club side and also England at Wembley. Two weeks before leading Villa out in the FA Cup final, Moss had been skipper for England when they played Scotland in the first International to be played at Wembley.

DIVISION ONE

MANAGER: Directors

MATCH	DATE	VENUE	OPPONENTS	RESULT	HT SCORE	SCORE	SCORERS	ATT
1	Aug 25	A	Birmingham	L	0 2	0 3		50,000
2	29	H	Manchester City	W	1 0	2 0	Walker, York	15,000
3	Sep 1	H	Birmingham	D	0 0	0 0		30,000
4	5	A	Manchester City	W	0 1	2 1	Capewell, Kirton	30,000
5	8	A	Chelsea	D	0 0	0 0		40,000
6	12	H	Everton	D	0 1	1 1	McBain (og)	15,000
7	15	H	Chelsea	D	0 0	0 0		30,000
8	19	A	Everton	L	0 0	0 2		15,000
9	22	A	Preston North End	D	1 1	2 2	Walker, Capewell	18,000
10	29	H	Preston North End	W	2 0	5 1	Walker 3 (2 pens), Kirton, Capewell	25,000
11	Oct 6	A	Burnley	W	1 0	2 1	Capewell, Walker	16,000
12	13	H	Burnley	D	0 1	1 1	Kirton	33,000
13	20	A	West Bromwich Albion	L	0 0	0 1		50,000
14	27	H	West Bromwich Albion	W	2 0	4 0	York, Walker 3	40,000
15	Nov 3	H	Notts County	D	0 0	0 0		25,000
16	10	A	Notts County	W	1 0	1 0	Kirton	15,000
17	17	H	Liverpool	D	0 0	0 0		20,000
18	24	A	Liverpool	W	0 0	1 0	Capewell	25,000
19	Dec 1	H	Middlesbrough	D	0 0	0 0		15,000
20	8	A	Middlesbrough	W	1 0	2 0	Dickson, Kirton	14,000
21	15	A	Sheffield United	L	1 2	1 2	Capewell	30,000
22	22	H	Sheffield United	D	1 1	2 2	Capewell 2	15,000
23	25	A	West Ham United	D	1 0	1 1	Capewell	40,000
24	26	H	West Ham United	L	0 0	0 1		30,000
25	29	H	Cardiff City	W	1 0	2 1	Capewell, Blair (og)	52,000
26	Jan 1	A	Newcastle United	L	1 2	1 4	Dorrell	45,000
27	5	A	Cardiff City	W	0 0	2 0	Walker, Capewell	38,000
28	19	A	Bolton Wanderers	L	0 1	0 1		26,972
29	26	H	Bolton Wanderers	W	1 0	1 0	Capewell	50,000
30	Feb 9	H	Sunderland	L	0 1	0 1		35,000
31	13	A	Sunderland	L	0 1	0 2		30,000
32	16	A	Arsenal	W	0 0	1 0	Dorrell	35,000
33	Mar 1	A	Blackburn Rovers	L	1 2	1 3	Capewell	20,000
34	12	H	Arsenal	W	0 1	2 1	Kirton, Dorrell	25,000
35	15	H	Tottenham Hotspur	D	0 0	0 0		22,000
36	22	A	Tottenham Hotspur	W	1 2	3 2	Capewell 3	35,000
37	Apr 2	H	Blackburn Rovers	W	0 0	1 0	Stephenson	8,000
38	5	A	Huddersfield Town	L	0 1	0 1		25,000
39	12	H	Nottingham Forest	D	0 0	0 0		10,000
40	19	H	Nottingham Forest	W	0 0	2 0	Capewell 2	16,000
41	21	H	Newcastle United	W	1 1	6 1	Hunter (og), Capewell, York, Walker 3	20,000
42	30	H	Huddersfield Town	W	2 1	3 1	Walker, Capewell, Dorrell	14,000

Final League Position: 5th in First Division

	Appearances	Goals
3 Own-goals		

FA CUP

1	Jan 12	A	Ashington	W	2 1	5 1	Blackburn, Walker 2, Capewell, Page (og)	11,837
2	Feb 2	A	Swansea Town	W	1 0	2 0	Capewell 2	19,035
3	23	H	Leeds United	W	2 0	3 0	Capewell 2, Walker	51,000
4	Mar 8	A	West Bromwich Albion	W	2 0	2 0	Capewell, Dorrell	43,743
SF	29	N	Burnley *	W	1 0	3 0	Kirton, York 2	54,531
F	Apr 26	N	Newcastle United **	L	0 0	0 2		91,695

	Appearances	Goals
1 Own-goal		

* Played at Bramall Lane, Sheffield
** Played at Wembley Stadium

FINAL LEAGUE TABLE

	P	W	D	L	F	A	P
Huddersfield Town	42	23	11	8	60	33	57
Cardiff City	42	22	13	7	61	34	57
Sunderland	42	22	9	11	71	54	53
Bolton Wanderers	42	18	14	10	68	34	50
Sheffield United	42	19	12	11	69	49	50
Aston Villa	**42**	**18**	**13**	**11**	**52**	**37**	**49**
Everton	42	18	13	11	62	53	49
Blackburn Rovers	42	17	11	14	54	50	45
Newcastle United	42	17	10	15	60	54	44
Notts County	42	14	14	14	44	49	42
Manchester City	42	15	12	15	54	71	42
Liverpool	42	15	11	16	49	48	41
West Ham United	42	13	15	14	40	43	41
Birmingham City	42	13	13	16	41	49	39
Tottenham Hotspur	42	12	14	16	50	56	38
West Bromwich A	42	12	14	16	51	62	38
Burnley	42	12	12	18	55	60	36
Preston North End	42	12	10	20	52	67	34
Arsenal	42	12	9	21	40	63	33
Nottingham Forest	42	10	12	20	42	64	32
Chelsea	42	9	14	19	31	53	32
Middlesbrough	42	7	8	27	37	60	22

1924/25

SEASON SNIPPETS

The 3-3 draw with Bury on 1 September was the last game for Alex McClure.

Walter Harris made his debut on 18 October.

Joe Eccles played his first match on 15 November. His ten appearances during the season were his only Villa games.

Tommy Muldoon made his debut on 13 December.

'Ginger' Phoenix scored twice on his Boxing Day debut against Leeds United, but only played three more games, his last appearance coming on 29 April.

Les Dennington made his only appearance on 7 February.

George Jakeman made his debut in the 4-1 defeat by West Bromwich Albion on 28 February. George Clarke made his only appearance in this game.

Tommy Jones and Billy Dinsdale both made their debut in the 4-0 win against Arsenal on 1 April.

Albert Surtees played his last game on 4 April.

Percy Varco scored the only goal of the match when he played his last Villa game against Preston on 18 April.

DIVISION ONE

MANAGER: Directors

MATCH	DATE	VENUE	OPPONENTS	RESULT	HT SCORE	SCORE	SCORERS	ATT
1	Aug 30	A	Liverpool	W	3 0	4 2	Walker 2, Dorrell, Kirton	45,000
2	Sep 1	H	Bury	D	1 3	3 3	York, Kirton, Capewell	35,000
3	6	H	Newcastle United	D	0 0	0 0		45,000
4	8	A	Bury	L	1 2	3 4	Moss, Dorrell, Walker	23,000
5	13	A	Sheffield United	D	1 2	2 2	Capewell, Walker	15,000
6	20	H	West Ham United	D	1 1	1 1	Walker	30,000
7	27	A	Blackburn Rovers	D	1 1	1 1	Walker	20,000
8	Oct 2	A	Nottingham Forest	W	0 0	2 0	Kirton, Walker	12,000
9	4	H	Huddersfield Town	D	0 0	1 1	Walker	30,000
10	11	A	Birmingham	L	0 1	0 1		45,000
11	18	A	Arsenal	D	0 0	1 1	Walker	40,000
12	25	H	West Bromwich Albion	W	1 0	1 0	Dorrell	50,000
13	Nov 1	A	Tottenham Hotspur	W	2 1	3 1	Stephenson, Capewell, Moss	15,000
14	8	H	Bolton Wanderers	D	1 2	2 2	Kirton, Walker	25,000
15	15	A	Notts County	D	0 0	0 0		24,000
16	22	H	Everton	W	2 1	3 1	Walker, Dorrell, Varco	25,000
17	29	A	Sunderland	D	1 1	1 1	Blackburn	25,000
18	Dec 6	A	Cardiff City	L	0 1	1 2	Walker	30,000
19	13	H	Preston North End	L	1 1	2 3	Walker, Dorrell	7,000
20	20	H	Burnley	W	0 0	3 0	Kirton, Surtees, Walker (pen)	24,000
21	25	A	Leeds United	L	0 0	0 6		24,000
22	26	H	Leeds United	W	1 0	2 1	Phoenix 2	50,000
23	Jan 3	A	Newcastle United	L	0 0	1 4	Kirton	15,000
24	17	H	Sheffield United	D	0 0	1 1	York	24,000
25	21	A	Liverpool	L	0 1	1 4	Capewell	14,000
26	24	A	West Ham United	L	0 0	0 2		20,000
27	Feb 7	A	Huddersfield Town	L	1 1	1 4	Walker	15,000
28	14	H	Birmingham	W	0 0	1 0	Capewell	60,000
29	28	A	West Bromwich Albion	L	1 1	1 4	York	28,000
30	Mar 7	H	Tottenham Hotspur	L	0 0	0 1		25,000
31	14	A	Bolton Wanderers	L	0 2	0 4		18,900
32	21	H	Notts County	D	0 0	0 0		15,000
33	28	A	Everton	L	0 1	0 2		30,000
34	Apr 1	H	Arsenal	W	1 0	4 0	York 2, Walker, Dorrell	10,000
35	4	H	Sunderland	L	1 2	1 4	Dorrell	20,000
36	10	H	Manchester City	W	1 0	2 1	Stephenson, Walker	20,000
37	11	A	Cardiff City	L	1 1	1 2	York	18,000
38	13	A	Manchester City	L	0 0	0 1		25,000
39	18	H	Preston North End	W	0 0	1 0	Varco	20,000
40	25	A	Burnley	D	0 0	1 1	Walker	10,000
41	29	H	Blackburn Rovers	W	4 0	4 3	Stephenson 2, Dorrell, Walker	10,000
42	May 2	H	Nottingham Forest	W	1 0	2 0	Stephenson, Morgan (og)	12,000

Final League Position: 15th in First Division

1 Own-goal

Appearances
Goals

FA CUP

1	Jan 10	H	Port Vale	W	0 0	7 2	Walker 3, Capewell 4	35,600
2	31	A	Swansea Town	W	1 1	3 1	Walker 2, York	20,000
3	Feb 21	A	West Bromwich Albion	D	0 1	1 1	Walker	64,612
R	25	H	West Bromwich Albion	L	1 1	1 2	Phoenix	60,015

Appearances
Goals

358

FINAL LEAGUE TABLE

	P	W	D	L	F	A	P
Huddersfield Town	42	21	16	5	69	28	58
West Bromwich A	42	23	10	9	58	34	56
Bolton Wanderers	42	22	11	9	76	34	55
Liverpool	42	20	10	12	63	55	50
Bury	42	17	15	10	54	51	49
Newcastle United	42	16	16	10	61	42	48
Sunderland	42	19	10	13	64	51	48
Birmingham City	42	17	12	13	49	53	46
Notts County	42	16	13	13	42	31	45
Manchester City	42	17	9	16	76	68	43
Cardiff City	42	16	11	15	56	51	43
Tottenham Hotspur	42	15	12	15	52	43	42
West Ham United	42	15	12	15	62	60	42
Sheffield United	42	13	13	16	55	63	39
Aston Villa	**42**	**13**	**13**	**16**	**58**	**71**	**39**
Blackburn Rovers	42	11	13	18	53	66	35
Everton	42	12	11	19	40	60	35
Leeds United	42	11	12	19	46	59	34
Burnley	42	11	12	19	46	75	34
Arsenal	42	14	5	23	46	58	33
Preston North End	42	10	6	26	37	74	26
Nottingham Forest	42	6	12	24	29	65	24

1925/26

SEASON SNIPPETS

Len Capewell scored after only 20 seconds on 29 August and went on to score five goals in the 10-0 win against Burnley - Villa's record opening-day league victory. Capewell, the third Villa player to score five goals in a league match, was the first to do so in the opening league fixture.

Reg Chester made his debut on 7 September.

When he netted against Birmingham on 17 October, Len Capewell set a record by scoring in eight consecutive Villa league games.

On Saturday 5 December, Mr Edmund Wallis Strange, who had been with Villa for 30 years, had an accident on Snow Hill Station when returning from Cardiff where he had been to look at a player. Mr Strange was taken to the General Hospital and then transferred to Dudley Road Infirmary, but did not regain consciousness, and died at 4.00pm on Friday 18 December. Mr Stange first joined the Club as a player in August 1895, but his playing career was cut short by a knee injury in 1901. He was then appointed Assistant Secretary to the Club and Manager of the Reserve Team.

Cecil Harris made his last appearance on New Year's Day.

George Blackburn played his last game on 27 February.

Billy Dinsdale's last game was on 13 March.

Fred Norris made his debut on 5 April.

On 17 April Villa won 3-0 against Tottenham Hotspur without three of their players who were playing for England in the international with Scotland. Billy Walker was England's captain, Tommy Mort and Dicky York were also in the side.

DIVISION ONE

MANAGER: Directors

MATCH	DATE	VENUE	OPPONENTS	RESULT	HT SCORE	SCORE	SCORERS	ATT
1	Aug 29	H	Burnley	W	4 0	10 0	Capewell 5, Walker 3, York, Stephenson	37,025
2	Sep 2	A	Manchester United	L	0 3	0 3		41,717
3	5	A	Leeds United	D	1 1	2 2	Dorrell, Walker	29,501
4	7	H	Manchester United	D	1 2	2 2	Capewell, York	29,701
5	12	H	Newcastle United	D	1 0	2 2	Capewell, Walker (pen)	38,819
6	19	A	Bolton Wanderers	W	3 0	3 1	Capewell, York 2	16,982
7	26	H	Notts County	W	1 0	2 1	Capewell, Milne	22,382
8	Oct 3	A	West Bromwich Albion	D	0 1	1 1	Capewell	43,267
9	5	H	Sunderland	W	2 0	4 2	Capewell 2, Walker 2	18,593
10	10	A	Leicester City	W	1 0	2 1	Capewell, Walker	37,483
11	17	H	Birmingham	D	2 0	3 3	Walker 2, Capewell	52,254
12	24	A	Bury	W	1 2	3 2	York 3	13,127
13	31	H	Cardiff City	L	0 1	0 2		33,161
14	Nov 7	A	Sheffield United	L	1 3	1 4	Capewell	8,452
15	14	H	Huddersfield Town	W	0 0	3 0	Capewell 3	33,401
16	21	A	Everton	D	1 1	1 1	Capewell	27,037
17	28	H	Manchester City	W	1 0	3 1	Walker, Capewell 2	21,988
18	Dec 5	A	Tottenham Hotspur	D	1 1	2 2	Capewell 2	28,821
19	12	H	Blackburn Rovers	L	1 1	1 2	Walker (pen)	24,162
20	19	A	Sunderland	L	1 1	2 3	Walker, Capewell	14,707
21	25	A	West Ham United	L		2 5	Walker, York	22,218
22	26	H	West Ham United	W	1 0	2 0	Capewell, Dorrell	45,538
23	Jan 1	A	Liverpool	L	0 3	1 3	Capewell	23,587
24	2	A	Burnley	W	1 1	3 2	Capewell, York 2	22,329
25	23	A	Newcastle United	D	0 1	2 2	York, Walker	39,305
26	Feb 3	H	Leeds United	W	3 1	3 1	Dorrell, Capewell 2	11,573
27	6	A	Notts County	L	0 0	0 1		18,426
28	13	H	West Bromwich Albion	W	2 1	2 1	Walker, Capewell	42,714
29	27	A	Birmingham	L	0 1	1 2	Walker	38,231
30	Mar 6	H	Bury	D	1 0	1 1	Mort	29,947
31	10	H	Leicester City	D	1 1	2 2	York 2	9,037
32	13	A	Cardiff City	L	0 0	0 2		21,982
33	20	H	Sheffield United	D	2 1	2 2	Dorrell, Capewell	18,017
34	27	A	Huddersfield Town	L	0 2	1 5	York	28,442
35	Apr 2	H	Arsenal	W	1 0	3 0	York, Stephenson, Walker	26,177
36	3	H	Everton	W	2 1	3 1	York 2, Walker (pen)	20,555
37	5	A	Arsenal	L	0 1	0 2		28,490
38	6	H	Liverpool	W	2 0	3 0	Norris 2, Chester	16,496
39	10	A	Manchester City	L	1 2	2 4	Dorrell, Walker	34,537
40	17	H	Tottenham Hotspur	W	2 0	3 0	Capewell 2, Stephenson	11,774
41	24	A	Blackburn Rovers	L	0 2	1 3	Walker (pen)	15,258
42	26	H	Bolton Wanderers	D	1 1	2 2	Capewell, Smart (pen)	13,093

Final League Position: 6th in First Division

Appearances
Goals

FA CUP

3	Jan 9	A	Hull City	W	2 0	3 0	York, Capewell 2	26,000
4	30	A	West Bromwich Albion	W	0 0	2 1	Walker, Kirton	52,160
5	Feb 20	H	Arsenal	D	0 0	1 1	Kirton	71,390
R	24	A	Arsenal	L	0 2	0 2		55,400

Appearances
Goals

360

FINAL LEAGUE TABLE

	P	W	D	L	F	A	P
Huddersfield Town	42	23	11	8	92	60	57
Arsenal	42	22	8	12	87	63	52
Sunderland	42	21	6	15	96	80	48
Bury	42	20	7	15	85	77	47
Sheffield United	42	19	8	15	102	82	46
Aston Villa	**42**	**16**	**12**	**14**	**86**	**76**	**44**
Liverpool	42	14	16	12	70	63	44
Bolton Wanderers	42	17	10	15	75	76	44
Manchester United	42	19	6	17	66	73	44
Newcastle United	42	16	10	16	84	75	42
Everton	42	12	18	12	72	70	42
Blackburn Rovers	42	15	11	16	91	80	41
West Bromwich A	42	16	8	18	79	78	40
Birmingham City	42	16	8	18	66	81	40
Tottenham Hotspur	42	15	9	18	66	79	39
Cardiff City	42	16	7	19	61	76	39
Leicester City	42	14	10	18	70	80	38
West Ham United	42	15	7	20	63	76	37
Leeds United	42	14	8	20	64	76	36
Burnley	42	13	10	19	85	108	36
Manchester City	42	12	11	19	89	100	35
Notts County	42	13	7	22	54	74	33

361

1926/27

SEASON SNIPPETS

Aston Villa undertook their first ever Continental Tour from 21 May to 9 June. The club played six games in Sweden, Norway and Denmark, winning four games with two matches lost. 28 goals were scored and 16 conceded. Recent signing Joe Nicholson was held up by rail problems, failed to arrive in time to join the party, and missed the tour.

The 4-0 defeat at Newcastle United on the opening day of the season was Joe Nicholson's only match.

Cyril Spiers made his last appearance on 30 August.

Billy Kingdon made his debut at home to Burnley on 4 September.

Tommy Muldoon played his last game at home to Bury on 18 September.

Goalkeeper Bill Johnson made his debut in a 5-3 win against Everton on 4 December.

The home game against Cardiff on 31 January was the last match for both Fred Norris and Joe Corbett.

Billy Cook made his debut at Bolton on 12 February.

The 5-1 home defeat by West Ham United on 2 April was the last of Billy Kirton's 261 games.

'Jock' Johnstone played his last game at home to Arsenal on 18 April.

On 30 April, Aston Villa paid a record transfer fee of £7,500 to Patrick Thistle for Jimmy Gibson.

DIVISION ONE

MANAGER: Directors

MATCH	DATE	VENUE	OPPONENTS	RESULT	HT SCORE	SCORE	SCORERS	ATT
1	Aug 28	A	Newcastle United	L	0 1	0 4		36,057
2	30	H	Liverpool	D	0 1	1 1	Capewell	19,544
3	Sep 4	H	Burnley	D	1 1	1 1	Capewell	30,386
4	8	A	Liverpool	L	0 2	1 2	Stephenson	22,945
5	11	A	Cardiff City	W	2 2	3 2	York, Capewell, Kingdon	20,081
6	15	A	Leeds United	L	1 2	1 3	Kirton	13,792
7	18	H	Bury	L	0 0	1 2	Stephenson	22,929
8	25	H	Bolton Wanderers	L	2 4	3 4	York, Harris, Walker	20,696
9	Oct 2	A	Manchester United	L	0 0	1 2	York	31,234
10	9	H	Derby County	W	2 1	3 1	Dorrell, Harris, Stephenson	22,386
11	16	A	Sunderland	D	1 1	1 1	Stephenson	17,155
12	23	H	West Bromwich Albion	W	0 0	2 0	Harris, Walker	44,744
13	30	A	Birmingham	W	1 1	2 1	Dorrell, Walker	48,104
14	Nov 6	H	Tottenham Hotspur	L	0 3	2 3	Walker 2 (1pen)	19,496
15	13	A	West Ham United	L	1 2	1 5	Dorrell	7,647
16	20	H	Sheffield Wednesday	D	2 1	2 2	York, Kingdon	14,889
17	27	A	Leicester City	L	0 2	1 5	Walker	29,423
18	Dec 4	H	Everton	W	1 3	5 3	Capewell 3, Dorrell, Stephenson	23,082
19	11	A	Blackburn Rovers	W	0 0	2 0	Capewell 2	15,701
20	18	H	Huddersfield Town	W	2 0	3 0	Dorrell, Walker, Stephenson	31,236
21	25	H	Sheffield United	W	2 0	4 0	York, Capewell, Stephenson 2	36,777
22	27	A	Sheffield United	L	1 3	1 3	Capewell	47,105
23	28	H	Leeds United	W	3 1	5 1	Capewell, Dorrell, Walker, York, Stephenson	43,963
24	Jan 15	H	Newcastle United	L	1 1	1 2	Dorrell	46,723
25	22	A	Burnley	L	1 1	3 6	Capewell 2, Stephenson	18,081
26	29	H	Blackburn Rovers	W	2 0	4 3	Walker 2, Capewell 2	16,455
27	31	H	Cardiff City	D	0 0	0 0		10,481
28	Feb 5	A	Bury	W	1 0	1 0	Capewell	14,974
29	12	A	Bolton Wanderers	W	2 0	2 0	York 2	17,745
30	19	H	Manchester United	W	1 0	2 0	Cook, York	12,467
31	26	A	Derby County	W	1 0	3 2	Stephenson, Cook 2	22,328
32	Mar 5	H	Sunderland	W	2 0	3 1	Walker 2, Cook	33,847
33	12	A	West Bromwich Albion	L	0 1	2 6	York 2	43,996
34	19	H	Birmingham	W	2 1	4 2	Cook, Stephenson, York 2	49,334
35	26	A	Tottenham Hotspur	W	0 0	1 0	Cook	30,614
36	Apr 2	H	West Ham United	L	0 3	1 5	Cook	22,413
37	9	A	Sheffield Wednesday	L	0 1	1 2	Cook	9,020
38	15	H	Arsenal	L	0 1	1 2	Walker	38,096
39	16	A	Leicester City	W	0 0	2 0	Cook, Johnstone	30,857
40	18	H	Arsenal	L	2 3	2 3	Walker, Stephenson	22,542
41	23	A	Everton	D	1 1	2 2	Walker 2	33,394
42	May 7	A	Huddersfield Town	D	0 0	0 0		10,603

Final League Position: 10th in First Division

Appearances
Goals

FA CUP

| 3 | Jan 8 | A | Cardiff City | L | 0 0 | 1 2 | Dorrell | 31,000 |

Appearances
Goals

Player Appearances by Match

Match	Spiers CH	Smart T	Mort T	Johnstone JC	Talbot AD	Muddoon TP	York RE	Norris FH	Nicholson JR	Capewell LK	Dorrell AR	Milne Dr VE	Moss F	Kirton WJ	Stephenson GT	Jackson T	Kingdon WIG	Walker WH	Bowen SE	Harris WH	Jakeman GJW	Johnson WWF	Armfield WCW	Corbett J	Cook GW	Chester RA	Gibson JD
1	2	3	4	5	6	7	8	9	10	11																	
2	1	2	3	4			7		9	11	5	6	8	10													
3		2	3				7		9	11	5	6	8		1	4	10										
4		2			5		7		9	11		6	8	10	1	4		3									
5		2					7		9	11	5	6	8		1	4		3	10								
6		2				6	7			11	5	4	8	10	1			3	9								
7		2				6	4	8	9	11	5			7	1		10	3									
8			4				7			11	5	6	8		1		10	3	9	2							
9		2	4				7	8		11	5	6			1		10	3	9								
10		2	4						10	11	5	6		8	1			3	9								
11		2	3				7			11	5	6	8		1	4	10		9								
12		2	3				7			11	5	6	8		1	4	10		9								
13			3				7			11	5	6	8		1	4	10	2	9								
14		2	3				7			11	5	6	8		1	4	10		9								
15		2	3				7			11	5	6	8		1	4	10		9								
16		2	3				7			11	5	4	8		1	6	10		9								
17		2	3				7			11	5	6	8		1	4	10		9								
18			3	4			7		9	11	5	6	8				10	2			1						
19			3	4			7		9	11	5	6	8		1		10	2									
20			3	4			7		9	11	5	6	8		1		10	2									
21			3	4			7		9	11	5	6	8		1		10	2									
22			3	4			7		9	11	5	6	8					2		10							
23			3	4			7		9	11	5	6	8				10	2			1						
24			3	4			7		9	11	5	6	8		1		10	2									
25			3	4			7		9	11	5		8		1	6	10	2									
26		2					4		9	11	5		8		1	6	10	3				7					
27		2					7	8	9	11	5				1	4	10	3					6				
28		2					7		9	11	5	6			1	4		3									
29		2	6				7		9		5		8		1	4		3							10		
30		2					7			11	5	6	8		1	4	10	3							9		
31		2					7			11	5	6	8		1	4		3							9		
32		2					7			11	5	6	8		1	4	10	3							9		
33		2					7			11	5	6	8		1	4	10	3							9		
34		2			5		7			11		6	8	10	1	4									9		
35		2			5		7			11		6			1	4	10	3							9		
36		2					7			11		6	8	10	1	4	5	3							9		
37		2					7				5	6	8		1	4	10	3							9	11	
38		2	3	4			7				5	6	8		1		10								9	11	
39			3	4			7				5		8		1	6	10	2							9	11	
40		2	6	4			7		9		5		8		1		10	3								11	
41			3		5		7			11		6	8		1	4	10	2							9		
42		2	3				7			11		6	8		1	4	10								9		5

| Totals | 2 | 30 | 24 | 16 | 6 | 2 | 42 | 3 | 21 | 38 | 35 | 34 | 36 | 8 | 38 | 26 | 33 | 31 | 13 | 1 | 2 | 1 | 1 | 13 | 4 | 1 | |
| Goals | | | | 1 | | | 13 | | 16 | 7 | | | 1 | 13 | | 2 | 16 | | 3 | | | | | 9 | | | |

Goals: 3 | 4 | 7 | 9 | 11 | 5 | 6 | 8 | 1 | 10 | 2 | 3
1 | 1 | 1 | 1 | 1 | 1 | 1 | 1 | 1 | 1 | 1
| | | | 1

FINAL LEAGUE TABLE

	P	W	D	L	F	A	P
Newcastle United	42	25	6	11	96	58	56
Huddersfield Town	42	17	17	8	76	60	51
Sunderland	42	21	7	14	98	70	49
Bolton Wanderers	42	19	10	13	84	62	48
Burnley	42	19	9	14	91	80	47
West Ham United	42	19	8	15	86	70	46
Leicester City	42	17	12	13	85	70	46
Sheffield United	42	17	10	15	74	86	44
Liverpool	42	18	7	17	69	61	43
Aston Villa	**42**	**18**	**7**	**17**	**81**	**83**	**43**
Arsenal	42	17	9	16	77	86	43
Derby County	42	17	7	18	86	73	41
Tottenham Hotspur	42	16	9	17	76	78	41
Cardiff City	42	16	9	17	55	65	41
Manchester United	42	13	14	15	52	64	40
Sheffield Wednesday	42	15	9	18	75	92	39
Birmingham City	42	17	4	21	64	73	38
Blackburn Rovers	42	15	8	19	77	96	38
Bury	42	12	12	18	68	77	36
Everton	42	12	10	20	64	90	34
Leeds United	42	11	8	23	69	88	30
West Bromwich A	42	11	8	23	65	86	30

1927/28

SEASON SNIPPETS

George T Stephenson played his last game at Portsmouth on 31 August. George was the youngest of three Stephenson brothers who played for Villa and when he departed for Derby County on 11 November, it ended a connection going back to March 1910 when Clem joined the Club followed by brother Jimmy in May 1913.

Joe Beresford made his debut on 3 September.

Walter Harris played his last game on 19 November.

John Yates played his first game on 3 December.

Harry Goddard's only Villa game came on 17 December.

Goalkeeper Joe Hickman conceded nine goals in his two Villa games, his debut being a 5-4 win against Sheffield Wednesday on Christmas Eve followed by a 5-0 defeat by Derby County on a snow covered pitch on Boxing Day.

Joe Tate made his debut in the Boxing Day game.

Fred Tully played his first game on 27 December, but it was Bill Johnson's last appearance.

Ben Olney made his debut on New Year's Eve.

While Villa were playing at Arsenal in the FA Cup on 18 February, Tom 'Pongo' Waring, who was already cup tied, made his Villa debut in a reserve team game and netted a first-half hat-trick in a 6-2 demolition of Birmingham. A crowd of 23,600 were at Villa Park for the game.

On 25 February, 'Pongo' Waring scored on his Villa league debut, a 3-2 win at Sunderland. John Brittleton also played his first match.

On 28 April, Billy Armfield scored in his last game.

DIVISION ONE

MANAGER: Directors

MATCH	DATE	VENUE	OPPONENTS	RESULT	HT SCORE	SCORE	SCORERS	ATT
1	Aug 27	H	Leicester City	L	0 1	0 3		47,288
2	31	A	Portsmouth	L	1 1	1 3	Walker	32,050
3	Sep 3	A	Liverpool	D	0 0	0 0		42,196
4	5	H	Portsmouth	W	4 1	7 2	Cook 2, Dorrell, Beresford 3 (1 pen), Walker	20,624
5	10	H	Arsenal	D	1 2	2 2	Beresford, Cook	42,136
6	17	A	Burnley	L	2 2	2 4	Cook 2	19,523
7	24	H	Bury	W	1 0	1 0	York	25,538
8	Oct 1	A	Sheffield United	W	1 0	3 0	Dorrell, Cook, Beresford	12,327
9	8	H	Middlesbrough	W	2 1	5 1	Walker, Dorrell, Cook 3	38,180
10	15	H	Sunderland	W	3 2	4 2	York, Cook, Walker 2	38,116
11	22	A	Huddersfield Town	D	0 1	1 1	Cook	14,679
12	29	H	Newcastle United	W	1 0	3 0	Dorrell, Walker, Spencer (og)	50,797
13	Nov 5	A	Birmingham	D	0 0	1 1	Walker	47,605
14	12	H	Tottenham Hotspur	L	0 0	1 2	Cook	30,759
15	19	A	Manchester United	L	0 3	1 5	Cook	25,991
16	26	H	Blackburn Rovers	W	0 0	2 0	Walker, Beresford	27,281
17	Dec 3	A	Cardiff City	L	1 1	1 2	Cook	14,264
18	10	H	Everton	L	1 2	2 3	Cook, Chester	40,353
19	17	A	Bolton Wanderers	L	1 1	1 3	Dorrell	14,852
20	24	H	Sheffield Wednesday	W	4 3	5 4	Beresford 3, Cook 2	12,345
21	26	A	Derby County	L	0 3	0 5		23,303
22	27	H	Derby County	L	0 0	0 1		43,228
23	31	A	Leicester City	L	0 1	0 3		25,233
24	Jan 7	H	Liverpool	L	2 3	3 4	Chester 2, Capewell	29,505
25	21	A	Arsenal	W	0 0	3 0	Dorrell, Smart (pen), Cook	32,505
26	Feb 4	A	Bury	D	0 0	0 0		9,814
27	8	H	Burnley	W	2 0	3 1	Cook, Capewell 2	18,602
28	11	H	Sheffield United	W	0 0	1 0	Cook	27,231
29	25	A	Sunderland	W	3 2	3 2	Cook, Waring, York	29,444
30	Mar 10	A	Newcastle United	L	2 4	5 7	Cook, Waring 2, Dorrell, York	23,053
31	17	H	Birmingham	D	0 1	1 1	Smart (pen)	59,367
32	21	A	Middlesbrough	D	0 0	0 0		15,698
33	24	A	Tottenham Hotspur	L	1 0	1 2	Capewell	21,537
34	31	H	Manchester United	W	1 0	3 1	Smart (pen), Waring, Cook	24,691
35	Apr 6	A	West Ham United	D	0 0	0 0		31,469
36	7	A	Blackburn Rovers	W	1 0	1 0	Armfield	21,432
37	9	H	West Ham United	W	0 0	1 0	Dorrell	31,059
38	14	H	Cardiff City	W	1 0	3 1	Beresford, Smart (pen), Waring	22,428
39	21	A	Everton	L	0 2	2 3	Waring, Gibson	39,825
40	28	H	Bolton Wanderers	D	0 2	2 2	Walker, Armfield	22,895
41	May 2	H	Huddersfield Town	W	2 0	3 0	Walker, Dorrell, Waring	30,173
42	5	A	Sheffield Wednesday	L	0 0	0 2		36,636

Final League Position: 8th in First Division

1 Own-goal

Appearances
Goals

FA CUP

3	Jan 14	A	Burnley	W	0 0	2 0	Walker, Beresford	26,150
4	28	H	Crewe Alexandra	W	2 0	3 0	Cook 3	41,000
5	Feb 18	A	Arsenal	L	0 2	1 4	Cook	58,505

Appearances
Goals

364

FINAL LEAGUE TABLE

	P	W	D	L	F	A	P
Everton	42	20	13	9	102	66	53
Huddersfield Town	42	22	7	13	91	68	51
Leicester City	42	18	12	12	96	72	48
Derby County	42	17	10	15	96	83	44
Bury	42	20	4	18	80	80	44
Cardiff City	42	17	10	15	70	80	44
Bolton Wanderers	42	16	11	15	81	66	43
Aston Villa	**42**	**17**	**9**	**16**	**78**	**73**	**43**
Newcastle United	42	15	13	14	79	81	43
Arsenal	42	13	15	14	82	86	41
Birmingham City	42	13	15	14	70	75	41
Blackburn Rovers	42	16	9	17	66	78	41
Sheffield United	42	15	10	17	79	86	40
Sheffield Wednesday	42	13	13	16	81	78	39
Sunderland	42	15	9	18	74	76	39
Liverpool	42	13	13	16	84	87	39
West Ham United	42	14	11	17	81	88	39
Manchester United	42	16	7	19	72	80	39
Burnley	42	16	7	19	82	98	39
Portsmouth	42	16	7	19	66	90	39
Tottenham Hotspur	42	15	8	19	74	86	38
Middlesbrough	42	11	15	16	81	88	37

1928/29

SEASON SNIPPETS

Frank Moss was sent off in his last match on 27 August following a tackle on Hugh McLenahan. United's Jim Hanson was also later sent off. Moss was suspended for a month from 18 September and joined Cardiff City on 15 January 1929.

John Yates played his last game on 15 September.

Fred Tully's last appearance came on 22 September.

George Jakeman played his last game on 5 January.

Len Capewell, who had scored on his debut on 1 April, also scored on his last game on 1 April - exactly seven years later. It was his 100th Villa goal.

In addition to Capewell, the Leicester City game on 1 April was also the last match for both Dr Victor Milne and Billy Cook.

Norman Swales made his debut in the FA Cup fourth-round match against Clapton Orient on 26 January. Swales was the only player to make his debut during the season.

DIVISION ONE

MANAGER: Directors

MATCH	DATE	VENUE	OPPONENTS	RESULT	HT SCORE	SCORE	SCORERS	ATT
1	Aug 25	A	Leeds United	L	0 2	1 4	York	26,588
2	27	H	Manchester United	D	0 0	0 0		16,000
3	Sep 1	H	Liverpool	W	2 1	3 1	Beresford, York, Capewell	30,356
4	8	A	West Ham United	L	1 2	1 4	Capewell	26,110
5	15	H	Newcastle United	D	1 1	1 1	Chester	33,811
6	22	A	Burnley	L	0 4	1 4	Chester	19,147
7	29	H	Cardiff City	W	1 0	1 0	York	30,190
8	Oct 6	A	Sheffield United	W	1 0	3 1	Waring 2, Dorrell	23,200
9	13	H	Bury	W	4 0	7 1	Walker, Waring 2, Dorrell, York 3	29,163
10	20	H	Bolton Wanderers	L	3 2	3 5	Walker 2, Dorrell	29,827
11	27	A	Birmingham	W	1 2	4 2	Waring, Walker 2, Beresford	36,261
12	Nov 3	H	Derby County	L	0 0	2 3	Walker, Dorrell	43,086
13	10	A	Sunderland	W	2 1	3 1	Talbot, Walker 2	21,250
14	17	H	Blackburn Rovers	W	1 1	2 1	Beresford 2	31,212
15	24	A	Arsenal	W	4 0	5 2	Waring 3, York, Talbot	30,491
16	Dec 1	H	Everton	W	1 0	2 0	Waring, Walker	45,416
17	8	A	Huddersfield Town	L	0 1	0 3		16,406
18	19	H	Manchester City	W	4 1	5 1	Gibson, Beresford 2, York 2	8,496
19	22	A	Sheffield Wednesday	L	0 3	1 4	Gibson	24,822
20	25	A	Portsmouth	L	2 2	2 3	Dorrell, Beresford	24,679
21	26	H	Portsmouth	W	3 1	3 2	Waring, Beresford, Walker	54,331
22	29	H	Leeds United	W	1 0	1 0	Waring	31,565
23	Jan 1	A	Manchester United	D	2 1	2 2	Waring 2	25,935
24	5	A	Liverpool	L	0 1	0 4		31,146
25	19	H	West Ham United	W	2 1	5 2	Beresford, Chester 2, Walker, York	28,838
26	Feb 2	H	Burnley	W	2 1	4 2	Waring 3, York	21,277
27	9	A	Cardiff City	W	2 0	2 0	Beresford, Cook	15,978
28	20	H	Sheffield United	W	0 1	3 2	Waring, York 2	14,022
29	23	A	Bury	D	1 1	2 2	Smart (pen), Walker	14,679
30	Mar 9	H	Birmingham	L	1 1	1 2	Waring	56,528
31	13	A	Newcastle United	L	1 1	1 2	York	30,168
32	16	A	Derby County	L	0 0	0 1		18,835
33	25	H	Sunderland	W	2 1	3 1	England (og), Cook, Waring (pen)	8,573
34	30	A	Blackburn Rovers	W	1 1	5 2	Walker 2, Dorrell, Waring, Cook	15,690
35	Apr 1	H	Leicester City	L	1 0	1 4	Capewell	35,744
36	2	H	Leicester City	W	4 1	4 2	Walker 2, Chester, Waring	31,901
37	6	H	Arsenal	W	3 1	4 2	Beresford, York, Walker, Waring	26,664
38	13	A	Everton	W	1 0	1 0	Waring	20,594
39	17	A	Bolton Wanderers	L	1 1	1 3	Waring	10,271
40	20	H	Huddersfield Town	W	2 0	4 1	Chester 3, Walker	23,811
41	27	A	Manchester City	L	0 2	0 3		30,154
42	May 4	H	Sheffield Wednesday	W	2 1	4 1	Chester, York, Waring, Walker	25,075

Final League Position: 3rd in First Division

1 Own-goal

Appearances
Goals

FA CUP

3	Jan 12	H	Cardiff City	W	2 0	6 1	Tate, Dorrell, Beresford 2, Waring, York	51,242
4	26	H	Clapton Orient	D	0 0	0 0		53,086
R	30	A	Clapton Orient	W	2 0	8 0	Waring 3, Swales, Beresford, Cook, Dorrell, York	27,532
5	Feb 16	A	Reading	W	2 1	3 1	Dorrell, Waring 2	23,703
6	Mar 2	H	Arsenal	W	0 0	1 0	Waring	73,686
SF	23	N	Portsmouth *	L	0 1	0 1		36,147

Appearances
Goals

* Played at Highbury Stadium, London

366

Player Appearances by Match

Match	Olney BA	Smart T	Mort T	Kingdon WIG	Gibson JD	Moss F	York RE	Beresford J	Waring T	Walker WH	Dorrell AR	Talbot AD	Jackson T	Milne Dr VE	Yates J	Capewell LK	Chester RA	Bowen SE	Tully FC	Cook GW	Tate JT	Jakeman GJW	Swales N	Brittleton JT
1	1	2	3	4	5	6	7	8	9	10	11													
2		2	3	4		6	7	8	9	10	11	5	1											
3		2	3	4			7	8		10			1	5	6	9	11							
4	1	2	3	4			7	8		10				5	6	9	11							
5	1	2	3	4			7	10	8					5	6	9	11							
6	1	2		6			4	10	8					5		9	11	3	7					
7	1	2		4			7	10	9	6				5			11	3		8				
8	1	2		4			7	8	9	10	11			5				3		6				
9	1	2		4			7	8	9	10	11			5				3		6				
10	1	2		4			7	8	9	10	11			5				3		6				
11	1	2		4			7	8	9	10	11			5				3		6				
12	1	2		4			7	8	9	10	11			5				3		6				
13		2		4			7	8	9	10	11	5	1					3		6				
14	1	2		4			7	8	9	10	11	5						3		6				
15	1	2		4			7	8	9	10	11	5						3		6				
16	1	2		4			7	8	9	10	11	5						3		6	4			
17	1	2		4			7	8	9	10	11	5						3		6				
18	1	2		4	9		7	8		10	11	5						3		6				
19	1	2		4	9		7	8		10	11			5				3		6				
20	1	2		4			7	8	9	10	11	5						3		6				
21	1	2		4			7	8	9	10	11	5						3		6				
22	1	2		4			7	8	9	10	11	5						3		6	4			
23	1	2		4			7	8	9	10		5					11	3		6				
24		2		6			7	8	9	10		5	1				11	3			4			
25	1	2		4			7	8	9			5					11	3		6				
26	1	2		4			7	8	9		11	5						3	10		6			
27		2	3	4			7	8	9		11	5							10	6				
28	1	2	3	4			7	8	9		11	5							10	6				
29	1	2		4			7	8	9	10				5			11	3		6				
30	1	2	3		4		7	8	9	10	11	5								6				
31	1		3	4			7	8	9		11	5							10	6				
32	1	2		4	9		7			10				5			11	3	8		6			
33	1		3	4			7		9	10	11	5						2	8	6				
34	1			4			7			10	11	5						3	8		6	2		
35	1			4			7			10	11	5			9			3	8		6	2		
36	1						7	8	9	10		5					11	3		6	4	2		
37	1		3	4			7	8	9	10		5					11	2		6				
38	1			4			7	8	9	10		5					11	3		6			2	
39	1			4			7	8	9	10		5					11	3		6				
40	1		3	4			7	8	9	10		5					11	2		6			2	
41	1			4			7	8	9	10		5					11	3		6			2	
42				4			7	8	9	10		5	1				11	3		6			2	

Totals: 37 | 31 | 12 | 38 | 5 | 2 | 42 | 38 | 36 | 36 | 25 | 25 | 5 | 16 | 3 | 5 | 17 | 34 | 1 | 9 | 30 | 3 | 5 | 7
Goals: | | | 1 | | | 2 | 16 | 11 | 25 | 19 | 6 | | 2 | | | 3 | 9 | | 3 | | | |

FA Cup

	Olney	Smart	Mort	Kingdon	York	Beresford	Waring	Walker	Dorrell	Talbot	Milne	Chester	Bowen	Tate										Rnd
	1	2		4	7	8	9	10	11	5			3	6										3
	1	2		4	7	8	9	10		5	11	3		6										4
	1	2		4	7	8	9		11	5		3	10	6										R
	1	2	3	4	7	8	9	10	11	5				6										5
	1	2	3	4	7	8	9	10	11	5	11			6										6
	1		3	4	7	8	9	10	11	5		2		6										SF

Goals: 6 | 5 | 3 | 6 | | | 6 | 6 | 6 | 5 | 4 | 6 | | | | 2 | 4 | | 1 | 4 | | 2 | |
| | | | | | | 2 | 3 | 7 | | 3 | | | | | | | 1 | 1 | | 1 | |

FINAL LEAGUE TABLE

	P	W	D	L	F	A	P
Sheffield Wednesday	42	21	10	11	86	62	52
Leicester City	42	21	9	12	96	67	51
Aston Villa	**42**	**23**	**4**	**15**	**98**	**81**	**50**
Sunderland	42	20	7	15	93	75	47
Liverpool	42	17	12	13	90	64	46
Derby County	42	18	10	14	86	71	46
Blackburn Rovers	42	17	11	14	72	63	45
Manchester City	42	18	9	15	95	86	45
Arsenal	42	16	13	13	77	72	45
Newcastle United	42	19	6	17	70	72	44
Sheffield United	42	15	11	16	86	85	41
Manchester United	42	14	13	15	66	76	41
Leeds United	42	16	9	17	71	84	41
Bolton Wanderers	42	14	12	16	73	80	40
Birmingham City	42	15	10	17	68	77	40
Huddersfield Town	42	14	11	17	70	61	39
West Ham United	42	15	9	18	86	96	39
Everton	42	17	4	21	63	75	38
Burnley	42	15	8	19	81	103	38
Portsmouth	42	15	6	21	56	80	36
Bury	42	12	7	23	62	99	31
Cardiff City	42	8	13	21	43	59	29

1929/30

SEASON SNIPPETS

George Brown made his debut in a 2-1 home win over Birmingham on 31 August.

The match at Birmingham on 28 December was the last of Arthur Dorrell's 390 appearances.

Eric Houghton missed a penalty when making his debut at home to Leeds United on 4 January.

Tommy Jackson, who had made his debut at Sunderland in February 1921, played his last game at Sunderland on 1 February 1930.

Fred Biddlestone and Bob Brocklebank both made their debut at home to Burnley on 5 February, but Norman Swales played his last game.

The collapse of two goalposts at Everton on 5 March resulted in the kick-off being delayed for eight minutes.

Jack Mandley scored on his debut in a 5-3 win against Huddersfield Town on 15 March.

John Brittleton made his final appearance at home to West Ham United on 26 April.

Villa were drawn away in round four of the FA Cup, but the Walsall directors asked the FA's permission to transfer the fixture to Villa Park and the request was granted.

The sixth-round FA Cup defeat at home to Huddersfield Town on 1 March was Ben Olney's last game.

DIVISION ONE

MANAGER: Directors

MATCH	DATE	VENUE	OPPONENTS	RESULT	HT SCORE	SCORE	SCORERS	ATT
1	Aug 31	H	Birmingham	W	1 1	2 1	Chester, York	36,834
2	Sep 4	A	Derby County	L	0 3	0 4		21,971
3	7	A	Leeds United	L	1 3	1 4	Beresford	23,649
4	9	H	Derby County	D	1 0	2 2	Brown, York	23,556
5	14	H	Sheffield Wednesday	L	0 1	1 3	Chester (pen)	36,209
6	21	A	Burnley	W	3 0	4 1	Brown 2, Chester, Walker	14,062
7	25	A	Arsenal	W	3 1	5 2	Gibson, Brown 3, Beresford	33,850
8	28	H	Sunderland	W	1 1	2 1	Chester, York	41,919
9	Oct 5	A	Bolton Wanderers	L	0 1	0 3		19,187
10	12	H	Everton	W	2 1	5 2	Brown 3, Chester (pen), Walker	35,243
11	19	A	Leicester City	W	2 0	3 0	Brown 2, Tate	37,813
12	26	A	Grimsby Town	W	1 0	2 0	Chester 2	20,225
13	Nov 2	H	Manchester United	W	0 0	1 0	Chester	24,292
14	9	A	Huddersfield Town	D	0 1	1 1	Walker	18,183
15	16	H	Liverpool	L	1 2	2 3	Brown, Beresford	21,837
16	23	A	Middlesbrough	W	2 0	3 2	Brown 2, Beresford	16,051
17	30	H	Blackburn Rovers	W	2 0	3 0	York, Brown, Beresford	25,910
18	Dec 7	A	Newcastle United	D	0 1	2 2	Chester, Brown	30,758
19	14	H	Sheffield United	W	3 1	5 1	Walker 4, Beresford	26,821
20	21	A	West Ham United	L	1 2	2 5	Smart (pen), Brown (pen)	14,624
21	25	H	Manchester City	L	0 0	0 2		39,778
22	26	A	Manchester City	W	0 1	2 1	Brown, Heinemann (og)	68,704
23	28	A	Birmingham	D	0 0	1 1	Walker	33,228
24	Jan 4	H	Leeds United	L	1 4	3 4	Brown 2, Talbot	32,476
25	18	A	Sheffield Wednesday	L	0 1	0 3		34,911
26	Feb 1	H	Sunderland	L	0 1	1 4	Brown (pen)	8,909
27	5	H	Burnley	L	1 1	1 2	Beresford	13,378
28	8	H	Bolton Wanderers	W	2 0	2 0	Beresford, Brown	26,235
29	22	A	Leicester City	L	2 1	3 4	Houghton, York 2	26,701
30	Mar 5	A	Everton	W	2 2	4 3	Houghton 2, Brown, Waring	15,946
31	8	A	Manchester United	W	0 2	3 2	Waring 2, Beresford	25,407
32	15	H	Huddersfield Town	W	3 2	5 3	Mandley, Brown, Waring 2, Houghton	18,084
33	22	A	Liverpool	L	0 1	0 2		34,018
34	29	H	Middlesbrough	W	1 2	4 2	Waring 2, Brown 2	26,986
35	Apr 2	H	Grimsby Town	W	2 1	4 1	Houghton 2, Waring, Brown	8,965
36	5	A	Blackburn Rovers	L	0 1	0 2		14,136
37	12	H	Newcastle United	W	0 0	2 0	Houghton, Brown	25,801
38	18	A	Portsmouth	W	1 0	2 1	Houghton, Waring	28,687
39	19	A	Sheffield United	D	1 2	3 3	Beresford, Houghton 2	11,953
40	21	H	Portsmouth	L	0 1	0 1		28,208
41	26	H	West Ham United	L	2 2	2 3	Brown (pen), Houghton	18,047
42	May 3	A	Arsenal	W	3 0	4 2	Houghton, Brown, Waring 2	37,020

Final League Position: 4th in First Division

1 Own-goal

Appearances
Goals

FA CUP

MATCH	DATE	VENUE	OPPONENTS	RESULT	HT SCORE	SCORE	SCORERS	ATT
3	Jan 11	H	Reading	W	2 0	5 1	Houghton 2, Brown, Walker (pen), York	39,000
4	25	H	Walsall	W	2 1	3 1	Walker 2, Brown	74,626
5	Feb 15	H	Blackburn Rovers	W	2 0	4 1	Brown 3 (1 pen), Beresford	69,884
6	Mar 1	H	Huddersfield Town	L	1 1	1 2	Brown (pen)	65,732

Appearances
Goals

																							MATCH
Olney BA	Smart T	Mort T	Kingdon WIG	Gibson JD	Tate JT	York RE	Brown G	Waring T	Walker WH	Chester RA	Bowen SE	Beresford J	Talbot AD	Dorrell AR	Houghton WE	Jackson T	Biddlestone TF	Swales N	Brocklebank RE	Mandley J	Brittleton JT		
1	2	3	4	5	6	7	8	9	10	11													1
1	2	3	4	5	6	7	8	9	10	11													2
1		3	4	5	6		9	7	10	11	2	8											3
1		3	4		6	7	8	9	10	11	2		5										4
1		3		4	6	7	8	9	10	11	2		5										5
1	2	3		4	6	7	9		10	11		8	5										6
1	2	3		4	6	7	9		10	11		8	5										7
1	2	3		4	6	7	9		10	11		8	5										8
1	2	3		4	6	7	9		10	11		8	5										9
1	2	3		4	6	7	9		10	11		8	5										10
1	2	3		4	6	7	9		10	11		8	5										11
1	2	3	4		6	7	9		10	11		8	5										12
1	2	3		4	6	7		9	10	11		8	5										13
1	2	3		4	6	7	9		10	11		8	5										14
1	2	3		4	6	7	9		10	11		8	5										15
1	2	3		4	6	7	9		10	11		8	5										16
1	2	3	4		6	7	9		10	11		8	5										17
1	2	3	4		6	7	9		10	11		8	5										18
1	2	3	4		6	7	9		10	11		8	5										19
1	2	3	4		6	7	9		10	11		8	5										20
1		3	4		6	7	8	9	10		2		5	11									21
1		3	4		6	7	9	8	10		2		5	11									22
		3	4		6	7	9	8	10		2		5	11									23
1		3	4		6	7	9		10		2	8	5	11									24
1		3	4		6	7	9	8	10		2		5	11									25
		3	4	8	6		9		10		2	7	5	11	1								26
		3	4		6		9		10		2	7	5	11		1	6	8					27
1	2			4	6	7	9		10		3	8	5	11									28
1	2	3	4		6	7	9		10			8	5	11									29
		3		4	6	7	10	9			2	8	5	11	1								30
	3	6	4			7	10	9			2	8	5	11	1								31
		3		4	6		10	9			2	8	5	11	1			7					32
		3		4	6		10	9			2	8	5	11	1			7					33
		3		4	6		10	9			2	8	5	11	1			7					34
		3	4		6		10	9			2	8	5	11	1			7					35
		3	4		6		10	9			2	8	5	11	1			7					36
		3		4	6		10	9			2	8	5	11	1			7					37
	2		4	6			10	9			3	8	5	11	1			7					38
	2		4	6			10	9			3	8	5	11	1			7					39
	2		4	6			10	9			3	8	5	11	1			7	2				40
			4	6			8	9	10		3		5	11	1			7					41
		3	4	6			8	9	10		2		5		1			7					42
27	22	37	21	26	40	28	41	23	31	20	24	32	39	3	19	1	14	1	1	11	1		
	1			1		1	6	30	11	8	9		10	1	12					1			

																							3
1		3	4		6	7	9		10		2	8	5	11									4
1	2	3		4	6	7	9		10			8	5	11									5
1	2	3		4	6	7	9		10			8	5	11									6
1	2	3		4	6	7	9		10			8	5	11									

| 4 | 3 | 4 | 1 | 3 | 4 | 4 | | 4 | | 1 | 4 | 4 | | 4 | | | | | | | | | |
| | | | | | | 1 | 6 | | 3 | | 1 | | 2 | | | | | | | | | | |

FINAL LEAGUE TABLE

	P	W	D	L	F	A	P
Sheffield Wednesday	42	26	8	8	105	57	60
Derby County	42	21	8	13	90	82	50
Manchester City	42	19	9	14	91	81	47
Aston Villa	**42**	**21**	**5**	**16**	**92**	**83**	**47**
Leeds United	42	20	6	16	79	63	46
Blackburn Rovers	42	19	7	16	99	93	45
West Ham United	42	19	5	18	86	79	43
Leicester City	42	17	9	16	86	90	43
Sunderland	42	18	7	17	76	80	43
Huddersfield Town	42	17	9	16	63	69	43
Birmingham City	42	16	9	17	67	62	41
Liverpool	42	16	9	17	63	79	41
Portsmouth	42	15	10	17	66	62	40
Arsenal	42	14	11	17	78	66	39
Bolton Wanderers	42	15	9	18	74	74	39
Middlesbrough	42	16	6	20	82	84	38
Manchester United	42	15	8	19	67	88	38
Grimsby Town	42	15	7	20	73	89	37
Newcastle United	42	15	7	20	71	92	37
Sheffield United	42	15	6	21	91	96	36
Burnley	42	14	8	20	79	97	36
Everton	42	12	11	19	80	92	35

1930/31

SEASON SNIPPETS

Pongo Waring scored in each of the first seven games by which time he had netted 13 goals.

Villa's total of 128 league goals is still a top flight record.

Waring's total of 50 goals for the season is still a Villa record.

Dicky York played the last of his 390 Villa games against Grimsby Town on 15 September while Percy Maggs made his debut.

Tommy Wood's first appearance came at home to Blackburn Rovers on 1 November.

Villa drew a league game 5-5 for the first time on 3 January.

On 14 January, a mid-week record crowd of 73,632 saw the FA Cup third-round replay with Arsenal.

Reg Miles made his debut at Liverpool on 24 January and played in the last sixteen games, but these were his only Villa appearances.

Percy Maggs played his last game against Bolton Wanderers on 17 January.

DIVISION ONE

MANAGER: Directors

MATCH	DATE	VENUE	OPPONENTS	RESULT	HT SCORE	SCORE	SCORERS	ATT
1	Aug 30	A	Manchester United	W	1 2	4 3	Waring 4	18,004
2	Sep 1	H	Sheffield Wednesday	W	0 0	2 0	Waring, Brown	27,622
3	6	H	West Ham United	W	3 1	6 1	Houghton, Walker, Waring 4	35,897
4	9	A	Grimsby Town	W	2 1	2 1	Waring, Houghton	19,224
5	13	A	Bolton Wanderers	D	0 1	1 1	Waring	17,207
6	15	H	Grimsby Town	W	2 0	2 0	Houghton, Waring	22,301
7	20	H	Liverpool	W	3 1	4 2	Houghton, Brown, Walker, Waring	31,993
8	27	A	Middlesbrough	L	1 1	1 3	Beresford	19,260
9	Oct 4	H	Huddersfield Town	W	2 0	6 1	Houghton 2, Walker 3, Waring	43,235
10	11	A	Sunderland	D	1 0	1 1	Houghton	34,847
11	18	H	Birmingham	D	1 1	1 1	Waring	55,482
12	25	A	Leicester City	L	0 2	1 4	Waring	32,029
13	Nov 1	H	Blackburn Rovers	W	3 1	5 2	Waring 2, Houghton 2 (1 pen), Beresford	29,032
14	8	A	Arsenal	L	1 3	2 5	Waring 2	56,417
15	15	H	Derby County	L	2 3	4 6	Houghton 2 (1 pen), Talbot, Waring	37,563
16	22	A	Blackpool	D	1 2	2 2	Chester, Mandley	12,054
17	Dec 3	H	Portsmouth	D	1 2	2 2	Gibson, Mandley	20,169
18	6	A	Sheffield United	W	3 1	4 3	Waring 2, Houghton, Beresford	17,540
19	13	H	Leeds United	W	3 1	4 3	Mandley, Houghton, Waring, Walker	26,272
20	20	A	Manchester City	L	0 1	1 3	Waring	29,342
21	25	A	Chelsea	W	0 0	2 0	Waring, Walker	40,990
22	26	H	Chelsea	D	1 1	3 3	Waring 2, Houghton (pen)	53,580
23	27	H	Manchester United	W	3 0	7 0	Mandley 2, Houghton 2 (2 pens), Brown 2, Beresford	32,505
24	Jan 1	A	Newcastle United	L	0 0	0 2		45,045
25	3	A	West Ham United	D	3 5	5 5	Beresford 2, Walker, Brown, Houghton (pen)	18,810
26	17	H	Bolton Wanderers	W	1 0	3 1	Houghton, Waring, Mandley	21,950
27	24	A	Liverpool	D	0 0	1 1	Walker	30,503
28	31	H	Middlesbrough	W	5 0	8 1	Beresford, Waring 2, Walker 2, Houghton 2 (1 pen), Mandley	15,947
29	Feb 7	A	Huddersfield Town	W	1 1	6 1	Waring 2, Houghton 2, Gibson, Beresford	14,296
30	18	H	Sunderland	W	4 1	4 2	Waring 4	10,875
31	21	A	Birmingham	W	1 0	4 0	Tate, Mandley, Houghton, Beresford	49,609
32	28	H	Leicester City	W	2 1	4 2	Waring, Beresford 3	23,531
33	Mar 7	A	Blackburn Rovers	W	1 0	2 0	Beresford, Waring	11,222
34	14	H	Arsenal	W	3 1	5 1	Waring 2, Walker, Houghton 2	60,997
35	21	A	Derby County	D	0 0	1 1	Houghton	24,466
36	28	H	Blackpool	W	2 1	4 1	Waring 3, Houghton	27,245
37	Apr 4	A	Portsmouth	L	0 3	0 5		26,677
38	7	H	Newcastle United	W	2 3	4 3	Walker 2, Houghton (pen), Waring	29,975
39	11	H	Sheffield United	W	1 0	4 0	Walker, Houghton (pen), Waring 2	26,952
40	18	A	Leeds United	W	1 0	2 0	Waring, Chester	10,388
41	25	H	Manchester City	W	2 0	4 2	Chester, Beresford, Waring, Houghton	13,272
42	May 2	A	Sheffield Wednesday	L	0 2	0 3		12,419

Final League Position: 2nd in First Division

Appearances
Goals

FA CUP

3	Jan 10	A	Arsenal	D	2 1	2 2	Brown, Walker	40,864
R	14	H	Arsenal	L	0 1	1 3	Waring	73,632

Appearances
Goals

FINAL LEAGUE TABLE

	P	W	D	L	F	A	P
Arsenal	42	28	10	4	127	59	66
Aston Villa	**42**	**25**	**9**	**8**	**128**	**78**	**59**
Sheffield Wednesday	42	22	8	12	102	75	52
Portsmouth	42	18	13	11	84	67	49
Huddersfield Town	42	18	12	12	81	65	48
Derby County	42	18	10	14	94	79	46
Middlesbrough	42	19	8	15	98	90	46
Manchester City	42	18	10	14	75	70	46
Liverpool	42	15	12	15	86	85	42
Blackburn Rovers	42	17	8	17	83	84	42
Sunderland	42	16	9	17	89	85	41
Chelsea	42	15	10	17	64	67	40
Grimsby Town	42	17	5	20	82	87	39
Bolton Wanderers	42	15	9	18	68	81	39
Sheffield United	42	14	10	18	78	84	38
Leicester City	42	16	6	20	80	95	38
Newcastle United	42	15	6	21	78	87	36
West Ham United	42	14	8	20	79	94	36
Birmingham City	42	13	10	19	55	70	36
Blackpool	42	11	10	21	71	125	32
Leeds United	42	12	7	23	68	81	31
Manchester United	42	7	8	27	53	115	22

1931/32

SEASON SNIPPETS

The line-up for the first eight games was unchanged, but then both Waring and Houghton were called up for England's game against Ireland on 17 October. Dai Astley made his debut as Waring's replacement and scored in a 3-1 win at Portsmouth while Reg Chester stood in for Houghton. Meanwhile Waring and Houghton each scored twice in a 6-2 England victory in Belfast.

Danny Blair made his debut at home to Blackpool on 7 November.

Goalkeeper Harry Morton made his debut at Manchester City on 28 November. Villa were three goals down with only fifteen minutes to play, but came back to draw 3-3.

On 25 December, Villa recorded their highest Christmas Day victory with a 7-1 home win against Middlesbrough

On 2 January, George Brown became the first Villa player to score five goals in an away league game.

George H Stephenson made his debut in the FA cup third-round win at West Bromwich Albion on 9 January and scored on his league debut, a 6-1 win against Liverpool, the following week.

Billy Simpson's first game was against Chelsea on 30 January.

On 7 May, Tommy Moore scored in his only game.

DIVISION ONE

MANAGER: Directors

MATCH	DATE	VENUE	OPPONENTS	RESULT	HT SCORE	SCORE	SCORERS	ATT
1	Aug 29	H	Leicester City	W	0 1	3 2	Houghton, Waring 2	41,606
2	31	A	Huddersfield Town	D	0 1	1 1	Waring	13,188
3	Sep 5	A	Liverpool	L	0 2	0 2		32,909
4	12	H	Grimsby Town	W	3 0	7 0	Beresford, Houghton 2, Mandley 2, Walker, Waring	18,753
5	19	A	Chelsea	W	3 1	6 3	Waring 4, Houghton 2	56,698
6	26	H	West Ham United	W	2 0	5 2	Waring 4, Houghton	39,619
7	Oct 3	A	Sheffield Wednesday	L	0 1	0 1		28,798
8	10	H	Bolton Wanderers	W	1 1	2 1	Houghton, Walker	39,673
9	17	A	Portsmouth	W	0 0	3 0	Walker, Beresford, Astley	20,915
10	24	H	Everton	L	1 2	2 3	Houghton, Mandley	61,663
11	31	A	Arsenal	D	0 0	1 1	Waring	54,951
12	Nov 7	H	Blackpool	W	2 0	5 1	Waring 3, Houghton, Beresford	40,448
13	14	A	West Bromwich Albion	L	0 1	0 3		59,674
14	21	H	Birmingham	W	2 0	3 2	Walker, Waring 2	44,948
15	28	A	Manchester City	D	0 0	3 3	Smart (pen), Waring 2	27,334
16	Dec 5	H	Derby County	W	1 0	2 0	Houghton 2	32,871
17	12	A	Sheffield United	L	1 3	4 5	Gibson, Waring, Walker, Houghton	24,831
18	19	H	Blackburn Rovers	L	0 3	1 5	Walker	9,263
19	25	H	Middlesbrough	W	4 1	7 1	Houghton 3, Beresford 3, Mort	33,774
20	26	A	Middlesbrough	D	1 1	1 1	Chester	28,006
21	28	H	Newcastle United	W	1 0	3 0	Chester, Waring, Houghton	42,441
22	Jan 1	A	Newcastle United	L	1 1	1 3	Beresford	43,391
23	2	A	Leicester City	W	5 2	8 3	Brown 5, Beresford, Walker 2	13,714
24	16	H	Liverpool	W	2 0	6 1	Houghton, Brown 4, Stephenson	32,041
25	30	H	Chelsea	L	0 2	1 3	Houghton	35,993
26	Feb 2	A	Grimsby Town	D	0 2	2 2	Mandley, Waring	11,132
27	6	A	West Ham United	L	0 2	1 2	Beresford	25,438
28	20	A	Bolton Wanderers	L	0 2	1 2	Waring	12,682
29	24	H	Sheffield Wednesday	W	2 1	3 1	Walker, Houghton, Waring	12,045
30	27	H	Portsmouth	L	0 0	0 1		29,360
31	Mar 5	A	Everton	L	0 2	2 4	Astley, Waring	39,190
32	19	A	Blackpool	W	1 1	3 1	Waring 2, Houghton (pen)	15,585
33	25	A	Sunderland	D	0 1	1 1	Astley	44,866
34	26	H	West Bromwich Albion	W	1 0	2 0	Astley, Houghton	43,347
35	28	H	Sunderland	W	2 0	2 0	Brown, Houghton	25,401
36	Apr 2	A	Birmingham	D	1 1	1 1	Houghton	35,671
37	9	H	Manchester City	W	1 1	2 1	Chester (pen), Brown	18,170
38	16	A	Derby County	L	1 2	1 3	Chester	14,967
39	23	H	Sheffield United	W	3 0	5 0	Talbot, Waring, Astley 2, Mandley	14,937
40	25	H	Arsenal	D	1 1	1 1	Mandley	25,959
41	30	A	Blackburn Rovers	L	0 1	0 2		9,116
42	May 7	H	Huddersfield Town	L	1 1	2 3	Waring, Moore	19,383

Final League Position: 5th in First Division

Appearances
Goals

FA CUP

3	Jan 9	A	West Bromwich Albion	W	0 1	2 1	Houghton, Brown	49,232
4	23	A	Portsmouth	D	0 0	1 1	Beresford	36,956
R	27	H	Portsmouth	L	0 0	0 1		55,080

Appearances
Goals

FINAL LEAGUE TABLE

	P	W	D	L	F	A	P	
Everton	42	26	4	12	116	64	56	
Arsenal	42	22	10	10	90	48	54	
Sheffield Wednesday	42	22	6	14	96	82	50	
Huddersfield Town	42	19	10	13	80	63	48	
Aston Villa	**42**	**19**	**8**	**15**	**104**	**72**	**46**	
West Bromwich A	42	20	6	16	77	55	46	
Sheffield United	42	20	6	16	80	75	46	
Portsmouth	42	19	7	16	62	62	45	
Birmingham City	42	18	8	16	78	67	44	
Liverpool	42	19	6	17	81	93	44	
Newcastle United	42	18	6	18	80	87	42	
Chelsea	42	16	8	18	69	73	40	
Sunderland	42	15	10	17	67	73	40	
Manchester City	42	13	12	17	83	73	38	
Derby County	42	14	10	18	71	75	38	
Blackburn Rovers	42	16	6	20	89	95	38	
Bolton Wanderers	42	17	4	21	72	80	38	
Middlesbrough	42	15	8	19	64	89	38	
Leicester City	42	15	7	20	74	94	37	
Blackpool	42	12	9	21	65	102	33	
Grimsby Town	42	13	6	23	67	98	32	
West Ham United	42	12	7	23	62	107	31	R

1932/33

SEASON SNIPPETS

On 22 October, Villa set a record for their best start to a league season, remaining undefeated in the first eleven games.

In 1932, Alec Talbot set a new record for consecutive Villa league games. Talbot's run started on 9 September 1929 and by 5 November 1932, Talbot had made 136 consecutive league appearances. This run only ended when he was called up to play for the Football League against the Scottish League at Manchester on 12 November when Villa were playing at Everton. Ironically, Talbot had to leave the field with a twisted knee in the representative match and missed three further Villa games.

Dennis Watkin made his debut at Leeds United on 10 December.

Joe Nibloe's first game came at Wolverhampton Wanderers on 27 December.

Ernie 'Mush' Callaghan made his debut in the FA Cup third-round replay against Bradford City on 18 January.

Oliver Tidman made his only appearance in a 1-0 win at Chelsea on 11 February.

Goalkeeper Ken Tewkesbury kept a clean sheet in his only Villa game, a 3-0 win against Newcastle United on 18 April.

Villa stunned the football world at the beginning of May with the purchase of Ronnie Dix and Arthur Cunliffe from Blackburn Rovers. Both made their debut in the final game on 6 May, Cunliffe scored in a 2-0 win against Derby County.

The 6-2 defeat at Blackpool on 18 March was the last of Tommy Smart's 451 Villa games.

DIVISION ONE

MANAGER: Directors

MATCH	DATE	VENUE	OPPONENTS	RESULT	HT SCORE	SCORE	SCORERS	ATT
1	Aug 27	A	Middlesbrough	W	0 0	2 0	Brown, Walker	18,909
2	29	H	Sunderland	W	1 0	1 0	Brown	23,802
3	Sep 3	H	Bolton Wanderers	W	4 1	6 2	Brown 4, Beresford 2	31,296
4	7	A	Sunderland	D	1 0	1 1	Brown	22,214
5	10	A	Liverpool	D	0 0	0 0		33,387
6	17	H	Leicester City	W	1 1	4 2	Brown 2, Walker, Houghton	35,322
7	24	A	Portsmouth	W	1 1	4 2	Brown 2, Astley 2	29,949
8	Oct 1	H	Chelsea	W	2 0	3 1	Gibson, Astley 2	32,684
9	8	A	Huddersfield Town	D	0 0	0 0		13,342
10	15	H	Sheffield United	W	2 0	3 0	Walker, Houghton, Brown	31,536
11	22	H	Birmingham	W	0 0	1 0	Houghton	52,191
12	29	A	West Bromwich Albion	L	0 2	1 3	Houghton	42,105
13	Nov 5	H	Blackpool	W	4 1	6 2	Houghton 2, Mandley, Walker 2, Brown	29,371
14	12	A	Everton	D	1 2	3 3	Astley, Brown, Mandley	38,769
15	19	H	Arsenal	W	2 2	5 3	Gibson, Houghton 2, Mandley, Brown	58,066
16	26	A	Manchester City	L	1 3	2 5	Astley, Houghton	35,025
17	Dec 3	H	Sheffield Wednesday	L	2 3	3 6	Brown, Astley 2	31,518
18	10	A	Leeds United	D	0 1	1 1	Houghton (pen)	23,794
19	17	H	Blackburn Rovers	W	4 0	4 0	Astley 2, Brown 2	23,518
20	24	A	Derby County	D	0 0	0 0		26,043
21	26	H	Wolverhampton Wanderers	L	1 2	1 3	Astley	48,080
22	27	A	Wolverhampton Wanderers	W	0 0	4 2	Brown 2, Mandley, Beresford	52,110
23	31	H	Middlesbrough	W	1 0	3 1	Houghton (pen), Mandley, Beresford	22,309
24	Jan 7	A	Bolton Wanderers	W	1 0	1 0	Mandley	17,624
25	21	H	Liverpool	W	3 2	5 2	Waring 2, Houghton, Gibson, Beresford	29,937
26	Feb 4	A	Portsmouth	W	2 0	4 1	Brown, Watkin, Waring 2	28,701
27	9	A	Leicester City	L	0 3	0 3		13,806
28	11	A	Chelsea	W	0 0	1 0	Mandley	34,378
29	18	H	Huddersfield Town	L	0 2	0 3		25,243
30	Mar 8	A	Birmingham	L	0 1	2 3	Brown, Mandley	24,868
31	11	H	West Bromwich Albion	W	1 1	3 2	Astley 2, Brown	47,523
32	18	A	Blackpool	L	0 5	2 6	Chester, Simpson	15,729
33	25	H	Everton	W	1 1	2 1	Brown, Beresford	27,463
34	Apr 1	A	Arsenal	L	0 3	0 5		54,265
35	8	H	Manchester City	D	1 0	1 1	Brown	20,998
36	15	A	Sheffield Wednesday	W	1 0	2 0	Wood, Brown	16,445
37	17	A	Newcastle United	L	1 1	1 3	Brown	21,649
38	18	H	Newcastle United	W	1 0	3 0	Wood, Brown 2	23,700
39	22	H	Leeds United	D	0 0	0 0		21,238
40	24	A	Sheffield United	L	0 1	0 1		7,781
41	29	A	Blackburn Rovers	W	0 0	5 0	Brown 4, Houghton	3,624
42	May 6	H	Derby County	W	0 0	2 0	Cunliffe, Astley	32,738

Final League Position: 2nd in First Division

Appearances
Goals

FA CUP

3	Jan 14	A	Bradford City	D	2 1	2 2	Mandley, Brown	26,852
R	18	H	Bradford City	W	1 1	2 1	Brown, Tate	35,000
4	28	H	Sunderland	L	0 1	0 3		53,686

Appearances
Goals

FINAL LEAGUE TABLE

	P	W	D	L	F	A	P
Arsenal	42	25	8	9	118	61	58
Aston Villa	**42**	**23**	**8**	**11**	**92**	**67**	**54**
Sheffield Wednesday	42	21	9	12	80	68	51
West Bromwich A	42	20	9	13	83	70	49
Newcastle United	42	22	5	15	71	63	49
Huddersfield Town	42	18	11	13	66	53	47
Derby County	42	15	14	13	76	69	44
Leeds United	42	15	14	13	59	62	44
Portsmouth	42	18	7	17	74	76	43
Sheffield United	42	17	9	16	74	80	43
Everton	42	16	9	17	81	74	41
Sunderland	42	15	10	17	63	80	40
Birmingham City	42	14	11	17	57	57	39
Liverpool	42	14	11	17	79	84	39
Blackburn Rovers	42	14	10	18	76	102	38
Manchester City	42	16	5	21	68	71	37
Middlesbrough	42	14	9	19	63	73	37
Chelsea	42	14	7	21	63	73	35
Leicester City	42	11	13	18	75	89	35
Wolverhampton W	42	13	9	20	80	96	35
Bolton Wanderers	42	12	9	21	78	92	33
Blackpool	42	14	5	23	69	85	33

375

1933/34

SEASON SNIPPETS

On 19 August, former Villa winger Billy Armfield suffered a broken leg when playing in a practice match for Brierley Hill. On 11 September, Villa sent a team to Brierley Hill to play a Benefit Match. Two months after the accident his leg was amputated.

Teddy Bowen's last Villa game was at home to Sunderland on 23 September.

Billy Walker played the last of his 531 Villa games at Portsmouth on 30 September.

Joe Tate played his last game at home to Newcastle United on 25 November.

Jack Mandley's final appearance came in a 5-1 defeat at home to Tottenham Hotspur on 6 January.

Tommy Gardner made his Villa league debut at home to Stoke City on 24 February.

Joe Nibloe played his last Villa game at Everton on 5 May.

DIVISION ONE

MANAGER: Directors

MATCH	DATE	VENUE	OPPONENTS	RESULT	HT SCORE	SCORE	SCORERS	ATT
1	Aug 26	H	Leicester City	L	0 2	2 3	Astley, Waring	42,555
2	28	A	Sheffield Wednesday	W	1 1	2 1	Houghton, Astley	19,185
3	Sep 2	A	Tottenham Hotspur	L	0 2	2 3	Waring, Astley	44,974
4	4	H	Sheffield Wednesday	W	1 0	1 0	Waring	22,581
5	9	H	Liverpool	W	2 1	4 2	Astley, Houghton 2 (1 pen), Talbot	33,105
6	16	A	Chelsea	L	0 0	0 1		44,679
7	23	H	Sunderland	W	1 0	2 1	Houghton, Astley	39,137
8	30	A	Portsmouth	L	1 2	2 3	Astley, Cunliffe	25,750
9	Oct 7	H	Huddersfield Town	W	2 1	4 3	Houghton 2, Astley, Waring	29,491
10	14	A	Stoke City	D	1 0	1 1	Cunliffe	37,517
11	21	A	Manchester City	L	0 0	0 1		35,387
12	28	H	Arsenal	L	0 1	2 3	Waring 2	54,323
13	Nov 4	A	Leeds United	W	1 0	4 2	Waring 2, Houghton, Astley	20,148
14	11	H	Middlesbrough	W	1 0	3 0	Houghton (pen), Beresford, Cunliffe	27,740
15	18	A	Blackburn Rovers	L	1 1	1 2	Cunliffe	19,450
16	25	H	Newcastle United	L	1 1	2 3	Waring, Astley	25,009
17	Dec 2	A	Birmingham	D	0 0	0 0		34,718
18	9	H	Derby County	L	0 1	0 2		30,478
19	16	A	West Bromwich Albion	L	1 0	1 2	Astley	25,522
20	23	H	Everton	W	0 0	2 1	Astley, Houghton	24,438
21	25	H	Wolverhampton Wanderers	W	4 0	6 2	Mandley 2, Astley, Waring 2, Dix	57,070
22	26	A	Wolverhampton Wanderers	L	1 3	3 4	Chester 2, Dix	45,556
23	30	A	Leicester City	D	0 1	1 1	Astley	20,387
24	Jan 1	H	Sheffield United	D	1 2	3 3	Houghton 2 (1 pen), Waring	23,841
25	6	H	Tottenham Hotspur	L	0 4	1 5	Astley	35,296
26	20	A	Liverpool	W	2 1	3 2	Dix, Waring 2	25,890
27	Feb 3	A	Sunderland	L	1 3	1 5	Astley	15,582
28	7	H	Chelsea	W	1 0	2 0	Astley, Houghton	15,688
29	10	H	Portsmouth	D	0 1	1 1	Astley	32,573
30	21	A	Huddersfield Town	L	1 1	1 2	Cunliffe	8,074
31	24	H	Stoke City	L	1 2	1 2	Beresford	34,950
32	Mar 7	H	Manchester City	D	0 0	0 0		20,643
33	10	A	Arsenal	L	2 1	2 3	Dix, Houghton	41,169
34	24	A	Middlesbrough	W	1 1	2 1	Houghton, Astley	13,156
35	31	H	Blackburn Rovers	D	0 0	1 1	Talbot	30,966
36	Apr 2	A	Sheffield United	W	0 0	3 0	Astley, Houghton, Beresford	25,052
37	7	A	Newcastle United	D	0 1	1 1	Houghton	30,344
38	14	H	Birmingham	D	1 1	1 1	Dix	34,196
39	21	A	Derby County	D	1 0	1 1	Astley	14,149
40	28	H	West Bromwich Albion	D	1 3	4 4	Astley, Houghton 2 (1 pen), Beresford	16,554
41	30	H	Leeds United	W	1 0	3 0	Astley 3	9,849
42	May 5	A	Everton	D	1 1	2 2	Astley, Houghton	12,610

Final League Position: 13th in First Division

Appearances
Goals

FA CUP

3	Jan 13	A	Chesterfield	D	2 1	2 2	Cunliffe 2	23,878
R	17	H	Chesterfield	W	0 0	2 0	Astley, Beresford	25,400
4	27	H	Sunderland	W	4 1	7 2	Astley 4, Houghton 3	57,268
5	Feb 17	A	Tottenham Hotspur	W	0 0	1 0	Astley	44,365
6	Mar 3	H	Arsenal	W	2 0	2 1	Astley, Houghton	67,366
SF	17	N	Manchester City *	L	0 4	1 6	Astley	45,473

Appearances
Goals

* Played at Leeds Road, Huddersfield

Morton H	Blair D	Niblo J	Gibson JD	Talbot AD	Simpson WS	Houghton WE	Astley DJ	Waring T	Dix RW	Cunliffe A	Kingdon WIG	Walker WH	Bowen SE	Beresford J	Mort T	Tate JT	Brown G	Wood T	Mandley J	Chester RA	Callaghan E	Brocklebank RE	Gardner T	MATCH
1	2	3	4	5	6	7	8	9	10	11														1
1	2	3	4	5		7	8	9	10	11	6													2
1	2	3	4	5		7	8	9	10	11	6													3
1	2	3	4	5		7	8	9		11	6	10												4
1	2	3	4	5		7	8	9		11	6	10												5
1		3	4	5		7	8	9		11	6	10	2											6
1		3	4	5	6	7	8	9		11		10	2											7
1	2	3	4	5	6	7	8	9		11		10												8
1	2	3	4	5	6	7	10	9		11			8											9
1	2	3	4	5	6	7	10	9		11			8											10
1		3		5	6	7	10	9		11	4		8	2										11
1				5	6	7	10	9		11	4		8	2										12
1		3		5	6	7	10	9		11	4		8	2										13
1	2	3	4	5	6	7	10	9		11			8											14
1	2	3	4	5		7	10	9		11	6		8											15
1	2	3	4	5		7	10	9		11			8		6									16
1	3			5	4	11	8	9		7	6				10	2								17
1	2			5	6	11	10	7	8		4					3	9							18
1	2		4	5		11	10	7	8							3	9	6						19
1	2	3	4			11	10	9	8		5							6	7					20
1	2	3	4			11	10	9	8		5							6	7					21
1	2	3	4				10	9	8		5							6	7	11				22
1	2		4			11	10	9	8		5				3			6	7					23
1	2		4			11	10	9	8		5				3			6	7					24
1	2		4			11	10	9	8		5				3			6	7					25
1	2	3		5		7		9	10	11	4		8					6						26
1		3		5		7	9		10	11	4		8	2				6						27
1	2	3	4			7	9		10	11	5				8			6						28
1	2	3				7	9		10		4				8			6		11	5			29
1		3				7			10	11	4			2	9			6		5	8			30
1		3		5		7	9		10	11			8	2				6				4		31
1		3		5		7	9		10	11			8	2		9	6					4		32
1	2	3	5			7		9	10	11	4		8									4		33
1	2	3		5		7	9		10	11	6		8									4		34
1	2	3		5		7	9		10	11	6		8									4		35
1	2	3		5		7	9		10	11	6		8									4		36
1	2	3	5			7	9		10	11	6									8		4		37
1	2	3	5			7	9		10	11	6									8		4		38
1	2	3		5		7	9		10	11	6											4		39
1	2	3	5			7	9		10	11	6		8									4		40
1	2	3	5			7	9		10	11	6		8									4		41
1	2	3	5			7	9		10	11	6		8									4		42
42	33	36	27	27	11	41	38	27	28	33	32	5	21	13	1	6	14	6	2	2	3	12		
				2		19	25	14	5	5			4					2	2					

1	2		4	5		7	9		10	11			8	3			6							
1	2			5		7	10	9		11	4		8	3			6							
1		2		5		7	9		10	11	4		8	3			6							
1	2	3		5		7	9		10	11	4		8				6							
1	2	3		5		7	9		10	11	4		8				6							
1	2	3		5		7	9		10	11	4		8				6							
6	5	4		1		6	6	1	5	6	5		6	3			6							
							4	8			2			1										

FINAL LEAGUE TABLE

	P	W	D	L	F	A	P
Arsenal	42	25	9	8	75	47	59
Huddersfield Town	42	23	10	9	90	61	56
Tottenham Hotspur	42	21	7	14	79	56	49
Derby County	42	17	11	14	68	54	45
Manchester City	42	17	11	14	65	72	45
Sunderland	42	16	12	14	81	56	44
West Bromwich A	42	17	10	15	78	70	44
Blackburn Rovers	42	18	7	17	74	81	43
Leeds United	42	17	8	17	75	66	42
Portsmouth	42	15	12	15	52	55	42
Sheffield Wednesday	42	16	9	17	62	67	41
Stoke City	42	15	11	16	58	71	41
Aston Villa	**42**	**14**	**12**	**16**	**78**	**75**	**40**
Everton	42	12	16	14	62	63	40
Wolverhampton W	42	14	12	16	74	86	40
Middlesbrough	42	16	7	19	68	80	39
Leicester City	42	14	11	17	59	74	39
Liverpool	42	14	10	18	79	87	38
Chelsea	42	14	8	20	67	69	36
Birmingham City	42	12	12	18	54	56	36
Newcastle United	42	10	14	18	68	77	34
Sheffield United	42	12	7	23	58	101	31

1934/35

SEASON SNIPPETS

Aston Villa appointed their first Team Manager, Mr James McMullan, who was introduced at the Annual General Meeting on Friday 29 June.

In June, Villa paid a British record transfer fee of £10,775 to bring Jimmy Allen from Portsmouth. Allen made his debut against Birmingham on 25 August, as did George Beeson.

Fred Butcher made his debut on 22 September, but his last first-team match came the following week. Both games were won. On 23 January, Butcher suffered a fractured leg in a mid-week league game at Derby County.

Jimmy McLuckie made his debut on 15 December following a £6,500 move from Manchester City.

Billy Simpson's last game was against Grimsby Town on 6 October.

Alec Talbot played his last game on 29 December.

The FA Cup defeat by Bradford City on 12 January was Reg Chester's last game.

Tommy Mort played his last game on 19 January.

Frank Broome made his debut at Portsmouth on 6 April.

DIVISION ONE

MANAGER: James McMullan

MATCH	DATE	VENUE	OPPONENTS	RESULT	HT SCORE	SCORE	SCORERS	ATT
1	Aug 25	A	Birmingham	L	0 1	1 2	Waring	53,930
2	27	H	Wolverhampton Wanderers	W	1 0	2 1	Astley, Dix	34,666
3	Sep 1	H	Derby County	W	1 1	3 2	Houghton, Waring 2	44,267
4	3	A	Wolverhampton Wanderers	L	1 2	2 5	Dix, Houghton	29,147
5	8	A	Leicester City	L	0 1	0 5		28,548
6	15	H	Sunderland	D	1 0	1 1	Astley	45,138
7	22	A	Tottenham Hotspur	W	1 0	2 0	Waring, Houghton	42,088
8	29	H	Preston North End	W	1 1	4 2	Astley 3, Waring	28,781
9	Oct 6	A	Grimsby Town	L	1 4	1 5	Astley	17,732
10	13	H	Everton	D	1 1	2 2	Astley, Waring	37,707
11	20	A	Stoke City	L	0 0	1 4	Waring	33,744
12	27	H	Manchester City	W	4 1	4 2	Astley, Waring 2, Houghton	38,136
13	Nov 3	A	West Bromwich Albion	D	1 2	2 2	Richardson (og), Houghton	44,644
14	10	H	Sheffield Wednesday	W	2 0	4 0	Waring 2, Astley 2	25,205
15	17	A	Arsenal	W	0 0	2 1	Houghton, Brocklebank	54,226
16	26	H	Portsmouth	W	2 1	5 4	Chester 2, Houghton 2 (1 pen), Brocklebank	17,309
17	Dec 1	A	Liverpool	L	1 0	1 3	Waring	23,646
18	8	H	Leeds United	D	1 0	1 1	J Milburn (og)	31,682
19	15	A	Middlesbrough	L	0 2	1 4	Astley	16,245
20	22	H	Blackburn Rovers	D	0 1	1 1	Waring	25,633
21	25	A	Chelsea	L	0 1	0 2		46,746
22	26	H	Chelsea	L	0 1	0 3		52,886
23	29	A	Birmingham	D	1 2	2 2	Astley, Waring	40,785
24	Jan 5	A	Derby County	D	1 1	1 2	Houghton	24,674
25	19	H	Leicester City	W	3 0	5 0	Astley 3, Cunliffe, Beresford	27,608
26	Feb 2	H	Tottenham Hotspur	W	0 0	1 0	Dix	36,973
27	6	A	Sunderland	D	2 2	3 3	Cunliffe, Beresford, Dix	14,904
28	9	A	Preston North End	D	0 0	0 0		32,536
29	16	H	Grimsby Town	W	3 1	3 2	Houghton, Kingdon, Astley	32,020
30	23	A	Everton	D	1 1	2 2	Astley 2	30,772
31	Mar 2	H	Stoke City	W	1 1	4 1	Dix, Astley 3	33,308
32	9	A	Manchester City	L	1 0	1 4	Houghton	33,367
33	23	H	Sheffield Wednesday	L	1 2	1 2	Cunliffe	12,495
34	30	H	Arsenal	L	0 3	1 3	Houghton	59,572
35	Apr 3	H	West Bromwich Albion	L	1 1	2 3	Dix, Watkin	19,549
36	6	A	Portsmouth	W	0 0	1 0	Watkin	20,813
37	13	H	Liverpool	W	2 1	4 2	Cunliffe, Watkin, Broome 2	23,637
38	19	H	Huddersfield Town	D	1 1	1 1	Watkin	27,505
39	20	A	Leeds United	D	1 0	1 1	Kingdon	16,234
40	24	A	Huddersfield Town	D	0 0	1 1	Broome	7,727
41	27	H	Middlesbrough	L	0 1	0 3		15,685
42	May 4	A	Blackburn Rovers	L	0 1	0 5		5,921

Final League Position: 13th in First Division

Appearances

2 Own-goals   Goals

FA CUP

3	Jan 12	H	Bradford City	L	0 2	1 3	Hamilton (og)	30,795

Appearances

1 Own-goal   Goals

378

Players (columns)

Morton H | Beeson GW | Mort T | Gardner T | Allen JP | Gibson JD | Houghton WE | Astley DJ | Waring T | Dix RW | Cunliffe A | Kingdon WIG | Beresford J | Wood T | Blair D | Watkin AD | Brown G | Butcher FW | Simpson WS | Talbot AD | Brocklebank RE | Chester RA | McLuckie JS | Callaghan E | Broome FH

Match	Lineup
1	1 2 3 4 5 6 7 8 9 10 11
2	1 2 3 4 5 6 7 8 9 10 11
3	1 2 3 4 5 — 11 — 9 10 7 6 8
4	1 2 3 — 5 — 11 — 9 10 7 6 8 4
5	1 2 — — 5 4 11 — 8 10 — 6 — — — 3 7 9
6	1 2 — — 4 5 6 11 10 9 — — 8 — — 3 7
7	1 — — 4 5 — 11 10 9 — — — 8 — — 2 7 — 3 6
8	1 — — — 5 4 11 10 9 — — — 8 — — 2 7 — 3 6
9	1 2 — 4 5 — 11 10 9 — — — 8 — — — 3 7 — — 6
10	1 2 — 4 5 — — 7 10 9 — 11 6 8 — 3
11	1 2 — 4 — — 11 10 9 8 7 6 — 3 — — — 5
12	1 2 — 4 — — 11 10 9 — 7 6 — 3 — — — 5 8
13	1 2 — 4 — — 11 10 9 — 7 6 — 3 — — — 5 8
14	1 2 — 4 — — — 10 9 — 7 6 — 3 — — — 5 8 11
15	1 2 — 4 — — 7 10 9 — — 6 — 3 — — — 5 8 11
16	1 2 — 4 — — 7 10 9 — — 6 — 3 — — — 5 8 11
17	1 2 — 4 — — 7 10 9 — — 6 — 3 — — — 5 8 11
18	1 2 — 4 — — 7 10 9 — — 6 — 3 — — — 5 8 11
19	1 2 — — 5 — 7 10 9 — — 4 8 3 — — — — — 11 6
20	1 2 — — 5 4 7 10 9 — — 6 8 3 — — — — — 11
21	1 2 — 4 5 — 11 10 9 — — 6 — 3 7
22	1 2 — 4 — — 11 10 9 — — 6 — 3 7 — — 5 8
23	1 2 — 4 — — 7 10 9 — — 6 — 3 — — — 5 8 11
24	1 2 — 4 — — 7 10 9 — — 6 — 3 — — — — 8 11
25	1 2 3 4 5 — 7 — 9 10 11 6 8
26	1 2 — 4 5 — 7 — 9 10 11 6 8 3
27	1 2 — 4 5 — 7 — 9 10 11 6 8
28	1 2 — 4 5 — 7 — 9 10 11 6 8
29	1 2 — 4 5 — 7 — 9 10 11 6 8 3
30	1 2 — 4 5 — 7 — 9 10 11 6 8
31	1 2 — — 5 4 7 — 9 10 11 6 8 3
32	1 2 — — 5 4 7 — 9 10 11 6 8 3
33	1 2 — 4 5 — 9 — 7
34	1 2 — — 5 4 7 — 9 10 11 6 8 3
35	1 2 — — 5 4 8 — 9 10 11 6 3 7
36	1 2 — — — 5 — 8 — 10 11 6 3 7 — — — — — — 4 9
37	1 2 — 4 5 — 8 — — 10 11 6 3 7 — — — — — — — 9
38	1 2 — 4 5 — 8 — — 10 11 6 3 7 — — — — — — — 9
39	1 2 — 4 5 — 7 — — 10 11 6 8 3 — — — — — — — 9
40	1 2 — 4 5 — 7 — — 10 11 6 — 3 — — — — — — — 9
41	1 2 — 4 5 — 7 — — 10 11 6 8 3 — — — — — — — 9
42	1 2 — 4 5 — — — 11 9 10 6 — 3 — — — — — — — 7

Totals: 42 40 5 31 33 11 41 28 24 24 26 36 23 1 37 11 1 2 3 10 11 9 1 1 7
         — — — — — — 12 21 14 6 4 2 2 — — 4 — — — — 2 2 — — 3

Cup: 1 2 — 4 5 — 7 10 9 — 6 — 3 — — — — — — 8 11 (3)

Sub: 1 1 — — 1 1 — — 1 1 1 — 1 — 1 — — — — — 1 1

FINAL LEAGUE TABLE

	P	W	D	L	F	A	P
Arsenal	42	23	12	7	115	46	58
Sunderland	42	19	16	7	90	51	54
Sheffield Wednesday	42	18	13	11	70	64	49
Manchester City	42	20	8	14	82	67	48
Grimsby Town	42	17	11	14	78	60	45
Derby County	42	18	9	15	81	66	45
Liverpool	42	19	7	16	85	88	45
Everton	42	16	12	14	89	88	44
West Bromwich A	42	17	10	15	83	83	44
Stoke City	42	18	6	18	71	70	42
Preston North End	42	15	12	15	62	67	42
Chelsea	42	16	9	17	73	82	41
Aston Villa	**42**	**14**	**13**	**15**	**74**	**88**	**41**
Portsmouth	42	15	10	17	71	72	40
Blackburn Rovers	42	14	11	17	66	78	39
Huddersfield Town	42	14	10	18	76	71	38
Wolverhampton W	42	15	8	19	88	94	38
Leeds United	42	13	12	17	75	92	38
Birmingham City	42	13	10	19	63	81	36
Middlesbrough	42	10	14	18	70	90	34
Leicester City	42	12	9	21	61	86	33
Tottenham Hotspur	42	10	10	22	54	93	30

1935/36

SEASON SNIPPETS

On 14 September, Norman Young, who had signed for the Club in April 1926 from Redditch United, came in for his first game, a 5-1 home win against Preston North End.

In the evening of 7 October, George Burrell Ramsay died while staying at Llandrindod Wells.

The home game against Bolton Wanderers on 12 October was Tom 'Pongo' Waring's last game.

Manager James McMullan left the Club prior to the game with Leeds United on 26 October, Frank Barson was appointed coach. Pongo Waring requested a transfer.

George Cummings made his debut against Chelsea on 16 November along with Jackie Palethorpe and Charlie Drinkwater. For Tom Griffiths, who had first played at Liverpool the previous week, it was his home debut.

Jackie Williams scored twice on his debut in a 4-0 win against Stoke on 30 November.

It was not a happy debut for Alex Massie at Manchester on 7 December - Villa lost 5-0.

Jack Maund came in for his first game on 18 January when Villa played Preston North End as did Gordon Hodgson who arrived from Liverpool.

Charlie Phillips came from Wolves in January and sealed his debut against Derby County on 1 February by scoring Villa's equalising goal in a 3-1 away win.

In addition to Waring, Joe Beresford, Dennis Watkin, Arthur Cunliffe, Charlie Drinkwater, Norman Young, Bob Brocklebank, Jackie Palethorpe, Jimmy McLuckie, Danny Blair, Jimmy Gibson, Billy Kingdon and Jackie Williams all played their last Villa games during the season.

DIVISION ONE

MANAGER: James McMullan (to October 1935)

MATCH	DATE	VENUE	OPPONENTS	RESULT	HT SCORE	SCORE	SCORERS	ATT
1	Aug 31	H	Sheffield Wednesday	L	0 0	1 2	Cunliffe	48,637
2	Sep 4	A	Middlesbrough	W	1 0	2 1	Waring, Houghton	22,421
3	7	A	Portsmouth	L	0 1	0 3		33,775
4	9	H	Middlesbrough	L	0 5	2 7	Dix 2	19,109
5	14	H	Preston North End	W	2 1	5 1	Houghton (pen), Astley 2, Waring, Kingdon	31,501
6	16	H	Sunderland	D	1 1	2 2	Waring 2	24,717
7	21	A	Brentford	W	2 1	2 1	Waring, Astley	29,781
8	28	H	Derby County	L	0 1	0 2		49,474
9	Oct 5	A	Everton	D	0 2	2 2	Broome 2	26,682
10	12	H	Bolton Wanderers	L	0 1	1 2	Houghton (pen)	36,297
11	19	H	West Bromwich Albion	L	0 4	0 7		43,411
12	26	A	Leeds United	L	2 1	2 4	Astley, Dix (pen)	19,358
13	Nov 2	H	Grimsby Town	L	0 3	2 6	McLuckie, Houghton	35,311
14	9	A	Liverpool	L	1 2	2 3	Houghton, Broome	31,898
15	16	H	Chelsea	D	1 0	2 2	Palethorpe, Drinkwater	58,717
16	23	A	Birmingham	D	2 2	2 2	Astley 2	59,971
17	30	H	Stoke City	W	1 0	4 0	Dix, Williams 2, Houghton	43,283
18	Dec 7	A	Manchester City	L	0 3	0 5		40,588
19	14	H	Arsenal	L	0 3	1 7	Palethorpe	58,469
20	21	A	Blackburn Rovers	L	0 2	1 5	Broome	5,664
21	25	H	Huddersfield Town	W	2 1	4 1	Astley 3, Houghton	46,095
22	26	A	Huddersfield Town	L	1 2	1 4	Dix	19,316
23	28	A	Sheffield Wednesday	L	2 2	2 5	Houghton (pen), Williams	25,371
24	Jan 1	A	Sunderland	W	1 0	3 1	Dix 2, Massie	34,476
25	4	H	Portsmouth	W	2 1	4 2	Astley 2, Houghton 2 (2 pens)	44,152
26	18	A	Preston North End	L	0 0	0 3		23,178
27	25	H	Brentford	D	1 0	2 2	Williams, Astley	40,328
28	Feb 1	A	Derby County	W	2 1	3 1	Phillips, Williams, Astley	30,087
29	8	H	Everton	D	1 1	1 1	Astley	53,837
30	15	A	Bolton Wanderers	L	1 3	3 4	Hodgson, Astley, Houghton (pen)	30,834
31	29	H	Liverpool	W	1 0	3 0	Hodgson, Maund, Astley	18,703
32	Mar 7	A	Stoke City	W	3 1	3 2	Astley 2, Phillips	16,744
33	14	H	Leeds United	D	2 2	3 3	Astley, Massie, Maund	37,382
34	21	A	Chelsea	L	0 1	0 1		48,761
35	28	H	Birmingham	W	0 0	2 1	Hughes (og), Broome	49,531
36	Apr 1	H	West Bromwich Albion	W	1 0	3 0	Broome 2, Astley	28,821
37	4	A	Grimsby Town	L	1 2	1 4	Broome	10,413
38	10	H	Wolverhampton Wanderers	W	2 1	4 2	Houghton, Broome 2, Astley	50,164
39	11	H	Manchester City	D	2 1	2 2	Houghton, Hodgson	41,638
40	13	A	Wolverhampton Wanderers	D	2 1	2 2	Hodgson, Houghton	44,579
41	18	A	Arsenal	L	0 0	0 1		55,431
42	25	H	Blackburn Rovers	L	1 3	2 4	Broome, Houghton (pen)	27,378

Final League Position: 21st in First Division

1 Own-goal

Appearances
Goals

FA CUP

3	Jan 11	H	Huddersfield Town	L	0 0	0 1		62,600

Appearances
Goals

Player Appearances

Match	Morton H	Beeson GW	Blair D	Kingdon WIG	Allen JP	McLuckie JS	Houghton WE	Waring T	Astley DJ	Dix RW	Cunliffe A	Beresford J	Gardner T	Young NJ	Watkin AD	Gibson JD	Broome FH	Biddlestone TF	Brocklebank RE	Griffiths TP	Cummings GW	Wood T	Palethorpe JT	Drinkwater CJ	Williams JJ	Massie AC	Maund JH	Hodgson G	Callaghan E	Phillips C
1	1	2	3	4	5	6	7	8	9	10	11																			
2	1	2	3	4	5	6	7	9	8	10	11																			
3	1	2	3	4	5	6	7	9		10	11	8																		
4	1	2		3	5	6	7	9		10	11	8	4																	
5	1	2		4	5	6	11	8	9	10				3	7															
6	1	2		6	5		11	8	9	10			4	3	7															
7	1	2		6	5		11	9	8	10				3	7	4														
8	1	2	3	6	5			8	9	10	11		4		7															
9	1	2	3	6	5	10	11	9	8				4		7															
10	1	2	3	6	5	10	11	9	8				4		7															
11		2	3		5	6	7		10		11		4	9	1	8														
12	1	2		6	5	10		9	8	11		3	4		7															
13	1	2	3	6	5	10	7	9	8	11			4																	
14	1				6	7		8	10	11		4	2		9		5													
15	1		3			7		8	10			4	2				5	3	6	9	11									
16	1					7		8	10			4	2				5	3	6	9	11									
17	1				6			8	10		11		2				5	3	4	9		7								
18	1				6			8	10		11		2				5	3		9		7	4							
19	1	2						8	10		11						5	3		9		7	4							
20	1	2						8	10		11			9			5	3	6			7	4							
21				5			11	9	10							1	8	2	3	6		7	4							
22				5			11	9	10							1	8	2	3	6		7	4							
23				5			11	9	10							1	8	2	3	6		7	4							
24			4	5			11		10									2	3	6	9	7	8							
25	1		4	5			11	9	10									2	3	6		7	8							
26			4	5			11		10							1		2	3	6		8	7	9						
27				5			11	9	10							1		2	3	6		7	4	8						
28	2						11	9								1			3	6		7	4		10	5	8			
29	2						11	9								1			3	6		7	4		10	5	8			
30							11	9	10							1		2	3			4			10	5	7			
31							11	9								1		2	3	6		4	7		10	5	8			
32							11	9								1		2	3	6		4	7		10	5	8			
33							11	9								1		2	3	6		4	7		10	5	8			
34				5	10	11		9										2	3	6		4		7			8			
35							11		10						9	1		2	3	6		4			8	5	7			
36							11		10						9	1		2	3	6			4		8	5	7			
37		3	6				11		10			4			9	1		2							8	5	7			
38			6				11		10						9	1		2	3			4			8	5	7			
39							11		10					4	9	1		2	3			7	6		8	5				
40							11		10					4	9	1		2	3			7	4		8	5				
41							11		10						9	1		2	3			7	4		8	5				
42				6	5		11		10	8					9	1		2	3			7	4							
	21	15	12	19	22	14	40	10	38	26	9	2	5	9	2	10	16	21	4	27	27	21	6	2	17	24	4	15	13	11
						1		1	15	5	21	7	1				11						1		5	4	2	4		2

Bottom rows (cup/other):

| 1 | | | 4 | 5 | | 11 | | 9 | 10 | | | 7 | | | 2 | 3 | 6 | | | 8 | | | | | | | | | | |
| 1 | | | 1 | 1 | | 1 | | 1 | 1 | | | 1 | | | 1 | 1 | 1 | | | 1 | | | | | | | | | | |

FINAL LEAGUE TABLE   3

	P	W	D	L	F	A	P
Sunderland	42	25	6	11	109	74	56
Derby County	42	18	12	12	61	52	48
Huddersfield Town	42	18	12	12	59	56	48
Stoke City	42	20	7	15	57	57	47
Brentford	42	17	12	13	81	60	46
Arsenal	42	15	15	12	78	48	45
Preston North End	42	18	8	16	67	64	44
Chelsea	42	15	13	14	65	72	43
Manchester City	42	17	8	17	68	60	42
Portsmouth	42	17	8	17	54	67	42
Leeds United	42	15	11	16	66	64	41
Birmingham City	42	15	11	16	61	63	41
Bolton Wanderers	42	14	13	15	67	76	41
Middlesbrough	42	15	10	17	84	70	40
Wolverhampton W	42	15	10	17	77	76	40
Everton	42	13	13	16	89	89	39
Grimsby Town	42	17	5	20	65	73	39
West Bromwich A	42	16	6	20	89	88	38
Liverpool	42	13	12	17	60	64	38
Sheffield Wednesday	42	13	12	17	63	77	38
Aston Villa	**42**	**13**	**9**	**20**	**81**	**110**	**35**
Blackburn Rovers	42	12	9	21	55	96	33

1936/37

SEASON SNIPPETS

Prior to Villa's first league game outside the top flight at Swansea on 29 August, the teams lined up in the centre while the Welsh National Anthem was sung. Albert Kerr made his debut.

On 14 September, South African-born Gordon Hodgson became the first player born outside the British Isles to score a league hat-trick for Villa.

Three players made their debut in the match with Coventry City on 3 October, Bill Cobley, George Hardy and Jackie Martin.

The record attendance of 43,596 at Home Park for the match on 10 October still stands. Receipts were £2,672.

James Robey and Matt Moralee made their debut at Bradford Park Avenue on 17 October.

Bob Iverson and Freddie Haycock both made their debut in the 3-0 win against Norwich City on 19 December.

Ronnie Starling's first game was against Burnley on 9 January.

George Pritty's debut was against Blackpool on 20 March.

The 4-0 home defeat by Bury on 3 April was Freddie Goss' first game and the 2-0 home defeat by West Ham two weeks later was his last match.

Goss was one of ten players who made their final Villa appearance during the season, the others were Tommy Wood, Dai Astley, James Robey, Gordon Hodgson, Ronnie Dix, Harry Morton, Matt Moralee and Tom Griffiths.

DIVISION TWO

MANAGER: James Hogan (from August 1936)

MATCH	DATE	VENUE	OPPONENTS	RESULT	HT SCORE	SCORE	SCORERS	ATT
1	Aug 29	A	Swansea Town	W	1 0	2 1	Broome 2	25,189
2	Sep 2	A	Nottingham Forest	D	0 1	1 1	Broome	35,122
3	5	H	Southampton	W	1 0	4 0	Broome, Astley, Hodgson, Dix	41,934
4	7	H	Nottingham Forest	D	1 1	1 1	Astley	27,882
5	12	A	Burnley	W	2 1	2 1	Broome, Hodgson	16,098
6	14	H	Bradford City	W	3 1	5 1	Dix, Hodgson 3, Astley	21,979
7	19	H	Fulham	L	0 1	0 3		48,589
8	26	A	Doncaster Rovers	L	0 0	0 1		23,426
9	Oct 3	H	Coventry City	D	0 0	0 0		63,686
10	10	A	Plymouth Argyle	D	1 1	2 2	Broome, Astley	43,596
11	17	A	Bradford Park Avenue	D	1 1	3 3	Houghton, Broome, Johnstone (og)	12,001
12	24	H	Barnsley	W	1 1	4 2	Broome 2, Astley, Houghton	37,951
13	31	H	Sheffield United	L	1 1	1 5	Houghton (pen)	30,480
14	Nov 7	H	Tottenham Hotspur	D	0 1	1 1	Moralee	37,220
15	11	A	Bradford City	D	0 0	2 2	Griffiths, Dix	7,883
16	14	A	Blackpool	W	1 2	3 2	Houghton 2 (1 pen), Hodgson	15,694
17	21	H	Blackburn Rovers	D	1 1	2 2	Dix, Houghton	32,153
18	28	A	Bury	L	0 2	1 2	Hodgson	23,325
19	Dec 5	A	Leicester City	L	0 1	1 3	Massie	29,981
20	19	H	Norwich City	W	2 0	3 0	Broome, Dix, Maund	23,763
21	25	A	Chesterfield	L	0 1	0 1		19,795
22	26	H	Swansea Town	W	0 0	4 0	Dix 3, Allen	54,163
23	28	H	Chesterfield	W	2 0	6 2	Broome 2, Dix 2, Allen, Iverson	29,217
24	Jan 2	A	Southampton	D	1 1	2 2	Dix 2	20,853
25	9	H	Burnley	D	0 0	0 0		37,691
26	23	H	Fulham	L	1 2	2 3	Haycock, Gardner	15,840
27	30	H	Doncaster Rovers	D	0 1	1 1	Phillips	13,252
28	Feb 6	A	Coventry City	L	0 1	0 1		39,828
29	13	H	Plymouth Argyle	W	2 3	5 4	Houghton 3 (2 pens), Broome 2	40,956
30	20	H	Bradford Park Avenue	W	2 0	4 1	Houghton 2, Broome 2	28,775
31	27	A	Barnsley	W	2 0	4 0	Starling 2, Broome, Haycock	16,485
32	Mar 6	A	Sheffield United	W	2 1	2 1	Broome 2	32,009
33	13	A	Tottenham Hotspur	D	1 2	2 2	Haycock, Starling	35,652
34	20	H	Blackpool	W	2 0	4 0	Broome 3, Haycock	54,860
35	26	A	Newcastle United	W	1 0	2 0	Broome 2	46,213
36	27	A	Blackburn Rovers	W	3 2	4 3	Broome 3, Houghton	25,394
37	30	H	Newcastle United	L	0 1	0 2		65,437
38	Apr 3	H	Bury	L	0 2	0 4		46,872
39	10	A	Leicester City	L	0 0	0 1		37,112
40	17	H	West Ham United	L	0 0	0 2		19,908
41	24	A	Norwich City	L	0 3	1 5	Broome	25,052
42	May 26	A	West Ham United	L	0 2	1 2	Starling (pen)	11,558

Final League Position: 9th in Second Division

1 Own-goal

Appearances
Goals

FA CUP

3	Jan 16	H	Burnley	L	1 2	2 3	Houghton, Broome	43,668

Appearances
Goals

382

FINAL LEAGUE TABLE

	P	W	D	L	F	A	P
Leicester City	42	24	8	10	89	57	56
Blackpool	42	24	7	11	88	53	55
Bury	42	22	8	12	74	55	52
Newcastle United	42	22	5	15	80	56	49
Plymouth Argyle	42	18	13	11	71	53	49
West Ham United	42	19	11	12	73	55	49
Sheffield United	42	18	10	14	66	54	46
Coventry City	42	17	11	14	66	54	45
Aston Villa	**42**	**16**	**12**	**14**	**82**	**70**	**44**
Tottenham Hotspur	42	17	9	16	88	66	43
Fulham	42	15	13	14	71	61	43
Blackburn Rovers	42	16	10	16	70	62	42
Burnley	42	16	10	16	57	61	42
Barnsley	42	16	9	17	50	64	41
Chesterfield	42	16	8	18	84	89	40
Swansea Town	42	15	7	20	50	65	37
Norwich City	42	14	8	20	63	71	36
Nottingham Forest	42	12	10	20	68	90	34
Southampton	42	11	12	19	53	77	34
Bradford Park Av	42	12	9	21	52	88	33
Bradford City	42	9	12	21	54	94	30
Doncaster Rovers	42	7	10	25	30	84	24

1937/38

SEASON SNIPPETS

On 18 September, Frank Shell made his debut at Sheffield Wednesday.

Goalkeeper Bill Carey kept a clean sheet on his debut against Newcastle United on 16 October. It was also Jim Clayton's first Villa game.

The home game against Burnley on 13 November was the first of Jeff Barker's three Villa appearances.

On Christmas Eve, the presentation of a smoker's cabinet was made by the captain, Jimmy Allen, on behalf of the first-team to Mr James Hogan.

Villa's Christmas Day home game against Bradford Park Avenue was postponed because of fog.

Mr James Hogan presented ties to each of the players on Christmas morning.

Charlie Phillips made his last appearance against West Ham on New Year's Day.

Tommy Gardner played his last game against Newcastle United on 26 February.

George Hardy scored his only Villa goal in his last game, at home to Nottingham Forest on 9 March.

The 1-0 win at Coventry on 12 March was George Pritty's last game.

Jack Maund's last match was at Swansea Town on 18 April.

DIVISION TWO

MANAGER: James Hogan

MATCH	DATE	VENUE	OPPONENTS	RESULT	HT SCORE	SCORE	SCORERS	ATT
1	Aug 28	H	West Ham United	W	2 0	2 0	Haycock, Maund	50,539
2	Sep 1	A	Luton Town	L	1 2	2 3	Maund, Massie	25,349
3	4	A	Southampton	D	0 0	0 0		25,670
4	6	H	Luton Town	W	4 1	4 1	Broome 2, Phillips 2	30,439
5	11	H	Blackburn Rovers	W	2 1	2 1	Haycock, Maund	44,008
6	16	A	Norwich City	L	0 0	0 1		23,039
7	18	A	Sheffield Wednesday	W	1 1	2 1	Haycock, Iverson	20,663
8	25	H	Fulham	W	1 0	2 0	Broome, Haycock	42,224
9	Oct 2	A	Plymouth Argyle	W	1 0	3 0	Broome 2, Houghton	29,922
10	9	H	Chesterfield	L	0 0	0 2		50,621
11	16	H	Newcastle United	W	0 0	2 0	Houghton 2	50,192
12	23	A	Nottingham Forest	W	0 0	2 0	Broome, Houghton	24,254
13	30	A	Coventry City	D	0 1	1 1	Houghton	67,271
14	Nov 6	A	Bury	D	1 1	1 1	Haycock	17,221
15	13	H	Burnley	D	0 0	0 0		37,167
16	20	A	Manchester United	L	0 2	1 3	Iverson	33,193
17	27	H	Sheffield United	W	1 0	1 0	Clayton	39,138
18	Dec 4	A	Tottenham Hotspur	L	0 1	1 2	Houghton	37,238
19	11	H	Stockport County	W	4 1	7 1	Shell 3, Houghton (pen), Haycock, Broome 2	27,500
20	18	A	Barnsley	W	1 0	1 0	Shell	15,500
21	27	A	Bradford Park Avenue	W	0 1	2 1	Shell, Haycock	20,129
22	28	H	Barnsley	W	1 0	3 0	Massie, Broome 2	40,360
23	Jan 1	A	West Ham United	D	0 0	1 1	Weare (og)	30,408
24	15	H	Southampton	W	1 0	3 0	Haycock 2, Houghton	31,279
25	27	A	Blackburn Rovers	L	0 0	0 1		11,919
26	29	H	Sheffield Wednesday	W	2 1	4 3	Starling 2, Houghton (pen), Broome	35,603
27	Feb 5	A	Fulham	D	1 0	1 1	Houghton	38,608
28	19	A	Chesterfield	W	0 0	1 0	Broome	18,454
29	23	H	Plymouth Argyle	W	2 0	3 0	Broome, Maund, Haycock	21,214
30	26	A	Newcastle United	L	0 2	0 2		48,434
31	Mar 9	H	Nottingham Forest	L	0 0	1 2	Hardy	22,596
32	12	A	Coventry City	W	0 0	1 0	Starling	44,930
33	19	H	Bury	W	0 1	2 1	Broome, Haycock	51,364
34	Apr 2	H	Manchester United	W	1 0	3 0	Broome, Maund, Houghton (pen)	54,654
35	5	A	Burnley	L	0 1	0 3		16,704
36	9	A	Sheffield United	D	0 0	0 0		29,155
37	16	H	Tottenham Hotspur	W	1 0	2 0	Broome 2	53,730
38	18	A	Swansea Town	L	0 1	1 2	Starling	25,250
39	19	H	Swansea Town	W	1 0	4 0	Iverson, Shell 2, Houghton	47,070
40	23	A	Stockport County	W	2 1	3 1	Haycock, Broome 2	19,987
41	27	H	Bradford Park Avenue	W	2 0	2 0	Broome, Haycock	41,966
42	May 7	H	Norwich City	W	0 0	2 0	Shell, Haycock	42,021

Final League Position: 1st in Second Division

Appearances
Goals

FA CUP

3	Jan 8	A	Norwich City	W	2 1	3 2	Houghton, Haycock, Iverson	32,172
4	22	H	Blackpool	W	1 0	4 0	Houghton, Broome, Starling, Shell	69,000
5	Feb 12	A	Charlton Athletic	D	1 0	1 1	Shell	76,031
R	16	H	Charlton Athletic *	D	0 1	2 2	Broome, Shell	61,530
2R	21	N	Charlton Athletic **	W	0 1	4 1	Broome 3, Haycock	64,782
6	Mar 5	H	Manchester City	W	0 0	3 2	Broome, Haycock, Shell	75,500
SF	26	N	Preston North End ***	L	1 2	1 2	Shell	55,129

Appearances
Goals

* After extra-time
** Played at Highbury, London
*** played at Bramall Lane, Sheffield

Player appearances

	Biddlestone TF	Callaghan E	Cummings GW	Massie AC	Allen JP	Iverson RTJ	Phillips C	Haycock FJ	Broome FH	Starling RW	Maund JH	Shell FH	Houghton WE	Gardner T	Kerr AW	Carey WJ	Clayton JGT	Cobley WA	Barker J	Martin JR	Hardy G	Pritty GJ	MATCH
1	2	3	4	5	6	7	8	9	10	11													1
1	2	3	4	5	6	7	8	9	10	11													2
1	2	3	4	5	6	7	8	9	10	11													3
1	2	3	4	5	6	7	8	9	10	11													4
1	2	3	4	5	6	7	8	9	10	11													5
1	2	3	4	5	6	7	8	9	10	11													6
1	2	3	4	5	6	7	8		10				9	11									7
1	2	3		5	6		8	9	10					11	4	7							8
1	2	3	4	5	6		8	9	10					11		7							9
1	2	3		5	6	7	8	9	10					11									10
	2	3	4	5	6		8	7	10					11		1	9						11
1	2	3	4	5			8	7	10					11			9						12
1	2			5	6		8	7	10					11	4		9	3					13
1	2	3	4	5	6		8	7	10					11			9						14
1	2	3	4	5			8	7	10					11			9		6				15
1	2	3	4	5	6		8	7	10					11			9						16
1	2	3	4	5	9			7	8					11			10		6				17
1	2	3	4	5	9			7	8					11			10		6				18
1	2	3	4	5	6		8	7	10	9	11												19
1	2	3	4	5	6		8	7	10	9	11												20
1	2	3	4	5	6		8	7	10		11												21
1	2	3	4	5	6		8	7	10	9	11												22
1	2	3	4	5	6	9		7	10		11						8						23
1		3	4	5	6		8		10	9	11		7			2							24
			4	5			8	7	10	9	11					3							25
1	2		4	5	6		8	7	10	9	11					3							26
1	2	3	4	5	6		8	7	10	9	11												27
			4	5	6		8	7	10	9	11			1		3							28
	2	3	4	5	6		8	7	10	11	9			1									29
1	2	3	4	5			8	7	10		11	6				9							30
1	2		4				8	7	10	9	11					3		5	6				31
1	2		4				8	7	10	9	11					3			5				32
1	2	3	4	5	6		8	7	10	11	9												33
1	2	3	4	5	6		8	9	10	7	11												34
1	2	3	4	5	6		8		10	7	9	11											35
1	2	3	4	5	6		8		10	7	9	11											36
1	2	3	4	5	6		8	9	10	7	11												37
1	2	3	4	5	6		8	9	10	7	11												38
1	2	3	4	5	6		8	7	10		11	9											39
1	2	3	4	5	6		8	7	10		11	9											40
1	2	3	4	5	6		8	7	10		11	9											41
1		3	4	5	6		8	7	10		11	9				2							42
39	40	36	40	40	39	9	39	38	42	13	20	34	3	3	3	9	8	3	1	1	2		
			2		3	2	14	20	4	5	8	12				1			1				

FA Cup

1	2	3	4	5	6		8	7	10			9	11										3
1	2	3	4	5	6		8	7	10			9	11										4
1	2	3	4	5	6		8	7	10			9	11										5
1	2	3	4	5	6		8	7	10			9	11										R
	2	3	4	5	6		8	7	10			9	11					1					2R
1	2		4	5			8	7	10			9	11			3			6				6
1	2	3	4	5	6		8	7	10			9	11										SF
6	7	6	7	7	6		7	7	7			7	7		1	1		1	1				
					1		3	6	1			5	2										

FINAL LEAGUE TABLE

	P	W	D	L	F	A	P
Aston Villa	42	25	7	10	73	35	57
Manchester United	42	22	9	11	82	50	53
Sheffield United	42	22	9	11	73	56	53
Coventry City	42	20	12	10	66	45	52
Tottenham Hotspur	42	19	6	17	76	54	44
Burnley	42	17	10	15	54	54	44
Bradford Park Avenue	42	17	9	16	69	56	43
Fulham	42	16	11	15	61	57	43
West Ham United	42	14	14	14	53	52	42
Bury	42	18	5	19	63	60	41
Chesterfield	42	16	9	17	63	63	41
Luton Town	42	15	10	17	89	86	40
Plymouth Argyle	42	14	12	16	57	65	40
Norwich City	42	14	11	17	56	75	39
Southampton	42	15	9	18	55	77	39
Blackburn Rovers	42	14	10	18	71	80	38
Sheffield Wednesday	42	14	10	18	49	56	38
Swansea Town	42	13	12	17	45	73	38
Newcastle United	42	14	8	20	51	58	36
Nottingham Forest	42	14	8	20	47	60	36
Barnsley	42	11	14	17	50	64	36
Stockport County	42	11	9	22	43	70	31

1938/39

SEASON SNIPPETS

On Saturday 20 August, Villa played West Bromwich Albion for the benefit of The Football League Jubilee Trust. Frank Broome was on target in a 1-1 draw before a Villa Park crowd of 26,640. Receipts were £1,514 1s 9d.

Jim Clayton played his last game was on 3 September.

On 5 September Frank Moss (Junior) made his league debut at centre-forward.

George Edwards made his debut at home to Manchester United on 5 November.

On 10 November, Frank O'Donnell was signed for £10,500 from Blackpool and made his debut two days later at Stoke.

Bob Iverson set a record by scoring on 9.6 seconds of the game against Charlton Athletic on 3 December.

Alan Wakeman made his debut in goal on 10 December.

Joe Rutherford made his debut at home to Birmingham on 4 March 1939. Rutherford was the last player to make his Villa league debut before World War Two.

On Monday 8 May, Villa won 3-2 with an O'Donnell hat-trick against Ipswich Town away to win the Ipswich Hospital Cup.

DIVISION ONE

MANAGER: James Hogan

MATCH	DATE	VENUE	OPPONENTS	RESULT	HT SCORE	SCORE	SCORERS	ATT
1	Aug 27	A	Grimsby Town	W	1 0	2 1	Broome 2	19,117
2	31	A	Middlesbrough	D	0 1	1 1	Houghton (pen)	29,281
3	Sep 3	H	Derby County	L	0 0	0 1		49,604
4	5	H	Everton	L	0 2	0 3		34,105
5	10	A	Blackpool	W	2 2	4 2	Haycock, Kerr, Martin 2	29,128
6	17	H	Brentford	W	1 0	5 0	Martin 2, Kerr 2, Houghton (pen)	49,092
7	24	A	Arsenal	D	0 0	0 0		66,456
8	Oct 1	H	Portsmouth	W	1 0	2 0	Kerr, Starling	49,282
9	8	A	Huddersfield Town	D	0 1	1 1	Broome	20,639
10	15	A	Liverpool	L	0 3	0 3		41,224
11	22	H	Leicester City	L	0 0	1 2	Haycock	46,233
12	29	A	Birmingham	L	0 0	0 3		55,301
13	Nov 5	H	Manchester United	L	0 0	0 2		38,357
14	12	A	Stoke City	L	1 1	1 3	Kirton (og)	29,633
15	19	H	Chelsea	W	3 1	6 2	Broome, Haycock 2, O'Donnell 2, Houghton (pen)	41,678
16	26	A	Preston North End	L	2 3	2 3	Haycock, Broome	21,002
17	Dec 3	H	Charlton Athletic	W	1 0	2 0	Iverson, O'Donnell	39,505
18	10	A	Bolton Wanderers	W	0 1	2 1	Houghton, Broome	22,552
19	17	H	Leeds United	W	1 0	2 1	O'Donnell, Houghton (pen)	28,990
20	24	H	Grimsby Town	L	0 0	0 2		25,195
21	26	A	Sunderland	W	1 0	5 1	O'Donnell, Broome 2, Haycock, Houghton	38,612
22	27	H	Sunderland	D	0 1	1 1	Broome	61,221
23	31	A	Derby County	L	0 1	1 2	Houghton	25,759
24	Jan 14	H	Blackpool	W	2 1	3 1	Houghton 2 (1 pen), Haycock	34,190
25	28	H	Arsenal	L	0 1	1 3	O'Donnell	57,453
26	Feb 4	A	Portsmouth	D	0 0	0 0		27,649
27	8	A	Brentford	W	1 0	4 2	Broome 2, O'Donnell, Haycock	21,162
28	15	H	Huddersfield Town	W	1 0	4 0	Broome, O'Donnell 2, Martin	22,820
29	18	H	Liverpool	W	2 0	2 0	Broome 2	39,705
30	25	A	Leicester City	D	1 0	1 1	O'Donnell	22,266
31	Mar 4	H	Birmingham	W	2 0	5 1	Martin 3, Houghton 2 (1 pen)	40,874
32	11	A	Manchester United	D	0 0	1 1	Broome	28,292
33	18	H	Stoke City	W	1 0	3 0	Broome, O'Donnell, Houghton	43,762
34	25	A	Chelsea	L	0 0	1 2	Haycock	31,225
35	Apr 1	H	Preston North End	W	1 0	3 0	Martin, O'Donnell 2	41,894
36	8	A	Charlton Athletic	L	0 1	0 1		35,540
37	10	A	Wolverhampton Wanderers	L	1 0	1 2	O'Donnell	50,962
38	15	H	Wolverhampton Wanderers	D	1 1	2 2	Iverson, Starling	51,311
39	15	A	Bolton Wanderers	L	0 1	1 3	Starling	23,160
40	22	A	Leeds United	L	0 0	0 2		14,241
41	29	H	Everton	L	0 3	0 3		23,667
42	May 6	H	Middlesbrough	D	0 0	1 1	Haycock	20,149

Final League Position: 12th in First Division

1 Own-goal

Appearances
Goals

FA CUP

3	Jan 7	H	Ipswich Town	D	0 0	1 1	Allen	34,910
R	11	A	Ipswich Town	W	0 0	2 1	Haycock 2	28,194
4	21	A	Preston North End	L	0 1	0 2		37,548

Appearances
Goals

Player Appearances Table

	Biddlestone TF	Callaghan E	Cummings GW	Massie AC	Allen JP	Iverson RTJ	Broome FH	Haycock FJ	Shell FH	Starling RW	Houghton WE	Kerr AW	Martin JR	Clayton JGT	Moss F (junr)	Cobley WA	Edwards GR	O'Donnell FJ	Wakeman AD	Rutherford JHH	MATCH
1	2	3	4	5	6	7	8	9	10	11											1
1	2	3	4	5	6				10	11	7	8	9								2
1	2	3	4	5	6				10	11	7	8	9								3
1	2	3	4	5	6		8		10	11	7		9								4
1	2	3	4	5	6		8		10	11	7	9									5
1	2	3	4	5	6	10	8			11	7	9									6
1	2	3	4	5	6		8		10	11	7	9									7
1	2	3	4	5	6	11	8		10		7	9									8
1	2		4	5	6	11	8		10		7	9									9
1	2	3	4	5	6		7	8	10			9									10
1	2	3	4	5	6		8		10	11	7	9									11
1	2	3	4	5	6	7	8	9	10	11											12
1	2	3	4	5	6	7	8	9			11			10							13
1	2	3	4	5	6	7	8		10	11					9						14
1	2	3	4	5	6	7	8		10	11					9						15
1	2	3	4	5	6	7	8		10	11					9						16
1	2	3	4	5	6	7	8		10	11					9						17
	2	3	4	5	6	7	8		10	11					9	1					18
	2	3	4	5	6	7	8		10	11					9	1					19
	2	3	4	5	6	7	8		10	11					9	1					20
	2	3	4	5	6	7	8		10	11					9	1					21
	2	3	4	5	6	7	8		10	11					9	1					22
	2	3	4	5	6	7	8		10	11					9	1					23
1	2	3	4	5	6	7	8		10	11					9						24
1	2	3	4		6	7	8		10	11			5		9						25
1	2	3	4	5	6	7	10				11	8			9						26
1	2	3	4	5	6	7	10				11	8			9						27
1	2	3	4	5	6	7	10				11	8			9						28
1	2	3	4	5	6	7	10				11	8			9						29
1	2	3	4	5	6	7	10				11	8			9						30
	2	3	4	5	6	7	10				11	8			9	1					31
	2	3	4	5	6	7	10				11	8			9	1					32
	2	3	4	5	6	7	10				11	8			9	1					33
1	2	3	4	5	6	7	10				11	8			9						34
	2	3	4	5	6	7			10	11		8			9	1					35
	2	3	4	5	6					11		8			9						36
	2	3	4	5	6		10				11	7	8		9						37
	2	3	4	5	6				10	11	7	8			9	1					38
	2	3	4	5	6		8		10	11	7			3	9	1					39
	2	3	4	5	6	7	8		10			11			9	1					40
	2	3	4	5	6	7	10		11						9	1	8				41
	2	3	4	5	6	11	10		7						9	1	8				42

25	42	40	42	41	42	33	38	3	28	35	16	22	2	2	2	3	29	6	11	
				2	16	10		3	12	4	9					14				

FA Cup

1	2	3	4	5	6	7	8		10	11					9						3 R
1	2	3	4	5	6	7	8		10	11					9						4
1	2	3	4	5	6	7	8	9	10	11											

| 3 | 3 | 3 | 3 | 3 | | 3 | 3 | 3 | 1 | 3 | 3 | | | | 2 | | | | | |
| | | | | | 1 | | | 2 | | | | | | | | | | | | |

FINAL LEAGUE TABLE

	P	W	D	L	F	A	P
Everton	42	27	5	10	88	52	59
Wolverhampton W	42	22	11	9	88	39	55
Charlton Athletic	42	22	6	14	75	59	50
Middlesbrough	42	20	9	13	93	74	49
Arsenal	42	19	9	14	55	41	47
Derby County	42	19	8	15	66	55	46
Stoke City	42	17	12	13	71	68	46
Bolton Wanderers	42	15	15	12	67	58	45
Preston North End	42	16	12	14	63	59	44
Grimsby Town	42	16	11	15	61	69	43
Liverpool	42	14	14	14	62	63	42
Aston Villa	**42**	**16**	**9**	**17**	**71**	**60**	**41**
Leeds United	42	16	9	17	59	67	41
Manchester United	42	11	16	15	57	65	38
Blackpool	42	12	14	16	56	68	38
Sunderland	42	13	12	17	54	67	38
Portsmouth	42	12	13	17	47	70	37
Brentford	42	14	8	20	53	74	36
Huddersfield Town	42	12	11	19	58	64	35
Chelsea	42	12	9	21	64	80	33
Birmingham City	42	12	8	22	62	84	32
Leicester City	42	9	11	22	48	82	29

1939/40

SEASON SNIPPETS

The home game against Middlesbrough on 26 August was the first time Aston Villa players had worn numbered shirts for a League match.

With the prospects of war looming, there were very few changes to the playing staff for the new season. Jack Maund had joined Nottingham Forest and Amos Moss had joined the professional ranks.

A friendly match was played at Leicester City on 16 September when Villa were defeated 3-0.

On 11 May, Aston Villa won a six-a-side Competition at St. Andrews. Villa Team: Wakeman, Callaghan, Lunn, Batty, Massie, Goffin.

The 15,000 attendance for the Harry Hibbs Testimonial was the maximum permitted wartime crowd for the ground.

On 27 April, Villa played a friendly at Chelmsford City, losing 2-1 with Albert Kerr was the Villa scorer.

DIVISION ONE

MANAGER: James Hogan

MATCH	DATE	VENUE	OPPONENTS	RESULT	HT SCORE	SCORE	SCORERS	ATT
1	Aug 26	H	Middlesbrough	W	1 0	2 0	Martin, Edwards	35,000
2	28	H	Everton	L	0 2	1 2	Cummings (pen)	30,000
3	Sep 2	A	Derby County	L	0 0	0 1		7,996

Final League Position:

Note: The Football League was suspended after the opening three games of the season
These three matches were later expunged from official records

Appearances
Goals

THE FOOTBALL LEAGUE JUBILEE TRUST FUND

	Aug 19	H	West Bromwich Albion	D	0 0	1 1	Houghton	15,000

Appearances
Goals

Game originally scheduled to be played at West Bromwich but switched to Villa Park because of alterations to the stand at The Hawthorns

HARRY HIBBS TESTIMONIAL MATCH

	Apr 13	A	Birmingham	L	0 1	1 2	Lunn	15,000

Appearances
Goals

Rutherford JHH	Callaghan E	Cummings GW	Massie AC	Allen JP	Iverson RTJ	Edwards GR	Martin JR	O'Donnell FJ	Haycock FJ	Broome FH	Carey WJ	Starling RW	Barker J	Kerr AW	Houghton WE	Billingsley G	Lunn G	Latham L		MATCH
1	2	3	4	5	6	7	8	9	10	11										1
	2	3	4	5	6	7	8	9		11	1	10								2
1	2	3	4	5	6	7	8	9		11		10								3

| 2 | 3 | 3 | 3 | 3 | 3 | 3 | 3 | 3 | 1 | 3 | 1 | 2 | | | | | | | |
| | 1 | | | | | 1 | 1 | | | | | | | | | | | | |

1	2	3	4	5			8	9	10		6	7	11						
1	1	1	1	1			1	1	1		1	1	1						
													1						

		3	4		6	8			10	9		7	11	1	2	5			
		1	1		1	1			1	1		1	1	1	1	1			
										1									

1940/41

SEASON SNIPPETS

The game against Revo Electric on 21 September was played at Tividale. Dickie Davis, who scored a hat-trick, was a former Sutton Town player who was on Sunderland's books.

Villa's first home game was played at Solihull Town Ground which was then situated in Shirley where, it was announced, Villa would play all home games.

When Villa played RAF Bridgnorth on 15 February, Corporal Eric Houghton was in the opposition team and pulled a goal back for the RAF after 65 minutes.

Villa travelled to Worcester on 21 December with only ten players. Worcester City's Player Manager Syd Gibbons helped out, playing right-half for Villa.

Villa travelled to Worcester a man short again on 15 March 1941. On the way they encountered Joe Carter, an ex-West Bromwich Albion international. Although it had been more than five years since Carter had last played, he was persuaded to turn out and scored Villa's second goal.

BIRMINGHAM & DISTRICT LEAGUE

MANAGER: Directors

MATCH	DATE	VENUE	OPPONENTS	RESULT	HT SCORE	SCORE	SCORERS	ATT
1	Sep 14	A	Hednesford	L		1 6	Goffin	2,000
2	21	A	Revo Electric	L	4 4	4 8	Davis 3, Goffin	1,500
3	Oct 12	H	R.A.F. Cosford	L		0 1		1,000
4	Nov 9	H	Wellington Town	L		1 4	Houghton	2,500
5	16	A	R.A.F. Cosford	L		1 3	Shell	7,000
6	Dec 14	H	R.A.F. Hednesford	L		3 4	Goffin 2, Edwards	2,000
7	21	A	Worcester City	L	0 1	2 3	Davis, Goffin	3,500
8	Feb 15	H	R.A.F. Bridgnorth	W	3 0	3 1	Davis 3	1,000
9	22	A	Revo Electric	W	1 0	4 1	Bate (pen), Davis 3	500
10	Mar 1	H	R.A.F. Hednesford	W		5 1	Bate, Shell, Parkes, Davis 2	1,200
11	15	A	Worcester City	L		3 5	Davis, Carter, Brown (og)	3,000
12	Apr 5	H	R.A.F. Bradford	W		8 1	Davis, Broome 3, Goffin 2, Parkes, Bate (pen)	1,000
13	12	A	Wellington Town	L		2 4	Davis, Goffin	2,500
14	14	A	West Bromwich Albion	L	1 3	3 4	Edwards, Broome, Haycock	4,500
15	26	H	West Bromwich Albion	W		6 1	Davis 3, Goffin, Kerr, Martin	3,500
16	May 3	A	Hednesford	L		0 2		1,500

Final League Position: 7th in Birmingham & District League

	Appearances
1 Own-goal	Goals

BIRMINGHAM LEAGUE CUP

1F	Oct 26	A	Worcester City	L		0 2		2,000
1S	Nov 2	H	Worcester City	D		2 2	Houghton, Bate	1,500

	Appearances
	Goals

WORCESTERSHIRE CUP

1	Dec 7	A	Revo Electric	L		1 2	Parkes	500

	Appearances
	Goals

WORCESTER INFIRMARY CUP

1	May 10	A	Worcester City	L		1 2	Parkes	2,500

	Appearances
	Goals

OTHER MATCHES

1	Sep 28	A	Birmingham	W	1 0	3 0	Beresford 2, Davis	3,000
2	May 17	A	Walsall	L		3 4	Broome 2, Parkes	2,000

	Appearances
	Goals

Wakeman AD	Callaghan E	Iverson RTJ	Airey L	Moss A	Aston WH	Knight W	Martin JR	Beresford RH	Parkes HA	Goffin WC	Hickman AH	Barker J	Bate J	Devonport W	Neville S	Davis RD	Parsons R	Billingsley G	Potts VE	Yorke A	Shell FH	Houghton WE	Kerr AW	Batty SG	Lunn G	Edwards GR	Gibbons S	Lowry	Massie AC	Broome FH	Carter J	Vinall A	Cummings GW	Perry	Haycock FJ	Rutherford JHH	Spencer H	King J	Godfrey LL	MATCH
1	2	3	4	5	6	7	8	9	10	11																														1
1				5		7				11	2	3	4	6	8	9	10			8																				2
				6	7					11	2	5				8		1	3	4	9	10																		3
	2		4							11		6				8		1	3		9	10		5	7															4
				6	7				10	11		5						1	3	4	9	2			8															5
1				2	6				10	11		5							3	4	9	8			7															6
1				5		7			10	11						8			3	2	9					4	6													7
1						7			10	11	5		6			9			3	2		8				4														8
1									10	11	5		6			9			3	2	7		8				4													9
1						7			10	11	5		6			9			3	2	8		4																	10
1					6	7			10		5		4			8			3	2									9	11										11
1									10	11	5		6			8			3		7		4						9		2									12
1									10	11			6			9			2		7		4			8			3	5										13
1	2	6							10		5											11				4	9		3		8		1							14
	5						8		10	11			6			9			2			7					4		3											15
1	5				6		8		10		5					9			2				4				3													16
12	5	2	1	5	6	8	3	1	13	13	8	5	9	1	1	12	1	3	13	8	9	5	7	1	5	1	4		4	1	1	4	1	1	1					
							1		2	9			3			18						2	1		2		1		4	1			1							

				6						11	5					8		1	3	4	9	2	7	10																1F
				4	6	7				11	5		10			8		1	3		9	2																		1S
				1	2	1				2	2		1			2		2	2	1	2	2	1	1																
													1			1																								

				2	6	7			10	11	5					8		1	3	4	9	8																		1
				1	1	1			1	1	1					1		1	1	1	1	1																		
																						1																		

| 1 | | | | | | | 8 | | 10 | | | 6 | | | 9 | | | 2 | | | 4 | | | | | 7 | | | 3 | | | | 5 | 11 | | | | | | 1 |
| 1 | | | | | | | | | 1 | | | 1 | | | 1 | | | 1 | | | 1 | | | | | 1 | | | 1 | | | | 1 | 1 | | | | | | |

				5	6		8		11	2		10			9		1		4			7							7		3			3						1
1	5						8		10			11			9				4		2						7			3	6									2
1	1			1	1		1		1	1		2			2		1		2	1	1	2	1				1		1	1		1								
															1				1								2													

391

1941/42

SEASON SNIPPETS

The match against RAF Hednesford on 13 September was the first competitive game to be played at Villa Park since the outbreak of the War.

The away Keys Cup match on 24 December 1941 with Worcester City was played at Villa Park 'by arrangement'.

Villa's 19-2 win against RAF Lichfield on 21 March 1942 is a record score for a game at Villa Park.

BIRMINGHAM & DISTRICT LEAGUE

MANAGER: Directors

MATCH	DATE	VENUE	OPPONENTS	RESULT	HT SCORE	SCORE	SCORERS	ATT
1	Sep 6	A	Hednesford	W		3 0	Davis 3	1,000
2	13	H	R.A.F. Hednesford	W		2 1	Houghton, Davis	1,500
3	20	A	Revo Electric	W	3 0	5 1	Davis 2, Martin, Pearce, Houghton	600
4	27	H	Wellington Town	W	4 1	5 1	Davis 3, Parkes, Martin	2,000
5	Oct 4	A	Wellington Town	L		0 5		2,000
6	11	H	West Bromwich Albion	L	1 1	2 3	Davis, Parkes	5,500
7	18	H	R.A.F. Cosford	W	1 0	3 0	Davis 2, Goffin	1,000
8	Nov 1	A	Worcester City	W	3 0	8 1	Davis 6, Parkes, Bate	3,000
9	Dec 25	A	West Bromwich Albion	W		2 0	Haycock, Edwards	5,000
10	Jan 3	A	Wolverhampton Wanderers	W	0 1	3 1	Broome 2, Iverson	6,000
11	10	H	Hednesford	W		8 0	Broome, Parkes, Iverson 2, Goffin 2, Houghton 2	2,000
12	Feb 14	H	R.A.F. Hednesford	W		7 0	Kerr 3, Broome, Edwards 2, Houghton	1,000
13	21	H	Revo Electric	W		3 0	Broome 3	850
14	Mar 21	H	R.A.F. Lichfield	W		19 2	Broome 4, Parkes 4, Goffin 4, Kerr 2, Houghton 2, Cummings 2, Iverson	750
15	Apr 11	H	Worcester City	W		2 0	Kerr, Broome	1,500
16	18	H	R.A.F. Lichfield	W		9 0	Canning 3, Edwards 2, Goffin 2, Kerr, Houghton	600
17	25	H	R.A.F. Cosford	D	0 0	0 0		400
18	May 16	H	Wolverhampton Wanderers	W		6 1	Houghton 2, Iverson, Kerr, Davis, Goffin	3,000

Final League Position: 1st in Birmingham & District League

Appearances
Goals

BIRMINGHAM LEAGUE CUP

1F	Nov 8	H	Wellington Town	W		5 0	Davis 2, Martin, Houghton 2	800
1S	22	A	Wellington Town	L		1 2	Davis	1,900
2	Jan 17	H	R.A.F. Hednesford	W		14 1	Massie 5, Broome 4, Houghton 2, Parkes 2, Kerr	1,000
SF	31	H	Hednesford Town	W		3 2	Broome 2, Preston (og)	1,200
F	May 9	H	Worcester City	W		4 2	Goffin 2, Davis, Houghton	

Appearances
1 Own-goal   Goals

KEYS CUP

1F	Dec 6	H	Worcester City	W		6 0	Davis 4, Goffin, Smith (og)	1,000
1S	24	A	Worcester City	W		4 1	Davis 2, Parkes, Cottrill (og)	1,000
SF	Feb 28	A	Revo Electric	W		2 1	Potts, Kerr	500
F	May 23	H	Hednesford Town	W		5 0	Kerr 3, Goffin 2	1,400

Appearances
2 Own-goals   Goals

WORCESTER CHARITY CUP

1	Dec 13	H	Revo Electric	L	0 0	1 2	Iverson	

Appearances
Goals

WORCESTER INFIRMARY CUP

F	May 2	A	Worcester City	W		3 0	Goffin 2, Davis	

Appearances
Goals

OTHER MATCHES

1	Nov 15	H	Birmingham	W	2 0	7 0	Davis 4, Parkes 2, Kerr	
2	29	A	Birmingham	W	1 0	1 0	Iverson	
3	Dec 27	H	Birmingham	W		4 1	Houghton 2, Kerr, Broome	
4	Mar 14	H	Birmingham	W		4 0	Houghton, Kerr, Iverson, Broome	
5	28	A	West Bromwich Albion	W		2 1	Parkes 2	
6	Apr 6	A	Birmingham	L		1 2	Broome	
7	May 25	A	West Bromwich Albion	W		4 3	Davis 2, Haycock, Houghton	
8	30	H	RAF XI	L		1 2	Iverson	

Appearances
Goals

Wakeman AD	Potts VE	Cummings GW	Massie AC	Callaghan E	Bate J	Kerr AW	Martin JR	Davis RD	Parkes HA	Houghton WE	Rutherford JHH	Vinall A	Pearce H	Gofhn WC	Aston WH	Iverson RTJ	Edwards GR	Haycock FJ	Broome FH	Lunn G	Canning L	Cooper R	Starling RW	Bentley G	Croom A	Carswell J	Hickman AH	Marrs B	Crooks SD	Duncan		MATCH
1	2	3	4	5	6	7	8	9	10	11																						1
	2	3	4	5	6	7	8	9	10	11	1																					2
		3		5	6	4	8	9		10		2	7	11																		3
1	2	3		5	6	4	8	9	10				7	11																		4
1	2	3		5	4	7		9	10	8				11	6																	5
	2	3	4	5	6	7	8	9	10	11	1																					6
	2	3	5		4	7	8	9	10		1			11		6																7
1	2	3	4	5	8	7		9	10	11						6																8
1	2	3	4	5					10	11						6	7	8	9													9
	2	3	4	5	8	7			10		1			11		6			9													10
1	2	3		5	4	8			10	7				11		6			9													11
1	2	3	4	5		7			10	11						6	8		9													12
1	2	3	4	5	7	8			10	11						6			9													13
1		3	4	5		7			10	8				11		6			9	2												14
1	2	3	4	5		7			10	8				11		6			9													15
1	2		4	5	6	7			10		3			11		6	9				8											16
1	2	3	4	5		7		9	8					11		6						10										17
	2	3		5		7	4	9		10				11		6	7				8	1										18
13	16	17	13	17	12	17	6	9	15	15	4	2	2	11	1	11	4	1	7	1	2	1	1									
			2			1	8	2	19	8		1	10			5	5	1	12		3											

1	2	3	4	5		7	8	9	10	11						6																1F
1	2	3		5	4	8		9	10	11						6					7											1S
1	2	3	8	5	4	7			10	11				9		6																2
1	2	3		5		7	8	10	11					9		6							4									SF
1	2	3		5		7	4	9		8						11	6					7				10						F
5	5	5	2	5	2	5	1	4	4	5				1		5	2				1	1	1									
			5			1	1	4	2	5				2		6																

1		3	4	5		7	8	9	10							11	6						2									1F
1	2	3		5	4			9	10	11						11	6	8					7									1S
1	2	3	4	5	7	8		9	10	11						6			9													SF
1	2	3	4	5		7		9		10						11	6				8				1							F
4	3	4	3	4	2	3	1	3	3	2				3	1	4		1			1		1		1							
		1					4		6	1				3																		

1		3	4	5	8			9	10	11		7				6			2													1
		1	1	1	1		1	1	1							1	1															
									1							1																

1	2	3	4	5	10	7		9		8						11	6															F
1	1	1	1	1	1	1		1		1						1	1															
								1		2						1																

	2	3	4	5		7	8	9	10	11	1					6																1
	2	3	4	5	8	7		9	10	11	1					6																2
	2	3	4	5	6	7			10	11	1					8			9													3
1	2	3	4	5		7			10	8				11		6			9													4
	2	3	4	5		7			10	11	1					6	8		9													5
1		3	4	5		7			10	8				11		6			9					2	6							6
1	2	3	4	5		7		9		10				11		6	8	7														7
	2	3	4	5	9				10	1						6										7	11					8
3	7	8	8	8	2	7	2	3	6	8	5		3			7	1	1	5					1	1	1	1					
						3		6	4	2						3		1	3													

393

1942/43

SEASON SNIPPETS

On 5 September Birmingham played Leicester at Villa Park winning 2-1 and this was then Blues home ground for the remainder of the season.

On 26 September it was announced that Ernest Callaghan had been awarded the British Empire Medal for courageous work during an air raid. George Edwards was given permission to play against Walsall with his arm in plaster.

On 13 January George Cummings was suspended sine die as from 18 January following incidents in the game against Leicester City on Christmas Day.

Matches 19 to 28 (inclusive) also counted as The War Cup qualifying rounds. Matches 29 to 36 also counted as The War Cup (Proper) Competition. Villa lost in the semi-final to Blackpool (matches 35 & 36). Each game counted towards the Second Championship. Matches 37 & 38 were League games only.

FOOTBALL LEAGUE (NORTH)

MANAGER: Directors

MATCH	DATE	VENUE	OPPONENTS	RESULT	HT SCORE	SCORE	SCORERS	ATT
1	Aug 29	H	Wolverhampton Wanderers	W	1 0	2 0	Parkes, Edwards	18,000
2	Sep 5	A	Wolverhampton Wanderers	W	1 0	2 1	Goffin, Cummings (pen)	8,000
3	12	A	Coventry City	L	1 2	1 2	Broome	14,720
4	19	H	Coventry City	D	0 1	1 1	Houghton	15,000
5	26	H	Walsall	D	2 1	2 2	Broome, Haycock	7,500
6	Oct 3	A	Walsall	L	0 2	0 3		5,200
7	10	A	West Bromwich Albion	L	0 4	2 6	Houghton, Haycock	12,000
8	17	H	West Bromwich Albion	W	3 0	8 2	Houghton 3 (1 pen), Davis 2, Parkes 2, Broome	15,000
9	24	H	Stoke City	W	4 0	4 0	Haycock 2, Parkes, Edwards	8,000
10	31	A	Stoke City	L	0 1	0 1		6,000
11	Nov 7	A	Northampton Town	W	1 1	5 3	Haycock, Houghton 2, Parkes, Davis	4,000
12	14	H	Northampton Town	W	3 1	4 1	Parkes, Broome 2, Houghton	5,000
13	21	H	Birmingham	W	1 1	2 1	Davis 2	15,000
14	28	A	Birmingham	L	1 1	1 2	Edwards	15,000
15	Dec 5	A	Derby County	L	1 3	2 4	Edwards, Parkes	7,000
16	12	H	Derby County	W	1 0	2 0	Broome 2	8,000
17	19	H	Leicester City	W	3 1	4 2	Broome, Houghton 3 (2 pens)	5,000
18	25	A	Leicester City	W		5 2	Kerr 2, Broome 2, Edwards	9,000

Final League Position: 14th in Football League North First Championship

Appearances
Goals

FOOTBALL LEAGUE WAR CUP & FOOTBALL LEAGUE (NORTH) - SECOND CHAMPIONSHIP

19	26	H	Wolverhampton Wanderers	W	0 0	1 0	Edwards	20,000
20	Jan 2	A	Wolverhampton Wanderers	W	4 0	4 0	Broome 3, Davis	6,000
21	9	A	Stoke City	L	0 1	0 1		3,000
22	16	H	Stoke City	W	2 0	3 0	Edwards 2, Broome	7,000
23	23	H	West Bromwich Albion	L	2 2	3 5	Broome, Davis, Iverson	10,000
24	30	A	West Bromwich Albion	L	0 1	1 2	Broome	12,000
25	Feb 6	A	Northampton Town	L	0 2	1 2	Davis	6,000
26	13	H	Northampton Town	W	2 0	2 1	Parkes, Haycock	7,000
27	20	H	Walsall	W	0 0	2 1	Haycock, Houghton	7,500
28	27	A	Walsall	W	2 0	4 1	Davis 3, Kerr	4,500
29	Mar 6	H	Wolverhampton Wanderers	W	3 1	5 2	Houghton 3 (2 pens), Broome	25,000
30	13	A	Wolverhampton Wanderers	W	4 1	5 3	Houghton, Davis 3, Haycock	15,000
31	20	A	Stoke City	W	1 0	3 1	Davis 2, Houghton (pen)	15,000
32	27	H	Stoke City	W	1 0	2 0	Edwards, Houghton	20,000
33	Apr 3	A	Bristol City	D	0 0	0 0		24,650
34	10	H	Bristol City	W	1 1	2 1	Houghton 2 (1 pen)	30,000
35	17	A	Blackpool	L	1 2	1 3	Davis	28,000
36	24	H	Blackpool	W	0 0	2 1	Callaghan, Iverson	50,000
37	26	H	Birmingham	W	0 0	1 0	Iverson	5,000
38	May 1	H	West Bromwich Albion	L	1 1	2 6	Haycock, Edwards	9,000

Appearances
Goals

CHARITY MATCH

| | May 8 | H | Portsmouth | D | | 1 1 | Davis | |

Appearances
Goals

394

Wakeman AD	Potts VE	Cummings GW	Massie AC	Callaghan E	Bate J	Edwards GR	Haycock FJ	Broome FH	Parkes HA	Houghton WE	Iverson RTJ	Starling RW	Goffin WC	Billingsley G	Shell FH	Godfrey LL	Davis RD	Guttridge R	Martin JR	Kerr AW																															MATCH
1	2	3	4	5	6	7	8	9	10	11																																									1
1	2	3	5			7	4	9	10		6	8	11																																						2
1	2	3	5			7	4	9	10		6	8	11																																						3
	2	3	4	5			8	7		11	6	10		1	9																																				4
	2	3	5			7	8	9	10		6	4	11	1																																					5
1		3	5			7	8	9	10		6	4	11			2																																			6
1		3	4	5			8	7		11	6	10				9	2																																	7
1	2	3	5			7		8	10	11	6	4					9																																	8
1	2	3	5			7	9	8	10	11	6	4																																						9
1	2	3	5			7	9	8	10	11	6	4																																						10
1	2	3		5			8		10	11	6	4	7				9																																	11
1	2	3		5		7	9	8	10	11	6	4																																						12
1		3		5					10	11	6	4					9	2	8																															13
1	2	3		5		7		9	10	8	6	4	11																																					14
		3	4	5		7		9	10	11	6	8					2																																	15
1	2	3	4	5		7		8	10	11	6						9																																	16
1	2	3	4	5		7		9	10	11	6	8																																						17
1	2	3	4	5		9		8	10	11	6									7																														18
16	14	18	14	11	1	15	11	16	16	14	17	15	6	2	2	3	4	1	1	1																															
			1			5	5	10	7	11			1				5			2																															
1	2	3	4	5	11	9		8	10		6									7																														19
1	2	3	4	5				7	10	11	6	8					9																																	20
1	2	3	4	5	9			7	10	11	6	8																																						21
1	2	3	4	5		9		7	10	11	6	8																																						22
1	2		5			7		8	10	11	6	4					9	3																																23
1	2		4	5		7		9	10	11	6	8					9	3																																24
1	2		4	5		7	8			11	6	10					9	3																																25
1	2		4	5		7	8		10	11	6			9				3																																26
1	2		4	5			8	7	10	11	6			9				3																																27
1	2		4	5			10			11	6						9	3	8	7																														28
1	2		4	5			10	7		11	6						9	3	8																															29
1	2		4	5			10	7		11	6						9	3																																30
1	2		4	5		7	8		10	11	6						9	3																																31
1	2		4	5		8	10	7		11	6						9	3																																32
1	2			5		8	10			11	6	4					9	3																																33
1	2		4	5			10	7		11	6						9	3	8																															34
1	2		4	5			10	7		11	6						9	3																																35
1	2		4	5		9	8			11	6	10						3		7																														36
1	2		4	5				9		10	11	6	8					3		7																														37
1	2		4	5		7	8			11	6	10					3	9																																38
20	20	4	18	20	2	11	14	13	10	19	12	19			2	1	12	15	5	3																														
				1		5	4	7	1	9	3						13			1																														
1	2		4	5			7	10	11		6						9	3	8																															
1	1		1	1			1	1	1		1						1	1	1																															
																	1																																	

1943/44

SEASON SNIPPETS

The sine die suspension on George Cummings was lifted on 20 August.

Villa lost their 100% record on 2 October despite leading 4-0 at half-time. Walsall scored four times in 12 minutes in an amazing second-half blitz.

In March 1944 the German Radio announced that W E Houghton, the English international and Aston Villa outside-left was a Prisoner of War in Germany. However Houghton, who was still playing for Aston Villa at the time, stated that there wasn't a word of truth in it.

All Cup games counted towards the Second Championship with matches 19 to 32 also being Cup qualifying rounds. Matches 33 & 34 were quarter-final Cup games. Matches 36 & 37 were Cup semi-finals, the final being games 38 & 39.

The second leg of Villa's League (North) Cup final against Blackpool on 6 May opened in spectacular fashion with two goals in the first 75 seconds and two more before the match was fifteen minutes old.

At the end of the second leg of the Football League War Cup final, all the players were presented with War Savings Certificates instead of medals.

Challenge Match - As winners of the Football League (North) Cup, Aston Villa met Charlton Athletic, the Football League (South) winners, in a Challenge match at Stamford Bridge. The First Lord of the Admiralty presented the captain of each side with a trophy after the match.

FOOTBALL LEAGUE (NORTH)

MANAGER: Directors

MATCH	DATE	VENUE	OPPONENTS	RESULT	HT SCORE	SCORE	SCORERS	ATT
1	Aug 28	A	Stoke City	W	1 0	2 0	Broome, Edwards	5,000
2	Sep 4	H	Stoke City	W	1 0	2 1	Houghton (pen), Broome	15,000
3	11	A	Wolverhampton Wanderers	W	2 0	4 2	Edwards, Houghton, Broome 2	10,000
4	18	H	Wolverhampton Wanderers	W	1 1	4 1	Broome 2, Houghton, Starling	14,500
5	25	A	Walsall	W	1 0	2 0	Broome, Houghton (pen)	7,000
6	Oct 2	H	Walsall	D	4 0	4 4	Broome, Houghton 2 (1 pen), Starling	15,000
7	9	A	Coventry City	D	0 0	0 0		15,000
8	16	A	Coventry City	W	0 0	1 0	Haycock	14,000
9	23	H	West Bromwich Albion	W	2 0	3 1	Broome, Davis, Houghton	15,000
10	30	A	West Bromwich Albion	L	2 3	4 5	Broome 2, Haycock, Iverson	23,500
11	Nov 6	H	Northampton Town	W	1 0	4 0	Broome, Houghton 2, Haycock	14,000
12	13	A	Northampton Town	L	0 1	0 5		6,000
13	20	H	Birmingham	L	0 2	1 2	Houghton	15,000
14	27	H	Birmingham	W	2 0	3 0	O'Donnell 2, Broome	15,000
15	Dec 4	H	Derby County	L	0 1	0 1		12,000
16	11	A	Derby County	D	0 2	3 3	Canning 2, Houghton	10,000
17	18	A	Leicester City	W	2 1	3 1	Parkes 2, Houghton	5,000
18	25	H	Leicester City	W	2 0	3 1	Houghton 2 (1 pen), Broome	10,000

Final League Position: 8th in Football League North First Championship

Appearances
Goals

FOOTBALL LEAGUE WAR CUP & FOOTBALL LEAGUE (NORTH) - SECOND CHAMPIONSHIP

MATCH	DATE	VENUE	OPPONENTS	RESULT	HT SCORE	SCORE	SCORERS	ATT
19	Dec 27	H	Northampton Town	W	0 0	2 1	Iverson, Houghton (pen)	24,000
20	Jan 1	H	Northampton Town	W	1 1	2 1	O'Donnell, Broome	8,000
21	8	A	Stoke City	L	0 4	3 6	O'Donnell, Haycock, Houghton	16,500
22	15	H	Stoke City	L	0 1	0 2		32,000
23	22	A	Wolverhampton Wanderers	W	2 0	4 0	Starling, Martin, Goffin, O'Donnell	12,000
24	29	H	Wolverhampton Wanderers	W	2 0	3 1	Goffin, McLean (og), Broome (pen)	16,000
25	Feb 5	H	Coventry City	W	3 0	4 0	O'Donnell, Broome 2, Starling	10,000
26	12	A	Coventry City	L	0 0	0 2		15,770
27	19	A	Birmingham	D	0 1	1 1	Iverson	18,000
28	26	H	Birmingham	L	1 0	1 2	Broome	21,000
29	Mar 4	A	Stoke City	W	3 4	5 4	Martin, Broome 2, Houghton 2	11,500
30	11	H	Stoke City	W	0 0	3 0	Houghton 2 (1 pen), Broome	20,000
31	18	A	Coventry City	W	2 0	2 1	Iverson, Broome	23,664
32	25	H	Coventry City	W	2 0	2 1	Broome, Guttridge	29,000
33	Apr 1	H	Bath City	W	1 0	1 0	O'Donnell	32,000
34	8	A	Bath City	D	2 2	3 3	Parkes 2, Iverson	16,000
35	10	A	West Bromwich Albion	W	3 0	4 1	Broome 3, Edwards	16,000
36	15	H	Sheffield United	W	3 0	3 2	Iverson 2, Houghton	44,000
37	22	A	Sheffield United	D	0 1	2 2	Broome (pen), Parkes	48,000
38	29	A	Blackpool	L	0 0	1 2	Goffin	30,000
39	May 6	H	Blackpool	W	3 2	4 2	Broome 2, Edwards, Iverson,	54,824
40	20	N	Charlton Athletic *	D	0 0	1 1	Houghton	38,840

Final League Position: 6th in Football League North Second Championship

| 1 Own-goal |

Appearances
Goals

* Played at Stamford Bridge, London

CHARITY MATCH IN AID OF THE RED CROSS FUND AND THE KING GEORGE V SAILORS' FUND

MATCH	DATE	VENUE	OPPONENTS	RESULT	HT SCORE	SCORE	SCORERS	ATT
1	May 13	H	Portsmouth	D	1 3	3 3	Iverson, Parkes, Starling	12,000

Appearances
Goals

Wakeman AD	Potts VE	Guttridge R	Massie AC	Callaghan E	Iverson RTJ	Edwards GR	Haycock FJ	Broome FH	Starling RW	Houghton WE	Cummings GW	Morby JH	Godfrey LL	Davis RD	Parkes HA	Billingsley G	O'Donnell FJ	Canning L	Martin JR	Goffin WC																								MATCH
1	2	3	4	5	6	7	8	9	10	11																																		1
1	2		4		6	7	8	9	10	11	3	5																																2
1	2		4		6	7	8	9	10	11	3	5																																3
1	2		4		6	7	8	9	10	11		5	3																															4
1	2		4		6	7	8	9	10	11	3	5																																5
1	2		4		6	7		8	10	11	3	5		9																														6
1	2		4		6	7	8	9	10	11	3	5																																7
1	2		4			8	7	9	11	3	5			10																														8
1	2		4		6			7	8	11	3	5		9	10																													9
1	2		5		6	7	10	8	4	11	3				9																													10
	2				6	8	9	7	4	11	3	5			10	1																												11
	2				6	8	9	7	4	11	3	5			10	1																												12
	2					6	9	7	8	11			4		10	1																												13
1	2		4		6		8	7	10	11	3	5				9																												14
1	2	3	4		6		8	7	10	11		5				9																												15
1	2	3	4	5	6			10	7	9	11						8																											16
1	2		4	5	6			10	7		11	3			9		8																											17
1	2		4		6			10	7	8	11	3	5			9																												18
15	18	3	15	3	18	10	16	18	17	18	14	14	2		3	7	3	2	2																									198
					1	2	3	14	2	14				1	2			2	2																									43
1	2		4		6		10	7	8	11	3	5		9																														19
1	2		4				10	7	6	11	3	5			8	9																												20
1	2				6		10	7	4	11	3	5			8	9																												21
1	2		4	5	6		10	7	8	11	3			9																														22
1	2		4	5	6			7	10		3					9		8	11																									23
1	2		4		6		8	7	10		3					9			11																									24
1	2		4		6			7	10	11	3	5				9	8																											25
1	2		4	5	6		9	8	10	11	3								7																									26
1	2		4		6			7	10	11	3	5				9	8																											27
1	2		4		6			7	10	11	3	5				9	8																											28
1	2		4	5	6			7	10	11	3					9	8																											29
1	2		4	5	6			7	8	11	3			10		9																												30
1	2	6	4	5	10			7	8	11	3					9																												31
1	2	6	4	5	10			7	8	11	3					9																												32
1	2		4	5	6			7	10	11	3					9	8																											33
1	2	6	4	5	10			7	8	11	3			9																														34
1	2	6	4	5	10	8		7	4	11	3			9																														35
1	2	6	4	5	10			7	8	11	3			9																														36
1	2	6	4	5	10			7	8		3			9						11																								37
1	2		4	5	6	8		7	10		3			9						11																								38
1	2		4	5	10	8		7	6	11	3			9																														39
1	2		4	5	10	8		7	6	11	3			9																														40
22	22	6	20	16	21	4	6	22	22	18	22	6		2	10		12		6	5																								242
						1		7	2	1	16	2			3		5		2	3																								50

| 1 | 2 | | 4 | 5 | 10 | 8 | | 7 | 6 | 11 | 3 | | | 9 | | | | | | | | | | | | | | | | | | | | | | | | | | | | | | 1 |

| 1 | 1 | | 1 | 1 | 1 | | 1 | 1 | 1 | 1 | | 1 | | | 1 | | | | | | | | | | | | | | | | | | | | | | | | | | | | | 11 |
| | | | | | 1 | | | | 1 | | | | | | 1 | | | | | | | | | | | | | | | | | | | | | | | | | | | | | 3 |

397

1944/45

SEASON SNIPPETS

A number of wounded soldiers were guests of Villa for the first game of the season against Stoke City and the Club announced that this would apply for all home games during the season.

The game against Birmingham City on 14 October was the first match the opposition had played under their new title, having previously been called "Birmingham".

At the beginning of December Harry Cooch died. He first came to Villa as a goalkeeper in 1901 and played for Villa until 1908, returning in 1919 as assistant trainer. Cooch later became first-team trainer.

The game with West Bromwich Albion on 26 December was abandoned ten minutes from time due to fog, but the 3-4 result was allowed to stand.

It was not really surprising the attendance for Villa's game with Coventry City on 3 February 1945 was disappointing. On the same day there were 66,000 at Villa Park to see England play Scotland.

Matches 37 to 41 and match 43 are also Midland Cup games. Matches 39 & 40 against Coventry City are semi-final ties with matches 41 & 43 against Derby County being a two-legged final.

Both teams were introduced to Mr Arthur Drewry, a member of the Football League Management Committee, before the second-leg against Derby. Mr Drewry later presented the Cup. With him was Mr E A Eden, secretary of Birmingham County FA. Peter Doherty scored five of Derby's six goals.

All Cup games also counted towards the Football League (North) Second Championship.

The War in Europe ended officially at 3.00pm on Tuesday 8 May 1945. The following day Villa played at Portsmouth as part of the peace celebrations with the proceeds going to the Lord Mayor's Royal Navy and Mercantile Marine Fund.

398

FOOTBALL LEAGUE (NORTH)

MANAGER: Directors

MATCH	DATE	VENUE	OPPONENTS	RESULT	HT SCORE	SCORE	SCORERS	ATT
1	Aug 26	H	Stoke City	W	1 0	4 0	Parkes 2, Iverson, Edwards	17,000
2	Sep 2	A	Stoke City	L	0 0	1 3	Parkes	10,000
3	9	A	Wolverhampton Wanderers	W	1 0	2 1	Haycock, Iverson	14,000
4	16	H	Wolverhampton Wanderers	W	2 1	3 1	Parkes, Iverson, Haycock	18,000
5	23	H	Walsall	D	0 1	1 1	Edwards	16,000
6	30	A	Walsall	W	1 0	2 0	Haycock, Broome	10,000
7	Oct 7	A	Birmingham	L	1 2	2 3	Broome, Houghton	22,000
8	14	H	Birmingham City	D	0 0	1 1	Houghton	23,000
9	21	H	West Bromwich Albion	D	2 1	2 2	Parkes, Iverson	25,000
10	28	A	West Bromwich Albion	W	4 1	5 1	Parkes, Iverson, Millard (og), Houghton, Haycock	25,000
11	Nov 4	A	Port Vale	L	0 0	1 2	Iverson	10,000
12	11	H	Port Vale	W	3 0	4 0	Houghton, Griffiths (og), Edwards, Haycock	9,000
13	18	H	Coventry City	W	2 0	4 0	Edwards 2, Houghton, Goffin	15,000
14	25	A	Coventry City	W	2 0	6 0	Goffin, Haycock 2, Massie, Edwards, Houghton (pen)	10,500
15	Dec 2	A	Leicester City	W	2 0	3 0	Edwards, Houghton 2	10,000
16	9	H	Leicester City	W	2 0	5 0	Goffin, Houghton 3, Haycock	13,000
17	16	H	Northampton Town	W	2 0	5 2	Houghton 2, Iverson, Edwards 2	9,000
18	23	A	Northampton Town	W	1 2	3 2	Shepherdson (og), Goffin 2	6,000

Final League Position: 4th in Football League North First Championship

3 Own-goals

Appearances
Goals

FOOTBALL LEAGUE WAR CUP & FOOTBALL LEAGUE (NORTH) - SECOND CHAMPIONSHIP

MATCH	DATE	VENUE	OPPONENTS	RESULT	HT SCORE	SCORE	SCORERS	ATT
19	26	H	West Bromwich Albion	L	2 3	3 4	Parkes 2, Iverson	6,000
20	30	A	Northampton Town	L	0 0	0 2		5,000
21	Jan 6	A	West Bromwich Albion	W	1 0	3 1	Massie, Iverson, Edwards	22,000
22	13	H	West Bromwich Albion	W	2 0	6 2	Haycock 2, Edwards 2, Iverson, Houghton	16,000
23	20	H	Birmingham City	W	1 1	3 1	Edwards, Houghton (pen), Iverson	17,000
24	27	A	Birmingham City	W	1 0	1 0	Edwards	17,000
25	Feb 3	A	Coventry City	W	2 1	3 2	Goffin, Edwards, Houghton	4,000
26	10	H	Coventry City	W	2 1	5 2	Edwards 2, Broome, Iverson 2	19,000
27	17	H	Walsall	W	3 1	6 1	Houghton 2, Edwards 2, Broome, Iverson	17,000
28	24	A	Walsall	W	1 0	2 0	Iverson, Edwards	8,000
29	Mar 3	A	Northampton Town	D	1 1	2 2	Houghton 2 (1 pen)	21,000
30	10	H	Birmingham City	W	2 0	5 0	Edwards 2, Iverson 2, Houghton	20,000
31	17	A	Birmingham City	W	2 0	3 0	Edwards, Iverson, Houghton (pen)	19,000
32	24	H	Wolverhampton Wanderers	L	0 1	1 2	Houghton	32,000
33	31	A	Wolverhampton Wanderers	L	0 0	0 1		40,000
34	Apr 2	A	West Bromwich Albion	W	1 1	4 2	Edwards 3, Iverson	15,000
35	7	A	Leicester City	L	0 1	0 2		7,000
36	14	H	Leicester City	W	2 1	7 2	Edwards 2, Houghton 3 (2 pens), Parkes, Goffin	7,500
37	21	A	Stoke City	L	0 1	0 1		6,000
38	28	H	Stoke City	W	1 0	2 0	Edwards, Goffin	15,000
39	May 5	H	Coventry City	W	5 0	9 2	Iverson, Parkes, Goffin, Houghton, Edwards 4, Massie	7,500
40	12	A	Coventry City	L	1 0	1 3	Iverson	5,000
41	19	A	Derby County	L	0 1	0 3		22,000
42	21	H	Wolverhampton Wanderers	D	1 1	4 4	Iverson, Broome 2, Houghton	7,000
43	26	A	Derby County	L	0 1	0 6		16,000

Final League Position: 6th in Football League North Second Championship

Appearances
Goals

CHARITY MATCH - VE + 1 DAY PEACE CELEBRATIONS

1	May 9	A	Portsmouth	W	3 2	4 3	Parkes, Iverson 2, Goffin	16,000

Appearances
Goals

Wakeman AD	Potts VE	Cummings GW	Massie AC	Callaghan E	Starling RW	Goffin WC	Edwards GR	Parkes HA	Iverson RTJ	Houghton WE	Haycock FJ	Morby JH	Broome FH	Guttridge R	Canning L	McConnon JE	Latham L	Godfrey LL	Martin JR																																																																	MATCH
1	2	3	4	5	6	7	8	9	10	11																																																														1
1	2	3	4	5	6	7		9		11	10																																																													2
1	2	3	4	5	6			7	9	10	11	8																																																												3
1	2	3	4		6			7	9	10	11	8	5																																																												4
1	2	3	4		6			8	9		11	10	5	7																																																												5
1		3		5	4			9	10	6	11	8		7	2																																																												6
1	2	3	4	5	6			9		10	11	8		7																																																												7
1	2			5	4			7	9	6	11	10			3	8																																																											8
1	2	3		5	4				9	10	11	8		7	6																																																												9
1	2	3		5	4				9	10	11	8		7	6																																																												10
1	2	3		5	4				9	10	11	8		7	6																																																												11
1	2	3	4	5	6		7	9	10	11	8																																																															12
1	2	3	4	5	6	7	9	10		11	8																																																															13
1	2	3	4	5	6	7	9	10		11	8																																																															14
1	2		4	5	6	7	9	10		11	8			3																																																												15
1	2		4	5	6	7	9	10		11	8			3																																																												16
1	2	3	4	5	6	7	9		10	11	8																																																														17
1	2	3	4	5	6	7	9		10	11	8																																																														18

| 18 | 17 | 15 | 13 | 16 | 18 | 8 | 15 | 15 | 12 | 18 | 17 | 2 | 6 | 7 | 1 | | | | | | | | | | | | | | | | | | | | | | | | | | | | | | | | | | | | | | | | | | | | | | | | | | | | | | | | | | | | | |
| | | | | 1 | | 5 | 9 | 6 | 7 | 13 | 8 | | 2 | | | | | | | | | | | | | | | | | | | | | | | | | | | | | | | | | | | | | | | | | | | | | | | | | | | | | | | | | | | | | |

1	2	3		5	6	7		9	10	11	8			4																																																												19
1	2	3	4	5	6	7		9	10	11	8																																																															20
1	2	3	4	5	6			9		10	11	8		7																																																												21
1	2	3	4	5	6			9		10	11	8		7																																																												22
1	2	3	4	5	6	7		9		10	11	8																																																														23
1	2	3	4	5	6			9		10	11	8		7																																																												24
1	2	3	4	5	6	7		9		10	11	8																																																														25
1	2	3	4		6			9		10	11	8		7		5																																																											26
1	2	3	4		6			9		10	11	8		7			5																																																											27
1	2	3	4	5	6			9		10	11	8		7																																																												28
1	2	3	4	5	6			9		10	11	8		7																																																												29
1	2	3	4	5	6			9		10	11	8		7																																																												30
1	2	3	4	5	6			9		10	11	8		7																																																												31
1	2	3	4	5	6	7	9		10	11	8																																																															32
1	2	3	4	5	6			9		10	11	8																																																															33
1	2	3		5			9	8	10	11	7			6			4																																																											34
1	2	3	4	5	6			9		10	11	8		7																																																												35
1		3	4	5	6	7	9	8	10	11						2																																																												36
1		3	4		6		9	8	10	11		5		7																																																												37
1	2	3	4	5	6	7	9	10		11									8																																																									38
1	2	3	4	5	6	7	9	8	10	11																																																																	39
1	2	3		5	6	7	9	8	10	11								4																																																										40
1	2	3	4	5	6		9	8	10	11				7																																																														41
1	2	3		5	6		9	8	10	11				7				4																																																											42
1	2	3	4	5	8			9		10	11			7	6																																																												43

| 25 | 24 | 25 | 21 | 22 | 24 | 10 | 22 | 11 | 24 | 25 | 17 | 1 | 14 | 2 | | 2 | 1 | 4 | 1 | | | | | | | | | | | | | | | | | | | | | | | | | | | | | | | | | | | | | | | | | | | | | | | | | | | | | | | | | | |
| | | | | 2 | | 4 | 24 | 4 | 15 | 15 | 2 | | 4 | | | | | | | | | | | | | | | | | | | | | | | | | | | | | | | | | | | | | | | | | | | | | | | | | | | | | | | | | | | | | | | |

| 1 | 2 | 3 | 4 | 5 | 8 | 7 | | 9 | 10 | 11 | | | 6 | | | | | | | | | | | | | | | | | | | | | | | | | | | | | | | | | | | | | | | | | | | | | | | | | | | | | | | | | | | | | | | | 1 |

| 1 | 1 | 1 | 1 | 1 | 1 | 1 | | 1 | 1 | 1 | | | 1 | | | | | | | | | | | | | | | | | | | | | | | | | | | | | | | | | | | | | | | | | | | | | | | | | | | | | | | | | | | | | | | | |
| | | | | | | | | 1 | 1 | 2 | | | | | | | | | | | | | | | | | | | | | | | | | | | | | | | | | | | | | | | | | | | | | | | | | | | | | | | | | | | | | | | | | | | |

1945/46

SEASON SNIPPETS

On 1 September, skipper Alex Massie played his last game - a 7 - 1 win against Luton Town - before taking over the duties as team manager on Monday 3 September 1945.

On 3 November, Leslie G F Smith made his debut in a 3-0 win at Plymouth Argyle following a £7,500 move from Brentford.

At the invitation of the Norwegian Football Association, Villa played three matches in Norway in May 1946, drawing 2-2 against a Norwegian XI on 28 May, winning 4-2 against Sarpsburgh on 30 May and winning 9-1 against Stravenger on 5 June.

Villa played an Edinburgh Select XI in Scotland on 8 June drawing 3-3.

The total gate receipts for the season taken at Villa Park (£101,692) was a record for any club in the Country.

The attendance for the FA Cup match with Derby County on 2 March (76,588) is still the record attendance at Villa Park. The match receipts were £8,651 2s 6d.

Johnny Dixon, who went on to captain Villa in the 1957 Cup final, made his first team debut on 6 April scoring in Villa's 4-1 win against Derby County.

FOOTBALL LEAGUE (SOUTH)

MANAGER: Alex Massie

MATCH	DATE	VENUE	OPPONENTS	RESULT	HT SCORE	SCORE	SCORERS	ATT
1	Aug 25	A	Luton Town	D	1 1	1 1	Edwards	11,788
2	29	A	West Bromwich Albion	L	0 1	0 1		16,000
3	Sep 1	H	Luton Town	W	2 0	7 1	Broome 2, Gager (og), Edwards 4	25,000
4	5	H	West Bromwich Albion	D	1 2	3 3	Edwards, Parkes (pen), Goffin	36,000
5	8	H	Swansea Town	W	2 1	6 3	Iverson 2, Goffin, Edwards, Kerr 2	20,000
6	10	A	West Ham United	W	1 1	2 1	Edwards, Martin	23,000
7	15	A	Swansea Town	L	1 2	4 5	Goffin, Iverson 2, Kerr	18,000
8	22	H	Arsenal	W	2 1	4 2	Iverson 2, Edwards, Kerr	35,000
9	29	A	Arsenal	W	2 0	5 1	Edwards 4, Broome	45,000
10	Oct 6	A	Charlton Athletic	D	0 0	0 0		50,000
11	13	H	Charlton Athletic	L	0 0	0 2		48,000
12	20	H	Fulham	W	2 0	3 0	Edwards, Broome, Iverson	20,000
13	27	A	Fulham	W	0 0	4 1	Edwards 2, Iverson 2	32,500
14	Nov 3	A	Plymouth Argyle	W	1 0	3 0	Edwards 3	33,038
15	10	H	Plymouth Argyle	W	3 1	4 2	Martin 2, Iverson, Edwards	25,000
16	17	H	Portsmouth	W	1 2	3 2	Iverson, Guthrie (og), Edwards	38,000
17	24	A	Portsmouth	W	2 1	3 2	Edwards 2, Martin	30,000
18	Dec 1	H	Nottingham Forest	W	0 1	3 1	Parkes, Smith, Edwards	20,000
19	8	A	Nottingham Forest	W	1 1	3 1	Martin, Edwards 2	30,000
20	19	H	Newport County	W	3 2	5 2	Graham, Broome 2, Parkes, Edwards	13,000
21	22	A	Newport County	W	3 0	4 0	Iverson, Martin, Smith, Edwards	18,000
22	25	A	Wolverhampton Wanderers	W	2 0	2 1	Iverson, Edwards	30,000
23	26	H	Wolverhampton Wanderers	D	1 0	1 1	Martin	60,000
24	29	H	West Ham United	D	2 1	2 2	Martin, Iverson	34,000
25	Jan 12	H	Birmingham City	D	2 1	2 2	Jennings (og), Edwards	64,000
26	19	A	Birmingham City	L	1 1	1 3	Edwards	40,000
27	Feb 2	H	Tottenham Hotspur	W	1 0	5 1	Edwards 2, Broome 2, Cummings	25,000
28	16	A	Brentford	W	1 0	1 0	Iverson	27,000
29	20	A	Tottenham Hotspur	L	0 2	0 3		19,000
30	23	H	Chelsea	D	1 1	2 2	Goffin, Iverson	45,000
31	Mar 16	A	Millwall	D	2 1	2 2	Soo (og), Broome	20,000
32	23	H	Southampton	W	1 0	5 3	Edwards 2, Broome 2, Goffin	20,000
33	27	H	Chelsea	L	0 0	0 3		18,000
34	30	H	Southampton	W	1 0	2 0	Smith, Edwards	25,000
35	Apr 6	H	Derby County	W	2 1	4 1	Broome 2, Edwards, Dixon	50,000
36	13	A	Derby County	W	0 0	1 0	Dixon	30,000
37	17	H	Brentford	D	0 1	1 1	Broome	20,000
38	20	H	Coventry City	D	0 0	0 0		38,000
39	22	H	Leicester City	W	2 0	3 0	Dixon, Goffin 2	30,000
40	23	A	Leicester City	W	0 0	1 0	Martin	22,000
41	27	A	Coventry City	D	2 0	2 2	Edwards, Houghton (pen)	14,000
42	May 1	H	Millwall	W	1 0	2 0	Houghton (pen), Edwards	20,000

Final League Position: 2nd in Football League (South)

4 Own-goals

Appearances
Goals

FA CUP

R3/1	Jan 5	A	Coventry City	L	0 1	1 2	Smith	27,197
R3/2	8	H	Coventry City	W	1 0	2 0	Smith, Goffin	30,000
R4/1	26	A	Millwall	W	2 1	4 2	Goffin, Edwards 2, Smith	30,000
R4/2	28	H	Millwall	W	5 1	9 1	Broome 3, Edwards, Smith, Iverson, Goffin 2, Parkes	28,000
R5/1	Feb 9	A	Chelsea	W	0 0	1 0	Broome	65,307
R5/2	12	H	Chelsea	W	0 0	1 0	Goffin	56,000
R6/1	Mar 2	H	Derby County	L	2 1	3 4	Edwards, Iverson, Broome	76,588
R6/2	9	A	Derby County	D	1 1	1 1	Broome	32,000

Appearances
Goals

400

Wakeman AD	Potts VE	Cummings GW	Massie AC	Callaghan E	Starling RW	Broome FH	Martin JR	Edwards GR	Iverson RTJ	Parkes HA	Goffin WC	Kerr AW	Haycock FJ	Godfrey LL	Houghton WE	Graham JR	Morby JH	Lowe E	Smith LGF	Carey WJ	Scott RA	Beresford RM	Moss F (junr)	Rutherford JHH	Dixon JT	Shell FH	MATCH
1	2	3	4	5	6	7	8	9	10	11																	1
1	2	3	4	5	8	7		9	10	6	11																2
1	2	3	4	5	6	7	8	9	10	11																	3
1	2	3		5	4			9	10	6	11	7	8														4
1	2	3		5	4		8	9	10	6	11	7															5
1	2	3		5	4		8	9	10	6	11	7															6
1		3		5	4		8	9	10	6	11	7		2													7
1	2	3		5	6	7	8	9	10	4				11													8
1	2	3		5	6	7	8	9	10	4					11												9
1	2	3		5	6	7		9	10	4					11												10
1	2	3		5	6	7		9	10	4					11	8											11
1	2	3			6	7	8	9	10	4					11		5										12
1	2	3		5	6	7	8	9	10	4					11												13
1	2	3		5		7	8	9	10	4							6	11									14
1	2	3					8	9	10	4				7			6	11									15
	2	3		5	6		8	9	10	4				7				11	1								16
	2	3		5			8	9	10	4			7				6	11		1							17
	2	3		5		7	8	9	10	4							6	11		1							18
1	2	3		5		7	8	9	10	4							6										19
1	2	3		5				9	10	4						8	6	11									20
1	2	3		5		7	8	9	10	4							6	11									21
1	2	3		5		7	8	9	10	4							6	11									22
1	2	3		5			8	9	10	4				7			6	11									23
1	2	3		5	9		8		10	4		7					6	11									24
1	2	3					8	9	10	4		7					5	6									25
1		3					8	9	10	4		7	2	11			5	6									26
1	2	3			6	8		9	10	4	7						5	11									27
1	2	3		5		8		9	10	4	7			11			6										28
1	2	3		5			8		10	4		7					6	11			9						29
1	2	3				8		10	5	7						9	6	11				4					30
1	2	3			10		8		9		7						6	11				4					31
1	2	3			6	8		9	10		7					5		11				4					32
1	2	3			6	8		9	10		7					5		11				4					33
		3			10	7		9	6				2		8	5		11				4	1				34
	2	3			10	7		9	4		11					5	6						1	8			35
	2	3			10			4								5		11					1	8	9		36
	2	3			10	8			4		7					6		11		5			1		9		37
	2	3			10	7			4							6		11		5			1	8			38
	2	3			10	7			4		11					6		9		5			1	8			39
	2	3			10	7	9		4							11		6		5			1	8			40
	2	3			10			9	4							11		6		5			1	8	7		41
	2	3			10		8	9	4		7					11		6		5	1						42
30	39	42	3	26	28	28	24	34	41	30	16	10	1	3	13	4	9	24	23	1	2	1	11	9	6	4	
		1				14	9	39	16	3	7	4		2	1			3									
1	2	3		5			8	9	10	4		7					6	11									R3/1
1	2	3		5				9	10	4	8	7					6	11									R3/2
1	2	3		5		8		9	10	4	7						6	11									R4/1
1	2	3				8		9	10	4	7				5	6	11										R4/2
1	2	3				8		9	10	4	7				5	6	11										R5/1
1	2	3				8		9	10	4	7					6	11										R5/2
1	2	3				8		9	10	5	7					6	11			4							R6/1
1	2	3		5		8		9	10	4	7					6	11										R6/2
8	8	8		4		6	1	8	8	8	7	2			3	8	8			1							
						6		4	2	1	5					4											

1946/47

SEASON SNIPPETS

Alex Massie held a private trial for local youths at Villa Park prior to the season opening from which A T Davies, Roy Oakley, Charles Herbert and Jeffrey C Jackson were signed on amateur forms.

Three weeks after the season opened, Villa made their first big signing since the Football League was resume with the capture of Dickie Dorsett from Wolves.

On 26 December 1946, Eric Houghton played his last game for Aston Villa, a Central League match against Huddersfield Town, scoring a penalty with the last kick of the game. Houghton was transferred to Notts County after the match, but returned as Manager in September 1953 and led Villa to FA Cup glory in 1957. Houghton signed professional forms for Villa on 24 August 1927 and played a total of 724 games at all levels for the Club, scoring 345 goals in the process, 72 goals coming from the penalty spot and 32 from free-kicks.

Trevor Ford was signed from Swansea Town for a club record £12,000 in January and made his debut in the 2-0 away win at Arsenal on 18 January.

DIVISION ONE

MANAGER: Alex Massie

MATCH	DATE	VENUE	OPPONENTS	RESULT	HT SCORE	SCORE	SCORERS	ATT
1	Aug 31	H	Middlesbrough	L	0 0	0 1		49,246
2	Sep 2	H	Everton	L	0 0	0 1		35,618
3	7	A	Derby County	W	1 1	2 1	Dixon, Edwards	28,454
4	11	A	Wolverhampton Wanderers	W	2 1	2 1	Smith, Goffin	49,661
5	14	H	Arsenal	L	0 2	0 2		53,778
6	16	H	Wolverhampton Wanderers	W	3 0	3 0	Smith, Edwards 2	35,738
7	21	A	Blackpool	L	0 1	0 1		27,452
8	28	H	Brentford	W	2 1	5 2	GC Smith (og), Martin, Goffin 2, Graham	45,350
9	Oct 5	A	Blackburn Rovers	W	0 0	1 0	Edwards	22,619
10	12	H	Portsmouth	D	1 0	1 1	Smith	45,308
11	19	H	Charlton Athletic	W	2 0	4 0	Dorsett, Edwards, Dixon 2	43,523
12	26	A	Preston North End	L	1 1	1 3	Iverson	27,778
13	Nov 2	H	Manchester United	D	0 0	0 0		53,668
14	9	A	Stoke City	D	0 0	0 0		38,238
15	16	H	Bolton Wanderers	D	0 1	1 1	Dorsett (pen)	40,399
16	23	A	Chelsea	W	1 1	3 1	Edwards, Martin, Smith	63,896
17	30	H	Sheffield United	L	1 1	2 3	Edwards, Martin	43,051
18	Dec 7	A	Grimsby Town	W	1 0	3 0	Martin, Edwards, Dorsett	18,275
19	14	H	Leeds United	W	2 0	2 1	Dorsett, Smith	29,410
20	21	A	Liverpool	L	1 2	1 4	Dorsett	35,389
21	25	H	Huddersfield Town	D	2 0	2 2	Parkes, Martin	29,906
22	26	A	Huddersfield Town	L	0 0	0 1		39,606
23	28	A	Middlesbrough	W	1 0	2 1	Smith, Edwards	41,299
24	Jan 1	A	Everton	L	0 0	0 2		49,665
25	4	A	Derby County	W	0 0	2 0	Martin, Graham	50,254
26	18	A	Arsenal	W	2 0	2 0	Smith, Dorsett	57,524
27	25	H	Blackpool	D	0 1	1 1	Ford	32,541
28	Feb 1	A	Brentford	W	0 0	2 0	Ford 2	21,692
29	15	A	Portsmouth	L	2 1	2 3	Martin, Ford	26,791
30	22	A	Charlton Athletic	D	0 1	1 1	Campbell (og)	25,231
31	Mar 8	A	Manchester United	L	1 0	1 2	Dorsett	37,555
32	22	A	Bolton Wanderers	L	1 1	1 2	Martin	26,417
33	29	H	Chelsea	W	2 0	2 0	Ford, Dorsett	37,627
34	Apr 4	A	Sunderland	L	1 3	1 4	Dixon	53,796
35	5	A	Sheffield United	W	1 1	2 1	Dorsett 2	31,997
36	8	H	Sunderland	W	3 0	4 0	Ford 2, Iverson, Dorsett	30,686
37	12	H	Grimsby Town	D	3 0	3 3	Ford 2, Edwards	37,741
38	19	A	Leeds United	D	0 0	1 1	Dorsett	22,291
39	26	H	Liverpool	L	1 2	1 2	Evans	35,429
40	May 10	H	Blackburn Rovers	W	0 1	2 1	Dorsett, Dixon	22,413
41	17	H	Preston North End	W	2 1	4 2	Evans 2, Iverson, Dixon	26,197
42	26	H	Stoke City	L	0 1	0 1		39,947

Final League Position: 8th in First Division

2 Own-goals

Appearances
Goals

FA CUP

3	Jan 11	A	Burnley	L	0 2	1 5	Graham	38,532

Appearances
Goals

402

Player Appearances Table

Rutherford JHH	Potts VE	Cummings GW	Parkes HA	Callaghan E	Lowe E	Broome FH	Dixon JT	Edwards GR	Dodds TB	Smith LGF	Iverson RTJ	Goffin WC	Houghton WE	Moss F (junr)	Martin JR	Ashton DO	Haynes AET	Graham JR	Kerr AW	Dorset R	Wakeman AD	Moss A	Guttridge R	Ford T	Starling RW	Evans WE	MATCH
1	2	3	4	5	6	7	8	9	10	11																	1
1	2	3	10	5	6		8	9		11	4	7															2
1	2	3	4	5	6		8	9		10		7	11														3
1	2	3	4		6			9		11		7	10	5	8												4
1	2	3	4		6			9		11		7	10	5	8												5
1	2	3	4		6			9		11		7	10	5	8												6
1		3			6		8	9		10	4	11		5		2	7										7
1	2	3			6					10	4	11		5	8		7	9									8
1	2	3			6			9		10	4	11		5	8		7										9
1	2	3		5	6			9		11	4			8					7	10							10
1	2	3		5	6		7			11	4			8						10							11
	2	3			6		7	9		11	4		5	8						10	1						12
1	2	3			6		7	9		11	4		5	8						10							13
1	2	3			6		7	9		11	4		5	8						10							14
1	2	3			6			9		11	4	7	5	8						10							15
1	2	3	9		6			7		11	4		5	10			8										16
1	2	3			6			7		11	4		5	10			8	9									17
1	2	3	8		6			7		11	4		5	10				9									18
1	2	3	8		6			7		11	4		5	10				9									19
1	2	3	8		6			7		11	4		5	10				9									20
1	2	3	9		6			7		11			5	8						10	4						21
1	2	3			6		8	7		11			5	10							4						22
		3	9	2	6			7		11			5	8						10	4						23
1		3	6	2				10		11			5	8			7			9	4						24
1		3	6	2				9		11			5	8			7			10	4						25
	2		5		6			7		11				8						10	4	3	9				26
1	2	3	5		6		8	7		11										10	4		9				27
1	2	3	5		6			7		11			8							10	4		9				28
1	2	3	5					7		11	4		8							10			9				29
1	2	3	6					7		11			5	8						10			9				30
1	2	3			6			7		11	4		5	8				9		10							31
1	2				6			7		11	4		5	8				9		10		3					32
1	2				6		8	7		11	4		5							10		3	9				33
1	2	3			6		7	8		11	4		5							10			9				34
1	2				6		8	9		11	4		5		7					10		3					35
1			6	2				7		11	4		5	8						10		3	9				36
1			6	2				7		11	4		5							10		3	9	8			37
1	2		9		6		8	7		11	4		5							10		3					38
1	2				6			7		11	4		5	8						10					9		39
1	2		7		6		8			11	4		5							10		3			9		40
1	2				6			8	7	11	4		5							10		3			9		41
1	2				6			8	7	11	4		5							10		3			9		42
41	36	31	26	10	35	1	17	40	1	42	29	9	33	29	1	4	7	1	31	1	8	11	9	1	4		
			1				6	10			7	3	3		8		2		13				9		3		

1	2		4	3			7	11			5	8		9			10				6						3
1	1		1	1			1				1	1		1	1		1				1						
															1												

FINAL LEAGUE TABLE

	P	W	D	L	F	A	P
Liverpool	42	25	7	10	84	52	57
Manchester United	42	22	12	8	95	54	56
Wolverhampton W	42	25	6	11	98	56	56
Stoke City	41	24	7	10	89	51	55
Blackpool	42	22	6	14	71	70	50
Sheffield United	41	20	7	14	87	74	47
Preston North End	42	18	11	13	76	74	47
Aston Villa	**42**	**18**	**9**	**15**	**67**	**53**	**45**
Sunderland	42	18	8	16	65	66	44
Everton	42	17	9	16	62	67	43
Middlesbrough	42	17	8	17	73	68	42
Portsmouth	42	16	9	17	66	60	41
Arsenal	42	16	9	17	72	70	41
Derby County	42	18	5	19	73	79	41
Chelsea	42	16	7	19	69	84	39
Grimsby Town	42	13	12	17	61	82	38
Blackburn Rovers	42	14	8	20	45	53	36
Bolton Wanderers	42	13	8	21	57	69	34
Charlton Athletic	42	11	12	19	57	71	34
Huddersfield Town	42	13	7	22	53	79	33
Brentford	42	9	7	26	45	88	25
Leeds United	42	6	6	30	45	90	18

1947/48

SEASON SNIPPETS

A number of Rugby matches have been staged at Villa Park and it was at the ground that the fastest try ever recorded in Britain was scored on 17 September 1947. Australia played a Midland Counties XV and immediately after the Australians had kicked off, their captain W M McLean picked up a loose ball and sprinted straight to the by-line. McLean's touchdown was recorded at thirteen seconds. Australia went on to win 22-14.

Bob Iverson played his last League game on 30 August.

Albert 'Sailor' Brown was transferred from Nottingham Forest and made his debut on 18 October.

Keith Jones made his debut at Wolverhampton Wanderers on 27 December.

Albert Vinall and Harold Chapman both made their League debut on 26 March.

Harold Chapman made his last appearance on 10 April.

Vic Potts made his last appearance on 14 April.

On 28 June 1948, Villa Park hosted the British Middleweight Boxing Title fight between Dick Turpin and Vince Hawkins. Turpin won on points - the first black boxer ever to win a British boxing title.

DIVISION ONE

MANAGER: Alex Massie

MATCH	DATE	VENUE	OPPONENTS	RESULT	HT SCORE	SCORE	SCORERS	ATT
1	Aug 23	A	Grimsby Town	L	0 1	0 3		20,532
2	27	A	Sunderland	D	0 0	0 0		42,253
3	30	H	Manchester City	D	0 1	1 1	Dorsett	50,614
4	Sep 1	H	Sunderland	W	1 0	2 0	Goffin, Ford	31,271
5	6	A	Blackburn Rovers	D	0 0	0 0		24,772
6	8	H	Everton	W	2 0	3 0	Edwards, Ford, Dixon	28,764
7	13	H	Blackpool	L	0 1	0 1		56,004
8	17	A	Everton	L	0 3	0 3		32,537
9	20	A	Derby County	W	3 1	3 1	Edwards, Ford, Lowe	32,891
10	27	H	Huddersfield Town	W	1 1	2 1	Ford, Dixon	46,013
11	Oct 4	A	Chlsea	L	1 4	2 4	Dixon, Ford (pen)	67,789
12	11	A	Arsenal	L	0 1	0 1		60,427
13	18	H	Sheffield United	W	1 0	2 0	Ford 2	47,441
14	25	A	Manchester United	L	0 0	0 2		48,264
15	Nov 1	H	Preston North End	W	2 0	4 1	Brown, Martin 2, Dorsett	51,362
16	8	A	Portsmouth	W	2 2	4 2	Brown 2, Ford 2 (1 pen)	40,440
17	15	H	Bolton Wanderers	W	1 0	3 1	Smith, Edwards 2	43,531
18	22	A	Stoke City	W	2 1	2 1	Brown, Goffin	31,891
19	29	H	Burnley	D	0 2	2 2	Martin, F Moss	56,595
20	Dec 6	A	Liverpool	D	2 1	3 3	Ford, Martin, Brown	37,732
21	13	H	Middlesbrough	D	0 1	1 1	Smith	49,188
22	20	H	Grimsby Town	D	0 1	2 2	Brown, Dorsett (pen)	31,577
23	26	H	Wolverhampton Wanderers	L	0 1	1 2	Edwards	68,099
24	27	A	Wolverhampton Wanderers	L	0 0	1 4	Smith	54,677
25	Jan 3	A	Manchester City	W	1 0	2 0	Dorsett, Dixon	52,689
26	31	A	Blackpool	L	0 0	0 1		22,203
27	Feb 14	H	Hudersfield Town	W	1 0	1 0	Ford	20,571
28	21	H	Chelsea	W	1 0	3 0	Smith, Edwards, Ford	19,082
29	28	H	Arsenal	W	1 1	4 2	Ford 2, Smith, Dixon	65,690
30	Mar 6	A	Sheffield United	L	0 2	1 3	Dorsett (pen)	37,775
31	20	A	Preston North End	L	0 2	0 3		28,001
32	22	H	Manchester United	L	0 1	0 1		52,368
33	26	A	Charlton Athletic	D	1 1	1 1	Brown	39,072
34	27	H	Portsmouth	W	2 0	2 1	Brown, Edwards	36,786
35	30	H	Charlton Athletic	W	1 1	2 1	Phipps (og), Smith	32,105
36	Apr 3	A	Bolton Wanderers	L	0 0	0 1		26,468
37	7	H	Derby County	D	1 1	2 2	Vinall, Edwards	30,736
38	10	H	Stoke City	W	0 0	1 0	Smith	30,766
39	14	H	Blackburn Rovers	W	2 0	3 2	Edwards, Smith, Goffin	19,394
40	17	A	Burnley	L	0 1	0 1		25,671
41	24	H	Liverpool	W	0 1	2 1	Ford 2	22,668
42	May 1	A	Middlesbrough	W	2 1	3 1	Ford 2, Goffin	20,892

Final League Position: 6th in First Division

1 Own-goal

Appearances
Goals

FA CUP

| 3 | Jan 10 | H | Manchester United | L | 1 5 | 4 6 | Edwards 2, Smith, Dorsett (pen) | 58,683 |

Appearances
Goals

404

Player Appearances

Match	Rutherford JHH	Potts VE	Cummings GW	Iverson RTJ	Moss F (junr)	Lowe E	Goffin WC	Edwards GR	Ford T	Dorsett R	Smith LGF	Parkes HA	Martin JR	Guttridge R	Dixon JT	Brown RAJ	Evans WE	Jones K	Graham JR	Vinall A	Chapman H	Wakeman AD
1	1	2	3	4	5	6	7	8	9	10	11											
2	1	2	3	10	5	6	7	8	9		11	4										
3	1	2	3	4	5	6	7	8	9	10	11											
4	1	2	3		5	6	7	8	9		11	4	10									
5	1	2	3		5	6		7	9	8	11	4	10									
6	1		3			6		7	9	4	11	5	10	2	8							
7	1		3			6		7	9	4	11	5	10	2	8							
8	1	2	3		5	10		7	9	4	11	6			8							
9	1	2	3		5	10		7	9	4	11	6			8							
10	1	2	3		5	10		7	9	4	11	6			8							
11	1	2	3		5	10		7	9	4	11	6			8							
12	1	2	3		5		11	7	9	4	10	6	8									
13	1	2			5			7	9	4	11	6	8	3	10							
14	1	2			5			7	9	4	11	6	8	3	10							
15	1	2			5	6		7	9	4	11	3	8		10							
16	1	2			5	6		7	9	4	11	3	8		10							
17	1	2	3		5		7		9	4	11	6	8		10							
18	1	2			5	6	7		9	4	11	3	8		10							
19	1	2			5	6		7	9	4	11	3	8		10							
20	1	2			5	6		7	9	4	11	3	8		10							
21	1	2			5	6		7	9	4	11	3	8		10							
22	1	2			5	6	7		9	4	11	3	8		10							
23	1	2			5	6		7		4	11	3	9		10	8						
24					5	6	11	7		4	9	3	8			10	1					
25		2			5	6			9	4	11	3	8		7	10	1					
26		2	3		5	6		7	9	4	11		8			10	1					
27			3		2	6		7	9	4	11	5				10	1	8				
28			3		2	6		7	9	4	11	5			8	10	1					
29			3		2	6		7	9	4	11	5			8	10	1					
30			3		2	6		7	9	4	11	5			8	10	1					
31		2	3		5			7	9	4	11	6				10	1					
32			3		2	6		7	9	4	11	5			8	10	1					
33			2			6		7	9	10	11	5				8	1		3	4		
34			2			6		7	9	10	11	5			8		1		3	4		
35			2			6		7	9	10	11	5			8		1		3	4		
36			2			6	7	9			10	11	5				1		3	4		
37			2			6	11	7		9	4	10	5						3	8	1	
38			3		2	6			7	9	4	11	5	10			1			8		
39		2	3			6		7	10	9	4	11	5	8			1					
40			3		2	6		7	10	9	4	11	5	8			1					
41			3		2	6		7	10	9	4	11	5	8			1					
42			3		2	6		7	10	9	4	11	5	8			1					
	23	26	30	3	34	37	15	42	35	40	42	40	23	4	12	23	2	18	1	5	6	1
				1		1	4	9	18	5	8		4		5	8				1		

Goals: 2 5 6 7 9 4 11 3 8 10 1 3

1 1 1 1 1 1 1 1 1 1 1 1
2 1 1

FINAL LEAGUE TABLE

	P	W	D	L	F	A	P
Arsenal	42	23	13	6	81	32	59
Manchester United	42	19	14	9	81	48	52
Burnley	42	20	12	10	56	43	52
Derby County	42	19	12	11	77	57	50
Wolverhampton W	42	19	9	14	83	70	47
Aston Villa	**42**	**19**	**9**	**14**	**65**	**57**	**47**
Preston North End	42	20	7	15	67	68	47
Portsmouth	42	19	7	16	68	50	45
Blackpool	42	17	10	15	57	41	44
Manchester City	42	15	12	15	52	47	42
Liverpool	42	16	10	16	65	61	42
Sheffield United	42	16	10	16	65	70	42
Charlton Athletic	42	17	6	19	57	66	40
Everton	42	17	6	19	52	66	40
Stoke City	42	14	10	18	41	55	38
Middlesbrough	42	14	9	19	71	73	37
Bolton Wanderers	42	16	5	21	46	58	37
Chelsea	42	14	9	19	53	71	37
Huddersfield Town	42	12	12	18	51	60	36
Sunderland	42	13	10	19	56	67	36
Blackburn Rovers	42	11	10	21	54	72	32
Grimsby Town	42	8	6	28	45	111	22

1948/49

SEASON SNIPPETS

Ambrose 'Jock' Mulraney made his first Villa appearance against Newcastle United on 13 September.

Robert 'Sailor' Brown was injured in the game against Portsmouth on 9 October. Brown never fully recovered and announced his retirement in June 1949.

Jackie Martin played his last game against Arsenal on 11 September 1948. Martin retired at the end of the season.

Versatile Con Martin made his Villa debut at centre-half against Sheffield United on 2 October after moving from Leeds United.

Centre-forward Syd Howarth made his debut against Charlton Athletic on 23 October as Trevor Ford was leading the attack for Wales in the international against Scotland.

Miller Craddock made his debut in a 6-0 defeat at Middlesbrough on 11 December.

Ivor Powell made his debut at Liverpool on 18 December following a record £17,500 move from Queens Park Rangers.

Herbie Smith made his first-team debut in the Third Round FA Cup replay with Bolton Wanderers on 15 January 1949.

Villa again paid £17,500 this time for Colin H Gibson who arrived from Newcastle United in February, making his Villa debut in a 1-0 win at Huddersfield Town.

George Cummings retired in May and was appointed Villa's third-team coach.

DIVISION ONE

MANAGER: Alex Massie

MATCH	DATE	VENUE	OPPONENTS	RESULT	HT SCORE	SCORE	SCORERS	ATT
1	Aug 21	H	Liverpool	W	2 0	2 1	Ford 2	42,193
2	25	A	Bolton Wanderers	L	0 0	0 3		24,774
3	28	A	Blackpool	L	0 1	0 1		29,815
4	30	H	Bolton Wanderers	L	1 1	2 4	J Martin, Graham	26,890
5	Sep 4	H	Derby County	D	0 0	1 1	Dorsett (pen)	50,791
6	8	A	Newcastle United	L	1 1	1 2	Dixon	56,510
7	11	A	Arsenal	L	0 2	1 3	Edwards	54,144
8	13	H	Newcastle United	L	1 2	2 4	Dixon, Edwards	30,981
9	18	H	Huddersfield Town	D	1 0	3 3	Edwards, Brown, Smith	42,843
10	25	A	Manchester United	L	1 2	1 3	Edwards	53,820
11	Oct 2	H	Sheffield United	W	3 0	4 3	Ford 2, Edwards 2	49,629
12	9	H	Portsmouth	D	0 0	1 1	Mulraney	57,649
13	16	A	Manchester City	L	1 1	1 4	Smith	41,240
14	23	H	Charlton Athletic	W	2 2	4 3	Mulraney, Dorsett 2, Edwards	49,769
15	30	A	Stoke City	L	1 3	2 4	Dorsett (pen), Edwards	37,313
16	Nov 6	H	Burnley	W	1 1	3 1	Dorsett, Smith, Ford	43,323
17	13	A	Preston North End	W	1 0	1 0	Edwards	22,289
18	20	H	Everton	L	0 0	0 1		43,382
19	27	A	Chelsea	L	1 1	1 2	Smith	32,920
20	Dec 4	H	Birmingham City	L	0 1	0 3		62,424
21	11	A	Middlesbrough	L	0 2	0 6		21,184
22	18	A	Liverpool	D	1 1	1 1	Lowe	23,866
23	25	A	Wolverhampton Wanderers	L	0 3	0 4		39,640
24	27	H	Wolverhampton Wanderers	W	1 0	5 1	Howarth, Ford 4 (1 pen)	63,769
25	Jan 1	H	Blackpool	L	1 4	2 5	Edwards, Goffin	48,392
26	22	H	Arsenal	W	1 0	1 0	Goffin	69,191
27	Feb 12	A	Huddersfield Town	W	1 0	1 0	Ford	15,401
28	19	H	Manchester United	W	0 0	2 1	Dixon, Ford	68,354
29	26	A	Sheffield United	W	0 0	1 0	Howarth	33,268
30	Mar 5	A	Portsmouth	L	0 1	0 3		34,264
31	12	H	Manchester City	W	0 0	1 0	Goffin	41,952
32	19	A	Everton	W	1 1	3 1	Gibson, Dixon 2	50,201
33	26	H	Chelsea	D	0 1	1 1	Dorsett (pen)	40,954
34	Apr 2	A	Burnley	D	1 1	1 1	Dorsett	24,709
35	9	H	Preston North End	W	1 0	2 0	Smith, Ford	37,526
36	15	A	Sunderland	D	0 0	0 0		51,374
37	16	A	Charlton Athletic	W	1 0	2 0	Edwards, Dorsett	32,071
38	19	H	Sunderland	D	1 0	1 1	Ford	46,476
39	23	A	Stoke City	W	1 0	2 1	Edwards, Dixon	39,184
40	27	A	Derby County	D	1 2	2 2	Dixon, Dorsett (pen)	23,405
41	30	A	Birmingham City	W	1 0	1 0	Craddock	45,120
42	May 7	H	Middlesbrough	D	0 1	1 1	Dorsett	38,051

Final League Position: 10th in First Division

Appearances
Goals

FA CUP

3	Jan 8	H	Bolton Wanderers *	D	1 0	1 1	Ford	53,459
R	15	A	Bolton Wanderers *	D	0 0	0 0		38,706
2R	17	H	Bolton Wanderers *	W	0 0	2 1	Edwards, Smith H	49,709
4	29	H	Cardiff City	L	1 0	1 2	Dorsett	70,718

Appearances
Goals

* After extra-time

Jones K	Moss F (junr)	Cummings GW	Dorsett R	Parkes HA	Lowe E	Goffin WC	Brown RAJ	Ford T	Edwards GR	Smith LGF	Martin JR	Dixon JT	Graham JR	Canning L	Mulraney AA	Ashton DO	Martin CJ	Rutherford JHH	Howarth S	Moss A	Craddock LM	Powell IV	Evans WE	Gibson CH	Smith HH	MATCH
1	2	3	4	5	6	7	8	9	10	11																1
1	2	3	4	5	6	7	8	9	10	11																2
1	2	3	4	5	6	7		9	10	11	8															3
1	2	3	4	5	6			9	11	8	7	10														4
1	5	3	2	4	6		10	9	11	8	7															5
1	5	3	2	4	6		10	9	11	8	7															6
1	5	3	2	4	6			10	11	8	7		9													7
1	5	3	2	4	6				10	11	8		9	7												8
1	5		4	2	6		10		9	11	8			7	3											9
1		3	4	5	6			9	10	11		8		7	2											10
1		3	4		6		8	9	10	11				7	2	5										11
1		3	4	5	6		8	9	10	11				7	2											12
1		3	4	8	6			9	10	11				7	2	5										13
		3	8	6	4				10	11				7	2	5	1	9								14
		3	8	6	4			9	7	11					2	5	1	10								15
	5	3	8	6	4			9	10	11				7	2	1										16
	4	3	8	5	6				10	11				7	2	1	9									17
	4	3	8	5	6			9	10	11				7	2	1										18
	4	3	10	5	6			9		11				7	2	1	8									19
	5	3	8		6			9	10	11				7	2	1		4								20
	4	3	8	5	6	10		9		11					2	1			7							21
	5	3		6	10	8		9	7	11					2	1		4								22
	5	3		6	10	8		9	7	11					2	1		4								23
		3		2	6	11		9	7		10				5	1	8	4								24
		3		2	6	11		9	7		10				5	1	8	4								25
	6	3	10	2		11		9			7				5	1		4	8							26
	6	3	10	2					11		8				5	1		4	7							27
	6	3	10	2				9		11	8				5	1		4	7							28
		3	2		10				11		8				5	1	9	4	7							29
	6	3	10	2				9		11	8				5	1		4	7							30
	6		3	2		7		9		11	10				5	1		4	8							31
	6		3	2		7		9		11	10				5	1		4	8							32
	6		3	2				9		11	10				5	1		4	8							33
	6		3	2		7		9		11	10				5	1		4	8							34
	6		3	2		7		9		11	10				5	1		4	8							35
	6		3	2		7		9		11	10				5	1		4								36
	6	3	8	2				9	7	11	10				5	1		4								37
	6	3	8	2				9	7	11	10				5	1		4								38
	6	3	8	2				9	7	11	10				5	1		4								39
	6	3	8	2					7	11	10				5	1		4								40
	6	3	8	2					7	11	10				5	1		9	4							41
	6	3	10	2	4			11			9				5	1		7			8					42

| 13 | 34 | 34 | 38 | 40 | 26 | 16 | 7 | 31 | 29 | 38 | 5 | 25 | 2 | 2 | 12 | 7 | 31 | 29 | 7 | 1 | 3 | 20 | 1 | 11 | | |
| | | | 10 | | | 1 | 3 | 1 | 13 | 12 | 5 | 1 | 7 | 1 | 2 | | 2 | | 1 | | | 1 | | 1 | | |

		3		2	6	11		9	7		10				5	1	8		4							3 R
	6	3	10	2		11		9	8						5	1			4			7				2R
	6	3	10	2		11		9	8						5	1			4			7				4
	6	3	8	2		11		9	7	10					5	1			4							

| | | 3 | 4 | 3 | 4 | 1 | 4 | | 4 | 4 | 1 | | 1 | | | | 4 | 4 | 1 | | | 4 | | 2 | | |
| | | | | | | 1 | | | 1 | 1 | | | | | | | | | | | | | | 1 | | |

FINAL LEAGUE TABLE

	P	W	D	L	F	A	P
Portsmouth	42	25	8	9	84	42	58
Manchester United	42	21	11	10	77	44	53
Derby County	42	22	9	11	74	55	53
Newcastle United	42	20	12	10	70	56	52
Arsenal	42	18	13	11	74	44	49
Wolverhampton W	42	17	12	13	79	66	46
Manchester City	42	15	15	12	47	51	45
Sunderland	42	13	17	12	49	58	43
Charlton Athletic	42	15	12	15	63	67	42
Aston Villa	**42**	**16**	**10**	**16**	**60**	**76**	**42**
Stoke City	42	16	9	17	66	68	41
Liverpool	42	13	14	15	53	43	40
Chelsea	42	12	14	16	69	68	38
Bolton Wanderers	42	14	10	18	59	68	38
Burnley	42	12	14	16	43	50	38
Blackpool	42	11	16	15	54	67	38
Birmingham City	42	11	15	16	36	38	37
Everton	42	13	11	18	41	63	37
Middlesbrough	42	11	12	19	46	57	34
Huddersfield Town	42	12	10	20	40	69	34
Preston North End	42	11	11	20	62	75	33
Sheffield United	42	11	11	20	57	78	33

1949/50

SEASON SNIPPETS

Villa played all season without a manager following the shock resignation of Alex Massie during the summer.

Soon after making Trevor Ford's fifth-minute goal against Derby County on 31 August, Leslie G F Smith suffered a broken collar bone that would keep him out of action until November.

The 4-1 home defeat to Manchester United on 15 October was Syd Howarth's last Villa game.

Alan Wakeman made his last senior appearance in the 4-1 defeat at home to Wolves on 27 December.

Pat Daly made his debut at Blackpool on 14 January having been signed from Shamrock Rovers two months earlier, but Daly went on to play only four first-team games before returning home in May 1951.

Eddie Lowe made his last senior appearance in the FA Cup third round second replay against Middlesbrough at Leeds on 16 January. In May Lowe left for Fulham along with brother Reg.

DIVISION ONE

MANAGER: Directors

MATCH	DATE	VENUE	OPPONENTS	RESULT	HT SCORE	SCORE	SCORERS	ATT
1	20	A	Manchester City	D	1 1	3 3	L Smith, Goffin 2	43,196
2	23	H	Derby County	D	1 0	1 1	Ford	53,080
3	27	H	Fulham	W	2 0	3 1	L Smith, Goffin, Ford	47,785
4	31	A	Derby County	L	1 2	2 3	Ford, Goffin	31,748
5	Sep 3	A	Newcastle United	L	1 2	2 3	Lowe, Ford	57,669
6	5	H	Portsmouth	W	0 0	1 0	Powell	38,360
7	10	H	Blackpool	D	0 0	0 0		60,337
8	17	A	Middlesbrough	W	1 0	2 0	Goffin 2	30,525
9	24	H	Everton	D	1 1	2 2	Goffin, Ford	47,186
10	Oct 1	A	Huddersfield Town	L	0 1	0 1		20,636
11	8	A	West Bromwich Albion	D	0 0	1 1	Ford	53,690
12	15	H	Manchester United	L	0 3	0 4		47,483
13	22	A	Chelsea	W	2 1	3 1	Ford, Dixon, Craddock	44,705
14	29	H	Stoke City	D	0 0	1 1	Dixon	40,290
15	Nov 5	A	Burnley	L	0 1	0 1		24,030
16	12	H	Sunderland	W	2 0	2 0	Ford, Craddock	42,160
17	19	A	Liverpool	L	0 1	1 2	Dixon	50,293
18	26	H	Arsenal	D	1 0	1 1	Ford	45,863
19	Dec 3	A	Bolton Wanderers	D	0 0	1 1	Harrison	22,861
20	10	H	Birmingham City	D	1 1	1 1	Ford	45,008
21	17	A	Manchester City	W	0 0	1 0	F Moss	27,622
22	24	A	Fulham	L	0 2	0 3		30,663
23	26	A	Wolverhampton Wanderers	W	2 1	3 2	Powell, Edwards, Ford	54,571
24	27	H	Wolverhampton Wanderers	L	0 1	1 4	Dixon	64,937
25	31	H	Newcastle United	L	0 1	0 1		40,909
26	Jan 14	A	Blackpool	L	0 1	0 1		23,743
27	21	H	Middlesbrough	W	2 0	4 0	Goffin 2, Ford, Craddock	32,387
28	Feb 4	A	Everton	D	1 0	1 1	Gibson	43,634
29	18	H	Huddersfield Town	W	2 0	2 1	Ford 2	35,119
30	25	H	West Bromwich Albion	W	0 0	1 0	Gibson	47,539
31	Mar 8	A	Manchester United	L	0 1	0 7		24,072
32	11	H	Liverpool	W	1 0	2 0	Goffin, Dixon	40,820
33	25	H	Burnley	L	0 0	0 1		29,923
34	29	A	Arsenal	W	2 1	3 1	Gibson, Dixon 2	24,736
35	Apr 1	A	Sunderland	L	0 1	1 2	Edwards	36,293
36	7	A	Charlton Athletic	W	1 1	4 1	Ford, Martin (pen), Goffin, Dixon	37,917
37	8	H	Chelsea	W	1 0	4 0	Powell, Dixon, Ford, Goffin	37,730
38	11	H	Charlton Athletic	D	0 1	1 1	L Smith	41,854
39	15	A	Stoke City	L	0 0	0 0		20,660
40	22	H	Bolton Wanderers	W	2 0	3 0	Goffin, Dixon 2	29,820
41	29	A	Birmingham City	D	1 0	2 2	Ford 2	24,866
42	May 6	A	Portsmouth	L	0 2	1 5	Dorsett (pen)	41,638

Final League Position: 12th in First Division

Appearances
Goals

FA CUP

3	Jan 7	H	Middlesbrough	D	1 0	2 2	Gibson, Dorsett (pen)	50,097
R	11	A	Middlesbrough *	D	0 0	0 0		49,876
2R	16	N	Middlesbrough **	L	0 2	0 3		43,011

Appearances
Goals

* After extra-time
** Played at Elland Road, Leeds

Player Appearances

Match	Rutherford JHH	Parkes HA	Harrison JC	Powell IV	Martin CJ	Moss F (junr)	Gofrin WC	Dorsett R	Ford T	Gibson CH	Smith LGF	Dixon JT	Lowe E	Craddock LM	Jones K	Moss A	Howarth S	Smith HH	Edwards GR	Wakeman AD	Daly P
1	1	2	3	4	5	6	7	8	9	10	11										
2	1	2	3	4	5	6	7	10	9	8	11										
3	1	2	3	4	5	6	7	10	9	8	11										
4	1	2		4	5	6	7	3	9	8	11	10									
5		2		4	5	6	11	3	9	7		8	10								
6	1	2	10	4	5	6	11	3		7		8		9							
7		2		4	5	6	11	3	9	8		10		7	1						
8		2		4	5	6	11	3	9	8		10		7	1						
9		2		4	5	6	11	3	9	8		10		7	1						
10		2		4	5	6	11	3	9	8		10		7	1						
11		2		4	5	6	11	3	9			10	5	7	1						
12		2		4	5	6	11	3		8	10		7	1		9					
13		2		4	5	6	11	3	9	8		10		7	1						
14		2		4	5	6	11	3	9	8		10		7	1						
15		2		4	5	6		3	9	8		10		7	1		11				
16		2		4	5	6		3	9	8	11	10		7	1						
17	1	2		4	5	6		3	9	7	11	10	8								
18	1	2		4	5	6		3	9	7	11	10						8			
19	1	2	8	4	5	6		3		7	11	10						9			
20	1	2	8	4	5	6		3	9		11	7						10			
21		2	8	4	5	6		3	9		11	7						10	1		
22				2	5	6	7	3	9		11	8	4					10	1		
23		2		4	5		7	3	9		11	10						8	1		
24				4	5	2	7	3	9		11	10	6		1			8	1		
25	1	2		4	5	6		3	9	7	11	10	8								
26	1	2		4	5	6			9	7	11	10	8							3	
27	1	2		4	5	6	10		9	8	11		7							3	
28		2		4	5	6	10		9	8	11		7							3	
29	1	2		4	5	6	10	3	9	8	11	7									
30	1	2		4	5	6	10	3	9	8	11	7									
31	1	2	9	4		6	10	3		8	11	7			5						
32	1	2		4	5	6	10	3	9	8	11	7									
33	1	2		4	5	6	10	3	9	8	11	7									
34		2		4	5	6	10	3	9	8	11	7									
35	1	2		4	5	6		11		3	8		7			9			10		
36	1	2		4	5	6	10	3	9		11	7							8		
37	1	2		4	5	6	10	3	9		11	7							8		
38	1	2		4	5	6	10	3	9		11	7							8		
39	1	2		4	5	6	10	3	9		11	7							8		
40	1	2		4	5	6	10	3	9	8	11	7									
41	1	2		4	5	6	10	3	9	8	11	7									
42	1	2		4	5	6	11	3		8		7			9				10		
	28	40	8	42	40	42	33	39	36	32	29	37	6	16	10	2	1	1	13	4	3
			1		3	1	1	13	1	18	3	3	11	1	3				2		

FA Cup

3	1	2		4	5	6		3	9	7	11	10	8									
R	1	2		4	5	6		3	9	7	11	10	8									
2R	1	2		4	5	6	7		9		11	10	8							3		
	3	3		3	3	3	1	2	3	2	3	3	3							1		
							1			1												

FINAL LEAGUE TABLE

	P	W	D	L	F	A	P
Portsmouth	42	22	9	11	74	38	53
Wolverhampton W	42	20	13	9	76	49	53
Sunderland	42	21	10	11	83	62	52
Manchester United	42	18	14	10	69	44	50
Newcastle United	42	19	12	11	77	55	50
Arsenal	42	19	11	12	79	55	49
Blackpool	42	17	15	10	46	35	49
Liverpool	42	17	14	11	64	54	48
Middlesbrough	42	20	7	15	59	48	47
Burnley	42	16	13	13	40	40	45
Derby County	42	17	10	15	69	61	44
Aston Villa	**42**	**15**	**12**	**15**	**61**	**61**	**42**
Chelsea	42	12	16	14	58	65	40
West Bromwich A	42	14	12	16	47	53	40
Huddersfield Town	42	14	9	19	52	73	37
Bolton Wanderers	42	10	14	18	45	59	34
Fulham	42	10	14	18	41	54	34
Everton	42	10	14	18	42	66	34
Stoke City	42	11	12	19	45	75	34
Charlton Athletic	42	13	6	23	53	65	32
Manchester City	42	8	13	21	36	68	29
Birmingham City	42	7	14	21	31	67	28

409

1950/51

SEASON SNIPPETS

Villa again started the season without a manager, but on 15 December it was announced that Newcastle United boss George Martin was taking over as club manager at Villa park.

In October, Trevor Ford departed for Sunderland for a fee of £30,000, signing off with a goal against Huddersfield Town which gave him a Villa strike rate of 60 goals in 120 league games.

Dave Walsh arrived from West Bromwich Albion in December, Villa paying a record £25,000.

Ivor Powell was injured in the 3-3 draw at home to Everton on 2 December and played at outside-right in the second half. It was his last senior Villa game.

Miller Craddock's last game was at home to Derby on 23 December and Jack Hindle made his last appearance against Charlton Athletic on Boxing Day.

After thirteen years with the club, George Edwards made his last senior appearance at Bolton on 20 January.

Northern Ireland international half-back Danny Blanchflower arrived from Barnsley in March for a fee of £15,000.

DIVISION ONE

MANAGER: George Martin (from 15 December 1950)

MATCH	DATE	VENUE	OPPONENTS	RESULT	HT SCORE	SCORE	SCORERS	ATT
1	Aug 19	H	West Bromwich Albion	W	1 0	2 0	Dixon, Gibson	58,804
2	21	H	Sunderland	W	2 1	3 1	Craddock, Dixon, Gibson	37,143
3	26	A	Derby County	L	2 3	2 4	Craddock, L Smith	26,865
4	30	A	Sunderland	D	1 2	3 3	Powell, Dixon, Craddock	40,893
5	Sep 2	H	Liverpool	D	0 1	1 1	F Moss	45,127
6	4	H	Manchester United	L	0 1	1 3	Ford	42,724
7	9	A	Fulham	L	1 2	1 2	Goffin	35,817
8	13	A	Manchester United	D	0 0	0 0		34,824
9	16	H	Bolton Wanderers	L	0 0	0 1		32,817
10	23	A	Blackpool	D	0 1	1 1	Goffin	33,298
11	30	H	Tottenham Hotspur	L	1 1	2 3	Thompson, L Smith	36,538
12	Oct 7	H	Newcastle United	W	1 0	3 0	Powell, Craddock, Thompson	41,989
13	14	A	Huddersfield Town	L	0 3	2 4	Edwards, Ford	25,903
14	21	H	Arsenal	D	0 1	1 1	Canning	53,111
15	28	A	Burnley	L	0 1	0 2		26,471
16	Nov 4	H	Middlesbrough	L	0 1	0 1		36,542
17	11	A	Sheffield Wednesday	L	0 2	2 3	Craddock, Gibson	37,080
18	18	H	Chelsea	W	2 2	4 2	Dixon 2, Craddock, Thompson	27,609
19	25	A	Portsmouth	D	0 2	3 3	Dixon 2, Thompson	30,399
20	Dec 2	H	Everton	D	1 2	3 3	L Smith 2, Dorsett (pen)	27,133
21	9	A	Stoke City	L	0 1	0 1		19,291
22	16	A	West Bromwich Albion	L	0 1	0 2		27,599
23	23	H	Derby County	D	1 1	1 1	Lynn	28,129
24	25	A	Charlton Athletic	D	1 1	2 2	Thompson, L Smith	17,192
25	26	H	Charlton Athletic	D	0 0	0 0		32,837
26	Jan 13	H	Fulham	W	1 0	3 0	Lynn (pen), Dixon, Quested (og)	39,994
27	20	A	Bolton Wanderers	L	0 1	0 1		29,233
28	Feb 3	H	Blackpool	L	0 1	0 3		55,093
29	17	A	Tottenham Hotspur	L	0 1	2 3	Dixon, Gibson	47,842
30	Mar 3	H	Huddersfield Town	L	0 1	0 1		36,083
31	10	A	Arsenal	L	0 0	1 2	Lynn (pen)	39,747
32	17	H	Burnley	W	2 2	3 2	Canning, Pace, Dixon	26,347
33	24	A	Middlesbrough	L	1 0	1 2	Dixon	28,580
34	26	H	Wolverhampton Wanderers	W	2 0	3 2	Dixon, Parkes (pen), Short (og)	38,340
35	27	A	Wolverhampton Wanderers	W	1 0	1 0	Thompson	60,102
36	31	H	Sheffield Wednesday	W	1 0	2 1	Walsh, Thompson	29,321
37	Apr 4	A	Newcastle United	W	1 0	1 0	Thompson	38,543
38	7	A	Chelsea	D	0 0	1 1	H Smith	28,569
39	14	H	Portsmouth	D	1 0	3 3	H Smith, Dixon, Parkes (pen)	33,560
40	21	A	Everton	W	1 1	2 1	Dixon, H Smith	45,245
41	25	A	Liverpool	D	1 0	0 0		23,061
42	May 5	H	Stoke City	W	1 1	6 2	Thompson 2, Walsh 2, Dixon, J Sellars (og)	24,739

Final League Position: 15th in First Division

3 Own-goals

Appearances
Goals

FA CUP

3	Jan 6	H	Burnley	W	1 0	2 0	Thompson, L Smith	37,806
4	27	A	Wolverhampton Wanderers	L	0 2	1 3	Dixon	53,148

Appearances
Goals

410

Players and Appearances

	Jones K	Parkes HA	Dorsett R	Powell IV	Martin CJ	Moss F (junr)	Dixon JT	Gibson CH	Craddock LM	Goffin WC	Smith LGF	Edwards GR	Ford T	Hindle JR	Canning L	Thompson T	Lynn S	Sellars G	Moss A	Smith HH	Walsh DJ	Rutherford JHH	Jeffries RJ	Aldis BP	Blanchflower RD	Pace DJ	MATCH
	1	2	3	4	5	6	7	8	9	10	11																1
	1	2	3	4	5	6	7	8	9	10	11																2
	1	2	3	4	5	6	7	8	9	10	11																3
	1	2	3	4	5	6	10	8	9	11		7															4
	1	2	3	4	5	6		8	10	11		7	9														5
	1	2	3	4	5	6		8	10	11		7	9														6
	1	2	3	4	5	6	7	8	10	11			9														7
		2	3	8	5	6	10	7		11			9	1	4												8
		2	3	8	5	6	10	7		11			9	1	4												9
		2	3	4	5	6	10	7		11			9	1		8											10
		2	3	4	5	6		8	7	11			9	1		10											11
		2	3	4	5	6		8	7	11			9	1		10											12
		2		4	5	6		8		10	11	7	9	1			3										13
		2	3		5	6	10	8		11	9			1	4			7									14
		2	3	4	5	6		7		11	9			1	8	10											15
		2	3		5	6	7	8		11	9			1	4	10											16
	1	2	3		5	6	10	7	9	11				4		8											17
	1	2	3	4	5	6	10	7	9	11						8											18
	1	2	3	4	5	6	10	7	9	11						8											19
		2	3	4	5	6	10	7	9	11				1		8											20
		2	3			6	10			11				1	4	8			5	7							21
		2	3		5		10		9	11				1	4	8	9	7		6							22
		2	3		5		10		7	11				1	4	8	9			6							23
		2	3		5			7	11	10				1	4	8	9			6							24
		2	3		5			7	11	10				1	4	8	9			6							25
	1	3			5		7	10		11					4	8	2			6	9						26
	1	3			5		7		11		10				4	8	2			6	9						27
	1	2	3		5		10		7	11					4	8				6	9						28
		3	10		5	6	7	11							4	8	2				1	9					29
		2	3		5	6	7	10			11				4	8					9	1					30
		6	10		5		7	11							4	8	2				1	9	3				31
			3		5		10	7							11	8	2	6			1		5	4	9		32
		2	6		5		10		11						8				7		1		3	4	9		33
		2	6			5	10		11						8				7	9	1		3	4			34
		2	6			5	10		11						8				7	9	1		3	4			35
		2	6			5	10		11						8				7	9	1		3	4			36
		2	6			5	10		11						8				7	9	1		3	4			37
		2	6			5	10		11						8				7	9	1		3	4			38
		2	6			5	10		11						8				7	9	1		3	4			39
		2	6			5	10		11						8				7	9	1		3	4			40
		2	6			5	10		11						8				7	9	1		3	4			41
		2	6			5	10		11						8				7	9	1		3	4			42
	13	41	39	17	31	32	34	25	15	24	22	11	9	15	18	31	9	2	9	11	13	14	2	12	11	2	
		2	1	2		1	15	4	6	2	5	1	2		2	10	3			3	3				1		

FINAL LEAGUE TABLE

	P	W	D	L	F	A	P
Tottenham Hotspur	42	25	10	7	82	44	60
Manchester United	42	24	8	10	74	40	56
Blackpool	42	20	10	12	79	53	50
Newcastle United	42	18	13	11	62	53	49
Arsenal	42	19	9	14	73	56	47
Middlesbrough	42	18	11	13	76	65	47
Portsmouth	42	16	15	11	71	68	47
Bolton Wanderers	42	19	7	16	64	61	45
Liverpool	42	16	11	15	53	59	43
Burnley	42	14	14	14	48	43	42
Derby County	42	16	8	18	81	75	40
Sunderland	42	12	16	14	63	73	40
Stoke City	42	13	14	15	50	59	40
Wolverhampton W	42	15	8	19	74	61	38
Aston Villa	**42**	**12**	**13**	**17**	**66**	**68**	**37**
West Bromwich A	42	13	11	18	53	61	37
Charlton Athletic	42	14	9	19	63	80	37
Fulham	42	13	11	18	52	68	37
Huddersfield Town	42	15	6	21	64	92	36
Chelsea	42	12	8	22	52	65	32
Sheffield Wednesday	42	12	8	22	64	83	32
Everton	42	12	8	22	48	86	32

1951/52

SEASON SNIPPETS

On 9 June 1951, Villa Park enjoyed its second royal visit when Princess Elizabeth - later to become Queen Elizabeth II - attended a display of physical exercise and games on the pitch organised as part of the Festival of Britain celebrations. Princess Elizabeth took tea in the Oak Room before returning home.

Villa's haul of 13 points from the first eight matches represented the club's best start to a season since 1932/33.

Just after going top of the table with a 2-0 home win over Liverpool, Villa hosted a midweek afternoon friendly against Shamrock Rovers. The game against the Irish club was drawn 1-1.

The 5-2 home defeat against Manchester United on 13 October was goalkeeper Joe Rutherford's last game.

Leslie G F Smith made his last appearance on 10 November against Charlton Athletic.

Villa's FA Cup dreams were shattered by three Newcastle United goals in as many minutes at St James' Park. Johnny Dixon had put Villa two goals up inside 13 minutes and with only nine minutes remaining Villa still led - only to lose 4-2.

Villa and Portsmouth players observed a minute's silence before the game at Villa Park on Saturday 9 February 1952 to mourn the death of King George VI.

A 7-1 thrashing of Chelsea on 15 April was the club's biggest win in the First Division for 21 years.

DIVISION ONE

MANAGER: George Martin

MATCH	DATE	VENUE	OPPONENTS	RESULT	HT SCORE	SCORE	SCORERS	ATT
1	Aug 18	A	Bolton Wanderers	L	2 2	2 5	Thompson, H Smith	30,253
2	25	H	Derby County	W	3 0	4 1	Dixon 2, L Smith, Walsh	37,548
3	27	H	Sunderland	W	2 0	2 1	Pace, Dixon	42,295
4	Sep 1	A	Manchester City	D	2 0	2 2	Pace, L Smith	32,515
5	5	A	Sunderland	W	2 1	3 1	Dixon, McLain (og), Hudgell (og)	44,107
6	8	H	Arsenal	W	1 0	1 0	Thompson	56,860
7	10	H	Huddersfield Town	W	0 0	1 0	Goffin	37,233
8	15	A	Blackpool	W	0 0	3 0	Dixon 2, Thompson	31,783
9	19	A	Huddersfield Town	L	0 1	1 3	A Moss	19,994
10	22	H	Liverpool	W	2 0	2 0	Thompson, Goffin	47,056
11	29	H	Portsmouth	L	0 2	0 2		37,283
12	Oct 6	A	Stoke City	L	0 3	1 4	Dixon	37,565
13	13	H	Manchester United	L	2 1	2 5	Goffin, H Smith	47,765
14	20	A	Tottenham Hotspur	L	0 0	0 2		49,247
15	27	H	Preston North End	W	2 0	3 2	L Smith, Dixon, Gibson	40,504
16	Nov 3	A	Burnley	L	0 1	1 2	Thompson	17,680
17	10	H	Charlton Athletic	L	0 1	0 2		34,894
18	17	A	Fulham	D	2 0	2 2	Lynn, Dixon	15,397
19	24	H	Middlesbrough	W	1 0	2 0	Dixon 2	25,415
20	Dec 1	A	West Bromwich Albion	W	1 1	2 1	Gibson 2	47,633
21	8	H	Newcastle United	D	2 1	2 2	Thompson, Dixon	32,220
22	15	H	Bolton Wanderers	D	0 1	1 1	Goffin	28,907
23	22	A	Derby County	D	1 0	1 1	Thompson	21,833
24	25	H	Wolverhampton Wanderers	D	2 1	3 3	Walsh, Dixon, Goffin	38,656
25	26	A	Wolverhampton Wanderers	W	2 0	2 1	H Smith, Thompson	45,803
26	29	H	Manchester City	L	1 1	1 2	Dixon	37,319
27	Jan 5	A	Arsenal	L	1 1	1 2	Dixon	51,540
28	19	H	Blackpool	W	1 0	4 0	Thompson 2, Dixon, Walsh	33,613
29	26	A	Liverpool	W	2 1	2 1	Dixon, Gibson	39,774
30	Feb 9	H	Portsmouth	W	0 0	2 0	Walsh, Dixon	51,179
31	16	H	Stoke City	L	1 2	2 3	A Martin (og), Walsh	38,200
32	Mar 1	A	Manchester United	D	1 1	1 1	Dixon	41,717
33	8	H	Tottenham Hotspur	L	0 0	0 3		56,475
34	15	A	Preston North End	D	1 1	2 2	Thompson, Dixon	30,192
35	22	H	Burnley	W	2 0	4 1	Dixon, Roberts, Walsh, Thompson	31,128
36	Apr 5	H	Fulham	W	2 0	4 1	Dixon, Goffin, Thompson, Walsh	17,251
37	12	A	Middlesbrough	L	0 2	0 2		26,880
38	14	A	Chelsea	D	2 2	2 2	Dorsett, Dixon	28,005
39	15	H	Chelsea	W	3 0	7 1	Gibson 2, Dixon, Goffin 3, Walsh	29,649
40	19	H	West Bromwich Albion	W	1 0	2 0	Dixon 2	47,294
41	24	A	Charlton Athletic	W	0 0	1 0	H Smith	15,544
42	26	A	Newcastle United	L	0 4	1 6	Goffin	36,852

Final League Position: 6th in First Division

3 Own-goals

Appearances
Goals

FA CUP

| 3 | Jan 12 | A | Newcastle United | L | 2 1 | 2 4 | Dixon 2 | 56,177 |

Appearances
Goals

Rutherford JHH	Parkes HA	Martin CJ	Blanchflower RD	Moss F (junr)	Dorsett R	Smith HH	Thompson T	Walsh DJ	Dixon JT	Smith LGF	Aldis BP	Pace DJ	Goffin WC	Moss A	Canning L	Cordell JG	Gibson CH	Lynn S	Jones K	Roberts K	MATCH
1	2	3	4	5	6	7	8	9	10	11											1
	2	1	4	5	6	7	8	9	10	11	3										2
	2	1	4	5	6	7	8		10	11	3	9									3
	2	1	4	5	6	7	8		10	11	3	9									4
	2	1	4	5	6	7	8		10		3	9	11								5
	2	1	4	5	6	7	8		10		3	9	11								6
	2	1	4	5	6	7	8		10		3	9	11								7
	2	1	4	5	6	7	8		10		3		11	9							8
	2	1	4	5	6	7	8		10				11	9							9
	2	1	4	5	6	7	8		10		3		11	9							10
	2	1	4	5	6	7	8		10		3		11	9							11
	2	1	4	5	6	7	8	9	10		3		11								12
1	2		4	5	10	7	8		9		3		11		6						13
	2		4	5	6	7		8	11	3	9	10			1						14
	2		4	5			8	9	10	11	3		6		1	7					15
	2		4	5			8	9	10	11	3		6		1	7					16
	2	1	4	5			8		10	11	3	9	6			7					17
	2	1	4	5		7	8		10		3		11	6			9				18
	3	1	4	5	6	7	8		10				11				9	2			19
	3	1	4	5	6	7	8		10				11				9	2			20
	3	1	4	5	6	7	8		10				11				9	2			21
	3	1	4	5	6	7	8		10				11				9	2			22
	3	1	4		6	7	8	9	10				11	5				2			23
	3	1	4	5	6	7	8	9	10				11					2			24
	3	1	4	5		7	8	9	10				11					2			25
	3	1	4		6	7	8	9	10				11	5				2			26
	3	1	4		6	7	8	9	10				11	5				2			27
	3	1	4	5	6		8	9	10				11					2	7		28
	3	1	4	5	6		8	9	10				11					2	7		29
	3	1	4	5	6		8	9	10				11					2	7		30
	3	1	4	5	6		8	9	10				11					2	7		31
	3		4	5	6		8	9	10				11					2	7	1	32
	3		4	5	6		8	9	10				11					2	7	1	33
	3		4	5	6		8	9	10				11					2	7	1	34
	3		4	5	6		8	9	10				11					2	1	7	35
	3		4	5	6		8	9	10				11					2	1	7	36
	3		4	5	6		8	9	10				11					2	1	7	37
	3		4	5	6			9	10				11				7	2	1	8	38
	3		4	5	6			9	10				11				7	2	1	8	39
	3		4	5	6			9	10				11				7	2	1	8	40
	3		4	5		7			10				11				9	2	1	8	41
	3		4	5	6	7			10				11				9	2	1	8	42

2	42	27	42	39	38	26	36	23	42	8	17	7	35	11	1	3	19	25	11	8
					1	4	13	8	26	3		2	10	1			6	1		1

	3	1	4	5	6	7	8		10		11			9	2						3
	1	1	1	1	1	1	1		1		1			1	1						
									2												

FINAL LEAGUE TABLE

	P	W	D	L	F	A	P
Manchester United	42	23	11	8	95	52	57
Tottenham Hotspur	42	22	9	11	76	51	53
Arsenal	42	21	11	10	80	61	53
Portsmouth	42	20	8	14	68	58	48
Bolton Wanderers	42	19	10	13	65	61	48
Aston Villa	**42**	**19**	**9**	**14**	**79**	**70**	**47**
Preston North End	42	17	12	13	74	54	46
Newcastle United	42	18	9	15	98	73	45
Blackpool	42	18	9	15	64	64	45
Charlton Athletic	42	17	10	15	68	63	44
Liverpool	42	12	19	11	57	61	43
Sunderland	42	15	12	15	70	61	42
West Bromwich A	42	14	13	15	74	77	41
Burnley	42	15	10	17	56	63	40
Manchester City	42	13	13	16	58	61	39
Wolverhampton W	42	12	14	16	73	73	38
Derby County	42	15	7	20	63	80	37
Middlesbrough	42	15	6	21	64	88	36
Chelsea	42	14	8	20	52	72	36
Stoke City	42	12	7	23	49	88	31
Huddersfield Town	42	10	8	24	49	82	28
Fulham	42	8	11	23	58	77	27

1952/53

SEASON SNIPPETS

Peter Aldis scored with a header from almost 35 yards in the 3 - 0 home win over Sunderland in September. The ball bounced over goalkeeper Harry Threadgold, who was distracted by a challenge by Dave Walsh. The bizarre effort was the only goal scored by Aldis in 295 appearances for the club.

Villa Park suffered its first postponement for 15 years when the game against Cardiff City in early December was called off because of ice. During the preceding week, the players even posed for photos of them 'skating' on the sheet of ice which covered the pitch.

To mark the Queen's Coronation, Villa and Birmingham City played a friendly in May, drawing 1-1 in front of a crowd estimated at around 25,000. On the end of season trip to Ireland, Villa won 8-1 against a Waterford Select XI and drew 1-1 against Shamrock Rovers.

The home game against Newcastle on 1 May was Dickie Dorsett's last league appearance.

DIVISION ONE

MANAGER: George Martin

MATCH	DATE	VENUE	OPPONENTS	RESULT	HT SCORE	SCORE	SCORERS	ATT
1	Aug 23	H	Arsenal	L	1 1	1 2	Walsh	50,930
2	30	A	Derby County	W	1 0	1 0	Gibson	22,010
3	Sep 1	H	Sunderland	W	0 0	3 0	H Smith, Aldis, Dixon	37,240
4	6	H	Blackpool	L	1 2	1 5	Dixon	52,688
5	8	A	Wolverhampton Wanderers	L	0 1	1 2	Pace	37,652
6	13	A	Chelsea	L	0 2	0 4		56,653
7	15	H	Wolverhampton Wanderers	L	0 1	0 1		33,050
8	20	H	Manchester United	D	1 1	3 3	Lockhart, Pace, Roberts	43,490
9	27	A	Portsmouth	D	1 0	1 1	Roberts	35,935
10	Oct 4	H	Bolton Wanderers	D	1 1	1 1	A Moss	32,242
11	11	A	Middlesbrough	W	1 0	1 0	Gibson	30,280
12	18	A	Liverpool	W	0 0	2 0	Hughes (og), Roberts	42,573
13	25	H	Manchester City	D	0 0	0 0		30,370
14	Nov 1	A	Stoke City	W	0 0	4 1	Dixon 3, Blanchflower	26,659
15	8	H	Preston North End	W	0 0	1 0	Gibson	41,990
16	15	A	Burnley	L	0 0	0 1		24,750
17	22	H	Tottenham Hotspur	L	0 1	0 3		32,265
18	29	A	Sheffield Wednesday	D	1 2	2 2	Lynn, Pace	29,785
19	Dec 13	H	Newcastle United	L	0 1	1 2	Dixon	38,046
20	20	A	Arsenal	L	0 2	1 3	Thompson	30,064
21	26	H	Charlton Athletic	D	0 1	1 1	Thompson	39,949
22	Jan 1	A	Sunderland	D	1 1	2 2	Dixon, Thompson	41,821
23	3	H	Derby County	W	1 0	3 0	Thompson, Dixon, Roberts	27,425
24	17	A	Blackpool	D	0 1	1 1	Gibson	21,258
25	24	H	Chelsea	D	0 0	1 1	Thompson	30,376
26	Feb 7	A	Manchester United	L	1 2	1 3	Walsh	36,134
27	18	H	Portsmouth	W	2 0	6 0	Stephen (og), Walsh 2, Dixon, Thompson, Goffin	15,181
28	21	A	Bolton Wanderers	D	0 0	0 0		34,446
29	Mar 4	A	Middlesbrough	L	0 0	0 1		13,176
30	7	H	Liverpool	W	2 0	4 0	Walsh, Dorsett, Dixon, Thompson	26,122
31	14	A	Manchester City	L	0 1	1 4	Thompson	32,552
32	18	A	Charlton Athletic	L	0 2	1 5	Walsh	10,382
33	25	H	Stoke City	D	1 0	1 1	Roberts	10,802
34	28	A	Preston North End	W	1 0	3 1	Pace 2, Walsh	21,385
35	Apr 4	H	Burnley	W	1 0	2 0	A Moss, Canning	32,404
36	6	A	West Bromwich Albion	L	1 1	2 3	Blanchflower, Walsh (pen)	32,580
37	7	H	West Bromwich Albion	D	0 1	1 1	Walsh	46,821
38	11	A	Tottenham Hotspur	D	1 0	1 1	Blanchflower	39,217
39	18	H	Sheffield Wednesday	W	1 3	4 3	Dixon 2, Gibson, Thompson	26,654
40	25	A	Cardiff City	W	1 1	2 1	Dixon, A Moss	29,917
41	29	H	Cardiff City	W	2 0	2 0	Blanchflower, Walsh	18,876
42	May 1	H	Newcastle United	L	0 1	0 1		16,809

Final League Position: 11th in First Division

2 Own-goals

Appearances
Goals

FA CUP

3	Jan 10	H	Middlesbrough	W	2 0	3 1	Dixon, Thompson, Gibson	41,996
4	31	H	Brentford	D	0 0	0 0		40,627
R	Feb 4	A	Brentford	W	1 1	2 1	Walsh, Thompson	21,735
5	14	A	Rotherham United	W	2 1	3 1	Goffin, Walsh 2	19,964
6	28	H	Everton	L	0 0	0 1		60,658

Appearances
Goals

Players

Jones K, Parkes HA, Aldis BP, Blanchflower RD, Moss F (junr), Dorsett R, Gibson CH, Moss A, Walsh DJ, Dixon JT, Goffin WC, Smith HH, Martin CJ, Roberts K, Pace DJ, Cordell JG, Lynn S, McParland PJ, Lockhart N, Thompson T, Parsons DR, Vinall A, Canning L

Match Appearances

Match	Jones K	Parkes HA	Aldis BP	Blanchflower RD	Moss F (junr)	Dorsett R	Gibson CH	Moss A	Walsh DJ	Dixon JT	Goffin WC	Smith HH	Martin CJ	Roberts K	Pace DJ	Cordell JG	Lynn S	McParland PJ	Lockhart N	Thompson T	Parsons DR	Vinall A	Canning L
1	1	2	3	4	5	6	7	8	9	10	11												
2	1	2	3	4	5	6	8		9	10	11	7											
3	1	2	3	4		6	8		9	10	11	7	5										
4	1	2	3	4		6			9	10	11	7	5	8									
5	1	2	3	4		6			9	10	11	7	5		8								
6	1	2	3	4		6	10		9		11	7	5		8								
7			3	4	10	6	8		9				5	7		1	2	11					
8			3	4		6	8			7			5	10	9	1	2	11					
9	1		3	4	5	6	8		10		7				9		2	11					
10	1		3		5	6	7	4	9						10		2	11	8				
11	1	3		4	5	6	9			10	7			8			2	11					
12	1	3		4	5	6	9			10	7			8			2	11					
13	1	3		4	5	6	9			10	7			8			2	11					
14	1	3		4	5	6	9		10	11	7			8			2						
15	1	3		4	5	6	9			10	11			7			2		8				
16	1	3		4	5	6			9	10				7			2	11	8				
17	1	3		4	5	6			9	10				7			2	11	8				
18	1	3		4	5	6			8	10	7					9	2	11					
19	1	3		4	5	6	7		9	10							2	11	8				
20	1	3		4	5	6	7		9	10							2	11	8				
21		3		4	5		9	6		10	11			7			2		8	1			
22		3		4	5	6	7			10	11			9			2		8	1			
23		3		4	5		7	6		10	11			9			2		8	1			
24		3		4	5	6	9			10	11			7			2		8	1			
25		3	2	4		6	9			10		5	7					11	8	1			
26		3	2	4	5	6	7		9									11	8	1			
27		3	2	4	5	6			9	10	11			7					8	1			
28		3	2	4	5	6			9	10	11			7					8	1			
29		3	2	4	5	6			9	10	11			7					8				
30	1	3	2	4		6	7		9	10		5		11					8				
31		3	2	4		6	7		9		11	5		10					8	1			
32		3	2	4		6			9			7	5	11					8	1			
33		3	2	4	5	6	8			11	7			10	9					1			
34		2		8	5		6	9						7	10			11		1	3	4	
35		2		8	5		6	9		11				7	10					1	3	4	
36		2		8	5		6	9		11				7	10					1	3	4	
37		2	3	8	5		6	9	10					11	7					1		4	
38		2	3	8	5		11	6	9	7								10	1			4	
39		2	3	8	5		11	6	9	7								10	1			4	
40		2	3	8	5		11	6	9	7								10	1			4	
41		2	3	8	5		11	6	9	7								10	1			4	
42		2	3	8	5	6	11		9					7				10	1			4	

Appearances: 20, 40, 23, 41, 33, 32, 30, 12, 30, 27, 23, 12, 10, 29, 11, 2, 18, 1, 14, 22, 20, 3, 9
Goals: 1, 4, 1, 5, 3, 10, 13, 1, 1, 5, 5, 1, 9, 1

FA Cup

Round																								
3			3		4	5	6	9			10	11			7			2		8	1			
4			3	2	4	5	6			9	10			7					11	8	1			
R			3	2	4	5	6	7		9	10								11	8	1			
5			3	2	4	5				9	10	11		7						8	1			
6			3	2	4	5	6			9	10	11		7						8	1			

Appearances: 5, 4, 5, 5, 5, 2, , 4, 5, 3, , , 4, , , 1, , , 2, 5, 5, ,
Goals: , , , , , , , 1, , 3, 1, 1, , , , , , , , , 2, ,

FINAL LEAGUE TABLE

	P	W	D	L	F	A	P
Arsenal	42	21	12	9	97	64	54
Preston North End	42	21	12	9	85	60	54
Wolverhampton W	42	19	13	10	86	63	51
West Bromwich A	42	21	8	13	66	60	50
Charlton Athletic	42	19	11	12	77	63	49
Burnley	42	18	12	12	67	52	48
Blackpool	42	19	9	14	71	70	47
Manchester United	42	18	10	14	69	72	46
Sunderland	42	15	13	14	68	82	43
Tottenham Hotspur	42	15	11	16	78	69	41
Aston Villa	**42**	**14**	**13**	**15**	**63**	**61**	**41**
Cardiff City	42	14	12	16	54	46	40
Middlesbrough	42	14	11	17	70	77	39
Bolton Wanderers	42	15	9	18	61	69	39
Portsmouth	42	14	10	18	74	83	38
Newcastle United	42	14	9	19	59	70	37
Liverpool	42	14	8	20	61	82	36
Sheffield Wednesday	42	12	11	19	62	72	35
Chelsea	42	12	11	19	56	66	35
Manchester City	42	14	7	21	72	87	35
Stoke City	42	12	10	20	53	66	34
Derby County	42	11	10	21	59	74	32

1953/54

SEASON SNIPPETS

Two weeks before the start of the season, George Martin was sacked as manager. He was succeeded the following month by former Villa player Eric Houghton.

Herbie Smith's last game was against Tottenham Hotspur on 19 August.

Billy Goffin made his last appearance against Huddersfield Town on 3 October.

Kenneth 'Shunter' Roberts played his last game against Cardiff City on 19 December.

On 30 December 1953 Villa Park hosted a Rugby match between a Midland XI and New Zealand All Blacks.

The New Year's Day match against Sunderland was Albert Vinall's last game.

The match against Arsenal at Highbury in January was abandoned after 22 minutes because of fog - with Villa trailing 3-0. A week later, Villa were back at Highbury for a third round FA Cup tie and were on the receiving end of a 5-1 drubbing. But when the league fixture was re-staged in April, a Peter McParland goal earned a 1-1 draw.

Seventeen-year-old Welsh winger Kenneth Owen Roberts became the youngest ever player to turn out for the club when he made his debut at Blackpool on 23 January 1954. Roberts then scored on his home debut against Chelsea the following week.

Larry Canning played his last game against Sheffield Wednesday on 31 March.

Villa made an end of season tour of Germany, losing 3-1 to Nuremburg, but beating St. Pauli 3-2 and Preussen 1-0.

DIVISION ONE

MANAGER: Eric Houghton (from 3 September)

MATCH	DATE	VENUE	OPPONENTS	RESULT	HT SCORE	SCORE	SCORERS	ATT
1	Aug 19	A	Tottenham Hotspur	L	0 1	0 1		50,202
2	22	A	Cardiff City	L	0 2	1 2	Dixon	36,671
3	24	H	Manchester City	W	1 0	3 0	Blanchflower, Thompson 2	21,194
4	29	H	Arsenal	W	2 1	2 1	Walsh, Dixon	33,731
5	Sep 2	A	Manchester City	W	1 0	1 0	Walsh	24,918
6	5	A	Portsmouth	L	0 2	1 2	Walsh	31,871
7	12	H	Blackpool	W	1 0	2 1	Thompson, Walsh	37,284
8	14	H	Sunderland	W	1 0	3 1	Thompson, Dixon 2	35,722
9	19	A	Chelsea	W	1 0	2 1	Walsh, Lockhart	47,487
10	26	H	Sheffield United	W	3 0	4 0	Walsh 2, Thompson, Lockhart	39,586
11	Oct 3	A	Huddersfield Town	L	0 3	0 4		36,534
12	10	A	Liverpool	L	1 1	1 6	Walsh	37,759
13	17	H	Newcastle United	L	1 0	1 2	Thompson	38,366
14	24	A	Manchester United	L	0 1	0 1		32,106
15	31	H	Bolton Wanderers	D	1 2	2 2	K Roberts, Walsh	25,325
16	Nov 7	A	Sheffield Wednesday	L	0 2	1 3	Thompson	30,687
17	14	H	Middlesbrough	W	4 2	5 3	Thompson 3, Walsh, Chapman	20,735
18	21	A	Burnley	L	1 2	2 3	Chapman 2	26,868
19	28	H	Charlton Athletic	W	0 2	2 1	Dixon, Thompson	30,205
20	Dec 5	A	Preston North End	D	0 1	1 1	Thompson	20,590
21	12	H	Tottenham Hotspur	L	0 0	1 2	Blanchflower	27,480
22	19	H	Cardiff City	L	0 2	1 2	Dixon	27,012
23	24	A	Wolverhampton Wanderers	W	1 0	2 1	Dixon, McParland	40,536
24	26	H	Wolverhampton Wanderers	L	1 1	1 2	Thompson	49,123
25	Jan 1	A	Sunderland	L	0 1	0 2		44,337
26	16	H	Portsmouth	D	0 0	1 1	Thompson	24,802
27	23	A	Blackpool	L	2 1	2 3	Thompson 2	16,629
28	Feb 6	H	Chelsea	D	1 1	2 2	K O Roberts, Blanchflower (pen)	20,625
29	20	H	Huddersfield Town	D	1 1	2 2	Thompson 2	24,451
30	27	H	Liverpool	W	1 0	2 1	Thompson, K O Roberts	25,973
31	Mar 6	A	Newcastle United	W	0 0	1 0	Walsh	36,847
32	13	H	Manchester United	D	1 2	2 2	Thompson, Baxter	26,023
33	20	A	Bolton Wanderers	L	0 2	0 3		26,292
34	31	H	Sheffield Wednesday	W	2 1	2 1	Thompson, Dixon	9,609
35	Apr 3	A	Middlesbrough	L	0 1	1 2	McParland	21,142
36	6	A	Arsenal	D	1 0	1 1	McParland	14,619
37	10	H	Burnley	W	2 0	5 1	Baxter, McParland, Gibson, Pace 2	23,043
38	17	A	Charlton Athletic	D	1 1	1 1	Pace	22,226
39	19	A	West Bromwich Albion	D	0 0	1 1	McParland	45,816
40	20	H	West Bromwich Albion	W	5 1	6 1	Pace 2, Tyrell 2, Dixon, Blanchflower	57,899
41	24	H	Preston North End	W	0 0	1 0	Tyrell	31,495
42	26	A	Sheffield United	L	0 1	1 2	Pace	12,796

Final League Position: 13th in First Division

Appearances
Goals

FA CUP

3	Jan 9	A	Arsenal	L	1 3	1 5	McParland	50,990

Appearances
Goals

416

Player appearances table

Match	Parsons DR	Parkes HA	Aldis BP	Blanchflower RD	Moss F (junr)	Moss A	Smith HH	Thompson T	Walsh DJ	Dixon JT	Gibson CH	Canning L	Lockhart N	Jones K	Martin CJ	Pace DJ	Goffin WC	Roberts K	Chapman RC	Baxter W	Lynn S	Vinall A	McParland PJ	Roberts KO	Tyrell JJ
1	1	2	3	4	5	6	7	8	9	10	11														
2	1	2	3	4	5	6		8	9	10		7	11												
3	1	2	3	8	5	6		10	9	7		4	11												
4		2	3	8	5	6		10	9	7		4	11	1											
5		2	3	8	5	6		10	9	7		4	11	1											
6		2	3	8		6		10	9	7		4	11	1	5										
7		2	3	4	5	6		8	9	10	7		11	1											
8		2	3	4	5	6		8	9	10	7		11	1											
9		2	3	4	5	6		8	9	10	7		11	1											
10		2	3	4	5	6		8	9	10	7		11	1											
11		2	3		5	6		8		10	7	4			9	11									
12		2	3	4	5	6		8	9	10	7		11	1											
13	1	2	3	4	5	6		8	9	10	7						11								
14	1	2	3	4	5	6		8	9		7		11			10									
15	1	2	3	4	5	6		8	9	10			11				7								
16	1	2	3	4	5	6		8	9	10			11				7								
17	1	2	3	4	5			8	9		7	6	11					10							
18	1	2	3	4	5			8	9		7	6	11					10							
19		2	3	4	5			8	9	7	11			1				10	6						
20		2	3	4	5			8	9	10	7			1			11		6						
21			3	4	5	6		8	9	10	7		11	1						2					
22		2	3	4	5			8		7	9		11	1		10			6						
23		2			8	5	6		10	9	7						4		3	11					
24				8		6		10	9	7		1	5				4	2	3	11					
25				8	5	6		10	9	7			1				4	2	3	11					
26		2		4	5			8	10	7			1	3			9	6		11					
27		2	3	8		6		10	9			1	5				4			11	7				
28		2	3	4	5			10	9	8		1					6			11	7				
29		2	3	4	5			10	9	8		1					6			11	7				
30		2	3	4	5			10	9	8		1					6			11	7				
31		2	3	4	5			10	9	8		1					6			11	7				
32		2	3	4	5			10	9	8		1					6			11	7				
33		2	3	4	5			10	9	8		1					6			11	7				
34		2	3		5			10	9	8	4	11	1				6				7				
35		2	3	4	5				9	10	8		1				6			11	7				
36		2	3	4	5				9	10	8		1				6			11	7				
37		2	3	4	5				10	8			1	9			6			11	7				
38		2	3	4	5				10	8			1	9			6			11	7				
39		2	3	4	5				10				1	9			6			11	7	8			
40		2	3	4	5				10				1	9			6			11	7	8			
41		2	3	4	5				10				1	9			6			11	7	8			
42		2	3	4	5				10				1	9			6			11	7	8			
	9	39	38	40	39	21	1	34	30	39	22	9	18	33	4	8	1	5	4	23	3	3	19	16	4
				4				21	11	9	1		2			6		1	3	2			5	2	3

Match																		
3		3	4	5	6		8	9	10	7		1			2	11		
		1	1	1	1		1	1	1		1				1	1		
																1		

FINAL LEAGUE TABLE

	P	W	D	L	F	A	P
Wolverhampton W	42	25	7	10	96	56	57
West Bromwich A	42	22	9	11	86	63	53
Huddersfield Town	42	20	11	11	78	61	51
Manchester United	42	18	12	12	73	58	48
Bolton Wanderers	42	18	12	12	75	60	48
Blackpool	42	19	10	13	80	69	48
Burnley	42	21	4	17	78	67	46
Chelsea	42	16	12	14	74	68	44
Charlton Athletic	42	19	6	17	75	77	44
Cardiff City	42	18	8	16	51	71	44
Preston North End	42	19	5	18	87	58	43
Arsenal	42	15	13	14	75	73	43
Aston Villa	**42**	**16**	**9**	**17**	**70**	**68**	**41**
Portsmouth	42	14	11	17	81	89	39
Newcastle United	42	14	10	18	72	77	38
Tottenham Hotspur	42	16	5	21	65	76	37
Manchester City	42	14	9	19	62	77	37
Sunderland	42	14	8	20	81	89	36
Sheffield Wednesday	42	15	6	21	70	91	36
Sheffield United	42	11	11	20	69	90	33
Middlesbrough	42	10	10	22	60	91	30
Liverpool	42	9	10	23	68	97	28

1954/55

SEASON SNIPPETS

Danny Blanchflower scored Villa's first goal of the season, a penalty in a 4-2 home defeat by Tottenham Hotspur. On 8 December 1954 Blanchflower moved to White Hart Lane for £30,000. Ten days later the teams met and when Spurs were awarded a penalty Alf Ramsey invited Blanchflower to take the kick. He declined and, taking the penalty kick himself, Ramsey shot wide of the goal.

A goal from Trevor Birch gave Villa a 1-0 friendly win over a British Army XI in October.

Tommy Southren signed for Villa at midnight on Christmas Eve on platform 6 at Euston Station and made his debut at Manchester United on 27 December.

Villa led Portsmouth 2-1 after 79 minutes in January when the game at Fratton Park was abandoned because of fog.

Ken 'Shunter' Roberts was forced to retire from the professional game in January, having played 46 games for Villa.

The 6-1 defeat at Charlton on 5 February was the last game for Frank Moss junior. It was also Nobby Clarke's only Villa league match.

Chairman Fred Normansell, a club director since 1933, died on 21 February 1955 at the age of 68.

Dave Walsh played his last Villa league game at Wolves on 11 April.

Tommy 'Toucher' Thompson signed off by scoring the only goal of the match in his last Villa game on 4 May.

Defender Harry Parkes, who had turned professional just after the war, retired in June 1955 after 345 games for Villa.

DIVISION ONE

MANAGER: Eric Houghton

MATCH	DATE	VENUE	OPPONENTS	RESULT	HT SCORE	SCORE	SCORERS	ATT
1	Aug 21	H	Tottenham Hotspur	L	1 2	2 4	Blanchflower (pen), Baxter	44,193
2	23	H	Sunderland	D	1 1	2 2	McParland, Pace	32,983
3	28	A	Sheffield Wednesday	L	1 5	3 6	Dixon 2, Pace	32,914
4	Sep 1	A	Sunderland	D	0 0	0 0		50,562
5	4	H	Portsmouth	W	0 0	1 0	Pace	28,284
6	8	A	Newcastle United	L	1 4	3 5	Pace, Dixon, Cowell (og)	39,960
7	11	A	Blackpool	W	1 0	1 0	Pace	31,417
8	13	H	Newcastle United	L	0 1	1 2	Blanchflower (pen)	20,370
9	18	H	Charlton Athletic	L	0 1	1 2	Chapman	24,651
10	25	A	Bolton Wanderers	D	3 1	3 3	Dixon 2, Pace	28,335
11	Oct 2	H	Huddersfield Town	D	0 0	0 0		22,392
12	9	A	Everton	L	0 1	0 2		30,702
13	16	H	Manchester City	W	1 1	4 2	Walsh, Thompson 3	36,384
14	23	A	Arsenal	W	0 0	2 1	Lockhart, Lynn (pen)	38,038
15	30	A	West Bromwich Albion	W	1 0	3 2	Thompson 2, McParland	51,662
16	Nov 6	H	Leicester City	L	1 0	2 5	Walsh, Lockhart	28,181
17	13	A	Burnley	L	0 2	0 2		19,186
18	20	H	Preston North End	L	1 1	1 3	Follan	25,187
19	27	A	Sheffield United	W	0 0	3 1	Dixon, Follan, Pace	25,154
20	Dec 4	H	Cardiff City	L	0 2	0 2		25,186
21	11	A	Chelsea	L	0 1	0 4		36,162
22	18	A	Tottenham Hotspur	D	1 1	1 1	Dixon	28,131
23	27	A	Manchester United	W	1 0	1 0	Dixon	50,941
24	28	H	Manchester United	W	1 0	2 1	Dixon, Lockhart	48,718
25	Jan 1	H	Sheffield Wednesday	D	0 0	0 0		22,990
26	22	H	Blackpool	W	2 0	3 1	Thompson 2, Pace	30,161
27	Feb 5	A	Charlton Athletic	L	1 3	1 6	Gibson	23,988
28	12	H	Bolton Wanderers	W	2 0	3 0	Lynn (pen), Dixon, Southren	21,447
29	23	A	Huddersfield Town	W	1 1	2 1	Lynn (pen), Dixon	5,287
30	Mar 5	H	Chelsea	W	2 1	3 2	Walsh 2, McParland	24,467
31	12	A	Arsenal	L	0 1	0 2		30,136
32	19	H	West Bromwich Albion	W	2 0	3 0	Walsh, Lynn (pen), Dixon	39,960
33	26	A	Leicester City	L	1 3	2 4	Southren, Dixon	19,200
34	Apr 2	H	Burnley	W	2 1	3 1	Follan, Dixon, McParland	19,950
35	9	A	Cardiff City	W	1 0	1 0	Follan	20,720
36	11	A	Wolverhampton Wanderers	L	0 0	0 1		33,765
37	12	H	Wolverhampton Wanderers	W	1 0	4 2	Thompson 3, Follan	44,334
38	16	H	Sheffield United	W	0 0	3 1	Thompson, Lynn, Gibson	21,149
39	23	A	Preston North End	W	1 0	3 0	Thompson 2, Follan	15,147
40	27	A	Portsmouth	D	1 2	2 2	Gibson, Follan	18,801
41	30	H	Manchester City	W	0 0	2 0	Lynn 2	27,788
42	May 4	A	Everton	W	1 0	1 0	Thompson	20,503

Final League Position: 6th in First Division

1 Own-goal

Appearances
Goals

FA CUP

3	Jan 8	A	Brighton & Hove Albion	D	2 1	2 2	Thompson 2	25,291
R	10	H	Brighton & Hove Albion	W	3 1	4 2	Lockhart 2, Southren, Thompson	13,609
4	29	H	Doncaster Rovers	D	0 0	0 0		27,767
R	Feb 2	H	Doncaster Rovers *	D	1 1	2 2	Thompson 2	36,872
2R	7	N	Doncaster Rovers **	D	0 1	1 1	Thompson	15,047
3R	14	N	Doncaster Rovers ***	D	0 0	0 0		16,117
4R	15	N	Doncaster Rovers ****	L	0 1	1 3	Dixon	17,155

Appearances
Goals

* After extra-time
** After extra-time - Played at Maine Road, Manchester
*** Abandoned after 90 minutes - Played at Hillsborough, Sheffield
**** Played at The Hawthorns, West Bromwich

Jones K	Parkes HA	Aldis BP	Blanchflower RD	Moss F (junr)	Baxter W	Roberts KO	Dixon JT	Pace DJ	Thompson T	McParland PJ	Parsons DR	Lynn S	Martin CJ	Gibson CH	Tyrell JJ	Lockhart N	Chapman RC	Pinner MJ	Moss A	Crowe VH	Walsh DJ	Follan EH	Proudler A	Birch T	Southren TC	Clarke NFM	Hogg AR	MATCH
1	2	3	4	5	6	7	8	9	10	11																		1
1	2	3	4	5	6	7	8	9	10	11																		2
	2	3	4	5	6	7	8	9	10	11	1																	3
	3		4	5	6	7	10	9	8	11	1	2																4
	3		4		6	7	10	9	8	11	1	2	5															5
	3		4	5	6		10	9	8	11	1	2		7														6
	3		4		6		10	9		11	1	2	5	7	8													7
	3		4		6		10	9		11	1	2	5	7	8													8
	3		4		6		8	9		11	1	2	5			7	10											9
	3		4				10	9		11		2	5			7		1										10
1	3				6	11	10	9	8			2	5			7			4									11
1	3		4		6		10	9	8	11		2	5			7												12
1		3			4			8	11			2	5			7				6	9	10						13
1		3	4		6			8	11			2	5			7					9	10						14
1		3	4		6			8	11			2	5			7					9	10						15
1		3			4			8	11			2				7				6	9	10	5					16
1		3			4		10	8	11			2	5			7				6	9							17
1		3			4	7		8	11			2	5							6	9	10						18
1		3			4		8	9		11		2	5			7						10						19
1		3	4		6		8	9		11		2	5			7						10						20
1		3		5			8	9		11		2				7				6		10		4				21
1		3		5			9		8	11		2				7			4	6		10						22
1		3		5			9		8			2				11			4	6		10			7			23
1		3					9		8			2	5			11			4	6		10			7			24
1		3		4			10	9	8			2	5			11			6						7			25
1		3					10	9				2	5			11			6						7			26
1		3		5			10	9		11				8		7				6				4				27
1		3			4		9		8			2	5			11				6		10			7			28
1		3			4		10			11		2	5	8						6	9				7			29
1		3			4		10			11		2	5	8						6	9				7			30
1		3			4		8			11		2	5							6	9	10			7			31
1		3					10			11		2	5						6	4	9	8			7			32
1		3					10	9		11		2	5						6			8			7	4		33
1		3					10			11		2	5	9					6	4		8			7			34
1		3					10			11		2	5	9					6	4					7			35
1		3					10			11		2	5						6	4	9	8						36
1		3			9			8	11			2	5		7	11			6	4		10						37
1		3			9			8				2	5	7		11			6	4		10						38
1		3			9			8				2	5			11			6	4		10						39
1		3			9			8				2	5	7		11			6	4		10						40
1		3				7	9	8				2	5			11			6	4		10						41
1		3					9	8				2	5			11			6	4					7			42
34	12	33	14	9	25	8	36	18	26	32	7	39	32	12	2	25	1	1	17	25	12	25	1	1	13	1	1	
			2		1		13	8	14	4		7		4		3	1			5	7				2			

1		3			6		9		8	10		2	5			11			4						7			3
1		3			6		9		8			2	5			11			4			10			7			R
1		3					9		8	10		2	5			11			6						7			4
1		3		5	4		9		8	10		2				11			6						7			R
1		3			4		10	9	8			2				11				6					7			2R
1		3			4		9	8				2	5			11				6		10			7			3R
1		3			4		9	8				2	5	10		11				6					7			4R
7		7		1	7		7	1	7	3		7	6	1		7			4	3		2			7			
								1	6					2								1			1			

FINAL LEAGUE TABLE

	P	W	D	L	F	A	P
Chelsea	42	20	12	10	81	57	52
Wolverhampton W	42	19	10	13	89	19	48
Portsmouth	42	18	12	12	74	62	48
Sunderland	42	15	18	9	64	54	48
Manchester United	42	20	7	15	84	74	47
Aston Villa	**42**	**20**	**7**	**15**	**72**	**73**	**47**
Manchester City	42	18	10	14	76	69	46
Newcastle United	42	17	9	16	89	77	43
Arsenal	42	17	9	16	69	63	43
Burnley	42	17	9	16	51	48	43
Everton	42	16	10	16	62	68	42
Huddersfield Town	42	14	13	15	63	68	41
Sheffield United	42	17	7	18	70	86	41
Preston North End	42	16	8	18	83	64	40
Charlton Athletic	42	15	10	17	76	75	40
Tottenham Hotspur	42	16	8	18	72	73	40
West Bromwich A	42	16	8	18	76	96	40
Bolton Wanderers	42	13	13	16	62	69	39
Blackpool	42	14	10	18	60	64	38
Cardiff City	42	13	11	18	62	76	37
Leicester City	42	12	11	19	74	86	35
Sheffield Wednesday	42	8	10	24	63	100	26

1955/56

SEASON SNIPPETS

Wing-half Pat Saward arrived from Millwall in August, while centre-forward Dave Hickson joined Villa from Everton in September. Hickson played only 12 matches, scoring in the 4-4 draw against Manchester United, before moving on to Huddersfield Town.

The game at West Bromwich Albion on 8 October was Colin H Gibson's last Villa match.

The club were again busy in the transfer market that winter, signing Jackie Sewell, Les Smith and Jimmy Dugdale - who had won an FA Cup medal with West Bromwich Albion in 1954.

Eddie Fullan played his last Villa game on 17 December.

Amos Moss made his last appearance against Blackpool on 14 January.

The FA Cup defeat at Arsenal was Con Martin's last game.

Villa just beat the transfer deadline to sign goalkeeper Nigel Sims from Wolverhampton Wanderers.

Norman Lockhart played his last game against Sheffield United on 14 April.

First Division survival was secured as Villa beat West Bromwich Albion 3-0 on the final day while Sheffield United lost 3-1 at Tottenham and were relegated along with Yorkshire rivals Huddersfield Town.

DIVISION ONE

MANAGER: Eric Houghton

MATCH	DATE	VENUE	OPPONENTS	RESULT	HT SCORE	SCORE	SCORERS	ATT
1	Aug 20	A	Manchester City	D	2 1	2 2	Dixon 2	37,999
2	24	A	Sunderland	L	0 1	1 5	Dixon	33,761
3	27	H	Cardiff City	W	1 0	2 0	Dixon, McParland	32,893
4	29	H	Sunderland	L	0 1	1 4	Lockhart	28,276
5	Sep 3	A	Huddersfield Town	D	1 1	1 1	McParland	19,805
6	5	H	Birmingham City	D	0 0	0 0		56,935
7	10	H	Blackpool	D	1 0	1 1	Kelly(og)	51,166
8	17	A	Chelsea	D	0 0	0 0		35,221
9	21	A	Birmingham City	D	1 1	2 2	Southren, Baxter	32,642
10	24	H	Bolton Wanderers	L	0 1	0 2		28,418
11	Oct 1	A	Arsenal	L	0 0	0 1		43,864
12	8	A	West Bromwich Albion	L	0 1	0 1		37,243
13	15	H	Manchester United	D	2 3	4 4	Dixon 2, Hickson, Saward	29,478
14	22	A	Everton	L	0 2	1 2	Dixon	55,431
15	29	H	Newcastle United	W	1 0	3 0	Dixon, Crowe, Lockhart	25,386
16	Nov 5	A	Burnley	L	0 0	0 2		20,592
17	12	H	Luton Town	W	0 0	1 0	Dixon	29,761
18	19	A	Charlton Athletic	L	1 0	1 3	Lockhart	19,830
19	26	H	Tottenham Hotspur	L	0 0	0 2		23,836
20	Dec 3	A	Sheffield United	D	1 0	2 2	Sewell, Pace	21,835
21	10	H	Preston North End	W	2 0	3 2	Baxter, Moss, Lockhart	27,814
22	17	H	Manchester City	L	0 2	0 3		19,215
23	24	A	Cardiff City	L	0 0	0 1		20,384
24	26	H	Portsmouth	L	1 2	1 3	Dixon	21,404
25	27	A	Portsmouth	D	0 2	2 2	McParland, Sewell	31,116
26	31	H	Huddersfield Town	W	2 0	3 0	Dixon 2, Lynn	25,746
27	Jan 14	A	Blackpool	L	0 3	0 6		15,844
28	21	H	Chelsea	L	1 1	1 4	Lynn	22,059
29	Feb 11	H	Arsenal	D	1 1	1 1	Dixon	28,060
30	18	A	Bolton Wanderers	L	0 1	0 1		19,737
31	25	A	Manchester United	L	0 0	0 1		36,476
32	Mar 3	H	Charlton Athletic	D	0 0	1 1	Pace	27,317
33	10	A	Newcastle United	W	2 1	3 2	McParland, Pace, Dixon	34,647
34	19	H	Burnley	W	2 0	2 0	Dixon, Smith	15,120
35	24	A	Luton Town	L	1 1	1 2	Southren	17,126
36	31	H	Everton	W	1 0	2 0	Pace, Dixon	28,052
37	Apr 2	A	Wolverhampton Wanderers	D	0 0	0 0		33,633
38	3	H	Wolverhampton Wanderers	D	0 0	0 0		39,122
39	7	A	Tottenham Hotspur	L	1 2	3 4	Smith, Pace, Dugdale	36,235
40	14	H	Sheffield United	W	3 1	3 2	Pace 3	23,407
41	21	A	Preston North End	W	0 0	1 0	Pace	16,175
42	28	H	West Bromwich Albion	W	3 0	3 0	Smith 2, Millard (og)	42,876

Final League Position: 20th in First Division

2 Own-goals

Appearances
Goals

FA CUP

3	Jan 7	H	Hull City	D	1 1	1 1	McParland	33,284
R	12	A	Hull City	W	1 0	2 1	Dixon, Sewell	15,685
4	28	A	Arsenal	L	0 3	1 4	Dixon	43,052

Appearances
Goals

Players

Jones K, Lynn S, Aldis BP, Crowe VH, Martin CJ, Baxter W, Southren TC, Gibson CH, Dixon JT, Follan EH, McParland PJ, Moss A, Lockhart N, Pace DJ, Tyrell JJ, Hickson D, Saward P, Birch T, Sewell J, Roberts KO, Hogg AR, Ashfield GO, Pritchard RT, Dugdale JR, Smith JL, Pinner MJ, Sims DN

FINAL LEAGUE TABLE

	P	W	D	L	F	A	P
Manchester United	42	25	10	7	83	51	60
Blackpool	42	20	9	13	86	62	49
Wolverhampton W	42	20	9	13	89	65	49
Manchester City	42	18	10	14	82	69	46
Arsenal	42	18	10	14	60	61	46
Birmingham City	42	18	9	15	75	57	45
Burnley	42	18	8	16	64	54	44
Bolton Wanderers	42	18	7	17	71	58	43
Sunderland	42	17	9	16	80	95	43
Luton Town	42	17	8	17	66	64	42
Newcastle United	42	17	7	18	85	70	41
Portsmouth	42	16	9	17	78	85	41
West Bromwich A	42	18	5	19	58	70	41
Charlton Athletic	42	17	6	19	75	81	40
Everton	42	15	10	17	55	69	40
Chelsea	42	14	11	17	64	77	39
Cardiff City	42	15	9	18	55	69	39
Tottenham Hotspur	42	15	7	20	61	71	37
Preston North End	42	14	8	20	73	72	36
Aston Villa	**42**	**11**	**13**	**18**	**52**	**69**	**35**
Huddersfield Town	42	14	7	21	54	83	35
Sheffield United	42	12	9	21	63	77	33

1956/57

SEASON SNIPPETS

Villa changed in a bus for their match at Leeds in September after the main stand at Elland Road - where the dressing rooms were situated - had been destroyed by fire the previous week.

The FA Cup final was not the only time Manchester United players cursed Villa in 1956/57 season. In October, an Army team, including Duncan Edwards, Bobby Charlton and Bill Foulkes were beaten 7-1 in a friendly.

Ray Hogg's last game was at Arsenal on 3 November.

Bill Baxter played his last match at Sheffield Wednesday on 1 December.

Billy Myerscough, who arrived from Walsall in an exchange deal for Dave Walsh, made his debut on 15 December.

1956 was the last year that matches were played on Christmas Day, but there was no festive cheer for Villa. They lost 1-0 to Sunderland at Roker Park, after the teams had travelled by rail together for the return match on Boxing Day. That game was postponed because there were eight inches of snow on the Villa Park pitch.

The FA Cup home replays against Luton Town and Burnley were both played on mid-week afternoons, as was the semi-final replay against West Bromwich Albion at St. Andrews. Neither ground had floodlights at the time.

Keith Jones made his last appearance at Tottenham on 19 January.

Dennis Jackson made his debut in a 2-1 win at Birmingham City on 10 April.

Goalkeeper Arthur Sabin made his debut in a 5-0 win against Sheffield Wednesday on 13 April.

Amateur International goalkeeper Mike Pinner made the last of his four Villa league appearances at Wolves on 23 April.

DIVISION ONE

MANAGER: Eric Houghton

MATCH	DATE	VENUE	OPPONENTS	RESULT	HT SCORE	SCORE	SCORERS	ATT
1	Aug 18	H	Charlton Athletic	W	1 0	3 1	Dixon, Baxter, O'Linn (og)	32,372
2	22	A	West Bromwich Albion	L	0 1	0 2		37,118
3	25	H	Manchester City	D	1 0	1 1	Smith	24,326
4	27	H	West Bromwich Albion	D	0 0	0 0		31,785
5	Sep 1	H	Blackpool	W	2 1	3 2	McParland 2, Sewell	44,374
6	5	A	Luton Town	D	0 0	0 0		21,171
7	8	A	Everton	W	0 0	4 0	Sewell 2, Dixon, Smith	43,762
8	15	H	Tottenham Hotspur	L	2 2	2 4	McParland, Pace	43,947
9	22	A	Leeds United	L	0 1	0 1		35,388
10	29	H	Bolton Wanderers	D	0 0	0 0		34,402
11	Oct 6	A	Portsmouth	L	0 2	1 5	Smith	23,613
12	13	H	Newcastle United	W	3 1	3 1	Sewell, Smith 2	35,144
13	27	H	Birmingham City	W	3 0	3 1	Lynn, Roberts, Sewell	54,927
14	Nov 3	A	Arsenal	L	1 2	1 2	McParland	40,045
15	10	H	Burnley	W	1 0	1 0	Sewell	22,420
16	17	A	Preston North End	D	0 2	3 3	Smith, Lynn (pen), McParland	19,270
17	24	H	Chelsea	D	0 0	1 1	Sewell	26,949
18	Dec 1	A	Sheffield Wednesday	L	1 1	1 2	McParland	23,560
19	8	H	Manchester United	L	0 1	1 3	Saward	42,530
20	15	A	Charlton Athletic	W	1 0	2 0	McParland, Dixon	13,452
21	25	A	Sunderland	L	0 0	0 1		18,543
22	29	A	Blackpool	D	0 0	0 0		16,777
23	Jan 12	H	Everton	W	3 1	5 1	Dixon, Pace 2, Sewell, Smith	25,274
24	19	A	Tottenham Hotspur	L	0 0	0 3		38,934
25	Feb 2	H	Leeds United	D	0 1	1 1	Pace	39,432
26	4	A	Manchester City	D	1 0	2 2	Smith, McParland	10,593
27	9	A	Bolton Wanderers	D	0 0	0 0		21,012
28	18	H	Portsmouth	D	1 0	2 2	Sewell 2	10,787
29	Mar 9	A	Manchester United	D	0 1	1 1	Dixon	55,686
30	13	H	Cardiff City	W	2 1	4 1	McParland, Sewell 2, Lynn (pen)	12,567
31	16	H	Arsenal	D	0 0	0 0		39,893
32	30	H	Preston North End	W	1 0	2 0	Myerscough, Sewell	33,185
33	Apr 3	A	Cardiff City	L	0 0	0 1		18,354
34	6	A	Chelsea	D	0 1	1 1	Sewell	28,025
35	8	H	Sunderland	D	1 1	2 2	Pace, Myerscough	8,930
36	10	A	Birmingham City	W	2 1	2 1	Chapman 2	29,853
37	13	H	Sheffield Wednesday	W	2 0	5 0	Sewell, Myerscough, Smith, McParland 2	28,134
38	15	A	Burnley	L	1 2	1 2	Pace	17,381
39	20	A	Newcastle United	W	0 1	2 1	Sewell, McParland	28,453
40	22	H	Wolverhampton Wanderers	W	1 0	4 0	Dixon, Smith 2, Sewell	34,063
41	23	A	Wolverhampton Wanderers	L	0 1	0 3		35,585
42	27	H	Luton Town	L	0 0	1 3	Smith	28,524

Final League Position: 10th in First Division

1 Own-goal

Appearances
Goals

FA CUP

3	Jan 5	A	Luton Town	D	1 0	2 2	Dixon, McParland	20,108
R	7	H	Luton Town	W	0 0	2 0	Dixon 2	28,536
4	26	A	Middlesbrough	W	1 2	3 2	Pace, Smith, Dixon	42,396
5	Feb 16	H	Bristol City	W	1 0	2 1	Pace, Sewell	63,099
6	Mar 2	A	Burnley	D	0 1	1 1	McParland	49,346
R	6	H	Burnley	W	1 0	2 0	Dixon, McParland	46,531
SF	23	N	West Bromwich Albion *	D	1 2	2 2	McParland 2	55,549
R	28	N	West Bromwich Albion **	W	1 0	1 0	Myerscough	58,067
F	May 4	N	Manchester United ***	W	0 0	2 1	McParland 2	100,000

Appearances
Goals

* Played at Molineux, Wolverhampton
** Played at St Andrews, Birmingham
*** Played at Wembley Stadium

FINAL LEAGUE TABLE

	P	W	D	L	F	A	P
Manchester United	42	28	8	6	103	54	64
Tottenham Hotspur	42	22	12	8	104	56	56
Preston North End	42	23	10	9	84	56	56
Blackpool	42	22	9	11	93	65	53
Arsenal	42	21	8	13	85	69	50
Wolverhampton W	42	20	8	14	94	70	48
Burnley	42	18	10	14	56	50	46
Leeds United	42	15	14	13	72	63	44
Bolton Wanderers	42	16	12	14	65	65	44
Aston Villa	**42**	**14**	**15**	**13**	**65**	**55**	**43**
West Bromwich A	42	14	14	14	59	61	42
Chelsea	42	13	13	16	73	73	39
Birmingham City	42	15	9	18	69	69	39
Sheffield Wednesday	42	16	6	20	82	88	38
Everton	42	14	10	18	61	79	38
Luton Town	42	14	9	19	58	76	37
Newcastle United	42	14	8	20	67	87	36
Manchester City	42	13	9	20	78	88	35
Portsmouth	42	10	13	19	62	92	33
Sunderland	42	12	8	22	67	88	32
Cardiff City	42	10	9	23	53	88	29
Charlton Athletic	42	9	4	29	62	120	22

423

1957/58

SEASON SNIPPETS

Bill Moore, Villa's trainer and Eric Houghton's right-hand man during the previous season's FA Cup success, left the club at the end of October.

Sixteen-year-old ground staff boy Walter Hazelden became the youngest player to score a league goal for Villa when he hit the opening goal of the match with West Bromwich Albion at The Hawthorns in November.

Gerry Hitchens joined Villa from Cardiff City on 20 December 1957, making his debut at home to Birmingham City the following afternoon.

The legendary Stanley Matthews was invited into Villa's dressing room before the 1-1 draw against Blackpool in February and presented with a briefcase as a gift for his 43rd birthday.

Although he had been cup-tied by playing for Villa in the third round against Stoke City, Stan Crowther was allowed to play for Manchester United in the competition after joining them just two weeks after the Munich air disaster. Only hours after signing, Crowther turned out for United in a 3-0 fifth-round victory over Sheffield Wednesday.

Villa's 19-year-old reserve goalkeeper Arthur Sabin died in Birmingham's Queen Elizabeth Hospital in March, having suffered kidney problems since mid-January. Sabin's last first-team game was against Spurs on 16 November.

Roy Pritchard, Jack Hinchcliffe, Roy Chapman, Kenneth Owen Roberts, Derek Pace, George Ashfield and Les Jones also made their last Villa appearances during the season.

DIVISION ONE

MANAGER: Eric Houghton

MATCH	DATE	VENUE	OPPONENTS	RESULT	HT SCORE	SCORE	SCORERS	ATT
1	Aug 24	A	Birmingham City	L	1 2	1 3	McParland	50,780
2	26	H	Leeds United	W	0 0	2 0	McParland, Sewell	25,693
3	31	H	Everton	L	0 1	0 1		37,759
4	Sep 4	A	Leeds United	L	0 1	0 4		22,685
5	7	A	Sunderland	D	0 1	1 1	Chapman	43,901
6	14	H	Luton Town	W	1 0	2 0	McParland, Dixon	28,962
7	16	A	Wolverhampton Wanderers	L	1 1	1 2	McParland	26,033
8	21	A	Blackpool	D	1 1	1 1	McParland	31,079
9	23	H	Wolverhampton Wanderers	L	1 2	2 3	Wright (og), McParland (pen)	20,904
10	28	H	Leicester City	W	4 0	5 1	Sewell 2, Southren, Lynn (pen), McParland	31,691
11	Oct 2	A	Arsenal	L	0 3	1 4		18,482
12	5	A	Manchester United	L	0 2	1 4	Pace	43,332
13	12	H	Chelsea	L	0 2	2 4	Sewell, McParland	40,769
14	19	H	Newcastle United	W	3 1	4 3	Myerscough, Dixon, Pace, Scott (og)	29,395
15	26	A	Burnley	L	0 1	0 3		20,860
16	Nov 2	H	Portsmouth	W	2 1	2 1	Southren, Pace	28,773
17	9	A	West Bromwich Albion	L	1 1	2 3	Hazelden, Crowther	41,307
18	16	H	Tottenham Hotspur	D	0 0	1 1	Sewell	28,390
19	23	A	Nottingham Forest	L	1 2	1 4	Crowther	30,382
20	30	H	Preston North End	D	1 0	2 2	Lynn (pen), McParland	25,847
21	Dec 7	A	Sheffield Wednesday	W	3 0	5 2	Hazelden 2, Crowther 2, McParland	15,411
22	14	H	Manchester City	L	0 0	1 2	McParland	24,767
23	21	H	Birmingham City	L	0 0	0 2		41,118
24	26	H	Arsenal	W	2 0	3 0	Evans (og), Lynn, Hitchens	38,383
25	28	A	Everton	W	1 0	2 1	Hitchens 2	41,195
26	Jan 11	A	Sunderland	W	5 2	5 2	Lynn 3 (2 pens), Myerscough, Sewell	22,645
27	18	A	Luton Town	L	0 0	0 3		16,619
28	Feb 1	H	Blackpool	D	1 0	1 1	McParland	47,499
29	8	A	Leicester City	L	1 4	1 6	Southren	25,535
30	22	H	Chelsea	L	0 2	1 3	McParland	20,358
31	Mar 1	A	Newcastle United	W	2 2	4 2	Smith, Hitchens 2, Dugdale	40,135
32	8	H	Burnley	W	2 0	3 0	Lynn (pen), McParland 2	25,679
33	15	A	Portsmouth	L	0 0	0 1		23,164
34	29	H	Tottenham Hotspur	L	1 4	2 6	Sewell, McParland	34,102
35	31	H	Manchester United	W	1 1	3 2	Hitchens, Myerscough, Sewell	16,631
36	Apr 4	A	Bolton Wanderers	L	0 1	0 4		19,026
37	5	H	West Bromwich Albion	W	1 0	2 1	Myerscough, McParland	31,406
38	8	H	Bolton Wanderers	W	2 0	4 0	Lynn, Hitchens, Sewell, Higgins (og)	32,745
39	12	A	Preston North End	D	1 1	1 1	Myerscough	21,053
40	19	H	Sheffield Wednesday	W	0 0	2 0	Hitchens 2	25,995
41	26	A	Manchester City	W	2 1	2 1	Smith, Sewell	28,275
42	30	H	Nottingham Forest	D	1 0	1 1	Hitchens	21,043

Final League Position: 14th in First Division

4 Own-goals

Appearances
Goals

FA CUP

3	Jan 4	A	Stoke City	D	1 0	1 1	McParland	45,800
R	8	H	Stoke City *	D	1 2	3 3	Sewell, Lynn, Hitchens	38,939
2R	13	N	Stoke City **	L	0 0	0 2		37,702

* After extra-time
** Played at Molineux, Wolverhampton

Appearances
Goals

FA CHARITY SHIELD

	Oct 22	A	Manchester United	L	0 0	0 4		27,923

Appearances
Goals

Players

Match	Sims DN	Lynn S	Aldis BP	Crowther S	Dugdale JR	Saward P	Smith JL	Sewell J	Myerscough WH	Dixon JT	McParland PJ	Southren TC	Chapman RC	Birch T	Jackson DL	Crowe VH	Pace DJ	Hinchliffe J	Pritchard RT	Ashfield GO	Roberts KO	Hazelden W	Sabin AH	Hitchens GA	Jones LC
1	1	2	3	4	5	6	7	8	9	10	11														
2	1	2	3	4	5	6	7	8	9	10	11														
3	1	2	3	4	5	6		8	9	10	11	7													
4	1	2	3	4	5	6		8	9	10	11	7													
5	1	2	3	4	5	6	7	8		9	11		10												
6	1	2	3	4	5	6	7	8		9	11		10												
7	1	2	3		5	6		8	7	9	11		10	4											
8	1	2	3		5	6		8	7	9	11		10												
9	1		3		5	6		8	7	9	11		10		2	4									
10	1	2	3	4	5	6		8		10	11	7					9								
11	1	2	3	4	5			8		10	11	7			6	9									
12	1	2	3	4	5	6		8	11						10	9	7								
13	1	2		4		6		8	9		11		10					7	3	5					
14	1		2	4	5	6		8	7	10	11					9				3					
15	1	2	3	4	5	6	7		8		11		10			9									
16	1	2		4	5	6	7				11	8				9				3	10				
17	1	2		4	5	6				11		7	10			9				3		8			
18		2		4	5	6		8		11		7				9				3	10		1		
19	1	2		4	5	6	7	10		11		8				9				3					
20	1	2	3	4	5	6	7	8	10	11						9									
21	1	2	3	8	5	6	7			11					4						10				
22	1	2	3	8	5	6	7			11					4	9					10				
23	1	2	3	8	5	6	7		10	11					4										
24	1	2	3	4	5	6	7	8		11											10			9	
25	1	2	3	4	5	6	7	8	10	11														9	
26	1	2		5		6	7	8	10	11					4				3					9	
27	1	2		6			8	10		11	7		5		4				3					9	
28	1	2		4		5	7	8		11					6						10			9	3
29	1	2		4			5	7	8		11	10			6									9	3
30	1	2			5	6	7	10		11		8			4									9	3
31	1	2	3		5	6	7	9		11					4						10			8	
32	1	2	3		5	6	7	9		11					4						10			8	
33	1	2	3		5	6	7	9		11					4						10			8	
34	1	2			5	6	7	9		11					4						10			8	
35	1	2			5	6	7	9	10	11					4									8	3
36	1			5	6	7	9	10		11					4									8	3
37	1	2	3		5	6	7	9	10	11					4									8	
38	1	2	3		5	6	7	9	10	11					4						8				
39	1	2	3		5	6	7	9	10	11					4						8				
40	1	2			5	6	7	9	10	11					4						8				
41	1	2			5	6	7	9		11					4						8				
42	1	2	3		5	6	7	9		11					4						8				

Appearances: 41 40 30 26 38 40 29 36 22 14 41 11 8 2 23 12 2 1 8 2 9 1 20 5
Goals: 8 4 1 2 10 5 2 17 3 1 3 3 10

Cup matches

1	2	3	6	5		7	8	9		11			4						10						3
1	2	3		5	6	7	8			11			4						10	9					R
1	2		6		5	7	8	10		11			4		3					9					2R

Goals: 3 3 2 2 2 2 3 2 3 3 1 2 2 1
        1 1 1 1

| 1 | 2 | 3 | 4 | 5 | 6 | 7 | 8 | 10 | | 11 | | | | | | 9 | | | | | | | | |

Goals: 1 1 1 1 1 1 1 1 1 1 1

FINAL LEAGUE TABLE

	P	W	D	L	F	A	P
Wolverhampton W	42	28	8	6	103	47	64
Preston North End	42	26	7	9	100	51	59
Tottenham Hotspur	42	21	9	12	93	77	51
West Bromwich A	42	18	14	10	92	70	50
Manchester City	42	22	5	15	104	100	49
Burnley	42	21	5	16	80	74	47
Blackpool	42	19	6	17	80	67	44
Luton Town	42	19	6	17	69	63	44
Manchester United	42	16	11	15	85	75	43
Nottingham Forest	42	16	10	16	69	63	42
Chelsea	42	15	12	15	83	79	42
Arsenal	42	16	7	19	73	85	39
Birmingham City	42	14	11	17	76	89	39
Aston Villa	**42**	**16**	**7**	**19**	**73**	**86**	**39**
Bolton Wanderers	42	14	10	18	65	87	38
Everton	42	13	11	18	65	75	37
Leeds United	42	14	9	19	51	63	37
Leicester City	42	14	5	23	91	112	33
Newcastle United	42	12	8	22	73	81	32
Portsmouth	42	12	8	22	73	88	32
Sunderland	42	10	12	20	54	97	32
Sheffield Wednesday	42	12	7	23	69	92	31

1958/59

SEASON SNIPPETS

The club's new £35,000 floodlights were switched on for the first time at half-time in the 3-2 win over Portsmouth on Monday 25 August 1958. Villa were drawing 1-1 at the time and nine minutes into the second half, Johnny Dixon became the first player to score under the lights when he put Villa ahead. The official opening took place on 29 October when Swedish club GAIS Gothenburg became the first continental visitors to play under the lights. Villa won 3-0 and then drew 3-3 against Heart of Midlothian in another floodlit friendly three weeks later.

Ron Wylie joined Villa from Notts County in November linking up with Eric Houghton who had also been his manager at Meadow Lane, but before he made his league debut, Houghton had parted company with the club 'by mutual consent'.

Sheffield United manager Joe Mercer took over at Villa Park on Christmas Eve and Dick Taylor was appointed as his assistant early in the New Year.

Ron Atkinson was not retained at the end of the season and joined Headington United - later re-named Oxford United - without playing a senior game for Villa. In July 1991 Atkinson returned as manager.

Peter Aldis, Leslie J Smith and Billy Myerscough - all FA Cup winners - played their last Villa league game during the season, as did Tommy Southren, John Willis, Ken Barrett, John Sharples, Bill Beaton, Walter Hazelden and Dennis Jackson.

DIVISION ONE

MANAGER: Eric Houghton (to 19 November)   Joe Mercer (from 24 December)

MATCH	DATE	VENUE	OPPONENTS	RESULT	HT SCORE	SCORE	SCORERS	ATT
1	Aug 23	H	Birmingham City	D	0 1	1 1	Lynn (pen)	55,198
2	25	H	Portsmouth	W	1 1	3 2	Myerscough, Dixon, McParland	35,172
3	30	A	West Ham United	L	0 4	2 7	Sewell, Smith	30,263
4	Sep 3	A	Portsmouth	L	1 2	2 5	Hitchens, Smith	24,209
5	6	H	Nottingham Forest	L	0 2	2 3	Smith, Hitchens	31,014
6	8	H	Wolverhampton Wanderers	L	1 3	1 3	Hitchens	43,138
7	13	A	Chelsea	L	1 1	1 2	Hazelden	44,023
8	17	A	Wolverhampton Wanderers	L	0 2	0 4		41,845
9	20	H	Blackpool	D	1 1	1 1	Myerscough	28,821
10	27	A	Blackburn Rovers	W	2 1	3 2	McParland, Hitchens, Smith	28,172
11	Oct 4	H	Newcastle United	W	1 0	2 1	Barrett 2	29,801
12	11	A	West Bromwich Albion	L	1 2	1 4	Barrett	45,778
13	18	A	Leeds United	D	0 0	0 0		21,088
14	22	H	Arsenal	L	1 1	1 2	McParland	30,563
15	25	H	Bolton Wanderers	W	1 1	2 1	McParland, Lynn	28,740
16	Nov 1	A	Luton Town	L	1 0	1 2	Hitchens	18,714
17	8	H	Everton	L	0 3	2 4	Sewell, Hitchens	27,649
18	15	A	Leicester City	L	3 1	3 6	Sewell, Hitchens 2	20,864
19	22	H	Preston North End	W	2 0	2 0	Smith (pen), McParland	28,060
20	29	A	Burnley	L	0 0	1 3	Hitchens	14,923
21	Dec 6	H	Manchester City	D	0 0	1 1	Myerscough	21,684
22	13	A	Arsenal	W	1 1	2 1	Myerscough, McParland	31,970
23	20	H	Birmingham City	L	1 0	1 4	Hazelden	31,857
24	26	A	Manchester United	L	1 1	1 2	Myerscough	63,098
25	27	H	Manchester United	L	0 0	0 2		56,450
26	Jan 3	H	West Ham United	L	0 0	1 2	McParland	29,334
27	31	H	Chelsea	W	2 1	3 1	Myerscough, Lynn, McParland	33,575
28	Feb 7	A	Blackpool	L	1 0	1 2	McParland	13,704
29	18	H	Blackburn Rovers	W	0 0	1 0	Sewell	30,050
30	21	A	Newcastle United	L	0 0	0 1		20,182
31	Mar 7	H	Leeds United	W	0 0	2 1	Sewell, Hitchens	27,631
32	18	A	Bolton Wanderers	W	2 0	3 1	Hitchens 3	21,808
33	21	H	Luton Town	W	0 1	3 1	Smith (pen), Hitchens 2	27,401
34	27	A	Tottenham Hotspur	L	1 1	2 3	McParland 2	45,059
35	28	A	Everton	L	1 1	1 2	McParland	34,986
36	30	H	Tottenham Hotspur	D	0 0	1 1	McParland	34,354
37	Apr 4	H	Leicester City	L	0 1	1 2	Dixon	39,963
38	11	A	Preston North End	L	2 1	2 4	Sewell, Myerscough	12,244
39	18	H	Burnley	D	0 0	0 0		27,097
40	20	A	Nottingham Forest	L	0 2	0 2		18,953
41	25	A	Manchester City	D	0 0	0 0		39,661
42	29	A	West Bromwich Albion	D	0 0	1 1	Hitchens	48,165

Final League Position: 21st in First Division

Appearances
Goals

FA CUP

3	Jan 10	H	Rotherham United	W	0 0	2 1	Sewell, Hitchens	33,923
4	24	A	Chelsea	W	2 1	2 1	Hitchens, Myerscough	55,944
5	Feb 14	A	Everton	W	3 0	4 1	Wylie 3, McParland	60,225
6	28	H	Burnley	D	0 0	0 0		60,145
R	Mar 3	A	Burnley	W	0 0	2 0	McParland 2	38,931
SF	14	N	Nottingham Forest *	L	0 0	0 1		64,882

Appearances
Goals

* Played at Hillsborough, Sheffield

Appearances

	Sims DN	Lynn S	Aldis BP	Birch T	Dugdale JR	Saward P	Southren TC	Hitchens GA	Dixon JT	Myerscough WH	McParland PJ	Smith JL	Crowe VH	Sewell J	Lee GF	Hazelden W	Sharples J	Willis JJ	Barrett KB	Beaton W	Jackson DL	Wylie RM	Winton GD	MATCH
	1	2	3	4	5	6	7	8	9	10	11													1
	1	2	3	4	5	6		8	9	10	11	7												2
	1	2	3		5	6		8		10	11	7	4	9										3
	1	2	3		5	6		8		10	11	7	4	9										4
	1	2	3			5		9			11	7	4	8	6	10								5
	1	2			5	6		8	9		11	7			4	10	3							6
	1	2			5	6		8	9		11	7			4	10	3							7
	1	2			5	6		8			11	7			4	10	3	9						8
	1	2			5	6		9		10	11	7		8	4		3							9
	1	2			5	6		8		10	11	7			9	4	3							10
	1	2			5	6		8			10	7			9	4	3		11					11
	1	2			5	6		8		9	10	7				4	3		11					12
	1	2			5					10	11		6	8	4	9	3		7					13
	1	2			5			8		11	7	6	9	4		3		10						14
	1	2			5					10	11	7	6	8	4		3		9					15
	1	2			5			9		10	11		6	8	4		3	7						16
	1	2			5			8		9	11	7	6	10	4		3							17
		2			5			8			11	7	6	10	4	9	3		1					18
	1		3		5			9	4		11	7	6	8						2	10			19
	1		3		5			8	4		11	7	6	10		9				2				20
	1		3		5			9	4	10	11	7	6	8						2				21
	1	2	3		5				4	9	11	7	6	8							10			22
	1	2	3		5				4	9	11	7	6	8			10							23
	1	2	3		5				4	9	11	7	6	8							10			24
	1		3		5			10	4	9	11	7	6							2	8			25
	1		3		5			8	4	9	11	7	6							2	10			26
	1	2	3		5			9	4	7	11		6	8							10			27
	1	2	3		5				4	7	11		6								10			28
	1		2		5			9	4	7	11		6	8							10	3		29
	1		2		5			9	4	7	11										10	3		30
	1		2		5			9	4		11	7	6	8							10	3		31
	1		2		5			9	4		11	7	6	8							10	3		32
	1		2		5			9	4		11	7	6	8							10	3		33
	1		2		5			9	4		11	7	6	8							10	3		34
	1		2		5			9	4		11	7	6	8							10			35
	1		2		5			9	4	10	11	7	6	8								3		36
	1		2		5			9	4	8	11	7	6								10	3		37
	1		2		5				4	9	11	7	6	8							10	3		38
	1		2		5				4	9	11	7	6	8							10	3		39
	1		2		5			9	4		11	7	6	8							10	3		40
	1	2			5	6		9	8	7	11		4								10	3		41
	1	2			5	6		9	8	7	11		4								10	3		42
	41	25	27	2	41	14	1	35	28	29	41	33	33	31	14	8	13	1	5	1	5	20	14	
		3						16	2	7	13	6		2			3							

FA Cup

	1	2	3		5			9	4	7	11		6	8							10			3
	1	2	3		5			9	4	7	11		6	8							10			4
	1		2		5			9	4	7	11		6	8							10	3		5
	1		2		5			9	4	7	11		6	8							10	3		6
	1		2		5				4	9	11	7	6								10	3		R
	1		2		5				4	9	11	7	6	8							10	3		SF
	6	2	6		6			6	6	6	6	2	6	6							6	4		
								2		1	3			1							3			

FINAL LEAGUE TABLE

	P	W	D	L	F	A	P
Wolverhampton W	42	28	5	9	110	49	61
Manchester United	42	24	7	11	103	66	55
Arsenal	42	21	8	13	88	68	50
Bolton Wanderers	42	20	10	12	79	66	50
West Bromwich A	42	18	13	11	88	68	49
West Ham United	42	21	6	15	85	70	48
Burnley	42	19	10	13	81	70	48
Blackpool	42	18	11	13	66	49	47
Birmingham City	42	20	6	16	84	68	46
Blackburn Rovers	42	17	10	15	76	70	44
Newcastle United	42	17	7	18	80	80	41
Preston North End	42	17	7	18	70	77	41
Nottingham Forest	42	17	6	19	71	74	40
Chelsea	42	18	4	20	77	98	40
Leeds United	42	15	9	18	57	74	39
Everton	42	17	4	21	71	87	38
Luton Town	42	12	13	17	68	71	37
Tottenham Hotspur	42	13	10	19	85	95	36
Leicester City	42	11	10	21	67	98	32
Manchester City	42	11	9	22	64	95	31
Aston Villa	**42**	**11**	**8**	**23**	**58**	**87**	**30**
Portsmouth	42	6	9	27	64	112	21

1959/60

SEASON SNIPPETS

Villa started the season with four new players: Jimmy MacEwan, Bobby Thomson, John Neal and Jimmy Adam, who had been signed during the summer at a combined cost of £30,000.

Thomson missed the first three matches because he was serving a suspension held over from the previous season, when he was with Wolverhampton Wanderers.

Jackie Sewell made his last first-team appearance at Sunderland on 26 August.

The 11-1 league victory over Charlton Athletic, featuring five goals from Gerry Hitchens was a record Villa Park win.

Villa were 2-1 winners in a Villa Park floodlit friendly against top Austrian side Rapid Vienna in October. Later that month, they also beat Raith Rovers in a game organised as part of Jimmy MacEwan's transfer from the Scottish club.

Villa lost only once at home all season, when their former striker Derek Pace scored a hat-trick as Sheffield United won 3-1 in February.

The 4-4 draw against Liverpool on 30 March was Trevor Birch's last game.

Brian Handley made his last appearance at Charlton on 2 April.

DIVISION TWO

MANAGER: Joe Mercer

MATCH	DATE	VENUE	OPPONENTS	RESULT	HT SCORE	SCORE	SCORERS	ATT
1	Aug 22	A	Brighton & Hove Albion	W	1 1	2 1	MacEwan, Sewell	31,484
2	26	A	Sunderland	L	0 1	0 1		29,860
3	29	H	Swansea Town	W	1 0	1 0	McParland	35,829
4	31	H	Sunderland	W	2 0	3 0	Hitchens 2, Thomson	32,891
5	Sep 5	A	Bristol Rovers	D	1 1	1 1	Hitchens	26,731
6	9	A	Portsmouth	W	2 1	2 1	Hitchens, Thomson	19,910
7	12	H	Ipswich Town	W	3 0	3 1	McParland 2, Wylie	33,747
8	14	H	Portsmouth	W	3 2	5 2	Thomson, McParland 2, MacEwan 2	34,623
9	19	A	Huddersfield Town	W	0 0	1 0	McParland	22,522
10	26	H	Leyton Orient	W	0 0	1 0	Hitchens	40,860
11	30	H	Stoke City	D	0 0	3 3	K Thomson (og), McParland 2	27,208
12	Oct 3	A	Lincoln City	D	0 0	0 0		13,812
13	10	A	Sheffield United	D	0 0	1 1	Hitchens	25,146
14	17	H	Middlesbrough	W	0 0	1 0	Lynn	35,362
15	24	A	Derby County	D	0 1	2 2	McParland 2	26,394
16	31	H	Plymouth Argyle	W	2 0	2 0	MacEwan, McParland	35,341
17	Nov 7	A	Liverpool	L	0 0	1 2	McParland	49,981
18	14	H	Charlton Athletic	W	4 1	11 1	Hitchens 5, Thomson 2, Wylie, MacEwan, McParland 2	21,291
19	21	A	Bristol City	W	2 0	5 0	Hitchens 3, Wylie, McParland	29,985
20	28	H	Scunthorpe United	W	3 0	5 0	McParland 2, Hitchens 2, Thomson	37,367
21	Dec 5	A	Rotherham United	L	1 1	1 2	Adam	20,537
22	12	H	Cardiff City	W	0 0	2 0	Adam, Hitchens	50,039
23	19	A	Brighton & Hove Albion	W	0 0	3 1	McParland 2, Hitchens	25,428
24	26	A	Hull City	W	0 0	1 0	McParland	29,399
25	28	H	Hull City	D	0 1	1 1	Lynn (pen)	33,386
26	Jan 2	H	Swansea Town	W	1 1	3 1	Thomson 2, Hitchens	24,848
27	16	H	Bristol Rovers	W	1 0	4 1	Thomson 2, Adam, Crowe	29,726
28	23	A	Ipswich Town	L	0 0	1 2	Dugdale	19,283
29	Feb 6	H	Huddersfield Town	W	2 0	4 0	Thomson 3, Hitchens	42,304
30	13	A	Leyton Orient	D	0 0	0 0		16,993
31	27	H	Sheffield United	L	0 2	1 3	Thomson	42,742
32	Mar 1	H	Lincoln City	D	0 0	1 1	Thomson	33,962
33	5	A	Middlesbrough	W	1 0	1 0	Hitchens	39,432
34	15	H	Derby County	W	1 2	3 2	Lynn (pen), McParland, Crowe	37,672
35	19	A	Scunthorpe United	W	1 0	2 1	Hitchens 2	13,084
36	30	H	Liverpool	D	0 3	4 4	McParland, Thomson 2, Lynn (pen)	25,216
37	Apr 2	A	Charlton Athletic	L	0 2	0 2		28,629
38	9	H	Bristol City	W	0 1	2 1	Lynn 2 (2 pens)	33,556
39	16	A	Cardiff City	L	0 1	0 1		52,364
40	18	H	Stoke City	W	0 0	2 1	Lynn (pen), Thomson	25,200
41	23	H	Rotherham United	W	0 0	3 0	Thomson 2, Wylie	32,860
42	30	A	Plymouth Argyle	L	0 3	0 3		29,895

Final League Position: 1st in Second Division

1 Own-goal

Appearances
Goals

FA CUP

3	Jan 9	H	Leeds United	W	1 1	2 1	McParland, Wylie	43,474
4	30	A	Chelsea	W	2 0	2 1	McParland, Thomson	66,671
5	Feb 20	A	Port Vale	W	0 1	2 1	Hitchens, Thomson	49,768
6	Mar 12	H	Preston North End	W	1 0	2 0	Hitchens, McParland	69,732
SF	26	N	Wolverhampton Wanderers *	L	0 1	0 1		55,596

Appearances
Goals

* Played at The Hawthorns, West Bromwich

428

Player	Apps	Goals

FINAL LEAGUE TABLE

	P	W	D	L	F	A	P
Aston Villa	42	25	9	8	89	43	59
Cardiff City	42	23	12	7	90	62	58
Liverpool	42	20	10	12	90	66	50
Sheffield United	42	19	12	11	68	51	50
Middlesbrough	42	19	10	13	90	64	48
Huddersfield Town	42	19	9	14	73	52	47
Charlton Athletic	42	17	13	12	90	87	47
Rotherham United	42	17	13	12	61	60	47
Bristol Rovers	42	18	11	13	72	78	47
Leyton Orient	42	15	14	13	76	61	44
Ipswich Town	42	19	6	17	78	68	44
Swansea Town	42	15	10	17	82	84	40
Lincoln City	42	16	7	19	75	78	39
Brighton and HA	42	13	12	17	67	76	38
Scunthorpe United	42	13	10	19	57	71	36
Sunderland	42	12	12	18	52	65	36
Stoke City	42	14	7	21	66	83	35
Derby County	42	14	7	21	61	77	35
Plymouth Argyle	42	13	9	20	61	89	35
Portsmouth	42	10	12	20	59	77	32
Hull City	42	10	10	22	48	76	30
Bristol City	42	11	5	26	60	97	27

429

1960/61

SEASON SNIPPETS

Gerry Hitchens scored Villa's first goal in the new League Cup competition when he opened the scoring against Huddersfield Town on 12 October.

Alan O'Neill joined the club from Sunderland for £10,000, and was on target after just 25 seconds of his debut, in a 6-2 thrashing of Birmingham City.

Villa signed goalkeeper Geoff Sidebottom from Wolverhampton Wanderers for £15,000 in February, but old Pat Saward, a member of the 1957 FA Cup-winning team, to Huddersfield Town the following month.

Johnny Dixon, who had made his debut in 1946, brought the curtain down on his one-club career when he made his only senior appearance of the season against Sheffield Wednesday at Villa Park. It was an eventful send-off for the 1957 FA Cup winning captain - he scored in a 4 - 1 win, but also broke his nose!

Charlie Aitken, who would go on to become the club's record appearance holder, made his debut in the same match.

Villa were beaten 2-0 by both Moscow Dynamo and Dinamo Tbilisi on their Russian tour in May.

Gerry Hitchens left Villa to sign a lucrative contract with Italian giants Inter Milan.

Kevin Keelan, Terry Morrall, Fred Potter, Jimmy Adam, Doug Winton and Mike Kenning also played their last Villa league games during the season.

DIVISION ONE

MANAGER: Joe Mercer

MATCH	DATE	VENUE	OPPONENTS	RESULT	HT SCORE	SCORE	SCORERS	ATT
1	Aug 20	H	Chelsea	W	0 0	3 2	McParland, Hitchens, Thomson	42,247
2	22	A	West Ham United	L	2 3	2 5	Thomson, Hitchens	28,959
3	27	A	Blackpool	L	0 4	3 5	McParland, Hitchens 2	16,821
4	29	H	West Ham United	W	0 1	2 1	Hitchens, Thomson	32,098
5	Sep 3	H	Everton	W	3 1	3 2	Hitchens 2, Thomson	32,864
6	7	A	Cardiff City	D	1 0	1 1	Crowe	34,716
7	10	A	Blackburn Rovers	L	1 2	1 4	Hitchens	22,112
8	12	H	Cardiff City	W	2 1	2 1	Thomson, Burrows	32,901
9	17	H	Manchester United	W	1 0	3 1	Burrows, Thomson, MacEwan	43,593
10	24	A	Tottenham Hotspur	L	0 4	2 6	MacEwan, Hitchens	61,356
11	Oct 1	H	Leicester City	L	0 3	1 3	McParland	30,115
12	8	H	Newcastle United	W	1 0	2 0	Wylie, Crowe	25,336
13	15	A	Arsenal	L	0 0	1 2	MacEwan	33,828
14	22	H	Birmingham City	W	2 0	6 2	O'Neill 2, Hitchens 3, McParland	44,722
15	29	A	West Bromwich Albion	W	2 0	2 0	Hitchens, O'Neill	41,903
16	Nov 5	H	Burnley	W	1 0	2 0	Hitchens 2	35,923
17	12	A	Preston North End	D	0 1	1 1	McParland	11,093
18	19	H	Fulham	W	1 1	2 1	MacEwan, Wylie	31,506
19	26	A	Sheffield Wednesday	W	2 1	2 1	Megson (og), Hitchens	26,172
20	Dec 3	H	Manchester City	W	2 1	5 1	O'Neill, Hitchens 2(1 pen), McParland, Wylie	25,093
21	10	A	Nottingham Forest	L	0 0	0 2		23,349
22	17	A	Chelsea	W	2 1	4 2	MacEwan, Wylie, Thomson 2	23,805
23	24	H	Wolverhampton Wanderers	L	0 2	0 2		49,088
24	26	A	Wolverhampton Wanderers	L	0 1	2 3	Hitchens 2	43,558
25	31	H	Blackpool	D	2 0	2 2	Hitchens 2	31,145
26	Jan 21	A	Blackburn Rovers	D	2 2	2 2	Hitchens 2	31,113
27	Feb 4	A	Manchester United	D	0 0	1 1	Thomson	33,484
28	11	H	Tottenham Hotspur	L	0 0	1 2	Lynn (pen)	50,786
29	25	A	Newcastle United	L	0 1	1 2	McParland	21,275
30	Mar 4	H	Arsenal	D	1 2	2 2	McParland, MacEwan	34,772
31	11	A	Birmingham City	D	1 0	1 1	Hitchens	41,656
32	22	A	Everton	W	0 1	2 1	Deakin, Thomson	28,115
33	25	A	Burnley	D	0 0	1 1	Hitchens	17,726
34	28	H	West Bromwich Albion	L	0 0	0 1		41,033
35	Apr 1	H	Nottingham Forest	L	0 0	1 2	McParland	25,469
36	3	A	Bolton Wanderers	L	0 1	0 3		21,721
37	4	H	Bolton Wanderers	W	1 0	4 0	MacEwan 2, McParland, O'Neill	15,732
38	8	A	Fulham	D	1 0	1 1	Hitchens	23,042
39	15	H	Preston North End	W	1 0	1 0	Thomson	24,028
40	19	A	Leicester City	L	0 2	1 3	Hale	21,219
41	22	A	Manchester City	L	0 4	1 4	Crowe	25,235
42	29	H	Sheffield Wednesday	W	2 1	4 1	Hitchens 2, Thomson, Dixon	26,023

Final League Position: 9th in First Division

1 Own-goal

Appearances
Goals

FA CUP

3	Jan 7	A	Bristol Rovers	D	0 1	1 1	Thomson	34,061
R	9	H	Bristol Rovers	W	2 0	4 0	Thomson 2, Hitchens 2	26,542
4	28	A	Peterborough United	D	1 1	1 1	Banham (og)	28,266
R	Feb 1	H	Peterborough United	W	0 0	2 1	McParland 2	64,531
5	18	H	Tottenham Hotspur	L	0 2	0 2		69,672

1 Own-goal

Appearances
Goals

FOOTBALL LEAGUE CUP

2	Oct 12	H	Huddersfield Town	W	2 1	4 1	Hitchens, Wylie 2, Burrows	17,000
3	Nov 15	A	Preston North End	D	2 1	3 3	O'Neill, Hitchens, Thomson	7,577
R	23	H	Preston North End	W	1 1	3 1	Hitchens, Wylie, MacEwan	20,545
4	Dec 13	H	Plymouth Argyle	D	0 2	3 3	McParland 2, MacEwan	12,195
R	19	A	Plymouth Argyle *	D	0 0	0 0		11,006
2R	Feb 6	A	Plymouth Argyle	W	1 2	5 3	Burrows, O'Neill, Hitchens 3	13,548
5	22	H	Wrexham	W	0 0	3 0	Thomson, Hitchens 2	19,965
SF1	Apr 10	A	Burnley	D	1 1	1 1	Hitchens	15,908
SF2	26	H	Burnley **	D	2 0	2 2	Hitchens, Thomson	23,077
SFR	May 2	N	Burnley ***	W	0 0	2 1	Lynn (pen), Hitchens	7,953
F1	Aug 22	A	Rotherham United	L	0 0	0 2		12,226
F2	Sep 5	H	Rotherham United **	W	0 0	3 0	O'Neill, Burrows, McParland	31,201

Appearances
Goals

* Abandoned after 90 minutes
** After Extra Time
*** Played at Old Trafford, Manchester
Final played in season 1961/62 - Villa won 3-2 on aggregate after extra-time

430

FINAL LEAGUE TABLE

	P	W	D	L	F	A	P
Tottenham Hotspur	42	31	4	7	115	55	66
Sheffield Wednesday	42	23	12	7	78	47	58
Wolverhampton W	42	25	7	10	103	75	57
Burnley	42	22	7	13	102	77	51
Everton	42	22	6	14	87	69	50
Leicester City	42	18	9	15	87	70	45
Manchester United	42	18	9	15	88	76	45
Blackburn Rovers	42	15	13	14	77	76	43
Aston Villa	**42**	**17**	**9**	**16**	**78**	**77**	**43**
West Bromwich A	42	18	5	19	67	71	41
Arsenal	42	15	11	16	77	85	41
Chelsea	42	15	7	20	98	100	37
Manchester City	42	13	11	18	79	90	37
Nottingham Forest	42	14	9	19	62	78	37
Cardiff City	42	13	11	18	60	85	37
West Ham United	42	13	10	19	77	88	36
Fulham	42	14	8	20	72	95	36
Bolton Wanderers	42	12	11	19	58	73	35
Birmingham City	42	14	6	22	62	84	34
Blackpool	42	12	9	21	68	73	33
Newcastle United	42	11	10	21	86	109	32
Preston North End	42	10	10	22	43	71	30

1961/62

SEASON SNIPPETS

Villa's second game of the season was a cup final! The inaugural League Cup final had to be held over from the previous season, and although Villa were beaten 2-0 by Rotherham United in the first leg at Millmoor, they became the competition's first winners with a 3-0 extra-time success at Villa Park in the second-leg two weeks later.

Bobby Thomson and Derek Dougan were injured in a car crash in September. Thomson was out of action for two months while Dougan did not play again until December.

Stan Lynn played his last Villa game against Blackburn on 16 September and joined Birmingham City on 20 October.

Allan Jones played his only league game on 7 October.

The 3-1 defeat by Birmingham City on 28 October was the last Villa league game for Norman Ash.

More than two decades before the clubs met in the European Cup quarter-finals, Villa were 2-1 winners against Dynamo Kiev in a Villa Park friendly on 13 November.

Peter McParland, the club's 1957 FA Cup hero, left the club in January, joining Wolverhampton Wanderers for £25,000.

Tommy Ewing, a £20,000 buy from Partick Thistle, made his debut on 3 February against Blackburn Rovers.

Alfie Hale, who had arrived from Waterford in April 1961, made the last of his seven appearances on 24 February.

Jimmy Dugdale made his last appearance against Birmingham City on 17 March and Jimmy McMorran's last game came the following week against Burnley.

DIVISION ONE

MANAGER: Joe Mercer

MATCH	DATE	VENUE	OPPONENTS	RESULT	HT SCORE	SCORE	SCORERS	ATT
1	Aug 19	A	Everton	L	0 1	0 2		52,289
2	26	H	Chelsea	W	1 1	3 1	Thomson, Burrows, MacEwan	29,390
3	28	A	Wolverhampton Wanderers	D	0 2	2 2	Dougan 2	31,703
4	Sep 2	A	Sheffield United	W	1 0	2 0	Burrows, Dougan	21,336
5	9	H	West Ham United	L	0 0	2 4	Crowe, McParland	31,836
6	16	A	Blackburn Rovers	L	1 0	2 4	Tindall, Burrows	15,611
7	18	H	Manchester United	D	1 1	1 1	McParland	38,837
8	23	H	Blackpool	W	2 0	5 0	Burrows 2, McParland 3	31,711
9	30	A	Tottenham Hotspur	L	0 0	0 1		38,099
10	Oct 2	H	Wolverhampton Wanderers	W	1 0	1 0	MacEwan	43,298
11	7	A	Fulham	L	0 1	1 3	MacEwan	22,229
12	16	H	Sheffield Wednesday	W	1 0	1 0	McParland	34,932
13	21	A	West Bromwich Albion	D	1 1	1 1	S Jones (og)	39,071
14	28	H	Birmingham City	L	0 2	1 3	McParland	49,532
15	Nov 4	A	Burnley	L	0 2	0 3		22,487
16	11	H	Arsenal	W	1 0	3 1	Burrows, McParland, Thomson	24,178
17	18	A	Bolton Wanderers	D	0 1	1 1	Thomson	13,198
18	25	H	Manchester City	W	2 0	2 1	Burrows, McParland	26,617
19	Dec 2	A	Leicester City	W	1 0	2 0	Wylie, Dougan	22,651
20	9	H	Ipswich Town	W	1 0	3 0	McParland 2, Thomson	31,924
21	16	H	Everton	D	1 1	1 1	Thomson	34,939
22	23	A	Chelsea	L	0 0	0 1		20,538
23	26	A	Cardiff City	L	0 0	0 1		18,394
24	Jan 13	A	Sheffield United	D	0 0	0 0		26,350
25	15	A	Manchester United	L	0 2	0 2		20,807
26	20	A	West Ham United	L	0 2	0 2		20,284
27	Feb 3	H	Blackburn Rovers	W	1 0	1 0	Dougan	28,718
28	10	A	Blackpool	W	0 1	2 1	MacEwan, McMorran	13,039
29	21	H	Tottenham Hotspur	D	0 0	0 0		49,892
30	24	H	Fulham	W	0 0	2 0	MacEwan, Burrows	24,725
31	Mar 3	A	Sheffield Wednesday	L	0 2	0 3		21,888
32	14	H	West Bromwich Albion	W	0 0	1 0	Burrows	34,969
33	17	A	Birmingham City	W	2 0	2 0	Burrows, Wylie	43,489
34	24	H	Burnley	L	0 1	0 2		36,864
35	31	A	Arsenal	W	1 2	5 4	Thomson 2, Dougan, Crowe, Ewing	20,107
36	Apr 7	H	Bolton Wanderers	W	1 0	3 0	Ewing, Thomson, Dougan	23,571
37	14	A	Manchester City	L	0 0	0 1		18,564
38	21	H	Leicester City	W	4 2	8 3	Thomson 3, Dougan 2, Chalmers (og), Baker, Burrows	24,579
39	23	H	Nottingham Forest	W	4 1	5 1	Burrows 2 (1 pen), McKinlay (og), Thomson, Ewing	24,147
40	24	A	Nottingham Forest	L	0 0	0 2		25,118
41	28	A	Ipswich Town	L	0 0	0 2		28,932
42	May 1	H	Cardiff City	D	2 2	2 2	Rankmore (og), Dougan	22,174

Final League Position: 7th in First Division

4 Own-goals

Appearances
Goals

FA CUP

3	Jan 6	H	Crystal Palace	W	2 2	4 3	Burrows 2, McParland, Dougan	39,011
4	27	H	Huddersfield Town	W	1 0	2 1	Hale, Crowe	38,013
5	Feb 17	H	Charlton Athletic	W	0 0	2 1	Dougan, Burrows	42,057
6	Mar 10	A	Tottenham Hotspur	L	0 0	0 2		63,879

Appearances
Goals

FOOTBALL LEAGUE CUP

1	Sep 13	A	Bradford City	W	3 0	4 3	MacEwan, Wylie 2, Burrows	9,768
2	Oct 9	A	West Ham United	W	2 1	3 1	McParland, Burrows, Bond (og)	17,735
3	Nov 21	H	Ipswich Town	L	0 2	2 3	Burrows 2 (1 pen)	22,541

Appearances
Goals

432

FINAL LEAGUE TABLE

	P	W	D	L	F	A	P
Ipswich Town	42	24	8	10	93	67	56
Burnley	42	21	11	10	101	67	53
Tottenham Hotspur	42	21	10	11	88	69	52
Everton	42	20	11	11	88	54	51
Sheffield United	42	19	9	14	61	69	47
Sheffield Wednesday	42	20	6	16	72	58	46
Aston Villa	**42**	**18**	**8**	**16**	**65**	**56**	**44**
West Ham United	42	17	10	15	76	82	44
West Bromwich A	42	15	13	14	83	67	43
Arsenal	42	16	11	15	71	72	43
Bolton Wanderers	42	16	10	16	62	66	42
Manchester City	42	17	7	18	78	81	41
Blackpool	42	15	11	16	70	75	41
Leicester City	42	17	6	19	72	71	40
Manchester United	42	15	9	18	72	75	39
Blackburn Rovers	42	14	11	17	50	58	39
Birmingham City	42	14	10	18	65	81	38
Wolverhampton W	42	14	8	20	73	86	36
Nottingham Forest	42	13	10	19	63	79	36
Fulham	42	13	7	22	66	74	33
Cardiff City	42	9	14	19	50	81	32
Chelsea	42	9	10	23	63	94	28

433

1962/63

SEASON SNIPPETS

When Villa beat Tottenham Hotspur 2-1 in the opening week of the season, it was their first victory over the Londoners since the Second World War.

Winger Harry Burrows and West Bromwich Albion's Clive Clark were sent off for fighting during Villa's 2-0 home win over their neighbours in October.

Jimmy Dugdale, a veteran of the 1957 FA Cup triumph, ended his six-year association with the club, joining Queen's Park Rangers for £6,000 on 20 October.

Phil Woosnam joined Villa from West Ham United for £25,000 in November, while full-back John Neal left Villa Park for Southend United.

Cammie Fraser, a £24,500 buy from Dunfermline Athletic, made his debut in the 6-2 League Cup win against Preston on 12 November while Alan O'Neill moved to Plymouth Argyle on the 27th of the month.

The home game against Manchester City on the Saturday before Christmas was abandoned after 48 minutes because of fog. City led 1-0, but Villa won 3-1 when the game was re-staged in May.

Wilson Briggs played the second of his two games on 1 April.

Derek Dougan signed off with a goal against Leicester on 15 May, his last game before joining Peterborough United.

DIVISION ONE

MANAGER: Joe Mercer

MATCH	DATE	VENUE	OPPONENTS	RESULT	HT SCORE	SCORE	SCORERS	ATT
1	Aug 18	H	West Ham United	W	2 0	3 1	Dougan, MacEwan, Thomson	37,657
2	20	H	Tottenham Hotspur	W	0 1	2 1	Dougan 2	55,630
3	25	A	Manchester City	W	0 0	2 0	Thomson, Burrows	29,524
4	29	A	Tottenham Hotspur	L	0 3	2 4	Dougan, Deakin	55,650
5	Sep 1	H	Blackpool	D	1 1	1 1	MacEwan	35,084
6	4	A	Arsenal	W	2 0	2 1	Thomson 2	33,851
7	8	A	Blackburn Rovers	L	1 2	1 4	Burrows	13,953
8	10	H	Arsenal	W	3 1	3 1	Thomson, Burrows, MacEwan	36,866
9	15	H	Sheffield United	L	0 2	1 2	J Shaw (og)	29,564
10	22	A	Nottingham Forest	L	0 1	1 3	Burrows (pen)	32,434
11	29	H	Ipswich Town	W	2 1	4 2	Wylie, Thomson 2, Dougan	31,860
12	Oct 6	A	West Bromwich Albion	W	1 0	2 0	Baker, Burrows (pen)	43,583
13	13	A	Everton	D	0 1	1 1	Baker	53,035
14	20	H	Leyton Orient	W	0 0	1 0	Burrows	30,169
15	27	A	Birmingham City	L	0 0	2 3	O'Neill, Burrows (pen)	42,228
16	Nov 3	H	Fulham	L	0 1	1 2	Burrows (pen)	28,987
17	10	A	Sheffield Wednesday	D	0 0	0 0		18,625
18	17	H	Burnley	W	2 1	2 1	Burrows, Dougan	32,380
19	24	A	Manchester United	D	1 1	2 2	Cantwell (og), Dougan	37,747
20	Dec 1	H	Bolton Wanderers	W	1 0	5 0	Burrows, MacEwan 2, Thomson, Dougan	34,075
21	8	A	Leicester City	D	2 1	3 3	Chalmers (og), MacEwan, Burrows	26,783
22	26	A	West Ham United	D	0 1	1 1	Thomson	21,529
23	Jan 19	A	Blackburn Rovers	D	0 0	0 0		18,276
24	Feb 13	A	Liverpool	L	0 3	0 4		46,347
25	Mar 9	A	Leyton Orient	W	2 0	2 0	Woosnam, Wylie	11,509
26	16	H	Birmingham City	W	3 0	4 0	Woosnam, Deakin, Baker, Burrows (pen)	40,400
27	23	A	Fulham	L	0 0	0 1		22,508
28	29	A	Blackpool	L	0 1	0 4		10,690
29	Apr 1	H	Everton	L	0 0	0 2		31,377
30	6	A	Burnley	L	1 2	1 3	Crowe	19,605
31	9	H	Manchester United	L	0 1	1 2	Thomson	26,895
32	13	H	Sheffield Wednesday	L	0 0	0 2		23,014
33	15	A	Wolverhampton Wanderers	L	1 0	1 3	R A Thomson (og),	26,299
34	16	H	Wolverhampton Wanderers	L	0 1	0 2		31,474
35	20	A	Bolton Wanderers	L	0 3	1 4	Burrows	13,411
36	May 1	A	Sheffield United	L	1 1	1 2	Burrows	17,111
37	4	H	Nottingham Forest	L	0 2	0 2		21,268
38	8	H	Manchester City	W	3 0	3 1	Baker, Burrows 2 (2 pens)	20,418
39	11	A	West Bromwich Albion	L	0 1	0 1		25,916
40	15	H	Leicester City	W	0 0	3 1	Fraser, Dougan, Lee	21,305
41	18	H	Liverpool	W	0 0	2 0	Graham, Thomson	21,017
42	21	A	Ipswich Town	D	0 1	1 1	Thomson	17,230

Final League Position: 15th in First Division

4 Own-goals

Appearances
Goals

FA CUP

3	Jan 16	A	Bristol City	D	0 1	1 1	Burrows (pen)	22,176
R	Mar 7	H	Bristol City	W	1 2	3 2	Burrows, Baker, Thomson	23,178
4	11	A	Manchester United	L	0 1	0 1		52,265

Appearances
Goals

FOOTBALL LEAGUE CUP

2	Sep 24	H	Peterborough United	W	4 0	6 1	Dougan 3, Ewing, Burrows, Wylie	17,392
3	Oct 17	H	Stoke City	W	2 0	3 1	Thomson, Ewing, Burrows (pen)	20,218
4	Nov 12	H	Preston North End	W	2 0	6 2	Burrows 2 (1 pen), Baker 2, O'Neill	16,704
5	Dec 3	H	Norwich City	W	1 1	4 1	Thomson 2, MacEwan, Dougan	14,862
SF1	Jan 12	A	Sunderland	W	2 0	3 1	Crowe, Thomson, Dougan	33,237
SF2	Apr 22	H	Sunderland	D	0 0	0 0		22,102
F1	May 23	A	Birmingham City	L	1 1	1 3	Thomson	31,902
F2	27	H	Birmingham City	D	0 0	0 0		37,949

Appearances
Goals

434

	Sims DN	Lee GF	Aitken CA	Crowe VH	Sleeuwenhoek JC	Deakin AR	MacEwan J	Baker AR	Dougan AD	Thomson RGM	Burrows H	Tindall MC	Sidebottom G	Neal J	Wylie RM	Ewing T	O'Neill A	Fraser JC	Woosnam PA	Gavan JT	Briggs WW	Chatterley LC	Graham G	Fencott KS		MATCH
	1	2	3	4	5	6	7	8	9	10	11															1
	1	2	3	4	5	6	7	8	9	10	11															2
	1	2	3	4	5	6	7	8	9	10	11															3
	1	2	3	4	5	6	7	8	9	10	11															4
	1	2	3	4	5		7	8	9	10	11	6														5
			3	4	5		7	8		9	11	6	1	2	10											6
		2	3	4	5		7	8	9	10	11	6	1													7
	1	6	3	4	5		7		9	10	11			2	8											8
	1	4	3		5	6	7	8	9	10	11			2												9
		2	3	4	5	6	7		9	8	11	1			10											10
		2	3	4	5	6			9	8	11	1			10	7										11
		2	3	4	5	6		8	9	10	11	1				7										12
		2	3	4	5	6		8		9	11	1			10	7										13
	1	4	3		5				9	11		6		2	10	7	8									14
		2	3	4	5	6				9	11	1			10	7	8									15
		2	3	4	5	6			9	8	11	1			10	7										16
		2	3	4	5		7	8		9	11	1						10								17
			3	4	5		7	8	9		11	6	1					10	2							18
			3	4	5		7	8	9		11	6	1					10	2							19
			3	4	5	6	7		9	8	11	1							2	10						20
			3	4	5	6	7		9	8	11	1							2	10						21
			3	4	5	6	7		9	8	11	1							2	10						22
			3	4	5	6	7	8		9	11	1							2	10						23
			3	4	5	6	7		9	8	11	1							2	10						24
			3		5		6		8		11	4	1		10	7		2		9						25
			3	4	5	6			9	11		1							2	10						26
			3	4	5	6	7	8	9			1					11		2	10	1					27
			3	4	5	6			9		11	8	1			7			2	10						28
			3	4	5	6		7	9	8	11	1								10	1	2				29
		10	3	4	5			7	9	8	11	6							2		1					30
			3	4	5			7	9	8	11	6							2	10	1					31
			3		5	6		9		11	4	1		10					2	8						32
			3		5	6			9	7	11		1		10				2	8						33
			3	4	5		7		9	6	11	1			8				2	10						34
			3	4	5		7		9		11	6	1		10											35
			3	4		5	6		7		8		9		10	11										36
		2	3	4		6			9	8	11	1			10	7				5						37
	1	6	3	4			7		9		11				10				2	8	5					38
	1	6	3	4			7		9		11				10				2	8	5					39
	1	6	3	4			7		9		11				10				2	8	5					40
	1		4	3		6	7		9		11				10				2		5	8				41
	1		4	3		6	7		9						10	11			2		5	8				42
	13	24	42	36	35	27	19	30	28	34	39	15	25	4	20	13	5	22	18	4	1	6	2			
		1		1		2	6	4	9	12	16			2		1	1	2				1				

		3	4	5	6	7		9	8	11		1						2	10						3
		2	3	4	5	6	7	8		9	11	1							2	10						R
			3	5		6	7		9	11	4	1		8					2	10						4

| | | 1 | 3 | 3 | 2 | 3 | 3 | 1 | 3 | 3 | 1 | 3 | | | | 1 | | | 2 | 3 | | | | | |
| | | | | | | | | 1 | | 1 | 2 | | | | | | | | | | | | | | |

		2	3	4	5	6			9	8	11	1			10	7										2
		2	3	4	5			8	9		11	6	1		10	7										3
			3	4	5			8	9		11	6	1					10	2					7		4
			3	4	5	6	7	8	9	10	11	1							2							5
			3	4	5	6	7	8	9	10	11	1							2							SF1
		2	3	4	5			8		9	11	6	1		10	7						11				SF2
	1	6	3	4	5			7		9	11				10				2		8					F1
	1	6	3	4				7		9	11				10				2		5	8				F2
	2	5	8	7	8	7	3	2	7	4	6	8	3	6		5	3	1	5		1	2	2			
				1			1	2	5	5	4					1	2	2								

FINAL LEAGUE TABLE

	P	W	D	L	F	A	P
Everton	42	25	11	6	84	42	61
Tottenham Hotspur	42	23	9	10	111	62	55
Burnley	42	22	10	10	78	57	54
Leicester City	42	20	12	10	79	53	52
Wolverhampton W	42	20	10	12	93	65	50
Sheffield Wednesday	42	19	10	13	77	63	48
Arsenal	42	18	10	14	86	77	46
Liverpool	42	17	10	15	71	59	44
Nottingham Forest	42	17	10	15	67	69	44
Sheffield United	42	16	12	14	58	60	44
Blackburn Rovers	42	15	12	15	79	71	42
West Ham United	42	14	12	16	73	69	40
Blackpool	42	13	14	15	58	64	40
West Bromwich A	42	16	7	19	71	79	39
Aston Villa	**42**	**15**	**8**	**19**	**62**	**68**	**38**
Fulham	42	14	10	18	50	71	38
Ipswich Town	42	12	11	19	59	78	35
Bolton Wanderers	42	15	5	22	55	75	35
Manchester United	42	12	10	20	67	81	34
Birmingham City	42	10	13	19	63	90	33
Manchester City	42	10	11	21	58	102	31
Leyton Orient	42	6	9	27	37	81	21

1963/64

SEASON SNIPPETS

Villa won their opening game of the season for the second year running, Tony Hateley scoring the only goal at Nottingham Forest following his £22,000 summer move from Notts County. Villa would have to wait another seven years before they again won on the opening day, by which time they were in the Third Division!

Michael Wright made his debut in the 4-0 away win at Blackpool on 7 September.

Dave Pountney joined the club in a £20,000 move from Shrewsbury Town, making his debut on 26 October.

Villa hosted a testimonial match for Vic Crowe in November, a London XI beating a Birmingham XI 6-1. Crowe joined Peterborough United the following summer.

Police insisted that Denis Law leave Villa Park before the end of the match after Manchester United's Scottish star had been sent off for kicking Alan Deakin as the Villa player lay on the ground.

Long-serving goalkeeper Nigel Sims left after eight years, joining Nuneaton Borough on a free transfer. Sims was the last of Villa's 1957 FA Cup-winning team.

It was Joe Mercer's last season in charge. He left the club in July and was replaced by Dick Taylor. Tommy Ewing returned to Partick Thistle while George Graham was sold to Chelsea for £5,950.

DIVISION ONE

MANAGER: Joe Mercer

MATCH	DATE	VENUE	OPPONENTS	RESULT	HT SCORE	SCORE	SCORERS	ATT
1	Aug 24	A	Nottingham Forest	W	1 0	1 0	Hateley	29,505
2	26	H	Stoke City	L	0 2	1 3	Hateley	40,147
3	31	H	Blackburn Rovers	L	0 1	1 2	England (og)	23,629
4	Sep 4	A	Stoke City	D	1 1	2 2	Burrows, Hateley	37,537
5	7	A	Blackpool	W	2 0	4 0	Deakin, Burrows 3	16,885
6	10	A	Arsenal	L	0 2	0 3		29,139
7	14	H	Chelsea	W	1 0	2 0	MacEwan, Hateley	23,681
8	16	H	Tottenham Hotspur	L	1 0	2 4	P Baker (og), A Baker	36,643
9	21	A	West Ham United	W	1 0	1 0	Burrows	20,346
10	28	H	Sheffield United	L	0 1	0 1		22,212
11	Oct 5	A	Liverpool	L	2 2	2 5	Hateley 2	39,106
12	7	H	Everton	L	0 0	0 1		23,999
13	12	A	West Bromwich Albion	L	2 1	3 4	Crawford (og), Tindall, Hateley	28,602
14	19	H	Arsenal	W	0 1	2 1	Hateley 2 (1 pen)	22,958
15	26	A	Sheffield Wednesday	L	0 1	0 1		19,843
16	Nov 2	H	Bolton Wanderers	W	0 0	3 0	Ewing, Burrows 2	18,847
17	9	A	Fulham	L	0 0	0 2		15,060
18	16	H	Manchester United	W	2 0	4 0	Hateley 2, Deakin, Burrows	36,276
19	23	A	Burnley	L	0 1	0 2		13,606
20	30	H	Ipswich Town	D	0 0	0 0		16,353
21	Dec 7	A	Leicester City	D	0 0	0 0		21,420
22	14	H	Nottingham Forest	W	3 0	3 0	Burrows, MacEwan, Whitefoot (og)	14,216
23	21	A	Blackburn Rovers	L	0 1	0 2		17,095
24	26	A	Wolverhampton Wanderers	D	0 0	3 3	Pountney, Crowe, Hateley	27,569
25	28	H	Wolverhampton Wanderers	D	1 1	2 2	Burrows 2	34,187
26	Jan 11	H	Blackpool	W	1 0	3 1	Woosnam 2, Hateley	14,191
27	18	A	Chelsea	L	0 0	0 1		23,968
28	25	A	Tottenham Hotspur	L	0 2	1 3	Burrows (pen)	36,394
29	Feb 1	H	West Ham United	D	1 1	2 2	Burrows, Woosnam	16,721
30	8	A	Sheffield United	D	1 0	1 1	Wylie	14,740
31	19	H	Liverpool	D	2 2	2 2	Wylie, Burrows	13,793
32	22	A	West Bromwich Albion	W	0 0	1 0	Woosnam	27,723
33	28	A	Everton	L	1 1	2 4	Burrows, Graham	50,292
34	Mar 7	H	Sheffield Wednesday	D	1 1	2 2	Hateley, Aitken	13,875
35	21	H	Fulham	D	1 0	2 2	Tindall, Burrows	11,427
36	28	A	Bolton Wanderers	D	1 1	1 1	Hateley	8,348
37	30	H	Birmingham City	L	0 1	0 3		25,797
38	31	A	Birmingham City	D	3 2	3 3	Chatterley 2, Tindall	28,069
39	Apr 4	H	Burnley	W	0 0	2 0	Hateley 2	14,269
40	6	A	Manchester United	L	0 1	0 1		26,072
41	11	A	Ipswich Town	L	1 1	3 4	Pountney 2, Wylie	11,658
42	18	H	Leicester City	L	0 2	1 3	Deakin	18,322

Final League Position: 19th in First Division

4 Own-goals

Appearances
Goals

FA CUP

3	Jan 4	H	Aldershot	D	0 0	0 0		21,912
R	8	A	Aldershot	L	0 0	1 2	Hateley	13,566

Appearances
Goals

FOOTBALL LEAGUE CUP

2	Sep 25	H	Barnsley	W	2 0	3 1	Hateley, Baker, Burrows	10,679
3	Oct 16	H	West Ham United	L	0 0	0 2		11,194

Appearances
Goals

436

FINAL LEAGUE TABLE

	P	W	D	L	F	A	P
Liverpool	42	26	5	11	92	45	57
Manchester United	42	23	7	12	90	62	53
Everton	42	21	10	11	84	64	52
Tottenham Hotspur	42	22	7	13	97	81	51
Chelsea	42	20	10	12	72	56	50
Sheffield Wednesday	42	19	11	12	84	67	49
Blackburn Rovers	42	18	10	14	89	65	46
Arsenal	42	17	11	14	90	82	45
Burnley	42	17	10	15	71	64	44
West Bromwich A	42	16	11	15	70	61	43
Leicester City	42	16	11	15	61	58	43
Sheffield United	42	16	11	15	61	64	43
Nottingham Forest	42	16	9	17	64	68	41
West Ham United	42	14	12	16	69	74	40
Fulham	42	13	13	16	58	65	39
Wolverhampton W	42	12	15	15	70	80	39
Stoke City	42	14	10	18	77	78	38
Blackpool	42	13	9	20	52	73	35
Aston Villa	**42**	**11**	**12**	**19**	**62**	**71**	**34**
Birmingham City	42	11	7	24	54	92	29
Bolton Wanderers	42	10	8	24	48	80	28
Ipswich Town	42	9	7	26	56	121	25

437

1964/65

SEASON SNIPPETS

New manager Dick Taylor broke Villa's transfer record in early September when he paid £40,000 for Arsenal winger John MacLeod, who had scored one goal and made another in the Gunners' 3-1 victory over Villa at Highbury the previous Saturday.

Goalkeeper Colin Withers joined the club in November, arriving from Birmingham City for £18,000. The deal was concluded just half an hour after the club paid £20,000 for striker Barry Stobart from Manchester City.

Geoff Sidebottom's last game was the 7-1 League Cup win against Bradford City on 23 November.

The three games against Wolverhampton Wanderers in the fifth round of the FA Cup attracted a combined total attendance of 137,473.

Harry Burrows played his last game on 27 February and was then transferred to Stoke City.

Gordon Lee's final game was against West Ham on 31 March.

Villa's players spent a week on the south coast at the end of the season. Their break included a friendly with Bournemouth, which was drawn 1-1. Tony Hateley, who had scored 34 goals in competitive matches throughout the campaign, was the man on target for Villa at Dean Court.

Ron Wylie joined Birmingham City in June.

DIVISION ONE

MANAGER: Dick Taylor

MATCH	DATE	VENUE	OPPONENTS	RESULT	HT SCORE	SCORE	SCORERS	ATT
1	Aug 22	H	Leeds United	L	1 1	1 2	Woosnam	25,502
2	26	A	Chelsea	L	0 1	1 2	Hateley	30,389
3	29	A	Arsenal	L	0 1	1 3	Hateley	28,832
4	31	H	Chelsea	D	0 1	2 2	Hateley, Wylie	19,757
5	Sep 5	H	Blackburn Rovers	L	0 2	0 4		21,785
6	9	A	Sunderland	D	2 1	2 2	Burrows, Hateley	44,099
7	12	A	Blackpool	L	1 1	1 3	Hateley	22,795
8	14	H	Sunderland	W	2 0	2 1	Aitken, Hateley	18,756
9	19	A	Sheffield Wednesday	W	1 0	2 0	Burrows, Hateley	18,841
10	26	A	Liverpool	L	1 2	1 5	Hateley	38,940
11	Oct 5	H	Everton	L	0 0	1 2	Pountney	23,115
12	10	A	West Ham United	L	0 1	0 3		20,703
13	17	H	West Bromwich Albion	L	0 0	0 1		26,091
14	24	A	Manchester United	L	0 2	0 7		37,233
15	31	H	Fulham	W	1 0	2 0	MacEwan, Lee	14,845
16	Nov 7	A	Nottingham Forest	L	1 3	2 4	Hateley, Burrows (pen)	26,200
17	14	H	Stoke City	W	1 0	3 0	Burrows 2, Tindall	19,334
18	21	A	Tottenham Hotspur	L	0 2	0 4		29,724
19	28	H	Burnley	W	0 0	1 0	Stobart	18,177
20	Dec 5	A	Sheffield United	L	0 1	2 4	Pountney, Burrows	12,892
21	12	A	Leeds United	L	0 1	0 1		27,339
22	19	H	Arsenal	W	0 1	3 1	Baker 2, MacLeod	15,497
23	26	A	Wolverhampton Wanderers	W	1 0	1 0	Baker	30,829
24	Jan 2	A	Blackburn Rovers	L	0 3	1 5	Stobart	18,292
25	16	H	Blackpool	W	1 2	3 2	Hateley, Baker, MacLeod	17,411
26	Feb 6	H	Liverpool	L	0 1	0 1		24,366
27	13	A	Birmingham City	W	1 0	1 0	Stobart	32,491
28	27	A	West Bromwich Albion	L	0 0	1 3	Stobart	26,615
29	Mar 13	A	Everton	L	1 2	1 3	Hateley	32,525
30	15	H	Sheffield Wednesday	L	0 1	1 3	Chatterley	11,526
31	20	H	Nottingham Forest	W	1 0	2 1	Hateley 2	14,433
32	22	H	Wolverhampton Wanderers	W	3 1	3 2	Baker, Chatterley 2	28,805
33	27	A	Stoke City	L	0 1	1 2	Hateley	20,380
34	31	H	West Ham United	L	2 0	2 3	Hateley, Aitken	19,966
35	Apr 3	H	Tottenham Hotspur	W	1 0	1 0	Baker	24,930
36	10	A	Burnley	D	1 1	2 2	Hateley, Aitken	10,105
37	12	H	Birmingham City	W	2 0	3 0	Woosnam, Chatterley, Hateley	36,871
38	17	H	Sheffield United	W	1 0	2 1	Hateley 2 (1 pen)	19,823
39	19	A	Leicester City	D	1 1	1 1	Woosnam	14,607
40	20	H	Leicester City	W	0 0	1 0	Chatterley	22,213
41	24	A	Fulham	D	0 0	1 1	Hateley	13,494
42	28	H	Manchester United	W	2 0	2 1	Baker, Park	36,005

Final League Position: 16th in First Division

Appearances

Goals

FA CUP

3	Jan 9	H	Coventry City	W	1 0	3 0	Hateley 2, MacLeod	47,656
4	30	A	Sheffield United	W	2 0	2 0	Hateley, Stobart	31,655
5	Feb 20	H	Wolverhampton Wanderers	D	0 1	1 1	Hateley	52,010
R	24	A	Wolverhampton Wanderers *	D	0 0	0 0		47,929
2R	Mar 1	N	Wolverhampton Wanderers **	L	0 1	1 3	Park	37,534

Appearances

Goals

* After extra-time
** Played at The Hawthorns, West Bromwich

FOOTBALL LEAGUE CUP

2	Sep 23	A	Luton Town	W	1 0	1 0	Park	9,011
3	Oct 14	A	Leeds United	W	1 1	3 2	Burrows, Park, Hateley	10,656
4	Nov 4	H	Reading	W	2 0	3 1	Hateley 2, Burrows	7,964
5	23	H	Bradford City	W	4 0	7 1	Chatterley, Hateley 4, Wylie, Burrows	7,882
SF1	Jan 20	H	Chelsea	L	0 2	2 3	Hateley 2	12,022
SF2	Feb 10	A	Chelsea	D	1 0	1 1	Hateley	17,425

Appearances

Goals

438

FINAL LEAGUE TABLE

	P	W	D	L	F	A	P
Manchester United	42	26	9	7	89	39	61
Leeds United	42	26	9	7	83	52	61
Chelsea	42	24	8	10	89	54	56
Everton	42	17	15	10	69	60	49
Nottingham Forest	42	17	13	12	71	67	47
Tottenham Hotspur	42	19	7	16	87	71	45
Liverpool	42	17	10	15	67	73	44
Sheffield Wednesday	42	16	11	15	57	55	43
West Ham United	42	19	4	19	82	71	42
Blackburn Rovers	42	16	10	16	83	79	42
Stoke City	42	16	10	16	67	66	42
Burnley	42	16	10	16	70	70	42
Arsenal	42	17	7	18	69	75	41
West Bromwich A	42	13	13	16	70	65	39
Sunderland	42	14	9	19	64	74	37
Aston Villa	**42**	**16**	**5**	**21**	**57**	**82**	**37**
Blackpool	42	12	11	19	67	78	35
Leicester City	42	11	13	18	69	85	35
Sheffield United	42	12	11	19	50	64	35
Fulham	42	11	12	19	60	78	34
Wolverhampton W	42	13	4	25	59	89	30
Birmingham City	42	8	11	23	64	96	27

439

1965/66

SEASON SNIPPETS

The attendance of 40,694 for Villa's League Cup quarter-final against West Bromwich Albion at The Hawthorns was, at the time, a record for the competition.

Graham Parker became Villa's first substitute when he replaced Tony Hateley during the 3-2 win against Tottenham on 25 September.

Two Villa games were abandoned in December. The game against West Bromwich Albion at The Hawthorns was stopped after 53 minutes because of monsoon-like conditions, while the Boxing Day clash against West Ham United at Villa Park lasted just half an hour because of a frozen pitch.

Villa were 2-1 winners against Dutch club Twente Enschede at Villa Park on 21 March 1966.

The club were forced to call off an end-of-season tour to Germany and Denmark following the re-arrangement of their final match at Chelsea.

Jimmy MacEwan played his last match on 27 April at Sheffield Wednesday.

The 6-1 defeat by Manchester United on 9 May was Allan Baker's last game.

The Villa Lions club was officially opened in June 1996 by club president Sir Theodore Pritchett.

In July 1966, three World Cup games were staged at Villa Park, Argentina won 2-1 against Spain on the 13th and played a goalless draw with West Germany on 16 July. West Germany won 2-1 against Spain on 20 July.

DIVISION ONE

MANAGER: Dick Taylor

MATCH	DATE	VENUE	OPPONENTS	RESULT	HT SCORE	SCORE	SCORERS	ATT
1	Aug 21	A	Sheffield United	L	0 0	0 1		15,575
2	23	H	Leeds United	L	0 1	0 2		33,940
3	28	H	Leicester City	D	0 0	2 2	Hateley (pen), Aitken	21,119
4	Sep 1	A	Leeds United	L	0 2	0 2		33,575
5	4	A	Blackburn Rovers	W	2 0	2 0	Hateley 2	9,367
6	6	H	Sunderland	W	0 0	3 1	Hamilton, Park, Hateley	25,905
7	11	H	Blackpool	W	1 0	3 0	Hamilton, Woosnam, Park	21,640
8	15	A	Sunderland	L	0 2	0 2		37,961
9	18	A	Fulham	W	2 1	6 3	Hateley 2, Woosnam, Tindall, MacLeod, Hamilton	12,634
10	25	H	Tottenham Hotspur	W	2 0	3 2	Park, Woosnam, Hamilton	29,856
11	Oct 2	A	Liverpool	L	0 1	1 3	Woosnam	43,859
12	9	A	Newcastle United	L	0 0	0 1		31,382
13	16	H	West Bromwich Albion	D	0 0	1 1	Pountney	41,379
14	23	A	Nottingham Forest	W	1 1	2 1	Woosnam, Hateley	20,833
15	30	H	Sheffield Wednesday	W	1 0	2 0	Scott, Hateley	23,222
16	Nov 6	A	Northampton Town	L	0 2	1 2	Park	18,836
17	13	H	Stoke City	L	0 0	0 1		22,836
18	20	A	Burnley	L	1 0	1 3	Hateley	14,281
19	27	H	Chelsea	L	1 2	2 4	Scott, Pountney	16,414
20	Dec 4	A	Arsenal	D	1 1	3 3	Hateley, Parker, Hamilton	25,890
21	11	H	Everton	W	3 0	3 2	Woosnam, Hateley 2	18,826
22	Jan 1	H	Newcastle United	W	2 1	4 2	MacLeod, Woosnam 2, Hamilton	19,423
23	8	A	Everton	L	0 1	0 2		34,641
24	15	H	Nottingham Forest	W	1 0	3 0	Hamilton, Woosnam 2	14,993
25	29	H	Sheffield United	L	0 1	0 2		15,318
26	Feb 5	A	Leicester City	L	0 1	1 2	Hateley	21,073
27	7	H	West Ham United	L	0 1	1 2	Hateley (pen)	13,450
28	11	A	West Bromwich Albion	D	1 1	2 2	Hateley 2	17,089
29	19	H	Blackburn Rovers	W	2 0	3 1	Deakin, Hateley, MacLeod	15,117
30	26	A	Blackpool	W	0 0	1 0	Hamilton	11,075
31	Mar 5	A	West Ham United	L	0 2	2 4	MacLeod, Hateley	22,074
32	12	H	Fulham	L	1 2	2 5	Hateley, Woosnam	13,793
33	19	A	Tottenham Hotspur	D	1 4	5 5	Hateley 4, Deakin	28,371
34	26	H	Liverpool	L	0 1	0 3		23,298
35	Apr 2	A	Northampton Town	L	1 0	1 2	Hamilton	10,438
36	6	H	Manchester United	D	0 0	1 1	MacEwan	28,222
37	9	A	Stoke City	L	0 0	0 2		15,165
38	16	H	Burnley	W	1 2	2 1	Hateley, Woosnam	14,100
39	27	A	Sheffield Wednesday	L	0 0	0 2		27,259
40	30	H	Arsenal	W	2 0	3 0	Hateley 2, Woosnam	19,039
41	May 9	A	Manchester United	L	0 3	1 6	Woosnam	23,205
42	16	A	Chelsea	W	1 0	2 0	Hateley (pen), Woosnam	16,232

Final League Position: 16th in First Division

Appearances
Subs
Goals

FA CUP

3	Jan 22	H	Leicester City	L	1 0	1 2	Woosnam	38,015

Appearances
Subs
Goals

FOOTBALL LEAGUE CUP

2	Sep 21	A	Swansea Town	W	1 1	3 2	MacLeod, Woosnam 2	9,858
3	Oct 13	A	Sunderland	W	2 0	2 1	Tindall, Woosnam	19,723
4	Nov 3	A	Fulham	D	0 1	1 1	Stobart	10,083
R	8	H	Fulham	W	0 0	2 0	Woosnam 2	18,536
5	17	A	West Bromwich Albion	L	0 2	1 3	Hateley	40,694

Appearances
Subs
Goals

440

																								MATCH
Withers CC	Wright JM	Aitken CA	Tindall MC	Pountney DH	Deakin AR	Baker AR	Park RC	Hateley A	Woosnam PA	MacLeod JM	Hamilton WM	Stobart BH	Sleeuwenhoek JC	Parker GS	Scott AJE	Gavan JT	Bloomfield RG	Roberts D	MacEwan J	Bradley K				
1	2	3	4	5	6	7	8	9	10	11														1
1	2	3	4	5	6	7	10	9		11	8													2
1	2	3	4	5	6			9	10	7	8	11												3
1	2	3	4	6				9	10	7	8	11	5											4
1	2	3	4	6				9		7	8	11	5	10										5
1	2	3	4	6			11	9	10	7	8		5											6
1	2	3	4	6			11	9	10	7	8		5											7
1	2	3	4	6			11	9	10	7	8		5											8
1	2	3	4	6			11	9	10	7	8		5											9
1	2	3	4	6			11	9[1]	10	7	8		5		12[1]									10
1	2	3	4		6		11		9	7	10		5		8									11
1	2	3	4	9	6					10	7	8	5			11								12
1	2	3	4	9	6					10	7	8	5			11								13
1	2	3	4		6			9		10	7	8	5			11								14
1	2	3	4	12[1]	6			9		10[1]	7	8	5			11								15
1	2	3	4		6		10	9			7	8	5			11								16
	2	3		12[1]	6[1]			9	10	7	8		5		4	11	1							17
	2	3			6		8	9	10	12[1]			5			11[1]	1	4	7					18
	2	3			6		12[1]	9[1]	10	7	8		5			11	1	4						19
1	2	3			6			9	10	7	8		5		4	11								20
1	2	3			6			9	10	7	8		5		4	11								21
1	2	3			6			9	10	7	8		5		4	11								22
1	2	3			6			9	10	7	8			5	4[1]	11								23
1	2	3			6		12[1]	9	10	7	8				4	11								24
1	2	3			6			9			8	10	5		4	11								25
1	2	3	4	12[1]	6[1]	7		9	10	11	8		5											26
1	2	3	4	6				9	10	7	8[1]		5	12[1]		11								27
1	2	3	4		6		8	9	10	7			5			11								28
1	2	3	4		6			9	10	7	8		5			11								29
1	2	3	4		6			9	10	7	8		5			11								30
1	2	3	4		6			9	10	7	8		5			11								31
1	2	3	4	12[1]	6		10	9		7			5	8		11[1]								32
1	2	3		4	6	10	11	9					8	5					7					33
1	2	3	4	6		10	7	9					8			11								34
	2	3	4		6	12[1]		9	10	7[1]			8			11	1							35
1			4	6			9	10		8			5			11			7	2				36
1		3	4	6			9	10		8			5			11			7	2				37
1	12[1]	3	4	6			9	10		8			5			11[1]				2				38
1		3	4	6			9	10	11	8			5						7	2				39
1	2	3	4	6		7	9	10	11	8			5											40
1		3	4	6		7	9	10	11	8			5							2				41
1		3	4	6			8	9	10	11				7	5	2								42

38	36	42	26	30	26	8	13	39	35	36	37	5	38	4	8	25	4	2	1	4	5			
	1			4		1	2			1	1				1	1								
			1	1	2	3		4	27	14	4	9			1	2			1					

| 1 | 2 | 3 | | 6 | | | | 9 | 10 | 7 | 8 | | 5 | | 4 | 11 | | | | | | | 3 | |

| 1 | 1 | 1 | | 1 | | | | 1 | 1 | 1 | 1 | | 1 | | 1 | 1 | | | | | | | | |
| | | | | | | | | | | 1 | | | | | | | | | | | | | | |

1	2	3	4	6			11	9	10	7	8		5										2	
1	2	3	4	9	6		11		10	7	8		5										3	
1	2	3	4			6	8	10	9				7	5		11							4	
	2	3			6			9	10	7	8		5		4	11	1						R	
	2	3		6				9	10	7	8		5		4	11	1						5	

| 3 | 5 | 5 | 3 | 3 | 3 | 1 | 3 | 4 | 4 | 4 | 4 | 1 | 5 | | 2 | 3 | 2 | | | | | | | |
| | | | | 1 | | | | 1 | 5 | 1 | | 1 | | | | | | | | | | | | |

FINAL LEAGUE TABLE

	P	W	D	L	F	A	P	
Liverpool	42	26	9	7	79	34	61	
Leeds United	42	23	9	10	79	38	55	
Burnley	42	24	7	11	79	47	55	
Manchester United	42	18	15	9	84	59	51	
Chelsea	42	22	7	13	65	53	51	2
West Bromwich A	42	19	12	11	91	69	50	3
Leicester City	42	21	7	14	80	65	49	4
Tottenham Hotspur	42	16	12	14	75	66	44	R
Sheffield United	42	16	11	15	56	59	43	5
Stoke City	42	15	12	15	65	64	42	
Everton	42	15	11	16	56	62	41	
West Ham United	42	15	9	18	70	83	39	
Blackpool	42	14	9	19	55	65	37	
Arsenal	42	12	13	17	62	75	37	
Newcastle United	42	14	9	19	50	63	37	
Aston Villa	**42**	**15**	**6**	**21**	**69**	**80**	**36**	
Sheffield Wednesday	42	14	8	20	56	66	36	
Nottingham Forest	42	14	8	20	56	72	36	
Sunderland	42	14	8	20	51	72	36	
Fulham	42	14	7	21	67	85	35	
Northampton Town	42	10	13	19	55	92	33	
Blackburn Rovers	42	8	4	30	57	88	20	

1966/67

SEASON SNIPPETS

Wales international Phil Woosnam left the club to become manager-coach of Atlanta in the new American Soccer League.

Villa signed striker John Woodward from Stoke City for £30,000 at the end of September and two weeks later paid around £8,000 to Shrewsbury Town for former Wolverhampton Wanderers and England international Peter Broadbent. By the end of October, though, Tony Hateley had departed, joining Chelsea for £100,000. Woodward, unfortunately, played only three games before being ruled out for the rest of the season by injury.

Willie Hamilton played his last game on 19 November.

Lew Chatterley made a small piece of football history when his booking in a 2-1 victory over Manchester United on 3 December was expunged from the records by the FA Disciplinary Committee. It was the first time such action had been taken.

In January, winger Willie Anderson joined Villa from Manchester United for £20,000.

Villa Park hosted the FA Amateur Cup quarter-final between local side Highgate and Enfield. A crowd of 31,570 saw the Londoners win 6-0.

Manager Dick Taylor was sacked before the final match, along with chief scout Jimmy Easson and assistant trainer Johnny Dixon.

DIVISION ONE

MANAGER: Dick Taylor

MATCH	DATE	VENUE	OPPONENTS	RESULT	HT SCORE	SCORE	SCORERS	ATT
1	Aug 20	H	Newcastle United	D	1 0	1 1	Chatterley	17,673
2	22	H	Sheffield Wednesday	L	0 0	0 1		15,013
3	27	A	Arsenal	L	0 1	0 1		26,762
4	31	A	Sheffield Wednesday	L	0 1	0 2		25,184
5	Sep 3	H	Manchester City	W	1 0	3 0	Chatterley, Hateley, Wright	15,552
6	5	H	Southampton	L	0 0	0 1		18,253
7	10	A	Blackpool	W	1 0	2 0	MacLeod, Chatterley	15,238
8	17	H	Chelsea	L	0 4	2 6	MacLeod, Hateley	18,259
9	24	A	Leicester City	L	0 1	0 5		22,065
10	Oct 1	H	Liverpool	L	1 1	2 3	Hateley 2 (1pen)	24,920
11	8	H	Leeds United	W	2 0	3 0	Chatterley, Woodward 2	19,125
12	15	A	West Bromwich Albion	L	0 2	1 2	Park	31,128
13	22	H	Sheffield United	D	0 0	0 0		20,911
14	29	A	Tottenham Hotspur	W	1 0	1 0	Chatterley	31,014
15	Nov 5	H	West Bromwich Albion	W	3 0	3 2	MacLeod 2, Roberts	23,984
16	12	A	Fulham	L	0 0	1 5	Tindall	16,072
17	19	H	Nottingham Forest	D	1 1	1 1	MacLeod	18,165
18	26	A	Burnley	L	1 0	2 4	MacLeod, Chatterley	14,935
19	Dec 3	H	Manchester United	W	1 0	2 1	Scott, Chatterley	40,016
20	10	A	Stoke City	L	1 3	1 6	MacLeod	20,240
21	17	A	Newcastle United	W	1 0	3 0	Bradley, Scott, Chatterley	25,406
22	26	A	Sunderland	L	0 1	1 2	Harvey (og)	31,262
23	27	H	Sunderland	W	1 0	2 1	Chatterley (pen), Bradley	26,612
24	31	H	Arsenal	L	0 1	0 1		19,440
25	Jan 14	A	Blackpool	W	1 1	3 2	Stobart 2, Chatterley	16,913
26	21	A	Chelsea	L	1 3	1 3	Stobart	30,922
27	Feb 4	H	Leicester City	L	0 1	0 1		26,589
28	11	A	Liverpool	L	0 1	0 1		45,745
29	25	A	Leeds United	W	1 0	2 0	Chatterley, Stobart	34,498
30	Mar 4	H	Tottenham Hotspur	D	1 1	3 3	Chatterley, Anderson, Stobart	31,718
31	18	A	Sheffield United	D	1 1	3 3	Anderson (pen), Stobart 2	15,656
32	24	A	West Ham United	L	1 1	1 2	Anderson	28,715
33	25	H	Stoke City	W	0 0	2 0	Anderson (pen), Sleeuwenhoek	21,006
34	28	H	West Ham United	L	0 1	0 2		22,011
35	Apr 1	A	Everton	L	0 3	1 3	MacLeod	36,619
36	8	H	Fulham	D	1 1	1 1	Stobart	13,723
37	15	A	Nottingham Forest	L	0 1	0 3		41,468
38	19	A	Manchester City	D	0 0	1 1	Chatterley	26,252
39	22	H	Burnley	L	0 1	0 1		19,010
40	29	A	Manchester United	L	1 0	1 3	Anderson	55,763
41	May 6	H	Everton	L	1 1	2 4	Stobart 2	25,302
42	13	A	Southampton	L	1 2	2 6	Walker (og), Stobart	20,855

Final League Position: 21st in First Division

2 Own-goals

Appearances
Subs
Goals

FA CUP

3	Jan 28	A	Preston North End	W	0 0	1 0	Roberts	26,385
4	Feb 18	A	Liverpool	L	0 0	0 1		52,477

Appearances
Subs
Goals

FOOTBALL LEAGUE CUP

2	Sep 14	A	West Bromwich Albion	L	0 3	1 6	Hateley (pen)	25,039

Appearances
Subs
Goals

442

FINAL LEAGUE TABLE

	P	W	D	L	F	A	P
Manchester United	42	24	12	6	84	45	60
Nottingham Forest	42	23	10	9	64	41	56
Tottenham Hotspur	42	24	8	10	71	48	56
Leeds United	42	22	11	9	62	42	55
Liverpool	42	19	13	10	64	47	51
Everton	42	19	10	13	65	46	48
Arsenal	42	16	14	12	58	47	46
Leicester City	42	18	8	16	78	71	44
Chelsea	42	15	14	13	67	62	44
Sheffield United	42	16	10	16	52	59	42
Sheffield Wednesday	42	14	13	15	56	47	41
Stoke City	42	17	7	18	63	58	41
West Bromwich A	42	16	7	19	77	73	39
Burnley	42	15	9	18	66	76	39
Manchester City	42	12	15	15	43	52	39
West Ham United	42	14	8	20	80	84	36
Sunderland	42	14	8	20	58	72	36
Fulham	42	11	12	19	71	83	34
Southampton	42	14	6	22	74	92	34
Newcastle United	42	12	9	21	39	81	33
Aston Villa	**42**	**11**	**7**	**24**	**54**	**85**	**29**
Blackpool	42	6	9	27	41	76	21

443

1967/68

SEASON SNIPPETS

Tommy Cummings, the former Burnley defender, was unveiled as Villa's new manager on Friday 6 July.

A combined total of more than 95,000 spectators watched the two Second City derbies - both of them won by Birmingham City.

Tommy Mitchinson became Cummings' first signing when he arrived from Mansfield Town for £18,000. He was followed to Villa Park in September by Preston North End's Brian Godfrey and Brian Greenhalgh for a combined fee of £35,000. Just before the transfer deadline in March, Cummings snapped up another Mansfield player, Dick Edwards, for £30,000, but the biggest signing of the campaign was Mike Ferguson, who arrived from Blackburn for a club record of £55,000.

Centre-half John Sleeuwenhoek was picked for both Villa and Birmingham City on Friday 3 November 1967. Sleeuwenhoek was named in the Villa side to face Carlisle United the following day, but later that afternoon joined Birmingham City for £45,000 and was selected for their game against Derby County.

Dave Pountney, John Inglis, Tony Scott, Barry Stobart, Graham Parker, Mike Tindall, Dave Roberts and John MacLeod all played their last Villa games during the season while Barry Ansell made his only appearance.

The Aston Villa board defeated a move by the Shareholders Association to have all five directors removed by an overwhelming margin of 303.

DIVISION TWO

MANAGER: Tommy Cummings

MATCH	DATE	VENUE	OPPONENTS	RESULT	HT SCORE	SCORE	SCORERS	ATT
1	Aug 19	A	Norwich City	L	0 1	0 1		19,408
2	23	A	Plymouth Argyle	L	0 2	1 2	Stobart	20,295
3	26	H	Rotherham United	W	2 0	3 1	Rudge, Stobart, Anderson	13,673
4	28	H	Plymouth Argyle	L	0 1	0 1		15,123
5	Sep 2	A	Derby County	L	1 0	1 3	Stobart	22,967
6	5	A	Queen's Park Rangers	L	0 2	0 3		21,438
7	9	H	Preston North End	W	1 0	1 0	Park	13,285
8	16	A	Charlton Athletic	L	0 3	0 3		12,499
9	23	H	Crystal Palace	L	0 1	0 1		12,862
10	30	A	Middlesbrough	D	1 1	1 1	Godfrey	20,534
11	Oct 7	A	Birmingham City	L	2 2	2 4	Greenhalgh, Godfrey	50,067
12	14	A	Millwall	W	1 0	2 1	Godfrey, Greenhalgh	13,392
13	21	H	Blackpool	W	2 1	3 2	Anderson, Greenhalgh, Mitchinson	21,628
14	Nov 4	H	Carlisle United	W	1 0	1 0	Mitchinson	17,767
15	11	A	Ipswich Town	L	1 0	1 2	Godfrey	17,748
16	18	H	Hull City	L	1 0	2 3	Greenhalgh 2	19,675
17	25	A	Bolton Wanderers	W	1 0	3 2	Greenhalgh, Godfrey, Tindall	13,064
18	Dec 2	H	Huddersfield Town	D	0 0	0 0		19,507
19	16	A	Norwich City	W	2 2	4 2	Mitchinson 2, Woodward, Greenhalgh	16,508
20	23	A	Rotherham United	W	0 0	2 0	Greenhalgh, Mitchinson	10,252
21	26	A	Cardiff City	L	0 1	0 3		18,180
22	30	H	Cardiff City	W	0 1	2 1	Greenhalgh, Anderson	17,667
23	Jan 6	H	Derby County	W	0 1	2 1	Greenhalgh, MacLeod	23,805
24	20	H	Charlton Athletic	W	1 0	4 1	MacLeod, Greenhalgh, Godfrey, Woodward	19,560
25	Feb 3	A	Crystal Palace	W	1 0	1 0	Godfrey	10,214
26	10	H	Middlesbrough	L	0 0	0 1		22,724
27	24	A	Birmingham City	L	1 1	1 2	Godfrey	45,283
28	27	A	Bristol City	D	0 0	0 0		17,138
29	Mar 2	H	Millwall	W	2 1	3 1	Anderson 2 (1 pen), Mitchinson	14,886
30	13	A	Blackburn Rovers	L	0 1	1 2	Rudge	10,026
31	16	A	Blackpool	L	0 0	0 1		14,361
32	18	H	Preston North End	L	1 2	1 2	Greenhalgh	17,043
33	23	H	Blackburn Rovers	L	1 1	1 2	Mitchinson	14,111
34	30	A	Carlisle United	W	2 1	2 1	Rudge, Godfrey	8,861
35	Apr 6	H	Ipswich Town	D	2 1	2 2	Mitchinson, Godfrey	19,874
36	13	A	Hull City	L	0 0	0 3		15,965
37	15	A	Portsmouth	D	2 0	2 2	Haydock (og), Godfrey	26,045
38	16	H	Portsmouth	W	0 0	1 0	Rudge	16,774
39	20	H	Bolton Wanderers	D	0 1	1 1	Chatterley	16,860
40	27	A	Huddersfield Town	D	0 0	0 0		7,489
41	May 4	H	Bristol City	L	2 3	2 4	Godfrey, Chatterley	15,301
42	11	H	Queen's Park Rangers	L	1 0	1 2	Mitchinson	33,835

Final League Position: 16th in Second Division

1 Own-goal

Appearances
Subs
Goals

FA CUP

| 3 | Jan 27 | H | Millwall | W | 1 0 | 3 0 | Godfrey, Anderson, Woodward | 34,703 |
| 4 | Feb 17 | H | Rotherham United | L | 0 0 | 0 1 | | 33,442 |

Appearances
Subs
Goals

FOOTBALL LEAGUE CUP

| 2 | Sep 13 | A | Northampton Town | L | 0 1 | 1 3 | Scott | 11,832 |

Appearances
Subs
Goals

444

Withers CC	Wright JM	Aitken CA	Chatterley LC	Sleeuwenhoek JC	Tindall MC	MacLeod JM	Park RC	Stobart BH	Broadbent PF	Anderson WJ	Inglis JF	Rudge DH	Pountney DH	Mitchinson TW	Deakin AR	Roberts D	Scott AJE	Bradley K	Martin LJ	Turnbull F	Godfrey BC	Greenhalgh BA	Parker GS	Woodward J	Ansell B	Dunn JA	Edwards RT	MATCH
1	2	3	4	5	6	7	8	9	10	11																		1
1	2	3	4	5	6	7		9	10	11	8¹		12¹															2
1	2	3	4	5	6	7		9	10	11	8																	3
1	2	3	4	5	6	7		9	10¹	11	12¹	8																4
1	2	3	4	5		7		9		11		8	6	10														5
1	2	3	4	5		7				11				10	6	8												6
1	2	3	4	5										10¹	6			11	12¹									7
1	2	3	4	5			8	9	10	7					6				11		8							8
1	2	3	4	5		7	8	9		11				10	6			12¹		5	8	9						9
1	2¹	3	4					7		11				10	6			12¹		5	8	9						10
1		3	4	5	6		12¹		8	11		7¹					2				10	9						11
1		3	4	5			12¹			11		7			8		2				10	9	6¹					12
1		3	4	5		7	6			11					8		2				10	9						13
1		3	4			7	6			11					8		2	5			10	9						14
1		3	4¹			7	6			11	12¹				8		2	5			10	9						15
1		3	5			7	6			11					8		2				10	9	4					16
1		3	5		12¹		6		11¹						8	4	2				10	9						17
1		3	5			7	6			11					8	4	2				10	9						18
1	2	3	5						4	11					8	6					10	9	7					19
1	2	3	5						4	11					8	6					10	9	7					20
1	2		5				12¹		4	11					8	6					10	9	7¹	3				21
1	2	3	5			7	4			11					8	6					10	9						22
1	2	3	5			7	4			11					8¹	6					10	9	12¹					23
1	2	3	5			7	4			11					8	6					10¹	9	12¹		1			24
	2	3	5			7	4			11					8	6					10	9						25
1	2	3	5			7	4			11					8	6					10	9						26
1		3	5				6			11					8	4	7		2		10		9					27
	3		5				4			11					8	6	7		2		10		9	1				28
	3	12¹	5				4¹			11	7				8	6			2		10		9	1				29
	3¹	12¹	5				4			11	7				8	6			2		10		9	1				30
		3	5					12¹		11	7¹				8	6	2				10	9			1		4	31
		3	5							11	7				8	6	2				10	9			1		4	32
		3¹	5			7	4			12¹	11				8	6	2				10		9		1			33
1	3		4							11			7		8	6		5			10						2	34
1	3		4							11			7¹		8	6		5	12¹		10						2	35
1	3		4							11			7		8	6		5	10		9						2	36
1	3		4							11			7		8	6¹		5	12¹		10	9					2	37
1	3		4				6			11			7		8			5	10		9						2	38
1	3		4							11			7		8			5	12¹		10	9¹					2	39
1	3¹		4			7	6		12¹	11					8	6		5	10		9						2	40
1		3	4							11			7		8	6		5	10		9						2	41
		3		5			6			11			7		8				2		10	9				1	4	42
34	29	30	42	12	5	20	25	10	8	42	1	15	1	36	28	3	2	16	1	11	33	28	2	8	1	8	11	
		2				1	1	4			1	1	1		5								2					
			2		1	2	1	3		5		4		9				12	12				2					

FINAL LEAGUE TABLE

	P	W	D	L	F	A	P	
Ipswich Town	42	22	15	5	79	44	59	
Queens Park Rangers	42	25	8	9	67	36	58	
Blackpool	42	24	10	8	71	43	58	
Birmingham City	42	19	14	9	83	51	52	
Portsmouth	42	18	13	11	68	55	49	
Middlesbrough	42	17	12	13	60	54	46	2
Millwall	42	14	17	11	62	50	45	
Blackburn Rovers	42	16	11	15	56	49	43	
Norwich City	42	16	11	15	60	65	43	
Carlisle United	42	14	13	15	58	52	41	
Crystal Palace	42	14	11	17	56	56	39	
Bolton Wanderers	42	13	13	16	60	63	39	
Cardiff City	42	13	12	17	60	66	38	
Huddersfield Town	42	13	12	17	46	61	38	
Charlton Athletic	42	12	13	17	63	68	37	
Aston Villa	**42**	**15**	**7**	**20**	**54**	**64**	**37**	
Hull City	42	12	13	17	58	73	37	
Derby County	42	13	10	19	71	78	36	
Bristol City	42	13	10	19	48	62	36	
Preston North End	42	12	11	19	43	65	35	
Rotherham United	42	10	11	21	42	76	31	
Plymouth Argyle	42	9	9	24	38	72	27	

1968/69

SEASON SNIPPETS

Arthur Cox, who would later manage Newcastle United and Derby County, was appointed trainer in succession to Bill Baxter, who returned to his native Scotland.

Oscar Arce became the first South American to sign for Villa, although he never played a first-team competitive match.

Welsh international Barrie Hole joined Villa from Blackburn Rovers in September for a club record fee of £65,000.

Goalkeeper Colin Withers played his last game, a 4-0 defeat by his old club, Birmingham City, on 21 September.

With the club rooted to the bottom of the table, manager Tommy Cummings and his assistant Malcolm Musgrove were sacked on 11 November 1968. Tommy Docherty was appointed manager on 18 December.

Before Doug Ellis was appointed Chairman in December, the Football League strongly opposed a proposed takeover of Villa by American soccer club Atlanta Chiefs.

Docherty's first signing was defender Brian Tiler from Rotherham United for £35,000. Tiler scored on his Boxing Day debut against Cardiff City.

Also in December, Brian Greenhalgh, John Chambers, John Woodward and Tommy Mitchinson all played their last Villa games.

Bobby Park's last Villa game came on 1 February.

Dave Simmons arrived from Arsenal and made his debut against Bury on 15 February.

Peter Broadbent's last game was at Hull City on 19 April.

DIVISION TWO

MANAGER: Tommy Cummings (to 11 November) Tommy Docherty (from 18 December)

MATCH	DATE	VENUE	OPPONENTS	RESULT	HT SCORE	SCORE	SCORERS	ATT
1	Aug 10	A	Sheffield United	L	0 3	1 3	Anderson (pen)	17,708
2	17	H	Fulham	D	0 1	1 1	Woodward	21,450
3	19	H	Millwall	D	1 0	1 1	Anderson (pen)	19,069
4	24	A	Blackburn Rovers	L	0 1	0 2		12,666
5	26	A	Bristol City	W	0 0	1 0	Woodward	17,685
6	31	H	Blackpool	L	0 1	0 1		18,938
7	Sep 7	A	Derby County	L	0 2	1 3	Ferguson	23,723
8	14	H	Hull City	D	0 0	1 1	Anderson	17,688
9	18	A	Bolton Wanderers	L	0 2	1 4	Godfrey	14,513
10	21	A	Birmingham City	L	0 0	0 4		40,527
11	28	H	Oxford United	W	1 0	2 0	Hole, Godfrey	17,101
12	Oct 5	A	Cardiff City	D	0 1	1 1	Godfrey	17,113
13	8	A	Bristol City	L	0 0	0 1		15,199
14	12	H	Crystal Palace	D	0 1	1 1	Anderson (pen)	15,887
15	19	A	Norwich City	D	1 1	1 1	Chatterley	14,579
16	26	H	Carlisle United	D	0 0	0 0		15,000
17	Nov 2	A	Huddersfield Town	L	1 0	1 3	Ferguson	9,346
18	9	H	Preston North End	L	0 0	0 1		13,388
19	16	A	Portsmouth	L	0 1	0 2		18,154
20	23	H	Middlesbrough	W	0 0	1 0	Rooks (og)	15,281
21	30	A	Bury	L	0 2	2 3	Woodward, Anderson	5,609
22	Dec 7	H	Charlton Athletic	D	0 0	0 0		12,758
23	14	A	Crystal Palace	L	0 0	2 4	Martin, Edwards	11,071
24	21	H	Norwich City	W	1 0	2 1	Edwards, Hole	20,111
25	26	H	Cardiff City	W	1 0	2 0	Hole, Tiler	41,296
26	28	A	Carlisle United	W	0 0	1 0	Anderson	12,554
27	Jan 11	H	Huddersfield Town	W	1 0	1 0	Hole	29,056
28	18	A	Preston North End	L	0 0	0 1		15,252
29	Feb 1	H	Portsmouth	W	0 0	2 0	Rudge, Godfrey	31,611
30	15	H	Bury	W	0 0	1 0	Rudge	28,042
31	22	A	Charlton Athletic	D	1 1	1 1	Simmons	21,959
32	Mar 1	H	Sheffield United	W	1 0	3 1	Hole, Simmons 2	27,498
33	4	A	Middlesbrough	D	0 0	0 0		29,824
34	8	A	Fulham	D	1 0	1 1	Roberts (og)	15,509
35	15	H	Blackburn Rovers	D	1 0	1 1	Simmons	27,644
36	22	A	Blackpool	D	1 0	1 1	Godfrey	12,148
37	29	H	Derby County	L	0 1	0 1		49,188
38	Apr 4	A	Millwall	W	0 0	1 0	Martin	15,168
39	5	A	Oxford United	L	0 1	0 1		17,170
40	8	H	Bolton Wanderers	D	1 0	1 1	Hulme (og)	25,442
41	12	H	Birmingham City	W	0 0	1 0	Simmons	53,647
42	19	A	Hull City	L	0 1	0 1		10,537

Final League Position: 18th in Second Division

3 Own-goals

Appearances
Subs
Goals

FA CUP

3	Jan 4	H	Queen's Park Rangers	W	1 1	2 1	Godfrey, Martin	39,854
4	25	A	Southampton	D	2 0	2 2	Godfrey, Hole	27,581
R	29	H	Southampton	W	1 1	2 1	Broadbent, Martin	59,084
5	Feb 12	A	Tottenham Hotspur	L	0 0	2 3	Hole, Broadbent	49,986

Appearances
Subs
Goals

FOOTBALL LEAGUE CUP

2	Sep 4	H	Tottenham Hotspur	L	0 1	1 4	Martin	24,775

Appearances
Subs
Goals

446

Withers CC	Edwards RT	Aitken CA	Park RC	Chatterley LC	Deakin AR	Ferguson MK	Mitchinson TW	Greenhalgh BA	Godfrey BC	Anderson WJ	Wright JM	Turnbull F	Woodward J	Chambers JF	Dunn JA	Rudge DH	Bradley K	Martin LJ	Hole BG	Broadbent PF	Tiler B	Simmons DJ	Lynch BJ	Griffiths J	MATCH
1	2	3	4	5	6¹	7	8	9	10	11	12¹														1
1	4	3	12¹			7	10	9	6¹	11	2	5	8												2
1	4	3	12¹			7	10	9	6¹	11	2	5	8												3
1	4	3				7	10	9	6	11	2	5	8¹	12¹											4
	4	3	6			7	8	12¹	10		2	5	9		1	11¹									5
	4	3	6			7	8	12¹	10	11¹		5	9		1		2								6
	4	3			6	7	8	9		11¹	2	5	12¹		1			10							7
1	4	3				7	8¹	9	10	11	2	5							6	12¹					8
1	4	3¹	12¹	9		7	8		10	11	2	5							6						9
1	4	3				7		8	10	11	2	5	9						6						10
	9	3			4	7	8		10	11	2	5			1				6						11
	4	3						9	8	7	2	5			1	11¹		12¹	6	10					12
	4	3				7¹		9	8	11	2	5			1			12¹	6	10					13
	4	3	12¹					8	7	2	5	9¹			1	11			6	10					14
	4	3		9					10	7	2	5			1			11	6	8					15
	4	3		9		7			10	11	2¹	5			1			12¹	6	8					16
	3	4				7	8			11		2	5		1			9	6	10					17
	4	3		12¹		7	8		11		2	5	9		1				6¹	10					18
	4	3			6	7			10	11	2	5	9		1					8					19
	4	3			6	7			10	11	2	5	9		1					8					20
	4	3			6	7			10	11	2	5	9		1					8					21
	4	3		6¹		7		12¹	9	11	2	5			1			10		8					22
	4	3				7			9	11	2	5		6	1			10		8					23
	4	3				7			9¹	11	2	5	12¹		1			10	6	8					24
	5	3				7			9	11	2				1			10	4	8	6				25
	5	3				7	8		9	11	2				1	10			4	8	6				26
	5	3				7¹			9	11	2				1	12¹		10	4	8	6				27
	5	3				7			9	11	2				1			10	4	8	6				28
	5	3	12¹						9	11¹	2				1	7		10	4	8	6				29
	5	3							9	11	2				1	7		10	4	8¹	6	12¹			30
	5	3								11¹	2	12¹			1	7		4	8	6	10				31
	5	3							9	11	2				1	7		4	8	6	10				32
	5¹	3					9			11	2	10			1	7	12¹	8	4	6					33
		3					10			11	2	5			1	7	8	9	4	6					34
	5	3				7				11	2	10			1	8			4¹	12¹	6	9			35
	5	3							8	11	2	10			1	7		4		6	9				36
	5	3							8¹	11	2	10			1	7		12¹	4	6	9				37
	5	3								8	11	2			1	7		12¹	4¹	10	6	9			38
	5	3								8	11	2			1	7		4		10	6	9			39
	5	3						10		8	11				1	7	2	12¹	4		6	9¹			40
	5	3			6			7		8	11				1		2		4		10	9			41
	5	3			6				9			2			1	7				8	10		4	11	42

7	40	42	4	6	7	30	13	9	37	38	38	28	11	1	35	17	4	15	28	23	18	9	1	1	
			5	1				3				1	2	1		1	1	6		2		1			
	2			1		2			5	6			3			2		2	5		1	5			

	5	3				7			9	11	2	6			1	10		8	4						3
	5	3							9	11	2¹	6			1	7	12¹	10	4	8					4
	5	3							9	11		6			1	7	2	10	4	8					R
	5	3¹							9	11	2	6			1	7	12¹	10	4	8					5

	4	4					1		4	4	3	4			4	4	1	4	4	3					
																	2								
								2											2	2	2				

| | 4 | 3¹ | 12¹ | | 6 | 7 | 8 | | | 11 | 2 | 5 | 9 | | 1 | | | 10 | | | | | | | 2 |

	1	1			1	1	1		1	1	1	1		1		1									
			1																						
																				1					

FINAL LEAGUE TABLE

	P	W	D	L	F	A	P
Derby County	42	26	11	5	65	32	63
Crystal Palace	42	22	12	8	70	47	56
Charlton Athletic	42	18	14	10	61	52	50
Middlesbrough	42	19	11	12	58	49	49
Cardiff City	42	20	7	15	67	54	47
Huddersfield Town	42	17	12	13	53	46	46
Birmingham City	42	18	8	16	73	59	44
Blackpool	42	14	15	13	51	41	43
Sheffield United	42	16	11	15	61	50	43
Millwall	42	17	9	16	57	49	43
Hull City	42	13	16	13	59	52	42
Carlisle United	42	16	10	16	46	49	42
Norwich City	42	15	10	17	53	56	40
Preston North End	42	12	15	15	38	44	39
Portsmouth	42	12	14	16	58	58	38
Bristol City	42	11	16	15	46	53	38
Bolton Wanderers	42	12	14	16	55	67	38
Aston Villa	**42**	**12**	**14**	**16**	**37**	**48**	**38**
Blackburn Rovers	42	13	11	18	52	63	37
Oxford United	42	12	9	21	34	55	33
Bury	42	11	8	23	51	80	30
Fulham	42	7	11	24	40	81	25

1969/70

SEASON SNIPPETS

Villa started the season with the most expensive side in the Second Division after spending more than £200,000 on new players, including £110,000 for brothers Bruce and Neil Rioch from Luton Town and 'Chico' Hamilton for £40,000 from Southend United.

The Second City derby attracted 54,470 to Villa Park - the country's biggest crowd of the day.

Tommy Docherty was sacked as manager on 19 January 1970, with his assistant and former Villa player Vic Crowe taking over in a caretaker capacity.

Wales international Barrie Hole staged a month-long strike after being fined by Docherty, but returned to the side after the manager's departure.

Andy Lochhead was signed in February, the striker costing £35,000 from Leicester City.

The club staged a testimonial match at the end of the season to mark Charlie Aitken's ten years' service but, with Villa relegated, only 9,512 turned up. The campaign finally closed with a 1-1 friendly draw against Italian club Napoli.

John Griffiths, Alan Deakin, Evan Williams, Mike Ferguson, Dick Edwards, Barry Lynch, Dave Rudge, John Phillips, Emment Kapengweand Barrie Hole all played their last Villa games during the season while Brian Rowan and Freddie Mwila made their only Villa appearances.

DIVISION TWO

MANAGER: Tommy Docherty (to 19 January)   Vic Crowe (from 19 January)

MATCH	DATE	VENUE	OPPONENTS	RESULT	HT SCORE	SCORE	SCORERS	ATT
1	Aug 9	H	Norwich City	L	0 0	0 1		32,601
2	16	A	Huddersfield Town	L	0 2	0 2		13,364
3	19	A	Carlisle United	D	0 0	1 1	Hamilton	12,504
4	23	H	Swindon Town	L	0 2	0 2		29,833
5	27	H	Leicester City	L	0 0	0 1		34,816
6	30	A	Middlesbrough	L	0 1	0 1		19,438
7	Sep 6	H	Millwall	D	0 0	2 2	Rudge 2	23,800
8	13	A	Watford	L	0 0	0 3		19,351
9	17	A	Bolton Wanderers	L	0 2	1 2	B Rioch	11,700
10	20	H	Hull City	W	1 2	3 2	Godfrey, Chatterley, Rudge	23,666
11	27	A	Portsmouth	D	0 0	0 0		17,884
12	Oct 4	H	Preston North End	D	0 0	0 0		25,445
13	8	H	Huddersfield Town	W	2 1	4 1	Godfrey, Tiler, Hole, Martin	23,215
14	11	A	Cardiff City	L	0 1	0 4		25,871
15	18	A	Birmingham City	D	0 0	0 0		54,405
16	25	A	Oxford United	D	2 1	2 2	McMahon 2	14,474
17	Nov 1	H	Queen's Park Rangers	D	0 1	1 1	Simmons	31,525
18	8	A	Bristol City	L	0 1	0 1		16,165
19	12	H	Carlisle United	W	0 0	1 0	Rudge	24,469
20	15	H	Blackpool	D	0 0	0 0		24,993
21	19	H	Bolton Wanderers	W	1 0	3 0	Martin, B Rioch, Anderson	22,951
22	22	A	Sheffield United	L	0 1	0 5		17,266
23	Dec 6	A	Blackburn Rovers	L	0 0	0 2		12,008
24	13	H	Watford	L	0 1	0 2		20,152
25	26	A	Swindon Town	D	0 1	1 1	Curtis	23,220
26	Jan 17	H	Portsmouth	L	2 2	3 5	B Rioch 2, Anderson	21,170
27	31	H	Preston North End	D	1 1	1 1	Chatterley	14,182
28	Feb 7	H	Cardiff City	D	0 0	1 1	B Rioch	27,024
29	14	A	Norwich City	L	1 1	1 3	Anderson	10,080
30	21	H	Bristol City	L	0 0	0 2		26,870
31	25	A	Charlton Athletic	W	1 0	1 0	Went (og)	23,992
32	28	A	Queen's Park Rangers	L	1 2	2 4	Anderson (pen), Chatterley	17,057
33	Mar 10	A	Hull City	L	0 2	1 3	Curtis	9,688
34	14	H	Charlton Athletic	L	0 1	0 1		9,979
35	16	A	Millwall	L	0 1	0 2		13,553
36	21	H	Blackburn Rovers	D	1 0	1 1	Curtis	18,840
37	28	A	Blackpool	L	0 1	1 2	Hamilton	17,352
38	30	A	Birmingham City	W	1 0	2 0	B Rioch, McMahon	41,696
39	31	H	Oxford United	D	0 0	0 0		29,360
40	Apr 4	A	Leicester City	L	0 0	0 1		27,481
41	8	H	Middlesbrough	W	1 0	2 0	Anderson, Godfrey	22,805
42	13	H	Sheffield United	W	1 0	1 0	McMahon	32,316

Final League Position: 21st in Second Division

1 Own-goal

Appearances
Subs
Goals

FA CUP

3	Jan 3	H	Charlton Athletic	D	0 0	1 1	Martin	30,742
R	12	A	Charlton Athletic	L	0 1	0 1		23,798

Appearances
Subs
Goals

FOOTBALL LEAGUE CUP

1	Aug 13	A	Chester	W	1 1	2 1	McMahon, Hamilton	10,510
2	Sep 3	H	West Bromwich Albion	L	0 1	1 2	Hole	40,303

Appearances
Subs
Goals

FINAL LEAGUE TABLE

	P	W	D	L	F	A	P
Huddersfield Town	42	24	12	6	68	37	60
Blackpool	42	20	13	9	56	45	53
Leicester City	42	19	13	10	64	50	51
Middlesbrough	42	20	10	12	55	45	50
Swindon Town	42	17	16	9	57	47	50
Sheffield United	42	22	5	15	73	38	49
Cardiff City	42	18	13	11	61	41	49
Blackburn Rovers	42	20	7	15	54	50	47
Queens Park Rangers	42	17	11	14	66	57	45
Millwall	42	15	14	13	56	56	44
Norwich City	42	16	11	15	49	46	43
Carlisle United	42	14	13	15	58	56	41
Hull City	42	15	11	16	72	70	41
Bristol City	42	13	13	16	54	50	39
Oxford United	42	12	15	15	35	42	39
Bolton Wanderers	42	12	12	18	54	61	36
Portsmouth	42	13	9	20	66	80	35
Birmingham City	42	11	11	20	51	78	33
Watford	42	9	13	20	44	57	31
Charlton Athletic	42	7	17	18	35	76	31
Aston Villa	**42**	**8**	**13**	**21**	**36**	**62**	**29**
Preston North End	42	8	12	22	43	63	28

1970/71

SEASON SNIPPETS

The club's major signings were David Gibson from Leicester City and Geoff Vowden from Birmingham City.

Dave Simmons scored in his last game, a 1-1 draw at Barnsley on 12 September.

The FA Cup defeat at Torquay on 21 November was Lew Chatterley's last game.

The highest home attendance by far was 62,500 for the second leg of the League Cup semi-final on 23 December.

Goalkeeper John Dunn made his last appearance as Villa went down 4-3 at home to Wrexham on 1 May.

The victory over Reading in the final match condemned the Royals to relegation to Division 4 and preserved Walsall's place. It was Brian Godfrey's last game.

Villa were undefeated in games against the teams who were promoted, winning home and away against Fulham, with a victory against Preston North End at Villa Park and a draw at Deepdale.

The club were charged with misconduct by the FA for having two players sent off and 19 booked. They received a £3,000 fine, suspended for three years.

Other Third Division clubs were delighted when Villa missed out on promotion - for financial reasons. Wherever Villa played, their travelling army of fans usually doubled their opponents average home attendance.

DIVISION THREE

MANAGER: Vic Crowe

MATCH	DATE	VENUE	OPPONENTS	RESULT	HT SCORE	SCORE	SCORERS	ATT
1	Aug 15	A	Chesterfield	W	2 1	3 2	McMahon, B Rioch 2	16,689
2	22	H	Plymouth Argyle	D	1 1	1 1	McMahon	29,230
3	29	A	Swansea City	W	0 1	2 1	Hamilton, McMahon	13,535
4	31	H	Mansfield Town	L	0 0	0 1		30,862
5	Sep 5	H	Doncaster Rovers	W	1 1	3 2	Lochhead 2, McMahon	23,619
6	12	A	Barnsley	D	0 0	1 1	Simmons	13,644
7	19	H	Preston North End	W	2 0	2 0	Lochhead 2	26,896
8	23	H	Gillingham	W	2 0	2 1	Hamilton, McMahon	29,416
9	26	A	Wrexham	W	2 1	3 2	Lochhead, Gibson, Hamilton (pen)	18,536
10	30	H	Bristol Rovers	D	1 0	1 1	Lochhead	32,103
11	Oct 3	H	Brighton & Hove Albion	D	0 0	0 0		26,092
12	10	A	Rochdale	D	1 1	1 1	Lochhead	7,537
13	17	H	Chesterfield	D	0 0	0 0		27,042
14	19	A	Port Vale	L	0 1	0 2		11,224
15	24	H	Tranmere Rovers	W	0 0	1 0	Hamilton	20,569
16	31	A	Reading	W	3 0	5 3	Lochhead, Tiler, McMahon, Anderson (pen), Butler (og)	13,479
17	Nov 7	H	Torquay United	L	0 0	0 1		28,112
18	11	H	Bury	W	1 0	1 0	Hamilton	17,029
19	14	A	Halifax Town	L	0 2	1 2	Turnbull	5,845
20	28	A	Fulham	W	0 0	2 0	Hamilton, McMahon	16,021
21	Dec 5	H	Bradford City	W	1 0	1 0	Hamilton	23,589
22	19	A	Plymouth Argyle	D	1 1	1 1	Lochhead	12,996
23	26	H	Shrewsbury Town	W	0 0	2 0	McMahon, B Rioch	31,177
24	Jan 2	A	Walsall	L	0 2	0 3		19,203
25	9	A	Bristol Rovers	W	1 0	2 1	B Rioch, Parsons (og)	25,486
26	16	H	Port Vale	W	1 0	1 0	B Rioch	28,933
27	23	A	Rotherham United	D	0 1	1 1	Hamilton	12,817
28	30	H	Fulham	W	0 0	1 0	Anderson (pen)	33,344
29	Feb 6	A	Bradford City	L	0 0	0 1		10,029
30	13	H	Rotherham United	W	0 0	1 0	Anderson	27,211
31	20	A	Bury	L	0 1	1 3	Allen (og)	7,516
32	Mar 5	A	Tranmere Rovers	D	0 1	1 1	Hamilton	6,579
33	10	A	Gillingham	D	0 0	0 0		10,812
34	13	H	Halifax Town	D	1 0	1 1	Turnbull	33,533
35	17	H	Walsall	D	0 0	0 0		37,640
36	20	A	Torquay United	D	1 1	1 1	Vowden	6,963
37	26	A	Doncaster Rovers	L	1 2	1 2	Gregory	7,879
38	Apr 3	H	Swansea City	W	2 0	3 0	Vowden 2, Gregory	23,510
39	9	A	Brighton & Hove Albion	L	0 0	0 1		22,613
40	10	A	Shrewsbury Town	L	0 1	1 2	Turnbull	13,636
41	12	H	Barnsley	D	0 0	0 0		20,718
42	17	H	Rochdale	W	1 0	1 0	Vowden	18,406
43	24	A	Preston North End	D	0 0	0 0		22,616
44	26	A	Mansfield Town	L	0 1	0 2		9,655
45	May 1	H	Wrexham	L	2 2	3 4	Vowden, Godfrey 2	17,302
46	4	H	Reading	W	1 0	2 1	Anderson, Bell (og)	16,694

Final League Position: 4th in Division Three

4 Own-goals

Appearances
Subs
Goals

FA CUP

| 1 | Nov 21 | A | Torquay United | L | 1 3 | 1 3 | Aitken | 9,227 |

Appearances
Subs
Goals

FOOTBALL LEAGUE CUP

1	Aug 19	H	Notts County	W	3 0	4 0	Anderson, McMahon, B Rioch, Hamilton	17,843
2	Sep 9	H	Burnley	W	0 0	2 0	Hamilton, Martin	28,341
3	Oct 6	A	Northampton Town	D	1 1	1 1	Hamilton	15,072
R	13	H	Northampton Town	W	1 0	3 0	Lochhead 2, Anderson	25,822
4	28	H	Carlisle United	W	0 0	1 0	Tiler	26,779
5	Nov 17	A	Bristol Rovers	D	1 1	1 1	McMahon	28,780
R	25	H	Bristol Rovers	W	0 0	1 0	McMahon	37,525
SF1	Dec 16	H	Manchester United	D	1 1	1 1	Lochhead	49,000
SF2	23	H	Manchester United	W	1 1	2 1	Lochhead, McMahon	62,500
F	27	N	Tottenham Hotspur *	L	0 0	0 2		97,024

* Played at Wembley Stadium, London

Appearances
Subs
Goals

450

		Dunn JA	Wright JM	Aitken CA	Godfrey BC	Curtis GW	Chatterley LC	McMahon P	Rioch BD	Lochhead AL	Hamilton IM	Anderson WJ	Tiler B	Brown JK	Turnbull F	Simmons DJ	Martin LJ	Gibson DW	Rioch N	Gregory GH	Bradley K	Crudgington G	Vowden GA	MATCH
		1	2	3	4	5	6	7	8	9	10	11												1
		1	2	3	4	5	6	7	8	9	10	11												2
		1	2	3	4	5	6	7	8	9	10	11												3
		1	2	3	4	5	6	7¹	8	9	10	11	12¹											4
		1	2	3	8	5¹	6	7		9	10	11	4	12¹										5
		1	2	3	8			7		9			4	6	5	10	11							6
		1	2	3	8			7		9	10	11	4	6	5									7
		1	2	3	8			7		9	10	11¹	4	6	5		12¹							8
		1	2	3	8			7		9	10		4	6	5		11							9
		1	2¹	3	8		12¹	7		9	10		4	6	5		11							10
		1	2	3			6	7		9	10	8	4		5		11							11
		1	2	3	7¹		6			9	10	8	4		5		11	12¹						12
		1	2	3	4					9	10	11	6	7¹	5		12¹	8						13
		1	2¹	3	4					9	10	11	6	8	5		12¹	7						14
		1		3	4	5		7		9	10	11			6			8	2					15
	1			3	4	5		7		9¹	10	11	8		6			12¹	2					16
		1		3	4	5		7		9	10	11	8		6				2					17
		1	2	3	4	5		7		9¹	10	11	8		6			12¹						18
		1	2	3	4		5	7			10	11	8		6			9						19
		1		3	4			7		9	10	11	6	8	5				2					20
		1		3	4			7		9	10	11	6		5		8		2					21
		1		3	4			7		9	10	11	6		5				2					22
		1		3	4			7	12¹	9	10	11	6		5		8¹		2					23
		1		3	4			7	12¹	9	10	11	6		5		8¹		2					24
				3	4			7	8	9	10	11	6		5				2					25
				3	4			7	8	9	10	11	6		5				2	1				26
		1			3			7	8	9	10	11	6	4¹	5			12¹	2					27
		1		3	4			7	8	9	10	11	6		5				2					28
		1		3	4			7	8	9	10	11	6		5				2					29
		1		3	4			7	8	9	10¹	11	6		5			12¹	2					30
		1		3	4			7	8	9	10	11	6		5			12¹	2					31
		1		3	4			7	8	9	10¹	11	6		5				2					32
		1		3	4			7	8	9	10¹	11	6		5				2				12¹	33
		1		3	4¹			7	12¹	9	10	11	6		5				2				8	34
		1		3	4			7		9	10¹	11	6			7		12¹	2				8	35
		1		3	4			7			10	11	6					9	2				8	36
		1		3	4			7	12¹		10	11	6					9	2				8¹	37
		1		3	4					9	10		6		5		11		7				8	38
		1		3	4				12¹		11		6		5		10¹		7				8	39
		1		3	4				4	10	9	12¹	11		5				7¹				8	40
		1		3	4			12¹		9	10	11¹	6		5			7	2				8	41
		1		3	4					9	10	11	6		5			7	2				8	42
		1		3	4					9	10	11	6		5				7	2			8	43
	1		3				7		9	10	11	6		5¹			12¹	2					8	44
		1	2	3	4					9	10	11	6		5								8	45
			2	3	4				9	7		10	11	6	5						1		8	46
		43	19	44	44	9	8	36	17	41	43	42	41	9	41	1	1	13		10	28	3	13	
						1	1	5		1		1		1		3	1		1	6		1		
					2			8	5	9	9	4	1		3	1		1		2			5	

FINAL LEAGUE TABLE

	P	W	D	L	F	A	P
Preston North End	46	22	17	7	63	39	61
Fulham	46	24	12	10	68	41	60
Halifax Town	46	22	12	12	74	55	56
Aston Villa	**46**	**19**	**15**	**12**	**54**	**46**	**53**
Chesterfield	46	17	17	12	66	38	51
Bristol Rovers	46	19	13	14	69	50	51
Mansfield Town	46	18	15	13	64	62	51
Rotherham United	46	17	16	13	64	60	50
Wrexham	46	18	13	15	72	65	49
Torquay United	46	19	11	16	54	57	49
Swansea City	46	15	16	15	59	56	46
Barnsley	46	17	11	18	49	52	45
Shrewsbury Town	46	16	13	17	58	62	45
Brighton and HA	46	14	16	16	50	47	44
Plymouth Argyle	46	12	19	15	63	63	43
Rochdale	46	14	15	17	61	68	43
Port Vale	46	15	12	19	52	59	42
Tranmere Rovers	46	10	22	14	45	55	42
Bradford City	46	13	14	19	49	62	40
Walsall	46	14	11	21	51	57	39
Reading	46	14	11	21	48	85	39
Bury	46	12	13	21	52	60	37
Doncaster Rovers	46	13	9	24	45	66	35
Gillingham	46	10	13	23	42	67	33

1971/72

SEASON SNIPPETS

Pat McMahon suffered a stress fracture and dislocation to his right ankle after scoring in the opening-day victory over Plymouth Argyle, and didn't make the starting line-up again until February.

The 4-3 win against Wrexham at The Hawthorns on 31 August was Geoff Crudgington's last game.

The FA Cup defeat at Southend United on 20 November was the last game for Tommy Hughes, Keith Bradley and David Gibson.

The 6-0 victory over Oldham Athletic at Boundary Park, featuring an Andy Lochhead hat-trick, was Villa's biggest away win since the Second World War. Jim Cumbes made his debut.

Polish club Gornik Zabrze, who would meet Villa in the UEFA Cup six years later, drew 1-1 in a Villa Park friendly on 1 December. Chico Hamilton scored Villa's goal.

The 2-1 home win over fellow promotion contenders Bournemouth in February was watched by 48,110, a record for the Third Division.

There was an even bigger turn-out, 54,437, for the friendly against Brazilian club Santos, featuring the legendary Pele, on 21 February.

The substitute appearance by Lionel Martin on 19 January was his last game.

Harry Gregory made his last appearance against York City on 5 February.

George Curtis played his last game on 24 April.

On 25 April, Aston Villa won the FA Youth Cup for the first time, beating Liverpool 5 - 2 on aggregate after extra time.

DIVISION THREE

MANAGER: Vic Crowe

MATCH	DATE	VENUE	OPPONENTS	RESULT	HT SCORE	SCORE	SCORERS	ATT
1	Aug 14	H	Plymouth Argyle	W	2 1	3 1	Vowden, McMahon, Anderson (pen)	26,343
2	21	A	Walsall	D	1 1	1 1	Vowden	13,092
3	28	H	Rochdale	W	2 0	2 0	Lochhead, Graydon	24,280
4	Sep 4	A	Bolton Wanderers	L	0 1	0 2		11,782
5	11	H	Brighton & Hove Albion	W	0 0	2 0	Graydon, Hamilton	25,812
6	18	A	Halifax Town	W	0 0	1 0	Graydon	7,462
7	22	H	Mansfield Town	L	0 0	0 1		28,112
8	25	H	Wrexham	W	1 0	2 0	Anderson (pen), Graydon	23,004
9	28	A	Barnsley	W	1 0	4 0	Lochhead 2, Hamilton 2	8,632
10	Oct 2	A	Bristol Rovers	W	0 0	1 0	Anderson	20,442
11	9	H	Rotherham United	L	1 1	1 2	Lochhead	30,251
12	16	A	Plymouth Argyle	L	0 2	2 3	B Rioch, Vowden	18,570
13	20	H	Tranmere Rovers	W	1 0	2 0	B Rioch, Lochhead	24,231
14	23	A	Bournemouth	L	0 2	0 3		20,305
15	30	H	Blackburn Rovers	W	4 1	4 1	N Rioch 2, Hamilton, Anderson	25,558
16	Nov 6	A	Port Vale	D	3 2	4 4	Hamilton, Anderson (pen), Cross (og), Graydon	11,118
17	13	H	Notts County	W	1 0	1 0	Graydon	37,462
18	27	A	Oldham Athletic	W	3 0	6 0	Lochhead 3, Anderson, B Rioch 2,	12,175
19	Dec 4	H	Bradford City	W	2 0	3 0	Anderson (pen), B Rioch 2	27,847
20	18	H	Bolton Wanderers	W	2 2	3 2	Lochhead, Graydon, Aitken	27,767
21	27	A	Swansea City	W	0 1	2 1	Aitken, Graydon	24,404
22	Jan 1	H	Halifax Town	W	0 0	1 0	Graydon	32,749
23	8	A	Rochdale	L	0 0	0 1		5,874
24	19	H	Shrewsbury Town	W	2 0	3 0	Hamilton, Graydon, Lochhead	27,140
25	22	H	Barnsley	W	1 0	2 0	Lochhead, B Rioch	30,531
26	28	A	Tranmere Rovers	W	0 0	1 0	Aitken	12,054
27	Feb 5	A	York City	W	0 0	1 0	Anderson (pen)	26,905
28	12	H	Bournemouth	W	0 1	2 1	Vowden, Lochhead	48,110
29	19	A	Blackburn Rovers	D	1 0	1 1	Lochhead	15,562
30	26	H	Port Vale	W	0 0	2 0	Lochhead, McMahon	32,806
31	Mar 4	A	Notts County	W	0 0	3 0	McMahon 2, Graydon	34,208
32	11	A	Rotherham United	W	2 0	2 0	Lochhead, Graydon	15,743
33	15	A	Shrewsbury Town	D	0 1	1 1	Nicholl	16,336
34	18	H	Walsall	D	0 0	0 0		45,953
35	25	A	Brighton & Hove Albion	L	0 1	1 2	B Rioch	28,833
36	31	A	Wrexham	W	2 0	2 0	Anderson, Graydon	17,162
37	Apr 1	H	Swansea City	W	0 0	2 0	Anderson, McMahon	33,394
38	3	A	Bristol Rovers	W	1 0	2 1	Lochhead 2	41,518
39	8	A	York City	W	1 0	1 0	B Rioch	9,419
40	10	H	Oldham Athletic	W	0 0	1 0	Graydon	32,226
41	12	A	Torquay United	L	0 1	1 2	Vowden	9,928
42	19	A	Chesterfield	W	2 0	4 0	Lochhead, Vowden 2, Hamilton	12,510
43	22	A	Bradford City	W	1 0	1 0	Aitken	9,285
44	24	A	Mansfield Town	D	0 0	1 1	Vowden	12,476
45	29	H	Torquay United	W	4 1	5 1	Vowden 2, Lochhead, Jackson (og), Little	37,179
46	May 5	H	Chesterfield	W	0 0	1 0	Ross	45,714

Final League Position: 1st in Division Three

2 Own-goals

Appearances
Subs
Goals

FA CUP

1	Nov 20	A	Southend United	L	0 1	0 1		16,929

Appearances
Subs
Goals

FOOTBALL LEAGUE CUP

1	Aug 18	H	Wrexham	D	0 0	2 2	Lochhead, Anderson (pen)	24,552
R	23	A	Wrexham *	D	0 0	1 1	Anderson	12,113
2R	31	N	Wrexham **	W	1 1	4 3	Lochhead 2, Anderson (pen), Ingle (og)	20,697
2	Sep 8	A	Chesterfield	W	2 1	3 2	Lochhead, Vowden, Anderson (pen)	14,000
3	Oct 5	A	Crystal Palace	D	0 1	2 2	Hamilton, Lochhead	21,179
R	13	H	Crystal Palace	W	0 0	2 0	Lochhead, Graydon	24,978
4	26	A	Blackpool	L	0 1	1 4	Anderson	20,193

1 Own-goal

Appearances
Subs
Goals

* After extra-time
** played at The Hawthorns, West Bromwich

452

FINAL LEAGUE TABLE

	P	W	D	L	F	A	P
Aston Villa	46	32	6	8	85	32	70
Brighton and HA	46	27	11	8	82	47	65
AFC Bournemouth	46	23	16	7	73	37	62
Notts County	46	25	12	9	74	44	62
Rotherham United	46	20	15	11	69	52	55
Bristol Rovers	46	21	12	13	75	56	54
Bolton Wanderers	46	17	16	13	51	41	50
Plymouth Argyle	46	20	10	16	74	64	50
Walsall	46	15	18	13	62	57	48
Blackburn Rovers	46	19	9	18	54	57	47
Oldham Athletic	46	17	11	18	59	63	45
Shrewsbury Town	46	17	10	19	73	65	44
Chesterfield	46	18	8	20	57	57	44
Swansea City	46	17	10	19	46	59	44
Port Vale	46	13	15	18	43	59	41
Wrexham	46	16	8	22	59	63	40
Halifax Town	46	13	12	21	48	61	38
Rochdale	46	12	13	21	57	83	37
York City	46	12	12	22	57	66	36
Tranmere Rovers	46	10	16	20	50	71	36
Mansfield Town	46	8	20	18	41	63	36
Barnsley	46	9	18	19	32	64	36
Torquay United	46	10	12	24	41	69	32
Bradford City	46	11	10	25	45	77	32

1972/73

SEASON SNIPPETS

Kidderminster-born striker Alun Evans, who started his career with Wolverhampton Wanderers, was signed from Liverpool for £70,000 on 5 August.

Doug Ellis was deposed as chairman just before the start of the season and was replaced by vice-chairman Jim Hartley. But Ellis was subsequently re-elected as a director and was back in the chair by October.

Michael Wright played his last game on 19 August.

Brian Tiler's last game was on 26 August.

Former Liverpool apprentice John Gidman made his debut against Carlisle on 29 August.

On 7 October, Keith Leonard, a signing from Highgate United, made his debut at Fulham.

In December, manager Vic Crowe beat off competition from neighbours Birmingham City and Wolverhampton Wanderers to sign England under-23 international full-back John Robson from Derby County. Malcolm Beard played his last game against Orient on 16 December.

The FA Cup defeat by Everton on 13 January was Willie Anderson's last game.

Villa drew 1-1 with Bayern Munich in a Villa Park friendly on 23 January. Nine years and four months later the teams would meet again in Rotterdam in the European Cup Final.

Andy Lochhead netted at Carlisle on 28 April - his last game.

DIVISION TWO

MANAGER: Vic Crowe

MATCH	DATE	VENUE	OPPONENTS	RESULT	HT SCORE	SCORE	SCORERS	ATT
1	Aug 12	A	Preston North End	W	0 0	1 0	Anderson	17,371
2	19	H	Huddersfield Town	W	1 0	2 0	Vowden, Graydon	34,843
3	26	A	Burnley	L	1 3	1 4	Hamilton	14,941
4	29	H	Carlisle United	W	0 0	1 0	B Rioch	29,047
5	Sep 2	H	Brighton & Hove Albion	D	0 0	1 1	Lochhead	30,750
6	9	A	Cardiff City	W	2 0	2 0	B Rioch, Lochhead	16,707
7	16	H	Swindon Town	W	0 1	2 1	Evans, Lochhead	30,775
8	23	A	Nottingham Forest	D	0 0	1 1	Cottam (og)	18,082
9	27	H	Sunderland	W	1 0	2 0	Evans, B Rioch	29,918
10	30	H	Millwall	W	0 0	1 0	B Rioch (pen)	31,451
11	Oct 7	A	Fulham	L	0 2	0 2		17,576
12	14	H	Queen's Park Rangers	L	0 0	0 1		34,045
13	17	A	Blackpool	D	1 0	1 1	Evans	15,043
14	21	H	Portsmouth	W	1 0	1 0	Vowden	13,524
15	28	A	Middlesbrough	D	1 1	1 1	Vowden	30,345
16	Nov 4	A	Sunderland	D	1 1	2 2	B Rioch, Little	18,717
17	11	H	Blackpool	D	0 0	0 0		31,651
18	18	H	Luton Town	L	0 1	0 2		29,044
19	25	A	Oxford United	L	0 1	0 2		13,647
20	Dec 2	H	Hull City	W	1 0	2 0	Graydon (pen), Hamilton	21,213
21	16	H	Orient	W	1 0	1 0	Evans	20,572
22	23	A	Sheffield Wednesday	D	2 1	2 2	Graydon 2	20,561
23	26	H	Nottingham Forest	D	0 2	2 2	Lochhead, Evans	37,000
24	30	A	Huddersfield Town	D	0 1	1 1	Evans	9,719
25	Jan 6	H	Burnley	L	0 2	0 3		38,637
26	20	A	Brighton & Hove Albion	W	1 0	3 1	Evans, Graydon, Brown	12,212
27	27	H	Cardiff City	W	1 0	2 0	Graydon (pen), B Rioch	28,856
28	Feb 10	A	Swindon Town	W	1 0	3 1	Evans, Graydon 2	13,855
29	17	H	Preston North End	D	1 1	1 1	Aitken	27,717
30	24	A	Orient	L	0 1	0 4		9,085
31	Mar 3	H	Fulham	L	1 0	2 3	Little, B Rioch	24,007
32	10	A	Queen's Park Rangers	L	0 0	0 1		21,578
33	17	H	Portsmouth	W	2 0	2 0	Vowden, McMahon	18,432
34	24	H	Middlesbrough	D	0 0	1 1	McMahon	9,776
35	27	A	Bristol City	L	0 1	0 3		15,654
36	31	H	Oxford United	W	1 1	2 1	McMahon, Vowden	15,902
37	Apr 7	A	Hull City	W	1 0	2 1	Hamilton, Little	8,072
38	14	H	Bristol City	W	0 0	1 0	N Rioch	19,545
39	21	A	Luton Town	D	0 0	0 0		10,981
40	23	A	Millwall	D	1 1	1 1	Graydon	9,932
41	24	H	Sheffield Wednesday	W	0 1	2 1	Lochhead, Hamilton	20,710
42	28	A	Carlisle United	D	1 2	2 2	Lochhead, Hamilton	6,178

Final League Position: 3rd in Division Two

1 Own-goal

Appearances
Subs
Goals

FA CUP

| 3 | Jan 13 | A | Everton | L | 1 3 | 2 3 | Vowden, Evans | 42,222 |

Appearances
Subs
Goals

FOOTBALL LEAGUE CUP

1	Aug 16	H	Hereford United	W	1 0	4 1	B Rioch, Graydon, Vowden, Evans	32,113
2	Sep 5	A	Nottingham Forest	W	1 0	1 0	Evans	17,665
3	Oct 4	H	Leeds United	D	0 1	1 1	B Rioch	46,185
R	11	A	Leeds United	L	0 2	0 2		28,894

Appearances
Subs
Goals

FA CHARITY SHIELD

| | Aug 5 | H | Manchester City | L | 0 0 | 0 1 | | 34,890 |

Appearances
Subs
Goals

454

	Cumbes J	Wright JM	Aitken CA	Rioch BD	Nicholl CJ	Ross I	Graydon RJ	McMahon P	Lochhead AL	Vowden GA	Anderson WJ	Evans AW	Tiler B	Hamilton IM	Gidman J	Turnbull F	Leonard KA	Rioch N	Little B	Beard M	Robson JD	Brown JK	McDonald RW	MATCH
1	2	3	4	5	6	7	8	9	10	11														1
1	2	3	4¹	5	6	7	8	9	10	11	12¹													2
1		3		5	6	7	8	9	10	11		2	4											3
1		3	4	5	6	7	8¹	9	10	11	12¹	2												4
1		3	4	5	6	7	8	9	10	11¹	12¹	2												5
1		3	4	5	6	7	10	9¹	8	11	12¹	2												6
1		3	4	5	6	7	8	9	10	11¹	12¹	2												7
1		3	4	5	6	7	8	9	10	11		2												8
1		3	4	5	6	7¹	8	9	10	11		12¹	2											9
1			4	5	3		8	9	10	11		7	2	6										10
1		3	4	5	6		8	9¹	10	11		7	2	6	12¹									11
1		3	4	5	6	7		9¹	10	11	8		2	6	12¹									12
1		3	4	5¹	9	7			10	11	8	12¹	2	6										13
1		3	4		9	7¹			10	11	8		2	6		5	12¹							14
1		3	4	5	9				10	11	8	2		6			7							15
1		3	4	5	9				10	11	8	2		6			7							16
1		3	4	5	2	7		12¹	10	11¹	8			6			9¹							17
1		3	4	5	2	7	12¹	9	10	11	8			6										18
1		3	4	5	2	7	11	9	10		8			6										19
1		3	4	5	2	7	11	9	10¹		8	12¹		6										20
1		3	4	5	2	7	11	9			8			6				10						21
1		3	4	5	10	7	11	9			8			6					2					22
1		3	4	5	10	7	11¹	9			8			6			12¹		2					23
1		3	4	5	10	7	11				8			6					2					24
1		3¹	4	5	10	7	11	9			8	12¹		6					2					25
1		3	4	5	6	7		10			9						11		2	8				26
1		3	4	5	6	7		10			9	12¹					11¹		2	8				27
1		3	4	5	6	7		10			9						11		2	8				28
1		3	4	5	6	7		10			9						11		2	8				29
1		3	4	5	6¹	7	12¹	10¹			9						11		2	8				30
1		3	4	5		7	12¹	10¹			9			6			11		2	8				31
1		3				7	4	10			9			6			11		2	8				32
1				5		7	4	11	10		9			6					2	8	3			33
1			4	5			7	11	10		9			6					2	8	3			34
1			4	5			7	11	10		9			6					2	8	3			35
1		3		5			7	11	10		9			6					2	8	4			36
1				5	6		7	9	10						11				12¹	8	2	4		37
1		3¹		5			7	9	10						11				6	8	3	4		38
1				5	2		7	9	10						11				6	8	3	4		39
1				5	2	10	7	9							11				6	8	3	4		40
1				5	6	10	7¹	9							11				12¹	8	2	4	3	41
1				5	2	7¹		9	10			12¹			11		6			8	3	4		42
42	2	33	32	41	36	32	28	30	35	14	29	1	9	13	21		6	17	1	19	17	4		
			1	7				9	3	6	5		2		2	2		1	3		1			
								3	6	5	1	8	5					1	3		1			

FINAL LEAGUE TABLE

	P	W	D	L	F	A	P	
Burnley	42	24	14	4	72	35	62	
Queens Park Rangers	42	24	13	5	81	37	61	
Aston Villa	**42**	**18**	**14**	**10**	**51**	**47**	**50**	
Middlesbrough	42	17	13	12	46	43	47	
Bristol City	42	17	12	13	63	51	46	1
Sunderland	42	17	12	13	59	49	46	2
Blackpool	42	18	10	14	56	51	46	3
Oxford United	42	19	7	16	52	43	45	R
Fulham	42	16	12	14	58	49	44	
Sheffield Wednesday	42	17	10	15	59	55	44	
Millwall	42	16	10	16	55	47	42	
Luton Town	42	15	11	16	44	53	41	
Hull City	42	14	12	16	64	59	40	
Nottingham Forest	42	14	12	16	47	52	40	
Orient	42	12	12	18	49	53	36	
Swindon Town	42	10	16	16	46	60	36	
Portsmouth	42	12	11	19	42	59	35	
Carlisle United	42	11	12	19	50	52	34	
Preston North End	42	11	12	19	37	64	34	
Cardiff City	42	11	11	20	43	58	33	
Huddersfield Town	42	8	17	17	36	56	33	
Brighton and HA	42	8	13	21	46	83	29	

1973/74

SEASON SNIPPETS

Villa signed football nomad Trevor Hockey from Norwich City in June 1973, but he rejoined one of his former clubs, Bradford City, a year later.

Sammy Morgan, a £25,000 signing from Port Vale, made his debut against Oxford on 8 September.

A share issue in November, designed to increase the club's spending power on new players, raised £65,000.

With the nation in the grip of a power crisis, Villa hired two generators in order to play their fourth round FA Cup replay against Arsenal under floodlights. It was worth the effort, Villa winning 2-0 in front of nearly 48,000 spectators.

Leading scorer Bruce Rioch was sold to Derby County for £200,000 on 22 February.

Villa won 3-0 in a friendly against First Division Southampton on 9 March, but the game attracted only 3,881 to Villa Park. Another friendly against Feyenoord on 30 April also failed to pull in the crowd, just 7,596 watching a 7-1 romp against the Dutch club.

Trevor Hockey made his last appearance on 2 March against West Bromwich Albion.

Former FA Youth Cup-winning captain Roy Stark made his second and final appearance on 6 April against Swindon.

Fred Turnbull's last game was on 24 April against Nottingham Forest.

Geoff Vowden played his last game on 27 April.

Having failed to take Villa into the top flight for their centenary season, manager Vic Crowe and his assistant Ron Wylie were sacked on Monday 6 May 1974.

DIVISION TWO

MANAGER: Vic Crowe

MATCH	DATE	VENUE	OPPONENTS	RESULT	HT SCORE	SCORE	SCORERS	ATT
1	Aug 25	H	Preston North End	W	0 0	2 0	Aitken, Hockey	28,861
2	Sep 1	A	Millwall	D	1 0	1 1	Little	12,009
3	8	H	Oxford United	W	0 0	2 0	B Rioch (pen), Vowden	28,078
4	11	A	Crystal Palace	D	0 0	0 0		20,838
5	15	A	Middlesbrough	D	0 0	0 0		14,742
6	19	H	Fulham	D	0 0	1 1	B Rioch	30,162
7	22	H	Orient	D	2 2	2 2	B Rioch, Vowden	26,685
8	29	A	Notts County	L	0 1	0 2		15,872
9	Oct 2	A	Fulham	L	0 0	0 1		11,776
10	6	H	Cardiff City	W	2 0	5 0	Woodruff (og), Graydon, B Rioch 2, Morgan	24,483
11	13	A	Bolton Wanderers	W	1 0	2 1	Evans 2	19,496
12	20	H	Bristol City	D	1 2	2 2	Little, Graydon	26,918
13	23	H	Crystal Palace	W	1 1	2 1	Little, Graydon	26,670
14	27	A	Nottingham Forest	W	1 1	2 1	Graydon, Aitken	17,718
15	Nov 3	H	Sheffield Wednesday	W	1 0	1 0	Little	28,599
16	10	A	Portsmouth	L	0 1	0 2		12,678
17	17	H	Hull City	D	1 1	1 1	Little	23,773
18	24	A	Swindon Town	L	0 0	0 1		8,666
19	Dec 8	A	Sunderland	L	0 1	0 2		20,784
20	15	A	Luton Town	L	0 0	0 1		10,020
21	22	H	Notts County	D	0 0	1 1	B Rioch	20,825
22	26	A	West Bromwich Albion	L	0 1	0 2		43,029
23	29	A	Oxford United	L	1 1	1 2	Graydon	10,390
24	Jan 1	H	Millwall	D	0 0	0 0		20,905
25	12	A	Middlesbrough	D	0 0	1 1	B Rioch	26,906
26	19	A	Preston North End	D	0 0	0 0		10,766
27	Feb 2	H	Luton Town	L	0 0	0 1		26,180
28	23	A	Cardiff City	W	1 0	1 0	Graydon	12,184
29	27	H	Bolton Wanderers	D	1 0	1 1	McMahon	18,952
30	Mar 2	A	West Bromwich Albion	L	1 3	1 3	Morgan	37,323
31	13	A	Carlisle United	W	1 0	2 1	Evans, Hamilton (pen)	12,007
32	16	A	Bristol City	W	0 0	1 0	Morgan	12,759
33	23	H	Portsmouth	W	0 1	4 1	McMahon 2, Morgan 2	15,517
34	Apr 1	A	Sheffield Wednesday	W	2 1	4 2	Little 2, McMahon, Leonard	22,504
35	6	H	Swindon Town	D	0 0	1 1	Little	20,709
36	13	A	Hull City	D	0 1	1 1	Deere (og)	7,810
37	15	H	Blackpool	L	0 1	0 1		18,351
38	20	A	Blackpool	L	0 1	1 2	Hamilton	10,707
39	20	H	Sunderland	L	1 1	1 2	McMahon	17,321
40	24	H	Nottingham Forest	W	3 1	3 1	Hamilton, Campbell, Graydon	12,439
41	27	A	Carlisle United	L	0 1	0 2		12,494
42	May 3	A	Orient	D	0 0	1 1	Graydon (pen)	29,766

Final League Position: 14th in Division Two

Appearances
Subs
2 Own-goals Goals

FA CUP

3	Jan 5	H	Chester	W	1 1	3 1	Nicholl, Morgan 2	16,545
4	26	A	Arsenal	D	1 0	1 1	Morgan	41,682
R	30	H	Arsenal	W	1 0	2 0	Morgan, Evans	47,821
5	Feb 16	A	Burnley	L	0 1	0 1		29,301

Appearances
Subs
Goals

FOOTBALL LEAGUE CUP

2	Oct 9	A	York City	A	0 0	0 1		7,981

Appearances
Subs
Goals

	Cumbes J	Robson JD	Aitken CA	Rioch BD	Nicholl CJ	Ross I	Brown JK	Hockey T	Evans AW	Vowden GA	Little B	Hamilton IM	Morgan SJ	Graydon RJ	Gidman J	McMahon P	Rioch N	McDonald RW	Turnbull F	Leonard KA	Stark RH	Findlay JW	Campbell RM		MATCH
	1	2	3	4	5	6	7	8	9	10¹	11	12¹													1
	1	2	3	4	5	6	8	7	9	10	11														2
	1	2	3	4	5	6	8	7¹	9	10	11	12¹													3
	1	2	3	4	5	6	8	7	9	10	11														4
	1	2	3	4	5	6	7	8	9	10	11														5
	1	2	3	4	5	6	7	8	9	10¹			11	12¹											6
	1	2	3	4	5	6	7	8	9¹	10			11	12¹											7
	1	2	3	4	5	6	7¹	8		10	11		9	12¹											8
	1	2	3	4	5	6	7	8		10	11		9												9
	1	2	3	4	5	6		8		10	11		9	7											10
	1		3	4	5	6	8	10	9		11			7	2										11
	1		3		5	6	8	4	9	10¹	11		12¹	7	2										12
	1		3		5	6	8		9		11	10		7	2	4									13
	1		3		5	6	8		9		11	10		7¹	2	4	12¹								14
	1		3		5	6	8	4	9		11	10	12¹	7¹	2										15
	1		3		5	6	8	4	9		11	10			2	7									16
	1		3		5	6	8¹	4	9		11	10	12¹		2	7									17
	1		3		5	6	8	4	12¹	7	11	10	9¹		2										18
	1		3		5	6	8	4	9	7¹	11	10			2		12¹								19
	1		3		5	6	8	4			11	10			2	7	9								20
	1		3	7	5	6	8¹	4			11	10	12¹	2		9									21
	1		3	8	5	6		4			11	10		2		9									22
	1		3		5	6		4	9		11¹	10		2		7	12¹								23
	1		3	4	5	6	8		9		11	10		2		7									24
	1		3	4	5	6			12¹	8¹	11	10	9	7	2										25
	1		3	4	5	6		11		8		10	9	7	2										26
	1		3	4	5	6	8		11		12¹	10	9	7¹	2										27
	1		3		5	6		4	11			10	9	7	2	8									28
	1		3		5	6		4	9		11	10		7	2	8									29
	1		3		5	6		4	11			10	9	7	2	8									30
	1				5	8			11			7	10	9	2	4		3	6						31
	1		3		5	4			11			8	10	9	2	7		6	8						32
	1		3		5	8						7	10	9	2	4		6	11						33
	1		3			8						7	10	9	2	4		6	11	5					34
	1		3			8						7	10	9	2	4		6	11	5					35
	1		3		5	8						7	10	9	2	4		6							36
	1		3		5	8		12¹				7	10	9¹	2	4		6	11						37
	1		3		5	8			9			7	10		2	4		6	11						38
					5	8			9¹				11	10	2	4					1	12¹			39
	1				5	8						11	10	9	7	2	4		3	6¹			12¹		40
	1	2			5	6				12¹	11	10	9	7		4	3						8¹		41
	1	2	3		5	6	8				11	10	9	7		4									42
	41	12	38	18	40	42	24	24	24	15	36	30	21	19	30	20	3	4	10	7	2	1	1		
										3	1	1	4			3						2			
		2	7				1	3	2	8	3	5	4	8		5					1				

	1		3	4	5	6	8		9¹		11	10	12¹	7	2									3
	1		3	4	5	6			11	8		10	9		2	7									4
	1		3	4	5	6			11	8¹	12¹	10	9		2	7									R
	1		3	4	5	6			11			10	9	7	2	8									5
	4		4	4	4	4	1		4	2	1	4	3	2	4	3									
											1			1											
						1			1				4												

	1	2	3	4	5	6	8				10	11	9	7											2
	1	1	1	1	1	1	1				1	1	1	1											

FINAL LEAGUE TABLE

	P	W	D	L	F	A	P
Middlesbrough	42	27	11	4	77	30	65
Luton Town	42	19	12	11	64	51	50
Carlisle United	42	20	9	13	61	48	49
Orient	42	15	18	9	55	42	48
Blackpool	42	17	13	12	57	40	47
Sunderland	42	19	9	14	58	44	47
Nottingham Forest	42	15	15	12	57	43	45
West Bromwich A	42	14	16	12	48	45	44
Hull City	42	13	17	12	46	47	43
Notts County	42	15	13	14	55	60	43
Bolton Wanderers	42	15	12	15	44	40	42
Millwall	42	14	14	14	51	51	42
Fulham	42	16	10	16	39	43	42
Aston Villa	**42**	**13**	**15**	**14**	**48**	**45**	**41**
Portsmouth	42	14	12	16	45	62	40
Bristol City	42	14	10	18	47	54	38
Cardiff City	42	10	16	16	49	62	36
Oxford United	42	10	16	16	35	46	36
Sheffield Wednesday	42	12	11	19	51	63	35
Crystal Palace	42	11	12	19	43	56	34
Preston North End	42	9	14	19	40	62	31
Swindon Town	42	7	11	24	36	72	25

1974/75

SEASON SNIPPETS

Ron Saunders was appointed manager on Tuesday 4 June 1974 in succession to Vic Crowe. The new manager's first signing was Frank Carrodus from Manchester City for £95,000 on 15 August.

The club celebrated their Centenary with a special pre-season friendly against Leeds United, losing 2-1 to the league champions in front of 29,481.

Midfielder Leighton Phillips was signed from Cardiff City for £100,000 on 18 September.

The 2-0 defeat at Bristol Rovers on 14 September was the last game for Pat McMahon and on-loan goalkeeper Graham Moseley.

Tony Betts made his last appearance on 16 November.

Alan Little's last game was on 7 December.

The Boxing Day win against Bristol Rovers was Bobby Campbell's last game and two days later, at Cardiff, Jimmy Brown played his last Villa game.

The FA Cup defeat at Ipswich Town was the last appearance for Alun Evans who signed off with a goal.

Neil Rioch's last game was at Portsmouth on 18 February.

Former boss Tommy Docherty brought his Manchester United side to Villa Park on 22 February, the first time he had managed a team at the ground since his departure. But Villa beat the league leaders 2-0 with goals from Ray Graydon and Charlie Aitken.

Villa won the League Cup for the second time in their history, and for the first time at Wembley, as Ray Graydon's goal clinched victory over Norwich City.

A helicopter was used to dry out the rain-sodden pitch before Villa's 3-0 home win over Southampton on 15 March.

Promotion was clinched by a 4-0 mid-week success against Sheffield Wednesday at Hillsborough on 23 April.

DIVISION TWO

MANAGER: Ron Saunders

MATCH	DATE	VENUE	OPPONENTS	RESULT	HT SCORE	SCORE	SCORERS	ATT
1	Aug 17	A	York City	D	1 1	1 1	Graydon	9,396
2	20	A	Hull City	D	0 0	1 1	Robson	8,712
3	24	H	Norwich City	D	0 0	1 1	Graydon	23,297
4	28	H	Hull City	W	1 0	6 0	Morgan 3, Graydon, B Little, Hamilton	18,973
5	31	A	Bolton Wanderers	L	0 0	0 1		13,265
6	Sep 7	H	Orient	W	2 0	3 1	Morgan, Graydon 2 (1 pen)	16,902
7	14	A	Bristol Rovers	L	0 0	0 2		14,045
8	21	H	Millwall	W	1 0	3 0	Graydon 3 (1 pen)	21,375
9	28	A	Southampton	D	0 0	0 0		18,599
10	Oct 2	H	Nottingham Forest	W	2 0	3 0	Graydon, Hamilton, Leonard	20,357
11	5	A	Oldham Athletic	W	0 0	2 1	Hicks (og), Graydon	15,574
12	12	H	Blackpool	W	0 0	1 0	Graydon	25,763
13	19	A	Sunderland	D	0 0	0 0		33,232
14	26	H	Sheffield Wednesday	W	3 1	3 1	Phillips, Nicholl, Graydon (pen)	23,977
15	Nov 2	A	Fulham	L	0 1	1 3	B Little	10,979
16	9	H	Notts County	L	0 1	0 1		22,182
17	16	A	Manchester United	L	0 1	1 2	Hamilton	55,615
18	23	H	Portsmouth	W	2 0	2 0	Hamilton, B Little	16,821
19	29	H	Oxford United	D	0 0	0 0		18,554
20	Dec 7	A	Bristol City	L	0 1	0 1		13,390
21	14	H	York City	W	2 0	4 0	Graydon, Nicholl, B Little, Hamilton	15,840
22	21	A	West Bromwich Albion	L	0 1	0 2		29,614
23	26	H	Bristol Rovers	W	0 0	1 0	Graydon	21,556
24	28	A	Cardiff City	L	0 3	1 3	Hamilton	11,060
25	Jan 11	H	Bristol City	W	1 0	2 0	B Little, Hamilton	22,422
26	18	A	Oxford United	W	0 0	2 1	B Little, Nicholl	10,064
27	Feb 1	H	Notts County	W	1 1	3 1	B Little 2, Carrodus	16,651
28	8	H	Fulham	D	0 1	1 1	Nicholl	28,551
29	18	A	Portsmouth	W	3 2	3 2	Carrodus, Graydon, B Little	13,355
30	22	H	Manchester United	W	2 0	2 0	Graydon, Aitken	39,156
31	Mar 5	H	Bolton Wanderers	D	0 0	0 0		39,322
32	8	A	Nottingham Forest	W	2 2	3 2	Graydon 2, B Little	20,205
33	15	H	Southampton	W	0 0	3 0	Leonard, Graydon, Holmes (og)	31,859
34	22	A	Orient	L	0 0	0 1		9,719
35	29	H	West Bromwich Albion	W	0 1	3 1	Leonard 2, Hamilton	47,574
36	Apr 1	A	Millwall	W	1 1	3 1	Hamilton (pen), Leonard, B Little	13,115
37	9	H	Cardiff City	W	0 0	2 0	B Little 2	32,748
38	12	H	Oldham Athletic	W	2 0	5 0	B Little 3, Hicks (og), Hamilton	36,244
39	19	A	Blackpool	W	2 0	3 0	Phillips, Hatton (og), B Little	20,762
40	23	A	Sheffield Wednesday	W	2 0	4 0	Leonard, B Little 2, Ross (pen)	23,770
41	26	H	Sunderland	W	0 0	2 0	Ross (pen), B Little	57,266
42	30	A	Norwich City	W	2 0	4 1	Leonard, Gidman, McDonald, Carrodus	35,943

Final League Position: 2nd in Division Two

4 Own-goals

Appearances
Subs
Goals

FA CUP

3	Jan 4	A	Oldham Athletic	W	1 0	3 0	B Little, Nicholl, Graydon	14,510
4	25	H	Sheffield United	W	1 0	4 1	Leonard 2, Nicholl, Graydon	35,881
5	Feb 15	A	Ipswich Town	L	1 0	2 3	McDonald, Evans	31,297

Appearances
Subs
Goals

FOOTBALL LEAGUE CUP

2	Sep 11	H	Everton	D	1 0	1 1	Nicholl	29,640
R	18	A	Everton	W	0 0	3 0	Morgan, Carrodus, Graydon	24,595
3	Oct 9	A	Crewe Alexandra	D	1 0	2 2	Morgan, Leonard	12,290
R	16	H	Crewe Alexandra	W	0 0	1 0	Hamilton	24,007
4	Nov 12	A	Hartlepool	D	1 0	1 1	Aitken	12,305
R	25	H	Hartlepool	W	2 0	6 1	Hamilton 2 (1 pen), B Little 2, Graydon 2 (1 pen)	17,686
5	Dec 3	A	Colchester United	W	2 0	2 1	A Little, Graydon	11,871
SF1	Jan 15	A	Chester	D	1 1	2 2	McDonald, Graydon	19,000
SF2	22	H	Chester	W	2 1	3 2	Leonard 2, B Little	47,632
F	Mar 1	N	Norwich City *	W	0 0	1 0	Graydon	100,000

Appearances
Subs
Goals

* Played at Wembley Stadium, London

458

FINAL LEAGUE TABLE

	P	W	D	L	F	A	P
Manchester United	42	26	9	7	66	30	61
Aston Villa	**42**	**25**	**8**	**9**	**79**	**32**	**58**
Norwich City	42	20	13	9	58	37	53
Sunderland	42	19	13	10	65	35	51
Bristol City	42	21	8	13	47	33	50
West Bromwich A	42	18	9	15	54	42	45
Blackpool	42	14	17	11	38	33	45
Hull City	42	15	14	13	40	53	44
Fulham	42	13	16	13	44	39	42
Bolton Wanderers	42	15	12	15	45	41	42
Oxford United	42	15	12	15	41	51	42
Orient	42	11	20	11	28	39	42
Southampton	42	15	11	16	53	54	41
Notts County	42	12	16	14	49	59	40
York City	42	14	10	18	51	55	38
Nottingham Forest	42	12	14	16	43	55	38
Portsmouth	42	12	13	17	44	54	37
Oldham Athletic	42	10	15	17	40	48	35
Bristol Rovers	42	12	11	19	42	64	35
Millwall	42	10	12	20	44	56	32
Cardiff City	42	9	14	19	36	62	32
Sheffield Wednesday	42	5	11	26	29	64	21

1975/76

SEASON SNIPPETS

On 1 September Doug Ellis resigned as Chairman of Aston Villa and was replaced by Sir William Dugdale.

Keith Leonard suffered an injury against Arsenal on 13 September that ended his career.

The club's first venture into European competition was a big disappointment, Villa losing 5-1 on aggregate to Belgian club Royal Antwerp. Jim Cumbes played his last game in the first leg while the second leg was Sammy Morgan's last match.

Villa spent more than £200,000 on two players in late September and early October. Manager Ron Saunders signed goalkeeper John Burridge from Blackpool for £100,000 and followed up with a £110,000 swoop for Dundee United's 19 year old striker Andy Gray.

Dennis Mortimer joined Villa from Coventry City for £175,000 just before Christmas, making his debut in a 4-1 Boxing Day victory over West Ham United.

Charlie Aitken made the last of his 660 appearances on 31 January.

Chris Nicholl scored all four goals in a 2-2 draw against Leicester City at Filbert Street in March. Nicholl twice put the Foxes ahead, but responded with equalisers on each occasion – the second just four minutes from time.

Chico Hamilton played his last game on 3 April and the 2-0 win against Middlesbrough on 24 April was the last game for both Bobby McDonald and Ian Ross.

Frank Pimblett and John Overton also made their last appearances during the season.

DIVISION ONE

MANAGER: Ron Saunders

MATCH	DATE	VENUE	OPPONENTS	RESULT	HT SCORE	SCORE	SCORERS	ATT
1	Aug 16	H	Leeds United	L	1 1	1 2	Phillips	46,026
2	19	A	Queen's Park Rangers	D	0 0	1 1	Leonard	21,986
3	23	A	Norwich City	L	1 4	3 5	Graydon 2 (1 pen), Aitken	21,195
4	27	H	Manchester City	W	0 0	1 0	Leonard	35,712
5	30	H	Coventry City	W	0 0	1 0	Graydon	41,026
6	Sep 6	A	Newcastle United	L	0 2	0 3		35,604
7	13	H	Arsenal	W	0 0	2 0	Phillips, Leonard	34,474
8	20	A	Liverpool	L	0 0	0 3		42,779
9	23	A	Wolverhampton Wanderers	D	0 0	0 0		33,344
10	27	H	Birmingham City	W	0 1	2 1	Hamilton, Little	53,782
11	Oct 4	A	Middlesbrough	D	0 0	0 0		24,102
12	11	H	Tottenham Hotspur	D	0 0	1 1	Gray	40,048
13	18	A	Everton	L	0 2	1 2	Nicholl	30,376
14	25	H	Burnley	D	0 0	1 1	Noble (og)	35,204
15	Nov 1	A	Ipswich Town	L	0 1	0 3		24,687
16	8	H	Sheffield United	W	1 0	5 1	Gray, Hamilton 2, Deehan, Graydon (pen)	30,053
17	15	A	Manchester United	L	0 1	0 2		51,682
18	22	H	Everton	W	1 0	3 1	Gray 2, McNaught (og)	33,949
19	29	H	Leicester City	D	0 1	1 1	Graydon	36,388
20	Dec 6	A	Stoke City	D	1 1	1 1	Graydon	28,515
21	13	H	Norwich City	W	2 1	3 2	Graydon, Deehan 2	30,478
22	20	A	Leeds United	L	0 1	0 1		29,118
23	26	H	West Ham United	W	2 1	4 1	Deehan 2, Gray, Hamilton	51,250
24	27	A	Derby County	L	0 0	0 2		36,230
25	Jan 10	A	Arsenal	D	0 0	0 0		24,539
26	17	H	Newcastle United	D	1 1	1 1	Mahoney (og)	36,387
27	31	H	Queen's Park Rangers	L	0 0	0 2		32,223
28	Feb 7	A	Manchester City	L	1 0	1 2	Gray	32,331
29	14	A	Sheffield United	L	1 1	1 2	Graydon	21,152
30	21	H	Manchester United	W	1 1	2 1	McDonald, Gray	50,094
31	24	H	Wolverhampton Wanderers	D	0 0	1 1	Graydon (pen)	47,693
32	28	A	Burnley	D	2 1	2 2	Graydon, Gray	17,174
33	Mar 6	H	Ipswich Town	D	0 0	0 0		32,477
34	13	A	Tottenham Hotspur	L	1 3	2 5	Graydon, Gray	24,169
35	20	A	Leicester City	D	1 1	2 2	Nicholl 2	24,663
36	27	H	Stoke City	D	0 0	0 0		32,359
37	Apr 3	A	Birmingham City	L	1 1	2 3	Gray, Graydon (pen)	46,251
38	10	H	Liverpool	D	0 0	0 0		44,250
39	13	A	Coventry City	D	0 1	1 1	Nicholl	27,569
40	17	A	West Ham United	D	2 1	2 2	Deehan, Hunt	21,642
41	19	H	Derby County	W	0 0	1 0	McDonald	39,241
42	24	H	Middlesbrough	W	1 1	2 1	Deehan, Carrodus	33,241

Final League Position: 16th in Division One

3 Own-goals

Appearances
Subs
Goals

FA CUP

3	Jan 3	A	Southampton	D	0 0	1 1	Gray	24,138
4	7	H	Southampton *	L	1 1	1 2	Graydon	44,623

Appearances
Subs
Goals

* After extra-time

FOOTBALL LEAGUE CUP

2	Sep 10	H	Oldham Athletic	W	0 0	2 0	Leonard, Nicholl	23,041
3	Oct 8	H	Manchester United	L	0 0	1 2	Gray	41,447

Appearances
Subs
Goals

UEFA CUP

1F	Sep 17	A	Royal Antwerp	L	0 4	1 4	Graydon	21,000
1S	Oct 1	H	Royal Antwerp	L	0 1	0 1		31,513

Appearances
Subs
Goals

FINAL LEAGUE TABLE

	P	W	D	L	F	A	P
Liverpool	42	23	14	5	66	31	60
Queens Park Rangers	42	24	11	7	67	33	59
Manchester United	42	23	10	9	68	42	56
Derby County	42	21	11	10	75	58	53
Leeds United	42	21	9	12	65	46	51
Ipswich Town	42	16	14	12	54	48	46
Leicester City	42	13	19	10	48	51	45
Manchester City	42	16	11	15	64	46	43
Tottenham Hotspur	42	14	15	13	63	63	43
Norwich City	42	16	10	16	58	58	42
Everton	42	15	12	15	60	66	42
Stoke City	42	15	11	16	48	50	41
Middlesbrough	42	15	10	17	46	45	40
Coventry City	42	13	14	15	47	57	40
Newcastle United	42	15	9	18	71	62	39
Aston Villa	**42**	**11**	**17**	**14**	**51**	**59**	**39**
Arsenal	42	13	10	19	47	53	36
West Ham United	42	13	10	19	48	71	36
Birmingham City	42	13	7	22	57	75	33
Wolverhampton W	42	10	10	22	51	68	30
Burnley	42	9	10	23	43	66	28
Sheffield United	42	6	10	26	33	82	22

461

1976/77

SEASON SNIPPETS

Mr Pat Matthews, President of Aston Villa since the club was re-organised in December 1968 resigned his position due to business reasons and was replaced by Mr A Trevor Gill.

Gordon Smith, Villa's £80,000 signing from St Johnstone, made his first appearance as Villa beat Royal Antwerp 3-1 in a pre-season friendly at Villa Park.

Scottish midfielder Alex Cropley was signed from Arsenal in September for a fee of £125,000.

A friendly match against Glasgow Rangers on Saturday 9 October 1976 was abandoned after 53 minutes when Rangers supporters invaded the pitch after Frank Carrodus had put Villa two goals up. There were scenes of violence at and around Villa Park and in Birmingham City centre.

In November, Villa beat Eintracht Frankfurt 3-1 in another Villa Park friendly.

Striker Keith Leonard's 15-month battle to overcome a knee injury ended when he was forced to retire from football in December at the age of 26.

David T Hughes played his last game on 25 April at Arsenal. Ray Graydon and Keith Masefield both made their last appearance at Tottenham on 30 April.

Charles Young's last game was on 14 May at Newcastle.

The 4-0 win against WBA on 23 May was the last game for both John Burridge and Chris Nicholl.

DIVISION ONE

MANAGER: Ron Saunders

MATCH	DATE	VENUE	OPPONENTS	RESULT	HT SCORE	SCORE	SCORERS	ATT
1	Aug 21	H	West Ham United	W	0 0	4 0	Gray 2, Graydon 2 (1 pen)	39,012
2	25	A	Manchester City	L	0 2	0 2		41,007
3	28	A	Everton	W	2 0	2 0	Little, Lyons (og)	32,055
4	Sep 4	H	Ipswich Town	W	1 1	5 2	Little, Gray 3, Graydon	39,916
5	11	A	Queen's Park Rangers	L	1 1	1 2	Gray	23,602
6	18	H	Birmingham City	L	1 2	1 2	Gray	50,084
7	25	A	Leicester City	W	1 0	2 0	Graydon (pen), Gray	36,652
8	Oct 2	H	Stoke City	L	0 1	0 1		29,602
9	16	A	Sunderland	W	0 0	1 0	Cropley	31,578
10	20	H	Arsenal	W	2 1	5 1	Mortimer, Graydon (pen), Gray 2, Little	33,860
11	23	H	Bristol City	W	0 1	3 1	Nicholl, Gidman, Graydon	37,094
12	30	A	Liverpool	L	0 0	0 3		51,751
13	Nov 6	H	Manchester United	W	1 1	3 2	Mortimer, Gray 2	44,789
14	10	A	West Bromwich Albion	D	1 0	1 1	Mortimer	41,867
15	20	H	Coventry City	D	1 0	2 2	Gidman, Gray	40,047
16	27	A	Norwich City	D	1 1	1 1	Little	22,110
17	Dec 11	H	Leeds United	W	1 0	3 1	Gray 2, Cropley	31,232
18	15	H	Liverpool	W	5 1	5 1	Gray 2, Deehan 2, Little	42,851
19	18	H	Newcastle United	W	1 1	2 1	Deehan 2	33,982
20	27	A	Middlesbrough	L	1 3	2 3	Gray, Hughes	31,451
21	Jan 1	A	Manchester United	L	0 2	0 2		55,446
22	22	H	West Ham United	W	1 0	1 0	Gray	27,577
23	Feb 5	H	Everton	W	1 0	2 0	Gray, Little	41,305
24	12	A	Ipswich Town	L	0 1	0 1		29,766
25	Mar 2	H	Derby County	W	3 0	4 0	Mortimer, Gidman, Little, Cowans	37,396
26	5	A	Leicester City	D	1 1	1 1	Deehan	22,038
27	23	H	Sunderland	W	2 0	4 1	Gidman, Gray, Deehan 2	34,458
28	Apr 2	A	Bristol City	D	0 0	0 0		27,266
29	5	H	Middlesbrough	W	1 0	1 0	Deehan	32,646
30	9	A	Derby County	L	0 1	1 2	Little	28,061
31	16	H	Coventry City	W	1 2	3 2	Cowans, Deehan, Little	31,288
32	20	H	Tottenham Hotspur	W	2 0	2 1	Little, Deehan	42,047
33	23	H	Norwich City	W	1 0	1 0	Little	35,899
34	25	A	Arsenal	L	0 2	0 3		24,011
35	30	A	Tottenham Hotspur	L	1 1	1 3	Deehan	30,690
36	May 4	H	Manchester City	D	0 0	1 1	Little	36,190
37	7	H	Leeds United	W	0 1	2 1	Deehan, Cropley	38,205
38	10	A	Birmingham City	L	0 0	1 2	Deehan	43,721
39	14	A	Newcastle United	L	1 3	2 3	Little 2	29,873
40	16	H	Stoke City	W	1 0	1 0	Gray (pen)	28,936
41	20	H	Queen's Park Rangers	D	0 0	1 1	Cowans	28,056
42	23	A	West Bromwich Albion	W	2 0	4 0	Nicholl, Gray 3	42,532

Final League Position: 4th in Division One

1 Own-goal

Appearances
Subs
Goals

FA CUP

3	Jan 8	A	Leicester City	W	0 0	1 0	Gray	27,112
4	29	H	West Ham United	W	0 0	3 0	Deehan 2, Mortimer	46,954
5	Feb 26	H	Port Vale	W	1 0	3 0	Nicholl, Little, Deehan	46,872
6	Mar 19	A	Manchester United	L	1 1	1 2	Little	57,089

Appearances
Subs
Goals

FOOTBALL LEAGUE CUP

2	Sep 1	H	Manchester City	W	1 0	3 0	Little 2, Graydon	34,585
3	21	H	Norwich City	W	1 0	2 1	Gray 2	31,295
4	Oct 27	A	Wrexham	W	2 1	5 1	Little 2, Carrodus, Nicholl, Gray	41,428
5	Dec 1	H	Millwall	W	1 0	2 0	Nicholl, Little	37,947
SF1	Feb 1	H	Queen's Park Rangers	D	0 0	0 0		28,739
SF2	16	H	Queen's Park Rangers *	D	0 0	2 2	Deehan 2	48,429
SFR	22	N	Queen's Park Rangers **	W	2 0	3 0	Little 3	40,438
F	Mar 12	N	Everton ***	D	0 0	0 0		100,000
R	16	N	Everton ****	D	0 0	1 1	Kenyon (og)	55,000
2R	Apr 13	N	Everton *****	W	0 1	3 2	Nicholl, Little 2	54,749

Appearances
Subs
1 Own-goal
Goals

* After extra-time ** Played at Highbury Stadium, London
*** Played at Wembley Stadium, London **** After extra-time - Played at Hillsborough, Sheffield
***** After extra-time - Played at Old Trafford, Manchester

462

Burridge J	Gidman J	Smith GM	Phillips L	Nicholl CJ	Mortimer DG	Graydon RJ	Little B	Gray AM	Robson JD	Carrodus F	Cowans GS	Hunt SK	Cropley AJ	Findlay JW	Deehan JM	Young CF	Buttress MD	Hughes DT	Masefield KL	Linton I	MATCH
1	2	3	4	5	6	7	8	9	10	11											1
1	2	3	4	5	6	7	8	9	10	11											2
1	2	3	4	5	6	7	8	9	10	11											3
1	2	3	4	5	6	7	8	9	10	11											4
1	2	3	4	5	6	7	8	9	10¹	11	12¹										5
1	2	3	4	5	6	7	8	9	10¹	11	12¹										6
1	2	3	4	5	6	7	8	9		11		10									7
1	2	3	4	5	6	7	8	9		11		10									8
1	2	3	4	5	6	7	8	9		11		10									9
1	2	3	4	5	6	7	8	9		11		10									10
1	2	3	4	5	6	7	8	9		11		10									11
1	2	3	4	5	6	7	8	9		11		10									12
1	2	3	4	5	6	7	8	9		11		10									13
1	2	3	4	5	6	7¹	8	9	12¹	11		10									14
	2	3	4	5	6		8	9		11		10	1	7							15
	2	3	4	5	6		8	9	7	11		10	1								16
	2		4		6		8	9	3	11		10	1	7	5						17
	2		4		6		8	9	3	11		10¹	1	7	5	12¹					18
		2	4		6		8	9	3	11		10¹	1	7	5	12¹					19
		2	4		6		8	9	3	11			1	7	5	10					20
1		2	4	5	6		8	9	3	11		10		7							21
1	2	12¹	4	5	6		8	9	3	11		10¹		7							22
1	2		4	5	6		8	9¹	3	11	12¹	10		7							23
1	2		4	5	6			3	11	9		10		7							24
1	2	12¹	4	5	6		8		3	11	9			7		10¹					25
	2	10	4	5	6		8		3	11	9		1	7							26
1	2			4	6		8	9	3	11	10			7	5						27
1	2			5	6		8	9	3	11		10		7	4						28
1	2		4	5	6		8	9	3	11		10		7							29
1	2		4	5	6		8	9	3	11¹	12¹	10		7							30
1		2	4	5	6	7	8		3		11	10		9							31
1		2	4	5¹	6	7	8		3		11	10		9	12¹						32
1		2	4		6¹	7	8		3		11	10		9	5	12¹					33
1		2	4				8	9	3		11	10		7	5	6¹	12¹				34
1		3	4		6	7	8	9				10		11			2				35
1	2		4	5	6		8	9	3		11	10		7							36
1	2		4	5	6		8	9	3		11	10		7							37
1	2		4	5	6		8	9	3		11	10		7							38
1	2			5	6		8	9	3		11	10		7	4						39
1	2		4	5	6		8	9	3		11	10		7¹				12¹			40
1	2		4	5	6		8	9	3		11	10		7							41
1	2		4	5	6		8	9¹	3		11	10		7				12¹			42

35	27	32	40	35	41	18	42	36	32	30	15	32	7	27	9	3	1			
		2							1		1				1	2	1	1	2	
	4			2	4	6	14	25		3	3		13		1					

FINAL LEAGUE TABLE

	P	W	D	L	F	A	P
Liverpool	42	23	11	8	62	33	57
Manchester City	42	21	14	7	60	34	56
Ipswich Town	42	22	8	12	66	39	52
Aston Villa	**42**	**22**	**7**	**13**	**76**	**50**	**51**
Newcastle United	42	18	13	11	64	49	49
Manchester United	42	18	11	13	71	62	47
West Bromwich A	42	16	13	13	62	56	45
Arsenal	42	16	11	15	64	59	43
Everton	42	14	14	14	62	64	42
Leeds United	42	15	12	15	48	51	42
Leicester City	42	12	18	12	47	60	42
Middlesbrough	42	14	13	15	40	45	41
Birmingham City	42	13	12	17	63	61	38
Queens Park Rangers	42	13	12	17	47	52	38
Derby County	42	9	19	14	50	55	37
Norwich City	42	14	9	19	47	64	37
West Ham United	42	11	14	17	46	65	36
Bristol City	42	11	13	18	38	48	35
Coventry City	42	10	15	17	48	59	35
Sunderland	42	11	12	19	46	54	34
Stoke City	42	10	14	18	28	51	34
Tottenham Hotspur	42	12	9	21	48	72	33

463

1977/78

SEASON SNIPPETS

Scottish central defender Ken McNaught, who had played against Villa for Everton in the marathon League Cup final the previous season, was signed for a club record £200,000. McNaught effectively took over from Chris Nicholl who was transferred to Southampton.

Manager Ron Saunders also started the season with two other new signings, goalkeeper Jimmy Rimmer from Arsenal for £70,000 and midfielder John Gregory from Northampton Town for £40,000

The North Stand was opened, replacing the old Witton End terrace.

Alex Cropley suffered a broken leg on 10 December in a challenge by West Bromwich Albion's Alistair Brown, and was out of action for more than a year.

John Robson was diagnosed with Multiple Sclerosis - his last game had been at Nottingham Forest on 17 September.

Jake Findlay's last game was on 19 October.

Michael Buttress played his last game on 14 January.

Gary Shelton was signed from Walsall on 18 January.

Villa's transfer record was smashed again on 25 January when Tommy Craig arrived from Newcastle United for £270,000.

DIVISION ONE

MANAGER: Ron Saunders

MATCH	DATE	VENUE	OPPONENTS	RESULT	HT SCORE	SCORE	SCORERS	ATT
1	Aug 20	A	Queen's Park Rangers	W	0 0	2 1	Webb (og), Carrodus	25,431
2	24	H	Manchester City	L	1 2	1 4	Deehan	40,121
3	27	H	Everton	L	1 0	1 2	Gray	37,806
4	Sep 3	A	Bristol City	D	1 0	1 1	Little	22,359
5	10	A	Arsenal	W	0 0	1 0	Cropley	36,929
6	17	A	Nottingham Forest	L	0 1	0 2		31,016
7	23	H	Wolverhampton Wanderers	W	0 0	2 0	Brazier (og), Deehan	39,403
8	Oct 1	H	Birmingham City	L	0 0	0 1		45,436
9	5	A	Leeds United	D	1 0	1 1	Gray	27,797
10	8	A	Leicester City	W	0 0	2 0	Cowans, Gray	20,276
11	15	H	Norwich City	W	1 0	3 0	Gray, Cowans, Little	32,978
12	22	A	West Ham United	D	1 1	2 2	McNaught, Gray	26,599
13	29	H	Manchester United	W	2 0	2 1	Gray, Cropley	39,144
14	Nov 5	A	Liverpool	W	1 0	2 1	Gray 2	50,436
15	12	H	Middlesbrough	L	0 1	0 1		31,837
16	19	A	Chelsea	D	0 0	0 0		31,764
17	Dec 3	A	Ipswich Town	L	0 2	0 2		20,908
18	10	H	West Bromwich Albion	W	2 0	3 0	Cowans, Gray, Gidman	43,196
19	17	A	Middlesbrough	L	0 0	0 1		14,999
20	26	H	Coventry City	D	0 0	1 1	Deehan	43,671
21	27	A	Derby County	W	2 0	3 0	Little, Gray, Deehan	30,395
22	31	A	Manchester City	L	0 0	0 2		46,074
23	Jan 2	H	Queen's Park Rangers	D	1 0	1 1	Little	34,750
24	14	A	Everton	L	0 1	0 1		40,630
25	28	H	Bristol City	W	0 0	1 0	Deehan	29,676
26	Feb 4	A	Arsenal	W	1 0	1 0	Macdonald (og)	30,127
27	25	A	Birmingham City	L	0 0	0 1		33,679
28	Mar 4	H	Leicester City	D	0 0	0 0		29,971
29	11	A	Norwich City	L	0 1	0 1		18,575
30	18	H	West Ham United	W	2 1	4 1	Gregory 2, Deehan, Mortimer	28,275
31	21	A	Coventry City	W	2 0	3 2	Little, McNaught, Gray	30,920
32	25	H	Derby County	D	0 0	0 0		32,793
33	29	A	Manchester United	D	0 0	1 1	Deehan	41,625
34	Apr 1	H	Liverpool	L	0 3	0 3		40,190
35	5	H	Nottingham Forest	L	0 0	0 1		44,215
36	8	A	Newcastle United	D	1 1	1 1	A Evans	19,330
37	15	H	Chelsea	W	0 0	2 0	Cowans, Wicks (og)	27,375
38	17	H	Newcastle United	W	1 0	2 0	Cowans, Gray	25,493
39	22	A	West Bromwich Albion	W	3 0	3 0	Deehan, Cowans, Mortimer	35,112
40	26	H	Leeds United	W	1 0	3 1	Deehan, Little, Mortimer	30,524
41	29	H	Ipswich Town	W	4 0	6 1	Deehan 2, Gray, Little, Carrodus, Cowans	30,955
42	May 2	A	Wolverhampton Wanderers	L	1 2	1 3	Carrodus	30,644

Final League Position: 8th in Division One

| | | | | | | | 4 Own-goals | Appearances
Subs
Goals |

FA CUP

3	Jan 7	A	Everton	L	1 3	1 4	Gray	46,320

| | | | | | | | | Appearances
Subs
Goals |

FOOTBALL LEAGUE CUP

2	Aug 31	A	Exeter City	W	1 0	3 1	Gray 3	13,768
3	Oct 26	H	Queen's Park Rangers	W	1 0	1 0	Gray (pen)	34,481
4	Nov 29	A	Nottingham Forest	L	0 3	2 4	Little, Carrodus	29,333

| | | | | | | | | Appearances
Subs
Goals |

UEFA CUP

1F	Sep 14	H	Fenerbahce	W	2 0	4 0	Gray, Deehan 2, Little	30,351
1S	28	A	Fenerbahce	W	1 0	2 0	Deehan, Little	18,000
2F	Oct 19	H	Gornik Zabrze	W	1 0	2 0	McNaught 2	34,138
2S	Nov 2	A	Gornik Zabrze	D	0 1	1 1	Gray	15,000
3F	23	H	Athletic Club Bilbao	W	1 0	2 0	Iribar (og), Deehan	32,973
3S	Dec 7	A	Athletic Club Bilbao	D	1 0	1 1	Mortimer	39,000
4F	Mar 1	H	Barcelona	D	0 1	2 2	McNaught, Deehan	49,619
4S	15	A	Barcelona	L	0 0	1 2	Little	80,000

| | | | | | | | | Appearances
Subs
Goals |
| | | | | | | | 1 Own-goal | |

FINAL LEAGUE TABLE

	P	W	D	L	F	A	P
Nottingham Forest	42	25	14	3	69	24	64
Liverpool	42	24	9	9	65	34	57
Everton	42	22	11	9	76	45	55
Manchester City	42	20	12	10	74	51	52
Arsenal	42	21	10	11	60	37	52
West Bromwich A	42	18	14	10	62	53	50
Coventry City	42	18	12	12	75	62	48
Aston Villa	**42**	**18**	**10**	**14**	**57**	**42**	**46**
Leeds United	42	18	10	14	63	53	46
Manchester United	42	16	10	16	67	63	42
Birmingham City	42	16	9	17	55	60	41
Derby County	42	14	13	15	54	59	41
Norwich City	42	11	18	13	52	66	40
Middlesbrough	42	12	15	15	42	54	39
Wolverhampton W	42	12	12	18	51	64	36
Chelsea	42	11	14	17	46	69	36
Bristol City	42	11	13	18	49	53	35
Ipswich Town	42	11	13	18	47	61	35
Queens Park Rangers	42	9	15	18	47	64	33
West Ham United	42	12	8	22	52	69	32
Newcastle United	42	6	10	26	42	78	22
Leicester City	42	5	12	25	26	70	22

465

1978/79

SEASON SNIPPETS

The club made no signings nor sold any players during the summer of 1978. The closest they came to a piece of transfer business was when manager Ron Saunders turned down a bid from West Bromwich Albion for striker John Deehan.

Villa were the first visitors to White Hart Lane following the arrival of Tottenham Hotspur's Argentine duo Osvaldo Ardiles and Ricardo Villa, and came away with the points, winning 4-1 on 23 August.

The League Cup win at Coventry against Crystal Palace on 16 October was the last game for Frank Carrodus.

Leighton Phillips played his last game on 4 November.

The 1-0 win at Chelsea on 9 December was the last game for Gordon Smith.

Kenny Swain was signed from Chelsea for £100,000 on 14 December and Joe Ward arrived from Clyde a week later.

The coldest winter for years meant that no games were played at Villa Park from Boxing Day until the first weekend of March. Villa's only action during January and February comprised an FA Cup defeat at Nottingham Forest, plus draws at Everton and Manchester United.

Tommy Craig's last game was 4 April at Nottingham.

By wearing the number eight shirt against Liverpool on 16 April, John Gregory achieved the feat of playing in all ten outfield positions for Villa. However, Gregory made his last Villa appearance on 15 May.

David Evans and Willie Young also played their last games during the season.

DIVISION ONE

MANAGER: Ron Saunders

MATCH	DATE	VENUE	OPPONENTS	RESULT	HT SCORE	SCORE	SCORERS	ATT
1	Aug 19	H	Wolverhampton Wanderers	W	0 0	1 0	Gray	43,922
2	23	A	Tottenham Hotspur	W	1 0	4 1	A Evans, Gregory, Little, Shelton	47,892
3	26	A	Bristol City	L	0 0	0 1		23,881
4	Sep 2	H	Southampton	D	1 1	1 1	Gray	34,067
5	9	A	Ipswich Town	W	1 0	2 0	Gregory, Gray (pen)	22,189
6	16	H	Everton	D	1 1	1 1	Craig	38,636
7	23	A	Queen's Park Rangers	L	0 0	0 1		16,410
8	30	H	Nottingham Forest	L	1 0	1 2	Craig (pen)	36,735
9	Oct 7	A	Arsenal	D	0 1	1 1	Gregory	34,537
10	14	H	Manchester United	D	2 0	2 2	Gregory 2	36,204
11	21	H	Birmingham City	W	1 0	1 0	Gray	36,145
12	27	H	Middlesbrough	L	0 1	0 2		32,614
13	Nov 4	H	Manchester City	D	0 0	1 1	Deehan	32,724
14	11	A	Wolverhampton Wanderers	W	2 0	4 0	Shelton, McNaught, Deehan, Mortimer	23,289
15	18	H	Bristol City	W	0 0	2 0	Deehan, Cowans	27,621
16	21	A	Southampton	L	0 2	0 2		20,616
17	25	A	West Bromwich Albion	D	0 1	1 1	A Evans	35,166
18	Dec 9	A	Chelsea	W	1 0	1 0	A Evans	19,636
19	16	H	Norwich City	D	0 0	1 1	McGuire (og)	26,228
20	23	A	Derby County	D	0 0	0 0		20,109
21	26	H	Leeds United	D	2 0	2 2	Gregory 2	40,973
22	Jan 31	A	Everton	D	0 0	1 1	Shelton	29,079
23	Feb 24	A	Manchester United	D	0 0	1 1	Swain	44,437
24	Mar 3	H	Birmingham City	W	0 0	1 0	Cowans	42,419
25	7	H	Bolton Wanderers	W	3 0	3 0	Gray, Swain, Jones (og)	28,053
26	10	A	Middlesbrough	L	0 0	0 2		16,558
27	20	H	Queen's Park Rangers	W	1 0	3 1	A Evans, Gidman (pen), Mortimer	24,310
28	24	H	Tottenham Hotspur	L	2 0	2 3	Gidman (pen), Gray	35,486
29	28	H	Coventry City	D	0 0	1 1	A Evans	25,670
30	Apr 4	A	Nottingham Forest	L	0 1	0 4		27,056
31	7	A	Coventry City	D	0 1	1 1	Deehan	23,668
32	11	H	Derby County	D	1 2	3 3	Cowans 2, Gidman (pen)	21,884
33	14	A	Leeds United	L	0 1	0 1		24,281
34	16	H	Liverpool	W	2 0	3 1	A Evans, Thompson (og), Deehan	44,029
35	21	A	Norwich City	W	1 1	2 1	Shelton, Cropley	13,421
36	25	H	Arsenal	W	0 1	5 1	Shelton 3 (1 pen), Deehan 2	26,168
37	28	H	Chelsea	W	0 1	2 1	G Wilkins (og), Swain	29,219
38	May 2	H	Ipswich Town	D	2 1	2 2	Swain, Deehan	26,636
39	5	A	Bolton Wanderers	D	0 0	0 0		17,394
40	8	A	Liverpool	L	0 2	0 3		50,576
41	11	H	West Bromwich Albion	L	0 1	0 1		35,991
42	15	A	Manchester City	W	0 1	3 2	Cropley, Mortimer, Deehan	30,028

Final League Position: 8th in Division One

Appearances
Subs
4 Own-goals   Goals

FA CUP

3	Jan 10	A	Nottingham Forest	L	0 0	0 2		29,550

Appearances
Subs
Goals

FOOTBALL LEAGUE CUP

2	Aug 30	H	Sheffield Wednesday	W	1 0	1 0	Shelton	31,152
3	Oct 4	H	Crystal Palace	D	1 0	1 1	Little	30,690
R	10	A	Crystal Palace *	D	0 0	0 0		33,155
2R	16	N	Crystal Palace **	W	2 0	3 0	Gray 2, Gregory	25,455
4	Nov 8	H	Luton Town	L	0 0	0 2		32,727

Appearances
Subs
Goals

* After extra-time
** Played at Highfield Road, Coventry

466

Player appearances

	Rimmer JJ	Gidman J	Smith GM	Evans AJ	McNaught K	Mortimer DG	Shelton G	Little B	Gray AM	Cowans GS	Carrodus F	Gregory JC	Shaw GR	Craig TB	Jenkins LR	Evans DG	Williams G	Deehan JM	Phillips L	Young WJ	Linton I	Gibson CJ	Cropley AJ	Swain K	Ward J	Ormsby BTC		MATCH
	1	2	3	4	5	6	7	8	9¹	10	11	12¹																1
	1	2	3	4	5	6	7	8		10	11	9																2
	1	2	3	4	5	6	7¹	8		10	11	9	12¹															3
	1	2	3	4	5	6	7	8	9	10	11																	4
	1	2¹	3	4	5	6		8	9	10		7		11	12¹													5
	1			4	5	6	11¹	8	9	10		3		7		2	12¹											6
	1			4	5	6	11	8		10		3		7		2		9¹	12¹									7
	1			4	5	6	11	8		10¹		2		7	12¹	3		9										8
	1			4	5	6		8			11	2		7		3		9	10									9
	1	2			5				9		11	6		7		3	8	4	10									10
	1	2		4	5	6			9			10		7		3			11									11
	1	2		4	5	6		8	9			10		7		3			12¹	11¹								12
	1	2¹		12¹	5	6		8	9			11		7		3	10	4										13
	1	2		4	5	6	7	8		10		11				3	9											14
	1	2		4¹	5	6	7			10		11				3	9		8	12¹								15
	1	2	12¹	4	5	6	7¹			10		11				3	9		8									16
	1	2		4	5	6				10		11	8	7		3	9											17
	1	2	3	4	5	6				10		11	8¹	7			9			12¹								18
	1	2		4	5	6				10		11		7		3	9		8									19
	1	2		4	5	6	11			10				7		3	9		8									20
	1	2		4	5	6				10		11		7		3	9		8									21
	1	2		9	5	6	11¹			10		4		7		3				12¹	8							22
	1	2		5		6	11			10		4		7		3					8	9						23
	1	2		5		6		8	9	10		4		7		3					11							24
	1	2		5		6		8	9¹	10		4		7		3	12¹			6	11							25
	1			5		6		8	9			4		7		3			2	6	11							26
	1	2		5		6		8¹	9	10		4		7		3			12¹		11							27
	1	2		5		6		8	9	10		4		7		3				2	11							28
	1			5		6		8	9	10		4		7		3				2	11							29
	1	2		4	5	6		8	9			3		7							11							30
	1	2		4	5	6			7	3						9					10	11						31
	1	2			5	6¹		8	7							12¹	9			3	10	11		4				32
	1	2		4	5			8	7			6					9			3	10	11						33
	1	2		4	5	6			7	8							9			3	10	11						34
	1	2			5¹	6	8		7	4							9			12¹	3	10	11					35
	1	2				6	8		7	4							9				3	10	11	5				36
	1	2		5		6	8		7	4							9				3	10	11					37
	1	2		5		6	8		7	4							9				3	10	11					38
	1	2			8	6			7	4							9				3	10	11					39
	1	2			8	5	6			7	4						9			12¹	3	10¹	11					40
	1	2		4¹	5	6	7			8							9			12¹	3	10	11					41
	1	2				5	6	7	8								9				3	10	11					42
	42	36	6	36	32	38	19	24	15	34	6	38	2	23		2	21	25	3	4	11	15	24	1	2			
			1	1							1		2				2		1			2						
		3		6		1	3	7	1	6		4		7	2			1	2			2	4					

FA Cup

| | 1 | 2 | | 4 | 5 | 6 | | | | 10 | | 11 | | 7 | | 3 | 9 | | | | 8 | | | | | | | 3 |

FA Cup replays

| | 1 | 1 | | 1 | 1 | 1 | | | | 1 | | 1 | | 1 | | 1 | 1 | | | | 1 | | | | | | | |

League Cup

	1	2	3	4	5	6	7	8	9	10	11																	2
	1			4	5	6	10¹	8			11	2		7		3	9	12¹										3
	1			4	5¹	6			9		11	2		7		3	8	10							12¹			R
	1	2		4	5	6		8	9	11	10			7		3		4										2R
	1	2		4	5	6		8	9¹	12¹	11			7		3	10											4

Goals

| | 5 | 3 | 1 | 4 | 5 | 5 | 2 | 4 | 4 | 4 | | 4 | | | | 4 | | | | 4 | 3 | 2 | | | | 1 | | |
| | | | | | | | | 1 | 1 | 2 | | 1 | | | | | | | | | | 1 | | | | | | |

FINAL LEAGUE TABLE

	P	W	D	L	F	A	P
Liverpool	42	30	8	4	85	16	68
Nottingham Forest	42	21	18	3	61	26	60
West Bromwich A	42	24	11	7	72	35	59
Everton	42	17	17	8	52	40	51
Leeds United	42	18	14	10	70	52	50
Ipswich Town	42	20	9	13	63	49	49
Arsenal	42	17	14	11	61	48	48
Aston Villa	**42**	**15**	**16**	**11**	**59**	**49**	**46**
Manchester United	42	15	15	12	60	63	45
Coventry City	42	14	16	12	58	68	44
Tottenham Hotspur	42	13	15	14	48	61	41
Middlesbrough	42	15	10	17	57	50	40
Bristol City	42	15	10	17	47	51	40
Southampton	42	12	16	14	47	53	40
Manchester City	42	13	13	16	58	56	39
Norwich City	42	7	23	12	51	57	37
Bolton Wanderers	42	12	11	19	54	75	35
Wolverhampton W	42	13	8	21	44	68	34
Derby County	42	10	11	21	44	71	31
Queens Park Rangers	42	6	13	23	45	73	25
Birmingham City	42	6	10	26	37	64	22
Chelsea	42	5	10	27	44	92	20

467

1979/80

SEASON SNIPPETS

Two new players arrived at Villa Park in the summer of 1979 - winger Tony Morley from Burnley for £200,000 and striker Terry Donovan from Grimsby Town for £90,000. John Gregory and Tommy Craig, meanwhile, left for Brighton & Hove Albion and Swansea City respectively.

The opening home game, against Brighton was the last appearance for Alex Cropley. Having battled back from a broken leg, Cropley broke his ankle early in the game. It was also the last appearance for Lee Jenkins.

Andy M Gray, one of the most popular players ever to pull on a claret and blue shirt, was sold to Wolverhampton Wanderers for a transfer fee of £1.469m, on 12 September.

John Deehan moved to West Bromwich Albion for a fee of £500,000 on 21 September. Deehan's last game on 15 September was also Joe Ward's last appearance.

Manager Ron Saunders used the windfall from those sales to finance the purchase of Mike Pejic from Everton, Des Bremner from Hibernian and David Geddis (for a club record £300,000) from Ipswich Town.

On 18 October John Gidman was transferred to Everton in a deal worth around £750,000, with Pat Heard moving to Villa Park in part exchange.

Terry Bullivant arrived from Fulham on 15 November.

Mike Pejic suffered a serious groin injury against Liverpool on 8 December from which he never recovered, forcing his retirement from playing in June.

On 23 April, Brian Little played his last game. In February 1981, Little was given the news that he would not play again due to injury to his right knee.

DIVISION ONE

MANAGER: Ron Saunders

MATCH	DATE	VENUE	OPPONENTS	RESULT	HT SCORE	SCORE	SCORERS	ATT
1	Aug 18	A	Bolton Wanderers	D	0 0	1 1	Cowans	19,795
2	22	H	Brighton & Hove Albion	W	1 1	2 1	A Evans (pen), Morley	28,803
3	25	H	Bristol City	L	0 1	0 2		25,526
4	Sep 1	A	Everton	D	1 0	1 1	Morley	29,271
5	8	H	Manchester United	L	0 1	0 3		34,859
6	15	A	Crystal Palace	L	0 1	0 2		28,428
7	22	H	Arsenal	D	0 0	0 0		27,277
8	29	A	Middlesbrough	D	0 0	0 0		16,017
9	Oct 6	H	Southampton	W	2 0	3 0	Bremner, Mortimer, A Evans (pen)	24,377
10	13	H	West Bromwich Albion	D	0 0	0 0		36,007
11	20	A	Derby County	W	1 1	3 1	Little, Shaw, Mortimer	20,162
12	27	A	Wolverhampton Wanderers	D	1 1	1 1	Shaw	36,267
13	Nov 3	H	Bolton Wanderers	W	2 0	3 1	Shaw, A Evans, Mortimer	24,744
14	10	A	Ipswich Town	D	0 0	0 0		17,795
15	17	H	Stoke City	W	1 1	2 1	Mortimer, A Evans (pen)	27,086
16	24	H	Leeds United	D	0 0	0 0		29,736
17	Dec 1	A	Norwich City	D	1 0	1 1	A Evans	15,257
18	8	H	Liverpool	L	0 0	1 3	Little	41,160
19	15	A	Tottenham Hotspur	W	1 0	2 1	Geddis, Cowans (pen)	30,555
20	19	H	Coventry City	W	1 0	3 0	Donovan, Little 2	24,446
21	26	A	Nottingham Forest	L	0 0	1 2	Shaw	32,072
22	29	A	Bristol City	W	0 0	3 1	Shaw 3	18,799
23	Jan 12	H	Everton	W	0 0	2 1	Gibson, Donovan	31,108
24	Feb 2	H	Crystal Palace	W	1 0	2 0	Cowans, Mortimer	29,469
25	9	A	Arsenal	L	0 1	1 3	Mortimer	33,816
26	23	A	West Bromwich Albion	W	0 1	2 1	McNaught, Little	33,618
27	27	H	Manchester City	D	1 0	2 2	Shaw, Donachie (og)	29,139
28	Mar 1	H	Derby County	W	1 0	1 0	A Evans	28,956
29	3	A	Brighton & Hove Albion	D	1 1	1 1	A Evans	23,077
30	10	H	Wolverhampton Wanderers	L	1 3	1 3	Shaw	30,432
31	15	A	Southampton	L	0 1	0 2		20,735
32	19	H	Middlesbrough	L	0 1	0 2		15,319
33	22	H	Ipswich Town	D	0 1	1 1	Morley	22,836
34	26	H	Norwich City	W	0 0	2 0	Cowans (pen), Hopkins	17,956
35	29	A	Stoke City	L	0 1	0 2		16,558
36	Apr 5	H	Nottingham Forest	W	2 1	3 2	Bremner, A Evans, Lloyd (og)	29,156
37	7	A	Manchester City	D	1 0	1 1	Geddis	32,943
38	19	A	Leeds United	D	0 0	0 0		15,840
39	23	A	Manchester United	L	0 1	1 2	Bremner	45,201
40	26	H	Tottenham Hotspur	W	0 0	1 0	Cowans	29,549
41	29	A	Coventry City	W	1 0	2 1	Gibson, Cowans (pen)	17,932
42	May 3	A	Liverpool	L	1 1	1 4	Cohen (og)	51,541

Final League Position: 7th in Division One

3 Own-goals

Appearances
Subs
Goals

FA CUP

3	Jan 4	A	Bristol Rovers	W	1 0	2 1	Shaw, Cowans	16,060
4	26	A	Cambridge United	D	1 1	1 1	Donovan	12,000
R	30	H	Cambridge United	W	2 1	4 1	Donovan 2, A Evans, Little	36,835
5	Feb 16	A	Blackburn Rovers	D	1 0	1 1	Geddis	29,468
R	20	H	Blackburn Rovers	W	0 0	1 0	A Evans	42,161
6	Mar 8	A	West Ham United	L	0 0	0 1		36,393

Appearances
Subs
Goals

FOOTBALL LEAGUE CUP

2F	Aug 28	A	Colchester United	W	1 0	2 0	Shaw 2	6,221
2S	Sep 5	H	Colchester United *	L	0 1	0 2		19,473
3	25	H	Everton	D	0 0	0 0		22,635
R	Oct 9	A	Everton	L	0 2	1 4	Swain	22,098

Appearances
Subs
Goals

* After extra-time - Aston Villa won 9-8 on penalties

FINAL LEAGUE TABLE

	P	W	D	L	F	A	P
Liverpool	42	25	10	7	81	30	60
Manchester United	42	24	10	8	65	35	58
Ipswich Town	42	22	9	11	68	39	53
Arsenal	42	18	16	8	52	36	52
Nottingham Forest	42	20	8	14	63	43	48
Wolverhampton W	42	19	9	14	58	47	47
Aston Villa	**42**	**16**	**14**	**12**	**51**	**50**	**46**
Southampton	42	18	9	15	65	53	45
Middlesbrough	42	16	12	14	50	44	44
West Bromwich A	42	11	19	12	54	50	41
Leeds United	42	13	14	15	46	50	40
Norwich City	42	13	14	15	58	66	40
Crystal Palace	42	12	16	14	41	50	40
Tottenham Hotspur	42	15	10	17	52	62	40
Coventry City	42	16	7	19	56	66	39
Brighton and HA	42	11	15	16	47	57	37
Manchester City	42	12	13	17	43	66	37
Stoke City	42	13	10	19	44	58	36
Everton	42	9	17	16	43	51	35
Bristol City	42	9	13	20	37	66	31
Derby County	42	11	8	23	47	67	30
Bolton Wanderers	42	5	15	22	38	73	25

469

1980/81

SEASON SNIPPETS

The club's transfer record was smashed during the summer by one of the most significant signings in Villa's history, when Peter Withe arrived from Newcastle United for £500,000.

Villa won their first trophy of the season on 26 November when they lifted the Daily Express Five-a-side Championship trophy at Wembley. Villa triumphed with wins over Tottenham Hotspur and Manchester United followed by a 7-1 victory over Arsenal before beating Chelsea 3-0 in the final. The Villa squad comprised of Kevin Poole (goal), Kenny Swain (captain), Allan Evans, Des Bremner, Peter Withe and Noel Blake.

Villa won the First Division title with a squad of just 14 players, of whom seven - Jimmy Rimmer, Kenny Swain, Ken McNaught, Des Bremner, Gordon Cowans, Dennis Mortimer and Tony Morley - were ever-present. Peter Withe, meanwhile, headed the score chart with 20 goals, with Gary Shaw finding the net 18 times.

Despite a 2-0 defeat against Arsenal at Highbury on the final day, Villa became champions by virtue of Ipswich Town's 2-1 defeat at Middlesbrough.

Ron Saunders was elected Manager of the Year in the Bell's Scotch whisky awards.

DIVISION ONE

MANAGER: Ron Saunders

MATCH	DATE	VENUE	OPPONENTS	RESULT	HT SCORE	SCORE	SCORERS	ATT
1	Aug 16	A	Leeds United	W	1 1	2 1	Morley, Shaw	23,401
2	20	H	Norwich City	W	0 0	1 0	Shaw	25,970
3	23	A	Manchester City	D	1 0	2 2	Withe 2	30,017
4	30	H	Coventry City	W	0 0	1 0	Shaw	26,050
5	Sep 6	A	Ipswich Town	L	0 0	0 1		23,163
6	13	H	Everton	L	0 2	0 2		25,673
7	20	H	Wolverhampton Wanderers	W	1 0	2 1	Hughes (og), Geddis	26,881
8	27	A	Crystal Palace	W	0 0	1 0	Shaw	18,885
9	Oct 4	H	Sunderland	W	1 0	4 0	Evans 2, Morley, Shaw	26,914
10	8	A	Manchester United	D	1 2	3 3	Withe, Cowans (pen), Shaw	38,831
11	11	A	Birmingham City	W	1 0	2 1	Cowans (pen), Evans	33,879
12	18	H	Tottenham Hotspur	W	1 0	3 0	Morley 2, Withe	30,940
13	22	H	Brighton & Hove Albion	W	1 1	4 1	Mortimer, Withe, Bremner, Shaw	27,367
14	25	A	Southampton	W	1 0	2 1	Morley, Withe	21,239
15	Nov 1	H	Leicester City	W	0 0	2 0	Shaw, Cowans	29,953
16	8	A	West Bromwich Albion	D	0 0	0 0		34,195
17	12	A	Norwich City	W	0 1	3 1	Shaw 2, Evans	16,388
18	15	H	Leeds United	D	1 1	1 1	Shaw	29,106
19	22	A	Liverpool	L	0 0	1 2	Evans	48,114
20	29	H	Arsenal	D	0 0	1 1	Morley	30,140
21	Dec 6	A	Middlesbrough	L	0 0	1 2	Shaw	15,721
22	13	H	Birmingham City	W	0 0	3 0	Geddis 2, Shaw	41,101
23	20	A	Brighton & Hove Albion	L	0 1	0 1		16,429
24	26	H	Stoke City	W	1 0	1 0	Withe	34,658
25	27	A	Nottingham Forest	D	1 1	2 2	Lloyd (og), Shaw	33,930
26	Jan 10	H	Liverpool	W	1 0	2 0	Withe, Mortimer	47,960
27	17	A	Coventry City	W	0 0	2 1	Morley, Withe	27,094
28	31	H	Manchester City	W	1 0	1 0	Shaw	33,682
29	Feb 7	A	Everton	W	2 1	3 1	Morley, Mortimer, Cowans (pen),	31,480
30	21	H	Crystal Palace	W	1 0	2 1	Withe 2	27,203
31	28	A	Wolverhampton Wanderers	W	0 0	1 0	Withe	34,693
32	Mar 7	A	Sunderland	W	2 0	2 1	Evans, Mortimer	27,278
33	14	H	Manchester United	D	2 0	3 3	Withe 2, Shaw	42,182
34	21	A	Tottenham Hotspur	L	0 1	0 2		35,091
35	28	H	Southampton	W	2 1	2 1	Morley, Geddis	32,467
36	Apr 4	A	Leicester City	W	2 2	4 2	Withe 2, Bremner, Morley	26,032
37	8	H	West Bromwich Albion	W	0 0	1 0	Withe	47,998
38	14	H	Ipswich Town	L	0 1	1 2	Shaw	47,495
39	18	H	Nottingham Forest	W	2 0	2 0	Cowans (pen), Withe	34,707
40	20	A	Stoke City	D	1 1	1 1	Withe	23,537
41	25	H	Middlesbrough	W	1 0	3 0	Shaw, Withe, Evans	38,018
42	May 2	A	Arsenal	L	0 2	0 2		57,472

Final League Position: 1st in Division One

2 Own-goals

Appearances
Subs
Goals

FA CUP

3	Jan 3	A	Ipswich Town	L	0 1	0 1		27,721

Appearances
Subs
Goals

FOOTBALL LEAGUE CUP

2F	Aug 27	H	Leeds United	W	1 0	1 0	Morley	23,622
2S	Sep 3	A	Leeds United	W	2 1	3 1	Withe, Shaw 2	12,236
3	Sep 23	A	Cambridge United	L	1 2	1 2	Morley	7,608

Appearances
Subs
Goals

Player Appearances

Rimmer JJ	Swain K	Deacy ES	Williams G	McNaught K	Mortimer DG	Bremner DG	Shaw GR	Withe P	Cowans GS	Morley WA	Gibson CJ	Evans AJ	Geddis D	MATCH
1	2	3	4	5	6	7	8	9	10	11				1
1	2			5	6	7	8	9	10	11	3	4		2
1	2			5	6	7	8	9	10	11	3	4		3
1	2			5	6	7	8	9	10	11	3	4		4
1	2			5	6	7	8	9	10	11	3	4		5
1	2			5	6	7	8	9	10	11	3	4		6
1	2			5	6	7		9	10	11	3	4		7
1	2			5	6	7	8	9	10	11	3	4	8	8
1	2	12¹		5	6	7	8	9	10	11	3¹	4		9
1	2	3		5	6	7	8	9	10	11		4		10
1	2	3		5	6	7	8	9	10	11				11
1	2			5	6	7	8	9	10	11	3	4		12
1	2			5	6	7	8	9	10	11	3	4		13
1	2	12¹		5	6	7	8	9	10	11¹	3	4		14
1	2	3¹	12¹	5	6	7	8	9	10	11		4		15
1	2		3	5	6	7	8	9	10	11		4		16
1	2		3	5	6	7	8	9	10	11		4		17
1	2		3	5	6	7	8	9	10	11		4		18
1	2		3	5	6	7	8	9	10	11		4		19
1	2		3	5	6	7	8	9	10	11		4		20
1	2	12¹	3	5	6	7	8		10	11		4	9¹	21
1	2		3	5	6	7	8		10	11		4	9	22
1	2	12¹	3	5	6	7			10	11		4	9¹	23
1	2		3	5	6	7	8	9	10	11		4		24
1	2		3	5	6	7	8		10	11		4	9	25
1	2			5	6	7	8	9	10	11	3	4		26
1	2			5	6	7	8	9	10	11	3	4		27
1	2	3		5¹	6	7	8	9	10	11		4	12¹	28
1	2		3	5	6	7	8	9	10	11		4		29
1	2		3¹	5	6	7	8	9	10	11	12¹	4		30
1	2		3	5	6	7	8	9	10	11		4		31
1	2		3	5¹	6	7	8	9	10	11	12¹	4		32
1	2		3	5	6	7	8	9	10	11		4		33
1	2		3	5	6	7	8		10	11		4	9	34
1	2		3	5	6	7	8		10	11		4	9	35
1	2		3	5	6	7	8	9	10	11		4		36
1	2			5	6	7		9	10	11	3	4	8	37
1	2		4	5	6	7	8	9	10	11	3			38
1	2		4	5	6	7	8	9	10	11	3			39
1	2	12¹		5	6	7	8¹	9	10	11	3	4		40
1	2			5	6	7	8	9	10	11	3	4		41
1	2			5	6	7	8	9	10	11	3	4		42

42	42	5	21	42	42	42	40	36	42	42	19	39	8	
		5	1								2		1	
				4	2	18	20	5	10		7	4		

| 1 | 2 | | 3 | 5 | 6 | 7 | 8 | 9 | 10 | 11¹ | | 4 | 12¹ | 3 |
| 1 | 1 | | 1 | 1 | 1 | 1 | 1 | 1 | 1 | 1 | | 1 | 1 | |

1	2			5	6	7	8	9	10	11	3	4		2F
1	2	12¹		5	6	7	8¹	9	10	11	3	4		2S
1	2			5	6	7	12¹	9	10	11¹	3	4	8	3

3	3			3	3	3	2	3	3	3	3	1		
		1					1			2				
							2	1		2				

FINAL LEAGUE TABLE

	P	W	D	L	F	A	P
Aston Villa	42	26	8	8	72	40	60
Ipswich Town	42	23	10	9	77	43	56
Arsenal	42	19	15	8	61	45	53
West Bromwich A	42	20	12	10	60	42	52
Liverpool	42	17	17	8	62	42	51
Southampton	42	20	10	12	76	56	50
Nottingham Forest	42	19	12	11	62	44	50
Manchester United	42	15	18	9	51	36	48
Leeds United	42	17	10	15	39	47	44
Tottenham Hotspur	42	14	15	13	70	68	43
Stoke City	42	12	18	12	51	60	42
Manchester City	42	14	11	17	56	59	39
Birmingham City	42	13	12	17	50	61	38
Middlesbrough	42	16	5	21	53	61	37
Everton	42	13	10	19	55	58	36
Coventry City	42	13	10	19	48	68	36
Sunderland	42	14	7	21	52	53	35
Wolverhampton W	42	13	9	20	43	55	35
Brighton and HA	42	14	7	21	54	67	35
Norwich City	42	13	7	22	49	73	33
Leicester City	42	13	6	23	40	67	32
Crystal Palace	42	6	7	29	47	83	19

1981/82

SEASON SNIPPETS

The only summer signing was midfielder Andy Blair, who arrived from Coventry City for £350,000. Alex Cropley, meanwhile, moved to Portsmouth.

Villa drew 2-2 against F.A. Cup holders Tottenham Hotspur in the FA Charity Shield at Wembley. Both teams held the trophy for six months each.

On 16 September, Peter Withe and Terry Donovan netted twice in Villa's first ever European Cup tie, a 5-0 home win against Valur of Iceland, after Tony Morley had opened the scoring.

Ivor Linton's last game was at Swansea on 15 December.

Noel Blake made his last appearance on 19 December.

Gary Shelton played his last game on 2 February.

Terry Donovan's last match was at Ipswich on 20 March.

Terry Bullivant made his last appearance on 27 March.

Manager Ron Saunders resigned on 9 February and was succeeded by his assistant Tony Barton who led the team to European glory.

Villa used only 17 players in the whole of their European Cup-winning campaign, including Ivor Linton and Nigel Spink who each made just one substitute appearance.

Goalkeeper Nigel Spink had played only one senior game when he replaced Jimmy Rimmer after 9 minutes of the European Cup Final.

DIVISION ONE

MANAGER: Ron Saunders (to 9 February)   Tony Barton (from 9 February)

MATCH	DATE	VENUE	OPPONENTS	RESULT	HT SCORE	SCORE	SCORERS	ATT
1	Aug 29	H	Notts County	L	0 1	0 1		30,097
2	Sep 2	A	Sunderland	L	1 1	1 2	Donovan	29,372
3	5	A	Tottenham Hotspur	W	3 0	3 1	Donovan 2, Mortimer	31,265
4	12	H	Manchester United	D	1 1	1 1	Cowans	37,661
5	19	A	Liverpool	D	0 0	0 0		37,474
6	23	H	Stoke City	D	1 0	2 2	Withe 2	25,637
7	26	H	Birmingham City	D	0 0	0 0		41,098
8	Oct 3	A	Leeds United	D	1 0	1 1	Shaw	21,065
9	10	A	Coventry City	D	1 1	1 1	Shaw	16,306
10	17	H	West Ham United	W	3 1	3 2	Morley, Geddis, Mortimer	32,064
11	24	A	Wolverhampton Wanderers	W	2 0	3 0	Shaw 2, Palmer (og)	19,942
12	31	H	Ipswich Town	L	0 1	0 1		32,652
13	Nov 7	A	Arsenal	L	0 2	0 2		27,316
14	21	A	Middlesbrough	D	1 1	3 3	Withe, Cowans, Shaw	12,522
15	28	H	Nottingham Forest	W	2 0	3 1	Bremner 2, Withe	26,847
16	Dec 5	A	Manchester City	L	0 0	0 1		32,487
17	15	A	Swansea City	L	1 2	1 2	Thompson (og)	15,191
18	19	H	Everton	L	0 1	0 2		16,544
19	28	A	Brighton & Hove Albion	W	0 0	1 0	Morley	24,259
20	Jan 16	H	Notts County	L	0 0	0 1		9,590
21	30	H	Liverpool	L	0 2	0 3		35,947
22	Feb 2	H	Sunderland	W	0 0	1 0	Geddis	19,916
23	6	A	Manchester United	L	1 1	1 4	Geddis	43,184
24	10	A	Southampton	D	0 1	1 1	Withe	24,287
25	17	H	Tottenham Hotspur	D	0 0	1 1	Withe	23,877
26	20	A	Birmingham City	W	0 0	1 0	Withe	32,817
27	27	H	Coventry City	W	2 1	2 1	Cowans (pen), Shaw	24,474
28	Mar 6	A	West Ham United	D	1 1	2 2	Cowans, Withe	26,894
29	13	H	Wolverhampton Wanderers	W	2 1	3 1	Donovan, Morley, Shaw	26,790
30	20	A	Ipswich Town	L	0 2	1 3	McNaught	21,016
31	27	A	Arsenal	L	2 2	3 4	Shaw, Morley, Heard	24,756
32	30	H	West Bromwich Albion	W	0 1	2 1	Shaw, Withe	28,440
33	Apr 10	A	Southampton	W	0 0	3 0	Nicholl (og), McNaught, Morley	22,801
34	12	H	Brighton & Hove Albion	W	0 0	3 0	Geddis 2, Evans	22,731
35	17	H	Middlesbrough	W	1 0	1 0	Evans	21,098
36	24	A	Nottingham Forest	D	0 1	1 1	Cowans (pen)	18,213
37	28	H	Leeds United	L	1 1	1 4	Geddis	20,566
38	May 1	H	Manchester City	D	0 0	0 0		22,150
39	5	A	Stoke City	L	0 1	0 1		10,363
40	8	A	West Bromwich Albion	W	0 0	1 0	Heard	19,556
41	15	H	Everton	L	1 1	1 2	Cowans	20,446
42	21	H	Swansea City	W	2 0	3 0	Morley, Bremner, Withe	18,294

Final League Position: 11th in Division One

Appearances
Subs
3 Own-goals | Goals

FA CUP

3	Jan 5	A	Notts County	W	4 0	6 0	Richards (og), Shaw, Geddis 3, Cowans (pen)	12,312
4	23	A	Bristol City	W	0 0	1 0	Shaw	20,279
5	Feb 13	A	Tottenham Hotspur	L	0 1	0 1		42,950

Appearances
Subs
1 Own-goal | Goals

FOOTBALL LEAGUE CUP

2F	Oct 7	H	Wolverhampton Wanderers	W	0 1	3 2	Bremner, Blair, Morley	26,353
2S	27	A	Wolverhampton Wanderers	W	1 0	2 1	Cowans 2 (1 pen)	19,491
3	Nov 11	A	Leicester City	D	0 0	0 0		19,806
R	25	H	Leicester City	W	2 0	2 0	Cowans (pen), Withe	23,136
4	Dec 1	A	Wigan Athletic	W	0 1	2 1	Cowans (pen), Withe	15,362
5	Jan 20	H	West Bromwich Albion	L	0 1	0 1		35,197

Appearances
Subs
Goals

EUROPEAN CUP

1F	Sep 16	H	FC Valur	W	3 0	5 0	Morley, Withe 2, Donovan 2	20,481
1S	30	A	FC Valur	W	1 0	2 0	Shaw 2	3,500
2F	Oct 21	A	Dynamo Berlin	W	1 0	2 1	Morley 2	25,000
2S	Nov 4	H	Dynamo Berlin	L	0 1	0 1		28,175
3F	Mar 3	A	Dynamo Kiev	D	0 0	0 0		20,000
3S	17	H	Dynamo Kiev	W	2 0	2 0	Shaw, McNaught	38,579
SF1	Apr 7	H	Anderlecht	W	1 0	1 0	Morley	38,539
SF2	21	A	Anderlecht	D	0 0	0 0		38,040
F	May 26	N	Bayern Munich *	W	0 0	1 0	Withe	39,776

Appearances
Subs
Goals

* Played at Feyenoord Stadium, Rotterdam

FA CHARITY SHIELD

	Aug 22	N	Tottenham Hotspur *	D	1 1	2 2	Withe 2	92,500

Appearances
Subs
Goals

* Played at Wembley Stadium, London   Each club retained the shield for six months

FINAL LEAGUE TABLE

	P	W	D	L	F	A	P	
Liverpool	42	26	9	7	80	32	87	2F
Ipswich Town	42	26	5	11	75	53	83	2S
Manchester United	42	22	12	8	59	29	78	3 R
Tottenham Hotspur	42	20	11	11	67	48	71	4
Arsenal	42	20	11	11	48	37	71	5
Swansea City	42	21	6	15	58	51	69	
Southampton	42	19	9	14	72	67	66	
Everton	42	17	13	12	56	50	64	
West Ham United	42	14	16	12	66	57	58	1F
Manchester City	42	15	13	14	49	50	58	1S
Aston Villa	42	15	12	15	55	53	57	2F 2S
Nottingham Forest	42	15	12	15	42	48	57	3F
Brighton and HA	42	13	13	16	43	52	52	3S
Coventry City	42	13	11	18	56	62	50	SF1 SF2
Notts County	42	13	8	21	61	69	47	F
Birmingham City	42	10	14	18	53	61	44	
West Bromwich A	42	11	11	20	46	57	44	
Stoke City	42	12	8	22	44	63	44	
Sunderland	42	11	11	20	38	58	44	
Leeds United	42	10	12	20	39	61	42	
Wolverhampton W	42	10	10	22	32	63	40	
Middlesbrough	42	8	15	19	34	52	39	

1982/83

SEASON SNIPPETS

Villa players wore advertising on their shirts for the first time as part of a sponsorship deal with local brewers Davenports.

The 5-0 defeat at Everton on 31 August was Kenny Swain's last game.

Villa's first round European Cup match against Turkish club Besiktas was played behind closed doors at Villa Park as a punishment for crowd trouble in Brussels at the previous season's semi-final against Anderlecht.

Pat Heard played his last game on 7 December.

Villa lost 2-0 to Penarol of Uruguay in the World Club Championship in Tokyo on 12 December. The line-up was: Rimmer, Jones, Evans, McNaught, Williams, Bremner, Mortimer, Cowans, Morley, Shaw and Withe.

Jimmy Rimmer played his last game on 27 December.

Alan Curbishley became Tony Barton's first signing in a £100,000 move from Birmingham City in March with Robert Hopkins moving in the opposite direction.

Ray Walker made his debut at West Ham on 23 April.

The 2-1 win against Arsenal on 14 May was the last match for both Ken McNaught and David Geddis.

DIVISION ONE

MANAGER: Tony Barton

MATCH	DATE	VENUE	OPPONENTS	RESULT	HT SCORE	SCORE	SCORERS	ATT
1	Aug 28	H	Sunderland	L	1 0	1 3	Cowans	22,945
2	31	A	Everton	L	0 3	0 5		24,029
3	Sep 4	A	Southampton	L	0 1	0 1		17,943
4	8	H	Luton Town	W	3 0	4 1	Mortimer, Withe, Cowans 2 (2 pens)	18,823
5	11	H	Nottingham Forest	W	2 1	4 1	Mortimer, Withe 2, Cowans (pen)	21,224
6	18	A	Manchester City	W	1 0	1 0	Shaw	28,650
7	25	H	Swansea City	W	2 0	2 0	Mortimer, Evans	21,246
8	Oct 2	A	West Bromwich Albion	L	0 0	0 1		25,165
9	9	H	Notts County	L	0 2	1 4	Shaw	8,977
10	16	H	Watford	W	1 0	3 0	Withe, Morley 2	21,572
11	23	A	Norwich City	L	0 0	0 1		14,986
12	30	H	Tottenham Hotspur	W	0 0	4 0	Cowans 2 (1 pen), Morley, Shaw	25,992
13	Nov 6	A	Coventry City	D	0 0	0 0		12,199
14	13	H	Brighton & Hove Albion	W	0 0	1 0	Withe	18,834
15	20	H	Manchester United	W	1 1	2 1	Shaw, Withe	35,487
16	27	A	Stoke City	W	1 0	3 0	Parkin (og), Shaw 2	18,797
17	Dec 4	H	West Ham United	W	0 0	1 0	Cowans (pen)	24,658
18	7	A	Arsenal	L	1 2	1 2	McNaught	17,384
19	18	H	Liverpool	L	2 3	2 4	Shaw, Withe	34,568
20	27	A	Birmingham City	L	0 1	0 3		43,864
21	29	H	Ipswich Town	D	1 1	1 1	Withe	21,912
22	Jan 1	A	Manchester United	L	1 1	1 3	Cowans (pen)	41,545
23	3	H	Southampton	W	1 0	2 0	Cowans (pen), Evans	19,925
24	15	A	Sunderland	L	0 0	0 2		16,052
25	22	H	Manchester City	D	1 1	1 1	Shaw	20,415
26	Feb 5	H	Nottingham Forest	W	1 1	2 1	Withe 2	16,352
27	12	H	Everton	W	1 0	2 0	Morley, Withe	21,117
28	26	A	Watford	L	1 1	1 2	Walters	19,318
29	Mar 5	H	Norwich City	W	1 1	3 2	Withe, Deacy, Shaw	18,624
30	8	H	Notts County	W	1 0	2 0	Withe, Shaw	17,452
31	19	H	Coventry City	W	3 0	4 0	Shaw, Withe 2, Evans	20,509
32	23	A	Tottenham Hotspur	L	0 1	0 2		22,455
33	26	A	Brighton & Hove Albion	D	0 0	0 0		14,648
34	Apr 2	A	Ipswich Town	W	1 1	2 1	Shaw, Withe	20,945
35	4	H	Birmingham City	W	0 0	1 0	Shaw	40,897
36	9	A	Luton Town	L	1 1	1 2	Shaw	10,924
37	19	H	West Bromwich Albion	W	1 0	1 0	Mortimer	26,921
38	23	A	West Ham United	L	0 0	0 2		21,822
39	30	H	Stoke City	W	1 0	4 0	Cowans, McNaught, Morley, Evans	20,944
40	May 2	A	Swansea City	L	1 1	1 2	Shaw	9,173
41	7	A	Liverpool	D	1 0	1 1	Shaw (pen)	39,939
42	14	H	Arsenal	W	1 0	2 1	Shaw, Gibson	24,647

Final League Position: 6th in Division One

1 Own-goal

Appearances
Subs
Goals

FA CUP

3	Jan 8	A	Northampton Town	W	1 0	1 0	Walters	14,529
4	29	H	Wolverhampton Wanderers	W	1 0	1 0	Withe	43,121
5	Feb 19	A	Watford	W	2 0	4 1	Shaw, Morley, Gibson, Cowans	34,330
6	Mar 12	A	Arsenal	L	0 2	0 2		41,774

Appearances
Subs
Goals

FOOTBALL LEAGUE CUP

2F	Oct 6	H	Notts County	L	1 0	1 2	Withe	16,312
2S	26	A	Notts County	L	0 0	0 1		6,921

Appearances
Subs
Goals

EUROPEAN CUP

1F	Sep 15	H	Besiktas	W	3 0	3 1	Withe, Morley, Mortimer	*
1S	29	A	Besiktas	D	0 0	0 0		45,000
2F	Oct 20	A	Dinamo Bucharest	W	1 0	2 0	Shaw 2	80,000
2S	Nov 3	H	Dinamo Bucharest	W	1 1	4 2	Shaw 3, Walters	22,244
3F	Mar 2	H	Juventus	L	0 1	1 2	Cowans	45,531
3S	16	A	Juventus	L	0 2	1 3	Withe	70,000

* Played behind closed doors

Appearances
Subs
Goals

EUROPEAN SUPER CUP

F	Jan 19	A	Barcelona	L	0 0	0 1		45,000
S	26	H	Barcelona *	W	0 0	3 0	Shaw, Cowans, McNaught	31,570

* after extra time

Appearances
Subs
Goals

WORLD CLUB CHAMPIONSHIP

	Dec 12	N	Penarol *	L	0 1	0 2		62,000

* Played at The Tokyo National Stadium

Appearances
Subs
Goals

FINAL LEAGUE TABLE

	P	W	D	L	F	A	P	
Liverpool	42	24	10	8	87	37	82	
Watford	42	22	5	15	74	57	71	
Manchester United	42	19	13	10	56	38	70	
Tottenham Hotspur	42	20	9	13	65	50	69	
Nottingham Forest	42	20	9	13	62	50	69	
Aston Villa	**42**	**21**	**5**	**16**	**62**	**50**	**68**	1F / 1S
Everton	42	18	10	14	66	48	64	2F
West Ham United	42	20	4	18	68	62	64	2S
Ipswich Town	42	15	13	14	64	50	58	3F / 3S
Arsenal	42	16	10	16	58	56	58	
West Bromwich A	42	15	12	15	51	49	57	
Southampton	42	15	12	15	54	58	57	
Stoke City	42	16	9	17	53	64	57	
Norwich City	42	14	12	16	52	58	54	
Notts County	42	15	7	20	55	71	52	
Sunderland	42	12	14	16	48	61	50	
Birmingham City	42	12	14	16	40	55	50	
Luton Town	42	12	13	17	65	84	49	
Coventry City	42	13	9	20	48	59	48	
Manchester City	42	13	8	21	47	70	47	
Swansea City	42	10	11	21	51	69	41	
Brighton and HA	42	9	13	20	38	68	40	

1983/84

SEASON SNIPPETS

Steve McMahon was signed from Everton for £250,000 while 19-year-old striker Paul Rideout arrived from Swindon Town for £350,000, Villa beating off competition from Liverpool to sign the former England schoolboy International.

Members of Villa's triumphant European Cup squad were moving on. Ken McNaught joined West Bromwich Albion on 23 August with David Geddis moving to Barnsley on 24 September.

Villa fans were delighted when Gordon Cowans' proposed move to Italian club Napoli broke down - and then distraught when he suffered a badly broken leg in a pre-season tournament and was ruled out for the whole campaign.

Mervyn Day arrived from Leyton Orient on 11 August.

Paul Birch made his league debut on 29 August.

Mark Jones played his last game on 26 November.

Tony Morley left for West Bromwich Albion on 8 December.

Dean Glover made his debut on 11 January.

The 3-1 home defeat by Liverpool on Friday 20th January was the first league match to be broadcast live on TV from Villa Park.

Steve Foster was transferred from Brighton and made his debut on 14 April with Paul Kerr also playing his first game.

Eamonn Deacy played his last game on 12 May.

DIVISION ONE

MANAGER: Tony Barton

MATCH	DATE	VENUE	OPPONENTS	RESULT	HT SCORE	SCORE	SCORERS	ATT
1	Aug 27	H	West Bromwich Albion	W	3 3	4 3	Evans, Walters, Shaw, Ormsby	30,590
2	29	H	Sunderland	W	0 0	1 0	Walters	21,969
3	Sep 3	A	Queen's Park Rangers	L	0 1	1 2	Withe	16,922
4	7	A	Nottingham Forest	D	1 1	2 2	Withe, Shaw	16,379
5	10	H	Norwich City	W	1 0	1 0	Mortimer	18,887
6	17	A	Liverpool	L	0 0	1 2	Gibson	34,246
7	24	H	Southampton	W	1 0	1 0	Withe	21,209
8	Oct 1	A	Luton Town	L	0 0	0 1		12,747
9	15	H	Birmingham City	W	1 0	1 0	Withe	39,318
10	23	H	Wolverhampton Wanderers	D	1 0	1 1	Withe	13,202
11	29	H	Arsenal	L	1 4	2 6	Morley, Evans (pen)	23,678
12	Nov 5	A	Manchester United	W	1 0	2 1	Withe 2	45,077
13	12	H	Stoke City	D	0 1	1 1	Withe	19,272
14	19	H	Leicester City	W	2 1	3 1	Withe, Rideout, McMahon	19,024
15	26	A	Notts County	L	0 2	2 5	Mortimer, Evans (pen)	8,960
16	Dec 3	H	West Ham United	W	0 0	1 0	Rideout	21,297
17	10	A	Everton	D	0 0	1 1	Rideout	15,814
18	17	H	Ipswich Town	W	1 0	4 0	Withe, Rideout, McMahon, Evans (pen)	16,548
19	26	A	Watford	L	0 2	2 3	Curbishley, Walters	18,276
20	27	H	Tottenham Hotspur	D	0 0	0 0		30,125
21	31	H	Queen's Park Rangers	W	0 0	2 1	Evans (pen), McMahon	19,978
22	Jan 2	A	Southampton	D	1 0	2 2	McMahon, Shaw	18,963
23	14	A	West Bromwich Albion	L	0 0	1 3	Shaw	20,359
24	20	H	Liverpool	L	1 0	1 3	Mortimer	19,566
25	Feb 4	H	Luton Town	D	0 0	0 0		18,656
26	11	A	Norwich City	L	0 0	1 3	Shaw	13,658
27	Feb 18	A	Arsenal	D	0 1	1 1	Evans (pen)	26,640
28	25	H	Wolverhampton Wanderers	W	1 0	4 0	Withe 2, Birch, Walters	18,257
29	Mar 3	A	Manchester United	L	0 1	0 3		32,874
30	10	A	Stoke City	L	0 0	0 1		13,968
31	13	A	Coventry City	D	2 2	3 3	Evans (pen), Withe, Rideout	11,106
32	17	H	Nottingham Forest	W	0 0	1 0	McMahon	16,270
33	24	A	Sunderland	W	1 0	1 0	Walters	11,908
34	31	A	Birmingham City	L	1 1	1 2	Withe	23,993
35	Apr 7	H	Coventry City	W	1 0	2 0	Ormsby, Birch	15,318
36	14	A	Leicester City	L	0 1	0 2		13,366
37	18	A	Tottenham Hotspur	L	1 2	1 2	Walters	18,668
38	21	H	Watford	W	1 1	2 1	Mortimer, Foster	16,110
39	28	H	Notts County	W	1 1	3 1	Walters 2, Withe	13,052
40	May 5	A	West Ham United	W	1 0	1 0	Mortimer	17,393
41	7	H	Everton	L	0 0	0 2		16,792
42	12	A	Ipswich Town	L	1 1	1 2	Withe	19,985

Final League Position: 10th in Division One

Appearances
Subs
Goals

FA CUP

3	Jan 7	H	Norwich City	D	1 1	1 1	Withe	21,454
R	11	A	Norwich City	L	0 1	0 3		16,420

Appearances
Subs
Goals

FOOTBALL LEAGUE CUP

2F	Oct 4	A	Portsmouth	D	0 1	2 2	Gibson, Evans	18,484
2S	26	H	Portsmouth *	W	0 1	3 2	Evans (pen), Withe, Walters	20,898
3	Nov 9	H	Manchester City	W	1 0	3 0	Gibson, Evans, Mortimer	23,922
4	30	A	West Bromwich Albion	W	1 1	2 1	Walters, Mortimer	31,114
5	Jan 17	A	Norwich City	W	2 0	2 0	Shaw, Rideout	21,568
SF1	Feb 15	A	Everton	L	0 1	0 2		40,006
SF2	22	H	Everton	W	0 0	1 0	Rideout	42,426

Appearances
Subs
Goals

* After extra-time

EUFA CUP

1F	Sep 14	A	Vitoria Guimaraes	L	0 0	0 1		28,750
1S	28	H	Vitoria Guimaraes	W	1 0	5 0	Withe 3, Ormsby, Gibson	23,732
2F	Oct 19	A	Moscow Spartak	D	0 0	2 2	Gibson, Walters	50,400
2S	Nov 2	H	Moscow Spartak	L	1 0	1 2	Withe	29,511

Appearances
Subs
Goals

476

FINAL LEAGUE TABLE

	P	W	D	L	F	A	P	
Liverpool	42	22	14	6	73	32	80	
Southampton	42	22	11	9	66	38	77	
Nottingham Forest	42	22	8	12	76	45	74	
Manchester United	42	20	14	8	71	41	74	
Queens Park Rangers	42	22	7	13	67	37	73	2F
Arsenal	42	18	9	15	74	60	63	2S
Everton	42	16	14	12	44	42	62	3
Tottenham Hotspur	42	17	10	15	64	65	61	4
West Ham United	42	17	9	16	60	55	60	SF1
Aston Villa	**42**	**17**	**9**	**16**	**59**	**61**	**60**	SF2
Watford	42	16	9	17	68	77	57	
Ipswich Town	42	15	8	19	55	57	53	
Sunderland	42	13	13	16	42	53	52	
Norwich City	42	12	15	15	48	49	51	
Leicester City	42	13	12	17	65	68	51	
Luton Town	42	14	9	19	53	66	51	1F
West Bromwich A	42	14	9	19	48	62	51	1S
Stoke City	42	13	11	18	44	63	50	2F
Coventry City	42	13	11	18	57	77	50	2S
Birmingham City	42	12	12	18	39	50	48	
Notts County	42	10	11	21	50	72	41	
Wolverhampton W	42	6	11	25	27	80	29	

477

1984/85

SEASON SNIPPETS

Tony Barton's reign as manager came to an end on 18 June 1984 when he sacked and replaced by Shrewsbury Town boss Graham Turner who, at 36 years of age, became the youngest manager in the club's history.

American evangelist Billy Graham held a week long crusade at Villa Park during the summer, attracting crowds totalling 257,181 and included a visit by Cliff Richard.

Villa lost 2-1 to Bayern Munich and 2-0 to Boca Juniors in a pre-season Tournament in Barcelona.

Andy Blair joined Sheffield Wednesday on 7 August.

Eamonn Deacy returned to Ireland.

Des Bremner joined Birmingham City on 27 September.

Didier Six, one of the stars of France's European Championship triumph, joined Villa from Mulhouse on 4 October on a loan deal for the rest of the season.

Steve Foster was transferred to Luton Town on 29 November.

European Cup-winning captain Dennis Mortimer played his last Villa game on 20 October when he substituted Steve McMahon.

Alan Curbishley's last game was on 15 December.

Mervyn Day moved to Leeds United on 1 February.

Peter Withe and Paul Rideout both played their last Villa League game on 11 May.

Villa faced an England XI at the end of the season in a testimonial match for Dennis Mortimer, while George Best turned out in claret and blue against West Bromwich Albion in a match in aid of the Bradford City fire disaster fund.

DIVISION ONE

MANAGER: Graham Turner

MATCH	DATE	VENUE	OPPONENTS	RESULT	HT SCORE	SCORE	SCORERS	ATT
1	Aug 25	H	Coventry City	W	0 0	1 0	Bremner	20,970
2	27	A	Stoke City	W	2 1	3 1	Walters 2, Withe	12,505
3	Sep 1	A	Newcastle United	L	0 0	0 3		31,591
4	5	H	Nottingham Forest	L	0 1	0 5		17,730
5	8	H	Chelsea	W	3 0	4 2	Withe 2, Foster, Rideout	21,494
6	15	A	Watford	D	1 2	3 3	Foster, Withe, McMahon	16,440
7	22	H	Tottenham Hotspur	L	0 0	0 1		22,409
8	29	A	Ipswich Town	L	0 1	0 3		15,378
9	Oct 6	H	Manchester United	W	2 0	3 0	Withe, Evans, Rideout	37,132
10	13	A	Everton	L	1 1	1 2	Withe	25,043
11	20	H	Norwich City	D	1 2	2 2	Withe 2	14,149
12	27	A	Leicester City	L	0 4	0 5		11,885
13	Nov 3	H	West Ham United	D	0 0	0 0		15,709
14	10	A	Arsenal	D	1 1	1 1	Birch	33,193
15	17	H	Southampton	D	2 0	2 2	Withe, Six	13,937
16	24	A	Queen's Park Rangers	L	0 1	0 2		11,689
17	Dec 1	H	Sunderland	W	0 0	1 0	Rideout	14,669
18	8	A	Luton Town	L	0 1	0 1		7,696
19	15	H	Liverpool	D	0 0	0 0		24,007
20	22	H	Newcastle United	W	2 0	4 0	Evans (pen), Rideout 3	14,491
21	26	A	Sheffield Wednesday	D	1 0	1 1	Rideout	30,971
22	29	A	Nottingham Forest	L	2 1	2 3	Gibson, Rideout	17,676
23	Jan 1	H	West Bromwich Albion	W	1 1	3 1	Gibson, Birch, Rideout	31,710
24	19	A	Coventry City	W	1 0	3 0	Walters 2, Rideout	15,290
25	Feb 2	H	Ipswich Town	W	1 0	2 1	Cowans, Gibson	15,051
26	23	A	West Ham United	W	0 0	2 1	Walters, Ormsby	14,855
27	Mar 2	H	Leicester City	L	0 0	0 1		16,285
28	9	A	Norwich City	D	0 0	2 2	Evans 2 (2 pens)	21,120
29	13	H	Arsenal	D	0 0	0 0		15,487
30	16	H	Everton	D	0 1	1 1	Evans (pen)	22,625
31	23	A	Manchester United	L	0 3	0 4		40,941
32	27	H	Stoke City	W	0 0	2 0	Berry (og), Six	10,874
33	30	A	Tottenham Hotspur	W	1 0	2 0	Rideout, Walters	27,971
34	Apr 6	H	Sheffield Wednesday	W	1 0	3 0	Rideout, Ormsby, Evans (pen)	18,308
35	8	A	West Bromwich Albion	L	0 1	0 1		20,936
36	16	A	Chelsea	L	0 2	1 3	Walters	13,267
37	20	A	Southampton	L	0 1	0 2		15,736
38	24	H	Watford	D	1 1	1 1	Walters	11,493
39	27	H	Queen's Park Rangers	W	3 1	5 2	Rideout 2, Withe 2, Walters	12,023
40	May 4	A	Sunderland	W	2 0	4 0	Gibson, Walters, McMahon, Withe	12,467
41	6	H	Luton Town	L	0 1	0 1		14,130
42	11	A	Liverpool	L	0 0	1 2	Birch	33,001

Final League Position: 10th in Division One

1 Own-goal

Appearances
Subs
Goals

FA CUP

3	Jan 5	A	Liverpool	L	0 1	0 3		36,877

Appearances
Subs
Goals

FOOTBALL LEAGUE CUP

2F	Sep 24	A	Scunthorpe United	W	1 0	3 2	Kerr 2, Gibson	6,212
2S	Oct 10	H	Scunthorpe United	W	1 1	3 1	Cowans, Gibson, Rideout	11,421
3	30	A	Queen's Park Rangers	L	0 0	0 1		12,547

Appearances
Subs
Goals

478

Day MR	Williams G	Gibson CJ	Evans AJ	Foster SB	McMahon S	Bremner DG	Walters ME	Withe P	Cowans GS	Mortimer DG	Rideout PD	Dorigo AR	Birch P	Ormsby BTC	Kerr PA	Six D	Spink NP	Curbishley LC	Norton DW	Glover DV	Bradley DM	Walker R	Poole K	Daley AM	MATCH
1	2	3	4	5	6	7	8	9	10	11															1
1	2	3	4	5	6	7	8	9	10	11															2
1	2	3	4	5	6	7	8	9	10	11															3
1	2	3	4	5	6	7	8	9	10	11¹	12¹														4
1		2	4	5	6		11	9	10			8	3	7											5
1		2	4	5	6		11	9	10			8	3	7											6
1	9	2	4	5	6		11		10			8	3	7											7
1	2	3	4				11¹	9	10	6		8		7	5	12¹									8
1	2	3	4		6		12¹	9	10			8	3	7	5		11¹								9
1	2		4		6			9	10			8	3	7	5	12¹	11¹								10
1	2	3		4	6¹			9	10	12¹	8		7	5		11									11
1	2	3	4		6			9	10		8¹		7	5	12¹	11									12
1	2	3	4		6			9	10				7	5	8	11									13
1	2	3	4		6			9	10			12¹	7	5	8	11¹									14
1	2	3	4		6			9	10			12¹	7	5	8¹	11									15
1	2	3	4				8	9	10				7	5		11									16
	2¹	3	4		6		11	9	10		8	12¹		5			1	7							17
	2	3	4		6¹		11		10		8	12¹		5			1	7							18
	2	10	4				11	9			8	3	7	5			1	6							19
	2	10	4		6¹		11	9			8	3	7	5		12¹	1								20
	2	10	4		6		11				8¹	3	7	5		12¹	1								21
	2	10	4		6		11	9			8	3	7	5			1								22
	2	10	4¹		6		11	9	12¹		8	3	7	5			1								23
	2		4		6		11	9			8	3	7	5			1		2	4					24
		7	4		6		11	9	10		8	3		5			1		2						25
	2	6	4				11	9			8	3		5			1								26
	2	6	4		12¹		11	9	10		8¹	3	7	5			1								27
	2	7	4		6¹		11	9	10			3		5	8		1			12¹					28
	2	7	4				11	9	10			3		5	8		1			6					29
	2		4		6		11	9	10			3		5	8	12¹	1			7¹					30
	2	7	4		6		11	9	10			3		5	8		1								31
	2	10	4¹		6		11	9			8	3		5		7	1			12¹					32
	2	10			6		11	9			8	3¹		5		7			4	12¹	1				33
	2	3	4		6		11	9	10		8			5		7				12¹	1				34
	2	10	4		6		11	9			8	3		5		7¹					1				35
	2	10	4		6		11	9			8	3	7	5			1	5							36
	2	10	4				11				9	3	7	5		1				6		8			37
	2	10	4				11	9			8	3		5		1				6		7			38
	2	7	4				11	9	10		8	3		5							1	6			39
	2	8			6		11¹	9	10			3	7		12¹			5	4		1				40
	2	8	4		6		11¹	9	10			3	7					5			1	12¹			41
	2	10	4				11	9			8	3	12¹	5							1	7¹			42
16	38	40	38	8	34	4	35	40	29	5	28	27	24	32	6	13	19	3	2	5	1	4	7	4	
					1		1			1	1		4		4	3				1	3			1	
		4	6	2	1		10	12	1		14			3	2										

| | 4 | 2 | | | 6 | | 11 | 9 | 10 | | 8 | 3 | 7 | 5 | | 1 | | | | | | | | | |
| | 1 | 1 | | | 1 | | 1 | 1 | 1 | | 1 | 1 | 1 | 1 | | 1 | | | | | | | | | |

1	2	3	4	5	6¹		11		10			9	12¹	7		8									
1	2	3			4	6	8¹	9	10		12¹		7	5											2F
1	2	3	4		6			9	10			11	7	5	8¹	12¹									2S
																									3
3	3	3	2	2	3		2	2	3		1	1	3	2	2	1									
											1		1		1	1									
		2							1		1			2											

FINAL LEAGUE TABLE

	P	W	D	L	F	A	P
Everton	42	28	6	8	88	43	90
Liverpool	42	22	11	9	68	35	77
Tottenham Hotspur	42	23	8	11	78	51	77
Manchester United	42	22	10	10	77	47	76
Southampton	42	19	11	12	56	47	68
Chelsea	42	18	12	12	63	48	66
Arsenal	42	19	9	14	61	49	66
Sheffield Wednesday	42	17	14	11	58	45	65
Nottingham Forest	42	19	7	16	56	48	64
Aston Villa	**42**	**15**	**11**	**16**	**60**	**60**	**56**
Watford	42	14	13	15	81	71	55
West Bromwich A	42	16	7	19	58	62	55
Luton Town	42	15	9	18	57	61	54
Newcastle United	42	13	13	16	55	70	52
Leicester City	42	15	6	21	65	73	51
West Ham United	42	13	12	17	51	68	51
Ipswich Town	42	13	11	18	46	57	50
Coventry City	42	15	5	22	47	64	50
Queens Park Rangers	42	13	11	18	53	72	50
Norwich City	42	13	10	19	46	64	49
Sunderland	42	10	10	22	40	62	40
Stoke City	42	3	8	31	24	91	17

1985/86

SEASON SNIPPETS

Having helped Wolverhampton Wanderers to win the League Cup in 1980 and Everton to FA Cup glory in 1984, Scottish striker Andy Gray returned to Villa Park on 15 July for another spell in claret and blue.

On 27 August, Villa signed midfielder Steve Hodge from Nottingham Forest for £400,000.

Steve McMahon departed for Liverpool on 12 September.

On 24 September, Simon Stainrod arrived from Sheffield Wednesday - and scored four goals on his debut, a 4-1 League Cup win at St James' Park against Exeter City.

Brendan Ormsby and Ray Walker both made his last appearances on 26 October.

Colin Gibson left the club on 29 November, moving to Manchester United for £275,000. Manager Graham Turner put the money towards the £400,000 purchase of Paul Elliott from Luton Town.

Brian Little resigned as Villa's youth team coach in January with another former player, Ron Wylie, replacing him.

The attendance of 8,456 against Southampton was the lowest for a league match at Villa Park for 29 years.

Darren Bradley's last game was on 8 March.

Two former players, Andy Blair and Steve Hunt, returned to the club on 14 March.

DIVISION ONE

MANAGER: Graham Turner

MATCH	DATE	VENUE	OPPONENTS	RESULT	HT SCORE	SCORE	SCORERS	ATT
1	Aug 17	A	Manchester United	L	0 0	0 4		49,743
2	21	H	Liverpool	D	1 1	2 2	Shaw, Walters	20,197
3	24	H	Queen's Park Rangers	L	0 1	1 2	Walters	11,896
4	27	A	Southampton	D	0 0	0 0		14,220
5	31	H	Luton Town	W	3 0	3 1	Walters, Hodge, Norton	10,524
6	Sep 4	A	West Bromwich Albion	W	2 0	3 0	Evans (pen), Daley, Walters	17,267
7	7	A	Birmingham City	D	0 0	0 0		24,971
8	14	H	Coventry City	D	1 1	1 1	Hodge	12,198
9	21	A	Ipswich Town	W	2 0	3 0	Walters, Hodge, Birch	11,882
10	28	H	Everton	D	0 0	0 0		22,048
11	Oct 5	A	Arsenal	L	1 2	2 3	Stainrod, Walters	18,869
12	12	H	Nottingham Forest	L	0 0	1 2	Gibson	15,315
13	19	A	West Ham United	L	1 2	1 4	Stainrod	15,034
14	26	H	Newcastle United	L	1 1	1 2	Gray	12,633
15	Nov 2	H	Oxford United	W	1 0	2 0	Evans (pen), Stainrod	12,922
16	9	A	Watford	D	1 0	1 1	Gray	14,085
17	16	H	Sheffield Wednesday	D	1 1	1 1	Gibson	13,849
18	23	A	Chelsea	L	1 1	1 2	Gray	17,509
19	30	H	Tottenham Hotspur	L	0 0	1 2	Walters	14,099
20	Dec 7	A	Liverpool	L	0 1	0 3		29,418
21	14	H	Manchester United	L	1 1	1 3	Hodge	27,626
22	17	A	Queen's Park Rangers	W	1 0	1 0	Birch	8,237
23	26	A	Leicester City	L	1 2	1 3	Walters	13,752
24	28	H	West Bromwich Albion	D	1 0	1 1	Kerr	18,796
25	Jan 1	H	Manchester City	L	0 0	0 1		14,215
26	11	A	Coventry City	D	1 3	3 3	Stainrod, Gray, Elliott	10,326
27	18	A	Luton Town	L	0 1	0 2		10,217
28	Feb 1	H	Southampton	D	0 0	0 0		8,456
29	Mar 1	A	Everton	L	0 0	0 2		32,171
30	8	H	Arsenal	L	0 0	1 4	Walters	10,584
31	15	A	Nottingham Forest	D	0 0	1 1	Walters	12,933
32	19	H	West Ham United	W	1 1	2 1	Hodge 2	11,567
33	22	H	Birmingham City	L	0 2	0 3		26,694
34	29	A	Manchester City	D	1 0	2 2	Hodge, Stainrod	20,935
35	31	H	Leicester City	W	0 0	1 0	Stainrod	12,200
36	Apr 5	A	Oxford United	D	0 0	1 1	Stainrod	11,406
37	9	A	Newcastle United	D	1 1	2 2	Daley, Hunt	20,435
38	12	H	Watford	W	0 1	4 1	Dorigo, Evans (pen), Gray, Stainrod	12,781
39	16	H	Ipswich Town	W	0 0	1 0	Hodge	13,611
40	19	A	Sheffield Wednesday	L	0 1	0 2		19,782
41	26	H	Chelsea	W	1 0	3 1	Norton, Hunt, Stainrod	17,770
42	May 3	A	Tottenham Hotspur	L	1 1	2 4	Stainrod, Elliott	14,854

Final League Position: 16th in Division One

Appearances
Subs
Goals

FA CUP

3	Jan 4	A	Portsmouth	D	1 0	2 2	Kerr, Birch	17,732
R	13	H	Portsmouth *	W	1 0	3 2	Evans (pen), Stainrod 2	14,958
4	25	H	Millwall	D	1 1	1 1	Hodge	12,205
R	29	A	Millwall	L	0 0	0 1		10,273

Appearances
Subs
Goals

* After extra-time

FOOTBALL LEAGUE CUP

2F	Sep 25	A	Exeter City	W	2 0	4 1	Stainrod 4	5,325
2S	Oct 9	H	Exeter City	W	6 0	8 1	Gray 2, Stainrod 2, Ormsby 2, Williams 2, Birch	7,678
3	30	A	Leeds United	W	1 0	3 0	Walters, Stainrod 2	15,444
4	Nov 20	H	West Bromwich Albion	D	0 1	2 2	Evans (pen), Stainrod	20,204
R	27	A	West Bromwich Albion	W	1 0	2 1	Hodge, Walters	18,629
5	Jan 22	H	Arsenal	D	0 1	1 1	Glover	26,093
R	Feb 4	A	Arsenal	W	1 0	2 1	Birch, Evans	33,091
SF1	Mar 4	H	Oxford United	D	1 1	2 2	Birch, Stainrod	23,098
SF2	12	A	Oxford United	L	0 0	1 2	Walters	13,989

Appearances
Subs
Goals

480

FINAL LEAGUE TABLE

	P	W	D	L	F	A	P
Liverpool	42	26	10	6	89	37	88
Everton	42	26	8	8	87	41	86
West Ham United	42	26	6	10	74	40	84
Manchester United	42	22	10	10	70	36	76
Sheffield Wednesday	42	21	10	11	63	54	73
Chelsea	42	20	11	11	57	56	71
Arsenal	42	20	9	13	49	47	69
Nottingham Forest	42	19	11	12	69	53	68
Luton Town	42	18	12	12	61	44	66
Tottenham Hotspur	42	19	8	15	74	52	65
Newcastle United	42	17	12	13	67	72	63
Watford	42	16	11	15	69	62	59
Queens Park Rangers	42	15	7	20	53	64	52
Southampton	42	12	10	20	51	62	46
Manchester City	42	11	12	19	43	57	45
Aston Villa	**42**	**10**	**14**	**18**	**51**	**67**	**44**
Coventry City	42	11	10	21	48	71	43
Oxford United	42	12	12	20	62	80	42
Leicester City	42	10	12	20	54	76	42
Ipswich Town	42	11	8	23	32	55	41
Birmingham City	42	8	5	29	30	73	29
West Bromwich A	42	4	12	26	35	89	24

481

1986/87

SEASON SNIPPETS

Despite the summer arrival of striker Garry Thompson from Sheffield Wednesday, defender Martin Keown from Arsenal and midfielder Neale Cooper from Aberdeen at a combined cost of £920,000, Villa were quoted at only 50-1 by bookmakers Corals for the First Division title.

On 26 August, Villa were the first team to visit Plough Lane for a top flight match, which they lost to newly-promoted Wimbledon. The Dons had fought their way from the Southern League in the space of nine years.

Manager Graham Turner was sacked after the 6-0 defeat at the City Ground against Nottingham Forest, and was replaced by Manchester City boss Billy McNeill MBE. Ironically, both Villa and Manchester City were relegated.

Unsettled midfielder Steve Hodge moved to Tottenham Hotspur for £650,000 on 23 December.

Striker Warren Aspinall became McNeill's only signing, arriving from Everton for £350,000 on 19 February.

Mark Burke made his debut on 18 April.

McNeill was sacked on Friday 8 May, four days after relegation had been confirmed by a 2-1 home defeat at the hands of Sheffield Wednesday. This was the last match for Gary Williams, Kevin Poole and Paul Elliott.

Frank Upton was in charge of the team for the final match of the season, a 3-1 defeat by Manchester United at Old Trafford. Bernard Gallacher made his debut, substitute Stuart Ritchie made his only appearance and it was the last game for Andy M Gray, Tony Dorigo, Phil Robinson and Dean Glover.

DIVISION ONE

MANAGER: Graham Turner (to 14 September) Billy McNeill MBE (from 22 September - 8 May)

MATCH	DATE	VENUE	OPPONENTS	RESULT	HT SCORE	SCORE	SCORERS	ATT
1	Aug 23	H	Tottenham Hotspur	L	0 2	0 3		24,712
2	26	A	Wimbledon	L	1 2	2 3	Evans (pen), Thompson	6,372
3	30	A	Queen's Park Rangers	L	0 0	0 1		10,011
4	Sep 3	H	Luton Town	W	1 0	2 1	Kerr 2	13,122
5	6	H	Oxford United	L	0 0	1 2	Stainrod (pen)	14,668
6	13	A	Nottingham Forest	L	0 2	0 6		17,045
7	20	H	Norwich City	L	0 2	1 4	Stainrod	12,304
8	27	A	Liverpool	D	2 2	3 3	Hodge, Thompson, Evans (pen)	38,322
9	Oct 4	A	Coventry City	W	0 0	1 0	Thompson	19,047
10	11	H	Southampton	W	1 0	3 1	Elliott 2, Evans (pen)	16,211
11	18	A	Watford	L	0 0	2 4	Walters Stainrod	16,420
12	25	H	Newcastle United	W	2 0	2 0	Hodge 2	14,614
13	Nov 1	H	Leicester City	W	0 0	2 0	Stainrod 2	14,529
14	8	A	Manchester City	L	0 1	1 3	Daley	22,875
15	15	H	Chelsea	D	0 0	0 0		17,737
16	22	A	West Ham United	D	0 1	1 1	Thompson	21,959
17	29	H	Arsenal	L	0 1	0 4		21,658
18	Dec 6	A	Sheffield Wednesday	L	1 1	1 2	Evans (pen)	21,144
19	13	H	Manchester United	D	1 1	3 3	Hodge, Thompson, Evans (pen)	29,205
20	20	A	Oxford United	D	2 1	2 2	Thompson, Walters	8,362
21	26	H	Charlton Athletic	W	0 0	2 0	Birch, Daley	16,692
22	27	A	Chelsea	L	0 2	1 4	Elliott	14,637
23	Jan 1	A	Everton	L	0 0	0 3		40,219
24	3	H	Nottingham Forest	D	0 0	0 0		19,159
25	24	A	Tottenham Hotspur	L	0 1	0 3		19,121
26	Feb 7	H	Queen's Park Rangers	L	0 0	0 1		13,109
27	14	A	Luton Town	L	0 2	1 2	Evans (pen)	9,174
28	21	H	Liverpool	D	2 1	2 2	Lawrenson (og), Elliott	32,093
29	28	A	Norwich City	D	1 0	1 1	Elliott	14,849
30	Mar 4	H	Wimbledon	D	0 0	0 0		12,484
31	7	A	Newcastle United	L	1 1	1 2	Daley	21,365
32	21	A	Southampton	L	0 4	0 5		13,686
33	25	H	Watford	D	0 1	1 1	Hunt	12,575
34	28	H	Coventry City	W	0 0	1 0	Birch	18,689
35	Apr 4	A	Manchester City	D	0 0	0 0		18,241
36	11	A	Leicester City	D	0 1	1 1	Walters	11,933
37	18	H	Everton	L	0 0	0 1		31,218
38	20	A	Charlton Athletic	L	U 2	U 3		6,595
39	25	H	West Ham United	W	2 0	4 0	Hunt, Aspinall 2, Stainrod	13,584
40	May 2	A	Arsenal	L	1 2	1 2	Aspinall	18,462
41	4	H	Sheffield Wednesday	L	0 2	1 2	Robinson	15,007
42	9	A	Manchester United	L	0 0	1 3	Birch	35,179

Final League Position: 22nd in Division One

Appearances
Subs
1 Own-goal Goals

FA CUP

3	Jan 10	H	Chelsea	D	0 1	2 2	Cooper, Hunt	21,997
R	21	A	Chelsea *	L	1 0	1 2	Hunt	13,473

Appearances
Subs
Goals

* after extra time

FOOTBALL LEAGUE CUP

2F	Sep 24	A	Reading	D	1 1	1 1	Hodge	9,363
2S	Oct 8	H	Reading	W	2 1	4 1	Hodge, Gray 2, Walters	12,484
3	29	A	Derby County	D	1 0	1 1	Daley	19,374
R	Nov 4	H	Derby County	W	1 1	2 1	Birch, Thompson	19,477
4	18	A	Southampton	L	0 1	1 2	Evans (pen)	13,402

Appearances
Subs
Goals

FOOTBALL LEAGUE FULL MEMBERS' CUP

2	Nov 12	H	Derby County	W	3 1	4 1	Shaw 2, Evans, Daley	5,124
3	Dec 2	A	Ipswich Town	L	0 0	0 1		8,244

Appearances
Subs
Goals

482

FINAL LEAGUE TABLE

	P	W	D	L	F	A	P	
Everton	42	26	8	8	76	31	86	
Liverpool	42	23	8	11	72	42	77	
Tottenham Hotspur	42	21	8	13	68	43	71	
Arsenal	42	20	10	12	58	35	70	
Norwich City	42	17	17	8	53	51	68	
Wimbledon	42	19	9	14	57	50	66	
Luton Town	42	18	12	12	47	45	66	
Nottingham Forest	42	18	11	13	64	51	65	2F
Watford	42	18	9	15	67	54	63	2S
Coventry City	42	17	12	13	50	45	63	3
Manchester United	42	14	14	14	52	45	56	R
Southampton	42	14	10	18	69	68	52	4
Sheffield Wednesday	42	13	13	16	58	59	52	
Chelsea	42	13	13	16	53	64	52	
West Ham United	42	14	10	18	52	67	52	
Queens Park Rangers	42	13	11	18	48	64	50	
Newcastle United	42	12	11	19	47	65	47	2
Oxford United	42	13	18	44	69	46		3
Charlton Athletic	42	11	11	20	45	55	44	
Leicester City	42	11	9	22	54	76	42	
Manchester City	42	8	15	19	36	57	39	
Aston Villa	**42**	**8**	**12**	**22**	**45**	**79**	**36**	

483

1987/88

SEASON SNIPPETS

New manager Graham Taylor had a busy summer in the transfer market. His first signings were defender Steve Sims from his former club Watford for £50,000 and midfielder David Hunt on a free transfer from Notts County. Those two were followed by full-back Kevin Gage from Wimbledon for £110,000 and striker Alan McInally from Celtic for £225,000. Tony Dorigo, meanwhile, joined Chelsea, Paul Elliott moved to Italian club Pisa and Gary Williams linked up with Leeds United.

Taylor's dealings continued into the season, with the arrival of Mark Lillis from Derby County, Andy A Gray from Crystal Palace and Stuart Gray from Barnsley, while Scottish striker Andy M Gray joined West Bromwich Albion and Mark Walters made a £615,000 move to Glasgow Rangers.

Villa won six consecutive away matches in September and early October - a record the club last achieved 90 years earlier.

Gary Shaw's last game was against Ipswich on 16 January.

Graham Taylor described the £200,000 fee he paid Crewe Alexandra for David Platt on 2 February as 'over-the-top' after having to increase his offer because of competition from Watford, by then managed by Taylor's former assistant Steve Harrison.

David Norton's last game was on 4 April.

Gareth Williams made his debut on 9 April.

Warren Aspinall's last Villa league game was on 7 May.

Steve Hunt, who scored in his last game on 21 October, was forced to retire at the end of the season due to a badly-damaged knee.

DIVISION TWO

MANAGER: Graham Taylor

MATCH	DATE	VENUE	OPPONENTS	RESULT	HT SCORE	SCORE	SCORERS	ATT
1	Aug 15	A	Ipswich Town	D	1 1	1 1	O'Donnell (og)	14,805
2	22	H	Birmingham City	L	0 0	0 2		30,870
3	29	A	Hull City	L	1 1	1 2	Aspinall (pen)	8,315
4	31	H	Manchester City	D	1 0	1 1	Gage	16,282
5	Sep 5	A	Leicester City	W	1 0	2 0	Walters, Lillis	10,288
6	8	H	Middlesbrough	L	0 0	0 1		12,665
7	12	H	Barnsley	D	0 0	0 0		12,621
8	16	A	West Bromwich Albion	W	0 0	2 0	Aspinall 2	22,072
9	19	A	Huddersfield Town	W	1 0	1 0	S Hunt	6,884
10	26	H	Sheffield United	D	1 0	1 1	Gage	14,761
11	30	H	Blackburn Rovers	D	1 1	1 1	Aspinall	11,772
12	Oct 3	A	Plymouth Argyle	W	3 1	3 1	Walters 2, Lillis	10,515
13	10	A	Leeds United	W	1 1	3 1	Rennie (og), Aspinall 2	20,698
14	17	H	Bournemouth	D	1 0	1 1	Walters	15,145
15	21	H	Crystal Palace	W	2 1	4 1	Walters 3 (1 pen), S Hunt	12,755
16	24	A	Stoke City	D	0 0	0 0		13,494
17	31	H	Reading	W	0 0	2 1	Blair, Lillis	13,413
18	Nov 3	A	Shrewsbury Town	W	1 1	2 1	Keown, Aspinall	7,089
19	7	H	Millwall	L	1 2	1 2	Keown	13,255
20	14	A	Oldham Athletic	W	1 0	1 0	McInally	6,484
21	28	A	Bradford City	W	2 1	4 2	S Gray 2, Birch, Thompson	15,006
22	Dec 5	H	Swindon Town	W	0 0	2 1	Thompson 2	16,127
23	12	A	Birmingham City	W	1 1	2 1	Thompson 2	27,789
24	18	H	West Bromwich Albion	D	0 0	0 0		24,437
25	26	A	Sheffield United	D	0 0	1 1	Thompson	15,809
26	28	H	Huddersfield Town	D	1 1	1 1	Birch	20,948
27	Jan 1	H	Hull City	W	1 0	5 0	S Gray, Aspinall 2, AA Gray, McInally	19,236
28	2	A	Barnsley	W	1 0	3 1	Aspinall, Birch, McInally	11,542
29	16	A	Ipswich Town	W	1 0	1 0	Keown	20,201
30	23	A	Manchester City	W	1 0	2 0	Daley, Thompson	24,668
31	Feb 6	H	Leicester City	W	2 0	2 1	Lillis, Evans	18,867
32	14	A	Middlesbrough	L	1 0	1 2	Daley	16,957
33	20	A	Blackburn Rovers	L	0 1	2 3	Platt, Thompson	17,356
34	27	H	Plymouth Argyle	W	3 1	5 2	S Gray (pen), Platt, Birch 2, Thompson	16,142
35	Mar 5	A	Bournemouth	W	1 0	2 1	Daley, Platt	10,057
36	12	H	Leeds United	L	0 2	1 2	McInally	19,677
37	19	A	Reading	W	1 0	2 0	Birch, Thompson	10,255
38	26	H	Stoke City	L	0 0	0 1		20,392
39	Apr 2	A	Millwall	L	1 1	1 2	Thompson	13,697
40	4	H	Oldham Athletic	L	1 0	1 2	S Gray	19,138
41	9	A	Crystal Palace	D	1 0	1 1	Platt	16,476
42	23	H	Shrewsbury Town	W	1 0	1 0	Aspinall	18,396
43	May 2	H	Bradford City	W	1 0	1 0	Platt	36,423
44	7	A	Swindon Town	D	0 0	0 0		10,959

Final League Position: 2nd in Division Two

Appearances
Subs
2 Own-goals Goals

FA CUP

| 3 | Jan 9 | A | Leeds United | W | 1 0 | 2 1 | McInally, AA Gray | 29,002 |
| 4 | 31 | H | Liverpool | L | 0 0 | 0 2 | | 46,324 |

Appearances
Subs
Goals

FOOTBALL LEAGUE CUP

2F	Sep 23	A	Middlesbrough	W	1 0	1 0	Aspinall	11,424
2S	Oct 7	H	Middlesbrough	W	1 0	1 0	Birch	11,702
3	28	H	Tottenham Hotspur	W	1 0	2 1	McInally, Aspinall	29,114
4	Nov 18	H	Sheffield Wednesday	L	1 1	1 2	Thompson	25,302

Appearances
Subs
Goals

SIMOD CUP

| 1 | Nov 11 | H | Bradford City | L | 0 3 | 0 5 | | 4,217 |

Appearances
Subs
Goals

484

FINAL LEAGUE TABLE

	P	W	D	L	F	A	P	
Millwall	44	25	7	12	72	52	82	
Aston Villa	**44**	**22**	**12**	**10**	**68**	**41**	**78**	3
Middlesbrough	44	22	12	10	63	36	78	4
Bradford City	44	22	11	11	74	54	77	
Blackburn Rovers	44	21	14	9	68	52	77	
Crystal Palace	44	22	9	13	86	59	75	
Leeds United	44	19	12	13	61	51	69	
Ipswich Town	44	19	9	16	61	52	66	
Manchester City	44	19	8	17	80	60	65	2F / 2S
Oldham Athletic	44	18	11	15	72	64	65	3
Stoke City	44	17	11	16	50	57	62	4
Swindon Town	44	16	11	17	73	60	59	
Leicester City	44	16	11	17	62	61	59	
Barnsley	44	15	12	17	61	62	57	
Hull City	44	14	15	15	54	60	57	
Plymouth Argyle	44	16	8	20	65	67	56	
AFC Bournemouth	44	13	10	21	56	68	49	1
Shrewsbury Town	44	11	16	17	42	54	49	
Birmingham City	44	11	15	18	41	66	48	
West Bromwich A	44	12	11	21	50	69	47	
Sheffield United	44	13	7	24	45	74	46	
Reading	44	10	12	22	44	70	42	
Huddersfield Town	44	6	10	28	41	100	28	

485

1988/89

SEASON SNIPPETS

Defenders Derek Mountfield and Chris Price arrived from Everton and Blackburn Rovers respectively for a combined £600,000 while Gordon Cowans returned from Bari for £250,000. Gary Shaw, meanwhile, was released on a free transfer, as was Andy Blair.

A pre-season testimonial game was staged for long-serving defender Allan Evans, Villa beating Walsall 4-2.

Villa scored 13 goals without reply against Birmingham City, recording 7-0 aggregate success in the League Cup and beating their rivals 6-0 in the Simod Cup.

Ian Olney scored on his debut on 12 October

Lee Butler made his debut on 9 November.

The team headed off to the Holy Land in December, losing 1-0 to the Israel national side in a friendly.

Two strikers left the club. Warren Aspinall moved to Portsmouth and Garry Thompson joined Watford.

Ian Ormondroyd became the club's £650,000 record signing, arriving from Bradford City on 2 February, the same day Nigel Callaghan was transferred from Derby County for a similar fee and Andy A Gray joined Queen's Park Rangers.

The defeat at Derby on 6 May was the only game played by Darrell Duffy and the last for Mark Lillis and David Hunt.

On 13 May, Allan Evans, Martin Keown, Steve Sims and Alan McInally all played their last Villa league game.

DIVISION ONE

MANAGER: Graham Taylor

MATCH	DATE	VENUE	OPPONENTS	RESULT	HT SCORE	SCORE	SCORERS	ATT
1	Aug 27	H	Millwall	D	2 2	2 2	S Gray (pen), McInally	22,449
2	Sep 3	A	Arsenal	W	1 0	3 2	McInally 2, AA Gray	37,417
3	10	H	Liverpool	D	1 0	1 1	McInally	41,409
4	17	A	West Ham United	D	2 0	2 2	McInally 2	19,186
5	24	H	Nottingham Forest	D	1 0	1 1	Gage	23,029
6	Oct 1	A	Sheffield Wednesday	L	0 1	0 1		18,301
7	8	H	Wimbledon	L	0 0	0 1		15,416
8	15	A	Charlton Athletic	D	0 1	2 2	McInally, Platt	7,594
9	22	H	Everton	W	1 0	2 0	Daley, Platt	26,636
10	29	H	Tottenham Hotspur	W	0 0	2 1	Fenwick (og), Daley	26,238
11	Nov 5	A	Manchester United	D	0 1	1 1	Cowans	44,804
12	12	A	Southampton	L	1 1	1 3	Daley	16,107
13	19	H	Derby County	L	0 0	1 2	Mountfield	23,489
14	26	A	Coventry City	L	0 1	1 2	McInally	19,880
15	Dec 3	H	Norwich City	W	1 1	3 1	Gage 2, Platt	19,653
16	10	A	Middlesbrough	D	2 1	3 3	AA Gray, McInally 2	18,096
17	17	A	Luton Town	D	0 1	1 1	M Johnson (og)	8,785
18	26	H	Queen's Park Rangers	W	2 0	2 1	McInally 2	25,106
19	31	H	Arsenal	L	0 2	0 3		32,486
20	Jan 3	A	Liverpool	L	0 0	0 1		39,014
21	14	H	Newcastle United	W	1 1	3 1	AA Gray, Daley, McInally	21,010
22	21	A	Nottingham Forest	L	0 1	0 4		22,662
23	Feb 4	H	Sheffield Wednesday	W	2 0	2 0	Callaghan, Platt	19,334
24	11	A	Wimbledon	L	0 1	0 1		6,201
25	14	A	Everton	D	1 1	1 1	Ormondroyd	20,116
26	25	H	Charlton Athletic	L	1 1	1 2	Cowans	16,481
27	Mar 1	A	Tottenham Hotspur	L	0 1	0 2		19,090
28	12	H	Manchester United	D	0 0	0 0		28,332
29	18	A	Millwall	L	0 1	0 2		13,206
30	25	H	West Ham United	L	0 1	0 1		22,471
31	27	A	Queen's Park Rangers	L	0 0	0 1		11,382
32	Apr 1	H	Luton Town	W	2 1	2 1	Daley, Olney	15,640
33	8	A	Newcastle United	W	1 0	2 1	S Gray, Platt	20,464
34	22	A	Norwich City	D	0 0	2 2	Olney, McInally	14,550
35	29	H	Middlesbrough	D	0 0	1 1	S Gray	18,590
36	May 2	H	Southampton	L	0 2	1 2	S Gray	15,218
37	6	A	Derby County	L	1 1	1 2	Platt	18,121
38	13	H	Coventry City	D	1 0	1 1	Platt	29,906

Final League Position: 17th in Division One

2 Own-goals

Appearances
Subs
Goals

Match 16: Birch replaced Gage on 41 minutes, but was then replaced by Mountfield on 70 minutes

FA CUP

3	Jan 7	A	Crewe Alexandra	W	0 2	3 2	Platt, Gage, McInally	5,500
4	28	H	Wimbledon	L	0 0	0 1		25,043

Appearances
Subs
Goals

FOOTBALL LEAGUE CUP

2F	Sep 27	A	Birmingham City	W	2 0	2 0	Gage, AA Gray	21,177
2S	Oct 12	H	Birmingham City	W	4 0	5 0	Mountfield, Gage 2, Olney, Daley	19,753
3	Nov 2	H	Millwall	W	2 1	3 1	McInally 2, Platt	17,648
4	30	H	Ipswich Town	W	2 0	6 2	McInally 2, Platt 4	16,284
5	Jan 18	A	West Ham United	L	0 1	1 2	Platt	30,110

Appearances
Subs
Goals

SIMOD CUP

1	Nov 9	H	Birmingham City	W	5 0	6 0	Platt, Gallacher, Mountfield, McInally 2, Evans	8,324
2	23	A	Derby County	L	1 1	1 2	McInally	10,086

Appearances
Subs
Goals

FINAL LEAGUE TABLE

	P	W	D	L	F	A	P
Arsenal	38	22	10	6	73	36	76
Liverpool	38	22	10	6	65	28	76
Nottingham Forest	38	17	13	8	64	43	64
Norwich City	38	17	11	10	48	45	62
Derby County	38	17	7	14	40	38	58
Tottenham Hotspur	38	15	12	11	60	46	57
Coventry City	38	14	13	11	47	42	55
Everton	38	14	12	12	50	45	54
Queens Park Rangers	38	14	11	13	43	37	53
Millwall	38	14	11	13	47	52	53
Manchester United	38	13	12	13	45	35	51
Wimbledon	38	14	9	15	50	46	51
Southampton	38	10	15	13	52	66	45
Charlton Athletic	38	10	12	16	44	58	42
Sheffield Wednesday	38	10	12	16	34	51	42
Luton Town	38	10	11	17	42	52	41
Aston Villa	**38**	**9**	**13**	**16**	**45**	**56**	**40**
Middlesbrough	38	9	12	17	44	61	39
West Ham United	38	10	8	20	37	62	38
Newcastle United	38	7	10	21	32	63	31

1989/90

SEASON SNIPPETS

Striker Alan McInally and defender Martin Keown had left the club during the summer, joining Bayern Munich and Everton respectively.

The club's two big summer signings were Danish defender Kent Nielsen from Brondby for £500,000 and Republic of Ireland international Paul McGrath from Manchester United for £425,000. Striker Adrian Heath was also snapped up from Espanyol, but played only eight league matches, plus one substitute appearance, before moving on to Manchester City.

Andy Comyn made his debut on 23 August.

In September, Villa gave trials to two youngsters from Trinidad and Tobago - Colvin Hutchinson and Dwight Yorke. Three months later Yorke signed his first professional contract.

Mark Blake played his first match on 14 October.

Striker Tony Cascarino became the club's £1.5m record signing when he arrived from Millwall on 16 March.

Gareth Williams made his last appearance on 5 May.

David Platt was voted PFA's Player of the Year.

DIVISION ONE

MANAGER: Graham Taylor

MATCH	DATE	VENUE	OPPONENTS	RESULT	HT SCORE	SCORE	SCORERS	ATT
1	Aug 19	A	Nottingham Forest	D	1 0	1 1	Mountfield	26,766
2	23	H	Liverpool	D	0 1	1 1	Platt	35,796
3	26	H	Charlton Athletic	D	1 1	1 1	Olney	15,236
4	29	H	Southampton	L	0 0	1 2	Platt	14,301
5	Sep 9	H	Tottenham Hotspur	W	2 0	2 0	Olney 2	24,769
6	16	A	Sheffield Wednesday	L	0 1	0 1		17,509
7	23	H	Queen's Park Rangers	L	1 2	1 3	Platt	14,170
8	30	H	Derby County	W	1 0	1 0	Platt	16,245
9	Oct 14	A	Luton Town	W	1 0	1 0	Mountfield	9,433
10	22	H	Manchester City	W	1 0	2 0	Daley, Olney	23,354
11	28	A	Crystal Palace	W	0 0	2 1	Platt 2	15,724
12	Nov 5	H	Everton	W	3 0	6 2	Cowans, Olney 2, Platt 2, Nielsen	17,637
13	11	A	Norwich City	L	0 0	0 2		18,186
14	18	H	Coventry City	W	2 1	4 1	Ormondroyd 2, Peake (og), Platt (pen)	22,803
15	25	A	Wimbledon	W	1 0	2 0	Platt, Daley	5,981
16	Dec 2	H	Nottingham Forest	W	1 1	2 1	Olney, Platt	25,757
17	9	A	Liverpool	D	1 0	1 1	Olney	37,435
18	16	A	Millwall	L	0 0	0 2		10,536
19	26	H	Manchester United	W	0 0	3 0	Olney, Platt, Gage	41,247
20	30	H	Arsenal	W	1 0	2 1	Platt, Mountfield	40,665
21	Jan 1	A	Chelsea	W	1 0	3 0	Gage, Daley, Platt	23,990
22	13	A	Charlton Athletic	W	1 0	2 0	Mountfield, McLaughlin (og)	10,460
23	20	H	Southampton	W	1 0	2 1	Daley, Gage	33,118
24	Feb 10	H	Sheffield Wednesday	W	0 0	1 0	Platt	27,168
25	21	A	Tottenham Hotspur	W	0 0	2 0	Ormondroyd, Platt	32,472
26	24	H	Wimbledon	L	0 0	0 3		29,325
27	Mar 4	A	Coventry City	L	0 0	0 0		18,012
28	10	H	Luton Town	W	1 0	2 0	Daley, Platt	22,505
29	17	A	Derby County	W	0 0	1 0	Ormondroyd	20,062
30	20	H	Queen's Park Rangers	D	0 0	1 1	Nielsen	15,856
31	24	H	Crystal Palace	L	0 1	0 1		18,586
32	Apr 1	A	Manchester City	L	1 1	1 2	Cowans	24,797
33	11	A	Arsenal	W	0 0	1 0	Price	30,060
34	14	H	Chelsea	W	1 0	1 0	Cowans	28,361
35	17	A	Manchester United	L	0 2	0 2		44,080
36	21	H	Millwall	W	0 0	1 0	Platt	21,028
37	28	H	Norwich City	D	0 1	3 3	McGrath, Cascarino, Platt	28,988
38	May 5	A	Everton	D	0 1	3 3	Cascarino, Cowans, Daley	29,557

Final League Position: 2nd in Division One

	Appearances / Subs / Goals
2 Own-goals	

FA CUP

3	Jan 6	A	Blackburn Rovers	D	1 1	2 2	Olney, Ormondroyd	14,456
R	10	H	Blackburn Rovers	W	2 1	3 1	Ormondroyd, Daley, May (og)	31,169
4	27	H	Port Vale	W	2 0	6 0	Platt, Birch 2, Olney, S Gray 2	36,532
5	Feb 17	A	West Bromwich Albion	W	1 0	2 0	Mountfield, Daley	26,585
6	Mar 14	A	Oldham Athletic	L	0 1	0 3		19,490

	Appearances / Subs / Goals
1 Own-goal	

FOOTBALL LEAGUE CUP

2F	Sep 20	H	Wolverhampton Wanderers	W	1 0	2 1	Platt, S Gray	27,400
2S	Oct 4	A	Wolverhampton Wanderers	D	1 1	1 1	Mountfield	22,754
3	25	H	West Ham United	D	0 0	0 0		20,898
R	Nov 8	A	West Ham United	L	0 1	0 1		23,833

Appearances / Subs / Goals

ZENITH DATA SYSTEMS CUP

2	Nov 28	A	Hull City	W	0 0	2 1	Mountfield, Platt	2,888
3	Dec 22	H	Nottingham Forest	W	0 1	2 1	Platt (pen), Mountfield	6,530
4	Jan 17	A	Leeds United	W	0 0	2 0	S Gray, Platt (pen)	17,543
NF1	30	H	Middlesbrough *	L	1 1	1 2	Birch	16,457
NF2	Feb 6	A	Middlesbrough **	L	1 0	1 2	S Gray	20,806

Appearances / Subs / Goals

* Northern Area Final (1st leg)
** Northern Area Final (2nd leg) after extra time

488

FINAL LEAGUE TABLE

	P	W	D	L	F	A	P	
Liverpool	38	23	10	5	78	37	79	
Aston Villa	**38**	**21**	**7**	**10**	**57**	**38**	**70**	
Tottenham Hotspur	38	19	6	13	59	47	63	2F
Arsenal	38	18	8	12	54	38	62	2S
Chelsea	38	16	12	10	58	50	60	3
Everton	38	17	8	13	57	46	59	R
Southampton	38	15	10	13	71	63	55	
Wimbledon	38	13	16	9	47	40	55	
Nottingham Forest	38	15	9	14	55	47	54	
Norwich City	38	13	14	11	44	42	53	
Queens Park Rangers	38	13	11	14	45	44	50	2
Coventry City	38	14	7	17	39	59	49	3
Manchester United	38	13	9	16	46	47	48	4
Manchester City	38	12	12	14	43	52	48	NF1
Crystal Palace	38	13	9	16	42	66	48	NF2
Derby County	38	13	7	18	43	40	46	
Luton Town	38	10	13	15	43	57	43	
Sheffield Wednesday	38	11	10	17	35	51	43	
Charlton Athletic	38	7	9	22	31	57	30	
Millwall	38	5	11	22	39	65	26	

489

1990/91

SEASON SNIPPETS

With Graham Taylor appointed England coach, Czech National boss, Dr Jozef Venglos became the club's first overseas manager on Saturday 21 July.

Former manager Joe Mercer died on 9 August, his 76th birthday.

Along with Manchester United, Villa were the first club to return to European competition following a ban on English clubs which had operated for five years. While United played in the Cup Winners' Cup, Villa started their UEFA Cup campaign with a victory over Banik Ostrava on 19 September.

Bernard Gallacher played his last game on 3 November.

Villa made their UEFA Cup exit in round two, surrendering a 2-0 first leg advantage as they went down 3 - 2 on aggregate to Italian giants Inter Milan on 7 November.

Ivo Stas, who had impressed for Banik Ostrava in the first round, joined Villa for £500,000 on 15 November, but Stas was beset by injury problems and never played a competitive Villa match.

Assistant Manager John Ward left the club on 8 January and was replaced by European Cup hero Peter Withe.

Nigel Callaghan's last game was on 2 February.

On 4 February, Peter Withe, now 39 years old, played in a Central League match against Coventry City.

Neil Cox was signed from Scunthorpe United on 11 February, but his first-team debut would not come until March 1992.

On 9 March, Gary Penrice, signed from Watford for £1m, became the only player to make his debut during the season. The match was Stuart Gray's last.

Lee Butler made his last appearance on 13 April.

Andy Comyn's last game was on 23 April.

Kevin Gage, David Platt and Tony Cascarino all played their last game on 11 May.

Jozef Venglos stood down as Manager on 28 May after Villa had only narrowly avoided relegation.

490

DIVISION ONE

MANAGER: Dr Jozef Venglos

MATCH	DATE	VENUE	OPPONENTS	RESULT	HT SCORE	SCORE	SCORERS	ATT
1	Aug 25	H	Southampton	D	1 1	1 1	Cascarino	29,542
2	Sep 1	A	Liverpool	L	1 1	1 2	Platt	38,061
3	5	A	Manchester City	L	0 0	1 2	Platt (pen)	30,199
4	8	H	Coventry City	W	1 0	2 1	Platt (pen), Cascarino	27,001
5	15	A	Derby County	W	1 0	2 0	Daley, Platt	17,524
6	22	H	Queen's Park Rangers	D	2 2	2 2	Mountfield, Ormondroyd	23,301
7	29	A	Tottenham Hotspur	L	1 1	1 2	Platt	34,939
8	Oct 6	H	Sunderland	W	1 0	3 0	Olney, Daley, Platt	26,017
9	20	A	Wimbledon	D	0 0	0 0		6,946
10	27	H	Leeds United	D	0 0	0 0		24,219
11	Nov 3	A	Chelsea	L	0 1	0 1		23,555
12	10	H	Nottingham Forest	D	0 0	1 1	Nielsen	25,797
13	17	A	Norwich City	L	0 1	0 2		17,243
14	24	A	Luton Town	L	0 1	0 2		10,071
15	Dec 1	H	Sheffield United	W	1 0	2 1	Platt, Price	21,713
16	15	A	Southampton	D	0 1	1 1	Platt (pen)	15,128
17	23	H	Arsenal	D	0 0	0 0		22,687
18	26	A	Everton	L	0 0	0 1		27,816
19	29	A	Manchester United	D	1 1	1 1	Pallister (og)	47,485
20	Jan 1	H	Crystal Palace	W	0 0	2 0	Platt 2	25,523
21	12	A	Liverpool	D	0 0	0 0		40,026
22	19	A	Coventry City	L	0 0	1 2	Platt	15,696
23	Feb 2	H	Derby County	W	1 1	3 2	Cowans, Cascarino, Yorke	21,852
24	23	A	Nottingham Forest	D	0 1	2 2	Cascarino, Mountfield	22,036
25	Mar 2	A	Sheffield United	L	0 0	1 2	Mountfield	22,074
26	9	H	Luton Town	L	0 2	1 2	Cascarino	20,587
27	16	H	Tottenham Hotspur	W	2 0	3 2	Platt 3	32,638
28	23	A	Sunderland	W	1 0	3 1	Cascarino 2, Platt	21,182
29	30	H	Everton	D	0 1	2 2	Platt, Olney	27,660
30	Apr 3	A	Arsenal	L	0 1	0 5		41,867
31	6	H	Manchester United	D	0 0	1 1	Cascarino	33,307
32	10	A	Queen's Park Rangers	L	1 0	1 2	Platt	11,539
33	13	A	Crystal Palace	D	0 0	0 0		18,331
34	20	H	Wimbledon	L	1 1	1 2	Olney	17,001
35	23	H	Manchester City	L	0 2	1 5	Platt (pen)	24,168
36	May 4	A	Leeds United	L	1 2	2 5	Nielsen, Mountfield	29,188
37	8	H	Norwich City	W	1 1	2 1	Bowen (og), Yorke	16,697
38	11	H	Chelsea	D	1 2	2 2	Cascarino, Platt (pen)	27,866

Final League Position: 17th in Division One

	Appearances
	Subs
2 Own-goals	Goals

FA CUP

3	Jan 5	H	Wimbledon	D	0 1	1 1	S Gray	19,305
R	9	A	Wimbledon *	L	0 0	0 1		7,382

	Appearances
	Subs
	Goals

* After extra-time

FOOTBALL LEAGUE CUP

2F	Sep 26	H	Barnsley	W	0 0	1 0	Platt	14,471
2S	Oct 9	A	Barnsley	W	1 0	1 0	Daley	13,924
3	31	H	Millwall	W	0 0	2 0	Cascarino, Platt (pen)	15,117
4	Nov 28	H	Middlesbrough	W	1 0	3 2	Ormondroyd, Daley, Platt (pen)	17,317
5	Jan 16	A	Leeds United	L	0 1	1 4	Ormondroyd	28,176

	Appearances
	Subs
	Goals

UEFA CUP

1F	Sep 19	H	Banik Ostrava	W	1 1	3 1	Platt, Mountfield, Olney	27,317
1S	Oct 3	A	Banik Ostrava	W	0 1	2 1	Mountfield, Stas (og)	25,000
2F	Oct 24	H	Internazionale Milan	W	1 0	2 0	Nielsen, Platt	36,461
2S	Nov 7	A	Internazionale Milan	L	0 1	0 3		75,580

	Appearances
	Subs
1 Own-goal	Goals

Appearances

	Spink NP	Price CJ	Gray S	McGrath P	Mountfield DN	Nielsen K	Daley AM	Platt DA	Olney ID	Cowans GS	Cascarino AG	Gage KW	Gallacher B	Yorke D	Ormondroyd I	Birch P	Comyn AJ	Blake MA	Butler LS	Callaghan NI	Penrice GK	MATCH
	1	2	3	4	5	6	7	8	9	10	11											1
	1	2	3	4	5	6	7	8		10	11	9										2
	1	2	3	4	5¹	6	7	8	12¹	10	11	9										3
	1	2		4	5	6	7	8	9¹	10	11		3	12¹								4
	1	2	3	4	5	6	7	8	9	10	11	9										5
	1	2	3	4	5	6	7	8	9¹	10				12¹	11							6
	1	2	3	4	5	6	7	8	9¹	10				12¹	11							7
	1	2	3	4	5	6	7	8	9²	10	13²			12¹	11¹							8
	1	2	3		5	6	7	8		10	11			9¹	12¹	4						9
	1	2	3		5	6	7	8		10	11				9	4						10
	1	2		4	5	6	7¹	8		10	11		3	12¹	9							11
	1	2	3	4	5	6	7	8	9	10	11											12
	1	2	3	4	5	6	7	8	9	10	11											13
	1	2	3	4	5²	6	7	8		10	11			13²	12¹		9¹					14
	1	2	3	4		6	7	8	9¹	10	12¹			11		5						15
	1	2	3	4		6	7	8		10	11			12¹	9¹	5²	13²					16
	1	2	3	4		6	7	8		10	11				9	5						17
	1	2	3		5¹	6	7	8		10	11			12¹	9							18
	1	2	3	4	5	6	7¹	8		10	11			9	12¹							19
		2	3	4	5	6		8		10	9			7	11				1			20
	1	2		4		6		8		10	9	3		7			5		11			21
	1	2	3	4		6		8		10	9	11¹		12¹	13²	7	5²					22
	1	2	3	4	5	6	7			10	9	8		12¹	11		5		11¹			23
	1	2		4	5	6				10	9	3		7¹	11		12¹	8				24
	1	2	11	4	5	6			12¹	10	9	3		7			8¹					25
	1	2	3	4	5²	6¹		8	13²	10	9	12¹		7					11			26
	1	2		4	5	6		8	12¹	10	9	3		7¹					11			27
	1	2		4	5	6		8		10	9	3					11		7			28
	1	2		4	5	6¹		8	12¹	10	9	3					11		7			29
	1¹	2		4	5			8		10	9	3			11		6	12¹	7			30
		2		4	5	6		8	7¹	10	9	3		12¹	11				1			31
		2		4	5¹	6		8	7	10	9	3			11				1			32
		2		4	5	6		8	7¹	10	9	3			11				12¹			33
	1	2			5	6	12¹	8	7	10	9	3		11¹			4²		13²			34
	1	2		4		6	7	8	9	10	12¹	3					5¹		11			35
	1	2		4	5¹	6		8	7¹	10		3		12¹	11							36
	1	2		4	5	6	7¹	8		10	9	3		12¹			11¹		7			37
	1	2		4	5	6		8		10	9	3		11					7			38
	34	38	22	35	32	37	22	35	13	38	33	20	2	8	13	6	9	6	4	2	9	
							1		5		3	1		10	5	2	2	1			3	
			1		4	2	2	19	3	1	9			2	1							

| | 1 | 2 | 3 | 4 | | 6 | | 8 | | 10 | 9 | | 7 | 11 | 13² | 5² | | | 12¹ | | | 3 |
| | 1 | 2 | 3¹ | 4 | | 6 | | 8 | | 10 | 9 | | 7 | | 12¹ | 5 | | | 11 | | | R |

| | 2 | 2 | 2 | 2 | | 2 | | 2 | | 2 | 2 | | 1 | 2 | | 2 | | | 1 | | | |
| | | | 1 | | | | | | | | | | | | 2 | | | | 1 | | | |

	1	2	3	4		6		8		10	9			7	11¹	13²	5²		12¹			3
	1	2	3	4		5		7		9¹	10	12¹			11		6					2F
	1	2	3¹		5	6	7	8	9	10	11			9	12¹	4						2S
	1	2	3	4	5	6	7	8¹	9	10					11	12¹						4
	1	2	3	4		6		8		10	9		7	12¹	5¹				11			5
	5	5	5	4	4	4	4	5	3	5	2		1	3	2	2	1					
									1		1			1	3							
					2	3			1					2								

	1	2	3	4	5	6	7	8	13²	10	11²	9¹			12¹							1F
	1	2	3	4	5	6	7	8	9	10				11								1S
	1	2	3		5	6	7	8		10	11				9	4						2F
	1	2	3	4	5¹	6	7	8	12¹	10	11				9							2S
	4	4	4	3	4	4	4	4	1	4	3	1			2	1						
					1				2		1				1							
								2	1		2	1										

FINAL LEAGUE TABLE

	P	W	D	L	F	A	P	
Arsenal	38	24	13	1	74	18	83	
Liverpool	38	23	7	8	77	40	76	2F
Crystal Palace	38	20	9	9	50	41	69	2S
Leeds United	38	19	7	12	65	47	64	3
Manchester City	38	17	11	10	64	53	62	4
Manchester United	38	16	12	10	58	45	59	5
Wimbledon	38	14	14	10	53	46	56	
Nottingham Forest	38	14	12	12	65	50	54	
Everton	38	13	12	13	50	46	51	
Tottenham Hotspur	38	11	16	11	51	50	49	
Chelsea	38	13	10	15	58	69	49	1F
Queens Park Rangers	38	12	10	16	44	53	46	1S
Sheffield United	38	13	7	18	36	55	46	2F
Southampton	38	12	9	17	58	69	45	2S
Norwich City	38	13	6	19	41	64	45	
Coventry City	38	11	11	16	42	49	44	
Aston Villa	**38**	**9**	**14**	**15**	**46**	**58**	**41**	
Luton Town	38	10	7	21	42	61	37	
Sunderland	38	8	10	20	38	60	34	
Derby County	38	5	9	24	37	75	24	

491

1991/92

SEASON SNIPPETS

Ron Atkinson arrived from Sheffield Wednesday to replace the sacked Jozef Venglos and immediately set about reshaping the team. Atkinson's summer spending spree featured Dalian Atkinson for £1.6m, Kevin Richardson for £450,000 from Spanish club Real Sociedad, Steve Staunton at a cost £1.1m from Liverpool, Shaun Teale from Bournemouth for £300,000, Cyrille Regis was signed on a free transfer from Coventry City, Ugo Ehiogu from West Bromwich Albion for £40,000, Paul Mortimer for a fee of £350,000 from Charlton Athletic, Dariusz Kubicki from Legia Warsaw for £200,000 and Les Sealey from Manchester United on a free transfer.

David Platt joined Italian club Bari for £5.5m and Tony Cascarino headed to Celtic for £1.1m.

Cyrille Regis, Dalian Atkinson and Steve Staunton each scored when making their debut in the opening day's 3-2 win at Sheffield Wednesday.

Paul Mortimer's Villa career lasted only until 18 October when he was sold to Crystal Palace for £500,000.

Bryan Small made his debut on 19 October.

Gordon Cowans joined Blackburn Rovers on 28 November.

Alan McLoughlin, on loan from Southampton, played in the Zeneth Data Systems Cup win on 23 October.

On 29 November, Garry Parker arrived from Nottingham Forest in a £650,000 deal.

Steve Froggatt made his debut in the Boxing Day win.

On 3 February Derek Mountfield joined Wolverhampton Wanderers for £150,000.

Earl Barrett became Villa's £1.7m record signing when he arrived from Oldham Athletic on 25 February.

Villa lost 1-0 at home to Bari on 17 March in a friendly organised as part of David Platt's move to Italy. Ian Olney missed a penalty and Richard Crisp made his first-team debut.

Ian Olney was booked after just 15 seconds on 31 March following a foul on Sheffield United goalkeeper Mel Rees.

Nine of the twelve players against Tottenham in the FA Cup third-round game on 5 January were making their FA Cup debuts for Villa. Only McGrath, Daley and Yorke had previously represented Villa in this competition.

Other players making their Villa debut during the season included Matthias Breitkreutz, Martin Carruthers, Neil Cox, Stefan Beinlich and Mark Bosnich.

492

DIVISION ONE

MANAGER: Ron Atkinson

MATCH	DATE	VENUE	OPPONENTS	RESULT	HT SCORE	SCORE	SCORERS	ATT
1	Aug 17	A	Sheffield Wednesday	W	1 2	3 2	Regis, Atkinson, Staunton	36,749
2	21	H	Manchester United	L	0 1	0 1		39,995
3	24	H	Arsenal	W	1 1	3 1	Staunton (pen), Penrice, Daley	29,684
4	28	A	West Ham United	L	0 0	1 3	Daley	23,644
5	31	A	Southampton	D	1 1	1 1	Richardson	15,113
6	Sep 4	H	Crystal Palace	L	0 1	0 1		20,740
7	7	H	Tottenham Hotspur	D	0 0	0 0		33,096
8	14	A	Liverpool	D	1 1	1 1	Richardson	38,400
9	18	A	Chelsea	L	0 1	0 2		17,182
10	21	H	Nottingham Forest	W	0 1	3 1	Blake, Richardson, Yorke	28,506
11	28	A	Coventry City	L	0 1	0 1		17,831
12	Oct 5	H	Luton Town	W	1 0	4 0	Richardson, Regis, Yorke, Mortimer	18,722
13	19	A	Everton	W	1 0	2 0	Regis, Daley	28,116
14	26	H	Wimbledon	W	2 0	2 1	Olney, Yorke	16,928
15	Nov 2	A	Queen's Park Rangers	W	1 0	1 0	Yorke	10,642
16	16	H	Notts County	W	1 0	1 0	Yorke	23,020
17	24	A	Leeds United	L	0 1	1 4	Yorke	23,713
18	30	H	Oldham Athletic	L	1 1	2 3	Blake, Regis	15,370
19	Dec 7	H	Manchester City	W	2 0	3 1	Regis, Yorke, Daley	26,265
20	14	A	Sheffield United	L	0 1	0 2		18,401
21	26	H	West Ham United	W	2 0	3 1	Yorke, Daley, Richardson	31,959
22	28	H	Southampton	W	1 0	2 1	Regis, Yorke	23,094
23	Jan 1	A	Norwich City	L	0 0	1 2	Regis	15,318
24	11	A	Arsenal	D	0 0	0 0		31,406
25	18	H	Sheffield Wednesday	L	0 0	0 1		28,036
26	22	A	Manchester United	L	0 0	0 1		45,022
27	Feb 2	H	Everton	D	0 0	0 0		17,451
28	8	A	Wimbledon	L	0 1	0 2		5,034
29	22	H	Oldham Athletic	W	0 0	1 0	Regis	20,609
30	29	A	Manchester City	L	0 1	0 2		28,268
31	Mar 3	A	Leeds United	D	0 0	0 0		29,655
32	10	A	Notts County	D	0 0	0 0		8,391
33	14	H	Queen's Park Rangers	L	0 0	0 1		19,630
34	21	A	Crystal Palace	D	0 0	0 0		15,368
35	28	H	Norwich City	W	0 0	1 0	Staunton	16,985
36	31	H	Sheffield United	D	0 0	1 1	Regis	15,745
37	Apr 4	A	Tottenham Hotspur	W	2 2	5 2	Richardson, Olney, Yorke, Daley, Regis	26,370
38	11	H	Liverpool	W	0 0	1 0	Daley	35,755
39	18	A	Nottingham Forest	L	0 1	0 2		22,800
40	20	H	Chelsea	W	1 0	3 1	Staunton, McGrath, Parker	19,269
41	25	A	Luton Town	L	0 1	0 2		11,178
42	May 2	H	Coventry City	W	2 0	2 0	Regis, Yorke	31,984

Final League Position: 7th in Division One

Appearances
Subs
Goals

FA CUP

3	Jan 5	H	Tottenham Hotspur	D	0 0	0 0		29,316
R	14	A	Tottenham Hotspur	W	1 0	1 0	Yorke	25,462
4	Feb 5	A	Derby County	W	4 2	4 3	Yorke 3, Parker	22,452
5	16	A	Swindon Town	W	0 1	2 1	Yorke, Froggatt	16,402
6	Mar 8	A	Liverpool	L	0 0	0 1		29,109

Appearances
Subs
Goals

FOOTBALL LEAGUE CUP

2F	Sep 25	A	Grimsby Town	D	0 0	0 0		13,835
2S	Oct 9	H	Grimsby Town *	D	0 0	1 1	Teale	15,338

Appearances
Subs
Goals

* After extra-time - Aston Villa lost on away goals rule

ZENITH DATA SYSTEMS CUP

2	Oct 23	A	Coventry City	W	1 0	2 0	Olney, Yorke	6,447
3	Nov 19	H	Nottingham Forest	L	0 1	0 2		7,859

Appearances
Subs
Goals

FINAL LEAGUE TABLE

	P	W	D	L	F	A	P
Leeds United	42	22	16	4	74	37	82
Manchester United	42	21	15	6	63	33	78
Sheffield Wednesday	42	21	12	9	62	49	75
Arsenal	42	19	15	8	81	46	72
Manchester City	42	20	10	12	61	48	70
Liverpool	42	16	16	10	47	40	64
Aston Villa	**42**	**17**	**9**	**16**	**48**	**44**	**60**
Nottingham Forest	42	16	11	15	60	58	59
Sheffield United	42	16	9	17	65	63	57
Crystal Palace	42	14	15	13	53	61	57
Queens Park Rangers	42	12	18	12	48	47	54
Everton	42	13	14	15	52	51	53
Wimbledon	42	13	14	15	53	53	53
Chelsea	42	13	14	15	50	60	53
Tottenham Hotspur	42	15	7	20	58	63	52
Southampton	42	14	10	18	39	55	52
Oldham Athletic	42	14	9	19	63	67	51
Norwich City	42	12	12	19	47	63	45
Coventry City	42	11	11	20	35	44	44
Luton Town	42	10	12	20	38	71	42
Notts County	42	10	10	22	40	62	40
West Ham United	42	9	11	22	37	59	38

493

1992/93

SEASON SNIPPETS

On 15 August Dalian Atkinson scored Villa's first ever Premier League goal in the 84th minute of the 1-1 draw at Portman Road. Ray Houghton made his Villa league debut.

On 8 September, Villa beat Birmingham City 2-0 in a testimonial match for Jimmy Dugdale. Villa gave a trial to Canadian international Alec Bunbury.

Frank McAvennie was taken on trial and made his debut on 22 August. McAvennie set up Villa's equalising goal, but his last appearance came on 5 September.

Dean Saunders made his debut on 13 September. Villa paid a club record £2.3m for Saunders from Liverpool and on his home debut against the Merseysiders on 19 September, he scored twice in a 4-2 win.

Mark Blake's last appearance came on 26 September.

Dalian Atkinson scored a spectacular solo goal against Wimbledon at Selhurst Park on 3 October which was voted BBC 'Goal of the Month' and later 'Goal of the Season'.

David Farrell made his debut on 24 October.

On 20 February, Mark Bosnich and Jason Kearton were the first Australian goalkeepers to face each other in an English league match. Villa beat Everton 2-1.

Cyrille Regis played his last game on 24 March.

Martin Carruthers made his last appearance on 9 May.

On 10 May, Villa beat Stoke City 4-1 in a testimonial match for Gordon Cowans who was a Blackburn Rovers player at the time, but returned on 1 June for a third spell at Villa Park.

PREMIER LEAGUE

MANAGER: Ron Atkinson

MATCH	DATE	VENUE	OPPONENTS	RESULT	HT SCORE	SCORE	SCORERS	ATT
1	Aug 15	A	Ipswich Town	D	0 1	1 1	Atkinson	16,977
2	19	H	Leeds United	D	0 0	1 1	Atkinson	29,151
3	22	H	Southampton	D	0 0	1 1	Atkinson	17,894
4	25	A	Everton	L	0 0	0 1		22,373
5	29	A	Sheffield United	W	1 0	2 0	Parker 2	18,773
6	Sep 2	H	Chelsea	L	1 2	1 3	Richardson	19,125
7	5	H	Crystal Palace	W	2 0	3 0	Yorke, Staunton, Froggatt	17,120
8	13	A	Leeds United	D	1 0	1 1	Parker	27,815
9	19	H	Liverpool	W	1 1	4 2	Saunders 2, Atkinson, Parker	37,863
10	26	A	Middlesbrough	W	1 0	3 2	Saunders 2, Atkinson	20,905
11	Oct 3	A	Wimbledon	W	2 1	3 2	Saunders 2, Atkinson	6,849
12	19	H	Blackburn Rovers	D	0 0	0 0		30,398
13	24	A	Oldham Athletic	D	0 1	1 1	Atkinson	13,457
14	Nov 1	H	Queen's Park Rangers	W	1 0	2 0	Saunders, Atkinson	20,140
15	7	H	Manchester United	W	1 0	1 0	Atkinson	39,063
16	21	A	Tottenham Hotspur	D	0 0	0 0		32,852
17	28	H	Norwich City	L	0 0	1 2	Houghton, Parker	28,837
18	Dec 5	A	Sheffield Wednesday	W	1 1	2 1	Atkinson 2	29,964
19	12	H	Nottingham Forest	W	1 1	2 1	Regis, McGrath	29,015
20	19	A	Manchester City	D	1 0	1 1	Parker	23,525
21	26	A	Coventry City	L	0 0	0 3		24,135
22	28	H	Arsenal	W	1 0	1 0	Saunders (pen)	35,170
23	Jan 9	A	Liverpool	W	0 1	2 1	Parker, Saunders	40,826
24	17	A	Middlesbrough	W	3 0	5 1	Parker, McGrath, Yorke, Saunders, Teale	19,977
25	27	H	Sheffield United	W	0 0	3 1	McGrath, Kamara (og), Richardson	20,266
26	30	A	Southampton	L	0 1	0 2		19,087
27	Feb 6	H	Ipswich Town	W	2 0	2 0	Yorke, Saunders	25,395
28	10	A	Crystal Palace	L	0 1	0 1		12,270
29	13	A	Chelsea	W	1 0	1 0	Houghton	20,081
30	20	H	Everton	W	2 1	2 1	Cox, Barrett	32,913
31	27	H	Wimbledon	W	0 0	1 0	Yorke	34,496
32	Mar 10	H	Tottenham Hotspur	D	0 0	0 0		37,727
33	14	A	Manchester United	D	1 1	1 1	Staunton	36,163
34	20	H	Sheffield Wednesday	W	1 0	2 0	Yorke 2	38,024
35	24	A	Norwich City	L	0 0	0 1		19,528
36	Apr 4	A	Nottingham Forest	W	0 0	1 0	McGrath	26,742
37	10	H	Coventry City	D	0 0	0 0		38,543
38	12	A	Arsenal	W	0 0	1 0	Daley	27,125
39	18	H	Manchester City	W	0 1	3 1	Saunders, Parker (pen), Houghton	33,108
40	21	A	Blackburn Rovers	L	0 3	0 3		15,127
41	May 2	H	Oldham Athletic	L	0 1	0 1		37,247
42	9	A	Queen's Park Rangers	L	1 0	1 2	Daley	18,904

Final League Position: 2nd in Premier League

Appearances
Subs
1 Own-goal   Goals

FA CUP

3	Jan 2	H	Bristol Rovers	D	1 0	1 1	Cox	27,048
R	20	A	Bristol Rovers	W	1 0	3 0	Saunders 2, Houghton	8,880
4	23	H	Wimbledon	D	1 1	1 1	Yorke	21,088
R	Feb 3	A	Wimbledon *	D	0 0	0 0		8,048

Appearances
Subs
Goals

*After extra-time: Aston Villa lost 5-6 on penalties

FOOTBALL LEAGUE CUP

2F	Sep 23	A	Oxford United	W	0 0	2 1	McGrath, Teale	8,837
2S	Oct 7	H	Oxford United	W	1 0	2 1	Atkinson, Richardson	19,808
3	28	H	Manchester United	W	1 0	1 0	Saunders	35,964
4	Dec 2	H	Ipswich Town	D	0 0	2 2	Atkinson, Saunders	21,545
R	15	A	Ipswich Town	L	0 0	0 1		19,196

Appearances
Subs
Goals

From the start of the Premier League in 1992 pitch time minutes for each player are shown

Spink NP (GK)	Barrett ED	Staunton S	Teale S	McGrath P	Richardson K	Daley AM	Parker GS	Houghton RJ	Atkinson DR	Froggatt SJ	Regis C	Yorke D	McAvennie F	Ehiogu U	Saunders DN	Blake MA	Small B	Farrell DW	Bosnich MJ (GK)	Cox NJ	Breitkreutz M	Beinlich S	Carruthers MG	Kubicki D	MATCH
90	90	90	90	90	52	90	90	90	90	90	38¹														1
90	90	90	90	90	90	90	90	90	90		61¹	29													2
90	90	90	90	90		90	90	90	76		37	53¹	14²												3
90	90	90	90	90	90	89	90	90	90		1¹														4
90	90	90	90	90		90	90	90	90	72			18¹												5
90	90	90	90	90		90	90	90	90	70		20¹													6
90	90	90	90	90		90	90	90	90		73	17¹													7
90	90	90	90	90		90	90	90	90					90											8
90	90	90	90	90		90	90	90	90					90											9
90	90	90	90	90		87	90	90	71		19¹			90	3²										10
90	90	90	90	90		90	90	90	45		45¹			90											11
90	90	90	90	90		90	90	90	45					90	45¹										12
90	90	90	90	90		90	90				74			90	90	1¹ 1									13
90	90	90	90	90		90	90	89			1²			90	30¹	60									14
90	90	90	90	90		90	90	90						90	90										15
90	90	90	71	90		84	90	90		6²		19¹		90	90										16
90	90	90		90		90	90	90		7¹		83		90	90										17
	90	90	90	90		90		90			90			90	90		90	90							18
90	90	90	90	90		90	90			90				90	90		90								19
90	90	90	90	90		90	90	61			90			90	90		29¹								20
90	90	90	90	90		84	90			67				90	90		6²	23¹							21
90	90	90	90	90		90	90		74	90				90			16¹								22
90	90	90	90	90		90	90	45	42¹	90				90			3²								23
90	90	90	90	81		90	90		71	90				90			9²	19¹							24
90	90	90	90	90		90				75				90	90		10²	80	15¹						25
90	90	90	90	90		90				90				90	70		21¹	69	20²						26
	90	90	90	90		90	90		80	86				90			90	10¹	4²						27
	90	90	90	90		78	90		90	90				90			90	12¹							28
	90	90	90	90		82	90	60	90	30¹				90			90	8²							29
	90	90	90	90		90				90				90			90	90	90						30
	90	90	90	90		90			90	90				90			90	90							31
	90	90	90	90	85	90			5¹	90				90			90								32
	90	90	90	90	24¹	66	90			90				90	90		90								33
90	90	90	90	90		90	90		90	90				90			90								34
90	90	90	90	90	8¹	82	90		90	90				90			90								35
90	90	90	90	90	14¹	90	90	90		76				90			90								36
90	90	90	90	90	7¹	90	90	90		83				90			90								37
	90	90	90	90		75	90	90		90				90	15¹		90	90							38
	90	90		90	90	90	77	90	90					90	13¹		90	90							39
	90	90	90	90		90		90	90		29¹			90	61		90								40
	90	90	90	90	30¹	60	90	90		90				90			90								41
	90	80	90	90		90	90	79	90					90			90	10²		11¹					42

25	42	42	39	42	42	8	37	39	28	16	7	22		1	35		10	17	6	2	1				
						5				1	6	5	3	3		1	4	1	9	1	6	1			
	1	2	1	4	2	2	9	3	11	1	1	6			12				1						

90	90	17	90	90	90		90	90		90	16²	74			90			73¹							3 R
90	90	90	90	90	90		84	90		6¹	6²	84			90			90							4 R
90	90	90	90	90	90		90	90		90		90			90										
	120	120	120	120	120		120	120				120			120			120	120						

3	4	4	4	4	4		4	4		2		4			4			1	2						
										1	2								1						
								1			1				2				1						

FINAL LEAGUE TABLE

	P	W	D	L	F	A	P	
Manchester United	42	24	12	6	67	31	84	
Aston Villa	**42**	**21**	**11**	**10**	**57**	**40**	**74**	
Norwich City	42	21	9	12	61	65	72	
Blackburn Rovers	42	20	11	11	68	46	71	
Queens Park Rangers	42	17	12	13	63	55	63	
Liverpool	42	16	11	15	62	55	59	
Sheffield Wednesday	42	15	14	13	55	51	59	
Tottenham Hotspur	42	16	11	15	60	66	59	
Manchester City	42	15	12	15	56	51	57	
Arsenal	42	15	11	16	40	38	56	
Chelsea	42	14	14	14	51	54	56	
Wimbledon	42	14	12	16	56	55	54	
Everton	42	15	8	19	53	55	53	
Sheffield United	42	14	10	18	54	53	52	
Coventry City	42	13	13	16	52	57	52	
Ipswich Town	42	12	16	14	50	55	52	
Leeds United	42	12	15	15	57	62	51	
Southampton	42	13	11	18	54	61	50	
Oldham Athletic	42	13	10	19	63	74	49	
Crystal Palace	42	11	16	15	48	61	49	
Middlesbrough	42	11	11	20	54	75	44	
Nottingham Forest	42	10	10	22	41	62	40	

2F
2S
3
4
R

90	90	90	90	90	90		90	90	83	90		7¹			90										
90	90	90	90		90		90	90	90			90		90	90										
90	90	90	90	90	90		90	90	90			90			90										
90	90		90		90		77	84	90		6²				90		90	13¹		90					
90	90	90	90	90	90		71	90			12	78¹			90			90	19²						

5	5	5	4	4	5		5	5	4	1	1	2		1	5			1			1				
											1	2						1	1						
			1	1				2				2													

495

1993/94

SEASON SNIPPETS

Villa's summer signings were midfielder Andy Townsend who cost £2.1m from Chelsea and striker Guy Whittingham for a fee of £1.3m from Portsmouth.

Andy Townsend made his debut on 14 August.

Goalkeeper Mark Bosnich missed the start of the season after being suspended by FIFA for two weeks after declining to play for Australia against Canada.

Guy Whittingham made his debut on 23 August.

Dariusz Kubicki made his last appearance on 24 November.

Former Villa player Danny Blanchflower, who captained Tottenham Hotspur to the first 'double' since Villa achieved the feat in 1897, died on 9 December at the age of 67.

Gordon Cowans played his last Villa game on 11 December. Cowans left the club for a third time, joining Derby County on 3 February.

Dean Saunders scored the first Premier League hat-trick by a Villa player on 12 February.

Graham Fenton made his debut on 22 February.

Mark Bosnich made three saves during the penalty shoot-out in the League Cup semi-final against Tranmere Rovers on 27 February - and kept out two more spot kicks at Tottenham Hotspur three days later.

Stephen Froggatt played his last game on 30 March.

Neil Cox made his last appearance on 30 April and it was also the last game for Matthias Breitkreutz.

On 7 May, both Tony Daley and Stefan Beinlich played their last match.

PREMIER LEAGUE

MANAGER: Ron Atkinson

MATCH	DATE	VENUE	OPPONENTS	RESULT	HT SCORE	SCORE	SCORERS	ATT
1	Aug 14	H	Queen's Park Rangers	W	1 1	4 1	Atkinson 2, Saunders, Staunton	32,944
2	18	A	Sheffield Wednesday	D	0 0	0 0		28,450
3	21	A	Wimbledon	D	1 1	2 2	Richardson, Staunton	7,564
4	23	H	Manchester United	L	1 1	1 2	Atkinson	39,624
5	28	H	Tottenham Hotspur	W	0 0	1 0	Staunton (pen)	32,498
6	31	A	Everton	W	1 0	1 0	Whittingham	24,067
7	Sep 11	H	Coventry City	D	0 0	0 0		31,181
8	18	A	Ipswich Town	W	1 1	2 1	Saunders, Townsend	16,858
9	25	H	Oldham Athletic	D	0 1	1 1	Saunders	12,836
10	Oct 2	H	Newcastle United	L	0 0	0 2		37,336
11	16	A	West Ham United	D	0 0	0 0		20,416
12	23	H	Chelsea	W	1 0	1 0	Atkinson	29,706
13	30	A	Swindon Town	W	1 1	2 1	Teale, Atkinson	16,322
14	Nov 6	H	Arsenal	W	1 0	2 1	Whittingham, Townsend	31,773
15	20	H	Sheffield United	W	0 0	1 0	Whittingham	24,686
16	24	H	Southampton	L	0 0	0 2		16,180
17	28	A	Liverpool	L	0 1	1 2	Atkinson	38,484
18	Dec 4	A	Queen's Park Rangers	D	1 2	2 2	Richardson, Parker	14,915
19	8	H	Sheffield Wednesday	D	1 1	2 2	Cox, Saunders (pen)	20,304
20	11	H	Wimbledon	L	0 0	0 1		17,940
21	19	A	Manchester United	L	0 1	1 3	Cox	44,499
22	29	A	Norwich City	W	0 1	2 1	Houghton, Saunders	20,650
23	Jan 1	H	Blackburn Rovers	L	0 1	0 1		40,903
24	15	A	West Ham United	W	2 1	3 1	Richardson, Atkinson 2	28,869
25	22	A	Chelsea	D	1 0	1 1	Saunders	14,348
26	Feb 6	H	Leeds United	W	0 0	1 0	Townsend	26,919
27	12	H	Swindon Town	W	1 0	5 0	Saunders 3 (2 pens), Froggatt, Richardson	27,637
28	22	H	Manchester City	D	0 0	0 0		19,254
29	Mar 2	A	Tottenham Hotspur	D	1 0	1 1	Parker	17,452
30	6	A	Coventry City	W	1 0	1 0	Daley	14,323
31	12	H	Ipswich Town	L	0 1	0 1		23,732
32	16	A	Leeds United	L	0 1	0 2		33,126
33	19	H	Oldham Athletic	L	0 0	1 2	Redmond (og)	21,214
34	30	H	Everton	D	0 0	0 0		36,044
35	Apr 2	A	Manchester City	L	0 2	0 3		26,075
36	4	H	Norwich City	D	0 0	0 0		25,416
37	11	A	Blackburn Rovers	L	0 1	0 1		19,287
38	16	A	Sheffield United	W	2 1	2 1	Richardson, Fenton	18,402
39	23	H	Arsenal	L	0 1	1 2	Houghton	31,580
40	27	A	Newcastle United	L	1 3	1 5	Beinlich	32,217
41	30	A	Southampton	L	0 2	1 4	Saunders	18,803
42	May 7	H	Liverpool	W	0 1	2 1	Yorke 2	45,347

Final League Position: 10th in Premier League

Match 41: Nigel Spink sent off 78 minutes | 1 Own-goal

Appearances
Subs
Goals

FA CUP

3	Jan 8	A	Exeter City	W	0 0	1 0	Saunders (pen)	10,570
4	29	A	Grimsby Town	W	1 0	2 1	Houghton, Yorke	15,771
5	Feb 20	A	Bolton Wanderers	L	0 0	0 1		18,817

Appearances
Subs
Goals

FA Cup Round Four: Shaun Teale sent off 16 minutes

FOOTBALL LEAGUE CUP

2F	Sep 21	A	Birmingham City	W	0 0	1 0	Richardson	27,815
2S	Oct 6	H	Birmingham City	W	0 0	1 0	Saunders	35,856
3	26	A	Sunderland	W	2 0	4 1	Atkinson, Richardson, Houghton	23,672
4	Nov 30	A	Arsenal	W	1 0	1 0	Atkinson	26,453
5	Jan 12	H	Tottenham Hotspur	W	0 0	2 1	Houghton, Barrett	31,408
SF1	Feb 16	A	Tranmere Rovers	L	0 1	1 3	Atkinson	17,148
SF2	27	H	Tranmere Rovers *	W	2 1	3 1	Saunders, Teale, Atkinson	40,593
F	Mar 27	N	Manchester United **	W	1 0	3 1	Atkinson, Saunders 2 (1 pen)	77,231

*after extra time Aston Villa won 5-4 on penalties **Played at Wembley Stadium, London

Appearances
Subs
Goals

UEFA CUP

1F	Sep 15	A	Slovan Bratislava	D	0 0	0 0		10,886
1S	29	H	Slovan Bratislava	W	2 0	2 1	Atkinson, Townsend	24,461
2F	Oct 19	A	Deportivo La Coruna	D	0 0	1 1	Saunders	27,500
2S	Nov 3	H	Deportivo La Coruna	L	0 1	0 1		26,737

Appearances
Subs
Goals

496

FINAL LEAGUE TABLE

	P	W	D	L	F	A	P	
Manchester United	42	27	11	4	80	38	92	
Blackburn Rovers	42	25	9	8	63	36	84	
Newcastle United	42	23	8	11	82	41	77	
Arsenal	42	18	17	7	53	2	71	
Leeds United	42	18	16	8	65	39	70	
Wimbledon	42	18	11	13	56	53	65	2F / 2S
Sheffield Wednesday	42	16	16	10	76	54	64	3
Liverpool	42	17	9	16	59	55	60	4
Queens Park Rangers	42	16	12	14	62	61	60	5
Aston Villa	**42**	**15**	**12**	**15**	**46**	**50**	**57**	SF1 / SF2
Coventry City	42	14	14	14	43	45	56	F
Norwich City	42	12	17	13	65	61	53	
West Ham United	42	13	13	16	47	58	52	
Chelsea	42	13	12	17	49	53	51	
Tottenham Hotspur	42	11	12	19	54	59	45	
Manchester City	42	9	18	15	38	49	45	1F / 1S
Everton	42	12	8	22	42	63	44	
Southampton	42	12	7	23	49	66	43	2F
Ipswich Town	42	9	16	17	35	58	43	2S
Sheffield United	42	8	18	16	42	60	42	
Oldham Athletic	42	9	13	20	42	68	40	
Swindon Town	42	5	15	22	47	100	30	

1994/95

SEASON SNIPPETS

John Fashanu, a £1.35m signing from Wimbledon, scored on his debut on 20 August. Phil King also made his debut.

Nii Lamptey, signed on a loan deal from Anderlecht, scored on his debut against Wigan Athletic on 21 September.

Michael Oakes played his first game on 5 October.

Ron Atkinson was sacked on 10 November.

Jim Barron was in charge for the 4-3 win at Tottenham Hotspur on 19 November.

Brian Little was appointed manager on 25 November. Little would go on to install two more former players, Allan Evans and John Gregory, to his backroom staff.

David Farrell played his last game on 30 November.

Chris Boden's only appearance came on 3 December.

Guy Whittingham and Nii Lamptey both made their last appearance on 10 December.

Garry Parker's final Villa game came on 19 December.

Ian Taylor became Brian Little's first signing, arriving from Sheffield Wednesday on 21 December in an exchange deal which saw Guy Whittingham moving to Hillsborough.

On 6 January, Tommy Johnson and Gary Charles were signed from Derby County for a combined fee of £2.9m.

Kevin Richardson's last game was on 2 January.

Former manager Dick Taylor died in January aged 76.

Earl Barrett's last game was on 28 January.

John Fashanu suffered serious knee ligament damage at Old Trafford on 4 February which ended his career.

Franz Carr made his first appearance on 22 February.

On 18 March, Alan Wright made his debut following a £900,000 move from Blackburn Rovers while Ray Houghton made his final appearance.

Dalian Atkinson's last game was on 17 April.

On 9 May Aston Villa beat Birmingham City 2-0 in a testimonial match for Paul McGrath.

Shaun Teale, Dean Saunders and Phil King made their final Villa appearance on 14 May.

PREMIER LEAGUE

MANAGER: Ron Atkinson (to 10 November 1994)   Brian Little (from 25 November 1994)

MATCH	DATE	VENUE	OPPONENTS	RESULT	HT SCORE	SCORE	SCORERS	ATT
1	Aug 20	A	Everton	D	0 1	2 2	Fashanu, Saunders	35,552
2	24	H	Southampton	D	1 0	1 1	Saunders	24,179
3	27	H	Crystal Palace	D	0 0	1 1	Staunton	23,305
4	29	A	Coventry City	W	1 0	1 0	Yorke	12,218
5	Sep 10	H	Ipswich Town	W	1 0	2 0	Staunton, Saunders	22,241
6	17	A	West Ham United	L	0 0	0 1		18,326
7	24	A	Blackburn Rovers	L	0 1	1 3	Ehiogu	22,694
8	Oct 1	H	Newcastle United	L	0 0	0 2		29,960
9	8	A	Liverpool	L	1 2	2 3	Whittingham, Staunton	32,158
10	15	H	Norwich City	D	0 0	1 1	Saunders	22,468
11	22	H	Nottingham Forest	L	0 1	0 2		29,217
12	29	A	Queen's Park Rangers	L	0 1	0 2		16,073
13	Nov 6	H	Manchester United	L	1 1	1 2	Atkinson	32,136
14	9	A	Wimbledon	L	2 1	3 4	Parker, Saunders 2	6,221
15	19	A	Tottenham Hotspur	W	3 1	4 3	Atkinson, Fenton 2, Saunders	26,899
16	27	H	Sheffield Wednesday	D	1 0	1 1	Atkinson	25,082
17	Dec 3	A	Leicester City	D	0 1	1 1	Whittingham	20,896
18	10	H	Everton	D	0 0	0 0		29,678
19	19	A	Southampton	L	0 1	1 2	Houghton	13,874
20	26	A	Arsenal	D	0 0	0 0		34,452
21	28	H	Chelsea	W	2 0	3 0	Sinclair (og), Yorke, Taylor	32,901
22	31	A	Manchester City	D	0 1	2 2	Brightwell I (og), Saunders	22,513
23	Jan 2	H	Leeds United	D	0 0	0 0		35,038
24	14	H	Queen's Park Rangers	W	1 0	2 1	Fashanu, Ehiogu	26,578
25	21	A	Nottingham Forest	W	1 0	2 1	Fashanu, Saunders	24,598
26	25	H	Tottenham Hotspur	W	1 0	1 0	Saunders	40,017
27	Feb 4	A	Manchester United	L	0 1	0 1		43,795
28	11	H	Wimbledon	W	4 1	7 1	Reeves (og), Johnson 3, Saunders 2 (1 pen), Yorke	23,982
29	18	A	Sheffield Wednesday	W	2 0	2 1	Saunders 2	24,063
30	22	H	Leicester City	D	2 0	4 4	Saunders, Staunton, Yorke, Johnson	30,825
31	25	A	Newcastle United	L	1 1	1 3	Townsend	34,637
32	Mar 4	H	Blackburn Rovers	L	0 1	0 1		40,114
33	6	A	Coventry City	D	0 0	0 0		26,186
34	18	H	West Ham United	L	0 1	0 2		26,682
35	Apr 1	A	Ipswich Town	W	0 0	1 0	Swailes (og)	15,895
36	4	A	Crystal Palace	D	0 0	0 0		12,949
37	15	A	Chelsea	L	0 1	0 1		17,015
38	17	H	Arsenal	L	0 2	0 4		32,005
39	29	A	Leeds United	L	0 0	0 1		32,973
40	May 3	H	Manchester City	D	1 0	1 1	Ehiogu	30,133
41	6	H	Liverpool	W	2 0	2 0	Yorke 2	40,154
42	14	A	Norwich City	D	1 0	1 1	Staunton	19,374

Final League Position: 18th in Premier League

Appearances
Subs
4 Own-goals   Goals

Match 14: Andy Townsend sent off 40 minutes   Match 20: Andy Townsend sent off 60 minutes   Match 39: Mark Bosnich sent off 87 minutes

FA CUP

| 3 | Jan 7 | A | Barnsley | W | 0 0 | 2 0 | Yorke, Saunders | 11,469 |
| 4 | 28 | A | Manchester City | L | 0 1 | 0 1 | | 21,177 |

Appearances
Subs
Goals

FOOTBALL LEAGUE CUP

2F	Sep 21	H	Wigan Athletic	W	2 0	5 0	Yorke, Atkinson 2, Saunders, Lamptey	12,433
2S	Oct 5	A	Wigan Athletic	W	1 0	3 0	Lamptey 2, Whittingham	2,633
3	26	H	Middlesbrough	W	1 0	1 0	Townsend	19,254
4	Nov 30	H	Crystal Palace	L	1 0	1 4	Atkinson	12,653

Appearances
Subs
Goals

League Cup Round 4: Ugo Ehiogu sent off 26 minutes

UEFA CUP

1F	Sep 15	A	Internazionale Milan	L	0 0	0 1		22,639
1S	29	H	Internazionale Milan *	W	1 0	1 0	Houghton	30,533
2F	Oct 18	A	Trabzonspor	L	0 0	0 1		30,000
2S	Nov 1	H	Trabzonspor **	W	0 0	2 1	Atkinson, Ehiogu	23,858

Appearances
Subs
Goals

* After extra-time - Aston Villa won 4-3 on penalties   ** Trabzonspor won on away goals rule

498

FINAL LEAGUE TABLE

	P	W	D	L	F	A	P	
Blackburn Rovers	42	27	8	7	80	39	89	
Manchester United	42	26	10	6	77	28	88	
Nottingham Forest	42	22	11	9	72	43	77	
Liverpool	42	21	11	10	65	37	74	
Leeds United	42	20	13	9	59	38	73	
Newcastle United	42	20	12	10	67	47	72	
Tottenham Hotspur	42	16	14	12	66	58	62	2F
Queens Park Rangers	42	17	9	16	61	59	60	2S
Wimbledon	42	15	11	16	48	65	56	3
Southampton	42	12	18	12	61	63	54	4
Chelsea	42	13	15	14	50	55	54	
Arsenal	42	13	12	17	52	49	51	
Sheffield Wednesday	42	13	12	17	49	57	51	
West Ham United	42	13	11	18	44	48	50	
Everton	42	11	17	14	44	51	50	1F
Coventry City	42	12	14	16	44	62	50	1S
Manchester City	42	12	13	17	53	64	49	2F
Aston Villa	42	11	15	16	51	56	48	2S
Crystal Palace	42	11	12	19	34	49	45	
Norwich City	42	10	13	19	37	54	43	
Leicester City	42	6	11	25	45	80	29	
Ipswich Town	42	7	6	29	36	93	27	

499

1995/96

SEASON SNIPPETS

Villa's transfer record was smashed twice in the space of three days. On 23 June it was announced at a Villa Park press conference that Gareth Southgate has been signed from Crystal Palace for £2.5m and then on 26 June came the news of an agreed £3.5m deal for Savo Milosevic from Partizan Belgrade.

On 12 August, Partizan Belgrade were beaten 2-0 in a Villa Park friendly organised as part of the Milosevic deal.

On 19 August, Southgate and Milosevic made their Villa league debut along with Mark Draper, a £3.25m signing from Leicester City, who scored in a 3-1 win, while substitute Riccardo Scimeca made his first appearance.

Gareth Farrelly made his first appearance on 20 September.

On 21 October, Graham Fenton made his final appearance.

On 28 October, Carl Tiler was taken off injured after 75 minutes of his debut and did not play again all season.

On 23 December, substitute Lee Hendrie was sent off for two cautions on his debut. Goalkeeper Nigel Spink had to go on as an outfield player, replacing the injured Ian Taylor. It was Spink's 460th and last Villa game.

Julian Joachim made his debut on 24 February.

On 13 March, Franz Carr's goal at Nottingham Forest took the club to their first FA Cup semi-final for 36 years, but his last Villa game came three days later at Hillsborough.

Neil Davis made his first appearance on 13 March and his last on 27 April.

Scott Murray made his debut on 19 March.

Paul Browne played the first of two games on 19 March, his second match coming on 5 May.

Club legend Eric Houghton died on 1 May at the age of 85.

Villa beat Birmingham City 6-0 at St Andrews on 1 May in a testimonial match for John Frain.

Villa were drawn away to Gravesend & Northfleet in the third round of the F.A. Cup but the tie was switched to Villa Park.

Four Euro '96 Championship matches were staged at Villa Park from 11 June to 23 June 1996.

PREMIER LEAGUE

MANAGER: Brian Little

MATCH	DATE	VENUE	OPPONENTS	RESULT	HT SCORE	SCORE	SCORERS	ATT
1	Aug 19	H	Manchester United	W	3 0	3 1	Taylor, Draper, Yorke (pen)	34,655
2	23	A	Tottenham Hotspur	W	0 0	1 0	Ehiogu	26,598
3	26	A	Leeds United	L	0 1	0 2		35,086
4	30	H	Bolton Wanderers	W	0 0	1 0	Yorke	31,770
5	Sep 9	A	Blackburn Rovers	D	1 0	1 1	Milosevic	27,084
6	16	H	Wimbledon	W	1 0	2 0	Draper, Taylor	26,928
7	23	H	Nottingham Forest	D	0 0	1 1	Townsend	33,972
8	30	H	Coventry City	W	1 0	3 0	Yorke, Milosevic 2	21,004
9	Oct 14	A	Chelsea	L	0 0	0 1		34,922
10	21	A	Arsenal	L	0 0	0 2		38,271
11	28	H	Everton	W	0 0	1 0	Yorke	32,792
12	Nov 4	A	West Ham United	W	1 0	4 1	Milosevic 2, Johnson, Yorke	23,637
13	18	H	Newcastle United	D	1 0	1 1	Johnson	39,167
14	20	A	Southampton	W	1 0	1 0	Johnson	13,582
15	25	A	Manchester City	L	0 0	0 1		28,027
16	Dec 2	H	Arsenal	D	0 0	1 1	Yorke	37,770
17	10	A	Nottingham Forest	D	0 0	1 1	Yorke	25,790
18	16	H	Coventry City	W	1 0	4 1	Johnson, Milosevic 3	28,486
19	23	A	Queen's Park Rangers	L	0 0	0 1		14,778
20	Jan 1	A	Middlesbrough	W	2 0	2 0	Wright, Johnson	28,523
21	13	A	Manchester United	D	0 0	0 0		42,667
22	21	H	Tottenham Hotspur	W	1 1	2 1	McGrath, Yorke	35,666
23	31	H	Liverpool	L	0 0	0 2		39,332
24	Feb 3	H	Leeds United	W	2 0	3 0	Yorke 2, Wright	35,982
25	10	A	Bolton Wanderers	W	1 0	2 0	Yorke 2	18,099
26	24	A	Wimbledon	D	0 1	3 3	Reeves (og), Yorke (pen), Cunningham (og)	12,193
27	28	H	Blackburn Rovers	W	0 0	2 0	Joachim, Southgate	28,008
28	Mar 3	A	Liverpool	L	0 3	0 3		39,508
29	6	H	Sheffield Wednesday	W	0 1	3 2	Milosevic 2, Townsend	27,893
30	9	A	Queen's Park Rangers	W	1 0	4 2	Milosevic, Yorke 2, Yates (og)	28,221
31	16	A	Sheffield Wednesday	L	0 0	0 2		22,964
32	19	H	Middlesbrough	D	0 0	0 0		23,933
33	Apr 6	A	Chelsea	W	1 1	2 1	Miosevic, Yorke	23,530
34	8	H	Southampton	W	0 0	3 0	Taylor, Charles, Yorke	34,059
35	14	A	Newcastle United	L	0 0	0 1		36,546
36	17	H	West Ham United	D	1 0	1 1	McGrath	26,768
37	27	H	Manchester City	L	0 0	0 1		39,336
38	May 5	A	Everton	L	0 0	0 1		40,127

Final League Position: 4th in Premier League

Appearances
Subs
3 Own-goals   Goals

Match 7: Andy Townsend sent off 70 minutes
Match 19: substitute Lee Hendrie sent off 90 minutes

FA CUP

3	Jan 6	A	Gravesend & Northfleet *	W	1 0	3 0	Draper, Milosevic, Johnson	26,021
4	28	A	Sheffield United	W	0 0	1 0	Yorke (pen)	18,749
5	Feb 17	A	Ipswich Town	W	2 0	3 1	Draper, Yorke, Taylor	20,748
6	Mar 13	A	Nottingham Forest	W	1 0	1 0	Carr	21,067
SF	31	N	Liverpool **	L	0 1	0 3		39,072

Appearances
Subs
Goals

* Played at Villa Park
** Played at Old Trafford, Manchester

FOOTBALL LEAGUE CUP

2F	Sep 20	H	Peterborough United	W	3 0	6 0	Draper, Yorke 2 (2 pens), Johnson, Heald (og), Southgate	19,602
2S	Oct 3	A	Peterborough United	D	0 1	1 1	Staunton	5,745
3	25	H	Stockport County	W	0 0	2 0	Ehiogu, Yorke	17,679
4	Nov 29	H	Queen's Park Rangers	W	0 0	1 0	Townsend	24,951
5	Jan 10	A	Wolverhampton Wanderers	W	0 0	1 0	Johnson	39,277
SF1	Feb 14	A	Arsenal	D	1 2	2 2	Yorke 2	37,562
SF2	21	H	Arsenal *	D	0 0	0 0		39,334
F	Mar 24	N	Leeds United **	W	1 0	3 0	Milosevic, Taylor, Yorke	77,065

Appearances
Subs
1 Own-goal   Goals

* After extra-time – Aston Villa won on away goals rule
** Played at Wembley Stadium, London

FINAL LEAGUE TABLE

	P	W	D	L	F	A	P
Manchester United	38	25	7	6	73	35	82
Newcastle United	38	24	6	8	66	37	78
Liverpool	38	20	11	7	70	34	71
Aston Villa	**38**	**18**	**9**	**11**	**52**	**35**	**63**
Arsenal	38	17	12	9	49	32	63
Everton	38	17	10	11	64	44	61
Blackburn Rovers	38	18	7	13	61	47	61
Tottenham Hotspur	38	16	13	9	50	38	61
Nottingham Forest	38	15	13	10	50	54	58
West Ham United	38	14	9	15	43	52	51
Chelsea	38	12	14	12	46	44	50
Middlesbrough	38	11	10	17	35	50	43
Leeds United	38	12	7	19	40	57	43
Wimbledon	38	10	11	17	55	70	41
Sheffield Wednesday	38	10	10	18	48	61	40
Coventry City	38	8	14	16	42	60	38
Southampton	38	9	11	18	34	52	38
Manchester City	38	9	11	18	33	58	38
Queens Park Rangers	38	9	6	23	38	57	33
Bolton Wanderers	38	8	5	25	39	71	29

501

1996/97

SEASON SNIPPETS

On 12 July, Fernando Nelson was signed from Sporting Lisbon for £1.75m.

Scott Murray played his last game on 17 August.

On 24 August, Serbian midfielder Sasa Curcic, a record £4m signing from Bolton Wanderers, made his debut. Substitute Fernando Nelson also made his first appearance.

Paul McGrath made his last appearance on 24 September.

On 30 September, Dwight Yorke scored a hat-trick, but finished on the losing side as Villa went down 4-3.

On 10 October, after 323 games for the club, Paul McGrath joined Derby County.

On 22 October, first-team coach John Gregory left the club to become manager of Wycombe Wanderers.

Villa's undersoil heating system, installed in the summer, was used for the first time in December to ensure the game against Wimbledon went ahead three days before Christmas.

Carl Tiler played his last game on 1 February.

David Hughes made his debut on 2 March.

Tommy Johnson scored in his last game on 22 March. Johnson joined Celtic for £2.4m five days later.

David Hughes made his last appearance on 19 April.

3 May was Gareth Farrelly's last appearance.

PREMIER LEAGUE

MANAGER: Brian Little

MATCH	DATE		VENUE	OPPONENTS	RESULT	HT SCORE		SCORE		SCORERS	ATT
1	Aug	17	A	Sheffield Wednesday	L	0	0	1	2	Johnson	26,861
2		21	H	Blackburn Rovers	W	0	0	1	0	Southgate	32,457
3		24	H	Derby County	W	1	0	2	0	Joachim, Johnson (pen)	34,646
4	Sep	4	A	Everton	W	0	0	1	0	Ehiogu	39,115
5		7	H	Arsenal	D	1	0	2	2	Milosevic 2	37,944
6		15	A	Chelsea	D	1	1	1	1	Townsend	27,729
7		21	H	Manchester United	D	0	0	0	0		39,339
8		30	A	Newcastle United	L	1	3	3	4	Yorke 3	36,400
9	Oct	12	A	Tottenham Hotspur	L	0	0	0	1		32,840
10		19	H	Leeds United	W	0	0	2	0	Yorke, Johnson	39,051
11		26	A	Sunderland	L	0	1	0	1		21,032
12	Nov	2	H	Nottingham Forest	W	1	0	2	0	Tiler, Yorke	35,310
13		16	A	Leicester City	L	1	2	1	3	Yorke	36,193
14		23	A	Coventry City	W	1	0	2	1	Joachim, Staunton	21,335
15		30	H	Middlesbrough	W	1	0	1	0	Yorke (pen)	39,053
16	Dec	4	A	West Ham United	W	1	0	2	0	Ehiogu, Yorke	19,105
17		7	A	Southampton	W	1	0	1	0	Townsend	15,232
18		22	H	Wimbledon	W	2	0	5	0	Yorke 2, Milosevic, Taylor, Blackwell (og)	28,875
19		26	H	Chelsea	L	0	0	0	2		39,339
20		28	A	Arsenal	D	0	1	2	2	Milosevic, Yorke	38,130
21	Jan	1	A	Manchester United	D	0	0	0	0		55,133
22		11	H	Newcastle United	D	1	2	2	2	Yorke, Milosevic	39,339
23		18	A	Liverpool	L	0	0	0	3		40,489
24		29	H	Sheffield Wednesday	L	0	0	0	1		26,726
25	Feb	1	H	Sunderland	W	1	0	1	0	Milosevic	32,491
26		19	H	Coventry City	W	1	0	2	1	Yorke 2	30,409
27		22	A	Nottingham Forest	D	0	0	0	0		25,239
28	Mar	2	H	Liverpool	W	0	0	1	0	Taylor	39,339
29		5	A	Leicester City	L	0	0	0	1		20,626
30		15	H	West Ham United	D	0	0	0	0		35,992
31		22	A	Blackburn Rovers	W	0	0	2	0	Johnson, Yorke	24,274
32	Apr	5	H	Everton	W	1	1	3	1	Milosevic, Staunton, Yorke	39,339
33		9	A	Wimbledon	W	1	0	2	0	Milosevic, Wright	9,015
34		12	A	Derby County	L	0	2	1	2	Joachim	18,071
35		19	H	Tottenham Hotspur	D	0	0	1	1	Yorke	39,339
36		22	A	Leeds United	D	0	0	0	0		26,884
37	May	3	A	Middlesbrough	L	0	2	2	3	Ehiogu, Milosevic	30,012
38		11	H	Southampton	W	1	0	1	0	Dryden (og)	39,339

Final League Position: 5th in Premier League

Appearances
Subs
2 Own-goals | Goals

Match 8: Mark Draper sent off 42 minutes
Match 37: Steve Staunton sent off 80 minutes

FA CUP

3	Jan	14	A	Notts County	D	0	0	0	0		13,315
R		22	H	Notts County	W	1	0	3	0	Yorke 2, Ehiogu	25,006
4		25	A	Derby County	L	0	2	1	3	Curcic	17,977

Appearances
Subs
Goals

FOOTBALL LEAGUE CUP

3	Oct	23	A	Leeds United	W	0	0	2	1	Taylor, Yorke (pen)	15,803
4	Nov	26	A	Wimbledon	L	0	1	0	1		7,573

Appearances
Subs
Goals

UEFA CUP

1F	Sep	10	H	Helsingborgs IF	D	1	0	1	1	Johnson	25,818
1S		24	A	Helsingborgs IF *	D	0	0	0	0		10,103

Appearances
Subs
Goals

* Helsingborgs IF won on away goals rule

502

		Bosnich MJ (GK)	Staunton S	Southgate G	McGrath P	Townsend AD	Taylor IK	Draper MA	Milosevic S	Yorke D	Johnson T	Joachim JK	Oakes MC (GK)	Wright AG	Nelson FJ	Ehiogu U	Hendrie LA	Tiler C	Farrelly G	Scimeca R	Murray SG	Curcic S	Hughes RD		
		1	3	4	5	6	7	8	9	10	11	12	13	14	15	16	17	18	19	20	24	26	27		MATCH
			90	90		90	90	90		90	90	27¹	90	90		90					63				1
			90	90		90	90	90		90	84	90	90	90							6¹				2
			90	90		90	90	90	15	90	75¹	90	90	90	11²	90					79				3
			90	90		90	15¹	90	86	90	4²		90	90	89	90				1³	75				4
			90	90		90	30¹	90	84	90	6²		90	60	90						90				5
			90	90		90	15²	90	65	90	25¹		90	90	90						75				6
			90	90		90	6¹	90	90	90			90	90	90						84				7
			90	90			90	42	90	90			90	90	90						90				8
		90	90			80	90	80	80	90	10¹	10²		90	90		10³				90				9
		90	41			90	90			90	81	9²		90	90	90	90				49¹	90			10
		57		90		90	90	61		90	90	29²	33¹	90		90	29³	90				61			11
				90		90	90			90	90		90	90	90	90						90			12
				90		90	90	34¹		90	90	30²	90	90	56	90	90					60			13
			90	90		90	30¹	89	14²		90	76	90	90			1³					60			14
			90			90	90	90	90		90		90	90	90		90								15
			90			90	90	90	90		90		90	90	90		90								16
			90			90	90	90	54		36¹	90	90	90	90		90								17
		90	73			90	90	80	90	90			90	90	90		17¹		90		10²				18
		90	90			90	90	61	61	90	29¹		90	90	90		90				29²				19
		90	90			90	90	88	90	90	2¹		90	90			90								20
		90	90			90	84	90	90	90	6¹		90	90	90										21
		90	90	90		90		90	67	90	23²		90	34	90		90				56¹				22
		90		90		90		90	90	90			90	90			90				90				23
		90	90	90		90		90	90		14¹		90	90	14²	76	90				76				24
		90	90	90		90		90	90				90	90	12¹	90	90				78				25
		90	90	90		90	90	90	90		90	90	90	90			90								26
		90	46	90		90	90	90	90		90	90	90	90		44¹									27
		90	45	90		90	90	90	90		90	90	90	90							45¹				28
		90		90		90	90	90	74		74	16¹	16²	90							90				29
		90		90		90	90	71		90	16²	74		90	90	90	19¹				90				30
		90	90			90	90	90	59	90	31¹		90	90	90		90								31
			55	90			81	90	90	90			90	90	90		90		90		9²	35¹			32
				90			90	90	90				90	90			90					90			33
				90		90	90	61	90		17²	90	90	90							29³	73			34
			90	45		90	90	65	90		90		90	90	90		90				25²	45¹			35
		90	90		90	90	45	90		90			90	90		45¹					90				36
		75	80	90	90		90	85		90	33¹	15²	90	90		5¹					57				37
		90	90	90	90	90		90	90	90			90	90	90		90								38
		20	30	28		34	29	28	29	37	10	3	18	38	33	38		9	1	11	1	17	4		
			2					5	1		10	12	2			1		4	2	2		5	3		
			1				2	2		9	17	4	3		1			3	1						

FINAL LEAGUE TABLE

	P	W	D	L	F	A	P
Manchester United	38	21	12	5	76	44	75
Newcastle United	38	19	11	8	73	40	68
Arsenal	38	19	11	8	62	32	68
Liverpool	38	19	11	8	62	37	68
Aston Villa	**38**	**17**	**10**	**11**	**47**	**34**	**61**
Chelsea	38	16	11	11	58	55	59
Sheffield Wednesday	38	14	15	9	50	51	57
Wimbledon	38	15	11	12	49	46	56
Leicester City	38	12	11	15	46	54	47
Tottenham Hotspur	38	13	7	18	44	51	46
Leeds United	38	11	13	14	28	38	46
Derby County	38	11	13	14	45	58	46
Blackburn Rovers	38	9	15	14	42	43	42
West Ham United	38	10	12	16	39	48	42
Everton	38	10	12	16	44	57	42
Southampton	38	10	11	17	50	56	41
Coventry City	38	9	14	15	38	54	41
Sunderland	38	10	10	18	35	53	40
Middlesbrough	38	10	12	16	51	60	39
Nottingham Forest	38	6	16	16	31	59	34

1997/98

SEASON SNIPPETS

On 13 May, Villa smashed their transfer record with the £7m signing of Stan Collymore from Liverpool.

On 27 June, Leicester City's Player of the Year, Simon Grayson, joined his former manager at Villa.

On 1 July, Gareth Farrelly joined Everton.

On 12 July, it was announced that Ugo Ehiogu would take over the No.5 shirt previously worn by Paul McGrath.

On 9 August, Stan Collymore made his Villa league debut.

Simon Grayson made his debut on 13 August, but Villa suffered their biggest ever defeat for an opening home fixture.

The defeat at Tottenham on 27 August gave Villa their worst ever start to a league campaign. It was Andy Townsend's last game.

Sasa Curcic made his last appearance on 6 December.

On 9 December, Scott Murray moved to Bristol City.

On 28 December Darren Byfield and Richard Walker made their debut.

Brian Little resigned as manager on 24 February.

On 25 February John Gregory was appointed manager.

On 27 February assistant manager Allan Evans was sacked.

On 2 March, Steve Harrison was re-appointed to the coaching staff ten years after leaving to manage Watford.

Savo Milosevic played his last Villa game on 25 April.

Gareth Barry came in for his first game on 2 May.

On 10 May, Fernando Nelson played his last match.

PREMIER LEAGUE

MANAGER: Brian Little (to 24 February 1998)   John Gregory (from 25 February 1998)

MATCH	DATE	VENUE	OPPONENTS	RESULT	HT SCORE	SCORE	SCORERS	ATT
1	Aug 9	A	Leicester City	L	0 1	0 1		20,304
2	13	H	Blackburn Rovers	L	0 3	0 4		37,122
3	23	A	Newcastle United	L	0 1	0 1		36,783
4	27	A	Tottenham Hotspur	L	1 1	2 3	Yorke, Collymore	26,316
5	30	H	Leeds United	W	0 0	1 0	Yorke	39,027
6	Sep 13	H	Barnsley	W	1 0	3 0	Ehiogu, Draper, Taylor	18,649
7	20	H	Derby County	W	0 1	2 1	Yorke, Joachim	35,444
8	22	A	Liverpool	L	0 0	0 3		34,843
9	27	H	Sheffield Wednesday	D	1 2	2 2	Staunton, Taylor	32,044
10	Oct 4	A	Bolton Wanderers	W	1 0	1 0	Milosevic	24,196
11	18	H	Wimbledon	L	1 1	1 2	Taylor	32,087
12	26	A	Arsenal	D	0 0	0 0		38,061
13	Nov 1	H	Chelsea	L	0 1	0 2		39,372
14	8	A	Crystal Palace	D	0 1	1 1	Joachim	21,097
15	22	H	Everton	W	1 1	2 1	Milosevic, Ehiogu	36,389
16	29	A	West Ham United	L	1 1	1 2	Yorke	24,976
17	Dec 6	H	Coventry City	W	1 0	3 0	Collymore, Hendrie, Joachim	33,250
18	15	A	Manchester United	L	0 0	0 1		55,175
19	20	H	Southampton	D	0 0	1 1	Taylor	29,343
20	26	A	Tottenham Hotspur	W	1 0	4 1	Draper 2, Collymore 2	38,644
21	28	A	Leeds United	D	0 0	1 1	Milosevic	36,909
22	Jan 10	H	Leicester City	D	0 0	1 1	Joachim	36,429
23	17	A	Blackburn Rovers	L	0 2	0 5		24,834
24	Feb 1	H	Newcastle United	L	0 0	0 1		38,266
25	7	A	Derby County	W	0 0	1 0	Yorke	30,251
26	18	H	Manchester United	L	0 0	0 2		39,372
27	21	A	Wimbledon	L	1 2	1 2	Milosevic	13,131
28	28	H	Liverpool	W	1 1	2 1	Collymore 2	39,372
29	Mar 8	A	Chelsea	W	0 0	1 0	Joachim	33,018
30	11	H	Barnsley	L	0 1	0 1		29,519
31	14	H	Crystal Palace	W	3 0	3 1	Taylor, Milosevic 2 (1 pen)	33,781
32	28	A	Everton	W	1 1	4 1	Joachim, Charles, Yorke 2 (1 pen)	36,471
33	Apr 4	A	West Ham United	W	0 0	2 0	Joachim, Milosevic	39,372
34	11	A	Coventry City	W	1 0	2 1	Yorke 2	22,790
35	18	A	Southampton	W	1 1	2 1	Hendrie, Yorke	15,238
36	25	H	Bolton Wanderers	L	0 2	1 3	Taylor	38,392
37	May 2	A	Sheffield Wednesday	W	2 0	3 1	Yorke, Hendrie, Joachim	34,177
38	10	H	Arsenal	W	1 0	1 0	Yorke (pen)	39,372

Final League Position: 7th in Premier League

Appearances
Subs
Goals

Match 10: Stan Collymore sent off 90 minutes
Match 38: Ugo Ehiogu sent off 24 minutes

FA CUP

3	Jan 3	A	Portsmouth	D	1 2	2 2	Staunton, Grayson	16,013
R	14	H	Portsmouth	W	1 0	1 0	Milosevic	25,355
4	24	H	West Bromwich Albion	W	1 0	4 0	Grayson, Yorke 2, Collymore	39,372
5	Feb 14	H	Coventry City	L	0 0	0 1		36,979

Appearances
Subs
Goals

FOOTBALL LEAGUE CUP

3	Oct 15	A	West Ham United	A	0 2	0 3		20,360

Appearances
Subs
Goals

UEFA CUP

1F	Sep 16	A	Girondins de Bordeaux	D	0 0	0 0		16,000
1S	30	H	Girondins de Bordeaux *	W	0 0	1 0	Milosevic	33,072
2F	Oct 21	A	Athletic Bilbao	D	0 0	0 0		46,000
2S	Nov 4	H	Athletic Bilbao	W	1 0	2 1	Taylor, Yorke	35,915
3F	25	A	Steaua Bucharest	L	0 2	1 2	Yorke	24,000
3S	Dec 9	H	Steaua Bucharest	W	0 0	2 0	Milosevic, Taylor	35,102
4F	Mar 3	A	Atletico Madrid	L	0 1	0 1		47,000
4S	17	H	Atletico Madrid **	W	0 1	2 1	Taylor, Collymore	39,163

Appearances
Subs
Goals

* After extra-time   ** Atletico Madrid won on away goals rule

504

FINAL LEAGUE TABLE

	P	W	D	L	F	A	P
Arsenal	38	23	9	6	68	33	78
Manchester United	38	23	8	7	73	26	77
Liverpool	38	18	11	9	68	42	65
Chelsea	38	20	3	15	71	43	63
Leeds United	38	17	8	13	57	46	59
Blackburn Rovers	38	16	10	12	57	52	58
Aston Villa	**38**	**17**	**6**	**15**	**49**	**48**	**57**
West Ham United	38	16	8	14	56	57	56
Derby County	38	16	7	15	52	49	55
Leicester City	38	13	14	11	51	41	53
Coventry City	38	12	16	10	46	44	52
Southampton	38	14	6	18	50	55	48
Newcastle United	38	11	11	16	35	44	44
Tottenham Hotspur	38	11	11	16	44	56	44
Wimbledon	38	10	14	14	34	46	44
Sheffield Wednesday	38	12	8	18	52	67	44
Everton	38	9	13	16	41	56	40
Bolton Wanderers	38	9	13	16	41	61	40
Barnsley	38	10	5	23	37	82	35
Crystal Palace	38	8	9	21	37	71	33

1998/99

SEASON SNIPPETS

Midfielder Alan Thompson arrived from Bolton Wanderers for £4.5m and made his debut on 15 August.

David Unsworth arrived on 24 July from West Ham for £4m, but departed to Everton on 20 August for the same fee without playing a competitive match.

On 15 August, Dwight Yorke played his last match. Yorke was transferred to Manchester United on 20 August for £12.6m - a new Villa record.

Darius Vassell made his first appearance on 23 August.

Paul Merson joined Villa for £6.75m from Middlesbrough and made his debut on 12 September.

Fabio Ferraresi made his debut on 29 September.

Steve Watson was transferred from Newcastle United for £3.5m and made his first appearance on 24 October.

Tommy Jaszczun made his only appearance on 28 October.

It was Darren Byfield's last game.

Dion Dublin arrived from Coventry City on 5 November at a cost of £5.75m and made his debut two days later.

Dublin set a club record by scoring a total of seven goals in his first three league games.

A 12-match unbeaten run to 14 November represented the club's best ever start to a league campaign.

On 26 December, substitute goalkeeper Adam Rachel made his only appearance after Michael Oakes was sent off.

On 2 January, Aaron Lescott made his only Villa appearance when he substituted Lee Hendrie after 76 minutes. It was the last appearance for Gary Charles.

Steve Stone made his debut on 13 March.

Stan Collymore played his last Villa game on 21 March.

Colin Calderwood played his first game on 2 April.

Mark Bosnich played his last game on 17 April. Bosnich signed for Manchester United on a free transfer on 2 June.

Michael Oakes, Riccardo Scimeca and Simon Grayson all played their last Villa game on 16 May.

PREMIER LEAGUE

MANAGER: John Gregory

MATCH	DATE	VENUE	OPPONENTS	RESULT	HT SCORE	SCORE	SCORERS	ATT
1	Aug 15	A	Everton	D	0 0	0 0		40,112
2	23	H	Middlesbrough	W	1 0	3 1	Joachim, Charles, Thompson	29,559
3	29	A	Sheffield Wednesday	W	1 0	1 0	Joachim	25,989
4	Sep 9	A	Newcastle United	W	0 0	1 0	Hendrie (pen)	39,241
5	12	H	Wimbledon	W	1 0	2 0	Merson, Taylor	32,959
6	19	A	Leeds United	D	0 0	0 0		33,162
7	26	H	Derby County	W	1 0	1 0	Merson	38,007
8	Oct 3	A	Coventry City	W	2 0	2 1	Taylor 2	22,650
9	17	A	West Ham United	D	0 0	0 0		26,002
10	24	H	Leicester City	D	0 1	1 1	Ehiogu	39,241
11	Nov 7	H	Tottenham Hotspur	W	2 0	3 2	Dublin 2, Collymore	39,241
12	14	A	Southampton	W	1 0	4 1	Dublin 3, Merson	15,242
13	21	H	Liverpool	L	0 2	2 4	Dublin 2	39,241
14	28	A	Nottingham Forest	D	0 2	2 2	Joachim 2	25,753
15	Dec 5	H	Manchester United	D	0 0	1 1	Joachim	39,241
16	9	A	Chelsea	L	1 1	1 2	Hendrie	34,765
17	13	H	Arsenal	W	0 2	3 2	Joachim, Dublin 2	39,217
18	21	A	Charlton Athletic	W	1 0	1 0	Rufus (og)	20,043
19	26	A	Blackburn Rovers	L	0 1	1 2	Scimeca	27,536
20	28	H	Sheffield Wednesday	W	1 1	2 1	Southgate, Ehiogu	39,217
21	Jan 9	A	Middlesbrough	D	0 0	0 0		34,643
22	18	H	Everton	W	1 0	3 0	Joachim 2, Merson	32,488
23	30	A	Newcastle United	L	0 2	1 2	Merson	36,766
24	Feb 6	H	Blackburn Rovers	L	0 1	1 3	Joachim	37,404
25	17	H	Leeds United	L	0 2	1 2	Scimeca	37,510
26	21	A	Wimbledon	D	0 0	0 0		15,582
27	27	H	Coventry City	L	0 1	1 4	Dublin (pen)	38,799
28	Mar 10	A	Derby County	L	1 2	1 2	Thompson	26,836
29	13	H	Tottenham Hotspur	L	0 0	0 1		35,963
30	21	H	Chelsea	L	0 0	0 3		39,217
31	Apr 2	H	West Ham United	D	0 0	0 0		36,813
32	5	A	Leicester City	D	1 0	2 2	Hendrie, Joachim	20,652
33	10	H	Southampton	W	1 0	3 0	Draper, Joachim, Dublin	32,203
34	17	A	Liverpool	W	1 0	1 0	Taylor	44,306
35	24	H	Nottingham Forest	W	1 0	2 0	Draper, Barry	34,492
36	May 1	A	Manchester United	L	1 1	1 2	Joachim	55,189
37	8	H	Charlton Athletic	L	1 1	3 4	Barry, Joachim 2	37,705
38	16	A	Arsenal	L	0 0	0 1		38,308

Final League Position: 6th in Premier League

1 Own-goal

Appearances
Subs
Goals

Match 13: Stan Collymore sent off 67 minutes
Match 19: Michael Oakes sent off 55 minutes
Match 27: Draper, who came on as a substitute was then replaced by Collymore
Match 37: Steve Watson sent off 89 minutes

FA CUP

3	Jan 2	H	Hull City	W	1 0	3 0	Collymore 2, Joachim	39,217
4	23	H	Fulham	L	0 2	0 2		35,260

Appearances
Subs
Goals

FOOTBALL LEAGUE CUP

3	Oct 28	A	Chelsea	L	1 1	1 4	Draper	26,790

Appearances
Subs
Goals

UEFA Cup

1F	Sep 15	H	Stromsgodset IF	W	0 2	3 2	Charles, Vassell 2	28,893
1S	29	A	Stromsgodset IF	W	2 0	3 0	Collymore 3	4,835
2F	Oct 20	A	RC Celta Vigo	W	1 0	1 0	Joachim	30,000
2S	Nov 3	H	RC Celta Vigo	L	1 2	1 3	Collymore (pen)	29,910

Appearances
Subs
Goals

Aston Villa — Appearances & Final League Table

Player	1	2	3	4	5	6	7	8	9	10	11	12	13	14	15	16	17	18	20	21	22	24	26	28	30	32	34	MATCH
	Bosnich MJ (GK)	Charles GA	Wright AG	Southgate G	Ehiogu U	Watson SC	Taylor IK	Draper MA	Collymore SV	Yorke D	Merson PC	Thompson A	Joachim JK	Oakes MC (GK)	Dublin D	Barry G	Grayson SN	Hendrie LA	Ferraresi F	Scimeca R	Byfield D	Vassell D	Delaney MA	Stone SB	Jaszczun AJ	Rachel A (GK)	Lescott AA	Calderwood C	
	90	90	90	90			90	16¹		90	74		90		90													1
	90	90	90	90	90		90	7³			90	80			90	22¹	83		68	10²								2
	90	90	90	90				78	90		90	90			90	12¹	90											3
	90	90	90	90	90		23¹	67			80	90			90	10²	90		86	4³								4
	90	90	90	90	90		88	2²		89	74	90			90	16¹	90		1³									5
	90	82	90	90	90		90	29¹		90	61	90			90	8²	90											6
	90	90	90	90	90		90	18²	3³	90	72	87			64	26¹	90											7
	90	69	90	90	90		90		90	69	90	21¹			90	21²	90											8
		90	90	90	90		90		90	90	90		90		90		90											9
		62	90	90	90	7²	90		90	83	90	28¹	90		90		90											10
			90	90	90	90	90	9¹		90			90	81	90		90											11
			90	90	90	90	90	11¹	79	83		7²	90	90	90		90											12
		3³	75	90	90	87		52	67		90	38¹	15²	90	90	90	90											13
			90	90	90	90	90				45	45¹	90	90	90		90											14
			90	90	90	90	90				90	90	90	90	90		90											15
			90	90	90	90	90	7¹			90	83	90	90	90		90											16
			90	90	90	90	90	37¹			90	86	90	90	53	4²	90											17
			90	90	90	90	90		55		90	90	90	90		90		35¹										18
			90	90	90	70		20²			90	82	55	90		8³	57	90				35¹						19
			90	90	90	90	52	38¹	38²		90	90	90	90	90		52											20
			90	90	90	90					90	90	90	90		20¹	70											21
			90	90	90	90	58	10³	45¹	32²	90	90	45	90			80											22
			90	90	40	84	90			90		90	90	90		50¹	90		6²									23
			90	90		90	90			90	12¹	90	90	90	78	90	90											24
			90	90		90	90		19²		90	25¹	90	90	71	65		90										25
			90	90		90	90		14¹		90	76	90	90		90		90										26
			90	90		44	31	25¹	34³		90		90	90	90	46²	90	90										27
90		90	90					90		90	90	14¹		90	90		90		76									28
90		90	90					90	90	90	67	90	23¹		90		90		90									29
90		90	90		90	7³		74		16¹	90	16²		74	90		83		90				90					30
		90	90		90	90	90			4¹	86	90		90									90		90			31
		90	90		75	90	90					90		90	15¹		90						90		90			32
90		90	90		90	90	57			33²	5	90		89	1³		85¹		69				90		90			33
90		90			90	90	90			21¹		89		90	1²								90		90			34
		90	90	18²	72	90	90			90		90	90	45	45¹		90					8³	82		90			35
		90	90		90	90	90			90	23¹	90	90	75								15²	90		90			36
		90	90	29¹	89	90	61			90		90	90	90								29²	90		61			37
		90	90	90	72		90			90		90	90						72		90	18¹	18²	9³		81		38
15	10	38	38	23	26	31	13	11	1	21	20	29	23	24	27	4	31		16			9				8	
	1			2	1	2	10	9		5	5	7		5	11	1		2		6	2	1		1			
	1		1	2		4	2	1		5	2	14		11	2		3		2								

20²	90	90	90	70		58	90			90	90		90	32¹	76		90				14³		3
	58	90	90	90	90				90		90	90		90		90			90	32¹			4
	2	2	2	2	1	1	1		1	2	2		2	2		2			1	1	1	
1							2				1			1								
	75	73		90	90	90	90			33¹	90	90			90			57	90	15³		17²	
	1	1		1	1	1				1	1		1			1		1	1		1		
							1			1													
90	90	90	90		53¹	67				90	90			90	37	90		23²	80	10³			
90	51	90	90		70	90	90			90	66			90		20³	39¹	24²					
90	90	90	90			90	90				90	90		90		90							
	45	90	90		90	45¹	90			82	90	90		63	8³	90		27²					
2	4	4	3		2	3			3	4	2		3	2	3	1	1						
					1						1				1	2		3					
	1						4			1								2					

FINAL LEAGUE TABLE

	P	W	D	L	F	A	P
Manchester United	38	22	13	3	80	37	79
Arsenal	38	22	12	4	59	17	78
Chelsea	38	20	15	3	57	30	75
Leeds United	38	18	13	7	62	34	67
West Ham United	38	16	9	13	46	53	57
Aston Villa	**38**	**15**	**10**	**13**	**51**	**46**	**55**
Liverpool	38	15	9	14	68	49	54
Derby County	38	13	13	12	40	45	52
Middlesbrough	38	12	15	11	48	54	51
Leicester City	38	12	13	13	40	46	49
Tottenham Hotspur	38	11	14	13	47	50	47
Sheffield Wednesday	38	13	7	18	41	42	46
Newcastle United	38	11	13	14	48	54	46
Everton	38	11	10	17	42	47	43
Coventry City	38	11	9	18	39	51	42
Wimbledon	38	10	12	16	40	63	42
Southampton	38	11	8	19	37	64	41
Charlton Athletic	38	8	12	18	41	56	36
Blackburn Rovers	38	7	14	17	38	52	35
Nottingham Forest	38	7	9	22	35	69	30

1999/00

SEASON SNIPPETS

The club's major summer signings were David James from Liverpool for £1.8m and George Boateng from Coventry City at a fee of £4.5m. Both players made their debut on 7 August.

Mark Draper's brief appearance on 21 August was his last.

Peter Enckelman made his debut on 11 September.

Najwan Ghrayib, who had arrived from Israeli club Hapoel Haifa, made his debut on 14 September.

Jlloyd Samuel made his debut on 21 September.

On 20 October, Italian midfielder Benito Carbone joined Villa from Sheffield Wednesday on a short-term contract until the end of the season.

Villa were drawn against 'lucky losers' Darlington in the third round of the FA Cup. The Quakers had been knocked out in round two, but were re-admitted after Manchester United withdrew to take part in a tournament in Brazil.

Despite losing on penalties in a League Cup quarter-final at West Ham on 15 December, Villa were given a second chance after it was discovered the Hammers had fielded an ineligible player. Villa won the re-staged tie 3-1.

Colin Calderwood played his last game on 5 February.

On 10 February, Stan Collymore joined Leicester City.

On 14 February, Neil Cutler made his only Villa appearance.

On 15 April, Jonathan Bewers substituted Mark Delaney in the last minute of the game - it was Bewers only appearance.

Steve Watson played his last game on 22 April.

Najwan Ghrayib played his last game on 29 April.

The FA Cup final on 20 May was the last game for Benito Carbone.

PREMIER LEAGUE

MANAGER: John Gregory

MATCH	DATE	VENUE	OPPONENTS	RESULT	HT SCORE	SCORE	SCORERS	ATT
1	Aug 7	A	Newcastle United	W	0 0	1 0	Joachim	36,376
2	11	H	Everton	W	1 0	3 0	Joachim, Dublin, Taylor	30,337
3	16	H	West Ham United	D	1 1	2 2	Dublin 2	26,250
4	21	A	Chelsea	L	0 0	0 1		35,071
5	24	A	Watford	W	0 0	1 0	Delaney	19,161
6	28	H	Middlesbrough	W	1 0	1 0	Dublin	28,728
7	Sep 11	A	Arsenal	L	1 1	1 3	Joachim	38,093
8	18	H	Bradford City	W	0 0	1 0	Dublin	28,083
9	25	A	Leicester City	L	0 1	1 3	Dublin	19,917
10	Oct 2	H	Liverpool	D	0 0	0 0		39,217
11	18	A	Sunderland	L	0 0	1 2	Dublin	39,866
12	23	H	Wimbledon	D	1 1	1 1	Dublin	27,160
13	30	A	Manchester United	L	0 2	0 3		55,211
14	Nov 6	H	Southampton	L	0 0	0 1		26,474
15	22	A	Coventry City	L	1 1	1 2	Dublin	20,174
16	27	A	Everton	D	0 0	0 0		34,750
17	Dec 4	H	Newcastle United	L	0 0	0 1		34,531
18	18	H	Sheffield Wednesday	W	0 1	2 1	Merson, Taylor	23,885
19	26	A	Derby County	W	0 0	2 0	Boateng, Taylor	33,222
20	29	H	Tottenham Hotspur	D	0 1	1 1	Taylor	39,217
21	Jan 3	A	Leeds United	W	1 0	2 1	Southgate 2	40,027
22	15	A	West Ham United	D	1 0	1 1	Taylor	24,237
23	22	H	Chelsea	D	0 0	0 0		33,704
24	Feb 5	A	Watford	W	0 0	4 0	Stone, Merson 2, Walker	27,647
25	14	A	Middlesbrough	W	1 0	4 0	Carbone, Summerbell (og), Joachim 2	31,571
26	26	A	Bradford City	D	1 0	1 1	Merson	18,276
27	Mar 5	H	Arsenal	D	0 0	1 1	Walker	36,930
28	11	H	Coventry City	W	1 0	1 0	Ehiogu	33,177
29	15	A	Liverpool	D	0 0	0 0		43,615
30	18	A	Southampton	L	0 1	0 2		15,218
31	25	H	Derby County	W	1 0	2 0	Carbone, Boateng	28,613
32	Apr 5	A	Sheffield Wednesday	W	0 0	1 0	Thompson	18,136
33	9	H	Leeds United	W	1 0	1 0	Joachim	33,889
34	15	A	Tottenham Hotspur	W	0 1	4 2	Dublin 2 (1 pen), Carbone, Wright	35,304
35	22	H	Leicester City	D	1 1	2 2	Thompson, Merson	31,229
36	29	H	Sunderland	D	0 0	1 1	Barry	33,949
37	May 6	A	Wimbledon	D	0 1	2 2	Hendrie, Dublin	19,188
38	14	H	Manchester United	L	0 0	0 1		39,217

Final League Position: 6th in Premier League

1 Own-goal

Appearances / Subs / Goals

Match 9: Gareth Southgate sent off 65 minutes

FA CUP

3	Dec 11	H	Darlington	W	1 0	2 1	Carbone, Dublin	22,101
4	Jan 8	H	Southampton	W	1 0	1 0	Southgate	25,487
5	30	H	Leeds United	W	1 2	3 2	Carbone 3	30,026
6	Feb 20	A	Everton	W	2 1	2 1	Stone, Carbone	35,331
SF	Apr 2	N	Bolton Wanderers *	D	0 0	0 0		62,828
F	May 20	N	Chelsea **	L	0 0	0 1		78,217

* Played at Wembley Stadium, London - after extra-time - Aston Villa won 4-1 on penalties
** Played at Wembley Stadium, London
FA Cup Sixth Round: Benito Carbone sent off 89 minutes
FA Cup Semi-final: Mark Delaney sent off 110 minutes

Appearances / Subs / Goals

FOOTBALL LEAGUE CUP

2F	Sep 14	A	Chester City	W	0 0	1 0	Hendrie	4,364
2S	21	H	Chester City	W	2 0	5 0	Boateng, Taylor, Hendrie 2, Thompson	22,613
3	Oct 13	A	Manchester United	W	1 0	3 0	Joachim, Taylor, Stone	33,815
4	Dec 1	H	Southampton	W	1 0	4 0	Watson, Joachim, Dublin 2	17,608
5	Jan 11	A	West Ham United *	W	0 0	3 1	Taylor 2, Joachim	25,592
SF1	25	H	Leicester City	D	0 0	0 0		28,037
SF2	Feb 2	A	Leicester City	L	0 1	0 1		21,843

Appearances / Subs / Goals

* After extra-time - score 90 minutes 1-1 - restaged match after West Ham United fielded an ineligible player

508

FINAL LEAGUE TABLE

	P	W	D	L	F	A	P
Manchester United	38	28	7	3	97	45	91
Arsenal	38	22	7	9	73	43	73
Leeds United	38	21	6	11	58	43	69
Liverpool	38	19	10	9	51	30	67
Chelsea	38	18	11	9	53	34	65
Aston Villa	**38**	**15**	**13**	**10**	**46**	**35**	**58**
Sunderland	38	16	10	12	57	56	58
Leicester City	38	16	7	15	55	55	55
West Ham United	38	15	10	13	52	53	55
Tottenham Hotspur	38	15	8	15	57	49	53
Newcastle United	38	14	10	14	63	54	52
Middlesbrough	38	14	10	14	46	52	52
Everton	38	12	14	12	59	49	50
Coventry City	38	12	8	18	47	54	44
Southampton	38	12	8	18	45	62	44
Derby County	38	9	11	18	44	57	38
Bradford City	38	9	9	20	38	68	36
Wimbledon	38	7	12	19	46	74	33
Sheffield Wednesday	38	8	7	23	38	70	31
Watford	38	6	6	26	35	77	24

2000/01

SEASON SNIPPETS

Both home Intertoto Cup-ties were played at The Hawthorns as work was under way on rebuilding the Trinity Road Stand. Kick-off time for the Marila Pribram tie was brought forward one hour because of a wedding reception at the stadium.

Belgium striker Luc Nilis made his Villa debut on 22 July.

On 2 August, Alan Thompson was sent off in his final game.

Flamboyant French winger David Ginola, signed from Tottenham Hotspur for £3m, made his debut on 19 August along with Alpay Ozalan a £5.6 signing from Fenerbahce.

After just five games for Villa, in which he scored twice, Luc Nilis saw his career ended when he suffered a double fracture of his right leg in a collision with Ipswich Town goalkeeper Richard Wright on 9 September.

Ugo Ehiogu played his last Villa game on 9 September.

Gilles De Bilde, on loan from Sheffield Wednesday, made his debut on 5 November.

Irish defender Steve Staunton returned from Liverpool for a second spell with Villa on 6 December.

John McGrath made his first appearance on 1 January, but his third and last appearance came on 3 February.

Gilles De Bilde played his last game on 1 January.

Thomas Hitzlsperger made debut on 13 January.

Richard Walker made his last appearance on 17 January.

Columbian Juan Pablo Angel, at £9.5m a club record signing from River Plate (Argentina) made his debut on 20 January.

Julian Joachim made his last appearance on 28 April.

David James and Gareth Southgate played their final Villa game on 19 May.

Graham Taylor returned to Villa Park as non-executive director in July 2001.

PREMIER LEAGUE

MANAGER: John Gregory

MATCH	DATE	VENUE	OPPONENTS	RESULT	HT SCORE	SCORE	SCORERS	ATT
1	Aug 19	A	Leicester City	D	0 0	0 0		21,455
2	27	H	Chelsea	D	1 1	1 1	Nilis	27,056
3	Sep 6	A	Liverpool	L	0 3	1 3	Stone	43,360
4	9	A	Ipswich Town	W	1 0	2 1	Hendrie, Dublin	22,064
5	16	H	Bradford City	W	1 0	2 0	Southgate, Dublin (pen)	27,849
6	23	A	Middlesbrough	D	0 0	1 1	Joachim	27,556
7	30	H	Derby County	W	2 0	4 1	Joachim 2, Merson, Wright	27,941
8	Oct 14	A	Arsenal	L	0 0	0 1		38,046
9	22	H	Sunderland	D	0 0	0 0		27,215
10	28	H	Charlton Athletic	W	2 0	2 1	Taylor, Merson	27,461
11	Nov 5	A	Everton	W	0 0	1 0	Merson	27,670
12	11	H	Tottenham Hotspur	W	1 0	2 0	Taylor 2	33,608
13	18	A	Southampton	L	0 2	0 2		14,979
14	25	A	Coventry City	D	1 0	1 1	Dublin	21,455
15	Dec 2	H	Newcastle United	D	1 0	1 1	Dublin	34,255
16	9	A	West Ham United	D	1 1	1 1	Hendrie	25,888
17	16	H	Manchester City	D	0 0	2 2	Dublin, Ginola	29,281
18	23	A	Leeds United	W	1 0	2 1	Southgate, Boateng	39,714
19	26	H	Manchester United	L	0 0	0 1		40,889
20	Jan 1	A	Chelsea	L	0 1	0 1		33,159
21	13	H	Liverpool	L	0 2	0 3		41,366
22	20	A	Manchester United	L	0 0	0 2		67,533
23	24	H	Leeds United	L	1 1	1 2	Merson	29,335
24	Feb 3	A	Bradford City	W	0 0	3 0	Vassell 2, Joachim	19,591
25	10	H	Middlesbrough	D	1 0	1 1	Stone	28,912
26	24	A	Derby County	L	0 1	0 1		27,289
27	Mar 5	A	Sunderland	D	0 0	1 1	Joachim	44,114
28	10	H	Ipswich Town	W	0 1	2 1	Joachim 2	28,216
29	18	H	Arsenal	D	0 0	0 0		36,111
30	31	A	Manchester City	W	2 1	3 1	Merson, Dublin, Hendrie	34,243
31	Apr 4	H	Leicester City	W	1 1	2 1	Dublin, Hendrie	29,043
32	7	H	West Ham United	D	0 0	2 2	Ginola, Hendrie	31,432
33	14	H	Everton	W	1 1	2 1	Dublin, Taylor	31,272
34	17	A	Charlton Athletic	D	0 2	3 3	Ginola, Vassell, Hendrie	20,043
35	21	H	Southampton	D	0 0	0 0		29,336
36	28	A	Tottenham Hotspur	D	0 0	0 0		36,096
37	May 5	H	Coventry City	W	0 2	3 2	Vassell, Angel, Merson	39,761
38	19	A	Newcastle United	L	0 2	0 3		51,306

Final League Position: 8th in Premier League

Appearances
Subs
Goals

Match 8: Lee Hendrie sent off 65 minutes Match 17: Lee Hendrie sent off 77 minutes Match 38: Ian Taylor sent off 85 minutes

FA CUP

3	Jan 7	A	Newcastle United	D	0 0	1 1	Stone	37,862
R	17	H	Newcastle United	W	0 0	1 0	Vassell	25,387
4	27	H	Leicester City	L	0 1	1 2	Joachim	26,383

Appearances
Subs
Goals

FA Cup Round Four: Darius Vassell sent off 34 minutes

FOOTBALL LEAGUE CUP

2	Nov 1	H	Manchester City	L	0 0	0 1		24,138

Appearances
Subs
Goals

INTERTOTO CUP

3F	Jul 16	A	Marila Pribram	D	0 0	0 0		7,852
3S	22	H	Marila Pribram *	W	1 1	3 1	Dublin, Taylor, Nilis	8,200
SF1	26	A	Celta Vigo	L	0 0	0 1		14,000
SF2	Aug 2	H	Celta Vigo *	L	1 1	1 2	Barry (pen)	11,909

Appearances
Subs
Goals

* Played at The Hawthorns, west Bromwich
Intertoto Cuo Round 3F: Mark Delaney sent off 80 minutes
Intertoto Cup Round 3S: Paul Merson sent off 60 minutes
Intertoto Cup semi-final 2: Ian Taylor sent off 47 minutes
Intertoto Cup semi-final 2: Alan Thompson sent off 90 minutes

FINAL LEAGUE TABLE

	P	W	D	L	F	A	P	
Manchester United	38	24	8	6	79	31	80	
Arsenal	38	20	10	8	63	38	70	
Liverpool	38	20	9	9	71	39	69	
Leeds United	38	20	8	10	64	43	68	2
Ipswich Town	38	20	6	12	57	42	66	
Chelsea	38	17	10	11	68	45	61	
Sunderland	38	15	12	11	46	41	57	
Aston Villa	**38**	**13**	**15**	**10**	**46**	**43**	**54**	
Charlton Athletic	38	14	10	14	50	57	52	3F
Southampton	38	14	10	14	40	48	52	3S
Newcastle United	38	14	9	15	44	50	51	SF1
Tottenham Hotspur	38	13	10	15	47	54	49	SF2
Leicester City	38	14	6	18	39	51	48	
Middlesbrough	38	9	15	14	44	44	42	
West Ham United	38	10	12	16	45	50	42	
Everton	38	11	9	18	45	59	42	
Derby County	38	10	12	16	37	59	42	
Manchester City	38	8	10	20	41	65	34	
Coventry City	38	8	10	20	36	63	34	
Bradford City	38	5	11	22	30	70	26	

511

2001/02

SEASON SNIPPETS

It was a busy summer in the transfer market, with Villa signing Swede Olof Mellberg from Spanish club Racing Santander for £5.6m, Moroccans Moustapha Hadji and Hassan Kachloul from Coventry City and Southampton respectively, Danish goalkeeper Peter Schmeichel from Sporting Lisbon and Croatian striker Bosko Balaban from Dinamo Zagreb.

Gareth Southgate moved to Middlesbrough, David James joined West Ham United and Julian Joachim signed for Coventry City as part of the Hadji deal.

Peter Schmeichel, Hassan Kachloul and Moustapha Hadji all made their debut on 21 July.

Olof Mellberg made his debut on 18 August.

On 21 August Villa won the Intertoto Cup and thereby qualified for the UEFA Cup.

Bosko Balaban's first appearance came on 26 August.

On 20 October Peter Schmeichel became the first Villa goalkeeper to score a competitive goal when he netted at Everton. In doing so, he also became the oldest scorer in Villa's history.

The new Trinity Road stand was officially opened by Prince Charles on 12 November.

On 1 December substitute David Ginola was sent off in his final Villa game. Ginola joined Everton on 8 February.

Peter Crouch, signed from Portsmouth for £4.5m, made his debut on 30 March.

On 6 April Peter Schmeichel played his last Villa game.

Bosko Balaban made his last appearance on 20 April.

George Boateng played his last game on 11 May.

PREMIER LEAGUE

MANAGER: John Gregory (to 24 January) Graham Taylor (from 4 February)

MATCH	DATE	VENUE	OPPONENTS	RESULT	HT SCORE	SCORE	SCORERS	ATT
1	Aug 18	A	Tottenham Hotspur	D	0 0	0 0		36,059
2	26	H	Manchester United	D	1 0	1 1	Vassell	42,632
3	Sep 8	A	Liverpool	W	1 0	3 1	Dublin, Hendrie, Vassell	44,102
4	16	A	Sunderland	D	0 0	0 0		31,688
5	24	A	Southampton	W	2 1	3 1	Boateng, Angel, Hadji	26,794
6	30	H	Blackburn Rovers	W	0 0	2 0	Angel, Vassell	28,623
7	Oct 14	H	Fulham	W	0 0	2 0	Vassell, Taylor	28,579
8	20	A	Everton	L	0 1	2 3	Hadji, Schmeichel	33,352
9	24	H	Charlton Athletic	W	1 0	1 0	Kachloul	27,701
10	27	H	Bolton Wanderers	W	2 1	3 2	Angel 2 (1 pen), Vassell	33,599
11	Nov 3	A	Newcastle United	L	0 1	0 3		51,057
12	17	H	Middlesbrough	D	0 0	0 0		35,424
13	25	A	Leeds United	D	1 1	1 1	Kachloul	40,159
14	Dec 1	H	Leicester City	L	0 1	0 2		30,711
15	5	A	West Ham United	D	1 0	1 1	Dublin	28,377
16	9	A	Arsenal	L	2 0	2 3	Merson, Stone	38,074
17	17	H	Ipswich Town	W	1 1	2 1	Angel 2	29,320
18	22	H	Derby County	L	1 1	1 3	Angel	28,001
19	26	H	Liverpool	L	1 1	1 2	Hendrie	42,602
20	29	H	Tottenham Hotspur	D	0 1	1 1	Angel (pen)	41,134
21	Jan 1	A	Sunderland	D	0 0	1 1	Taylor	45,324
22	12	H	Derby County	W	2 1	2 1	Vassell, Angel	28,881
23	21	A	Charlton Athletic	W	2 0	2 1	Vassell, Angel	25,681
24	30	H	Everton	D	0 0	0 0		32,460
25	Feb 2	A	Fulham	D	0 0	0 0		20,041
26	9	H	Chelsea	D	1 0	1 1	Merson	41,137
27	23	A	Manchester United	L	0 0	0 1		67,592
28	Mar 2	H	West Ham United	W	1 1	2 1	Angel, Vassell	37,341
29	5	A	Blackburn Rovers	L	0 1	0 3		21,988
30	17	H	Arsenal	L	0 1	1 2	Dublin	41,520
31	23	A	Ipswich Town	D	0 0	0 0		25,247
32	30	A	Bolton Wanderers	L	2 2	2 3	Warhurst (og), Taylor	24,600
33	Apr 2	H	Newcastle United	D	1 1	1 1	Crouch	36,597
34	6	A	Middlesbrough	L	0 1	1 2	Angel	26,003
35	13	H	Leeds United	L	0 1	0 1		40,039
36	20	A	Leicester City	D	2 1	2 2	Vassell, Hitzlsperger	18,125
37	27	H	Southampton	W	2 0	2 1	Vassell 2	35,255
38	May 11	A	Chelsea	W	1 0	3 1	Crouch, Vassell, Dublin	40,709

Final League Position: 8th in Premier League

Match 5: Dion Dublin sent off 57 minutes   **Match 14:** David Ginola sent off 85 minutes

Appearances
Subs
1 Own-goal   Goals

FA CUP

3	Jan 6	H	Manchester United	L	0 0	2 3	Taylor, P Neville (og)	38,444

Appearances
Subs
1 Own-goal   Goals

FOOTBALL LEAGUE CUP

3	Oct 10	H	Reading	W	1 0	1 0	Dublin	23,431
4	Nov 28	H	Sheffield Wednesday	L	0 1	0 1		26,526

Appearances
Subs
Goals

INTERTOTO CUP

3F	Jul 14	A	Slaven Belupo	L	0 0	1 2	Ginola	3,000
3S	21	H	Slaven Belupo	W	2 0	2 0	Hendrie 2	27,850
SF1	25	A	Stade Rennais	L	0 1	1 2	Vassell	15,753
SF2	Aug 1	H	Stade Rennais *	W	1 0	1 0	Dublin	30,782
F1	7	A	FC Basel	D	0 0	1 1	Merson	25,879
F2	21	H	FC Basel	W	1 1	4 1	Vassell, Angel 2, Ginola	39,593

Appearances
Subs
* Aston Villa won on away-goals rule   NOTE: SQUAD NUMBERS WERE NOT USED FOR THE INTERTOTO CUP GAMES   Goals

UEFA CUP

1F	Sep 20	H	NK Varteks	L	0 1	2 3	Angel 2	27,132
1S	27	A	NK Varteks	W	0 0	1 0	Hadji	9,000

Appearances
Subs
Goals

512

FINAL LEAGUE TABLE

	P	W	D	L	F	A	P
Arsenal	38	26	9	3	79	36	87
Liverpool	38	24	8	6	67	30	80
Manchester United	38	24	5	9	87	45	77
Newcastle United	38	21	8	9	74	52	71
Leeds United	38	18	12	8	53	37	66
Chelsea	38	17	13	8	66	38	64
West Ham United	38	15	8	15	48	57	53
Aston Villa	38	12	14	12	46	47	50
Tottenham Hotspur	38	14	8	16	49	53	50
Blackburn Rovers	38	12	10	16	55	51	46
Southampton	38	12	9	17	46	54	45
Middlesbrough	38	12	9	17	35	47	45
Fulham	38	10	14	14	36	44	44
Charlton Athletic	38	10	14	14	38	49	44
Everton	38	11	10	17	45	57	43
Bolton Wanderers	38	9	13	16	44	62	40
Sunderland	38	10	10	18	29	51	40
Ipswich Town	38	9	9	20	41	64	36
Derby County	38	8	6	24	33	63	30
Leicester City	38	5	13	20	30	64	28

513

2002/03

SEASON SNIPPETS

Bosko Balaban spent the season on loan at his former club Dinamo Zagreb.

Michael Boulding made his debut on 21 July, but it was the last appearance for Hassan Kachloul.

Swedish striker Marcus Allback, who joined Villa from Dutch club Heerenveen for £2m, made his debut on 27 July.

Stefan Moore also played his first game on 27 July, but it was the last match for Michael Boulding, who scored, and Paul Merson who then joined Portsmouth.

On 31 July, Stefan Postma made his debut while Steve Stone made his last appearance.

Ecuador international Ulises de la Cruz, who had arrived from Hibernian for £1.5m, made his debut on 18 August.

Mark Kinsella made his debut on 24 August.

Ronny Johnsen arrived from Manchester United and made his debut on 11 September.

Oyvind Leonhardsen made his debut on 22 September.

Rob Edwards made his debut on 28 December.

The League Cup quarter-final on 18 December started eighty minutes late because of ticketing problems.

The FA Cup match on 4 January was Liam Ridgewell's first appearance.

Icelandic midfielder Joey Gudjonsson who was signed on loan from Spanish club Real Betis scored on his debut on 28 January.

Alan Wright played his last game on 22 March.

Peter Whittingham's first match was on 21 April.

On 26 April, Rob Edwards played his last game.

Steve Staunton and Oyvind Leonhardsen both played their last game on 3 May.

Ian Taylor, Peter Enckelman, Stephen Cooke and Joey Gudjonsson all played their last game on 11 May.

Manager Graham Taylor resigned on 14 May after Villa had narrowly avoided relegation.

PREMIER LEAGUE

MANAGER: Graham Taylor

MATCH	DATE	VENUE	OPPONENTS	RESULT	HT SCORE	SCORE	SCORERS	ATT
1	Aug 18	H	Liverpool	L	0 0	0 1		41,183
2	24	A	Tottenham Hotspur	L	0 1	0 1		35,384
3	28	H	Manchester City	W	0 0	1 0	Vassell	33,494
4	Sep 1	A	Bolton Wanderers	L	0 0	0 1		22,500
5	11	H	Charlton Athletic	W	0 0	2 0	De la Cruz, S Moore	26,483
6	16	A	Birmingham City	L	0 1	0 3		29,505
7	22	H	Everton	W	1 0	3 2	Hendrie 2, Dublin	30,023
8	28	A	Sunderland	L	0 0	0 1		40,492
9	Oct 6	H	Leeds United	D	0 0	0 0		33,505
10	21	H	Southampton	L	0 0	0 1		25,817
11	26	A	Manchester United	D	1 0	1 1	Mellberg	67,619
12	Nov 3	A	Blackburn Rovers	D	0 0	0 0		23,004
13	9	H	Fulham	W	1 0	3 1	Angel, Allback, Leonhardsen	29,563
14	16	A	West Bromwich Albion	D	0 0	0 0		27,091
15	23	H	West Ham United	W	1 0	4 1	Hendrie, Leonhardsen, Dublin, Vassell	33,279
16	30	A	Arsenal	L	0 1	1 3	Hitzlsperger	38,090
17	Dec 7	H	Newcastle United	L	0 0	0 1		35,446
18	14	H	West Bromwich Albion	W	1 1	2 1	Vassell, Hitzlsperger	40,391
19	21	A	Chelsea	L	0 1	0 2		38,284
20	26	A	Manchester City	L	1 1	1 3	Dublin	33,991
21	28	H	Middlesbrough	W	1 0	1 0	Dublin	33,637
22	Jan 1	H	Bolton Wanderers	W	1 0	2 0	Dublin, Vassell	31,838
23	11	A	Liverpool	D	0 1	1 1	Dublin (pen)	43,210
24	18	H	Tottenham Hotspur	L	0 0	0 1		38,576
25	28	A	Middlesbrough	W	2 2	5 2	Vassell 2, Gudjonsson, Barry, Dublin	27,546
26	Feb 2	H	Blackburn Rovers	W	2 0	3 0	Dublin 2, Barry	29,171
27	8	A	Fulham	L	1 2	1 2	Barry	17,092
28	22	A	Charlton Athletic	L	0 0	0 3		26,257
29	Mar 3	H	Birmingham City	L	0 0	0 2		42,602
30	15	H	Manchester United	L	0 1	0 1		42,602
31	22	A	Southampton	D	2 1	2 2	Hendrie, Vassell	31,888
32	Apr 5	H	Arsenal	D	0 0	1 1	Toure (og)	42,602
33	12	A	West Ham United	D	1 1	2 2	Vassell (pen), Leonhardsen	35,029
34	19	H	Chelsea	W	1 0	2 1	Allback 2	39,358
35	21	A	Newcastle United	D	0 1	1 1	Dublin	52,015
36	26	A	Everton	L	0 0	1 2	Allback	40,167
37	May 3	H	Sunderland	W	0 0	1 0	Allback	36,963
38	11	A	Leeds United	L	1 1	1 3	Gudjonsson	40,205

Final League Position: 16th in Premier League

1 Own-goal

Appearances
Subs
Goals

Match 10: Peter Enckelman sent off 47 minutes
Match 18: Steve Staunton sent off 69 minutes
Match 29: Dion Dublin sent off 50 minutes
Match 29: Joey Gudjonsson sent off 80 minutes

FA CUP

3	Jan 4	H	Blackburn Rovers	L	1 1	1 4	Angel	23,884

Appearances
Subs
Goals

FOOTBALL LEAGUE CUP

2	Oct 2	H	Luton Town	W	2 0	3 0	De la Cruz, Dublin 2	20,883
3	Nov 6	A	Oxford United	W	0 0	3 0	Taylor, Barry, Dublin	12,177
4	Dec 4	H	Preston North End	W	1 0	5 0	Vassell 2, Dublin, Angel, Hitzlsperger	23,042
5	18	H	Liverpool	L	1 1	3 4	Vassell (pen), Hitzlsperger, Dublin	38,530

Appearances
Subs
Goals

INTERTOTO CUP

3F	Jul 21	A	FC Zurich	L	0 1	0 2		4,500
3S	27	H	FC Zurich	W	1 0	3 0	Boulding, Allback, Staunton	18,349
SF1	31	A	Lille OSC	D	0 0	1 1	Taylor	14,437
SF2	Aug 7	H	Lille OSC	L	0 1	0 2		26,192

Appearances
Subs
Goals

Intertoto Cup Round 3F: Jlloyd Samuel sent off 85 minutes
NOTE: SQUAD NUMBERS WERE NOT USED FOR THE INTERTOTO CUP GAMES

FINAL LEAGUE TABLE

	P	W	D	L	F	A	P	
Manchester United	38	25	8	5	74	34	83	
Arsenal	38	23	9	6	85	42	78	
Newcastle United	38	21	6	11	63	48	69	
Chelsea	38	19	10	9	68	38	67	2
Liverpool	38	18	10	10	61	41	64	3
Blackburn Rovers	38	16	12	10	52	43	60	4
Everton	38	17	8	13	48	49	59	5
Southampton	38	13	13	12	43	46	52	
Manchester City	38	15	6	17	47	54	51	
Tottenham Hotspur	38	14	8	16	51	62	50	
Middlesbrough	38	13	10	15	48	44	49	
Charlton Athletic	38	14	7	17	45	56	49	3F
Birmingham City	38	13	9	16	41	49	48	3S
Fulham	38	13	9	16	41	50	48	SF1
Leeds United	38	14	5	19	58	57	47	SF2
Aston Villa	**38**	**12**	**9**	**17**	**42**	**47**	**45**	
Bolton Wanderers	38	10	14	14	41	51	44	
West Ham United	38	10	12	16	42	59	42	
West Bromwich A	38	6	8	24	29	65	26	
Sunderland	38	4	7	27	21	65	19	

2003/04

SEASON SNIPPETS

New manager David O'Leary's summer signings were Thomas Sorensen and Gavin McCann, who cost £2m each from Sunderland.

Paul McGrath topped a poll on the official club website as the most popular character in the club's history, pipping Dennis Mortimer into second place.

On 16 August, Villa became the first team to visit Portsmouth for a Premier League fixture. Thomas Sorensen and Gavin McCann both made their debut.

Moustapha Hadji played his last game on 14 September.

Alpay Ozalan played his last match on 5 October. Ozalan's contract was terminated on 23 October after he had insulted David Beckham during a Turkey v England international.

Mark Kinsella made his last appearance on 25 October.

On 3 December, Busku Balaban's contract was terminated. The Croatian striker moved to Belgian club Bruges.

Peter Enckelman was transferred to Blackburn Rovers on 7 January after a two months loan deal.

Peru international Nolberto Solano, signed from Newcastle United for £1.5m, made his debut on 31 January.

Luke Moore made his debut on 22 February.

On 8 May, Ronny Johnsen played his last game.

Dion Dublin, released by the club after reaching the end of his contract, was given a standing ovation by supporters after his final game on 15 May. It was also the last Villa match for Peter Crouch and Marcus Allback.

PREMIER LEAGUE

MANAGER: David O'Leary

MATCH	DATE	VENUE	OPPONENTS	RESULT	HT SCORE	SCORE	SCORERS	ATT
1	Aug 16	A	Portsmouth	L	0 1	1 2	Barry (pen)	20,101
2	24	H	Liverpool	D	0 0	0 0		42,573
3	27	A	Arsenal	L	0 0	0 2		38,010
4	30	H	Leicester City	W	3 0	3 1	Thatcher (og), Angel 2	32,274
5	Sep 14	A	Manchester City	L	1 0	1 4	Angel	46,687
6	20	H	Charlton Athletic	W	1 0	2 1	Ozalan, Samuel	31,410
7	27	A	Chelsea	L	0 1	0 1		41,182
8	Oct 5	H	Bolton Wanderers	D	0 0	1 1	Angel	30,229
9	19	A	Birmingham City	D	0 0	0 0		29,546
10	25	H	Everton	D	0 0	0 0		36,146
11	Nov 1	A	Newcastle United	D	1 1	1 1	Dublin	51,975
12	8	H	Middlesbrough	L	0 1	0 2		29,898
13	23	A	Tottenham Hotspur	L	0 0	1 2	Allback	33,140
14	29	H	Southampton	W	1 0	1 0	Dublin	31,285
15	Dec 6	A	Manchester United	L	0 2	0 4		67,621
16	14	H	Wolverhampton Wanderers	W	2 1	3 2	Angel 2, Barry	36,964
17	20	A	Blackburn Rovers	W	0 0	2 0	S Moore, Angel	20,722
18	26	A	Leeds United	D	0 0	0 0		38,513
19	28	H	Fulham	W	1 0	3 0	Angel, Vassell 2	35,617
20	Jan 6	H	Portsmouth	W	1 0	2 1	Angel, Vassell	28,625
21	10	A	Liverpool	L	0 1	0 1		43,771
22	18	H	Arsenal	L	0 1	0 2		39,380
23	31	A	Leicester City	W	0 0	5 0	Vassell 2, Crouch 2, Dublin	31,056
24	Feb 7	H	Leeds United	W	1 0	2 0	Angel (pen), Johnsen	39,171
25	11	A	Fulham	W	2 1	2 1	Angel, Vassell	16,153
26	22	H	Birmingham City	D	1 0	2 2	Vassell, Hitzlsperger	40,061
27	28	A	Everton	L	0 0	0 2		39,353
28	Mar 14	A	Wolverhampton Wanderers	W	3 0	4 0	Hitzlsperger, Mellberg, Angel 2	29,386
29	20	H	Blackburn Rovers	L	0 2	0 2		37,532
30	27	A	Charlton Athletic	W	1 1	2 1	Vassell, Samuel	26,250
31	Apr 4	H	Manchester City	D	1 0	1 1	Angel	37,602
32	10	A	Bolton Wanderers	D	1 0	2 2	Crouch, Hendrie	26,374
33	12	H	Chelsea	W	1 1	3 2	Vassell (pen), Hitzlsperger, Hendrie	41,112
34	18	H	Newcastle United	D	0 0	0 0		40,786
35	24	A	Middlesbrough	W	1 1	2 1	Barry, Crouch	31,322
36	May 2	H	Tottenham Hotspur	W	1 0	1 0	Angel	42,573
37	8	A	Southampton	D	1 1	1 1	Angel (pen)	32,054
38	15	H	Manchester United	L	0 2	0 2		42,573

Final League Position: 6th in Premier League

Appearances
Subs
1 Own-goal Goals

Match 1: Gareth Barry sent off 87 minutes
Match 11: Gavin McCann sent off 69 minutes
Match 35: Nolberto Solano sent off 58 minutes

FA CUP

3	Jan 4	H	Manchester United	L	1 0	1 2	Barry		40,371

Appearances
Subs
Goals

FOOTBALL LEAGUE CUP

2	Sep 23	A	Wycombe Wanderers	W	2 0	5 0	Whittingham, Angel 3 (1 pen), Vassell (pen)		6,072
3	Oct 29	H	Leicester City	W	0 0	1 0	Hitzlsperger		26,729
4	Dec 3	H	Crystal Palace	W	1 0	3 0	Symons (og), McCann, Angel		24,258
5	17	H	Chelsea	W	1 0	2 1	Angel, McCann		30,414
SF1	Jan 21	A	Bolton Wanderers	L	1 3	2 5	Angel 2		16,302
SF2	27	H	Bolton Wanderers	W	1 0	2 0	Hitzlsperger, Samuel		36,883

Appearances
Subs
1 Own goal Goals

League Cup Semi-final 2: Gavin McCann sent off 40 minutes

Player Appearances

	Sorensen T (GK)	Delaney MA	Samuel J	Mellberg EO	Ozalan A	Barry G	Hendrie LA	McCann GP	Dublin D	Vassell D	Solano NA	Hitzlsperger T	Postma S (GK)	Allback M	De la Cruz BU	Crouch PJ	Whittingham PM	Angel JP	Hadji M	Moore S	Ridgewell LM	Kinsella MA	Johnsen R	Moore LI	MATCH
	1	2	3	4	5	6	7	8	9	10	11	12	13	14	15	16	17	18	20	23	24	26	27	31	
	90	90	90		90	87	90	90			30[1]		90			14[2]	60	76			90				1
	90	90	90	90		90	87	90	1[2]	90				3[1]			90	89					90		2
	90	90	90		90	90				30[1]				90			90	90		60			90		3
	90	90	90	90	13[1]		83	90	7[2]	83		90			7[3]		90	90					77		4
	90	90	90	38	52[1]		90	90	14[2]		90		90				90	76	24[2]				66		5
	90	90	90		90	90	90		26[1]					64	90		90	90					90		6
	90	90			90	90	90	90	37[1]						90		53	90							7
	45	90	90	90	90	90	90		90			45[1]	33[2]				57	90							8
	90	90	90	90		90	41	90		90							49[1]	90					90		9
	90	90	90	90		82		90	90	90		45[1]			8[2]		90	90				45			10
	90	90					90	69		90			28[2]		50		90	62		40[1]			90		11
	90	90	90	90		52	52	90	19[3]	38[1]		38[2]		71			90	90					90		12
	90	81	90	90		90	87		9[1]	90		90		90			90			3[2]			90		13
	90		90	90		90	65	90	90	90		5[3]		13[2]	90		85	77		25[1]					14
	90	90	90			90	90	90	90		17[2]			26[1]			73	64					90		15
	51	90	90	90		90		90	90	90		90	39[1]	57	33[2]			90							16
	90	90	90	90		79	89	90	90	22[1]			11[2]		1[3]		90	90	68						17
	90	90	90	90		90	67	90	90	23[1]			23[2]				90	90	67						18
	90	62	90	90		90	75	90		90		15[2]					90	84		6[3]	28[1]		90		19
	90	90	90	90		90	90	90	90	86		24[1]					90	66	82	4[3]					20
	90	90	90			90	69	40	90	45		50[1]					90	90		45[2]			21[3]		21
	90	90	90	90		86	86					90		86	4[1]	4[2]	90	90			4[3]		90		22
	90	81	90	90		90		90	90	70		90		70		20[1]	9[3]	90	20[2]						23
	90		90	90		90	86		48	86	90	90			90	4[2]		90			4[3]		42[1]		24
	90	76	90			80	88			90	90	90			14[1]		10[2]	90			2[3]		90		25
	90		90	90		56	82		38[1]	90	90	90			90		34[2]	90					52	8[3]	26
	90		90	90		90				78	90	90			90	12[1]		90					90		27
	90		90	90		90	83			60	90	90			90	12[2]	7[3]	78					90	30[1]	28
	90		90	90		29	90			81	45	90			90	9[3]	61[1]	90			90			45[2]	29
	90		90	90		85	90		89		90				90			90			5[1]		90	1[2]	30
	90		90	90		90	90		67		90				90	45[1]		45					90	23[2]	31
	90		90	90		90	79	90	21[2]	65	90				90	69	11[3]			90			25[1]		32
	90		90	90		90	55	90	2[3]	88	90				90	82	35[1]				1[3]		90	8[2]	33
	90		90	90		90	90		90	69	90			28[1]	90	62	21[2]						89		34
	90	31[2]	90	90		54		90		59	58	90			90	16[3]	36[1]	74			90				35
	90	1[3]	90	90		90		90	10[2]		89	90		21[1]	90	80		69			90				36
	90		90			90	89	90	5[2]	68	90				90	22[1]	1[3]	85			90		90		37
	90		90	90		82	75	90	8[3]		90			33[1]	90	57	15[2]	90			90				38
	38	23	38	33	4	36	32	28	12	26	10	22		7	20	6	20	33		2	5	2	21	
		2			2				11	6		10	2	8	8	10	12		1	6	6		2	7
			2	1	1	3	2		3	9		3		1		4	16			1			1	

FINAL LEAGUE TABLE

	P	W	D	L	F	A	P	
Arsenal	38	26	12	0	73	26	90	
Chelsea	38	24	7	7	67	30	79	
Manchester United	38	23	6	9	64	35	75	2
Liverpool	38	16	12	10	55	37	60	3
Newcastle United	38	13	17	8	52	40	56	4
Aston Villa	**38**	**15**	**11**	**12**	**48**	**44**	**56**	5
Charlton Athletic	38	14	11	13	51	51	53	SF1
Bolton Wanderers	38	14	11	13	48	56	53	SF2
Fulham	38	14	10	14	52	46	52	
Birmingham City	38	12	14	12	43	48	50	
Middlesbrough	38	13	9	16	44	52	48	
Southampton	38	12	11	15	44	45	47	
Portsmouth	38	12	9	17	47	54	45	
Tottenham Hotspur	38	13	6	19	47	57	45	
Blackburn Rovers	38	12	8	18	51	59	44	
Manchester City	38	9	14	15	55	54	41	
Everton	38	9	12	17	45	57	39	
Leicester City	38	6	15	17	48	65	33	
Leeds United	38	8	9	21	40	79	33	
Wolverhampton W	38	7	12	19	38	77	33	

2004/05

SEASON SNIPPETS

Martin Laursen was Villa's major summer signing at a cost of £3m from AC Milan. Laursen made his debut on 14 August along with Carlton Cole who was on loan from Chelsea, and who scored on his debut.

Vaclav Drobny, who arrived from RC Strasbourg on loan for the season on 2 August, did not play a competitive game.

Steven Davis made his debut on 18 September.

Mathieu Berson, a £1.6m signing from Nantes made his debut on 22 September.

Peter Whittingham's goal against Portsmouth on 6 November made a small piece of history - it was the first scored with the Premier League's new high-visibility yellow and blue ball.

Stefan Moore played his last game on 28 December.

Cameroon international Eric Djemba-Djemba, signed from Manchester United for £1.35m, made his debut on 2 February.

Mathieu Berson played his last game on 20 March.

On 2 April, three Newcastle United players were sent off during Villa's 3-0 win at St James' Park - including Kieron Dyer and Lee Bowyer for fighting each other!

Stefan Postma played his last game on 1 May.

Thomas Hitzlsperger played his last game on 7 May.

Darius Vassell and Carlton Cole both played their last match on 15 May.

PREMIER LEAGUE

MANAGER: David O'Leary

MATCH	DATE	VENUE	OPPONENTS	RESULT	HT SCORE	SCORE	SCORERS	ATT
1	Aug 14	H	Southampton	W	2 0	2 0	Vassell, Cole	36,690
2	22	A	West Bromwich Albion	D	1 1	1 1	Mellberg	26,601
3	25	A	Charlton Athletic	L	0 2	0 3		26,190
4	28	H	Newcastle United	W	1 2	4 2	Mellberg, Cole, Barry, Angel	36,305
5	Sep 11	H	Chelsea	D	0 0	0 0		36,691
6	18	A	Norwich City	D	0 0	0 0		23,805
7	25	H	Crystal Palace	D	1 1	1 1	Hendrie	34,843
8	Oct 2	A	Blackburn Rovers	D	1 1	2 2	Angel, Mellberg	20,502
9	16	A	Arsenal	L	1 2	1 3	Hendrie	38,137
10	23	H	Fulham	W	1 0	2 0	Solano, Hendrie	34,460
11	30	A	Everton	D	1 1	1 1	Hendrie	37,816
12	Nov 6	H	Portsmouth	W	3 0	3 0	Whittingham, Angel, Solano	32,633
13	13	A	Bolton Wanderers	W	1 1	2 1	McCann, Hitzlsperger	25,779
14	22	H	Tottenham Hotspur	W	0 0	1 0	Solano	35,702
15	27	A	Manchester City	L	0 2	0 2		44,530
16	Dec 4	H	Liverpool	D	1 1	1 1	Solano	42,593
17	12	H	Birmingham City	L	0 1	1 2	Barry	41,329
18	18	A	Middlesbrough	L	0 1	0 3		31,338
19	26	A	Chelsea	L	0 1	0 1		41,950
20	28	H	Manchester United	L	0 1	0 1		42,593
21	Jan 1	H	Blackburn Rovers	W	0 0	1 0	Solano	34,265
22	3	A	Crystal Palace	L	0 1	0 2		24,140
23	15	H	Norwich City	W	2 0	3 0	Ashton (og), Hendrie, Solano	38,172
24	22	A	Manchester United	L	0 1	1 3	Barry	67,859
25	Feb 2	A	Fulham	D	0 0	1 1	Angel	17,624
26	5	H	Arsenal	L	0 3	1 3	Angel	42,593
27	12	A	Portsmouth	W	1 1	2 1	De Zeeuw (og), Hitzlsperger	20,160
28	26	H	Everton	L	0 1	1 3	Solano	40,248
29	Mar 5	A	Middlesbrough	W	0 0	2 0	Laursen, L Moore	34,201
30	20	A	Birmingham City	L	0 0	0 2		29,382
31	Apr 2	A	Newcastle United	W	1 0	3 0	Angel, Barry 2 (2 pens)	52,306
32	10	H	West Bromwich Albion	D	1 0	1 1	Vassell	39,402
33	16	A	Southampton	W	0 2	3 2	Cole, Solano, Davis	31,926
34	20	H	Charlton Athletic	D	0 0	0 0		31,312
35	23	H	Bolton Wanderers	D	1 0	1 1	Hierro (og)	36,053
36	May 1	A	Tottenham Hotspur	L	1 3	1 5	Barry (pen)	36,078
37	7	H	Manchester City	L	0 2	1 2	Angel	39,645
38	15	A	Liverpool	L	0 2	1 2	Barry	43,406

Final League Position: 10th in Premier League

3 Own-goals

Appearances
Subs
Goals

Match 15: Lee Hendrie sent off 90 minutes
Match 32: Liam Ridgewell sent off 60 minutes

FA CUP

3	Jan 8	A	Sheffield United	L	0 0	1 3	Barry	14,003

Appearances
Subs
Goals

FOOTBALL LEAGUE CUP

2	Sep 22	H	Queen's Park Rangers	W	2 0	3 1	Vassell, Angel, Solano	26,975
3	Oct 26	A	Burnley	L	0 1	1 3	Angel	11,184

Appearances
Subs
Goals

Players (by squad number)

1	Sorensen T (GK)
2	Delaney MA
3	Samuel J
4	Mellberg EO
5	Laursen M
6	Barry G
7	Hendrie LA
8	McCann GP
9	Angel JP
10	Vassell D
11	Solano NA
12	Hitzlsperger T
13	Postma S (GK)
14	Djemba-Djemba ED
15	De la Cruz BU
16	Berson M
17	Whittingham PM
18	Cole CM
19	Ridgewell LM
22	Moore LI
24	Davis S
26	Moore S

Match appearances (minutes / goals)

Match	1	2	3	4	5	6	7	8	9	10	11	12	13	14	15	16	17	18	19	22	24	26
1	90	90	90	90	90	22	90			85		90			15²		53¹	90		5³		
2	90	90	90	90	90		90		90	19¹	71	80			10²		10³	90				
3	45	90	90	90	90			90	18²	90	90	90	45¹					72				
4	90	90	90	90		90	30¹	90	20²	86	90	60			90			70		4³		
5	90	90	90	90		90	33¹	90	67	89	57	90			90		1³	90		23²		
6	90	90	90	90			90		33¹	90	57	78			90		12³	57		33²		
7	90	90	90	90	81	55	90	90	90	61	90	35¹			90		9³	29²				
8	90	90			76	90	90	90	14¹	76	14²				90			90				
9		90	90		8	90	90	32³		90		45	90		90		82¹	58		45²		
10	90	90	90	90		87	90	90	62	90	3³				90		78	28¹		12²		
11	90	58	90	90			90	90	90	77	60				90		13³	90	32¹	30²		
12	90	90	90	90			78	90	90		85	5³			90		90	68		22¹	12²	
13	90	90	90				89	90		75	27¹				90		63	90	1³	15²		
14	90	90	90	90	14¹		90	90		86	76				90			90		4²	90	
15	90	90	90		61	90	90	90		90	29¹				90			61		29²		
16	90	90	90	90			69	90		90					90	21²		35		55¹	90	
17	90	90	90	90			90	90	90	90					90	45¹	45	14²		90		
18	90	90	90	90		76	90		90						90	90	90		90	10²		
19	90	45		90	80		90	45¹		90					90	90		90	10²			
20	90	90	90	90	67		90			90					90	87	23²	54	90	36¹	90	3³
21		90	90	90	90	90	90			90					90			90	89	1¹	90	
22	90	90		90	66	90				90					90			90	24¹	90		
23	90	90	90	90	90		90			82	13²						77	74	90	16¹	8³	
24	90	11	90	90			90			74	45²				79¹		45		90	16³	90	
25	90		90				90	64		79	90			11³	90	90		45	90	45¹	26²	
26	90		62	90			90			90	28¹			66	90	24²			90	90	90	
27	90		90	90		90	53		90					75	37¹	90	90	1³		90	15²	
28	90		90	90	90	34¹		90	28²	90	90			56	90			90	62			
29	90		90	90	90			57	90						90	90			33¹	90		
30	90		71	90	90	90		30¹	19³						90	60		30²	60	90		
31	90	90		45	90	84		88	90	6²	90						2³	45¹		90		
32	90	90	90		90	90	90	80	90	64					26¹		10²	60		90		
33	90	90	90	45	90	90		77	36	45²	90				90		54¹			13³	90	
34	90	90	90		90	72		90	18¹	90	90				90			84		6²	90	
35	90	90	90		90			90	90	79	90				90			11¹			90	
36		90	90	90	90		31¹		59	90	90	59	90					90	31²	90		
37	90	90	45		90	90	78		90	90	45¹	45		45²	90			90		12³	90	
38	90	90	42²		90	90	48		64	45	90			90	90			26³		45¹	90	
	36	30	34	30	12	33	25	20	30	17	32	17	2	4	30	7	15	18	12	5	19	1
				1		1	4		5	4	4	11	1	2	4	4	8	9	3	20	9	1
			3		1	7	5	1	7	2	8	2				1	3			1	1	

FINAL LEAGUE TABLE

	P	W	D	L	F	A	P
Chelsea	38	29	8	1	72	15	95
Arsenal	38	25	8	5	87	36	83
Manchester United	38	22	11	5	58	26	77
Everton	38	18	7	13	45	46	61
Liverpool	38	17	7	14	52	41	58
Bolton Wanderers	38	16	10	12	49	44	58
Middlesbrough	38	14	13	11	53	46	55
Manchester City	38	13	13	12	47	39	52
Tottenham Hotspur	38	14	10	14	47	41	52
Aston Villa	**38**	**12**	**11**	**15**	**45**	**52**	**47**
Charlton Athletic	38	12	10	16	42	58	46
Birmingham City	38	11	12	15	40	46	45
Fulham	38	12	8	18	52	60	44
Newcastle United	38	10	14	14	47	57	44
Blackburn Rovers	38	9	15	14	32	43	42
Portsmouth	38	10	9	19	43	59	39
West Bromwich A	38	6	16	16	36	61	34
Crystal Palace	38	7	12	19	41	62	33
Norwich City	38	7	12	19	42	77	33
Southampton	38	6	14	18	45	66	32

2005/06

SEASON SNIPPETS

History was created on the opening day when all four goals in the match against Bolton Wanderers were scored in the first nine minutes. Aaron Hughes and Kevin Phillips made their debut with Phillips scoring in the fourth minute.

On 23 August, Nolberto Solano was sent off in his last Villa game. Solano returned to his former club, Newcastle United, on 31 August.

Czech striker Milan Baros arrived from Liverpool for £7m and scored on his debut on 27 August. It was the first game also for substitute Patrik Berger.

James Milner and Wilfred Bouma made their debut on 12 September.

Gary Cahill made his debut on 20 September.

Luke Moore netted on 24 September and won £10,000 for charity from The Sun newspaper as the first player to score against Chelsea. Moore was also the only player to score a Premier League goal at home and away against Chelsea in the season.

On 2 October, Eirik Bakke made his debut.

On 16 October, Villa gained their first Premier League victory over neighbours Birmingham City.

On 31 October, Stuart Taylor made his debut when Thomas Sorensen was injured in the warm-up.

Craig Gardner made his debut on 26 December.

Eirik Bakke played his last game on 14 January.

On 4 February, Luke Moore became the first teenager to score a Premier League hat-trick for Villa.

Gabriel Agbonlahor scored on his debut on 18 March.

On 18 April, Ulises De La Cruz played his last game.

On 19 February, Mark Delaney played his last game.

Kevin Phillips played his last game on 7 May. It was James Milner's last match on loan before returning to Newcastle United.

PREMIER LEAGUE

MANAGER: David O'Leary

MATCH	DATE	VENUE	OPPONENTS	RESULT	HT SCORE	SCORE	SCORERS	ATT
1	Aug 13	H	Bolton Wanderers	D	2 2	2 2	Phillips, Davis	33,263
2	20	A	Manchester United	L	0 0	0 1		67,934
3	23	A	Portsmouth	D	1 1	1 1	Hughes (og)	19,778
4	27	H	Blackburn Rovers	W	1 0	1 0	Baros	31,010
5	Sep 12	A	West Ham United	L	0 2	0 4		29,582
6	17	H	Tottenham Hotspur	D	1 0	1 1	Milner	33,686
7	24	A	Chelsea	L	1 1	1 2	Moore	42,146
8	Oct 2	H	Middlesbrough	L	0 1	2 3	Moore, Davis	29,719
9	16	A	Birmingham City	W	1 0	1 0	Phillips	29,312
10	22	H	Wigan Athletic	L	0 1	0 2		32,294
11	31	H	Manchester City	L	0 2	1 3	Ridgewell	42,069
12	Nov 5	H	Liverpool	L	0 0	0 2		42,551
13	19	A	Sunderland	W	0 0	3 1	Phillips, Barry, Baros	39,707
14	26	H	Charlton Athletic	W	0 0	1 0	Davis	30,023
15	Dec 3	A	Newcastle United	D	0 1	1 1	McCann	52,267
16	10	A	Bolton Wanderers	D	0 0	1 1	Angel	23,646
17	17	H	Manchester United	L	0 1	0 2		37,128
18	26	A	Everton	W	1 0	4 0	Baros 2, Delaney, Angel	32,432
19	28	A	Fulham	D	1 2	3 3	Moore, Ridgewell 2	20,446
20	31	H	Arsenal	D	0 0	0 0		37,114
21	Jan 2	A	West Bromwich Albion	W	0 0	2 1	Davis, Baros (pen)	27,073
22	14	H	West Ham United	L	1 0	1 2	Hendrie	36,700
23	21	A	Tottenham Hotspur	D	0 0	0 0		36,243
24	Feb 1	H	Chelsea	D	0 1	1 1	Moore	38,562
25	4	A	Middlesbrough	W	2 0	4 0	Moore 3, Phillips	27,299
26	11	H	Newcastle United	L	1 2	1 2	Moore	37,140
27	25	A	Charlton Athletic	D	0 0	0 0		26,594
28	Mar 4	H	Portsmouth	W	1 0	1 0	Baros	30,194
29	11	A	Blackburn Rovers	L	0 0	0 2		21,932
30	18	A	Everton	L	0 3	1 4	Agbonlahor	36,507
31	25	H	Fulham	D	0 0	0 0		32,605
32	Apr 1	A	Arsenal	L	0 2	0 5		38,183
33	9	A	West Bromwich Albion	D	0 0	0 0		33,303
34	16	H	Birmingham City	W	1 1	3 1	Baros 2, Cahill	40,158
35	18	A	Wigan Athletic	L	0 1	2 3	Angel, Ridgewell	17,330
36	25	A	Manchester City	L	0 0	0 1		26,422
37	29	A	Liverpool	L	0 1	1 3	Barry	44,479
38	May 7	H	Sunderland	W	1 0	2 1	Barry, Ridgewell	33,820

Final League Position: 16th in Premier League

Appearances
Subs
1 Own-goal
Goals

Match 3: Nolberto Solano sent off 9 minutes
Match 23: Gareth Barry sent off 83 minutes
Match 26: Llloyd Samuel left the field injured 88 minutes

FA CUP

3	Jan 7	A	Hull City	W	0 0	1 0	Barry	17,051
4	28	H	Port Vale	W	0 0	3 1	Barros 2, Davis	30,434
5	Feb 19	H	Manchester City	D	0 0	1 1	Barros	23,847
R	Mar 14	A	Manchester City	L	0 1	1 2	Davis	33,006

Appearances
Subs
Goals

FOOTBALL LEAGUE CUP

2	Sep 20	A	Wycombe Wanderers	W	1 3	8 3	Davis 2, Baros, Milner 2, Easton (og), Barry 2	5,365
3	Oct 25	H	Burnley	W	1 0	1 0	Phillips	26,872
4	Nov 29	A	Doncaster Rovers	L	0 1	0 3		10,590

Appearances
Subs
1 Own-goal
Goals

520

Sorensen T (GK)	Delaney MA	Samuel J	Mellberg EO	Laursen M	Barry G	Hendrie LA	McCann GP	Angel JP	Baros M	Solano NA	Milner JP	Davis S	Taylor SJ (GK)	Djemba-Djemba ED	De la Cruz BU	Bouma W	Whittingham PM	Hughes AW	Ridgewell LM	Phillips KM	Cahill GJ	Moore LI	Berger P	Bakke E	Gardner C	Agbonlahor G		MATCH
1	2	3	4	5	6	7	8	9	10	11	12	13	14	15	16	17	18	19	20	21	22	23	24	26	30			
90		90	90	90	90		90	90		90		90				90	90		17³									1
90	20	90		90		90	90	90		17²		90		70¹	73		73	90	90		16²							2
90		90		90		90	74	9		90		90			53¹		90	90	37									3
90		90	90	90		90		90			90	90			69	90	90	90		21¹								4
90				90		62	9³	81	33¹	90		90			90	90	90		57		28²							5
90	18¹	90		90			90	90		90	90				72	90	90				90							6
90	23¹	90		85	5³		90			90	90			17²		73	90	90			90	67						7
90	45¹	90		90			90			90	90			45	76		90				90	90	14²					8
90		90		63			26²			90				6³			90		64		90	27¹	84					9
90		90	90	90			36¹			90	90						90	90	90		54	21²	69					10
	90	45		90						90	90		90	15³				90			70	30¹	20²					11
90	90		90		90	8²	90	29¹	90		90	90						90	61			82						12
90			90	90		1²	90		89	90	89				90		90	90	68		22¹		1³					13
90			90			90		89		90	90				90		90	90	90		1¹							14
90			90			90	90	62	90		61				90		90	90			28²	29¹						15
90			90			90	84	6³	76		81	9²			90		90	90			14³	90						16
90	90			90			90	45¹	90		45	90			90		90	90				90						17
90	90			90			90	16²	90		61	84			90		90				74		29¹	6³				18
90				90			90	20¹	90		90	90				76		90			70		14²					19
90	90			90			90	14¹	90		90	90			90		90	90			76		90					20
	90		90	90			90	27¹	90		90	90	90				90				85		63	5²				21
90	90	90	90			77¹	90	29²	90		90	90					90				61		13					22
90		5¹		83		90	90	80		90	90						90				5²							23
90	90	90	90			90	90	15¹	75		90	90					90		75		15²							24
90	90	82	79		90	8²	6³		90	90						90	11¹	90			84							25
90	90	88	90		90	55		35¹	35²						90	90	31³	55			90		59					26
90		90	90			90		90	65	90		90				45	90	25²			45¹							27
90		23		90		90		59		90	90			67¹	90		90	90	90		31²							28
90			90	90		9¹	90	8²	81		90				90		90	90	82		90							29
90		61¹	90		90	33²	90			90							29	90			90		57	90				30
90				90	58	90	17²			90		90			90		90	90	90		73					32¹		31
90				52	90		45¹			90				52	90		90	45	38²	90						38³		32
90					33	90			90		90						90	74	90		16²					57¹	90	33
90	90			90		90	29²	90		85	25						90	90	61	90						65¹	5³	34
90	90			90			90	90		90				24²			66	90		90						45	45¹	35
90		90	90			90	90	90	58		90				90		90	75	15²	90							32¹	36
90			90		82		90	45¹	45		90	86			90		90		8²	90						4³	90	37
90					90	8²	90	90		82	90				90		90	90	66	90						24¹		38
36	12	14	27	1	36	7	32	12	24	27	34	2	0	4	20	4	35	30	20	6	16	3	8	3	3			
		5				9		19	1		1			4	3			2	3		11	5	6	5	6			
		1				3	1	1	3		0	1		1				5	4	1	8				1			

90	90		90		90	90	90		90			90		90			3
90	90	90	90		90	90	69	90	90	90		90	21¹				4
90	45	90	90		90	90	26²	90	90	90		90	45¹	64			5
		90	90		90		40		90		90	90	90	90	50¹		R

FINAL LEAGUE TABLE

	P	W	D	L	F	A	P
Chelsea	38	29	4	5	72	22	91
Manchester United	38	25	8	5	72	34	83
Liverpool	38	25	7	6	57	25	82
Arsenal	38	20	7	11	68	31	67
Tottenham Hotspur	38	18	11	9	53	38	65
Blackburn Rovers	38	19	6	13	51	42	63
Newcastle United	38	17	7	14	47	42	58
Bolton Wanderers	38	15	11	12	49	41	56
West Ham United	38	16	7	15	52	55	55
Wigan Athletic	38	15	6	17	45	52	51
Everton	38	14	8	16	34	49	50
Fulham	38	14	6	18	48	58	48
Charlton Athletic	38	13	8	17	41	55	47
Middlesbrough	38	12	9	17	48	58	45
Manchester City	38	13	4	21	43	48	43
Aston Villa	**38**	**10**	**12**	**16**	**42**	**55**	**42**
Portsmouth	38	10	8	20	37	62	38
Birmingham City	38	8	10	20	28	50	34
West Bromwich A	38	7	9	22	31	58	30
Sunderland	38	3	6	29	26	69	15

2006/07

SEASON SNIPPETS

Martin O'Neill was appointed manager two weeks before the start of the season following the summer sacking of David O'Leary.

Bulgarian midfielder Stiliyan Petrov became O'Neill's first signing when he was snapped up from Celtic for £6.5m, while Ulises de la Cruz joined Reading, Kevin Phillips moved to West Bromwich Albion and Mathieu Berson linked up with Spanish club Levante.

Didier Agathe was signed on a short-term contract on 12 September and made his debut as a substitute against Tottenham Hotspur on 14 October. Agathe departed on 11 January 2007.

Chris Sutton was signed on a free transfer from Celtic in October, but was forced to retire at the end of the season because of a problem with his vision.

Olof Mellberg scored the first competitive goal at Arsenal's new Emirates Stadium on 19 August.

Villa were busy in the January transfer window, signing Ashley Young from Watford for £8m, Shaun Maloney from Celtic for £1m and John Carew from Lyon in exchange for Milan Baros.

Phil Bardsley was signed on a loan-deal until the end of the season from Manchester United on 8 January and made his debut against Watford on 20 January.

PREMIER LEAGUE

MANAGER: Martin O'Neill

MATCH	DATE	VENUE	OPPONENTS	RESULT	HT SCORE	SCORE	SCORERS	ATT
1	Aug 19	A	Arsenal	D	0 0	1 1	Mellberg	60,023
2	23	H	Reading	W	1 1	2 1	Angel (pen), Barry	37,329
3	27	H	Newcastle United	W	2 0	2 0	Moore, Angel	35,141
4	Sep 10	A	West Ham United	D	1 0	1 1	Ridgewell	34,576
5	16	A	Watford	D	0 0	0 0		18,620
6	23	H	Charlton Athletic	W	1 0	2 0	Agbonlahor, Moore	35,513
7	30	A	Chelsea	D	1 1	1 1	Agbonlahor	41,951
8	Oct 14	H	Tottenham Hotspur	D	0 0	1 1	Barry	42,551
9	21	A	Fulham	D	1 1	1 1	Barry (pen)	30,919
10	28	A	Liverpool	L	0 3	1 3	Agbonlahor	44,117
11	Nov 5	H	Blackburn Rovers	W	1 0	2 0	Barry (pen), Angel	30,089
12	11	A	Everton	W	1 0	1 0	Sutton	36,376
13	19	A	Wigan Athletic	D	0 0	0 0		18,455
14	25	H	Middlesbrough	D	1 1	1 1	Barry (pen)	33,612
15	29	H	Manchester City	L	0 2	1 3	McCann	30,124
16	Dec 2	A	Portsmouth	D	1 0	2 2	Barry (pen), Angel	20,042
17	11	H	Sheffield United	D	1 0	2 2	Petrov, Baros	30,957
18	16	H	Bolton Wanderers	L	0 0	0 1		27,450
19	23	H	Manchester United	L	0 0	0 3		42,551
20	26	A	Tottenham Hotspur	L	1 0	1 2	Barry	35,293
21	30	H	Charlton Athletic	L	1 0	1 2	Barry (pen)	26,699
22	Jan 2	H	Chelsea	D	0 0	0 0		41,006
23	13	A	Manchester United	L	0 3	1 3	Agbonlahor	76,073
24	20	H	Watford	W	0 0	2 0	Mahon (og), Agbonlahor	35,892
25	31	A	Newcastle United	L	1 2	1 3	Young	49,201
26	Feb 3	H	West Ham United	W	1 0	1 0	Carew	41,202
27	10	A	Reading	L	0 1	0 2		24,122
28	Mar 3	A	Fulham	D	1 1	1 1	Carew	24,552
29	14	H	Arsenal	L	0 1	0 1		39,968
30	18	H	Liverpool	D	0 0	0 0		42,551
31	Apr 2	H	Everton	D	0 1	1 1	Agbonlahor	36,407
32	7	A	Blackburn Rovers	W	1 1	2 1	Berger, Agbonlahor	24,211
33	9	H	Wigan Athletic	D	0 1	1 1	Agbonlahor	31,920
34	14	A	Middlesbrough	W	1 1	3 1	Gardner, Moore, Petrov	26,959
35	22	H	Portsmouth	D	0 0	0 0		31,745
36	28	A	Manchester City	W	1 0	2 0	Carew, Maloney	40,799
37	May 5	H	Sheffield United	W	2 0	3 0	Agbonlahor, Young, Berger	42,551
38	13	A	Bolton Wanderers	D	1 1	2 2	Gardner, Moore	26,255

Final League Position: 11th in Premier League

1 Own-goal

Appearances
Subs
Goals

Match 21: Gareth Barry sent off 61 minutes

FA CUP

3	Jan 7	A	Manchester United	L	0 0	1 2	Baros	74,924

Appearances
Subs
Goals

FOOTBALL LEAGUE CUP

2	Sep 20	A	Scunthorpe United	W	1 0	2 1	Angel 2	6,502
3	Oct 24	A	Leicester City *	W	2 1	3 2	Angel, Barry (pen), Agbonlahor	27,288
4	Nov 8	A	Chelsea	L	0 1	0 4		41,516

Appearances
Subs
Goals

* After extra-time

Appearances and Goals

	Sorensen T (GK)	Delaney MA	Samuel J	Mellberg EO	Laursen M	Barry G	Hendrie LA	McCann GP	Angel JP	Baros M	Carew JA	Petrov SA	Davis S	Taylor SJ (GK)	Djemba-Djemba ED	Agbonlahor G	Bouma W	Whittingham PM	Young AS	Hughes AW	Ridgewell LM	Phillips KM	Sutton CR	Cahill GJ	Moore LI	Berger P	Bardsley PA	Gardner C	Osbourne I	Kiraly GF (GK)	Maloney SR	Agathe FD	MATCH
	1	2	3	4	5	6	7	8	9	10	11	12	13	14	15	16	17	18	19	20	20	21	22	23	24	26	27	28	31				
	90	90	90	1²	90	7¹	90	89			83		1³		90		90	90			89												1
	90	59	90		90	90	90	90			90		90		31¹		90	90			90												2
	90		90		90	90	90	90			90		90		90		90	90			90												3
	90		90	90	90		90	81	9¹		90		90		85			90			90		72		5²								4
	90		90	90	90		90	90	18¹		90		90		85			90			90		90										5
	90		90	90	90		90	90	8¹		90		90		90		90	90			90		82										6
	90		90	7²	90		90	90	50¹		90		83		90		90	90			90		40										7
			90		90		90	90	65		90		77	90	90		90	90			90			13²				25¹					8
	90		90	90	90			75	45		90		83		90		90	90	15²			90	7³		45¹								9
	90		90	90	90			45	45		90		16³		90			90	45¹		89		74		45¹								10
	90		90	90	90		90	90	1¹		90		90		90	90		90															11
	90		90		90		90	76		90	1²		90		90	90		90			89		90		90			14¹					12
	90		90		90			68			22²		90		90	51		90			90	90			90			39¹					13
	70		90		90		90	61	29¹		90	29²	20³		90	90		90				90		61									14
			90		90		90	90		90	90	27¹	90		90	63		90															15
			90		90		90	90	12¹	78		89	90		90		1²	90			90			90									16
			90		90		90	7³	90		75	90	90		67		23¹	90	83		90												17
			90		90		45	19²	71		90		90		90			90	90		90		45¹		90								18
			90		90		90	77	13¹		90		90				90	90			90		90		90								19
			45		90			90		90			45		90		36	54¹			90				90	45³	90						20
			90		61			63			70		90		90	27¹		90							90	20²	90						21
			90					90	90	15²		90	75		90		90	90			90				27	63¹	90						22
			90						90		90		90		45²		90	45			45	90			90								23
	90	45¹	90		90		90			90			90		90	90		90			90		18¹	90									24
	90	11²	90		90		90	72	79		90		90		90	90		90			90		21¹	90									25
			90		90		90	5²		69	90				90	85	90				90		17¹	90									26
	90		90		90				73	90			90		90	90	89		1²		90		15¹	90					90				27
	90		90		90					90	90	2²			75		88				90			90					67				28
	90		90		90	56	90			90	90				23²	90		90			34¹		90										29
	90		90		90		90	75		90	90				90	90		90			90		15¹	90									30
	90		90		90		90	90		90	90				76	90		90			90		14¹	90									31
	90		90		90		90	45		90	90				90	90		41					45²	90				49³					32
	90		90	90	90			14¹		90	6³		90		90		10²				90		84	80	90			76					33
	90		90	90	90			90		90			90		39	51¹					17²		90	90	90			73					34
	90		90		90			90		90	9²		90		90	90	81	5³			24¹		90	85				66					35
	90		90		90				75	90			90		90	90	13²				15¹	80	77	90				10³					36
			90		90				71	90			86		90	90					4²	90	90	90				19¹					37
	90		90	90	90		7³		79		18¹		83		90	90		90			11²	90		90									38
	45		90	90	90						90		90		13¹	45¹		83	90		77			15²	75			90					

29	2	38	12	35		28	18	10	11	30		17	4	37	23	2	11	15		19		6	19	7	5	13	11	6	5	5		
	2		2		1	2	5	7		4		11	2	1	2		4	2		1	2	1	6	8	2	5		3	5			
			1		8		1	4	1	3	2		9					2			2		4	2			1					

	24²		90		90	53	37¹		66					90	90			90	90			90				90	90					3
		1			1		1		1		1			1				1			1					1	1					
							1											1														
								1																								

90		90		90		43	90	22²		90	90			90		47¹		90	90			68						107		30²	2
		120		120				66		120	90	120		120	13³			120	120			54¹										3
90		90	45	45		90	90	19³		90	71			90	90			90	45¹			90				45²					4

2		3	1	3		2	3	1		3	3	1		3	2	1		3	2			1				1		1		1	
							1	2			1				1	1			1			1				1					
				1				3							1			1													

FINAL LEAGUE TABLE

	P	W	D	L	F	A	P	
Manchester United	38	28	5	5	83	27	89	
Chelsea	38	24	11	3	64	24	83	
Liverpool	38	20	8	10	57	27	68	
Arsenal	38	19	11	8	63	35	68	
Tottenham Hotspur	38	17	9	12	57	54	60	
Everton	38	15	13	10	52	36	58	
Bolton Wanderers	38	16	8	14	47	52	56	
Reading	38	16	7	15	52	47	55	
Portsmouth	38	14	12	12	45	42	54	
Blackburn Rovers	38	15	7	16	52	54	52	
Aston Villa	**38**	**11**	**17**	**10**	**43**	**41**	**50**	
Middlesbrough	38	12	10	16	44	49	46	
Newcastle United	38	11	10	17	38	47	43	
Manchester City	38	11	9	18	29	44	42	
West Ham United	38	12	5	21	35	59	41	
Fulham	38	8	15	15	38	60	39	
Wigan Athletic	38	10	8	20	37	59	38	
Sheffield United	38	10	8	20	32	55	38	
Charlton Athletic	38	8	10	20	34	60	34	
Watford	38	5	13	20	29	59	28	

523

2007/08

SEASON SNIPPETS

Nigel Reo-Coker arrived from West Ham for £7.5m on 5 July 2007 and by the end of August he had been joined by Marlon Harewood, also from the Hammers, Zat Knight from Fulham and Moustapha Salifou from Wil 1900.

Villa played Inter Milan in a pre-season friendly on Saturday 4 August 2007, winning 3-0, before a crowd of 36,239. It was the first time for 12 years that Villa Park had hosted a pre-season friendly.

Scott Carson was signed on a season-long loan deal on 10 August and Curtis Davies on loan from West Bromwich Albion for the season on 31 August.

On 15 August, Mark Delaney was forced to retire through injury.

Wayne Routledge arrived from Tottenham for £1.25 million on 30 January.

Stiliyan Petrov scored from 45 yards against Derby County on 12 April. No Villa player had scored from a longer distance previously. The goal was voted Goal of the Month by BBC Match of the Day and also Match magazine.

Two members of Villa's 1957 FA Cup winning side died during the season, centre-half Jimmy Dugdale died at the age of 76 in February and winger Leslie Smith died the following month, age 80.

PREMIER LEAGUE

MANAGER: Martin O'Neill

MATCH	DATE	VENUE	OPPONENTS	RESULT	HT SCORE	SCORE	SCORERS	ATT
1	Aug 11	H	Liverpool	L	0 1	1 2	Barry (pen)	42,640
2	18	A	Newcastle United	D	0 0	0 0		51,049
3	25	H	Fulham	W	0 1	2 1	Young, Maloney	36,638
4	Sep 2	H	Chelsea	W	0 0	2 0	Knight, Agbonlahor	37,714
5	16	A	Manchester City	L	0 0	0 1		38,363
6	23	H	Everton	W	1 0	2 0	Carew, Agbonlahor	38,235
7	Oct 1	A	Tottenham Hotspur	D	3 1	4 4	Laursen 2, Agbonlahor, Gardner	36,094
8	6	H	West Ham United	W	1 0	1 0	Gardner	40,842
9	20	H	Manchester United	L	1 3	1 4	Agbonlahor	42,640
10	28	A	Bolton Wanderers	D	0 1	1 1	Moore	18,413
11	Nov 3	H	Derby County	W	0 0	2 0	Laursen, Young	40,938
12	11	A	Birmingham City	W	1 0	2 1	Ridgewell (og), Agbonlahor	26,539
13	24	A	Middlesbrough	W	1 0	3 0	Carew, Mellberg, Agbonlahor	23,900
14	28	A	Blackburn Rovers	W	1 0	4 0	Carew, Barry (pen), Young, Harewood	20,776
15	Dec 1	H	Arsenal	L	1 2	1 2	Gardner	42,018
16	8	H	Portsmouth	L	0 2	1 3	Barry (pen)	35,790
17	15	A	Sunderland	D	0 1	1 1	Maloney	43,248
18	22	H	Manchester City	D	1 1	1 1	Carew	41,455
19	26	A	Chelsea	D	2 1	4 4	Maloney 2, Laursen, Barry (pen)	41,686
20	29	A	Wigan Athletic	W	0 1	2 1	Davies, Agbonlahor	18,806
21	Jan 1	H	Tottenham Hotspur	W	1 0	2 1	Mellberg, Laursen	41,609
22	12	H	Reading	W	1 0	3 1	Carew 2, Laursen	32,288
23	21	A	Liverpool	D	0 1	2 2	Harewood, Fabio Aurelio (og)	42,590
24	26	H	Blackburn Rovers	D	0 0	1 1	Young	39,602
25	Feb 3	A	Fulham	L	0 0	1 2	Hughes (og)	24,760
26	9	H	Newcastle United	W	0 1	4 1	Bouma, Carew 3 (1 pen),	42,640
27	24	A	Reading	W	1 0	2 1	Young, Harewood	23,889
28	Mar 1	A	Arsenal	D	1 0	1 1	Senderos (og)	60,097
29	12	H	Middlesbrough	D	0 1	1 1	Barry (pen)	39,874
30	15	A	Portsmouth	L	0 2	0 2		20,388
31	22	H	Sunderland	L	0 0	0 1		42,640
32	29	A	Manchester United	L	0 2	0 4		75,932
33	Apr 5	H	Bolton Wanderers	W	1 0	4 0	Barry 2, Agbonlahor, Harewood	37,773
34	12	A	Derby County	W	3 0	6 0	Young, Carew, Petrov, Barry, Agbonlahor, Harewood	33,036
35	20	H	Birmingham City	W	2 0	5 1	Young 2, Carew 2, Agbonlahor	42,584
36	27	A	Everton	D	0 0	2 2	Agbonhahor, Carew	37,936
37	May 3	H	Wigan Athletic	L	0 0	0 2		42,640
38	11	A	West Ham United	D	1 1	2 2	Young, Barry	34,969

Final League Position: 6th in Premier League

4 Own-goals

Appearances
Subs
Goals

Match 9: Nigel Reo-Coker sent off 60 minutes
Match 9: Scott Carson sent off 67 minutes
Match 19: Zat Knight sent off 45 minutes
Match 30: Olof Mellberg sent off 89 minutes

FA CUP

3	Jan 5	H	Manchester United	L	0 0	0 2		33,630

Appearances
Subs
Goals

FOOTBALL LEAGUE CUP

2	Aug 28	A	Wrexham	W	1 0	5 0	Maloney 2, Moore, Reo-Coker, Harewood	8,221
3	Sep 26	H	Leicester City	L	0 0	0 1		25,956

Appearances
Subs
Goals

524

Aston Villa — Player Appearances

	Sorensen T (GK)	Bouma W	Mellberg EO	Laursen M	Barry G	Young AS	Moore LI	Harewood MA	Carew JA	Agbonlahor G	Taylor SJ (GK)	Davies CE	Knight Z	Salifou M	Routledge WNA	Petrov SA	Reo-Coker NSA	Cahill GJ	Carson SP (GK)	Berger P	Gardner C	Osbourne I	Maloney SR	MATCH
	1	3	4	5	6	7	8	9	10	11	13	15	16	17	18	19	20	21	22	23	26	27	28	
	71	90	45	90	90	90	19²		90	90		90				90	90	45¹		90				1
	90	90	90	90	90	24¹		66	90			90				90	90			90				2
	83	90	90	90	90	45¹	11²	79	90							45	90			90		7³		3
	90	90	90	90	90			79	90			90				11¹	90	90						4
	82	90	90	90	90			66	90			90				8²	82	90		8³		24¹		5
	90	90	90	90	90	80	10²	53	90			90					90	90		37¹				6
	90	90	90	90	90	66	24¹		90			90				17²	90	90		73				7
	90	90	90	90	90	67		90	90			90				12²	90	90		78		23¹		8
	90	90	90	90	90	53			90	23³		67					60	90		53	37¹	37²		9
	90	90	90	90	90	45¹			90	90		90				90		90			45	45		10
	90	90	90	90	69	77			90			2³	88			90	90	90		13²		21¹		11
	90	90	90	90	90	21¹		69	90				90			90	90	90						12
	90	90	84	90	90			75	90			6³	90			79	90	90		11²		15¹		13
	90	90	90	90		5²	90	85	90				90			82	90	90		8¹				14
	76	90	90	90			90	90	90				90			32		90	14²	90		58¹		15
	54	90	90	90	90		19²	90	90				90				90	90	36¹	71				16
	90	90	90	90	90			90	90				90				90	90		67		23¹		17
	90	90	90	90	90			90	90				90			15¹	90	90				75		18
	89	90	90	90	90	12²	1³	78	90	45¹		45				90		90				45		19
	90	90	90	90	89	79¹		11	90	90						1³	90			30²		60		20
	84	90	90	90	90	74			90				90			90	90	90		16¹		6²		21
	90		90	90	89		1¹	89	89		90		1²			90	90	90		90		1³		22
	90		90		90		24¹	89	90	90		1²				90	90			66				23
	90	90	90	90	90	30¹	90	90	90				90			60	90	90						24
	87	90	90	90			45¹	90	45	89			90			90	90	90		3²	1³	90		25
	90	45	90	90	89		45¹	90		90						45	90	90		45²	1³	90		26
	90		90	90	90		17¹	90	90	90							86	90		90	4²	73		27
	90		90	90	90		18³	90	90	39		58¹					32	90		90	51²	72		28
	90	45¹	90	90	90		45²	90	90				90				90	90		45		45		29
	79	89		90	90		33¹	90	90				90	11²			90	90				57		30
		90	90	90	90		33¹	90	90				90			57				90	16²	74		31
	80	90	90	90			69	41	90					21²		90	90				10³	49¹		32
	90	90	90	90	83		13¹	77	90			90		4³		86	90			90	7²			33
	90	90	90	80	80		17¹	73	90					90	10²	90	90			90	10³			34
	90	85	90	90	90		5¹	90	90				90			90	90	90						35
	78	90	90	90			12²	90	90				75			90	90			90	15¹			36
	69	90	90	90	90		21²	90	90				60			90	90			90	30¹			37
	90	90	90	90			3¹	87	90				90			90	90	90						38
	38	33	38	37	37	8	1	32	37	3	9	25				22	36		35		15	1	11	
		1				7	22			1	3	2	4	1	6		1		8	8	7	11		
	3	1			2	6	1	9	11	13	9	1			5	4	1		1					

	83	90	90	90	90	26¹		64	90		90					75	90		90	7³		15²	
	1	1	1	1	1	1		1	1		1					1	1		1			1	
						1														1			

		90		90		90	90		90	90						24¹	66	90			90	90	90	
	90		90	90	19¹	14²	76		90	90	80	90				90	90			10³		71	90	
		2		2		1	2		2	2	1	1				1	2	1		1	2	2	
					1	1										1							
						1	1															2	

FINAL LEAGUE TABLE

	P	W	D	L	F	A	P	
Manchester United	38	27	6	5	80	22	87	
Chelsea	38	25	10	3	65	26	85	
Arsenal	38	24	11	3	74	31	83	
Liverpool	38	21	13	4	67	28	76	2
Everton	38	19	8	11	55	33	65	3
Aston Villa	**38**	**16**	**12**	**10**	**71**	**51**	**60**	
Blackburn Rovers	38	15	13	10	50	48	58	
Portsmouth	38	16	9	13	48	40	57	
Manchester City	38	15	10	13	45	53	55	
West Ham United	38	13	10	15	42	50	49	
Tottenham Hotspur	38	11	13	14	66	61	46	
Newcastle United	38	11	10	17	45	65	43	
Middlesbrough	38	10	12	16	43	53	42	
Wigan Athletic	38	10	10	18	34	51	40	
Sunderland	38	11	6	21	36	59	39	
Bolton Wanderers	38	9	10	19	36	54	37	
Fulham	38	8	12	18	38	60	36	
Reading	38	10	6	22	41	66	36	
Birmingham City	38	8	11	19	46	62	35	
Derby County	38	1	8	29	20	89	11	

2008/09

SEASON SNIPPETS

On 3 July, Curtis Davies' loan was made permanent with Villa paying West Bromwich Albion £8m for his services, Steve Sidwell arrived from Chelsea a week later and Brad Friedel was signed from Blackburn Rovers on the 28th.

Nicky Shorey arrived from Reading on 8 August and Luke Young from Middlesbrough on the same day. Four days later Carlos Cuellar was transferred from Glasgow Rangers.

Nathan Delfouneso made his debut against Hafnarfjodur on 14 August.

Gabriel Agbonlahor became the first Villa player for 78 years to score a hat-trick in the opening League game of a season, notching a treble in a 4-2 win over Manchester City.

USA International goalkeeper Bradley Guzan made his Villa debut in the League Cup match against QPR on 24 September after representing his Country in the Olympic Games in Beijing.

Starting with the 2-0 win at Arsenal on 15 November, Villa went on a record-breaking sequence of seven consecutive away league wins, that only ended at Manchester City on 4 March.

Barry Bannan made his debut at SV Hamburg on 17 December.

Emile Heskey arrived from Wigan on 23 January for £3.5m and scored the only goal of the game on making his debut four days later at Portsmouth.

Marc Albrighton made his debut against CSK Moscow on 26 February.

On 15 May, Martin Laursen announced his retirement due to a serious knee injury. Laursen's last game was against West Bromwich Albion on 10 January.

Gareth Barry played the last of his 440 Villa games against Newcastle United on 24 May and joined Manchester City in a £12m deal on 2 June.

Former Villa players Johnny Dixon, Peter Aldis, Paul Birch, Vic Crowe, Harry Parkes, Eddie Lowe, Geoff Sidebottom, and Bert 'Sailor' Brown all died during the season.

PREMIER LEAGUE

MANAGER: Martin O'Neill

MATCH	DATE	VENUE	OPPONENTS	RESULT	HT SCORE	SCORE	SCORERS	ATT
1	Aug 17	H	Manchester City	W	0 0	4 2	Carew, Agbonlahor 3	39,955
2	23	A	Stoke City	L	0 1	2 3	Carew, Laursen	27,500
3	31	H	Liverpool	D	0 0	0 0		41,647
4	Sep 15	A	Tottenham Hotspur	W	1 0	2 1	Reo-Coker, A Young	36,075
5	21	A	West Bromwich Albion	W	2 1	2 1	Carew, Agbonlahor	26,011
6	27	H	Sunderland	W	2 1	2 1	A Young, Carew	38,706
7	Oct 5	A	Chelsea	L	0 2	0 2		41,593
8	18	H	Portsmouth	D	0 0	0 0		37,660
9	26	A	Wigan Athletic	W	1 0	4 0	Barry (pen), Agbonlahor, Carew, Sidwell	20,249
10	29	H	Blackburn Rovers	W	1 1	3 2	L Young, Barry, Agbonlahor	35,985
11	Nov 3	A	Newcastle United	L	0 0	0 2		44,567
12	9	H	Middlesbrough	L	1 1	1 2	Sidwell	36,672
13	15	A	Arsenal	W	0 0	2 0	Clichy (og), Agbonlahor	60,047
14	22	H	Manchester United	D	0 0	0 0		42,585
15	29	H	Fulham	D	0 0	0 0		36,625
16	Dec 7	A	Everton	W	1 1	3 2	Sidwell, A Young 2	31,922
17	13	H	Bolton Wanderers	W	2 1	4 2	Agbonlahor 2, Davies (og), A Young	35,134
18	20	A	West Ham United	W	0 0	1 0	Neill (og)	31,353
19	26	H	Arsenal	D	0 1	2 2	Barry (pen), Knight	42,585
20	30	A	Hull City	W	0 0	1 0	Zayatte (og)	24,747
21	Jan 10	H	West Bromwich Albion	W	2 0	2 1	Davies, Agbonlahor	41,757
22	17	A	Sunderland	W	0 1	2 1	Milner, Barry (pen)	40,350
23	27	A	Portsmouth	W	1 0	1 0	Heskey	19,073
24	31	H	Wigan Athletic	D	0 0	0 0		41,766
25	Feb 7	A	Blackburn Rovers	W	1 0	2 0	Milner, Agbonlahor	24,267
26	21	H	Chelsea	L	0 1	0 1		42,585
27	Mar 1	H	Stoke City	D	1 0	2 2	Petrov, Carew	39,641
28	4	A	Manchester City	L	0 1	0 2		40,137
29	15	H	Tottenham Hotspur	L	0 1	1 2	Carew	41,205
30	22	A	Liverpool	L	0 3	0 5		44,131
31	Apr 5	A	Manchester United	L	1 1	2 3	Carew, Agbonlahor	75,409
32	12	H	Everton	D	1 2	3 3	Carew, Milner, Barry (pen)	40,188
33	18	H	West Ham United	D	1 0	1 1	Heskey	39,534
34	25	A	Bolton Wanderers	D	1 0	1 1	A Young	21,709
35	May 4	H	Hull City	W	1 0	1 0	Carew	39,607
36	9	A	Fulham	L	1 1	1 3	A Young	25,660
37	16	A	Middlesbrough	D	0 1	1 1	Carew	27,621
38	24	H	Newcastle United	W	1 0	1 0	Duff (og)	42,585

Final League Position: 6th in Premier League

Match 22: Ashley Young sent off 72 minutes **Match 30:** Brad Friedel sent off 64 minutes

Appearances
Subs
Goals

FA CUP

3	Jan 4	A	Gillingham	W	1 0	2 1	Milner 2 (1 pen)	10,107
4	24	A	Doncaster Rovers	D	0 0	0 0		13,517
R	Feb 4	H	Doncaster Rovers	W	2 1	3 1	Sidwell, Carew, Delfouneso	24,203
5	15	A	Everton	L	1 2	1 3	Milner (pen)	32,979

Appearances
Subs
Goals

FOOTBALL LEAGUE CUP

3	Sep 24	H	Queen's Park Rangers	L	0 0	0 1		21,541

Appearances
Subs
Goals

INTERTOTO CUP

3F	Jul 19	A	Odense BK	D	1 1	2 2	Carew, Laursen	11,393
3S	26	H	Odense BK	W	0 0	1 0	A Young	31,423

Appearances
Subs
Goals

UEFA CUP

QF	Aug 14	A	FH Hafnarfjordur	W	3 1	4 1	Barry, A Young, Agbonlahor, Laursen	8,686
QS	28	H	FH Hafnarfjordur	D	1 1	1 1	Gardner	25,415
1F	Sep 18	A	PFC Litex Lovech	W	1 1	3 1	Reo-Coker, Barry (pen), Petrov	7,000
2S	Oct 2	H	PFC Litex Lovech	D	1 0	1 1	Harewood	27,230
MD1	23	H	Ajax	W	2 1	2 1	Laursen, Barry	36,657
MD2	Nov 6	A	Slavia Prague	W	1 0	1 0	Carew	20,302
MD4	Dec 4	A	MSK Zilina	L	1 2	1 2	Delfouneso	28,797
MD5	17	H	SV Hamburg	L	0 2	1 3	Delfouneso	49,121
32F	Feb 18	H	CSKA Moscow	D	0 1	1 1	Carew	38,038
32S	26	A	CSKA Moscow	L	0 0	0 2		25,650

Appearances
Subs
Goals

Match MD5: Steve Sidwell sent off 83 minutes

FINAL LEAGUE TABLE

	P	W	D	L	F	A	P
Manchester United	38	28	6	4	68	24	90
Liverpool	38	25	11	2	77	27	86
Chelsea	38	25	8	5	68	24	83
Arsenal	38	20	12	6	68	37	72
Everton	38	17	12	9	55	37	63
Aston Villa	**38**	**17**	**11**	**10**	**54**	**48**	**62**
Fulham	38	14	11	13	39	34	53
Tottenham Hotspur	38	14	9	15	45	45	51
West Ham United	38	14	9	15	42	45	51
Manchester City	38	15	5	18	58	50	50
Wigan Athletic	38	12	9	17	34	45	45
Stoke City	38	12	9	17	38	55	45
Bolton Wanderers	38	11	8	19	41	53	41
Portsmouth	38	10	11	17	38	57	41
Blackburn Rovers	38	10	11	17	40	60	41
Sunderland	38	9	9	20	34	54	36
Hull City	38	8	11	19	39	64	35
Newcastle United	38	7	13	18	40	59	34
Middlesbrough	38	7	11	20	28	57	32
West Bromwich A	38	8	8	22	36	67	32

527

2009/10

SEASON SNIPPETS

Prior to the start of the season, Aston Villa won the Peace Cup. After Group games against Malaga and Atlante, Villa defeated Porto 2-1 in the semi-final. The final against Juventus in the Stadio Olimpico Stadium in Seville on 2 August was deadlocked at 0-0 after extra-time and Villa won 4-3 penalties. Ashley Young was named Player of the Tournament.

On 8 August, Villa won 1-0 against Fiorentina in a pre-season friendly at Villa Park, Emile Heskey scoring the goal.

Fabian Delph, Habib Beye and substitute Marc Albrighton all made their Villa league debut against Wigan Athletic on 15 August.

Ciaran Clark made his debut on 30 August.

Richard Dunne, Stephen Warnock and James Collins made their Villa league debut in the 1-0 win against Birmingham City on 13 September.

Stewart Downing made his Villa league debut at Burnley on 21 November.

The 1-0 win against Birmingham City on 25 April gave Villa a record six consecutive wins in games between the clubs.

The three points earned from the win at Hull on 21 April brought Villa's total Premier League haul to 1,000 points.

Bradley Guzan saved three spot-kicks in the penalty shoot-out at Sunderland in the League Cup on 27 October. Guzan also saved a penalty from Kenwyne Jones in normal time.

John Carew became only the second Villa player to score a hat-trick in an FA Cup quarter-final - the first being Harry Hampton in 1913 - when he hit three goals at Reading on 7 March.

Wilfred Bouma, who had not played in the first team since being carried off with an horrific ankle injury in an Intertoto Cup match with Odense on 26 July 2008, was given a free transfer in May 2010.

PREMIER LEAGUE

MANAGER: Martin O'Neill

MATCH	DATE	VENUE	OPPONENTS	RESULT	HT SCORE	SCORE	SCORERS	ATT
1	Aug 15	H	Wigan Athletic	L	0 1	0 2		35,578
2	24	A	Liverpool	W	2 0	3 1	Lucas (og), Davies, A Young	43,667
3	30	H	Fulham	W	1 0	2 0	Pantsil (og), Agbonlahor	32,917
4	Sep 13	A	Birmingham City	W	0 0	1 0	Agbonlahor	25,196
5	19	H	Portsmouth	W	2 0	2 0	Milner, Agbonlahor,	35,979
6	26	A	Blackburn Rovers	L	1 1	1 2	Agbonlahor	25,172
7	Oct 5	H	Manchester City	D	1 0	1 1	Dunne	37,924
8	17	H	Chelsea	W	1 1	2 1	Dunne, Collins	39,047
9	24	A	Wolverhampton Wanderers	D	0 0	1 1	Agbonlahor	28,734
10	31	A	Everton	D	0 1	1 1	Carew	36,648
11	Nov 4	H	West Ham United	L	0 1	1 2	A Young	30,024
12	7	H	Bolton Wanderers	W	2 1	5 1	A Young, Agbonlahor, Carew, Milner, Cuellar	38,101
13	21	A	Burnley	D	0 1	1 1	Heskey	21,178
14	28	A	Tottenham Hotspur	D	1 0	1 1	Agbonlahor	39,866
15	Dec 5	H	Hull City	W	2 0	3 0	Dunne, Milner, Carew (pen)	39,748
16	12	A	Manchester United	W	1 0	1 0	Agbonlahor	75,130
17	15	A	Sunderland	W	1 0	2 0	Heskey, Milner	34,821
18	19	H	Stoke City	W	0 0	1 0	Carew	35,852
19	27	A	Arsenal	L	0 0	0 3		60,056
20	29	H	Liverpool	L	0 0	0 1		42,788
21	Jan 17	H	West Ham United	D	0 0	0 0		35,646
22	27	H	Arsenal	D	0 0	0 0		39,601
23	30	A	Fulham	W	2 0	2 0	Agbonlahor 2	25,408
24	Feb 6	A	Tottenham Hotspur	D	0 0	0 0		35,899
25	10	A	Manchester United	D	1 1	1 1	Cuellar	42,788
26	21	H	Burnley	W	1 1	5 2	A Young, Downing 2, Heskey, Agbonlahor	38,709
27	Mar 13	A	Stoke City	D	0 0	0 0		27,598
28	16	A	Wigan Athletic	W	1 1	2 1	J McCarthy (og), Milner	16,186
29	20	H	Wolverhampton Wanderers	D	1 2	2 2	Carew 2	37,562
30	24	H	Sunderland	D	1 1	1 1	Carew	37,473
31	27	A	Chelsea	L	1 2	1 7	Carew	41,825
32	Apr 3	A	Bolton Wanderers	W	1 0	1 0	A Young	21,111
33	14	H	Everton	D	0 1	2 2	Agbonlahor, Jagielka (og)	38,729
34	18	A	Portsmouth	W	1 1	2 1	Carew, Delfouneso	16,523
35	21	A	Hull City	W	1 0	2 0	Agbonlahor, Milner (pen)	23,842
36	25	H	Birmingham City	W	0 0	1 0	Milner (pen)	42,788
37	May 1	A	Manchester City	L	1 2	1 3	Carew	47,102
38	9	H	Blackburn Rovers	L	0 0	0 1		41,799

Final League Position: 6th in Premier League

Match 10: Carlos Cuellar sent off 89 minutes   Match 11: Habib Beye sent off 85 minutes   4 Own-goals

Appearances
Subs
Goals

FA CUP

3	Jan 2	H	Blackburn Rovers	W	2 0	3 1	Delfouneso, Cuellar, Carew (pen)	25,453
4	23	H	Brighton & Hove Albion	W	1 1	3 2	Delfouneso, A Young, Delph	39,725
5	Feb 14	A	Crystal Palace	D	1 1	2 2	Collins, Petrov	20,686
R	24	H	Crystal Palace	W	1 0	3 1	Agbonlahor, Carew 2 (2 pens)	31,874
6	Mar 7	A	Reading	W	0 2	4 2	A Young, Carew 3 (2 pens)	23,175
SF	Apr 10	N	Chelsea **	L	0 0	0 3		85,897

Appearances
Subs
Goals

** Played at Wembley Stadium, London

FOOTBALL LEAGUE CUP

3	Sep 23	H	Cardiff City	W	1 0	1 0	Agbonlahor	22,527
4	Oct 27	A	Sunderland *	D	0 0	0 0		27,666
5	Dec 2	H	Portsmouth	W	2 1	4 2	Heskey, Milner, Downing, A Young	17,034
SF1	Jan 14	A	Blackburn Rovers	W	1 0	1 0	Milner	18,595
SF2	20	H	Blackburn Rovers	W	2 2	6 4	Warnock, Milner (pen), Nzonzi (og), Agbonlahor, Heskey, A Young	40,406
F	Feb 28	N	Manchester United **	L	1 1	1 2	Milner (pen)	88,596

Appearances
Subs
Goals

* After extra-time - Aston Villa won 3-1 on penalties   ** Played at Wembley Stadium, London   1 Own-goal

UEFA EUROPA LEAGUE

QR1	Aug 20	A	Rapid Vienna	L	0 1	0 1		17,800
QR2	27	H	Rapid Vienna	W	1 0	2 1	Milner (pen), Carew	22,563

Appearances
Subs
Goals

Rapid Vienna won on away goals rule

528

FINAL LEAGUE TABLE

	P	W	D	L	F	A	P	
Chelsea	38	27	5	6	103	32	86	
Manchester United	38	27	4	7	86	28	85	
Arsenal	38	23	6	9	83	41	75	
Tottenham Hotspur	38	21	7	10	67	41	70	3
Manchester City	38	18	13	7	73	45	67	4
Aston Villa	**38**	**17**	**13**	**8**	**52**	**39**	**64**	5 / SF1
Liverpool	38	18	9	11	61	35	63	SF2
Everton	38	16	13	9	60	49	61	
Birmingham City	38	13	11	14	38	47	50	F
Blackburn Rovers	38	13	11	14	41	55	50	
Stoke City	38	11	14	13	34	48	47	
Fulham	38	12	10	16	39	46	46	
Sunderland	38	11	11	16	48	56	44	
Bolton Wanderers	38	10	9	19	42	67	39	QR1
Wolverhampton W	38	9	11	18	32	56	38	QR2
Wigan Athletic	38	9	9	20	37	79	36	
West Ham United	38	8	11	19	47	66	35	
Burnley	38	8	6	24	42	82	30	
Hull City	38	6	12	20	34	75	30	
Portsmouth	38	7	7	24	34	66	19	

2010/11

SEASON SNIPPETS

Martin O'Neill resigned five days before the opening match of the season. Reserve team coach Kevin MacDonald was put in charge.

James Milner played his last Villa game against West Ham United on 14 August, when he scored in a 3-0 home win, before joining Manchester City four days later.

Stephen Ireland made his debut in Villa's 6-0 defeat at Newcastle United on 22 August.

Although Gerard Houllier was appointed manager on 8 September, his first match in charge was not until 22 September owing to his prior commitments to the French Football Federation.

Curtis Davies played his last Villa game on 22 September when he substituted Ciaran Clarke on 76 minutes in a 3-1 League Cup home win against Blackburn Rovers. The central defender moved to Birmingham City four months later.

Darren Bent arrived from Sunderland for a record £18m and scored when making his debut on 22 January to provide a 1-0 home win against Manchester City.

On 20 April, manager Gerard Houllier was admitted to hospital with chest pains and the club announced that his assistant Gary McAllister would take charge in the manager's absence.

On 28 April, the manager was discharged from the coronary care unit at Birmingham's Queen Elizabeth Hospital.

On 27 May, it was announced that Isaiah Osbourne had been released by the club.

On 1 June, it was announced that Gerard Houllier had stepped down as manager by mutual consent.

PREMIER LEAGUE

MANAGER: Gerard Houllier (from 8 September)

MATCH	DATE	VENUE	OPPONENTS	RESULT	HT SCORE	SCORE	SCORERS	ATT
1	Aug 14	H	West Ham United	W	2 0	3 0	Downing, Petrov, Milner	36,604
2	22	A	Newcastle United	L	0 3	0 6		43,546
3	29	H	Everton	W	1 0	1 0	L Young	34,725
4	Sep 13	A	Stoke City	L	1 0	1 2	Downing	25,899
5	18	H	Bolton Wanderers	D	1 1	1 1	A Young	34,655
6	26	A	Wolverhampton Wanderers	W	1 0	2 1	Downing, Heskey	27,511
7	Oct 2	A	Tottenham Hotspur	L	1 1	1 2	Albrighton	35,871
8	16	H	Chelsea	D	0 0	0 0		40,122
9	23	A	Sunderland	L	0 1	0 1		41,506
10	31	H	Birmingham City	D	0 0	0 0		40,688
11	Nov 6	A	Fulham	D	1 0	1 1	Albrighton	23,654
12	10	H	Blackpool	W	1 1	3 2	Downing, Delfouneso, Collins	34,330
13	13	H	Manchester United	D	0 0	2 2	A. Young (pen), Albrighton	40,073
14	21	A	Blackburn Rovers	L	0 1	0 2		21,848
15	27	H	Arsenal	L	0 2	2 4	Clark 2	38,544
16	Dec 6	A	Liverpool	L	0 2	0 3		39,079
17	11	H	West Bromwich Albion	W	1 0	2 1	Downing, Heskey	37,015
18	26	A	Tottenham Hotspur	L	0 1	1 2	Albrighton	39,411
19	28	H	Manchester City	L	0 3	0 4		46,716
20	Jan 2	A	Chelsea	D	1 1	3 3	A. Young (pen), Heskey, Clark	41,222
21	5	H	Sunderland	L	0 0	0 1		32,627
22	16	A	Birmingham City	D	0 0	1 1	Collins	22,287
23	22	H	Manchester City	W	1 0	1 0	Bent	37,315
24	25	A	Wigan Athletic	W	0 0	2 1	Agbonlahor, A. Young (pen)	15,574
25	Feb 1	A	Manchester United	L	0 2	1 3	Bent	75,256
26	5	H	Fulham	D	1 0	2 2	Pantsil (og), Walker	35,899
27	12	A	Blackpool	D	1 1	1 1	Agbonlahor	16,000
28	26	H	Blackburn Rovers	W	0 0	4 1	A. Young 2 (1 pen), Hanley (og), Downing	34,309
29	Mar 5	A	Bolton Wanderers	L	1 1	2 3	Bent, Albrighton	22,533
30	19	H	Wolverhampton Wanderers	L	0 1	0 1		38,965
31	Apr 2	A	Everton	D	0 1	2 2	Bent 2	37,619
32	10	H	Newcastle United	W	1 0	1 0	Collins	37,090
33	16	A	West Ham United	W	1 1	2 1	Bent, Agbonlahor	34,604
34	23	H	Stoke City	D	1 1	1 1	Bent	35,235
35	30	A	West Bromwich Albion	L	1 0	1 2	Meite (og)	25,889
36	May 7	A	Wigan Athletic	D	1 1	1 1	A Young	36,293
37	15	A	Arsenal	W	2 0	2 1	Bent 2	60,023
38	22	H	Liverpool	W	1 0	1 0	Downing	62,785

Final League Position: 9th in Premier League

Appearances
Subs
3 Own-goals Goals

Match 21: Emile Heskey sent off 69 minutes
Match 27: Jean II Makoun sent off 70 minutes

FA CUP

3	Jan 8	A	Sheffield United	W	2 0	3 1	Walker, Albrighton, Petrov	16,888
4	29	H	Blackburn Rovers	W	3 1	3 1	Clark, Pires, Delfouneso	26,067
5	Mar 2	A	Manchester City	L	0 2	0 3		25,570

Appearances
Subs
Goals

FA Cup third round: Ashley Young sent off 77 minutes
FA Cup fourth round: Nathan Baker sent off 62 minutes

FOOTBALL LEAGUE CUP

3	Sep 22	H	Blackburn Rovers	W	0 1	3 1	Heskey, A Young 2	18,753
4	Oct 27	H	Burnley *	W	0 0	2 1	Heskey, Downing	34,618
5	Dec 1	A	Birmingham City	L	1 1	1 2	Agbonlahor	27,679

Appearances
Subs
Goals

League Cup Round 4: Marc Albrighton sent off 100 minutes
* After extra-time - score 90 minutes 1-1

UEFA EUROPA LEAGUE

QR1	Aug 19	A	Rapid Vienna	D	1 1	1 1	Bannan	
QR2	26	H	Rapid Vienna	L	1 0	2 3	Agbonlahor, Heskey	

Appearances
Subs
Goals

530

FINAL LEAGUE TABLE

	P	W	D	L	F	A	P
Manchester United	38	23	11	4	78	37	80
Chelsea	38	21	8	9	69	33	71
Manchester City	38	21	8	9	60	33	71
Arsenal	38	19	11	8	72	43	68
Tottenham Hotspur	38	16	14	8	55	46	62
Liverpool	38	17	7	14	59	44	58
Everton	38	13	15	10	51	45	54
Fulham	38	11	16	11	49	43	49
Aston Villa	**38**	**12**	**12**	**14**	**48**	**59**	**48**
Sunderland	38	12	11	15	45	56	47
West Bromwich A	38	12	11	15	56	71	47
Newcastle United	38	11	13	14	56	57	46
Stoke City	38	13	7	18	46	48	46
Bolton Wanderers	38	12	10	16	52	56	46
Blackburn Rovers	38	11	10	17	46	59	43
Wigan Athletic	38	9	15	14	40	61	42
Wolverhampton W	38	11	7	20	46	66	40
Birmingham City	38	8	15	15	37	58	39
Blackpool	38	10	9	19	55	78	39
West Ham United	38	7	12	19	43	70	33

531

2011/12

SEASON SNIPPETS

On 17 June, former Scotland boss Alex McLeish was appointed manager having resigned from Birmingham City the previous weekend.

The new manager's first signing was Shay Given who arrived from Manchester City on 18 July.

On 31 August, Alex McLeish signed two players from Tottenham Hotspur, Scotland international right-back Alan Hutton plus Jermaine Jenas on a season-long loan.

A service of re-dedication was held at St Mary's Church, Handsworth, on 20 December to mark the 100th Anniversary of the death of Villa legend and founder of the Football League, William McGregor.

Marc Albrighton scored the 20,000th Premier League goal when he netted in the 54th minute against Arsenal on 21 December.

Robbie Keane arrived on a two month loan deal from American Club LA Galaxy on 14 January.

Darren Bent scored his 100th Premier League goal in a 2-2 draw with Queens Park Rangers on 1 February.

On 30 March, it was announced that captain Stiliyan Petrov, who had been feeling unwell all week, had been diagnosed with acute leukemia.

On 14 May, Alex McLeish's contract was terminated by the club.

PREMIER LEAGUE

MANAGER: Alex McLeish

MATCH	DATE	VENUE	OPPONENTS	RESULT	HT SCORE	SCORE	SCORERS	ATT
1	Aug 13	A	Fulham	D	0 0	0 0		25,700
2	20	H	Blackburn Rovers	W	2 0	3 1	Agbonlahor, Heskey, Bent	32,319
3	27	H	Wolverhampton Wanderers	D	0 0	0 0		30,766
4	Sep 10	A	Everton	D	0 1	2 2	Petrov, Agbonlahor	32,736
5	17	H	Newcastle United	D	1 0	1 1	Agbonlahor	34,248
6	25	A	Queens Park Rangers	D	0 0	1 1	Bannan (penalty)	16,707
7	Oct 1	H	Wigan Athletic	W	1 0	2 0	Agbonlahor, Bent	30,744
8	15	A	Manchester City	L	0 1	1 4	Warnock	47,019
9	22	H	West Bromwich Albion	L	1 1	1 2	Bent (penalty)	34,152
10	29	A	Sunderland	D	1 1	2 2	Petrov, Dunne	37,062
11	Nov 5	H	Norwich City	W	1 1	3 2	Bent 2, Agbonlahor	35,290
12	21	A	Tottenham Hotspur	L	0 2	0 2		35,818
13	27	A	Swansea City	D	0 0	0 0		20,404
14	Dec 3	H	Manchester United	L	0 1	0 1		40,053
15	10	A	Bolton Wanderers	W	2 0	2 1	Albrighton, Petrov	20,285
16	18	H	Liverpool	L	0 2	0 2		37,460
17	21	H	Arsenal	L	0 1	1 2	Albrighton	35,818
18	26	A	Stoke City	D	0 0	0 0		27,739
19	31	A	Chelsea	W	1 1	3 1	Ireland, Petrov, Bent	41,332
20	Jan 2	H	Swansea City	L	0 1	0 2		35,642
21	14	A	Everton	D	0 0	1 1	Bent	31,853
22	21	A	Wolverhampton Wanderers	W	1 2	3 2	Bent (penalty), Keane 2	27,084
23	Feb 1	H	Queens Park Rangers	D	1 2	2 2	Bent, N'Zogbia	32,063
24	5	A	Newcastle United	L	1 1	1 2	Keane	48,569
25	12	H	Manchester City	L	0 0	0 1		35,132
26	25	A	Wigan Athletic	D	0 0	0 0		20,601
27	Mar 3	H	Blackburn Rovers	D	1 0	1 1	N'Zogbia	20,717
28	10	H	Fulham	W	0 0	1 0	Weimann	32,372
29	24	A	Arsenal	L	0 2	0 3		60,108
30	31	H	Chelsea	L	0 1	2 4	Collins, Lichaj	34,740
31	Apr 7	A	Liverpool	D	1 0	1 1	Herd	44,321
32	9	H	Stoke City	D	1 0	1 1	Weimann	30,100
33	15	A	Manchester United	L	0 2	0 4		75,138
34	21	H	Sunderland	D	0 0	0 0		32,557
35	24	H	Bolton Wanderers	L	0 0	1 2	Warnock	32,260
36	28	A	West Bromwich Albion	D	0 0	0 0		25,784
37	May 6	H	Tottenham Hotspur	D	1 0	1 1	Clark	36,008
38	13	A	Norwich City	L	0 2	0 2		26,803

Final League Position: 16th in Premier League

Appearances
Subs
Goals

Match 9: Chris Herd sent off 36 minutes
Match 17: Alan Hutton sent off 89 minutes

FA CUP

3	Jan 7	A	Bristol Rovers	W	1 0	3 1	Albrighton, Agbonlahor, Clark	10,883
4	29	A	Arsenal	L	2 0	2 3	Dunne, Bent	60,009

Appearances
Subs
Goals

FOOTBALL LEAGUE CUP

2	Aug 23	H	Hereford United	W	0 0	2 0	Lichaj, Delfouneso	21,058
4	Sep 27	H	Bolton Wanderers	L	0 0	0 2		22,261

Appearances
Subs
Goals

532

Appearances Table

	Given SJ (GK)	Young LP	Hutton A	Warnock S	Dunne RP	Collins JM	Ireland SJ	Jenas JA	Bent DA	N'Zogbia C	Agbonlahor G	Albrighton MK	Delfouneso N	Delph F	Makoun J	Heskey EWI	Petrov SA	Keane RD	Clark C	Guzan BE (GK)	Beye H	Cuellar CJ	Bannan B	Weimann A	Lichaj E	Herd C	Baker N	Gardner G	Carruthers SB	MATCH
	1	2	3	5	6	7	8	9	10	11	12	14	16	17	18	19	20	21	22	23	24	25	26	30	31	32	38	40		
	90	90		90	90	90			90	67	90	23¹		90	89			1²												1
	90	55		90	90	90			90	90	45	45¹		90	66	90		35²			24³									2
	90			90	90	90			90	74	90	6²		84	90	90					16¹		90							3
	90		90	90	90	90	10¹		90	72	90	18²		80	17	90					73¹									4
	90		90	90	90	90	22²		85	90	90	23¹	5³	90		68					67									5
	90		90	90	90	90				85	90	18¹		90		90					72	5²								6
	90		90	90	90	90	57		74	16²	85			90	33¹	90					90	5³								7
	90		90	90	90		55		90	35¹	90	14³		76	63	90		90			27²									8
	90	41	90	90	90				90	60	90	12³			30²	90				49¹	78			36						9
	90	90	90	90	90				90	87	90	3¹			90	90					90			90						10
	90	90	90	90	90	14²	23¹		90	90	90				67	76					90			90						11
	90	90	90	90	90				90	90			3²		90	90				64	26¹			87						12
	90	90	90	90			21¹		90	90	90		79		69						11²			90						13
	38	90	90	90	90		63	90	90	90	90				27³	31²		52¹			90			59						14
		90	90	90	90			81	90	90	90				9¹		90							90						15
		90	90	90	90				90		90	90	80		56	90		90			34¹	10²								16
		89	90		44				90	90	88	2²			90		90	90		90	46¹									17
		90	90	90					90	90	90	45¹		45	90		90	90		90										18
		90	90		90		12¹	78	90	78					84		90	90		90	6³			12²						19
		35¹	90	90	68		90	90	90	22²				90		85	90		55	5³									20
	90	90	81	90	90		90		90	90				90	9¹	90														21
	90	90	45¹	90		90			45	90				90	89	90				3²	1³			87						22
	90	90	90	90	90		90		90	90				90	90	70			90	20¹										23
	90	90	90	90		46		90	66					24²	90	90	84		90	44¹			6³							24
	90	90		89	90	13²		90	21¹		77			69	90	90		90				1³	90							25
	90	90			90	16²		79	11³	90	70			20¹		90			90				74							26
	90	90		90	90				75	90	89				90				90	15¹	1³		75	15⁷						27
	90	90	90		90	90			71	90	90				89				90	8²	19¹		82	1³						28
	90	78	90		90									65	90				90		25²	12³	52	38¹						29
	90		90		90	90			90	20¹				8²					90	82	90	70	90	90						30
	90	90	90		90	90								58						86	17²	90	73	90	32¹	4³				31
	90	90	59		90				16²	90				2²						74	90	90	88	90	31¹					32
	90	90			90	74			7³	90				26¹		64				90	83	90		90	90	16²				33
	90	47¹			43	90			83	48	90			42²					90	7³	90	90	90	90						34
	90	90	90						90	19¹	77	2³		71					90	13²	90	90	88	90						35
	90	90	90	90					74	90				90		89					90	90		90	16¹	1²				36
	90	53	90	90	37¹	90			90		20³			51		90				90	19³	90	90							37
	90		81	90	90	90				90				90		90			66	45¹		90	45	9³	24¹					38
	32	2	29	34	28	31	19	1	21	24	32	15	1	10	18	26	5	13	6	17	10	5	9	19	6	5				
		2		1		1	5	2	6	11	5	11	5	1	10	1	1	2	1	1	18	9	1	6	2	9	3			
				2	1	1	1		9	2	5	2			1	4	3	1			1	2	1	1						

	90	90	90	74	90		90		45¹	90				45	82		90	90		8³				16²					3
90		90	90	90		90		90		71				82	90	90			90	8²				19¹					4
1		2	2	2	1	2		2		1	1		1	2	1	2	1		1	2			2					2
								1		1	1			1	1					1								4
				1																			2					

				90		90		72	58		90	32¹		90					90	90	3³		90	18²	90	87		2
90		90	90	90	90				17¹	90	73	90		90					90				90					4
1		1	1	2	1	2		1	1	1	2	1		1			1		1	1	1		2	1	1		
									1			1									1			1			
												1															

FINAL LEAGUE TABLE

	P	W	D	L	F	A	P
Manchester City	38	28	5	5	93	29	89
Manchester United	38	28	5	5	89	33	89
Arsenal	38	21	7	10	74	49	70
Tottenham Hotspur	38	20	9	9	66	41	69
Newcastle United	38	19	8	11	56	51	65
Chelsea	38	18	10	10	65	46	64
Everton	38	15	11	12	50	40	56
Liverpool	38	14	10	14	47	40	52
Fulham	38	14	10	14	48	51	52
West Bromwich A	38	13	8	17	45	52	47
Swansea City	38	12	11	15	44	51	47
Norwich City	38	12	11	15	52	66	47
Sunderland	38	11	12	15	45	46	45
Stoke City	38	11	12	15	36	53	45
Wigan Athletic	38	11	10	17	42	62	43
Aston Villa	**38**	**7**	**17**	**14**	**37**	**53**	**38**
Queens Park Rangers	38	10	7	21	43	66	37
Bolton Wanderers	38	10	6	22	46	77	36
Blackburn Rovers	38	8	7	23	48	78	31
Wolverhampton W	38	5	10	23	40	82	25

2012/13

SEASON SNIPPETS

Paul Lambert was appointed manager on 2 June and the new boss was given a rousing reception at a supporters' forum at the Holte Suite on 14 August.

Summer signings Brett Holman, Matt Lowton, Karim El Ahmadi, and Ron Vlaar all made their debuts at West Ham United on 18 August.

Enda Stevens and Graham Burke made their debuts in a second round League Cup win against Tranmere Rovers on 28 August.

Joe Bennett arrived from Middlesbrough on 29 August and two days later Christian Benteke signed from Belgian club Genk, Jordan Bowery joined from Chesterfield and Ashley Westwood transferred from Crewe.

Villa suffered a club record defeat at Chelsea on 23 December, losing 8-0.

On 31 January, Villa made two transfer deadline-day signings, Yacouba Sylla from French club Clermont Foot and Simon Dawkins on loan from Tottenham Hotspur while Stephen Warnock joined Leeds United.

On 5 June, Richard Dunne, Eric Lichaj, Jean Makoun and Andy Marshall were all released.

On 22 June, Brett Holman's contract was cancelled by mutual consent.

PREMIER LEAGUE

MANAGER: Paul Lambert

MATCH	DATE	VENUE	OPPONENTS	RESULT	HT SCORE	SCORE	SCORERS	ATT
1	Aug 18	A	West Ham United	L	0 1	0 1		34,172
2	25	H	Everton	L	0 3	1 3	El Ahmadi	36,565
3	Sep 2	A	Newcastle United	D	1 0	1 1	Clark	48,245
4	15	H	Swansea City	W	1 0	2 0	Lowton, Benteke	34,005
5	22	A	Southampton	L	1 0	1 4	Bent	30,713
6	30	H	West Bromwich Albion	D	0 0	1 1	Bent	34,489
7	Oct 7	A	Tottenham Hotspur	L	0 0	0 2		35,802
8	20	A	Fulham	L	0 0	0 1		25,693
9	27	H	Norwich City	D	1 0	1 1	Benteke	33,184
10	Nov 3	A	Sunderland	W	0 0	1 0	Agbonlahor	41,515
11	10	H	Manchester United	L	1 0	2 3	Weimann 2	40,538
12	17	A	Manchester City	L	0 1	0 5		47,072
13	24	H	Arsenal	D	0 0	0 0		34,607
14	27	H	Reading	W	0 0	1 0	Benteke	28,692
15	Dec 1	A	Queens Park Rangers	D	1 1	1 1	Holman	17,387
16	8	H	Stoke City	D	0 0	0 0		30,110
17	15	A	Liverpool	W	2 0	3 1	Benteke 2, Weimann	44,607
18	23	A	Chelsea	L	0 3	0 8		41,363
19	26	H	Tottenham Hotspur	L	0 0	0 4		36,863
20	29	H	Wigan Athletic	L	0 1	0 3		33,374
21	Jan 1	A	Swansea City	D	1 1	2 2	Weimann, Benteke (pen)	20,406
22	12	H	Southampton	L	0 1	0 1		32,500
23	19	A	West Bromwich Albion	D	2 0	2 2	Benteke, Agbonlahor	25,583
24	29	H	Newcastle United	L	0 2	1 2	Benteke (pen)	30,334
25	Feb 2	A	Everton	D	2 1	3 3	Benteke 2, Agbonlahor	38,121
26	10	H	West Ham United	W	0 0	2 1	Benteke (pen), N'Zogbia	30,503
27	23	A	Arsenal	L	0 1	1 2	Weimann	60,079
28	Mar 4	H	Manchester City	L	0 1	0 1		33,217
29	9	A	Reading	W	2 1	2 1	Benteke, Agbonlahor	24,102
30	16	H	Queens Park Rangers	W	1 1	3 2	Agbonlahor, Weimann, Benteke	38,594
31	31	H	Liverpool	L	1 0	1 2	Benteke	42,037
32	Apr 6	A	Stoke City	W	1 0	3 1	Agbonlahor, Lowton, Benteke	27,544
33	13	H	Fulham	D	0 0	1 1	N'Zogbia	37,011
34	22	A	Manchester United	L	0 3	0 3		75,591
35	29	A	Sunderland	W	2 1	6 1	Vlaar, Weimann, Benteke 3, Agbonlahor	37,428
36	May 4	A	Norwich City	W	0 0	2 1	Agbonlahor 2,	26,842
37	11	H	Chelsea	L	1 0	1 2	Benteke	42,004
38	19	A	Wigan Athletic	D	1 2	2 2	Bent, Vlaar	23,001

Final League Position: 15th in Premier League

Appearances
Subs
Goals

Match 2: Ciaran Clark sent off 58 minutes
Match 7: Joe Bennett carried off on stretcher 77 minutes
Match 9: Joe Bennett sent off 52 minutes
Match 37: Christian Benteke sent off 58 minutes

FA CUP

3	Jan 5	H	Ipswich Town	W	0 1	2 1	Bent, Weimann	24,854
4	25	A	Millwall	L	1 1	1 2	Bent	15,007

Appearances
Subs
Goals

FOOTBALL LEAGUE CUP

2	Aug 28	H	Tranmere Rovers	W	1 0	3 0	Delph, Herd, Bent	15,319
3	Sep 25	A	Manchester City *	W	0 1	4 2	Barry (og), Agbonlahor 2, N'Zogbia	28,015
4	Oct 30	A	Swindon Town	W	2 0	3 2	Benteke 2, Agbonlahor	14,434
5	Dec 11	H	Norwich City	W	1 1	4 1	Holman, Weimann 2, Benteke	26,142
SF1	Jan 8	A	Bradford City	L	0 1	1 3	Weimann	22,245
SF2	22	H	Bradford City	W	1 0	2 1	Benteke, Weimann	40,193

Appearances
Subs
1 Own-goal Goals

* After extra-time

534

FINAL LEAGUE TABLE

	P	W	D	L	F	A	P
Manchester United	38	28	5	5	86	43	89
Manchester City	38	23	9	6	66	34	78
Chelsea	38	22	9	7	75	39	75
Arsenal	38	21	10	7	72	37	73
Tottenham Hotspur	38	21	9	8	66	46	72
Everton	38	16	15	7	55	40	63
Liverpool	38	16	13	9	71	43	61
West Bromwich A	38	14	7	17	53	57	49
Swansea City	38	11	13	14	47	51	46
West Ham United	38	12	10	16	45	53	46
Norwich City	38	10	14	14	41	58	44
Fulham	38	11	10	17	50	60	43
Stoke City	38	9	15	14	34	45	42
Southampton	38	9	14	15	49	60	41
Aston Villa	**38**	**10**	**11**	**17**	**47**	**69**	**41**
Newcastle United	38	11	8	19	45	68	41
Sunderland	38	9	12	17	41	54	39
Wigan Athletic	38	9	9	20	47	73	36
Reading	38	6	10	22	43	73	28
Queens Park Rangers	38	4	13	21	30	60	25

535

2013/14

SEASON SNIPPETS

On 7 June, Aleksandar Tonev became Villa's first summer signing when he arrived from Polish club Lech Poznan.

Villa won 3-1 in a pre-season friendly at home to Spanish club Malaga on 10 August.

Barry Bannan was transferred to Crystal Palace on 2 September.

Libor Kozak made his Villa league debut when he went on as a substitute for Karim El Ahmadi on 67 minutes against Newcastle United on 14 September.

HRH the Duke of Cambridge attended his first match at Villa Park on 30 November.

On 14 January, Grant Holt arrived from Wigan Athletic on a loan deal until the end of the season.

Ryan Bertrand, on loan from Chelsea, made his Villa debut in a 2-2 draw at Liverpool on 18 January.

Jack Grealish made his Villa debut as an 88th-minute substitute for Ryan Bertrand at Manchester City on 7 May.

On 20 May, Villa announced that both Marc Albrighton and Nathan Delfouneso had been released from their contracts and would be free agents for the start of the 2014/15 season.

Albrighton joined Leicester City on a four-year contract, while Delfouneso signed for Blackpool.

PREMIER LEAGUE

MANAGER: Paul Lambert

MATCH	DATE	VENUE	OPPONENTS	RESULT	HT SCORE	SCORE	SCORERS	ATT
1	Aug 17	A	Arsenal	W	1 1	3 1	Benteke 2 (1 pen), Luna	60,003
2	21	A	Chelsea	L	1 1	1 2	Benteke	41,527
3	24	H	Liverpool	L	0 1	0 1		42,098
4	Sep 14	H	Newcastle United	L	0 1	1 2	Benteke	37,554
5	21	A	Norwich City	W	1 0	1 0	Kozak	26,813
6	28	H	Manchester City	W	0 1	3 2	El Ahmadi, Bacuna, Weimann	34,063
7	Oct 5	A	Hull City	D	0 0	0 0		24,396
8	20	H	Tottenham Hotspur	L	0 1	0 2		35,391
9	26	H	Everton	L	0 0	0 2		35,154
10	Nov 2	A	West Ham United	D	0 0	0 0		34,977
11	9	H	Cardiff City	W	0 0	2 0	Bacuna, Kozak	35,809
12	25	A	West Bromwich Albion	D	0 0	2 2	El Ahmadi, Westwood	24,902
13	30	H	Sunderland	D	0 0	0 0		33,036
14	Dec 4	A	Southampton	W	1 0	3 2	Agbonlahor, Kozak, Delph	29,814
15	8	A	Fulham	L	0 2	0 2		22,288
16	15	H	Manchester United	L	0 2	0 3		42,682
17	21	A	Stoke City	L	0 0	1 2	Kozak	26,003
18	26	H	Crystal Palace	L	0 0	0 1		37,752
19	28	H	Swansea City	D	1 1	1 1	Agbonlahor	37,028
20	Jan 1	A	Sunderland	W	1 0	1 0	Agbonlahor	39,757
21	13	A	Arsenal	L	0 2	1 2	Benteke	36,097
22	18	A	Liverpool	D	2 1	2 2	Weimann, Benteke	44,737
23	28	H	West Bromwich Albion	W	3 3	4 3	Weimann, Bacuna, Delph, Benteke (pen)	36,083
24	Feb 1	A	Everton	L	1 0	1 2	Bacuna	39,469
25	8	H	West Ham United	L	0 0	0 2		36,261
26	11	A	Cardiff City	D	0 0	0 0		27,597
27	23	A	Newcastle United	L	0 0	0 1		50,417
28	Mar 2	H	Norwich City	W	4 1	4 1	Benteke 2, Bacuna, Bassong (og)	30,303
29	15	H	Chelsea	W	0 0	1 0	Delph	40,084
30	23	H	Stoke City	L	1 3	1 4	Benteke	30,292
31	29	A	Manchester United	L	1 2	1 4	Westwood	75,368
32	Apr 5	H	Fulham	L	0 0	1 2	Holt	33,532
33	12	A	Crystal Palace	L	0 0	0 1		25,564
34	19	H	Southampton	D	0 0	0 0		35,134
35	26	A	Swansea City	L	1 2	1 4	Agbonlahor	20,701
36	May 3	H	Hull City	W	3 1	3 1	Westwood, Weimann 2	37,182
37	7	A	Manchester City	L	0 0	0 4		47,023
38	11	A	Tottenham Hotspur	L	0 2	0 3		35,826

Final League Position: 15th in Premier League

1 Own-goal

Appearances
Subs
Goals

FA CUP

3	Jan 4	H	Sheffield United	L	0 1	1 2	Helenius	24,038

Appearances
Subs
Goals

FOOTBALL LEAGUE CUP

2	Aug 28	H	Rotherham United	W	2 0	3 0	Weimann, Benteke, Delph	22,447
3	Sep 24	H	Tottenham Hotspur	L	0 1	0 4		22,975

Appearances
Subs
Goals

FINAL LEAGUE TABLE

	P	W	D	L	F	A	P
Manchester City	38	27	5	6	102	37	86
Liverpool	38	26	6	6	101	50	84
Chelsea	38	25	7	6	71	27	82
Arsenal	38	24	7	7	68	41	79
Everton	38	21	9	8	61	39	72
Tottenham Hotspur	38	21	6	11	55	51	69
Manchester United	38	19	7	12	64	43	64
Southampton	38	15	11	12	54	46	56
Stoke City	38	13	11	14	45	52	50
Newcastle United	38	15	4	19	43	59	49
Crystal Palace	38	13	6	19	33	48	45
Swansea City	38	11	9	18	54	54	42
West Ham United	38	11	7	20	40	51	40
Sunderland	38	10	8	20	41	60	38
Aston Villa	**38**	**10**	**8**	**20**	**39**	**61**	**38**
Hull City	38	10	7	21	38	53	37
West Bromwich A	38	7	15	16	43	59	36
Norwich City	38	8	9	21	28	62	33
Fulham	38	9	5	24	40	85	32
Cardiff City	38	7	9	22	32	74	30

2014/15

SEASON SNIPPETS

On 1 July, former Republic of Ireland international Roy Keane was appointed as assistant manager to Paul Lambert.

Villa's pre-season programme included a trip to USA where they played FC Dallas on 23 July, winning 2-0, and a match against Houston Dynamo the following Saturday when Joe Bennett headed his first Villa goal to provide a 1-0 win.

Philippe Senderos, Aly Cissokho and Kieran Richardson all made their debuts in a 1-0 win at Stoke City on 16 August.

Carlos Sanchez made his debut as a 62nd-minute substitute for Charles N'Zogbia at home to Newcastle United on 23 August.

On 21 August, Villa announced that Tom Fox, formally Arsenal's chief commercial officer, had been appointed as their new chief executive.

Joe Cole played his first Villa game on 27 August in the League Cup when Villa lost 1-0 at home to Leyton Orient.

On 1 September, Tom Cleverley was signed on loan from Manchester United while Karim El Ahmadi returned to Feyenoord.

On 13 November, former Villa chairman Sir William Dugdale died at the age of 92.

A commemorative founding lamp to mark the club's 140th anniversary was unveiled outside the Holte Suite at Villa Park before the home game with Southampton on 24 November.

On 13 January, Spanish midfielder Carles Gill was signed from Valencia.

Scott Sinclair arrived on loan from Manchester City on 30 January.

On 11 February, Villa parted company with manager Paul Lambert.

Tim Sherwood was appointed manager on a three-and-a-half year contract on 14 February.

Scott Sinclair's loan deal became a permanent transfer on a four year deal on 19 May.

On 8 June, both Darren Bent and Enda Stevens were released by the club and ten days later Andreas Weimann left for Derby County.

Micah Richards joined Villa from Manchester City on 17 June.

Matt Lowton moved to Burnley on 22 June while Yacouba Sylla joined French club Stade Rennais.

538

PREMIER LEAGUE

MANAGER: Paul Lambert (to 11 February) Tim Sherwood (from 14 February)

MATCH	DATE	VENUE	OPPONENTS	RESULT	HT SCORE	SCORE	SCORERS	ATT
1	Aug 16	A	Stoke City	W	0 0	1 0	Weimann	27,478
2	23	H	Newcastle United	D	0 0	0 0		30,267
3	31	H	Hull City	W	2 0	2 1	Agbonlahor, Weimann	28,336
4	Sep 13	A	Liverpool	W	1 0	1 0	Agbonlahor	44,689
5	20	H	Arsenal	L	0 3	0 3		40,013
6	27	A	Chelsea	L	0 1	0 3		41,616
7	Oct 4	H	Manchester City	L	0 0	0 2		32,964
8	18	A	Everton	L	0 1	0 3		39,505
9	27	A	Queens Park Rangers	L	0 1	0 2		18,022
10	Nov 2	H	Tottenham Hotspur	L	1 0	1 2	Weimann	32,049
11	8	A	West Ham United	D	0 0	0 0		34,857
12	24	H	Southampton	D	1 0	1 1	Agbonlahor	25,311
13	29	A	Burnley	D	1 0	1 1	Cole	19,910
14	Dec 2	A	Crystal Palace	W	1 0	1 0	Benteke	23,935
15	7	H	Leicester City	W	1 1	2 1	Clark, Hutton	27,692
16	13	A	West Bromwich Albion	L	0 0	0 1		24,684
17	20	H	Manchester United	D	1 0	1 1	Benteke	41,273
18	26	A	Swansea City	L	0 1	0 1		20,683
19	28	H	Sunderland	D	0 0	0 0		35,436
20	Jan 1	H	Crystal Palace	D	0 0	0 0		29,047
21	10	A	Leicester City	L	0 1	0 1		31,728
22	17	H	Liverpool	L	0 1	0 2		39,758
23	Feb 1	A	Arsenal	L	0 1	0 5		59,958
24	7	H	Chelsea	L	0 1	1 2	Okore	35,969
25	10	A	Hull City	L	0 1	0 2		21,467
26	21	H	Stoke City	L	1 1	1 2	Sinclair	31,880
27	28	A	Newcastle United	L	0 1	0 1		51,573
28	Mar 3	H	West Bromwich Albion	W	1 0	2 1	Agbonlahor, Benteke (pen)	31,272
29	14	A	Sunderland	W	4 0	4 0	Benteke 2, Agbonlahor 2	45,746
30	21	H	Swansea City	L	0 0	0 1		35,598
31	Apr 4	A	Manchester United	L	0 1	1 3	Benteke	75,397
32	7	H	Queens Park Rangers	D	2 1	3 3	Benteke 3	33,708
33	11	A	Tottenham Hotspur	W	1 0	1 0	Benteke	35,687
34	25	A	Manchester City	L	0 1	2 3	Cleverley, Sanchez	45,036
35	May 2	H	Everton	W	2 0	3 2	Benteke 2, Cleverley	37,859
36	9	A	West Ham United	W	1 0	1 0	Cleverley	39,294
37	16	A	Southampton	L	1 5	1 6	Benteke	31,636
38	24	H	Burnley	L	0 1	0 1		40,792

Final League Position: 17 in Premier League

Appearances
Subs
Goals

Match 10: Christian Benteke sent off 65 minutes
Match 16: Kieran Richardson sent off 22 minutes
Match 17: Gabriel Agbonlahor sent off 65 minutes
Match 19: Fabian Delph sent off 49 minutes
Match 21: Kieran Clark sent off 89 minutes
Match 26: Ron Vlaar sent off 89 minutes
Match 33: Carlos Sanchez sent off 89 minutes

FA CUP

3	Jan 4	H	Blackpool	W	0 0	1 0	Benteke	21,837
4	25	H	Bournemouth	W	0 0	2 1	Gil, Weimann	27,415
5	Feb 15	A	Leicester City	W	0 0	2 1	Bacuna, Sinclair	28,098
6	Mar 7	H	West Bromwich Albion	W	0 0	2 0	Delph, Sinclair	39,592
SF	Apr 19	N	Liverpool	W	1 1	2 1	Benteke, Delph	85,416
F	May 30	N	Arsenal *	L	0 0	0 4		89,283

Appearances
Subs
Goals

FA Cup 6: Jack Grealish sent off 88 minutes
* Played at Wembley Stadium, London

FOOTBALL LEAGUE CUP

2	Aug 27	H	Leyton Orient	L	0 0	0 1		17,918

Appearances
Subs
Goals

Aston Villa – Player Appearances

	Guzan B (GK)	Baker N	Bennett J	Vlaar R	Okore J	Clark C	Bacuna L	Sinclair SA	Cleverley T	Weimann A	Agbonlahor G	Cole J	Steer J (GK)	Senderos P	Westwood AR	Delph F	Richardson K	Bent D	Benteke C	Hutton A	Cissokho A	Sanchez C	Gil C	N'Zogbia C	Hepburn-Murphy R	Given S (GK)	Lowton M	Grealish J	MATCH
1	2	3	4	5	6	7	8	9	10	11	12	13	14	15	16	18	19	20	21	23	24	25	28	29	31	34	40	
90		90			8²				82	90			90	90	90	90		90			71						19¹	1
90	8³	90							90	90			90	90	90	76	14²	90	82	28¹	62							2
90		90							90	85			90	90	90	75	5³	90	90	26¹	64						15²	3
90	90						86		72	89			90	90	90	90	1³	90	90	4²	18¹							4
90				90	4³	90			45	90			90		90	77		90	90	86			13²				45¹	5
90	90								69	90			90	90	90	69	21¹		90	90	21²							6
90	90					19²	90		61				90	90	90	71		29¹	90	90	71						19³	7
90	26			64¹			90		27²	90	9³		90		90			81	90	90	63							8
90			90		90				70	90	20¹		70			20²		90	90	90		90						9
90	90	90					90		86	16¹			90		4²	1³	65		89	90	74		90					10
90	88		90		1²				90	90		2¹	90			90		90	90	89	90		1³					11
90		90	90						90	90			90		26¹	16²		90	90	74	64							12
90			90	89			90		78	90	67		90		12²			90	90	90			1³	23¹				13
90			90	90			89		90	90	9		90		1²			90	90	81								14
90			90	90	14³	62			90				44		46¹			90	90	90	76			28²				15
90		12²	90	90		90			12³	90				45¹	22			90	90	78	78		45					16
90			90	90	90	10¹			80	65			90					90	88	90	10²		90					17
90			90	90				77					45¹	90				90		90	45		90				13²	18
90			90	29²	61	33¹	68		90					49				90	90	90	57			22³				19
90		15	90	75¹	90	64			83	90	7³							90	90	90	90			26²				20
90			90	89					18¹	90	72			90		14²		90	90	89	76		1³					21
90	90		90			59			31¹	90			59	90				90	90	90	90	31²						22
90			90	90		66			24¹	66	24²		90	90		90		90		76	90							23
90			90	90		74	16²	80	68	10³			90	90				22¹	90	90			90					24
90			90	90				59	45	90	31²		90					45¹	90	90	90							25
90			89						90	32²	90					90	42		90	90	48¹	90	58					26
90				90	90	8³	90		17²	73			90	90				90	90		24¹			82				27
90				90	90	13²	77		8³	82			90	90				90	90		59			90	31¹			28
90				90	64	90	90		11²	90			90	90				83			79	7³		90				29
90				90	90	90	25	90	15³	90			22²	90				75	90		65¹			68				30
90	29²			90	90	45¹			77	90	13³			90				90	45		61			90				31
90			90				90	75	81				90	20¹				90	90		90	9³		15²	70			32
90	72¹			90		18	90	90					27²	70	20³			90	90		89			3²	63			33
90				90	90		87		90				68	90				90			90	22¹			90			34
			90	90		81	90			1³			75	90	90			90	9²	15¹	89	90		90				35
			90	90		77	90			19¹			90	90	90			90	13²	1³	71	90		89				36
			90	90		67	90	8³		33¹			90	90				90			57		90	23²	82			37
	90		90			80	72	18¹		90		90	90	90				90	10²		90				90			38
34	8		19	22	22	10	31	5	20	30	3	1	25	27	16		26	27	24	20	4	19		3	8	7		
	3		1	1	3	9			4	11	4		1	2	1		6		7	3	3	1	8	1	1	4	10	
					1	1		3	1	3	6			1						13	1	1						

FINAL LEAGUE TABLE

	P	W	D	L	F	A	P	
Chelsea	38	26	9	3	73	32	87	3
Manchester City	38	24	7	7	83	38	79	4
Arsenal	38	22	9	7	71	36	75	5
Manchester United	38	20	10	8	62	37	70	6
Tottenham Hotspur	38	19	7	12	58	53	64	SF
Liverpool	38	18	8	12	52	48	62	F
Southampton	38	18	6	14	54	33	60	
Swansea City	38	16	8	14	46	49	56	
Stoke City	38	15	9	14	48	45	54	
Crystal Palace	38	13	9	16	47	51	48	
Everton	38	12	11	15	48	50	47	
West Ham United	38	12	11	15	44	47	47	
West Bromwich A	38	11	11	16	38	51	44	2
Leicester City	38	11	8	19	46	55	41	
Newcastle United	38	10	9	19	40	63	39	
Sunderland	38	7	17	14	31	53	38	
Aston Villa	**38**	**10**	**8**	**20**	**31**	**57**	**38**	
Hull City	38	8	11	19	33	51	35	
Burnley	38	7	12	19	28	53	33	
Queens Park Rangers	38	8	6	24	42	73	30	

2015/16

SEASON SNIPPETS

Ray Wilkins was appointed assistant manager on 29 June, Goalkeeper Mark Bunn was signed from Norwich City on 9 July and the following day, Idrissa Gueye arrived from French club Lille OSC, while Shay Given left for Stoke City.

On 11 July, Fabian Delph issued a statement insisting he was staying with Aston Villa.

On 17 July, Fabian Delph activated a release clause in his contract and signed for Manchester City.

Jordan Amavi arrived from French club Nice on 18 July.

Christian Benteke activated a release clause in his contract and departed for Liverpool on 22 July.

Villa signed Jordan Ayew from French club Lorient on 27 July and a day later Spanish defender Jose Angel Crespo arrived from Cordoba.

On 31 July, two more French players were signed, Jordan Veretout from Nantes and Rudy Gestede from Blackburn Rovers.

Adama Traore was transferred from Barcelona on 13 August.

Joleon Lescott arrived from West Bromwich Albion on 1 September along with Tiago Ilori on loan from Liverpool.

Tim Sherwood was sacked as manager on 25 October following a run of six consecutive defeats. Kevin MacDonald was appointed caretaker manager.

Remi Garde was appointed manager on 2 November and three days later, former French striker Reginald Ray joined Villa from Bastia as assistant manager.

Joe Cole moved to Coventry City on 7 January and Tiago Ilori returned to Liverpool.

On 14 January, the club announced that Steven Hollis been appointed as Villa's new chairman.

Eric Black was appointed first team coach on 26 January.

Former governor of the Bank of England, Sir Mervyn King, was appointed to Villa's board of directors on 4 February.

Former Villa chairman Harry Kartz died at the age of 102 on 12 March.

On 29 March, manager Remi Garde left the club and two days later it was announced that assistant manager Reginald Ray had also departed. Eric Black was appointed as acting manager.

Relegation from the Premier League was confirmed on 16 April following a 1-0 defeat at Manchester United.

Charles N'Zogbia and Kieran Richardson were both released by Villa on 10 June.

PREMIER LEAGUE

MANAGER: Tim Sherwood (to 25 October)
Remi Garde (from 2 November to 29 March then Eric Black as acting manager)

MATCH	DATE	VENUE	OPPONENTS	RESULT	HT SCORE	SCORE	SCORERS	ATT
1	Aug 8	A	Bournemouth	W	0 0	1 0	Gestede	11,155
2	14	H	Manchester United	L	0 1	0 1		42,200
3	22	A	Crystal Palace	L	0 0	1 2	Souare (og)	25,295
4	29	H	Sunderland	D	2 1	2 2	Sinclair 2 (1 pen)	35,399
5	Sep 13	A	Leicester City	L	1 0	2 3	Grealish, Gil	31,733
6	19	H	West Bromwich Albion	L	0 1	0 1		36,321
7	26	A	Liverpool	L	0 1	2 3	Gestede 2	44,228
8	Oct 3	H	Stoke City	L	0 0	0 1		33,189
9	17	A	Chelsea	L	0 1	0 2		41,596
10	24	H	Swansea City	L	0 0	1 2	Ayew	33,324
11	Nov 2	A	Tottenham Hotspur	L	0 2	1 3	Ayew	34,882
12	8	H	Manchester City	D	0 0	0 0		36,757
13	21	A	Everton	L	0 3	0 4		38,424
14	28	H	Watford	L	1 1	2 3	Richards, Ayew	35,057
15	Dec 5	A	Southampton	D	1 0	1 1	Lescott	29,645
16	13	H	Arsenal	L	0 2	0 2		33,285
17	19	A	Newcastle United	D	0 1	1 1	Ayew	48,234
18	26	H	West Ham United	D	0 1	1 1	Ayew (pen)	38,193
19	28	A	Norwich City	L	0 1	0 2		27,071
20	Jan 2	A	Sunderland	L	0 1	1 3	Gil	41,535
21	12	H	Crystal Palace	W	0 0	1 0	Hennessy (og)	28,245
22	16	H	Leicester City	D	0 1	1 1	Gestede	32,763
23	23	A	West Bromwich Albion	D	0 0	0 0		26,165
24	Feb 2	A	West Ham United	L	0 0	0 2		34,914
25	6	H	Norwich City	W	1 0	2 0	Klose (og), Agbonlahor	32,472
26	14	A	Liverpool	L	0 2	0 6		35,798
27	27	A	Stoke City	L	0 0	1 2	Bacuna	27,703
28	Mar 1	H	Everton	L	0 2	1 3	Gestede	29,755
29	5	A	Manchester City	L	0 0	0 4		53,892
30	13	H	Tottenham Hotspur	L	0 1	0 2		32,393
31	19	A	Swansea City	L	0 0	0 1		20,454
32	Apr 2	H	Chelsea	L	0 2	0 4		31,120
33	9	H	Bournemouth	L	0 1	1 2	Ayew	31,057
34	16	A	Manchester United	L	0 1	0 1		75,411
35	23	H	Southampton	L	1 2	2 4	Westwood 2	29,729
36	30	A	Watford	L	1 1	2 3	Clark, Ayew	20,653
37	May 7	H	Newcastle United	D	0 0	0 0		33,055
38	15	A	Arsenal	L	0 1	0 4		60,007

Final League Position: 20th in Premier League

3 Own-goals

Appearances
Subs
Goals

Match 24: Jordan Ayew sent off 17 minutes
Match 32: Alan Hutton sent off 85 minutes
Match 36: Aly Cissokho sent off 73 minutes

FA CUP

3	Jan 9	A	Wycombe Wanderers	D	1 0	1 1	Richards	9,298
3R	19	H	Wycombe Wanderers	W	0 0	2 0	Clark, Gana	20,706
4	30	H	Manchester City	L	0 2	0 4		23,636

Appearances
Subs
Goals

FOOTBALL LEAGUE CUP

2	Aug 25	H	Notts County	W	1 2	5 3	Traore, Sinclair 3 (1 pen), Bennett	21,430
3	Sept 22	H	Birmingham City	W	0 0	1 0	Gestede	34,442
4	Oct 28	A	Southampton	L	0 0	1 2	Sinclair (pen)	31,314

Appearances
Subs
Goals

540

	Guzan B (GK)	Baker N	Bennett J	Richards M	Okore J	Clark C	Bacuna L	Gana I	Sinclair SA	Agbonlahor G	Cole J	Steer J (GK)	Westwood AR	Lescott J	Veretout J	Richardson K	Ayew J	Traore A	Hutton A	Amavi J	Sanchez C	Gil C	Kozak L	NZogbia C	Hepburn-Murphy R	Green A	Bunn M (GK)	Crespo JA	Lyden J	Gestede R	Grealish J	Cissokho A	Toner K	MATCH
	1	2	3	4	5	6	7	8	9	11	12	13	15	16	17	18	19	20	21	23	24	25	27	28	29	30	31	33	38	39	40	43	46	
	90		90		90	90	90	78	90				90		71	12²	59			90	19²					31¹								1
	90		90		90	90	59	90					90		78		90			90	12²					31¹								2
	90		90		90		90						90			21¹			90	69						90	90							3
	90		90		90	68	90	90					90					90	90	90	22¹					90								4
	90		90			86		90	75				90	90		24¹		4³	90	66						15²	90							5
	90		90			14²		45	90				90	90	8³			90	82	76						45¹	90							6
	90		90				90	90					90	90	30¹		21²	90	90	60						90	69							7
	90		90				90	59					75	45	90		31²		90		15³				90	90	45¹							8
	90		90					90					90			64	68	22²	90	26¹	90					90	90							9
	90		90			90	90		85				90		90		90	5²	90		16¹					90	74							10
	90		90			90	90		45				38	90		90	52¹		90		90	25³				45²	65							11
	90		90		90	18²	90	72					90			90	84		90	90	90	65	25¹			6³								12
	90		90			90	45						90		90	90	90		90		45¹	57	16²			33²	74							13
	90		90			90	82	90					90	90	90	22¹	90		90	68						8²								14
	90			90		78	90	90	1³				15¹	90	90	12²	90		90	89						75								15
	90			90		90	78	87					90	90		90	90	3³	90		90	33¹				57	12²							16
	90			90		90	90	60					90	90		90	90		90							30¹								17
	90			90		90	90						90	90	83		90	7²	90		38	52¹				90								18
	90			90		90	69	90	58				90		81	90	90	32¹	90							21²	9³							19
	90			90			90	1³					90		90		32¹	76								90	57	90						20
				90	1¹	90	90						90	90		90			89		90	14²		90				90						21
				90		90	90	1²					90	90		89			67	90			90			23¹		90						22
				90		90	90						90	90	10²		90			90	64			90		16¹		90						23
				90		90	90	10³	80				90	90	19¹	17			71		90			90				90						24
			89	90	1¹	90	90						90	90	90				90					90				90						25
			85	90		66	90	32¹	58				90	90	90			5³		90				90		24²		90						26
				90		90	90	32²	90				90	90	77			90		58				90		13²		90						27
	90			90	90	90	90		66				71	90	19²		90		90							24¹		90						28
	90			90		90	16²	90	10³	70			90	90	74		80		90							20¹		90						29
			90			90	20²		90	90			90	90	62		90		90		70			28¹		90		90						30
				90			90		16²				90	90	61		90		90		74			29¹		90		90						31
	90		90			23²	82						90	90		90	90		85		67	66				8³	90	24¹	90					32
	90					90	90	71					90	90		84	90	19²	90							45	45¹	6³	90					33
	90					90	90	90					90	90		82	90		90							8¹		90						34
	90		45			90	90	90					90	90		59		90	90		68					31²	22³	90	45¹					35
						90	90	88	2²				90		90		79		90		11¹				90			73	90					36
						90	90	90	89				90		90		90		90		90			1¹		90		90						37
			25¹				90	90	90				90	65		90			90		90					90	75		15²	90	90			38
	28		23	12	16	27	35	19	13				31	30	21	8	27		26	9	16	17	3			10	2	14	9	18	3			
			1			2	4		8	2					4	3	3	10	2	1	4	6	1	2	1	2		2	18	7	1			
			1			1	1		2	1			2	1			7				1		2					5	1					

FINAL LEAGUE TABLE

	P	W	D	L	F	A	P
Leicester City	38	23	12	3	68	36	81
Arsenal	38	20	11	7	65	36	71
Tottenham Hotspur	38	19	13	6	69	35	70
Manchester City	38	19	9	10	71	41	66
Manchester United	38	19	9	10	49	35	66
Southampton	38	18	9	11	59	41	63
West Ham United	38	16	14	8	65	51	62
Liverpool	38	16	12	10	63	50	60
Stoke City	38	14	9	15	41	55	51
Chelsea	38	12	14	12	59	53	50
Everton	38	11	14	13	59	55	47
Swansea City	38	12	11	15	42	52	47
Watford	38	12	9	17	40	50	45
West Bromwich A	38	10	13	15	34	48	43
Crystal Palace	38	11	9	18	39	51	42
AFC Bournemouth	38	11	9	18	45	67	42
Sunderland	38	9	12	17	48	62	39
Newcastle United	38	9	10	19	44	65	37
Norwich City	38	9	7	22	39	67	34
Aston Villa	**38**	**3**	**8**	**27**	**27**	**76**	**17**

2016/17

SEASON SNIPPETS

On 3 June, Roberto Di Matteo was appointed manager followed by Steve Clarke as assistant manager and Kevin Bond as first-team coach.

On 14 June, Villa confirmed the sale of the club to Recon Group owned by Dr Tony Xia, and the following day Keith Wyness was appointed chief executive.

Tommy Elphick became the new manager's first signing on 20 June when he arrived from Bournemouth.

Goalkeeper Pierluigi Gollini was signed from Italian club Hellas Verona on 8 July.

Aaron Tshibola arrived from Reading on 10 July.

Carles Gil joined Spanish club Deportivo La Coruna on a season-long loan deal on 22 July and seven days later, Brad Guzan left for Middlesbrough.

In August Ross McCormack was signed from Fulham, James Chester arrived from West Bromwich Albion, Mile Jedinak from Crystal Palace, Ritchie De Laet from Leicester City, Jonathan Kodjia from Bristol City and Albert Adomah from Middlesbrough.

On 7 September, Gordon Cowans stepped down from his coaching role thereby parting company with the club.

On 3 October, Villa announced they had parted company with Roberto Di Matteo. Assistant Steve Clarke took over on a caretaker basis.

Steve Bruce was appointed manager on 12 October following which Steve Clarke departed.

Colin Calderwood was appointed assistant manager on 21 November.

Ruddy Gestede left for Middlesbrough on 4 January.

Keeper Sam Johnstone arrived on loan from Manchester United until the end of the season.

Former Villa and England manager Graham Taylor died on 12 January at the age of 72.

Henri Lansbury from Nottingham Forest, James Bree and Conor Hourihane from Barnsley, Birkir Bjarnason from Swiss club Basel, Scott Hogan from Brentford, Neil Taylor from Swansea and Jacob Bedeau from Bury also arrived in January.

Ugo Ehiogu died on 22 April at the age of 44 after suffering a cardiac arrest while coaching at Tottenham Hotspur the previous day.

On 8 May, Libor Kozak was released at the end of his contract.

EFL CHAMPIONSHIP

MANAGER: Roberto Di Matteo (to 3 October)   Steve Bruce (from 12 October)

MATCH	DATE	VENUE	OPPONENTS	RESULT	HT SCORE	SCORE	SCORERS	ATT
1	Aug 7	A	Sheffield Wednesday	L	0 0	0 1		30,060
2	13	H	Rotherham United	W	2 0	3 0	Gestede 2, Grealish	33,286
3	16	H	Huddersfield Town	D	1 0	1 1	McCormack	34,924
4	20	A	Derby County	D	0 0	0 0		31,205
5	27	A	Bristol City	L	1 0	1 3	Grealish	21,099
6	Sep 11	H	Nottingham Forest	D	0 0	2 2	McCormack, Gestede	30,619
7	14	H	Brentford	D	1 0	1 1	Kodjia	29,752
8	17	A	Ipswich Town	D	0 0	0 0		19,249
9	24	H	Newcastle United	D	0 1	1 1	Tshibola	32,062
10	27	A	Barnsley	D	0 0	1 1	Ayew	15,830
11	Oct 1	A	Preston North End	L	0 2	0 2		17,696
12	15	H	Wolverhampton Wanderers	D	1 1	1 1	Kodjia (pen)	32,533
13	18	A	Reading	W	1 0	2 1	Kodjia, Ayew (pen)	20,331
14	22	H	Fulham	W	0 0	1 0	Kodjia	32,201
15	30	A	Birmingham City	D	1 0	1 1	Gardner	29,656
16	Nov 5	H	Blackburn Rovers	W	0 0	2 1	Kodjia 2 (1 pen)	29,712
17	18	A	Brighton & Hove Albion	D	1 1	1 1	Baker	30,107
18	26	H	Cardiff City	W	2 1	3 1	Adomah, Kodjia, Gestede (pen)	31,484
19	Dec 3	A	Leeds United	L	0 0	0 2		32,648
20	10	H	Wigan Athletic	W	0 0	1 0	Grealish	29,392
21	13	A	Norwich City	L	0 0	0 1		26,044
22	18	A	Queens Park Rangers	W	0 0	1 0	Kodjia	16,285
23	26	H	Burton Albion	W	1 1	2 1	Bacuna, McCormack	41,337
24	29	H	Leeds United	D	0 0	1 1	Kodjia (pen)	37,078
25	Jan 2	A	Cardiff City	L	0 1	0 1		21,391
26	14	A	Wolverhampton Wanderers	L	0 1	0 1		27,255
27	21	H	Preston North End	D	2 0	2 2	Adomah 2 (1 pen)	32,415
28	31	A	Brentford	L	0 2	0 3		10,016
29	Feb 4	A	Nottingham Forest	L	1 1	1 2	Kodjia	19,866
30	11	H	Ipswich Town	L	0 0	0 1		30,796
31	14	H	Barnsley	L	1 2	1 3	Kodjia	26,435
32	20	A	Newcastle United	L	0 1	0 2		50,024
33	25	H	Derby County	W	1 0	1 0	Chester	30,935
34	28	H	Bristol City	W	0 0	2 0	Kodjia, Hourihane	28,119
35	Mar 4	A	Rotherham United	W	0 0	2 0	Vaulks (og), Kodjia	10,720
36	7	A	Huddersfield Town	L	0 0	0 1		20,584
37	11	H	Sheffield Wednesday	W	1 0	2 0	Kodjia 2	31,143
38	18	A	Wigan Athletic	W	0 0	2 0	Chester, Hogan	14,811
39	April 1	H	Norwich City	W	1 0	2 0	Kodjia 2	32,605
40	4	H	Queens Park Rangers	W	1 0	1 0	Kodjia	27,154
41	8	A	Burton Albion	D	1 0	1 1	Kodjia	6,716
42	15	H	Reading	L	1 1	1 3	Chester	30,742
43	17	A	Fulham	L	0 1	1 3	Grealish	23,891
44	23	H	Birmingham City	W	0 0	1 0	Agbonlahor	40,884
45	29	A	Blackburn Rovers	L	0 0	0 1		21,884
46	May 7	H	Brighton & Hove Albion	D	0 0	1 1	Grealish	32,856

Final League Position: 13th in EFL Championship

1 Own-goal

Appearances
Subs
Goals

Match 29: Jack Grealish sent off 78 minutes
Match 32: Scott Hogan carried off on stretcher 86 minutes
Match 33: Leandro Bacuna sent off 88 minutes
Match 43: Jonathan Kodjia sent off 22 minutes
Match 46: Nathan Baker sent off 63 minutes

FA CUP

3	Jan 8	A	Tottenham Hotspur	L	0 0	0 2		31,182

Appearances
Subs
Goals

FOOTBALL LEAGUE CUP

1	Aug 10	A	Luton Town	L	1 1	1 3	Ayew	7,412

Appearances
Subs
Goals

FINAL LEAGUE TABLE

	P	W	D	L	F	A	P
Newcastle United	46	29	7	10	85	40	94
Brighton and HA	46	28	9	9	74	40	93
Reading	46	26	7	13	68	64	85
Sheffield Wednesday	46	24	9	13	60	45	81
Huddersfield Town	46	25	6	15	56	58	81
Fulham	46	22	14	10	85	57	80
Leeds United	46	22	9	15	61	47	75
Norwich City	46	20	10	16	85	69	70
Derby County	46	18	13	15	54	50	67
Brentford	46	18	10	18	75	65	64
Preston North End	46	16	14	16	64	63	62
Cardiff City	46	17	11	18	60	61	62
Aston Villa	**46**	**16**	**14**	**16**	**47**	**48**	**62**
Barnsley	46	15	13	18	64	67	58
Wolverhampton W	46	16	10	20	54	58	58
Ipswich Town	46	13	16	17	48	58	55
Bristol City	46	15	9	22	60	66	54
Queens Park Rangers	46	15	8	23	52	66	53
Birmingham City	46	13	14	19	45	64	53
Burton Albion	46	13	13	20	49	63	52
Nottingham Forest	46	14	9	23	62	72	51
Blackburn Rovers	46	12	15	19	53	65	51
Wigan Athletic	46	10	12	24	40	57	42
Rotherham United	46	5	8	33	40	98	23

2017/18

SEASON SNIPPETS

In July, former Chelsea and England central defender John Terry joined Villa on a one year contract, Ahmed Elmohamady signed from Hull City, and Glenn Whelan arrived from Stoke City. They were joined by Chris Samba, who had been training at Bodymoor Heath since being released by Greek club Panathananaikos in January.

On 23 July, Villa won the Cup of Traditions tournament in Germany, after beating MSV Duisburg 3-0 in the semi-final followed by a 2-0 win against Hertha Berlin in the final.

On 28 July, Nathan Baker made a permanent move to Bristol City.

Villa and Watford paid tribute to their former manager, Graham Taylor, in a friendly at Villa Park on 29 July, The game ended goalless.

On 4 August Josh Onomah joined Villa on a season-long loan deal from Tottenham Hotspur.

When he scored against Hull City on 5 August, Gabriel Agbonlahor achieved the feat of scoring Villa league goals for 13 consecutive seasons.

Jordan Amavi moved to Marseille on 10 August.

Leandro Bacuna departed for Reading on 13 August.

Their Royal Highnesses the Duke and Duchess of Cambridge visited Villa Park for a Royal Foundation event on 22 November.

Axel Tuanzebe arrived on loan from Manchester United on 25 January.

Lewis Grabban arrived on loan from Bournemouth on 31 January.

The league game against QPR due to be played on 3 March was postponed - the first time since December 2000 that a first-team match at Villa Park had been called off because of weather conditions.

HRH The Duke of Cambridge returned to Villa Park, along with John Carew, on 10 April to see Villa win 1-0 against Cardiff City.

On 28 April, Gabriel Agbonlahor was presented with a special long service award before the Derby County game.

Goalkeeper Pierluigi Gollini moved permanently to Italian club Atalanta on 10 June.

EFL CHAMPIONSHIP

MANAGER: Steve Bruce

MATCH	DATE	VENUE	OPPONENTS	RESULT	HT SCORE	SCORE	SCORERS	ATT
1	Aug 5	H	Hull City	D	1 0	1 1	Agbonlahor	31,241
2	12	A	Cardiff City	L	0 1	0 3		23,899
3	15	A	Reading	L	0 0	1 2	Hourihane	20,144
4	19	H	Norwich City	W	2 0	4 2	Hourihane 3, Green	29,157
5	25	A	Bristol City	D	0 0	1 1	Onomah	21,542
6	Sep 9	H	Brentford	D	0 0	0 0		29,799
7	12	H	Middlesbrough	D	0 0	0 0		26,631
8	16	A	Barnsley	W	2 0	3 0	Adomah 2 (1 pen), Davis	14,633
9	23	H	Nottingham Forest	W	1 0	2 1	Adomah, Hourihane	28,554
10	26	A	Burton Albion	W	3 0	4 0	Davis, Adomah, Snodgrass, Onomah	5,786
11	30	H	Bolton Wanderers	W	1 0	1 0	Kodjia (pen)	31,451
12	Oct 14	A	Wolverhampton Wanderers	L	0 0	0 2		30,239
13	21	H	Fulham	W	1 1	2 1	Terry, Adomah	30,724
14	29	A	Birmingham City	D	0 0	0 0		24,408
15	Nov 1	A	Preston North End	W	2 0	2 0	Chester, Snodgrass	14,212
16	4	H	Sheffield Wednesday	L	0 2	1 2	Samba	33,154
17	18	A	Queens Park Rangers	W	1 1	2 1	Adomah 2 (1 pen)	16.934
18	21	H	Sunderland	W	1 0	2 1	Adomah, Onomah	27,622
19	25	H	Ipswich Town	W	1 0	2 0	Adomah 2	30,427
20	Dec 1	A	Leeds United	D	0 1	1 1	Lansbury	30,547
21	9	H	Millwall	D	0 0	0 0		29,628
22	16	A	Derby County	L	0 0	0 1		28,118
23	23	H	Sheffield United	D	2 2	2 2	Adomah (pen), Jedinak	35,210
24	26	A	Brentford	L	1 1	1 2	Onomah	11,341
25	30	A	Middlesbrough	W	0 0	1 0	Snodgrass	29,422
26	Jan 1	H	Bristol City	W	2 0	5 0	Hogan, Snodgrass 2, Bjarnason, Hourihane	32,604
27	13	A	Nottingham Forest	W	1 0	1 0	Hogan	25,433
28	20	H	Barnsley	W	3 1	3 1	Hogan 2, Hourihane	31,869
29	30	A	Sheffield United	W	0 0	1 0	Snodgrass	26,477
30	Feb 3	H	Burton Albion	W	1 0	3 2	Hogan, Adomah, Grealish	33,022
31	11	A	Birmingham City	W	0 0	2 0	Adomah, Hourihane	41,233
32	17	A	Fulham	L	0 0	0 2		24,547
33	20	H	Preston North End	D	0 1	1 1	Grabban (pen)	30,894
34	24	A	Sheffield Wednesday	W	1 2	4 2	Grabban, Whelan, Hourihane, Snodgrass (pen)	28,604
35	Mar 6	A	Sunderland	W	2 0	3 0	Grabban, Chester, Oviedo (og)	26,081
36	10	H	Wolverhampton Wanderers	W	1 1	4 1	Adomah, Chester, Grabban, Bjarnason	37,836
37	13	H	Queens Park Rangers	L	0 2	1 3	Chester	30,224
38	17	A	Bolton Wanderers	D	0 1	0 1		19,304
39	31	H	Hull City	D	0 0	0 0		16,133
40	April 3	H	Reading	W	0 0	3 0	Bjarnason, Hourihane, Hogan	29,223
41	7	A	Norwich City	L	0 1	1 3	Grealish	26,278
42	10	H	Cardiff City	W	0 0	1 0	Grealish	32,560
43	13	A	Leeds United	W	1 0	1 0	Grabban	33,374
44	21	A	Ipswich Town	W	1 0	4 0	Hourihane, Grabban 2, Lansbury	20,034
45	28	H	Derby County	D	0 1	1 1	Grabban	41,745
46	May 6	A	Millwall	L	0 1	0 1		17,195

Final League Position: 4th in EFL Championship

Appearances
Subs
1 Own-goal Goals

Match 7: Henri Lansbury sent off 64 minutes   **Match 11:** Neil Taylor sent off 89 minutes

CHAMPIONSHIP PLAY OFF GAMES

	May 12	A	Middlesbrough	W	1 0	1 0	Jedinak	29,233
	15	H	Middlesbrough	D	0 0	0 0		40,505
	26	N	Fulham *	N	0 1	0 1		85,243

Appearances
Subs
Goals

* Played at Wembley Stadium, London

FA CUP

3	Jan 6	H	Peterborough United	L	1 0	1 3	Davis	21,677

Appearances
Subs
Goals

FOOTBALL LEAGUE CUP

1	Aug 9	A	Colchester United	W	2 1	2 1	Hogan, Kent (og)	6,603
2	Aug 22	H	Wigan Athletic	W	3 1	4 1	Hogan 2, Adomah, Bjarnason	18,108
3	Sep 19	H	Middlesbrough	L	0 0	0 2		11,197

Appearances
Subs
1 Own-goal Goals

League Cup 3: Tommy Elphic sent off 58 minutes

FINAL LEAGUE TABLE

	P	W	D	L	F	A	P
Wolverhampton W	46	30	9	7	82	39	99
Cardiff City	46	27	9	10	69	39	90
Fulham	46	25	13	8	79	46	88
Aston Villa	**46**	**24**	**11**	**11**	**72**	**42**	**83**
Middlesbrough	46	22	10	14	67	45	76
Derby County	46	20	15	11	70	48	75
Preston North End	46	19	16	11	57	46	73
Millwall	46	19	15	12	56	45	72
Brentford	46	18	15	13	62	52	69
Sheffield United	46	20	9	17	62	55	69
Bristol City	46	17	16	13	67	58	67
Ipswich Town	46	17	9	20	57	60	60
Leeds United	46	17	9	20	59	64	60
Norwich City	46	15	15	16	49	60	60
Sheffield Wednesday	46	14	15	17	59	60	57
Queens Park Rangers	46	15	11	20	58	70	56
Nottingham Forest	46	15	8	23	51	65	53
Hull City	46	11	16	19	70	70	49
Birmingham City	46	13	7	26	38	68	46
Reading	46	10	14	22	48	70	44
Bolton Wanderers	46	10	13	23	39	74	43
Barnsley	46	9	14	23	48	72	41
Burton Albion	46	10	11	25	38	81	41
Sunderland	46	7	16	23	52	80	37

2018/19

SEASON SNIPPETS

On 21 July, Villa won the Bass Vase with a 4-0 win at Burton Albion.

In August, goalkeeper Andre Moreira arrived on a season-long loan deal from Atletico Madrid, Axel Tuanzebe returned for a second spell on loan from Manchester United, goalkeeper Orjan Nyland was signed from German club Ingolstadt, John McGinn arrived from Hibernian, Jed Steer moved to Charlton Athletic, Gary Gardner was signed on loan by Birmingham City, Anwar El Ghazi joined Villa on a season-long loan from French club Lille, Yannick Bolasie arrived on loan from Everton, Aaron Tshibola returned to Kilmarnock on loan, striker Tammy Abraham was acquired on loan from Chelsea while Tommy Elphick was loaned to Hull City and Jordan Lyden loaned to Oldham Athletic.

On 30 August, Christian Purslow was appointed CEO.

Ross McCormack joined Australian club Central Coast Mariners on loan on 19 September.

On 3 October, Steve Bruce was relieved of his duties as manager with his contract being terminated along with members of his backroom staff. Kevin MacDonald was placed in temporary charge.

Dean Smith was appointed head coach on 10 October with John Terry as his assistant.

Sir Doug Ellis died at the age of 94 on 11 October.

Richard O'Kelly was appointed assistant head coach alongside John Terry on 12 October.

Outgoing loans in January included Ross McCormack (Motherwell), Rushian Hepburn Murphy (Cambridge United), Callum O'Hare (Carlisle United), Scott Hogan (Sheffield United), James Bree (Ipswich Town), Harry McKirdy (Cambridge United) and Corey Blackett-Taylor (Walsall). Jacob Bedeau moved to Scunthorpe United on a free transfer.

Yannick Bolasie returned to Everton on 21 January.

Andre Moreira returned to Atletico Madrid on 23 January.

On January transfer deadline day, Tyrone Mings arrived on loan from Bournemouth and Tom Carroll signed on loan from Swansea City.

Villa also signed Frederic Guilbert from French club Caen, but he was then loaned back until the end of the season.

On 28 March Gabriel Agbonlahor officially announced his retirement from professional football.

In beating Millwall 1-0 on 22 April Villa extended their winning league sequence to ten consecutive games - a club record.

EFL CHAMPIONSHIP

MANAGER: Steve Bruce (to 3 October)   Dean Smith (from 10 October)

MATCH	DATE	VENUE	OPPONENTS	RESULT	HT SCORE	SCORE	SCORERS	ATT
1	Aug 6	A	Hull City	W	1 1	3 1	Elphick, Elmohamady, Hutton	14,071
2	11	H	Wigan Athletic	W	1 1	3 2	Chester, Dunkley (og), Bjarnason	34,331
3	18	A	Ipswich Town	D	1 1	1 1	Kodjia	17,824
4	22	H	Brentford	D	1 1	2 2	Kodjia	30,011
5	25	H	Reading	D	0 0	1 1	Elmohamady	33,405
6	Sep 1	A	Sheffield United	L	0 3	1 4	El Ghazi	26,030
7	15	A	Blackburn Rovers	D	0 0	1 1	Hourihane	15,982
8	18	H	Rotherham United	W	1 0	2 0	Abraham, Bolasie	27,991
9	22	H	Sheffield Wednesday	L	0 0	1 2	McGinn	35,572
10	28	A	Bristol City	D	1 1	1 1	Bjarnason	24,224
11	Oct 2	H	Preston North End	D	2 0	3 3	Kodjia, Abraham, Bolasie	27,331
12	6	A	Millwall	L	1 1	1 2	Abraham	14,491
13	20	H	Swansea City	W	1 0	1 0	Abraham	41,326
14	23	A	Norwich City	L	1 0	1 2	Chester	24,977
15	26	A	Queens Park Rangers	L	0 1	0 1		16,036
16	Nov 2	H	Bolton Wanderers	W	1 0	2 0	Grealish, Chester	30,802
17	10	A	Derby County	W	0 0	3 0	McGinn, Abraham, Hourihane	30,400
18	25	H	Birmingham City	W	2 1	4 2	Kodjia, Grealish, Abraham (pen), Hutton	41,200
19	28	H	Nottingham Forest	D	3 3	5 5	Abraham 4, (1 pen), El Ghazi	32,868
20	Dec 1	A	Middlesbrough	W	1 0	3 0	Chester, Abraham, Whelan	23,424
21	8	A	West Bromwich Albion	D	1 1	2 2	El Ghazi 2	26,513
22	15	H	Stoke City	D	0 0	2 2	Abraham (pen), Kodjia	36,999
23	23	H	Leeds United	L	2 0	2 3	Abraham, Hourihane	41,411
24	26	A	Swansea City	W	0 0	1 0	Hourihane	20,775
25	29	A	Preston North End	D	1 0	1 1	Abraham	19,126
26	Jan 1	H	Queens Park Rangers	D	1 1	2 2	Abraham 2	37,760
27	12	A	Wigan Athletic	L	0 1	0 3		13,882
28	19	H	Hull City	D	1 2	2 2	Chester, Abraham	33,619
29	26	A	Ipswich Town	W	1 0	2 1	Abraham 2 (1 pen)	33,653
30	Feb 2	A	Reading	D	0 0	0 0		17,458
31	8	H	Sheffield United	D	0 1	3 3	Mings, Abraham, Green	34,892
32	13	A	Brentford	L	0 0	0 1		9,636
33	16	H	West Bromwich Albion	L	0 2	0 2		39,263
34	23	A	Stoke City	D	0 1	1 1	Adomah	27,975
35	Mar 2	H	Derby County	W	4 0	4 0	Hourihane 2, Abrraham, Grealish	37,273
36	10	A	Birmingham City	W	0 0	1 0	Grealish	26,631
37	13	A	Nottingham Forest	W	2 1	3 1	McGinn 2, Hause	29,224
38	16	H	Middlesbrough	W	2 0	3 0	El Ghazi, McGinn, Adomah	36,263
39	30	H	Blackburn Rovers	W	1 0	2 1	Abraham, Mings	39,687
40	April 6	A	Sheffield Wednesday	W	1 1	3 1	McGinn, Adomah, Abraham	29,458
41	10	A	Rotherham United	W	0 1	2 1	Kodjia (pen), Adomah	10,558
42	13	H	Bristol City	W	0 0	2 1	Abraham (pen) Hourihane	41,418
43	19	A	Bolton Wanderers	W	0 0	2 0	Grealish, Abraham	17,344
44	22	H	Millwall	W	1 0	1 0	Kodjia	39,839
45	28	A	Leeds United	D	0 0	1 1	Adomah	36,786
46	May 5	H	Norwich City	D	1 1	1 2	Kodjia	41,696

Final League Position: 5th in EFL Championship

Appearances
Subs
1 Own-goal   Goals

Match 11: James Chester sent off 54 minutes   **Match 41:** Tyrone Mings sent off 34 minutes   **Match 45:** Anwar El Ghazi sent off 75 minutes

CHAMPIONSHIP PLAY OFF GAMES

	May 11	H	West Bromwich Albion	W	0 1	2 1	Hourihane, Abraham (pen)	40,754
	14	A	West Bromwich Albion*	L	0 1	0 1		25,702
	27	N	Derby County **	W	1 0	2 1	El Ghazi, McGinn	85,,826

Appearances
Subs
Goals

* Aston Villa won 4-3 on penalties   ** Played at Wembley Stadium, London

F.A. CUP

3	Jan 5	H	Swansea City	L	0 1	0 3		30,572

Appearances
Subs
Goals

FOOTBALL LEAGUE CUP

1	Aug 14	A	Yeovil Town	W	0 0	1 0	Hourihane	6,123
2	28	A	Burton Albion	L	0 0	0 1		3,411

Appearances
Subs
Goals

FINAL LEAGUE TABLE

	P	W	D	L	F	A	P
Norwich City	46	27	13	6	93	57	94
Sheffield United	46	26	11	9	78	41	89
Leeds United	46	25	8	13	73	50	83
West Bromwich A	46	23	11	12	87	62	80
Aston Villa	**46**	**20**	**16**	**10**	**82**	**61**	**76**
Derby County	46	20	14	12	69	54	74
Middlesbrough	46	20	13	13	49	41	73
Bristol City	46	19	13	14	59	53	70
Nottingham Forest	46	17	15	14	61	54	66
Swansea City	46	18	11	17	65	62	65
Brentford	46	17	13	16	73	59	64
Sheffield Wednesday	46	16	16	14	60	62	64
Hull City	46	17	11	18	66	68	62
Preston North End	46	16	13	17	67	67	61
Blackburn Rovers	46	16	12	18	64	69	60
Stoke City	46	11	22	13	45	52	55
Birmingham City	46	14	19	13	64	58	52
Wigan Athletic	46	13	13	20	51	64	52
Queens Park Rangers	46	14	9	23	53	71	51
Reading	46	10	17	19	46	69	47
Millwall	46	10	14	22	48	64	44
Rotherham United	46	8	16	22	52	83	40
Bolton Wanderers	46	8	8	30	29	78	32
Ipswich Town	46	5	16	25	36	77	31

547

2019/20

SEASON SNIPPETS

On 1 June, the club announced the release of eight players – Alan Hutton, Albert Adomah, Mile Jedinak, Glenn Whelan, Tommy Elphick, Mark Bunn, Ritchie De Laet and Micah Richards.

On 3 June, Ross McCormack was released.

Spanish winger Jota arrived from Birmingham City on 5 June with Gary Gardner moving to St Andrews.

Other summer signings included Brazilian striker Wesley from Belgian club Brugge, Matt Targett from Southampton, Ezri Konsa from Brentford, Bjorn Engels from Reims, Douglas Luiz from Manchester City, Tom Heaton from Burnley and Marvelous Nakamba from Club Brugge, while Egypt international Trezeguet arrived from Turkish club Kasimpasa.

Anwar El Ghazi, Kortney Hause and Tyrone Mings, who had all previously been on loan, signed permanent contracts.

On 8 August, Birkir Bjarnason's contract was terminated by mutual agreement.

On 29 November, Aston Villa announced that Dean Smith had signed a new four year contract.

On 7 December former manager Ron Saunders died at the age of 87.

Danny Drinkwater arrived on loan from Chelsea on 7 January followed by Pepe Reina on loan from AC Milan six days later.

Jonathan Kodjia signed for Qatar Stars League club Al-Gharafa on 19 January and scored a hat-trick on his debut four days later.

Mbwana Samatta signed from Belgium club Genk on 20 January while keeper Lovre Kalinic moved on loan to French club Toulouse until the end of the season.

Borja Baston arrived from Swansea City on 31 January while former captain James Chester joined Stoke City on loan.

The Premier League and the EFL announced that all football was postponed due to the spread of coronavirus on 13 March and six days later all professional football was put on hold.

Villa resumed fixtures on 17 June with a home game against Sheffield United played behind closed doors.

548

PREMIER LEAGUE

MANAGER: Dean Smith

MATCH	DATE	VENUE	OPPONENTS	RESULT	HT SCORE	SCORE	SCORERS	ATT
1	Aug 10	A	Tottenham Hotspur	L	1 0	1 3	McGinn	60,407
2	17	H	Bournemouth	L	0 2	1 2	Luiz	40,996
3	23	H	Everton	W	1 0	2 0	Wesley, El Ghazi	41,922
4	31	A	Crystal Palace	L	0 0	0 1		25,248
5	Sep 16	H	West Ham United	D	0 0	0 0		42,010
6	22	A	Arsenal	L	1 0	2 3	McGinn, Wesley	60,331
7	28	H	Burnley	D	1 0	2 2	El Ghazi, McGinn	41,546
8	Oct 5	A	Norwich City	W	2 0	5 1	Wesley 2, Grealish, Hourihane, Luiz	27,045
9	19	H	Brighton & Hove Albion	W	1 1	2 1	Grealish, Targett	41,826
10	26	A	Manchester City	L	0 0	0 3		54,506
11	Nov 2	H	Liverpool	L	1 0	1 2	Trezeguet	41,878
12	10	A	Wolverhampton Wanderers	L	0 1	1 2	Trezeguet	31,607
13	25	H	Newcastle United	W	2 0	2 0	Hourihane, El Ghazi	41,821
14	Dec 1	A	Manchester United	D	1 1	2 2	Grealish, Mings	73,381
15	4	A	Chelsea	L	1 1	1 2	Trezeguet	40,628
16	8	H	Leicester City	L	1 2	1 4	Grealish	41,908
17	14	A	Sheffield United	L	0 0	0 2		30,396
18	21	H	Southampton	L	0 2	1 3	Grealish	41,834
19	26	H	Norwich City	W	0 0	1 0	Hourihane	41,289
20	28	A	Watford	L	0 1	0 3		21,348
21	Jan 1	A	Burnley	W	2 0	2 1	Wesley, Grealish	19,561
22	12	H	Manchester City	L	0 4	1 6	El Ghazi (pen)	41,823
23	18	A	Brighton & Hove Albion	D	0 1	1 1	Grealish	30,551
24	21	H	Watford	W	0 1	2 1	Luiz, Mings	40,867
25	Feb 1	A	Bournemouth	L	0 2	1 2	Samatta	10,722
26	16	H	Tottenham Hotspur	L	1 2	2 3	Alderweireld (og), Engels	41,874
27	22	A	Southampton	L	0 1	0 2		31,478
28	Mar 9	A	Leicester City	L	0 1	0 4		32,125
29	June 17	H	Sheffield United	D	0 0	0 0		N/A
30	21	H	Chelsea	L	1 0	1 2	Hause	N/A
31	24	A	Newcastle United	D	0 0	1 1	Elmohamady	N/A
32	27	H	Wolverhampton Wanderers	L	0 0	0 1		N/A
33	July 5	A	Liverpool	L	0 2	0 2		N/A
34	9	H	Manchester United	L	0 2	0 3		N/A
35	12	A	Crystal Palace	W	1 0	2 0	Trezeguet 2	N/A
36	15	A	Everton	D	0 0	1 1	Konsa	N/A
37	18	H	Arsenal	W	1 0	1 0	Trezeguet	N/A
38	26	A	West Ham United	D	0 0	1 1	Grealish	N/A

Final League Position: 17 in Premier League

Appearances
Subs
1 Own-goal   Goals

Match 4: Mahmoud Trezeguet sent off 54 minutes

FA CUP

| 3 | Jan 4 | A | Fulham | L | 0 0 | 1 2 | El Ghazi | 12,980 |

Appearances
Subs
Goals

FOOTBALL LEAGUE CUP

1	Aug 27	A	Crewe Alexandra	W	3 0	6 1	Konsa, Hourihane 2, Davis, Guilbert, Grealish	7,173
2	Sept 25	A	Brighton & Hove Albion	W	2 0	3 1	Jota, Hourihane, Grealish	14,982
3	Oct 30	H	Wolverhampton Wanderers	W	1 0	2 1	El Ghazi, Elmohamady	34,962
4	Dec 17	H	Liverpool	W	4 0	5 0	Hourihane, Boyes (e.g.), Kodjia 2, Wesley	30,323
SF1	Jan 8	A	Leicester City	D	1 0	1 1	Guilbert	31,280
SF2	28	H	Leicester City	W	1 0	2 1	Targett, Trezeguet	39,300
F	Mar 1	N	Manchester City *	L	1 2	1 2	Samatta	82,145

Appearances
Subs
1 Own-goal   Goals

* Played at Wembley Stadium, London

FINAL LEAGUE TABLE

	P	W	D	L	F	A	P	
Liverpool	38	32	3	3	85	33	99	1
Manchester City	38	26	3	9	102	35	81	2
Manchester United	38	18	12	8	66	36	66	3
Chelsea	38	20	6	12	69	54	66	4
Leicester City	38	18	8	12	67	41	62	SF1
Tottenham Hotspur	38	16	11	11	61	47	59	SF2
Wolverhampton W	38	15	14	9	51	40	59	F
Arsenal	38	14	14	10	56	48	56	
Sheffield United	38	14	12	12	39	39	54	
Burnley	38	15	9	14	43	50	54	
Southampton	38	15	7	16	51	60	52	
Everton	38	13	10	15	44	56	49	
Newcastle United	38	11	11	16	38	58	44	
Crystal Palace	38	11	10	17	31	50	43	
Brighton and HA	38	9	14	15	39	54	41	
West Ham United	38	9	12	17	49	62	39	
Aston Villa	**38**	**9**	**8**	**21**	**41**	**67**	**35**	
AFC Bournemouth	38	9	7	22	40	65	34	
Watford	38	8	10	20	36	64	34	
Norwich City	38	5	6	27	26	75	21	

2020/21

SEASON SNIPPETS

On 1 September, James Bree moved to Luton Town and two days later Matty Cash arrived from Nottingham Forest on a five-year contract.

Ollie Watkins was signed from Brentford on 9 September.

Goalkeeper Emiliano Martinez joined Villa from Arsenal and saved a penalty in a 1-0 win on his debut against Sheffield United on 21 September.

Bertrand Traore arrived from French club Olympique Lyonnais on 18 September and Ally Samatta was transferred to Turkish club Fenerbahce the following week.

Ross Barkley scored on his debut - a 7-2 win over the champions Liverpool on 4 October - after arriving on a season-long loan deal from Chelsea.

Jacob Ramsey made his Villa league debut when he replaced Conor Hourihane on 76 minutes at Fulham on 28 September.

Jota's contract was cancelled by mutual consent on 2 October and three days later, Orjan Nyland left the club.

Villa won their opening four league games of the season for the first time since 1930/31.

On 15 January, Dean Smith was presented with the Barclays Manager of the Month award for December, when Villa were unbeaten.

On 18 January, Conor Hourihane joined Swansea City on loan for the remainder of the season.

On 26 January, the signing was announced of French midfielder Morgan Sanson from Marseille and two days later, Henri Lansbury's contract was cancelled by mutual consent.

The game against Chelsea on 23 May was Villa's 1,000th in the Premier League - and the 500th at Villa Park.

On 7 January, the Bodymoor Heath training ground was closed due to an outbreak of Covid-19 among first-team players and coaching staff. Villa were forced to field a team of under-18 and under-23 players for the third-round FA Cup tie against Liverpool. The team was managed by Mark Delaney.

PREMIER LEAGUE

MANAGER: Dean Smith

MATCH	DATE	VENUE	OPPONENTS	RESULT	HT SCORE	SCORE	SCORERS	ATT
1	Sep 21	H	Sheffield United	W	0 0	1 0	Konsa	N/A
2	28	A	Fulham	W	2 0	3 0	Grealish, Hourihane, Mings	N/A
3	Oct 4	H	Liverpool	W	4 1	7 2	Watkins 3, McGinn, Barkley, Grealish 2	N/A
4	18	A	Leicester City	W	0 0	1 0	Barkley	N/A
5	23	A	Leeds United	L	0 0	0 3		N/A
6	Nov 1	H	Southampton	L	0 3	3 4	Mings, Watkins (pen) Grealish	N/A
7	8	A	Arsenal	W	1 0	3 0	Saka (og), Watkins 2	N/A
8	21	H	Brighton & Hove Albion	L	0 1	1 2	Konsa	N/A
9	30	A	West Ham United	L	1 1	1 2	Grealish	N/A
10	Dec 12	A	Wolverhampton Wanderers	W	0 0	1 0	El Ghazi (pen)	N/A
11	17	H	Burnley	D	0 0	0 0		N/A
12	20	A	West Bromwich Albion	W	1 0	3 0	El Ghazi 2, (1 pen), Traore	N/A
13	26	H	Crystal Palace	W	1 0	3 0	Traore, Hause, El Ghazi	N/A
14	28	A	Chelsea	D	0 1	1 1	El Ghazi	N/A
15	Jan 2	A	Manchester United	L	0 1	1 2	Traore	N/A
16	20	A	Manchester City	L	0 0	0 2		N/A
17	23	H	Newcastle United	W	2 0	2 0	Watkins, Traore	N/A
18	27	A	Burnley	L	1 0	2 3	Watkins, Grealish	N/A
19	30	A	Southampton	W	1 0	1 0	Barkley	N/A
20	Feb 3	H	West Ham United	L	0 0	1 3	Watkins	N/A
21	6	H	Arsenal	W	1 0	1 0	Watkins	N/A
22	13	A	Brighton & Hove Albion	D	0 0	0 0		N/A
23	21	H	Leicester City	L	0 2	1 2	Traore	N/A
24	27	A	Leeds United	W	1 0	1 0	El Ghazi	N/A
25	Mar 3	A	Sheffield United	L	0 1	0 1		N/A
26	6	H	Wolverhampton Wanderers	D	0 0	0 0		N/A
27	12	A	Newcastle United	D	0 0	1 1	Clark (og)	N/A
28	21	H	Tottenham Hotspur	L	0 1	0 2		N/A
29	April 4	A	Fulham	W	0 0	3 1	Trezeguet 2, Watkins	N/A
30	10	A	Liverpool	L	1 0	1 2	Watkins	N/A
31	21	H	Manchester City	L	1 2	1 2	McGinn	N/A
32	25	A	West Bromwich Albion	D	1 1	2 2	El Ghazi (pen), Davis	N/A
33	May 1	H	Everton	W	1 1	2 1	Watkins, El Ghazi	N/A
34	9	H	Manchester United	L	1 0	1 3	Traore	N/A
35	13	H	Everton	D	0 0	0 0		N/A
36	16	A	Crystal Palace	L	2 1	2 3	McGinn, El Ghazi	N/A
37	19	A	Tottenham Hotspur	W	2 1	2 1	Reguilon (og), Watkins	10,000
38	23	H	Chelsea	W	1 0	2 1	Traore, El Ghazi (pen)	10,000

Appearances
Subs
Goals

Match 10: Douglas Luiz sent off 85 minutes **Match 13:** Tyrone Mings sent off 45 minutes
Match 31: Matty Cash sent off 57 minutes **Match 34:** Ollie Watkins sent off 89 minutes

FA CUP

3	Jan 8	H	Liverpool	L	1 1	1 4	Barry	N/A

Appearances
Subs
Goals

FOOTBALL LEAGUE CUP

2	Sept 15	A	Burton Albion	W	1 1	3 1	Watkins, Grealish, Davis	N/A
3	24	A	Bristol City	W	2 0	3 0	El Ghazi, Traore, Watkins	N/A
4	Oct 1	H	Stoke City	L	0 1	0 1		N/A

Appearances
Subs
1 Own-goal Goals

FINAL LEAGUE TABLE

	P	W	D	L	F	A	P
Manchester City	38	27	5	6	83	32	86
Manchester United	38	21	11	6	73	44	74
Liverpool	38	20	9	9	68	42	69
Chelsea	38	19	10	9	58	36	67
Leicester City	38	20	6	12	68	50	66
West Ham United	38	19	8	11	62	47	65
Tottenham Hotspur	38	18	8	12	68	45	62
Arsenal	38	18	7	13	55	39	61
Leeds United	38	18	5	15	62	54	59
Everton	38	17	8	13	47	48	59
Aston Villa	**38**	**16**	**7**	**15**	**55**	**46**	**55**
Newcastle United	38	12	9	17	46	62	45
Wolverhampton W	38	12	9	17	36	52	45
Crystal Palace	38	12	8	18	41	66	44
Southampton	38	12	7	19	47	68	43
Brighton and HA	38	9	14	15	40	46	41
Burnley	38	10	9	19	33	55	39
Fulham	38	5	13	20	27	53	28
West Bromwich A	38	5	11	22	35	76	26
Sheffield United	38	7	2	29	20	63	23

551

2021/22

SEASON SNIPPETS

Jack Grealish ended his long association with the club when Manchester City paid a British record £100million for the England international.

The club's summer signings were Emi Buendia from Norwich City, Leon Bailey from Bayer Leverkusen and Danny Ings from Southampton, while Ashley Young returned for a second spell at Villa Park.

Bjorn Engels joined Royal Antwerp, while Lovre Kalinic, Wesley and Conor Hourihane linked up with Hajduk Split, Club Brugge and Sheffield United on loan deals.

John Terry left the club after four years as a player and a coach, and assistant head coach Richard O'Kelly also departed.

Teenager Cameron Archer netted a hat-trick on his debut as Villa beat Barrow 6-0 away in the second round of the Carabao Cup.

Douglas Luiz won a gold medal at the Tokyo Olympics, helping Brazil to victory over Spain in the football final.

Villa beat Manchester United for the first time since 2009, a Kortney Hause header clinching a 1-0 success at Old Trafford.

Head coach Dean Smith was dismissed in November following a run of five straight defeats. He was replaced by former Liverpool and England midfielder Steve Gerrard. Gary McAllister returned to Villa Park as Gerrard's right-hand man.

Former Liverpool star Philippe Coutinho joined Villa on loan from Barcelona during the January transfer window, while France international Lucas Digne was signed from Everton and Calum Chambers arrived from Arsenal. Coutinho scored on his debut in a 2-2 home draw against Manchester United.

Swedish goalkeeper Robin Olsen was signed on loan from Roma as back-up to Emi Martinez, who signed a five-year contract extension.

Wesley returned from Bruges before joining Brazilian club Internacional on a 12-month loan agreement.

552

PREMIER LEAGUE

MANAGER / HEAD COACH: Dean Smith (to 7 November)   Steven Gerrard (from 11 November)

MATCH	DATE	VENUE	OPPONENTS	RESULT	HT SCORE	SCORE	SCORERS	ATT
1	Aug 14	A	Watford	L	0 2	2 3	McGinn, Ings (pen)	20,051
2	21	H	Newcastle United	W	1 0	2 0	Ings, El Ghazi (pen)	41,964
3	28	H	Brentford	D	1 1	1 1	Buendia	42,045
4	Sep 11	A	Chelsea	L	0 1	0 3		39,969
5	18	H	Everton	W	0 0	3 0	Cash, Digne (og), Bailey	41,888
6	25	A	Manchester United	W	0 0	1 0	Hause	72,922
7	Oct 3	A	Tottenham Hotspur	L	0 1	1 2	Watkins	53,076
8	16	H	Wolverhampton Wanderers	L	0 0	2 3	Ings, McGinn	41,951
9	22	A	Arsenal	L	0 2	1 3	Ramsey	59,496
10	31	H	West Ham United	L	1 2	1 4	Watkins	41,874
11	Nov 5	A	Southampton	L	0 1	0 1		30,178
12	20	H	Brighton & Hove Albion	W	0 0	2 0	Watkins, Mings	41,925
13	27	A	Crystal Palace	W	1 0	2 1	Targett, McGinn	25,203
14	Dec 1	H	Manchester City	L	0 2	1 2	Watkins	41,400
15	5	H	Leicester City	W	1 1	2 1	Konsa 2	41,572
16	11	A	Liverpool	L	0 0	0 1		53,093
17	14	A	Norwich City	W	1 0	2 0	Ramsey, Watkins	26,836
18	26	H	Chelsea	L	1 1	1 3	James (og)	41,907
19	Jan 2	H	Brentford	L	1 1	1 2	Ings	16,876
20	15	H	Manchester United	D	0 1	2 2	Ramsey, Coutinho	41,968
21	22	A	Everton	W	1 0	1 0	Buendia	38,203
22	Feb 9	H	Leeds United	D	3 2	3 3	Coutinho, J Ramsey 2	41,927
23	13	A	Newcastle United	L	0 1	0 1		52,207
24	19	H	Watford	L	0 0	0 1		41,936
25	26	A	Brighton & Hove Albion	W	1 0	2 0	Cash, Watkins	31,475
26	Mar 5	H	Southampton	W	2 0	4 0	Watkins, Luiz, Coutinho, Ings	41,855
27	10	A	Leeds United	W	1 0	3 0	Coutinho, Cash, Chambers	36,400
28	13	A	West Ham United	L	0 0	1 2	J Ramsey	59,957
29	19	H	Arsenal	L	0 1	0 1		41,956
30	Apr 2	A	Wolverhampton Wanderers	L	0 2	1 2	Watkins (pen)	31,012
31	9	H	Tottenham Hotspur	L	0 1	0 4		41,949
32	23	A	Leicester City	D	0 0	0 0		32,185
33	30	H	Norwich City	W	1 0	2 0	Watkins, Ings	40,290
34	May 7	A	Burnley	W	2 0	3 1	Ings, Buendia, Watkins	20,891
35	10	H	Liverpool	L	1 1	1 2	Luiz	41,919
36	15	H	Crystal Palace	D	0 0	1 1	Watkins	41,136
37	19	H	Burnley	D	0 1	1 1	Buendia	40,468
38	22	A	Manchester City	L	1 0	2 3	Cash, Coutinho	53,395

2 Own-goals   Appearances
                                  Subs
                                  Goals

Match 10: Ezri Konsa sent off 50 minutes
Match 22: Ezri Konsa sent off 87 minutes.

FA CUP

3	Jan 10	A	Manchester United	L	0 1	0 1		72,911

                                  Appearances
                                  Subs
                                  Goals

FOOTBALL LEAGUE CUP

2	Aug 24	A	Barrow	W	3 0	6 0	Archer 3, El Ghazi 2 (1 pen), Guilbert	5,349
3	Sep 22	A	Chelsea*	L	0 0	1 1	Archer	35,892

1 Own-goal   Appearances
                                  Subs
                                  Goals

* Chelsea won 4-3 on penalties

FINAL LEAGUE TABLE

	P	W	D	L	F	A	P
Manchester City	38	29	6	3	99	26	93
Liverpool	38	28	8	2	94	26	92
Chelsea	38	21	11	6	76	33	74
Tottenham Hotspur	38	22	5	11	69	40	71
Arsenal	38	22	3	13	61	48	69
Manchester United	38	16	10	12	57	57	58
West Ham United	38	16	8	14	60	51	56
Leicester City	38	14	10	14	62	59	52
Brighton and HA	38	12	15	11	42	44	51
Wolverhampton W	38	15	6	17	38	43	51
Newcastle United	38	13	10	15	44	62	49
Crystal Palace	38	11	15	12	50	46	48
Brentford	38	13	7	18	48	56	46
Aston Villa	**38**	**13**	**6**	**19**	**52**	**54**	**45**
Southampton	38	9	13	16	43	67	40
Everton	38	11	6	21	43	66	39
Leeds United	38	9	11	18	42	79	38
Burnley	38	7	14	17	34	53	35
Watford	38	6	5	27	34	77	23
Norwich City	38	5	7	26	23	84	22

CLUB HONOURS & RECORDS

ASTON VILLA MAJOR HONOURS

EUROPEAN CUP
Winners: 1982

EUROPEAN SUPER CUP
Winners: 1983

WORLD CLUBS CHAMPIONSHIP
Runners-up: 1982

INTERTOTO CUP
Winners: 2001

FOOTBALL LEAGUE
Champions: 1893/94 · 1895/96 · 1896/97 · 1898/99 · 1899/1900 · 1909/10 · 1980/81
Runners-up: 1888/89 · 1902/03 · 1907/08 · 1910/11 · 1912/13 · 1913/14 · 1930/31 · 1932/33 · 1989/90

FOOTBALL LEAGUE DIVISION TWO
Champions: 1937/38 · 1959/60
Runners-up: 1974/75 · 1987/88

FOOTBALL LEAGUE DIVISION THREE
Champions: 1971/72

PREMIER LEAGUE
Runners-up: 1992/93

CHAMPIONSHIP
Play-Off winners: 2019

FA CUP
Winners: 1887 · 1895 · 1897 · 1905 · 1913 · 1920 · 1957
Runners-up: 1892 · 1924 · 2000 · 2015

LEAGUE CUP
Winners: 1961 · 1975 · 1977 · 1994 · 1996
Runners-up: 1963 · 1971 · 2010 · 2020

European Cup winners 1982

FA Cup winners 1957

CLUB RECORDS

Record scorer: Billy Walker · 244

Record League scorer: Harry Hampton · 215

Record number of League goals in a season: 128
1930/31 (a top-flight record)

Highest individual scorer in one season:
Tom 'Pongo' Waring · 50   1930/31 (49 League, 1 FA Cup)

Most goals in a single match: 5

Harry Hampton v Sheffield Wednesday (H) 1912

Harold Halse v Derby County (H) 1912

Len Capewell v Burnley (H) 1925

George Brown v Leicester City (A) 1932

Gerry Hitchens v Charlton Athletic (H) 1959

Most appearances: Charlie Aitken · 660
(657 plus 3 sub)

Record victory: 13-0
v Wednesbury Old Athletic (FA Cup, 1886)

Record League victory: 12-2 v Accrington (1892)

Highest post-war victory: 11-1 v Charlton Athletic (1959)

Record home attendance: 76,588
v Derby County, FA Cup (1946)

Most League wins in a season: 32
1971/72 (Division 3)

Most wins in a top-flight season: 26   1980/81

Most away wins in a season: 13   1987/88 (Division 2)

Undefeated at home in a season:
1895/96 · 1898/99 · 1909/10

Youngest League player: Jimmy Brown
15 years 349 days v Bolton Wanderers (A) 1969

Youngest League scorer: Walter Hazelden
16 years 269 days v West Bromwich Albion (A) 1957

Charlie Aitken - 660 games

Walter Hazelden - Villa's youngest League scorer

APPEARANCES DURING WW2

INITIALS	SURNAME	DATES	FOOTBALL LEAGUE (NORTH), FOOTBALL LEAGUE (SOUTH) & FOOTBALL LEAGUE WAR CUP GAMES	GOALS	BIRMINGHAM & DISTRICT LEAGUE GAMES	GOALS	OTHER MATCHES GAMES	GOALS	TOTAL GAMES	GOALS
L	Airey	1940-1941	0	0	1	0	0	0	1	0
WH	Aston	1940-1942	0	0	7	0	5	0	12	0
J	Barker	1940-1941	0	0	5	0	1	0	6	0
J	Bate	1940-1943	3	0	21	4	12	1	36	5
SG	Batty	1940-1941	0	0	0	0	1	0	1	0
G	Bentley	1941-1942	0	0	0	0	2	0	2	0
RM	Beresford	1940-1946	1	0	1	0	1	2	3	2
G	Billingsley	1940-1944	5	0	3	0	4	0	12	0
FH	Broome	1940-1946	116	67	11	16	13	11	140	94
E	Callaghan	1940-1946	113	1	22	0	24	0	159	1
L	Canning	1941-1945	3	2	2	3	1	0	6	5
W.J	Carey	1945-1946	1	0	0	0	0	0	1	0
J	Carswell	1941-1942	0	0	0	0	1	0	1	0
J	Carter	1940-1941	0	0	1	1	0	0	1	1
R	Cooper	1941-1942	0	0	1	0	1	0	2	0
SD	Crooks	1941-1942	0	0	0	0	1	0	1	0
A	Croom	1941-1942	0	0	0	0	1	0	1	0
GW	Cummings	1940-1946	139	2	21	2	24	0	184	4
RD	Davis	1940-1944	21	19	21	37	18	19	60	75
W	Devenport	1940-1941	0	0	1	0	0	0	1	0
JT	Dixon	1945-1946	6	3	0	0	0	0	6	3
	Duncan	1941-1942	0	0	0	0	1	0	1	0
GR	Edwards	1940-1946	110	86	9	7	3	0	122	93
S	Gibbons	1940-1941	0	0	1	0	0	0	1	0
LL	Godfrey	1940-1946	13	0	0	0	1	0	14	0
WC	Goffin	1940-1946	45	20	24	19	13	8	82	47
JR	Graham	1945-1946	4	1	0	0	0	0	4	1
R	Guttridge	1942-1944	34	1	0	0	2	0	36	1
FJ	Haycock	1940-1946	82	23	2	2	2	1	86	26
AH	Hickman	1940-1942	0	0	8	0	5	0	13	0
WE	Houghton	1940-1946	124	71	20	11	24	11	168	93
RTJ	Iverson	1940-1946	144	49	13	5	21	7	178	61

APPEARANCES DURING WW2

NOTE: For League games which also counted towards Cup matches, appearances and goals have been included against League games only. Other Matches include Birmingham League Cup, Keys Cup, Worcestershire Cup, Worcester Infirmary Cup, Charity, Peace Celebrations and other games. Appearances and goals for FA Cup matches played in 1946 are not included. These are included in the main appearance and goals grid.

INITIALS	SURNAME	DATES	FOOTBALL LEAGUE (NORTH), FOOTBALL LEAGUE (SOUTH) & FOOTBALL LEAGUE WAR CUP GAMES	GOALS	BIRMINGHAM & DISTRICT LEAGUE GAMES	GOALS	OTHER MATCHES GAMES	GOALS	TOTAL GAMES	GOALS
AW	Kerr	1940-1946	14	7	24	9	20	8	58	24
J	King	1940-1941	0	0	0	0	1	0	1	0
W	Knight	1940-1941	0	0	8	0	2	0	10	0
L	Latham	1944-1945	1	0	0	0	0	0	1	0
E	Lowe	1945-1946	24	0	0	0	0	0	24	0
	Lowry	1940-1941	0	0	1	0	0	0	1	0
G	Lunn	1940-1942	0	0	2	0	2	0	4	0
B	Marrs	1941-1942	0	0	0	0	1	0	1	0
JR	Martin	1940-1946	37	11	9	3	7	1	53	15
AC	Massie	1940-1946	103	3	17	0	19	5	139	8
JE	McConnon	1944-1945	2	0	0	0	0	0	2	0
JH	Morby	1943-1946	32	0	0	0	0	0	32	0
A	Moss	1940-1941	0	0	5	0	3	0	8	0
F	Moss (Jnr)	1945-1946	11	0	0	0	0	0	11	0
S	Neville	1940-1941	0	0	1	0	0	0	1	0
FJ	O'Donnell	1943-1944	14	7	0	0	0	0	14	7
HA	Parkes	1940-1946	98	26	28	10	21	12	147	48
R	Parsons	1940-1941	0	0	1	0	0	0	1	0
H	Pearce	1941-1942	0	0	2	1	1	0	3	1
	Perry	1940-1941	0	0	1	0	0	0	1	0
VE	Potts	1940-1946	153	0	29	0	24	1	206	1
JHH	Rutherford	1940-1946	9	0	5	0	5	0	19	0
RA	Scott	1945-1946	2	0	0	0	0	0	2	0
FH	Shell	1940-1946	8	0	9	2	3	0	20	2
LGF	Smith	1945-1946	23	3	0	0	0	0	23	3
H	Spencer	1940-1941	0	0	0	0	1	0	1	0
RW	Starling	1941-1946	142	4	1	0	4	1	147	5
A	Vinall	1940-1942	0	0	3	0	0	0	3	0
AD	Wakeman	1940-1946	145	0	25	0	20	0	190	0
A	Yorke	1940-1941	0	0	8	0	3	0	11	0
	Own goals	1940-1946	0	8	0	1	0	3	0	12

ASTON VILLA PLAYER RECORDS

				LEAGUE			
PLAYER	SURNAME	BORN	SEASONS	SL	SUB	PL	GLS
Tammy	Abraham	Camberwell, London	2018-2019	37	0	37	25
Jimmy	Adam	Glasgow, Scotland	1959-1961	24	0	24	3
Albert	Adomah	Lambeth, London	2016-2019	86	27	113	21
Didier	Agathe	Saint-Pierre, Reunion	2006-2007	0	5	5	0
Gabriel	Agbonlahor	Birmingham	2005-2018	298	43	341	76
Charlie	Aitken	Edinburgh, Scotland	1960-1976	559	2	561	14
Marc	Albrighton	Tamworth, Staffordshire	2008-2014	48	38	86	7
Peter	Aldis	Birmingham	1950-1959	262	0	262	1
Albert	Aldridge	Walsall	1889-1890	17	0	17	0
Marcus	Allback	Gothenburg, Sweden	2002-2004	16	19	35	6
Albert	Allen	Aston, Birmingham	1887-1891	45	0	45	30
Jimmy	Allen	Poole	1934-1939	147	0	147	2
Malcolm	Allen	Caernarfon, Wales	1987-1988	4	0	4	0
WB (Barney)	Allen	Hockley, Birmingham	1905-1906	3	0	3	1
Jordan	Amavi	Toulon, France	2015-2017	35	9	44	0
David	Anderson	Birmingham	1882-1883	0	0	0	0
Willie	Anderson	Liverpool	1966-1973	229	2	231	36
Juan Pablo	Angel	Medellin, Columbia	2000-2007	134	41	175	44
Barry	Ansell	Birmingham	1967-1968	1	0	1	0
Brendel	Anstey	Bristol	1910-1915	42	0	42	0
Charles	Apperley	Birmingham	1882-1884	0	0	0	0
Cameron	Archer	Walsall	2019-2022	0	3	3	0
Billy	Armfield	Handsworth, Birmingham	1923-1928	12	0	12	2
Norman	Ashe	Bloxwich	1959-1962	5	0	5	0
George	Ashfield	Manchester	1955-1958	9	0	9	0
Walter	Ashmore	West Smethwick	1888-1889	1	0	1	0
Derek	Ashton	Worksop	1946-1949	8	0	8	0
Billy	Askew	Marybone	1911-1912	2	0	2	0
Warren	Aspinall	Wigan	1986-1988	40	4	44	14
Dai	Astley	Dowlais, South Wales	1931-1937	165	0	165	92
Charlie	Aston	Bilston	1897-1901	23	0	23	0
WC (Charlie)	Athersmith	Bloxwich	1890-1901	270	0	270	75
Dalian	Atkinson	Shrewsbury	1991-1995	79	8	87	23
Jordan	Ayew	Marseille, France	2015-2017	44	7	51	9
Joe	Bache	Stourbridge	1900-1915	431	0	431	167
Leandro	Bacuna	Groningen, Netherlands	2013-2018	88	28	116	7
Leon	Bailey	Kingston, Jamaca	2021-2022	7	11	18	1
John	Baird	Alexandria, Scotland	1891-1895	61	0	61	0
Allan	Baker	Tipton	1960-1966	92	1	93	13
Nathan	Baker	Worcester	2010-2017	103	8	111	1
Eirik	Bakke	Sogndal, Norway	2005-2006	8	6	14	0
Bosko	Balaban	Rijeka, Croatia	2001-2002	0	8	8	0
John	Ball	Birmingham	1879-1880	0	0	0	0
Tommy	Ball	Chester-le-Street	1919-1924	74	0	74	0
Herbert (Bert)	Banks	Coventry	1901-1902	5	0	5	0
Barry	Bannan	Airdrie, Scotland	2008-2013	35	29	64	1

ASTON VILLA PLAYER RECORDS

LEAGUE GAMES: The Football League and FA Premier League.
EUROPE: European Cup, European Super Cup, UEFA Cup, Intertoto Cup, UEFA Europa League.
OTHER GAMES: World Club Championship, Sheriff of London Charity Shield, FA Charity Shield, Full Members' Cup, Simod Cup, Zenith Data Systems Cup.

FA CUP				LEAGUE CUP				EUROPEAN				OTHER				TOTAL			
SL	SUB	PL	GLS	SL	SUB	PL	GLS	SL	SUB	PL	GLS	SL	SUB	PL	GLS	SL	SUB	PL	GLS
0	0	0	0	0	0	0	0	0	0	0	0	3	0	3	1	40	0	40	26
0	0	0	0	0	0	0	0	0	0	0	0	0	0	0	0	24	0	24	3
2	0	2	0	4	0	4	1	0	0	0	0	5	1	6	0	97	28	125	22
0	0	0	0	0	1	1	0	0	0	0	0	0	0	0	0	0	6	6	0
12	4	16	2	21	1	22	7	9	3	12	2	0	0	0	0	340	51	391	87
34	1	35	1	61	0	61	1	2	0	2	0	1	0	1	0	657	3	660	16
5	1	6	2	4	2	6	0	2	2	4	0	0	0	0	0	59	43	102	9
32	0	32	0	0	0	0	0	0	0	0	0	1	0	1	0	295	0	295	1
0	0	0	0	0	0	0	0	0	0	0	0	0	0	0	0	17	0	17	0
0	0	0	0	1	5	6	0	3	0	3	1	0	0	0	0	20	24	44	7
9	0	9	6	0	0	0	0	0	0	0	0	0	0	0	0	54	0	54	36
13	0	13	1	0	0	0	0	0	0	0	0	0	0	0	0	160	0	160	3
0	0	0	0	0	0	0	0	0	0	0	0	0	0	0	0	4	0	4	0
0	0	0	0	0	0	0	0	0	0	0	0	0	0	0	0	3	0	3	1
1	0	1	0	3	0	3	0	0	0	0	0	0	0	0	0	39	9	48	0
5	0	5	0	0	0	0	0	0	0	0	0	0	0	0	0	5	0	5	0
11	1	12	1	23	0	23	7	0	0	0	0	1	0	1	0	264	3	267	44
8	1	9	1	14	3	17	13	2	2	4	4	0	0	0	0	158	47	205	62
0	0	0	0	0	0	0	0	0	0	0	0	0	0	0	0	1	0	1	0
3	0	3	0	0	0	0	0	0	0	0	0	0	0	0	0	45	0	45	0
8	0	8	0	0	0	0	0	0	0	0	0	0	0	0	0	8	0	8	0
0	0	0	0	2	1	3	4	0	0	0	0	0	0	0	0	2	4	6	4
0	0	0	0	0	0	0	0	0	0	0	0	0	0	0	0	12	0	12	2
0	0	0	0	0	0	0	0	0	0	0	0	0	0	0	0	5	0	5	0
1	0	1	0	0	0	0	0	0	0	0	0	0	0	0	0	10	0	10	0
0	0	0	0	0	0	0	0	0	0	0	0	0	0	0	0	1	0	1	0
0	0	0	0	0	0	0	0	0	0	0	0	0	0	0	0	8	0	8	0
0	0	0	0	0	0	0	0	0	0	0	0	0	0	0	0	2	0	2	0
1	1	2	0	4	0	4	2	0	0	0	0	0	0	0	0	45	5	50	16
8	0	8	8	0	0	0	0	0	0	0	0	0	0	0	0	173	0	173	100
0	0	0	0	0	0	0	0	0	0	0	0	1	0	1	0	24	0	24	0
38	0	38	10	0	0	0	0	0	0	0	0	3	0	3	1	311	0	311	86
4	0	4	0	15	0	15	11	7	0	7	2	1	0	1	0	106	8	114	36
2	1	3	0	2	2	4	1	0	0	0	0	0	0	0	0	48	10	58	10
42	0	42	17	0	0	0	0	0	0	0	0	1	0	1	0	474	0	474	184
8	2	10	1	5	0	5	0	0	0	0	0	0	0	0	0	101	30	131	8
0	0	0	0	0	0	0	0	0	0	0	0	0	0	0	0	7	11	18	1
9	0	9	0	0	0	0	0	0	0	0	0	0	0	0	0	70	0	70	0
4	0	4	1	13	0	13	3	0	0	0	0	0	0	0	0	109	1	110	17
4	0	4	0	7	0	7	0	0	0	0	0	0	0	0	0	114	8	122	1
0	0	0	0	0	0	0	0	0	0	0	0	0	0	0	0	8	6	14	0
0	0	0	0	1	1	2	0	1	0	1	0	0	0	0	0	2	9	11	0
2	0	2	0	0	0	0	0	0	0	0	0	0	0	0	0	2	0	2	0
3	0	3	0	0	0	0	0	0	0	0	0	0	0	0	0	77	0	77	0
0	0	0	0	0	0	0	0	0	0	0	0	0	0	0	0	5	0	5	0
4	3	7	0	9	0	9	0	2	1	3	1	0	0	0	0	50	33	83	2

LEAGUE

PLAYER	SURNAME	BORN	SEASONS	SL	SUB	PL	GLS
Tommy	Barber	West Stanley	1912-1915	57	0	57	9
Peter	Bardsley	Salford	2006-2007	13	0	13	0
Jeff	Barker	Scunthorpe	1937-1938	3	0	3	0
Ross	Barkley	Liverpool	2020-2021	18	6	24	3
Dr William Ewart	Barnie-Adshead	Dudley	1922-1923	2	0	2	1
Milan	Baros	Valasske Mezirici, Czech Republic	2005-2007	34	8	42	9
Earl	Barrett	Rochdale	1991-1995	118	1	119	1
Ken	Barrett	Bromsgrove	1958-1959	5	0	5	3
Gareth	Barry	Hastings	1997-2009	353	12	365	41
Louie	Barry	Sutton Coldfield	2020-2021	0	0	0	0
Frank	Barson	Grimesthorpe	1919-1922	92	0	92	10
Borja	Baston	Madrid, Spain	2019-2020	0	2	2	0
Bill	Baxter	Methil, Fife, Scotland	1953-1957	98	0	98	6
Malcolm	Beard	Cannock	1971-1973	5	1	6	0
Bill	Beaton	Kincardine-on-Forth, Scotland	1958-1959	1	0	1	0
Frank	Bedingfield	Sunderland	1898-1899	1	0	1	1
George	Beeson	Clay Cross	1934-1937	69	0	69	0
Stefan	Beinlich	Berlin, Germany	1991-1994	7	9	16	1
Joe	Bennett	Rochdale	2012-2016	24	6	30	0
Darren	Bent	Tooting, London	2010-2015	45	16	61	21
Christian	Benteke	Kinshasa, Zaire	2012-2015	82	7	89	42
Lou	Benwell	Birmingham	1893-1894	1	0	1	0
Joe	Beresford	Chesterfield	1927-1936	224	0	224	66
Patrik	Berger	Prague, Czech Republic	2005-2008	8	21	29	2
Mathieu	Berson	Vannes, France	2004-2005	7	4	11	0
Ryan	Bertrand	Southwark, London	2013-2014	16	0	16	0
Tony	Betts	Sandiacre, Nr Derby	1974-1975	1	3	4	0
Jonathan	Bewers	Kettering	1999-2000	0	1	1	0
Habib	Beye	Suresnes, France	2009-2012	7	2	9	0
Fred	Biddlestone	Pensnett	1929-1939	151	0	151	0
Jimmy	Birch	Blackwell	1911-1912	3	0	3	2
Paul	Birch	West Bromwich	1982-1991	153	20	173	16
Trevor	Birch	West Bromwich	1954-1960	22	0	22	0
Birkir	Bjarnason	Akureyri, Iceland	2016-2019	27	21	48	5
George	Blackburn	Wilesden Green, London	1920-1926	133	0	133	1
Robert Ernest (Ernie)	Blackburn	Crawshaw Booth, Manchester	1921-1922	32	0	32	0
Corey	Blackett-Taylor	Erdington, Birmingham	2016-2019	0	1	1	0
Andy	Blair	Kircaldy, Scotland	1981-1984 1986-1988	43	11	54	1
Danny	Blair	Parkhead, Scotland	1931-1936	129	0	129	0
Mark	Blake	Nottingham	1989-1993	26	5	31	2
Noel	Blake	Kingston, Jamaca	1979-1982	4	0	4	0
Danny	Blanchflower	Belfast, Northern Ireland	1950-1955	148	0	148	10
Ray	Bloomfield	Kensington	1964-1966	3	0	3	0
George	Boateng	Nkawkaw, Ghana	1999-2003	96	7	103	4
Chris	Boden	Wolverhampton	1994-1995	0	1	1	0
John	Boden	Norwich	1905-1906	17	0	17	2
Lamare	Bogarde	Rotterdam, Netherlands	2020-2021	0	0	0	0
Yannick	Bolasie	Lyon, France	2018-2019	9	12	21	2
Mark	Bosnich	Fairfield, Australia	1991-1999	179	0	179	0

ASTON VILLA PLAYER RECORDS

FA CUP				LEAGUE CUP				EUROPEAN				OTHER				TOTAL			
SL	SUB	PL	GLS	SL	SUB	PL	GLS	SL	SUB	PL	GLS	SL	SUB	PL	GLS	SL	SUB	PL	GLS
11	0	11	1	0	0	0	0	0	0	0	0	0	0	0	0	68	0	68	10
0	0	0	0	0	0	0	0	0	0	0	0	0	0	0	0	13	0	13	0
0	0	0	0	0	0	0	0	0	0	0	0	0	0	0	0	3	0	3	0
0	0	0	0	0	0	0	0	0	0	0	0	0	0	0	0	18	6	24	3
0	0	0	0	0	0	0	0	0	0	0	0	0	0	0	0	2	0	2	1
3	1	4	4	3	2	5	1	0	0	0	0	0	0	0	0	40	11	51	14
9	0	9	0	15	0	15	1	7	0	7	0	0	0	0	0	149	1	150	2
0	0	0	0	0	0	0	0	0	0	0	0	0	0	0	0	5	0	5	3
19	2	21	3	28	0	28	4	22	4	26	4	0	0	0	0	422	18	440	52
1	0	1	1	0	0	0	0	0	0	0	0	0	0	0	0	1	0	1	1
16	0	16	0	0	0	0	0	0	0	0	0	0	0	0	0	108	0	108	10
0	0	0	0	0	0	0	0	0	0	0	0	0	0	0	0	0	2	2	0
9	0	9	0	0	0	0	0	0	0	0	0	0	0	0	0	107	0	107	6
0	0	0	0	1	0	1	0	0	0	0	0	0	0	0	0	6	1	7	0
0	0	0	0	0	0	0	0	0	0	0	0	0	0	0	0	1	0	1	0
0	0	0	0	0	0	0	0	0	0	0	0	0	0	0	0	1	0	1	1
1	0	1	0	0	0	0	0	0	0	0	0	0	0	0	0	70	0	70	0
0	0	0	0	0	0	0	0	0	0	0	0	0	1	1	0	7	10	17	1
2	0	2	0	5	1	6	1	0	0	0	0	0	0	0	0	31	7	38	1
4	0	4	3	4	3	7	1	0	0	0	0	0	0	0	0	53	19	72	25
6	0	6	2	6	0	6	5	0	0	0	0	0	0	0	0	94	7	101	49
0	0	0	0	0	0	0	0	0	0	0	0	0	0	0	0	1	0	1	0
27	0	27	7	0	0	0	0	0	0	0	0	0	0	0	0	251	0	251	73
0	0	0	0	1	2	3	0	0	0	0	0	0	0	0	0	9	23	32	2
0	1	1	0	0	1	1	0	0	0	0	0	0	0	0	0	7	6	13	0
0	0	0	0	0	0	0	0	0	0	0	0	0	0	0	0	16	0	16	0
0	0	0	0	0	1	1	0	0	0	0	0	0	0	0	0	1	4	5	0
0	0	0	0	0	0	0	0	0	0	0	0	0	0	0	0	0	1	1	0
2	0	2	0	2	1	3	0	4	0	4	0	0	0	0	0	15	3	18	0
9	0	9	0	0	0	0	0	0	0	0	0	0	0	0	0	160	0	160	0
0	0	0	0	0	0	0	0	0	0	0	0	0	0	0	0	3	0	3	2
11	5	16	3	23	4	27	5	2	1	3	0	3	1	4	1	192	31	223	25
1	0	1	0	0	0	0	0	0	0	0	0	0	0	0	0	23	0	23	0
1	0	1	0	3	0	3	1	0	0	0	0	0	2	2	0	31	23	54	6
12	0	12	1	0	0	0	0	0	0	0	0	0	0	0	0	145	0	145	2
1	0	1	0	0	0	0	0	0	0	0	0	0	0	0	0	33	0	33	0
0	0	0	0	0	1	1	0	0	0	0	0	0	0	0	0	0	2	2	0
3	0	3	0	1	2	3	1	6	1	7	0	1	1	2	0	54	15	69	2
9	0	9	0	0	0	0	0	0	0	0	0	0	0	0	0	138	0	138	0
2	0	2	0	1	1	2	0	0	0	0	0	2	0	2	0	31	6	37	2
0	0	0	0	0	0	0	0	0	0	0	0	0	0	0	0	4	0	4	0
7	0	7	0	0	0	0	0	0	0	0	0	0	0	0	0	155	0	155	10
0	0	0	0	0	0	0	0	0	0	0	0	0	0	0	0	3	0	3	0
9	0	9	0	8	1	9	1	13	0	13	0	0	0	0	0	126	8	134	5
0	0	0	0	0	0	0	0	0	0	0	0	0	0	0	0	0	1	1	0
1	0	1	0	0	0	0	0	0	0	0	0	0	0	0	0	18	0	18	2
1	0	1	0	0	0	0	0	0	0	0	0	0	0	0	0	1	0	1	0
0	0	0	0	0	0	0	0	0	0	0	0	0	0	0	0	9	12	21	2
17	0	17	0	20	1	21	0	11	0	11	0	0	0	0	0	227	1	228	0

LEGAUE

PLAYER	SURNAME	BORN	SEASONS	SL	SUB	PL	GLS
Michael	Boulding	Sheffield	2002-2003	0	0	0	0
Wilfred	Bouma	Helmond, Holland	2005-2009	81	2	83	1
Hubert	Bourne	Bromsgrove	1919-1921	7	0	7	2
Teddy	Bowen	Hednesford	1923-1934	191	0	191	0
Jordan	Bowery	Nottingham	2012-2014	5	14	19	0
Tommy	Bowman	Ayr, Scotland	1897-1901	101	0	101	2
Walter 'Dick'	Boyman	Richmond, Surrey	1919-1922	22	0	22	11
Reg	Boyne	Leeds	1913-1915	8	0	8	0
Darren	Bradley	Birmingham	1984-1986	16	4	20	0
Keith	Bradley	Ellesmere Port	1964-1972	115	7	122	2
Michael	Bradley	Princeton, New Jersey, USA	2010-2011	0	3	3	0
Billy	Brawn	Wellingborough	1901-1906	96	0	96	20
James	Bree	Wakefield	2016-2019	15	6	21	0
Matthias	Breitkreutz	Crivitz, Germany	1991-1994	10	3	13	0
Des	Bremner	Aberchirder, Scotland	1979-1985	170	4	174	9
Mungo	Bridge	Daventry, Northamptonshire	2020-2021	0	0	0	0
Wilson	Briggs	Gorebridge, Edinburgh, Scotland	1961-1963	2	0	2	0
John	Brittleton	Winsford	1927-1930	10	0	10	0
Peter	Broadbent	Dover	1966-1969	60	3	63	0
Bob	Brocklebank	Finchley	1929-1936	19	0	19	2
Frank	Brooks	Aston, Birmingham	1881-1882	0	0	0	0
Frank	Broome	Berkhamsted	1934-1947	133	0	133	78
Albert A	Brown	Aston, Birmingham	1884-1894	86	0	86	35
Albert Γ	Brown	Tamworth	1900-1901	2	0	2	2
Albert 'Sailor'	Brown	Great Yarmouth	1947-1948	30	0	30	9
Arthur	Brown	Aston, Birmingham	1880-1886	0	0	0	0
George	Brown	Mickley, Northumberland	1929-1935	116	0	116	79
James R	Brown	Birmingham	1890-1893	51	0	51	4
Jimmy	Brown	Musselburgh, Scotland	1969-1975	72	4	76	1
Ralph	Brown	Ilkeston	1960-1961	0	0	0	0
Walter George	Brown	Cheadle	1904-1906	12	0	12	0
Paul	Browne	Glasgow, Scotland	1995-1996	2	0	2	0
Tom	Bryan	Walsall	1882-1883	0	0	0	0
Chris	Buckley	Urmston, Manchester	1906-1913	136	0	136	3
Emiliano	Buendia	Mar del Plata, Argentina	2021-2022	22	13	35	4
Terry	Bullivant	Lambeth, London	1979-1982	10	3	13	0
Mark	Bunn	Camden, London	2015-2019	17	1	18	0
Graham	Burke	Dublin, Ireland	2012-2013	0	0	0	0
Mark	Burke	Solihull	1986-1988	5	2	7	0
John	Burridge	Workington	1975-1977	65	0	65	0
Harry	Burrows	Haydock	1959-1965	147	0	147	53
GF (Frank)	Burton	Aston, Birmingham	1892-1898	52	0	52	2
JH (Jack)	Burton	Handsworth, Birmingham	1885-1891	28	0	28	1
Fred	Butcher	Hemmingfield	1934-1935	2	0	2	0
Lee	Butler	Sheffield	1988-1991	8	0	8	0
Mike	Buttress	Peterborough	1976-1978	1	2	3	0
Darren	Byfield	Sutton Coldfield	1997-1999	1	6	7	0
Gary	Cahill	Dronfield	2005-2008	25	3	28	1
Colin	Calderwood	Glasgow, Scotland	1998-2000	23	3	26	0
Ernie 'Mush'	Callaghan	Birmingham	1932-1947	125	0	125	0

ASTON VILLA PLAYER RECORDS

	FA CUP				LEAGUE CUP				EUROPEAN				OTHER				TOTAL			
SL	SUB	PL	GLS	SL	SUB	PL	GLS	SL	SUB	PL	GLS	SL	SUB	PL	GLS	SL	SUB	PL	GLS
0	0	0	0	0	0	0	0	2	0	2	1	0	0	0	0	2	0	2	1
3	0	3	0	1	1	2	0	2	0	2	0	0	0	0	0	87	3	90	1
0	0	0	0	0	0	0	0	0	0	0	0	0	0	0	0	7	0	7	2
12	0	12	0	0	0	0	0	0	0	0	0	0	0	0	0	203	0	203	0
1	1	2	0	0	1	1	0	0	0	0	0	0	0	0	0	6	16	22	0
13	0	13	0	0	0	0	0	0	0	0	0	3	0	3	0	117	0	117	2
0	0	0	0	0	0	0	0	0	0	0	0	0	0	0	0	22	0	22	11
0	0	0	0	0	0	0	0	0	0	0	0	0	0	0	0	8	0	8	0
0	0	0	0	3	0	3	0	0	0	0	0	0	0	0	0	19	4	23	0
6	2	8	0	14	0	14	0	0	0	0	0	0	0	0	0	135	9	144	2
1	0	1	0	0	0	0	0	0	0	0	0	0	0	0	0	1	3	4	0
12	0	12	1	0	0	0	0	0	0	0	0	0	0	0	0	108	0	108	21
2	0	2	0	3	1	4	0	0	0	0	0	1	0	1	0	21	7	28	0
0	0	0	0	0	1	1	0	0	0	0	0	0	0	0	0	10	4	14	0
14	0	14	0	17	1	18	1	19	0	19	0	2	0	2	0	222	5	227	10
1	0	1	0	0	0	0	0	0	0	0	0	0	0	0	0	1	0	1	0
0	0	0	0	0	0	0	0	0	0	0	0	0	0	0	0	2	0	2	0
0	0	0	0	0	0	0	0	0	0	0	0	0	0	0	0	10	0	10	0
5	0	5	2	0	0	0	0	0	0	0	0	0	0	0	0	65	3	68	2
1	0	1	0	0	0	0	0	0	0	0	0	0	0	0	0	20	0	20	2
1	0	1	0	0	0	0	0	0	0	0	0	0	0	0	0	1	0	1	0
18	0	18	13	0	0	0	0	0	0	0	0	0	0	0	0	151	0	151	91
28	0	28	24	0	0	0	0	0	0	0	0	0	0	0	0	114	0	114	59
0	0	0	0	0	0	0	0	0	0	0	0	0	0	0	0	2	0	2	2
1	0	1	0	0	0	0	0	0	0	0	0	0	0	0	0	31	0	31	9
22	0	22	15	0	0	0	0	0	0	0	0	0	0	0	0	22	0	22	15
10	0	10	10	0	0	0	0	0	0	0	0	0	0	0	0	126	0	126	89
4	0	4	1	0	0	0	0	0	0	0	0	0	0	0	0	55	0	55	5
4	0	4	0	8	0	8	0	0	0	0	0	0	0	0	0	84	4	88	1
0	0	0	0	1	0	1	0	0	0	0	0	0	0	0	0	1	0	1	0
0	0	0	0	0	0	0	0	0	0	0	0	0	0	0	0	12	0	12	0
0	0	0	0	0	0	0	0	0	0	0	0	0	0	0	0	2	0	2	0
2	0	2	0	0	0	0	0	0	0	0	0	0	0	0	0	2	0	2	0
7	0	7	0	0	0	0	0	0	0	0	0	1	0	1	0	144	0	144	3
1	0	1	0	1	0	1	0	0	0	0	0	0	0	0	0	24	13	37	4
1	0	1	0	0	1	1	0	0	0	0	0	0	0	0	0	11	4	15	0
1	0	1	0	2	0	2	0	0	0	0	0	0	0	0	0	20	1	21	0
0	0	0	0	0	2	2	0	0	0	0	0	0	0	0	0	0	2	2	0
0	0	0	0	0	0	0	0	0	0	0	0	0	1	1	0	5	3	8	0
6	0	6	0	9	0	9	0	0	0	0	0	0	0	0	0	80	0	80	0
11	0	11	5	23	0	23	15	0	0	0	0	0	0	0	0	181	0	181	73
2	0	2	1	0	0	0	0	0	0	0	0	0	0	0	0	54	0	54	3
21	0	21	2	0	0	0	0	0	0	0	0	0	0	0	0	49	0	49	3
0	0	0	0	0	0	0	0	0	0	0	0	0	0	0	0	2	0	2	0
0	0	0	0	0	0	0	0	0	0	0	0	2	0	2	0	10	0	10	0
0	0	0	0	0	0	0	0	0	0	0	0	0	0	0	0	1	2	3	0
0	1	1	0	1	0	1	0	1	0	1	0	0	0	0	0	3	7	10	0
1	0	1	0	2	0	2	0	0	0	0	0	0	0	0	0	28	3	31	1
0	0	0	0	3	1	4	0	0	0	0	0	0	0	0	0	26	4	30	0
17	0	17	0	0	0	0	0	0	0	0	0	0	0	0	0	142	0	142	0

LEAGUE

PLAYER	SURNAME	BORN	SEASONS	SL	SUB	PL	GLS
Nigel	Callaghan	Singapore	1988-1991	24	2	26	1
Archie	Campbell	Crook, Co. Durham	1923-1925	4	0	4	0
Bobby	Campbell	Belfast, Northern Ireland	1973-1975	7	3	10	1
George	Campbell	Ayr, Scotland	1890-1893	50	0	50	1
Johnny	Campbell	Glasgow, Scotland	1895-1897	55	0	55	38
Lewis	Campbell	Edinburgh, Scotland	1889-1893	40	0	40	20
Larry	Canning	Cowdenbeath, Scotland	1948-1954	39	0	39	3
Jimmy	Cantrell	Sheepbridge	1904-1908	49	0	49	23
Len	Capewell	Birmingham	1921-1929	144	0	144	88
Benito	Carbone	Bagnara Calabra, Italy	1999-2000	22	2	24	3
John	Carew	Strommen, Norway	2006-2011	89	24	113	37
Bill	Carey	Manchester	1937-1938	3	0	3	0
Franz	Carr	Preston	1994-1996	1	2	3	0
Frank	Carrodus	Altrincham	1974-1979	151	0	151	7
Tom	Carroll	Watford	2018-2019	0	2	2	0
Martin	Carruthers	Nottingham	1991-1993	2	2	4	0
Samir	Carruthers	Islington, London	2011-2012	0	3	3	0
Scott	Carson	Whitehaven	2007-2008	35	0	35	0
Arthur	Cartlidge	Stoke-on-Trent	1908-1911	52	0	52	0
Tony	Cascarino	Orpington, Kent	1989-1991	43	3	46	11
Matthew (Matty)	Cash	Slough	2020-2022	66	0	66	4
Calum	Chambers	Petersfield	2021-2022	9	2	11	1
John	Chambers	Birmingham	1968-1969	1	1	2	0
Robert	Chandler	Calcutta, India	1913-1914	1	0	1	0
Harold	Chapman	Liverpool	1947-1948	6	0	6	0
Roy	Chapman	Birmingham	1953-1958	19	0	19	7
Fred	Chapple	Treharris, South Wales	1906-1908	9	0	9	3
Gary	Charles	Newham	1994-1999	72	7	79	3
Bob	Chatt	Barnard Castle	1892-1898	86	0	86	20
Lew	Chatterley	Birmingham	1962-1971	149	6	155	26
James	Chester	Warrington	2015-2020	119	0	119	12
Reg	Chester	Long Eaton	1925-1935	93	0	93	34
Ben	Chrisene	Exeter	2020-2021	0	0	0	0
Caleb	Chukwuemeka	Eisenstadt, Austria	2021-2022	0	0	0	0
Carney	Chukwuemeka	Eisenstadt, Austria	2020-2022	2	12	14	0
Aly	Cissokho	Blois, France	2014-2017	53	2	55	0
Ciaran	Clark	Harrow, London	2009-2016	119	15	134	7
Mitch	Clark	Nuneaton	2017-2018	0	0	0	0
Billy	Clarke	Walsall	1881-1884	0	0	0	0
George	Clarke	Bolsover	1924-1925	1	0	1	0
Norman (Nobby)	Clarke	Birmingham	1954-1955	1	0	1	0
Willie	Clarke	Mauchline, Scotland	1901-1905	41	0	41	5
Thomas	Clarkson	Stourbridge	1889-1893	17	0	17	0
Jim	Clayton	Sunderland	1937-1939	11	0	11	1
Tom	Cleverley	Basingstoke	2014-2015	31	0	31	3
Bill	Cobley	Leicester	1936-1939	44	0	44	0
Rowland	Codling	Durham	1905-1909	77	0	77	0
Carlton	Cole	Croydon, Surrey	2004-2005	18	9	27	3
Joe	Cole	Paddington, London	2014-2016	3	9	12	1
James	Collins	Newport, Wales	2009-2012	88	3	91	5

ASTON VILLA PLAYER RECORDS

	FA CUP				LEAGUE CUP				EUROPEAN				OTHER				TOTAL			
SL	SUB	PL	GLS	SL	SUB	PL	GLS	SL	SUB	PL	GLS	SL	SUB	PL	GLS	SL	SUB	PL	GLS
1	1	2	0	2	1	3	0	0	0	0	0	0	0	0	0	27	4	31	1
0	0	0	0	0	0	0	0	0	0	0	0	0	0	0	0	4	0	4	0
0	0	0	0	2	0	2	0	0	0	0	0	0	0	0	0	9	3	12	1
2	0	2	0	0	0	0	0	0	0	0	0	0	0	0	0	52	0	52	1
8	0	8	4	0	0	0	0	0	0	0	0	0	0	0	0	63	0	63	42
8	0	8	4	0	0	0	0	0	0	0	0	0	0	0	0	48	0	48	24
2	0	2	0	0	0	0	0	0	0	0	0	0	0	0	0	41	0	41	3
3	0	3	1	0	0	0	0	0	0	0	0	0	0	0	0	52	0	52	24
13	0	13	12	0	0	0	0	0	0	0	0	0	0	0	0	157	0	157	100
6	0	6	5	0	0	0	0	0	0	0	0	0	0	0	0	28	2	30	8
6	2	8	7	3	2	5	0	5	0	5	4	0	0	0	0	103	28	131	48
1	0	1	0	0	0	0	0	0	0	0	0	0	0	0	0	4	0	4	0
1	0	1	1	0	0	0	0	0	0	0	0	0	0	0	0	2	2	4	1
9	0	9	0	27	0	27	3	10	0	10	0	0	0	0	0	197	0	197	10
0	0	0	0	0	0	0	0	0	0	0	0	0	0	0	0	0	2	2	0
0	1	1	0	0	0	0	0	0	0	0	0	0	1	1	0	2	4	6	0
0	0	0	0	0	0	0	0	0	0	0	0	0	0	0	0	0	3	3	0
1	0	1	0	0	0	0	0	0	0	0	0	0	0	0	0	36	0	36	0
2	0	2	0	0	0	0	0	0	0	0	0	1	0	1	0	55	0	55	0
2	0	2	0	2	1	3	1	3	0	3	0	0	0	0	0	50	4	54	12
1	0	1	0	1	0	1	0	0	0	0	0	0	0	0	0	68	0	68	4
0	0	0	0	0	0	0	0	0	0	0	0	0	0	0	0	9	2	11	1
0	0	0	0	0	0	0	0	0	0	0	0	0	0	0	0	1	1	2	0
0	0	0	0	0	0	0	0	0	0	0	0	0	0	0	0	1	0	1	0
0	0	0	0	0	0	0	0	0	0	0	0	0	0	0	0	6	0	6	0
0	0	0	0	0	0	0	0	0	0	0	0	0	0	0	0	19	0	19	7
0	0	0	0	0	0	0	0	0	0	0	0	0	0	0	0	9	0	9	3
5	2	7	0	9	1	10	0	6	3	9	1	0	0	0	0	92	13	105	4
9	0	9	7	0	0	0	0	0	0	0	0	0	0	0	0	95	0	95	27
4	0	4	0	7	0	7	1	0	0	0	0	0	0	0	0	160	6	166	27
2	0	2	0	2	0	2	0	0	0	0	0	3	0	3	0	126	0	126	12
4	0	4	0	0	0	0	0	0	0	0	0	0	0	0	0	97	0	97	34
1	0	1	0	0	0	0	0	0	0	0	0	0	0	0	0	1	0	1	0
0	0	0	0	0	1	1	0	0	0	0	0	0	0	0	0	0	1	1	0
0	0	0	0	1	1	2	0	0	0	0	0	0	0	0	0	3	13	16	0
3	0	3	0	0	0	0	0	0	0	0	0	0	0	0	0	56	2	58	0
15	1	16	3	10	0	10	0	0	0	0	0	0	0	0	0	144	16	160	10
0	0	0	0	1	0	1	0	0	0	0	0	0	0	0	0	1	0	1	0
7	0	7	0	0	0	0	0	0	0	0	0	0	0	0	0	7	0	7	0
0	0	0	0	0	0	0	0	0	0	0	0	0	0	0	0	1	0	1	0
0	0	0	0	0	0	0	0	0	0	0	0	0	0	0	0	1	0	1	0
1	0	1	0	0	0	0	0	0	0	0	0	0	0	0	0	42	0	42	5
0	0	0	0	0	0	0	0	0	0	0	0	0	0	0	0	17	0	17	0
0	0	0	0	0	0	0	0	0	0	0	0	0	0	0	0	11	0	11	1
6	0	6	0	0	0	0	0	0	0	0	0	0	0	0	0	37	0	37	3
2	0	2	0	0	0	0	0	0	0	0	0	0	0	0	0	46	0	46	0
5	0	5	0	0	0	0	0	0	0	0	0	0	0	0	0	82	0	82	0
1	0	1	0	1	1	2	0	0	0	0	0	0	0	0	0	20	10	30	3
1	1	2	0	1	1	2	0	0	0	0	0	0	0	0	0	5	11	16	1
6	2	8	1	7	1	8	0	1	0	1	0	0	0	0	0	102	6	108	6

ASTON VILLA · THE COMPLETE RECORD

PLAYER	SURNAME	BORN	SEASONS	LEAGUE SL	SUB	PL	GLS
Stan	Collymore	Stone, Staffordshire	1997-1999	34	11	45	7
Andy	Comyn	Wakefield	1989-1991	12	3	15	0
James	Connor	Birmingham	1889-1891	4	0	4	0
Harry	Cooch	Birmingham	1901-1908	25	0	25	0
Billy	Cook	Evenwood	1926-1929	57	0	57	35
Stephen	Cooke	Walsall	2000-2003	0	3	3	0
Neale	Cooper	Darjeeling, India	1986-1988	19	1	20	0
George	Copley	Birmingham	1880-1882	0	0	0	0
Joseph	Corbett	Brierley Hill	1923-1927	7	0	7	0
Walter	Corbett	Wellington	1904-1907	13	0	13	0
John	Cordell	Walsall	1951-1953	5	0	5	0
Frank	Cornan	Sunderland	1908-1909	16	0	16	0
Frank	Coulton	Walsall	1886-1894	35	0	35	0
Philippe	Coutinho	Rio de Janeiro, Brazil	2021-2022	16	3	19	5
James	Cowan	Jamestown, Scotland	1889-1902	315	0	315	22
John	Cowan	Dumbarton, Scotland	1895-1899	65	0	65	23
Gordon	Cowans	Durham	1975-1985 1988-1992 1993-1994	399	15	414	49
Gershom	Cox	Birmingham	1887-1893	87	0	87	0
Neil	Cox	Scunthorpe	1991-1994	26	16	42	3
Jimmy	Crabtree	Burnley	1895-1902	178	0	178	7
Miller	Craddock	Newent, Herefordshire	1948-1951	34	0	34	10
Tommy	Craig	Glasgow, Scotland	1977-1979	27	0	27	2
Jose Angel	Crespo	Lora del Rio, Spain	2015-2016	1	0	1	0
Alex	Cropley	Aldershot	1976-1980	65	2	67	7
William	Crossland	West Bromwich	1879-1882	0	0	0	0
Peter	Crouch	Macclesfield	2001-2004	20	17	37	6
Vic	Crowe	Abercynon, Wales	1954-1964	294	0	294	10
Stan	Crowther	Bilston	1956-1958	50	0	50	4
Geoff	Crudgington	Wolverhampton	1970-1972	4	0	4	0
Carlos	Cuellar	Madrid, Spain	2008-2012	87	7	94	2
Jim	Cumbes	Manchester	1971-1976	157	0	157	0
George	Cummings	Falkirk, Scotland	1935-1949	210	0	210	0
Arthur	Cunliffe	Blackrod, Nr Wigan	1932-1936	69	0	69	11
Alan	Curbishley	Forest Gate, London	1982-1985	34	2	36	1
Sasa	Curcic	Belgrade, Yugoslavia	1996-1998	20	9	29	0
George	Curtis	Dover	1969-1972	51	0	51	3
Neil	Cutler	Birmingham	1999-2000	0	1	1	0
Tony	Daley	Birmingham	1984-1994	189	44	233	31
Pat	Daly	Dublin, Republic of Ireland	1949-1950	3	0	3	0
Curtis	Davies	Waltham Forest, London	2007-2011	45	4	49	3
Arthur	Davis	Birmingham	1919-1922	5	0	5	1
Elisha	Davis	Dudley	1879-1885	0	0	0	0
George	Davis	Birmingham	1889-1890	1	0	1	0
George A	Davis	Handsworth, Birmingham	1892-1893	1	0	1	1
Keinan	Davis	Stevenage	2016-2022	22	51	73	3
Neil	Davis	Bloxwich	1995-1996	0	2	2	0
Richmond	Davis	Walsall	1885-1887	0	0	0	0
Steven	Davis	Ballymena, Northern Ireland	2004-2007	70	21	91	5

ASTON VILLA PLAYER RECORDS

	FA CUP				LEAGUE CUP				EUROPEAN				OTHER				TOTAL			
SL	SUB	PL	GLS	SL	SUB	PL	GLS	SL	SUB	PL	GLS	SL	SUB	PL	GLS	SL	SUB	PL	GLS
5	0	5	3	1	0	1	0	9	1	10	5	0	0	0	0	49	12	61	15
2	0	2	0	2	1	3	0	1	0	1	0	0	0	0	0	17	4	21	0
0	0	0	0	0	0	0	0	0	0	0	0	0	0	0	0	4	0	4	0
0	0	0	0	0	0	0	0	0	0	0	0	0	0	0	0	25	0	25	0
4	0	4	5	0	0	0	0	0	0	0	0	0	0	0	0	61	0	61	40
0	0	0	0	0	0	0	0	0	1	1	0	0	0	0	0	0	4	4	0
2	0	2	1	0	0	0	0	0	0	0	0	0	0	0	0	21	1	22	1
5	0	5	0	0	0	0	0	0	0	0	0	0	0	0	0	5	0	5	0
0	0	0	0	0	0	0	0	0	0	0	0	0	0	0	0	7	0	7	0
0	0	0	0	0	0	0	0	0	0	0	0	0	0	0	0	13	0	13	0
0	0	0	0	0	0	0	0	0	0	0	0	0	0	0	0	5	0	5	0
0	0	0	0	0	0	0	0	0	0	0	0	0	0	0	0	16	0	16	0
20	0	20	0	0	0	0	0	0	0	0	0	0	0	0	0	55	0	55	0
0	0	0	0	0	0	0	0	0	0	0	0	0	0	0	0	16	3	19	5
39	0	39	5	0	0	0	0	0	0	0	0	2	0	2	0	356	0	356	27
5	0	5	2	0	0	0	0	0	0	0	0	0	0	0	0	70	0	70	25
28	1	29	3	40	4	44	5	29	1	30	2	9	1	10	0	505	22	527	59
15	0	15	0	0	0	0	0	0	0	0	0	0	0	0	0	102	0	102	0
4	2	6	1	5	2	7	0	1	0	1	0	1	0	1	0	37	20	57	4
22	0	22	1	0	0	0	0	0	0	0	0	2	0	2	0	202	0	202	8
0	0	0	0	0	0	0	0	0	0	0	0	0	0	0	0	34	0	34	10
1	0	1	0	4	0	4	0	0	0	0	0	0	0	0	0	32	0	32	2
0	0	0	0	1	0	1	0	0	0	0	0	0	0	0	0	2	0	2	0
2	0	2	0	9	0	9	0	5	0	5	0	0	0	0	0	81	2	83	7
6	0	6	0	0	0	0	0	0	0	0	0	0	0	0	0	6	0	6	0
0	0	0	0	1	1	2	0	4	0	4	0	0	0	0	0	25	18	43	6
34	0	34	1	23	0	23	1	0	0	0	0	0	0	0	0	351	0	351	12
11	0	11	0	0	0	0	0	0	0	0	0	1	0	1	0	62	0	62	4
0	0	0	0	1	0	1	0	0	0	0	0	0	0	0	0	5	0	5	0
9	0	9	1	9	0	9	0	9	0	9	0	0	0	0	0	114	7	121	3
8	0	8	0	16	0	16	0	1	0	1	0	1	0	1	0	183	0	183	0
22	0	22	0	0	0	0	0	0	0	0	0	0	0	0	0	232	0	232	0
6	0	6	2	0	0	0	0	0	0	0	0	0	0	0	0	75	0	75	13
0	0	0	0	5	0	5	0	2	0	2	0	0	0	0	0	41	2	43	1
2	0	2	1	1	1	2	0	0	1	1	0	0	0	0	0	23	11	34	1
3	0	3	0	4	0	4	0	0	0	0	0	0	0	0	0	58	0	58	3
0	0	0	0	0	0	0	0	0	0	0	0	0	0	0	0	0	1	1	0
15	1	16	2	22	2	24	4	6	0	6	0	9	2	11	1	241	49	290	38
1	0	1	0	0	0	0	0	0	0	0	0	0	0	0	0	4	0	4	0
5	1	6	0	1	1	2	0	9	1	10	0	0	0	0	0	60	7	67	3
0	0	0	0	0	0	0	0	0	0	0	0	0	0	0	0	5	0	5	1
22	0	22	2	0	0	0	0	0	0	0	0	0	0	0	0	22	0	22	2
0	0	0	0	0	0	0	0	0	0	0	0	0	0	0	0	1	0	1	0
0	0	0	0	0	0	0	0	0	0	0	0	0	0	0	0	1	0	1	1
1	2	3	1	5	4	9	2	0	0	0	0	0	1	1	0	28	58	86	6
0	1	1	0	0	0	0	0	0	0	0	0	0	0	0	0	0	3	3	0
12	0	12	3	0	0	0	0	0	0	0	0	0	0	0	0	12	0	12	3
4	1	5	2	6	0	6	2	0	0	0	0	0	0	0	0	80	22	102	9

PLAYER	SURNAME	BORN	SEASONS	SL	SUB	PL	GLS
Simon	Dawkins	London	2012-2013	0	4	4	0
Frederick H (Frankie)	Dawson	Birmingham	1883-1889	3	0	3	0
James	Dawson	Stoke-on-Trent	1881-1882	0	0	0	0
Mervyn	Day	Chelmsford	1983-1985	30	0	30	0
Gilles	De Bilde	Zellik, Belgium	2000-2001	4	0	4	0
Ulises	De la Cruz	Piqulucho, Ecuador	2002-2006	66	23	89	1
Ritchie	De Laet	Antwerp, Belgium	2016-2019	4	4	8	0
Eamonn	Deacy	Galway, Republic of Ireland	1979-1984	27	7	34	1
Alan	Deakin	Birmingham	1959-1970	230	1	231	9
John	Deehan	Solihull	1975-1980	107	3	110	40
Mark	Delaney	Haverfordwest, Wales	1998-2006	144	14	158	2
Nathan	Delfouneso	Birmingham	2008-2013	4	27	31	2
Fabian	Delph	Bradford	2009-2015	97	15	112	3
Les	Dennington	West Bromwich	1924-1925	1	0	1	0
Harry	Devey	Birmingham	1887-1893	73	0	73	1
John	Devey	Birmingham	1891-1902	271	0	271	166
William	Devey	Perry Barr, Birmingham	1892-1894	10	0	10	2
William	Dickie	Wednesbury	1889-1890	0	0	0	0
Ian	Dickson	Maxwell Town, Dumfries, Scotland	1920-1924	76	0	76	30
William (Billy)	Dickson	Crail, Fife, Scotland	1889-1892	58	0	58	31
Lucas	Digne	Meaux, France	2021-2022	16	0	16	0
Billy	Dinsdale	Guisborough	1924-1926	8	0	8	0
Edwin	Diver	Cambridge	1891-1892	3	0	3	0
Ronnie	Dix	Bristol	1932-1937	97	0	97	30
Arthur	Dixon	Matlock	1888-1889	3	0	3	1
Johnny	Dixon	Hebburn-on-Tyne	1946-1961	392	0	392	132
Eric	Djemba-Djemba	Douala, Cameroon	2004-2007	4	7	11	0
Arthur	Dobson	Chesterton, Staffordshire	1912-1915	6	0	6	0
Tommy	Dodds	South Shields, Co. Durham	1946-1947	1	0	1	0
Stuart	Doncaster	Gainsborough	1912-1913	2	0	2	1
Terry	Donovan	Liverpool	1979-1982	17	0	17	6
Tony	Dorigo	Melbourne, Australia	1983-1987	106	5	111	1
Arthur	Dorrell	Birmingham	1919-1930	355	0	355	60
William (Billy)	Dorrell	Leicester	1894-1896	10	0	10	5
Dickie	Dorsett	Brownhills	1946-1953	257	0	257	32
Derek	Dougan	Belfast, Northern Ireland	1961-1963	51	0	51	19
Peter	Dowds	Johnstone, Renfrewshire, Scotland	1892-1893	19	0	19	3
Stewart	Downing	Middlesbrough	2009-2011	61	2	63	9
Jake	Doyle-Hayes	Ballyjamesduff, Ireland	2017-2019	0	0	0	0
Mark	Draper	Long Eaton	1995-2000	108	12	120	7
Charlie	Drinkwater	Willesden	1935-1936	2	0	2	1
Danny	Drinkwater	Manchester	2019-2020	4	0	4	0
Dion	Dublin	Leicester	1998-2004	120	35	155	48
Andy	Ducat	Brixton	1912-1921	74	0	74	4
Darrell	Duffy	Birmingham	1988-1989	1	0	1	0
Jimmy	Dugdale	Liverpool	1955-1962	215	0	215	3
John	Dunn	Barking	1967-1971	101	0	101	0
Richard	Dunne	Tallaght, Dublin, Ireland	2009-2012	95	0	95	4
J William (Bill)	Dunning	Perth, Scotland	1892-1895	64	0	64	0
Thomas	Dutton	West Bromwich	1891-1892	1	0	1	0

ASTON VILLA PLAYER RECORDS

\multicolumn{4}{c	}{FA CUP}	\multicolumn{4}{c	}{LEAGUE CUP}	\multicolumn{4}{c	}{EUROPEAN}	\multicolumn{4}{c	}{OTHER}	\multicolumn{4}{c}{TOTAL}
SL	SUB	PL	GLS	SL	SUB	PL	GLS	SL	SUB	PL	GLS	SL	SUB	PL	GLS	SL	SUB	PL	GLS
0	0	0	0	0	0	0	0	0	0	0	0	0	0	0	0	0	4	4	0
17	0	17	2	0	0	0	0	0	0	0	0	0	0	0	0	20	0	20	2
5	0	5	1	0	0	0	0	0	0	0	0	0	0	0	0	5	0	5	1
0	0	0	0	3	0	3	0	0	0	0	0	0	0	0	0	33	0	33	0
0	0	0	0	0	0	0	0	0	0	0	0	0	0	0	0	4	0	4	0
2	0	2	0	6	2	8	1	0	0	0	0	0	0	0	0	74	25	99	2
1	0	1	0	4	1	5	0	0	0	0	0	0	0	0	0	9	5	14	0
1	0	1	0	2	3	5	0	0	1	1	0	0	0	0	0	30	11	41	1
17	0	17	0	22	0	22	0	0	0	0	0	0	0	0	0	269	1	270	9
7	1	8	3	14	0	14	2	7	0	7	5	0	0	0	0	135	4	139	50
8	1	9	0	10	3	13	0	13	0	13	0	0	0	0	0	175	18	193	2
6	2	8	4	1	4	5	1	3	5	8	2	0	0	0	0	14	38	52	9
12	0	12	3	7	2	9	2	1	0	1	0	0	0	0	0	117	17	134	8
0	0	0	0	0	0	0	0	0	0	0	0	0	0	0	0	1	0	1	0
11	0	11	0	0	0	0	0	0	0	0	0	0	0	0	0	84	0	84	1
38	0	38	17	0	0	0	0	0	0	0	0	2	0	2	0	311	0	311	183
0	0	0	0	0	0	0	0	0	0	0	0	0	0	0	0	10	0	10	2
1	0	1	0	0	0	0	0	0	0	0	0	0	0	0	0	1	0	1	0
7	0	7	8	0	0	0	0	0	0	0	0	0	0	0	0	83	0	83	38
6	0	6	2	0	0	0	0	0	0	0	0	0	0	0	0	64	0	64	33
0	0	0	0	0	0	0	0	0	0	0	0	0	0	0	0	16	0	16	0
0	0	0	0	0	0	0	0	0	0	0	0	0	0	0	0	8	0	8	0
0	0	0	0	0	0	0	0	0	0	0	0	0	0	0	0	3	0	3	0
7	0	7	0	0	0	0	0	0	0	0	0	0	0	0	0	104	0	104	30
0	0	0	0	0	0	0	0	0	0	0	0	0	0	0	0	3	0	3	1
38	0	38	12	0	0	0	0	0	0	0	0	0	0	0	0	430	0	430	144
0	0	0	0	0	0	0	0	0	0	0	0	0	0	0	0	4	7	11	0
1	0	1	0	0	0	0	0	0	0	0	0	0	0	0	0	7	0	7	0
0	0	0	0	0	0	0	0	0	0	0	0	0	0	0	0	1	0	1	0
0	0	0	0	0	0	0	0	0	0	0	0	0	0	0	0	2	0	2	1
6	0	6	3	0	0	0	0	1	0	1	2	0	0	0	0	24	0	24	11
7	0	7	0	14	1	15	0	0	0	0	0	2	0	2	0	129	6	135	1
35	0	35	5	0	0	0	0	0	0	0	0	0	0	0	0	390	0	390	65
1	0	1	2	0	0	0	0	0	0	0	0	0	0	0	0	11	0	11	7
14	0	14	3	0	0	0	0	0	0	0	0	0	0	0	0	271	0	271	35
5	0	5	2	4	0	4	5	0	0	0	0	0	0	0	0	60	0	60	26
1	0	1	0	0	0	0	0	0	0	0	0	0	0	0	0	20	0	20	3
6	3	9	0	5	1	6	2	1	0	1	0	0	0	0	0	73	6	79	11
0	0	0	0	3	0	3	0	0	0	0	0	0	0	0	0	3	0	3	0
10	0	10	2	11	1	12	2	12	1	13	0	0	0	0	0	141	14	155	11
0	0	0	0	0	0	0	0	0	0	0	0	0	0	0	0	2	0	2	1
0	0	0	0	0	0	0	0	0	0	0	0	0	0	0	0	4	0	4	0
5	2	7	1	13	2	15	8	10	2	12	2	0	0	0	0	148	41	189	59
13	0	13	0	0	0	0	0	0	0	0	0	0	0	0	0	87	0	87	4
0	0	0	0	0	0	0	0	0	0	0	0	0	0	0	0	1	0	1	0
27	0	27	0	12	0	12	0	0	0	0	0	1	0	1	0	255	0	255	3
5	0	5	0	12	0	12	0	0	0	0	0	0	0	0	0	118	0	118	0
8	0	8	1	8	0	8	0	0	0	0	0	0	0	0	0	111	0	111	5
5	0	5	0	0	0	0	0	0	0	0	0	0	0	0	0	69	0	69	0
0	0	0	0	0	0	0	0	0	0	0	0	0	0	0	0	1	0	1	0

LEAGUE

PLAYER	SURNAME	BORN	SEASONS	SL	SUB	PL	GLS
Archie	Dyke	Newcastle-under-Lyme	1913-1915	9	0	9	0
Joe	Eccles	Stoke-on-Trent	1924-1925	10	0	10	0
Harold	Edgley	Crewe	1911-1920	75	0	75	16
Alfred	Edwards	Coventry	1911-1912	6	0	6	0
Dick	Edwards	Kirby-in-Ashfield	1967-1970	68	0	68	2
George	Edwards	Great Yarmouth	1938-1951	138	0	138	34
Rob	Edwards	Telford	2002-2003	7	1	8	0
Ugo	Ehiogu	Hackney, London	1991-2001	223	14	237	12
Karim	El Ahmadi	Enschede, Netherlands	2012-2014	38	13	51	3
Anwar	El Ghazi	Barendrecht, Netherlands	2018-2022	72	30	102	20
James	Elliott	Middlesbrough	1893-1896	19	0	19	0
Paul	Elliott	Lewisham	1985-1987	56	1	57	7
Ahmed	Elmohamady	El-Mahalla El-Kubra, Egypt	2017-2021	87	26	113	3
Tommy	Elphick	Brighton	2016-2019	34	7	41	1
Arthur	Elston	Liverpool	1905-1906	1	0	1	0
Peter	Enckelman	Turku, Finland	1999-2003	51	1	52	0
Bjorn	Engels	Kaprijke, Belgium	2019-2021	15	2	17	1
Albert	Evans	Barnard Castle	1896-1906	179	0	179	0
Allan	Evans	Polbeth, Scotland	1977-1989	374	6	380	51
Alun	Evans	Bewdley, Worcestershire	1972-1975	53	9	62	11
David	Evans	West Bromwich	1977-1979	2	0	2	0
Orlando	Evans	Hednesford	1902-1903	2	0	2	0
Robert	Evans	Chester	1906-1908	16	0	16	4
Walter	Evans	Builth Wells, Wales	1890-1893	61	0	61	0
William	Evans	Aston, Birmingham	1946-1949	7	0	7	3
Tommy	Ewing	Larkhall, Scotland	1961-1964	39	0	39	4
Edmund	Eyre	Worksop	1908-1911	44	0	44	8
David	Farrell	Birmingham	1992-1995	5	1	6	0
Gareth	Farrelly	Dublin, Republic of Ireland	1995-1997	2	6	8	0
John	Fashanu	Kensington	1994-1995	11	2	13	3
Kenny	Fencott	Walsall	1961-1964	3	0	3	0
Graham	Fenton	Wallsend	1993-1996	16	16	32	3
Mike	Ferguson	Burnley	1968-1970	38	0	38	2
Fabio	Ferraresi	Fano, Italy	1998-1999	0	0	0	0
Jake	Findlay	Blairgowrie, Perth, Scotland	1973-1978	14	0	14	0
Albert James (James)	Fisher	Denny, Scotland	1897-1898	17	0	17	5
Albert William	Fisher	Birmingham	1902-1903	1	0	1	0
James	Fleming	Leith, Scotland	1892-1893	4	0	4	2
Eddie	Follan	Greenock, Scotland	1954-1956	34	0	34	7
Trevor	Ford	Swansea, Wales	1946-1951	120	0	120	60
Steve	Foster	Portsmouth	1983-1985	15	0	15	3
Cammie	Fraser	Blackford, Perthshire, Scotland	1962-1964	33	0	33	1
Brad	Friedel	Lakewood, Ohio, USA	2008-2011	114	0	114	0
Stephen	Froggatt	Lincoln	1991-1994	30	5	35	2
Kevin	Gage	Chiswick	1987-1991	113	2	115	8
Bernard	Gallacher	Johnstone, Perthshire, Scotland	1986-1991	55	2	57	0
Idrissa	Gana Gueye	Dakar, Senegal	2015-2016	35	0	35	0
Craig	Gardner	Solihull	2005-2010	32	27	59	5
Gary	Gardner	Solihull	2011-2018	23	19	42	1
Tommy	Gardner	Huyton	1933-1938	74	0	74	1

ASTON VILLA PLAYER RECORDS

| FA CUP |||| LEAGUE CUP |||| EUROPEAN |||| OTHER |||| TOTAL ||||
SL	SUB	PL	GLS	SL	SUB	PL	GLS	SL	SUB	PL	GLS	SL	SUB	PL	GLS	SL	SUB	PL	GLS
0	0	0	0	0	0	0	0	0	0	0	0	0	0	0	0	9	0	9	0
0	0	0	0	0	0	0	0	0	0	0	0	0	0	0	0	10	0	10	0
11	0	11	2	0	0	0	0	0	0	0	0	0	0	0	0	86	0	86	18
2	0	2	0	0	0	0	0	0	0	0	0	0	0	0	0	8	0	8	0
6	0	6	0	3	0	3	0	0	0	0	0	0	0	0	0	77	0	77	2
14	0	14	7	0	0	0	0	0	0	0	0	0	0	0	0	152	0	152	41
1	0	1	0	0	0	0	0	0	0	0	0	0	0	0	0	8	1	9	0
22	2	24	1	22	1	23	1	17	0	17	1	1	0	1	0	285	17	302	15
0	0	0	0	5	0	5	0	0	0	0	0	0	0	0	0	43	13	56	3
2	1	3	1	11	0	11	4	0	0	0	0	3	0	3	1	88	31	119	26
6	0	6	0	0	0	0	0	0	0	0	0	0	0	0	0	25	0	25	0
4	0	4	0	7	0	7	0	0	0	0	0	1	0	1	0	68	1	69	7
1	0	1	0	8	2	10	1	0	0	0	0	5	0	5	0	101	28	129	4
1	0	1	0	4	0	4	0	0	0	0	0	0	0	0	0	39	7	46	1
0	0	0	0	0	0	0	0	0	0	0	0	0	0	0	0	1	0	1	0
1	0	1	0	6	0	6	0	7	1	8	0	0	0	0	0	65	2	67	0
1	0	1	0	1	0	1	0	0	0	0	0	0	0	0	0	17	2	19	1
24	0	24	0	0	0	0	0	0	0	0	0	3	0	3	0	206	0	206	0
26	0	26	3	42	2	44	6	18	1	19	0	6	0	6	2	466	9	475	62
6	0	6	3	3	2	5	2	0	0	0	0	0	1	1	0	62	12	74	16
0	0	0	0	0	0	0	0	1	0	1	0	0	0	0	0	3	0	3	0
0	0	0	0	0	0	0	0	0	0	0	0	0	0	0	0	2	0	2	0
1	0	1	0	0	0	0	0	0	0	0	0	0	0	0	0	17	0	17	4
7	0	7	0	0	0	0	0	0	0	0	0	0	0	0	0	68	0	68	0
0	0	0	0	0	0	0	0	0	0	0	0	0	0	0	0	7	0	7	3
2	0	2	0	4	0	4	2	0	0	0	0	0	0	0	0	45	0	45	6
1	0	1	0	0	0	0	0	0	0	0	0	0	0	0	0	45	0	45	8
0	0	0	0	2	0	2	0	0	0	0	0	0	0	0	0	7	1	8	0
0	0	0	0	0	1	1	0	0	0	0	0	0	0	0	0	2	7	9	0
2	0	2	0	0	0	0	0	1	0	1	0	0	0	0	0	14	2	16	3
0	0	0	0	2	0	2	0	0	0	0	0	0	0	0	0	5	0	5	0
0	0	0	0	2	5	7	0	0	0	0	0	0	0	0	0	18	21	39	3
1	0	1	0	2	1	3	0	0	0	0	0	0	0	0	0	41	1	42	2
0	0	0	0	0	0	0	0	0	1	1	0	0	0	0	0	0	1	1	0
0	0	0	0	2	0	2	0	1	1	2	0	0	0	0	0	17	1	18	0
0	0	0	0	0	0	0	0	0	0	0	0	0	0	0	0	17	0	17	5
0	0	0	0	0	0	0	0	0	0	0	0	0	0	0	0	1	0	1	0
0	0	0	0	0	0	0	0	0	0	0	0	0	0	0	0	4	0	4	2
2	0	2	0	0	0	0	0	0	0	0	0	0	0	0	0	36	0	36	7
8	0	8	1	0	0	0	0	0	0	0	0	0	0	0	0	128	0	128	61
0	0	0	0	2	0	2	0	0	0	0	0	0	0	0	0	17	0	17	3
2	0	2	0	5	0	5	0	0	0	0	0	0	0	0	0	40	0	40	1
9	0	9	0	3	0	3	0	5	0	5	0	0	0	0	0	131	0	131	0
5	2	7	1	1	1	2	0	0	0	0	0	0	0	0	0	36	8	44	3
9	0	9	1	13	0	13	3	1	0	1	0	7	0	7	0	143	2	145	12
3	0	3	0	8	1	9	0	0	0	0	0	3	0	3	1	69	3	72	1
2	1	3	1	0	0	0	0	0	0	0	0	0	0	0	0	37	1	38	1
3	3	6	0	3	0	3	0	11	1	12	1	0	0	0	0	49	31	80	6
0	0	0	0	2	0	2	0	0	0	0	0	0	0	0	0	25	19	44	1
2	0	2	0	0	0	0	0	0	0	0	0	0	0	0	0	76	0	76	1

571

PLAYER	SURNAME	BORN	SEASONS	SL	SUB	PL	GLS
James	Garfield	Canterbury	1899-1900	1	0	1	1
George	Garratt	Byker	1905-1906	13	0	13	0
Billy	Garraty *	Saltley, Birmingham	1897-1908	225	1	226	96
Batty Walter	Garvey	Aston, Birmingham	1888-1890	7	0	7	4
Richard	Gaudie	Sheffield	1898-1899	5	0	5	1
John	Gavan	Walsall	1962-1966	9	0	9	0
David	Geddis	Carlisle	1979-1983	43	4	47	12
Billy	George	Atcham	1897-1911	360	0	360	0
Billy	Gerrish	Bristol	1909-1912	55	0	55	17
Rudy	Gestede	Essey-les-Nancy, France	2015-2017	22	28	50	9
Najwan	Ghrayib	Nazareth, Israel	1999-2000	1	4	5	0
Colin H	Gibson	Normanby-on-Tees	1948-1956	158	0	158	24
Colin J	Gibson	Bridport	1978-1986	181	4	185	10
Dave	Gibson	Winchburgh, Scotland	1970-1972	16	3	19	1
Jimmy	Gibson	Larkhall, Scotland	1926-1936	215	0	215	10
John	Gidman	Liverpool	1972-1980	196	1	197	9
Carles	Gil	Valencia, Spain	2014-2016	21	7	28	2
James	Gillan	Derby	1893-1894	3	0	3	0
TA (Alf)	Gilson	Lichfield	1900-1901	2	0	2	0
David	Ginola	Gassin, Nr St. Tropez, France	2000-2002	14	18	32	3
Alfred	Gittins	Manchester	1908-1909	1	0	1	0
Shay	Given	Lifford, County Donegal, Ireland	2011-2015	37	0	37	0
Dean	Glover	West Bromwich	1983-1987	25	3	28	0
Howard Vincent (Harry)	Coddard	Warsop Vale	1927-1928	1	0	1	0
Brian	Godfrey	Flint, North Wales	1967-1971	139	4	143	22
Billy	Goffin	Amington	1945-1954	156	0	156	36
Pierluigi	Gollini	Bologna, Italy	2016-2017	20	0	20	0
Archie	Goodall	Belfast, Northern Ireland	1888-1889	14	0	14	7
Bert	Goode	Chester	1911-1912	7	0	7	3
Robert (Bob)	Gordon	Leith, Scotland	1894-1895	4	0	4	2
Freddie	Goss	Draycott	1936-1937	2	0	2	0
Lewis	Grabban	Croydon, Surrey	2017-2018	10	5	15	8
George	Graham	Bargeddie, Lanarkshire, Scotland	1962-1964	8	0	8	2
Jack	Graham	Smethwick	1889-1892	19	0	19	5
John	Graham	Leyland	1946-1949	10	0	10	3
Andy A	Gray	Lambeth, London	1987-1989	34	3	37	4
Andy M	Gray	Glasgow, Scotland	1975-1979 1985-1987	165	2	167	59
Frank	Gray	Oldbury	1889-1890	2	0	2	0
Josiah	Gray	Bristol	1904-1905	7	0	7	0
Stuart	Gray	Withernsea	1987-1991	102	4	106	9
Ray	Graydon	Bristol	1971-1977	189	4	193	68
Simon	Grayson	Ripon	1997-1999	32	16	48	0
Jack	Grealish	Birmingham	2013-2021	146	39	185	29
Andre	Green	Solihull	2015-2019	16	24	40	2
Tommy	Green	Worcester	1887-1889	21	0	21	13
Brian	Greenhalgh	Chesterfield	1967-1969	37	3	40	12
Sam	Greenhalgh	Eagley	1905-1908	46	0	46	2
Harry	Gregory	Buckhurst Hill, Essex	1970-1972	18	6	24	2
John	Gregory	Scunthorpe	1977-1979	59	6	65	10

ASTON VILLA PLAYER RECORDS

	FA CUP				LEAGUE CUP				EUROPEAN				OTHER				TOTAL			
	SL	SUB	PL	GLS	SL	SUB	PL	GLS	SL	SUB	PL	GLS	SL	SUB	PL	GLS	SL	SUB	PL	GLS
	0	0	0	0	0	0	0	0	0	0	0	0	0	0	0	0	1	0	1	1
	4	0	4	1	0	0	0	0	0	0	0	0	0	0	0	0	17	0	17	1
	31	0	31	15	0	0	0	0	0	0	0	0	3	0	3	1	259	1	260	112
	0	0	0	0	0	0	0	0	0	0	0	0	0	0	0	0	7	0	7	4
	0	0	0	0	0	0	0	0	0	0	0	0	0	0	0	0	5	0	5	1
	0	0	0	0	3	0	3	0	0	0	0	0	0	0	0	0	12	0	12	0
	4	1	5	4	4	0	4	0	0	0	0	0	1	0	1	0	52	5	57	16
	40	0	40	0	0	0	0	0	0	0	0	0	3	0	3	0	403	0	403	0
	3	0	3	1	0	0	0	0	0	0	0	0	1	0	1	0	59	0	59	18
	2	0	2	0	2	1	3	1	0	0	0	0	0	0	0	0	26	29	55	10
	0	0	0	0	1	0	1	0	0	0	0	0	0	0	0	0	2	4	6	0
	9	0	9	2	0	0	0	0	0	0	0	0	0	0	0	0	167	0	167	26
	12	0	12	1	26	0	26	4	13	1	14	2	1	0	1	0	233	5	238	17
	1	0	1	0	4	0	4	0	0	0	0	0	0	0	0	0	21	3	24	1
	12	0	12	0	0	0	0	0	0	0	0	0	0	0	0	0	227	0	227	10
	12	0	12	0	25	0	25	0	9	0	9	0	0	0	0	0	242	1	243	9
	3	2	5	1	1	0	1	0	0	0	0	0	0	0	0	0	25	9	34	3
	0	0	0	0	0	0	0	0	0	0	0	0	0	0	0	0	3	0	3	0
	0	0	0	0	0	0	0	0	0	0	0	0	0	0	0	0	2	0	2	0
	1	0	1	0	1	1	2	0	3	3	6	2	0	0	0	0	19	22	41	5
	0	0	0	0	0	0	0	0	0	0	0	0	0	0	0	0	1	0	1	0
	9	0	9	0	7	0	7	0	0	0	0	0	0	0	0	0	53	0	53	0
	3	0	3	0	7	0	7	1	0	0	0	0	1	0	1	0	36	3	39	1
	0	0	0	0	0	0	0	0	0	0	0	0	0	0	0	0	1	0	1	0
	8	0	8	3	9	0	9	0	0	0	0	0	0	0	0	0	156	4	160	25
	17	0	17	6	0	0	0	0	0	0	0	0	0	0	0	0	173	0	173	42
	0	0	0	0	0	0	0	0	0	0	0	0	0	0	0	0	20	0	20	0
	0	0	0	0	0	0	0	0	0	0	0	0	0	0	0	0	14	0	14	7
	0	0	0	0	0	0	0	0	0	0	0	0	0	0	0	0	7	0	7	3
	0	0	0	0	0	0	0	0	0	0	0	0	0	0	0	0	4	0	4	2
	0	0	0	0	0	0	0	0	0	0	0	0	0	0	0	0	2	0	2	0
	0	0	0	0	0	0	0	0	0	0	0	0	3	0	3	0	13	5	18	8
	0	0	0	0	2	0	2	0	0	0	0	0	0	0	0	0	10	0	10	2
	0	0	0	0	0	0	0	0	0	0	0	0	0	0	0	0	21	0	21	7
	2	0	2	2	0	0	0	0	0	0	0	0	0	0	0	0	11	0	11	4
	1	0	1	1	0	0	0	0	0	0	0	0	0	2	2	0	40	6	46	6
	3	1	4	1	3	0	3	1	0	0	0	0	0	0	0	0				
	10	2	12	3	25	0	25	14	5	0	5	2	1	0	1	0	206	4	210	78
	0	0	0	0	0	0	0	0	0	0	0	0	0	0	0	0	2	0	2	0
	0	0	0	0	0	0	0	0	0	0	0	0	0	0	0	0	7	0	7	0
	5	1	6	3	11	0	11	1	4	0	4	0	3	2	5	2	125	7	132	15
	10	0	10	3	25	1	26	9	2	0	2	1	1	0	1	0	227	5	232	81
	4	1	5	2	1	1	2	0	6	3	9	0	0	0	0	0	43	21	64	2
	5	5	10	0	7	5	12	3	0	0	0	0	6	0	6	0	164	49	213	32
	1	1	2	0	3	0	3	0	0	0	0	0	1	2	3	0	21	27	48	2
	7	0	7	5	0	0	0	0	0	0	0	0	0	0	0	0	28	0	28	18
	1	0	1	0	0	0	0	0	0	0	0	0	0	0	0	0	38	3	41	12
	2	0	2	0	0	0	0	0	0	0	0	0	0	0	0	0	48	0	48	2
	0	0	0	0	5	0	5	0	0	0	0	0	0	0	0	0	23	6	29	2
	2	0	2	0	5	0	5	1	3	1	4	0	0	0	0	0	69	7	76	11

573

| | | | | LEAGUE | | | |
PLAYER	SURNAME	BORN	SEASONS	SL	SUB	PL	GLS
Harry	Griffin	Dudley	1902-1903	1	0	1	0
Jeremiah	Griffiths	Birmingham	1895-1897	2	0	2	0
John	Griffiths	Oldbury	1968-1970	1	2	3	0
Tom	Griffiths	Moss, North Wales	1935-1937	66	0	66	1
Willie	Groves	Leith, Scotland	1893-1894	22	0	22	3
Joey	Gudjonsson	Akranes, Iceland	2002-2003	9	2	11	2
Frederic	Guilbert	Valognes, France	2019-2022	22	3	25	0
Ronald (Roy)	Guttridge	Widnes	1946-1948	15	0	15	0
Bradley	Guzan	Evergreen Park, USA	2008-2016	142	2	144	0
Moustapha	Hadji	Ifrane, Morocco	2001-2004	24	11	35	2
George	Hadley	West Bromwich	1919-1920	4	0	4	0
Harry	Hadley	Barrow-in-Furness	1905-1906	11	0	11	0
William	Haggart	Edinburgh, Scotland	1898-1900	2	0	2	0
Alfie	Hale	Waterford, Republic of Ireland	1960-1962	5	0	5	1
Albert	Hall	Stourbridge	1903-1914	195	0	195	51
Harold	Halse	Leytonstone	1912-1913	30	0	30	21
Ian 'Chico'	Hamilton	Streatham, London	1969-1976	189	18	207	40
Willie	Hamilton	Chapelhall, Airdrie, Scotland	1965-1967	49	0	49	9
John	Hampson	Oswestry	1919-1921	14	0	14	0
George	Hampton	Wellington, Shropshire	1914-1915	3	0	3	0
Harry	Hampton	Wellington, Shropshire	1904-1920	338	0	338	215
Brian	Handley	Wakefield	1959-1960	3	0	3	0
George	Hardy	Newbold, Derbyshire	1936-1938	6	0	6	1
Sam	Hardy	Newbold, Derbyshire	1912-1921	159	0	159	0
Charlie	Hare	Birmingham	1891-1895	26	0	26	13
Marlon	Harewood	Hampstead, London	2007-2009	1	28	29	5
George	Harkus	Newcastle-on-Tyne	1921-1923	4	0	4	0
Charles	Harley	Wednesbury	1890-1891	1	0	1	0
Rowland	Harper	Lichfield	1907-1908	2	0	2	0
Cecil	Harris	Grantham	1922-1926	26	0	26	0
Edward	Harris	Willenhall	1895-1896	1	0	1	0
George	Harris	Halesowen	1901-1908	20	0	20	1
Walter	Harris	Plymouth	1924-1928	20	0	20	3
James	Harrison	Leicester	1949-1950	8	0	8	1
Thomas	Harrison	Birmingham	1888-1889	2	0	2	0
Jimmy	Harrop	Heeley, Sheffield	1912-1921	152	0	152	4
Howard	Harvey	Wednesbury	1897-1898	11	0	11	3
Richard	Harvey	Nottingham	1882-1883	0	0	0	0
Walter	Harvey	Derby	1884-1885	0	0	0	0
Tony	Hateley	Derby	1963-1967	127	0	127	68
Kortney	Hause	Goodmayes	2018-2022	38	25	43	4
Freddie	Haycock	Bootle, Liverpool	1936-1939	99	0	99	28
Arthur	Haynes	Birmingham	1946-1947	4	0	4	0
Walter	Hazelden	Ashton-in-Makerfield	1957-1959	17	0	17	5
Pat	Heard	Hull	1979-1983	20	5	25	2
Adrian	Heath	Stoke-on-Trent	1989-1990	8	1	9	0
Tom	Heaton	Chester	2019-2021	20	0	20	0
Nicklas	Helenius	Svenstrup, Denmark	2013-2014	0	3	3	0
Lee	Hendrie	Birmingham	1995-2007	202	49	251	27
Horace	Henshall	Hednesford	1910-1912	45	0	45	7

ASTON VILLA PLAYER RECORDS

	FA CUP				LEAGUE CUP				EUROPEAN				OTHER				TOTAL			
SL	SUB	PL	GLS	SL	SUB	PL	GLS	SL	SUB	PL	GLS	SL	SUB	PL	GLS	SL	SUB	PL	GLS
0	0	0	0	0	0	0	0	0	0	0	0	0	0	0	0	1	0	1	0
1	0	1	0	0	0	0	0	0	0	0	0	0	0	0	0	3	0	3	0
0	0	0	0	1	0	1	0	0	0	0	0	0	0	0	0	2	2	4	0
2	0	2	0	0	0	0	0	0	0	0	0	0	0	0	0	68	0	68	1
4	0	4	0	0	0	0	0	0	0	0	0	0	0	0	0	26	0	26	3
0	0	0	0	0	0	0	0	0	0	0	0	0	0	0	0	9	2	11	2
0	0	0	0	6	1	7	3	0	0	0	0	0	0	0	0	28	4	32	3
0	0	0	0	0	0	0	0	0	0	0	0	0	0	0	0	15	0	15	0
7	0	7	0	11	0	11	0	9	0	9	0	0	0	0	0	169	2	171	0
0	1	1	0	3	0	3	0	4	5	9	1	0	0	0	0	31	17	48	3
0	0	0	0	0	0	0	0	0	0	0	0	0	0	0	0	4	0	4	0
1	0	1	0	0	0	0	0	0	0	0	0	0	0	0	0	12	0	12	0
0	0	0	0	0	0	0	0	0	0	0	0	0	0	0	0	2	0	2	0
2	0	2	1	0	0	0	0	0	0	0	0	0	0	0	0	7	0	7	2
19	0	19	10	0	0	0	0	0	0	0	0	1	0	1	0	215	0	215	61
6	0	6	7	0	0	0	0	0	0	0	0	0	0	0	0	36	0	36	28
12	0	12	0	31	0	31	8	2	0	2	0	0	0	0	0	234	18	252	48
1	0	1	0	4	0	4	0	0	0	0	0	0	0	0	0	54	0	54	9
1	0	1	0	0	0	0	0	0	0	0	0	0	0	0	0	15	0	15	0
0	0	0	0	0	0	0	0	0	0	0	0	0	0	0	0	3	0	3	0
34	0	34	27	0	0	0	0	0	0	0	0	0	0	0	0	372	0	372	242
0	0	0	0	0	0	0	0	0	0	0	0	0	0	0	0	3	0	3	0
0	0	0	0	0	0	0	0	0	0	0	0	0	0	0	0	6	0	6	1
24	0	24	0	0	0	0	0	0	0	0	0	0	0	0	0	183	0	183	0
1	0	1	0	0	0	0	0	0	0	0	0	0	0	0	0	27	0	27	13
0	1	1	0	3	0	3	1	5	2	7	1	0	0	0	0	9	31	40	7
0	0	0	0	0	0	0	0	0	0	0	0	0	0	0	0	4	0	4	0
0	0	0	0	0	0	0	0	0	0	0	0	0	0	0	0	1	0	1	0
0	0	0	0	0	0	0	0	0	0	0	0	0	0	0	0	2	0	2	0
0	0	0	0	0	0	0	0	0	0	0	0	0	0	0	0	26	0	26	0
0	0	0	0	0	0	0	0	0	0	0	0	0	0	0	0	1	0	1	0
1	0	1	0	0	0	0	0	0	0	0	0	0	0	0	0	21	0	21	1
0	0	0	0	0	0	0	0	0	0	0	0	0	0	0	0	20	0	20	3
0	0	0	0	0	0	0	0	0	0	0	0	0	0	0	0	8	0	8	1
0	0	0	0	0	0	0	0	0	0	0	0	0	0	0	0	2	0	2	0
18	0	18	0	0	0	0	0	0	0	0	0	0	0	0	0	170	0	170	4
0	0	0	0	0	0	0	0	0	0	0	0	0	0	0	0	11	0	11	3
4	0	4	1	0	0	0	0	0	0	0	0	0	0	0	0	4	0	4	1
4	0	4	0	0	0	0	0	0	0	0	0	0	0	0	0	4	0	4	0
8	0	8	5	13	0	13	13	0	0	0	0	0	0	0	0	148	0	148	86
0	0	0	0	10	1	11	0	0	0	0	0	0	0	0	0	48	7	55	4
11	0	11	5	0	0	0	0	0	0	0	0	0	0	0	0	110	0	110	33
0	0	0	0	0	0	0	0	0	0	0	0	0	0	0	0	4	0	4	0
2	0	2	0	0	0	0	0	0	0	0	0	0	0	0	0	19	0	19	5
0	0	0	0	0	1	1	0	1	0	1	0	0	0	0	0	21	6	27	2
0	1	1	0	1	1	2	0	0	0	0	0	0	0	0	0	9	3	12	0
0	0	0	0	0	0	0	0	0	0	0	0	0	0	0	0	20	0	20	0
0	1	1	1	0	2	2	0	0	0	0	0	0	0	0	0	0	6	6	1
12	8	20	0	15	3	18	3	14	5	19	2	0	0	0	0	243	65	308	32
5	0	5	3	0	0	0	0	0	0	0	0	0	0	0	0	50	0	50	10

PLAYER	SURNAME	BORN	SEASONS	SL	SUB	PL	GLS
Rushian	Hepburn-Murphy	Birmingham	2014-2019	0	13	13	0
Chris	Herd	Melbourne, Australia	2010-2014	31	5	36	1
Emile	Heskey	Leicester	2008-2012	56	36	92	9
Joe	Hickman	County Durham	1927-1928	2	0	2	0
Dave	Hickson	Ellesmere Port	1955-1956	12	0	12	1
Arthur	Hickton	Birmingham	1889-1890	1	0	1	0
Albert	Hinchley	Warwick	1891-1892	11	0	11	0
John (Jackie)	Hinchliffe	Tillicoultry, Scotland	1957-1958	2	0	2	0
Jack	Hindle	Preston	1950-1951	15	0	15	0
Joe	Hisbent	Plymouth	1905-1906	2	0	2	0
Percy	Hislop	Glasgow, Scotland	1891-1892	7	0	7	4
Gerry	Hitchens	Rawnsley, Staffordshire	1957-1961	132	0	132	78
Thomas	Hitzlsperger	Munich, Germany	2000-2005	74	25	99	8
Charles	Hobson	Walsall	1885-1886	0	0	0	0
Trevor	Hockey	Keighley	1973-1974	24	0	24	1
Steve	Hodge	Nottingham	1985-1987	53	0	53	12
Dennis	Hodgetts	Birmingham	1886-1896	181	0	181	64
Gordon	Hodgson	Johannesburg, South Africa	1935-1937	28	0	28	11
Scott	Hogan	Salford	2016-2019	28	28	56	7
Jonathan	Hogg	Middlesbrough	2010-2011	5	0	5	0
Ray	Hogg	Lowick, Northumberland	1954-1957	21	0	21	0
Barrie	Hole	Swansea, Wales	1968-1970	47	0	47	6
Brett	Holman	Bankstown, Sydney, Australia	2012-2013	16	11	27	1
Grant	Holt	Carlisle	2013-2014	3	7	10	1
Robert	Hopkins	Birmingham	1979-1983	1	2	3	1
Stan	Horne	Clanfield, Oxfordshire	1963-1964	6	0	6	0
Tommy	Horton	Dudley Port	1881-1882	0	0	0	0
Eric	Houghton	Billingborough, Lincolnshire	1929-1947	361	0	361	160
Ray	Houghton	Glasgow, Scotland	1992-1995	83	12	95	6
Conor	Hourihane	Bandon, County Cork, Ireland	2016-2022	107	25	132	23
Syd	Howarth	Newport, Wales	1948-1950	8	0	8	2
Aaron	Hughes	Cookstown, Northern Ireland	2005-2007	50	4	54	0
David (RD)	Hughes	Wrexham, Wales	1996-1997	4	3	7	0
David T	Hughes	Birmingham	1976-1977	3	1	4	1
Tommy	Hughes	Dalmuir, Scotland	1971-1972	16	0	16	0
Howard	Humphries	Aston, Birmingham	1914-1922	20	0	20	2
David	Hunt	Leicester	1987-1989	12	1	13	0
Steve	Hunt	Birmingham	1974-1977 1985-1988	65	4	69	7
Andy	Hunter	Joppa, Ayrshire, Scotland	1879-1883	0	0	0	0
Archie	Hunter	Joppa, Ayrshire, Scotland	1879-1890	32	0	32	9
George	Hunter	Peshawur, India	1908-1912	91	0	91	1
Alan	Hutton	Glasgow, Scotland	2011-2019	172	13	185	3
John	Inglis	Leven, Fife, Scotland	1967-1968	1	1	2	0
Danny	Ings	Winchester	2021-2022	22	8	30	7
Stephen	Ireland	Cork, Ireland	2010-2013	34	13	47	1
Tim	Iroegbunam	Great Barr, Birmingham	2021-2022	1	2	3	0
Bob	Iverson	Folkestone	1936-1948	135	0	135	9
Dennis	Jackson	Birmingham	1956-1959	8	0	8	0
Tommy	Jackson	Newcastle-upon-Tyne	1920-1930	172	0	172	0

ASTON VILLA PLAYER RECORDS

	FA CUP				LEAGUE CUP				EUROPEAN				OTHER				TOTAL			
SL	SUB	PL	GLS	SL	SUB	PL	GLS	SL	SUB	PL	GLS	SL	SUB	PL	GLS	SL	SUB	PL	GLS
0	1	1	0	2	1	3	0	0	0	0	0	0	0	0	0	2	15	17	0
2	0	2	0	4	1	5	1	0	0	0	0	0	0	0	0	37	6	43	2
6	1	7	0	5	2	7	4	4	0	4	1	0	0	0	0	71	39	110	14
0	0	0	0	0	0	0	0	0	0	0	0	0	0	0	0	2	0	2	0
0	0	0	0	0	0	0	0	0	0	0	0	0	0	0	0	12	0	12	1
0	0	0	0	0	0	0	0	0	0	0	0	0	0	0	0	1	0	1	0
0	0	0	0	0	0	0	0	0	0	0	0	0	0	0	0	11	0	11	0
0	0	0	0	0	0	0	0	0	0	0	0	0	0	0	0	2	0	2	0
0	0	0	0	0	0	0	0	0	0	0	0	0	0	0	0	15	0	15	0
0	0	0	0	0	0	0	0	0	0	0	0	0	0	0	0	2	0	2	0
0	0	0	0	0	0	0	0	0	0	0	0	0	0	0	0	7	0	7	4
18	0	18	7	10	0	10	11	0	0	0	0	0	0	0	0	160	0	160	96
0	1	1	0	4	6	10	4	4	0	4	0	0	0	0	0	82	32	114	12
2	0	2	0	0	0	0	0	0	0	0	0	0	0	0	0	2	0	2	0
0	0	0	0	0	0	0	0	0	0	0	0	0	0	0	0	24	0	24	1
4	0	4	1	12	0	12	3	0	0	0	0	1	0	1	0	70	0	70	16
37	0	37	26	0	0	0	0	0	0	0	0	0	0	0	0	218	0	218	90
0	0	0	0	0	0	0	0	0	0	0	0	0	0	0	0	28	0	28	11
1	0	1	0	3	0	3	3	0	0	0	0	0	1	1	0	32	29	61	10
0	0	0	0	1	0	1	0	1	0	1	0	0	0	0	0	7	0	7	0
0	0	0	0	0	0	0	0	0	0	0	0	0	0	0	0	21	0	21	0
4	0	4	2	2	0	2	1	0	0	0	0	0	0	0	0	53	0	53	9
0	0	0	0	1	1	2	1	0	0	0	0	0	0	0	0	17	12	29	2
0	0	0	0	0	0	0	0	0	0	0	0	0	0	0	0	3	7	10	1
0	0	0	0	0	0	0	0	0	0	0	0	0	0	0	0	1	2	3	1
0	0	0	0	0	0	0	0	0	0	0	0	0	0	0	0	6	0	6	0
1	0	1	0	0	0	0	0	0	0	0	0	0	0	0	0	1	0	1	0
31	0	31	10	0	0	0	0	0	0	0	0	0	0	0	0	392	0	392	170
7	0	7	2	11	2	13	2	4	2	6	1	0	0	0	0	105	16	121	11
2	0	2	0	8	3	11	5	0	0	0	0	5	1	6	1	122	29	151	29
1	0	1	0	0	0	0	0	0	0	0	0	0	0	0	0	9	0	9	2
5	0	5	0	5	0	5	0	0	0	0	0	0	0	0	0	60	4	64	0
0	0	0	0	0	0	0	0	0	0	0	0	0	0	0	0	4	3	7	0
0	0	0	0	0	0	0	0	0	0	0	0	0	0	0	0	3	1	4	1
1	0	1	0	6	0	6	0	0	0	0	0	0	0	0	0	23	0	23	0
1	0	1	0	0	0	0	0	0	0	0	0	0	0	0	0	21	0	21	2
0	0	0	0	2	0	2	0	0	0	0	0	0	0	0	0	14	1	15	0
2	0	2	2	8	0	8	0	0	1	1	0	1	0	1	0	76	5	81	9
11	0	11	4	0	0	0	0	0	0	0	0	0	0	0	0	11	0	11	4
42	0	42	34	0	0	0	0	0	0	0	0	0	0	0	0	74	0	74	43
6	0	6	0	0	0	0	0	0	0	0	0	1	0	1	0	98	0	98	1
8	0	8	0	5	1	6	0	0	0	0	0	3	0	3	0	188	14	202	3
0	0	0	0	1	0	1	0	0	0	0	0	0	0	0	0	2	1	3	0
1	0	1	0	0	0	0	0	0	0	0	0	0	0	0	0	23	8	31	7
2	1	3	0	6	1	7	0	1	0	1	0	0	0	0	0	43	15	58	1
0	0	0	0	0	0	0	0	0	0	0	0	0	0	0	0	1	2	3	0
18	0	18	3	0	0	0	0	0	0	0	0	0	0	0	0	153	0	153	12
0	0	0	0	0	0	0	0	0	0	0	0	0	0	0	0	8	0	8	0
14	0	14	0	0	0	0	0	0	0	0	0	0	0	0	0	186	0	186	0

LEAGUE

PLAYER	SURNAME	BORN	SEASONS	SL	SUB	PL	GLS
George	Jakeman	Small Heath, Birmingham	1924-1929	8	0	8	0
David	James	Welwyn Garden City	1999-2001	67	0	67	0
Tommy	Jaszczun	Kettering	1998-1999	0	0	0	0
Mile	Jedinak	Sydney, Australia	2016-2019	62	13	75	1
Ron	Jeffries	Birmingham	1950-1951	2	0	2	0
Jermaine	Jenas	Nottingham	2011-2012	1	2	3	0
Lee	Jenkins	West Bromwich	1978-1980	0	3	3	0
Julian	Joachim	Boston	1995-2001	90	51	141	39
Ronny	Johnsen	Sandefjord, Norway	2002-2004	46	3	49	1
Tommy	Johnson	Newcastle	1994-1997	38	19	57	13
William	Johnson	Bradley, Staffordshire	1926-1928	4	0	4	0
George	Johnson *	West Bromwich	1897-1905	99	1	100	38
Charles	Johnstone	Birmingham	1879-1881	0	0	0	0
Jock	Johnstone	Dundee, Scotland	1921-1927	106	0	106	1
Sam	Johnstone	Preston	2016-2018	66	0	66	0
Allan	Jones	Burton-on-Trent	1961-1962	1	0	1	0
Keith	Jones	Nantyglo, Ebbw Vale, Wales	1947-1957	185	0	185	0
Les	Jones	Mountain Ash, Wales	1957-1958	5	0	5	0
Mark	Jones	Oldbury	1981-1984	24	0	24	0
Percy	Jones	Aston, Birmingham	1921-1924	15	0	15	0
Tommy	Jones	Birmingham	1924-1926	5	0	5	0
Walter	Jones	Wellington, Shropshire	1910-1911	2	0	2	1
Walter A	Jones	Wednesfield	1885-1886	0	0	0	0
Romallo	Jota	A Pobra do Caramiñal, Spain	2019-2021	4	6	10	0
Hassan	Kachloul	Agadir, Morocco	2001-2003	17	5	22	2
Lovre	Kalinic	Split, Croatia	2018-2019	7	0	7	0
Emment	Kapengwe	Zambia	1969-1970	3	0	3	0
Robbie	Keane	Dublin, Ireland	2011-2012	5	1	6	3
John	Kearns	Nuneaton	1908-1912	40	0	40	0
Kevin	Keelan	Calcutta, India	1959-1961	5	0	5	0
Mike	Kenning	Birmingham	1960-1961	3	0	3	0
Martin	Keown	Oxford	1986-1989	109	3	112	3
Albert	Kerr	Lanchester, County Durham	1936-1947	29	0	29	4
Paul	Kerr	Portsmouth	1983-1987	16	8	24	3
Kaine	Kesler	Birmingham	2020-2021	0	0	0	0
Walter	Kimberley	Aston, Birmingham	1907-1909	7	0	7	0
Phil	King	Bristol	1994-1995	13	3	16	0
Bert	Kingaby	London	1905-1906	4	0	4	0
Billy	Kingdon	Worcester	1926-1936	224	0	224	5
Mark	Kinsella	Dublin, Republic of Ireland	2002-2004	17	4	21	0
George	Kinsey	Burton-on-Trent	1894-1895	3	0	3	0
Gabor	Kiraly	Szombathely, Hungary	2006-2007	5	0	5	0
Billy	Kirton	Newcastle-on-Tyne	1919-1927	229	0	229	54
Zat	Knight	Solihull	2007-2009	38	2	40	2
Jonathan	Kodjia	Paris, France	2016-2020	67	29	96	29
Ezri	Konsa	Newham, London	2019-2022	88	2	90	5
Libor	Kozak	Opava, Czech Republic	2013-2017	11	9	20	4
Dariusz	Kubicki	Kozuchow, Poland	1991-1994	24	1	25	0
Peter	Kyle	Cadder, Scotland	1907-1909	5	0	5	0
John	Laidlaw	Muirkirk, Scotland	1913-1914	2	0	2	0

ASTON VILLA PLAYER RECORDS

	FA CUP				LEAGUE CUP				EUROPEAN				OTHER				TOTAL			
SL	SUB	PL	GLS	SL	SUB	PL	GLS	SL	SUB	PL	GLS	SL	SUB	PL	GLS	SL	SUB	PL	GLS
0	0	0	0	0	0	0	0	0	0	0	0	0	0	0	0	8	0	8	0
8	0	8	0	5	0	5	0	4	0	4	0	0	0	0	0	84	0	84	0
0	0	0	0	0	1	1	0	0	0	0	0	0	0	0	0	0	1	1	0
1	0	1	0	0	0	0	0	0	0	0	0	3	1	4	1	66	14	80	2
0	0	0	0	0	0	0	0	0	0	0	0	0	0	0	0	2	0	2	0
0	0	0	0	0	0	0	0	0	0	0	0	0	0	0	0	1	2	3	0
0	0	0	0	0	0	0	0	0	0	0	0	0	0	0	0	0	3	3	0
8	4	12	2	9	1	10	3	6	3	9	1	0	0	0	0	113	59	172	45
1	0	1	0	5	1	6	0	0	0	0	0	0	0	0	0	52	4	56	1
5	2	7	1	5	0	5	2	1	1	2	1	0	0	0	0	49	22	71	17
0	0	0	0	0	0	0	0	0	0	0	0	0	0	0	0	4	0	4	0
9	0	9	9	0	0	0	0	0	0	0	0	2	0	2	0	110	1	111	47
2	0	2	0	0	0	0	0	0	0	0	0	0	0	0	0	2	0	2	0
10	0	10	0	0	0	0	0	0	0	0	0	0	0	0	0	116	0	116	1
1	0	1	0	0	0	0	0	0	0	0	0	3	0	3	0	70	0	70	0
0	0	0	0	0	0	0	0	0	0	0	0	0	0	0	0	1	0	1	0
14	0	14	0	0	0	0	0	0	0	0	0	0	0	0	0	199	0	199	0
0	0	0	0	0	0	0	0	0	0	0	0	0	0	0	0	5	0	5	0
1	0	1	0	3	0	3	0	4	0	4	0	1	0	1	0	33	0	33	0
0	0	0	0	0	0	0	0	0	0	0	0	0	0	0	0	15	0	15	0
0	0	0	0	0	0	0	0	0	0	0	0	0	0	0	0	5	0	5	0
0	0	0	0	0	0	0	0	0	0	0	0	0	0	0	0	2	0	2	1
2	0	2	0	0	0	0	0	0	0	0	0	0	0	0	0	2	0	2	0
1	0	1	0	3	2	5	1	0	0	0	0	0	0	0	0	8	8	16	1
0	0	0	0	2	0	2	0	6	2	8	0	0	0	0	0	25	7	32	2
1	0	1	0	0	0	0	0	0	0	0	0	0	0	0	0	8	0	8	0
0	0	0	0	0	0	0	0	0	0	0	0	0	0	0	0	3	0	3	0
1	0	1	0	0	0	0	0	0	0	0	0	0	0	0	0	6	1	7	3
1	0	1	0	0	0	0	0	0	0	0	0	0	0	0	0	41	0	41	0
0	0	0	0	0	0	0	0	0	0	0	0	0	0	0	0	5	0	5	0
0	0	0	0	0	0	0	0	0	0	0	0	0	0	0	0	3	0	3	0
6	0	6	0	12	0	12	0	0	0	0	0	2	0	2	0	129	3	132	3
2	0	2	0	0	0	0	0	0	0	0	0	0	0	0	0	31	0	31	4
2	0	2	1	5	2	7	2	0	0	0	0	0	2	2	0	23	12	35	6
1	0	1	0	0	0	0	0	0	0	0	0	0	0	0	0	1	0	1	0
0	0	0	0	0	0	0	0	0	0	0	0	0	0	0	0	7	0	7	0
0	0	0	0	3	0	3	0	4	0	4	0	0	0	0	0	20	3	23	0
0	0	0	0	0	0	0	0	0	0	0	0	0	0	0	0	4	0	4	0
18	0	18	0	0	0	0	0	0	0	0	0	0	0	0	0	242	0	242	5
1	0	1	0	2	2	4	0	0	0	0	0	0	0	0	0	20	6	26	0
0	0	0	0	0	0	0	0	0	0	0	0	0	0	0	0	3	0	3	0
1	0	1	0	0	0	0	0	0	0	0	0	0	0	0	0	6	0	6	0
32	0	32	6	0	0	0	0	0	0	0	0	0	0	0	0	261	0	261	60
3	0	3	0	2	0	2	0	9	0	9	0	0	0	0	0	52	2	54	2
1	1	2	0	1	2	3	2	0	0	0	0	0	5	5	0	69	37	106	31
1	0	1	0	6	2	8	1	0	0	0	0	0	0	0	0	95	4	99	6
0	0	0	0	1	1	2	0	0	0	0	0	0	0	0	0	12	10	22	4
4	1	5	0	3	0	3	0	0	0	0	0	1	0	1	0	32	2	34	0
0	0	0	0	0	0	0	0	0	0	0	0	0	0	0	0	5	0	5	0
0	0	0	0	0	0	0	0	0	0	0	0	0	0	0	0	2	0	2	0

PLAYER	SURNAME	BORN	SEASONS	SL	SUB	PL	GLS
Nii	Lamptey	Accra, Ghana	1994-1995	1	5	6	0
Henri	Lansbury	Enfield	2016-2021	26	15	41	2
Martin	Laursen	Silkeborg, Denmark	2004-2009	82	2	84	8
Samuel (Sammy)	Law	Birmingham	1879-1882	0	0	0	0
Jimmy	Lawrence	Earlestown	1919-1920	13	0	13	0
Arthur	Layton	Gornal	1908-1911	16	0	16	0
Jimmy	Leach	Spennymoor, County Durham	1912-1922	66	0	66	3
Alex	Leake	Small Heath, Birmingham	1902-1908	127	0	127	8
Edward (Ted)	Lee	Harborne, Birmingham	1879-1883	0	0	0	0
Gordon	Lee	Hednesford	1958-1965	118	0	118	2
Jimmy	Lee	Brierley Hill	1919-1921	18	0	18	0
Walter	Leigh	Yardley, Birmingham	1898-1899	1	0	1	0
Keith	Leonard	Birmingham	1972-1976	36	2	38	11
Oyvind	Leonhardsen	Kristiansund, Norway	2002-2003	13	6	19	3
Aaron	Lescott	Birmingham	1998-1999	0	0	0	0
Joleon	Lescott	Birmingham	2015-2016	30	0	30	1
Eric	Lichaj	Downers Grove, Illinois, USA	2010-2013	21	11	32	1
Mark	Lillis	Manchester	1987-1989	30	1	31	4
Hayden	Lindley	Huddersfield	2020-2022	0	0	0	0
Albert	Lindon	King's Norton, Birmingham	1911-1912	1	0	1	0
Ivor	Linton	West Bromwich	1976-1982	16	11	27	0
Alan	Little	Horden	1974-1975	2	1	3	0
Brian	Little	Newcastle-upon-Tyne	1971-1980	242	5	247	60
William	Littlewood	Aston, Birmingham	1911-1915	50	0	50	0
Frank	Lloyd	London	1900-1902	5	0	5	1
Arthur	Loach	West Bromwich	1886-1887	0	0	0	0
Andy	Lochhead	Milngavie, Scotland	1969-1973	127	4	131	34
Arthur	Lockett	Alsagers Bank	1902-1905	41	0	41	5
Norman	Lockhart	Belfast, Northern Ireland	1952-1956	74	0	74	10
Alec	Logan	Barrhead, Scotland	1906-1909	24	0	24	11
James	Logan	Troon, Scotland	1892-1894	14	0	14	8
James L	Logan	Barrhead, Scotland	1905-1912	146	0	146	4
Eddie	Lowe	Halesowen	1945-1950	104	0	104	3
Shane	Lowry	Perth, Western Australia	2009-2010	0	0	0	0
Matthew	Lowton	Chesterfield	2012-2015	63	9	72	2
Douglas	Luiz	Rio de Janeiro, Brazil	2019-2022	91	12	103	5
Antonio	Luna	Son Servera, Spain	2013-2014	16	1	17	1
Jordan	Lyden	Perth, Australia	2015-2018	2	2	4	0
Barry	Lynch	Northfield, Birmingham	1968-1970	2	0	2	0
Stan	Lynn	Bolton	1950-1962	281	0	281	36
Tommy	Lyons	Hednesford	1907-1915	216	0	216	0
Willie	Macaulay	Glasgow, Scotland	1900-1901	4	0	4	0
Jimmy	MacEwan	Dundee, Scotland	1959-1966	143	0	143	28
Norman	Mackay	Edinburgh, Scotland	1923-1924	2	0	2	0
John	MacLeod	Edinburgh, Scotland	1964-1968	123	3	126	16
Percy	Maggs	Clutton	1930-1931	12	0	12	0
Walter	Maiden	Kidderminster	1919-1920	1	0	1	0
Jean II	Makoun	Yaounde, Cameroon	2010-2012	7	0	7	0
Shaun	Maloney	Miri, Sarawak, Malaysia	2006-2009	16	14	30	5
Jack	Mandley	Hanley, Staffordshire	1929-1934	106	0	106	25

ASTON VILLA PLAYER RECORDS

	FA CUP				LEAGUE CUP				EUROPEAN				OTHER				TOTAL			
SL	SUB	PL	GLS	SL	SUB	PL	GLS	SL	SUB	PL	GLS	SL	SUB	PL	GLS	SL	SUB	PL	GLS
0	0	0	0	2	1	3	3	0	0	0	0	0	0	0	0	3	6	9	3
1	2	3	0	8	1	9	0	0	0	0	0	0	0	0	0	35	18	53	2
1	0	1	0	1	0	1	0	5	0	5	3	0	0	0	0	89	2	91	11
11	0	11	1	0	0	0	0	0	0	0	0	0	0	0	0	11	0	11	1
1	0	1	0	0	0	0	0	0	0	0	0	0	0	0	0	14	0	14	0
1	0	1	0	0	0	0	0	0	0	0	0	0	0	0	0	17	0	17	0
9	0	9	0	0	0	0	0	0	0	0	0	0	0	0	0	75	0	75	3
15	0	15	2	0	0	0	0	0	0	0	0	0	0	0	0	142	0	142	10
12	0	12	0	0	0	0	0	0	0	0	0	0	0	0	0	12	0	12	0
8	0	8	0	16	0	16	0	0	0	0	0	0	0	0	0	142	0	142	2
0	0	0	0	0	0	0	0	0	0	0	0	0	0	0	0	18	0	18	0
0	0	0	0	0	0	0	0	0	0	0	0	0	0	0	0	1	0	1	0
3	0	3	2	6	0	6	4	0	0	0	0	0	0	0	0	45	2	47	17
0	0	0	0	3	1	4	0	0	0	0	0	0	0	0	0	16	7	23	3
0	1	1	0	0	0	0	0	0	0	0	0	0	0	0	0	0	1	1	0
0	0	0	0	1	0	1	0	0	0	0	0	0	0	0	0	31	0	31	1
2	0	2	0	6	1	7	1	1	0	1	0	0	0	0	0	30	12	42	2
2	0	2	0	4	0	4	0	0	0	0	0	1	0	1	0	37	1	38	4
0	1	1	0	0	1	1	0	0	0	0	0	0	0	0	0	0	2	2	0
0	0	0	0	0	0	0	0	0	0	0	0	0	0	0	0	1	0	1	0
1	0	1	0	0	0	0	0	0	2	2	0	0	0	0	0	17	13	30	0
0	0	0	0	2	0	2	1	0	0	0	0	0	0	0	0	4	1	5	1
15	1	16	4	29	1	30	15	9	0	9	3	0	0	0	0	295	7	302	82
2	0	2	0	0	0	0	0	0	0	0	0	0	0	0	0	52	0	52	0
1	0	1	0	0	0	0	0	0	0	0	0	0	0	0	0	6	0	6	1
3	0	3	3	0	0	0	0	0	0	0	0	0	0	0	0	3	0	3	3
2	0	2	0	20	0	20	10	0	0	0	0	1	0	1	0	150	4	154	44
0	0	0	0	0	0	0	0	0	0	0	0	0	0	0	0	41	0	41	5
11	0	11	2	0	0	0	0	0	0	0	0	0	0	0	0	85	0	85	12
1	0	1	1	0	0	0	0	0	0	0	0	0	0	0	0	25	0	25	12
1	0	1	0	0	0	0	0	0	0	0	0	0	0	0	0	15	0	15	8
11	0	11	0	0	0	0	0	0	0	0	0	0	0	0	0	157	0	157	4
13	0	13	0	0	0	0	0	0	0	0	0	0	0	0	0	117	0	117	3
0	0	0	0	0	0	0	0	0	2	2	0	0	0	0	0	0	2	2	0
3	0	3	0	7	0	7	0	0	0	0	0	0	0	0	0	73	9	82	2
1	0	1	0	6	1	7	0	0	0	0	0	0	0	0	0	98	13	111	5
1	0	1	0	0	0	0	0	0	0	0	0	0	0	0	0	17	1	18	1
1	1	2	0	0	2	2	0	0	0	0	0	0	0	0	0	3	5	8	0
1	0	1	0	0	0	0	0	0	0	0	0	0	0	0	0	3	0	3	0
36	0	36	1	6	0	6	1	0	0	0	0	1	0	1	0	324	0	324	38
20	0	20	0	0	0	0	0	0	0	0	0	1	0	1	0	237	0	237	0
0	0	0	0	0	0	0	0	0	0	0	0	0	0	0	0	4	0	4	0
20	0	20	0	18	0	18	4	0	0	0	0	0	0	0	0	181	0	181	32
0	0	0	0	0	0	0	0	0	0	0	0	0	0	0	0	2	0	2	0
8	0	8	1	6	0	6	1	0	0	0	0	0	0	0	0	137	3	140	18
2	0	2	0	0	0	0	0	0	0	0	0	0	0	0	0	14	0	14	0
0	0	0	0	0	0	0	0	0	0	0	0	0	0	0	0	1	0	1	0
0	0	0	0	1	0	1	0	0	0	0	0	0	0	0	0	8	0	8	0
0	1	1	0	2	0	2	2	0	0	0	0	0	0	0	0	18	15	33	7
6	0	6	1	0	0	0	0	0	0	0	0	0	0	0	0	112	0	112	26

LEAGUE

PLAYER	SURNAME	BORN	SEASONS	SL	SUB	PL	GLS
Christopher	Mann	West Smethwick	1899-1901	10	0	10	0
Frank	Mann	Newark	1911-1912	1	0	1	0
William (Bill)	Marriott	Northampton	1901-1902	8	0	8	0
Fred	Marshall	Walsall	1890-1891	3	0	3	0
Con	Martin	Dublin, Republic of Ireland	1948-1956	194	0	194	1
John	Martin	Ashington	1964-1965	1	0	1	0
John (Jackie)	Martin	Hamstead, Birmingham	1936-1949	81	0	81	22
Lionel	Martin	Ludlow	1966-1972	36	12	48	4
Emiliano	Martinez	Mar del Plata, Argentina	2020-2022	74	0	74	0
Keith	Masefield	Birmingham	1974-1977	1	3	4	0
Tommy	Mason	Burton-on-Trent	1882-1883	0	0	0	0
William B	Mason	Birmingham	1879-1880	0	0	0	0
Alex	Massie	Possilpark, Glasgow, Scotland	1935-1939	141	0	141	5
William (Billy)	Matthews	Derby	1903-1907	26	0	26	12
Jack	Maund	Hednesford	1935-1938	47	0	47	8
Frank	McAvennie	Glasgow, Scotland	1992-1993	0	3	3	0
Gavin	McCann	Blackpool	2003-2007	108	2	110	3
Alex	McClure	Workington	1923-1925	7	0	7	0
Ross	McCormack	Glasgow, Scotland	2016-2018	13	7	20	3
Bobby	McDonald	Aberdeen, Scotland	1972-1976	33	6	39	3
Charlie	McEleny	Glasgow, Scotland	1899-1900	1	0	1	0
John	McGinn	Glasgow, Scotland	2018-2022	138	2	140	15
John	McGrath	Limerick, Republic of Ireland	2000-2001	0	3	3	0
Paul	McGrath	Ealing, London	1989-1997	248	5	253	8
Alan	McInally	Ayrshire, Scotland	1987-1989	50	8	58	18
John	McKenzie	Montrose, Scotland	1908-1909	5	0	5	0
Tom	McKnight	Lichfield	1890-1891	10	0	10	1
Albert	McLachlan	Kirkcudbright, Scotland	1913-1914	3	0	3	0
John	McLachlan	Dumfries, Scotland	1912-1915	17	0	17	3
John	McLaverty	South Shields, Co. Durham	1913-1914	2	0	2	0
Alan	McLoughlin	Manchester	1991-1992	0	0	0	0
Jasper	McLuckie	Glasgow, Scotland	1901-1904	57	0	57	41
Jimmy	McLuckie	Stonehouse, Lanarkshire, Scotland	1934-1936	15	0	15	1
Pat	McMahon	Glasgow, Scotland	1969-1975	121	9	130	25
Steve	McMahon	Liverpool	1983-1986	74	1	75	7
Jimmy	McMorran	Muirkirk, Scotland	1960-1962	11	0	11	1
Ken	McNaught	Kirkcaldy, Fife, Scotland	1977-1983	207	0	207	8
Peter	McParland	Newry, Northern Ireland	1952-1962	293	0	293	98
Olof	Mellberg	Gullspang, Sweden	2001-2008	231	1	232	8
Paul	Merson	Northolt, Middlesex	1998-2003	101	16	117	18
Freddie	Miles	Aston, Birmingham	1903-1914	248	0	248	0
Reg	Miles	Enfield	1930-1931	16	0	16	0
Arthur	Millar	Montrose, Scotland	1900-1902	11	0	11	0
Charlie	Millington	Lincoln	1905-1908	35	0	35	10
Dr Victor	Milne	Aberdeen, Scotland	1923-1929	157	0	157	1
James	Milner	Leeds	2005-2006 2008-2011	95	5	100	12
Savo	Milosevic	Bijeljina, Yugoslavia	1995-1998	84	6	90	28
Tyrone	Mings	Bath	2018-2022	119	1	120	7
Tommy	Mitchinson	Sunderland	1967-1969	49	0	49	9

ASTON VILLA PLAYER RECORDS

\multicolumn{4}{c	}{FA CUP}	\multicolumn{4}{c	}{LEAGUE CUP}	\multicolumn{4}{c	}{EUROPEAN}	\multicolumn{4}{c	}{OTHER}	\multicolumn{4}{c}{TOTAL}
SL	SUB	PL	GLS	SL	SUB	PL	GLS	SL	SUB	PL	GLS	SL	SUB	PL	GLS	SL	SUB	PL	GLS
0	0	0	0	0	0	0	0	0	0	0	0	1	0	1	0	11	0	11	0
0	0	0	0	0	0	0	0	0	0	0	0	0	0	0	0	1	0	1	0
0	0	0	0	0	0	0	0	0	0	0	0	0	0	0	0	8	0	8	0
0	0	0	0	0	0	0	0	0	0	0	0	0	0	0	0	3	0	3	0
19	0	19	0	0	0	0	0	0	0	0	0	0	0	0	0	213	0	213	1
0	0	0	0	0	0	0	0	0	0	0	0	0	0	0	0	1	0	1	0
3	0	3	0	0	0	0	0	0	0	0	0	0	0	0	0	84	0	84	22
6	0	6	3	2	3	5	2	0	0	0	0	0	0	0	0	44	15	59	9
1	0	1	0	0	0	0	0	0	0	0	0	0	0	0	0	75	0	75	0
0	0	0	0	0	0	0	0	0	0	0	0	0	0	0	0	1	3	4	0
3	0	3	0	0	0	0	0	0	0	0	0	0	0	0	0	3	0	3	0
2	0	2	2	0	0	0	0	0	0	0	0	0	0	0	0	2	0	2	2
11	0	11	0	0	0	0	0	0	0	0	0	0	0	0	0	152	0	152	5
0	0	0	0	0	0	0	0	0	0	0	0	0	0	0	0	26	0	26	12
1	0	1	0	0	0	0	0	0	0	0	0	0	0	0	0	48	0	48	8
0	0	0	0	0	0	0	0	0	0	0	0	0	0	0	0	0	3	3	0
7	0	7	0	12	0	12	2	0	0	0	0	0	0	0	0	127	2	129	5
0	0	0	0	0	0	0	0	0	0	0	0	0	0	0	0	7	0	7	0
0	1	1	0	1	2	3	0	0	0	0	0	0	0	0	0	14	10	24	3
3	0	3	1	3	0	3	1	1	0	1	0	0	0	0	0	40	6	46	5
0	0	0	0	0	0	0	0	0	0	0	0	0	0	0	0	1	0	1	0
2	0	2	0	1	1	2	0	0	0	0	0	3	0	3	1	144	3	147	16
0	0	0	0	0	0	0	0	0	0	0	0	0	0	0	0	0	3	3	0
23	1	24	0	29	1	30	1	11	1	12	0	4	0	4	0	315	8	323	9
4	0	4	2	6	0	6	5	0	0	0	0	3	0	3	3	63	8	71	28
0	0	0	0	0	0	0	0	0	0	0	0	0	0	0	0	5	0	5	0
2	0	2	2	0	0	0	0	0	0	0	0	0	0	0	0	12	0	12	3
0	0	0	0	0	0	0	0	0	0	0	0	0	0	0	0	3	0	3	0
0	0	0	0	0	0	0	0	0	0	0	0	0	0	0	0	17	0	17	3
0	0	0	0	0	0	0	0	0	0	0	0	0	0	0	0	2	0	2	0
0	0	0	0	0	0	0	0	0	0	0	0	1	0	1	0	1	0	1	0
5	0	5	5	0	0	0	0	0	0	0	0	0	0	0	0	62	0	62	46
0	0	0	0	0	0	0	0	0	0	0	0	0	0	0	0	15	0	15	1
4	0	4	0	15	0	15	5	0	0	0	0	1	0	1	0	141	9	150	30
3	0	3	0	9	0	9	0	4	0	4	0	0	0	0	0	90	1	91	7
2	0	2	0	1	0	1	0	0	0	0	0	0	0	0	0	14	0	14	1
13	0	13	0	17	0	17	0	21	0	21	5	2	0	2	0	260	0	260	13
36	0	36	19	11	0	11	4	0	0	0	0	1	0	1	0	341	0	341	121
9	0	9	0	17	0	17	0	5	0	5	0	0	0	0	0	262	1	263	8
11	0	11	0	5	2	7	0	8	1	9	1	0	0	0	0	125	19	144	19
20	0	20	0	0	0	0	0	0	0	0	0	1	0	1	0	269	0	269	0
0	0	0	0	0	0	0	0	0	0	0	0	0	0	0	0	16	0	16	0
0	0	0	0	0	0	0	0	0	0	0	0	0	0	0	0	11	0	11	0
3	0	3	4	0	0	0	0	0	0	0	0	0	0	0	0	38	0	38	14
18	0	18	0	0	0	0	0	0	0	0	0	0	0	0	0	175	0	175	1
10	1	11	3	9	0	9	6	5	1	6	1	0	0	0	0	119	7	126	22
10	0	10	2	8	1	9	1	8	0	8	2	0	0	0	0	110	7	117	33
1	0	1	0	4	0	4	0	0	0	0	0	3	0	3	0	127	1	128	7
2	0	2	0	1	0	1	0	0	0	0	0	0	0	0	0	52	0	52	9

583

PLAYER	SURNAME	BORN	SEASONS	SL	SUB	PL	GLS
Isaac	Moore	Tipton	1889-1890	5	0	5	3
Luke	Moore	Birmingham	2003-2008	36	51	87	14
Stefan	Moore	Birmingham	2002-2005	9	13	22	2
Tommy	Moore	Dudley Port	1931-1932	1	0	1	1
Wesley	Moraes	Juiz de Fora, Brazil	2019-2022	21	4	25	5
Matthew	Moralee	Mexborough	1936-1937	12	0	12	1
John	Morby	Wednesfield	1945-1946	0	0	0	0
Andre	Moreira	Ribeirao, Portugal	2018-2019	0	0	0	0
Sammy	Morgan	Belfast, Northern Ireland	1973-1976	35	5	40	9
Tony	Morley	Ormskirk	1979-1984	128	9	137	25
Terry	Morrall	Smethwick	1959-1961	8	0	8	0
William	Morris	Danesmoor, Derbyshire	1911-1915	51	0	51	0
Tommy	Mort	Kearsley	1921-1935	338	0	338	2
Dennis	Mortimer	Liverpool	1975-1985	316	1	317	31
Paul	Mortimer	Kensington	1991-1992	10	2	12	1
Harry	Morton	Oldham	1931-1937	192	0	192	0
Graham	Moseley	Manchester	1974-1975	3	0	3	0
Amos	Moss	Aston, Birmingham	1946-1956	102	0	102	5
Arthur	Moss	Crewe	1909-1912	5	0	5	0
Frank	Moss (Junior)	Aston, Birmingham	1938-1955	297	0	297	3
Frank	Moss (Senior)	Aston, Birmingham	1914-1929	253	0	253	8
Derek	Mountfield	Liverpool	1988-1992	88	2	90	9
Tommy	Muldoon	Athlone, Republic of Ireland	1924-1927	33	0	33	0
Ambrose (Jock)	Mulraney	Wishaw, Nr Motherwell, Scotland	1948-1949	12	0	12	2
Jimmy	Murray	Benwhat, Scotland	1900-1902	2	0	2	0
Scott	Murray	Aberdeen, Scotland	1995-1997	4	0	4	0
Freddie	Mwila	Kasama, Zambia	1969-1970	1	0	1	0
Billy	Myerscough	Bolton	1956-1959	64	0	64	15
Marvelous	Nakamba	Hwange, Zimbabwe	2019-2022	38	20	58	0
Harry	Nash	Fishponds, Wales	1914-1920	12	0	12	5
John	Neal	Seaham	1959-1963	96	0	96	0
Fernando	Nelson	Porto, Portugal	1996-1998	54	5	59	0
Tommy	Niblo	Dunfermline, Scotland	1901-1904	45	0	45	9
Joe	Nibloe	Corkerhill, Scotland	1932-1934	48	0	48	0
Chris	Nicholl	Wilmslow	1971-1977	210	0	210	11
Joe	Nicholson	Ryhope	1926-1927	1	0	1	0
Kent	Nielsen	Frederiksberg, Denmark	1989-1992	74	5	79	4
Luc	Nilis	Hasselt, Belgium	2000-2001	3	0	3	1
Michael	Noon	Burton-on-Trent	1899-1906	76	0	76	1
Fred	Norris	Aston, Birmingham	1925-1927	9	0	9	2
David	Norton	Cannock	1984-1988	42	2	44	2
Orjan	Nyland	Volda, Norway	2018-2021	28	2	30	0
Charles	N'Zogbia	Harfleur, France	2011-2016	54	26	80	4
Michael	Oakes	Northwich	1994-1999	49	2	51	0
Frank	O'Donnell	Buckhaven, Fife, Scotland	1938-1939	29	0	29	14
Callum	O'Hare	Solihull	2017-2019	0	4	4	0
Jores	Okore	Abidjan, Ivory Coast	2013-2017	36	2	38	1
Ben	Olney	Holborn, London	1927-1930	84	0	84	0
Ian	Olney	Luton	1988-1992	62	26	88	16
Robin	Olsen	Malmo, Sweden	2021-2022	1	0	1	0

ASTON VILLA PLAYER RECORDS

| FA CUP |||| LEAGUE CUP |||| EUROPEAN |||| OTHER |||| TOTAL ||||
SL	SUB	PL	GLS	SL	SUB	PL	GLS	SL	SUB	PL	GLS	SL	SUB	PL	GLS	SL	SUB	PL	GLS
1	0	1	0	0	0	0	0	0	0	0	0	0	0	0	0	6	0	6	3
3	2	5	0	2	4	6	1	0	0	0	0	0	0	0	0	41	57	98	15
0	1	1	0	2	3	5	0	0	2	2	0	0	0	0	0	11	19	30	2
0	0	0	0	0	0	0	0	0	0	0	0	0	0	0	0	1	0	1	1
0	0	0	0	0	1	1	1	0	0	0	0	0	0	0	0	21	5	26	6
0	0	0	0	0	0	0	0	0	0	0	0	0	0	0	0	12	0	12	1
3	0	3	0	0	0	0	0	0	0	0	0	0	0	0	0	3	0	3	0
0	0	0	0	2	0	2	0	0	0	0	0	0	0	0	0	2	0	2	0
3	1	4	4	5	0	5	2	1	1	2	0	0	0	0	0	44	7	51	15
8	0	8	1	14	0	14	3	18	1	19	5	2	0	2	0	170	10	180	34
0	0	0	0	1	0	1	0	0	0	0	0	0	0	0	0	9	0	9	0
3	0	3	1	0	0	0	0	0	0	0	0	0	0	0	0	54	0	54	1
31	0	31	0	0	0	0	0	0	0	0	0	0	0	0	0	369	0	369	2
21	0	21	1	38	0	38	2	28	0	28	2	2	0	2	0	405	1	406	36
0	0	0	0	2	0	2	0	0	0	0	0	0	0	0	0	12	2	14	1
15	0	15	0	0	0	0	0	0	0	0	0	0	0	0	0	207	0	207	0
0	0	0	0	0	0	0	0	0	0	0	0	0	0	0	0	3	0	3	0
7	0	7	0	0	0	0	0	0	0	0	0	0	0	0	0	109	0	109	5
0	0	0	0	0	0	0	0	0	0	0	0	0	0	0	0	5	0	5	0
17	0	17	0	0	0	0	0	0	0	0	0	0	0	0	0	314	0	314	3
28	0	28	0	0	0	0	0	0	0	0	0	0	0	0	0	281	0	281	8
6	0	6	1	13	0	13	2	4	0	4	2	7	0	7	3	118	2	120	17
1	0	1	0	0	0	0	0	0	0	0	0	0	0	0	0	34	0	34	0
0	0	0	0	0	0	0	0	0	0	0	0	0	0	0	0	12	0	12	2
0	0	0	0	0	0	0	0	0	0	0	0	0	0	0	0	2	0	2	0
0	0	0	0	0	0	0	0	0	0	0	0	0	0	0	0	4	0	4	0
0	0	0	0	0	0	0	0	0	0	0	0	0	0	0	0	1	0	1	0
9	0	9	2	0	0	0	0	0	0	0	0	1	0	1	0	74	0	74	17
1	0	1	0	9	0	9	0	0	0	0	0	0	0	0	0	48	20	68	0
0	0	0	0	0	0	0	0	0	0	0	0	0	0	0	0	12	0	12	5
10	0	10	0	8	0	8	0	0	0	0	0	0	0	0	0	114	0	114	0
1	1	2	0	3	0	3	0	7	2	9	0	0	0	0	0	65	8	73	0
6	0	6	0	0	0	0	0	0	0	0	0	0	0	0	0	51	0	51	9
4	0	4	0	0	0	0	0	0	0	0	0	0	0	0	0	52	0	52	0
12	0	12	4	27	0	27	5	2	0	2	0	1	0	1	0	252	0	252	20
0	0	0	0	0	0	0	0	0	0	0	0	0	0	0	0	1	0	1	0
6	0	6	0	6	1	7	0	4	0	4	1	6	0	6	0	96	6	102	5
0	0	0	0	0	0	0	0	2	0	2	1	0	0	0	0	5	0	5	2
8	0	8	0	0	0	0	0	0	0	0	0	0	0	0	0	84	0	84	1
0	0	0	0	0	0	0	0	0	0	0	0	0	0	0	0	9	0	9	2
2	1	3	0	8	0	8	0	0	0	0	0	2	0	2	0	54	3	57	2
1	0	1	0	5	0	5	0	0	0	0	0	0	0	0	0	34	2	36	0
5	1	6	0	4	3	7	1	0	0	0	0	0	0	0	0	63	30	93	5
2	0	2	0	3	0	3	0	5	0	5	0	0	0	0	0	59	2	61	0
2	0	2	0	0	0	0	0	0	0	0	0	0	0	0	0	31	0	31	14
2	0	2	0	3	0	3	0	0	0	0	0	0	0	0	0	5	4	9	0
5	2	7	0	2	0	2	0	0	0	0	0	0	0	0	0	43	4	47	1
13	0	13	0	0	0	0	0	0	0	0	0	0	0	0	0	97	0	97	0
5	1	6	2	8	2	10	1	1	2	3	1	7	0	7	1	83	31	114	21
0	0	0	0	0	0	0	0	0	0	0	0	0	0	0	0	1	0	1	0

	LEAGUE			

PLAYER	SURNAME	BORN	SEASONS	SL	SUB	PL	GLS
Alan	O'Neill	Leadgate	1960-1963	23	0	23	6
Akos	Onodi	Gyor, Hungary	2020-2021	0	0	0	0
Joshua	Onomah	Enfield	2017-2018	20	13	33	4
Ian	Ormondroyd	Bradford	1988-1992	41	15	56	6
Brendan	Ormsby	Birmingham	1978-1986	115	2	117	4
Isaiah	Osbourne	Birmingham	2006-2011	7	12	19	0
John	Overton	Rotherham	1975-1976	2	1	3	0
Alpay	Ozalan	Karisyaled, Turkey	2000-2004	56	2	58	1
Derek	Pace	Bloxwich	1950-1958	98	0	98	40
Jackie	Palethorpe	Leicester	1935-1936	6	0	6	2
Tom	Pank	Aston, Birmingham	1879-1882	0	0	0	0
Bobby	Park	Edinburgh, Scotland	1964-1969	60	15	75	7
Garry	Parker	Oxford	1991-1995	91	4	95	13
Graham	Parker	Coventry	1963-1968	16	1	17	1
Harry	Parkes	Birmingham	1945-1955	320	0	320	3
Dennis	Parsons	Birmingham	1952-1955	36	0	36	0
Daniel	Paton	Auchencorrach Moor, Scotland	1889-1891	3	0	3	1
James	Paton	Glasgow, Scotland	1892-1893	1	0	1	0
Joe	Pearson	Brierley Hill	1900-1907	103	0	103	4
Mike	Pejic	Chesterton, Staffordshire	1979-1980	10	0	10	0
Jack	Pendleton	Liverpool	1919-1920	6	0	6	0
Gary	Penrice	Bristol	1990-1992	14	6	20	1
Tom	Perry	West Bromwich	1901-1903	28	0	28	1
Stiliyan	Petrov	Sofia, Bulgaria	2006-2012	174	11	185	9
Charlie	Phillips	Victoria, Monmouthshire, Wales	1935-1938	22	0	22	5
John	Phillips	Shrewsbury	1969-1970	15	0	15	0
Kevin	Phillips	Hitchin	2005-2006	20	3	23	4
Leighton	Phillips	Briton Ferry, Wales	1974-1979	134	6	140	4
Jaden	Philogene-Bidace	London	2020-2022	0	2	2	0
Arthur 'Ginger'	Phoenix	Manchester	1924-1925	3	0	3	2
Frank	Pimblett	Liverpool	1974-1976	9	0	9	0
Mike	Pinner	Boston	1954-1957	4	0	4	0
Robert	Pires	Reims, France	2010-2011	2	7	9	0
David	Platt	Chadderton	1987-1991	121	0	121	50
William	Podmore	Derby	1894-1895	0	0	0	0
Kevin	Poole	Bromsgrove	1984-1987	28	0	28	0
Stefan	Postma	Utrecht, Holland	2002-2005	7	4	11	0
Fred	Potter	Cradley Heath	1960-1961	3	0	3	0
Vic	Potts	Birmingham	1945-1948	62	0	62	0
Dave	Pountney	Baschurch, Shropshire	1963-1968	109	6	115	7
Ivor	Powell	Gilfach, Wales	1948-1951	79	0	79	5
Chris	Price	Hereford	1988-1992	109	2	111	2
Lew	Price	Caersws, Wales	1920-1922	10	0	10	0
Robert	Price	Hereford	1883-1886	0	0	0	0
Roy	Pritchard	Dawley	1955-1958	3	0	3	0
George	Pritty	Birmingham	1936-1938	3	0	3	0
Arthur	Proudler	Kingswinford	1954-1955	1	0	1	0
Thomas	Purslow	Perry Barr, Birmingham	1894-1895	1	0	1	1
Adam	Rachel	Birmingham	1998-1999	0	1	1	0
Arjan	Raikhy	Wolverhampton	2020-2021	0	0	0	0

ASTON VILLA PLAYER RECORDS

	FA CUP				LEAGUE CUP				EUROPEAN				OTHER				TOTAL			
SL	SUB	PL	GLS	SL	SUB	PL	GLS	SL	SUB	PL	GLS	SL	SUB	PL	GLS	SL	SUB	PL	GLS
3	0	3	0	8	0	8	5	0	0	0	0	0	0	0	0	34	0	34	11
1	0	1	0	0	0	0	0	0	0	0	0	0	0	0	0	1	0	1	0
1	0	1	0	2	0	2	0	0	0	0	0	0	0	0	0	23	14	37	4
5	0	5	2	4	2	6	2	1	1	2	0	5	0	5	0	56	18	74	10
3	1	4	0	11	1	12	2	7	0	7	1	0	0	0	0	136	4	140	7
1	1	2	0	4	0	4	0	2	3	5	0	0	0	0	0	14	16	30	0
0	0	0	0	0	0	0	0	0	0	0	0	0	0	0	0	2	1	3	0
2	0	2	0	3	0	3	0	8	0	8	0	0	0	0	0	69	2	71	1
8	0	8	2	0	0	0	0	0	0	0	0	1	0	1	0	107	0	107	42
0	0	0	0	0	0	0	0	0	0	0	0	0	0	0	0	6	0	6	2
11	0	11	0	0	0	0	0	0	0	0	0	0	0	0	0	11	0	11	0
3	0	3	1	8	1	9	2	0	0	0	0	0	0	0	0	71	16	87	10
10	0	10	1	12	0	12	0	0	2	2	0	0	0	0	0	113	6	119	14
1	0	1	0	3	0	3	0	0	0	0	0	0	0	0	0	20	1	21	1
25	0	25	1	0	0	0	0	0	0	0	0	0	0	0	0	345	0	345	4
5	0	5	0	0	0	0	0	0	0	0	0	0	0	0	0	41	0	41	0
0	0	0	0	0	0	0	0	0	0	0	0	0	0	0	0	3	0	3	1
0	0	0	0	0	0	0	0	0	0	0	0	0	0	0	0	1	0	1	0
13	0	13	3	0	0	0	0	0	0	0	0	0	0	0	0	116	0	116	7
0	0	0	0	2	0	2	0	0	0	0	0	0	0	0	0	12	0	12	0
0	0	0	0	0	0	0	0	0	0	0	0	0	0	0	0	6	0	6	0
0	0	0	0	0	0	0	0	0	0	0	0	0	0	0	0	14	6	20	1
2	0	2	0	0	0	0	0	0	0	0	0	0	0	0	0	30	0	30	1
11	1	12	2	12	1	13	0	9	0	9	1	0	0	0	0	206	13	219	12
0	0	0	0	0	0	0	0	0	0	0	0	0	0	0	0	22	0	22	5
2	0	2	0	0	0	0	0	0	0	0	0	0	0	0	0	17	0	17	0
1	1	2	0	1	1	2	1	0	0	0	0	0	0	0	0	22	5	27	5
7	0	7	0	17	1	18	0	10	0	10	0	0	0	0	0	168	7	175	4
0	1	1	0	1	1	2	0	0	0	0	0	0	0	0	0	1	4	5	0
1	0	1	1	0	0	0	0	0	0	0	0	0	0	0	0	4	0	4	3
1	0	1	0	1	0	1	0	0	0	0	0	0	0	0	0	11	0	11	0
0	0	0	0	0	0	0	0	0	0	0	0	0	0	0	0	4	0	4	0
2	0	2	1	0	1	1	0	0	0	0	0	0	0	0	0	4	8	12	1
9	0	9	2	14	0	14	10	4	0	4	2	7	0	7	4	155	0	155	68
1	0	1	0	0	0	0	0	0	0	0	0	0	0	0	0	1	0	1	0
1	0	1	0	2	0	2	0	0	0	0	0	1	0	1	0	32	0	32	0
1	0	1	0	1	0	1	0	1	0	1	0	0	0	0	0	10	4	14	0
2	0	2	0	1	0	1	0	0	0	0	0	0	0	0	0	6	0	6	0
10	0	10	0	0	0	0	0	0	0	0	0	0	0	0	0	72	0	72	0
9	0	9	0	8	0	8	0	0	0	0	0	0	0	0	0	126	6	132	7
7	0	7	0	0	0	0	0	0	0	0	0	0	0	0	0	86	0	86	5
7	0	7	0	14	0	14	0	4	0	4	0	7	1	8	0	141	3	144	2
0	0	0	0	0	0	0	0	0	0	0	0	0	0	0	0	10	0	10	0
8	0	8	0	0	0	0	0	0	0	0	0	0	0	0	0	8	0	8	0
0	0	0	0	0	0	0	0	0	0	0	0	0	0	0	0	3	0	3	0
1	0	1	0	0	0	0	0	0	0	0	0	0	0	0	0	4	0	4	0
0	0	0	0	0	0	0	0	0	0	0	0	0	0	0	0	1	0	1	0
0	0	0	0	0	0	0	0	0	0	0	0	0	0	0	0	1	0	1	1
0	0	0	0	0	0	0	0	0	0	0	0	0	0	0	0	0	1	1	0
1	0	1	0	0	0	0	0	0	0	0	0	0	0	0	0	1	0	1	0

PLAYER	SURNAME	BORN	SEASONS	LEAGUE SL	SUB	PL	GLS
Albert	Ralphs	Nantwich	1911-1912	1	0	1	0
George Burrell	Ramsay	Glasgow, Scotland	1879-1880	0	0	0	0
Aaron	Ramsey	Great Barr, Birmingham	2021-2022	0	0	0	0
Jacob	Ramsey	Great Barr, Birmingham	2018-2022	35	22	57	6
John	Ramsey	Bordesley Green, Birmingham	1892-1893	4	0	4	0
Walter	Randle	Aston, Birmingham	1893-1894	1	0	1	0
George	Reeves	Hucknall	1907-1909	35	0	35	10
Cyrille	Regis	Maripasoula, French Guiana	1991-1993	46	6	52	12
Pepe	Reina	Madrid, Spain	2019-2020	12	0	12	0
William (Bill)	Renneville	Mullingar, Republic of Ireland	1910-1911	2	0	2	1
Nigel	Reo-Coker	Thornton Heath	2007-2011	85	17	102	1
Dominic	Revan	West Bromwich	2020-2021	0	0	0	0
Jack 'Baldy'	Reynolds	Blackburn	1893-1897	96	0	96	17
Leonard	Richards	Bilston	1911-1914	7	0	7	0
Micah	Richards	Birmingham	2015-2017	24	2	26	1
Kevin	Richardson	Newcastle-upon-Tyne	1991-1995	142	1	143	13
Kieran	Richardson	Greenwich, London	2014-2016	24	9	33	0
Thomas	Riddell	Handsworth, Birmingham	1883-1886	0	0	0	0
Paul	Rideout	Bournemouth	1983-1985	50	4	54	19
Liam	Ridgewell	Bexleyheath	2002-2007	66	13	79	6
Tom	Riley	Blackburn	1905-1908	15	0	15	0
Jimmy	Rimmer	Southport	1977-1983	229	0	229	0
Bruce	Rioch	Aldershot	1969-1974	149	5	154	34
Neil	Rioch	Paddington	1969-1975	17	6	23	3
Stuart	Ritchie	Southampton	1986-1987	0	1	1	0
Dave	Roberts	Birmingham	1964-1968	15	1	16	1
Ken 'Shunter'	Roberts	Crewe	1951-1954	42	0	42	7
Kenneth Owen	Roberts	Cefn Mawr, Wales	1953-1958	38	0	38	3
Robert (Bob)	Roberts	West Bromwich	1892-1893	4	0	4	0
Walter	Roberts	Stoubridge	1882-1884	0	0	0	0
Richard	Robertson	Hockley, Birmingham	1884-1887	0	0	0	0
James	Robey	Radcliffe	1936-1937	3	0	3	0
Callum	Robinson	Northampton	2013-2014	0	4	4	0
Phil	Robinson	Stafford	1986-1987	2	1	3	1
John	Robson	Consett	1972-1978	141	3	144	1
Dr Dick	Roose	Holt, Wales	1911-1912	10	0	10	0
Ian	Ross	Glasgow, Scotland	1971-1976	175	0	175	3
Wayne	Routledge	Sidcup	2007-2009	0	2	2	0
Brian	Rowan	Glasgow, Scotland	1969-1970	1	0	1	0
Callum	Rowe	Leicester	2020-2021	0	0	0	0
Edward (Teddy)	Rowe	Leamington Spa	2020-2021	0	0	0	0
John	Roxburgh	Granton, Scotland	1922-1923	12	0	12	3
Dave	Rudge	Wolverhampton	1966-1970	49	6	55	10
George	Russell	Ayrshire, Scotland	1893-1895	32	0	32	1
Joe	Rutherford	Fatfield	1938-1952	148	0	148	0
Arthur	Sabin	Kingstanding, Birmingham	1956-1958	2	0	2	0
Moustapha	Salifou	Lome, Togo	2007-2009	0	4	4	0
Mbwana	Samatta	Dar Es Salaam, Tanzania	2019-2020	11	3	14	1
Chris	Samba	Creteil, France	2017-2018	5	7	12	1
Jlloyd	Samuel	Trinidad	1999-2007	144	25	169	2

ASTON VILLA PLAYER RECORDS

	FA CUP				LEAGUE CUP				EUROPEAN				OTHER				TOTAL		
SL	SUB	PL	GLS	SL	SUB	PL	GLS	SL	SUB	PL	GLS	SL	SUB	PL	GLS	SL	SUB	PL	GLS
0	0	0	0	0	0	0	0	0	0	0	0	0	0	0	0	1	0	1	0
1	0	1	0	0	0	0	0	0	0	0	0	0	0	0	0	1	0	1	0
0	0	0	0	0	1	1	0	0	0	0	0	0	0	0	0	0	1	1	0
1	1	2	0	3	1	4	0	0	0	0	0	0	0	0	0	39	24	63	6
0	0	0	0	0	0	0	0	0	0	0	0	0	0	0	0	4	0	4	0
0	0	0	0	0	0	0	0	0	0	0	0	0	0	0	0	1	0	1	0
1	0	1	0	0	0	0	0	0	0	0	0	0	0	0	0	36	0	36	10
5	2	7	0	3	1	4	0	0	0	0	0	0	0	0	0	54	9	63	12
0	0	0	0	0	0	0	0	0	0	0	0	0	0	0	0	12	0	12	0
0	0	0	0	0	0	0	0	0	0	0	0	0	0	0	0	2	0	2	1
6	0	6	0	5	0	5	1	11	0	11	1	0	0	0	0	107	17	124	3
1	0	1	0	0	0	0	0	0	0	0	0	0	0	0	0	1	0	1	0
14	0	14	0	0	0	0	0	0	0	0	0	0	0	0	0	110	0	110	17
0	0	0	0	0	0	0	0	0	0	0	0	0	0	0	0	7	0	7	0
3	0	3	1	2	0	2	0	0	0	0	0	0	0	0	0	29	2	31	2
12	0	12	0	15	0	15	3	8	0	8	0	2	0	2	0	179	1	180	16
5	0	5	0	3	0	3	0	0	0	0	0	0	0	0	0	4	0	4	0
10	0	10	0	0	0	0	0	0	0	0	0	0	0	0	0	10	0	10	0
1	1	2	0	4	2	6	3	1	0	1	0	0	0	0	0	56	7	63	22
3	2	5	0	6	3	9	0	0	0	0	0	0	0	0	0	75	18	93	6
0	0	0	0	0	0	0	0	0	0	0	0	0	0	0	0	15	0	15	0
12	0	12	0	23	0	23	0	21	0	21	0	2	0	2	0	287	0	287	0
7	0	7	0	14	0	14	3	0	0	0	0	1	0	1	0	171	5	176	37
1	0	1	0	1	1	2	0	0	0	0	0	0	0	0	0	19	7	26	3
0	0	0	0	0	0	0	0	0	0	0	0	0	0	0	0	0	1	1	0
1	0	1	1	2	0	2	0	0	0	0	0	0	0	0	0	18	1	19	2
4	0	4	0	0	0	0	0	0	0	0	0	0	0	0	0	46	0	46	7
1	0	1	0	0	0	0	0	0	0	0	0	0	0	0	0	39	0	39	3
0	0	0	0	0	0	0	0	0	0	0	0	0	0	0	0	4	0	4	0
5	0	5	1	0	0	0	0	0	0	0	0	0	0	0	0	5	0	5	1
3	0	3	0	0	0	0	0	0	0	0	0	0	0	0	0	3	0	3	0
0	0	0	0	0	0	0	0	0	0	0	0	0	0	0	0	3	0	3	0
0	0	0	0	0	1	1	0	0	0	0	0	0	0	0	0	0	5	5	0
0	0	0	0	0	0	0	0	0	0	0	0	0	0	0	0	2	1	3	1
10	0	10	0	19	0	19	0	2	1	3	0	0	0	0	0	172	4	176	1
0	0	0	0	0	0	0	0	0	0	0	0	0	0	0	0	10	0	10	0
10	0	10	0	17	0	17	0	2	0	2	0	1	0	1	0	205	0	205	3
0	0	0	0	0	1	1	0	2	3	5	0	0	0	0	0	2	6	8	0
0	0	0	0	0	0	0	0	0	0	0	0	0	0	0	0	1	0	1	0
1	0	1	0	0	0	0	0	0	0	0	0	0	0	0	0	1	0	1	0
0	1	1	0	0	0	0	0	0	0	0	0	0	0	0	0	0	1	1	0
0	0	0	0	0	0	0	0	0	0	0	0	0	0	0	0	12	0	12	3
4	1	5	0	0	0	0	0	0	0	0	0	0	0	0	0	53	7	60	10
5	0	5	2	0	0	0	0	0	0	0	0	0	0	0	0	37	0	37	3
8	0	8	0	0	0	0	0	0	0	0	0	0	0	0	0	156	0	156	0
0	0	0	0	0	0	0	0	0	0	0	0	0	0	0	0	2	0	2	0
1	0	1	0	0	0	0	0	6	2	8	0	0	0	0	0	7	6	13	0
0	0	0	0	2	0	2	1	0	0	0	0	0	0	0	0	13	3	16	2
0	0	0	0	2	0	2	0	0	0	0	0	0	0	0	0	7	7	14	1
7	1	8	0	15	1	16	1	5	2	7	0	0	0	0	0	171	29	200	3

589

LEAGUE

PLAYER	SURNAME	BORN	SEASONS	SL	SUB	PL	GLS
Carlos	Sanchez	Quibdo, Colombia	2014-2016	36	12	48	1
Morgan	Sanson	Saint-Doulchard, France	2020-2022	6	13	19	0
Dean	Saunders	Swansea, Wales	1992-1995	111	1	112	37
Pat	Saward	Cobh, Republic of Ireland	1955-1961	152	0	152	2
Peter	Schmeichel	Gladsaxe, Denmark	2001-2002	29	0	29	1
Riccardo	Scimeca	Leamington Spa	1995-1999	50	23	73	2
Tony	Scott	St Neots	1965-1968	47	3	50	4
Les	Sealey	Bethnal Green	1991-1992	18	0	18	0
Geoff	Sellars	Stockport	1950-1951	2	0	2	0
Philippe	Senderos	Geneva, Switzerland	2014-2015	7	1	8	0
Jackie	Sewell	Whitehaven	1955-1960	123	0	123	36
Bertram	Sharp	Hereford	1897-1899	22	0	22	1
John (Jack)	Sharp	Hereford	1897-1899	23	0	23	14
John	Sharples	Wolverhampton	1958-1959	13	0	13	0
Gary	Shaw	Kingshurst	1978-1988	158	7	165	59
Frank	Shell	Hackney, London	1937-1939	23	0	23	8
Gary	Shelton	Nottingham	1978-1982	24	0	24	7
Nicky	Shorey	Romford	2008-2010	22	2	24	0
GH (Hartley)	Shutt	Burnley	1901-1904	40	0	40	0
Geoff	Sidebottom	Mapplewell	1960-1965	70	0	70	0
Steve	Sidwell	Wandsworth	2008-2011	24	21	45	3
Harry	Simmonds	Birmingham	1879-1882	0	0	0	0
Joseph	Simmonds	Birmingham	1882-1888	0	0	0	0
Dave	Simmons	Gosport	1968-1971	13	4	17	7
Billy	Simpson	Cowdenbeath, Scotland	1931-1935	29	0	29	1
Nigel	Sims	Coton-in-the-Elms	1955-1964	264	0	264	0
Steve	Sims	Lincoln	1987-1989	41	0	41	0
Scott	Sinclair	Bath	2014-2016	24	12	36	3
Herbert	Singleton	Manchester	1923-1924	2	0	2	0
Didier	Six	Lille, France	1984-1985	13	3	16	2
David	Skea	Arbroath, Scotland	1892-1893	1	0	1	1
Len	Skiller	Penzance	1908-1909	1	0	1	0
Charlie	Slade	Bath	1913-1914	3	0	3	0
John	Sleeuwenhoek	Wednesfield	1960-1968	226	0	226	1
Dick	Sloney	London	1919-1920	2	0	2	0
Bryan	Small	Birmingham	1991-1995	31	5	36	0
Herbert	Smart	Smethwick	1913-1914	1	0	1	0
Tommy	Smart	Blackheath, Staffordshire	1919-1933	405	0	405	8
George	Smith	Preston	1901-1902	5	0	5	0
Gordon	Smith	Partick, Scotland	1976-1979	76	3	79	0
Herbie	Smith	Birmingham	1948-1954	51	0	51	8
Les	Smith	Halesowen	1955-1959	115	0	115	24
Leslie GF	Smith	Ealing	1945-1952	181	0	181	31
Stephen	Smith	Abbots Bromley	1893-1901	162	0	162	36
Robert	Snodgrass	Glasgow, Scotland	2017-2018	38	2	40	7
Harrison	Sohna	Gloucester	2020-2021	0	0	0	0
Nolberto	Solano	Lima, Peru	2003-2006	44	5	49	8
Thomas	Sorensen	Fredericia, Denmark	2003-2007	139	0	139	0
Gareth	Southgate	Watford	1995-2001	191	0	191	7
Tommy	Southren	Sunderland	1954-1959	63	0	63	7

ASTON VILLA PLAYER RECORDS

FA CUP				LEAGUE CUP				EUROPEAN				OTHER				TOTAL			
SL	SUB	PL	GLS	SL	SUB	PL	GLS	SL	SUB	PL	GLS	SL	SUB	PL	GLS	SL	SUB	PL	GLS
3	2	5	0	3	0	3	0	0	0	0	0	0	0	0	0	42	14	56	1
0	0	0	0	1	0	1	0	0	0	0	0	0	0	0	0	7	13	20	0
9	0	9	4	15	0	15	7	8	0	8	1	0	0	0	0	143	1	144	49
16	0	16	0	1	0	1	0	0	0	0	0	1	0	1	0	170	0	170	2
1	0	1	0	2	0	2	0	4	0	4	0	0	0	0	0	36	0	36	1
9	1	10	0	4	3	7	0	5	2	7	0	0	0	0	0	68	29	97	2
2	0	2	0	5	0	5	1	0	0	0	0	0	0	0	0	54	3	57	5
4	0	4	0	0	0	0	0	0	0	0	0	2	0	2	0	24	0	24	0
0	0	0	0	0	0	0	0	0	0	0	0	0	0	0	0	2	0	2	0
0	0	0	0	1	0	1	0	0	0	0	0	0	0	0	0	8	1	9	0
21	0	21	4	0	0	0	0	0	0	0	0	1	0	1	0	145	0	145	40
1	0	1	0	0	0	0	0	0	0	0	0	0	0	0	0	23	0	23	1
1	0	1	0	0	0	0	0	0	0	0	0	0	0	0	0	24	0	24	14
0	0	0	0	0	0	0	0	0	0	0	0	0	0	0	0	13	0	13	0
11	0	11	4	16	2	18	5	16	0	16	9	3	0	3	2	204	9	213	79
8	0	8	5	0	0	0	0	0	0	0	0	0	0	0	0	31	0	31	13
0	0	0	0	2	1	3	1	0	0	0	0	0	0	0	0	26	1	27	8
3	0	3	0	2	0	2	0	10	0	10	0	0	0	0	0	37	2	39	0
2	0	2	0	0	0	0	0	0	0	0	0	0	0	0	0	42	0	42	0
4	0	4	0	13	0	13	0	0	0	0	0	0	0	0	0	87	0	87	0
5	3	8	1	2	3	5	0	6	0	6	0	0	0	0	0	37	27	64	4
10	0	10	0	0	0	0	0	0	0	0	0	0	0	0	0	10	0	10	0
22	0	22	0	0	0	0	0	0	0	0	0	0	0	0	0	22	0	22	0
0	2	2	0	0	0	0	0	0	0	0	0	0	0	0	0	13	6	19	7
0	0	0	0	0	0	0	0	0	0	0	0	0	0	0	0	29	0	29	1
31	0	31	0	14	0	14	0	0	0	0	0	1	0	1	0	310	0	310	0
0	0	0	0	5	0	5	0	0	0	0	0	1	0	1	0	47	0	47	0
4	2	6	2	2	1	3	4	0	0	0	0	0	0	0	9	30	15	45	9
0	0	0	0	0	0	0	0	0	0	0	0	0	0	0	0	2	0	2	0
0	0	0	0	1	1	2	0	0	0	0	0	0	0	0	0	14	4	18	2
0	0	0	0	0	0	0	0	0	0	0	0	0	0	0	0	1	0	1	1
1	0	1	0	0	0	0	0	0	0	0	0	0	0	0	0	2	0	2	0
0	0	0	0	0	0	0	0	0	0	0	0	0	0	0	0	3	0	3	0
12	0	12	0	22	0	22	0	0	0	0	0	0	0	0	0	260	0	260	1
0	0	0	0	0	0	0	0	0	0	0	0	0	0	0	0	2	0	2	0
2	1	3	0	2	0	2	0	2	0	2	0	2	0	2	0	39	6	45	0
0	0	0	0	0	0	0	0	0	0	0	0	0	0	0	0	1	0	1	0
46	0	46	0	0	0	0	0	0	0	0	0	0	0	0	0	451	0	451	8
0	0	0	0	0	0	0	0	0	0	0	0	0	0	0	0	5	0	5	0
1	0	1	0	8	1	9	0	7	0	7	0	0	0	0	0	92	4	96	0
3	0	3	1	0	0	0	0	0	0	0	0	0	0	0	0	54	0	54	9
14	0	14	1	0	0	0	0	0	0	0	0	1	0	1	0	130	0	130	25
16	0	16	6	0	0	0	0	0	0	0	0	0	0	0	0	197	0	197	37
22	0	22	7	0	0	0	0	0	0	0	0	3	0	3	0	187	0	187	43
0	0	0	0	0	0	0	0	0	0	0	0	3	0	3	0	41	2	43	7
0	1	1	0	0	0	0	0	0	0	0	0	0	0	0	0	0	1	1	0
1	0	1	0	2	0	2	1	0	0	0	0	0	0	0	0	47	5	52	9
6	0	6	0	13	0	13	0	0	0	0	0	0	0	0	0	158	0	158	0
20	0	20	1	16	0	16	1	15	0	15	0	0	0	0	0	242	0	242	9
9	0	9	1	0	0	0	0	0	0	0	0	0	0	0	0	72	0	72	8

591

LEAGUE

PLAYER	SURNAME	BORN	SEASONS	SL	SUB	PL	GLS
Howard	Spencer	Edgbaston, Birmingham	1894-1908	258	0	258	2
Cyril	Spiers	Witton, Birmingham	1920-1927	104	0	104	0
Nigel	Spink	Chelmsford	1979-1996	357	4	361	0
Simon	Stainrod	Sheffield	1985-1988	58	5	63	16
Roy	Stark	Nottingham	1973-1974	2	0	2	0
Ronnie	Starling	Pelaw-on-Tyne	1936-1947	88	0	88	11
Steve	Staunton	Drogheda, Republic of Ireland	1991-1998 2000-2003	270	11	281	17
Jed	Steer	Norwich	2013-2022	18	1	19	0
Clem	Stephenson	New Delaval	1910-1921	193	0	193	85
George H	Stephenson	Stillington	1931-1932	2	0	2	1
George T	Stephenson	New Delaval	1921-1928	93	0	93	22
Jimmy	Stephenson	New Delaval	1914-1921	31	0	31	2
Enda	Stevens	Dublin, Ireland	2012-2013	6	1	7	0
Barry	Stobart	Doncaster	1964-1968	45	0	45	18
Arthur	Stokes	West Bromwich	1892-1893	13	0	13	0
Steve	Stone	Gateshead	1998-2003	66	24	90	4
Edward	Strange	Bordsley Green, Birmingham	1897-1898	2	0	2	0
James	Suddick	Middlesbrough	1897-1898	2	0	2	1
Easah	Suliman	Birmingham	2017-2019	0	0	0	0
Albert	Surtees	Willington Quay	1923-1925	11	0	11	1
Chris	Sutton	Nottingham	2006-2007	6	2	8	1
Kenny	Swain	Birkenhead	1978-1983	148	0	148	4
Norman	Swales	New Marske	1928-1930	6	0	6	0
Sil	Swinkels	Sint-Oedenrode, Netherlands	2020-2021	0	0	0	0
Mamadou	Sylla	Barcelona, Spain	2020-2021	0	0	0	0
Yacouba	Sylla	Etampes, France	2012-2014	12	10	22	0
Alec	Talbot	Cannock	1923-1935	240	0	240	7
Matthew	Targett	Winchester	2019-2022	65	1	66	1
Joe	Tate	Old Hill	1927-1934	180	0	180	2
Ian	Taylor	Birmingham	1994-2003	202	31	233	28
Martin	Taylor	Annfield Plain	1921-1922	1	0	1	0
Neil	Taylor	Ruthin, Wales	2016-2021	80	9	89	0
Stuart	Taylor	Romford	2005-2009	9	3	12	0
Shaun	Teale	Southport	1991-1995	146	1	147	2
Robert (Bobby)	Templeton	Coylton, Scotland	1898-1903	64	0	64	10
John	Terry	Barking	2017-2018	32	0	32	1
Ken	Tewkesbury	Hove	1932-1933	1	0	1	0
Robert (Bob)	Thomas	Newtown, Birmingham	1888-1889	0	0	0	0
Alan	Thompson	Newcastle	1998-2001	36	10	46	4
Garry	Thompson	King's Heath, Birmingham	1986-1989	56	4	60	17
Jack	Thompson	Crewe	1919-1921	26	0	26	0
Tommy	Thompson	Fencehouses	1950-1955	149	0	149	67
Bobby	Thomson	Dundee, Scotland	1959-1964	140	0	140	56
Oliver	Tidman	Margate	1932-1933	1	0	1	0
Brian	Tiler	Rotherham	1968-1973	106	1	107	3
Carl	Tiler	Sheffield	1995-1997	10	2	12	1
Mike	Tindall	Birmingham	1959-1968	118	2	120	8
Kevin	Toner	Dublin, Ireland	2015-2016	3	1	4	0
Aleksandar	Tonev	Elin Pelin, Bulgaria	2013-2014	6	11	17	0

ASTON VILLA PLAYER RECORDS

FA CUP				LEAGUE CUP				EUROPEAN				OTHER				TOTAL			
SL	SUB	PL	GLS	SL	SUB	PL	GLS	SL	SUB	PL	GLS	SL	SUB	PL	GLS	SL	SUB	PL	GLS
35	0	35	0	0	0	0	0	0	0	0	0	1	0	1	0	294	0	294	2
8	0	8	0	0	0	0	0	0	0	0	0	0	0	0	0	112	0	112	0
28	0	28	0	45	0	45	0	18	1	19	0	7	0	7	0	455	5	460	0
6	0	6	2	11	1	12	9	0	0	0	0	1	0	1	0	76	6	82	27
0	0	0	0	0	0	0	0	0	0	0	0	0	0	0	0	2	0	2	0
11	0	11	1	0	0	0	0	0	0	0	0	0	0	0	0	99	0	99	12
23	1	24	1	22	2	24	1	20	1	21	1	0	0	0	0	335	15	350	20
2	0	2	0	12	0	12	0	0	0	0	0	3	0	3	0	35	1	36	0
24	0	24	11	0	0	0	0	0	0	0	0	0	0	0	0	217	0	217	96
2	0	2	0	0	0	0	0	0	0	0	0	0	0	0	0	4	0	4	1
2	0	2	0	0	0	0	0	0	0	0	0	0	0	0	0	95	0	95	22
1	0	1	0	0	0	0	0	0	0	0	0	0	0	0	0	32	0	32	2
0	0	0	0	1	1	2	0	0	0	0	0	0	0	0	0	7	2	9	0
6	0	6	1	2	0	2	1	0	0	0	0	0	0	0	0	53	0	53	20
1	0	1	0	0	0	0	0	0	0	0	0	0	0	0	0	14	0	14	0
5	5	10	2	5	2	7	1	10	4	14	0	0	0	0	0	86	35	121	7
0	0	0	0	0	0	0	0	0	0	0	0	0	0	0	0	2	0	2	0
0	0	0	0	0	0	0	0	0	0	0	0	0	0	0	0	2	0	2	1
0	0	0	0	0	1	1	0	0	0	0	0	0	0	0	0	0	1	1	0
0	0	0	0	0	0	0	0	0	0	0	0	0	0	0	0	11	0	11	1
0	0	0	0	0	1	1	0	0	0	0	0	0	0	0	0	6	3	9	1
10	0	10	0	12	0	12	1	8	0	8	0	1	0	1	0	179	0	179	5
2	0	2	1	0	0	0	0	0	0	0	0	0	0	0	0	8	0	8	1
0	1	1	0	0	0	0	0	0	0	0	0	0	0	0	0	0	1	1	0
1	0	1	0	0	0	0	0	0	0	0	0	0	0	0	0	1	0	1	0
0	0	0	0	1	1	2	0	0	0	0	0	0	0	0	0	13	11	24	0
23	0	23	0	0	0	0	0	0	0	0	0	0	0	0	0	263	0	263	7
0	0	0	0	4	0	4	1	0	0	0	0	0	0	0	0	69	1	70	2
13	0	13	2	0	0	0	0	0	0	0	0	0	0	0	0	193	0	193	4
14	3	17	2	19	2	21	7	18	1	19	5	0	0	0	0	253	37	290	42
0	0	0	0	0	0	0	0	0	0	0	0	0	0	0	0	1	0	1	0
3	0	3	0	8	0	8	0	0	0	0	0	3	0	3	0	94	9	103	0
0	0	0	0	3	0	3	0	2	0	2	0	0	0	0	0	14	3	17	0
13	0	13	0	15	0	15	3	4	0	4	0	2	0	2	0	180	1	181	5
7	0	7	0	0	0	0	0	0	0	0	0	0	0	0	0	71	0	71	10
1	0	1	0	0	0	0	0	0	0	0	0	3	0	3	0	36	0	36	1
0	0	0	0	0	0	0	0	0	0	0	0	0	0	0	0	1	0	1	0
1	0	1	0	0	0	0	0	0	0	0	0	0	0	0	0	1	0	1	0
1	0	1	0	3	3	6	1	4	1	5	0	0	0	0	0	44	14	58	5
4	0	4	0	6	0	6	2	0	0	0	0	3	0	3	0	69	4	73	19
2	0	2	0	0	0	0	0	0	0	0	0	0	0	0	0	28	0	28	0
16	0	16	9	0	0	0	0	0	0	0	0	0	0	0	0	165	0	165	76
14	0	14	6	18	0	18	8	0	0	0	0	0	0	0	0	172	0	172	70
0	0	0	0	0	0	0	0	0	0	0	0	0	0	0	0	1	0	1	0
2	1	3	0	17	0	17	1	0	0	0	0	0	0	0	0	125	2	127	4
2	0	2	0	1	0	1	0	0	0	0	0	0	0	0	0	13	2	15	1
3	0	3	0	13	0	13	1	0	0	0	0	0	0	0	0	134	2	136	9
0	0	0	0	0	0	0	0	0	0	0	0	0	0	0	0	3	1	4	0
1	0	1	0	1	1	2	0	0	0	0	0	0	0	0	0	8	12	20	0

LEAGUE

PLAYER	SURNAME	BORN	SEASONS	SL	SUB	PL	GLS
Andy	Townsend	Maidstone	1993-1998	133	1	134	8
George	Tranter	Quarry Bank	1906-1915	164	0	164	1
Adama	Traore	L'Hospitalet de Llobregat, Spain	2015-2017	0	11	11	0
Bertrand	Traore	Bobo-Dioulasso, Burkina Faso	2020-2022	30	15	45	7
James E (George)	Travers	Newtown, Birmingham	1908-1909	4	0	4	4
Mahmoud	Trezeguet	Kafr El-Sheikh, Egypt	2019-2022	32	24	56	8
Aaron	Tshibola	Newham	2016-2017	5	3	8	1
Axel	Tuanzebe	Bunia, DR Congo	2017-2019 2021-2022	34	5	39	0
Fred	Tully	St. Pancras	1927-1929	7	0	7	0
Fred	Turnbull	Wallsend-on-Tyne	1967-1974	160	1	161	3
Horace	Turner	Hall Green, Birmingham	1907-1911	15	0	15	0
Joe	Tyrell	Stepney	1953-1956	7	0	7	3
Archie	Vale	King's Heath, Birmingham	1883-1884	0	0	0	0
Percy	Varco	Fowey	1923-1925	10	0	10	2
Darius	Vassell	Birmingham	1998-2005	107	55	162	35
Indiana	Vassilev	Savannah, Georgia, USA	2019-2020	0	4	4	0
Oliver Howard	Vaughton	Aston, Birmingham	1880-1887	0	0	0	0
Jordan	Veretout	Ancenis, France	2015-2016	21	4	25	0
Albert	Vinall	Birmingham	1947-1954	11	0	11	1
Ron	Vlaar	Hensbroek, Netherlands	2012-2015	78	1	79	2
Geoff	Vowden	Barnsley	1970-1974	93	5	98	22
Alan	Wakeman	Walsall	1938-1950	12	0	12	0
Billy	Walker	Wednesbury	1919-1934	478	0	478	214
Jake	Walker	Shrewsbury	2020-2021	0	0	0	0
Kyle	Walker	Sheffield	2010-2011	15	0	15	1
Ray	Walker	North Shields	1982-1986	15	8	23	0
Richard	Walker	Birmingham	1997-2001	2	4	6	2
Charlie	Wallace	Southwick, County Durham	1907-1921	313	0	313	55
Dave	Walsh	Waterford, Republic of Ireland	1950-1955	108	0	108	37
Joe	Walters	Stoubridge	1905-1912	114	0	114	42
Mark	Walters	Birmingham	1981-1988	168	13	181	39
Joe	Ward	Glasgow, Scotland	1978-1980	2	1	3	0
Tom 'Pongo'	Waring	High Tranmere	1927-1936	215	0	215	159
Jimmy	Warner	Lozells, Birmingham	1886-1892	75	0	75	0
Stephen	Warnock	Ormskirk	2009-2012	83	1	84	2
Dennis	Watkin	Stapleford	1932-1936	21	0	21	5
Alfred Ernest (Fred)	Watkins	Llanwnnog, Wales	1899-1900	1	0	1	0
Olliver (Ollie)	Watkins	Torquay	2020-2022	70	2	72	25
WM (Martin)	Watkins	Caersws, Wales	1903-1905	6	0	6	1
Steve	Watson	North Shields	1998-2000	39	2	41	0
Walter	Watson	Sheffield	1911-1912	3	0	3	0
William (Bill)	Watts	Yardley, Birmingham	1880-1881	0	0	0	0
Andreas	Weimann	Vienna, Austria	2010-2015	82	31	113	17
Jimmy	Welford	Barnard Castle	1893-1897	79	0	79	1
Tommy	Weston	Halesowen	1911-1922	153	0	153	0
Ashley	Westwood	Nantwich	2012-2017	137	10	147	5
Oliver	Whateley	Coventry	1881-1886	0	0	0	0
Glenn	Whelan	Dublin, Ireland	2017-2019	53	15	68	2
Freddie	Wheldon	Langley Green	1896-1900	123	0	123	68

ASTON VILLA PLAYER RECORDS

	FA CUP				LEAGUE CUP				EUROPEAN				OTHER				TOTAL			
SL	SUB	PL	GLS	SL	SUB	PL	GLS	SL	SUB	PL	GLS	SL	SUB	PL	GLS	SL	SUB	PL	GLS
12	0	12	0	20	0	20	2	10	0	10	1	0	0	0	0	175	1	176	11
11	0	11	0	0	0	0	0	0	0	0	0	1	0	1	0	176	0	176	1
0	0	0	0	1	0	1	1	0	0	0	0	0	0	0	0	1	11	12	1
0	0	0	0	3	0	3	1	0	0	0	0	0	0	0	0	33	15	48	8
0	0	0	0	0	0	0	0	0	0	0	0	0	0	0	0	4	0	4	4
0	1	1	0	4	3	7	1	0	0	0	0	0	0	0	0	36	28	64	9
1	0	1	0	1	0	1	0	0	0	0	0	0	0	0	0	7	3	10	1
0	0	0	0	4	0	4	0	0	0	0	0	3	0	3	0	41	5	46	0
0	0	0	0	0	0	0	0	0	0	0	0	0	0	0	0	7	0	7	0
7	0	7	0	15	0	15	0	0	0	0	0	0	0	0	0	182	1	183	3
0	0	0	0	0	0	0	0	0	0	0	0	0	0	0	0	15	0	15	0
0	0	0	0	0	0	0	0	0	0	0	0	0	0	0	0	7	0	7	3
3	0	3	0	0	0	0	0	0	0	0	0	0	0	0	0	3	0	3	0
0	0	0	0	0	0	0	0	0	0	0	0	0	0	0	0	10	0	10	2
4	4	8	1	10	7	17	5	3	11	14	4	0	0	0	0	124	77	201	45
0	1	1	0	0	1	1	0	0	0	0	0	0	0	0	0	0	6	6	0
30	0	30	15	0	0	0	0	0	0	0	0	0	0	0	0	30	0	30	15
1	1	2	0	2	0	2	0	0	0	0	0	0	0	0	0	24	5	29	0
0	0	0	0	0	0	0	0	0	0	0	0	0	0	0	0	11	0	11	1
4	0	4	0	5	0	5	0	0	0	0	0	0	0	0	0	87	1	88	2
4	0	4	1	12	0	12	2	0	0	0	0	1	0	1	0	110	5	115	25
8	0	8	0	0	0	0	0	0	0	0	0	0	0	0	0	20	0	20	0
53	0	53	30	0	0	0	0	0	0	0	0	0	0	0	0	531	0	531	244
1	0	1	0	0	0	0	0	0	0	0	0	0	0	0	0	1	0	1	0
2	1	3	1	0	0	0	0	0	0	0	0	0	0	0	0	17	1	18	2
2	0	2	0	1	1	2	0	0	0	0	0	0	0	0	0	18	9	27	0
0	1	1	0	1	1	2	0	1	0	1	0	0	0	0	0	4	6	10	2
35	0	35	3	0	0	0	0	0	0	0	0	1	0	1	0	349	0	349	58
6	0	6	3	0	0	0	0	0	0	0	0	0	0	0	0	114	0	114	40
7	0	7	0	0	0	0	0	0	0	0	0	1	0	1	0	122	0	122	42
11	1	12	1	21	1	22	6	4	3	7	2	3	0	3	0	207	18	225	48
0	0	0	0	0	0	0	0	0	0	0	0	0	0	0	0	2	1	3	0
10	0	10	8	0	0	0	0	0	0	0	0	0	0	0	0	225	0	225	167
26	0	26	0	0	0	0	0	0	0	0	0	0	0	0	0	101	0	101	0
8	0	8	0	8	0	8	1	1	0	1	0	0	0	0	0	100	1	101	3
0	0	0	0	0	0	0	0	0	0	0	0	0	0	0	0	21	0	21	5
0	0	0	0	0	0	0	0	0	0	0	0	0	0	0	0	1	0	1	0
1	0	1	0	1	2	3	2	0	0	0	0	0	0	0	0	72	4	76	27
0	0	0	0	0	0	0	0	0	0	0	0	0	0	0	0	6	0	6	1
4	0	4	0	7	1	8	1	0	0	0	0	0	0	0	0	50	3	53	1
0	0	0	0	0	0	0	0	0	0	0	0	0	0	0	0	3	0	3	0
3	0	3	0	0	0	0	0	0	0	0	0	0	0	0	0	3	0	3	0
4	2	6	2	5	4	9	5	0	1	1	0	0	0	0	0	91	38	129	24
4	0	4	0	0	0	0	0	0	0	0	0	0	0	0	0	83	0	83	1
25	0	25	0	0	0	0	0	0	0	0	0	0	0	0	0	178	0	178	0
10	1	11	0	4	0	4	0	0	0	0	0	0	0	0	0	151	11	162	5
19	0	19	9	0	0	0	0	0	0	0	0	0	0	0	0	19	0	19	9
1	0	1	0	1	0	1	0	0	0	0	0	1	2	3	0	56	17	73	2
14	0	14	7	0	0	0	0	0	0	0	0	2	0	2	0	139	0	139	75

ASTON VILLA · THE COMPLETE RECORD

				LEAGUE			
PLAYER	**SURNAME**	**BORN**	**SEASONS**	**SL**	**SUB**	**PL**	**GLS**
Jimmy	Whitehouse	Birmingham	1896-1898	40	0	40	0
Jack	Whitley	Seacombe	1900-1902	9	0	9	0
Samson	Whittaker	Shelfield	1908-1915	62	0	62	6
Guy	Whittingham	Evesham	1993-1995	17	8	25	5
Peter	Whittingham	Nuneaton	2002-2007	32	24	56	1
John	Wilcox	Stourbridge	1907-1909	6	0	6	0
Albert	Wilkes	Birmingham	1898-1907	140	0	140	7
Tom	Wilkes	Alcester	1894-1899	64	0	64	0
Derrick	Williams	Hamburg, Germany	2012-2013	0	1	1	0
Evan	Williams	Dumbarton, Scotland	1969-1970	12	0	12	0
Gareth	Williams	Cowes, Isle of White	1987-1990	6	6	12	0
Gary	Williams	Wolverhampton	1978-1987	235	5	240	0
Jackie	Williams	Aberdare, Wales	1935-1936	17	0	17	5
William	Williams	Wrexham, Wales	1913-1914	1	0	1	0
John	Willis	Boldon	1958-1959	1	0	1	0
Bob	Wilson	Birmingham	1963-1964	9	0	9	0
Tom	Wilson	Preston	1900-1902	5	0	5	0
Jack	Windmill	Halesowen	1903-1909	42	0	42	1
Doug	Winton	Perth, Scotland	1958-1961	37	0	37	0
Peter	Withe	Liverpool	1980-1985	182	0	182	74
Colin	Withers	Erdington, Birmingham	1964-1969	146	0	146	0
Arthur	Wollaston	Shrewsbury	1888-1889	4	0	4	0
Alf	Wood	Smallthorne	1900-1905	102	0	102	8
Tommy	Wood	Wednesbury	1930-1937	62	0	62	2
John	Woodward	Stoke-on-Trent	1966-1969	22	4	26	7
Albert	Woolley	Hockley, Birmingham	1892-1895	20	0	20	13
Phil	Woosnam	Caersws, Wales	1962-1966	106	0	106	23
Joseph	Worrell	Stourbridge	1919-1920	4	0	4	0
Alan	Wright	Ashton-under-Lyne	1994-2003	255	5	260	5
Edmund	Wright	Leytonstone	1920-1921	2	0	2	0
Michael	Wright	Ellesmere Port	1963-1973	280	3	283	1
Ron	Wylie	Glasgow, Scotland	1958-1965	196	0	196	16
Harry	Yates	Walsall	1886-1890	14	0	14	0
John	Yates	Manchester	1927-1929	14	0	14	0
Dicky	York	Handsworth, Birmingham	1919-1931	356	0	356	80
Dwight	Yorke	Canaan, Tobago	1989-1998	195	36	231	73
Andrew	Young	Darlington	1919-1922	26	0	26	11
Ashley	Young	Stevenage	2006-2011 2021-2022	166	15	181	30
Brad	Young	Birmingham	2020-2021	0	0	0	0
Charles	Young	Nicosia, Cyprus	1976-1977	9	1	10	0
Luke	Young	Harlow	2008-2012	72	3	75	2
Norman	Young	King's Heath, Birmingham	1935-1936	9	0	9	0
Willie	Young	Glasgow, Scotland	1978-1979	3	0	3	0
	Own Goals		1883-2021	0	0	0	160

ASTON VILLA PLAYER RECORDS

	FA CUP				LEAGUE CUP				EUROPEAN				OTHER				TOTAL		
SL	SUB	PL	GLS	SL	SUB	PL	GLS	SL	SUB	PL	GLS	SL	SUB	PL	GLS	SL	SUB	PL	GLS
3	0	3	0	0	0	0	0	0	0	0	0	0	0	0	0	43	0	43	0
0	0	0	0	0	0	0	0	0	0	0	0	0	0	0	0	9	0	9	0
6	0	6	0	0	0	0	0	0	0	0	0	0	0	0	0	68	0	68	6
0	0	0	0	4	1	5	1	2	1	3	0	0	0	0	0	23	10	33	6
1	0	1	0	6	3	9	1	0	0	0	0	0	0	0	0	39	27	66	2
0	0	0	0	0	0	0	0	0	0	0	0	0	0	0	0	6	0	6	0
17	0	17	1	0	0	0	0	0	0	0	0	2	0	2	0	159	0	159	8
11	0	11	0	0	0	0	0	0	0	0	0	0	0	0	0	75	0	75	0
0	0	0	0	0	0	0	0	0	0	0	0	0	0	0	0	0	1	1	0
0	0	0	0	1	0	1	0	0	0	0	0	0	0	0	0	13	0	13	0
0	0	0	0	0	0	0	0	0	0	0	0	0	1	1	0	8	8	16	0
2	0	2	0	0	1	1	0	0	0	0	0	0	0	0	0	297	5	302	2
14	0	14	0	29	0	29	2	17	0	17	0	2	0	2	0	17	0	17	5
0	0	0	0	0	0	0	0	0	0	0	0	0	0	0	0	1	0	1	0
0	0	0	0	0	0	0	0	0	0	0	0	0	0	0	0	1	0	1	0
0	0	0	0	0	0	0	0	0	0	0	0	0	0	0	0	9	0	9	0
0	0	0	0	0	0	0	0	0	0	0	0	0	0	0	0	5	0	5	0
7	0	7	0	0	0	0	0	0	0	0	0	0	0	0	0	49	0	49	1
6	0	6	0	7	0	7	0	0	0	0	0	0	0	0	0	50	0	50	0
9	0	9	2	19	0	19	5	21	0	21	9	2	0	2	2	233	0	233	92
10	0	10	0	7	0	7	0	0	0	0	0	0	0	0	0	163	0	163	0
1	0	1	0	0	0	0	0	0	0	0	0	0	0	0	0	5	0	5	0
8	0	8	0	0	0	0	0	0	0	0	0	0	0	0	0	110	0	110	8
9	0	9	0	0	0	0	0	0	0	0	0	0	0	0	0	71	0	71	2
1	1	2	1	1	0	1	0	0	0	0	0	0	0	0	0	24	5	29	8
4	0	4	0	0	0	0	0	0	0	0	0	0	0	0	0	24	0	24	13
9	0	9	1	10	0	10	5	0	0	0	0	0	0	0	0	125	0	125	29
0	0	0	0	0	0	0	0	0	0	0	0	0	0	0	0	4	0	4	0
25	0	25	0	18	0	18	0	26	0	26	0	0	0	0	0	324	5	329	5
0	0	0	0	0	0	0	0	0	0	0	0	0	0	0	0	2	0	2	0
13	0	13	0	20	1	21	0	0	0	0	0	1	0	1	0	314	4	318	1
24	0	24	4	24	0	24	7	0	0	0	0	0	0	0	0	244	0	244	27
15	0	15	0	0	0	0	0	0	0	0	0	0	0	0	0	29	0	29	0
0	0	0	0	0	0	0	0	0	0	0	0	0	0	0	0	14	0	14	0
34	0	34	7	0	0	0	0	0	0	0	0	0	0	0	0	390	0	390	87
22	2	24	14	20	2	22	8	9	0	9	2	1	0	1	1	247	40	287	98
0	0	0	0	0	0	0	0	0	0	0	0	0	0	0	0	26	0	26	11
11	1	12	2	10	1	11	4	11	0	11	2	0	0	0	0	198	1	215	38
0	1	1	0	0	0	0	0	0	0	0	0	0	0	0	0	0	1	1	0
1	0	1	0	0	0	0	0	0	0	0	0	0	0	0	0	10	1	11	0
5	0	5	0	2	0	2	0	7	0	7	0	0	0	0	0	86	3	89	2
0	0	0	0	0	0	0	0	0	0	0	0	0	0	0	0	9	0	9	0
0	0	0	0	0	0	0	0	0	0	0	0	0	0	0	0	3	0	3	0
0	0	0	9	0	0	0	8	0	0	0	2	0	0	0	0	0	0	0	179

ROLL OF HONOUR

Thank you to these people for pre-ordering
Aston Villa · The Complete Record

Colin Abbott	Michael Barker
Samantha Allan	Rick Barley
Benjamin Allen	Andrew Barnes
Neil & Greg Allen	Steve Barney
Thomas Allmark	Joshua James Fred Barnwell
Alun Allsop	Dean Barratt
David Anchor	Adam Thomas Barrett
Sbalchiero Andrea	Nick Barter
Stefano Armellini	Paul Bate
Glenn Armstrong	Joshua James Bate
Stephen James Arnold	Rylan Batley-Thomsett
Paul Arnold	Michael Batsford
Tom Ashcroft	Deborah Beal
Michele Astbury	Zoe Beal
Michèle Asthury	Bedford Lions
Rhys Astley	Ian Edward Beesley
Ryan Astley	Joanne Bennett
Michael Atkinson	Steve Bennett
Eve Atterbury	Arthur Bent
Nathan Atterbury	Dean Beresford
Luke Atterbury	Lee Bickerton
Marco Baetens	Derek Bignell
Paul Bailey	Alissia Bird
Chris Bailey	David Birt
Richard Bailey	Jeff & Ann Bishop
Matthew Bailey	Helen Bishop
Connor Bailey	Jorgen Bolin
Stephen John Baker	Liana & Andrew Bolton
Lewis W Baker	David Borovský
Trevor John Baker	Karl Bowater
Stuart Ball	Liam Bowen
Chris Ballard	Adrian Bowley

ROLL OF HONOUR

Matt Braddock
Michael Brainsby
Robert E Brampton
Tony Braniff
Mark Branigan
Phil Daniel Niall Brennan
Dave Bridgewater
Pam Bridgewater
Mike Brown
Andy Bryan
Steve, Georgina, Jamie & Ian Buchan
Mr Paul Buckley
Paul 'Publunch' Buet
Michael Burbage
Alan Burdon
Stephen Burridge
Christopher Teague & Mary Butler
Dave Butler
Göran Bylund
Mark Byworth
Graham Byworth
Kayleigh Byworth
Lewis Byworth
Matt Caldwell
Stuart Caldwell
Brian Callaghan
Henry Callaghan
Robert Canning
Clive Capewell
Jonathan Capps
Matthew Carder
Adam Carlton-Gray
Matthew Carter
Philip Leslie Cashmore
Cormac Cassidy

Graham Cecil
Darren Chambers
Matt Chick
David Chick
Martin Childs
Ray & Linda Clarkson
David John Edward Clayton
Mark Clinton
Glen Clougher
Neil Codling
Simone Colaci
Phil Coldicott
Mark Colin
Sean Collins
Nick Connolly
John Connolly
Mark Cooksey
Roy Cooper
Jack Corbett
Jimmy Corbett
Matthew Corcoran
Martin Coughlan
Iain & Ace Courage
Martin Lawrence Cox
Ian Coxsey
Alan Crampton
Mark Crane
Adam Crawford
Mike Crockett
Rob Cronin
Gary Crook
Linley Cross
Stuart Cummings
Bob Curry
Benedict Curry

599

Lennon Cutler	Michael Dugmore
Jamie Cutteridge	Richard Duncombe
DanAdPee	Nigel Dunmore
Russell Dale	Neil Dunworth
Scott Dale	Adam Alexander Eagles
Russell Dale Junior	James Earp
Andy Dale	Adrian Earp
Kevin Daly	Will Earp
Gareth Davies	Neil Easto
Anthony Davies	Callum David Edmonds
James Davis	Richard John Edmonds
Kevin Davis	Andy Edmunds
Derek Day	Carol & Bob Edwards
Peter Day	Patrick Arran Edwards
Michael Dearn	Paul Alan Edwards
Gavin Delaney	Richard Elis
Stefano Denni	Anthony Ellerington
Craig Dewis	Stuart Ellis
Bob Dilworth	Vaughan Ellis
Luke Dodds	Andrew Elson
Hugh Doherty	John F Evans
Gary & Lisa Dolphin	Reg Evans
Tony Donnelly	Reg Evans (RIP)
Philip Doody	Elliot Evlyn-Bufton
Leigh Douglas	Roger Evlyn-Bufton
Ron Dovey	Dr Philip Fairchild
Chris Dovey	Jonathan Fairless
John Downes	Mark Farmer
Lee Downing	Joseph Farr
Clive Drinkwater	Dennis Farrell
Patrick Drummey	Mick Farrell
Marco Duarte	Jon Farrelly
Cliff Dubberley	Paul Farrington
Cliff Dubberley	The Fellows family (Annie, Ewan, Harry & Millie)
My Dad, Derek Duckers	Paddy Fenlon

ROLL OF HONOUR

Andrew Fernie	John 'Charlie' Gowen
James Field	Alan Graham (al bundy)
Bruce Firmstone	Samuel Graham
Paul Fitzpatrick	Paul Grant
Simon, Oliver, Toby & (hopefully) Henry Fitzpatrick	Philip Gray
James Fitzsimmons	Arthur Greaves
John Flanner	Richard Greaves
Charlie Foat	Steve Gregory
Nigel & Amy Follos	Joseph Gregory Jr
William Ford	Chris Grey
Rob Ford	Thomas Griffin
Nicholas Foskett	William Griffin
Guy Foster	John Griffiths
David, Thomas & William Foster	Dave Griffiths
John Foster	Kyle Grigg
Bob Fountain	Andrew Grigg
Ben & Finlay Fowler	Anthony Grimes
Kevin Fowler	Allan Grindrod
Ryan & Roy Fradley	Glenn Grove
Freddie Jack Frost	Nigel Groves & Jacob Groves
Peter Fryer	Jon Hackett
Sean Gallagher	Ben Haddrell
Daniel Gallagher	Raymond Hadley
James Garbett	Rob Hale
Joshua Garratt	Gordon Halfpenny
Brian Garratt	Andy Hall
John Gaunt	Damon Hall
Christopher Gautrey	Shaun Hall
Barry J S Gibbs	Alice Halman
Neil Gibson	Steven Hampton
Robert Giedt	Matt Hancox
Stuart Giles	Keith Handley
Roger Goldman	Martin Harcourt
Howard Goodman	Jack Harris
Robert Gough	Mark Harris

Graham Harris	Martin Horton
Edward Hartlebury	Tony Houghton
Trevor Hartley	Mr JJ Howard (Guinness)
Steve Hartley	Peter Howard
Paul Harvey	Glyn Howell
Rosalind Haswell	Howard Howes
Anais Rose Hattersley	Ronnie Hughes
Lee Hawkeswood	Paul Graham Hughes
Justin Hawthorne	Graham Humphreys
Olivia Hawthorne	Darren Hunt
Brooke Hawthorne	Damien Hutchinson
Beci Hawthorne	Steven Leonard Hutton
Rob Hayes	Matthew Idoine
Mathew Heard	Scott & Ian J
Robert Michael Henry	Jim & Nige
Tim Herlihy	Graham Jackson
Richard Herrett	Nigel Jackson
Owain Hedd Wyn Herron	Matt Jackson
Stephen Hill	Barry Jackson
Jake Hinde	Lee Andrew Jackson
Kris Hinde	Paul Richard Jackson
Paul Hindle	Oliver James
Stephen Hines	Bob James
Matt Hipkiss	David Jenkins
David Hockenhull	Darren Jenkins
David Hodges	Colin Jennings
John Holder	Phil Johnson
William Edwin Holloway	Fred Johnson
Harold (Hoppy) Holman	Rob Johnson
Harry Homer	Michael Johnston
Russell Homer	Ron Jones
Wayne Hopkins	Steve Jones
Nigel Horton	Stephen Jordan
Karla Horton	Oliver Jordan
Archie Horton	Connor Jordan

Mark Joyce
Tony Joyner
Keaveny Family
Ian Kenny
Mat Kendrick
Michael Kessissoglou
Thomas Kibble
James King
Andrew King
Steven King
Gary Kingscote
Kevin Kington
Colin Kinsella
Guido Kirfel
John Knibb
Stephen Knott
Steve Knott
Ari Koivuranta
Oscar Stephen Lamb
James R Lamond
Peter, Paul & Mark Lanni
Steve Lavery
Robert Law
Mark Lench
Rick Leong
Rick Leong
Crewe Lewis
John Leydon
Tom Leydon
Kevin Leydon
Peter Leydon
Pete Lindstrom
Stuart Loach
Malcolm Loach
Steve Lowden

Stuart Lowe
Martin Lugsdin
Evie-May Lynch
Matt Lynch
Fran MacDonald
Eric MacEwan
Ian Mackenzie
Alexis Madders
Rich Male
Joseph Manjaly
Geoff Mann
Georgia Mann
Sayali Marathe
Julie Marples
Michael Marshall
Heather Martin
Jason Matcham
Paul Mattey
Paul Matthews
Mark J Matthews
Paul Matthews
Michael John Mattimoe
Mark McCabe
Gary Douglas McCall
Noel McCreesh
Arthur Leonardo Antonio McDaniel
Warren, Maggie, Ellie & Harry McDivitt
Mark McIntosh
Gregory McKenzie
Dave McMahon
Edward McNeill
John Meechan
Keith Meek
Andrew Melley
Huw & Harry Millichip

Darrel Millington	Joe Oliver
Thomas Mooney	Alan Ostojitsch
David Moore	Graham Owen
Peter Moore	Phil Parkes - Timor Leste
Adam Moore	Darren Palin
Bob Moore	Steven Pallett
Arran Morgan	Richard Parker
Mark 'Crippler' Morgon-Shaw	Michael Parker
Luke Morris	Dave Parsons
Keith Morris	Kirk Pastre
Daniel Moss	Raks Patel
Richard Mullaney	Donald Patrick
Stacy Murphy	Alan Patterson
Paul & Roz Myles	Andrew Pattison
Chris Nason	Frank Pattison
Nathan	Ken Pattison
Pat Neenan	Michael Pattison
Phil Newell	Rick Payne
Nigel Newman	Geoff Pearce
David Nightingale	Mark Pearce
Christine Nightingale	Andrew Pearsall
William Nightingale	John Peniket
Gary Nolan	Richard E Perkins
Ross Norman	Jon Perks
Daniel O'Meara	Jim Perrins
Patrick O'Meara	David Phillips
Mark O'Neill	Simon Phillips
Dermot O'Sullivan	Sav Phillips
Tim O'Brien	Claire Pierce
Jeremiah Thomas O'Brien	Leo Pinnock
Des O'Donoghue	Philip Piper
Dan O'Grady	Mark Policarpo
Jack O'Meara	Andrew Poulton
Terence O'Neill	Keith Powell
Patrick F J O'Reilly	John Villa Power

ROLL OF HONOUR

Tom Preece
Cathy Price
Adam Proctor
Maureen & Ian Purvey
Vera Ellen Ragsdale
Gary Randell
William Rangeley
Rasp
Callum Reilly
Bob, Stu, Christopher & Rob Reynolds
Matt Reynolds
Natasha Rice
David Richardson
Pauline Richardson
Kyle Richardson
Iain / Arran Richmond
Steven Riddick
Brian Ridgway
Rosie Ries
Max Jack Riley
Paul Barrie John Rimmer
Max Rippington
Peter Roberts
Oakley Rodgers
Malcolm Rogers (RIP)
Kevin Rollason & John Rollason
Harry George Rollason
Charlie David Rollason
Colin Roscorla
Sam Rose
Christine Rossiter
Steve Round
Jamie Rowley
Marc Rowley
Kevin Rudge

Henry Rushall
Christian Russ
Matthew Rutherford
James Rutherford
Luca Rymkiewicz
Nick Salter
Keith Sammons
John Samways
Hamraj Singh Sandhu
Barry J Sarl
Elliot J E Sarl
Andrea Sbalchiero
Brian C Seadon
Richard Seers
Andy Seferta
Nimit Shah
Nigel Shaw
Anthony Shepherd
Dan Shepherd
Eddie Sheppard
Richard Sheppard
Darren Shotter
Owen Shrimplin
Gregory Shutt
Wayne Simmonds
Robert Slack
Trevor Slack
Rob (Essex Bob) Slater
Rob Slazenger
Simen Smestad
Paul Smith
Nigel Smith
Nico Smith
Michael Hanby Smith
Dan Hanby Smith

Abigail Elizabeth Smith	David & Jacob Tansey
Dave G Smith	Nathan Taroni
Keith Roger Smith	Roxanne Taroni
Anthony M Smith	Carl Taylor
Neil K Smith	Nick Taylor
Mick Smith	Gordon James Taylor
John B Smith	Peter Tennant
Paul Graham Smith	James Terry
Graham Smith	Tezza
Richard Smith	Paul Thomas-Humphreys
Jacob Davis Smith	Andrew Thompson
Mike Smith	Sue & Mick Tilt
George Sneddon-Coombes	Mick Tilt
Ben Spindler	Aiden Timperley
David Spinks	John Timperley
Robin Squelch	Kian Timperley
Tom Staggard	Mike Tomlin
Matt Stalker	Nolan J Tonks
Michael W Stanley	Allan R Tonks
Jake Aston Stevens	Ray Totty
Michael Stevens	Greg Trappett
Andy Stevenson	Samuel Trigger
Oliver Stokes	Ryan Trott
Hannah & Ross Storey	Bradley Jay Tucker
James Street	Julie Tully (nee Richardson)
Steve Stride	Harrison & Tommy Tunley
Matthew Stride	Paul Turland
Studio EXP	Simon Turner
Cal Sullivan	Matt Turner
Jeff Summers	Andy Turner
Jorn Sundby	Jan Turner
Teo Sutherland	Martin (Tally Ho) Turner
Tom Swain	Peter Turner
Ethan Sweet	Martin Turrell
Mark Tamplin	Mark Twomlow

Becki Tyler	Richard Whitehead
Gary Tyler	Simon Wiggin
George Tyrer	Owen Wilding
Andy 'Turnstile' Ullah	Robin Wilkes
Malcolm Upfold	Lyndon Willetts
Greg Upton	Paul Williams
Andrew & Matéo Vass	Stephen J Williams
Ian & Cathryn Vass	Bill Willis RIP
Stephen Armand Villa	Pamela Willock née Maneffa
Reece Wakeling	Simon Wilson
Robert Walford	Roy Wilson
Kieran Walker	Roy Wilson
Edward Walker	Bill Wilson
Noah Wall	Colin Wilson
Brendan Walsh	Tom Wilson
Paul C Walsh	Russ G Wilson
Gordon Ward	Lynne Wilson
John Ward	The Wilson Family 1955
Louise Ward	John Wilson
Gary Warner	Evelyn Winch
Colin Warren	Danielle Winch
Graham Watkiss	Mat Wolski
Martin Watson	Stuart Woods
Hugo & Monte Watts	Anthony Woolley
Rob Weake	Evie Woolridge
Jim Weaver	Stanley Wragg 1925-2022
Gary Weaver	Terry Wright
Jason 'Brummiewebbie' Webb	Geoffrey Wright
Tony, Angela, Craig & Charlie Webb	Simon Wykes
Michael Webber	Katie Wykes
Joe Welch	Phillip & Paul Yeomans
David Wells	Nick Yost
Simon 'Wilf' & Alfie Wheeler	Jake Young
Matthew Paul Wheeler	Mikael Zeiner
Joe White	Massimiliano Zoratti

UP THE VILLA!